# Plus, Exciting <u>New Material</u> for the Third Edition . . .

✔ Detailed focus on **spelling** highlights the connection between word recognition and written language, featuring a significantly revised chapter (Chapter 13). Includes a more **extensive discussion of orthography** and the reciprocal relationship between word knowledge in spelling and in reading.

✔ **Reviews of model tutoring programs** integrated throughout the book illustrate proven, exemplary teaching principles (Chapters 5 and 12).

✔ Now with more coverage of issues related to **English language learners** throughout the text, culminating in a new case study in Chapter 11.

✔ Expanded section on **literature discussion** deepens students' engagement with texts and improves comprehension both in and out of the classroom (Chapter 15).

✔ Valuable discussions of **leveled texts** help teachers tailor their instruction and improve the quality of assessment information (Chapters 6, 9, and 12).

✔ Analysis of contemporary **research about successful schools** examines factors that influence student achievement and offers sound strategies teachers can apply every day in their own classrooms.

✔ Increased attention to **fluency** in assessment and instruction sections (Chapters 8 and 13).

✔ Contains updated information about **phonological awareness** (Chapters 7, 10, and 13). This edition treats early word level knowledge and skill, including phonemic awareness and phonics comprehensively, **reflecting recent research findings** and the growing knowledge base in this area.

THIRD EDITION

# Assessment and Instruction of Reading and Writing Difficulty

## An Interactive Approach

**Marjorie Y. Lipson**
*The University of Vermont*

**Karen K. Wixson**
*The University of Michigan*

Boston     New York     San Francisco
Mexico City     Montreal     Toronto     London     Madrid     Munich     Paris
Hong Kong     Singapore     Tokyo     Cape Town     Sydney

**Series Editor:**  *Aurora Martínez Ramos*
**Series Editorial Assistant:**  *Beth Slater*
**Senior Marketing Manager:**  *Elizabeth Fogarty*
**Composition Buyer:**  *Linda Cox*
**Manufacturing Buyer:**  *JoAnne Sweeney*
**Editorial-Production Administrator:**  *Karen Mason*
**Editorial-Production Service:**  *Lauren Shafer*
**Cover Administrator:**  *Linda Knowles*
**Cover Designer:**  *Suzanne Harbison*

For related titles and support materials, visit our online catalog at www.ablongman.com.

A previous edition was published under the title *Assessment and Instruction of Reading and Writing Disability.*

***Library of Congress Cataloging-in-Publication Data***

Lipson, Marjorie Y.
    Assessment and instruction of reading and writing difficulty : an interactive approach / Marjorie Y. Lipson, Karen K. Wixson.— 3rd ed.
        p.   cm.
    Rev. ed. of: Assessment and instruction of reading and writing disability, c1997.
    Includes bibliographical references (p.) and index.
    ISBN 0-205-35540-4
    1. Reading disability.   2. Reading—Ability testing.   3. Reading comprehension.   4. Reading—Remedial teaching.   I. Wixson, Karen K. II. Lipson, Marjorie Y. Assessment and instruction of reading and writing disability.   III. Title.

LB1050.5 .L 54 2003
428'.42—dc21

                                                                    2002026140

Printed in the United States of America

10   9   8   7   6   5   4                    08   07   06   05   04

*To Michael, Nora, and Theo*
*who have been patient with my distraction (mostly),*
*made me laugh when I needed it (generally),*
*and who remind me that I am a lucky person (always).*

*MYL*


*To all the educators who have dedicated themselves*
*to helping struggling readers and writers.*

*KKW*

# BRIEF CONTENTS

# CONTENTS

**6  Instructional Resources    172**

# PREFACE

This text, like the earlier editions, is based on an interactive view of ability and disability. Since we first planned and wrote this text, the field has changed rapidly in its treatment of reading and writing and in its awareness of the importance of assessing and teaching struggling readers and writers. Some issues that were critically important in earlier versions are now well understood and do not require quite as much attention in this edition. For example, the deep interrelationships between reading and writing are taken for granted in current views of literacy, and although reading is often singled out for special attention, especially in the earliest years, knowledgeable professionals know that both young and struggling students benefit from careful attention to the reciprocal relationships between the two domains.

At the same time that some divisions have been put to rest, others have emerged, however. When the second edition of this text was published, there were only the softest whisperings that the field would be wrenched by a resurgence of the old "reading wars." Although our balanced and interactive perspective on reading and writing difficulties has always included careful attention to each of the components of skilled reading/writing, this edition contains a significantly revised Chapter 13, "Adapting Instruction to Focus on Word Recognition, Fluency, and Spelling," that treats early word level knowledge and skill, including phonemic awareness and phonics, somewhat more comprehensively, reflecting recent research findings and our growing knowledge base in this area. This edition also contains additional materials related to comprehension, fluency, and motivation.

This third edition has, of course, been updated in all areas. This has resulted in a more careful and extensive discussion of orthography and the reciprocal relationship between word knowledge in spelling and in reading. Similarly, more attention has been directed toward fluency, in both the assessment and instructional chapters. Strategies for leveling texts have added depth to Chapter 6, "Instructional Resources," and Chapter 8, "Informal Classroom-Based Assessment." Chapter 12, "Getting Started in Instruction," also addresses these ideas in a discussion of high-utility strategies. In order to provide more powerful instructional support for teachers in all settings, this edition also contains new information related to tutoring, flexible groupings, and literature discussion. Finally, there is considerably more discussion of English language learners throughout the text, culminating with a new case study in Chapter 11 of a bilingual student from a diverse cultural and linguistic background.

We continue to believe that the interactive view of reading and writing offers a productive alternative to the deficit view that still dominates textbooks on reading and writing disability. Deficit models suggest that the cause of reading or writing difficulties lies entirely within the reader. Instructional programs based on a deficit model focus primarily on what Sarason and Doris (1979) call the "search for pathology" within the reader. In contrast, an interactive view suggests that reading or writing disability is a relative concept, not a static state, and that the difficulty often lies in the match between the learner and the conditions of the learning situation. Recent research has provided converging evidence to strengthen this perspective (Spear-Swerling & Sternberg, 1998), and additional research suggests strongly that all but a small proportion of struggling readers can learn to read and write well (Vellutino et al., 1996).

Consistent with an interactive perspective, this text focuses on the process of evaluating the existing match between the learner and the instructional context and identifying an optimal match. The content of this text also reflects our belief that the most important factor in effective assessment and instruction is the knowledge base of the teacher. Accordingly, the first section of the text presents background information regarding reading, writing, and disability.

Section One, "Theory into Practice," contains three chapters that provide the knowledge base for using the remainder of the text. In Chapter 1, "Perspectives on Reading and Writing Ability," we describe a historical view and several theoretical views of reading and writing. We also discuss legal and political perspectives on reading and writing and examine the legal and social roots of special education. Chapter 2, "An Interactive View of Reading and Writing," details an interactive view of reading and writing, providing a detailed picture of the various elements of skilled performance and the factors that influence it. In Chapter 3, "Reading and Writing Disability and the Assessment-Instruction Process," we provide an overview of the assessment-instruction process that is used to guide the remainder of the text and provide a case study example.

The remaining chapters are organized in a manner that parallels the assessment-instruction process described in Chapter 3. Section Two, "Getting Started and Evaluating the Context," contains two subsections, one on "Getting Started with Assessment" (Chapter 4) and one on "Evaluating the Reading/Writing Context" (Chapters 5 and 6). Chapter 4, "Getting Started with Assessment," provides guidelines for gathering initial information. Chapter 5, "Evaluating the Instructional Environment/Context," is the first of two chapters related to evaluating context factors. It considers how the overall classroom setting and instructional practices (including instructional methods, routines, and assessments) may influence reading and writing performance and provides tools for evaluating these aspects of the context. Chapter 6, "Instructional Resources," describes how reading and writing performance can be affected by these factors and provides additional tools and strategies for assessing the context.

The next four chapters in Section Three, "Evaluating the Learner," are focused on assessment. Chapter 7, "The Foundations of Literacy," is devoted to an understanding of early and emergent literacy concepts and the assessment of young learners. Chapter 8, "Informal Classroom-Based Assessment," focuses on informal, continuous methods of assessing word recognition, comprehension, and writing. Chapter 9, "Structured Inventories and Assessments," provides an in-depth discussion of issues and practices in using information reading inventories (IRIs) and other more systematic assessment tools. Finally, Chapter 10, "Formal Assessment," addresses the understanding of important statistical concepts and provides a detailed description of the characteristics and types of tests that are commonly associated with assessment in reading and writing.

Section Four, "Interactions: Assessment as Inquiry," consists of a single chapter, Chapter 11, "Interactive Decision Making," emphasizing the juncture where assessment and instruction come together. The steps in the assessment-instruction process that involve evaluating the match between the learner and the context, reflecting and generating hypotheses about the source of interference with learning, and identifying an optimal instructional match are all described.

Section Five, "Instruction," contains two subsections. The first, "Getting Started in Instruction" (Chapter 12), describes high-utility instructional strategies and provides a rationale for making decisions about the instructional issues and techniques. The other section, containing Chapters 13, 14, and 15, provides support to teachers as they adapt their instructional program to focus on the specific areas of word recognition, fluency, and spelling (Chapter 13), vocabulary (Chapter 14), and comprehension, composition, and studying (Chapter 15).

The final section and chapter of the text, Section Six and Chapter 16, both entitled "Professional Roles and Responsibilities," place teachers and students in a broader context. This chapter provides techniques and frameworks for reporting information to others and addresses many of the ethical and legal responsibilities of reading professionals.

# Acknowledgments

We would like to acknowledge our appreciation to the many people who provided advice, encouragement, and assistance in the development of this text. We gratefully acknowledge the thoughtful reviews provided to us by Shane Templeton and Sheila Valencia, whose careful reading and clear insights improved this edition. Any failure to implement their helpful suggestions rests entirely with us. We greatly appreciate the comments of the following reviewers as well: Kathryn H. Au, University of Hawaii at Manoa; Patricia M. Britt, Crichton College; and Pamela Dunston, Clemson University. We would also like to thank Linda Mosteiro-Marshall, Deb Young, and Maria Chesley Fisk for their special assistance. Special thanks are extended to Molly McClasky for providing an inspiring teaching model and the entire teaching staff at Essex Elementary School for their professional commitment to literacy development. We also thank Kyle and his parents for allowing us to share in the excitement of learning to read. Finally, we would like to acknowledge the special contribution of the students in our graduate and undergraduate courses who offered us feedback and ideas based on the original text.

We have been grateful to the many individuals who have communicated with us about earlier versions of the text and hope that this revision keeps alive the dialogue. We look forward to our readers' responses to the challenges presented in this text.

Marjorie Y. Lipson<br>
Karen K. Wixson

# SECTION ONE

# Theory into Practice

In the first section of this book we provide a theoretical foundation and rationale for the remainder of the text. The section contains three chapters. In Chapter 1 we describe various views of reading and writing. We use available theory and research to advance an interactive perspective on reading and writing that lays the foundation for the remainder of the text. In the final part of this chapter we describe the legal and political aspects of special education and disability.

In Chapter 2 we discuss the component skills and strategies required to succeed in reading and writing tasks. This chapter may be a review for some students taking a graduate course in assessment and instruction, but the information is essential for teachers and clinicians to make sound decisions during assessment and to plan appropriate instruction. In addition, we discuss in detail how learner factors, text factors, and contextual factors influence student performance in reading and writing.

In Chapter 3 we show how an interactive model of reading and writing ability can and should be applied to reading and writing disability. This chapter also provides an overview of the assessment and instruction process. The overview simultaneously describes the way literacy assessment and instruction typically progress, and also provides a guided tour of the sequence of this text. The steps of the assessment-instruction process detailed in Chapter 3 are used throughout the remainder of the book. In introductory materials for subsequent sections we highlight the particular step(s) to be considered in that section.

# 1

# Perspectives on Reading and Writing Ability

Concerns about reading and writing instruction—and the number of children who are failing to learn to do them well—often dominate both public and professional conversation about education. Too often, these issues and what to do about them are argued from personal experience. One person favors a particular approach because it worked for her daughter. Others argue for a different approach because they feel more comfortable themselves with certain practices. Teachers, however, need to base their decisions on a broad base of data, looking for patterns and evidence of efficacy for many students. Personal experience and years of practice are one source of information about what works. Combined with empirical research, formal case studies, and structured observations, they form the basis for sound decision making.

Good teaching always involves adapting instruction to the needs of specific individuals or groups of students. Such adaptations are absolutely essential when we are concerned, as we are in this text, with students who are not learning to read and write easily and well. These students require thoughtfully planned and executed instruction, fitted to their particular needs. What is needed for one "disabled" or struggling learner may be quite different from what is required for another.

How can we make decisions about what to change, how to adapt existing practice, and what to do with these students who have failed to learn when given exposure to the usual and customary instruction? To make decisions, teachers need to consider theory. In reality, all teachers have some sort of theory, whether they realize it or not. Sometimes called "teacher beliefs" (Anders & Evans, 1994) and sometimes "perspective" (Gutierrez-Clellen, Pena, & Quinn, 1995), teachers' theories about reading and writing are extremely important because the particular theory a teacher holds determines, at least in part, what that teacher does in the name of reading and writing instruction. In fact, Robinson (1998) recently suggested that teachers generally hold "problem-solving-based theories." In other words, they ignore some sources of data (e.g., some types of research) if the data do not address the problems they face or the settings in which they work. Theories help us to simplify educational decisions because they often tell us how to behave.

In this chapter we describe the ways in which existing views of reading and writing have influenced both assessment and instruction over the years and provide information that will help you refine your own theories of reading and writing. In addition, we trace the legal and political roots of programs designed to address the needs of students with reading and writing difficulties. These various perspectives will help teachers to reflect on their existing knowledge and beliefs, setting the stage for a more extensive discussion in Chapter 2 of an interactive view of reading and writing.

# Understanding Reading and Writing

In this section we describe the historical contexts in which reading and writing came to be viewed separately in education. This is followed by a discussion of more recent cognitive and social perspectives that have resulted in more integration of reading and writing in educational theory and practice.

## Historical Perspectives on Reading and Writing

The field of literacy education as we know it today began as reading instruction in the public school at the primary grade levels. Public schooling was seen as a way to provide a growing population with the foundations of good citizenship, and reading was the way for students to acquire common moral and political principles. The first public schools gave instruction in reading brief Biblical passages and other moralistic texts; later, primers offered secular, patriotic readings with questions and answers for students to copy and recite (Clifford, 1984; Squire, 1991).

Writing was considered less important than oral communication, since most citizens of the new nation had no need to write except to sign their names. Like reading, writing was thought to be a simple matter, a way to put words that would otherwise be spoken into print; all students needed to know for that simple translation was handwriting and spelling (Clifford, 1984; Russell, 1991).

After the Civil War the growing commercial and professional class was divided into many separate communities. These communities were linked more by written texts, such as memos, reports, professional literature, and administrative records, than by geography or social class (Russell, 1991). The new professionals demanded that schools provide their children an education that would prepare them for roles in government, commerce, and the growing professions. The purposes for school literacy instruction expanded to serve the general population as well as the college-bound elite (Katz, 1987; Russell, 1991).

In 1894 a committee composed of university professors, professionals, and business-men issued the Report of the Committee of Ten on public high schools. The report called for greater emphasis on English literature, since literature was seen as a vehicle for transmitting common values and "uplifting" ordinary citizens (Applebee, 1974). Following this report, a National Conference on College Entrance Requirements produced a list of core readings—a literary canon that dominated the entire high school English curriculum for decades (Applebee, 1974).

The Committee of Ten also set standards for written expression that were accepted throughout the society (Heath, 1991; Russell, 1991). As a result, schools and other public institutions began emphasizing standard English in writing as well as speaking; correct spelling and grammar became a focus of instruction. Classroom writing activities typically consisted of copying texts, underlining, circling, and supplying one-word responses (Clifford, 1989; North, 1987). Graded reading books that matched children's age and ability level, first printed in 1836, became a standard by the late 1800s and established the pattern for the basal reading series still used today (Squire, 1991).

From the mid-1800s through the first decades of the twentieth century, a progressive philosophy of education gained influence among educators. The foremost progressive philosopher, John Dewey, advocated a public school system that functioned neither to preserve privileged traditions nor to prepare students for prevailing social conditions, but to improve students' lives and create a society whose benefits accrued to all citizens (Applebee, 1974; Cremin, 1989). Dewey rejected the literary canon and recommended curriculum materials that had relevance to students. He promoted cooperation and group work in the classroom to encourage a free exchange of ideas and saw schools as learning communities (Applebee, 1974; Hendley, 1986; Russell, 1991).

The scientific movement arose as a counterinfluence on schools during the progressive era. One of the early educational psychologists, Edward Thorndike, developed scientific theories that led to the development of objective measures of student achievement. These measures were used to sort students into ability groups so that teachers could provide instruction suited to particular needs. This movement came to exert the same control that the literary canon once had on curriculum and instruction in the form of skills instruction.

In the last thirty years our understanding of how students learn and our approach to studying reading and writing has been changed rather dramatically by two new ways of thinking about teaching and learning: the cognitive revolution and the "social turn" (Geertz, 1983). These two perspectives, described more fully in the next section, are important because they prompted researchers and educators to consider reading and writing together, rather than separately. In addition, they are the basis for the interactive view described in this text. In describing these perspectives, we are greatly indebted to the thinking of McCarthey and Raphael (1992) and Englert and Palincsar (1991).

## Cognitive Information-Processing Perspectives on Reading and Writing

During the World War II period, computer technology suggested new ways to model mental processes that influenced our views of learning. The new cognitive scientists viewed computers and the mind as similar: active, self-monitoring systems for processing information. Information-processing theories have been used to develop several models of both reading and writing processes (for example, Gough, 1972; Hayes & Flower, 1980; Kintsch & vanDijk, 1978; LaBerge & Samuels, 1974).

When an information-processing perspective is applied to reading and writing, three assumptions seem to operate: (1) reading and writing consist of a number of subprocesses used to perform specialized tasks, (2) readers and writers have limited capacity for attention so that trade-offs occur across the subprocesses, and (3) competence in reading and writing is determined by the degree of attention needed to operate subprocesses; the less memory needed, the more efficient the operation (McCarthey & Raphael, 1992).

***Subprocesses in Reading and Writing.***   Like the computer whose components perform specialized functions that interact to complete a task, information-processing models divide reading and writing processes into subprocesses, each with a different function. For example, Gough (1972) proposed a model of reading as a linear, hierarchical process. The reader works from the smallest units of analysis (letters) to the largest (text meaning), and each level of analysis triggers the next, with the sum of these analyses adding up to meaning. The subprocesses identified in this model include a visual or iconic image, moving toward letter identification, searching one's lexicon, and accessing memory for meaning.

In contrast, LaBerge and Samuels (1974) described reading in terms of the component processes that relate to the functions of different types of memory: visual, phonological, semantic, and episodic. At the heart of their model is attention, the process that allocates the reader's efforts to the subprocess or memory type needed for the task at hand. In this view, progress through the subprocesses may not be linear, since attention may be allocated to different memories in different patterns.

These "bottom-up" models of text processing have given way to interactive models (Rumelhart, 1977). Interactive models suggest that the processing of text is a flexible interaction of the different information sources available to the reader and that the information contained in "higher" stages of processing can influence, as well as be influenced by, the analysis that occurs at lower stages of analysis.

Information-processing models of writing are similar to those of reading. For example, Flower and Hayes (1981) described writing as consisting of three recursive phases: planning, in which writers set goals and make plans; translating, in which writers put ideas into written form; and reviewing, in which writers test the plans and translations. Similarly, Scardamalia, Bereiter, and Goelman (1982) distinguish between metacomponents, used to identify choices and make decisions, and performance components that allow writers to carry out their plans. Although these models differ in the division of tasks and specific definitions of the writing process, they share an emphasis on dividing the process into smaller components for analysis and description.

***Limited Capacity Processors.***    Information-processing theorists also use the computer metaphor to describe the limited capacity of readers and writers, who must often juggle several subprocesses at once (accessing background knowledge, organizing ideas, making decisions about relevant and redundant information, and monitoring). Just as the computer cannot attend to everything at once, humans also have limitations on their processing capacities. The juggling required for successful reading and writing performance is explained in terms of how much attention is actually necessary to engage in a given activity and how effectively individuals switch their attention to the process most useful for a particular task.

***Speed of Processing.***    The term *automaticity* has been used to describe the way skilled readers' subprocesses operate as instinctive routines (LaBerge & Samuels, 1974). Initially, subprocesses such as decoding in reading and handwriting in composition are so demanding of attentional resources that higher-level processes cannot be employed. Eventually, however, lower-level subprocesses are mastered to the point of automaticity, and new routines can be learned. Although not all subprocesses become automatic (comprehension and planning always involve some conscious attention), the more that do become automatic, the better able the reader or writer is to attend to more cognitively demanding activities.

***Implications.***    Information-processing models and research have provided us with an increased understanding of reading and writing processes in terms of their components. We also have a better understanding of the knowledge base of skilled readers and writers. However, current information-processing models do not account for the variability that occurs in reading and writing as a result of a host of contextual factors such as the nature of the task, goals, purposes, and instruction. Information-processing models also tend to overlook or dismiss larger social and cultural factors that influence an individual's reading and writing performance.

There has been little effort to detail the specific links between reading and writing from within the information processing perspective. Although there is some research dealing with how reading and writing may be related (for example, Ehri, 1989; Shanahan & Lomax, 1986), information-processing theory sheds little light on how to encourage their development or on how less successful or novice readers and writers become more skilled.

## Social Perspectives on Reading and Writing

At about the same time as the cognitive revolution, social scientists were developing an orientation that brings into focus the social and cultural contexts that shape language and thought. Social theories of language and learning suggest that meaning is not an individual construction, but a social negotiation that depends on supportive interaction and shared use of language.

The assumptions underlying various social perspectives on reading and writing are quite different from those described above: (1) reading and writing are social and cultural phenomena; (2) knowledge is constructed through the individual's interaction with the sociocultural environment; and (3) cognitive processes related to reading and writing are acquired through contextualized activity and assisted learning (Englert & Palincsar, 1991; McCarthey & Raphael, 1992).

*Sociocultural Nature of Reading and Writing.* The societies or cultures within which we live, learn, and work determine how reading and writing are defined, instructed, and evaluated. For example, at the district level, curriculum decisions such as the choice of literature-based versus traditional basal reading materials influence the instructional and assessment practices of teachers.

At the school level, the principal's and teachers' beliefs about learning and teaching have an effect on practices that determine, for example, the extent to which diverse groups of students are accorded equal opportunities to learn. Culture also manifests itself in classrooms in the form of patterns of social interactions and the sets of rules or routines that guide teachers' and students' social exchanges. These routines develop, in the participants, shared understandings about what it means to read and write, about "what counts" as reading and writing, and about appropriate uses of reading and writing (Dyson, 1999; Miller & Gadnow, 1995; Rogoff, 1990).

According to sociocultural theorists, the oral and written texts that students produce don't stand alone. Instead, they must be seen as related to all the activity and experience that have gone before for that teacher and classroom. Books have been read, ideas have been exchanged, and social interactions have occurred, all of which influence the types of oral and written exchanges that happen today (Cole, 1990).

Viewing reading and writing in terms of cultural practices means that we must understand the political and social, as well as cognitive dimensions, of literacy. When the classroom is viewed as a culture, we must be concerned with teachers' and students' beliefs about reading, writing, and the patterns of interactions occurring among students and between teachers and students rather than discrete activities. We must consider factors such as the ways in which reading and writing are represented to students and the occasions students have to participate as readers and writers within the classroom culture.

***Knowledge Construction through Interaction.***    The social perspective on learning asserts that learning to think, read, and write are not individual, independent activities. Instead, the acquisition of such functions begins with the interactions of parent and child, among siblings, or between teacher and students. The role of language and dialogue is critical, since it is through speech and social interaction that the learner acquires abilities such as reading and writing (Vygotsky, 1986).

Vygotsky (1978) proposed that in the early stages of development processes first appear between people on the social plane; they are jointly performed and constructed by teachers and students as they cooperatively engage in dialogue. Processes that begin as social and shared become internalized in a second phase. In this phase, students' performance is assisted by their own self-talk; social speech becomes internalized as egocentric speech and collaborative dialogue with oneself.

Finally, in a third phase, the self-directing speech of the learner goes underground as it becomes "inner speech." At this point, learners do not overtly vocalize or self-instruct, although self-talk may surface as the difficulty of the task increases. Learners do not simply take in information; they continually construct new, more complex meanings as they transform knowledge for application across a broad range of activities.

***Contextualized Activity and Assisted Learning.***    Vygotsky (1978) suggested that mental processes are context specific and are best situated and learned through practical activity. This implies that reading and writing instruction must engage students at all ability levels as participants in contextualized, authentic, and holistic activities. Vygotsky (1978) proposed that the difference between what a child can do alone and what he or she can do with the assistance of a more-capable other represents the "zone of proximal development" (ZPD) in which instruction should occur. The concept of the ZPD assumes that a deliberate transfer of control from the more knowledgeable to the less knowledgeable person takes place.

How the adult or more knowledgeable person assists the student in taking control of a process is integral to social views of learning. Assisted learning and instruction have been compared to a scaffold in that it provides support, but is also temporary and adjustable (Palincsar, 1984; Wood, Bruner, & Ross, 1976). This educational scaffolding involves structuring tasks through modeling, explaining, questioning, and feedback until the learner can operate independently and is essential to learning in a social view of reading and writing.

***Implications.***    Social perspectives on reading and writing address a number of the weaknesses identified in information-processing models. Specifically, they account for variations among cultures in literacy practices and in the ways students learn to read and write in different settings. They highlight the role of social context and bring our attention to the need to be sensitive to the values and practices of different cultural groups in schools. In addition, the focus on language as a cultural tool helps us understand how new learning is acquired and how important it is in developing new instructional strategies (McCarthey & Raphael, 1992).

Social perspectives emphasize that reading and writing are connected through their uses within the culture and through the role dialogue plays in the development of literacy. Although there is research on issues related to the role of culture in literacy practices and in cognition, little research has been done on the connections between reading and writing from this perspective.

## An Interactive Perspective on Reading and Writing

The interactive perspective on reading and writing described in this book is an amalgam of the cognitive information-processing and social views. It rests on several assumptions: (1) reading and writing are processes of constructing meaning; (2) the construction of meaning results from an interaction between the reader/writer and the context of the reading/writing situation; and (3) the interaction is dynamic, or variable, as a function of numerous reader/writer and contextual factors (see Figure 1.1). Meaning, in the form of skilled reading and writing performance, is generated from the interaction between the learner and the reading/writing context, and there are many factors that influence learners' ability to comprehend and compose. A general discussion of this perspective is provided below.

**FIGURE 1.1**
An Interactive View of Reading and Writing

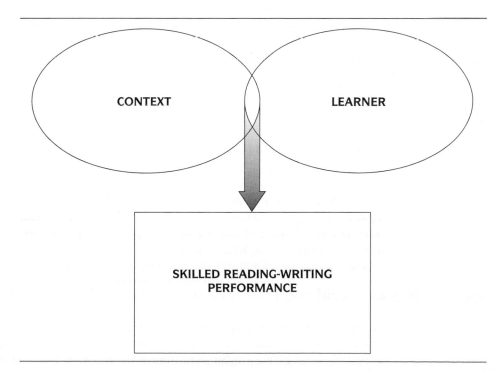

***Construction of Meaning in Reading and Writing.***   In addition, the interactive view acknowledges how development in reading and writing are interrelated. At both the word level (Bear & Templeton, 1998) and the discourse level (Tierney, 1992), writing informs reading and vice versa. An interactive perspective suggests that readers construct meaning when they comprehend in much the same way writers construct meaning when they compose. Meaning is created in the mind of the reader/writer as a function of the interplay between the cognitive information processing abilities of individuals and the context of the reading and/or writing event. As with the sociocultural perspective, skilled performance is viewed as the ability to use reading and writing for personal, recreational, academic, and civic purposes.

***Interactions.***   The interactive view argues that *both* cognitive information processing structures and sociocultural aspects of context influence reading and writing processes and performance. Reader/writer factors that affect reading and writing performance and processes include prior knowledge of content, knowledge about reading and writing processes, and attitudes and motivation. Context factors include the setting for learning, the reading and writing curriculum, and the instructional methods, materials, and tasks employed. Each of these factors has been shown to affect how people approach reading and writing tasks and also how well they perform.

***Dynamic Interactions.***   The term *dynamic* is used to indicate that reading and writing are variable processes, adapting to the specific demands of each particular reading/writing experience. Reading and writing ability are relative properties, not stable, static constructs. Each person may have several reading abilities and several writing abilities, depending on texts, tasks, and contexts. For example, we may be very good at writing friendly letters but do poorly at writing research papers, or we may devour romance novels with good comprehension but shudder at the thought of reading a book about the latest breakthroughs in physics.

***Implications.***   The variability within and across individuals means that reading and writing performance are a function of what learners *can* and *will* do at any given moment. Appropriate instruction requires that we understand the variability that exists within individual learners. Issues of linguistic background, motivation, and/or cultural understanding and values are each as relevant as whether the learner can read sight words or understands punctuation. Instruction that takes these issues into account focuses on providing students with a rich and diverse selection of reading materials and opportunities for ample self-selection during both reading and writing. In addition, students have opportunities to read and write for many different purposes.

## Understanding the Legal and Political Aspects of Reading and Writing

In this section we turn away from theoretical perspectives and toward legal and political perspectives on the acquisition of literacy among students who are struggling. Reading, especially early reading, has become a major topic of conversation and action in the political arena. The influence of policy on practice—at local, state, and national levels—has never been greater, and we examine some of the activity surrounding these issues. In addition, because they influence literacy instruction so strongly, we consider the legal and social basis for present-day *special education* programs and describe the specific provisions for meeting existing legal requirements in that arena.

## Questions of Early Reading and Reading Difficulty

Reading and literacy are at the heart of some of the most controversial debates about education. People care about how well students read and write. Some care about it because they are particularly concerned about reading and writing. Others care about it because they view it as a general indicator of the health of public schools. Finally, some care about it because the methods of reading instruction may be emblematic of philosophical or personal orientations toward larger issues such as student-centered versus curriculum-centered learning.

We cannot, of course, take on all of these issues in this book. However, we cannot avoid them either. Many of the theoretical and pedagogical arguments are not new (see Lemann, 1997, and Mathews, 1966, for a discussion of the "reading wars"). Certainly, old arguments have been resurrected in the current debate. However, the contemporary version of the debate is also an argument about which knowledge counts (and to whom) and also about who will decide.

To an extraordinary extent, the current debate is being conducted in state houses, legislative meeting rooms, and the halls of Congress. "This modern reform movement has been characterized by efforts to create new 'policy instruments' to elicit, encourage, or demand changes in teaching and learning" (Valencia & Wixson, 2000, p. 909). It should not be surprising, then, to see an entire section devoted to literacy policies in Volume III of *The Handbook of Reading Research* (see, e.g., Au, 2000; McGill-Franzin, 2000; Valencia & Wixson, 2000). Although states such as Texas and California stand out because their state legislatures have become involved in reading and reading instruction at the micro level, the influences of politics and policy can be observed in most states. Indeed, the most recent proposals for the Elementary and Secondary Education Act (ESEA) includes specific proposals for the content of reading instruction for early education. Whether by means of state-mandated assessments, statewide standards, or teacher preparation requirements, teachers and teacher educators find their ability to make decisions influenced or constrained (see Lipson, Mosenthal, Daniels, & Woodside-Jiron, 2000; McGill-Franzin, 2000; Valencia & Wixson, 2000).

This can have the positive effect of creating more coherent programs, providing support for less-skilled and knowledgeable teachers, and helping everyone to gain clarity about a state or community's shared goals. Depending on how policy is developed and implemented, it can also have the less positive effect of creating divisions among educators, promoting cynicism and distrust among the public, and calling into question the motives of the participants.

If they did not know this before, most teachers now understand that policies and practices can make a very big difference in the choices they have available to them. The political forays might seem distant from the classroom and from our work with individual students who are having reading difficulties. However, because these debates have become so public and so political, they affect instruction in significant ways. All states except Nebraska now have mandated state testing, for example (see McGill-Franzin, 2000). Similarly, most have state frameworks of standards. In many areas these debates have also influenced the nature of the programs or practices used to teach reading. Commercial publishers shape their programs to accommodate both the intellectual and political debates. Teachers might find that they *must* use a particular program to teach a specifically mandated component of reading using a predetermined methodology. Tests that assess only limited aspects of reading competence encourage teachers to address a narrower range of reading behaviors.

In other words, the policy perspective has moved into a central spot, governing (directly or indirectly) the decisions that teachers make every day. Debates rage about what types of text to use, whether students should be grouped or not, whether skills or literature should be taught, and whether to teach explicitly or implicitly.

These debates have recently triggered several significant attempts to specify the instructional imperatives for teaching reading. The National Academy of Sciences, through its Commission on Behavior and Social Sciences and Education, created a Committee on the Prevention of Reading Difficulties and charged the committee to synthesize research on early reading and reading difficulties. In 1998 this prestigious group published *Preventing Reading Difficulties* (Snow, Burns, & Griffin, 1998).

Shortly after that, Congress charged the director of the National Institute of Child Health and Human Development and the Secretary of Education to establish a panel of experts to synthesize and summarize the research-based knowledge related to teaching children to read. The charge was controversial, largely because the panel conceived of research so narrowly that it excluded a large amount of worthwhile literacy research and limited the usefulness of the findings for classroom teachers. The resulting document, Teaching Children to Read: An Evidence-Based Assessment of Scientific Research and Its Implications for Reading Instruction [National Reading Panel (NRP), 2000] was released amid significant debate (see, e.g., Garan, 2001; Shanahan, 2001). Although the summary of the NRP report has caused much concern, a reading of the full report suggests a complex perspective on reading and reading disability with few simple or simplistic answers.

Interestingly, each of these reports supports a balanced approach to instruction that is consistent with the interactive perspective described in this text. Throughout the book we will describe more fully our own interactive perspective, one that we believe successfully accounts for a wide array of research findings and provides a place in the dialogue for a perspective that honors both the findings of research and the diverse contexts of teaching and learning in U.S. schools.

## Legal and Social Roots of Special Education

During the 1950s and 1960s a combination of social and political factors combined to create an environment in which unusual and extensive attention was focused on students who were failing to learn easily and well in the public schools of the United States. National attention was captured by a series of legal battles initiated by a group of advocates who wanted to see that all students received appropriate public education.

Bricker (1986) relates the history of one such legal battle, *PARC* v. *Commonwealth of Pennsylvania* (1971), in which the court concluded that students had been excluded or excused from attendance in public schools simply because they were retarded and ordered the state to support public education for such students. As a result, "for the first time, any school-age child, no matter how impaired, was eligible to receive a free, appropriate public education" (Bricker, 1986, p. 106).

Access to public education was only one of the problems confronting the field at that time, however. The practices surrounding testing and labeling students were suspect for many reasons. For minority students the problems of abuses and inadequate protections were particularly apparent. Two other cases were directly related to practices in these areas. The decisions handed down by the court in *Diana* v. *Board of Education* (1970) and *Larry P.* v. *Riles* (which started in 1971 and concluded in 1979) required that the state of California test students in their primary language, reevaluate students from minority groups (African Americans, Latinos, and Asians) currently in classes for the mentally retarded, and develop and standardize IQ tests appropriate for minority groups.

A final concern among advocates in the area of special education involved the treatment and instruction provided to handicapped individuals once they were placed in specialized institutional settings. In two cases, *Wyatt* v. *Stickney* and *New York ARC* v. *Rockefeller,* judges ruled that residents of such placements had the right to appropriate treatment, and in the *Wyatt* case the judge specified that this treatment should occur in the least restrictive environment (Bricker, 1986).

The active round of legal rulings prompted both attention and concern and provided the basis for the legislative initiatives to follow. Beginning in the early 1960s, laws were passed that established federal programs related to service, training, and research designed specifically for the handicapped. These legislative actions culminated with the passage of Section 504 of the Rehabilitation Act of 1973 and the Education for All Handicapped Act (PL 94-142) in 1975. Replaced by the Individuals with Disabilities Education Act (PL 101-476, or IDEA) in 1990, it was further amended in 1997. Taken together, these legislative actions define disability, describe the roles of various individuals in the identification of students and the planning of instructional programs, and guide decisions about procedures for identification, placement, and programs of students with special needs.

Although Section 504 was actually passed before the other legislation, the regulations came out several years later, and many schools were slow to adopt the provisions of Section 504. On the other hand, all schools are well aware of the provisions of IDEA, which mandates the following:

- The right to education—all handicapped children are to be provided with free, appropriate, public education;
- The right to nondiscriminatory evaluation;
- The right to an IEP (Individualized Education Plan)—a clear statement of objectives for each child along with documentation of the child's current and expected performance;
- The right to education in the least restrictive environment;
- The right to due process;
- The right of parental participation (Gallagher, 1984).

## Special Education Identification

The actual procedures for implementing the mandates of IDEA vary somewhat from community to community, but the process must include provisions for meeting each mandate. Practically speaking, a teacher, administrator, or parent may make an initial referral in order to determine whether a student is entitled to special education services. Following this referral, the child's parents must be fully informed about the prospective assessment process and permission to proceed must be received from them. Only after these stages have been completed are assessment procedures initiated to determine whether the student meets federal and local guidelines for exceptionality. In addition, the assessment is usually designed to determine the category of handicap that will be used for purposes of classification.

IDEA clearly specifies procedures for the assessment phase. The procedures designed to address the mandate that students have "the right to nondiscriminatory evaluation" are as follows:

- Tests must be selected and administered so as to ensure that results "accurately reflect the child's aptitude and achievement . . . rather than reflecting the child's impaired sensory, manual, or speaking skills";
- No single testing procedure may be used for determining an appropriate educational program for the child;
- The evaluation must be conducted by a multidisciplinary team;
- The child must be assessed in all areas related to health, vision, hearing, social and emotional status, academic performance, communicative status, and motor abilities (see IDEA Regulations, C.F.R. § 300.532).

In addition, the law provides guidelines for the types of assessment instruments that may be used, stating that tests and other evaluation materials should:

- Be provided and administered in the child's native language;
- Have been validated for the specific purpose for which they are used;
- Be administered by trained personnel;
- Include materials tailored to assess specific areas of educational need and not merely those that are designed to provide a single general intelligence quotient (see IDEA Regulations, C.F.R. § 300.532).

When the assessment phase is completed, IDEA states clearly that there will be a meeting to develop the child's individualized education plan (IEP). As was previously noted, the IEP is mandated by the federal government and requires a clear statement of objectives for each child along with documentation of the child's current and expected performance. In addition, the IEP must contain a statement that specifies who will be responsible for each component of the plan and ensures periodic reevaluation of the child's status.

The most recent IDEA regulations require that the multidisciplinary team involved in developing the IEP must include a public education representative, who is qualified to provide or supervise the provision of special education, a regular education teacher, the child's teacher, one or both of the child's parents, the child where applicable, and other individuals at the discretion of the parent or agency (see IDEA Regulations, C.F.R. § 300.344).

The parent(s) must agree to the designation of the child under a particular handicapping condition and to the information provided in the IEP. If the parents do not agree with the recommendations of the team, a series of legal procedures are set in motion to settle the disagreement.

## Students with Disabilities

According to IDEA, a student's eligibility for special education services is determined by the type and degree of deficit in a particular area, following the guidelines developed through legal and judicial channels. There are currently nine categories of special needs students:

1. Mental impairment
2. Hearing impairment
3. Visual impairment
4. Speech impairment
5. Orthopedic impairment
6. Other health impairments (limited vitality, strength, or alertness due to chronic or acute health problems)
7. Multiply handicapped
8. Serious emotional impairment
9. Specific learning disability

In most respects the procedures and practical implications for students and schools is the same across IDEA and Section 504. All students who are eligible for special services under IDEA are also eligible for the protections of Section 504. However, Section 504 has a broader definition for eligibility, and some students may be eligible under Section 504 who would not meet the criteria for services under IDEA. Any student whose disability "substantially limits a major life activity or is regarded as a handicap by others" may be eligible. Thus, students with certain medical conditions (e.g., asthma, allergies, communicable diseases) or students with attention deficit hyperactivity disorder, behavior problems, or drug or alcohol problems may require support under Section 504.

Eligibility for children in many categories is established early and unequivocally because many handicapping conditions are apparent prior to a student's entrance into school. However, learning disability and the less-severe cases of mental and emotional impairment are often identified after a student has entered school and failed to meet certain academic expectations.

Reading and writing personnel are often involved with students who have been identified as having special needs in the area of learning disability because the referral is frequently made on the basis of a student's academic performance in the area of reading and writing. "Over 75–80% of school-age students with mild disabilities (i.e., learning disabilities, mild mental retardation, emotional disturbance, and behavioral disorders) experience significant problems in basic language and reading skills (Ellis & Cramer, 1994)" (quoted in Gaffney & Anderson, 2000, p. 71). Learning-disabled students currently account for well over half of the children served through special education programs (Allington, 1994).

Learning disability is defined by the federal government in the following manner:

> "Specific learning disability" means a disorder in one or more of the basic psychological processes involved in understanding or in using language, spoken or written, which may manifest itself in an imperfect ability to listen, think, speak, read, write, spell, or to do mathematical calculations. The term includes such conditions as perceptual handicaps, brain injury, minimal brain dysfunction, dyslexia, and developmental aphasia. The term does not include children who have learning problems which are primarily the result of visual, hearing, or motor handicaps, of mental retardation, of emotional disturbance, or of environmental, cultural, or economic disadvantage. (*Federal Register,* Dec. 29, 1977, 65083)

It is important to understand how learning disability is related to other controversial issues surrounding reading and writing disability. For example, the similarity between the definition of learning disability and the definition of dyslexia offered by the World Federation of Neurology has not been lost on most educators:

> [Dyslexia] is a disorder manifested by difficulty in learning to read despite conventional instruction, adequate intelligence, and sociocultural opportunity. It is dependent upon fundamental cognitive disabilities which are frequently of constitutional origin. (Critchley, 1975)

These definitions suggest that for all practical purposes *learning disability* and *dyslexia* are synonymous. What is most important is that both definitions clearly imply either a medical or nonspecified etiology within the learner. As Spear-Swerling and Sternberg (1998) note, the intrinsic perspective has dominated the field of reading and learning disability for many decades. In this view, the students' difficulties are seen as internal and intrinsic to the learner. The extrinsic perspective, drawing attention to the quality and nature of school experiences, poverty rate, or linguistic variations, has never taken root in the special education literature. The interactive view has only recently generated interest among educators and researchers in that field.

## The Implications for Practice

Although it may appear that special education determinations are straightforward, they are generally far from clear-cut. In addition, schools throughout the country are struggling to decide what programs to offer, who should deliver instruction, and who is eligible for various special programs. For reading and writing professionals and for students who need help in reading and writing, these issues can be troublesome. More than any other classification of handicap, that of learning disabilities has revived discussion about the source of disability. In the process, troubling sociological issues have been raised as well.

Until recently, the "learning disability" category was most likely to be used in identifying affluent and middle-class students. As a result, these students received federally mandated support through special education. Poor students and those from diverse backgrounds were more likely to receive support (when they received any additional help at all) from the nonmandated compensatory education system.

Chapter 1 of the Elementary and Secondary Education Act was originally passed in 1965 and was conceived as a program to provided additional educational assistance (compensatory education) to schools with large numbers of low-income families. It has been revised several times since then, presently providing services in eligible schools through Title I programs. Title I (previously Chapter 1) services are available in most elementary schools in the country, serving 25 percent of all primary-grade students (see McGill-Franzin, 2000).

More recently, researchers and educational policy experts have found that students from diverse backgrounds are disproportionately represented among both the special education and remedial populations (Donovan & Cross, 2002; Patton, 1998). There is some evidence that students who might have, in the past, received support through compensatory education programs are now being identified as "learning disabled" because the availability of other funds has diminished (McGill-Franzin, 1994). What is important to realize is that these decisions to label students or place them in remedial programs have specific and serious instructional consequences. According to Au (2000, p. 840), "Students of diverse backgrounds, who tend to be categorized as poor readers, are likely to spend more time working on skills in isolation and less time actually reading and writing."

Several studies have challenged the efficacy of Title I/Chapter 1 programs (see Allington & McGill-Franzin, 1989; Puma et al., 1997). However, recent studies of Title I/Chapter 1 suggest that schools can affect the reading performance of students in high-poverty areas. The implementation of a model that permits schoolwide classroom improvement projects (rather than individual remediation) and professional development for systemic reform appears to be central to success. Drawing on national data from the National Assessment of Education Progress (NAEP, 1996), McGill-Franzin (2000, p. 893) notes that, although still wide, "the achievement gap between Whites and minorities was reduced by one third during the (past) two decades, a time of increasing poverty for many families. This phenomenon has been attributed in part to federal educational interventions like Chapter 1."

Not surprisingly, perhaps, students whose first language is not English also receive instruction within a confusing context of policy and practice. The first Bilingual Education Acts (BEA) of 1968 initiated experimental demonstration projects for educating language minority students from low-income families. The reauthorization of the BEA in 1974 eliminated the requirement that students must be poor to qualify for services, and the 1978 reauthorization expanded services to include students with limited academic proficiency as well as those with limited English proficiency. Importantly, these early versions required schools to attend to students' native languages and cultures. Subsequent reauthorizations (1984, 1988, 1994) have not ensured that students receive appropriate instructional support and have directed resources toward English-only and/or transition programs.

Once again, the impact of these social and political influences on students' opportunity to learn is significant (Garcia, 2000). As summarized by Crawford (1997, p. 7), the problem is a serious one: "A substantial minority of LEP children—estimates range from 22 to 30 percent—receive no language assistance whatsoever (Crawford, 1997; Donly, Henderson, & Strang, 1995; Moss & Puma, 1995). That is, as many as 1.1 million children, depending on which estimate of the LEP population one uses may be receiving no (English language instruction)."

Research has consistently demonstrated that students benefit from receiving early reading instruction in their native language (Cummins, 1998; Snow, Burns, & Griffin, 1998), and the 1994 reauthorization of the Bilingual Education Act establishes "proficient bilingualism as a desirable goal, which can bring cognitive, academic, cultural, and economic benefits to individuals and to the nation" (Crawford, 1997, p. 1). However, strong opposition to bilingual education and a widespread advocacy for English-only schools has meant that "the political climate for bilingual education has never been chillier" (Crawford, 1997, p. 2).

The existence of two or even three distinct systems for handling reading, writing, and language difficulties creates an environment in which cohesive planning and intervention are often impossible. In many schools today, there are both special education and literacy professionals (Title I or locally supported developmental-reading teachers) serving students with reading and writing problems. In addition, teachers of ESL and ELL (English Language Learner) often encounter students with literacy difficulties, but these teachers rarely interact in coordinated ways with the other professionals.

Although special programs can bring badly needed resources to schools and classrooms, there are costs associated with the potential benefits. Too often, classroom teachers see children in terms of the classifications used to get them help. The funds that are used to provide compensatory education are associated with high-poverty students, who are not infrequently seen as "educationally deprived" or "without background knowledge." Similarly, English language learners have been viewed as "culturally deprived" or "linguistically deficient" (see Crawford, 1997). Finally, Coles (1978) argued many years ago that the "learning disabled" label is an example of "biologizing social problems." By positing biological bases for learning problems, the responsibility for failure is put "within the head of the child" rather than placed on the shoulders of schools, communities, and other institutions. "The classification plays its political role, moving the focus away from the general educational process, away from the need to change institutions, away from the need to appropriate more resources for social use toward the remedy of a purely medical problem" (Coles, 1978, p. 333).

In other words, these labels and classifications may encourage teachers to think that these students are no longer their primary responsibility. The cost to all of us may be greater than we realize. Allington (1994, pp. 104–105) suggests, "As schools have been expected to educate a greater proportion of children to increasingly higher standards of literacy, the regular education bureaucracy has put in place an increasing array of special programs and employed an expanding bevy of special personnel in attempts to minimize the roles and responsibilities of the regular education system in educating all children." He further argues that it is this sense of regular education's retreat from responsibility that has led the United States Department of Education to call for reducing exclusionary programs and set the stage for the current inclusionary education initiative for educating handicapped children (Will, 1986). This concern has also led to a shift in federal program guidelines indicating that the academic success of disadvantaged students is the responsibility of the whole school, not just the Title I/Chapter 1 program (LeTendre, 1991) or the bilingual program (August & Hakuta, 1994, 1997).

### Integration/Inclusion

It is clear that there are stronger and more frequent calls for addressing the instructional needs of students with special needs within the mainstream classroom setting. Although the pace and the effort vary considerably, movements for *full inclusion* mean that many special education students now often receive their education in the mainstream setting (Smith, Polloway, Patton, & Dowdy, 1995; Villa & Thousand, 1995). In addition, criticisms of pullout programs in Title I/Chapter 1 have also intensified (Allington & McGill-Franzen, 1989; Slavin, 1989). Although the majority of students in those programs still receive instruction in small-group settings out of the classroom, there is no doubt that this has changed and continues to change. Finally, there is no doubt that schools are serving an increasingly diverse student population (Crawford, 1997; Day, 1992).

Although there is little doubt that neurological or constitutional dysfunction plays a role in certain cases of reading and writing disability, the percentage of cases accounted for by identifiable neurological problems appears to be extremely small (Spear-Sweling & Sternberg, 1998; Vellutino et al., 1996). The majority of difficulties in reading and writing are more likely to result from a complex interaction between the learner and the reading and writing situation. It is this complex interaction to which we turn our attention for the remainder of the text.

All this means that all teachers, whether "special," "regular," or "remedial," need to consider individual differences among students. In addition, they need the skills and knowledge to work in multiple settings with other professionals. For many this means new roles and responsibilities.

## Chapter Summary

This chapter began with the idea that theories of reading and writing are important because they help us make decisions about assessment and instruction. We then suggested how reading and writing came to be treated separately in education and how the recent "cognitive revolution" and "social turn" have led to more integrated views of reading and writing.

Cognitive information-processing perspectives on reading and writing were described as emphasizing subprocesses in reading and writing, readers and writers as limited-capacity processors, and speed of processing. This view has increased our understanding of reading and writing processes in terms of their components and the knowledge base of skilled readers and writers but cannot account for the variability in performance that occurs as a result of a host of social and cultural factors.

Social perspectives on reading and writing were described as emphasizing reading and writing as social and cultural phenomena, knowledge as constructed through the individual's interaction with the sociocultural environment, and the acquisition of cognitive processes as related to reading and writing through contextualized activity and assisted learning. Social perspectives were seen as addressing some of the weaknesses observed in information-processing views and as helpful in formulating pedagogical goals and strategies for reading and writing.

The interactive view of reading and writing that serves as the basis for this text was characterized as an amalgam of the information-processing and social views. This perspective suggests that reading and writing are processes of constructing meaning through a dynamic interaction between the reader/writer and the context of the reading/writing situation. This means that reading and writing are not static but vary as a function of *contextual factors* such as setting, curriculum, and instructional conditions and *reader/writer factors* such as background knowledge, motivation, and interests. These interactions are described more fully in Chapter 2.

The second section of this chapter described the legal, social, and political influences on reading instruction and briefly discussed the contemporary disputes over reading instruction. Two recent syntheses of the research provide support for the interactive view proposed in this text. We then described the legislative and legal basis for special programs, including compensatory education and special education (IDEA and Section 504). The provisions and protections in IDEA for the rights of all handicapped children were noted, and the procedures for implementing these provisions were discussed. Criticisms were presented of all three "entitlement" programs—special education, Title I, and bilingual education—as mechanisms for minimizing the roles and responsibilities of regular education in educating all children. Responses to these criticisms have led to the inclusionary education movement in special education and the movement to schoolwide programs for addressing concerns about poor reading achievement.

# 2  An Interactive View of Reading and Writing

The interactive view of reading and writing described in the first chapter provides the framework for thinking about the nature of reading and writing. We now turn our attention to a discussion of skilled reading and writing and the factors that interact and influence performance in these areas. Throughout this chapter we describe evidence that even the most mechanical aspects of reading and writing are influenced by both contextual and learner factors.

As we examine the conventional components of reading and writing performance, we need to consider also how these learner and contextual factors interact to influence student performance. If a complex and dynamic view of reading and writing is not used during assessment, we run the risk of developing a distorted picture of the reading and writing processes. Inaccurate or incomplete conclusions may be drawn about students, and ineffective or harmful instruction may result.

## Understanding the Elements of Skilled Performance

It is easy to lose sight of the target of skilled reading and writing when we are working with less able readers and writers. In the past both assessment and instruction have too often focused on isolated aspects of students' knowledge and skill. Although we consider component aspects of reading and writing in the chapters that follow, we should always start with, and return to, questions of how these relate to skilled and motivated comprehension and composition.

So what is desirable performance in reading and writing? First and foremost, readers and writers read and write. They *use* their knowledge and skill to accomplish personal, recreational, academic, and civic purposes (Michigan Reading Association, 1993). This also means that reading and writing are not defined by classroom practices and texts but move out into authentic, real-world materials and tasks. Readers and writers can and do apply their knowledge and skill in flexible ways to accomplish meaningful tasks, suggesting that both reading and writing are adaptive and intentional activities (Dole, Duffy, Roehler, & Pearson, 1991). In addition, readers and writers from diverse backgrounds need to be able to perform appropriately in a wide range of contexts.

People generally associate literacy with the ability to read and write. This is the common dictionary definition, the mark of literacy in society at large, and the one generally thought of in regard to schooling. However, literacy can be viewed in a broader and educationally more productive way, as the ability to think and reason like a literate person, *within a particular society.* As Vygotsky (1978) suggested, because the practices of literacy and ways of understanding them depend upon the social conditions in which they are learned, the skills, concepts, and ways of thinking that an individual develops reflect the uses and approaches to literacy that permeate the particular society in which that person is a participant. (Langer, 1991, p. 11)

Over the past three decades we have come to know a great deal about the nature of skilled and motivated reading and writing performance and the learner and about the contextual factors that influence performance (see Figure 2.1). These are the elements and factors that we must examine in the assessment and instruction of students who are experiencing problems in reading and writing. We discuss first the elements of skilled performance and then the factors that influence it.

There is some risk in pulling out elements of skilled performance for discussion. In doing so, we may lead some to believe that these are isolated or entirely separable components of reading and writing. However, as we have already discussed and will demonstrate again a bit later, each of these elements interacts with others and is influenced by contextual and learner factors. In short, the whole of skilled performance is variable and dynamic. As educators and clinicians, though, we need to have some idea of the component elements so that we can consider which of these are targets for assess-

**FIGURE 2.1**
An Elaborated
Interactive View of
Reading and Writing

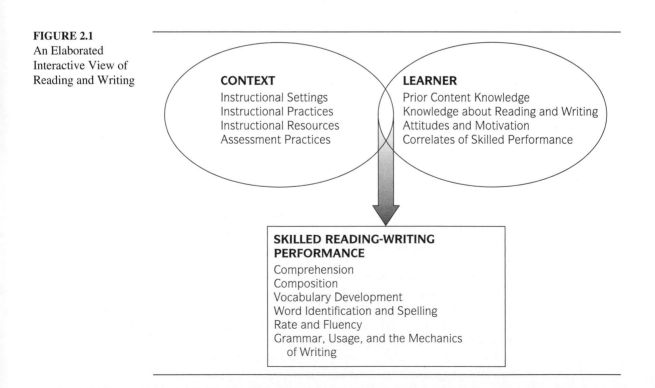

ment and instruction. Skilled reading and writing performance comprises the following elements.

## Comprehension

Comprehension is the ability to use previously acquired information to construct meaning for a given text. The two aspects of comprehension considered here are reading for understanding and reading to learn and/or remember.

*Reading for Understanding.* This area focuses primarily on readers' ability to reason their way through a text by integrating existing knowledge with new information, drawing inferences, and forming and testing hypotheses. The goal of comprehension is the construction of an integrated representation of the information suggested by a text that is appropriate for the reading purpose. Other activities that are critical to good comprehension include establishing purposes for reading, identifying important elements of information and their relations within text, monitoring one's comprehension, and dealing with failures to comprehend (Baker & Brown, 1984).

The successful accomplishment of the activities that comprise good comprehension requires the use of a variety of strategies (Dole, Duffy, Roehler, & Pearson, 1991). Although there is no comprehensive list of such strategies, we can identify a range of possible strategies that are appropriate for different activities. As in the case of word analysis strategies, no one strategy is necessarily more or less important than the others. Rather, the appropriateness of a given strategy is determined by its utility in the interaction between a reader and a specific reading situation (Duffy, 1993). What matters most is how effective and efficient a strategy is for accomplishing a specific purpose.

Rather than focusing on the mastery of prerequisite skills, the interactive approach focuses assessment and instruction on the behaviors or activities that characterize good comprehension. Skills and strategies are the means to achieving the goal of good comprehension, not the end itself. It is important to keep this in mind, lest our old lists of skills be replaced by new lists of strategies and our assessment and comprehension instruction remain unchanged from past practices.

*Reading to Remember/Learn.* Reading to learn and/or remember what has been comprehended or understood from text is often referred to as studying. Three primary activities are involved in effective studying. First, students must be able to preview text to familiarize themselves with its form and content and to make plans for reading. Second, students must be able to locate specific information within the text. Third, students must be able to identify the organization of information within the text.

As with comprehension, the successful accomplishment of studying activities requires the use of a variety of strategies. These strategies may include outlining, note taking, summarizing, self-questioning, diagramming or mapping text, and underlining, as well as many of the strategies that are used in comprehending. What is most important is students' ability to select and apply these strategies in a manner that is appropriate to the study task at hand. It is not a question of which study strategies are best, but of how effective a selected strategy is in a given study situation.

## Composition

Writing is essentially idea making. Drawing on their own knowledge of language and the conventions of various written genres, writers create texts for readers to use. The writing process refers to a series of nonlinear activities in which students engage to produce a finished piece of writing. These include prewriting, drafting, revising, editing, and publishing. To counteract the idea that these activities are discrete steps or stages, Pappas, Keifer, and Levstik (1995) refer to them as experiences of the composing process and provide descriptions of each of these writing experiences as follows.

*Prewriting Experiences.*    Prewriting is generating and exploring ideas, recalling and rehearsing ideas, relating and probing ideas, planning, thinking, and deciding. Prewriting experiences occur when we talk, listen, read, research, observe, and so forth. They often include writing itself in forms such as notes, brainstorming, and outlines. Prewriting is an ongoing experience rather than a distinct period of writing and can interact with other writing experiences.

*Drafting Experiences.*    Drafting involves attempts to get the ideas down and create a whole text. Writers try not to worry too much about spelling and punctuation during drafting because they know that the text will be reconsidered, rearranged, and revised. Drafting can be interrupted by prewriting and can occur simultaneously with revising.

*Revising Experiences.*    Revising has to do with attempts to rethink, review, remake, reconstruct, and reexamine the text. Revising is an ongoing activity that can occur during prewriting or during and after drafting. The writer becomes a reader when the text is reread and revised. This is also when other readers such as teachers and peers may interact with the text and provide feedback. Readers' responses to draft text may lead to more drafting as well as more prewriting.

*Editing Experiences.*    Editing is intended to clean up text so that its message is communicated by using the most appropriate language. It involves changing words and sentences, changing, deleting, or rearranging them to make the message more clear. The tone or style of the text, as well as the spelling, punctuation, and grammar, is also checked during editing.

*Publishing Experiences.*    Classroom publishing emphasizes sharing. The publishing of final drafts takes various forms in terms of the nature of the final product and how it is shared. Because publishing has to do with sharing in general, it can apply to any writing, not just final drafts. Publishing can also occur with a range of audiences within the classroom or beyond in the school, community, or even state and national newspapers and magazines.

In summary, writing is a social, constructive, meaning-making process that consists of a variety of writing experiences in the production of texts representing a variety of genres. Both the text product and the process of constructing text are important.

## Vocabulary Development

The importance of vocabulary development as a major contributor to reading comprehension has long been acknowledged and widely studied (Bauman & Kameenui, 1991; National Reading Panel, 2000). Skilled reading and writing require knowledge of the meanings of words and the ability to infer and learn the meanings of new words. Words are the labels for objects and ideas and provide an index of readers' and writers' prior knowledge. Readers and writers who do not have adequate knowledge of important words and concepts and/or are unable to determine word meanings will have difficulty successfully comprehending or composing texts.

The relationship between vocabulary development and reading apparently extends beyond its significant impact on comprehension. According to Snow, Burns, and Griffin (1998, p. 47), for example, there is a "well-documented link between vocabulary size and early reading ability: the development of fine within-word discrimination ability (phonemic representations) may be contingent on vocabulary size rather than age or general developmental level." In addition, but perhaps not surprisingly, vocabulary has been identified as a critical factor in second-language students' reading difficulties (Kim, 1995).

During the preschool years children's vocabulary grows at an average of seven words per day, or 2,500–3,000 words a year (Nagy & Herman, 1987). However, vocabulary development is not simply the number of dictionary definitions of words that students have acquired. The primary focus of this area is the depth, breadth, and organization of students' vocabulary knowledge which seems to be much more complex and interconnected than was previously thought.

Although students' knowledge of specific vocabulary is important, we must consider ability to infer and to learn the meanings of new words and concepts as well. Students are frequently confronted in their reading with new words for which they may not already have a concept. Students need to develop strategies, such as different types of contextual and morphemic analysis as described in the next section, for inferring the meanings of unfamiliar vocabulary and independently increasing their vocabulary learning. Indeed, humans appear to store and learn words using a highly elaborated mechanism for making connections. Word knowledge seems to grow because people establish relationships between new words and previously acquired words and concepts (Nagy & Scott, 2000). In addition, these newly acquired words change and influence the word meanings that were already stored in vocabulary.

## Word Identification and Spelling

Rapid word identification is an essential component of skilled reading. Students must be able to recognize familiar words quickly and to decode unfamiliar words rapidly enough that the process of meaning construction is not unduly interrupted. As they read, people use a repertoire of word identification strategies and recruit a wide array of knowledge and skill. This information and these skills are related to each other but also make separate contributions to performance. That is, although readers and writers who are strong in one component area are generally strong in others, these can and do vary among individuals and may produce difficulties in some readers or writers.

***Sight Word Recognition.***    The most efficient form of word identification occurs when students recognize words immediately on sight, without sounding them out or using any other strategy to help identify them. Words that can be recognized instantly are called *sight words* and are considered part of a student's *sight vocabulary.*

Sight words fall into several categories, especially in early reading. The first words that children can recognize in print are generally *"high-potency"* words (Hunt, n.d.), such as their own and other family members' names and words with heavy contextual support such as *McDonald's* (Hiebert, 1981). These words are relatively easy to remember because of their visual distinctiveness and/or because of the strong affect attached to them (Ashton-Warner, 1963).

A second type of sight words is the *high-frequency function* words (*the, of, but*) that appear over and over in written texts. These words are difficult to decode or figure out using word analysis strategies because they are irregular and may not follow basic decoding rules. They are often more difficult to remember than other words because many are similar in appearance (*where, there, here, when, then*). These words are usually learned as sight words when children are first learning how to read; however, many poor readers have not mastered these words even by seventh or eighth grade. Limited recognition of these high-frequency sight words affects fluency and comprehension.

The last type of sight words includes all of the other words that students have learned to recognize instantly. Many of these words are *content* words (*meal, bake, animal*) that are already part of a child's speaking or listening vocabularies. These words are often read initially through the application of various word analysis strategies and become sight words after repeated exposure through reading. Many poor readers simply do not read enough to acquire a sufficient number of these sight words. Others may rely too heavily on one or another of the word analysis strategies that are discussed in the next section. Either way, children who do not develop an adequate sight vocabulary are likely to have difficulty in all aspects of reading.

***Word Analysis Strategies.***    These strategies are used to identify printed words that we do not recognize immediately on sight. Unfortunately, word analysis has often been perceived as consisting only of (grapho)phonic analysis. Students may employ a variety of word analysis strategies, and no one strategy is necessarily any better or worse than another. Children who rely too heavily on only one strategy often produce distorted reading and have limited comprehension.

Although it might seem that skilled readers move through text so quickly that they must be recognizing every word at sight, it is clear that they actually do speed their word recognition by using graphophonic (letter–sound correspondence) cue systems within our language and by making predictions about words based on the context (meaning and sentence structure). For example, it is the contextual cue system that enables us to predict that the missing word in the sentence "The window in the kitchen of our new _____ is beautiful" could be either *house, home,* or *apartment.* However, it is the graphophonic cue system that assists you in determining that the missing word in the sentence "Our new h _ r _ _ is beautiful" is *horse* instead of *house* or *home.*

The utility of a given strategy depends on its effectiveness in the situation in which it is being applied. Therefore, children need to have a repertoire of word analysis strategies that are available for use in a variety of reading situations. *Contextual analysis* and *morphemic analysis* are both meaning-based word identification strategies. *Phonic analysis* is a strategy based on sound–symbol correspondence that results in approximate pronunciation of individual words.

*Contextual Analysis.*   Probably the most common method of word identification is to use the context of the sentence in which the unknown word appears and/or the context that surrounds the sentence to determine what the word is most likely to be. Mature readers make use of two sorts of context during reading: general and local context (Durkin, 1983). General context is provided by the central topic and general organization of a text. For example, one would expect a story about the circus to include words such as *ringmaster, clown, acrobat, elephant,* and *trapeze* or a chapter on heredity to include words such as *gene, meiosis,* and *chromosome.* Obviously, the use of general context requires prior knowledge about the topic of the text. Clues provided by the graphic aids in a text such as charts, maps, illustrations, titles, and subtitles, are also likely to contribute to the general context of a text.

Readers who use local context take their cue from the phrases and sentences that surround an unknown word. For example, if you read, "Nora wished she had a _____ so _____ could listen to her favorite station," you would expect the first word to be *radio* or possibly *Walkman,* because these are what we use to listen to a station. The possible choices are constrained by the syntactic and semantic cues provided by the local context. Skilled readers use context to derive word *meanings* but phonic analysis (see below) for word *recognition.*

*Morphemic Analysis.*   Morphemic analysis is a strategy in which the reader breaks down words into smaller meaning-bearing units as an aid to word identification and understanding. *Morpheme* is a linguistic term for the smallest unit of meaning in our language.

The meaning-bearing units used in morphemic analysis are root words, affixes, and inflections. For example, the word *returnables* can be divided into four meaningful parts: *re-, turn, -able,* and *-s.* The prefix *re-* and the suffix *-able* are affixes that change the function of the root word. The inflectional ending *-s* modulates the meaning of the root word without changing its function. Other common inflections signal possession (*-'s*), verb tense (*-ed, -ing*), or comparison (*-er, -est*). Finally, morphemic analysis can be used as an aid in the identification and understanding of compound words (for example, *fireman, breadbox*) and contractions (for example, *don't, he'll*).

*Phonic Analysis.*   The writing systems of some other languages are different, but English is an alphabetic language. Because it is, children must gain an understanding that what gets written (and read) is a representation of the sounds of the language. Specifically, they must learn which letters or letter combinations (graphemes) represent specific English sounds (phonemes). The ability to isolate *phonemes,* the linguistic term for the smallest unit of sound in our language, is central to successful application of phonic analysis. Words can be sounded out letter by letter or by using spelling patterns, letter clusters, or syllables that have predictable sounds.

This phonological knowledge is critical to skilled reading. As Barker, Torgeson, and Wagner (1992, p. 335) note,

> Skill at identifying words based on phonological information requires at least awareness of the phonological structure of words, knowledge of specific grapheme-phoneme correspondences, and skill in synthesizing the phonemes to produce a recognizable word. In many cases, phonological knowledge and skill can be used to identify words that have never before been encountered in print.

The specific graphophonic elements that are useful in phonic analysis are suggested by a framework for phonics instruction provided by Mason and Au (1990). These are consonant–sound relations in the initial, medial, and final positions in words; blends of two or three consonants in which each consonant retains its own sound (*spr, fl*); consonant digraphs, or combinations of two consonants that are pronounced as one sound (*ch, th*); and vowel–sound patterns represented by vowels followed by *r* or *l* (*ar*), and consonant–vowel–consonant (*sit*), consonant–vowel–consonant–silent *e* (*lake*), and consonant–vowel–vowel (*meal*).

The use of graphophonic information in longer words often requires *structural analysis.* In structural analysis, readers must recognize and segment by syllable boundaries (either through "rules" or by identifying recurrent spelling patterns) and then apply known graphophonic patterns to decode the segments (*seg/ment*) (see Figure 2.2).

Skilled readers most often decode unfamiliar words by comparing new, unknown words with known letter–sound combinations (Cunningham, 1975–76). Using knowledge of onsets and rimes and an analogy strategy is effective for readers with some knowledge of sound–symbol correspondence. However, some young children, especially those with very little phonological or letter knowledge, require specific instruction in individual phonemes and graphemes before they can use onsets and rhymes for decoding (Gaskins et al., 1996/1997; Vandervelden & Siegel, 1995).

***Orthographic Processes and Spelling.***    Most experts today agree that word identification in skilled readers involves two types of knowledge and skill: phonological and orthographic. Orthographic processes are linked to the appearance of specific words. "Orthographic knowledge involves memory for specific visual/spelling patterns that identify individual words, or word parts, on the printed page. Orthographic knowledge . . . would seem to be acquired by repeated exposure to printed words until a stable visual representation of the whole word, or meaningful subword units, has been acquired" (Barker, Torgeson, & Wagner, 1992, p. 336).

Although there are relatively strong relationships between orthographic and phonological skills in most individuals, it is also quite clear that these two abilities make unique and separate contributions to reading and writing performance (Juel, Griffith, & Gough, 1986; Olson, Wise, Conners, Rack, & Fulker, 1989). For example, orthographic skills appear to make a bigger difference in the reading of connected text (versus isolated word recognition) and also seem more highly related to fluency in reading (see below). It also appears that the relationships between phonological and orthographic skills are devel-

**FIGURE 2.2** The Synchrony of Literacy Development

**Reading and Writing Stages:**

| Emergent | | | Beginning | | | Transitional | | | Intermediate | | | Advanced | | |
|---|---|---|---|---|---|---|---|---|---|---|---|---|---|---|
| *Early* | *Middle* | *Late* | *Early* | *Middle* | *Late* | *Early* | *Middle* | *Late* | *Early* | *Middle* | *Late* | *Early* | *Middle* | *Late* |

Pretend read — Read aloud, word by word, fingerpoint reading — Approaching fluency, some expression in oral reading — Reads fluently with expression. Develops a variety of reading styles. Vocabulary grows with experience, reading, and writing.

Pretend write — Word-by-word writing, may write a few words or lines — Approaching fluency, more organization, several paragraphs — Writes fluently with expression and voice. Experiences different writing styles and genres. Writing shows personal problem solving and reflection.

**Spelling Stages:**

| Emergent ➔ | | | Letter Name— Alphabetic ➔ | | | Within Word Pattern ➔ | | | Syllables and Affixes ➔ | | | Derivational Relations ➔ | | |
|---|---|---|---|---|---|---|---|---|---|---|---|---|---|---|

*Examples:*

bed — b bd bad — bed

ship — s sp sep shep — ship

float — f ft fot flot flott — flowt floaut flote float

train — t trn jran tan chran trcn — teran traen trane train

cattle — c kd catl cadol — cotel catol cattel catol cattle

cellar — s sir sair celr — saler celer seler celler seller cellar

pleasure — p pjr plasr plager — plejer pleser plesher pleser plesher plesour pleasure pleasure

confident — confedent confiedret confedent confident confident

opposition — opasishan oppasishion oposision oposition oposition opposition

*Source:* From *Words Their Way*, 2nd ed., by D. R. Bear, M. Invernizzi, S. Templeton, and F. Johnston, p. 14. Copyright © 2000, 1996 by Prentice-Hall, Inc. Reprinted by permission of Pearson Education, Inc., Upper Saddle River, NJ.

opmental, with orthographic skill making a stronger contribution to word reading after first grade (that is, after the initial stages of reading acquisition).

What has become increasingly clear is the close relationship between early reading and spelling. Templeton recently emphasized the relationships between and among these abilities (personal communication, September 20, 2001):

> Research strongly suggests that a common core of word knowledge underlies the process of word identification in reading and the process of spelling words in writing . . . in fact, what students learn about words in appropriate spelling activities helps the developing process of reading more than reading helps the development of spelling knowledge (Bosman & van Orden, 1997; Ellis & Cataldo, 1990). Spelling supports the ability to read words in two ways: First, the memory for each specific word and its structure is reinforced; second, common spelling patterns across words are discerned and abstracted; the construct of pattern in turn supports recognition and identification of words during the reading process.

In short, the orthographic knowledge that students build up by studying word spellings and examining spelling patterns is precisely what helps them to move from decoding individual letters and sounds to storing and retrieving larger chunks (see the discussion of fluency in the next subsection).

It is likely that word study is initially more useful to reading than to spelling because the ability to spell appears to be a consequence of knowing about words in many ways—their visual or graphic characteristics, their phonological and structural properties, and their meanings. English does not have a one-to-one correspondence between graphemes (letters) and phonemes (sounds). The twenty-six letters of the alphabet represent approximately forty-four phonemes. To further complicate the situation, three letters—*c, q,* and *x*—do not represent unique phonemes, and there are anywhere between 500 and 2,000 spellings to represent the forty-four phonemes in English. The sheer number of spellings and the lack of fit between phonemes and graphemes suggest that children are unlikely to learn to spell simply through memorization or sounding out words.

Like learning to read and write, learning to spell is a developmental process. More than thirty years ago, the evidence began to show that young children, even preschoolers, use their knowledge of English phonology to invent spellings (Read, 1971, 1975, 1986). Since then, research has revealed that students move through stages in their spelling development and that these "stages are marked by broad, qualitative shifts in the types of spelling errors children commit" (Bear, Invernizzi, Templeton, & Johnston, 2000, p. 8). Students' knowledge and skill at each development stage are fairly predictable, although individual variation, the result of the sorts of interactions described earlier, are visible also (see Figure 2.2).

Not all children invent spellings in exactly the same way or at the same pace, but they do develop spelling strategies in roughly the same sequence (Henderson, 1980) and move through roughly the same stages to become conventional spellers (Gentry, 1981, 1982; Invernizzi, Abouzeid, & Gill, 1994). These stages are described more fully in Chapter 7 ("The Foundations of Literacy"). Generally, children move from early scribbles and letterlike forms to representing sounds without reference to conventional spelling combinations.

Eventually, children stop relying only on phonological information and begin to use morphological (word parts) and visual information to spell many words correctly.

Researchers continue to study children's spelling development in later years (see Bear & Barone, 1998; Bear & Templeton, 1998; Bear et al., 2000). For example, Firth (1980) found that older students who are good readers and spellers make spelling errors that are characteristic of the transitional stage, while students who are poor readers and spellers make errors that are characteristic of the semiphonetic and phonetic stages. Other studies indicate a developmental shift among better spellers from a reliance upon the phoneme–grapheme strategies used in the early school years toward a strategy of spelling words by analogy to other known words.

In summary, rapid and accurate word recognition is important to effective and efficient reading, and accurate spelling is important to effective communication in writing. A combination of strategies and abilities is useful, especially in the earliest stages of reading/writing acquisition. However, as quickly as possible, students need to acquire accurate and rapid word identification skills that appear dependent on both good phonologic and orthographic skills.

## Rate and Fluency

"Fluent readers can read text with speed, accuracy, and proper expression" (National Reading Panel, 2000, p. 3-1). Although accuracy and rate are related to fluency, they are not the same thing; oral fluency also involves readers' ability to group words into meaningful phrase units. Smoothness and the maintenance of comprehension are important as well (Harris & Hodges, 1995).

*Rate* of reading refers to the speed of oral and/or silent reading as measured in words per minute. Proficient reading requires *automaticity,* or the ability to identify words rapidly enough that sufficient resources are available for attention to comprehension. Research suggests that beginning readers who develop automatic word identification skills are better able to comprehend text (Perfetti & Hogaboam, 1975). How fast is fast enough and how slow is too slow are questions that are still open for debate, however. Norms for reading rate vary widely, and research designed to improve comprehension by teaching rapid word identification has produced equivocal results. It appears that reading rate may be a necessary but insufficient condition for proficient reading and that decisions about the adequacy of a student's reading rate may need to be made on an individual basis.

Allington (1983b) notes that fluency is often overlooked in assessment and instruction because it is mistakenly assumed that it is merely a symptom of poor word identification skills. Unfortunately, he argues further, this interpretation often leads to additional instruction in letters, sounds, or words in isolation in the mistaken belief that more attention to these areas will result in improved reading.

This is especially troubling because so many struggling readers are experiencing fluency difficulties. Evidence from a special study conducted along with the 1992 National Assessment of Educational Progress (NAEP) reading assessement suggests a strong relationship between oral fluency and silent reading comprehension (Pinnell et al., 1995). There is also evidence that high levels of fluency are related to ample opportunities to practice (Pinnell et al., 1995; Snow, Burns, & Griffin, 1998). This, in turn, is likely related to the fact that the development of good orthographic knowledge and skill seems to make a strong contribution to both rate and fluency. Perhaps, as Barker, Torgeson, and Wagner (1992) note, orthographic skills allow readers to recognize words in whole automatically, circumventing the need for more discrete levels of phonological analysis. This, in turn, allows readers to focus more attention on the other aspects of reading text, most notably, meaning.

## Grammar, Usage, and the Mechanics of Writing

Grammar is the description of the structure of a language based on principles of word and sentence formation. In the case of oral language, students will need to learn about the appropriate use of language in different social situations and contexts and the reasons for paying attention to appropriateness. In the case of written language, students will learn that most grammar and usage issues come into play during the revision and editing phases of the writing process. Through practice students gradually become more and more familiar with the conventions of grammar and usage, but at some point the "rules" of grammar and usage may need to be addressed directly. However, they must be viewed as part of a real social context or as part of the revising and editing phases of writing to be helpful.

*Grammar.*    Grammar can be defined as a system of rules by which words are arranged into meaningful units. Everyone who speaks and understands English knows the rules, even if they can't articulate them. For example, we know that *The dog chased the cat up the tree* is a grammatical sentence, while *Tree up cat dog the the chased the* is not, because it violates rules of English grammar. Because we are aware of the violations, we must, on some level, know the rules that have been violated, even if we can't state them clearly. Rules such as these are best characterized as *subconscious abstract concepts.*

In contrast, *explicit* rules have been created by individuals trying to describe English grammar as it is used. A perfect set of explicit rules would be one that described all of the sentences that most people would consider grammatical and excluded any that would not be considered grammatical. No one has ever developed a perfect set of rules, but linguists continue to try and in the process have developed different types of grammars. Elements of two kinds of grammar—structural and transformational—are most relevant to our concerns with grammar instruction and learning. These elements are: form classes or parts of speech; structures of common sentences; and transformation of sentences.

Structural grammar focuses on sentence patterns and the functions of words in sentences. It identifies four form classes resembling nouns, verbs, adjectives, and adverbs. All the words that can fill a particular slot in a sentence belong to the same class. Advocates of structural grammars describe patterns or basic sentence types. For example, Roberts (1962) developed a sequence of ten patterns that are frequently used in textbooks that use a structural approach (determiner–noun–verb [intransitive]–adverb).

Transformational grammar focuses on the process used to generate sentences and ideas. Using four or five basic sentence types (or kernels) as the starting point for making sentences, we add transformations to change our basic sentences into more complex ones. Three kinds of sentence transformations are those that (1) change one type of sentence into another, such as questions, negatives, and passive sentences; (2) conjoin elements of several sentences into compounds; and (3) reduce some sentences into fragments and insert them into other sentences (Malmstrom, 1968).

It appears that nearly all children can use the basic sentence types and that instruction in sentence combining is beneficial to a broad range of students, especially those who are less skilled (Hillocks, 1986). On the other hand, Applebee and his colleagues (Applebee et al., 1990), using data from the National Assessment of Educational Progress (NAEP), concluded that student writing among 9-, 13-, and 17-year-olds across the country revealed that very few have any significant difficulty with sentences or fragments.

*Usage.* Language usage concerns the various language standards considered appropriate for different occasions, audiences, and purposes. Everyone's language varies, depending on the formality of the occasion. The number of usage levels available differs according to different grammarians. One scheme suggests three possible levels of usage; nonstandard English, general English, and formal English (Lodge & Trett, 1968). However, it is important to recognize that language standards change from one group to another and with time. "In the final analysis, the appropriateness of usage must be determined within the social context in which the language is used" (Savage, 1977, p. 369).

*Mechanics of Writing.* The mechanics of writing include punctuation and capitalization. Punctuation and capitalization are important because they clarify meaning. During oral exchanges, listeners hear pauses, speech stops, and rising and falling intonation that help them construct meaning. Readers and writers replace these verbal signals with punctuation and capitalization.

Studies show that punctuation—particularly with commas and periods—is frequently a problem for elementary-age students (Porter, 1974). Most children seem to have fewer problems applying capitalization rules than applying punctuation rules. A recent NAEP report concluded that the writing of about 10 percent of the students reflected relatively serious problems with punctuation (Applebee et al., 1990). Thus, attention to punctuation will be an issue for some students or for many students in some settings.

## Understanding Contextual Factors That Influence Performance

Contextual factors are the least likely to be considered in any discussion of reading and writing performance. Indeed, the importance of context has only recently been realized. In the following sections we describe briefly several aspects of context that have been shown to influence reading and writing: the setting in which the reading and writing event occurs, the reading and writing curriculum, the instructional methods employed, and the instructional materials and tasks associated with reading and writing. This brief discussion serves only to introduce ideas that will be discussed at greater length in Chapters 5 and 6.

### Settings

The community and culture of students exert central, often critical, influence on achievement in reading and writing. It also appears that the willingness and ability of the school to respond to local and/or cultural characteristics has a powerful impact on reading and writing acquisition and performance and can determine the effectiveness of instruction and achievement (Gallego & Hollingsworth, 1992; Goldenberg & Gallimore, 1991). Home environments that are different from the dominant culture are not pathological. Students can be hopelessly handicapped, however, if the school expects and accepts only one type of entry experience from its students.

The setting in which reading and writing and their instruction take place affects reading and writing performance. Meaning making depends on the broader context in which a text is being written or read. For example, imagine that you are reading or writing a text on common antidotes to poisoning. Now imagine the effect that context would have in the following situations: the evening newspaper, a test of reading comprehension, at home after you believe your child has ingested some poisonous substance, and a first aid course.

Similarly, researchers have found differences in students' performance on the same task, depending on subtle changes in the classroom context, that is, whether students were asked to do the task as part of an informal lesson or as part of a formal testing situation (Mosenthal & Na, 1980). Indeed, several aspects of classroom settings have been examined and found to contribute to students' reading and writing achievement. For example, grouping patterns influence both teachers and students. Reviews of ability grouping for reading instruction suggest that instructional and social reading experiences differ for students in high- and low-ability reading groups and that these differences influence students' learning (Allington, 1983a; Hiebert, 1983). Grouping practices may also communicate information to students about their relative ability that eventually influences their learning (Opitz, 1998; Weinstein, 1976).

## Instructional Practices

***Standards and Curriculum.***   The standards and curriculum in particular school settings have a critical influence on student performance because they may influence access to instruction, dictate the type of instruction offered, and even determine what is counted as reading and writing performance. Teachers and schools decide what and how to teach by referring to the standards established by their district and/or state. The nature of these standards and the curriculum that grows out of them have often been controversial. In some places, standards setting has been an inclusive matter, leading to strengthened instruction and enhanced learning. In other places, standards appear to have been imposed, and the quality is uneven. In either case standards have the effect of making public what is valued in reading and writing (see Wixson & Dutro, 1999).

The reading curriculum has often been defined by commercially produced materials, typically basal reader series. A review of basal reading programs suggested that the curriculum presented by these programs had changed in the past decade (Hoffman et al., 1994). During the early 1990s, for example, the literature in anthologies was drawn from children's literature rather than contrived or commissioned pieces; the vocabulary was less stringently controlled; and there was a decreased focus on phonics and isolated skills instruction. Newer programs continue to emphasize good literature while providing controlled vocabulary options for early reading practice. In addition, they are likely to include more explicit phonics than was true just a short time ago.

For students who experience problems with reading and writing, the curriculum issue is even more complicated. When more children began attending school in the early part of the twentieth century, it was observed that not every student learned what they were supposed to learn at each grade level. In response to this observation American education adopted the position that it was not fair to hold all students to the same standards and searched for the most appropriate techniques for differentiating instruction and for setting differential educational goals (Allington, 1991).

Not until the 1970s and 1980s did people begin to suggest that what had been considered differentiation might actually be a form of discrimination (Carew & Lightfoot, 1979). It was observed that students with the least adaptive capacity were asked to make the greatest adjustments across the school day (Good, 1983), including exposure to multiple literacy curricula often representing divergent theories of reading and writing processes. Increasing evidence of the lack of efficacy of the "second system" programs that have evolved since the turn of the century (Allington, 1994) has resulted in the current movement toward establishing a common set of high-level curriculum standards for *all* students. Many believe that this is the only way to ensure that all students are provided equal opportunities to achieve.

The important point for this discussion is that the reading and writing curriculum has a tremendous impact on student performance. Many local school districts have their own curriculum as do many states. Curricula that reflect a more skills-based perspective are likely to promote very different procedures for instruction and assessment than curricula that reflect a more interactive or sociocultural perspective. The nature of the curriculum cannot be underestimated as a factor in students' reading and writing performance.

***Instructional Methods.***    Teachers and the lay public both are aware that instructional methods make a difference in students' learning. For example, there is evidence that instructional programs that focus on the processes of reading and writing have a powerful impact on students' awareness of what has been taught, awareness of comprehension and composing strategies, and performance on tasks that require strategic reading and writing (Duffy et al., 1986; Paris, Cross, & Lipson, 1984).

Differences in instructional methods that influence performance vary along a continuum from direct, or explicit, instruction to discovery, or implicit, learning. Direct instruction involves explaining or telling students the procedures involved in engaging in a particular reading or writing activity. Indirect methods instruct through repeated practice with activities that are examples of the desired reading behavior. Discovery methods emphasize placing students in a literate environment in which reading and writing will develop naturally. These different types of instruction are likely to have a major impact on reading and writing performance.

Other aspects of instructional method that influence student performance include the extent to which teachers support, or scaffold, students as they engage in reading and writing activities; the nature and content of instructional dialogue; and the level of instruciton offered. In addition, students' motivation for reading and writing is affected by specific instructional methods.

The purposes for which students read or write and/or the tasks they must complete in association with their reading and writing can also make a difference in performance. For example, questioning is probably the most frequently used task in reading instruction. The evidence suggests that the type of questions children are asked can influence their comprehension. It appears that implicit or inferential questions are more difficult for many children than explicit or literal questions (Pearson, Hansen, & Gordon, 1979). Furthermore, there is evidence that the type of questions asked influences the numbers and types of inferences students make. Specifically, questions with answers stated explicitly in the text result in fewer inferences, questions that require the integration of information in the text result in a larger number of text-based inferences, and questions that require students to draw heavily on their prior knowledge result in more knowledge-based inferences (Wixson, 1983a).

*Instructional Activities and Routines.*    The *instructional tasks* and *practice activities* that students perform define reading and writing for them. For example, in some classrooms students spend more time doing seatwork activities than they do reading and writing. It should be noted that these materials generally provide practice of separate component areas, not practice in the holistic act of reading or writing. This is especially true for students who are experiencing reading and writing difficulties (Allington, 1984; Allington, Stuetzel, Shake, & Lamarchi, 1986).

Alternatively, many classrooms contain other types of materials and tasks, including extensive quantities of specially created small paperback books that are accompanied by instructional frameworks. These materials include reading levels and suggestions for assessment. These program materials are often used by teachers who identify themselves as "whole-language" teachers and are exerting an influence on practice that is as substantial as basal programs. Similarly for writing, some programs are still defined by grammar books and teacher-assigned "creative writing" activities, and others involve writers' workshops, conferences, and self-selected topics. The students in these classrooms will think about reading and writing differently than students in classrooms where reading and writing are extensive and pervasive and where tasks are linked in authentic ways to the reading and writing products. These different tasks produce different types of writers.

*Assessment Practices.*    One of the truisms of education is that you get what you assess. For a variety of reasons teachers are likely to direct their instructional attention toward the types of performance that will be evaluated, especially if the evaluation is highly public or used for other high-stakes purposes.

Most educators have concluded that the standardized tests that are currently used in U.S. schools fail to adequately assess either sophisticated literacy skills or real-world literacy abilities. On the other hand, the nature of many classroom-based assessment efforts isn't adequate either, often failing to focus on important content, complex ideas, or high-level strategies.

Because assessment practices may exert such a strong influence on instruction, they should be examined carefully. Teachers should be aware that the ways in which information is gathered and the specific abilities that are tested can both influence student performance and affect their appraisal of student competence. For example, the form and content of external accountability measures can influence students' reading and writing performance. Specifically, students' performance is likely to suffer when the form and content of an external accountability measure is inconsistent with the form and content of classroom tasks.

These types of inconsistencies can also confuse students about their learning goals. For example, many accountability measures consist of multiple-choice and short-answer tasks that focus on decontextualized skills. Students who have little experience with these types of tasks are likely to do less well than are students who experience them on a regular basis. Furthermore, students who are evaluated in this manner are likely to evaluate their own competence in terms of their ability to perform a series of isolated skills tasks.

It is important to be aware of what types of assessments are being used and for what purposes within specific instructional contexts. If the only form of assessment is testing focused on isolated skills, then students are likely to be attending to skill mastery at the expense of integrated skill performances. In contrast, if the only form of assessment is student self-reflection, then students are likely to become more responsible for their own learning but may miss some important skills and not progress as rapidly as needed to perform at desirable levels. As can be seen, assessment practices can have a significant impact on students' reading and writing performance.

## Instructional Resources

Students are presented with an enormous array of materials and tasks during their development as readers and writers. Prominent among these are commercial instructional programs, trade materials, tutoring programs, and computer technology.

***Commercial Instructional Programs.***    In many classrooms students still work primarily from commercial programs, and teachers rely heavily on the published plans that accompany these materials. These materials inevitably become a part of a teacher's instructional set and often determine both what is read and written and what instructional activity is employed. Analyses of the lesson frames, materials, and instructional activities provided in most basal reading programs indicates that publishers have been responsive to earlier criticisms but that problems remain, especially when these materials are used nonselectively (Durkin, 1981; Wepner & Feeley, 1993). Too often, these materials still create an environment that involves mechanical completion of unconnected activities. Although there is variability, there is still too little reading in many programs and too little coherence in the skill work.

***Trade Materials.***    Students come into contact with a wide variety of trade materials in their daily lives as readers and writers: comic books, cereal boxes, instructions for constructing models, notes from friends, letters from relatives, and so forth. It is possible, and perhaps even desirable, to consider any or all of these materials as having instructional potential. However, the range of materials used for instruction in most classrooms is more constrained than this, and the materials to which students are exposed during instruction often differ from the materials they encounter in other contexts (Wage & Moje, 2000).

In almost every classroom students are asked to read various types of prose, or written texts. Prose selections used for instructional purposes come from a variety of sources, including basal readers, trade books (children's literature), subject area textbooks, magazines, reference materials, weekly readers, and the students' own writing. Research consistently demonstrates that the printed materials students encounter in instructional contexts influence reading and writing. In the past, one of the few text features that was given much attention was its difficulty or readability, as measured by factors such as the number of syllables in the words and the number of words in the sentences. Current research has demonstrated that a number of other factors have a significant impact on both how much and what students understand and learn from a text. The presence or absence of these factors determines the extent to which a given text can be considered "considerate" or "inconsiderate" (Armbruster, 1984).

*Considerate texts* are designed to enable the learner to gather appropriate information with minimal effort; *inconsiderate texts* require the learner to put forth extra effort to compensate for the inadequacies of the text. Inconsiderate texts are not necessarily incomprehensible, but they do require more effort, skill, and prior knowledge to comprehend. Two factors that determine the considerateness of a given text are its type and organization. For example, under certain circumstances students' oral reading and writing errors have been observed to vary according to the type of text they were reading and writing (stories versus informational articles, subject-area texts versus basal materials). Stories are more easily comprehended than informational texts for many students, and well-constructed stories are more easily comprehended than less well-organized stories (Brennan, Bridge, & Winograd, 1986; Olson, 1985).

The linguistic properties of texts including word usage, sentence structure, and sentence connectives are another factor influencing its comprehensibility. Each of these surface features influences performance on a variety of reading tasks. For example, texts that include a large proportion of words that occur with high frequency in our language are more easily comprehended than are texts with a large proportion of low-frequency words (Ruddell, 1965; Wittrock, Marks, & Doctorow, 1975).

The comprehensibility or considerateness of a text is also influenced by its structural characteristics, including all the features of texts that authors and editors use to aid organization and understanding such as headings, boldface type, illustrations, diagrams, and end-of-chapter questions and activities. For example, there is evidence that comprehension is enhanced when main idea statements are highlighted through the use of italics or headings (Baumann, 1986). It also appears that students are actually led to attend to unimportant ideas when structural features focus on trivial information. For example, if questions that follow reading focus on insignificant details, children are more likely to learn this information than the more important ideas in the text (Wixson, 1984).

***Tutoring Programs.***    Schools have for many years used a variety of tutorial models for addressing the instructional needs of struggling readers. Recently, however, there has been a distinct increase in the variety and number of programs designed to improve students' reading ability, especially that of young students. With this proliferation of new tutoring programs and tutoring models have come concerns about the effectiveness of tutoring as a response for remedial and/or intervention programs (Shanahan, 1998).

Not surprisingly, tutoring does appear to be an effective approach to improving reading performance, but it is not always effective, and it is not equally effective for all students. Educators need to evaluate the impact of tutoring on individual students. Factors that can affect student performance include the overall quality of the instructional program, the nature of the tutorial experience itself, and the knowledge and expertise of the tutors.

***Computer Technology.*** Although access to them varies considerably by school and district, multimedia and microcomputer activities are an important additional type of material. Careful examination of these programs is especially important for teachers who work with less-able readers and writers. There is continuing pressure to operate remedial settings through the use of diagnostic-prescriptive management systems that involve micro-computer testing, computer-generated profiles of skill needs, and computer programs for remedial instruction. There are also many other types of computer programs intended for assessment and instruction in reading, and their role in instruction may have an important effect on students' reading and writing performance.

# Understanding Learner Factors That Influence Performance

An interactive view of reading and writing suggests that a variety of learner factors influence reading and writing performance. These include prior content knowledge; knowledge about reading and writing, in particular, phonological awareness; attitudes and motivation; and the physical, cognitive, linguistic, and social-emotional correlates of reading and writing disability.

## Prior Content Knowledge

It is difficult to overestimate the influence of children's prior knowledge and their experience. In their review of children's learning from text, Alexander and Jetton (2000, p. 291), conclude, "Of all the factors (involved in learning from text), none exerts more influence on what students understand and remember than the knowledge they possess."

Research findings have consistently demonstrated how prior knowledge and experience influence reading comprehension (Lipson, 1982, 1983). Simply put, the more accurate and elaborated knowledge readers have about the ideas, concepts, or events described in the text, the better they will understand. On the other hand, limited information and/or misconceptions create obstacles to comprehension.

Comprehension proceeds so smoothly under ordinary circumstances that most adults are unaware of the process of constructing a model or interpretation of a text that fits with their knowledge of the world. It is instructive to try to understand material for which meaning is not immediately apparent. For example, take a moment to read and try to understand the paragraph in the following exercise, which was used in a classic study by Bransford and Johnson (1972, p. 722):

> The procedure is actually quite simple. First you arrange things into different groups. Of course, one pile may be sufficient depending on how much there is to do. If you have to go somewhere else due to lack of facilities that is the next step, otherwise you are pretty well set. It is important not to overdo things. That is, it is better to do too few things at once than too many. In the short run this may not seem important, but complications can easily arise. A mistake can be expensive as well. At first the whole procedure will seem complicated. Soon, however, it will become just another facet of life. It is difficult to foresee any end to the necessity for this task in the immediate future, but then one never can tell. After the procedure

is completed one arranges the materials into different groups again. Then they can be put into their appropriate places. Eventually they will be used once more and the whole cycle will then have to be repeated. However, that is part of life.

Were there any words you could not pronounce or for which you do not have some idea of the meaning? Is the syntax too complex? You probably did not have problems in either of these areas. Yet for most people this passage does not make much sense. However, it does become meaningful as soon as we use the title "Washing Clothes." Then the well-known concepts related to doing this job can be used to construct and assign meaning.

Learners also need to understand a great deal about social interactions and human relationships to connect ideas in texts. This type of prior knowledge seems to be especially important in inferential understanding (Lipson, Mosenthal, & Mekkelsen, 1999). Fragmented information and/or misconceptions can impede comprehension (Hynd & Alvermann, 1986; Lipson, 1982, 1983; Maria, 1986). This is especially troublesome when students attempt to learn from informational texts. People read unfamiliar text more slowly, they remember less, they construct meanings that are inconsistent with the author's intention, and they sometimes reject the text information outright. Misconceptions and limited information influence comprehension in a number of ways (see Guzzetti & Hynd, 1998).

There are many times when a text written for an audience with certain background knowledge is given to an audience with different or limited knowledge of the topic. For example, certain learners will have difficulties in trying to understand the materials in Figure 2.3, which were taken from newspapers in Vermont and Australia. Now suppose you were

**FIGURE 2.3**   Text Taken from Newspapers in Vermont and Australia

---

# NIGHT AUCTION

## Thursday, Oct. 9th   7:30 PM

Located on the so-called Harry Domina farm on Route #118 between East Berkshire and Montgomery, Vt. Watch for Auction Signs at Route Jct. #105 & #118 in East Berkshire, Vt.

## 50  Holstein Heifers   50

22 of the heifers are fresh within the last ten days and are milking between 50 to 60 lbs. of weighted milk, balance are all springing, 5 of these heifers are registered with papers that will be handed out the same night. Heifers have good size and condition and are going to be sold for cash regardless of price. Heifers have all been T.B., blood tested and inoculated from shipping fever and I.B.R. Heifers are open for inspection anytime on site where auction is to be held. Trucking available.

Auctioneer:                              Ringman:
Tel:                                          Berkshire, Vt.
**Sales held inside tent**              Tel:

**Owners:**
Berkshire, Vt.  Tel.:

# CRICKET MATCH
## AUSTRALIA vs. ENGLAND

A hair-raising century by Australian opener Graeme Wood on Friday set England back on its heels in the third test at the Melbourne Cricket Ground. Unfortunately, living dangerously eventually cost the Australians the match. Wood was caught out of his crease on the first over after lunch. Within ten more overs, the Australians were dismissed. Four were dismissed by dangerous running between creases. Two were dismissed when the English bowlers lifted the balls from the batsmen's wickets. The three remaining batsmen were caught by English fieldsmen. One was caught as he tried for a six. When the innings were complete the Australians had fallen short of the runs scored by the English.

asked to identify the main ideas of these texts. If you failed to complete this task successfully, would it mean that you do not know how to "get" a main idea? Obviously not; it simply means that you do not have sufficient background knowledge about the game of cricket, or about dairy cows, to be able to understand the most important points in these texts. Yet we rarely consider our students' prior knowledge in evaluating their performance on comprehension tasks.

Although there is little direct evidence regarding the role of prior knowledge as a factor in writing, common sense suggests that it would influence performance in analogous ways. Almost all views of the writing process, for example, involve a prewriting stage in which writers either activate existing topic knowledge or engage in experiences or information-gathering activities to expand knowledge. Authors can use only the voice they have or convey only the knowledge and experience they possess.

A basic fallacy of skills-based views of reading and writing is that skills are static across all reading and writing situations and that students' skill performance under one set of reading and writing conditions is indicative of their performance under all reading and writing conditions. Clearly, this is not the case for us or for our students. Children do not have the same experiential background as adults, and the meanings they construct for a given piece of text may be different from the meanings constructed by their adult teachers or authors of instructional materials.

## Knowledge about Reading and Writing

There are two major types of knowledge that influence students' acquisition of and facility with reading and writing: *phonological awareness* and *metacognitive awareness*. Both of these factors are developmental; that is, in general, younger people have both quantitatively less and qualitatively different knowledge than older people. Both of these factors are also strongly implicated in the reading difficulties experienced by many students.

*Metacognition.*  This term was introduced by developmental psychologists to refer to individuals' knowledge about and control over their own learning and thinking activities (Flavell & Wellman, 1977; Paris, Wasik, & Van der Westhuizen, 1988).

Metacognition in reading and writing refers to one's understanding of the reading and writing processes. This understanding is revealed in two ways. First, understanding involves the learner's knowledge of the nature of reading and writing; the purposes and goals of reading and writing; the various factors that influence reading and writing; and the what, how, when, and why of strategy usage in reading and writing. Second, learners' understanding is reflected in the control they have of their actions while reading and writing for different purposes. Active learners monitor their own state of learning, plan strategies, adjust efforts appropriately, and evaluate the success of their ongoing efforts (Brown, Armbruster, & Baker, 1986; Raphael, Kirschner, & Englert, 1988).

Research suggests that skilled learners know a great deal about reading and writing, and that this knowledge influences their ability to select and use appropriate strategies and skills in different reading and writing situations. It is becoming increasingly clear that learners need several types of knowledge in order to become proficient. First, they need to understand that a skill or strategy exists and is available to be used for reading/writing. For example, writers need to be aware that they can edit or revise their writing when it does not communicate their meaning as clearly. Many young and less-skilled writers seem unaware of this aspect of skilled writing. This type of knowledge is called *declarative knowledge* and requires only that the child know that a skill or strategy exists.

Knowing that a particular skill or tactic exists is not enough for successful performance. Learners also need to know how to perform the skill or strategy. To continue with our example, it is not sufficient to know that you can change your writing to clarify meaning; you must also understand how to go about editing and revising. This type of knowledge is called *procedural knowledge* because it refers to knowledge of the procedures necessary to execute and orchestrate the components of the reading process.

In the past, it was assumed that declarative and procedural knowledge would ensure application; that students who knew about the components and how to apply them would surely use this knowledge in the appropriate reading situations. Almost daily, however, teachers encounter students who appear to have mastered a skill or strategy sufficiently to employ it, but who fail to demonstrate any such competence during real reading situations. These children often fail to apply their existing skills and strategies because they lack a third type of knowledge, *conditional knowledge* (Paris, Lipson, & Wixson 1983). Simply stated, conditional knowledge is knowledge about when and why to employ a known strategy or skill. For example, skimming is obviously not a universally helpful approach to reading. Readers need to know when and why it is appropriate to use skimming. Conditional knowledge is essential for students to be able to apply the strategies and skills learned during reading instruction in other reading situations.

Skilled learners possess a wide range of knowledge related to reading and writing including knowledge of purposes and goals, knowledge of various text factors, knowledge of task requirements, and knowledge about the skills and strategies used in reading and writing. For example, they know that the purpose of reading and writing is "to make meaning" rather than "to say all of the words right" or "to write neatly." Skilled learners also realize that reading and writing will be easier if they know a great deal about the topic of the text they are reading or writing and if they are interested in it. These examples may seem incredibly obvious, but there are many young and poor learners who do not have even these basic understandings about reading and writing.

Skilled learners also understand how various text factors can influence their reading and writing. Before we ever open a book or write the first words in a text, our knowledge of the type of text we are reading or writing influences the way we will read or write that text. We know about different types of texts such as encyclopedias, cookbooks, letters from friends, novels, newspapers, and so forth. We have expectations for how these texts are organized and for the types of information they contain, and this knowledge guides us in the selection of appropriate reading and writing strategies. For example, if you were reading or writing about a miracle cure for baldness from or for *Scientific American,* you would be likely to approach the task differently than if you were reading or writing about it from or for the *National Enquirer.*

Knowledge about the tasks that learners will be asked to complete in the course of reading and writing also affects strategy selection and usage. When we asked a group of fifth grade students to tell us why they thought their teachers wanted them to work in their workbooks, one child responded indignantly, "Do you know what she [the teacher] did? She gave us a test on the workbook. You're not supposed to remember that stuff!" His response reflected his awareness that in many classrooms students need not remember the material in their workbooks; they must simply complete it and put it in the appropriate place.

Skilled learners also have knowledge about different skills and strategies for reading and writing and about how to use them (Paris, Wasik, & Turner, 1991). For example, they are aware of strategies for dealing with words and sentences they do not know (ask for help, use the dictionary, reread). They are also aware of the purposes for different strategies, such as planning or prewriting (it helps you get out all your ideas, you can see how your ideas go together). It is not sufficient to know what the strategies are and how to use them; learners must also know when and why to use them.

Skilled learners not only have a great deal of knowledge about reading and writing, but they can also apply that knowledge to monitor and regulate their reading and writing. There is evidence that they can adjust their strategies in response to different reading and writing situations (reading and writing for fun, reading and writing for specific ideas or for general impressions, studying) and that they use specific strategies to meet the demands of specific reading and writing situations (for example, using different styles depending on their relationship to the intended audience of their writing). In summary, it appears that students' knowledge and control of the reading and writing processes play an important role in their reading and writing performance.

*Phonological Awareness.* Over the course of their preschool years most children become increasingly aware of the phonological structure of their language (see Chapter 7, "The Foundations of Literacy," for a more comprehensive discussion of this aspect of reading development). Phonological awareness refers to children's ability to divide sentences into words, break words into syllables, and identify common phonemes (e.g., recognize rhyming words). As we have already noted, in an alphabetic language such as English, it is essential to attend to the phonology of the language. Initially, children are likely to attend to word play, rhymes, and then syllables as units of sound. Eventually, however, children need to be able to isolate individual phonemes, or sounds, within a word. This specialized aspect of phonological awareness is called *phonemic awareness* or *phonemic segmentation* (see Chapters 7 and 13). Because most children and adults attend primarily to meaning in spoken language, many young children do not acquire the idea that the sound structure is distinct from the meaning structure of the language until quite late in their preschool or early school years. The majority of children do not acquire the ability to isolate (segment) phonemes until the age of 5 or 6 (Liberman & Shankweiler, 1979). There is additional, emerging research that suggests that phonological awareness, like other correlates, may be quite stable and linked to innate individual differences. Vellutino and his colleagues, for example, have found that the vast majority of students who struggle in first and second grades can be taught to read with appropriate instruction (Vellutino et al., 1996; Vellutino, Scanlon, & Sipay, 1997). A very small number, however (called the "hardest to remediate" and totaling about 2 percent of all students), had a different profile of phonological awareness skills than other students. In particular, they were different in phoneme awareness and rapid naming tasks.

In their extensive review of research in this area the Committee on the Prevention of Reading Difficulties in Young Children described the development of phonological abilities (Snow et al., 1998), concluding that phonological awareness is a strong predictor of subsequent reading achievement. They also conclude that early tests of phonological awareness may not always provide definitive information:

> [P]honological awareness in kindergarten appears to have the tendency to be a more successful predictor of future *superior* reading than of future reading *problems*. That is, among children who have recently begun or will soon begin kindergarten, few of those with strong phonological awareness skills will stumble in learning to read, but many of those with weak phonological sensitivity will go on to become adequate readers [emphasis in the original]. (Snow et al., 1998, p. 112)

This is likely because researchers have also demonstrated that the relationship of phonological awareness to development is "bidirectional, involving reciprocal causation (Ehri, 1979, 1987; Perfetti et al., 1987)" (Snow et al., 1998, p. 56). That is, children with good phonological awareness abilities learn to read more easily and quickly. However, learning to read (experiencing instruction focused on reading and writing) results in improved phonological awareness. Thus, although very strongly related to reading ability (and to language development in general), good phonological awareness is not a prerequisite to reading and should not be used to limit students' access to good developmental instruction. On the other hand, there is also strong evidence to suggest that for students who need it "instruction that heightens phonological awareness and that emphasizes the connections to the alphabetic code promotes greater skill in word recognition; a skill essential to becoming a proficient reader" (Blachman, 2000, p. 495).

## Attitudes and Motivation

Whether children perform or learn in a particular situation depends on whether they can do what must be done and whether they choose to do it (Adelman & Taylor, 1977). Learning and performance require both skill and will (Paris, Lipson, & Wixson, 1983). Factors such as interest, the amount of time and effort required, willingness to take risks, or perceived competence can influence children's decisions whether to use their skills or not.

The student's attitude toward reading and writing is a central factor affecting reading and writing performance. Positive attitudes and motivation can compensate for relatively weak skills, and negative attitudes can prevent a student from applying existing knowledge or from acquiring new information (Paris, Olson, & Stevenson, 1983). However, researchers have argued recently that attitude is distinct from motivation, since students frequently report doing well on academic tasks (including reading) at the same time that they report disliking the activity (McKenna, Kear, & Ellsworth, 1995). These findings have caused us to look more broadly at the purposes for which people engage in reading and writing activities. It is clear that some people have an intrinsic motivation to read for enjoyment. At the same time, other purposes prevail, including a "learning goal orientation" and a "performance or ego orientation" (Guthrie & Wigfield, 2000). Readers with a learning goal orientation want to improve their reading skills, whereas readers with a performance orientation have a competitive desire to do better than others. Still other readers have social motivation for reading. Young children especially might want to spend time with their peers and interact with them in a common experience. Clearly, different goals might result in varied levels of motivation depending on the tasks and settings.

Although few educators would dispute the relationship between motivation and achievement, the research establishing these links is somewhat mixed, largely because of differences in definition, student population, and subject area. Recently, researchers have begun to think of motivation and student engagement as mediating factors in school success (Guthrie & Wigfield, 2000). They suggest that the individual classroom context factors might not influence performance directly. Instead, the instructional methods, materials, and tasks determine or effect student engagement, and it is this student engagement that directly impacts performance and achievement. According to Guthrie and Wigfield (2000), engagement is a combination of motivation, conceptual knowledge, social interaction, and strategy use.

Research indicates that positive self-perception (or self-efficacy) promotes achievement-oriented behavior, whereas low self-perception leads to decreased motivation. In addition, positive attitudes and self-perceptions are associated with a sense of control over reading and writing successes and failures. Perceived lack of control can grow out of repeated and prolonged failure experiences. This can have a debilitating effect, sometimes called *learned helplessness,* which in turn causes a general expectation that all events that happen to the person are uncontrollable. The end result can be passive behavior.

This cyclic pattern was demonstrated in a study by Butkowsky and Willows (1980). The poor learners in the study had significantly lower initial expectations for success than did average and good learners, and when confronted with failure, they persisted at the task for shorter periods of time. However, it also appears that children's beliefs about why they succeed or fail in reading and writing vary across reading and writing situations (Hiebert, Winograd, & Danner, 1984). Therefore, it is likely that learners' willingness to exert effort also will vary from situation to situation.

## Correlates of Reading and Writing Performance

There are a number of factors internal to the learner related to successful learning and achievement. These factors are frequently referred to as *correlates* of reading and writing ability/disability, because strengths and weaknesses in any of these areas are often correlated with reading and/or writing performance. When one or more of these correlates is strongly present in a student or a student population, these students may be considered *at risk* for school failure (Vacca & Padak, 1990). It is important to understand, however, that a high correlation between some learner factor and performance in reading and writing does not ensure that this factor is the *cause* of the high or low performance. The research thus far has yielded only equivocal findings regarding the causal relationships between most correlates and reading and writing success.

In addition, these factors are not biologically determined. They certainly can and often do influence students' reading, but they may be much less critical than had previously been imagined. As Snow, Burns, and Griffin (1998, p. 24) explain:

> [I]n all populations, reading ability occurs along a continuum, and biological factors are influenced by, and interact with, a reader's experiences. The findings of an anomalous brain

system say little about the possibility for change, for remediation, or for response to treatment. It is well-known that, particularly in children, neural systems are plastic and responsive to changed input.

In the following sections we describe briefly correlates of reading and writing performance in four major areas: social and emotional development, language development, physical development, and cognitive development.

***Social and Emotional Development.***   An area related to attitudes and motivation is students' social and emotional development. Students who have trouble adjusting to various social situations with peers and/or adults may experience academic difficulties. Students with emotional problems may also have difficulty concentrating in school, which often has a negative effect on their learning. However, it is frequently difficult to determine the extent to which emotional and social maladjustment are causes or results of reading and writing problems. "Every poor learner is at risk for psychological disturbance, almost always as a result of, rarely as the cause of, and frequently as a further contribution to, the poor reading [and writing]" (Eisenberg, 1975, p. 219).

Although Harris and Sipay (1985) note that studies have failed to demonstrate stable relationships between poor learners as a group and emotional or social difficulties, individual students may certainly exhibit reading and writing difficulties due largely to social or emotional problems (see Rock, Fessler, & Church, 1997). There are students for whom learning is made more difficult by family upheaval, by neglect, and by interpersonal problems in school. In addition, of course, physiologically based emotional problems (for example, from drug-related birth trauma) can lead to students who are easily discouraged or unable to relate to others, although it is increasingly clear that even students with these challenges can achieve high levels of success in literacy with the right instruction (Snow et al., 1998). Regardless of whether emotional or social problems are the cause or the result of reading and writing problems, if they are interfering with learning and performance, they must be considered in developing an instructional program.

***Language Development.***   The acquisition of language competence is a major factor influencing subsequent reading and writing achievement. Indeed, the researchers at the Center for the Improvement of Early Reading Achievement recently asserted that "oral language is the foundation on which reading is built, and it continues to serve this role as children develop as readers" (Hiebert et al., 1998, Topic 1, p. 1). As children learn language, they develop abilities in understanding and producing speech. This development involves learning how their language is structured, how humans use language to communicate, and the specific words and rules of their own language.

All languages have certain characteristics, described earlier in this chapter, that children must learn or acquire (see also Chapter 7). Humans use language for a variety of purposes, and understanding the functions embedded in language is critical to comprehending and composing messages. The communicative functions include regulating other people's behavior, expressing feelings, pretending and creating, conveying or obtaining information, and establishing and maintaining contact with others.

Children acquire language competence at varying rates and to varying degrees. With few exceptions children will have mastered the language and communication patterns of their own families before entering first grade. Not all language and communication patterns are equally good matches with the demands of school settings, however. Children with delayed, underdeveloped, or merely different language skills are likely to have difficulty with conventional reading and writing. Indeed, one factor that is likely to place students at risk of school failure is limited English proficiency. Children's knowledge of the structure of language forms the foundation for learning to read. If the child's language differs significantly from the language he or she is encountering in books, the resulting mismatch will make initial learning difficult.

Although it seems obvious to point out that children will not easily learn to read a language they cannot speak, not all schools are equipped to provide the foundations in oral language that may be required for many students. Nor are many schools prepared to offer a rich multilingual experience that capitalizes on the knowledge and expertise of the larger community (Moll & Gonzalez, 1994). Language and culture are strongly interrelated (Bernhardt, 2000; Ovando, 1988), which means that the aspects of context (culture, setting, etc.) influence learner factors as well as performance. The influence of context, in other words, can affect the learner directly or interact with learner factors (and other context factors) to influence performance. As Ruddell (1993, p. 325) has noted:

> Regardless of whether students are learning English as a second language or a third (or fourth) language, much of what they bring to school from their primary langauge is a part of the beliefs, attitudes, behaviors, and values of their primary culture as well. To teach bi- and multilingual students effectively, we need knowledge and understanding of their language and culture, and the relationships between the two.

These are particularly challenging concerns for two reasons. First, the number of children with limited English proficiency has increased in recent years. Estimates suggest that about 9 percent of school-aged children are classified as having limited English proficiency (Freeman & Freeman, 2000). Second, these students are far more likely to experience significant reading and learning difficulties leading to gaps in school achievement. For example, "despite the group's progress in achievement over the past 15 to 20 years, (Hispanic) students are about twice as likely as non-Hispanic whites to be reading below average for their age" (Snow et al., 1998, p. 28).

As young children are engaged in experiences with language, thought, and print, they gain an increasing awareness about what is required to accomplish literacy tasks. Learning reading and writing, like most cognitive tasks, requires some degree of reflective ability, yet not all children have acquired appropriate abilities in this area. Some abilities, though potentially useful, are late in developing in all children (phonemic segmentation, for example). Because the assessment-instruction process needs to take these factors into account, we will return to the issue of language development in Chapter 7.

***Physical Development.*** Within the area of physical development there are several factors that may influence reading and writing performance; hearing and vision are two of these.

*Hearing.* There are several types of hearing loss. Some make it difficult for students to hear all sounds (measured by the intensity or loudness of sounds); others result in loss of hearing for particular sounds (or frequencies). Both types of hearing loss can occur in the same person, and hearing loss can occur in one or both ears. According to Richek, Caldwell, Jennings, and Lerner (2002, p. 347), "even a moderate loss in the ability to hear may substantially affect the ability to read." Generally speaking, the vowel sounds of English are low-frequency sounds, and the consonants are high-frequency sounds; impairments in either area might affect students' word recognition development.

An appropriate referral should be made if there is any evidence of impaired hearing, and if at all possible, the loss should be corrected before any further specialized instruction occurs. Hearing loss resulting from more temporary physical conditions (for example, ear infections) can also interfere with learning and should prompt careful teachers to consider adapting their methods of instruction.

*Vision.* There are several types of visual impairments we need to be concerned about. People who are farsighted have difficulty in seeing objects up close, as when reading or writing. Nearsightedness, on the other hand, results in difficulties seeing distant objects, such as the chalkboard. Astigmatism results in distorted visual images, which could lead to problems such as keeping one's place while reading and writing. Other types of vision problems occur when the eye muscles do not work together in a smooth, coordinated fashion. These types of problems can result in fatigue and discomfort that interfere with reading and writing.

Research regarding the impact of these visual problems on reading and writing achievement appears to be equivocal. It seems that visual acuity and poor eye muscle coordination are "rarely the cause of poor reading" (Gunning, 2002, p. 52). In addition, visual problems that might make reading more difficult often go undetected because the eye test that is commonly used in school screenings, the Snellen Chart, is designed to detect only problems with far-point vision and not the near-point difficulties that might influence reading performance.

**Cognitive Development.** As children grow and mature, they acquire an increasingly sophisticated repertoire of cognitive abilities, including the ability to read and write. Developmental stages or shifts in perspective are often used to capture this changing and increasing knowledge base (Bruner, 1964; Piaget, 1960; Vygotsky, 1978). Both Piaget and Bruner describe growth during the preschool and school years as a process during which children are moving toward the ability to transcend the present and think flexibly about the world. Teachers need to understand how their students think about their world so that they can provide experiences that are appropriate to children's cognitive functioning and that move them to expand and restructure their knowledge.

Cognitive factors include development in the areas of perception, attention, and memory, as well as encompassing traditional notions of intelligence and verbal ability. Although it is beyond the scope of this text to consider each of these aspects in detail, each will be discussed briefly below to provide an awareness of the scope of the cognitive-developmental factors that may influence reading and writing achievement.

*Intelligence.* Intelligence generally refers to overall mental ability. Included in the construct of intelligence are such indicators of ability as speed of learning, ability to solve problems, and ability to engage in high-level thinking tasks. Although overall cognitive/developmental ability certainly influences students' learning, the specific impact on the acquisition of literacy should not be overestimated. Snow, Burns, and Griffin (1998, p. 24) conclude, for example, that "the child's intelligence, as long as it is in the normal range, does not have much of an impact on the ease of learning to read" (Stanovich, Cunningham, & Cramer, 1984).

Given the importance of judgments about intelligence in school settings, several points need to be made here. First, intelligence is a construct. That is, the components of intelligence are not readily observable. Indeed, there is substantial disagreement about what the components are. Most psychological authorities note that intelligence is actually grounded in culture and that different societies value different sets of skills and define intelligence accordingly (Okagaki & Sternberg, 1991). Recent conceptualizations of intelligence involve a more expansive consideration of the components involved in cognitive activity. Gardner's (1983) multiple intelligences have been joined by others. Sternberg (1999), for example, suggests that intelligence involves five components: metacognitive skills, learning skills, thinking skills, knowledge (declarative and procedural), and motivation.

As Bransford, Goldman, and Nye (1991, p. 152) point out:

A shift in the emphasis from academic intelligence to multiple intelligences carries with it the implication that intelligence is not a wholistic trait that characterizes an individual. Thus, an individual might be relatively intelligent in school but relatively unintelligent in other contexts such as the auto repair shop and vice versa.

This supports the notion of an interactive view of learning and ability, rejecting the older view that intelligence was a relatively stable characteristic and, as such, was not susceptible to change via instruction.

On the other hand, certain abilities that are frequently measured on tests of intelligence but are not part of everyday definitions of intelligence may have significant implications for student's reading development. For example, many poor readers complete rapid automatized naming (RAN) tasks, which require the ability to quickly name random letters or numerals, more slowly than capable readers. Increasingly, it appears that speed of processing, especially speed and flexibility in manipulating the phonological aspects of language, may affect students' reading (Wagner et al., 1997).

Given this situation, caution needs to be exercised in attributing reading and writing problems to limited overall congitive ability. In our multicultural society, it is possible for different types of behavior and knowledge to mean different things to different individuals. For example, some cultural groups take aggressive display of information as totally inappropriate behavior—the mark of someone who is either not very smart or not very polite. Other groups teach children to provide creative, but not necessarily factual, answers to situational questions. Conclusions generated about intelligence in the absence of appropriate cultural context can be misleading.

Increasingly, it appears that intelligence can be influenced by certain experiences and instruction (Carnegie Corporation, 1994; Slavin, 1991). More important, there is an increased interest, not in static measures of intelligence as traditionally assessed, but in measures of potential to learn. The evidence to date suggests that measures of potential can contribute important information to the process of assessment and instruction and we will return to these in Chapter 11.

*Information-Processing Abilities.*    Student learning is also associated with the ability to process information in either written or spoken form. *Attention, perception,* and *memory* are all factors that influence learning and performance.

Attention

The ability and willingness to pay attention to important stimuli is a major factor in school success (Gage & Berliner, 1988). Human beings are surrounded by stimuli, that is, all aspects of the environment that are present to be learned, enjoyed, and noticed. Some students appear to have an exceptionally difficult time attending to school tasks and concentrating on print-related activities. Many of these students are being diagnosed with attention deficit disorder (ADD), sometimes also with hyperactivity (ADHD). The evidence regarding either the validity or the prevalence of ADD is controversial and inconclusive. The research does suggest that attention is very selective and is influenced by a number of other

Vanessa →

factors, including motivation, maturity, context, and instruction. For example, people focus more attention on unusual or unique stimuli (larger print, boldface, etc). In other words, not all children who are inattentive have biologically based attention deficits. Clearly, whether because of biological disposition or for other reasons, if students cannot or do not attend to the parts of the environment that contain essential information, they cannot learn or retain new information and skills, and this issue should be examined during assessment.

Perception

The ability to impose order on sensory information is called *perception.* It too is central to student learning and performance in general. Perception, like attention and memory, is developmental. That is, important changes occur during childhood and adolescence. Older children have more experience and knowledge, and this allows them to impose order on a greater array of stimuli, thus enhancing perception. Because reading is clearly a cognitive-perceptual process, many educators have assumed that reading difficulties arise from deficits in visual-perceptual processing. However, decades of research have demonstrated unequivocally that reading problems are not caused by such weaknesses. In reviewing the research in this area, Klenk and Kibby (2000, p. 671) concluded:

> The validity of perceptual training programs as a method of improving reading has long been debunked . . . The conclusion from decades of research on this topic is abundantly clear: Perceptual training programs, although perhaps increasing perceptual ability, have no substantive affect on reading ability.

Memory

Finally, the development of memory is an important aspect of cognitive information-processing ability. *Memory* is the process of storing and retrieving information. "The ability to retain verbal information in working memory is essential for reading and learning" (Snow et al., 1998, p. 108). Indeed, recent research suggests that young children's ability to recall a short story that has been read aloud is more strongly related to their subsequent reading achievement that do scores on digit span, word span, or memory for pseudo-words (Scarborough, 1998).

As with all cognitive abilities, memory changes and develops over time. Older children are better at storing and retrieving information than younger children, and adults tend to be better at this than children. Older children and adults clearly have better concept formation and a more elaborate network connecting concepts that allows for better organization of new information. In addition, older children and adults tend to have better strategies for coping with information, and they are better at understanding what they need to do to remember information.

It is easy to see how individual differences in these areas of development can affect students' abilities to cope with school tasks. It is also becoming increasingly clear that these cognitive abilities are not static. Attention, perception, and memory operate in relation to *specific types of information.* It is misleading to talk of children's processing abilities without specifying exactly what it is they are trying to perceive and remember (Gage & Berliner, 1988). We see once again how culture, expectations, and experience can influence performance and potentially confound the measurement of these abilities.

## Chapter Summary

This chapter focused on the elements of skilled reading and writing performance and the contextual and learner factors that influence performance. The first section of the chapter described skilled performance as the ability to use reading and writing effectively and creatively for personal, recreational, academic, and civic purposes. The elements of skilled performance were defined as comprehension; composition; vocabulary development; word identification and spelling; rate and fluency; and grammar, usage, and the mechanics of writing.

The second and third sections of the chapter identified and described the contextual and learner factors that influence performance. The contextual factors were grouped according to settings, instructional practices, curriculum, and instructional resources. The learner factors were categorized as prior content knowledge, knowledge about reading and writing, attitudes and motivation, and correlates of skilled performance. The correlates of performance were defined as those social, emotional, linguistic, cognitive, and physical factors that are related to, but do not necessarily cause, strengths and weaknesses in reading and writing performance.

Consideration of the conventional aspects of reading and writing performance must be constrained by concerns for the ways in which learner and contextual factors interact to influence performance. Unless this complex and dynamic view of reading and writing is employed during assessment, we run the risk of developing a distorted picture of reading and writing processes. This poses serious problems for assessment but even more serious concerns about the quality of instruction.

# 3 Reading and Writing Disability and the Assessment-Instruction Process

Chapters 1 and 2 focused on understanding the reading and writing processes. In this chapter and in much of the remainder of the book we focus on understanding the nature of reading and writing disability and applying this understanding to the assessment and instruction of reading and writing. A plan for the assessment-instruction process is presented, and we explain the reasons for using this plan and describe each of the following steps:

## The Steps in the Assessment-Instruction Process

Step 1   Getting Started with Assessment
Step 2   Evaluating the Context
Step 3   Evaluating the Learner: Focusing on Reading and Writing
Step 4   Evaluating the Match between the Learner and the Context
Step 5   Reflection, Decision Making, and Planning
Step 6   Identifying a Better Match: Diagnostic Teaching
Step 7   Adapting Instruction: Continuous Monitoring and Modification
Step 8   Reporting

## Understanding an Interactive View of Reading and Writing Disability

In this text we use contemporary views of reading and writing ability and the lessons of history to detail an interactive perspective on reading and writing disability. We are suggesting that the interactive view of reading and writing *ability* be adopted for reading and writing difficulties or (dis)ability as well. This means that reading and writing disability, like ability, would no longer be viewed as an absolute property of the learner, but rather as a relative property of the interaction between specific learner and contextual factors (Lipson & Wixson, 1986).

An interactive view of reading and writing disability addresses several of the concerns we have about any theory of disability. First, we believe that a theory of disability should respond to recent conceptual and empirical evidence; it should account for the reading and writing behaviors of struggling students but should also suggest new areas of investigation. Second, we believe that theories of reading and writing disability should enhance instruction. We now turn our attention to these issues.

## A Theoretically Sound View of Disability

Current theory and research in reading and writing provide evidence that the ability to comprehend and/or compose varies for both able and disabled learners, as a function of various interactions with different reading and writing situations. For example, there is evidence that young children of all ability levels are better able to recognize words that contain regular phonic patterns and that they are also more successful when reading high-frequency words than low-frequency words (Juel, 1988). The results of such studies suggest that children's performance on measures of isolated word recognition can be expected to vary as a function of the particular words on a given test.

Small samples of oral reading errors are often used to characterize a student's word recognition ability in all reading contexts. However, studies of oral reading errors suggest that children's word recognition ability is highly variable and is influenced by many factors. These factors include instructional method, type of prose being read, the student's prior knowledge of the materials being read, and the difficulty of the text (Wixson, 1979). This means that oral reading errors reflect particular strategies a learner employs in interaction with a particular reading activity. As such, they may or may not be representative of the strategies used by a particular learner in other reading situations.

Comprehension performance is also subject to variability in both able and less-able learners. The two groups are similarly affected by differences in prior knowledge, by text organization, and by type of comprehension task. For example, Williams and her colleagues have demonstrated in a number of studies that both able and less-able students in grades 3 through 7 were better able to identify the main idea when they were asked to select the best title than when they were asked to write a summary sentence (Williams, Taylor, & deCani, 1984).

Finally, there is evidence that less-skilled learners perform like skilled learners under certain circumstances. For example, in an examination of the story comprehension patterns of sixth grade learners, McConaughy (1985) found no differences between good and poor learners in either the quality or the accuracy of their recall summaries. Specifically, McConaughy reports that poor learners' story organization is as good as that of good learners of the same age when the structure of the text is explicit and learners are required to summarize what they think is important rather than to recall as much as possible.

A related finding in the area of writing is that the relative difficulty of the expository text structures in writing tasks varies depending on the type of task that students are performing and the manner in which the writing is analyzed. If written productivity is evaluated, then an explanation text structure may be easier for students to produce than a comparison/constrast structure. If text organization is evaluated, then the comparison/contrast text structure might be easier for students to produce than the explanation text structure.

The foregoing suggests that the strategies students employ as they read and write should be expected to vary as a function of a number of factors. There is evidence that both the awareness and application of reading and writing strategies varies in relation to the difficulty of the text and task (Lipson, Mosenthal, & Mekkelsen, 1999). Evaluating strategic behavior in the absence of some consideration of potential sources of variability is problematic. As Jones (1983, p. 6) has noted, "learning strategies cannot be defined or understood without reference to the text to which they apply because the cognitive processes vary according to the text condition."

When reading and writing disability are viewed from an interactive perspective, it becomes clear how difficult, and probably fruitless, it is to search for a single causative factor within the learner. Yet this is the approach that continues to dominate assessment and instruction in reading and writing disability today. Despite the increased sophistication of perspectives on reading and writing ability, our views of reading and writing disability are still wedded to the historic "search for pathology" (Sarason & Doris, 1979).

An editorial in the *The Learning Disability Quarterly,* a journal that publishes much of today's research on reading and writing disability, summarized this view very well: "Our entire field is DEFICIT DRIVEN; we spend millions of dollars and hours looking for deficits, defining them, perseverating on them, imagining that we are exorcizing them, and sometimes even inventing them to rationalize our activities" (Poplin, 1984, p. 133). Research has amply demonstrated that variability in performance is a normal part of the reading and writing process. However, assessment and instruction for most disabled learners still depend on the use of commercial, standardized test instruments that assume that reading and writing processes are static and that reading and writing ability can be measured at some point in time, using one set of materials and tasks to predict performance on other materials in other settings. This is especially problematic given the tasks that comprise existing reading and writing tests. Many existing instruments are based on dated and incomplete notions about reading and writing. When a mismatch exists between the theories used to define reading and writing competence and those used to drive assessment and instruction, the assessment information is of little value (Valencia & Pearson, 1987; Wixson, Peters, Weber, & Roeber, 1987). We will discuss the problems and advantages of standardized testing in Chapter 10.

## An Instructionally Significant View of Disability

An interactive view is well suited to the understanding of reading and writing (dis)ability because it predicts variability in performance within individuals across texts, tasks, and settings. This perspective moves discussions of reading and writing disability away from simply specifying deficits and toward the specification of the conditions under which a student can and will learn. In this view, a student's performance on various reading and writing measures is considered an indication of what he or she can and will do under a specific set of conditions rather than as a set of fixed abilities and disabilities (Wixson & Lipson, 1986). The necessity for identifying the disability is eliminated, and our attention is refocused on how each student performs under different conditions and which set of conditions is most likely to facilitate learning.

An interactive view of reading and writing disability provides a unifying theoretical orientation for teachers and specialized support personnel. The clearest implication of such a reorientation is that the performance of both able and less-able students is subject to variability. The factors that influence the reading and writing process are the same for both populations of students. At present there is a tremendous need for coordination of assessment and instruction between classrooms and specialized programs. If different views of reading and writing underlie the programs in these two settings, problems inevitably arise for students, and the prospects for potential transfer and learning are limited. Both classroom teachers and specialists need to recognize that the student who is experiencing difficulty in reading and writing is only one component in the reading and writing process.

An interactive view of reading and writing also provides a basis for communication between teachers and support staff. Personnel involved in the education of students with reading and writing problems can begin to talk about the specific contributions of the learner, the text, and the context as determiners of reading and writing performance. All educators need to understand the importance of recognizing this so that we can begin to work together. Because learner performance is likely to be influenced by a wide array of factors, pull-out programs are unlikely to be effective unless there is coordination between the classroom and the clinic. Teachers must provide opportunities for classroom practice and application of the skills and techniques developed in the clinic. Similarly, clinicians can no longer ignore the content and context of classroom instruction, believing that remediation of some specific disability will transfer to other settings.

Finally, an interactive view makes clear the important contribution of context. Both classroom teachers and specialists must be sensitive to the influences of their distinct environments on learner performance. Thoughtful teachers have always realized that information collected in one situation is not entirely helpful in another. Unfortunately, we have sometimes rejected information from various sources as unreliable because it did not coincide with our own. Such apparently contradictory information can be valuable in planning optimal student instruction. For example, it should no longer surprise us when a student performs differently as an individual, in small group settings, and in large group settings. The documentation of these differences can provide the basis for genuinely collaborative professional relationships—relationships that will strengthen the prospects of learning for all students.

## Understanding the Assessment-Instruction Process

The problem of teaching and learning is the match between the student and the circumstances he or she encounters in the learning environment (Hunt, 1961). The notion of the proper match between student and circumstance is what we must grasp if we are to be effective evaluators and instructors. Assessment and instruction need to be focused on an evaluation of the existing match and the identification of the optimal match between a learner and the conditions of the reading and writing context.

The purpose of assessment, then, is to find patterns of interactions that allow us to make relatively good decisions about instruction. Because few standardized tests provide this kind of information, we suggest a number of assessment strategies that are needed to supplement existing measures. We are not suggesting that current testing instruments be abandoned altogether, but rather that assessment move forward from a different perspective. Nor are we suggesting that the individual student is not an important factor in the assessment process, but that we must look to the individual in interaction with specific texts, tasks, and methods. In the past such specification was incidental to the goal of identifying the learner's problem. This text is designed to help educators accomplish this in an intentional and thoughtful fashion.

The long-range goal of the entire assessment and instruction process is to produce strategic, motivated, reflective readers and writers and to develop mature readers and writers who can and will apply their skills and strategies independently and in a flexible manner— not to identify causes or provide labels. To achieve an interactive approach to assessment and instruction, we need to gather information about the demands of the context (for example, what is required to read and write using various methods or materials) and explore how the context may influence a student's performance and learning. We also need to gather information about what the learner knows and how he or she behaves during reading and writing. We must also examine the interaction between the areas within these two components of the assessment-instruction process.

The best way to become proficient at the assessment and instruction of reading and writing is to learn as much as possible about learners, the contexts in which reading and writing occur, and how they interact to influence reading and writing performance.

A plan for proceeding with the process of assessment and instruction is described in the next sections of this chapter. This is a decision-making approach to assessment and instruction. Throughout this text we provide information about areas to be assessed and also describe in detail tools and strategies for gathering information. In addition, however, we need to make decisions at every stage of the process because the complex of factors that interact is never quite the same for any two students. Effective decision making is dependent on knowing when and why we would engage in a particular activity, or use a particular test or instructional technique.

## Implementing the Assessment-Instruction Process

The components of effective assessment and instruction are similar whether they are conducted in the classroom or in a remedial/support setting, by a classroom teacher or a specialist. However, the amount of attention devoted to each component and the procedures used to evaluate them are likely to be different. The classroom teacher has the benefit of daily contact with the student or students in question but limited time to spend with individual students. The specialist or clinician has the benefit of individual time with the student but limited knowledge about the student's daily interactions with reading and writing in the classroom.

It is important for classroom teachers to develop a repertoire of assessment techniques that can be incorporated easily into their daily instruction. (These will be discussed in the chapters that follow.) Students who demonstrate difficulty on these assessments would then be seen individually or in smaller groups for further evaluation. The assessment of the methods and materials may be fairly straightforward for classroom teachers because of their daily access and repeated experience with them. Classroom teachers have the added benefit of being able to incorporate trial teaching procedures into the real context of their daily instruction.

The language arts specialist or clinician usually deals only with students who have already been identified by some means as having a problem. Specialists have the advantage of working closely in small settings with an individual student. This may provide in-depth information unavailable to the classroom teacher. However, if specialists do not work in the classroom, evaluating the learner in interaction with the reading and writing context may be more difficult because they do not have daily contact with the student(s) in question in the context in which the problem is occurring. They must rely on limited examinations of the materials, classroom observation, and interviews with the parents, the teacher, and the students for this evaluation. Furthermore, they must be aware of and sensitive to the teacher's style and the organization of the classroom to develop trial teaching procedures that would be appropriate for use in the student's classroom.

Specialists who are operating in pull-out programs need to be especially aware of the potential difficulties in this situation. Too often, the students who are most in need of consistent, coherent reading and writing instruction are the ones who receive the most fragmented instruction. What is most important, however, is that students may be practicing and acquiring skills and abilities in one setting that are neither valued nor applied in another. Communication between classroom and clinic is of the utmost importance.

Increasingly, the advantages of these different settings are being tapped by innovative staffing configurations. Many schools have implemented student support teams composed of classroom teachers, special educators, and content specialists. The members of these teams confer about individual students and pool their insights, knowledge, and resources. Many assessment and instruction strategies will be tried by the classroom teacher, others may be implemented in the classroom by a Title I or special education teacher, and still others may involve pulling the student out for individual assessment or instruction.

The remainder of this book is designed to provide information about the what, how, when, and why of the assessment-instruction process. The next section of this chapter provides a step-by-step plan for carrying out this process. The steps in this plan provide the framework for the subsequent sections of this book, and the procedures involved in each step are discussed in detail in at least one or more of the following chapters (see Figure 3.1). Within each chapter the specific information needed to implement the assessment-instruction process is provided in as much detail as possible, including examples of what procedures to use and how to use them and explanations of when and why they are appropriate for use.

## Steps in the Assessment-Instruction Process

The steps in the assessment-instruction process are guided by four questions that we have adapted over the years:

1. What is the current status of the interaction between the learner and the instructional context?
2. What variation do we see across texts, tasks, and contexts?
3. What is the primary source of interference with learning or performance?
4. How can learning or performance be established or improved?

The foundation of the assessment-instruction process rests on an accurate assessment of the existing match between the learner and the context. Using this information, our next task is to generate hypotheses about the primary source of interference with learning or performance. It is critical that the hypotheses generated in this phase of the process focus on problems

**FIGURE 3.1**
The Assessment-
Instruction Process

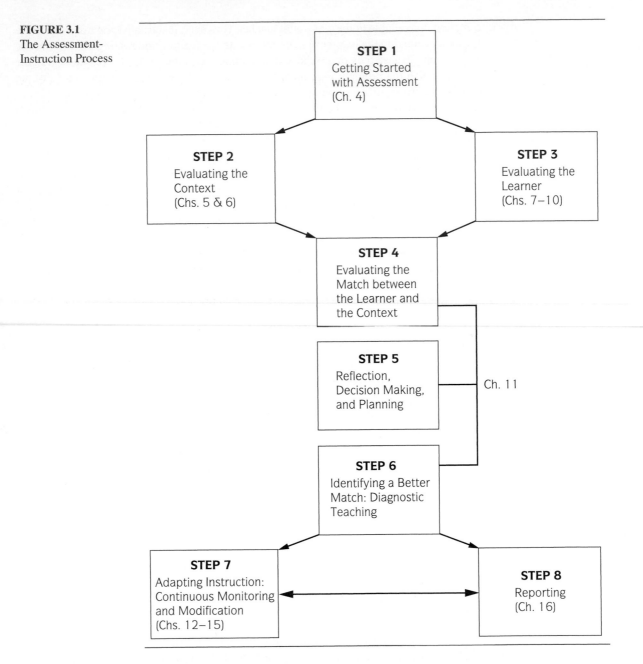

STEP 1
Getting Started
with Assessment
(Ch. 4)

STEP 2
Evaluating the
Context
(Chs. 5 & 6)

STEP 3
Evaluating the
Learner
(Chs. 7–10)

STEP 4
Evaluating the
Match between
the Learner and
the Context

STEP 5
Reflection,
Decision Making,
and Planning

Ch. 11

STEP 6
Identifying a Better
Match: Diagnostic
Teaching

STEP 7
Adapting Instruction:
Continuous Monitoring
and Modification
(Chs. 12–15)

STEP 8
Reporting
(Ch. 16)

of major importance. All readers and writers have minor difficulties with certain aspects of literacy, but these problems are rarely a primary source of interference with learning or performance. To ensure that we are focusing on major problems, it is sometimes helpful to ask ourselves, "If I corrected this problem, would the individual in question be likely to demonstrate improved reading and writing learning or performance?" The steps focus on identifying the means by which learning or performance may be established or improved.

The steps of the assessment-instruction process are summarized below. We follow a case study through all the steps to illustrate how the process was carried out with one student. Detailed information on how to proceed with each step is provided in subsequent chapters.

***Step 1: Getting Started with Assessment.*** The assessment-instruction process described here is not a standard set of tests and prescriptions to be used with all students. Rather, it is a dynamic process tailored to the needs of individual students and continually evolving as each additional piece of information is uncovered. The first step in the process involves identifying the presenting problem, gathering background information, and planning the initial evaluations of the learner and the learning context. Individuals are referred for, or seek out, help in reading and/or writing for a wide range of reasons. If there were only one or two sources of difficulty, our task would be relatively easy. Since that is not the case and unlimited time is rarely available to explore all possible avenues, the initial phase of assessment must provide a focus for subsequent steps in the process.

Background information provided by the individual, parents, school records, interviews, and visitations can yield valuable insights into possible sources of difficulty. Information about both the learner and the context should be gathered. Trying to complete an assessment for an individual is rather like reading a good mystery. No clues should be ignored, no information overlooked in the early stages of the story. We cannot be sure at the beginning just what will turn out to be important, even when the evidence seems to lead to an obvious conclusion. The task in this first phase is not to arrive at conclusions, but rather to generate hunches that may be tested. In short, you should try to avoid coming to any conclusions in the early stages and view your early findings as hypotheses to be tested against reality later on.

*Case Study.* Seth was referred to the clinic of one of the authors by Mr. Williams, his Title I teacher, who had several concerns. First, the available psychological data on Seth were not entirely helpful in planning an instructional program, and Mr. Williams wanted additional information to improve Seth's program. Seth had been referred for evaluation for special education services but was not currently receiving them because of parental resistance. Therefore, Mr. Williams wanted additional information so that he could make a recommendation about the appropriate placement for Seth. Finally, Seth was failing to make good progress despite receiving remedial reading help in school for the past two years. At the time he was referred, Seth was in the mid-third grade and had repeated first grade once. Seth lived in a state with no compulsory kindergarten, and he did not attend school at all before entering the first grade.

In gathering background data on Seth, we spoke to his mother and to his older sister, who was a teacher in his school district. Seth was the youngest of six children and lived on a farm in a rural county. He was small for his age and had limited use of his left hand and arm, which were underdeveloped and deformed. Both parents were busy with farm chores, and Seth was expected to help as well. Because of the family's responsibilities, little time was available for other activities. Family life seemed to revolve around their shared jobs.

Seth had little contact with children outside the school setting and had limited experiences with life off the farm.

The school records included annual report cards and a recent report by the school psychologist. The records suggested that Seth had been struggling with reading since he began his school career. At the time of the evaluation he was placed in regular third grade material in all areas except reading instruction, which was provided by a Title I reading program outside the regular classroom. Seth's written language abilities were also weak, but there was very little writing activity in the classroom, and he received no special support in writing.

The records also indicated that Seth was inattentive to assigned tasks and that he frequently failed to complete his work. On a norm-referenced achievement test administered four months before this evaluation, Seth scored in the first percentile in reading comprehension. The psychologist's report included an estimate of ability within the low-average to average range. In addition, the psychologist suggested that Seth's left-side paralysis might be impairing neurological functioning and argued strongly for a right-hemisphere approach to instruction, involving whole-word and whole-language experience activities.

*Case Discussion.*    In this first step we gathered and considered a variety of preexisting information. Briefly, we concluded that, with regard to reading and writing, Seth was not learning or performing as well as might be expected on the basis of his age, ability, and educational background. In addition, we had gathered enough background information to form some initial impressions that were used to guide subsequent evaluations of the learner and the learning context. These can be summarized as follows:

1. Seth's background and interests suggested that he may have had limited experience with and knowledge about reading and writing. This was an area we needed to pursue through interviews with Seth and his parents.
2. Seth's apparent lack of interest in many school-related activities and his failure to complete assignments suggested that he may have had little motivation for school in general and reading and writing in particular. This area needed to be pursued through observations and interviews with Seth, his teacher, and his parents.
3. Seth's history of poor performance, his test scores, and his difficulty completing assigned tasks suggested that his basic reading skills were very poor. This hypothesis needed to be tested, and assessment of sight word recognition, word analysis, and comprehension skills were all planned.
4. Seth's failure to complete assignments and his dependence on the teacher suggested that the work he was being given may have been too difficult for him. This was an area that needed to be examined through informal measures and an evaluation of the materials and methods being used.

***Step 2: Evaluating the Instructional Context.***    Despite wide recognition that teachers and teaching methods contribute to academic success, academic assessments rarely include evaluations of these factors. If teachers and methods are rarely considered, the contribution of materials or setting factors are examined even less frequently, especially the nonschool literacy abilities that may accompany students from diverse backgrounds. Failure to even consider such factors leaves the learner as the sole source of difficulty, and is something akin to blaming the victim (Coles, 1978; Stuckey, 1991).

A variety of procedures should be used to assess the learning context, including classroom observations, interviews, checklists, and visual inspection and analysis. Because most of these procedures are informal, care must be taken to examine this information systematically. Observation guidelines are helpful here, as are checklists. Great strides have also been made in the area of materials assessment, so a variety of procedures such as text analysis, comprehensibility checklists, and holistic scans have been added to traditional readability measures. Teachers, students, and parents can also provide invaluable information as they describe important aspects of the cultural and instructional setting for learning.

It is not always possible, or even desirable, to evaluate all possible contextual factors. However, it is imperative that the student's performance be examined from the perspective contexts in which he or she is expected to learn and perform. Not infrequently, students' reading or writing problems are exacerbated, if not actually caused, by contextual factors.

*Case Study.*   This step focuses on assessing the instructional context in which Seth was expected to perform and also the larger social context within which he was learning. During the interview with Seth's parents they indicated that he did read a farm journal occasionally and that he received *Humpty-Dumpty* magazine at home. They confirmed that reading aloud to Seth was not a practice in their home. Instead, Seth, like other members of the family, was oriented to outdoor activities and farm chores.

Information about the instructional context was gathered during a half-day classroom observation and interviews with Seth's teachers. Seth received instruction both in a regular classroom and outside the classroom in a Title I reading program. He was not part of a regular reading group within the classroom, although workbook tasks were assigned frequently. It appeared that he was rarely expected to read full-length texts in either setting. However, when longer selections were assigned, there was generally no prereading preparation or during-reading support.

Although the teacher read aloud as a daily part of the instructional program, Seth went to his Title I reading class during much of this period. Contrary to federal guidelines, Seth did not receive reading instruction in his regular classroom but only in the Title I classroom. His reading instruction was focused largely on word analysis, and work was assigned from a program that emphasized visual and auditory perception of letter clusters in words. The method of instruction used by this particular program emphasized the analysis of words into their constituent parts rather than beginning with word parts and blending them together to form a word.

The classroom teacher indicated that Seth was responsible for the same assigned work that was required of all other children in the class and that there was no differentiation of tasks among students. The language arts, spelling, and social studies books used in Seth's classroom were standard third grade texts with readability estimates ranging from a 2.5 to a 5.0 grade level. Seth was expected to complete all classroom assignments before going to recess. The teacher reported that Seth really liked recess and did not like to miss it, although he frequently did because his work was incomplete.

On the day we observed, Seth still had twelve math problems left to complete when recess time came, despite the fact that he had finished his art project earlier than most of the other children and returned to his seatwork and despite the fact that he worked industriously and without distraction for the entire period. He repeatedly asked the teacher for help—on every item, in fact. As we observed Seth, we were able to determine that he had little idea about how to approach the math problems that were assigned. Each time Seth approached the teacher for help, he was given information about how to do the specific problem he was working on, but he never received additional instruction targeted at his lack of understanding about how to do that *type* of problem. More troubling still was our observation that at least some of the assigned work was explained while Seth was involved in reading instruction outside of the classroom. In this particular case he had little recourse but to continue approaching the teacher for help.

Discussion with Seth provided additional information about his instructional context. After our visit to his classroom we asked him about his favorite part of the day, and he noted that he really enjoyed the time when his teacher read to the class. Seth had previously indicated that he enjoyed the period in the day when his teacher was reading *James and the Giant Peach.* During that earlier exchange we had been concerned because, despite his obvious interest, he was unable to accomplish a coherent retelling of the story. This time, Seth explained that he had to go to Title I reading class during read-aloud time and was able to hear only the initial portion of each day's reading!

*Case Discussion.*   Our evaluation of the learning context revealed the following: instructional materials written at a third grade level and above, little evidence of materials that Seth would be interested in and/or motivated to read, classroom assignments that emphasized task completion, no individualization of classroom assignments, large numbers of classroom assignments, lack of direction and explanation for classroom assignments caused in part by a pull-out reading program, no reading instruction in the regular classroom, Title I reading instruction focused on word analysis, and little opportunity to read longer texts for meaning.

### Step 3: *Evaluating the Learner.*

Each individual's abilities, skills, beliefs, interests, and instructional history influence reading and writing achievement. In Chapter 2 we outlined the components of reading and writing knowledge and skill that must be considered in any assessment. As in the evaluation of the context a variety of sources should be used in evaluating the learner because each source of information provides only a small part of the picture. These include classroom observations; interviews with parents, teachers, and the student; formal assessments; and informal assessments.

In the chapters to follow we describe in detail the types of procedures that may be employed in evaluating the learner. Generally speaking, these procedures fall into three categories. First, *observational and interview data* are rich sources of information but are often considered unreliable or subjective (see Chapter 4). We discuss ways of increasing the reliability of data collected in these ways and describe the unique contributions to assessment that are made by such procedures. Second, more traditional types of information about the learner result from using various *informal assessment* instruments and techniques (Chapters 7, 8, and 9). Both familiar and less-familiar strategies are presented. The third and best-known source of information about learners is *formal assessment,* using standardized, norm-referenced tests (see Chapter 10). Although widely used, most formal tests have significant problems in terms of the value of the diagnostic information they yield. However, a consideration of individual assessment would not be complete without a serious discussion of the role of such instruments in the assessment-instruction process.

*Case Study.*   An initial interview with Seth confirmed that his life revolved around family and friends. He reported few other interests but became animated in his discussions of the animals and his exploits on his four-wheeler. Seth said that he didn't like television very much, that he didn't like "being cooped up," and that he would rather play outside. Although he said he enjoyed stories, he reported that neither he nor his family read at home.

In response to questions focused on his knowledge about reading, Seth could not give a reason why people read and said that he read because he wanted to be "smart." He appeared to believe that reading involved only accurate word recognition, naming only "sounding out" as a strategy for analyzing unknown words. Similarly, he used neatness as an indicator of "good writing" and seemed unaware of personal uses for writing. When asked what his teachers did to help him become a better reader and writer, he could think of nothing for writing but said that they helped him sound out the words in reading.

During the interview with Seth's parents, Mrs. C. reported that Seth's health history was normal except that he had had a series of ear infections during his first year of first grade. Tubes were inserted to correct this problem, and no further difficulty was reported. She also noted that Seth's left arm paralysis resulted from a forceps delivery during which nerves were damaged. Thus, it seemed unlikely to us that neurological impairment was implicated in his problems.

Seth's classroom teacher reported that Seth seemed much younger than the other children in the class and that he sometimes asked questions or made comments that were "babyish." She indicated that Seth asked for help frequently to get attention. Further, she felt that Seth acted "cute" when he could not do something or wanted help, which was often.

Seth's abilities and behaviors were observed in both the classroom and the clinic. In the clinical setting, Seth appeared highly motivated to work hard in the areas in which he felt he was competent and/or in which he was succeeding. He enjoyed several of the instructional activities that were used and was always anxious to try reading on his own if appropriate prereading support had been provided. Seth sought help when he perceived work to be too difficult for him, and in those situations he put forth little effort. When pressed, he would attempt difficult tasks, but if success was not immediate, he shrugged and said he could not do it.

As described previously, Seth was also observed in his classroom. At the beginning of the observation period, Seth's teacher was phasing children into a painting project. Seth was one of the first students done with his project. While the majority of the class continued to paint, Seth washed his hands and returned to work at his desk. After returning to his desk, Seth looked up from his work only occasionally. Despite the noise level and the proximity of two groups of children chatting, Seth seemed undistracted. However, he was very reliant on his teacher. He asked questions frequently, requiring her help on nearly every individual task on which the examiner observed him working.

Informal assessments of several types were also employed with Seth. Information was collected using informal tests of isolated word recognition, informal reading inventories, and tests of word analysis skill. Formal assessments, including norm-referenced tests of reading achievement and vocabulary knowledge, were administered to obtain estimates of Seth's performance as compared to other children his age. The pattern of results indicated that, overall, Seth's reading achievement was at least a year and a half below what we might reasonably expect given his age and school experience. His sight word recognition was inadequate, and his word analysis skills were limited to the ineffective use of phonic analysis. Although his vocabulary knowledge was appropriate for his age, both his listening comprehension and reading comprehension were generally poor. In addition, his oral reading errors reflected little attention to meaning or contextual cues. However, in situations in which he had adequate background knowledge and sufficient interest, he was able to answer questions successfully, retell a story, and/or generate a main idea. Finally, early informal work samples suggested that he was almost entirely unable to produce a written product. Even with considerable support, his ideas were disjointed, and his narratives were limited to three or four sentences.

*Case Discussion.*    At this point in the assessment-instruction process, several specific areas of difficulty had been identified. Seth's responses to interview questions and performance on informal measures suggested that both his reading and writing knowledge and skill were limited. For example, although Seth believed that he usually understood what he read, he had difficulty retelling stories in a coherent fashion, could not write coherent texts, and could neither identify nor generate a main idea. Seth did not appear to apply what skills and knowledge he had in a consistent way, so the products of his efforts were even less acceptable than might be expected. Although he was not actively resistant to reading or writing, Seth did not appear to be motivated to read or write nor to improve his skills; he greatly preferred to do other things. He worked hard when he experienced success, but application during difficult tasks was limited.

### Step 4: Evaluating the Match between the Learner and the Context.

The fourth step is to evaluate the match between the knowledge, performance, and motivation of the learner and the materials, methods, and settings within the learning context, using the information gathered in the previous steps. This is the culmination of the first phase of the assessment-instruction process. It provides the answer to the first and second questions guiding the assessment-instruction process: What is the current status of the interaction between the learner and the learning context and what variation do we see across texts, tasks, and contexts?

Because an interactive view of disability predicts variability, it becomes relatively easy to see why some students appear to thrive in the very environments that befuddle others. Our job in this stage of the assessment-instruction process is to pull together all that we know as the result of our professional efforts and experience and to evaluate how well existing demands, expectations, and supports of the context match the student's abilities, interests, knowledge, and level of independence.

*Case Study.*    As we reached this point in the assessment-instruction process with Seth, we began to see that the match between Seth's abilities, interests, knowledge, and level of independence and the demands, expectations, and supports of his present placement was problematic in several ways. First, it appeared that his daily classroom assignments were mismatched with his knowledge and skills. The quantity of work was more than he could reasonably complete in the allotted time. In addition, the level of work was too difficult. He could not complete any of this work without additional help. This situation was aggravating his already strong personal tendency toward dependency. Our assessment suggested that he was receiving no in-class support that might help to compensate for limited knowledge and skill.

Second, Seth's interests lay outside the academic setting. He was not internally motivated to complete classwork in order to reap the rewards of school success. The content of the school's instructional materials and tasks was largely devoid of references to lifestyles or interests similar to Seth's. His experiences were limited, and little prereading development was done to increase what appeared to be inadequate prior knowledge.

The emphasis on word analysis in Seth's remedial program appeared to represent a closer match to his existing needs and abilities; however, little attention was being given to his problems with comprehension. Finally, he was regularly denied access to the aspects of school life that he did enjoy—recess, book read-aloud time, and so on.

*Case Discussion.*   At this stage in the process, there were still many unanswered questions about the match between Seth's specific problems and particular instructional approaches. Although our assessment of the learner had revealed a number of problem areas, these needed to be prioritized and the most effective instructional approaches identified. The issue of instruction was especially critical, since it appeared that the existing match was not ideal.

### Step 5: Reflection, Decision Making, and Planning.

The fifth step is to generate hypotheses from the evaluation of the existing match regarding the third guiding question: What is the primary source of interference with learning or performance? Probably the most critical feature of skilled assessment is the ability to reflect on available data and realize what it means. Collecting information about learners is relatively easy, compared to thinking about it and making sense of it. The assessment-instruction process must include sufficient time to reflect on information gathered. Indeed, the inexperienced clinician may need to spend as much time reflecting on the information as has been spent gathering it. In later chapters we provide guidelines and formats for summarizing and reflecting on available data.

The answers we have generated in response to the question "What is the primary source of interference with learning or performance?" are then used to identify possible solutions to the hypothesized problems. Not all things are equally possible, given the realities of school life and the state of our current knowledge. Decision making is both a thoughtful consideration of instructional priorities (What does the student seem to need most?) and a consideration of the available resources and feasibility of change (How much control do we have over the mismatch?). During decision making, we must specify which components of the problem might be changed in some way, and how this might best be accomplished. These decisions form the basis of the plans for the next steps in the process.

There is a temptation at this stage to begin mapping out a detailed instructional program. However, we are often not ready to say with certainty exactly what needs to be done. As we reflect on available information, new questions are often raised that need to be addressed through further evaluation. Therefore, the focus of this step is to identify possible solutions that can be tried out in some systematic way.

*Case Study.*   As we reflected on Seth, we had several hunches about his strengths and weaknesses as a reader and the best use of our resources. First, Seth's word identification skills were inadequate. His knowledge of sight words was far from automatic, and his phonological awareness abilities were very undeveloped. He was unable to analyze whole words into their individual phonemes and typically could not recall the letter sequences in known words. Seth's failure to recognize that the whole was made up of parts was not limited to word analysis. For example, Seth seemed unable to analyze stories at a global level, often failing to see connections between one event in a text and another. His retellings were typically fragmented, and he seemed unable to remedy the problems, even with discussion. Not surprisingly, during oral reading, Seth was often content to leave nonsensical miscues uncorrected, suggesting that he was not attending to meaning.

Despite these serious difficulties, Seth's strengths were notable. He had no difficulties in the areas of hearing or discriminating letter sounds. He both knew and regularly applied sound–symbol information for initial and final consonants. Seth's overall reading behavior indicated that he was inattentive to meaning, but he did demonstrate ability in this area during isolated reading events. For example, while reading a selection about a boy's dog being hit by a car, Seth's miscues were consistently meaningful, and his responses to subsequent questions indicated a strong ability to bring relevant prior knowledge to bear on the text.

*Case Discussion.*   We identified the primary source of interference with Seth's learning or performance as inadequate word identification skills, coupled with limited background knowledge, interest, and motivation. Secondarily, we were concerned with his ability to read for meaning. Our best guess at this point was that Seth needed an approach that would help him see how the various parts fit into the larger whole of identifying words and understanding what was being read. Therefore, we decided to try a holistic, language-experience approach with Seth in an effort to address both his problems with word identification and comprehension and with background knowledge, interest, and motivation. We planned to try out several different methods for enhancing Seth's word identification skills within the context of this approach. The specifics of these diagnostic teaching procedures are described in greater detail in the next section.

### Step 6: Identifying a Better Match: Diagnostic Teaching.

The sixth step involves continued assessment, based on the hypotheses and possible solutions generated in the previous step. The primary method of assessment used in this step is called diagnostic teaching. The two major purposes of diagnostic teaching are to provide additional diagnostic information about the interaction between the learner and the instructional context, and to identify instructional procedures that are likely to be effective in improving learning and performance.

Diagnostic teaching is a combination of assessment and instruction that provides information about how students perform under classroomlike conditions and how they might perform if we altered some aspects of the instructional setting. Diagnostic teaching usually involves systematically manipulating one or more components of reading and/or writing processes. Teachers are often gratified to know that there is a name for what might look like "messing around" or "trying out this and that." All instruction can be viewed as diagnostic teaching, as long as it is thoughtfully planned using our best guesses about what may work for a given student and as long as we are prepared to monitor our work continually to see how adjustments have affected learning and performance.

*Case Study.*   Although we had a great deal of information about Seth, we also had several questions and concerns that needed to be addressed in order to be able to identify a better match:

1. What approach to instruction should be employed with Seth?
2. By what means does Seth learn most rapidly and retain most consistently?
3. Should the relative focus of instruction be placed on expanding Seth's repertoire of word recognition skills, or could some generic instruction improve both word analysis and passage comprehension abilities?
4. Could reading and writing inform each other in Seth's instructional program?

On the basis of our earlier reflections, we planned a series of diagnostic teaching episodes for Seth. The first component of instruction we manipulated involved word recognition and retention. Using three different approaches to instruction and three groups of five words, we systematically taught Seth to recognize the words instantly. We timed the instructional sequence so that we would know how long it took under each set of instructional circumstances for him to learn the five words in each set, and we also retested him on these words after one and one-half hours to see how many words he had retained from each sequence. Thus, we are able to evaluate both effectiveness and efficiency. Finally, we asked Seth to tell us which method he thought had been most effective for him.

At delayed retesting, Seth knew at sight (two-second flash) all fifteen new words. It appeared that all three instructional approaches were effective. However, using one approach, he learned the five new words in one and a half minutes, whereas using a different approach, it took ten minutes for him to learn the words! In terms of efficiency, Seth was likely to benefit from a phonics program that blends parts into wholes as opposed to a phonics program that breaks the whole into component parts. It should be noted, however, that he learned the words with equal ease when they were presented as sight words. The approach that was least efficient for Seth was the whole-to-part phonics approach that was similar to his current instructional program. Interestingly, Seth's perception conformed to these conclusions. He felt he had learned the words most easily in the part-to-whole phonics approach.

These results were a little disconcerting since, as noted earlier, we suspected that Seth could benefit from a holistic approach to instruction. To clarify issues related to approach and content, we initiated a language-experience activity designed to allow Seth to read and write about topics of interest to him. During the first diagnostic teaching segment we were chagrined to find that while Seth was enthusiastic about discussing a personal encounter with a "coydog" (half dog, half coyote), the story he dictated was sparse and incoherent. Subsequent work with a conference partner did nothing to improve the quality of the product. Two additional trials, yielding similar results, led us to conclude that this was not the most effective method for improving Seth's word recognition or comprehension skills at the present time.

*Case Discussion.*    Recall that the questions we wished to address in the diagnostic teaching step of the process included "What should be the focus on instruction for Seth?" and "What approach to instruction should be employed?" After several manipulations such as those described above, we concluded that Seth's program would need to contain strong elements of work in both word recognition and comprehension, and these might need to be somewhat separate for the time being. Despite our earlier conclusions, it appeared that Seth needed to develop a strong understanding of the component parts before he would benefit from more holistic instruction. For him the rather counterintuitive benefits of part-to-whole instruction were obvious. However, he also needed as much exposure as possible to whole texts and read-aloud sessions as a means of increasing his understanding of the purposes for reading and writing and to increase his motivation and interest.

### Step 7: Adapting Instruction: Continuous Monitoring and Modification.    The results of diagnostic teaching are used to plan an instructional program that is likely to respond to the most important needs of the individual reader. There are times when instruction will proceed before assessment is completed. At other times the individual responsible for assessment will not deliver instruction. Wherever possible, of course, the preferred arrangement is for both assessment and instruction to be conducted by the same person.

In either case initial instructional outcomes are established. Although attitude goals, content goals, and process goals may all be included in an individual's program, it is also possible that one or two of these will receive special emphasis. The information gathered in earlier portions of the process is used to inform decisions about what content to include and what delivery system to use. It is understood that these initial decisions may be changed or altered as further information is gathered.

Every instructional encounter with a particular reader is an opportunity for assessing and improving instruction. It is possible, and desirable, to continually monitor the effectiveness of the recommended instructional program and to make fine-tuning adjustments in the program as needed. Continuous monitoring of instructional progress is absolutely essential, and adaptive teaching involving modifications in texts, tasks, and materials is desirable. The full potential of this process can be realized only when it becomes part of daily practice.

*Case Study.*    Because there was increasing evidence to suggest that a more part-to-whole approach would be effective for Seth, he received daily work that focused on the individual constituent parts of words. For phonically regular words he received instruction in individual sounds and symbols and was supported as he blended these to form words and word parts. This focus on constituent parts was also used for high-frequency sight words. In this case, though, the tutor used a visual and kinesthetic approach, having Seth trace a new word four times with different colors. Then Seth was directed to "get a picture" of the word in his head, and the card was removed. As a next step, Seth was asked to talk about the word, in general: how many "tall letters," its shape, and any other unique features (for example double letters). Then Seth was encouraged to spell the word, checking against the card. Finally, the word was added to the practice pile and counted as "learned" when he could recognize it reliably in print.

The part-to-whole approach was also used to support comprehension through an adapted process writing approach. During the first phase, Seth dictated a story. When he believed it to be complete, the tutor then rewrote the story so that it included an introduction, episode, and conclusion. This revised piece was discussed, with the emphasis placed on the components of a strong story. Finally, one component (the introduction, episode, or conclusion) was deleted, and Seth was encouraged to write a replacement. This process was continued until Seth had rewritten the entire piece. This practice proved especially helpful to Seth and was later coupled with "story frames" (Fowler, 1982) to encourage Seth to construct whole texts that contained important component pieces. In addition, contact between school and clinic was maintained to good effect.

Although Seth continued to receive remedial reading support outside the classroom during the regularly scheduled reading instruction time, he no longer missed key components of the rest of the day. The support personnel in Seth's school also agreed to incorporate several of the recommended instructional procedures. For example, Seth's program was changed to include daily experiences with whole texts. He was read to daily, and these read-aloud sessions formed the basis for work in comprehension and writing. Similarly, direct instruction in word recognition was planned so that rapid application in text was featured.

*Case Discussion.* It is especially important to recognize that only parts of Seth's instructional program could really be accomplished in the clinic setting. Because some aspects of his progress in reading and writing were governed by the classroom and school setting, it was important to include teachers and specialists very early on in Seth's remedial program. He clearly needed, and could benefit from, some individualized instruction. However, he also needed a total instructional program that was more responsive to his needs.

*Step 8: Reporting.* This step involves the summarization of information obtained in the previous steps in written reports and/or oral conferences. It requires a clear statement of the presenting problem(s), a description of the information collected in the evaluations of the learner and the learning context and through diagnostic teaching, a synthesis of this information into a clear statement of the primary difficulty, and recommendations for future practice, including descriptions and examples of appropriate materials and methods.

Although procedures for writing and reporting vary, the reporting format should parallel as closely as possible the goals of the assessment-instruction process. For now it is important only to arrive at a general appreciation of how important clear, concise communication can be for students.

*Case Study.* As a result of the clinic's report, Seth's parents concluded that he did indeed need the help of special education placement and requested that he be evaluated for determination of eligibility. The school, in turn, was anxious to use the information obtained from Seth's assessment in the clinic. Conferences were conducted with the Title I teacher and with the special educator, and the school effectively implemented the suggestions detailed in the final report. The special educator was especially interested in the mapping activities that had been done and incorporated these activities into Seth's program. She also worked with the classroom teacher to find ways to provide prereading support activities for Seth in social studies and science.

You may also recall that there was reason to believe that Seth's daily classwork was not entirely appropriate. The final report recommended that Seth's program would need to be individualized to accommodate his specific needs and abilities. Therefore, Seth's fourth-grade classroom placement was made with an eye to teacher flexibility. In particular, the teacher's ability to provide consistent and appropriate support and willingness to adapt and individualize instruction were considered. He was placed with a teacher who had demonstrated these abilities in the past and who was also capable of ensuring that Seth took responsibility for his work.

*Case Discussion.*   In later chapters we discuss these aspects of communicating the results of the assessment-instruction process in some depth. In the meantime you can find Seth's final report in Appendix A. Continuous assessment is critical, of course. In Seth's case this will need to be done by the special education team as they conduct their periodic reevaluation of Seth's eligibility for their services. In addition, this will be done to make adjustments to the recommended program. It is likely that Seth will need continued support for some time to come. Only continuous assessment and adjustment will ensure his progress.

# Chapter Summary

This chapter considered an interactive view of reading and writing disability and its application to assessment and instruction. The first section of the chapter presented an interactive view of reading and writing *disability* that is consistent with the interactive view of reading and writing *ability* presented previously in Chapter 1 and that provides the theory that drives this text. An interactive view of disability suggests that students' performance on various reading and writing tasks is an indication of what they can and will do under specified conditions, rather than a set of fixed abilities and disabilities. Our attention is focused on how each student performs under different conditions and which conditions are most likely to facilitate learning rather than identifying the disability. The notion of the proper match between student and circumstance is what we must grasp if we are to be effective evaluators and instructors.

The second section of this chapter focused on an understanding of the assessment-instruction process. The long-range goal of the assessment-instruction process was described as the development of strategic, motivated, reflective learners who are able to apply their skills and strategies independently and in a flexible manner. Learning to read and write was characterized as a lifelong pursuit in which the knowledge gained from each reading/writing experience affects subsequent experiences. Because there are differences between instructional settings (classroom, resource room, clinic, etc.), different applications of the assessment-instruction process for these settings were discussed. Classroom teachers have the benefit of daily contact with students but limited time to spend with individual students. In contrast, the specialist or clinician has the benefit of individual time with the student but limited access to the student's daily interactions with reading and writing in the classroom. As a result, the amount of attention devoted to each component and the procedures used to evaluate them are likely to vary.

In the final section of this chapter we described *procedures* for implementing the assessment-instruction process. The steps in the assessment-instruction process are guided by four questions: What is the current status of the interaction between the learner and the context? What variation do we see across texts, tasks, and contexts? What is the primary source of interference with learning or performance? How can learning or performance be established or improved? The steps in the assessment-instruction process are as follows:

Step 1   Getting Started with Assessment
Step 2   Evaluating the Context
Step 3   Evaluating the Learner: Focusing on Reading and Writing
Step 4   Evaluating the Match between the Learner and the Context
Step 5   Reflection, Decision Making, and Planning
Step 6   Identifying a Better Match: Diagnostic Teaching
Step 7   Adapting Instruction: Continuous Monitoring and Modification
Step 8   Reporting

# SECTION TWO

# Getting Started and Evaluating the Context

In the first two chapters we provided both a theoretical and a practical framework for thinking about assessment-instruction. The theoretical framework provides the rationale for much of the remainder of the text. Frequent reference is made throughout to the ideas and concepts presented in Chapters 1 and 2.

Section Two is critical to creating a contextualized assessment that reflects the interactive model we advocate in this book. It is divided into two parts. The first, which comprises Chapter 4, is titled *Getting Started with Assessment*. As its name suggests, it includes a discussion of tools and strategies for initiating assessment. These include strategies for examining both the learner and the context as the assessment-instruction process is getting underway.

The second part contains two chapters. The discussions in these two chapters provide the basis for the execution of Step 2 of the assessment-instruction process: *Evaluating the Context*. In this section we describe more fully the contextual factors of setting, including both home and school; instructional environment, including methods and routines; and instructional resources, including texts and tasks. We discuss the contributions of these factors to reading and writing performance and describe ways in which these factors can be evaluated for individual students. The measures we suggest are designed to help summarize information about the setting, the specific instruction, the instructional materials, and the tasks students face in their literacy contexts. Each of these areas is considered in light of the most current research and also in terms of the desirable outcomes for reading and writing instruction.

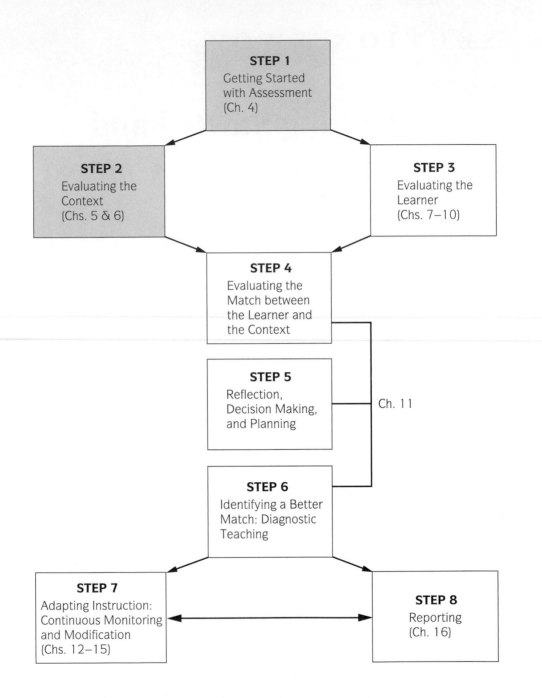

**STEP 1**
Getting Started
with Assessment
(Ch. 4)

**STEP 2**
Evaluating the
Context
(Chs. 5 & 6)

**STEP 3**
Evaluating the
Learner
(Chs. 7–10)

**STEP 4**
Evaluating the
Match between
the Learner and
the Context

**STEP 5**
Reflection,
Decision Making,
and Planning

Ch. 11

**STEP 6**
Identifying a Better
Match: Diagnostic
Teaching

**STEP 7**
Adapting Instruction:
Continuous Monitoring
and Modification
(Chs. 12–15)

**STEP 8**
Reporting
(Ch. 16)

# 4 Getting Started with Assessment

Assessments of student reading and writing ability must begin somewhere. In this chapter we provide a road map for the initial step of the assessment-instruction process: Getting Started. The procedures for collecting, interviewing, and observing described in this chapter are essential to a good beginning, but these activities don't end after this phase of the assessment-instruction process—as in "That's done, now let's move on to the next step." Talking and observing with an eye toward assessment should be continuous activities in every classroom and clinical setting. Because these are such powerful tools, they are useful in virtually every phase of the assessment-instruction process and are discussed in almost every chapter of this book.

This chapter begins with a brief discussion of the nature of assessment and some guidelines that are important for the entire assessment-instruction process. The idea of a *diagnostic portfolio* is also introduced. As we use the term, it is both a way to think about assessment and instruction and a way to manage information. Then we provide a rationale and describe procedures for collecting background information and conducting observations and interviews, including a discussion of the sources of information that are useful in the Getting Started phase.

In the Getting Started step of the assessment-instruction process, we are less concerned with gathering information about students' application of literacy skills than we are with obtaining a general picture of the factors that may be influencing the performance data we will gather later. In this chapter *observation, interviews,* and *work samples* are discussed as approaches to the problem of gathering *background information* for the purpose of getting started. We hope to gain an initial understanding of the learner and the context within which he or she is learning. The techniques described in this Getting Started step of assessment-instruction may save many hours of work later on.

## Understanding Assessment

### Contexts for Assessment Instruction

Most students learn to read and write in *developmental* programs at the elementary and middle school levels. These programs are based on materials and tasks that have been developed so that they increase in difficulty and complexity across age and grade levels and are designed for use with large numbers of students. The assumption underlying developmental reading and writing programs is that the same (or very similar) base materials, content, instructional plans, delivery systems, and sequence are appropriate for all "normally developing" students. Consequently, everyone proceeds through the program in the same order and in the same way, although the pace may vary for some students.

In most classrooms, however, there is a wide range of student achievement in reading and writing. Many teachers accommodate individual differences in their classroom by varying their instruction somewhat, within the parameters of the developmental program. When students fail to maintain the pace or make anticipated progress, they are generally referred for help.

Specialized programs of all sorts (often called *remedial* or *corrective* programs) exist to serve students who have not learned to read or write as well or as quickly as their peers or whose progress is slower than expected. Until quite recently, special programs almost invariably involved identifying students based on formal achievement/diagnostic tests and then removing them from their regular classroom for some period during the day/week so that they could work with a specialist. Most of the instruction for struggling students was delivered by someone other than the classroom teacher and in an area outside the regular classroom (often called the *pull-out model*).

Although these configurations are still quite common, many schools and classrooms have moved toward a new generation of procedures and processes for working with students at risk for failure. These alternatives generally provide additional diagnostic flexibility and also focus more attention on the role of the classroom and the teacher. There is an increased awareness that assessment and evaluation should be located in the classroom and be conducted by the classroom teacher whenever possible. The vast majority of diagnostic information needed to plan and evaluate instruction can be gathered in the course of normal literacy events, as long as the teacher is knowledgeable and skilled.

The instructional value of collaborative and contextualized assessment procedures is likely to be much greater than could be realized by conventional approaches. In many schools all teachers participate in team staffings that are designed to promote collaborative responses to individual strengths and needs. In this section and throughout the book we try to suggest strategies that are compatible with a more integrated approach to working with students' reading and writing problems. At the same time we recognize that traditional clinical settings and pull-out programs are still common, and we try to suggest ways to create the best assessment-instruction context possible.

## Guidelines for Assessment

Assessment must reflect our best and most current understandings of reading and writing. Certainly, it appears that many traditional assessment practices have not provided information about important aspects of literacy, but "We are seeing a dramatic shift in *what* is assessed as well as in *how* it is assessed. . . . [S]tudents are (being) asked to engage in complex and challenging tasks" (Valencia, 1998, pp. 4–5). The International Reading Association and the National Council of Teachers of English have jointly published a document that details the *Standards for the Assessment of Reading and Writing* (IRA/NCTE, 1994). The eleven standards are summarized in Figure 4.1. These standards are both implicitly and explicitly visible in the recommended practices we describe throughout the text. In addition to these

**FIGURE 4.1**
Standards for the
Assessment of
Reading and Writing

| Standards for the Assessment of Reading and Writing |
| --- |
| • **Standard 1:** The interests of the student are paramount in assessment.<br>• **Standard 2:** The primary purpose of assessment is to improve teaching and learning.<br>• **Standard 3:** Assessment must reflect and allow for critical inquiry into curriculum and instruction.<br>• **Standard 4:** Assessments must recognize and reflect the intellectually and socially complex nature of reading and writing and the important roles of school, home, and society in literacy development.<br>• **Standard 5:** Assessment must be fair and equitable.<br>• **Standard 6:** The consequences of an assessment procedure are the first, and most important, consideration in establishing the validity of the assessment.<br>• **Standard 7:** The teacher is the most important agent of assessment.<br>• **Standard 8:** The assessment process should involve multiple perspectives and sources of data.<br>• **Standard 9:** Assessment must be based in the school community.<br>• **Standard 10:** All members of the education community—students, parents, teachers, administrators, policy makers—must have a voice in the development, interpretation, and reporting of assessment.<br>• **Standard 11:** Parents must be involved as active essential participants in the assessment process. |

standards we offer the following few guidelines for assessment focused on students who are struggling in the areas of reading or writing.

For these students it is also essential that we assess directly the factors that are known to influence reading and writing, rather than ignoring them or attempting to create situations where they do not matter. What is needed is a structured approach to determine how an individual handles actual reading materials or writing tasks under conditions that simulate real reading and writing situations both in and out of the classroom. The following guidelines provide the basis for assessment practices that achieve these goals.

***Assess Meaningful Activities in Appropriate Contexts.*** To evaluate students' reading and writing abilities, we must assess students as they read and write real texts for real purposes. There are times when it may be reasonable to evaluate some component skill in isolation (for example, sight word vocabulary). However, we should avoid generating conclusions about the contribution of any single skill to overall reading and writing ability until we have also observed the component in context.

In addition, we must consider how relevant the component abilities are for real, or *authentic,* reading and writing activities. Authenticity describes both tasks and materials (Valencia, 1998). There should be a purpose for reading or writing that transcends assessment or instruction. School tasks and texts in reading and writing should be similar to those used by people in nonschool settings. If they are not, questions of authenticity are raised.

Similarly, the most informative assessments are those that occur within the everyday instructional context rather than artificial testing contexts. There is evidence that people are aware of the differences among contexts and alter their performance accordingly (Spiro & Myers, 1984). Anyone who has ever puzzled over the discrepancy between students' performance in the classroom and their test performance is aware of this problem.

In general, students tend to consider formal testing situations to be more important than everyday classroom tasks. However, this perception can have very different effects on different students. Some students perform better in the formal testing situations because of increased motivation to do well; others perform less well because of the anxiety created by the pressure to do well. Therefore, we do not want to collect information that tells us only how students perform in formal testing situations. We want to be able to make some predictions about students' performance in everyday instructional contexts.

***Match Assessment to Purpose and to Instruction.***    No single assessment tool or strategy can do everything. We must think carefully about what we want to know and why we are assessing. If we need comparative data on large numbers of students, then informal, classroom-based assessment probably is not practical. On the other hand, if we want information that will help us plan instruction for individuals or groups of students, then standardized, norm-referenced tests are not likely to be helpful.

Two general purposes for assessment are often contrasted: external and internal (Wixson, Valencia, & Lipson, 1994). The audience for external assessments is outside the classroom, even when the assessment is conducted inside. The audience for internal assessment is inside the classroom; teachers and students use the information to advance instructional goals. Even after these primary audiences have been defined, purposes can and should influence assessment decisions. For example, if we are interested in making placement decisions, then we do not need procedures that yield a fine-grained analysis of strengths and weaknesses. Alternatively, if we are trying to make decisions about whether to teach or reteach a particular component, then we will need a tool or strategy that provides an evaluation of a specific area. On the other hand, if we are concerned about evaluating whole reading programs, we still want to be sure that the reading assessments mimic authentic reading, since they are likely to become "curricular magnets" for both teachers and students, which encourage teachers to teach test content to the exclusion of all else (Popham, 1993).

Because tests can be such powerful influences on instruction, it is important to remember that decisions about instructional goals and outcomes should *precede* assessment decisions. At the very least, there should be good alignment between the assessment and the nature and goals of the instrucitonal program (Valencia, 1998). Similarly, the ways in which students demonstrate competence should be similar across the assessment and instructional contexts.

***Be Systematic.***    Whether we use formal, standardized tests or informal, classroom-based procedures, our assessments must be reliable or trustworthy indices of student performance (see Chapter 10). The results of an assessment would have little meaning if they fluctuated wildly from one administration to the next.

The reliability of formal test instruments typically is addressed through the standardization process and reported in the manual. The trustworthiness of informal assessments depends on the extent to which we are systematic and consistent in our use of these techniques (Valencia & Calfee, 1991). When making comparisons among individuals, we must attempt to evaluate all of our students under the same conditions, with the same level of support. For example, we should attempt to formalize at least some of the probing questions asked during story retellings. If the student is given additional assistance, then it is important to record the information provided to clarify the conditions under which the performance occurred. Otherwise, the information will not be instructionally useful.

***Assess Continuously.***   Multiple samples of students' performance are always preferable to a single sample. Not only does continuous evaluation improve the reliability of the procedure, it also permits us to observe the *patterns* of behavior that are most informative for assessment and instruction. In addition, it casts assessment and instruction in their proper roles—as interacting elements of teaching. Viewing every instructional interaction with a student as an assessment opportunity enhances our diagnostic powers.

We have found that continuous assessment helps us to view both our own teaching and the students' abilities in a different light. A student's failure to perform can be viewed as an opportunity to gather information rather than a reflection of some static and inherent ability (in either the teacher or the child). Teacher evaluations must be taken seriously. Indeed, the majority of assessments in reading and writing can and should be done continuously and in conjunction with the daily instructional program as an aid to planning, adapting, and refining instruction.

***Promote Reflection and Self-Assessment.***   Most educators do not think of assessment as an opportunity to promote student independence and self-evaluation. Nor do most of us think of assessment as an opportunity to reflect on our own teaching practices and glean insights for self-improvement. Indeed, most of us think of assessment as something that is done "to us." However, contemporary views of literacy assessment acknowledge an important truth: Appropriate self-assessment and the ability to set appropriate goals lead to learning and improved performance—for both teachers and students.

As Valencia (1998, p. 20), has noted:

> Reflection grows naturally out of classroom assessment because instruction and assessment are integrated. Both teachers and students learn that people improve by judging their own performance against exemplars and clearly defined standards. In turn, they become more expert at understanding what good work looks like, more likely to be self-directed, and more invested in their own learning and progress—all of which leads to success.

Many, perhaps most, struggling readers and writers have ceded the responsibility for judgment to the teachers. They acquire a passive approach to learning that is harmful to their progress. Teachers and students alike need to acquire the skills related to self-reflection.

## The Diagnostic Portfolio and the Thumbnail Sketch

Thoughtful reflection and good records are essential when a variety of standardized and informal procedures are used to plan instruction, evaluate progress, and communicate with parents and administrators. We suggest creating and using a *diagnostic portfolio* as a way to support and promote the ongoing and multisource type of assessment advocated in this text. According to Valencia, McGinley, and Pearson (1990, p. 126), the term *portfolio* has both a physical and philosophical sense:

> As a concept, the "idea" of a portfolio forces us to expand the range of "things" we would consider as data to use in instructional decision-making. It is also an attitude suggesting that assessment is a dynamic rather than a static process reflected most accurately in multiple snapshots taken over time. All who have a stake in contributing to the portfolio (students, teachers, and parents) have a right to visit it whenever they wish—to reflect on and analyze its contents. But it is also a physical entity, a container in which we can store the artifacts of our literacy—the examples, documents, and observations that serve as evidence of growth and development—so that they are available for visitation and reflection.

Diagnostic portfolios, like other types of portfolios, are *organized* and *intentional* collections. Also like other portfolios, they include materials that exemplify the depth and breadth of a student's expertise. They include a variety of different types of information collected over time as indicators of growth in reading and writing, which make it easier for teachers, clinicians, and students to plan the experiences that will encourage additional progress.

The contents of the portfolio will vary in relation to the particular program of assessment and instruction in effect. As Valencia (1990a) notes, the range of items that can be included in a portfolio is almost limitless; some items are written responses to reading, reading logs, selected daily work, pieces of writing at various stages of completion, classroom tests, observational checklists, unit projects, and audio or video tapes. An important addition to these suggestions, for those who follow the assessment-instruction process outlined in this book, is the inclusion of measures designed to evaluate various aspects of the instructional context. "The key is to ensure a variety of types of indicators of learning so that teachers, parents, students, and administrators can build a complete picture of the student's development" (Valencia, 1990a, p. 339).

There will also be information in a diagnostic portfolio that is unlikely to appear in conventional portfolios. Most contemporary descriptions of portfolios suggest that portfolios should be embedded in classroom instruction and that students should play a pivotal role in selecting, maintaining, and reflecting upon the portfolio contents.

A diagnostic portfolio has somewhat different functions and forms and the degree of student involvement will be quite dependent on the age and maturity of the student. The diagnostic portfolio is designed to improve teacher decision making through more comprehensive and representative assessment and to get a richer and more authentic view of the student's literacy knowledge and use in order to rethink and/or reshape instruction. As a result, the teacher is likely to have a more central role in the diagnostic portfolio than is typical for classroom-based portfolios. Because the purpose of this portfolio is much more highly focused, it is likely to contain at least some conventional assessment information and there will be many more pieces of evidence that speak to the teacher and to the specialist (see Figure 4.2).

We recommend that the contents of the portfolio be organized into several layers of information: the actual evidence, or raw data, and one or more levels of summary or profile

**FIGURE 4.2**   The Diagnostic Portfolio

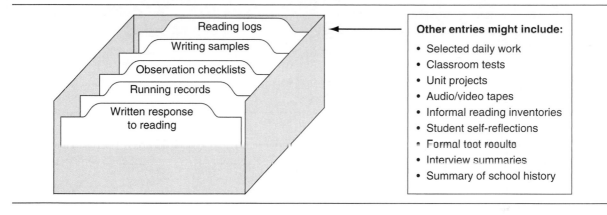

sheets to help synthesize the information. Inclusion of the raw data enables us to examine students' actual work and progress notes, rather than relying simply on a number or grade.

Summary or profile sheets assist us in analyzing and synthesizing the information in ways that help us make decisions and communicate with parents and administrators. We have found it helpful to use a summary chart that we call the *thumbnail sketch* to facilitate and monitor decision making as we work through the steps of the assessment-instruction process (see Figure 4.3). This chart, or any form of written summary for that matter, forces us to think carefully about the important factors operating in individual cases. It can also identify areas about which we need more information. In this chapter we describe some of the tools and strategies for gathering information in Step 1.

## Sources of Information

All students, even very young children, come to us with a personal and educational history. Students' physical, cognitive, affective, and sociocultural histories have a profound influence on what and how they learn. In some cases assessments of reading or writing ability can be speeded immeasurably by the careful and thoughtful gathering and analysis of background information regarding these areas.

In the Getting Started phase of the assessment-instruction process, it is important to gather as much background information as possible from the home, the school, and the learner because we cannot know what information might be significant. There are several reasons to collect background information. First, it is helpful at the onset of assessment to establish that the primary source of difficulty is *not* a correlate (see Chapter 2), since some correlates should receive attention before assessment is continued (for example, poor vision). Second, we want to avoid, where possible, duplicating assessment information and efforts. Some students have already received a great deal of attention and testing. Unless there is a good reason to do so, we would not want to duplicate efforts. Finally, we want to gather as much information as possible in order to make good decisions as we proceed with the assessment-instruction process.

**FIGURE 4.3** The Thumbnail Sketch

| Getting Started (Step 1) | About the Reading and Writing Context (Step 2) | About the Learner (Step 3) | Decision Making (Steps 4 and 5) | Diagnostic Teaching (Step 6) |
|---|---|---|---|---|
| *Background*<br><br>Name:<br>Age:<br>Grade:<br><br>Key Correlates: | *Resources* | *Knowledge about Reading and Writing* | *Evaluating the Match* (What is the existing match?) | *Planning and Implementing* (What is most likely to (re)establish learning?) |
| *Information about the Learner*<br><br>Knowledge about Reading and Writing:<br><br>Motivation: | *Instruction* | *Reading and Writing Performance* | | |
| | *Settings* | *Motivation* | *Reflection and Generating Hypotheses* (What does the learner need?) | *Evaluating the Diagnostic Teaching Sessions* |
| *Information about the Context*<br><br>School History:<br><br>Instructional Approaches:<br><br>Experiences, linguistic and cultural context: | *Tasks* | *Reflection and Independence* | | |

It is important not to leap to conclusions about etiology at this early stage. For example, although the failing marriage of a student's parents may be contributing to reading or writing problems, a great many students whose families are experiencing stress read and write well and prosper academically. The purpose of gathering background information is not to attribute cause but to provide insights that will allow us to make good decisions about instruction.

Background information can be examined from a number of points of view, reflecting the contributions to reading and writing of both learner and context. The school gathers and reports information on students from a point of view that is different from a parent's. Similarly, the student's view of his or her history is likely to be different from either of these other sources of background information. Each of these points of view can provide important insights during the Getting Started phase. Using several sources of information allows us to examine performance from several perspectives. As Anthony et al. (1991) point out, this increases our confidence in the information and deepens our understanding of the student's reading and writing.

***Home/Parents.***   Parents are particularly good sources of information about a student's background, because they have enduring contact with their child. They have information about the child's overall experiential background and developmental history that includes knowledge about physical, cultural, linguistic, affective, and cognitive factors. Parents are likely to have a somewhat different perspective about students than school personnel. It is often more personal and more graphic, including critical cultural, motivational, and attitudinal information.

Parents also have a longer-range view of their child's school experience. They will remember and describe, for example, how first grade was such "a waste" because the teacher got sick in the middle of the year and they couldn't find a substitute teacher. Or they will know, even if the school records don't reveal it, that their daughter's problems in writing started in third grade, when the school started a new approach to writing. Although this information does not necessarily inform us about the specific difficulties that the student is experiencing right now, it can help our understanding of the overall context of the reading or writing problem.

Home and community expectations for learning and achievement have a profound effect on students, and these should be explored as fully as possible with parents (Snow et al., 1998). Coming to understand how parents use reading and writing, what they believe about the value and nature of literacy, whether English is a primary language in the home, and how they try to teach knowledge and skills can be helpful in both assessment and instruction.

In addition to the value of the information itself, it is important to enlist parental support as early as possible. Their involvement and understanding is often necessary to achieve lasting change in reading or writing performance. Some parents are unaware of the need to provide continuous and supported reading and writing practice in the home or believe that only school personnel should work with their child. Some parents are literate and supportive in their first language but not in English. Others are distrustful of schools. Recent research suggests that students are less likely to be motivated to learn to read when their parents do not value reading or schooling (Baker, Scher, & Mackler, 1997). An initial interview can provide information about the amount and type of reading and writing activity that takes place in the home and about how literacy and schooling are viewed there.

*School.*    Sometimes teachers are reluctant to seek background information because they are worried that such knowledge will color their perceptions and treatment of students. They are aware of studies about the effects of teacher expectations on student achievement, often called *Pygmalion effects* (Rosenthal & Jacobson, 1968). This is a more serious concern when reading or writing disability is viewed as a problem located entirely within the learner (see Chapter 3) than it is when disability is viewed from an interactive and contextual perspective.

From an interactive perspective, patterns observed in the past are not invariable or static, nor are they the only patterns possible. Past history merely reflects the student's performance in a specific setting, using particular materials, instructional approaches, and so on. Consequently, teachers and clinicians must have access to background knowledge so that they can begin to determine what their students have experienced and how they responded to these experiences—information about both the learner *and* the learning context.

In addition, of course, there is some information that is very straightforward and important to know. For example, if Jennifer missed a great deal of school because of illness, we know that she has not had the opportunity to acquire particular knowledge and skills. This background is different from the history of Jason, of the same age and disability, who was present during all instructional periods. Although we cannot know immediately why Jason has failed to benefit from instruction, we know that he was exposed to it.

*School Records.*    All schools keep records on students' progress and achievement, although the amount and type of information available from schools vary widely from one school district to another. Today, most schools maintain and retain little except the most standardized information. In some areas, support personnel (for example, reading teachers, speech therapists) keep their own records, and this information might not be included in the overall school records. Permanent records normally contain only the results of standardized achievement tests, copies of periodic grading results, and perhaps a list of the curricular materials used by the student (for example, a listing of basal criterion test results). Some schools have established minimum competencies, or benchmarks, and student progress in these areas would be noted.

When students have been tested for eligibility for a special education placement, however, the school records probably contain a great deal more information. There would probably be an evaluation by a school psychologist, including the results of one or several individual intelligence and aptitude tests. In addition, there would normally be some sort of report from the classroom teacher regarding academic progress and overall functioning. It is important to note the dates associated with these types of information as an aid to interpretation. When comprehensive in-school assessment has taken place, the school records can eliminate the need for gathering certain types of information, although it is often necessary to supplement this formal information before drawing specific diagnostic or instructional conclusions.

Although this type of records review can be extremely helpful, it is important to examine the data from within our interactive perspective. This is especially true in getting started with students from diverse backgrounds. As Burne (2001, p. 2) notes,

While valuable information can be obtained from standardized tests, their nature and cultural specificity make them useful as only part of an assessment. Informal testing, such as curriculum-based assessments, observations, interviews, and play-based assessments can provide information unavailable through standardized testing. When reviewing the assessment information, the team should look for corroboration among the results of various types of assessment data.

*Teachers.*   If the classroom teacher is not the person leading the assessment, then he or she is an obvious source of information about the student who is experiencing difficulty. Classroom teachers can quickly and efficiently provide information about students' performance in reading and writing and about the types of instructional programs or opportunities that the student has experienced. Less obvious is that teachers can also provide insight into the types of tasks that are considered important in their classrooms. In addition, they can describe the criteria used to evaluate students in this context. Students are rarely required or expected to do the same things in all settings, and teachers can help us to understand the richer details of the instructional context.

Similarly, it is important to gather information from all teachers who work with a student. Recently, a Title I reading teacher with whom we work discovered that one of her students worked with five different teachers in the course of each week (in five different places in the building!). Each of these teachers had somewhat different expectations and programs. It turned out that no one had realized this until they began a close assessment using a thumbnail sketch to pull the information together.

*Learner.*   Probably the most neglected source of information regarding a student's performance is the student. Poor readers or writers are often surprisingly insightful about their difficulties. For this reason we have devoted a large segment of this chapter to student interviews and observation.

In later chapters we will describe how the learner provides very direct performance information. Here we want to suggest how student interviews, work samples, and observation can help us to gather information about their background knowledge, their reading and writing knowledge and skill, and their attitudes and motivations about reading and writing. These approaches can also help us get started by providing us with student self-evaluation information and with information about how the student perceives his or her instructional setting.

This is always important but is especially so when the learner's primary culture or language are divergent from the school's expectations and values. Ovando (1993) has argued that "Because teaching practices are not always linguistically enlightened, language can become a main source of inequality surrounding the lives of students who come to school marked with a stigmatized speech variety" (p. 223). Students can help us to understand their cultural, linguistic, or ethnic background and to make some early inferences about how these might interact during reading and writing events.

*Work Samples.*   Unlike the other sources just described, work samples may seem an unfamiliar source of assessment information. Teachers have always used students' own products and behaviors to make decisions about instruction, further assessment, and/or referral. However, until recently, these sources of information have not been viewed as centrally important for appropriate, effective, and efficient assessment. Consequently, both teachers and specialists have tended to downplay their usefulness and even ignore the information altogether.

Work samples that provide evidence about students' understanding and interpretation of texts are especially useful. In particular, work samples can and should be selected so that they reveal students' *growth,* not just their present level of functioning. Some students who are not reading or writing at age-appropriate levels have, nevertheless, made great strides. Where possible, the same or similar tasks or products should be selected from several points in a student's school history. This can reveal quite vividly dramatic changes in students' performance or troubling evidence of failure to develop. They can also provide insight into the experiences provided by the instructional context and the task expectations encountered there.

# Tools and Strategies for Getting Started

## Interviews

Although interviews are widely used in our society for a variety of purposes, these tools are not used often in the area of literacy assessment. Interviews can be time-consuming to conduct, but professionals have begun to realize that information elicited from interviews can enhance the diagnostic value of the overall assessment. Even when teachers talk to students and others, the information gleaned is rarely reported. This may be because many teachers and administrators are distrusting of interview information.

In part, this distrust results from the fact that interview information is *self-reported.* In the past, both school personnel and researchers have been troubled by a number of issues surrounding self-reported information (see Afflerbach, 2000). First, there is a possibility that students or parents might report information that is an inaccurate reflection of their true ideas, beliefs, or inclinations. In particular, it has been argued that students are likely to report what they think the teacher/adult wants to hear.

A second concern revolves around the ability of individuals, especially children, to talk about their ideas or abilities. This is a particular concern when students are either very young or have speech/language differences or difficulties. Of course, similar concerns arise when English is not the primary language in the home. It is clear that we must consider these potentially confounding factors just as we would the factors that can influence performance on other types of assessment instruments, and seek multiple indicators to confirm or validate their findings. However, it is also important to remember that research suggests that interviews and other types of self-report strategies can provide both reliable and valid information that is difficult, perhaps impossible, to glean otherwise (Ericsson & Simon, 1980; Lipson, Irwin, & Poth, 1986).

Interviewing, like other informal assessment tools, requires a knowledgeable and skilled professional eye. It is important for teachers and specialists to structure interviews and to try to gather information in systematic ways, recording data in a consistent manner. Structured procedures, including tape recording, can increase the reliability of interview information and ensure that teachers interpret thoughtfully the results of such assessments. There is also an argument for collecting information in less formal contexts, by attending to the nature and content of everyday talk with students. These multiple and repeated conversations can provide both new and confirming ideas about students' reading and writing performance (Lipson, 1995).

*Parents.* During the Getting Started phase of the assessment-instruction process, it is imperative to gather information about family background, parental expectations, health history, and support for reading and writing in the home. We prefer to do this through personal interviews. We try to be informal, using an interview form to remind us of important areas of discussion. It is usually sufficient to start the interview by asking the parent, "Tell me about your child's school experience," or "Tell me about your child's reading/writing problems." This is generally enough to launch parents into a long monologue, because few people ever get enough time to talk specifically about their children.

Cultural differences among parents can obviously influence interviews. The expectations of immigrant parents, even well-educated ones, may differ considerably from those of native-born Americans (Valdes, 1996). Understanding something about how authority figures are viewed by the cultural group of the parents and acquiring knowledge about appropriate conversational rules is professionally responsible. It can also help you to interpret more accurately the information you get. Of course, when parents' primary language is not English, you will need an interpreter if you are not fluent in their language.

Even if there are no apparent cultural or linguistic differences, parents are often confused and intimidated by professionals and their jargon. In addition, many parents of poor readers and writers are frightened and dismayed by their child's apparent inability to acquire these critical abilities. For many this is interpreted to mean that their daughter or son is not very bright. Sometimes they are concerned that they have done or not done something that has caused the problem. It is important to be positive and supportive while working with parents, without raising any unrealistic hopes about magic remedies.

Several authors have suggested helpful guidelines for parent interviewing (McCloughlin, 1987; McGinnis & Smith, 1982). These include the following:

1. Meet in a private and confidential setting.
2. Avoid jargon.
3. Listen attentively and avoid talking too much.
4. Keep note taking to a minimum, although it's a good idea to summarize major points with the parents at the end.
5. When in doubt, clarify what was said to avoid misunderstandings.
6. Follow cues provided by the parents and be aware of variation in cultural expectations and rules for interaction.
7. Avoid making judgmental remarks.
8. Be tactful.
9. Encourage less talkative people by asking open-ended questions.
10. Do not be afraid of silences. They often elicit important information.
11. Respond forthrightly to parents' anxiety; try to reassure without painting an overly optimistic picture.

12. Remain relaxed and avoid defensiveness and sarcasm, at all costs.
13. Assure parents that the information will be treated confidentially and then make sure that it is.

A family information form is presented in Figure 4.4 that can be used either as an interview guide or, in cases when a personal interview is not possible or practical, as a written form to be completed at home by the student's family. It is important to remember that completing a written form can be intimidating to some parents. In particular, be alert to the possibility that the parents may not be literate themselves. This may be the case when forms are repeatedly "lost" or "forgotten," suggesting that an extra effort may be needed to make personal contact. It is entirely possible, for example, to have a satisfactory phone interview to gather key background information.

Although most parents do not mind sharing family history, some will be concerned. It may be necessary or desirable to explain certain questions, particularly those that refer to family history of academic success and early developmental and health history. Simply telling parents that these can be factors in students' achievement is usually enough.

Parents are often unaware of the potential influence of routine childhood experiences. For example, chronic ear infections can have an inhibiting effect on both language development and phonological awareness. Similarly, unreasonable parental expectations, competition with older, successful siblings, or early entrance into academic programs can cause students to avoid reading tasks. Parents rarely offer this information spontaneously, but an interview should elicit it.

Some parents attribute their child's difficulties to poor teaching and schooling. School history can, of course, be a critical factor in students' reading and writing development. Unsatisfactory initial instruction, poor classroom management, or simply lack of readiness for the program offered in the school can result in learning difficulties. It is important not to fuel this discontent, since the student (and the parents) will probably continue to depend on the school and teacher in question. On the other hand, being an empathic listener and an advocate for students is a responsibility you bear. If schools or teachers appear to be a factor in the student's problem, it is important to be tactful in responding to parents' concern, frustration, and anger, while also working to remove barriers to successful performance.

Finally, parents are potential sources of information about students' development in specific areas of reading and writing. Asking parents to report on their own observations of key literacy outcomes can be enormously informative. Figure 4.5 shows a sample of the information that parents can provide and a notation about the outcomes related to those items. Parents would not, of course, receive the annotated version but would respond only to the prompts in the left-hand column. Again, information about student performance from several perspectives can help us gain confidence in the emerging picture we have of an individual learner.

*School.*    As with parent information, we seek information from the school that is uniquely its to offer. School records and personnel can suggest how well a student has functioned in an academic setting, what instructional materials have been used, and how far he or she has progressed in acquiring age-appropriate reading and writing knowledge and skill. School records can also help us avoid the duplication of previous assessment efforts. When available,

**FIGURE 4.4**
Family
Information
Form

*General Information:* _____

_____

    Languages spoken: _____
    Preferred language: _____
    Primary language spoken at home: _____

*Family Members:*
    Mother's name, occupation, and age: _____
    Father's name, occupation, and age: _____
    Marital status: _____
    Siblings' names and ages: _____
    Has a family member experienced any health or learning problems? ___ If so,
    please describe _____
    Is there anything in the home that may be a source of difficulty for your child
    (e.g., moving, separation, remarriage, illness, financial problems)? ___ If so, please
    describe _____

    _____

*Educational History:* _____

_____

_____

*Health History and Development:* _____

_____

_____

*Reading and Writing Development:*
    What are your child's attitudes toward reading? writing? school? _____
    What do you feel are your child's special learning needs? _____
    What does your child do very well? _____
    Does your child have any special interests? ___ What are they? _____
    How does your child spend leisure time? _____
    When did you first notice that your child seemed to be having some trouble in
    reading or writing? _____
    How do you feel your child's special needs have been handled? _____
    What do you expect for your child's future? _____

*Comments:*
    Please write about any other attitudes, behaviors, or information that you feel are
    important for us to know. _____

    _____

**FIGURE 4.5**   Observation Guide for Parents (Primary) Signifying Important Learning Behaviors

| MY CHILD AS A LEARNER | | | |
|---|---|---|---|
| Name _____    Date _____<br>Grade _____<br>Indicate your observation of your child's learning in the following areas. Please comment where appropriate. | | | |
| | Yes | No | Comments/Examples |
| 1. My child likes to listen to me read to him/her | ☐ | ☐ | |
| 2. My child likes to read to me. | ☐ | ☐ | |
| 3. My child tries to read in everyday situations (street signs, cereal boxes, store signs). | ☐ | ☐ | |
| 4. It is clear from the way my child talks that a book has been understood. | ☐ | ☐ | |
| 5. My child tries to figure out new words for him/herself when reading. | ☐ | ☐ | |
| 6. My child sometimes guesses at words but they usually make sense. | ☐ | ☐ | |
| 7. My child sometimes chooses to write. | ☐ | ☐ | |
| 8. My child likes to talk about & share what was written. | ☐ | ☐ | |
| 9. My child voluntarily tries out new words or forms of writing. | ☐ | ☐ | |
| Questions: _____<br>_____<br>_____ | | | |

ATTITUDE

INDEPENDENT APPLICATION

FOCUS ON COMPREHENSION

STRATEGY

RISK-TAKING

SELF-INITIATED ACTIVITY

*Source:* Reprinted by permission from *Evaluating Literacy: A Perspective for Change* by Robert Anthony, Terry D. Johnson, Norma Mickelson, and Alison Preece. Copyright © 1991 by Heinemann Educational Books. Published by Heinemann, a division of Reed Elsevier Inc., Portsmouth, NH.

recent test results and observational data may provide invaluable direction for preparing an assessment plan. In the best cases information is obtained about what has worked instructionally and what has not.

Student information should be accessed and handled discretely. Schools are sometimes sensitive to the permanence of student records, which are always available to parents at their request. Students may view their own records at the age of majority (Family Educational Rights and Privacy Act/Buckley Amendment, PL 93-380, 1974). If you are a teacher in the building, you may access and discuss any student information as long as you are planning instruction or making decisions. Schools are not permitted to distribute this information to any outside professionals without explicit parental consent, and most schools and school employees do not discuss individual students without it either. If there is any question about whether a parent would be concerned about the assessment processes being used, it is a good idea to obtain written parental consent before reviewing student records.

There appears to be a tremendous lack of coordination in many schools between the regular classroom reading program and resource or remedial room instruction (Walmsley & Allington, 1995). Consequently it is important to gather information from both settings when students are involved in pull-out programs.

Personal conversations or written summary forms from key school personnel can add immeasurably to our understanding of the student and his or her reading and writing history. Figure 4.6 presents a school information form that can be used either as a guide for interviewing teachers and support personnel or as a written form to be completed independently by them. We need to know as much as possible about the student's specific knowledge and skill. We also need to know exactly what types of instruction have been offered, how the instruction has been received, and the school's perception of this student.

***Student.*** Student interviews are especially important because they signal to students the importance and value of self-evaluation. They can help to establish a collaborative working relationship, and they send a message early in the assessment-instruction process that students are expected to take some responsibility for their own learning.

Current research reveals that measures of reading and writing knowledge are strongly related to reading comprehension or writing performance (Englert et al., 1991; Paris & Jacobs, 1984; Paris, Cross, & Lipson, 1984). Interviews or less formal classroom conversations offer considerable promise as a method of assessment because they provide us with rich information about students' knowledge, understanding, and beliefs.

Although students can provide essential insights into their own reading and writing strengths and weaknesses, interviewing them is not always easy. As Johnston (1997, p. 179) notes, "the principal message to be conveyed throughout is that the students are the experts from whom you wish to learn, and that you can be trusted with the information they give you." We have found that this can be demonstrated most clearly by listening intently to what students say when a few open-ended prompts are offered. For example, you might start with several general questions such as the following:

1. What kind of a reader (writer) are you?
2. What do you do when you read (write)?
3. What is the easiest part about reading (writing) for you?

**FIGURE 4.6**
School
Information
Form

## Student Background

Name: _____ Birthdate _____

Age: _____ Grade: _____ Teacher: _____

School district: _____ School: _____

School address: _____ Phone: _____

Principal: _____ Teacher: _____

Parent(s): _____ Phone: _____

Parent address _____

School attendance: Regular _____ Irregular _____ Reason _____

Ever repeated/skipped a grade? _____ If yes, what grade? _____

    What was result? _____

Is nonpromotion or special class placement now being considered? _____

What, if any, special services is this student now receiving? _____

_____

Describe the student's performance in reading, spelling, writing, math, science, and

    social studies: _____

_____

_____

What concerns, if any, do you have about this student's behavior and/or performance

    in the classroom? _____

_____

## Reading/Writing Instruction

Instructional personnel                    Materials and methods        Progress

Name: _____        _____    _____

Position: _____        _____    _____

Frequency of instruction: _____

Name: _____        _____    _____

Position: _____        _____    _____

Frequency of instruction: _____

Name: _____        _____    _____

Position: _____        _____    _____

Frequency of instruction: _____

Describe any special methods or materials used to help this student: _____

_____

What are this student's strengths? _____

    Weaknesses? _____

## Test Results

Type of test        Name of test        Date        Results        Examiner

Intelligence

Achievement

Vision

Hearing

Other

Other information relevant to this student's performance in school: _____

_____

_____

4. What is the most difficult part?
5. When you read (write) at school, what is that like?
6. What do your teachers/parents do to help you to be a better reader?
7. What could they do to help you more?

This type of initial interview sets the tone for a mutually supportive working relationship.

Subsequent interviews and conversations can focus on students' knowledge of the goals of reading and writing, the processes and skills involved in skilled reading and writing, and students' appraisal of their own reading and writing abilities (see Lipson, 1995). Each of these aspects is discussed below.

*Functions, Goals, and Purposes of Reading and Writing.*  When asked to talk about their knowledge of reading and writing and reflect on their abilities, students share with us their view of what it means to be competent. Several researchers report responses from students who possess mistaken notions about the goals of skilled reading (Paris & Jacobs, 1984; Wixson, Bosky, Yochum, & Alvermann, 1984). Our experience suggests that many struggling writers have similarly mistaken ideas about writing. When student theories of reading or writing are inaccurate, or their image of their own competence is askew, learning is difficult. Their theories compete for attention and can make them resistant to learning more efficient and effective strategies (see Johnston, 1985, for several powerful case studies of adults whose concepts of reading have interfered with acquisition of reading skill).

Consider the following responses to the question "Do you have trouble with reading?":

**JONATHON, AGE 10:**  "I have to tell you something. I'm in the fourth grade, but I'm only using a third grade reader. That's not very good."

**MICHAEL, AGE 13:**  "I must, my Mom's making me come here [the clinic]."

**JANE, AGE 11:**  "Yes, when I read, the stuff just seems to go out of my head."

**SARA, AGE 7:**  "Yes, I read too softly."

Embedded in these responses are theories about reading. In their daily interactions with teachers, parents, and print, students construct a vision of reading in general and their ability to perform in particular. In the quotations above, note that both Michael and Jonathon estimate their ability only in terms of external factors. Sara, on the other hand, estimates reading competence using a criterion appropriate only for public performance. Such definitions can interfere with the ability to learn the important elements of skilled reading, because students often fail to understand the reason for instructional activities. Only Jane has provided a response that suggests she may grasp the nature and demands of real reading and has recognized a serious limitation in her own ability. Not surprisingly, these students perform differently in and out of school. Although each was classified as "at risk" in reading and/or writing, their problems are quite different, and these first responses in an interview setting provided important information that was pursued in later sessions.

Asked to respond to the question "What makes a good writer?" students reveal their theories as well. The following samples from several third and fourth grade students suggest the range of responses to questions like these.

BRANDIE, AGE 10:    A good writer would put his experiences in the story. Try to make the story sound real, and put voice in it.

CHAD, AGE 9:    They write good; periods, capitals, full sentences. Put your apostrophes in and spell right.

HEIDI, AGE 10:    They write neatly. Spell almost every word right.

GREG, AGE 10:    Someone who has good thoughts, good description in their stories.

These students clearly have differing ideas about the goals and functions of writing. Both Brandie and Greg understand something about the personal value of writing as well as the variation in genre. Chad and Heidi, on the other hand, think in terms of mechanics and usage. Not surprisingly, their views of reading and writing are often, though not always, aligned. Greg thinks that a good reader, "is someone who knows what the book says, who really gets into the book and has a lot of feeling in the book." Heidi, on the other hand, thinks that a good reader is "someone that knows every word in the book."

It appears that many young students believe that the goal of reading is flawless word calling or that effective reading is equivalent to verbatim memory of text. As well, many students appear to equate writing with neat handwriting and/or accurate spelling. Such inappropriate assessments by students may lead to a corresponding application of inappropriate strategies (pay attention only to the graphic cues, read it over and over again, write using only words that can be spelled correctly, etc.). These beliefs may also provide insight into classroom practices that need to be explored more fully.

*Self-Appraisal and Goal-Setting.*    As was noted previously, it is often helpful to ask students to appraise their own reading and writing abilities and to establish goals for their instructional work. Open-ended interview questions can provide insight into students' abilities to engage in self-evaluation but also into the criteria they apply for responding.

In our experience students are frequently very accurate in their appraisals of their difficulties and often select appropriate goals as well. Self-appraisal is particularly important when working with older students and adults. These individuals are likely to have fairly sophisticated abilities to reflect on their actions and skills. We were reminded of this quite painfully as we recently observed a conversation between a seventh grade boy and his special educator. He angrily proclaimed in a planning meeting that "this year I want to learn to read!" She retorted that she wished he would feel better about himself as a reader, since he really could read. He countered that "reading like a first or second grader didn't count." She reiterated her belief that he should view himself as a reader.

Exchanges like this one can provide very useful information to teachers. Joe's desire to set ambitious goals are fueled by his self-consciousness over his limited reading ability. Although his teacher has good intentions, she may be inadvertently communicating that she doesn't think Joe can achieve the goal he desires. Many poor students are not skilled in setting goals and may do so inappropriately. Certainly, Joe's attitude in this exchange was challenging. On the other hand, a skilled teacher would use this interview information to help Joe set and meet short-term as well as long-term goals.

The types of scripted interview questions that are particularly effective are summarized in Figure 4.7. These are, of course, just questions to begin a conversation. A skilled interviewer will follow the leads offered by children as they reflect on learning experiences, as well as more specific reading knowledge, melding the critical components of skill and attitude (see Figure 4.7).

*Knowledge about Reading and Writing Skills and Strategies.* Information about students' knowledge and awareness can be gathered through interviews. Wixson et al. (1984) devel-

**FIGURE 4.7**
Student Interview

Questions designed to elicit students' awareness of various aspects of the reading and writing process might include:

*Functions, goals and purposes of reading and writing*
- What is reading (or writing)?
- What are some of the reasons people write (read)?
- Why do people read (or write)? (See Chapter 6 for additional suggestions.)

*Self-appraisal and goal-setting*
- Describe yourself as a reader (writer).
- Tell me two things you can do now in writing (reading) that you didn't used to be able to do.
- What would you like to do better as a reader (writer)?
- What is there about writing (reading) that you still don't understand?
- What kind of help do you think you need with reading? In writing?
- How long do you think it will take for you to read as well as you want or need to read?
- Who is the best writer (reader) you know?
- What does that person do that makes her/him such a good writer (reader)?
- How could you improve your reading (writing)?

*Knowledge about reading/writing skills and strategies*
- Do you read in a different way when you're reading different kinds of things?
- Are some things easier to write about than others?
- How do you decide what to read (write)?
- What do you do when you have trouble during reading and writing?
- How do you get started in writing?

*Attitudes and motivation*
- Do you write (read)? What?
- What are some titles of books that you've enjoyed?
- What topics do you enjoy writing about?
- Have you ever had a teacher who made reading/writing fun and exciting? Tell me about her/him.
- Have you ever learned something just by writing (reading) about it?
- Have you had some experiences that have made you want to read (write) about something?
- Do your parents (or someone else) read to you? How often?
- Do you have a library card? Books? Magazines?

oped an interview specifically designed to evaluate readers' awareness of the goals and purposes of reading activities, the demands imposed on them by specific reading activities, and the strategies they have available to carry out specific reading activities. We have adapted it here for use with writing as well as reading (see Figure 4.8). Because the interview is designed to be used with actual classroom materials (that is, a basal reader, a content-area text, workbook pages, writing samples), it reveals students' perceptions of their own abilities and the strategies they might employ in specific contexts they encounter daily.

Such systematic probing can lead to fairly detailed and differentiated profiles of students' understanding of the situations in which reading skills and strategies should be employed. For example, responses to the question "If your teacher told you to remember the information in this story (chapter), what would be the best way to do this?" asked in the context of several types of materials, such as a basal reader, a trade book, and a content-area text, can provide information about a reader's level of strategy development and sensitivity to the varying demands that the same task can impose in different reading contexts. Some students provide responses such as "try hard" or "think about it" in both contexts, which may indicate a generalized lack of awareness regarding task demands and strategy usage.

Other students' responses suggest that they have developed context-specific strategies for dealing with a particular task. Within the context of writing, responses such as "think about the plot" or "use voice" suggest an awareness of the properties of narrative text that make narrative writing effective. Similarly, responses in the context of a content-area text such as "take notes and study," "write out the questions," "have someone quiz you," and "break it up into small parts and memorize it" suggest an awareness that remembering in this context requires a conscious effort on the part of the reader.

*Attitudes and Motivation.*    We can learn a great deal by asking students about their reading- and writing-related experiences, interests, habits, and attitudes. These initial interviews are most effective when we listen carefully, clarify when needed, and assume a nonjudgmental attitude.

Teachers have long recognized that students differ in their attitudes and motivation toward reading and writing. That poor readers or writers are less motivated than good readers or writers is hardly surprising. However, we may not realize the depth of these feelings. Juel (1988) reported on the results of a longitudinal study in which readers were periodically asked to choose preferred activities, with reading listed as one of the choices. One poor reader spontaneously offered the comment "I'd rather clean scum off the bathtub than read!"

Interviews can also provide insights into learner motivations and attributions for success and failure. For example, Joey, age 9 and repeating the third grade, was recently referred to one of the authors' clinics. The results from interest inventories and unfinished sentence forms indicated that Joey did not read and would rather do almost anything else than read. As you read the following excerpt from an initial interview, think about what Joey is saying:

> **INTERVIEWER:**   "How do you think you do as a reader?"
>
> **JOEY:**   "I'd feel good about reading if I could learn how to read."
>
> **INTERVIEWER:**   "What do you think the problem is?"

**FIGURE 4.8**
Interview for
Assessing Students'
Perceptions of
Classroom Reading
and Writing Tasks

## Reading and Writing Interview

Name _____ Date _____

Classroom Teacher: _____ Reading Level: _____

Grade: _____

**Directions:** Introduce the procedure by explaining that you are interested in finding out what students think about various reading and writing activities. Tell the students that they will be asked questions about their reading and writing, that there are no right or wrong answers, and that you are only interested in knowing what they think. Tell students that if they do not know how to answer a question they should say so and you will go on to the next one.

General probes such as "Can you tell me more about that?" or "Anything else?" may be used. Keep in mind that the interview is an informal diagnostic measure and you should feel free to probe to elicit useful information.

1. What hobbies or interests do you have that you like to read or write about?
2. a. How often do you read in school?
   b. How often do you read at home?
3. a. How often do you write in school?
   b. How often do you write at home?
4. What school subjects do you like to read about?
5. What school subjects do you like to write about?

### Introduce reading and social studies books

**Directions:** For this section use the student's classroom basal reader and a content area textbook (social studies, science, etc.). If no basal is used in the classroom, select a piece of literature that is representative of classroom reading materials. Place these texts in front of the student. Ask each question twice, once with reference to the basal reader and once with reference to the content area textbook. Randomly vary the order of presentation (basal/literature, content). As each question is asked, open the appropriate text in front of the student to help provide a point of reference for the question.

6. a. What is the most important reason for reading this kind of material?
   b. Why does your teacher want you to read this book?
7. a. Who's the best reader you know _____ ?
   b. What does he/she do that makes him/her such a good reader?
8. a. How good are you at reading this kind of material?
   b. How do you know?
9. a. Do you write about this kind of material?
   b. Why does your teacher want you to write about this?
10. What do you have to do to get a good grade in reading?
11. a. If the teacher told you to remember the information in this story/chapter, what would be the best way to do this?
    b. Have you ever tried __(e.g. summarizing)_____ ?
12. a. If your teacher told you to find the answers to the questions in this book what would be the best way to do this? Why?
    b. Have you ever tried __(e.g. asking yourself questions)_____ ?

*(continued)*

**FIGURE 4.8**
(Continued)

13. a. What is the hardest part about answering questions like the ones in this book?
    b. What do you do to answer them?

### Introduce writing samples

**Directions:**   For this section use the student's own writing or, if not available, two different types of writing. An informal piece of writing, like a journal entry, and a more formal piece of writing, like a revised story or report (depending on age), should be used.

14. a. What is the most important reason for doing this kind of writing?
    b. Why does your teacher want you to write this?
15. a. Who's the best writer you know _____ ?
    b. What does he/she do that makes him/her such a good writer?
16. a. How good are you at writing this kind of material?
    b. How do you know?
17. What do you have to do to get a good grade in writing?
18. What did (would) you do to get ready to write this piece?
19. Do you ever reread your writing? Tell me about that.
20. Do you ever revise your writing? Tell me about that.

### Introduce at least two comprehension worksheets and two worksheets on written mechanics

**Directions:**   Select worksheets that are similar to those used by students in that grade and school. Show them to the student and ask questions 21 and 22. Ask the student to complete portions of each worksheet. Then ask questions 23 and 24. Next, show the student a worksheet designed to simulate the work of another student. Then ask question 25.

21. Why would your teacher want you to do worksheets like these (for what purpose)?
22. What would your teacher say you must do to get a good mark on worksheets like these? (What does your teacher look for?)

### Ask the student to complete portions of at least two worksheets.

23. Did you do this one differently from the way you did that one? How or in what way?
24. Did you have to work harder on one of these worksheets than the other? (Does one make you think more?)

### Present the simulated worksheet

**Directions:**   Present completed samples of worksheets and indicate that another student had done these. These simulated materials should vary along dimensions that students and teachers often use to evaluate work (i.e., neatness, degree of completion, accuracy, thoughtfulness, and combinations of these).

25. a. Look over this worksheet. If you were the teacher, what kind of mark would you give the worksheet? Why?
    b. If you were the teacher, what would you ask this person to do differently next time?

**FIGURE 4.8**
(Continued)

> ### *Summary Sheet*
>
> - What does the student perceive as the goal or purpose of classroom reading and writing activities? (see questions)
>
>   Basal reader or literature selections:
>   Content textbook: _____
>   Reading worksheets: _____
>   Writing samples: _____
>
> - What criteria does the student use to evaluate his/her reading and writing performance? (questions 7, 10, 11, 15, 17, 22, and 25)
>
>   Basal reader or literature selections:
>   Content textbook: _____
>   Reading worksheets: _____
>   Writing samples: _____
>
> - What strategies does the student indicate he/she use when engaging in different comprehension activities? (questions 11, 12, 13, 18, 19, 20, 23, and 24)
>
> - Remembering information?
>   Basal reader or literature selections:
>   Content textbook: _____
>
> - Answering questions?
>   Basal reader or literature selections:
>   Content textbook: _____
>   Reading worksheets: _____
>
> - Conveying information?
>   Journals: _____
>   Stories or reports: _____

*Source:* Adapted from "An Interview for Assessing Students' Perceptions of Classroom Reading Tasks" by Karen K. Wixson, Anita B. Bosky, M. Nina Yochum, and Donna E. Alvermann. (1984, January). *The Reading Teacher.* Reprinted with permission of Karen Wixson and the International Reading Association.

**JOEY:** "I don't know. Something inside me stops me when I try to read. I can't spell either."

**INTERVIEWER:** "What do you enjoy reading?"

**JOEY:** "Nothing. I'm embarrassed 'cause I can't read."

**INTERVIEWER:** "What do you think might help you to become a better reader?"

**JOEY:** "I don't really know."

Joey is clearly not motivated to read at this point. It would be easy to attribute his reading problem to lack of motivation. During this portion of the interview, however, Joey revealed a much more complex picture of his underlying motivations and attitudes. He appears to be suggesting that his lack of motivation for reading grows from his awareness that he cannot do it. What is especially troubling is the fact that he appears to doubt that he will ever be able to read well.

Over time, feelings such as those expressed by Joey may very well develop into the generalized pattern of learned helplessness (Dweck, 1975) described in Chapter 2. Importantly, the information gleaned through interviews can help teachers to understand the potentially conflicting goals of disabled readers and writers. As Johnston (1985) so powerfully documents, these students may want to learn to read or learn to read better, but other goals may inhibit their progress.

Many disabled readers and writers experience high anxiety about the task; many, like Joey, suspect that they cannot succeed in any event; and many may not want to admit to such "failure." Because discussions of motivation, attributions, and interest can be emotionally charged, we must proceed cautiously. Remember, it is important to have multiple indicators to interpret, confirm, and validate the information obtained through interviews.

As we are just getting started in the process, the value of these initial interviews lies in their ability to suggest hypotheses. These hypotheses can help to inform the evaluation process and may suggest directions that otherwise might never have been uncovered.

## Observation

Although much information can be obtained through talk and testing, no other single tool can provide such in-depth information about the learner's actual use and application of knowledge and skill as observation. No other tool can demonstrate so clearly whether the reader or writer is both skilled *and* motivated. Nor, of course, can any other tool provide such a quick view of the student's instructional setting—an overview of daily assignments, texts, and tasks, as well as the social environment for learning.

Observation, in the hands of an experienced evaluator, is one of the most powerful assessment tools a teacher or clinician can possess. Information about virtually every component of reading and writing can be collected by using observation. We have provided in-depth discussions of how to observe specific components in other portions of the book. In this section we limit our discussion to general observational guidelines and try to capture the power of this tool as a rich source of information about the learner and the general instructional context.

The quality and utility of observational information is subject to variation, since observational data may not be reliable. Reliability (Chapter 10) deals with the question of consistency. When we say that a measure is reliable, we mean that the results we attain tomorrow using this tool would be roughly the same as those we achieved today. Reliability "depends, for all practical purposes, on the adequacy of the behavior sample on which the score is based, which, in turn, depends on the stability of the behavior being measured. Our experience indicates that a score based on a single visit to a classroom seldom has adequate reliability. . . . Since reliability is primarily a function of the adequacy of the sample of behavior observed, reliabilities can be raised by increasing the number of visits" (Medley, 1985, p. 101).

Because teachers have many opportunities to observe student behavior, their estimates of student strengths and weaknesses are often quite trustworthy. External specialists who may observe students only once or twice need to exercise caution in generalizing the results, for either student performance or classroom context.

Other factors, such as observer (teacher) objectivity, may also influence the quality and reliability of observational information. Teachers must be aware that their observations are subject to personal bias. Like everyone else, teachers tend to see things from their own personal perspectives. Some teachers conclude that students are making satisfactory progress when they appear to be busy and attentive. Some teachers are prone to notice certain kinds of behavior and block out other kinds.

There are several ways to increase the reliability of observational data. First, teachers should determine exactly what will be noted before observing. Next, teachers plan how, when, and where to observe (Borich, 1994). If these observation categories are important and well defined, then observation accuracy will increase. Finally, teachers should use some type of format or observation guide that helps to systematize the observation.

The forms and ideas presented here are examples of the ways in which observations can be structured so that the information gathering is reasonably objective. Observing in a busy classroom requires fairly structured observations. This could involve making anecdotal records of what students say during different reading activities or during conversation or making notations regarding the interactions in groups. "The important thing is that teachers think of observation as a form of problem solving; it is a selective search for knowledge to guide instruction" (Jaggar, 1985, p. 6).

Perhaps the greatest strength of observation as an assessment tool is that students' performance and behavior can be evaluated in real settings as they are actually performing target tasks. Many teachers question the validity of standardized tests because they believe that students are being evaluated on tasks that are not meaningful or typical. Observation, of course, should normally avoid this problem. This is also a useful tool for those who are not the regular classroom teacher. Observations of a student functioning in the regular classroom can provide information that is not available in a one-to-one clinical setting.

As with all assessment instruments, the validity of observations is dependent on how carefully the behaviors to be assessed have been selected. Knowledge of the reading and writing processes is critical, since the validity of observation is related to what is worth noticing. In reading and writing, this means looking for authentic literacy behaviors where students are engaged in a variety of activities under a variety of conditions—engaged in independent seatwork, sustained silent reading, writing for a specified audience, cooperative work projects, teacher-guided lessons, and so forth.

Observation can be used as a tool in almost any phase of the assessment-instruction process. For example, observation can be used to get to know individual students, evaluate groups, assess progress, appraise teaching techniques, and identify problems. In the following chapters we provide specific and detailed ideas for evaluating the learning context (see Chapters 5 and 6), and observation plays a central role in these discussions.

In the Getting Started phase we use observation primarily to observe the student in context. No attempt is made to analyze or interpret detailed information about the setting or task or about the student's specific reading or writing difficulties. Instead, we want to gather information that helps us to interpret the interviews and work samples we are collecting at the same time, to gain insight into the school climate and culture, and to understand the organization and structure of the classroom.

***Teacher and Classroom.***    When students are struggling, it is critical to examine the context within which they function. Whether you are the student's classroom teacher responsible for the daily instructional setting or a support teacher responsible for planning and implementing a specialized program, it is important to understand what the student is expected to do and how. If you are observing in someone else's classroom, you should make it clear to the classroom teacher that your observation is intended to help you understand the student's instructional program and that the goal is to benefit the student. If you are the classroom teacher for the student, "observation" of your own classroom is, of course, impossible. However, you can take stock, using the questions and observation formats as guides for self-reflection.

If the student moves from one setting to another during the school day, your observations should include each one. Questions like the following can be used to organize your context assessment:

- What materials and tasks are used in teaching this student?
- What types of classroom organization, expectations, and interactions are apparent?
- What types of instructional groups does the student participate in?
- Does the instructional approach in each setting seem congruent with the others?

In the early stages of the assessment-instruction process, these types of questions can help us identify areas that may benefit from closer examination later. In Chapters 1 and 2 we introduced a number of context factors, or aspects of the classroom, that may influence learning. Observations or self-reflections that focus on these aspects can get us started in an efficient manner. A summary form may be helpful in conducting an initial classroom examination (see Figure 4.9).

As any experienced teacher knows, each classroom has its own personality. The learning climate that teachers establish with their students can be an influential factor in students' learning and achievement. As described by Borich (1994), the *learning climate* is a combination of the amount of teacher control (high–low) and teacher warmth (high–low). Teachers vary in the extent to which they praise students, use their ideas in instruction, teach responsively, or give encouragement. Similarly, they may vary in the extent to which they provide for student-centered activities, encourage a variety of responses, and engage students in active learning. Different behaviors result in different student outcomes.

Teacher attitudes and expectations are not the only things that contribute to this dimension, however. Others include student attitudes and self-concepts, the way faculty and staff overall deal and interact with students, and the involvement of parents. There is considerable evidence that students from different cultures react differently to aspects of the learning climate, but it is also the case that teachers of students from diverse settings, especially those serving children of poverty, often provide the least warmth and the most controlling learning environments (see Allington, 1991; Au, 2000).

The setting includes aspects of classroom management but also organizational issues related to grouping, access to literate activity, and integration of supportive instruction within the classroom context. Teaching and learning benefit from safe, orderly environments. When teachers and students spend too much time in transitions, in managing unruly behavior, or in explanations of routine tasks, less time is available for teaching and learning. These

**FIGURE 4.9**
Summary Form for
Observing Context

| Name: _____ Class: _____ Date: _____ |
|---|

| Observations: Classroom Dimensions | Comments |
|---|---|
| **Learning Climate:** | |
| **Setting:** | |
| **Curriculum:** | |
| **Instructional Methods:** | |
| **Instructional Materials:** | |
| **Instructional Tasks:** | |

management factors influence learning for all students, but for the student who is struggling, it is important to notice whether there are unique management issues operating. For example, these students are more likely to leave the room for instructional purposes. Is this time being used effectively? How much time is taken in transitions?

The instructional dimension, of course, is paramount. We will return to this issue in Chapter 6. In the Getting Started step, observation and self-reflection will function at a fairly global level. Issues that may be examined at this time could focus on the following:

- What types of assessments are done in this setting?
- How has the teacher used assessment information in planning the student's program?
- How does the teacher respond to individual differences in the classroom? (Is there evidence of accommodations, modifications, etc.?)

The context for instruction is of central importance, but different students interact with settings and materials differently. Observation of the student in the instructional setting provides the final, critical pieces of information as we get started.

*Learner.*    Skilled teachers know that conclusions should not be drawn from one or even two instances of a particular behavior. Instead, when using observation, we are looking for *patterns of performance.* Patterns emerge when the same (or similar) behaviors are observed repeatedly over time. Alternatively, patterns can emerge that reveal the circumstances that influence reading and writing. You can see how the student performs *in interaction* with various texts and contexts (that is, subject-area texts, children's magazines, library research, reading groups, and so on), watching for variability or stability. In this way it is possible to determine what students can and will do under different conditions.

It should be easy to remember important events, but by the end of a busy day we frequently have forgotten what we meant to remember. Finding a convenient and accurate way to record information is important. Many teachers find it useful to keep sticky notes close at hand. Whenever you observe something of interest, jot down the time, date, and student information. Then, at your leisure, you can put these memos in a notebook or portfolio tabbed for each student.

Many teachers use checklists such as the one in Figure 4.10 that provide a place to note students' overall interactions in the classroom. These should be created to facilitate observations of important classroom activities. The advantage here is that it focuses on multiple sources of information about students and can help us to establish patterns of behavior that can lead to fresh instructional approaches.

As we get started, it is unlikely that we will make detailed observations of students' application of reading and writing knowledge and skill. These are done as we get further into the assessment-instruction process. In the initial stages an observant teacher can find out a great deal about reading and writing interests by observing the students. Samples of the types of behavior we might want to look for to inform us about our students' knowledge of reading and writing are presented in Figure 4.10. More open-ended questions can be used to summarize our observations and are worth asking about all students:

**FIGURE 4.10** An Observation Guide for Reading and Writing

| | |
|---|---|
| ☐ Demonstrates flexibility in approach to reading tasks | ☐ Uses different approaches to writing tasks |
| ☐ Handles different genre with ease | ☐ Writes different genre with ease |
| ☐ Always seeks the same type of literature | ☐ Always writes in the same modes and genre |
| ☐ Reads about a range of topics | ☐ Writes about a range of topics |
| ☐ Adapts reading strategies to task demands | ☐ Adapts strategies to demands of writing and written stage (i.e., has strategies for planning, revising, and editing) |
| ☐ Selects books for recreation | |
| ☐ Can use books to find information | ☐ Writes for personal and recreational purposes |
| ☐ Checks books out of library | |
| ☐ Discusses books with others | ☐ Uses writing to learn |
| ☐ Uses literary references in informal conversation (e.g., "When I'm six I'll fix Matthew") | ☐ Shares and discusses writing |
| | ☐ Uses literary references in writing |

Comments:

- For what purposes does the student read/write: to accomplish classroom tasks or for pleasure?
- How does the student respond to different types of comprehension questions? Writing tasks?
- How does the student adjust his/her rate, strategy usage, and writing approach to meet the demands of different purposes, texts, and tasks?

As we have already discussed, students' attitudes can have a significant and cumulative effect on their achievement. Often people do not like to read or write because they are not skilled at these tasks. However, it is also the case that skilled reading and writing require practice. Teachers and clinicians are obliged to help students find reading material and writing activities that respond to their individual interests and that help them to see the functional value of reading and writing.

One of the simplest and most effective ways of finding out students' interests is to watch their daily behavior and listen to their conversations (see Lipson, 1995). The following are examples of the types of questions that can be used to guide these observations:

1. How do students approach reading and writing activities (active involvement or passive resistance)?
2. What types of reading and writing activities do students select during their spare time at school and at home?
3. Do students stick with reading and writing activities or give up easily?
4. Do students talk about reading? About writing? What is the content and tone of these remarks?

Gathering information in response to these questions will not provide a solution to the problems. It can, however, indicate whether a student understands and appreciates the value of reading or writing and is willing or able to use this knowledge to support the hard work of becoming a skilled reader and/or writer.

## Work Samples

Gathering work samples is relatively easy. In most classrooms teachers retain at least some student work, and in portfolio classrooms there will be a wide range of student work in work folders or showcase portfolios (Tierney, Carter, & Desai, 1991; Valencia, 1998). Not all work samples are equally useful in helping us to understand readers and writers, so we need some sense of *what to select*. In addition, once samples have been selected, we need to know *what to make of the work*. To be effective, work samples must be collected intentionally to represent dimensions you have decided are important. In other words, you should know what types of samples you will seek and what you will do with them when you have them.

In the Getting Started phase we will be trying to get a broad view of the student's experience with print and his or her abilities to respond to text. These may include story maps, illustrations, retellings, and literary reviews (Valencia, 1998). Work samples that are especially helpful in the Getting Started step include the following:

- Samples of the types of reading and writing work that are generally required in the student's classroom
- Writing samples—unsupported writing about self-selected topics (This can come from the classroom portfolio if there is one; otherwise, it should be collected.)
- Lists of books that the student has recently read in and out of the classroom
- Examples of work completed for projects or other content areas

Work samples like these can, of course, help you make some initial judgments about the student's knowledge and skills in key areas. For example, reading logs (see Figures 4.11a and 4.11b) can provide useful information about several aspects of students' literacy development, including the frequency and quantity of students' reading and the breadth of their experiences.

Similarly, writing samples from many contexts should be examined—journal entries, process writing folders, projects, letters, and notes. Not all of these reveal the same

**FIGURE 4.11a**
Sample Reading Log

| Name _____ Term _____ | | |
|---|---|---|
| **Date Completed** | **Title of Book** | **Author** |
|  |  |  |
|  |  |  |
|  |  |  |
|  |  |  |
|  |  |  |
|  |  |  |
|  |  |  |
|  |  |  |
|  |  |  |
|  |  |  |
|  |  |  |
|  |  |  |
|  |  |  |
|  |  |  |
|  |  |  |

*Source:* From *Authentic Assessment* by B. Hill and C. Rupic. Copyright © 1994 Christopher Gordon. Reprinted by permission.

FIGURE 4.11b  Sample Reading Log

Name _____                                                                                        Month/Year _____

| Title | Author | Start Date / Finish | Value High–Low | Genre | # of Pages | Response |
|-------|--------|---------------------|----------------|-------|------------|----------|
| | | | 1 2 3 4 5 | | | |
| | | | 1 2 3 4 5 | | | |
| | | | 1 2 3 4 5 | | | |
| | | | 1 2 3 4 5 | | | |
| | | | 1 2 3 4 5 | | | |
| | | | 1 2 3 4 5 | | | |
| | | | 1 2 3 4 5 | | | |
| | | | 1 2 3 4 5 | | | |
| | | | 1 2 3 4 5 | | | |
| | | | 1 2 3 4 5 | | | |
| | | | 1 2 3 4 5 | | | |
| | | | 1 2 3 4 5 | | | |
| | | | 1 2 3 4 5 | | | |
| | | | 1 2 3 4 5 | | | |
| | | | 1 2 3 4 5 | | | |

*Source:* From *Authentic Assessment* by B. Hill and C. Ruptic. Copyright © 1994 Christopher Gordon. Reprinted by permission.

information about students' knowledge and skill in writing nor about their motivation to write.

# Getting Started on the Diagnostic Portfolio

Finding the time to conduct in-depth assessments on individual students is problematic. One solution to the problem of achieving both in-depth and ongoing evaluation is to create strong collaborative working arrangements among classroom teachers and specialists or resource personnel. Classroom teachers can benefit from the assistance of specialists in obtaining more detailed information about students and how they perform in a variety of settings. Resource personnel can benefit from the assistance of classroom teachers in obtaining continuous assessments of students' knowledge, skills, and attitudes in various classroom contexts. This type of collaboration also allows teachers and specialists to coordinate their instructional efforts and to evaluate the extent to which students are able to transfer their knowledge and skills from one setting to another.

Teacher reflection is a critical component of successful assessment. The Getting Started step requires the gathering together of existing information and the initial collection of some new interview and observational data. Specific artifacts, such as work samples or written responses to interviews, should be used to begin the diagnostic portfolio.

## The Cases of Marvin and Kyle

Information gleaned from oral interviews, observations, and work samples should be summarized on the thumbnail sketch. Figure 4.12 gives two samples of what this looks like in the Getting Started step. The information in this figure is a summary of the information about Marvin and about Kyle, who will be used frequently throughout the book to illustrate ongoing assessment.

*Marvin.* Marvin's parents were concerned about his lack of progress in reading and writing. His classroom teacher was also concerned about "significant" reading difficulties. Marvin was referred to the University Reading Clinic.

Information gathered from his school records and his teachers revealed that he was 11 years old, he had recently begun fifth grade, and his reading level was at approximately the third grade level. In addition, there was no indication that any physical, linguistic, or cognitive correlates were implicated in his reading problem. Interviews with Marvin indicated that he understood the purposes of reading and that he believed his problem was comprehension. Observations in the classroom and in the clinical setting suggested a pleasant, cooperative individual whose behavior did not change dramatically under different contextual conditions. No useful work samples existed because Marvin's school records did not include these and he had been in the current setting so short a time. The nature and extent of Marvin's specific reading and writing abilities remained unclear.

Interviews with Marvin's parents suggested that frequent moves and variation in school settings could be a factor. These need to be explored more fully in an investigation of the instructional context.

**FIGURE 4.12a**
Marvin's
Thumbnail Sketch:
Getting Started

| Information about Marvin, gathered in the Getting Started step, is summarized here. (Other information will be added later.) | |
|---|---|
| **Getting Started (Step 1)** | **About the Reading and Writing Context (Step 2)** |
| ***Background*** | ***Resources*** |
| Name: Marvin<br>Age: 11    Grade: 5<br><br>Key Correlates:<br>• Above average IQ<br>• Normal vision, hearing, and overall health<br>• Interests are science, sports, "taking things apart" | ***Instruction*** |
| ***Information about the Learner*** | |
| Knowledge about Reading and Writing:<br>• Reports that people read to learn and for recreation: reports adjusting rate for text difficulty<br>• Reports that own reading problem is comprehension<br>• Names, "breaking words down" and "asking someone" as the only strategies for reading words that are unfamiliar | ***Settings***<br><br><br>***Tasks*** |
| Motivation:<br>• Pleasant, cooperative demeanor during the classroom and clinic sessions<br>• Talks freely about affective responses to text and persists without prompting on difficult tasks | |
| ***Information about the Context*** | |
| School History<br>• School-administered achievement tests place him in the 35th percentile in reading<br>• Multiple moves and family disruptions during K–1.<br><br>Instructional Approaches: Skills-based basal; highly structured<br><br>Experiences, Linguistic and Cultural Context:<br>• English spoken in the home. | |

**FIGURE 4.12b**
Kyle's Thumbnail
Sketch: Getting
Started

| Getting Started (Step 1) | About the Reading and Writing Context (Step 2) |
|---|---|
| ***Background*** | ***Resources*** |
| Name: Kyle | |
| Age: 6½   Grade: 2 | |
| Key Correlates: | |
| • Normal vision, hearing, and overall health/development | ***Instruction*** |
| • Difficult time "paying attention" | |
| ***Information about the Learner*** | |
| Knowledge about Reading and Writing: | |
| • Reports that own reading problem is knowing the words | ***Settings*** |
| • Is able to reflect on his own reading and writing abilities | |
| Motivation: | |
| • Says he doesn't really like to read, would rather play and build | ***Tasks*** |
| • Cooperative and willing to work both in school and in extra sessions | |
| ***Information about the Context*** | |
| School History: | |
| • Successful preschool experience | |
| • Same multi-age K–2 classroom since kindergarten | |
| • Lack of progress in reading and writing noted at end of grade 1 | |
| Instructional Approaches: | |
| • Literature-based instruction in an inquiry-oriented classroom | |
| • Daily reading and writing | |
| Experiences, Linguistic, and Cultural Context: | |
| • English spoken in the home | |
| • Both parents college graduates | |
| • Many books and book activities | |

***Kyle.*** Kyle's classroom teacher expressed concern about his slow progress. Kyle is in a multiage K–2 classroom. He had been with the same teacher, Ms. McIntyre, since kindergarten. She knew he had made progress but wanted to review and evaluate his literacy development to make the most of his last year, as well as to ask questions about possible referral for special services.

School records included literacy portfolios in Kyle's school. A review of these indicated that Kyle knows a great deal about his own emerging abilities (see Figure 4.13). These portfolios also supported the teacher's belief that Kyle had made progress. Writing samples from kindergarten and grade 1 clearly demonstrated his ability to apply his growing knowledge and skill (see Figures 4.14 and 4.15).

In addition, Ms. McIntyre had asked her students to think about their favorite activities, and this feedback provides insight into Kyle's motivation for reading and writing as well as his ownership of various activities. His self-knowledge was striking and powerful.

**FIGURE 4.13**
Kyle's Reflections on Writing Progress

name  Kyle                            date  February
                                            grade 1
                  Portfolio Reflection on Writing

| When I write I used to... | Now I know how to... |
|---|---|
| I used to be sloppy, | do longer stories |
|  | I put titles on my stories |
| and I didn't sound out the words | I sound out words better |
| I can't read my own words back, | I can read back my story better. |
| not make clear letters | now I know which way the letters go. |
| use one letter to spell a whole word |  |
| use all upper case letters | use lower case letters |
| not leave spaces |  |

**FIGURE 4.14**
Kyle's Preferences
for Tasks and
Projects

These clearly revealed that Kyle preferred action and choice to sitting and "paying attention." Not surprisingly, he readily noted in a casual conversation that he really didn't like to read.

An interview with Kyle's mother supported Kyle's view of himself. She noted that he would prefer riding his bike to reading. She also said that although his overall development was normal, he was a "fast mover." He was running at nine months, and his verbal development was very quick, "above normal," according to her. Kyle's family was supportive of literacy. He had "always been surrounded by books; they've always been there," and he read in bed every night. He had a younger sister who was reading well above grade level already.

As we move through the assessment-instruction process, further information about Marvin and Kyle can be added to their thumbnail sketches.

**FIGURE 4.15**
Kyle's Reflections
Re: Paying Attention

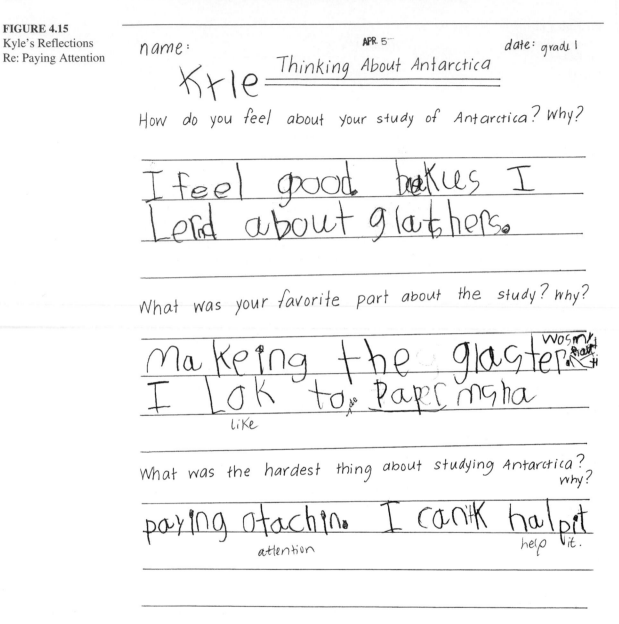

name: Kyle          APR. 5          date: grade 1

Thinking About Antarctica

How do you feel about your study of Antarctica? Why?

I feel good bekues I Lernd about glathers.

What was your favorite part about the study? Why?

Makeing the glaster wosn't rialy hard
I Lok to Paper msha
   like

What was the hardest thing about studying Antarctica? why?

paying otachin. I can'k halpit
      attention              help  it.

## Chapter Summary

The purpose of this chapter was to assist the reader by providing the knowledge and techniques necessary for getting started in the assessment-instruction process. We began with a set of guidelines that are important for the entire assessment-instruction process. These guidelines promote an approach to assessment that is contextualized; that examines how readers and writers perform in authentic classrooms or other real-world settings. They are as follows:

- Assess meaningful activities in appropriate contexts
- Match assessment to purpose
- Be systematic
- Assess continuously
- Promote reflection and self-assessment

In this chapter we also discussed the contexts for assessment and instruction and sources of information. We noted that students and teachers often work in more collaborative environments today, and although there still are some isolated remedial instructional settings, these are less common than in the past. Sources of information include the home, school (school records and teachers), and the learner. Finally, we advocate using a diagnostic portfolio to plan instruction, evaluate progress, and communicate with parents and administrators.

The second major section of this chapter describes the tools and strategies that are used in the Getting Started phase of assessment. Interviews and informational forms that can be used to gather information about both learner and context were described. Specific interviewing and observational techniques were described for the purpose of evaluating various aspects of students' knowledge about reading and writing and their attitudes and motivation toward reading and writing activities.

Finally, the chapter describes how to use a thumbnail sketch as a vehicle for summarizing information from the diagnostic portfolio. As we get started with assessment, Marvin and Kyle are used as examples.

# 5 Evaluating the Instructional Environment/Context

Traditional assessment looks only to the student as the source of reading and writing difficulties. Clearly, students' knowledge, skill, and motivation are crucial factors in reading and writing achievement. However, a growing body of research demonstrates that instructional context and methods can support learning or contribute to disability. Assessment that is intended to inform instruction requires careful descriptions of how different aspects of the instructional environment influence learning in general and how they match the needs of particular students.

School success and failure result from a complex interaction among many factors (Coles, 1987). Some factors that seem to negatively influence a particular student do not have the same effect on other students. Similarly, a program that has been successful in the past might not work for the student who is struggling now. The focus should be on assessing the context and method in terms of their likely impact on specific students' performance in reading and writing.

An analysis of fifty years of research suggests that "the different kinds of classroom instruction and climate had nearly as much impact on learning as the student aptitude categories" (Wang, Haertel, & Walberg, 1994, p. 74). Taken together, factors such as classroom management, climate, instruction, assessment, and social interaction influenced learning as much as the learner characteristics. In this and the next chapter we discuss how different aspects of the instructional environment influence reading and writing performance and describe methods of evaluating these factors (see Figure 5.1).

This chapter begins with a discussion of literacy and the role of cultural context in defining the goals of literacy and continues on to describe how subtle interactions between these factors and instructional settings and practices influence school achievement. Then we turn our attention to understanding and assessing the elements that make up instructional settings and practices, including classroom organization, instructional goals, methods, activities, and assessment practices.

## Understanding Literacy Learning Environments

Before turning our attention to the instructional setting, we briefly consider the relations among home/community and school settings. American children are often exposed to books in the home before they begin formal schooling, and many children participate in social

**FIGURE 5.1**
Components of the
Instructional Context

| Instructional Settings | Instructional Practice | Instructional Resources |
|---|---|---|
| • Teacher beliefs and literate environment<br>• Classroom interaction<br>• Classroom organization<br>• Grouping<br>• Congruence among settings | • Instructional goals<br>• Instructional methods<br>• Instructional activities<br>• Assessment practices | • Commercial programs<br>• Trade materials<br>• Technology |

groups devoted to story time or reading and writing in settings such as daycare, preschools, clubs, and church groups. Becoming literate occurs in social situations that shape purposes, conditions, constraints, audiences, standards, and motivation to engage in reading and writing activities (Paris & Wixson, 1987).

## Relations among Home/Community and School Settings

Every educator knows that literacy is not accomplished in schools alone. The children themselves contribute to learning and achievement, but so do parents, siblings, and the general community. Attributes that are important to consider regarding the larger literacy setting include the nature of the linguistic community (i.e., the language(s) spoken in the home/community), the literacy status of the home/community, the relationships between the home/community and school, and the socioeconomic status of the home/community. All of these factors affect individual and community literacy goals.

Identifying attributes that contribute to school achievement should not be a process of laying blame. Rather, careful examination and description of the settings children encounter can promote both understanding and adaptation. Poor instruction is a less prevalent problem than instruction that is unresponsive to the needs of individual students. The interactions among various setting features can be both extremely subtle and profoundly important, affecting student learning and motivation. Teachers and clinicians must consider the results of extensive research that offer insights into the ways in which home experiences can produce a mismatch between student and teacher expectations. One of the most illuminating of these is a study by Heath (1983).

Heath studied the patterns of language use in three communities in the southeastern United States and concluded that patterns of language use and social interaction differed strikingly among children in homes from these communities. In "Maintown," a middle-class, school-oriented community, the focus of literacy-related activities was on labeling, explaining, and learning appropriate interactional patterns of displaying knowledge. Children learned how to use language in literacy events and were socialized into the interactional sequences that are central features of classroom lessons.

Families in "Roadville," a white working-class community, also focused on labeling and explanations; however, they did not link these ways of taking meaning from books to other aspects of their environment. Consequently, children from these homes were well prepared for the literal tasks of early reading instruction but not for reading assignments that call for reasoning and personal responses.

The third group of homes was located in "Trackton," a black working-class community. The children in these homes were not taught labels or asked for explanations; rather, they were asked to provide reasons and express personal responses to events in their lives. As a consequence, these children were unprepared for the types of questions that are often used in beginning reading instruction and were unfamiliar with the interaction patterns used in reading lessons.

These differences resulted in mismatches in the patterning of teacher–pupil interactions during reading and writing instruction (Heath, 1981). For example, a predominant characteristic of teachers' questions was (and still is) to ask students to name the attributes of objects or events in isolated contexts. Trackton parents did not ask the children these kinds of questions, and Trackton children had different techniques for responding to questions. Teachers reported that it was difficult to get responses from Trackton students; Trackton parents reported that teachers did not listen, noting that "we don't talk to our children the way you do"; and Trackton children reported that teachers asked "dumb" questions they already knew about.

Heath then shared with the teachers examples of how Trackton children interacted at home, and teachers incorporated questions similar to those the children were familiar with in their instruction. As a result, the children participated much more frequently, and in time the teachers were able to involve them in more traditional question answering as well. The point here is that children from these homes were initially disabled by not having engaged in the type of interaction that is characteristic of classroom instruction but that their disabilities were remedied by the social interaction they subsequently experienced with their teachers (Gavelek & Palincsar, 1988). Subsequently, these findings and the conclusion that disability can best be viewed from an interactive perspective have been supported by any number of researchers (see, e.g., Au, 2000; Spear-Swerling & Sternberg, 1998).

## Goals for Learning Literacy

Teachers and schools are often frustrated by the apparent lack of motivation and achievement among some students. Recent research and reflection have led to a more complex conclusion: All children are motivated to achieve, but they may direct their actions toward different goals, under different conditions, and for different reasons. It must be recognized that at least some children are motivated toward different goals than those emphasized by educators.

It is also important to realize the existence of different definitions of achievement and motivation. Students' achievement and motivation can be understood only in relation to the cultural contexts in which they live. Different cultures and different contexts dictate norms of behavior that vary. Individual behavior reflects, and is constrained by, these different norms. To the extent to which subcultures define achievement goals differently, differences in observed motivation to achieve those goals would be expected.

Experts cannot agree on a single definition of literacy because the attributes and standards are relative to the context in which reading and writing are observed. An African boy chanting the Koran in a language he cannot understand, a teenager studying the driver's test manual, and a student in a classroom trying to pronounce words in a primer are all participating in literate activities. Literacy is a social and cultural phenomenon that encompasses much more than school-oriented values and practices. Furthermore, as cultures change, so do definitions of literacy. New technological advances require new knowledge and skills, and societies expect both more and different abilities from literate individuals.

Because literacy definitions vary, many scholars describe literacy activities in terms of how print is used and how reading and writing fit into the total fabric of a cultural group (Scribner & Cole, 1981). These uses and purposes partly determine the value that is placed on literacy by the community. They may also determine who has access to literacy within a particular culture. It is well known that literacy is given different levels of priority in various societies and that many cultures restrict access to literacy to certain portions of the population (Dyson, 1999; Gutierrez-Clellen, Pena, & Quinn, 1995).

Although it is relatively rare today for cultures to restrict access to literacy by law or stricture, there are other, less direct ways to control access to literacy. Cultures define the social functions of literacy, methods of instruction, and standards of competence. For example, Western societies historically restricted females' access to scientific and mathematical literacy by denying women entry into certain types of employment and by establishing certain norms of behavior. Less obvious are the ways in which cultural norms inform both boys and girls about "appropriate" topics, forms, and interactional patterns (Finders, 1997; Fleming, 1995; Henkin, 1995). The complicated nature of these relationships has recently been highlighted as researchers reexamine the issue in light of the comparatively poor performance of boys in the literacy domain (see Young & Borzo, 2001).

Similarly, the culture of the school informs students of acceptable forms of achievement behavior and motivation (Dreeben, 1968). Schools do vary in the way they operate, and these differences may result in differing expectations for students (Miller & Goodnow, 1995; Miller & Mehler, 1994). For example, a school may routinely provide excused absences from class and even classwork for certain students (e.g., athletes, student government representatives, job training participants). Features of the school such as its size, neighborhood, formal structure, and informal climate may also influence students' motivation and achievement by affecting their expectations for success, self-esteem, and time on task (Dyson, 1999).

Different cultural groups can have similar or dissimilar frames of reference for the functions and activities of literacy (Green & Bloome, 1983). When students do not have the same expectations or rules for communication and participation in the classroom as teachers do, the students often devalue literacy or exempt themselves from instruction, thereby diminishing their opportunities to become literate. Although cultural setting is a vague and general term, it is important to recognize at the outset that the functions, values, and frames of reference in particular contexts influence who has access to literate activities and the opportunity to learn to read and write (see Fraatz, 1987).

## Understanding the Role of Instructional Settings in Reading and Writing Performance

In this section we discuss how various aspects of instructional setting interact with cultural and home environments to influence students' learning. Setting factors do not operate in isolation from other aspects of the instructional environment; rather, they interact with each other and with other contextual factors. We have separated them somewhat for purposes of discussion and as a guide to the factors that must be considered in evaluating the instructional context. Wherever possible, however, we have tried to suggest the interrelationships between and among the elements of the instructional context.

## Teacher Beliefs and the Literate Environment

Perhaps no single factor influences the instructional setting more than a teacher's knowledge and beliefs about teaching and learning. As we noted in Chapter 1, teachers are often unaware of the extent to which their views about learning and literacy influence and shape classroom instruction and the learning experiences offered to students.

According to DeFord (1986, p. 166), "beliefs will serve as a frame of reference for a teacher in selecting materials for instruction and for presenting and guiding the use of these instructional materials. These values will be communicated to the students, both verbally and nonverbally. Students will adhere to and improvise upon the contextual demands, or will find ways to change the nature of those demands through active, or passive, negotiation." As a result, students' behavior and the degree to which they participate in academic tasks are often determined by what others expect of them.

Teachers' expectations are shaped by their beliefs about learning and literacy in general. In turn, these beliefs influence the type of classroom environment that is established (Lipson et al., 2000). Students attend to these subtle and not-so-subtle clues as they determine how to behave and what to learn. Evidence of how these beliefs and actions influence each other is provided by DeFord (1986), who studied three separate classroom literacy environments: traditional, literature-based, and mastery learning. The three teachers, who had all been identified as "exemplary," created dramatically different classroom settings.

The context in the *traditional* classroom was formed by the teacher. Within this curriculum model, the teacher set up a series of general rules for classroom participation, some explicitly stated and others implied. Lessons were thoroughly planned, allowing for a limited number of child-initiated decisions, and usually structured so that they could be completed in one work period. Reading groups were generally organized according to the basal program, with seatwork consisting of workbook pages and phonics worksheets. If the seatwork was a writing activity, the teacher assigned the topic; very little writing was student-initiated. The children in the traditional classroom were responsible and cooperative. They participated actively in discussions led by the teacher and worked diligently to complete their assignments. Verbal interactions were most commonly teacher–child or teacher–group conversations, although quiet child–child conversations were allowed during seatwork time to discuss assigned work.

Teacher goals and student goals were negotiated to produce the curriculum and context in the *literature-based* classroom. The rules, which were set by the teacher and children together, revolved around issues of productive work and social/child development. Reading and writing instruction were handled individually or in small-group situations, with the teacher assessing and teaching on a daily basis from information gathered during the work period. Instruction involved a variety of topics, materials, and methods, including numerous field trips that provided the content for reading and writing. Teacher planning for student projects usually extended from several days to several weeks, during which time progress was evaluated continuously until the projects were completed. The teacher structured open-ended activities and helped students make decisions about personal outcomes. The children were active, independent, and generally responsible for the social climate of the room. They helped each other and collaborated on projects. Child–child conversations and teacher–child conversations were most common, with fewer teacher–group interactions.

*mastery learning classroom*

In the *mastery learning* classroom, "the literacy context was directed by the curriculum, the teacher serving as mediator and manager of the reading and writing program" (DeFord, 1986, p. 174). Because the content of the curriculum was delivered within a highly structured management system, students worked independently at their seats a significant amount of the time. The teacher created an orderly and quiet work environment for the execution of these tasks. Reading groups met to receive teacher-directed instruction within the programmed materials. Assigned workbook and basal reader pages were executed independently, and tests were administered periodically. Writing activities and oral exchanges occurred almost exclusively at the initiation of the teacher. Planning occurred only within the prescribed program materials, and work was assigned so that it could be completed in a half-day block of time.

The observational research (DeFord, 1986; Lipson et al., 2000) highlights the extent to which classroom organization, activities, and discourse may vary as a function of teacher beliefs about literacy and literacy education. Teachers' differing beliefs lead them to make different judgments about materials, tasks, assessment criteria, and interactional patterns. In turn, students have different experiences and construct the purposes and forms of literacy differently. In these ways, the unique attributes of classroom settings influence students' literacy learning.

## Classroom Interaction

Teachers rely on verbal interactions to make many educational decisions and judgments. According to Cazden (1986, p. 432), "spoken language is the medium by which . . . students demonstrate to teachers much of what they have learned. Spoken language is also an important part of the identities of all participants."

Variation in ways of speaking is a universal fact. When the variation is significant, it can lead to painful mismatches for individual students or groups, and these mismatches can affect achievement (Cazden, 1986; Wilkinson & Silliman, 2000). Differences in how and when something is said may require only a temporary adjustment, or they can seriously impair effective teaching and accurate evaluation.

Teachers, like other groups of specialists, have unique ways of talking. Some of the more obvious features of teacher talk include asking known-answer questions and evaluating students' answers to questions. Teacher talk is often characterized by its preoccupation with control of behavior and of talk itself. Students must "learn how to participate in reading, what effective reading means, and the definitions of reading held by the teacher and school" (Green & Bloome, 1983, p. 23) to be regarded as skilled in literacy activities in school.

Studies of cultural differences also suggest that students would be better served if teachers took differences in prior experiences in the home community into account more than they now do (Au, 2000). Too often, "teachers now differentiate among their students in ways that may continue, even increase, the inequalities of information and skills that are present when students start school" (Cazden, 1986, p. 445). Research evidence suggests that some children come to school with an oral style of discourse that is inconsistent with that of the teachers. These children often do not gain access to the kind of instruction and practice that are required to develop a more literate discourse style, and as a result they perform less well in school-based literacy activities.

Linguistic and interaction patterns are important because teachers make judgments about students' abilities and behavior based on them. For example, Michaels (1981) studied first-grade "sharing-time" experiences and found that when children's narrative styles were very different from the teacher's expectations, the event was generally unsuccessful. In addition, the teacher frequently made negative assessments of the students' ability and sanctioned the students' performance.

Because interaction styles are so subtle and interwoven with individual identity, they can be difficult to assess. However, there is evidence that when instruction is shaped to respond to these differences, achievement and interaction improve. Research with native Hawaiians provides an example of the importance of cultural compatibility of communication styles in reading lessons.

Boggs (1985) learned that native Hawaiian adults rarely ask children questions for information, as white middle-class parents commonly do. Hawaiian parents use direct questions primarily when reprimanding their children. When telling a story, Hawaiians cooperate in taking turns to construct the story with voices overlapping, an activity called "talk story." In addition, Hawaiians delegate household chores to an older child, who is responsible for making certain that the work is done. Apprenticeship and observation, rather than explanation or discussion, are used to teach children new skills.

Consistent with this knowledge about the interaction patterns of native Hawaiians, Au (1980) observed that Hawaiian children were more successful in reading lessons using the participation structures of the talk story than with the conventional recitation pattern commonly used in reading lessons with children from the mainstream culture (Au & Mason, 1981). Teachers using these two participation structures clearly provided different kinds of social events, and Hawaiian students demonstrated much higher levels of achievement-related behavior in the lessons that incorporated the culturally compatible talk story pattern.

The convergence of evidence about the interactive effects of language led to calls for more "culturally congruent" or "culturally responsive" instruction (see Au & Kawakami, 1994). According to Au (2000, p. 839), a culturally responsive school environment would do the following:

1. Establish ownership of literacy as the overarching goal of the language arts curriculum
2. Recognize the importance of students' home language and promote biliteracy
3. Increase the use of multicultural literature in classrooms
4. Promote cultural responsiveness in classroom management and teachers' interactions with students
5. Make stronger links to the community
6. Provide students with authentic literacy activities and instruction in specific skills
7. Use forms of assessment that reduce bias and more accurately reflect students' literacy achievement

## Classroom Organization

Over the past several years research descriptions of classrooms have demonstrated what most classroom teachers know only too well: Classrooms are busy places, and teachers are very active participants in classroom events. Because the classroom environment is busy and demanding, organization is a major factor in classroom teaching. According to Doyle (1986), the activity is the basic unit of classroom organization. Activities take place in relatively short blocks of classroom time during which students are arranged in a particular way. Labels for activities reflect either their organizational focus (e.g., seatwork, discussion) or their focal content (e.g., reading, journal writing). More than thirty separate activities occur each day in the average elementary school class.

Teachers must also divide their attention among competing demands. For example, in a study of third grade classrooms, approximately half of the teachers' acts involved instructional activities such as questions, feedback, and imparting knowledge (Gump, 1969). The rest of the time the teachers were involved in organizing students for instruction and orienting them to tasks (23 percent), dealing with deviant behavior (14 percent), and handling individual problems and social arrangements (12 percent). Consequently, management of activity can take precedence over instructional content. Indeed, there is evidence to suggest that teachers and students often reduce subject matter to a set of procedures to be followed in completing assignments in order to satisfy management demands (Doyle, 1986). This disturbing finding is consistent with the evidence that while in class, students often focus a significant part of their attention on information about how to do the work they are assigned as well as what behavior they are to display (King, 1983). Clearly, the degree to which students have an opportunity to learn content or to practice significant literacy behaviors will depend, at least in part, on the types and quantity of classroom activity provided.

Differences among classrooms can and do account for differences in student performance and achievement (Au & Carrol, 1997; Mosenthal et al., 2001a, 2001b). Although classroom organization and management may vary within and among schools, the predominant pattern continues to be the teacher-directed classroom in which students are expected to work independently and to interact primarily with the teacher and the instructional materials. Increasingly, there are alternative classroom organizations in which teachers and students work more collaboratively, interact frequently about texts and tasks, and discuss reading and writing activities with peers in conferences and in literature groups. Different patterns of organization affect particular students in unique ways. Some may find the open-ended, workshop-oriented classroom structure difficult; others may find the traditional patterns of organization problematic.

Researchers contend that families and cultures vary considerably in the extent to which they prepare children for various settings (Fillion & Brause, 1987). Children who are accustomed to assisting others in accomplishing tasks, collaborating on projects, and generally working together are at ease in the cooperative classrooms in which these activities are rewarded but uncomfortable in more traditional classrooms. Hispanic homes have been characterized as fitting into the cooperative format (Tikunoff & Ward, 1983). Similarly, Philips (1982) found that Native American children were accustomed to independent activities and were unaccustomed to the noise and competition that are characteristic of many classrooms. Differences between cultural values and classroom values were so extreme as to alienate the children from their teachers and their classmates. These findings underscore the importance of examining the match between classroom organization and cultural or individual patterns of achievement.

***The Nature of Instructional Activities and Tasks.***    Activities and tasks consist of a goal and the set of cognitive operations required to meet the goal (cf. Doyle, 1983). They are defined by the products that students are required to create and the routes they can take to complete these products. Activities and tasks influence learners by directing their attention to particular aspects of content and promoting specific ways of processing information. They differ in both their content and their form, that is, in the procedures, social organization, and products they require. The elements of activities and tasks vary from simple to complex and combine in various ways to shape how students think and how they work by determining how information is obtained, how it is processed, and how it is presented to the teacher for evaluation.

The *content* of an activity refers to its cognitive complexity and reflects the objectives students are expected to attain. Different learning objectives vary in difficulty for students, because they require different levels of cognitive processing and different prerequisite skills (Doyle, 1983). Variations in the difficulty of activity content affect student learning and behavior. For example, moderately difficult activities produce greater motivation than do "easy" ones (Clifford, 1991). Moderately difficult activities help learners calibrate their progress toward a goal by providing information about progress as well as concrete evidence of accomplishments (Schunk, 1989). As a result, they enhance confidence and increase interest. Conversely, students may perceive minimally challenging situations or "safe" successes as evidence that others hold low expectations for them, which may reinforce a perception of their own low ability (Weiner, 1992).

Students' reactions to content are also influenced by their beliefs about its inherent appeal, its difficulty, and their familiarity with the topic (Blumenfeld et al., 1987). For example, students are more likely to be discouraged when they confront difficulties with new material because they are more uncertain about their ability. Because performance in the classroom is public and subject to evaluation, few children are likely to be strongly interested in new material that may cause them to be confused, make errors, or have to exert a great deal of effort unless they are fairly certain they will succeed (Brophy, 1983a).

The *form* of an activity also affects learning, irrespective of its content (Blumenfeld, Mergendoller, & Swarthout, 1987). As vehicles for the transmission of content, different forms vary in the extent to which learning objectives are evident to students. Forms differ in the obviousness of their purposes, the complexity of their procedures, the social organization in which they are carried out, and the products that result. For example, the purposes and procedures for completing worksheets are generally more straightforward than those surrounding a discussion.

Certain forms may exhibit more procedural complexity than others, but this can also vary within the same form. When activities are procedurally complex, students may spend more time carrying out procedures than focusing on the content to be learned. In addition, forms differ in the prerequisite skills they require. The more prerequisite knowledge and skill are required to accomplish the task, the more hesitant students may be to work at the activity

(Blumenfeld et al., 1987). Finally, difficulty is determined by the nature of the product students must complete for evaluation and by the clarity of the evaluation criteria.

When the product can be evaluated according to numerous criteria, students, particularly younger ones, tend to focus on aspects that are more objective and easier to identify and define (e.g., neatness or length) at the expense of concentrating on content or richness of ideas, clarity of explanations, or complexity of analysis (L. Anderson, 1981; Anderson, Brubaker, Alleman-Brooks, & Duffy, 1985). These tendencies are obviously strengthened when teachers' evaluative comments focus on neatness or effort. If teachers rely on assessment criteria that are ill matched to the original cognitive purpose of the activity, students will learn to process at the levels required by these criteria.

It is worth noting here the importance of employing authentic activities and tasks involving complex problems and projects as a means of promoting effective reading and writing. Newmann and Wehlage (1993; see also Newmann & Associates, 1996) use the word *authentic* to distinguish instruction and achievement that are significant and substantive from those that are trivial and meaningless. They use three criteria to define authenticity more precisely: "(1) students construct meaning and knowledge; (2) students use disciplined inquiry to construct meaning; and (3) students aim their work toward production of discourse, products, and performances that have value or meaning beyond success in school" (Newmann & Wehlage, 1993, p. 8).

Newmann and Wehlage (1993) caution that even activities that place students in the role of a more active, cooperative learner and that seem to respect student voices can be implemented in ways that do not produce authentic achievement. The challenge is not simply to adopt innovative teaching practices, but to work against two persistent problems that make conventional schooling inauthentic: The work students do often does not allow them to use their minds well, and the work frequently has no intrinsic meaning or value to students beyond achieving success in school.

***Cumulative Effects.***    Research suggests that students rely on prior experiences with lesson format and content as a guide to interpreting current activities. They construct knowledge, learning strategies, and representations of the subject itself according to their experience. Even when conditions make such approaches inappropriate, students' approach to activities is strongly influenced by their expectations about the form of the product and evaluative criteria to be used in assessment. If teachers do not provide information about product form or evaluation procedures, students will expect their performance to be assessed in the same way and at the same cognitive level as it was previously. So, for example, if students receive a steady diet of literal comprehension questions, they will tend to process the text at that level and attempt to answer more thoughtful questions in the same manner as they have learned to respond to literal questions.

Generally speaking, students have to do two things as part of academic tasks: obtain information from reading/listening and show teachers that they understand the information by producing a product. In some cases the form in which information is obtained is different from the form of the product required for evaluation. In some of these cases students will find it easier to obtain information than to display their knowledge or skill appropriately because the performance task is more complex. Blumenfeld et al. (1987) note that it is possible for students to possess the cognitive skills necessary to achieve the content goal but to be unable to negotiate successfully the form in which they are required to display their knowledge. The actual problem may be failure to understand the form rather than an inability to comprehend the content.

The more complex the task form, the more important it is for teachers to provide clear and specific explanation and feedback during the lesson to distinguish between the content- and form-related aspects of the learning activity. Otherwise, students may spend considerable time on aspects of the activity that are irrelevant to the learning objective. In such cases actual time on task may remain high, although much of it may be devoted to aspects of the activity that are irrelevant to the successful achievement of the objective.

The manner in which students approach and think about new information depends on their previous experience with the form of the activity. The more frequent the experience of similar activities across subject matter, classrooms, and grades, the greater is the consistency with which students approach and think about their work. If students are consistently exposed to activities with simple forms, they will have little practice in the form-related skills of planning, organizing, selecting among several alternative strategies, and monitoring their progress toward a goal. The result is limited opportunities to learn those self-regulation skills essential for accomplishing a variety of activities (Au, 1997; Corno & Mandinach, 1983; Darling-Hammond, 1995).

Similarly, this repeated exposure is likely to result in preferences for easy, clearly defined activities that require minimal time or involvement on the part of the learner. This problem is further compounded when the complexity of either the content or form of the activity differs by ability group. To the extent to which low achievers are assigned activities with simple content *and* form, opportunities to develop higher-level cognitive abilities become stratified and inequitable (Bowles & Gintis, 1976).

## Grouping

Grouping patterns in classrooms constitute a special type of organizational structure. Teachers need to exercise caution if they group students for instruction, because such arrangements have implications for student motivation and achievement. Key components of the grouping structure in the classroom include the size and number of groups, the basis for grouping, consistency of groups across content areas, stability of groups over time, labeling of groups, mobility of individuals between groups, the number of groups functioning as groups at one time, and the amount of time spent individual, group, or whole-class structure (Marshall & Weinstein, 1984).

Reviews of research on ability grouping for reading instruction suggest that instructional and social reading experiences differ for students in high- and low-ranked reading groups and that these differences influence student learning (e.g., Allington, 1983b; Hiebert, 1983). The social properties of ability groups are derived, at least in part, from the fact that students are grouped with those defined to be similar and separated from those defined to be different. Group placement is based on socially valued criteria, so that group membership immediately identifies some individuals as better than others. Therefore, high- and low-ranked reading groups are likely to form unique instructional-social contexts that influence the learning outcomes of the individuals within those groups.

As a consequence, students make judgments about their own and others' competence. Reading assessment can be enriched by a clear understanding of the types of social distinctions that accompany grouping patterns in the classroom. For example, when researchers ask students about how they learn how smart they are, students commonly refer to group membership (Marshall & Weinstein, 1984). We see this repeatedly when we interview students in our clinics. This type of awareness was displayed by 9-year-old Matthew who, when asked whether he liked to read, adamantly said he did not. But then he offered the following: "I'd like to read if I could learn how. . . ."

Student feelings of efficacy and motivation are affected by grouping decisions, but research suggests that students in different groups also receive distinctly different instruction. Students in low-ranked groups spend considerably less time in actual reading tasks than students in high-ranked groups do (McDermott, 1977). High-ability groups read silently more often than they read orally, whereas low-ability groups read orally much more frequently than silently (Allington, 1983b). In addition, teachers interrupt students following oral reading errors proportionally more often in low-ability groups than in high-ability groups and are more likely to emphasize word identification with low-ability groups and comprehension with high-ability groups (Allington, 1980).

The nature and extent of such differential treatment vary from teacher to teacher, and at least some of the variation can be seen as appropriate differential instruction (Brophy, 1983b; Haskins, Walden, & Ramey, 1983). Too often, however, low groups receive less exciting instruction, less emphasis on meaning and conceptualization, and more rote drill and practice activities (Good & Marshall, 1984).

The differential treatment, coupled with the simple fact of group membership, provides students with more messages about their potential for success in reading (Weinstein, 1986). Average- and low-ability students who are in ability groups give lower self-evaluations than those who are not in ability groups (Rosenbaum, 1980). Research suggests that most groups that are based on homogeneous ability levels are relatively stable over time with infrequent mobility of students from one group to another (Rosenbaum, 1980) and that membership in reading groups of different ability levels contributes significantly to the prediction of reading achievement beyond initial individual differences (Weinstein, 1976).

In sum, the evidence suggests that a low-group psychology develops wherever ability grouping is practiced, even in schools whose low-group students would be high-group students somewhere else (Good & Brophy, 2000). Such students may be prime candidates to become underachievers because it may be easier for them to remain passive and to pretend indifference rather than risk failure by trying their best.

Before leaving this topic, it is important to note that some groups are formed for reasons other than ability, such as grouping for student interests or specific skill needs; promoting interaction among students of varying backgrounds; and promoting learning in all students (Marshall & Weinstein, 1984). Research on cooperative learning groups has demonstrated a positive effect on achievement, race relations, and student self-esteem (Slavin, 1983). In contrast to stable and homogeneous groups, students have greater opportunity to work with more of their peers and to observe their own and others' strengths in a variety of areas when a flexible grouping strategy is used. Where external rewards are distributed, more children have the opportunity to receive recognition than where stable hierarchical grouping strategies result in the high-ability group consistently receiving more rewards and privileges.

In light of the foregoing, Good and Brophy (2000) offer the following guidelines for within-class ability grouping:

1. The number, size, and composition of groups should be determined by teacher goals.
2. Groups should not be formed for the sole purpose of altering the pace of instruction. Instead, they should promote differentiated instruction for individual students.
3. Assignments to groups should be flexible, not permanent.
4. The scheduling and instruction of groups should be subject to change as well.
5. Students should be assigned to a group for a specific purpose and should be managed in such a way as to limit the impact on their other activities, both academic and social. For example, members of the same reading group should not be seated together, nor should membership in a reading (or other group) dictate the students' grouping for other subjects.
6. The organization and instruction of groups should result in extra instruction for low achievers.

In writing instruction, permanent ability grouping is rare. As a result, students who are poor readers may be relatively enthusiastic writers. If grammar, usage, and mechanics are not emphasized unduly, these students escape the negative consequences that result from grouping practices in reading.

## Congruence within and across Instructional Settings

The school life of many poor readers involves not one, but several, instructional contexts. Until the 1990s most poor readers and writers received special instruction outside of the classroom (called pull-out programs), a configuration that is still not uncommon. However, many less-skilled readers and writers now receive their instruction via *inclusion* programs, receiving special instruction within the regular classroom. This instruction may still be planned and provided by a special teacher. In either arrangement it is likely that students are experiencing two settings, two teachers, and frequently two sets of program materials. Researchers such as Allington and Johnston have examined the relationships between supplemental reading and writing programs and regular classroom instruction (Allington & Johnston, 1989; Johnston, Allington, & Afflerbach, 1985). Their results revealed that an astonishing 80 percent of classroom teachers did not know what instructional materials were being used for the remedial students in their room. The data also indicated that only 50 percent of the specialists could specify the reading book used by classroom teachers. If classroom and supplemental teachers do not know this general information, it is, of course, extremely unlikely that they have coordinated any other aspects of the students' reading and writing instruction.

Examinations of the instruction students receive in the classroom and in the remedial setting suggests that there is little congruence. On a typical day, remedial students are receiving instruction on different skills, using different materials, and with a different focus in two different environments (Allington et al., 1986). As Johnston and his colleagues (1985) point out, this means that the students who have the most difficulty integrating information and transferring learned skills to new situations are receiving the most fragmented, least unified instruction of all.

The coordination of efforts between the classroom and the special teachers is at the heart of most definitions of what Walp and Walmsley (1989) call "procedural congruence." These authors note that organized mechanical coordination does little to ensure that students will encounter a coherent and well-conceived instructional environment. Simple inclusion programs will not assure congruent instruction either. "It is quite possible to have classroom and remedial teachers occupying the same space yet delivering unrelated programs" (Walp & Walmsley, 1989, p. 365). It seems likely that congruence between instructional settings for remedial readers will depend on teachers having serious discussion about the nature of reading and the rationale for delivering "more of the same" or "different" instruction.

## Understanding the Role of Instructional Practice in Reading and Writing Performance

In this section of the chapter we continue our examination of the instructional environment by focusing on the role of instructional practice in reading and writing performance. Specifically, we address the areas of instructional goals, instructional methods, reading and writing activities and tasks, and assessment practices.

### Instructional Goals

Reading and writing goals should be as consistent as possible with our understanding of the reading and writing processes. Both instructional activities and student outcomes should emanate from a definition of skilled reading and writing (see Chapter 1). Reading and writing goals in the United States have too often focused on easily measured subskills with too little attention directed toward the acquisition of important overall ability (Brown, Collins, & Duguid, 1989). In a well-designed literacy program, mastering the parts is not the end in itself, but a means to an end, and there is a balance between practice of the parts and practice of the whole (Anderson, Hiebert, Scott, & Wilkinson, 1985; Snow et al., 1998).

In addition to overall curricular goals, effective teachers establish specific instructional objectives for individual lessons and students. Students who are made aware of goals and objectives before reading and writing are more successful than those who do not have this information. Despite this fact, many teachers are not clear about their goals, and many schools do not have well-considered program outcomes.

Evaluating the instructional context requires consideration of both *overall curricular goals* and *specific instructional objectives*. The fundamental questions to be asked regarding goals and objectives are "What is being taught?" and "Is the student likely to be a better reader and/or writer because she or he has achieved this goal or objective?" The answers to these questions are explored for general curricular goals in the next section and for instructional objectives in the following section.

***Standards and Curriculum.*** Recent efforts to develop state and national content standards represent attempts to translate current theory and research into student outcomes

(Pearson, 1993). These efforts typically focus on reading, writing, listening, and speaking under the umbrella of English language arts. The outcomes or standards that are produced through these efforts are intended as guides for developing classroom or district curriculum and instruction.

There are likely as many different sets of English language arts standards as there are organizations, states, and districts formulating them. An example of one effort to describe the domain of K–12 English language arts curriculum comes from Peters and Wixson (in press), who identify four strands, which are then broken down further into content standards and benchmarks. The four strands are (1) genre, craft, and the conventions of language; (2) literature and understanding; (3) elements of effective communication; and (4) skills, strategies, processes, and dispositions.

Recognizing that every parsing of English language arts curriculum is arbitrary in some way, Peters and Wixson offer these four strands as one example of how to think about the domain. The genre, craft, and conventions of language strand describes specific genre to be read or listened to, which also serve as models for writing and speaking. The literature and understanding strand focuses on the key ideas, values, and beliefs in literature and the various interpretative perspectives (e.g., cultural and personal) associated with understanding. The elements of effective communication strand identifies the forms, audiences, and purposes of writing and speaking. The fourth and final strand describes the skills, strategies, processes, and dispositions required to use and apply the content within the other strands.

For the purposes of this text we have distilled current standards and outcomes such as those just described into the goal of developing *knowledgeable, strategic,* and *motivated* readers and writers. Knowledgeable readers and writers have a grasp of the content of reading and writing. Although there is no one agreed-upon set of content goals for reading and writing, most accounts assert that students need to understand the "what" of text content, literary elements, genre, and the craft of written language, as reflected in the first three strands of Peters and Wixson's domain description.

Strategic readers and writers use their knowledge and skills flexibly, adapting their approach for different purposes, tasks, and materials. They also develop and use their own standards to evaluate their reading and writing and the meanings they construct. They set personal goals for developing reading and writing abilities and for learning from reading and writing and are aware of both their efforts and their accomplishments. This goal is reflected in the fourth strand of Peters and Wixson's domain description.

Motivated readers and writers are those who not only *can* read and write, but also *choose* to do so for a variety of recreational and functional purposes. They generally understand the various purposes of reading and writing and are reasonably skilled at using reading and writing to meet their needs. Not all motivated readers and writers enjoy and select the same types of reading and writing activities, but they do have one thing in common: They read and write voluntarily. This goal is also reflected in the fourth strand.

In developing knowledgeable, motivated, and strategic readers and writers, much of the traditional content of reading and writing instruction will continue to be important, but students and teachers must not focus on the acquisition of knowledge and skill as an end in itself. Instead, the goal is for students to use their knowledge and skill as they read and write widely. The total reading and writing curriculum across ages and grades must attend to the interplay among these outcomes. A program that does not balance these primary aspects of reading and writing may produce students who can, but will not, read or write or students who enjoy books but cannot read them independently. Both breadth and depth are desirable in the developmental reading and writing program, but the relative attention to different aspects of the curriculum may vary across the developmental continuum.

Just as the emphasis on different outcomes may vary across the developmental continuum, it will also vary for individuals who are experiencing reading and writing difficulty. Some students will need to acquire knowledge about reading and writing; others will need ample opportunity to apply and adapt their reading and writing skills; still others will need to develop an increased appreciation for the functional value of reading and writing practice. The issue here is a critical one: Knowledge, skill, and motivation *are all factors in student achievement.*

***Specific Instructional Objectives.*** General curricular goals provide guidance and direction for the identification of more specific instructional objectives used for particular lessons and students at particular levels of development. It is important to understand that instructional objectives are not synonymous with activities (e.g., journal writing, dictating stories). When objectives are equated with activity completion, both teachers and students are likely to misconstrue the purpose of instruction. In addition, successful instruction is likely to be measured in terms of the number or levels of activities completed rather than the extent to which knowledge and/or competence has increased. This is an extremely important distinction that must be understood both to evaluate and to plan effective instructional programs.

The goal of developing knowledgeable, strategic, motivated readers and writers can be translated into three types of instructional objectives that relate to the outcomes required for students to become expert readers and writers (Duffy & Roehler, 1989). Sound instruction must contain provisions for each of the following types of objectives:

1. *Attitude objectives:* Students need to develop the motivation and desire to read and write for a variety of purposes.
2. *Content objectives:* Students need to learn the "what" of reading and writing and to understand the ideas they are reading and/or writing about.
3. *Process objectives:* Students need to acquire skill in using reading and writing processes.

Until recently, the most neglected area in reading and writing instruction has been that reflected by attitude objectives. Traditionally, many teachers have asserted that they want students to be motivated to read and write. However, few instructional programs have provided directly for the development of attitude objectives, and fewer still have included assessments of attitude. Just as students vary in their knowledge and skill, they may differ in their attitudes and motivation toward reading and writing. Some students find reading and writing gratifying and therefore read and write widely outside of school. Others do very little reading and writing and may come to view skilled reading and writing as tedious activities that are required to complete a number of discrete tasks.

Attitude objectives are important, legitimate concerns for all teachers. The relationship between positive attitudes and achievement suggest that students' expectations and values have a significant effect on both their effort and their achievement (Covington & Omelich, 1979; see Wigfield & Asher, 1984, for a complete review). To become effective readers and writers, students must demonstrate both *skill and will* (Paris, Lipson, & Wixson, 1983). If they are not willing to engage in independent reading and writing, students will not have sufficient opportunity to practice acquired skills, nor will they develop the facility to read and write flexibly for their own purposes.

If attitude outcomes have been neglected in the past, the same cannot be said about content outcomes, especially those focused on understanding what is being read. Many reading and literature lessons have traditionally focused almost exclusively on methods and techniques for helping students understand the content of specific texts. Teachers should not abandon their efforts to help students comprehend during reading. However, not all reading entails studying and a detailed understanding of the content of text, and students should not be led to believe that it does. Nor should instruction aimed at an understanding of specific content be divorced from instruction in the processes and values associated with a particular type of reading.

Instruction that is designed only to help students understand specific stories or textbooks aids comprehension but does little to develop comprehension ability (Johnston, 1997; Paris, Wixson, & Palincsar, 1986). Effective reading instruction must achieve the delicate balance between focusing on understanding content and developing the ability to process different types of materials for different purposes. Students must acquire the skills and strategies that will enable them to comprehend and learn *on their own,* and teachers need to think carefully about how they address these important process objectives. Similarly, effective writing instruction must balance attention to the content of writing with the skills and processes essential for effective writing in a variety of situations.

What we want to avoid is instruction that emphasizes content objectives at the expense of process objectives or vice versa. What is needed in both reading and writing instruction is a balance among attitude, content, and process objectives.

## Instructional Methods

In this portion of the chapter we summarize research on effective approaches to instructional practice. There are two ways in which this research can help in the assessment-instruction process. First, descriptions of effective instructional practice provide a framework for specifying the important attributes of the instructional context. Second, it is important to understand what characterizes good instruction to evaluate its contribution to the reading and writing process for individual students.

The question of what constitutes effective instruction has been of consuming interest to educators and researchers for decades. However, during the past thirty years there has been a great increase in efforts to specify the attributes of successful schools, classrooms, and teachers. The important lessons from research are that students need to be actively engaged in order to learn and that initial learning requires teacher modeling and explanation. There is also support for the general conclusion that students need multiple opportunities to learn (Cooley & Leinhardt, 1980). These findings suggest that the effects of instructional method are intimately connected to the classroom management practices and teacher expectations described previously. Unfortunately, the evidence also suggests that teachers are spending too much time managing and assessing children by assigning them activities and asking questions and too little time teaching (e.g., Durkin, 1978–79; Kane, 1994). Existing methods often encourage teachers to view instruction as placement in a program rather than a series of decisions to be made about what content should be taught or what methods might work best.

It is important to emphasize that research on effective instruction in reading and writing is far from definitive. Indeed, the research in this area is so diverse that it is possible to find evidence supporting contradictory practices. Effective teaching can occur within the context of many programs and many materials, but no one set of materials nor any single program is likely to address the needs of every student. Our instructional guidelines are derived from two sources of information: our conclusions about the best theoretical perspectives on the reading and writing process and our understanding of the best available research evidence regarding effective reading and writing practices, informed by several recent research syntheses (Bowman, Donovan, & Burns, 2000; Center for the Improvement of Early Reading Achievement, 2001; National Reading Panel, 2000; Snow et al., 1998).

Once important goals and objectives have been determined, attention can be directed to the best ways to help students meet these goals. This is the focus in the following sections, in which we move from *what* is being taught to the methods of instruction or *how* it is taught. We begin by describing an effective model of instruction and proceed to a discussion of instructional activities and tasks.

***Creating Knowledgeable, Strategic Readers and Writers.*** Good teaching must include instruction in how to read, write, remember, and think independently. This means both that students acquire reading and writing skill and that they are able to transfer this knowledge to a variety of reading and writing situations and tasks. The problem of how to maintain and transfer skilled and strategic behavior has been a major issue facing educators. The practice of teaching isolated component parts of reading and writing has proven less effective in improving reading and writing ability on transfer tests and on subsequent achievement tests than has instruction that is embedded in more meaningful events. On the other hand, the more recent attempts to provide instruction through immersion-only approaches have often been disappointing, for somewhat different reasons. As Au (2000, p. 846) concluded, "[M]otivation is a necessary but not sufficient condition for students to develop higher level thinking about text. . . . Research on constructivist approaches shows that the teaching of literacy can and should be motivating and responsive to children's backgrounds and interests, while at the same time providing them with systematic instruction in needed skills and strategies."

Current research suggests that it is possible to teach students how to be knowledgeable, strategic, motivated readers and writers. This research suggests a need for instruction based on the principle of gradually releasing responsibility for learning from the teacher to the student (Pearson & Gallagher, 1983). In the initial stages of acquisition the teacher has primary responsibility for students' learning. In the final stages of learning, the student has the primary responsibility for practicing and applying what has been learned. What comes between is a form of guided instruction that represents joint responsibility between the teacher and the student. These features are discussed at some length below.

During the acquisition phase of the instructional process, the teacher has the primary responsibility for student learning. Reviews of research by the Center for the Improvement of Early Reading Achievement (2001) and the National Reading Panel (2000) confirm that we know a great deal about how to help children learn to read. The attributes of teacher-based instruction that have demonstrably improved reading and writing performance include clear teacher presentations (Roehler & Duffy, 1984), good direct explanation (Paris et al., 1984), modeling and guided practice (Palincsar & Brown, 1984), high levels of active student involvement (Palincsar & Brown, 1984), and providing for review and feedback (Adams, Carnine, & Gersten, 1982). Using these techniques, researchers have demonstrated improvement in students' decoding abilities (e.g., Cunningham, 1990), vocabulary knowledge (e.g., Pany & Jenkins, 1978), and comprehension ability (e.g., Paris et al., 1984).

Although the relative contributions of these separate teaching practices have yet to be determined, it appears that clear, specific, teacher explanation is particularly important to students' improvement. Clear explanations provide students with knowledge about how to accomplish various reading and writing tasks. However, having knowledge about *how* to perform a skill or strategy does not ensure that students will use that knowledge.

To increase the likelihood that students will use their skills, teachers must provide students with information about when and why to use the skills they are learning. Research suggests that this is a critical factor in students' ability to transfer the skills they have learned to other reading and writing contexts (Cunningham, 1990; Paris, Lipson, & Wixson, 1983). Although it might seem obvious to teachers, students frequently do not understand how skills acquisition is related to real-life reading and writing. Effective reading and writing instruction must also involve feedback on the utility of the action (Lipson & Wickizer, 1989) and instruction in why, when, and where such activities should be applied (Paris, Cross, & Lipson, 1984).

As the student becomes more skilled, the responsibility for continued learning becomes shared between teacher and student. A study by Gordon and Pearson (1983) can be used to illustrate how this gradual release of responsibility might actually be accomplished. In this study, learning to make inferences was conceived as involving four tasks: (a) posing a question, (b) answering it, (c) finding evidence, and (d) giving the reasoning for how to get from the evidence to the answer. Release was accomplished through four stages of instruction. In stage 1 the teacher modeled all four tasks; in stage 2 the teacher did (a) and (b), and the students did (c) and (d); in stage 3 the teacher took responsibility for (a) and (c), and the students did (b) and (d); and in stage 4 the students did all but (a).

Once students have acquired sufficient knowledge and skill to work independently, the primary responsibility for learning is transferred to the student. Effective instruction provides students with many opportunities to advance their learning by using their literacy skills in productive and authentic ways. The effects of practicing reading and writing in holistic settings have become increasingly evident in recent years. Beginners can enjoy intensified gains when provided with increased opportunities to read and write large numbers of texts (Pinnell, 1985); 7- and 8-year-olds enjoy significant increases in meaning vocabulary when they listen to good books (Elley, 1989); individuals at many ages recognize more words after reading them in continuous text (Herman, Anderson, Pearson, & Nagy, 1987; Nagy, Herman, & Anderson, 1985); and both comprehension and vocabulary have been improved when students' recreational reading is increased (Anderson, Wilson, & Fielding, 1988).

We will return to these issues in later chapters, but the point should be made, since the evidence is quite impressive: Students need to read and write to become good readers and writers (Mosenthal et al., 2001a, 2001b). Simple workbook completion activities do not provide enough substantial practice and may actually contribute to students' lack of motivation for reading and writing authentic texts outside of school. The following sections discuss elements of practice related to the gradual release model of learning and instruction: scaffolding, social interaction or dialogue, level of instruction, and reflection.

*Scaffolding.* The hallmark of instruction involving the gradual release of responsibility is *scaffolding.* Scaffolding has been described as instructional assistance that enables someone to solve a problem, carry out a task, or achieve a goal that he or she could not accomplish without support (Wood, Bruner, & Ross, 1976). Wilkinson and Silliman (2000, p. 343) explain that a scaffold "is an external structure that braces another structure being built." The metaphor of a scaffold calls attention to a support system that is both temporary and adjustable. Teachers should expect students to need their support in moving from one level of competence to the next so that, in time, they will be able to apply problem-solving strategies independently and wisely (Paris et al., 1986).

Scaffolded instruction begins with selecting a learning task for the purpose of teaching a skill that is emerging in the learner's repertoire but is not yet fully developed. The task is evaluated to determine the difficulty it is likely to pose for the learner. This is done to facilitate decision making about how to make the task simpler and the learner more successful. Modeling, questioning, and explanation are used during instruction to make the task explicit and to represent appropriate approaches to the task (Palincsar, 1986).

There is considerable emphasis on student participation in the learning activity for the purposes of providing opportunities to use the skills being instructed and evaluating student performance. This evaluation is conducted to determine the level of difficulty of the task, make appropriate adjustments in the level of instructional support, and provide the learner with information regarding his or her performance. Finally, the aim of scaffolded instruction is generalization to less-structured contexts. Such generalization is facilitated by the gradual withdrawal of the scaffold as the learner demonstrates increased competence (Palincsar, 1986).

*Dialogue.* Instruction in the gradual release model is also characterized by the ongoing interplay between teacher and learner in the joint completion of a task. These dialogues are the means by which supports, or scaffolds, are provided and adjusted. When children engage in subsequent problem solving, they display the types of behaviors that are characteristic of dialogues they had when they were collaborating with a more expert individual. Palincsar (1986) suggests the following characteristics of dialogue:

1. The teacher supports students' contributions to the dialogue, eliciting and supporting responses at the idea level (versus asking for one-word, discrete responses).
2. The teacher uses student ideas and links those ideas to new information.

3. The dialogue has a focus and direction.
4. The teacher makes use of explicit instruction.
5. The teacher uses feedback constructively to help students improve their responses.

The relationship between teacher and learner in this supportive dialogue is to be contrasted with that observed when students are left to discover or invent strategies independently or when students are passive observers who receive demonstration and are talked at regarding strategy use. When this type of dialogue occurs with initial instruction, it "enables learners to participate in strategic activity even though they may not fully understand the activity and would most certainly not be able to exercise the strategy independently" (Palincsar, 1986, p. 75). The available evidence suggests that teachers often conduct monologues, not dialogues, and rarely use student ideas as the basis for discussion and teaching. Teachers are taught to "tell" and are rarely provided with instruction or guidance in conducting effective dialogues with students. Wilkinson and Silliman (2000) refer to these formal patterns of social interaction between teacher and students as "directive scaffolds." Question–answer evaluation sequences, for example, do serve an instructional purpose but do not support the aim of student responsibility for learning as directly as do the dialogue patterns inherent in the supportive scaffolds described in the previous section.

*Level of Instruction.*    A gradual release model of learning and instruction draws heavily on Vygotsky's (1978) view of the relationship between instruction and cognitive development. According to Vygotsky, instruction is best when it proceeds ahead of development and arouses those functions that are in the process of maturing. In other words, instruction leads development. Cognitive skills that are emerging but not yet fully mature are considered to lie within the zone of proximal or potential development. This zone is defined as the distance between the actual developmental level as determined by independent problem solving and the level of potential development as determined through problem solving under adult guidance or in collaboration with more capable peers (Vygotsky, 1978). This means that instruction is likely to be most effective when teachers identify the zone or levels at which students can perform with some assistance and guide them to higher levels of performance and then to the point of independent learning (Wilkinson & Silliman, 2000).

A familiar example offered by Au and Kawakami (1986) may be helpful in describing what instruction within the zone of proximal development might look like. They observed skilled teachers conducting reading comprehension lessons and noted that these teachers consistently posed questions that they knew their students were likely to have difficulty answering. This, the authors argue, demonstrates how the students were being challenged to perform at higher levels than they were able to achieve independently. They also observed that the teachers responded to incorrect answers by helping the students work out a better answer, rather than just giving them a correct response. Students were given the opportunity to carry out rather advanced comprehension skills, if only with considerable assistance.

The appropriate level of instruction may also be influenced by other factors, such as the difficulty of the materials that students are provided. Many poor readers are given materials that are so difficult that they cannot identify even 80 percent of the words correctly (Juel, 1988). Experts argue that 50 percent (Guthrie, 1980) to 60 percent (Ekwall & Shanker,

1985) of all elementary grade students are working with inappropriate instructional materials for reading. This and other factors influencing the appropriateness of the level of instruction are discussed in greater detail in Chapter 9.

*Reflection.* Without reflection neither knowledge nor the skills for applying knowledge are likely to be used intelligently (see Onosko & Newmann, 1994). Reflection encompasses a variety of traits, including a persistent desire to understand the reasons for one's own and other's thoughts and actions, a tendency to take time to think problems through for oneself rather than acting impulsively or automatically accepting the views of others, a flexibility to entertain alternative and original thoughts and actions, and a habit of examining one's own thinking processes and establishing personal goals. It is important that teachers design instruction explicitly to help students become reflective readers and writers. Central to reflection is the ability to monitor and evaluate one's own literate activity (Johnston, 1992). A common feature of students' having trouble with reading and writing is their failure to monitor and self-correct. They look to others to see whether they are "doing it right." They do not feel able to evaluate their own performance.

Johnston (1992) describes a variety of practices that encourage self-evaluation. For example, it is important to recognize self-evaluation when it occurs. When a student becomes aware of a problem, we can say, "I like the way you noticed that yourself. That is a sign of a good writer/reader." The information conveyed is that self-evaluation is important to becoming a better reader/writer, not that they have performed as you wanted.

Other practices that promote self-evaluation include encouraging students to give it a try, anticipate, and check their predictions and attempts. It can also be encouraged by reflective responses that turn questions back to learners. For example, a question such as "How could we check whether that is correct?" might provide assistance, since it opens up one or more strategies for self-checking. The student's response is also likely to give us information about the strategies the learner has available.

According to Tierney, Carter, and Desai (1991), students need opportunities to share their work with their peers. Reflecting on their work with other students becomes a vehicle for students to discover important ideas, explore new concepts, think in new ways, and refine their methods of communicating to different audiences. Charts can be created and updated as a way to record student thoughts about reading and writing. Samples of student work can be used as examples of a certain feature that students think is important to emphasize. Charts developed from student input become the beginning of criteria for quality work that students recognize.

Once students have a variety of samples and have generated ideas about criteria for reading and writing, they are ready to start to apply their criteria to their own reading and writing. Student comments will not be as sophisticated as teachers comments and may focus on features of reading and writing that are not that important at first when students are just beginning to develop the tools necessary to think critically about themselves as readers and writers. As they become increasingly responsible for judging the quality of their own work, they are learning to take control of their own reading and writing.

Self-evaluation and reflection can also be overtly valued by making portfolios a central part of classroom evaluation. A portfolio can include entries selected by the students to represent their growth. Each entry can have attached to it statements as to why the work is important, what has been learned, and future goals. This gives the teacher information about what the student values and requires the student to be reflective.

Walters, Seidel, and Gardner (1994) observe that as students work on projects and collect artifacts for their portfolios, they can also be engaged in a continuing discussion of standards of quality. How does a student come to understand that one essay is more articulate than another? How do these judgments go beyond the issues of simple accuracy in spelling and grammar? Even very young students are quite capable of setting standards for themselves (see Higgins, Harris, & Kuehn, 1994). Setting standards is an important ability in continuing to learn outside of school. We need to spend a greater portion of our time as teachers helping students set their own standards instead of always establishing those standards independently of the students and in advance of their experience.

For students to become reflective self-evaluators, they must feel themselves to be able knowers and evaluators. Students need to have confidence and self-respect and to value their own knowledge to be self-critical and develop reflective commitment to their reading and writing. These conditions are most likely to occur when students feel that they have something to contribute. Students are made to feel this way when people actually listen to them and communicate that their ideas are not less valuable than those of the teacher or others.

The way we talk as teachers can make us appear to have all the knowledge and be all-powerful arbiters of quality, or it can suggest that the students are knowledgeable and able to judge their own reading and writing. Students' thoughts about reading and writing need to be accepted. When we begin to understand what our students think, we can offer appropriate guidance that promotes individual progress.

***Creating Motivated Readers and Writers.***    Reading and writing achievement are powerfully influenced by motivation and attitudes (see Chapter 1). Good and Brophy (2000) concluded that most current research supports an expectancy × value theory of motivation. According to this theory, the effort that people will be willing to expend on an activity is a product of the degree to which they expect to be able to perform the task successfully if they apply themselves and the degree to which they value the rewards that successful performance will bring. This theory of motivation implies that teachers need both to help their students appreciate the value of school activities and to make certain that their students can achieve success in their school activities if they apply reasonable effort.

It is important that teachers use strategies designed to motivate their students to learn from academic activities. But Good and Brophy (2000) argue that certain preconditions must be in place for motivational strategies to be effective: (1) The teacher must create a classroom atmosphere that is supportive of students' learning efforts; (2) students must be given tasks of an appropriate difficulty level; (3) activities must be selected with worthwhile academic objectives in mind; and (4) the teacher must show moderation and variation in using motivational strategies. Once these preconditions are established, there are several different types of motivational strategies that teachers use to promote students' expectations for success and value of learning.

*Motivational Strategies.*    If they are to meet challenging goals, students must possess confidence and be willing to take risks; they must *expect to* be successful. Good and Brophy

(2000) describe strategies that teachers might use to promote students' expectations for success. Not surprisingly, the most basic strategy here involves assigning tasks on which students can succeed, if they apply reasonable effort, and instructing them thoroughly so that they know what to do and how to do it. Other strategies include helping students to set appropriate goals; commit themselves to these goals; use appropriate standards for appraising their levels of success; recognize the linkages between effort and outcome through modeling, socialization, and feedback; and view effort as an investment rather than a risk.

Although most teachers are aware of these strategies, they take considerable thought and often additional effort to apply. Good and Brophy (2000) point out that the class as a whole may respond to one level of motivational support, but students who have become discouraged to the point at which they give up at the first sign of difficulty or frustration need more intensive and individualized encouragement. Some students will require arranging instruction that virtually guarantees success. Such strategies are essential because students' expectations for success are often related to their judgments about why they succeed or fail, which affect their willingness to try difficult tasks. These judgments are called *attributions.*

Attributing success to ability and failure to lack of effort means that the person generally will expect to succeed and will be willing to try more challenging tasks. In contrast, attributing success to a variable factor (such as task ease) and failure to lack of ability means that the person will not expect to succeed. When the person fails, he or she will give up quickly, since extra effort will not overcome the person's perceived lack of ability (Wigfield & Asher, 1984, p. 425).

As a result, many less-able students may also benefit from "attribution retraining" (e.g., Fowler & Peterson, 1981). In this case instruction is aimed at teaching students to concentrate on the task at hand rather than worry about failure, cope by retracing their steps to find their mistakes or analyzing the problem to find an alternative approach, and attribute their failures to insufficient effort, lack of information, or reliance on ineffective strategies rather than lack of ability. It is important to understand that expectancy affects motivation. In addition, the degree of objective success that students achieve is less central than how they view their performance—that is, what they see as possible for them to achieve with reasonable effort, whether they define this achievement as successful or not, and whether they attribute their performance to controllable factors such as effective strategy usage or to uncontrollable factors such as ability.

Expectancy is not the only factor that influences student motivation. Remember that students must also value the activity. Good and Brophy (2000) suggest different strategies to address the *value* aspects of student motivation. These strategies emphasize motivation for *learning,* not merely performing. Much traditional instruction attempts to motivate students to learn in order to meet some performance standard (e.g., to take a test).

If students are motivated solely by grades or other extrinsic reward and punishment considerations, they are likely to adopt goals and associated strategies that concentrate on meeting minimum requirements that will entitle them to what they see as acceptable reward levels. They will do what they must to prepare for tests and then forget most of what they have learned (Good & Brophy, 2000). Strategies focused on learning, on the other hand, should motivate students to study and learn because they find the information or skill interesting, meaningful, or worthwhile. In this context it is not surprising that Gambrell

(1996) found that students' motivation was increased when teachers used literacy-related incentives such as books that reflected the value of reading.

Although the affective, emotional aspects of this approach to motivation are important, Good and Brophy (2000) argue that these will be insufficient for students in academic settings. Students should be focused on sensemaking and importance, not just enjoyment. This, they argue, will result in effective and motivated student effort. Teachers, especially teachers of older students, should attend to these distinctions.

Drawing from research by both Good and Brophy (2000) and Gambrell (1996), we conclude that the general features of classroom learning environments that support the development of student motivation to learn are as follows:

- Modeling of the thinking and actions associated with motivation to learn,
- Communicating expectations and attributions implying motivation to learn in students,
- Creating a supportive environment for learning by minimizing the role of factors that produce performance anxiety and creating many opportunities for students to read,
- Providing a book-rich classroom where teachers model reading and are familiar with many books,
- Promoting social interactions about books.

There are a number of other strategies for inducing student motivation to learn that are more situation-specific. For readers and writers who are struggling in school settings, the issue of motivation and the importance of communicating the value of becoming literate cannot be overemphasized. Effective teaching requires the acquisition of a sophisticated repertoire of ways to focus students on learning.

*Voluntary Reading and Writing.*    The cost of failing to address motivational issues is high. Too often, repeated experiences with failure or school experiences that do not make the value of reading and writing evident result in students with poor attitudes and limited willingness to attempt reading and writing tasks. Students with strong negative feelings about reading and writing are not likely to read or write voluntarily. These attitudes, in turn, influence ability.

There is a strong association between voluntary reading and writing and general reading and writing achievement (Greaney, 1980; Morrow, 1983; Stanovich, 1992). For example, children who demonstrate voluntary interest in books are rated significantly higher by teachers on school performance than are children with low interest in books (Morrow, 1986). They also score significantly higher on standardized tests and in work habits, social and emotional maturity, and language arts skills. Other evidence suggests that time spent in voluntary reading of books is the best predictor of reading achievement gains between second and fifth grade (Anderson, Wilson, & Fielding, 1988). Finally, research suggests that independent reading is one of the major determinants of vocabulary growth, especially during and after third grade (Nagy & Anderson, 1984).

It is clear that most reluctant learners will need experiences that go beyond the instruction provided in commercial programs if they are to become independent, voluntary readers and writers. Morrow (1983, 1986) has conducted a series of studies that examined instructional practice and its influence on students' motivation to read and its involvement in voluntary reading. Specifically, she has examined the influence of classroom environment (e.g., library corners) and literary activities like book talks on students' selection of reading as a voluntary activity. The following practices appear to influence students' voluntary reading (Morrow, 1989):

1. *Print-rich environment.* It appears that children need attractive and accessible library corners that provide a range of materials (books of all types, magazines, and so on).
2. *Active student involvement with reading.* Morrow suggests various teacher initiated activities and projects related to books. However, she also acknowledges the importance of ample practice time through recreational reading periods.
3. *Adult–child interactions focused on literature.* Teachers must invite children to interact with these materials by reading aloud and telling stories.

These practices are not new, but their importance has been reaffirmed. Teachers need to model their love of reading and writing, but they also need to consider the nature of their planned instructional activities. "If through a teacher's presentations, children learn to associate reading only with repetitious skill drills and testing, they will probably not be encouraged to reach for books on their own" (Morrow, 1989, p. 220). Reading and writing educators need to recognize how self-regard and motivation are influenced by instructional practices in order to avoid the negative consequences of repeated failure.

## Reading and Writing Activities and Tasks

Students are confronted with a wide variety of activities, tasks, and routines during the course of reading and writing instruction. In many classrooms they are expected to answer questions, complete seatwork activities, read stories and books, produce book reports, write reports, keep a journal, engage in educational games, and complete projects. As was discussed previously, activities and tasks influence how students interpret and experience the reading and writing curriculum and may be particularly powerful for students just beginning formal literacy instruction. They are the crucible in which student motivation, student cognition, instruction, and learning fuse (Turner, 1995). The activities and tasks within a particular classroom define for students what literacy is, why it is important, and what it can do. They influence students' literacy learning in two ways: by predisposing them to link literacy with specific cognitive strategies and by focusing students on certain uses and purposes for literacy (Turner, 1995).

A study by Turner (1995) in six basal and six whole-language first grade classrooms provides insight into the impact of literacy activities on students' voluntary strategy use, persistence, and attentional control during task completion. Literacy activities were classified as open (child-specified processes/goals, higher-order thinking required) or closed (other-designated processes/goals, recognition/memory skills required). The results indicated that there were both differences in the types of literacy activities employed in basal and whole-language classrooms and differences in the effects of open and closed literacy activities on student behavior.

Although student activities differed considerably between basal and whole-language classrooms, few classrooms were completely consistent in selecting activities that reflected a single type of instruction. The two most consistent structures in basal classrooms were individual seatwork and teacher-directed reading groups. The activities in basal rooms were primarily, although not exclusively, of the practice type as exemplified by copying, workbook, and worksheet assignments. Within basal classrooms, 77 percent of all activities observed were classified as closed.

Whole-language classroom structure consisted primarily of small groups. Activities were located at various centers in the classroom, such as the author's table, the library corner, and the listening center, and students were allowed some choice with regard to activities and order of completion. Within these classrooms 73 percent of all the activities observed were classified as open.

An interesting finding of the Turner (1995) study was that the type of literacy task students received was a stronger predictor of behavior than whether they were in a whole-language or basal classroom. Students used more strategies, persisted longer, and controlled their attention better during open than closed literacy tasks, regardless of the type of classroom in which these tasks occurred. The factors in open tasks that appear to influence students' motivated, strategic, reflective behavior are opportunities for challenge, personal control, satisfying interests, and collaboration (Turner & Paris, 1995).

In designing open tasks, teachers recast activities to emphasize the enjoyment and the value of literacy. They demonstrate to students the many ways in which a task can be done. Concrete examples of successful but different approaches to tasks are provided. Students are taught to assess the difficulty of a task and how to adjust their goals and strategies accordingly. They emphasize the positive aspects of help seeking and help giving. They teach students how to give clues rather than answers and group evaluation is a regular part of literacy instruction. These teachers help students see that real learning comes from error, since errors provide information about problems. By emphasizing the value of effort and refining strategies, they equip students to attempt increasingly difficult tasks and activities.

Turner (1995) notes that her study focused on average readers from white, middle-class populations and that her results may not apply to others outside this group. Hiebert and Fisher (1991) report, however, that an increasing number of studies describe growth in students' learning as a result of changes in activity structure such as increasing the diversity of the task "diet," student generation of oral and written language, use of students' prior knowledge, or authenticity of school activities.

For example, one program shifted from word-by-word reading of English texts to discussion of story content, allowing students and teachers to switch to Spanish when needed to clarify the meaning of the text (Moll & Diaz, 1987). By the third lesson, students were reading passages by themselves and answering comprehension questions at a level comparable to that of English monolingual readers at grade level. Similar results were reported in a case study of writing. It has also been demonstrated that integrating an activity such as teacher read-alouds on a regular basis can increase low-income students' involvement as readers and writers (Feitelson, Kita, & Goldstein, 1986), and increased participation of ESL students in reading trade books has resulted in reading and listening comprehension at twice the previous rate (Elley & Mangubhai, 1983).

Hiebert (1994a, p. 405) argues that open, or what she calls *authentic,* literacy activities allow students without extensive literacy experiences to participate more fully in literacy events:

> Students who depend on schools to become literate are probably most in need of authentic literacy tasks. A regimen of skill and drill for these students fails to help them become readers and writers who engage in thoughtful, avid literacy as a lifelong pursuit (Commins & Miramontes, 1989; Moll & Diaz, 1987; Moll et al., 1980). The opposite of the skill-and-drill syndrome, however, is not the answer either. As part of authentic tasks, students benefit from modeling and discussions about features of written language, including the graphophonic system.

Hiebert and Fisher (1991) argue that activity structures can be productively addressed in terms of the teaching and learning "diet" that students experience in schools. Although it may be tempting to view open tasks as always more preferable and closed structures as less preferable, the real issue is determining which activity structure(s) are most appropriate under different learning conditions. Because specific structures tend to promote or enhance some educational outcomes more than others, choice of literacy goals must drive instructional design. The situation is further complicated because the fit between activity and educational outcomes is not necessarily the same for students from different gender, racial, or sociocultural groups.

We agree with Hiebert's (1994a) conclusion that many models of literacy activities are needed, especially ones that attend to students of different ages and prior literacy experiences. The one-size-fits-all assumption that underlies many current authentic literacy practices, with the same activities recommended for all students, requires careful examination for the instruction of students who vary in developmental levels and literacy backgrounds. This one-size-fits-all assumption suggests that the same activities will be effective for students who have had well over 1,000 hours of literacy experiences before beginning kindergarten and those who enter first grade with the 100 hours or so of kindergarten literacy instruction. Hiebert (1994a, p. 407) indicates that this assumption is potentially damaging "because it encourages teachers to suspect that there is something wrong with children and their parents when immersion in literacy does not produce fast results."

The following discussion highlights several different types of activity structures that are commonly used in classrooms today, including reading comprehension questions, writing process, reading-writing workshop, and discussion. Other activities, such as independent seatwork and guided reading, are addressed in Chapter 6.

***Reading Comprehension Questions.*** Many different types of questions are used in a variety of ways each day in virtually every classroom. Questions are an integral part of teacher presentations, discussions, seatwork, examinations, homework assignments, and remedial instruction (Dillon, 1988). A variety of question taxonomies have been used to classify various types of questions. Traditional question taxonomies that classify questions separately from the text or information being questioned (e.g., Barrett, 1976; Bloom, 1956) are inadequate, given an interactive view of reading. Any interaction that occurs as a reader answers questions about a text will have a direct effect on comprehension and/or learning.

Indeed, a large body of literature indicates that the type, content, and use of questions all influence student comprehension and learning.

A taxonomy of question–answer relations proposed by Pearson and Johnson (1978) provides one means for examining questions in a more interactive manner. Questions are classified in the context of, rather than apart from, the text or information being questioned. Pearson and Johnson identify three types of questions based on the probable source of the information the reader will use to answer the question. When the information needed is stated explicitly in the text, the question is textually explicit (TE). When the answer is implied rather than explicitly stated, the question is textually implicit (TI). Finally, there are some questions for which the appropriate answer is neither explicitly stated nor implied in the text but relies heavily on the background information or prior knowledge the reader brings to the text. Pearson and Johnson (1978) call these types of questions scriptally implicit (SI), using *script* as a synonym for *schema* or *knowledge structure*.

Research by Wixson (1983a, 1983b, 1984) indicates that both the type and the content of questions promote different learning outcomes. Specifically, TE questions promote verbatim reproduction of the text, TI questions result in the generation of text-based inferences, and SI questions lead to the production of inferences based on prior knowledge. Furthermore, students learn and remember best the information they are questioned about, regardless of whether it is important or trivial to the important ideas in the text.

Indiscriminate use of questions can lead students away from, as well as toward, a desirable learning outcome. We must use questions in a manner consistent with the goals and purposes of our instruction. For example, in situations in which less inferential process-ing is desirable—such as reading directions or conducting science experiments—explicit questions may be the most appropriate. When the integration of the ideas within a text is desirable, as is often the case in subject area reading, textually implicit questions may be most helpful.

We must also remember that if we ask questions that focus on unimportant information, students are likely to learn this information at the expense of other, more important content. Furthermore, repeated use of similar types of questions shapes the way students approach their reading assignments. Hansen (1981) found that students who received a steady diet of inferential questions were able to answer those kinds of questions more easily than students who had been asked only literal level questions.

Students' performance is also affected by the pattern of question answering that teachers establish in the classroom. Effective questioning requires that students be allowed sufficient time to think about and to respond to questions, yet Rowe's (1974) study of *teacher* wait time provides stunning evidence that students often have little opportunity to produce thoughtful responses. Her observations indicate that after asking questions, teachers wait less than one second for a response before calling on someone. In addition, after calling on a student, they wait only about a second for the student to give the answer before supplying it themselves, calling on someone else, rephrasing the question, or giving clues. Following these observations, Rowe (1974) investigated what would happen if teachers were trained to extend their wait times to three to five seconds. The results of this study indicate that increased wait times leads to more active participation in lessons by a larger percentage of students and an increase in the quality of the participation.

Subsequent research indicates that pacing and wait time should be adjusted to the level of questions being asked and the objectives they are intended to address. A fast pace and short wait time are appropriate for drill or review activities covering specific facts. A slow pace and longer wait times are appropriate when students are expected to think about the material and formulate original responses, rather than simply retrieve information from memory.

At different times throughout the history of reading and writing instruction there has been a shift away from answering teacher-posed questions with their implied "right" answers. Instead, teachers may be advised to solicit personal responses to reading (Rosenblatt, 1978; Winograd & Johnston, 1987). Although the long-term effects of a heavy emphasis on personal response have yet to be determined, it appears that students can often respond to a piece of writing even though they cannot justify their responses (Galda, 1982). However, we do know that a steady diet of tasks that permit only literal, "correct" responses can result in students who are unengaged in reading and writing as personally important activities (Moffett, 1985; Parsons, 1990). The tension between these two approaches permeates much of educational practice today.

***Writing Process.***    Clearly, reading and writing development and instruction are intimately related. What children read will affect what and how they write. Eckhoff (1983), for example, found that the features of the basal texts read by children were reflected in their own writing. On the other hand, the writing instruction provided by teachers can, and often is, distinct from the reading program and this instructional program is likely to exert its own influence on students writing performance. According to Raphael, Englert, and Kirschner (1989, p. 265),

> The social context in which students engage in writing has a powerful impact on the type of writing they produce (DeFord, 1986). Key elements of successful writing programs include writing for a real purpose and a real audience in a supportive environment that provides frequent, if not daily, opportunities for sustained writing (Calkins, 1983; Graves, 1983).

Writing instruction today, like reading instruction, has undergone serious reconsideration. Historically, writing instruction was little more than assigning students to produce a written product and then evaluating it, with an emphasis on grammar, usage, and mechanics (Hoskisson & Tompkins, 1987). The written work was generally done during a single class period and was unrelated to the reading program.

In the elementary grades the focus was most often on producing narrative stories and writing time was often removed from spelling and grammar instruction. At higher levels, requests for products plus grammar instruction was *the* vehicle by which students were expected to improve their writing abilities.

Although these practices still exist to one degree or another, there is a general recognition that students' writing improves by writing and by viewing and discussing good models of written work (Hillocks, 1986). In addition, there is widespread interest in the process of writing. As Raphael, Englert, and Kirschner (1989, p. 265) note, "Research on this subject describes writing as a nonlinear process. That is, it does not begin with simple tasks and work toward more complex tasks; instead it consists of a number of more holistic activities."

The instructional program should provide daily writing opportunities to plan, draft, edit, revise, and/or publish written work. In addition, students need scaffolding during writing instruction in much the same way they do in reading. This support may take the form of conferences, modeling, and/or mini lessons. In recent years teachers have sometimes focused on the process approach too rigidly and have sometimes abandoned the role of teacher too completely. Graves (1994, p. xvi) remarks on this need for balance:

> [W]e've learned much more about the essentials of teaching writing and how to use our time more effectively. Readers of my earlier book will find *A Fresh Look at Writing* more assertive: although listening to children is still the heart of the book, I think we now know better when to step in, when to teach, and when to expect more of our students. . . . We've learned that, right from the start, teachers need to teach more.

Successful programs appear to have several common elements (Calkins, 1991; Graves, 1983, 1994; Lipson et al., 2000; Raphael, Englert, & Kirschner, 1989). First, the program provides for frequent, sustained time for writing that is both predictable and productive. Second, students write for real purposes and real audiences. Third, the environment is supportive, and students' are both challenged and encouraged. The environment is also organized so that students have access to materials and support. Finally, successful writing programs teach children the conventions of writing and are focused on improving students' writing abilities, not on the written product and/or the stages of the writing process (Graves, 1994; Lipson et al., 2000).

What is very apparent is that writing performance, like reading, is influenced by the opportunities presented in the classroom and by the context for learning established at home and at school. Most significantly, children's understanding of what it means to write will be influenced by the types of writing that are promoted in the classroom and by the focus of the instruction (Lipson et al., 2000).

***Reading-Writing Workshop.***    The Reading-Writing Workshop represents a comprehensive approach to reading and writing instruction that has been formalized into an approach advocated by Nancie Atwell (1987) and subsequently elaborated by others (see, e.g., Calkins, 1994; Taberski, 2000). The tasks associated with this approach are designed to engage students in meaningful literacy activities and to develop strategic approaches to reading and writing. Two main ideas behind the Reading-Writing Workshop are that students own their own reading and writing and the teacher's role is that of expert reader-writer and guide rather than evaluator. Students are responsible for selecting their own reading material and their own topics for writing. Teachers read and write for their own purposes along with the students and share their experiences with students. The four key elements of the Reading-Writing Workshop as defined by Atwell (1987) are as follows:

1. Time to read and write
2. Forums for response

3. Conferences with the teacher
4. Mini-lessons.

Reading and writing workshops provide extended time for students to read and write. Atwell (1987) provides guidelines for student behaviors that help all members of the class respect the reading and writing that are taking place and to keep reading and writing central to the activities in the classroom.

Guidelines for Reading Workshop time include that students are responsible for having a book in their possession at the beginning of the session; must read a book for the entire period (no magazines or newspapers), preferably one that tells a story (no books of lists or facts for which readers can't sustain attention or build speed and accuracy); cannot do homework or read material for another class; and may not talk to or disturb others. Guidelines for Writing Workshop time include that students should write on one side of the paper only to make it easier to cut and paste, are not to erase but are to save a record of their thinking by simply drawing a line through text they wish to change, and are to speak in quiet voices only so that others who are thinking will not be interrupted.

Along with time to read and write, Reading-Writing Workshop also provides forums for response to reading and writing. Responses can take both verbal and written forms. Verbal forms include literature response groups, peer conferencing, group sharing of writing, and conferencing with the teacher. Written forms include dialogue journals between teacher and student and note writing between students about their reading.

The primary basis for evaluation in the Reading-Writing Workshop are conferences between student and teacher that occur throughout the school year. Reading and writing conferences provide students with chances to review their progress toward old goals and to set new ones. Atwell (1987) describes four type of writing workshop conferences: status of the class, topic, draft writing, and evaluative.

The final element of Reading-Writing Workshop is mini-lessons to assist students with their reading and writing. Mini-lessons can include a variety of activities, from reading of poetry and literature through short discussions of an author to the presentation of reading strategies. The teacher makes choices about which mini-lessons to present based on students' dialogue journals and informal and formal conferencing. The key to mini-lessons is that they be relevant to students' actual reading or writing and that the topic can be addressed in a relatively short period of time.

Evidence of the impact of Reading-Writing Workshop comes from several sources. Atwell (1987) presents numerous examples of students who started reading in Reading Workshop because that was the expectation and ended up reading because they enjoyed it. Others have found that reading workshop has a positive effect on the attitude and involvement with reading of learning-disabled students (Oberlin & Shugerman, 1989). McAuliffe (1993) reports that the peer feedback available in writing workshop helped second grade students change their writing so that more of their classmates could engage with it.

Several issues have also been raised regarding Reading-Writing Workshop classrooms. Ash (1990) argues that although student ownership of reading is important, there is still an important role for whole-class or group readings of selected texts. Others point out that fiction and other narrative texts are privileged at the expense of great nonfiction with which students need to become familiar. It has also been suggested that such classrooms may actually limit students' engagement with diverse texts, since teachers tend to select mainstream literature (McCarthey, 1996). Similarly, there is some evidence that students may feel pressure to conform to certain content or modes of expression, thereby suppressing their engagement (see Finders, 1997; Moje, Willes, & Fassio, in press).

*Discussion.*    In a volume devoted to discussion as a means of promoting reading comprehension, Alvermann, Dillon, and O'Brien (1987) write that discussion is a curricular task selected by teachers for a variety of purposes. Some teachers may perceive discussion as a forum for raising important issues in relation to reading assignments. Others may see discussion as an opportunity for identifying and clarifying students' misconceptions. Still others may view discussion as a way of checking on whether students' read assigned material. Alvermann et al. (1987) indicate that discussion is important both as a communication skill and as the foundation for developing higher-level reading skills. As a means of defining discussion, they propose three criteria (Alvermann et al., 1987, p. 7):

> Discussants should put forth multiple points of view and stand ready to change their minds about the matter under discussion; students should interact with one another as well as with the teacher; and the interaction should exceed the typical two or three word phrase units common to recitation lessons.

Similarly, Goldenberg (1993) describes discussion as an interesting, engaging conversation that deals with an idea or a concept and has meaning and relevance for students. The focus remains discernible throughout, and there is a high level of participation without domination by any one person, especially the teacher. Teachers and students are responsive to what others say, so each statement builds on, challenges, or extends a previous one.

According to Goldenberg (1993), teachers or discussion leaders question, prod, challenge, coax, or remain silent. They clarify and instruct when necessary but without wasting time or words. They make certain that the discussion proceeds at an appropriate pace, knowing when to push to draw out an idea and when to ease up to allow for more thought and reflection. In essence, they are skilled at "weaving individual participants' comments into a larger tapestry of meaning" (Goldenberg, 1993, p. 318).

On the basis of the experiences of practicing teachers, Goldenberg (1993) identifies the basic elements of discussion as instructional and conversational (see Figure 5.2). In one sense, discussions are instructional because they are designed to promote learning. Teaching through discussion requires a deliberate and self-controlled agenda. In another sense, discussion is conversational in that it appears to be natural, spontaneous, and free from the didactic practices associated with formal teaching.

There is strong evidence that this type of discussion pattern is a more productive instructional approach for English language learners (ELL). In a follow-up study, Goldenberg and Patthey-Chavez (1995) found that ELL students both talked more and said more significant things during instructional conversations than they did in the more didactic pattern in which a teacher asks a question, the student responds, and then the teacher evaluates the response before asking another question.

**FIGURE 5.2**
Instructional
Conversation
Elements

| Elements of the Instructional Conversation |
| --- |

**Instructional Elements**

1. *Thematic focus.*   The teacher selects a theme or idea to serve as a starting point for forcusing the discussion and has a general plan for how the theme will unfold, including how to "chunk" the text to permit optimal exploration of the theme.

2. *Activation and use of background and relevant schemata.*   The teacher either "hooks into" or provides students with pertinent background knowledge and relevant schemata necessary for understanding a text. Background knowledge and schemata are then woven into the discussion that follows.

3. *Direct teaching.*   When necessary, the teacher provides direct teaching of a skill or concept.

4. *Promotion of more complex language and expression.*   The teacher elicits more extended student contributions by using a variety of elicitation techniques— invitations to expand (e.g., "tell me more about that"), questions (e.g., "what do you mean"), restatements (e.g., "in other words—"), and pauses.

5. *Elicitation of bases for statements or positions.*   The teacher promotes students' use of text, pictures, and reasoning to support an argument or position. Without overwhelming students, the teacher probes for the bases of students' statements— e.g., "How do you know?" "What makes you think that?" "Show us where it says _____."

**Conversational Elements**

6. *Fewer known-answer questions.*   Much of the discussion centers on questions and answers for which there might be more than one correct answer.

7. *Responsivity to student contributions.*   While having an initial plan and maintaining the focus and coherence of the discussion, the teacher is also responsive to students' statements and the opportunities they provide.

8. *Connected discourse.*   The discussion is characterized by multiple, interactive, connected turns; succeeding utterances build upon and extend previous ones.

9. *A challenging, but nonthreatening, atmosphere.*   The teacher creates a "zone of proximal development," where a challenging atmosphere is balanced by a positive affective climate. The teacher is more collaborator than evaluator and creates an atmosphere that challenges students and allows them to negotiate and construct the meaning of the text.

10. *General participation, including self-selected turns.*   The teacher encourages general participation among students. The teacher does not hold exclusive right to determine who talks, and students are encouraged to volunteer or otherwise influence the selection of speaking turns.

Before leaving the topic of discussion, it is important to heed the experiences of a group of educators attempting to improve their discussion practices (Villaume, Worder, Williams, Hopkins, & Rosenblatt, 1994). These educators observed a great deal of inconsistency in students' movement beyond the role of answer giver in their early discussions. Some students assumed an active, responsible role naturally, while others appeared uncomfortable and uncertain and still others used the opportunity to be disruptive and silly. They determined that modeling was not sufficient, as only a few students had accepted their subtle invitation to engage in the behaviors modeled. They determined that instruction about discussion was needed and developed a series of strategies to teach their students about discussion.

The experience of these educators suggests that without significant effort on the part of the teacher, many discussions are not likely to achieve the lofty goals articulated previously. Discussions that are not well developed are likely to have a variety of unanticipated consequences for students, especially those who are experiencing difficulty with reading and writing.

## Assessment Practices

This entire book deals with assessment in one way or another. This section focuses specifically on assessment practices as a feature of instructional contexts that influence reading and writing performance. Within this context we need to be concerned with at least two dimensions of classroom assessment: assessments required for external accountability purposes and assessments selected and/or created by the teacher for evaluation and to inform instruction.

***Impact of Assessment on Teaching and Learning.***   Both tests and alternative assessments often have some accountability function, whether to audiences who are external to the classroom or to the teacher and/or students themselves. It is the accountability functions of tests and assessments that result in the greatest impact on teaching and learning. Regardless of the form or frequency of assessment, to the extent to which performances of students and classrooms are made visible and have consequences ranging from prestige and shame to merit increases and management constraints, the nature of assessments tends to shape teachers' practice and therefore student learning and performance. We agree with Resnick and Resnick (1992) when they conclude the following:

> *You get what you assess*—Teachers will teach to the assessment if the tests matter in their own or their students' lives; and

> *You do not get what you do not assess*—What is not integral to classroom assessment tends to disappear from classrooms in time.

Given these principles, the type and focus of assessment can make a big difference. For example, because most traditional standardized tests focus on isolated skills rather than on complex performances, they can and do drive instruction in the wrong direction. When tests are used as arbiters of many school decisions about placement, graduation, advancement, and so forth, they often exert great influence on what is taught, leading to a narrowed curriculum. Teachers are pressured to teach what is tested and to teach these things in the particular forms and formats used on the tests. This leads to an overemphasis on superficial content coverage and drill on discrete skills at the expense of indepth projects and other complex tasks. It also leads to classwork in which students spend their time on testlike tasks, to shallow learning, and to misperceptions of students' abilities.

**Tests and Testing.**   Resnick and Resnick (1992) point out that tests are the heritage of earlier psychological theories that promoted a concept of learning as the development of routinized skill. Most standardized tests were developed at this same time and reflect the same theories. Thus, for example, two key assumptions of standardized tests are *decomposability* and *decontextualization.* Because they influence our ideas about teaching as well as testing, these concepts are discussed next.

*Decomposability.*   One part of earlier learning theories was that reading and writing are *decomposable,* that is, they can be separated into discrete components and that the parts would equal the whole. According to Resnick and Resnick (1992), built into the decomposability assumption is a metaphor that likens thought to a simple machine. A simple machine can be built by constructing each of the parts separately. When the parts are put together, if the design is good, the machine will run. It supports a notion of teaching and testing separate component skills, with the expectation that their composition into a complex performance will occur at some later time. This assumption has been seriously challenged by recent research that recognizes that complicated skills and competencies owe their complexity not just to the number of components they engage, but also to interactions among the components and strategies for calling upon them.

Complex competencies such as reading and writing cannot be defined just by listing all of their components. Efforts to assess reading and writing by identifying separate components of those abilities and testing them independently may interfere with effectively teaching such abilities. Assessing separate components encourages instructional activities in which isolated components are practiced. Because the components do not add up to reading and writing, students who practice only the components are unlikely to learn to do real reading and writing.

*Decontextualization.*   Closely linked to the decomposability assumption, decontextualization asserts that each component of a complex skill is fixed and that it will take the same form no matter where it is used. This assumption suggests that if students know how to get a main idea, for example, they know how to do so under all conditions of text type, prior knowledge, and so forth. However, recent theory and research suggest that we can no longer teach a skill component in one setting and expect it to be applied automatically in another. We cannot validly assess a competence in a context that is very different from the context in which it is practiced or used.

There is widespread agreement among educators, researchers, and policymakers that most standardized tests currently used in American schools do not tap many of the skills and abilities that students need to develop to be successful in later life and schooling (Darling-Hammond, Ancess, & Falk, 1995). Consistent with the decomposability and decontextualization assumptions, the most frequent criticism of these tests is that they do not evaluate higher-order skills and students' abilities to perform real-world tasks.

Although this discussion has focused primarily on standardized tests, it is worth noting that Chittenden (1991) defines tests as any situation in which the student is asked a question to which the questioner or examiner knows the answer. He also notes that although a lot of this type of interrogation goes on in our schools, whether under the guise of classroom discussion or standardized tests, it is not characteristic of normal, everyday conversations and interactions. Tests, then, can be anything from standardized measures to basal tests to teacher-made examination and questioning.

*Alternative Assessments.*    In response to the concerns about standardized tests, many educators and researchers are developing alternative assessment practices that look directly at students' work as a means of evaluating student performance. These alternative assessments are referred to by a variety of labels, including authentic and performance assessments, and take a variety of forms including portfolios, observation, and performance tasks.

According to Wiggins (1989) alternative assessments have four common characteristics. First, they are designed to be truly representative of performance in the field. For example, students actually do writing—for real audiences—rather than taking spelling tests or answering questions about writing. The tasks are contextualized, complex intellectual challenges involving the student's own research or use of knowledge. In addition, they allow student learning styles, aptitudes, and interests to serve as a source for developing competence and for the identification of strengths that may have been hidden previously.

Second, alternative assessments seek to evaluate "essentials" of performance against well-articulated criteria. These are openly expressed to students and others in the learning community, rather than kept "secure" in the tradition of tests. Learning and performance are both supported when teachers and students know ahead of time what an assessment will evaluate. Performance-based criteria guide teaching, learning, and evaluation in ways that place teachers in the role of coach and students in the role of performers.

Third, alternative assessments help students to develop the capacity to evaluate their own work against public standards. These assessments promote students' ability to revise, modify, and redirect their energies, taking initiative to assess their own progress.

Finally, alternative assessments involve students in presenting their work publicly. This deepens their learning by requiring that they reflect on what they know and frame it in a way that others can also understand; it ensures that their apparent mastery of a concept or topic is genuine.

According to Darling-Hammond et al. (1995), because most traditional tests provide only a limited measure of a narrow aspect of learning or development, they are poor predictors of how students will perform in other settings. This promotes a view of students as having deficits that need to be corrected rather than as having individual differences, approaches to learning, and strengths that can be supported and developed. Neither do traditional tests reflect or capture the diversity of students' backgrounds and experiences (Figueroa & Garcia, 1994). They often contain assumptions and facts that are grounded in the context of the dominant culture and fail to include relevant forms of knowledge from other cultures. This places students from nondominant cultures at a disadvantage in demonstrating what they know and can do (Garcia & Pearson, 1991).

In contrast, alternative assessments can, although may not if improperly designed, affect teaching and learning in more positive ways. Because students are involved in developing, exhibiting, and evaluating their own work, alternative assessments help them develop a sense of responsibility and ownership of their work and encourage them to analyze and reflect on their progress regularly. Alternative assessments can encourage an intelligent, rich curriculum, rather than the narrowed one fostered by teaching and coaching for tests.

So we need to be aware of what types of assessments are being used and for what purposes to determine their potential impact on reading and writing performance. For example, if the only form of assessment is testing focused on isolated skills, then students are likely to be attending to skill mastery at the expense of integrated skill performances. In contrast, if the only form of assessment is student self-reflection, then students are likely to become more responsible for their own learning but may miss some important skills or not progress as rapidly as needed to perform at desirable levels.

# Strategies and Tools for Assessing the Instructional Environment

In this chapter we are suggesting that it is important to observe the context for learning, not just the student in that context. Until recently, assessments of the instructional environment have been rare. Fortunately, there are now a sparse but growing number of strategies and tools for assessing instructional settings, methods, and materials.

Although some information may be collected by interviewing the teacher and/or the student and by examining materials and assignments (see also Chapter 6), reliable conclusions require some classroom observation. Because some teachers may be fearful about being observed (Stalling, Needels, & Sparks, 1987), it should be made quite clear that the purpose of the observation is not to pass judgment. Rather it is to try to determine what, if any, contextual factors might be altered to improve the match between what the student needs and what the classroom instruction provides.

## Assessing Instructional Setting

In this section we describe some techniques for examining and describing the general characteristics of instructional settings to determine how they may be contributing to a particular student's struggles or successes.

***The Literate Environment and Teacher Beliefs.*** As was suggested previously, the literate environment and teacher beliefs are important aspects of the instructional setting. The literate environment comprises the physical, social-emotional, and intellectual environments within a classroom, which often reflect teacher beliefs (Anders & Evans, 1994; Hoffman et al., 1998). We believe it is important to evaluate those aspects of the literate environment that directly influence the acquisition of reading and writing skills. To begin evaluating the literate environment, an overall observation can be helpful. The summary sheet in Figure 5.3 draws from a variety of sources and is designed to focus observation on the aspects of the instructional environment that are likely to influence reading and writing performance (Curry, 1993; Loughlin & Martin, 1987). This checklist provides an initial look

**FIGURE 5.3**
Checklist for
Evaluating the
Literate
Environment

| Classroom Resources | Comments |
|---|---|
| Many different kinds of books and other print materials | |
| Many different types of writing materials and tools | |
| Students' work, messages, labels, and stories are displayed | |
| Messages and/or plans for the current day | |
| Print materials displayed near objects, pictures, and other center displays | |
| Books or print displays about community, culture, or language | |
| Print has functional use—sign-ups, charts, etc. | |
| **Physical Arrangement** | **Comments** |
| Library—well stocked, accessible, and comfortable | |
| Writing/publishing center—well stocked and accessible | |
| Listening/viewing areas | |
| Group meeting places | |
| Conference areas | |
| Places for sharing, performing, etc. | |
| **Instructional Opportunities** | **Comments** |
| Daily opportunities for sustained reading and sustained writing | |
| Students read and write for a variety of purposes | |
| Students write for real audiences and for a variety of authentic purposes | |
| Students have choices about what to read or write | |
| Students confer with teacher and other students about reading/writing | |
| Support (scaffold) students during reading and writing | |
| Teach the fundamentals of writing and reading (conduct mini-lessons, teach conventions, provide spelling instruction) | |

at various aspects of the instructional setting that can be examined more closely by using other assessment tools described in this and the next chapter.

The literate environment can communicate to students both what is valued and what is acceptable. Inaccessible reading and/or writing centers and uninviting activities and spaces affect students' understanding of the value and purposes for reading and writing. They also influence student's voluntary reading and writing. Similarly, rigid seating arrangements do little to advance the cooperative or verbal interaction patterns that are necessary for many students' literacy development.

From time to time we all need to examine our beliefs and practices carefully in light of new information and new innovations. Several questionnaires and interviews have been developed to help identify teachers' beliefs and theories about reading and writing. Most of these are quite long and time consuming. Examinations of the literate environment often reveal what teachers believe about teaching, learning, and literacy. After examining the environment it would be useful to ask yourself (or ask the student's teacher) to talk about questions such as these:

*What does the teacher (or, do I) believe:*

- Is the purpose of reading and reading instruction? of writing and writing instruction?
- Is necessary for students to know and be able to do before they will become skilled readers and/or writers?
- Are appropriate activities to promote reading and writing competence?
- Are the most important priorities in literacy instruction?

Teachers are occasionally surprised to find that although they believe that something is important, they do not provide for it in their own program. For example, most teachers believe that prior knowledge influences reading and that building background is important, but many teachers actually do not include these features in their instruction. Recognizing mismatches between beliefs and practice helps teachers to more clearly identify what steps to take to help a student who is struggling to become literate.

A sound knowledge base and a commitment to literacy are extremely important, but teachers must also know how to maintain a functional learning environment for fairly large groups of children. The teacher's ability to organize the classroom and manage the daily routine influences the amount of time available for teaching and learning. Studies of successful schools suggest that effective teachers manage a variety of complex activity in their classrooms (Mosenthal et al., 2001b). Some key focus questions for assessing the management factors in classrooms are as follows:

- Do the routines help teachers address individual differences among students in the classroom? For example, are there multiple activities going on simultaneously?
- Are the practices designed to maximize students' engagement with authentic reading and writing tasks? For example, when children are not working with the teacher, are they engaged in sustained reading or writing?
- Do routines increase instructional time? For example, are there clearly understood classroom rules and routines and well-established procedures for seeking help and getting supplies?

- Are routine scheduling concerns handled smoothly and unobtrusively (e.g., movement by some students to special services or activities)?
- Are transitions between activities handled smoothly and quickly?

Any continuing factors or conditions that make it difficult to deliver instruction smoothly should also be identified. We are aware that there are a variety of constraints imposed on teachers that can influence the organization of their classrooms and their ability to make and execute good decisions. These should be identified and considered as the interactive case evaluation proceeds.

***Classroom Organization, Interaction, and Grouping.***    Other important aspects of the instructional setting are classroom organization, interaction, and grouping patterns. We are not only interested in the likely impact of these factors on reading and writing performance, but we also hope to gain insight into how they may influence a particular student's performance. According to Cambourne and Turbill (1994), teachers organize their reading and writing instruction in "episodes" consisting of various activities and routines such as sustained silent reading, teacher read-alouds, and reading/writing workshop. Within and across the instructional events or episodes that characterize a particular classroom or setting, we can examine both grouping and interaction patterns as well as the range of learning opportunities presented to individual students.

*Grouping.*    As we discussed previously, grouping practices can exert a strong influence on student achievement and motivation. Consequently, effective assessment must include a consideration of school and classroom grouping practices. Teachers often use a variety of organizational patterns in their classrooms. It will be particularly important to identify the variety of patterns and their associated purposes.

Both observation and interviews may be necessary to get a clear picture of the complex ways in which students are organized. For example, it is important to determine what information teachers use to make their placement decisions. Although most teachers make careful and intentional grouping decisions using some systematic procedure, others generate groupings on the basis of untested assumptions (Good & Brophy, 1987). An example of an untested assumption might be something like "Her brother had trouble in reading and writing, so she will too." Placement decisions that are based on this type of reasoning are obviously problematic, especially because teacher judgment is often used to make other educational decisions as well.

The assessment of grouping practices should also examine the extent to which membership in a group for one purpose (e.g., a reading or writing group) defines *access* to other tasks, activities, and levels of achievement. This is a problem especially in middle and junior high schools, where scheduling is complicated and the need to receive specialized instruction in reading and writing, for example, may dictate the classes and sections for all other subjects. To gather this information, it may be necessary to observe or inquire about the grouping arrangements and grouping characteristics for subjects other than language arts.

As we have already seen, one of the reasons this information about grouping is so important is that it influences the patterns of interaction that occur among peers and between teachers and students. The quantity and quality of these interactions may profoundly affect both achievement and motivation.

*Interactions.* It is important to recognize how difficult it may be to describe the features of classroom interaction, much less assess its impact. However, it may be helpful to apply the following set of focus questions to characterize the general pattern of interaction in a classroom:

- What are the notable characteristics of the linguistic community of the students you are assessing?
- Who typically initiates language exchanges, decides on the form and content of written work, or directs discussions?
- How often do oral and written interactions serve the purpose of eliciting set or known responses, in contrast to open discussion or divergent responses?

The answers to these global questions can give a sense of the amount and type of verbal interaction that occurs in the classroom and the demands and opportunities likely to be present for individual students. In particular, this general observation can reveal unusual linguistic, cultural, or classroom characteristics.

Occasionally, a much closer examination is desirable or necessary to gather in-depth information about the interactions between the teacher and a particular child or group of children. In this case careful and systematic classroom observation will be necessary. A procedure described by Page and Pinnell (1979) is useful in both classrooms and clinics. This procedure involves tape-recording a conversation with the student and then using a checklist to evaluate the types of exchanges that occur. The oral interactions are evaluated to see which conversational partner:

- Asks and/or answers questions,
- Gives personal information about self,
- Gives information about something other than self,
- Refers to past events,
- Make predictions,
- Draws conclusions,
- Makes evaluative statements,
- Gives orders,
- Makes requests.

The authors report that teachers are often chagrined at the analyses that result, since the patterns are not always what they intended: "Teachers only asked questions and students only gave answers. As a result, the language of both was limited" (Page and Pinnell, 1979, p. 62). When teachers use these initial results to shape subsequent interactions, there is often a dramatic increase in verbal *interaction* versus question–response patterns.

*Classroom Organization.* Using the episodes of instruction as a unit of analysis can provide an overview of reading and writing instruction within a particular classroom or setting.

Observational data can be gathered on the episodes of instruction that make up a typical class period, day and/or week in a particular setting along with information about the types of interactions and grouping they entail and the amount of time devoted to each (Good & Brophy, 2000). Completing a summary analysis such as the one provided in Figure 5.4 will quickly reveal what types of instructional activities are used regularly and the concomitant interaction and grouping patterns.

This type of observational system can provide useful information, especially if distinctions are made in terms of the amounts of actual reading and writing that are done. For example, one study of this type reported that students in the remedial classes observed spent only 10 to 20 percent of their time actually reading and writing connected text, even when a single paragraph is considered connected text (Allington et al., 1986). After completing a summary analysis such as the one provided in Figure 5.4, examine the information to determine how much time and/or what proportion of time the students spend:

- Reading connected text,
- Writing connected text,
- Listening to connected text,
- Interacting and working with other students, with or without the teacher, in whole- or small-group activities,
- Interacting and working individually with the teacher,
- Working individually/independently.

Ultimately, it is the relationship between student performance and classroom activities that is important to ascertain. For example, some teachers actually evaluate students' reading competence not according to their ability to read and write connected text but according to their ability to complete workbooks or other worksheets. On the other hand, there are classrooms in which students are regularly engaged in fruitful reading and writing activity for extended periods of time. To understand the experience of a particular student requires

**FIGURE 5.4**
Example of
Evaluating the
Instructional Setting

| Episode Setting | Time Frequency | Grouping | Interactive Patterns |
|---|---|---|---|
| Sustained Silent Reading (SSR) | 15 min per day | Individual | None |

a clear description of the kinds of activities and tasks that are used and an examination of the proportion of time that is spent on different types of activities and tasks.

## Assessing Instructional Practice

In the following sections we describe several ways to assess instructional goals, methods, and assessment practices.

***Instructional Goals and Methods.*** Most districts and/or schools now have published content standards and/or benchmarks for English language arts. These standards may exist for each grade level, or they may stipulate grade-level clusters such as K–2 or early elementary. Standards and benchmarks may also be quite general, in which case they really do not constitute a curriculum. Rather, schools or classroom teachers are expected to translate the standards into grade-level curricula. It is important to determine the role of standards in the schools and classrooms in which the students you are working with reside. This will help you know what is guiding the focus of instruction in the instructional environment.

It is also important to determine what role the instructional materials play in determining the focus of instruction. Many schools and classroom teachers still rely heavily on commercially prepared materials to specify their instructional program. If this is the case in the setting you are evaluating, it may be necessary to infer an instructional focus from the content of materials being used (see Chapter 6). The following focus questions can be used to examine general aspects of instructional goals and methods.

- Is the general approach to reading and writing basal-based? Literature-based? Based on subskills mastery learning curriculum? Based on some combination of these?
- Does the teacher attempt to meet individual needs by grouping? Altering content? Changing the tasks? Providing different levels of support? Or does the teacher not appear to differentiate instruction in any way?
- Does the teacher define language arts instruction in terms of a specific published program? Does the teacher and/or school draw from a variety of sources and define the reading and writing curriculum in terms of clearly established outcomes?
- What is the relationship between the goals and methods in this classroom and those of other teachers in the building?

Asking yourself or the teacher these questions results in useful descriptions of the instructional goals and methods employed by the teacher. In some schools these components of instructional goals and methods may be dictated by the administration of the school. In others these are informally decreed between and among teachers so that deviation from these practices may result in ostracism from the mainstream of professional contact. However, in most schools teachers have a great deal of discretion about how they deliver instruction, especially if they have demonstrated that they are reasonable, responsible professionals.

Increasingly, schools are using literacy coaches to help improve instruction, especially for the most struggling readers. Lyons and Pinnell (2001) have written a very useful book for educators who are involved in evaluating and supporting teachers. They suggest that coaches reflect before they make a classroom visit, asking questions such as these (Lyons & Pinnell, 2001, p. 249):

- What are your perceptions of the teacher's strengths?
- What are the differences between the way the teacher talks and what you observe in the classroom?
- What does the teacher say about children? To what degree does he or she describe children's behavior as evidence of learning?

Subsequently, they suggest using a structured observation device to look closely at teachers' instruction (see Figure 5.5). The tool they use is designed for observing student–teacher interactions and instruction within a guided reading format, but is well suited to assessing any text-based reading experience.

Other general aspects of instructional method that are worthy of attention include the use of scaffolding, dialogue, and motivational activities to promote reading and writing performance.

*Scaffolding and Dialogue.*    It is difficult to evaluate the use of scaffolding and the quantity and quality of dialogue within a particular setting without close observation in the classroom. Although no good tools are available to evaluate these critical features, there are some specific teaching behaviors we can look for as we observe in the classroom. For example,

- Does the teacher encourage students' acquisition of new or difficult material?
- Does the teacher support learning by modeling and/or providing guidance?
- Does the teacher engage in dialogue with students (as opposed to lecturing)?
- Does the teacher support students' contributions to dialogue?
- Does dialogue have focus and direction?
- Does the teacher use student ideas and link those ideas to new information?
- Does the teacher use feedback constructively to help students improve their responses?

Few teachers have been well trained in these methods, but some have developed these skills to a high degree. The presence or absence of these methods will most likely influence the achievement or involvement of some less-skilled students.

*Motivational Activities.*    As we have seen, instructional techniques and student motivation for learning are strongly related. Student interviews can be exceptionally useful in assessing the relationship between instruction and motivation. Some of the interviews we have already suggested may provide information about the quality and appropriateness of the instructional program (see Chapters 4 and 10), although these should clearly be designed or adapted to gather information about specific aspects of the setting or instruction that may be influencing the student.

For example, interviews can be structured to collect information about the motivational impact of units of instruction. Rogers and Stevenson (1988) asked students questions such as the following:

- What went well for you?
- What did you enjoy most?
- Should the study of _____ be a part of everyone's education?

**FIGURE 5.5**
Observation Summary Form

## Observation of Guided Reading

**Observer:** ____________ **Teacher:** ____________ **Date:** ____________

**Grade:** ____________ **Number of Children in Group:** ____________

| **Preparation** | **Independent Activities** |
|---|---|
| Text selected:<br>Level:<br>Notes: | Number: Engagement[1]: 1 2 3 4<br>Types represented: |

| **Introduction of Text** | **Engagement: 1 2 3 4** | **Start: End:** |
|---|---|---|
| *Teacher's Language* | *Children's Language* | *Other Observations* |
| | | |
| **Reading the Text** | **Engagement: 1 2 3 4** | **Start: End:** |
| *Teacher's Language* | *Children's Language* | *Other Observations* |
| | | |
| **After Reading the Text** | **Engagement: 1 2 3 4** | **Start: End:** |
| *Teacher's Language* | *Children's Language* | *Other Observations* |
| | | |
| *Word Work:* | | |
| *Extension/Assignment:* | | |

[1]RUBRIC FOR ENGAGEMENT: 1 = Only a few children are on task and attending to instruction. There are many distractions, including noise and movement. Instruction is severely undermined. 2 = About half of the children are on task and attending to the instruction, but there are many distractions, including noise and movement. Instruction is undermined. 3 = Most of the children are on task and attending to the instruction. There are occasional distractions and some children are moving about. Instruction, in general, is being provided most of the time. 4 = Almost all children are on task and attending to the instruction. Instruction is being provided most of the time. There are only a few distractions.

*Source:* Reprinted by permission from *Systems for Change in Literacy Education* by Carol A. Lyons and Gay Su Pinnell. Copyright © 2001 by Carol A. Lyons and Gay Su Pinnell. Published by Heinemann, a division of Reed Elsevier Inc., Portsmouth, NH. Material may not be reproduced for any purpose without the written permission of the publisher.

Interestingly, the last of these questions often provoked the most honest assessment of interest *and* learning. Perhaps asking a question that is more distant and less personal encourages richer thinking.

The interview information will, of course, be supplemented with data generated through observation. The instructional context should be examined for evidence of the motivational practices we described earlier (see Figure 5.6). Although these strategies cannot be quantified easily, this is not necessary. A strongly negative profile of instructional factors linked to motivation can provide important information about the achievement and progress of specific students.

***Assessment Practices.***   According to Chittenden (1991), assessment is an attitude before it is a method. Through his work in elementary classrooms, he observed four quite different attitudes or stances teachers adopt with respect to monitoring and evaluating students' learning, which he refers to as *keeping track, checking up, finding out,* and *summing up.* He notes that although these views are largely complementary, they sometimes conflict.

A *keeping track* stance is characterized by attention to what activities students have been involved in, such as what books a particular student has read or which students have not yet completed certain activities. Teachers devise many ways to make records to meet their keeping track needs. For example, they create informal checklists and inventories and gather material from student's journal entries. Over the year a fairly substantial record of activities and accomplishments is often compiled in the name of keeping track.

A *checking-up* stance is often approached both formally and informally. Informal checking up involves observing and asking student's questions. Formal checking up is focused on testing, defined as any situation in which the student is asked a question to which the questioner or examiner knows the answer. Chittenden (1991) notes that although a lot of this type of interrogation goes on in our schools, whether under the guise of classroom discussion or standardized tests, it is not characteristic of normal everyday conversations and interactions.

The *finding out* stance is focused on inquiry or figuring out what is going on. The teacher is attending to what a particular student response meant or what a student understood from a particular story. Teachers may be asking questions but clearly not with the intent of checking up. Chittenden (1991) believes that the finding out stance is most critical to successful teaching and learning.

Finally, completing the picture is the *summing up* stance. This stance directly addresses the needs of accountability through reporting to parents, districts, and students. Attention is focused on organizing information in ways that are meaningful outside the classroom.

The types of assessments used and the manner in which they are used are likely to vary according to these stances. In contexts in which all four stances are present, we would expect to see a full range of assessment instruments, including both tests and alternative assessments. These various assessments may complement each other in the sense that they reflect a consistent view of literacy learning. Alternatively, they may be in conflict in that some reflect a more traditional, isolated skills approach to literacy learning and others reflect a more interactive, constructivist view of literacy learning. This situation can be confusing to students and lead to difficulties and/or mixed impressions related to reading and writing performance.

**FIGURE 5.6**
Assessment of
Motivational
Strategies

| Motivational Analysis of Tasks and Activities |
|---|

Use: Whenever particular classroom tasks or activities are observed
Purpose: To identify the motivational elements built into the task or activity

Check each of the motivational elements that was included in the observed task or activity.

**A. Extrinsic motivational strategies**

_____ 1. Offers rewards as incentives for good performance
_____ 2. Calls attention to the instrumental value of the knowledge or skills developed in the activity (applications to present or future life outside of school)
_____ 3. Structures individual or group competition for prizes or recognition

**B. Intrinsic motivational features of the task or activity**

_____ 1. Opportunities for active response (beyond just watching and listening)
_____ 2. Opportunities to answer divergent questions or work on higher level objectives
_____ 3. Immediate feedback to students' responses (built into the task itself, rather than provided by the teacher as in C.8 below)
_____ 4. Gamelike features (the task is a game or contains gamelike features that make it more like a recreational activity than a typical academic activity)
_____ 5. Task completion involves creating a finished product for display or use
_____ 6. The task involves fantasy or simulation elements that engage students' emotions or allow them to experience events vicariously
_____ 7. The task provides opportunities for students to interact with their peers

**C. Teacher's attempts to stimulate students' motivation to learn**

_____ 1. Projects intensity (communicating that the material is important and deserves close attention)
_____ 2. Induces task interest or appreciation
_____ 3. Induces curiosity or suspense
_____ 4. Makes abstract content more personal, concrete, or familiar
_____ 5. Induces dissonance or cognitive conflict
_____ 6. Induces students to generate their own motivation to learn
_____ 7. States learning objectives or provides advance organizers
_____ 8. Provides opportunities for students to respond and get feedback (asks questions during group lessons, circulates to monitor performance during seatwork)
_____ 9. Models task-related thinking and problem solving ("thinks out loud" when working through examples)
_____ 10. Includes instruction or modeling designed to increase students' metacognitive awareness of their learning efforts in response to the task (includes information about mental preparation for learning, about the organization or structure built into the content, about how students can impose their own organizational structures on the content to help them remember it, or about how to monitor one's own comprehension and respond to confusion or mistakes)

Notes:

*Source:* From *Looking in Classrooms*, 4th ed. by Thomas L. Good and Jere E. Brophy. Copyright © 1987. Reprinted by permission of Allyn & Bacon.

Still other contexts may evidence heavy reliance on one or two stances. This situation is likely to direct curriculum and instruction in specific ways that may or may not support student literacy learning. For example, too much emphasis on checking up and/or summing up may lead to instructional practices that do not promote independence, motivation, and the problem-solving skills necessary for successful reading and writing performance. Heavy dependence on these stances can also lead to misperceptions of students' abilities. Determining the extent to which these stances are present or absent within a particular instructional context and their potential impact on a student's reading and writing performance provides valuable information in the evaluation of the instructional context.

***The Instructional Environment.***    The publication of *TIES: The Instructional Environment Scale* by Ysseldyke and Christenson (1987) was the first serious effort at systematically assessing the impact of instruction on student performance. Ysseldyke and Christenson developed TIES because they believe, as we do, that student performance in school is a function of an interaction between the student and the instructional environment. Their concern lies with the "goodness of fit" or match between the students and the instructional contexts they encounter each day. In 1993, Ysseldyke and Christenson extended the concept of instructional environment to include home contexts in TIES-II. Most recently, these authors have developed the Functional Assessment of Academic Behavior (FAAB) (Ysseldyke & Christenson, 2002), which maintains a focus on identifying and coordinating instructional, home, and home-school supports for the student of interest with the express purpose of designing feasible interventions to enhance academic success. The FAAB is a system designed to identify the presence or absence of environmental conditions that enhance a student's academic progress in school.

The authors describe four major purposes for the FAAB system: (a) gather information relevant to an individual student; (b) assess the instructional needs for the student, (c) assess supportive learning conditions, and (d) assist educators in designing instructional interventions. According to the authors, "FAAB is not to be used to evaluate or say what is wrong with the student, the classroom task, the teacher's instructional strategy, home support for learning, or the family-school relationship. It is designed to identify ways to change learning environments so that the student is responding to instruction more positively and to enhance a student's academic competence" (Ysseldyke & Christenson, 2002, p. 2).

FAAB consists of twenty-three "support for learning" components in three contexts: twelve classroom instruction components, five home components, and six home-school relationship components. These components focus on alterable variables associated with positive academic performance. The twelve instructional components are grouped into the four areas of planning, managing, delivering, and evaluating instruction; they are defined in Figure 5.7.

The authors assume that careful, systematic gathering of data about the student's learning context will allow for accurate or relevant judgment about the student's highest priority needs. In addition, they encourage individuals using this assessment system to maintain a focus on the individual student by addressing three questions: What does the student need to be successful on the task? What needs to be manipulated to produce a better student response? and What resources do teachers and parents desire to assist the student?

**FIGURE 5.7**  FAAB Instructional Support Components

---

*Instructional Planning:* Decisions are made about what to teach and how to teach the student. Realistic expectations are communicated to the student.

➤ *Instructional Match:* The student's needs are assessed accurately, and instruction is matched appropriately to the results of the instructional diagnosis.

➤ *Instructional Expectations:* There are realistic, yet high, expectations for both the amount and accuracy of work to be completed by the student, and these are communicated clearly to the student.

*Instructional Managing:* Effective instruction requires managing the complex mix of instructional tasks and student behaviors that are part of every classroom interaction. This means making decisions that control and support the orderly flow of instruction. To do this, teachers make decisions about classroom rules and procedures, as well as how to handle disruptions, how to organize classroom time and space to be most productive, and how to keep classrooms warm, positive, and accepting places for the student with different learning preferences and performances.

➤ *Classroom Environment:* The classroom management techniques used are effective for the student; there is a positive, supportive classroom atmosphere; and, time is used productively.

*Instructional Delivering:* Decisions are made about how to present information, as well as how to monitor and adjust presentations to accommodate individual differences and enhance the learning of the student.

➤ *Instructional Presentation:* Instruction is presented in a clear and effective manner; the directions contain sufficient information for the student to understand the kinds of behaviors or skills that are to be demonstrated; and, the student's understanding is checked.

➤ *Cognitive Emphasis:* Thinking skills and learning strategies for completing assignments are communicated explicitly to the student.

➤ *Motivational Strategies.* Effective strategies for heightening student interest and effort are used with the student.

➤ *Relevant Practice:* The student is given adequate opportunity to practice with appropriate materials and a high success rate. Classroom tasks are clearly important to achieving instructional goals.

➤ *Informed Feedback:* The student receives relatively immediate and specific information on his/her performance or behavior; when the student makes mistakes, correction is provided.

*Instructional Evaluating:* Effective instruction requires evaluating. Some evaluation activities occur during the process of instruction (i.e., when teachers gather data during instruction and use those data to make instructional decisions). Other evaluation activities occur at the end of instruction (e.g., when the teacher administers a test to determine whether a student has met instructional goals).

➤ *Academic Engaged Time:* The student is actively engaged in responding to academic content; the teacher monitors the extent to which the student is actively engaged and redirects the student when the student is unengaged.

➤ *Adaptive Instruction:* The curriculum is modified within reason to accommodate the student's unique and specific instructional needs.

➤ *Progress Evaluation:* There is direct, frequent measurement of the student's progress toward completion of instructional objectives; data on the student's performance and progress are used to plan future instruction.

➤ *Student Understanding:* The student demonstrates an accurate understanding of what is to be done and how it is to be done in the classroom.

---

*Source:* Reprinted with permission from Sopris West Educational Services. From Functional Assessment of Academic Behavior by James

The recommended steps for carrying out the portion of the FAAB that focuses on the assessment of the instructional environment are: (a) Identify and clarify the concern; (b) understand the student's instructional needs from the perspective of the teacher and the parents; and (c) collect data on the student's instructional environment. The FAAB system includes materials to assist in this process such as the *Instructional Needs Checklist,* which is designed to get information about the teacher's perspective of the student's instructional needs. The *Instructional Needs Checklist* asks for information in the following seven areas:

1. Referral concern
2. Instructional needs
3. Student responses to tasks
4. Instructional tasks and materials
5. Instructional modifications
6. If only two things could be done for this student, what would they be?
7. Other observations/relevant information

Areas two through five provide checklists with directions to the teacher to identify any aspects in which a change may be needed to provide the student with an optimal learning environment.

The FAAB also provides *Instructional Environment* checklists in both summary and annotated forms. These materials are designed to help identify the presence or absence of the components of the classroom, home, and home-school contexts that are likely to promote academic progress. The information needed to complete these checklists is intended to come from several sources, including classroom observation as well as student and parent interviews; additional materials are provided for data collection. The annotated *Instructional Environment Checklist* elaborates on the aspects of each of the twenty-three components that might be considered in determining if the component is one that might need some alteration. For example, the following items are listed under the Cognitive Emphasis component within the classroom/instructional context section of the inventory.

- The student understands the purpose of the lesson.
- The learning strategies that are used (e.g., memorizing, reasoning, concluding, and evaluating) are effective for the student.
- The student can explain the process used to solve problems or complete work.
- The student knows why and how his/her responses are correct/incorrect.

The FAAB and instruments like it are welcome additions to the repertoire of tools available for assessment, because they broaden the database upon which decisions about students are made. These types of instruments are also likely to play an educative role for teachers, consultants, and parents in improving the instructional environment for all students.

## Assessing Specific Activities and Episodes of Instruction

In addition to the assessment of general instructional goals, methods, and assessment practices, it is important to evaluate individual episodes of instruction to understand the performance of particular students within and across specific instructional events. The evaluation of individual instructional episodes involves an examination of specific instructional objectives, the methods of instruction and/or activities used, and the methods and/or opportunities for assessing student performance.

The examination of instructional objectives involves identifying the content, process, and attitude objectives as articulated by either the teacher or the materials or as inferred by the observer. The evaluation of an instructional episode also involves an examination of what both the teacher and students do in the context of each instructional event, along with an assessment of the methods used for evaluating student performance or, alternatively, the opportunities that exist for assessing student performance. Figure 5.8 presents a simple chart for use in evaluating the objectives, instruction/activities, and methods/opportunities for assessment that characterize individual instructional episodes or events.

In evaluating the objectives for a particular instructional episode, it is important to remember that the overarching goal of reading and writing instruction should be the development of knowledgeable, strategic, and motivated readers and writers. To do this, teachers must provide instruction aimed at specific content, process, and attitudinal instructional objectives. Although there may be times when instruction needs to be focused heavily on just one of these three areas, it is always a good idea to consider the role that each of these areas plays in every instructional episode or event. In reflecting on the information gathered for the chart in Figure 5.7, it may be helpful to ask the following questions:

1. Do the objectives clearly identify the *content* to be addressed through this reading/writing episode, the reading and writing *process* skills to be learned or practiced in this episode, and how the instructional episode is intended to help develop positive *attitudes* toward reading and writing?
2. Does the episode provide opportunities to read and/or write about important ideas and/or persistent issues found in the content of the curriculum?
3. Does the episode involve attention to the nature of the genre and craft of language used in the reading/writing activities?

**FIGURE 5.8**
Evaluating
Instructional
Episodes

| Objectives | Methods/Activities | Methods/Opportunities for Assessment |
|---|---|---|
| Content | | |
| Process | | |
| Attitude | | |

4. Does the episode provide opportunities to learn important information about the reading and writing processes?
5. Does the episode encourage students to recognize patterns in their reading and writing so that they can apply these in other contexts?
6. Does the episode encourage students to immerse themselves in reading, writing, and/or responding?
7. Does the event encourage students to share what they have read and/or written?
8. Is the episode authentic and relevant to students' needs and interests?

In thinking about how to assess the instructional methods and activities described on the chart, it may be helpful to consider the set of broad-based standards developed by Newmann and Wehlage for defining "authentic" instruction that engages "students in using their minds well" (1993, p. 8). The five standards developed by Newmann and Wehlage for evaluating the quality of instruction focus on higher-order thinking, depth of knowledge, connectedness to the world beyond the classroom, substantive conversation, and social support for student achievement. To evaluate these dimensions of instruction, Newmann and his colleagues (1996) developed a rating scale in which each standard is rated from 1 to 5 along a continuum from less to more (see Figure 5.9).

Scores on the higher-order thinking scale range from a 1, which represents lower-order thinking only, to a 5, which means that higher-order thinking is central to the instruction. A score of 3 means those students engage primarily in routine lower-order thinking, but there is at least one significant question or activity in which some students engage in some higher-order thinking. Lower-order thinking activities are defined as those that ask students to receive or recite factual information or to employ rules through repetitive routines. Students are in the role of information receivers and are asked to recall prespecified knowledge. In contrast, higher-order thinking activities require students to manipulate information and ideas in ways that transform their meaning and implications.

The depth of knowledge scale refers to the substantive character of the ideas in a lesson and to the level of understanding students demonstrate as they consider these ideas. Knowledge is thin or shallow when it does not deal with significant concepts and/or students have a trivial understanding of important concepts. Knowledge is deep or thick when it concerns important concepts and/or when students can make clear distinctions, develop arguments, solve problems, construct explanations, and otherwise work with relatively complex understandings. A score of 1 on this scale indicates that the student's knowledge is shallow, and a score of 5 indicates that the student's knowledge is deep. A score of 3 indicates

**FIGURE 5.9**
Research-Based
Standards for
Evaluating Quality
of Instruction

| Standards for Evaluating Quality of Instruction | | | |
|---|---|---|---|
| Focus on higher-order thinking | 1 ——————▶ | 3 ——————▶ | 5 |
| Depth of knowledge | 1 ——————▶ | 3 ——————▶ | 5 |
| Connectedness to the world | 1 ——————▶ | 3 ——————▶ | 5 |
| Substantive conversation | 1 ——————▶ | 3 ——————▶ | 5 |
| Social support for learning | 1 ——————▶ | 3 ——————▶ | 5 |

*Source:* Adapted from Newmann, Fred M., and Wehlage, Gary G., Five standards of authentic instruction. *Educational Leadership,* February 1993, Volume 50, No. 7, pp. 8–12, Figure 1. Reprinted with permission of the Association for Supervision and Curriculum Development. Copyright © 1993 by ASCD. All rights reserved.

that knowledge is treated unevenly during instruction; at least one significant idea may be presented in depth, but in general the focus is not sustained.

The third scale, connectedness to the world, measures the extent to which instruction has value and meaning beyond the school setting. A score of 1 is given to instruction with little or no value beyond the school; students' work has no impact on others and serves only to certify their success in the instructional context. A score of 5 is given to instruction that is connected to the world outside of school, and in which students address real-world problems and/or use personal experiences as a context for applying knowledge.

The fourth scale measures substantive conversation. A score of 1 indicates no substantive conversation, and a score of 5 indicates high-level substantive conversation. In classes with little or no conversation, interaction typically consists of teacher presentations that deviate little from a preplanned body of information and set of questions. The conversation is often choppy, rather than coherent, and there is often little or no discussion. High levels of substantive conversation are indicated by three features: considerable interaction about the ideas of a topic, sharing of ideas in exchanges that are not completely teacher-directed, and cohesive dialogue that builds on participants' ideas.

The fifth and final scale, social support for learning, involves high expectations, respect, and inclusion of all students in the learning process. Social support is low and earns a score of 1 when teacher or student behavior, comments, and actions tend to discourage effort or participation or when the overall atmosphere of the class is negative. Token acknowledgments of student actions or responses do not necessarily constitute evidence of social support. Social support is high and earns a score of 5 when the teacher conveys high expectations for all students, that it is necessary to take risks and try hard to master challenging work, that all members of the class can learn important knowledge and skills, and an understanding that a climate of mutual respect among all members of the class contributes to achievement by all.

The standards just described provide a framework through which to view instructional activities. Newmann and Wehlage (1993) caution that it is important to remember that these standards attempt only to represent the degree of authentic instruction observed within discrete class periods or episodes of instruction. Numerical ratings alone cannot portray how lessons relate to one another or how multiple lessons might accumulate into experiences that are more complex than the sum of individual lessons. The relative importance of the different standards also remains open for discussion.

Previous research indicates that teaching for thinking, problem solving, and understanding often has more positive effects on student performance than does traditional teaching. The effects of high levels of adherence to this specific set of standards are not well established. Many educators believe that there are appropriate times for traditional instructional practices such as memorizing, repetition, and quiet study without conversation. Clearly, the emphasis should be placed on moving instruction toward more authentic achievements for individual students, however that might best be accomplished.

## Congruence among Settings

Among the most critical aspects of an assessment of the instructional context will be the degree of congruence from one setting to another. In essence, it will be necessary to observe and collect information about multiple settings. A first step involves collecting information about the relationship between classroom instruction and any supplemental instruction. Shake (1989) suggests using a simple form that could be completed with relative ease by both the classroom teacher and specialists to summarize instruction across settings by the day of the week. Within two columns, one for the classroom teacher and one for the support classroom, each teacher writes a brief narrative for the day. A communication system such as this makes it easy to assess the degree of congruence between instructional settings for students who are receiving special services.

Once the instructional context for a particular student has been described, the information needs to be analyzed and evaluated. In particular, teachers need to examine the degree of similarity between instruction for average and above-average students and that received by lower-achieving readers and writers. For example, teachers need to consider how much text students with differing skill levels are exposed to each day and/or week. In addition, it is important to consider similarities and differences in the approaches used to teach students with differing skill levels. If there are substantial and significant variations in the two programs of the sort described previously in this chapter, teachers and assessment personnel should examine the assumptions and rationale for these programs and procedures very carefully. Some students may require unusual programs; however, such decisions should be based on careful consideration, not unsupported assumptions.

## Chapter Summary

Most textbooks on reading and writing assessment do not examine the types of context factors discussed in this chapter. However, contextual factors clearly contribute to students' literacy development and can enhance learning or lead to difficulty.

The first major section of this chapter describes how standards of competent performance are determined by culture. Next, we discuss how the instructional setting can influence student performance. For example, differing teacher beliefs result in the creation of diverse learning environments that can result in problems for students whose expectations and beliefs may be at odds with those of the teachers. Similarly, the differential treatment teachers frequently offer to members of different ability groups can have a negative effect on student performance and perceptions. Other, more subtle differences are also explored.

The third major section addresses instructional goals, instructional methods, reading and writing activities and tasks, and assessment practices that are evident within a particular instructional environment. As a means of translating general curricular goals into instruction, three types of instructional objectives are described: content, attitude, and process.

Motivated readers and writers are those who choose to read and write for a variety of recreational and informational purposes. Strategic readers and writers use their knowledge and skills flexibly, adapting their approach for different purposes, tasks, and materials, evaluating their reading and writing along the way.

Creating knowledgeable, strategic readers and writers involves authentic, complex projects and instructional practices based on the principle of gradually releasing responsibility for learning from the teacher to the student. Three notable characteristics of the gradual release model of learning and instruction are scaffolding, dialogue, and the level of difficulty.

Instructional practices that promote motivation are those that help students generate expectations for success and also help them focus on learning versus task completion as a valued endeavor. Key among these practices are activities that promote voluntary reading and writing.

Instructional methods also include classroom activities and tasks. Different types of tasks promote different student behaviors and need to be evaluated accordingly. Independent seatwork, reading comprehension questions, writing process, reading-writing workshop, and discussion are examined as examples of different types of literacy activities.

Finally, classroom assessment practices affect student performance because they so strongly influence the types of instruction offered to students—both by directing attention to what will be assessed and by limiting students' access to aspects of literacy that are *not* assessed. The tools and strategies section of the chapter describes techniques for assessing the instructional setting, general instructional practice, and specific instructional activities. These techniques include questionnaires and observational devices such as guiding questions, rating scales, and checklists. Most are informal and require some organization and reflection on the part of the person doing the evaluation. In addition, a relatively unique standardized instrument known as FAAB (Functional Assessment of Academic Behavior) is described and evaluated, with the conclusion that it adds an important tool to the repertoire of evaluation strategies for assessing context.

# 6 Instructional Resources

An increasing body of research suggests that the nature of the instructional materials used to teach reading and writing has a significant effect on students' performance. This realization has forced both educators and publishers to examine their assumptions about the sources of reading and writing difficulty and has encouraged special education practitioners to promote "curriculum-based evaluations" (see Howell & Morehead, 1987). A reading and writing assessment for any individual is incomplete until the characteristics of the materials that are regularly used for instruction have been identified.

Specifically addressed in this chapter are commercial reading/language arts programs, trade materials, and the use of technology in reading and writing instruction. The complexity of factors related to instructional environments makes assessment of instructional resources very difficult. We have attempted, however, to provide ways to evaluate the aspects of instructional resources that are known to influence reading and writing performance.

## Understanding the Role of Instructional Resources in Reading and Writing Performance

A survey conducted in the late 1990s revealed that 83 percent of teachers in the United States report using some combination of commercially prepared basal programs and trade books to teach reading (Baumann, Hoffman, Ro, & Duffy-Hester, 2000). The aspects of commercial reading/language arts programs that are known to influence student performance and are discussed here include student anthologies and texts for beginning readers, independent student activities, and teacher guides. Trade books are discussed from the perspective of the characteristics of narrative and informational text that influence comprehensibility. Computer technology is addressed in terms of its relationship to instruction in composition, work with special populations, and its relationship to student motivation and collaboration.

### Commercial Reading/Language Arts Programs

For a large number of teachers, commercial programs known as *basal series* constitute the bulk of their reading/language arts program. This makes it important to examine these materials to understand the nature of the instruction received by many of the students who are experiencing difficulty with reading and/or writing. It is also important to understand the changes that have occurred in basal programs over time, because it is not uncommon to find basal programs with outdated copyrights in many classrooms. It is even more common for old materials to be used in programs for students who are experiencing reading and writing difficulties.

Until the early 1990s basal programs reflected a skills-based approach to teaching reading/language arts, and the professional literature was critical of their use of contrived language, controlled vocabulary, and simplistic stories lacking in conflict, character development, and meaningful situations (Goodman, Shannon, Freeman, & Murphy, 1988). By 1989 skills-based approaches were giving way to a heavy emphasis on strategic reading in the form of metacomprehension strategies such as generating questions, summarizing, paraphrasing, predicting, verifying, and thinking aloud (Wepner & Feeley, 1993).

The late 1980s also brought changing market demands related to factors such as increased teacher involvement in decision making and policy initiatives to improve reading/language arts education (Hoffman et al., 1994). In the early 1990s basal publishers moved toward literature-based programs that were more aligned with the dominant sociocognitive theories and research related to reading and writing. As we write this in the early years of the twenty-first century, national concerns about levels of reading achievement have resulted in yet another wave of basal program reform that reflects a better balance between the skills-based approaches of the 1970s and 1980s and the literature-based approaches of the early 1990s. This brief overview of changes in basal programs over several decades suggests that the date of publication may be far more important to determining the nature of the instruction being provided than the publisher or the fact that it is a basal program.

Despite changes in philosophy, the basic components of basal programs have remained fairly constant. These include a multilevel series of materials for both the student and the teacher. At each level student materials consist of an anthology of reading selections of various types and a collection of independent activities. The primary material for the teacher at each level is a guide that includes detailed directions and suggestions for instruction. The one new addition to basal program materials in recent years has been the inclusion of "little books" as part of instruction in the early grades. The next sections consider separately the main components of basal reading programs.

*Basal Anthologies.*    The anthologies of reading material in basal programs contain a variety of different types of reading selections deemed appropriate for students at each grade or ability level. Although basal reading anthologies contain a variety of text types, poorly written and/or adapted narrative texts dominate the anthologies of basal programs that originated through the 1980s. The situation with informational text is even more serious. Older basal reading anthologies rarely include informational text, and when they do, the texts are not likely to represent the full range of informational materials students encounter in the real world of reading. For example, selections from subject-area textbooks were not (and still rarely are) included. In addition, the division between groupings of fiction and nonfiction selections in these anthologies results in limited use of the nonfiction material by teachers (Barr & Sadow, 1989).

Many students with reading and writing problems read only what is in their basal anthology. Consequently, the nature and organization of selections to which students are exposed in these materials can have a major impact on their reading and writing performance.

If basal anthologies are the primary instructional material, students might not have exposure to the full range of texts that students of a given age or ability are likely to encounter in school and nonschool settings. Students must have the opportunity to read many types of age-appropriate materials for a variety of purposes if they are to become competent readers and writers. More specific features of narrative and informational text that influence comprehensibility are considered in the section on trade materials in this chapter.

***Beginning Reading Materials.***    Given our focus in this text on students experiencing reading and writing difficulties, we want to pay special attention to the texts that are used to help students acquire reading skills. This will help us look at students' strengths and weaknesses in relation to the opportunities for learning. It will also help us understand some of our options in selecting materials that are likely to assist young students in becoming better readers.

Beginning reading texts occur within short anthologies and/or in the increasingly popular form known as "*little books*" or *leveled books*. The earliest levels of these books have one word per page for a total of perhaps five words, with the number of words increasing with each level. Multiple titles at each level provide teachers and students with choices and flexibility. Little books are popular with teachers who are concerned about the quality of selections in older basal anthologies and the difficulty of selections in the literature-based anthologies, although many, if not most, of these texts could hardly be considered good literature (see the section on narrative text structure later in the chapter for more on this). Particular strengths are the comfortable size of these materials and the fact that each contains its own unique text—a contrast to the heavy anthology of the typical basal program, even when it contains fine literature. Little or leveled books have become so popular that most basal programs now include them as part of the program, often in addition to the student anthology.

Hiebert and her colleagues (Hiebert, 1999; Hiebert & Martin, 2000; Hiebert & Raphael, 1998) have done extensive analyses of the early reading materials that have been most popular over time. They observed that older materials for beginning readers typically emphasize a particular feature of words and/or texts used to teach reading, often at the expense of other features. Specifically, the texts with copyrights before 1990 tend to emphasize either high-frequency words such as "boy," "go," and "look" or phonetically decodable words such as "can," "ran," and "pan" but not both types of words.

As Hiebert and her colleagues have observed, phonics and high-frequency texts provide different opportunities to learn word recognition strategies that can be generalized to words outside the beginning reading materials. Although a core group of high-frequency words accounts for a large percentage of the words in texts, these words account for only a small percentage of the words in text. In addition, many high-frequency words have irregular letter–sound relationships that do not reflect the common and consistent letter–sound patterns in English. A steady diet of texts consisting primarily of high-frequency words may make it difficult for beginning and poor readers to learn letter–sound principles that can be generalized to words not found in the beginning reading materials. On the other hand, a steady diet of phonics texts may lead beginning and poor readers to attempt to decode every word they encounter, which is likely to seriously impede fluency and attention to meaning.

As basal programs became more literature-based in the 1990s, so did beginning reading materials. Literature-based beginning reading materials emphasize the meaningfulness of the entire text, often in the form of "predictable" texts that repeat phrases and/or sentences. Hoffman et al. (1994) provide evidence of differences in beginning reading texts in basals with a 1986 or 1987 copyright and those with a 1993 copyright. Notably, in contrast to the 1986 and 1987 programs, the stories in the 1993 series are higher in quality, and there are fewer adaptations of literature. The evidence also indicates that vocabulary control and repetition are either substantially reduced or abandoned altogether in the 1993 programs. The total number of words in the 1993 programs is considerably less than those in the 1986 and 1987 programs; however, the 1993 programs include many more unique words. Just as with the high-frequency and phonics texts, a steady diet of literature-based texts is likely to pose certain difficulties for some beginning and poor readers (Hiebert & Martin, 2000).

As we write this, new textbook adoption standards in states such as Texas and California are guiding the development of early reading materials in texts with copyrights beginning around 2000. These materials are more likely to attend to multiple criteria, including the proportion of high-frequency and decodable words in addition to the meaningfulness of the entire text. Hiebert and Martin (2000) used the dimensions of (1) number of total and unique words; (2) proportion of unique words that are phonetically regular, multisyllabic, and highly frequent; and (3) "engagingness" to analyze these newer, "balanced" texts in comparison with earlier copyrights. The results of their analyses suggest that the newer texts may be more difficult on some dimensions and less difficult on others. Although the trend toward more balanced texts seems promising, "A 'perfect' sequence of books cannot be expected; rather, books need to be selected in relation to the existing strategies of particular readers and the strategies that are the focus of instruction" (Hiebert & Raphael, 1998, p. 129).

At present the materials that are available for beginning readers vary considerably on the dimensions we know are likely to influence young readers' ability to access text. One can certainly imagine that exposure only to materials that attend to a single dimension of words or text features could contribute to an individual student's early reading difficulties. Although many, if not most, students learn to read regardless of the types of materials used, others may struggle as a result of a particularly bad match between the materials used and their particular strengths and weaknesses. Understanding the types of texts students have used to learn reading may provide insight into their reading difficulties.

***Independent Student Activities.***   The anthologies are only one area requiring evaluation. The independent student activities often found in journals or workbooks that are part of each level of a basal series also require careful examination. Widely published reports from the 1980s suggest that on the average, elementary students spend fewer than ten minutes every school day reading connected text, and between 40 and 70 percent of their reading time doing seatwork (Anderson, 1984; Anderson et al., 1985; Fisher et al., 1980). Although the amount of time devoted to independent seatwork may have lessened since that time, we believe it still occupies a significant portion of instructional time. Because students spend so much time on seatwork, close examination of both the content and use of these activities is essential. As Osborn (1984) has noted, well-designed seatwork activities can facilitate the initial teaching of what is new and the maintenance of what has already been taught. On the other hand, poorly designed seatwork activities and practices force students to spend countless hours on boring and sometimes confusing activities that do not promote reading and writing competence.

Reviews of the content of traditional workbook and skill-sheet materials suggest that many of these materials are unlikely to benefit students in any significant way (R. C. Anderson et al., 1985). Criticisms of the content of traditional reading workbooks (Osborn, 1984; Scheu, Tanner, & Au, 1989) indicate that many of these materials involve very limited amounts of reading, focus on isolated drills of skills that are often only marginally useful in learning to read, involve little writing, and do not engage students in activities that promote comprehension.

Newer basal programs are clearly intended to promote reading/language arts abilities and prepare students to read a wide range of authentic material (novels, reference books, content-area textbooks, and so on). However, it is doubtful that this can occur with the steady diet of contrived texts that even today may appear in workbooks, since research suggests that the transfer of knowledge and skill from one context to another is far from automatic. Hare, Rabinowitz, and Schieble (1989) found that many students who could identify the main ideas in basallike skills texts were unable to construct main ideas in more complex, naturally occurring paragraphs.

Suggestions about how to improve seatwork tasks include helping students to access background knowledge and set purposes for reading, follow the structure of the reading selection, become increasingly independent in the use of comprehension strategies, and understand why they are doing the work and how it will help them be better readers. There are certainly better examples of seatwork in contemporary basal workbooks (see Figure 6.1).

In addition to the content of seatwork activities, we must be concerned with how seatwork materials are used. In an in-depth study of reading seatwork, L. M. Anderson et al. (1985) observed eight first-grade classrooms to determine what teachers and students do during the time devoted to seatwork and how students attempt to understand and complete assigned work. They observed that the same form of assignment often was used two to five times a week, and in six of the eight classes observed, over half of the seatwork assignments were given to the whole class, despite the fact that students were assigned to different groups. They also found that teacher instruction related to seatwork rarely included statements about what would be learned or how the assignment related to students' past learning. When teachers did attend to students doing seatwork, they most often monitored student behavior rather than their understanding or task performance. Teachers generally emphasized keeping busy and finishing assigned work, not understanding what was being taught.

The seatwork assignments that low achievers received were particularly inappropriate. These students did poorly on their assignments and often derived answers by using strategies that enabled them to complete the assignments without understanding them. These findings are compounded by the evidence that students assigned to lower-ability reading groups spend even more time on worksheet exercises and less time actually reading than students in higher-ability reading groups (Allington et al., 1986). It is not surprising that these students are especially likely to believe that reading is "finishing the workbook pages."

Contemporary studies of successful schools reinforce these ideas, suggesting that students in successful schools are much more likely than students in less successful schools to be engaged in seatwork that involves sustained reading and writing and written responses

**FIGURE 6.1**
Example of
Contemporary Basal
Workbook Activity

Name _____

# Off to Adventure!

**As you read each selection in *Off to Adventure!*, fill in the boxes of the chart that apply to the selection.**

| | How does the adventure begin? | How do the characters change by the end of the adventure? |
|---|---|---|
| **The Lost and Found** | | |
| **The Ballad of Mulan** | | |
| **The Waterfall** | | |

*Source:* From *Rewards* Practice Book in *Houghton Mifflin Reading: A Legacy of Literacy* by J. David Cooper and John J. Pikulski et al. Copyright © 2001 by Houghton Mifflin Company. Reprinted by permission of Houghton Mifflin Company. All rights reserved.

to authentic texts (Morrow, Tracey, Woo, & Pressley, 1999; Mosenthal, Lipson, Sortina, Russ, & Mekkelsen, 2001, Taylor, Pearson, Clark, & Walpole, 2000).

L. M. Anderson et al. (1985) suggest that poor seatwork habits developed in first grade may contribute to a subsequent passive learning style. Low achievers, who often work on assignments they do not understand, may come to believe that schoolwork does not have to make sense; therefore, it is not necessary to obtain additional information or assistance as an aid to understanding. In contrast, high-achieving students rarely have difficulty with seatwork, so that any problems they have are more likely to motivate them to seek help.

Scheu et al. (1989) suggest a general model for the development of seatwork activities that calls for teachers to act as decision makers who consider both their students' needs as developing readers and writers and the qualities of selections to be read. According to this model, teachers should design and assign seatwork tasks on the basis of the kinds of independent practice students need to understand specific selections and to become more proficient readers and writers in general. Activities need to be thoroughly integrated with the reading and writing lessons, because they give students the chance to work independently with the concepts and skills needed for a holistic understanding of a selection. The purposes of seatwork assignments should be explained and discussed.

Finally, completed seatwork assignments should often serve as the basis for starting a discussion of the selection. Rather than turning in their work for the teacher to grade, students should correct their own papers in the context of a discussion about the reading assignment and teach others by working together to complete their seatwork assignments (Cunningham, Moore, Cunningham, & Moore, 1989).

The increasing consensus among experts is reflected in the recommendations of the Commission on Reading: (1) Children should spend less time completing workbooks and skills sheets; (2) children should spend more time in independent reading; and (3) children should spend more time writing (R. C. Anderson et al., 1985). "Real" reading and writing activities should be a part of each student's daily seatwork. Unlike the time spent on traditional worksheet activities, time spent reading and writing has been shown to contribute to growth in literacy ability (Mosenthal et al., 2001).

***Teacher's Guides.***     The teacher's guides that accompany each level in a basal program are a significant feature of classroom practice that influences students' reading and writing performance. The instructional activities teachers choose are generally those described in the teacher's guides (Barr & Sadow, 1989; Durkin, 1984; Shannon, 1983). These guides provide a variety of information, including replicas of both the selections and the workbook pages that appear in the student's materials, organizational procedures to follow in implementing the program, specific directions for presenting prescribed skills, suggested questions to ask when discussing selections with students, enrichment activities for use as follow-up or culminating activities, and assessments that can be used to evaluate student progress. Perhaps the most important feature of teacher's guides, however, is the lesson design provided for each reading selection throughout the series.

*Directed Reading Activity.*     The instructional design, or framework, that has traditionally been used in basal reading programs is known as the *directed reading activity* (DRA). The DRA was first introduced by Betts in 1946 to give teachers a basic format for systematic group instruction, improve students' word recognition and comprehension skills, and guide students through a reading selection. It has remained remarkably unchanged since that time. Wepner and Feeley (1993) found that all seven basal programs they reviewed used a DRA framework, and although Hoffman et al. (1994) report some movement away from this model at the earliest levels, it is still a common feature of contemporary basals.

In a DRA framework, instruction is organized around before-, during-, and after-reading activities for each selection in the anthology:

- *Prereading activities* in a DRA often include providing relevant background, creating interest, introducing meanings and/or pronunciations for new vocabulary, and establishing purposes for reading.
- *During-reading activities* are intended to guide students' reading and often include silent reading focused on answering purpose-setting questions, oral reading and responding to questions dealing with short sections of the text, and/or oral rereading to clarify or verify a point.
- *Postreading activities* are of two types: activities focused on the reading selection, such as group discussion or end-of-selection questions, and activities focused on skill instruction and practice that may or may not be related to the reading selection.

Traditional basal lessons focus on content goals in teaching the reading selection, process or skill goals in separate skill lessons and activities, and largely ignore attitude goals. In copyrights before 1990, skills objectives often take precedence over content and attitude objectives; "that is, the stated purpose of each lesson is to learn a particular skill (which may or may not be relevant to understanding the reading selection). Students are often held accountable for their skill learning through practice exercises and end-of-unit or end-of-level tests. However, they are rarely held accountable for their comprehension of the reading selection, except through group questioning and discussion" (Wixson & Peters, 1989, p. 22). Similarly, Morrow's (1987) analysis of six sets of grade K–3 basal readers with older copyrights indicates that fewer than 5 percent of the overall instructional suggestions included activities designed to promote positive attitudes, to encourage book discussion, or to build knowledge of authors and illustrators.

The type of instruction that is typically associated with the traditional DRA promotes the role of the teacher as the presenter and the student as the receiver of information and encourages teacher-centered patterns of interaction. There is a lack of scaffolded instruction involving the progression from teacher modeling and explanation to independent student practice and application and there is little support for engaging in instructional dialogue (see Chapter 5). There is also little opportunity for student-initiated involvement, and students have little opportunity to monitor and regulate their own reading.

For example, Durkin's (1984) analysis of the teacher's guides of five major basal series revealed that they provide few suggestions for comprehension instruction but many for review, application, and practice. In addition, she reported that the teacher's guides "mention" the skills or strategy and then quickly move to brief examples available in application formats. Although there is little direct evidence regarding the effects of different instructional frameworks on student learning, it seems safe to assume that a steady diet of teacher-centered exchange would provide different results than more interactive patterns that place increased responsibility on the reader (see Palincsar & Brown, 1984).

Instructional design in the basal programs of the 1990s reflects the general shift that occurred in reading instruction from skills-based to literature-based instruction. This shift is evident in the increased importance given to content goals associated with comprehending the reading selection. Basal lessons in the 1990s copyrights also include many instructional choices and multiple opportunities for student-initiated activity. For example, in the Hoffman et al. (1994) comparison of early reading materials in 1986–1987 and 1993 programs, the tone of the teacher's guides was less prescriptive in the 1993 programs, moving in the direction of a teacher-as-decision-maker model. In addition the 1993 programs move toward a shared reading model and away from the directed reading model of the 1986 and 1987 programs. Vocabulary is introduced more in the context of the story in the 1993 editions, and fewer questions are provided in an effort to include more high-level questions. In addition assessment tools in the 1993 programs are broadened beyond the test-only model in the 1986 and 1987 programs.

Effective reading lessons focus simultaneously on content, process, and attitude objectives. The goal is not simply to teach the content of given selections, or to provide isolated skills instruction, but to promote knowledgeable, strategic, motivated reading of a variety of materials for a variety of purposes and tasks (see Chapter 5). Beginning with 2000 copyrights, we see yet another change in the lesson design of basal programs that attempts to meld the best of the literature and skills-based programs of the past. Time will tell whether the instructional frameworks of the twenty-first century will achieve a better balance in addressing the range of content and methods that we know are important for student learning.

***Alternative Frameworks.***    A variant of the DRA that has garnered a lot of attention in recent years is known as *guided reading* (Fountas & Pinnell, 1996; 2001a, 2001b). Guided reading is a framework for small-group instruction of students who read the same text. The groups are temporary and are homogenous in the sense that the students read at about the same level, demonstrate similar reading behaviors, and have similar instructional needs. The procedure begins with the introduction of a text that the teacher has selected in a way that is designed to support the students reading of the particular text. Students then read the text silently and independently, although the teacher may ask individual students to read orally at regular intervals and talk with them individually about the book. Following reading, the teacher discusses the meaning of the text with the students and asks them to revisit the text to make connections, search for information, and/or find evidence to support their thinking. Finally, the teacher uses the just-completed reading experience as the basis for teaching processing strategies that can be applied to other fiction and/or nonfiction materials. Fountas and Pinnell also describe a guided writing procedure with a similar structure to that of guided reading.

Another variant on the classic DRA used primarily by early elementary teachers is the shared reading approach. Modeled after a bedtime story reading time, the shared reading experience (Holdaway, 1979) encourages children to participate in reading and rereading activities in a supportive environment. Generally, teachers use a big book so that a group of students can see the print as the teacher reads the book through. After students have enjoyed the story, the teacher and students reread the book over several days, accomplishing a variety of tasks that may include comprehension and vocabulary work, concepts about print, phonics and decoding, or attention to narrative elements such as character or setting. Teachers provide scaffolded support through initial whole-text reading, choral reading, and rereading. Over time, students acquire the confidence to read this and similar stories in small book form.

To summarize, teachers need to examine the materials they use very carefully to determine what contributions to reading performance they may be making (see Hoffman, 2001). Examining the content and method of instruction used to teach reading can provide insight into what a particular student has had the opportunity to learn with regard to reading and writing. Not infrequently, students who have difficulty reading specific texts or with certain reading skills simply have not had the instructional or practice opportunities necessary to become competent. Such an evaluation can also provide information about what has *not* proved helpful in teaching individual children to read. When an analysis of the instruction and the instructional materials suggests ample opportunity to learn but the child has not benefited, further assessment and/or diagnostic teaching is needed (see Chapter 11).

## Trade Materials

Researchers have identified a number of text factors that influence readers' comprehension, fluency, memory, and enjoyment of selections. A major factor in determining students' reading performance is the type of text being read. Research in this area suggests that major differences exist between narrative (story) and expository (informational) text. Narrative text is often characterized by specific elements of information such as problem, conflict, and resolution. Expository text, by contrast, is usually described in terms of organizational structures such as cause/effect, compare/contrast, or descriptive. Generally speaking, the evidence suggests that narratives of all sorts (even unfamiliar ones) are easier to understand than expository texts (Graesser & Riha, 1984). Differences in text structure and organization, as well as purpose, probably contribute to the differences readers experience in reading narrative and expository texts. In the following section we describe separately what is known about the structure of stories and informational texts and its influence on reading performance.

*Narrative Text Structure.* A narrative tells a story about human events and actions. Researchers have concluded that narratives have an identifiable structure (see also Chapters 7 and 8). Although different types of narratives such as fables, mysteries, and adventures vary in specific ways, they also have some features in common. Common features of narrative include characters; setting or time placement; complications and major goals of main characters; plots and resolutions of complications; emotional patterns; and points, morals, and themes (Graesser, Golding, & Long, 1991).

The principal purpose for stories is often assumed to be entertainment, but "the range of purposes for telling a story is as varied as the motives that underlie human behavior. Thus, stories can be used to cause pain as well as pleasure (e.g., to embarrass, to humiliate, to parody, to flatter, to console, to teach, to arouse guilt, etc.)" (Stein & Policastro, 1984, p. 116). Readers and listeners use their knowledge of text purpose to anticipate text type and structure. For example, listeners expect different discourse features from a conversation or an amusing cocktail story than they do from a lecture.

Individuals build internal story structures and use them to aid comprehension during reading. Text organization helps readers predict, focus attention, and retain or recall content (McConaughy, 1982). Both children and adults comprehend better when story content is organized so that it conforms to expectations (Stein & Glenn, 1979; Stein & Nezworski, 1978). When stories contain missing segments (e.g., initiating events) or altered sequence, readers comprehend and remember less (Lipson, Mosenthal, & Mekkelsen, 1999; Thorndyke, 1977).

Because the internalized sense of story seems so central to comprehending narratives, it is important to understand something about its development. Even very young children appear to have a rather well-developed sense of story. Recent evidence also suggests that poor readers, at least by sixth grade, have as well-developed a sense of story as do good readers and that they use it to enhance comprehension (McConaughy, 1985). It should also be noted that these internal story structures appear to develop as children listen to and read well-formed stories. Thus it is extremely important that disabled readers are offered well-crafted stories containing strong story structures so that they can develop this sense of story early and make the most efficient use of this knowledge.

Unfortunately, many of the reading selections used in basal readers before 1990 and many of the remedial reading materials, even contemporary ones, are poorly written. Beck, McKeown, and McCaslin (1981) concluded as they analyzed basal stories that these types of selections can pose serious impediments to comprehension, because "the printed texts in the earliest school reading materials are not in themselves complete stories or even complete messages" (p. 780).

The "story" in Figure 6.2 is typical of a certain class of selections encountered in schools. It is hardly recognizable as the familiar story of the "Shoemaker and the Elves." Indeed, it does not conform to our expectations for either the content or organization of *any* story. In terms of content, for example, we expect that stories will revolve around some type of conflict—environmental conflict, interpersonal conflict, or internal conflict (Bruce, 1984). The segment in Figure 6.2 contains no such elements, and it is difficult to imagine what would pull a reader through the text. The structure and organization of this selection do not conform to traditional story grammar descriptions.

Reliance on this type of artificial text may actually make reading *more* difficult. Children find such texts uninteresting and difficult to comprehend, since they do not invite

**FIGURE 6.2**
"The Shoemaker and the Elves"

| Tap, Tap Story |
| --- |
| Tap, tap, tap. See me work. I make good things.<br>See the red ones. See the blue ones. See the yellow ones.<br>I want green ones.<br>No, no, no. I do not want big ones. I want little ones.<br>No, no, no. I do not want little ones. I want big ones.<br>Oh, my. Oh, my. No one wants my things. I will go to bed.<br>I will work in the morning. |

*Source:* Tap, Tap Story from *Learning to Read in American Schools* by R. C. Anderson, J. Osborn, and R. J. Tierney. Copyright © 1984 by Lawrence Erlbaum Associates, Inc., Publishers.

reader involvement (Bruce, 1984; Goldman & Rakestraw, 2000). Importantly, these texts probably affect students' writing development also. Children need good writing models if they are to improve their own writing. Hillocks (1986), who conducted an extensive review of research on writing, concluded that "research indicates that emphasis on the presentation of good pieces of writing as models is significantly more useful than the study of grammar" (p. 249).

***Informational Text Structure.***   Five common structures are used repeatedly in textbook writing, at least in the Western hemisphere (Armbruster, 1984):

1. *Simple listing:* Information is presented in an unordered list.
2. *Comparison/contrast:* Ideas are described in terms of their similarities and differences.
3. *Temporal sequence:* Time order of ideas or events is used to organize the text.
4. *Cause/effect:* The presentation of ideas or events focuses on the causal relationships between and among them.
5. *Problem/solution:* Relationship between and among ideas or events are linked so that one represents a problem and the other(s) represents a solution to that problem.

Whereas even young children seem able to recognize and use story structure, it appears that even middle grade students are either unaware of or unable to use informational or expository text structure to aid comprehension (Goldman & Rakestraw, 2000; Taylor & Samuels, 1983). Although the ability to use text organization to increase learning and promote comprehension improves with age, reading ability differences are also noted by the middle grades. In addition, struggling students are likely to be affected by different genre structures than good readers. In a recent review of research about learning from text, Alexander and Jetton (2000) concluded that "the quality of text becomes differentially important depending on the reader's stage of academic development. In short, competent and proficient learners are better equipped to deal with vagueness, incoherence, and other inconsiderate characteristics of (content) texts" (p. 302). Several factors probably account for this.

First, there are many ways to organize information in expository texts, and the patterns aren't so clearly defined. The research in this area suggests that not all of these text patterns are equally easy for less mature readers. For example, under some conditions simple listing is more difficult than compare/contrast because it requires readers to impose an organization, often by inferring the relationships between and among listed items (Meyer & Freedle, 1984).

A second reason why children may have less skill in reading expository text is that they typically have much less experience reading this type of material. Many schools do not use textbooks at the early levels for content area instruction, and basal reading programs have traditionally included more narrative than expository texts in their anthologies. In addition, differences between good and poor readers' ability to read exposition may be related to opportunity, since it appears that poor readers have even fewer opportunities to read informational text than good readers do (Allington, 1984).

Even when elementary students do have the opportunity to read, they are often offered poor examples of exposition. The quality of textual materials influences performance *for all readers* (see Shimmerlik, 1978). Studies designed to compare readers' comprehension of organized versus disorganized texts have consistently demonstrated that comprehension and recall are strongly affected by the organization of ideas in text. Well-organized text that highlights the overall structure and supports the relationships between ideas contributes to comprehension and enhances recall. Poor readers appear to be affected by these factors more seriously than good readers (Alexander & Jetton, 2000).

Well-structured text promotes the integration of knowledge so that more cognitive resources are available to process new, more complex information. In turn, these more organized knowledge structures promote complex comprehension activities such as generating inferences, summarizing, and evaluating. Poorly written text is difficult even for proficient readers to comprehend and remember. Students, especially those with reading problems, need to read *good* informational texts (Goldman & Rakestraw, 2000).

**Text Features That Influence Comprehensibility.**    The term *considerate texts* was coined by Armbruster and T. Anderson to describe texts that enable readers to gather appropriate information with minimal effort, as opposed to inconsiderate texts that require readers to put forth extra effort in order to compensate for the inadequacies of the text (Armbruster, 1984; Anderson & Armbruster, 1984a). Although the principles for analyzing considerate text were designed for subject-area textbooks, we believe that they apply equally well to narrative materials. The features of text that contribute to its considerateness are discussed briefly in the sections that follow. These features are coherence, unity, audience appropriateness, and adjunct instructional aids.

*Coherence.*    Coherence means "a sticking together" (Anderson & Armbruster, 1984a, p. 204). The ideas and concepts in texts are tied together by an underlying cohesive structure. According to Bateman and Rondhuis (1997), coherence establishes a meaning relationship between segments of a text that renders the segments, "more than the sum of its parts" (p. 2). In coherent writing, the author moves smoothly from one idea to the next, making it easier for readers to understand the big ideas. The author clarifies facts and helps the reader to understand the significance of these ideas or events.

According to Armbruster (1984), coherence is the text factor that exerts the strongest influence on comprehension and learning. When reading coherent (versus less coherent) text, readers take less time to read, they recall more, and the integration of ideas is improved (Gernsbacher, 1997; Goldman & Saul, 1990). Readers are better able to build a model of the meaning of text when it has a strong cohesive structure, which functions like a "roadmap to understanding" (Binkley, 1988, p. 104). For example, both reading time and recall are improved when authors repeatedly refer to key ideas (Goetz & Armbruster, 1980).

There are many ways that authors tighten relationships and increase the flow of ideas (Goldman & Rakestraw, 2000; Halliday & Hasan, 1976). Authors can make effective use of *reference* by using pronouns to link previous or forthcoming events, people, and things. Similarly, authors use *lexical repetition* and *synonyms* to tie ideas together—for example, by repeating key words several times or using other words with the same meaning (e.g., *elephant* and *lumbering animal*). Coherent text also makes effective use of *intersentential connectives* such as *therefore* and *obviously* to tie ideas together.

Stories for young or less-able readers are frequently inconsiderate because of attempts to control difficulty by using roundabout language or by omitting information completely.

This can result in highly contrived and incomplete selections such as the example in Figure 6.2. Although this excerpt is from a version of "The Shoemaker and the Elves," key words such as *shoemaker, elves,* and *shoes* are never used (see Figure 6.2).

Both able and less-able readers appear to take a very long time to recognize fully and use most cohesive ties in text (Bridge & Winograd, 1982). However, some aspects of cohesion seem to pose special problems for less-able readers. For example, although the absence of explicitly stated connectives makes reading more difficult for all readers, the need to infer connectives poses more serious problems for less-able readers (Marshall & Glock, 1978–79).

*Unity.* Although unity in text is closely related to coherence, they are not exactly the same thing. Unity refers to the degree to which the text addresses a single purpose. The author of a unified text has not strayed from the purpose by including irrelevant and distracting information. (Anderson & Armbruster, 1984a, p. 209). The importance of unity can be seen quite clearly in the sample fifth grade social studies text presented in Figure 6.3. Although this selection suffers from several problems, one of the greatest is its lack of unity. The reader is hard-pressed to know just what is important. Readers with little knowledge of the Civil War (most fifth grade students) will have a difficult time forming an integrated picture of the information in this section of text, since the selection moves from topic to topic so quickly. Similarly, poor readers will have trouble because there is little opportunity to use prior knowledge (either preexisting or garnered from text) as an aid to comprehension.

Text unity is likely to have an especially strong effect on both less-knowledgeable and less-able readers. For comprehension to occur, readers need to integrate text information with prior knowledge and also integrate the information from one part of the text with information from earlier parts. If this does not happen, readers' memory for the text will be limited because they will be forced to recall isolated facts rather than organized sets of information (Anderson & Armbruster, 1984a).

*Audience Appropriateness.* "Audience appropriateness refers to the extent to which the text matches the reader's knowledge base—knowledge both of the content and of discourse features such as syntactic and rhetorical structures" (Anderson & Armbruster, 1984a, p. 212). Authors of books for young people and the publishers who distribute the books have a responsibility to consider how appropriate both the content and structure of their materials are for those who are not yet expert in terms of either skill or knowledge.

Evaluating appropriateness can be extremely tricky for teachers who have had many more experiences in the world and are themselves often content experts. It is very clear that prior knowledge and expertise interact with structural cues in text, so more knowledgeable readers can cope better with inferior texts than poor readers can (Goldman & Rakestraw, 2000). Because teachers are so familiar with the content they teach, they may underestimate the processing demands required to understand the vocabulary, concepts, inferences, and metaphors.

Even when materials are generally appropriate for the intended audience, however, mismatches can occur. This is where the knowledgeable and thoughtful teacher will need to

**FIGURE 6.3** Social Studies Text

## The North and the South at War

*In 1861 Lincoln became the President of a divided United States.* He took the oath of office on a high platform in front of the capitol in Washington, D.C. He was dressed in a black suit, a stiff white shirt, and a high silk hat. He carried a cane with a gold handle.

Lincoln stepped forward and placed his left hand on a Bible. Raising his right hand, he promised to "preserve, protect, and defend the Constitution of the United States." People wondered how he would do this. Seven states had already left the United States. Would Lincoln try to punish them? What would he say about slavery?

Lincoln did not answer all of these questions in his Inaugural Address. He said that no state had the right to leave the United States. He warned that he would protect the forts and buildings which belonged to the United States government.

War broke out only a few weeks after Lincoln became President. It became known as the Civil War.

*The war began at Fort Sumter in South Carolina.* Fort Sumter was on a small island in Charleston harbor. Find it on the map. It belonged to the United States government. Union soldiers from the North held the fort. South Carolina, now a part of the Confederacy, ordered Fort Sumter to surrender. When the commander of the fort refused, the food supply was cut off.

Lincoln had food shipped to Fort Sumter. This made Confederate leaders angry. Southern soldiers fired on the fort. Northern soldiers fired back. A fierce battle took place. At last the Northern soldiers had to give up. This was the first battle of the Civil War.

Thousands offered to serve in the Union Army. Thousands rushed to join the Confederate forces, too. Everyone hoped the war would be over soon. But it wasn't. It dragged on for four years.

During the second year of the war, both sides ran short of troops. They then drafted, or ordered, people into the armies. This was the first time in United States history that soldiers were drafted.

Both sides needed money, supplies, and troops. Money-raising events were held in the Union and in the Confederacy. Groups were formed to help the families of soldiers.

Women who had never worked outside their homes went to work in offices and factories. Some women ran the family farms and businesses for the first time. Others knitted and sewed uniforms and made bandages to use in the hospitals.

Doctors and nurses went to serve on the battlefield. Mary Walker was one of the doctors. At first, she was allowed to work only as a nurse. Later, though, she became an Army officer and worked as a doctor.

*Clara Barton was called the "Angel of the Battlefield."* She was born on a Massachusetts farm on Christmas Day, 1821. For a while, she taught school near her home. Later she moved to Washington, D.C. She was a clerk in one of the government offices.

When the Civil War began, Clara Barton carried medicines and food to injured soldiers. The officers ordered her away. They said the battlefield was no place for a woman. But she did not give up. In fact, she got other women to join her. After a time, she ran a large hospital for wounded soldiers.

Clara Barton served suffering people the rest of her long life. She helped to find missing Union soldiers. She took care of the victims of wars in other parts of the world. She helped people who had lost homes in fires, floods, and storms. She founded the American Red Cross.

Dorothea Dix was another nurse during the Civil War. She had spent years trying to make life better for people in prisons and poorhouses. During the Civil War, though, she took time out from her work to care for wounded soldiers. She was in charge of all the nurses for the Union Army.

*Source:* From *Our Country* by Gertrude S. Browns, Ernest W. Tiegs, and Fay Adams. Copyright © 1979 by Ginn and Company. Reprinted by permission of Pearson Education, Inc.

exercise judgment. When working with special student populations or when the overall school curriculum does not support the content, we must make sure that we are judging the contribution of these materials to reader performance. Under some circumstances failure to comprehend has very little to do with reading skill.

*Adjunct Aids.* Adjunct aids are the structural features of texts that are intended to supplement or complement the information in the written text. They include features such as illustrations, headings and subheadings, boldfaced type, charts and figures, introductions and summaries, and questions either within or at the end of a reading selection. These features are included specifically to focus and guide readers' understanding and are common in materials used for instructional purposes.

As with other features of the text, adjunct aids have an impact on students' comprehension and learning. For example, when topic sentences are clearly present, readers comprehend and recall text content better (Bridge, Belmore, Moskow, Cohen, & Matthews, 1984). Furthermore, comprehension of main ideas is enhanced when they are stated explicitly at the beginning of paragraphs or text sections (Baumann, 1986) or are highlighted in some way (Doctorow, Wittrock, & Marks, 1978).

The mere presence of such features does not ensure enhanced comprehension. Students must be aware of these features and understand how they contribute to understanding. Many of the adjunct aids described above are unique to the materials used for instructional purposes, and students may need direct guidance and explanation from teachers to be able to take full advantage of these text features.

## Tutoring Programs

Tutoring programs are another instructional resource that can influence a student's reading and writing performance. Since the 1990s tutoring in the United States has come to mean "remedial instruction that is delivered by one teacher to one student, and this teacher is usually not the student's classroom teacher" (Shanahan, 1998, p. 218). The tutor may be another teacher, a paraprofessional, a parent or other volunteer, or another student. Shanahan (1998) poses a series of questions that help to organize the knowledge base that has accumulated on tutoring programs, which include the following: Is tutoring really effective? Does tutoring always work? Does tutoring work for all students? Do tutors need training? and How much tutoring is beneficial?

Research clearly supports the use of many forms of tutoring with a wide range of students. Drawing from eight literature reviews that summarize more than 100 studies, Shanahan (1998) concludes that there is a consistent pattern of tutored students doing better than students who do not receive tutoring. For example, Shanahan and Barr's (1995) examination of studies on Reading Recovery (RR) found that students who received RR instruction made sizable gains in reading achievement during the first grade year. These gains compared favorably with those of higher-achieving first graders who received only regular classroom instruction or such instruction along with compensatory support.

What is more important perhaps is the fact that tutoring is not always effective and is more effective in some instances than in others. Circumstances that might outweigh the benefits of tutoring include the instructional time lost in moving between classroom and compensatory instruction documented by Cunningham and Allington (1996). It may be difficult for tutoring, no matter how well designed and delivered, to compensate for the loss of ten to fifteen minutes of instructional time each day for movement from classroom to tutor and back again. The tutoring experience might also represent an incompatible change in the curriculum. Tutored students might receive instruction that contradicts what is offered in the regular classroom in ways that interfere with learning (see Wasik, 1998). Shanahan (1998) concludes that tutoring programs usually lead to at least small net gains in achievement beyond that accomplished through regular classroom instruction, but they in no way guarantee improved learning.

Tutoring is often proposed as a means to help low-achieving students catch up. However, research indicates that tutoring may not be especially effective with many low-achieving readers. For example, although generally effective, Reading Recovery fails to help a significant number of students. Many students are dropped from the program because of poor attendance or mobility problems. In addition, a large number of referrals are made by RR to special education simply because the students fail to make adequate progress even with this intensive instruction, indicating the ineffectiveness of even this program with certain low-achieving students (Hiebert, 1994b). Shanahan (1998) concludes that research does not yet allow us to reliably attribute differences in the effectiveness of tutoring across students to characteristics of those being tutored, qualities of the tutoring, or some interaction of these factors.

Research does, however, indicate that programs employing professional teachers as tutors produce more substantial gains than do programs involving peer tutoring, parent tutoring, or various volunteer models, although these are also successful. For example, Pinnell, Lyons, DeFord, Bryck, and Selzer (1994) found that the reading achievement of students taught by RR trained teachers improved more than that of students in a RR-style tutoring program taught by teachers without this training. It is worth noting, however, that programs using teachers as tutors that provide far less training are less effective than those providing more extensive training. There is also evidence that tutor training might not be as necessary in situations in which tutors are carefully supervised and instructional decisions are made by knowledgeable, professional teachers.

The amount of tutoring a student receives is also important, but the actual benefits are likely to depend on the tutors' level of knowledge and the supervision and management structures that are in place. Although some evidence suggests that less is more in terms of the optimal length of tutoring programs, there is also evidence that with well-trained tutors working with a well-structured curriculum, longer tutoring programs can continue to be effective even with nonprofessionals such as college students (Juel, 1996).

Clearly, tutoring can be an effective strategy for improving student achievement. Although it appears that tutors with more training and experience do best, even programs that employ less knowledgeable tutors are sometimes effective (see Morris, 1999; Santa & Hoien, 1999). An understanding of tutoring programs as an instructional resource will also likely include attention to the social dimensions of tutor–student relationship. Unfortunately, there is little research to guide our understanding of the interactions between the social and cognitive processes inherent in tutoring experiences.

## Computer Technology

The rapid growth in the use of personal computers for reading and writing instruction demands that separate attention be paid to these materials. Most educators and researchers do believe that computer technology can help students become better readers and writers but that teachers need to exercise both caution and judgment in selecting and using the available materials. The research on computer use in instruction that is most relevant to teachers' concerns centers on the topics of composition, special populations, motivation, and collaboration (Kamil & Intrator, 2000).

*Composition.*  Of all the uses of computer technology in literacy instruction, word processing is probably the best designed for the educational purposes to which it is put. The writing process as an educational concept predates the advent of word processors, but the two concepts seem to be so well matched that computer technology is the quintessential tool for the writing process. Word processing allows students and teachers to compose, edit, revise, and publish with little loss in the integrity of the process.

Word-processing studies fall into two categories: those in which technology is a simple replacement and those in which technology augments an older skill or practice (Kamil & Intrator, 2000). Bangert-Drowns (1993) reviewed thirty-two studies in which two groups of students received identical writing instruction but only one group was allowed to use word processing. The strong conclusion was that the quality of writing was higher for the word-processing groups.

Evidence on revisions is more mixed in that revisions might not automatically result from word processing. However, when revision prompts are added, word processing is also likely to result in more revision (Daiute, 1983). In general, it appears that adapting word-processing programs to instruction may make them even more effective. Word processing is one of the uses of computer technology that get a strong recommendation for implementation from the available research (Kamil & Intrator, 2000).

*Special Populations.*  Another body of work in computers and literacy reflects the use of computers to benefit individuals who may not learn as easily or effectively from traditional modes of instruction. Relevant here is the use of computer technology in an effort to remediate specific difficulties in literacy acquisition or to facilitate more rapid literacy acquisition. The computer has great potential with special populations because of its many functions and forms of output, including visual representations, print, and voice/communication capabilities.

One area of literacy that has been studied is the role of enhanced word-processing programs in helping to facilitate the writing process for students with learning disabilities. Advances in technology such as speech synthesis and word prediction provide benefits beyond those enjoyed from simple word processing. Speech synthesis, which allows the user to hear the computer pronounce the words that are typed into the program, has rendered some promising results in allowing students to detect a higher percentage of errors in their writing. Word prediction is another intervention that uses the computer to predict and offer choices of words as users begin to type. MacArthur (1998) found that young students with learning disabilities who used a word-processing program with speech synthesis and word prediction demonstrated increased spelling accuracy and legibility.

Another current trend involves the adaptive use of computers to help facilitate literacy acquisition with learners who face physical challenges. More conventional applications for learners with visual impediments have included using computers to increase the size of text, audio descriptions, Braille displays, and screen magnifiers. Computer technology is also used to develop literacy in children with severe speech and physical impairments. There are also potential benefits in using multimedia supports to help integrate sign, speech, and text for children with severe to profound hearing impairments.

There is also a growing body of literature on the extension and application of multimedia learning to benefit second-language learners, at-risk children, and very young, preliterate learners. For example, Plass, Chun, Mayer, and Leutner (1998) found that using computers to support verbal and visual learning preferences resulted in enhanced story comprehension and recall of word translations in students learning English as a second language. Liu and Reed (1995) also found positive gains in vocabulary and improvements in the correct use of words in context by a group of international students learning English using a hypermedia-assisted second-language learning program. After reviewing available research, Kamil and Intrator (2000) concluded that there does seem to be some evidence that teaching by computer raises achievement in special populations of students.

***Collaboration.***     Research that explores the role and impact of technology on literacy communities and on social interaction in the classroom is increasing. This area of research considers both the effects of collaborative literacy practices in the classroom and the effects of technology on the interaction patterns and relationships between teachers and students.

A long-standing concern about the use of the computer as a tool for learning involves the fear that learners will work in solitude without human interaction. However, research suggests that the use of computers fosters higher levels of interaction and collaboration, particularly in the domain of writing. For example, a study of the writing program in a first–second grade classroom showed that collaborative work at the computer created a new social organization that affected interaction patterns (Dickinson, 1986). During normal individual writing assignments students rarely spoke to each other; however, during collaborative computer writing, students spoke to each other about plans, revisions, and issues of meaning and style.

Other studies have found that the variety and complexity of language use increased during collaborative writing projects on the computer. For example, Gonzalez-Edfelt's (1990) study of limited English speakers discovered that the quantity and quality of oral discourse increased during collaborative computer activities. Still other studies indicate that collaborative work with computers improves the error monitoring of learning-disabled students (e.g., Hine, Goldman, & Cosden, 1990).

Despite concerns to the contrary, research suggests that computer use has either enhanced or left unchanged the frequency and/or quality of teacher–student interactions. It appears that teacher–student writing conferences involve more sophisticated interactions when a word processor is used, which may explain the enhanced writing of the word-processed compositions. Other studies have reported that the teacher's role and pattern of interaction with students undergo little change with the infusion of computers into their literacy practices once word-processing methods, programs, and instruction are introduced (Kamil & Intrator, 2000).

Most studies point to positive developments in the patterns of social interaction around writing with computers. However, several studies have highlighted ways in which collaborative work in technology environments occasionally results in interactions that do not approximate what is normally considered literate discourse (Kremers, 1990; Miller, 1993; Miller, & Olson, 1995).

*Motivation.*    The most consistently found effect of the impact of computer use on classrooms is an increase in motivation and closely related constructs such as interest and enjoyment of schoolwork, task involvement, persistence time on task, and retention in school. Lepper and his research group have conducted the most complete series of investigations into the impact of computers on motivation (Lepper & Chabay, 1985; Lepper & Malone, 1987). They concluded that computer-based educational activities can increase factors associated with the intrinsic motivation of students to the extent that they increase the opportunities to customize one's work and increase the control, curiosity, and challenge of the task. Specifically related to literacy development, computer use by children can increase their involvement in and enjoyment of writing and reading, thereby improving the quality of what they produce. For example, studies that compared word-processing revision versus handwritten revision commonly found that students were more highly motivated to revise, which led to more time spent on the revision process. Similarly, Daiute (1983) observed that children persisted on tasks longer when using word processing, which they found more fun than hand revision because it dispensed with recopying their writings.

Studies that have explored the motivational effects of technology environments on special populations of literacy learners suggest that context-specific learning activities will enhance learner motivation. For example, Scott, Kahlich, and Barker (1994) found that the rich context of a technology environment can provide the incentive required to invite at-risk students into literacy experiences, encouraging these students to persist at reading and writing by evoking self-interest and self-motivation.

Several studies have highlighted how heightened motivation in a technological environment can increase the sense of efficacy of students diagnosed with learning disabilities. For example, Cutler and Truss (1989) found that a program designed to immediately provide definitions for unknown words helped to increase reading rates and actively engaged junior high school remedial reading students in reading novels. Another study found that learners with writing and spelling difficulties who used word-processing and spell-checking programs were motivated to become more independent writers (Elkins, 1986).

## Assessing Instructional Resources

The idea that instructional resources might exert an independent influence on students' ability to read and write is not a new one. In this section we review some older tools and techniques and present some newer alternatives for assessing different instructional resources. The purpose for evaluating instructional resources in the assessment-instruction process is actually twofold: (1) to predict the likely impact of instructional factors on performance, that is, to assess the contributions of these factors to reading and writing ability, and (2) to gain insight regarding appropriate instructional materials, that is, to match the failing reader and writer with materials that result in effective teaching and efficient learning.

## Evaluating Text and Commercial Materials

Teachers have always been concerned about the materials their students read. They have generally recognized that "to teach reading effectively or to help students gain information from text requires a match between the difficulty of the reading material and the reading ability of the child" (Zakaluk & Samuels, 1988, p. 122). Unfortunately, achieving this match is not as easy as it sounds.

We have already described the many factors that can influence how difficult a particular text is for a particular individual, the complexity of which was recognized at least fifty years ago: "In its broadest sense, readability is the sum total—including interactions—of all those elements within a given piece of printed material that affect the success a group of readers have with it" (Dale & Chall, 1948, p. 15). The earliest discussions of "readability" assumed that factors such as the physical appearance and format of the print, the style of written expression, language usage, and the content of the text affected the difficulty of the text (Gray & Leary, 1935). In the intervening years researchers have demonstrated what teachers have long known: that interest, motivation, and prior knowledge also determine how readable a text will be.

Despite the early recognition that determining text difficulty was extremely complex, the tools used to measure readability have generally captured only limited aspects of text difficulty. No serious analysis of the forms and functions of narrative and expository text occurred until quite recently. Prompted by the desire to generate fast and efficient estimates of text difficulty, there has been a proliferation of "readability formulas." We are going to digress somewhat and present a fairly detailed discussion of them because these formulas still dominate the area of text assessment. We will then turn our attention to a variety of contemporary alternatives.

***Readability Formulas.***  Readability formulas are procedures that have been developed to assess difficulty objectively, generally by counting some text feature that can be easily identified. According to Klare (1988), Lively and Pressey developed the first readability formula in 1923. Since that time, over fifty readability formulas have been developed (Schuyler, 1982). To understand the appropriate use and potential misuse of readability formulas, it is important to understand something about their development and notable features.

*How Readability Formulas Are Developed.*  General procedures used in development are quite similar for all readability formulas (see Conrad, 1984, for a complete discussion). Readability formulas are derived from detailed analyses of a small set of passages, called *criterion passages.* The selection and validation of the original criterion passages make up a critical first step, since the difficulty of all other passages will be determined by comparison with these criterion passages and tasks. If the texts and tasks are not similar to those used by teachers or read by students, then the predictive power of the formula will be weak. Most of the existing readability formulas were validated by using extremely short criterion passages.

After the criterion passages are selected, they are examined for text elements that are likely to contribute to passage difficulty. Once the possible text elements have been identified and quantified, analyses are conducted to determine which are the best predictors of passage difficulty. Finally, a mathematical formula is generated that provides the best description of the relationship between text elements and text difficulty.

Even the earliest readability researchers assumed that critical elements would include text features such as conceptual density and quality of writing. However, these abstract factors proved difficult to measure and were often either not selected for study or dropped because they could not be counted reliably. The two elements that have proved to be the best predictors of text difficulty (at least using short criterion passages) are semantic difficulty and syntactic complexity of the sentences (Klare, 1984). Semantic difficulty is most often estimated using vocabulary, as measured by either frequency/familiarity or length of words; syntactic complexity is most often measured by sentence length.

Because different formulas have been developed using different criterion passages and different tasks, caution is needed in using any of the existing formulas. For example, the Spache Formula was developed so that it is appropriate only for primary grade passages, while the Dale-Chall is applicable only to materials above the fourth grade level. In addition, only some formulas examine elements that have theoretical or empirical support from current views of the reading process, and no formula provides a totally satisfactory assessment.

*How Readability Formulas Are Used.*    The greatest strength of readability formulas lies in their ease of use. But they must be used cautiously. One of the easiest and most frequently used formulas today is the Fry Formula (Fry, 1968). It assesses syntactic and semantic difficulty using only counts of syllables and sentence length (see Figure 6.4). Although this obviously provides a limited view of readability, at least the formula was developed using trade books and other real reading material.

The use of rich criterion passages makes readability formulas fairly reliable when used to rank real, noncontrived texts to be read by a general population (Klare, 1984). If materials are grossly unsuitable for use in a targeted grade, readability formulas can reveal this fact in a time-saving manner so that decisions about text appropriateness may be made more rapidly. However, as the Commission on Reading (R. C. Anderson et al., 1985) notes, "readability formulas are useful only as a rough check on the difficulty and appropriateness of books" (p. 81).

Studies suggest that interformula reliability is a cause for concern (McConnell, 1982) especially in the upper ranges of the readability estimates (high school and college level texts). Differences of two or more grade levels in the estimates generated are not unusual when several formulas are applied to the same piece of text. For placement purposes, the use of readability estimates alone clearly poses serious problems. When gross comparisons are needed, however, readability estimates can be helpful. If you are going to use these formulas, the tedium of analyzing text can be avoided by using one of the available computer software programs available (Schuyler, 1982).

**FIGURE 6.4**
Fry Readability
Formula

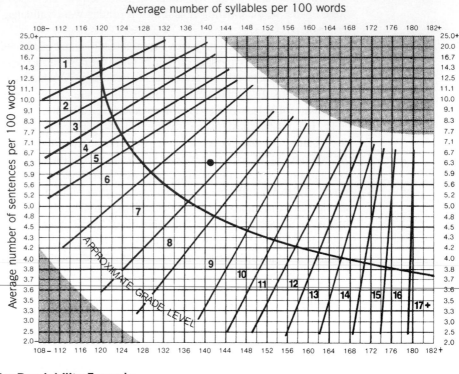

### Fry Readability Formula

(Description):
1. Select three 100-word selections from the beginning, middle, and end of the text. Don't count proper nouns.
2. Count the number of sentences in each selection. Estimate to the nearest tenth of a sentence.
3. Average sentence count.
4. Count the number of syllabes in each selection.
5. Average the syllable count.
6. Plot the two scores on the graph to get the grade level.

*Source:* From "A Readability Formula That Saves Time" by Edward Fry (1968, April). *Journal of Reading, 11*(7), 513. Copyright © International Reading Association. Reprinted with permission. All rights reserved.

*Criticisms and Misuses of Readability Formulas.*   Although formulas have proved quick and efficient, there are many concerns associated with them. Some of these have to do with the formulas themselves; others have to do with their use. As Cullinan and Fitzgerald (1984) note, it is not what is measured by formulas that causes concern; rather, it is what is *not* measured. Among the many factors that have been shown to influence text difficulty but that are not accounted for by typical formulas are text structure, interest, motivation, and prior knowledge (Entin & Klare, 1985; Fass & Schumacher, 1978). In combination, these factors may critically influence the relative difficulty of a selection. A text that may be difficult for one reader may be relatively easy for another of the same reading skill (see Alexander & Jetton, 2000; Goldman & Rakestraw, 2000).

One of the most serious concerns about readability formulas involves their misuse in rewriting existing materials, a practice that early formula developers promoted (Dale & Chall, 1948; Flesch, 1948). There has been an understandable temptation to revise text to make it easier and more accessible to readers. However, the indiscriminate use of readability indicators, such as sentence length, to rewrite text has often had the unexpected result of making text more, rather than less, difficult (Davison, 1984; Davison & Kantor, 1982).

Text "simplifications" based on readability formulas can and do lead to incoherence and increased text difficulty (Goldman & Rakestraw, 2000). In addition, such materials place a heavy burden on readers' prior knowledge because the text provides fewer clues for constructing meaning. Indeed, it may actually be necessary to lengthen text through elaboration, paraphrase, and example to enhance readability when topics are complex or less familiar.

The benefits gained from using readability formulas need to be measured carefully against the potential dangers of their use. The joint IRA/NCTE statement (see Figure 6.5) provides guidance in the appropriate use of readability formulas. These formulas should not be used to rewrite or write reading materials, and teachers should be cautious of texts that have been so produced. In addition, users need to be particularly alert to possible mismatches between the reader and the text; readers from nontraditional backgrounds may be influenced by factors that are not measured in the formula.

Finally, it is a good idea to remember that the purpose of these formulas is to *predict* the difficulty of materials. Formulas do not actually evaluate the relative difficulty that any individual reader experiences during reading of a particular text. As "tests" of reading materials (Chall, 1984), formulas fall short of providing comprehensive answers to our questions about text quality and appropriateness. We need other ways to evaluate these issues, and we consider alternatives in the next section.

***Evaluating Text Type and Comprehensibility.***   It should be quite clear by now that readability estimates alone are unlikely to provide all the information teachers need about the difficulty and appropriateness of textual materials for their students. First, not all text types pose the same difficulties; nor are all equally easy to read, even if the readability formula suggests otherwise. Second, the factors that are not accounted for by readability formulas require attention. In this section we suggest some strategies for evaluating narratives and expository texts to determine whether they are "comprehensible" or "understandable" versus "readable."

*Narrative Text.*   Two major issues must be addressed in evaluating narratives for comprehensibility. First, the text must be examined to determine whether it is well structured, conforming to conventional expectations for story structure and language use. Next, the narratives should be evaluated to find out whether they are interesting and enjoyable. The large class of narratives encompasses a wide range of genres, including realistic fiction, folktales, fables, fairy tales, myths, mystery, and science fiction (Buss & Karnowski, 2000).

**FIGURE 6.5** The IRA/NCTE Readability Statement

| Background Information Bulletin on the Use of Readability Formulae |
|---|

Textbook adoption committees and other educators face important decisions when deciding whether instructional materials are of appropriate difficulty for the students who will use them. Many factors enter into determining the readability of materials, including the syntactic complexity of sentences, density of concepts, abstractness of ideas, text organization, coherence and sequence of ideas, page format, length of type line, length of paragraphs, intricacy of punctuation, and the use of illustrations and color. In addition, research has shown that student interest in the subject-matter plays a significant role in determining the readability of materials.

Matching students with textbooks at appropriate levels of difficulty, therefore, is a complex and difficult task. Various pressures have forced publishers to use readability formulae to assure purchasers that their textbooks are properly "at grade level." Unfortunately, these formulae measure only average sentence and word length to determine the difficulty of passages. Although long words and sentences sometimes create problems of comprehension, they do not always do so. For example, the sentence "To be or not to be" is short, but it includes difficult concepts. This sentence, "The boy has a big, red apple for lunch and some cookies for a snack," is long but simple. Readability formulae would allow the first sentence but not the second.

Serious problems occur when publishers use readability formulae. Authors of materials who are required to write to "fit the formula" often produce choppy sentences full of short words. The language doesn't sound natural to the student, who is a sophisticated speaker and whose own language may be full of complex sentences and multisyllabic words. A second problem is that complex ideas, which depend on complex sentences, cannot be adequately written in the prose style dictated by readabiliy fomulae; consequently, learning of the content may be impaired.

Third, there is a real danger that makers of instructional materials will avoid using interesting and important works of literature because those works, which often contain long words and long sentences, don't "fit the formula." Not only the student's interest but also the beginnings of the student's literacy education are lost by such omissions.

Educators and publishers should use alternative approaches for measuring text difficulty. Procedures should include:

1. Teacher evaluation of proposed texts, based on teachers' knowledge of their students' prior information and experiences, and their reading ability and interests.
2. Teacher observations of students using proposed texts in instructional settings, in order to evaluate the effectiveness of the material.
3. Checklists for evaluating the readability of the proposed materials, involving attention to such variables as student interests, text graphics, the number and difficulty of ideas and concepts in the material, the length of lines in the text, and the many other factors which contribute to relative difficulty of text material.

If readability formulae are used at all, they MUST be used in conjunction with procedures that look at all the parts of a text which affect comprehension. Readability formulae are simply insufficient as a guide to matching students with books and other instructional material. It is not what readability formulae measure that concerns us; it is what they do NOT measure.

Informed educational consumers must demand that authors and publishers select and develop well-written, literate text materials for students, and all who are involved in preparing and selecting text materials for the schools should cease the practice of depending on readability formulae alone to determine what is readable.

*Source:* The IRA/NCTE Readability Statement (Bernice Cullinan and Shelia Fitzgerald, 1984). *The Reading Teacher.* Copyright © International

However, all narratives have something in common, and that must be captured in an evaluation of them: They are meant to be interesting and enjoyable.

When the characters and their relationships are well developed and their goals easily identifiable, children read with greater interest and understanding (Lipson, Mosenthal, & Mekkelsen, 1999; Sundbye, 1987). Because well-formed narratives are easier to read than more ambiguous ones, they should be evaluated for the common components of narrative texts (see also Chapter 8). The following set of questions adapted from Calfee (1987) might help to highlight these important, but more difficult to analyze, aspects of text:

- How does the story begin (setting, time)? How powerful, weak, or dull is the lead, or beginning of the story?
- Who are the main characters? Who is telling the story (point of view)? How much do we learn about the characters?
- What is/are the main problems or conflicts to be solved or resolved? Is the conflict interpersonal, with the environment, or internal to the character?
- How does the content of the story/plot teach a lesson or help readers learn about people, reasoning, problem solving, and so on?
- How does the story end (resolution)? Is the ending satisfying, interesting, and/or powerful?

In particular, the evaluation should identify the degree to which narratives have strong plots with well-defined characters whose motives and goals are clear. When these aspects of a narrative are obscure, poor readers have much more difficulty comprehending them.

*Expository Text.* As it has become clear how strongly text features can influence text difficulty, a number of guidelines for evaluating informational texts have been generated. One of the most comprehensive of these was offered by Irwin and Davis (1980) and is reproduced in Figure 6.6. An especially helpful feature of this checklist is that several dimensions of text difficulty are distinguished and evaluated separately. For example, learnability and understandability are evaluated separately. Consequently, teachers can evaluate the strengths and weaknesses of texts on the basis of the ways they wish to use them.

Expository text can be evaluated for understandability alone. However, when students are to be held accountable for learning and remembering information from textbooks, teachers need to evaluate texts somewhat differently. If students are having trouble learning information from text, an assessment of the textbook features may provide useful information about how to help them learn and remember more. Alternatively, an assessment may reveal the fact that the text obscures important or new information, making learning difficult.

A helpful procedure is described by Armbruster (1984), who suggests selecting a topic from the text and generating several questions that you would expect students to be able to answer after reading about such a topic. Then read the text and make sure that it is possible to answer these questions using *only* the textual information. When the text does not provide the information or makes it difficult to understand, teachers must be prepared to compensate for the text's inadequacies or elect not to use the text at all.

**FIGURE 6.6**
Readability
Checklist

This checklist is designed to help you evaluate the readability of your classroom texts. It can best be used if you rate your text while you are thinking of a specific class. Be sure to compare the textbook to a fictional idea rather than to another text. Your goal is to find out what aspects of the text are less than ideal. Finally, consider supplementary workbooks as part of the textbook and rate them together. Have fun!

Rate the questions below using the following rating system.

- 5 = Excellent
- 4 = Good
- 3 = Adequate
- 2 = Poor
- 1 = Unacceptable
- NA = Not applicable

Further comments may be written in the space provided.

Textbook title:
Publisher:
Copyright:

**Understandability**

A. _____ Are the assumptions about students' vocabulty knowledge appropriate?

B. _____ Are the assumptions about students' prior knowledge of this content area appropriate?

C. _____ Are the assumptions about students' general experiential backgrounds appropriate?

D. _____ Does the teacher's manual provide the teacher with ways to develop and review the students' conceptual and experiential background?

E. _____ Are new concepts explicitly linked to the students' prior knowledge or to their experiential backgrounds?

F. _____ Does the text introduce abstract concepts by accompanying them with many concrete examples?

G. _____ Does the text introduce new concepts one at a time with a sufficient number of examples for each one?

H. _____ Are definitions understandable and at a lower level of abstraction than the concept being defined?

I. _____ Is the level of sentence complexity appropriate for the students?

J. _____ Are the main ideas of paragraphs, chapters, and subsections clearly stated?

K. _____ Does the text avoid irrelevant details?

L. _____ Does the text explicitly state important complex relationships (e.g. causality, conditionality, etc.) rather than always expecting the reader to infer them from the context?

M. _____ Does the teacher's manual provide lists of accessible resources containing alternative readings for the very poor or very advanced readers?

N. _____ Is the readability level appropriate (according to a readability formula)?

**Learnability**
*Organization*

A. _____ Is an introduction provided for each chapter?

B. _____ Is there a clear and simple organization pattern relating the chapters to each other?

C. _____ Does each chapter have a clear, explicit, and simple organizational structure?

D. _____ Does the text include resources such as an index, glossary, and table of contents?

E. _____ Do questions and activities draw attention to the organizational pattern of the material (e.g., chronological, cause and effect, spatial, topical, etc.)?

**FIGURE 6.6**
(Continued)

F. _____ Do consumable materials interrelate well with the textbook?

*Reinforcement*

A. _____ Does the text provide opportunities for students to practice using new concepts?

B. _____ Are there summaries at appropriate intervals in the text?

C. _____ Does the text provide adequate iconic aids such as maps, graphs, illustrations, etc. to reinforce concepts?

D. _____ Are there adequate suggestions for usable supplementary activities?

E. _____ Do these activities provide for a broad range of ability levels?

F. _____ Are there literal questions provided for the students' self-review?

G. _____ Do some of the questions encourage the students to draw inferences?

H. _____ Are thee discussion questions which encourage creative thinking?

I. _____ Are questions clearly worded?

*Motivation*

A. _____ Does the teacher's manual provide introductory activities that will capture students' interests?

B. _____ Are chapter titles and subheadings concrete, meaningful, or interesting?

C. _____ Is the writing style of the text appealing to the students?

D. _____ Are the activities motivating? Will they make the student want to pursue the topic further?

E. _____ Does the book clearly show how the knowledge being learned might be used by the learner in the future?

F. _____ Does the text provide positive and motivating models for both sexes as well as for various racial, ethnic, and socioeconomic groups?

**Readability Analysis**

*Weaknesses*

1. On which items was the book rated lowest?
2. Did these items tend to fall in certain categories?
3. Summarize the weaknesses of this text.
4. What can you do in class to compensate for the weaknesses of this text?

*Assets*

1. On which items was the book rated the highest?
2. Did these items fall in certain categories?
3. Summarize the assets of this text.
4. What can you do in class to take advantage of the assets of this text?

*Source:* Chart from Irwin, Judith Westphal, & Davis, Carol A. (1980, November). Assessing readability: The checklist approach. *Journal of Reading, 24*(2), pp. 124–130. Reprinted with permission of the International Reading Association.

Careful examination of the text is absolutely essential. Checklists like the one in Figure 6.6 can provide important guidance for evaluating texts with specific student populations in mind. A text that is appropriate for some students might not be appropriate for others. Some texts will be used as supplements, while others will be used by all students as the primary source of information about a discipline. The readability checklist permits a consideration of different responses given different purposes and different students.

***Evaluating Anthologies and Sets of Books.***   Collections of stories, informational selections, poetry, and drama within a single volume or in a series of "little books" often provide students with the core of the material they will use in reading instruction. These anthologies and/or sets of books are often part of a larger set of instructional materials, but not always. For some students these anthologies and/or sets of books provide the only reading material they encounter, and the quality of their reading experience is determined by the content of these reading materials. For these reasons, such materials require careful evaluation.

Osborn (1989) suggests examining collections of reading selections for both the content and the appearance of the material. Others suggest examining the content for the types of thematic organization (Searfoss & Readence, 1989). Still others suggest evaluating the quality of the message, or the "ethos" content (Schmidt, Caul, Byers, & Buchman, 1984). Of course, we also need to be sure that the content is a reasonable fit with the goals and expectations of the school and its programs. In evaluating student anthologies and/or sets of books, Fountas and Pinnell (1996) suggest that the following features should be considered:

- Enjoyment, meaning, and interest to students;
- Accuracy and diversity in multicultural representation;
- Breadth and balance of type or genre;
- Depth in the number of titles or selections at each level of difficulty;
- Links across the collection of titles or selections (common characters, authors, settings, themes);
- The quality of the illustrations and their relations to the text;
- Content;
- Length; and
- Format.

Anthologies and/or sets of books are, of course, only as good as the selections that are included. So within these guidelines, we need to consider the qualities and characteristics of the narrative and expository selections themselves (see the sections on narrative and expository text). If students read *only* from an anthology or a particular set of books, the impact of exposure and practice must be carefully considered. For example, some children may have difficulty learning to read exposition because their materials provide limited experience with this type of text.

***Leveling Texts.***   It is also important to consider the relative difficulty of the selections that students are reading. Since so many struggling readers are placed in inappropriate, frustration-level materials, the assessment process should consider whether the books used by students are at an appropriate level of difficulty. In addition, the assessment process should consider whether students have been making appropriate progress in applying their knowledge and skill in increasingly difficult texts. There are any number of systems for "leveling" texts; the most commonly used were developed for Reading Recovery and subsequently applied to other texts and extended by Fountas and Pinnell (1996, 2001a, 2001b). They provide guidelines for creating what they call a *text gradient* that can be used to classify selections "along a continuum based on the combination of variables that support and confirm readers' strategic actions and offer the problem-solving opportunities that build the reading process" (1996, p. 113).

This process can be used both to create a leveled set of materials and to evaluate existing sets of materials. In establishing a text gradient, the following factors should be considered:

- Length;
- Size and layout of print;
- Vocabulary and concepts;
- Language structure;
- Text structure and genre;
- Predictability and pattern of language; and
- Illustration support.

A more in-depth discussion of some of these factors is provided in the next section, which focuses specifically on sets of books for beginning readers.

Even for readers who are beyond the initial stages of reading, however, leveled books may serve an important function in helping teachers to evaluate their instructional materials and make more refined judgments about their selection of instructional texts. In addition, when both classroom teachers and support personnel in school settings adopt a common framework for evaluating text difficulty, it improves communication across multiple contexts, and professionals are more likely to work together to plan for individual students (see Chapter 12).

It is beyond the scope of this text to provide an extensive discussion of the criteria used by Fountas and Pinnell and others. However, we have found it useful to refer to a set of "anchor" texts: lists of highly familiar and widely used books that have been leveled by using one or another system. For example, teachers who use the Pinnell and Fountas (2001) system would designate Brian Wildsmith's *The Cat on the Mat* at the very beginning level of first grade (Level B) and Frank Asch's *Just Like Daddy* at a level targeted for late first grade (Level F).

Similarly, books like *Leo the Late Bloomer* by Robert Kraus would provide an anchor for early grade 2 (Level I), while the *Cam Jensen* books by David Alder or James Marshall's *George and Martha* stories could help define reading performance at the end of that grade (Level L).

During grade 3, normally developing students would read books like *Freckle Juice* by Judy Blume (Level M) early in the year and *Ramona Quimby, Age 8* by Beverly Clearly (Level O) by the year's close.

Teachers using these anchors can begin to internalize a system for evaluating increasingly difficult texts since there is evidence that these text-leveling systems are quite accurate (Hoffman et al., 2000). It is more important that everyone using a text-leveling system agree on where to place the books than that everyone really like every decision. Educators should agree to use the commonly established levels for each text. In that way, when anyone refers to a particular level, everyone can agree about what texts would be read by students who had reached that level of proficiency. The Pinnell and Fountas (2001) system provides benchmarks for text-leveling right through the middle grades.

FIGURE 6.7
Dimensions of
Difficulty in Early
Reading Materials

**Number of total and unique words**

☐ Large number of unique words/100 running words
☐ Moderate number of unique words/100
☐ Few unique words/100

| Proportion of unique words that are: | | **1**<br>Low | **3**<br>Medium | **5**<br>High |
|---|---|---|---|---|
| Phonetically regular | | | | → |
| Multisyllabic | | | | → |
| Highly frequent | | | | → |

| Predictability | **None** | **1**<br>Small | **3**<br>Sizable | **5**<br>Large |
|---|---|---|---|---|
| Size of predictable unit | | | | → |

☐ Small (3–5 words)
☐ Sizable (6–10 words)
☐ Large (11–15) or more words

| Contextual Support | **None** | **1**<br>Weak | **3**<br>Moderate | **5**<br>Strong |
|---|---|---|---|---|
| (for recognizing words) | | | | |
| Picture support | | | | → |
| Content familiarity | | | | → |

| Engagingness | | **1**<br>Low | **3**<br>Medium | **5**<br>High |
|---|---|---|---|---|
| Design (illustrations, format) | | | | → |
| Content (familiarty, complexity) | | | | → |

*Source:* Adapted from Hiebert, E. H. & Raphael, T. E. (1998). *Early literacy instruction.* Fort Worth: Harcourt Brace, and Hiebert, E. H. & Martin, L. (2001). The texts of beginning reading instruction. In S. Neumann & D. K. Dickinson (Eds.), *Handbook of early literacy research* (pp. 361–376). New York: Guilford.

***Evaluating Beginning Reading Books.***    Evaluating the match between beginning reading books and the strengths and weaknesses of struggling readers is a task that has challenged educators for generations. Hiebert and Raphael (1998) identify five features of early reading materials that influence beginning readers' access to the text: (1) predictability, (2) contextual support, (3) word density, (4) proportion of decodable words, and (5) proportion of core high-frequency words. Figure 6.7 provides a checklist for evaluating beginning reading books in terms of these five features.

Books in which a phrase or sentence is repeated throughout the text are known as *predictable.* Beginning readers are usually able to recognize the repeated phrase or sentence after several readings of a predictable book with a more skilled reader. Although the concept is simple, the ways of making texts predictable are numerous and complicated. Both the size of the repeated unit and the proportion of the text accounted for by the repeated unit appear to influence children's reading acquisition with predictable texts (Hiebert & Raphael, 1998). The number of words repeated in a book constitute the unit size, and it is likely that larger sets of words are more difficult to remember than are shorter ones. Similarly, the larger the proportion of the text devoted to the predictable unit, the more likely it is that students will read along or attempt to read the book independently.

Contextual support refers to both the familiarity of concepts and the extent to which the illustrations are useful in identifying key words. The content of books for beginning readers varies from a focus on familiar objects and actions such as riding a bicycle to objects and actions that are much less familiar such as caring for exotic animals. Children's familiarity with a topic is clearly related to their abilities to decode unknown words related to the topic. Books in which illustrations support the identification of key words are also likely to be more accessible than those with illustrations unrelated to key words. Familiar concepts and supportive illustrations allow beginning readers to use what they already know about the world in combination with their emerging understanding of letter–sound correspondences to identify words.

According to Hiebert and Raphael (1998), children's success with an entire text depends on the number of words they find to be unique and their need to draw on word recognition strategies. Every time beginning readers encounter a new word in a book, they need to draw on their emerging repertoire of word recognition strategies. If there are many new words in a book, they may struggle and rely heavily on their ability to use contextual supports or on text predictability.

When at least some of the new words in a book contain common word patterns, or rimes, children have the opportunity to apply their emerging knowledge of letter–sound correspondences. However, selecting books that have some distinct words with common word patterns is quite different from selecting books in which words have almost perfect letter–sound relationships, such as *The Fat Cat*. Although consistency in the patterns of words in books read by beginning readers can be helpful, these types of materials will not help children generalize their knowledge of word patterns or develop an understanding of the variability of written English. Again, it is a matter of balance and of meeting the needs of particular students.

High-frequency words can be expected to occur often in text for beginning readers. Because the abstractness of these words makes learning to automatically recognize them difficult, a high level of these words can make a text too challenging. However, a steady diet of books that have too few high-frequency words makes it difficult for beginning readers to gain fluency with a core group of words.

The books that are currently available for beginning readers vary considerably in both the presence and the progression of the features that are known to influence the accessibility of a text. The checklist in Figure 6.7 provides a means for attending to these features. It is important to remember that there is no such thing as the perfect set or sequence of books. Rather, books should be chosen in relation to the strengths and weaknesses of particular readers and for use in introducing particular strategies.

***Evaluating Basal Lesson Design.*** In most commercial reading and language arts programs, the content, method, and tasks are dictated by the instructional framework used to teach the reading selections. As we have noted, this framework is divided roughly into prereading, reading, and postreading activities. It is especially important for teachers to evaluate the lesson frameworks and the content of commercially prepared lessons because these materials have been shown to have a powerful influence on classroom reading instruction.

Previously in this chapter we described the issues surrounding basal reading materials. Guidelines for evaluating basal lesson plans developed from a variety of critical reviews are provided in Figure 6.8. A program that does not meet most of these criteria is suspect, and its utility in promoting independent, motivated reading is doubtful. The use of these procedures can be time consuming. As Wixson and Peters (1989) point out, however, "over time, these procedures are likely to become more a 'mind set' than a series of discrete steps" (p. 60). In any event the degree to which detailed evaluations suggest the need for extensive modification provides one estimate of the quality of the commercial plans.

## Evaluating Tutoring Programs

Although research suggests that tutoring programs are generally effective, their impact on individual students is likely to vary dramatically. In a review of volunteer tutoring programs in reading, Wasik (1998) identified four factors that contributed to their effectiveness. These four factors provide the basis for the following set of questions, which can be used to evaluate reading and writing tutoring programs.

1. What are the knowledge and skill level of the designated coordinator of the language arts tutoring program?
2. How are the tutoring lessons structured and what is the quality of instruction?
3. What are the amount and quality of the training provided to tutors?
4. How is the tutoring program coordinated with classroom instruction?

Research reviewed by Wasik (1998) indicates that the effectiveness of language arts tutoring programs depends on a knowledgeable person to provide a basic understanding of the reading and writing processes to tutors and also to give them feedback on their tutoring sessions. Successful tutoring programs are also characterized by structure in the tutoring sessions and high-quality instruction. Among the successful tutoring programs reviewed by Wasik (1998), the following elements were apparent in the structure of the lessons:

- Reading of new materials by the student;
- Reading books in which either the words or the entire story were familiar to the student;
- An activity that emphasized word analysis and letter–sound relationships; and
- A writing activity that emphasized composing.

Students were less successful in tutoring sessions in which the tutor did most of the reading and writing activities than in those in which the student was a more active participant (Juel, 1996). Although these types of sessions were the most effective, others that provided "tutor-proof" materials have also shown positive effects.

**FIGURE 6.8**
Evaluating Basal
Lesson Plans

| Portion of the Lesson | Yes | No | Some |
|---|---|---|---|
| **Prereading** | | | |
| Evidence of process, content, attitude goals? | | | |
| Does instruction inform students about the type of text they are asked to read, its properties, the purposes for which it might be read, and the strategies for reading it? | | | |
| Are students encouraged to tap their own experiences, interests, and background knowledge? | | | |
| Are there provisions for individual differences? | | | |
| Are there suggestions for different grouping or reading options? | | | |
| | | | |
| **During Reading** | | | |
| Are there different levels of support for students? | | | |
| Do activities and questions help students achieve content, process, and attitude goals? | | | |
| Do instructional activities encourage students to become actively engaged in reading and to take responsibility for their reading? | | | |
| Is strategic reading modeled throughout? | | | |
| Are there suggestions for assessment during reading? | | | |
| Are students encouraged to engage in self-evaluation? | | | |
| Is the focus on teaching students how to comprehend or merely on checking whether a student has comprehended? | | | |
| | | | |
| **Postreading** | | | |
| Does the text ask students for personal response to the literature? | | | |
| Do questions focus on major text concepts and elements? | | | |
| Do activities and questions focus on theme concepts? | | | |
| Are students asked to make intertextual connections (to think about this text in terms of previously read material)? | | | |
| Does skill instruction clearly relate to the literature? | | | |
| Are reading and writing connections made visible? | | | |
| Is there an integrated model of reading and language arts? | | | |
| | | | |
| **Assessment** | | | |
| Are there multiple types of assessment provided? | | | |
| Is assessment clearly linked to the instruction provided? | | | |
| Does assessment promote an appropriate view of reading and writing? | | | |
| Are students, as well as teachers, involved in assessment? | | | |

Tutor training seems most needed for programs in which there is an emphasis on having the student actively involved in higher-level reading and writing activities and on the use of informed judgment on the part of the tutor. Programs that emphasize basic skills using "tutor-proof" materials require less training time. In addition to understanding the importance of training, it is necessary to know the specific techniques that the volunteers should be trained to use. Research suggests that the use of scaffolding and explicit modeling of reading and writing are effective strategies for tutors (Juel, 1996).

Finally, it appears that coordination between the tutoring programs and classroom experiences would benefit the child. This is most likely to be so if both experiences are of high quality. However, one must also consider the effect of any inconsistency between the instruction in these two settings. A lack of coordination might also affect a student's ability to keep pace in the classroom, although this must be weighed against individual students' needs to proceed at a slower pace.

In general, successful tutoring programs ensure adequate time on task for students, high quality of instruction, and appropriateness of curriculum (Shanahan, 1998). The ability of a tutoring program to deliver on these key elements is often a function of the knowledge and skill of the program coordinator and/or tutor. Examinations of the role of a tutoring program in a given student's reading and writing performance should emphasize these factors.

## Evaluating Computer Software and Web-Based Resources

Computer technology is used as a tool both for running site-based software programs and for exploring web-based resources. Site-based software runs on a computer that is networked to a computer server or installed directly on an individual computer within the classroom setting. Web-based resources are the innumerable web sites available throughout the World Wide Web. Regardless of the origin of a software program or a web site, the initial question to be asked in evaluating these materials should always be "How closely does the material match the philosophical and pedagogical frameworks of the larger reading and writing program?" In this section we provide guidelines for assessing the pedagogical and technical aspects of these instructional resources.

***Pedagogical Considerations.***   According to Ertmer, Gopalakrishnan, and Ross (2001), pedagogical beliefs and classroom practices strongly affect the way in which computer technology is integrated within the learning environment. It is important to understand the philosophical stances, purposes, and intended outcomes in a particular instructional environment (see Chapter 5) to evaluate the use of software programs and web-based resources in that context. In addition to being consistent with instructional reading and language arts objectives, pedagogically sound software should do the following:

- Provide for content modification by students or teachers;
- Include provisions for transfer from computer to off-screen reading situations; and
- Feature the unique capabilities of the medium rather than duplicate features of print media (Michigan Reading Association, 1993, p. 16).

Software programs and web-based resources should also be consistent with current research on reading and writing processes. As such, these programs and resources should have the following features:

- Include complete pieces of narrative or expository text;
- Present meaningful and useful information;
- Provide well-organized and logically developed materials;
- Engage readers and writers in active participation;
- Allow time for reflection and responses;
- Emphasize thinking rather than repetitive practice;
- Provide skills practice in real content with real purpose,
- Allow for rereading and/or editing;
- Take advantage of relationships between reading and writing; and
- Be free of bias regarding race, sex, age, handicaps, and ethics (Michigan Reading Association, 1993, p. 16).

These guidelines provide a basis for evaluating the quality of computer materials. The educational issues surrounding the use of computer technology should be paramount in evaluating computer materials.

***Software Considerations.*** A variety of software and web-based resources are used to promote reading and writing, including those that are developed specifically for this purpose as well as those that are aimed at specific subject-matter instruction. The best programs encourage the exploration and construction of knowledge, the communication of ideas (such as collaboration, information access, and self-expression), the development of metacognitive strategies, and the performance of real-life applications (Grabe & Grabe, 1986). Software programs that most effectively promote the manipulation of textual elements as ideas are examined, including word processors, conceptual mapping tools, desktop publishers, and presentation tools. To support a deeper exploration and richer representation of ideas requires software that allows students to add sounds, voice recordings, pictures, and video clips to their texts. These cognitive-based software programs encourage students to manipulate text, explore ideas, and produce evidence of their thinking that can be shared with others.

Software programs and web sites that assist students in accessing and interpreting data include databases and Internet search engines. Databases are organized computerized collections of information. Internet search engines are large databases. These collections can be searched and sorted rapidly and explored in different ways. Being able to access data effectively and efficiently to retrieve appropriate information on the Internet is a necessary skill in today's society. The inclusion of databases in reading and writing programs, however, involves more than developing the skills needed to gain access to information retrieved through Internet search engines. Thoughtful examination of the content in databases allows students to develop their abilities to identify key words, associate facts, draw conclusions, summarize data, organize information, and evaluate the accuracy and adequacy of sources.

Software programs and web sites for practicing word- and story-level comprehension provide opportunities for practicing phonemic elements, building vocabulary knowledge, and developing comprehension. Storybooks on CD-ROM are probably the most widely known software in this category, especially for young children and remedial readers. These storybooks are presented in a multimedia format. The speech capability of CD-ROM books allows students to choose to hear entire stories or hear only words that appear unfamiliar. Students can interact with any or all of the objects on each "page" of the story. These interactions may lead to developing conceptual knowledge about the story, exploring vocabulary meanings, examining story elements and characters, practicing phonic elements, and extending the reader's knowledge beyond the scope of the story.

As with any software or web-based resource, decisions about appropriate use should be made cautiously. For example, some links in CD-ROM storybooks have little educational value. These links connect with information, sounds, or graphic movements for the sake of pure fun. Exploring all the links, especially in hypermedia and web-based resources, may sidetrack students, causing them to forget their purposes. Students can become overwhelmed with all of the choices available to them. It is also important to be cautious about overassigning value to some of these computer-based activities. For instance, just because children can click on unfamiliar words in the CD-ROM storybooks does not necessarily mean that these children will exhibit an increase in their ability to decode other unfamiliar words (Leu, 2000). As with any instructional material, appropriate strategic behaviors need to be modeled and scaffolds need to be provided for students' ongoing uses of the technology by helping them to set purposes, understand outcomes, and intentionally use metacognitive strategies (Labbo, 2000).

***Technical Considerations.***  It is difficult to assess important aspects of software and web-based resources through program descriptions alone. Substantive evaluation of these materials requires a firsthand examination of the programs and resources, giving a variety of correct and incorrect responses. In this way it is possible to analyze the feedback and support structures that are provided for the students. It may also be helpful to ask students for their opinions about content, delivery style, and perceived friendliness. Observing students' reactions and interactions with the material can also provide useful information.

Computer software, like all educational material, should be accurate and free of errors. However, there are other technical factors to consider that are specific to software programs and web resources. One of the most comprehensive sets of guidelines available in this area is offered by the Michigan Reading Association (1993). The sections having to do with general technical evaluation are reproduced in Figure 6.9.

Some software is designed for more specialized purposes and requires careful inspection using other guidelines. For example, Michigan Reading Association (1985) has provided guidelines for assessing word processing and simulation programs (see Figure 6.10). Similarly, Balajthy (1989) has proposed guidelines for evaluating software with voice synthesizer features. In evaluating the voice synthesis program, he advises considering the following:

1. Evaluate the overall quality of the sound that is produced.
2. Is there a playback feature so that students can listen a second time to words or sentences that they have not understood?
3. Do informal tryouts with your students suggest that the voice recognition is adequate for your purposes?

**FIGURE 6.9**
Guidelines for
Evaluating Reading
Software

| Documentation and Support Features | Poor | | Good | | |
|---|---|---|---|---|---|
| 1. Clearly written user's manual for program operation | 1 | 2 | 3 | 4 | 5 |
| 2. Teacher's supplement with appropriate classroom uses and teaching activities | 1 | 2 | 3 | 4 | 5 |
| 3. Pre-requisite abilities indicated | 1 | 2 | 3 | 4 | 5 |
| 4. Objectives stated | 1 | 2 | 3 | 4 | 5 |
| 5. Sample screens illustrated | 1 | 2 | 3 | 4 | 5 |
| 6. Textual material printed for reference | 1 | 2 | 3 | 4 | 5 |
| 7. Cue card for commands unique to program | 1 | 2 | 3 | 4 | 5 |
| 8. Useful and efficient record-keeping capabilities, if appropriate | 1 | 2 | 3 | 4 | 5 |
| 9. Records easily printed on screen or on paper | 1 | 2 | 3 | 4 | 5 |
| 10. Teacher can monitor and modify individual assignments | 1 | 2 | 3 | 4 | 5 |
| Overall assessment of documentation and support features | 1 | 2 | 3 | 4 | 5 |

Comments:

| Technical Qualities | Poor | | Good | | |
|---|---|---|---|---|---|
| 1. Approach unique to computer capabilities | 1 | 2 | 3 | 4 | 5 |
| 2. Varied program to maintain interest over subsequent uses | 1 | 2 | 3 | 4 | 5 |
| 3. Positive feedback | 1 | 2 | 3 | 4 | 5 |
| 4. Student can operate independently | 1 | 2 | 3 | 4 | 5 |
| 5. Two or more students can interact cooperatively, if desired | 1 | 2 | 3 | 4 | 5 |
| 6. Clear directions | 1 | 2 | 3 | 4 | 5 |
| 7. Help screens available, if needed | 1 | 2 | 3 | 4 | 5 |
| 8. Option to quit and to save progress at any time | 1 | 2 | 3 | 4 | 5 |
| 9. Appropriate type size and attractive screen formatting | 1 | 2 | 3 | 4 | 5 |
| 10. Option to bypass sound and graphics | 1 | 2 | 3 | 4 | 5 |
| Overall assessment of technical qualities | 1 | 2 | 3 | 4 | 5 |

Comments:

**Summary and Recommendation**
Reviewer:
Program strengths:

Program weaknesses:

Recommendations:

*Source:* "Guidelines for Evaluating Reading Software." Copyright © 1985, *The Michigan Reading Journal, 18* (4). Reprinted by permission.

**4.** Is the voice synthesis feature an integral and important part of the program?
**5.** How many words are available in the system?
**6.** Is it possible to create new programs? How difficult is this?

The California Instructional Technology Clearinghouse (1998–2000) provides some pertinent guidelines for examining the navigational characteristics of software programs and web-based resources. These considerations are especially important for evaluating how

**FIGURE 6.10**   Evaluation of Related Software for Reading

| Word-Processing and Database Management Programs | Poor | | | | Good |
|---|---|---|---|---|---|
| 1. Size and spacing of characters appropriate for audience | 1 | 2 | 3 | 4 | 5 |
| 2. Options to vary print formats (e.g., page width, page length, spacing, type fonts) | 1 | 2 | 3 | 4 | 5 |
| 3. Words not split at ends of lines | 1 | 2 | 3 | 4 | 5 |
| 4. Actual format can be shown on screen before printing | 1 | 2 | 3 | 4 | 5 |
| 5. Command keys with logical names and minimal moves | 1 | 2 | 3 | 4 | 5 |
| 6. Easy editing features for erasing, inserting, centering, tabbing and underlining | 1 | 2 | 3 | 4 | 5 |
| 7. Ability to reorganize large blocks of text by moving, saving on disk, inserting in other places | 1 | 2 | 3 | 4 | 5 |
| 8. Provisions to restore previous action (e.g., return paragraph to original position) | 1 | 2 | 3 | 4 | 5 |
| 9. Warnings at critical points (e.g., You have not saved this text) | 1 | 2 | 3 | 4 | 5 |
| 10. Printer commands and capabilities available and easy for students to use | 1 | 2 | 3 | 4 | 5 |
| 11. Sturdy command cards for off-screen reference | 1 | 2 | 3 | 4 | 5 |
| 12. Adequate file functions including renaming, protecting, merging, and copying | 1 | 2 | 3 | 4 | 5 |
| 13. Related capabilities (e.g., idea processors, spelling checkers, grammar checkers, graphics) | 1 | 2 | 3 | 4 | 5 |
| 14. Ability to integrate text and illustrations | 1 | 2 | 3 | 4 | 5 |
| 15. Backup disks provided | 1 | 2 | 3 | 4 | 5 |
| 16. Support materials with useful teaching ideas | 1 | 2 | 3 | 4 | 5 |

| Authoring Systems and Other Utilities | Poor | | | | Good |
|---|---|---|---|---|---|
| 1. Clear directions for using program to create materials | 1 | 2 | 3 | 4 | 5 |
| 2. Easy to enter items | 1 | 2 | 3 | 4 | 5 |
| 3. Editing possible at any point | 1 | 2 | 3 | 4 | 5 |
| 4. Varied formats for developing materials (i.e., not limited to multiple-choice, true/false, or simple testing types) | 1 | 2 | 3 | 4 | 5 |
| 5. Can vary amount of text to be presented | 1 | 2 | 3 | 4 | 5 |
| 6. Clear directions for student use of the completed program | 1 | 2 | 3 | 4 | 5 |
| 7. Options for record-keeping | 1 | 2 | 3 | 4 | 5 |
| 8. Options for incorporating graphics | 1 | 2 | 3 | 4 | 5 |
| 9. Options for incorporating sound | 1 | 2 | 3 | 4 | 5 |
| 10. Support materials with useful teaching ideas | 1 | 2 | 3 | 4 | 5 |

| Simulations and Problem-Solving Programs | Poor | | | | Good |
|---|---|---|---|---|---|
| 1. Content consistent with local curriculum | 1 | 2 | 3 | 4 | 5 |
| 2. Realistic situations | 1 | 2 | 3 | 4 | 5 |
| 3. Motivating design | 1 | 2 | 3 | 4 | 5 |
| 4. Helpful feedback about user's decisions | 1 | 2 | 3 | 4 | 5 |
| 5. Supplementary bibliography available, indicating sources of content and related research possibilities for students | 1 | 2 | 3 | 4 | 5 |
| 6. Sample sheets provided for off-computer record-keeping, analysis and research | 1 | 2 | 3 | 4 | 5 |
| 7. Teaching suggestions for integrating content within curriculum | 1 | 2 | 3 | 4 | 5 |
| 8. Classroom management suggestions for using program within classroom with limited computer accessibility | 1 | 2 | 3 | 4 | 5 |

*Source:* "Guidelines for Evaluating Reading Software." Copyright © 1985, *The Michigan Reading Journal, 18* (4). Reprinted by permission.

students navigate or move around in multimedia, hypermedia, and web-based resources. These guidelines include the following:

- Menu choices are logical and are displayed clearly.
- Any icons used are logical, are easily understood, and represent metaphors from the real world whenever possible.
- The user interface is consistent throughout the program.
- Function keys are used effectively and consistently.
- One designated key is used consistently throughout to return learners to a previous menu.
- There is a cursor or other indicator to show where the response is to go.
- The teacher or the student, as appropriate, determines the pace at which the learner moves through the program.
- Introductory screens, including company logo and copyright statements, are kept to a minimum and/or can be bypassed by repeat learners.
- Program entry points are varied and are appropriate for the program.
- Menus or icons allow direct access to specific parts of the program.
- The learner can exit from any point in the program through a consistent routine.
- Keyboard templates, guides, labels, and/or displays are provided to assist the learner as appropriate.

In summary, evaluating software and web-based resources takes time and energy. For some struggling readers the computer may provide enough support and interest to encourage the persistence and effort that are needed to become more proficient. However, this is not likely to happen with repetitive, routinized activities that offer little after the initial novelty has worn off. In evaluating the resources that are at play in a particular instructional context, it is important to determine whether software programs and web-based resources are providing the type of supportive and interactive setting within which students' reading and writing are likely to thrive.

## Diagnostic Portfolio: The Instructional Context

In Chapter 4 we introduced the thumbnail sketch as a way to summarize information that is gathered throughout the assessment-instruction process. The thumbnail sketches for Marvin and Kyle have been updated on the basis of our evaluation of the context (see Figures 6.11a and 6.11b). This information provides the basis for our ongoing portfolio assessment.

## The Diagnostic Portfolio: The Cases of Marvin and Kyle

Both Marvin and Kyle live in middle-class communities with intact families. Both speak English as their primary and only language. Their parents are hard working, and each boy has a mother who has been deeply involved in his education from the beginning. Each currently attends a school that is highly regarded by the community.

**FIGURE 6.11a**
Marvin's
Thumbnail Sketch:
Evaluating the
Context

| Getting Started (Step 1) | About the Reading and Writing Context (Step 2) |
|---|---|
| **Background** | **Resources** |
| Name: Marvin | • Outdated basals and workbooks |
| Age: 11      Grade: 5 | • Until recently, no recreational reading at all |
| Key Correlates: | |
| • Above average IQ | **Instruction** |
| • Normal vision, hearing, and overall health | • Instruction focused on isolated phonics |
| • Interests are science, sports, "taking things apart" | • Reading assignments and practice without modeling |
| **Information about the Learner** | • No provision for development of motivation or strategies |
| Knowledge about Reading and Writing: | • Whole group basal instruction; little prereading support |
| • Reports that people read to learn and for recreation: reports adjusting rate for text difficulty | • No cooperative work, book sharing and little discussion, especially promoting higher-order thinking |
| • Reports that own reading problem is comprehension | • Limited reading outside the basal |
| • Names, "breaking words down" and "asking someone" as the only strategies for reading words that are unfamiliar | **Tasks** |
| Motivation: | • In both old and new school, most tasks are closed |
| • Pleasant, cooperative demeanor during the classroom and clinic sessions | • Workbooks, seatwork repetitive and isolated from instruction |
| • Talks freely about affective responses to text and persists without prompting on difficult tasks | • Questions used infrequently, most are text explicit, focused on detail |
| | • Almost no writing, except grammar worksheets and skills |
| **Information about the Context** | **Settings** |
| School History: | • English spoken in the home. Few reading materials, limited interest in reading at home |
| • School-administered achievement tests place him in the 35th percentile in reading | • Placed in private parochial school from grades 2–4. Large student–teacher ratio, no support services. Policy of placing all students in grade-appropriate materials. |
| • Multiple moves and family disruptions during K–1. | |
| Instructional Approaches: | |
| Experiences, Linguistic and Cultural Context: | |
| • English spoken in the home. | |

**FIGURE 6.11b**
Kyle's Thumbnail
Sketch: Evaluating
the Context

| Getting Started (Step 1) | About the Reading and Writing Context (Step 2) |
|---|---|
| **Background** | **Resources** |
| Name: Kyle<br>Age: 7½    Grade: 2 | • Beginning readers: "little books" and own writing |
| Key Correlates:<br>• Normal vision, hearing, and overall health/development<br>• Difficult time "paying attention" | • Emerging readers: commercially controlled vocabulary and then trade books, children's literature<br>• Journals, portfolios, theme booklets<br>• Process writing folders<br>• Many read alouds—literature |
| **Information about the Learner** | **Instruction** |
| Knowledge about Reading and Writing:<br>• Reports that own reading problem is knowing the words<br>• Is able to reflect on his own reading and writing abilities | • Child-centered curriculum<br>• Individual conferences and whole group meetings<br>• Inquiry-based theme work and choice time each day<br>• Cooperative and collaborative groups<br>• Problem-solving focus |
| Motivation:<br>• Says he doesn't really like to read, would rather play and build<br>• Cooperative and willing to work both in school and in extra sessions | **Tasks** |
| **Information about the Context** | • Almost all tasks are open<br>• Reading time spent in reading continuous texts, conferencing with teacher, responding in many ways |
| School History:<br>• Successful preschool experience<br>• Same multi-age K–2 classroom since kindergarten<br>• Lack of progress in reading and writing noted at end of grade 1 | • Writing time spent writing original texts and revising for publication—in books, on walls, in class<br>• Additional writing in journals, theme booklets, and correspondences<br>• Students reflect on own work as select portfolio entries and evaluate own learning |
| Instructional Approaches:<br>• Literature-based instruction in an inquiry-oriented classroom<br>• Daily reading and writing | **Settings** |
| Experiences, Linguistic, and Cultural Context:<br>• English spoken in the home<br>• Both parents college graduates<br>• Many books and book activities | • English only language spoken in home<br>• Considerable home emphasis on reading and writing<br>• Well-stocked library at school and home<br>• School and community emphasize achievement |

During the context evaluation, entries in a diagnostic portfolio are likely to be primarily narrative, anecdotal notes. Both work and text samples might, of course, provide useful information. Kyle's teacher, for example, regularly copies a page from students' texts to place in their portfolios, with a date, to show what is being read.

## Marvin

Before entering his current school, Marvin attended a private parochial school for three years. Parents and teachers in this school generally value a highly structured approach to teaching and learning. Skills are emphasized, and teachers generally believe that these "basics" must be acquired before students can move on to more challenging reading and writing tasks. The school uses a dated basal reading program, and both phonics and handwriting work are assigned often in the early grades.

The teachers in Marvin's previous school generally believe that all students should be doing "grade-level" work. This, coupled with a large student–teacher ratio, means that all students are placed in the same materials for instruction. The general instructional framework has involved whole-group instruction, with oral reading of stories from the basal and workbook and seatwork follow-up. Students sit in rows and move around the room very little.

The classroom environment in Marvin's new school is much more relaxed. Students' desks are arranged in clusters of four, and there is considerable movement around the room during the day. The teacher organizes instruction using ability groups, and Marvin has been placed in the lowest-ability group (with two other students) who are using the 3–2 basal from a dated reading program. Although Marvin's old school had no library and made no provisions for silent reading time during the day, in his new placement there is a well-stocked library, and the teacher has a fifteen-minute sustained silent reading time two or three times a week.

Students do very little writing in either school. What writing does occur is almost entirely closed task activity. In both settings there are some writing assignments, handwriting practice, and spelling tests.

Marvin has never received special services. The private school he attended did not make provisions for special needs, and his new school is just now exploring the options for Marvin.

Marvin's school experience, while changing, has been dominated by closed tasks and dated literacy resources. In Marvin's old school, whole-group oral reading followed by teacher directed questioning of content was the recurrent instructional frame. At no time during the day did Marvin make choices about what to read or write. The tasks that were assigned were almost entirely from commercially available instructional materials that focused on short-answer responses to content questions.

In his new setting, Marvin's reading group meets with the teacher periodically to do round-robin oral work and to correct workbook pages. In this new school also, each child in the class has a reading folder that contains differentiated seatwork activities to be completed independently. Although Marvin is now expected to choose books for silent reading and to work on book projects from time to time, his daily tasks are still mostly closed in nature.

The teacher does conduct discussions with the higher-ability reading groups, but since Marvin's group struggles with decoding, she focuses their independent seatwork on word-level assignments, and these are corrected together.

The only assessment that takes place in either setting is externally provided. In both schools the children are evaluated every year on a norm-referenced achievement test, and in Marvin's new setting, the teacher uses the end-of-level tests that accompany her basal reading program to evaluate student learning.

## Kyle

Kyle is in a multi-age K–2 classroom. He has been with the same teacher, Ms. McIntyre, since kindergarten. His mother volunteers in this room frequently. The literacy environment in this classroom is a rich one. As students enter each morning, they write their names in the sign-in book and also indicate with a check mark whether they want milk, hot lunch, or both. They sign up for their snack and make choices of activities each morning by moving their name tags to various activities being offered. There is a consistent message to students that they will read and they will write.

There are books of every sort. The library corner is attractive and accessible, teachers discuss books with children all the time, and book dialogue journals start early. There are also small teacher-made booklets for special purposes, such as tiny alphabet books for the youngest students and small handwriting booklets for everyone who needs to practice. There are big books, there are books in the science area, there are counting books next to the basket of nuts, and so on. There are different shapes of paper and many types of writing utensils.

Ms. McIntyre believes in a child-centered classroom and expects that students will learn to read and write by reading and writing. Her job is to ask the right question at the right time or to provide the right prompt when things get stalled. She can most often be found in corners and on the floor, having quiet but intense conversations with children about their work. Children interact with her and with each other continuously. The most frequent type of interactions involve discussions of ongoing work, activities, or personal responses. The children talk about their out-of-school experiences during share time and write about them in journals. The classroom is organized as a reading/writing workshop. There are no formal groupings of any sort, although Ms. McIntyre might call a group together to work on an area of interest or difficulty, and children frequently organize themselves into groups to accomplish tasks—to plan a puppet show, work on blocks, or read together, for example.

In addition, there are multiple types of formats for writing. The children in Ms. McIntyre's room write a great deal—in journals, in process writing folders, about their themes, to record their exploratory findings, and to communicate with each other. For reading, the youngest children read each other's writing and read from a set of early reading materials (predictable texts, picture-label books, etc.). Later, as they progress, they read from commercial "easy-to-read" controlled vocabulary books. There are also many children's literature trade books, and these are read by children as soon as they are able. By second grade most children are choosing easy "chapter books." These texts may be self-selected, negotiated between teacher and child, or assigned. In early second grade Kyle was reading from the easiest of the controlled vocabulary books (*Little Bear,* by Minarik, for example).

**FIGURE 6.12**
Kyle's Dialogue
Journal

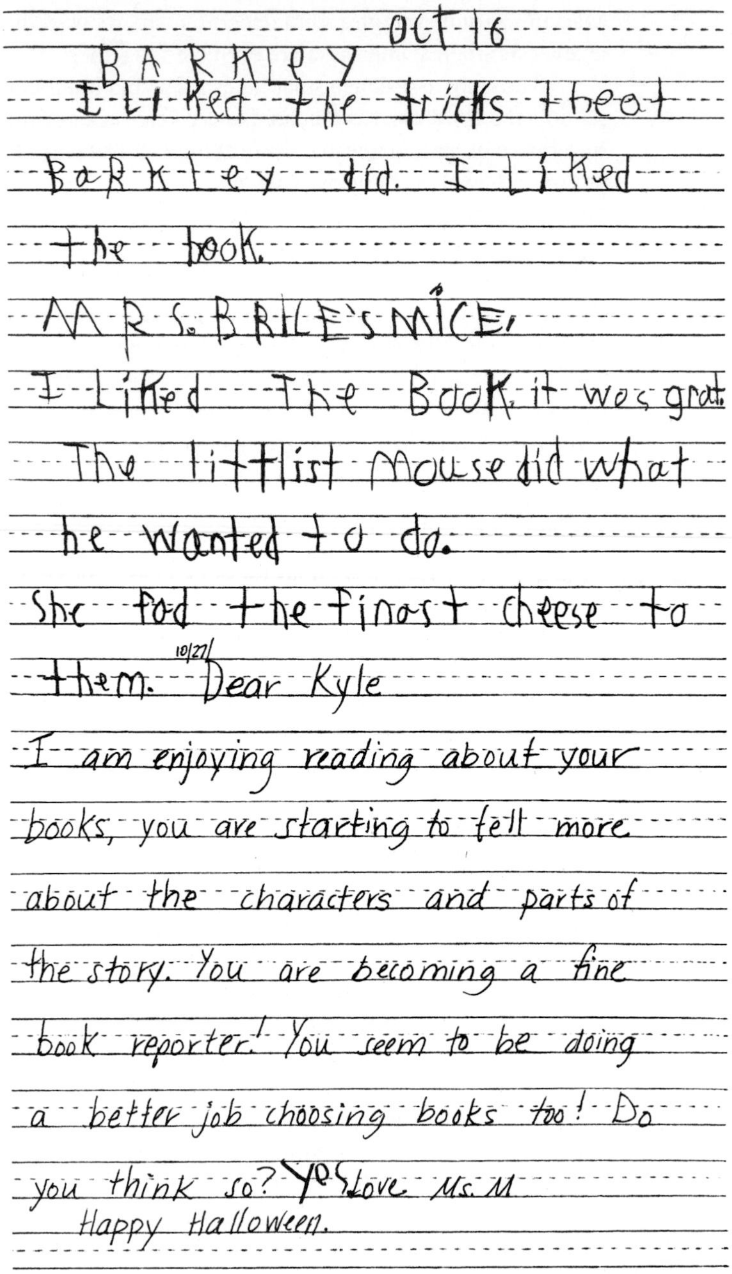

OCT 16

BARKLEY
I Liked the tricks theat
BaRkLey did. I Liked
the book.
MR.S. BRILE'S MICE.
I Liked The Book. it wes grat.
The littlist Mouse did what
he wanted to do.
She fed the finost cheese to
them. 10/27/ Dear Kyle
I am enjoying reading about your
books, you are starting to tell more
about the characters and parts of
the story. You are becoming a fine
book reporter! You seem to be doing
a better job choosing books too! Do
you think so? Yes Love Ms. M
    Happy Halloween.

Kyle's classroom is one of many like it in his district. The school district has a well-articulated curriculum design. The outcomes clearly focus on student's literature-based reading process writing.

Motivation to learn is shaped by the many activities and opportunities to explore personal issues. For example, Kyle wrote extensively throughout second grade about snakes; he conducted research, wrote a book, and made journal entries about snakes. There is a wide array of activities to engage students with different learning styles. Some will spend their time building with blocks during planning time, while others will work on a science experiment. However, everyone writes about what they have done when choice time is over.

Children expect to be successful because they see children of all ages around them being successful. Risk taking is supported through individual goal setting that Ms. McIntyre discusses with all students. In twice-daily class meetings, Ms. McIntyre models how to solve problems, how to establish goals, and encourages children to do the same. Older students frequently model by explaining how they think or what they learned or plan to do.

In this classroom there are very few whole-group or even small-group lessons. Students do not receive direct instruction in skills except in response to their own reading and their own questions about print. Ms. McIntyre does discuss reading skills and strategies with individual children as they read and write. Conversations are explicit, and the feedback to students about strategies (e.g., using picture cues, thinking about the middle and endings of words) is very focused and direct. Ms. McIntyre is adept at providing scaffolding for students through the selection of predictable books, through shared and repeated readings, and in the instructional dialogue that she and others provide.

The use of scaffolding and dialogue is perhaps most visible in the dialogue journals used by Ms. McIntyre and her students. In Figure 6.12, Kyle and Ms. McIntyre have an exchange. Ms. McIntyre's response supports Kyle's ideas, provides him with correct spelling models, and challenges him to take on a new task.

There are no workbooks or worksheets in this classroom. The classroom is organized as a reading/writing workshop, and most tasks in Ms. McIntyre's room are open ones. Students are expected to make good decisions during planning time and to write about the work they did during that time. They also read books, discuss them with their teachers, write responses to their reading in response logs, keep track of what they read in reading logs, write letters to their teachers in their dialogue journals, write about personal experiences in their journals. In their writing folders they create drafts, keep notes, have conferences, and rework some pieces, and they publish writing regularly in public displays and in bound books.

No norm-referenced tests are used in this school. Teachers have adopted a portfolio system and have also worked to put into place an assessment system that reflects and challenges their own instructional and curricular designs (see Chapters 8 and 9).

## Chapter Summary

The first half of this chapter addresses the role of instructional resources in reading and writing performance. We begin with an examination of the features of commercial reading/language arts programs that are likely to influence reading and writing performance, including the reading anthologies, independent student activities, and teachers' guides. We then consider how the types and structures of trade material texts can influence reading and learning and the features of text that influence comprehensibility—the aspects of text that can make reading easier or more difficult and learning more productive or more tedious. We also examine the important characteristics of tutoring programs and how they influence student performance. Finally, we discuss the role of computer technology in students' writing performance, motivation, and collaboration.

The second half of this chapter describes strategies and tools for assessing the instructional resources addressed in the first half of the chapter. Strategies and tools for assessing reading materials range from highly structured readability formulas to more informal checklists. In addition, we provide guidelines and evaluative questions for examining tutoring programs and computer software that may be among the resources used to assist students who are struggling with reading and writing.

# SECTION THREE

# Evaluating the Learner

This third section of the book, *Evaluating the Learner,* contains four chapters and is easily the longest section in the book. The traditional emphasis on the learner has resulted in the generation of many tools and strategies for assessment. Recent attention to other aspects of reading, writing, and learning has been helpful, but there is not nearly as large a body of knowledge. Each of the four chapters in this section contains information that will increase teachers' knowledge and understanding and also describes tools and strategies for assessment. These include norm-referenced tests and traditional informal measures (i.e., informal reading inventories), as well as innovative, teacher-based tools and strategies. In Chapter 7 we examine the foundations of literacy, with a close look at emergent reading and writing. In Chapters 8 and 9 we provide educators with an extensive array of tools for assessing students' reading and writing in classroom contexts. Finally, in Chapter 10 we examine formal assessment tools and review many of the most commonly used commercial tests. Using the strategies and approaches described in these chapters, teachers will be able to assess all major aspects of reading and writing performance.

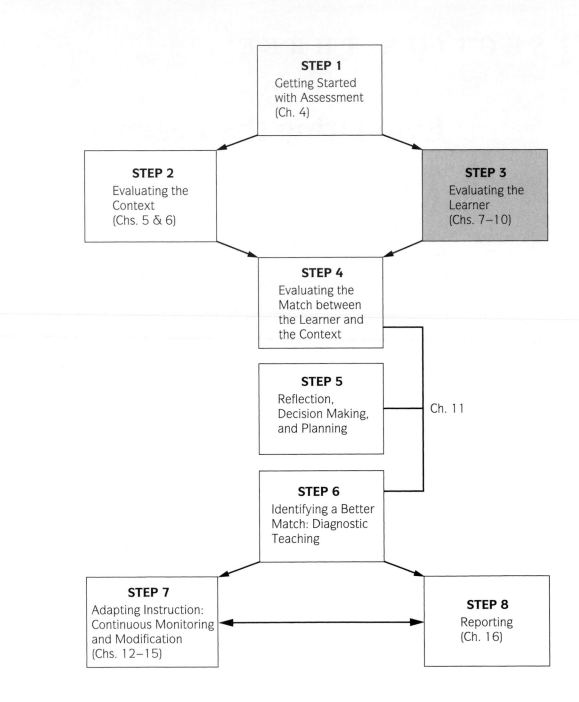

STEP 1
Getting Started
with Assessment
(Ch. 4)

STEP 2
Evaluating the
Context
(Chs. 5 & 6)

STEP 3
Evaluating the
Learner
(Chs. 7–10)

STEP 4
Evaluating the
Match between
the Learner and
the Context

STEP 5
Reflection,
Decision Making,
and Planning

Ch. 11

STEP 6
Identifying a Better
Match: Diagnostic
Teaching

STEP 7
Adapting Instruction:
Continuous Monitoring
and Modification
(Chs. 12–15)

STEP 8
Reporting
(Ch. 16)

# 7 The Foundations of Literacy

An understanding of the foundations of literacy is essential to the development of an appropriate program of assessment and instruction. A rich body of research produced over the last three decades has helped us to understand how the competence of young children emerges in the areas of reading and writing. These developments in the area of emergent literacy provide teachers and specialists with information that can be used to develop more effective assessment and instructional programs than have been possible with previous conceptualizations of readiness.

This chapter is divided into three major sections. The first section examines the historical context for thinking about beginning reading and writing, leading to the more contemporary perspective known as *emergent literacy*. The second section elaborates on two major areas of competence necessary for literacy learning derived from an emergent literacy perspective, language development and literacy experiences, which include developing print awareness, understanding the forms and functions of print, analyzing print, and controlling reading and writing processes. The last major section of this chapter describes strategies and tools for assessing the emergent abilities of young readers and writers.

## Understanding Emergent Literacy

### Background

Over the last century educators have differed in their views of how children learn to read and write. The ideas and beliefs associated with various perspectives are still present in the thinking of many teachers and administrators and in instructional programs provided to young children. Early educators argued that children simply grow into *readiness,* much the way a tree or plant develops. Later, some teachers and theorists asserted that readiness is either caused or facilitated by the environment. During a period beginning in the 1920s and extending through the 1980s there was a strongly held belief that "readiness" was an organically determined phenomenon. Mental age, perceptual-motor development, social maturity, and general physical development were all considered critical aspects of reading readiness. Students' readiness would unfold in a predetermined way and time.

These ideas led, perhaps unwittingly, to an instructional mandate for inaction. The implications for educational practice seemed straightforward: Instruction should be withheld until the child is "ready" (Teale & Sulzby, 1986). Even today, some educators argue that early print experiences or even the presence of print in the kindergarten environment is inappropriate.

McGill-Franzen (1992) has countered that this version of learning is "a trap for poor children" because the kinds of experiences that might lead children toward literacy are considered inappropriate for kindergarten settings although they are generally offered to middle-class children in their homes. The available evidence certainly suggests that development, and therefore readiness for school tasks, is influenced by both experience and instruction.

Recent research has led to a reconceptualization of readiness as *emergent literacy,* or the gradual emergence of written literacy skills in the context of general cognitive and oral language development (see Neuman & Dickinson, 2001). Educators and researchers who have studied young children's literacy development have come to understand that children begin to acquire literate knowledge, skills, and behaviors at home during their earliest years. Teale and Sulzby (1986) note that "the first years of the child's life represent a period when legitimate reading and writing development are taking place. These behaviors and knowledge are not *pre-* anything, as the term *pre-reading* suggests" (p. xix). From an emergent perspective, readiness is reconceptualized as the *process of becoming literate,* as opposed to a series of discrete, specifiable skills that must be developed before learning how to read.

An emergent perspective does not deny the developmental nature of literacy learning but places it in a framework that identifies children's early years as a period of high activity rather than passive waiting for readiness to unfold. More contemporary developmental views, informed by the work of Piaget (1960) and Vygotsky (1978), see children as active constructors of knowledge. This view acknowledges the critical role of the learner, but also highlights the role of engaged adults:

> By talking with grownups and capable peers as they go about doing the kinds of things literate people do, children are able to construct meanings for tasks that they could not understand on their own . . . such instruction actually transforms the child's development so that tomorrow the child is able to independently do what he could do only with assistance today. (McGill-Franzen, 1992, p. 58)

Of course, this also means that the concept of "literacy" is inextricably intertwined with the particular social and cultural contexts of the home and community. As Johnston and Rogers (2001) noted, "there is extraordinary variation in the languages and cultures that children bring to literacy learning and in the literacies into which they have been apprenticed prior to coming to school" (p. 386). In some low socioeconomic communities, for example, mothers and their children are very adept at reading and talking about newspaper ads, but they are not experienced in reading and talking about alphabet books (Pellegrini, 2001).

An emergent perspective also focuses our attention on all aspects of literacy, not just reading. Indeed, the relevant evidence suggests that many children will write before they read. At the very least the most recent research findings suggest that children are developing competence simultaneously in all aspects of literate behavior: reading, writing, listening, and speaking; and that children seem to acquire some of the readiness skills *in the process of learning to read and write* (Ehri, 1979). Thus, reading and writing are seen as a continuum of socio- and psycholinguistic development that begins long before the onset of formal schooling and lasts a lifetime.

Current research suggests that there are many abilities that provide the underpinnings for literacy learning. It appears that these abilities emerge more or less simultaneously and that none is mastered before children enter school. Even at age seven, children continue to refine their understanding and control of literacy tasks (Lomax & McGee, 1987). It is also clear that the acquisition of these early emerging abilities sets the stage for subsequent success or failure in school settings (Juel, 1988; Whitehurst & Lonigan, 2001).

In the sections that follow, we consider two important aspects of emergent literacy. First, we consider the nature of oral language development and how the acquisition of oral language competence prepares children for reading tasks and vice versa. Second, we discuss the types of literacy experiences necessary for effective emergence into conventional reading and writing. Four interrelated experiences are identified and discussed: developing print awareness, understanding the forms and functions of print, analyzing print, and controlling reading and writing processes.

## Learning to Talk

Learning to talk is one of the first productive cognitive tasks confronting young humans.

> There is much for children to learn: not just the words, but their pronunciation and the ways of combining them to express the relationships between the objects, attributes, and actions to which they refer. They also have to learn how the more subtle distinctions of intention are expressed—indirect and direct requests; questions of various kinds, and expression of different attitudes, such as sympathy, anger, apology, and so on—through different selections and orderings of words and structures and the use of different patterns of intonation and facial and bodily gestures. (Wells, 1986, p. 39)

The ways in which children accomplish this task can tell us a great deal about how humans learn to acquire cognitive competence in general.

Learning to read and write are highly correlated with oral language competence. This relationship probably exists for a number of reasons. First, reading and writing are language-based, cognitive tasks. Second, both written language and spoken language are communicative processes. That is, reading, writing, and talking are used to exchange ideas, request information, demand and elicit help, share feelings, and so forth. Finally, both oral language communication and written communication are interactive, taking place in a context that influences the active search for meaning. By studying how children learn language, we can gain tremendous insight into the cognitive structures and strategies they will use in learning to read and write.

The connections here are reinforced in an unexpected set of findings involving studies of learning to read and write among limited English proficiency (LEP) students. The research suggests that "LEP students who develop a strong sociocultural, linguistic, and cognitive base in their primary language (L1) tend to transfer those attitudes and skills to the other language and culture (L2)" (Ovando, 1993, p. 225) and are more successful at learning to read and write in English (Hudelson, 1987).

***What Children Must Learn about Language.***    There are some features common to all languages that must be learned. "Language has many subsystems having to do with sound, grammar, meaning, vocabulary, and knowing the right way to say something on a particular occasion in order to accomplish a specific purpose. Knowing the language entails knowing its *phonology, morphology, syntax,* and *sematics,* as well as its *pragmatics*" [emphasis in the original] (Gleason, 1997, p. 20). Thus, one of the first tasks that confronts babies is to figure out that the auditory sounds of humans are meaningful. The sounds of a language provide only the starting point, however. Children must learn how to express their intentions by using language. To accomplish this, they must figure out *how* to name the objects and ideas in their language and mark subtle changes of meaning (tense, number, etc.) by using additional morphemes. In addition, they must figure out the *grammar* of their language. This grammar is composed of the rules for mapping meaning onto words. The grammar typically dictates that various meaning relationships are described by particular word orders or syntactic structures (see Chapter 2).

Not all languages have the same rules for mapping meaning on strings of words. So, for example, in most romance languages (such as Spanish), adjectives follow the noun they are describing, whereas in English these modifiers are placed before the noun. Children must learn what word order is dictated by their particular grammar and the rules that tell them how to combine words.

There are other important skills and abilities required of the competent oral language user. For example, at very early ages children come to recognize a range of *language functions.* Halliday (1975) has studied and categorized the functions of language. In Figure 7.1, these functions are coupled with examples from a young child from the ages of eighteen to twenty months.

Language is learned to express certain intentions and to perform certain functions. These intentions and purposes are executed in the context of social interaction. It is our knowledge of language that allows us to translate the sounds speakers produce into a representation of the messages that they are trying to communicate. The end result of language learning is not simply mastering the language structures. Children master the forms of language to communicate. Mastery of vocabulary and word order results in nothing if the learner cannot use those forms for the purpose of producing and understanding thoughts, ideas, and feelings.

When individuals are competent in their primary or home language (L1), they know other things as well. According to Ovando (1993), there are five culture-related domains involved in learning a language. These include (1) *discourse,* or knowledge of how to organize the language in longer chunks; (2) *appropriateness,* involving knowledge of what types of language to use in different settings (for example, with friends versus in school); (3) *paralinguistics,* which captures the nonverbal aspects of communication such as gesture and distance from speaker; (4) *pragmatics,* or knowledge of the implicit norms governing communication in social settings, such as when to speak, how to pace talk, and politeness rules; and (5) *cognitive-academic language proficiency,* which describes the language skills needed to learn specialized content. The complexity of this knowledge and the ways in which it interacts in different languages and cultures highlight how culture-specific language acquisition really is.

**FIGURE 7.1**
Functions of
Language

| Language Function | Example |
|---|---|
| Instrumental language<br>the "I want" function; language used to satisfy needs | "I wanna the cookie too." Or, reaching for toy another child has, "Mine!" |
| Regulatory language<br>the "do as I tell you" function; language for controlling others | "I do it myself." |
| Interactional language<br>the "me and you" function; language for interacting with others | "What you doing?" (Said over and over to elicit response from adult) |
| Personal language<br>the "here I come" function; language for expressing feelings and personality | "I scared." |
| Imaginative language*<br>the "let's pretend" function; language used to create own environment. | (Putting a construction worker's hardhat on his head): "Going to work. Bye-bye." |
| Heuristic language<br>the "tell me why" function; language for exploring the environment | "Emma crying. What happened?" |
| Informative/representational language<br>the "I've got something to tell you" function; language for communicating | "It's darking." (at the end of the day) |

*As children get older, their use of language for imaginative play is very evident: "You pretend that you're sick and that's the hospital and I'll pretend I'm the mommy." (T's older sister, age 5).

*Source:* Functions of Language, as described by Halliday (1975). *Learning How to Mean* (pp. 18–21). New York: Elsevier North Holland, Inc.

Of course, the social conventions of language are an important determinant of school achievement (see Chapter 5). They dictate how we should speak to different individuals in different contexts. "Languages grow and develop as tools of communication within a given environment. In this sense, there is no such thing as 'right' or 'wrong' language, only language that is appropriate or inappropriate in a given context" (Ovando, 1993, p. 217). Mismatches between school conventions and the conventions that children have learned at home can lead to poor performance and wrong judgments about children's ability to learn in school.

***How Language Is Learned.*** Most humans appear to move toward oral language competence through a series of more or less similar stages. The presence of these developmental stages across cultural and linguistic boundaries provides strong evidence that humans have some biological basis for language production. It is clear that children learn to speak their language using differing types of information and interactive styles (see Gee, 2001). Thus, it seems that human babies have a biological predisposition toward learning language. However, it should also be noted that this predisposition is played out in environments where others interact through language and encourage children to participate (Wells, 1986; Wong-Fillmore, 1991).

Many parents would assert that they "taught their children to talk" and that children learn language largely through imitation and reinforcement/feedback. However, the available research evidence suggests otherwise. Children are not deliberately taught the language, and they don't learn to talk through imitation alone. Instead, it appears that children construct the grammar of their language through the internalization and generation of rules. What the child learns is not a set of utterances but a set of rules for processing utterances. For example, young children frequently produce utterances such as "He *goed* to the store," "It's *darking* outside," or "I'm going to school today, *amn't* I?" These examples demonstrate how children produce speech that could not have been imitated, as no competent speaker of English produces them. The child creates order by generating hypotheses, testing them, and then modifying them in the face of new evidence.

Children's mistakes reveal more about their knowledge than about their lack of knowledge. As children generate rules for the language they are learning, their speech reflects this growing knowledge. For example, when children come to know that nouns can be converted to verb forms (as in "That room is a mess" and "You're messing up my things"), they may create errors that are consistent with this knowledge, such as "We'll airplane to Florida" and "You're germing it all up." In these examples we see that children search for regularities, create rules, simplify the task, and overgeneralize and extend the information they have to new situations. In short, they are engaged in the development of strategies.

Attention to meaning is a striking feature of early language development. From the beginning young children's utterances reflect semantic intent. Their productions reflect an awareness that the functional purpose of language is to create and communicate meaning. This is most evident at the two-word utterance stage, when children seem capable of producing only two-word constructions. During this stage, researchers have observed what is termed *telegraphic* speech, so called because children leave out the words that are left out in telegrams and retain only those most essential to convey meaning, for example "baby ride" and "Mommy cookie."

Although it is clear that children are not taught language, they do not learn it without help. Children need to have language available to them so that they can work out the regularities. In addition, they need responsive conversational partners who will help them to see how the language works and provide feedback on their efforts.

> Learning to talk should thus be thought of as the result of a partnership: a partnership in which parents and other members of the community provide the evidence and then encourage children to work it out for themselves. Andrew Lock sums it all up in a single phrase when he describes the process as "the guided reinvention of language. (Wells, 1986, p. 51)

***Oral Language and Its Relationship to Reading and Writing.***    Although learning to read and write is not entirely dependent on oral language knowledge, it certainly is true that the development of oral language abilities lays the foundation for successful acquisition of reading and writing competence (Snow et al., 1998). Taking all the evidence together, oral language competence is important to reading and writing for these reasons:

1. In learning to talk, children develop (or demonstrate) a number of general cognitive strategies for learning.
2. In learning to talk (and listen), children acquire much that they will use to aid them in bringing meaning to print: vocabulary, understanding of syntax, the ways in which meaning is carried in language structures, and alternative structures for communicating similar and dissimilar ideas.
3. An extensive vocabulary appears to promote phonological analysis.
4. Children use known oral language structures in their writing.
5. Sophisticated vocabulary, syntax, phonological development, and word usage are all helpful in learning to read.

Recently, Watson (2001) reviewed a great deal of research on the relationship between oral language and literacy development. She concluded that when oral language is acquired and used in highly literate environments, it appears to exert a broad-based influence on literacy acquisition because children learn how to select and use specific linguistic and pragmatic forms to communicate and comprehend. In other words, there might not be a simple one to one relationship between learning language and learning to read, but children who learn both more language and more sophisticated language are better prepared for the types of literate skills they must acquire for learning to read and write in school settings.

## Literacy Experiences

The foundations of literacy begin with language acquisition, but also include learning that print and speech are related, print encodes a message, pictures are guides to the message, some language units are more likely to occur than others, certain words in certain orders reflect particular messages, and memory may be used as a guide to understanding (Clay, 1979).

These aspects of literacy are acquired in homes, parks, preschools, and stores—anywhere that children encounter and use print. Children are most likely to acquire useful and refined ideas about print as they observe and interact with literate adults. Researchers have consistently found that early and/or successful readers and writers share certain types of literacy experiences (Kastler, Roser, & Hoffman, 1987; Ollila & Mayfield, 1992):

1. Families provide a variety of writing materials.
2. Children observe others reading and writing.
3. Children are encouraged to experiment in writing.
4. Parents read aloud to their children.
5. Parents or others answer questions about reading and writing.
6. There are books in the home and/or children are taken to the library.

These experiences set the stage for learning to read and write but also promote the acquisition of specific knowledge and skill. They are important for developing print awareness, understanding the forms and functions of print, analyzing the task of reading, and gaining control of literacy behaviors/activities.

Importantly, it appears that different home and preschool experiences influence different aspects of children's emerging literacy. For example, shared storybook reading does not appear to have a significant impact on phonological skills, although it does have a significant impact on children's oral language (vocabulary) development (see Whitehurst & Lonigan, 2001). On the other hand, parental efforts to teach their children about print were significantly related to children's alphabet knowledge, word reading, and invented spelling in kindergarten and first grade (Senechal, LeFevre, Thomas, & Daley, 1998).

***Learning about the Forms and Functions of Print.***    Children understand the functional value and significance of literacy when they experience it directly—through lap reading with their parents and as they send cards or help to write grocery lists.

*Developing Print Awareness.*    Children in our society are surrounded by print—on doors, cereal boxes, signs, television, even clothing. It appears that they acquire, at an early age, a fairly sophisticated understanding that these symbols convey meaning. Although some researchers question the usefulness of this generalized awareness (for example, Ehri, 1987), it does appear that situational print awareness is part of a larger progression of acquired skill and knowledge. It is likely that most children understand something about the functions of print in environmental settings and use this information to arrive at key conclusions about the links between print and speech; however, it is also important to remember that some do not.

Just as children must come to understand the functional, meaningful nature of spoken language, they must come to appreciate that print is communicative, functional, and meaningful. Recent evidence suggests that most children in our society have a fairly well-developed "sense of print awareness in situational contexts" by the time they reach school age (Goodman, 1986; Heath, 1983). For example, Hiebert (1981) found that three-, four-, and five-year-old children were all sensitive to differences between print and drawing stimuli. In addition, when presented with words and letters in meaningful contexts, even very young children demonstrate competence in understanding concepts such as word and letter, provided they are not asked to use or understand specific terminology.

Children generally learn that print is meaningful before they begin formal schooling as they observe print on pizza and cereal boxes, for example, and as they watch more competent others write notes or letters to friends and relatives. Many young children engage in "scribble writing" at a very early age and announce, as three-year-old Theo did, "Oh, I think I'll write in cursive." What is especially revealing is that children's early scribbles vary from culture to culture—reflecting the characteristics of adult writing in that system. So, for example, although young U.S. children and young Egyptian and Israeli children all scribble, the physical appearance of the scribbles are very different, though the purpose and intent are remarkably similar (Harste, Woodward, & Burke, 1984).

Environmental print awareness is necessary for emergent literacy, but it clearly is not sufficient for success in conventional reading and writing. Children need to acquire much more specific ideas about how print is organized and why we read.

*Understanding the Language of Books.* Despite many commonalities, oral and written language are not identical, and young children need to learn the language of books. *Read-aloud transactions* provide a pleasurable and supportive environment for this type of literacy learning. The Commission on Reading concluded in its 1985 report that "the single most important activity for building the knowledge required for eventual success in reading is reading aloud to children" (R. C. Anderson et al., 1985). Perhaps because of this, storybook reading interactions have been well studied over the past two decades (Bus, 2001; Bus, van Ijzendoorn, & Pellegrini, 1995; Vernon-Feagans, Hammer, Miccio, & Manlove, 2001). The benefits of reading aloud to children and interacting with them about books are many; children's vocabularies are improved, they understand the language of books better, they acquire knowledge about literacy conventions, and it improves their metalinguistic awareness. Children also become familiar with the look of print, the direction of it, the ways in which pages are turned to move through text, the fact that pictures and text are generally related, and so forth (Clay, 1979). This knowledge is as useful for writing as for reading. For example, one of the most important differences between spoken and written language is that written language is "decontextualized" (Gleason, 1997). This means that written language is produced so that it does not require the writer and the reader to share a physical context. To accomplish this, authors use a variety of cohesive devices to link information together in a meaningful whole. Children must learn to attend to the cues and referents that authors use so that they can sort out events and motives and to use them intentionally in their own writing so that others can understand the messages they compose.

Increasingly, researchers are studying not only the specific knowledge gleaned during reading aloud, but also the lessons learned from the exchanges themselves. These events often provide opportunities for adults to model appropriate thinking and feeling responses. This active interaction with text is necessary, of course, if children are to become competent readers and skillful writers. In addition, these read-aloud transactions teach children to question the meaning of text and encourage them to begin to think and use language in ways that will later be critical for school success (Altwerger, Diehl-Faxon, & Dockstader-Anderson, 1985; Wells, 1982).

Of course, the lessons learned are highly dependent on the specific interactional styles modeled, and there is considerable evidence to suggest differences among parents from diverse socioeconomic and ethnic groups (Heath, 1983; Pellegrini, Perlmutter, Galda, & Brody, 1990; Vernon-Feagans et al., 2001). Not surprisingly, "parents' own literacy practices appeared to determine opportunities for young children to become involved in literacy-related interactions. Parents were more inclined to respond to their child's interest in books when they had a positive orientation toward literacy, which was manifested in mutually enjoyable book-reading sessions" (Bus, 2001, p. 186). The most experienced parents, regardless of socioeconomic or racial background, tended to shape the reading experience to their child's interests and abilities. Thus, with very young children the book events tended to include a great deal of picture discussion and labeling, whereas more experienced children and adults focused on comprehending the story, often with discussion throughout.

Nevertheless, researchers have also observed systematic differences between white parents' storybook readings and those of African American parents, even when socioeconomic background was considered. Vernon-Feagans et al. (2001) note that schools should become aware of the differences between home and school practices. In particular, African

American children have much less experience with question-and-answer formats. Clearly, this does not need to be a barrier to literacy development, but it is likely to be one if teachers misunderstand the sources of students' behavior.

*Understanding Story Structure.*    Research suggests that young children need a well-developed sense of story to comprehend text fully. In addition, story sense appears helpful in generating predictions about upcoming text and also in remembering (or reconstructing) stories.

Read-aloud transactions help children begin to internalize different structures for different types of text. Well-read-to youngsters generate a mental map for stories during the many interactions they have with this type of text (Mandler & Johnson, 1977; Stein & Glenn, 1979). These mental maps, or "story schema," are generalized structures that people use to comprehend and remember (McConaughy, 1982). Several types of story structures have been proposed. The stories children encounter in school settings typically contain the following elements:

- Setting—generally the physical setting and characters;
- Initiating event—"it all started when . . .";
- Internal response—how the main character reacts to the initiating event;
- Attempt—an action or series of actions by the character(s) to try to reach a goal or solve a problem;
- Consequence—what happens as a result of the attempt;
- Reaction—a final reaction or event that ties the rest of the story together (also called a resolution).

These elements actually describe the elements present in stories that come from the European folk and fable tradition (Stein & Glenn, 1979). Other stories have different types of arrangements and are reflected in the stories children tell and in their comprehension of stories heard or read (Gee, 1989; Minami & McCabe, 1991, 1995). Many experiences with different types of texts encourage children to see that stories have certain predictable features and that these can be relied upon to aid comprehension and memory.

Not surprisingly, children's ability to tell their own spontaneous narratives is also fueled by their language development and their experiences with stories. Recent research demonstrates that "the preferred way of telling stories varies from culture to culture . . . and children typically adopt the narrative style of their own community" (Gleason, 1997, p. 409). Students who have experienced stories that unfold in different ways or have symbols and meanings different from European folktales will have a different sense of story. They will have different mental maps available for comprehension. For example, Hispanic narratives revolve around personal and family relationships rather than events and what happened (McCabe, 1992; Rodino, Gimbert, Perez, Craddock-Willis, & McCabe, 1991), and the story structure of narratives told by African American children (especially girls) tends to differ from that of white, middle-class children (Gee, 1989). In addition, it is important to understand that children's primary language is a factor in assessment. Many L2 learners provide much more complete retellings if they are allowed to substitute their first language for key English vocabulary words they don't know or can't remember (Garcia, 1991).

Similarly, our experience suggests that even when students demonstrate weak ability to tell classic narrative stories, they may have very strong ability to narrate other types. In Figure 7.2, for example, you can see Ian's attempt at telling a story, which is weak and ill-formed. You can also see that when he is asked to tell a personal narrative ("tell a story about something that happened to you"), his knowledge and skill look far more impressive.

Ian is a young, first-grade child from an isolated rural community. His experiences with literature and formal school tasks were very scant. However, his large, extended family obviously provided considerable experience in telling and retelling personal narratives.

The oral and written stories of less-skilled readers and writers are often less coherent and well-developed than those told or written by their skilled classmates (Montague, Cleborne, Maddux, & Dereshiwsky, 1990). Research has consistently indicated that disabled readers produce poor narratives and have difficulty recalling narratives they have heard. In particular, they tend to delete causal and temporal connections from their stories (Dickinson & McCabe, 1991; Peterson, Jesso, & McCabe, 1999).

General literacy experiences such as read-aloud transactions provide children with the information they need to generate good hypotheses about conventional literacy. If children come to school without these experiences, the instructional program should build on the specific experiences children bring with them.

**FIGURE 7.2**
Ian's Storytelling and Personal Narrative

---

**IAN, grade 2**

**I. Story Narrative:** "Tell me a story"

Monster Meals. Monsters eat meals. Put some car doors, some old shoes, some nails. That's how monsters eat their meals. And I made that up.

**II. Personal Narrative:** "Sometimes people tell stories about a time when something exciting or sad happened; or about a good time with a friend. Did anything like that ever happen to you? Tell me a story about it."

When I was in kindergarten, my teacher told me to get off the ice. I didn't. I threw out a rock about this big and I went to go get it. I slipped and the rock landed on my thumb and I broke by thumb. And that hurt. (pause) They said my thumb was too small for a cast, so they said, "Gauze it up." So that's what my Mom and Dad put on it, gauze.

**III. Retelling:** "Now, tell *me* that story."

Dogger
There was this little boy that had a dog. He lost him. His parents and him were searching, but he didn't find him until they went to the fair and a little girl bought him. And he said, "Well," and his sister said, "Would you swap this teddy bear for my brother's dog back, please?" And she smiled. And then he said, "Did you like that teddy bear anyway?" She said, "No, I didn't like him because his eyes were too scary." And she said, "If I had another teddy in my bed, there wouldn't be room for me." They used to walk him like a real dog, and his mother showed him how to wash him. And sometimes he'd pull him in a wagon.

***Analyzing Speech and Print.***    In order to become successful readers and writers children also must acquire the ability to analyze and to control their interactions with print (Bialystok & Ryan, 1985). The special requirements of reading or writing print are not obvious to the novice. Young children typically demonstrate limited awareness of language itself. This *metalinguistic awareness,* or conscious knowledge of the linguistic elements of language, continues to develop throughout the school years. Yet children must develop linguistic awareness to learn to read and write.

*The Concept of Word.*    Because the strategy "pay attention to meaning" works so well for speech, young children seem not to be aware of the component pieces of language. For example, speech provides few cues to tell children about the word as a unit of analysis. Words that name objects are easily isolated, but in the flow of normal speech, individual words are not clearly marked. To be successful in reading and writing, though, children must acquire the ability to identify individual words in the context of other words, that is, they must acquire a *concept of word,* which is an "awareness of the match between the spoken word and the written word in the reading of text" (Morris, 1993).

The following example demonstrates how children who appear competent may have incorporated unanalyzed items into their language. A three-year-old sings, "Baa-baa, black sheep, *have you any* wool . . ." (a favorite song that she has sung for months). Then she asks, "Mom, what's *pabuany*?" What has been understood by the informed listener (Mom) as "have you any" has actually been perceived and produced by the child as a single unit: "pabuany." However, the child's question does indicate her growing demand for clarity in language.

As Downing (1978) points out, beginners must also learn what conventions are represented in print. For example, children must learn that words are bound configurations that are separated by white space in print and that the term *word* is used to refer to a specific aspect of language. The available evidence suggests that four- and five-year-old children have a difficult time selecting a word from among letters, numbers, phrases, and sentences (Ferriero & Teberosky, 1979, 1982; Hare, 1984). Reid (1966) interviewed five-year-old English children, asking them whether a variety of stimuli were "words." Some identified whole sentences as words, some made only random guesses, and some said that words, phrases, and sentences were all words. Even when children are asked about reading and words with a book in front of them, many four- and five-year-olds demonstrate substantial confusion about what constitutes a word and what people look at when they read (Morris, 1981).

Children do not acquire the concept of *word* in one flash of insight. As with all such knowledge and skill, the concept develops over time. In a longitudinal study of thirty children between the ages of three and six, Ferreiro (1980) examined the development of children's hypotheses and strategies for reading and writing. Her findings demonstrate that children's early "guesses" about the nature of these processes are quite different from those of older children. For example, children at first thought that similarities and differences between words were determined by the characteristics of the referent items, not by any similarities in sound. Thus, more letters were needed to write the name of a large item than were needed to write the name of a small one. Ferreiro (1980) provides the following marvelous example from a child in this stage:

> Maria (age four) was asked how many letters it would take to write her name. She said four (as many years as she was old). When asked how many letters it would take to write her mother's name, she responded six. But, for her father (a large man), she responded: "As many as a thousand."

There was considerable agreement among children as they moved through several stages. For example, at some point all the children she studied clearly evolved a "syllabic hypothesis." During this stage, the children believed that each letter represented one syllable. Clearly, when children arrive at the syllabic hypothesis, they have begun to see the formal relationships between speech and print. And, although the timing varied, all the children eventually realized that words are written with strings of graphemes.

Many researchers have concluded that children learn about the concept of word *during* the process of learning to read and write (Ehri, 1987; Sulzby, 1986). For example, it appears that children are better able to identify specific words, or "voice-point," when they can identify the initial consonants in words (Ehri & Sweet, 1991; Morris, 1993). Finger-point reading (the ability to match spoken words to print in memorized text) appears to play a linchpin role, according to Morris (1993), but it in turn is dependent on beginning consonant knowledge. The development of a concept of word is then used to develop and promote phoneme consciousness.

*Phonemic Awareness and Segmentation.* The ability to separate words into constituent sounds, or phonemic segmentation, is one ability that increasingly appears to distinguish children who have difficulty learning to read and write from those who make good progress (Juel, 1988; Stanovich, 1986; Yopp, 1988). For example, Juel's longitudinal study of a large group of at-risk children suggests that children who are poor readers in first grade remain poor readers in fourth grade. One hallmark of those poor first grade readers was very limited phonemic awareness. Indeed, Juel's findings suggest that although poor readers' phonemic awareness grew steadily in first grade, they left first grade with a little less phonemic awareness than the children who became average or good readers possessed upon entering first grade.

Clearly, children must be able to distinguish separate sound units in words before they will be able to identify letters in words that relate to these sounds. It is important to note that phonemic segmentation ability does not require that children know what letter stands for each sound they hear in a word. Phonemic segmentation is not the same as auditory discrimination, which refers to the ability to distinguish between two different sounds. Indeed, it appears that auditory discrimination tests are poor predictors of ability to segment speech (Yopp, 1988).

Research suggests that young children may take quite a long time to acquire phonemic awareness. Liberman and Shankweiler (1979), for example, report the results of a study investigating the ability of four-, five-, or six-year-old children to segment speech into constituent phonemes and syllables. None of the children at age four was able to segment by phoneme, although half of these children could segment by syllable. Only 20 percent of the five-year-old children were able to segment by phoneme and, even at age six, only 70 percent were able to do so. Other authors have reported similar findings based on a variety of criteria (Calfee, Lindamood, & Lindamood, 1973; Fox & Routh, 1976).

Although research suggests that there is a strong relationship between the rhyming abilities of children as young as three years old and their later success in reading (Bryant, MacLean, Bradley, & Crossland, 1990), more recent findings point to the greater importance of phonemic segmentation over rhyming for subsequent reading achievement (Muter, Hulme, Snowling, & Taylor, 1997; Naslund & Schneider, 1996). Despite these strong correlations, phonological awareness and phonemic segmentation should not be viewed as prerequisite to reading instruction. Instead, many researchers argue that this relationship is due to differences in children's ability to detect individual phonemes. Other researchers argue convincingly that children learn these individual phonemes when they receive instruction in school reading programs (Bowey & Frances, 1991; Ehri, 1987).

It is increasingly clear that there is a progression of phonological knowledge that children acquire in the preschool and kindergarten period. Yopp (1992) suggests the following stages:

1. Rhyming
2. Blending (individual sounds to form words)
3. Counting (*How many sounds do you hear in "man"?*)
4. Segmenting (*Tell me the sounds you hear in "man"*)
5. Deleting (*Say,* "man," *now take the /m/ away—what is the word?*)
6. Substituting (If I change the /m/ in "man" to /c/, what word do I have?)

Many existing readiness programs do not include instruction designed to help children segment words into either phonemes or onsets and rimes. Since the ability to segment speech into phonemic units appears to have strong predictive power, most researchers suggest that early instruction in this area is needed (Tunmer, Herriman, & Nesdale, 1988; Snow et al., 1948; National Reading Panel, 2000). Indeed, recent research suggests that direct instruction in phonemic segmentation (Cunningham, 1990) or onset and rimes (Goswami, 1986) may be related to reading achievement at the beginning stages of reading development.

However, caution is needed in this area. Although the ability to segment sounds is clearly important, most researchers have also concluded that phonological sensitivity is necessary, but not sufficient, for reading achievement (Tunmer et al., 1988). For most children good instruction in reading and writing leads to greater linguistic awareness. It is as though the child had never thought to analyze speech but, in learning to read and/or write, had been forced to recognize units and subdivisions (Francis, 1973). Thus, early successful experiences with print can develop students' abilities in this critical area (see Cunningham & Cunningham, 1992; National Reading Panel, 2000; Pikulski, 1994).

## The Development of Written Language

In the same way that reading experiences promote phonemic awareness, writing appears to develop print level awareness and skill. As DeFord (1991) has noted,

When young children write, the reading/writing process is conveniently slowed down; to form messages and print, children must work on a variety of levels. They have to think about what they want to say, what they hear and how they represent it, what they expect to see if they can't hear it and it doesn't look right, where they are in their message, and how they can make their message clear to other readers . . . As young writers focus in on smaller or physical aspects of writing, they learn certain principles about print formation, letter sound relationships, spelling patterns, and the meaning of certain morphological forms. (pp. 86, 88)

As children increase their understanding of the requirements of reading and writing, they begin to acquire more cognitive control over their own literacy skills.

***The Form and Function of Writing.*** It seems clear that young children acquire writing competence by writing—in much the same way that they become competent in speech by talking. This does not, of course, happen without a supportive and responsive environment. When children see others around them using writing for functional purposes, they will model their own behavior accordingly, writing lists and messages and signs during play and to signal wants and needs. Of course, these notes and signs will reflect the child's knowledge and skill in writing.

The following stages are evident in the writing development of most children (DeFord, 1980, p. 162):

1. Scribbling
2. Differentiation between drawing and writing
3. Concepts of linearity, uniformity, linear complexity, symmetry, placement, left-to-right motion, and top-to-bottom directionality
4. Development of letters and letterlike shapes
5. Combination of letters, possibly with spaces, indicating understanding of units (letters, words, sentences), but may not show letter/sound correspondence
6. Writing known, isolated words—developing letter–sound correspondence
7. Writing simple sentences with use of inventive spellings
8. Combining two or more sentences to express complete thoughts
9. Control of punctuation—periods, capitalization, use of upper- and lowercase letters
10. Form of discourse—stories, information material, letters, and so on

Caution should be exercised in interpreting this information, because many of these characteristics will be evident simultaneously as children gain control over written forms.

***Invented Spelling.*** The term *invented spelling* is a considered one. It is used to refer to a consistent phenomenon observed in young emergent readers/writers: the ability to invent spellings on their own. It is increasingly clear that children's developing spelling abilities reflect their growing linguistic knowledge and control. As children acquire the conventions and patterns of a language, these appear in their own writing. "Invented spelling appears to be a vehicle through which children grapple with and begin to understand the alphabetic principle (that letters represent sounds)" (Whitehurst & Lonigan, 2001, p. 18). Thus, spelling "errors" across children are not random, as can be seen from the sample in Figure 7.3. This sample demonstrates how Kelly's writing reflects a rather considerable knowledge base; they are *not* mistakes. She can already isolate all initial and final consonants and represent them appropriately in print. Indeed, she can also represent most medial sounds.

This ability to isolate and represent phonemes sets the stage for more advanced decoding work. Torgesen and Davis (1996), for example, found that the best predictor of

**FIGURE 7.3**
Writing Sample
(Age 6)

My brother and my sister are standing by my house

kindergarten children's success in a phonological training program was their pretest scores on a measure of invented spelling. Similarly, when first grade children were encouraged to use invented spellings in their writing, they made better progress in both spelling and decoding than did children without invented spelling encouragement (Clarke, 1988).

Emergent readers and writers proceed through distinctive developmental stages, moving from very immature spellings to those that approximate standard spellings (e.g., Henderson, 1990; Templeton & Bear, 1992). Although there are some disputes about the content of each stage, the following distinctions are generally made (see also Figure 2.2).

*Pre-Phonemic Spelling.*   Children use alphabetic symbols to "write" words, but these are generally unrelated to the target word. No sound–symbol relationship is present, and these are likely to reflect earlier notions about how the writing system works (see Ferreiro, 1978).

*Early Phonemic (or Semiphonemic) Spelling.*   Children exhibit a clear awareness that there is a relationship between phonemes and print. However, children represent very little of the phonemic information in print—sometimes the initial, sometimes the final, graphemes. The letters that are used represent specific phonemes from the word, but not all the phonemes are represented. Example: DR GML = Dear Grandma.

*Phonetic (and Letter Name) Spelling.*   Children hear and produce sequences of sounds in words. At this stage, children may produce spellings that are quite readable (*wns* for *once* and *bik* for *bike*). However, children at this stage are also often using a strategy that results in rather strange productions. As they try to represent more and more sounds in words, they begin to use a *letter-name strategy* (Beers & Henderson, 1977). That is, they analyze the word they want to spell into its component sounds and then find a letter name to represent each sound. They then spell each sound by choosing the letter name that most closely resembles the sound they want to represent (Gillet & Temple, 1982). Thus, children in this stage also produce such words as *lavatr* for *elevator* (Morris, 1981). This approach causes problems in correct production of vowels and certain consonant combinations, in particular.

*Transitional or Within-Word Pattern Spelling.*   Children's spellings bear a much closer resemblance to standard spellings. In this stage, children make use of visual as well as phonemic information (Gentry, 1982). Children generally represent short vowels appropriately in this stage and also mark long vowels, even though these often represent overgeneralizations of learned rules. Thus, spellings such as the following are typical of this stage: *dres* for *dress* and *rane* for *rain*. As Morris (1981) notes, "These transitional spellings, which begin to appear in late first grade or early second grade, are to be welcomed by the teacher, for they signal advancement in the child's understanding of English spelling. No longer does the child believe that spelling is a fixed, simple code in which letters map to sounds in a left-to-right, one-to-one fashion" (p. 664). As Templeton (1997) has noted, children in this phase understand the *patterns* that make up the letter–sound relationships.

Children's inventive spellings can provide a great deal of information about their emergent literacy skills. As Dear et al. (2000) have noted, there is a "synchrony of reading, writing, and spelling development. This means that development in one area is observed along with advances in other areas" (p. 13). As children learn how written language works in English and how the sounds are represented in print, they use that knowledge in both writing and reading. It is, of course, productive to continue to attend to students' spelling as it reflects their control in the writing process. Spelling continues to develop in a systematic way right through the early middle school years (see Chapter 9 for consideration of spelling development beyond the within-word phase).

# Strategies and Tools for Assessing Emergent Literacy

## Assessment of Emergent Literacy

Gathering dependable and useful information about the literacy abilities of young children can be a very tricky business. In the following section we briefly discuss the theoretical problems involved in using most existing formal assessment instruments, saving a discussion of specific standardized tools for later in the text (see Chapter 10). In this chapter we describe a number of informal assessment strategies for observation, structured informal assessment, and diagnostic teaching. Before we turn our attention to these specific practices, it is important to consider the problems associated with the assessment of early literacy.

The match between early literacy assessment and beginning reading and writing instruction has become increasingly poor as our knowledge and understanding of emergent literacy has continued to expand. Almost all of the readiness tests used today are variations of earlier tests that evolved from older, developmental views of reading readiness. Between 1930 and 1943, twelve readiness tests were published (Betts, 1946), several of which are still used widely today in revised versions. As Teale, Hiebert, and Chittenden (1987) note, "Young children's reading and writing are being measured in ways that do not reflect an adequate conceptualization of early literacy development or sensitivity to the fact that children of age 4 or 5 have special social and developmental characteristics" (p. 773). Few readiness tests, for example, evaluate children's awareness of the purposes for reading; nor, for that matter, do they evaluate students' phonemic awareness. Similarly, none ask children to write or permit teachers to assess whether children know how to handle a book, understand the conventions of print, or understand the language that will be used in beginning reading instruction (Day & Day, 1986).

In addition, many readiness tests include some tasks not directly related to the act of reading or writing (for example, identifying and/or matching geometric shapes). Finally, the demands of specific programs of beginning instruction have been ignored almost completely. "Because most (readiness tests) attempt to be nationally standardized tests, equally applicable to a variety of situations, none fully accounts for the questions of 'what methods' or 'what materials' will be used for instruction" (Nurss, 1979, p. 43).

Now, however, the climate seems much more hospitable for examining children's literacy knowledge and abilities in more authentic ways. Teale, Hiebert, and Chittenden (1987) describe the attributes necessary for good emergent literacy assessment:

1. Assessment is a part of instruction.
2. Assessment methods and instruments are varied.
3. Assessment focuses on a broad range of skills and knowledge reflecting the various dimensions of literacy.
4. Assessment occurs continuously.
5. Literacy is assessed in a variety of contexts.
6. Measures are appropriate for children's developmental levels and cultural background.

These characteristics are entirely consistent with our approach to *all* assessment, but they are critical in evaluating the knowledge and skill of very young children. Only a few formal assessments meet these standards (see Chapter 10), although a number of structured, developmental screening tools have appeared in the past decade (see Meisels et al., 1997) that can be exceptionally helpful in assessing early literacy. The majority of early literacy assessment will be conducted less formally, and as a result, the diagnostic portfolio is an especially useful tool in the assessment of young, or very disabled, readers and writers.

## Diagnostic Portfolio and Emergent Literacy

Gathering dependable and useful information about emergent literacy requires continuous observation of children in actual literacy settings. As assessment is planned, it is helpful to reflect on the following questions:

- What do I already know about this child?
- How do I know that?

- What do I still need to know to plan instruction?
- How can I find this out?

A summary form such as the one shown in Figure 7.4 should be used to organize information as it is gathered. This form can also be used to help determine what information is already available from sources such as those described in the Getting Started Phase (see Chapter 4).

Assessment strategies that can be conducted during everyday instructional exchanges are described in the following sections. These classroom-based strategies, sometimes called curriculum-embedded performance assessments (Meisels, 1998), involve both careful observation of children engaged in normal instructional events and observations of children in

**FIGURE 7.4**
Summary/Planning
Form: Emergent
Literacy Assessment

Student: _____ Age: _____ Date: _____
Examiner: _____

**I. Oral Language**
   A. First language
   B. Phonological development
   C. Vocabulary
   D. Syntactic sophistication
   E. Pragmatics (functions and uses of language)

**II. Literacy Knowledge/Experience**
   A. Family/home print-literacy environment
   B. Print awareness (environmental)
   C. Book concepts (language, directionality, etc.)
   D. Concept of word (boundaries and linearity)
   E. Speech-to-print match
   F. Phonemic segmentation
      1. rhyming          4. deleting
      2. blending         5. substituting
      3. segmenting

**III. Story Retelling**
   A. Story sense
   B. Dictated stories
   C. Language use

**IV. Writing**
   A. Forms and functions of writing
   B. Invented spelling

**V. Observations and Comments**

situations that have been structured by the teacher to assess specific components of literacy (see Figure 7.5). Thus, for each technique described here, we indicate the types of information that can be gathered.

Informal assessments can provide rich data about children, but it is important to guard against hasty judgments and assumptions. Conclusions *must* be documented. The strategies and forms provided below can help with this task and the role of the diagnostic portfolio is

**FIGURE 7.5**  Components of Emergent Literacy Assessment

### Components of Emergent Literacy Assessment by Various Informal Techniques

| Assessment Strategy | Developmentally appropriate articulation and syntax | Adequate vocabulary | Elaborated use of language | Wide range of language functions | Recognizes environmental print | Recognizes various functions of print | Print carries a message | Parts of book | Directionality/orientation | Language of book print (word/letter) | Punctuation | Recognizes/recalls story elements | Produces well-structured stories | Retains structure during recall | Segmentation of words (oral) | Segmentation of syllables (oral) | Segmentation of phonemes (oral) | Rhyming | Matches spoken words to print | Some sight vocabulary | Sound-symbol correspondence (initial) | Attempts reading/writing | Knows letter names | Knows some sound-symbols | Uses some invented spelling |
|---|---|---|---|---|---|---|---|---|---|---|---|---|---|---|---|---|---|---|---|---|---|---|---|---|---|
| | **Oral Language Competence** | | | | **Print Awareness** | | | **Concepts of Book Print** | | | | **Story Sense** | | | **Phonemic Awareness** | | | | **Speech-to-Print Match** | | | **Control of Reading/Writing** | | | |
| Informal Observation | X | X | X | X | X | X | X | ————————————————————————————————————→ | | | | | | | | | | | | | | | | | |
| Structured Interviews | X | X | X | X | X | X | X | X | X | X | X | | | | X | | | | | | X | | | | |
| Structured Observation | | | | | X | X | X | X | X | X | X | | | | | | | | | | | | | | |
| Retelling Guides | X | X | X | X | | | | | | | | X | X | X | | | | | | | | | | | |
| Dictated Stories | X | X | X | X | | | X | | | | | X | X | | | | | | X | X | X | | | | |
| Writing Samples | X | X | | | | | X | | | | | | | | X | X | X | X | X | X | X | X | X | X | X |
| DLTA | | | | | | X | X | X | X | X | | X | X | X | | | | | | | | | | | |

key here. Young children's work samples and the observation checklists provide the evidence you need.

## Observing Spontaneous Use of Knowledge and Skill

The procedures described in this section expand the focus of the observational techniques on knowledge and attitudes about reading, described in Chapter 4, to include observation of emergent literacy in the areas of oral language development and concepts about print.

***Teacher Rating of Oral Language and Literacy (TROLL).*** This research-based assessment tool has only recently been developed (see Dickinson, McCabe, & Sprague, 2001). It was designed to provide a research-based instrument for teachers to use in evaluating several critical aspects of students' early literacy development, including language, reading, and writing abilities. TROLL draws on benchmark abilities in speaking and listening that have been described for children at preK–grade 3 (New Standards project, Tucker & Codding, 1998). TROLL is designed for teacher use, with the expectation that teachers will track students' progress on a variety on language arts dimensions. Teachers rate students using a rubric related to specific abilities. Figure 7.6 presents a sample from TROLL.

In addition to language use in communicating personal experiences, as shown in Figure 7.6, TROLL items focus on other aspects of language use, vocabulary development, ability to engage in emergent reading and writing activities, and phonological segmentation abilities. These items yield several subtotals (writing, oral language, and reading) as well as a total TROLL score. The authors provide an extremely useful table transforming the total TROLL scores into percentiles and providing recommendations/interpretations of these scores for

**FIGURE 7.6**
Sample Assessment from TROLL

| Item 2 asks: "How well does the child *communicate personal experiences* in a clear and logical way?" Assign the score that best describes this child when he/she is attempting to tell an adult about events at home or some other place where you were not present. | | | |
|---|---|---|---|
| **1** | **2** | **3** | **4** |
| Child is very tentative, only offers a few words, requires you to ask questions. Has difficulty responding to questions you ask. | Child offers some information, but additional information needed to really understand the event (e.g., where or when it happened, who was present, the sequence of what happened). | Child offers information and sometimes includes the necessary information to really understand the event. | Child freely offers information and tells experiences in a way that is nearly always complete, well-sequenced, and comprehensible. |

*Source:* Based on material from Dickinson, D. K., McCabe, A., & Sprague, K. (2001). *Teacher rating of oral language and literacy (TROLL): A research-based tool* (CIERA Report #3-016, p. 15). Ann Arbor, MI: Center for the Improvement of Early Reading Achievement.

children ages 3, 4, and 5. Because the tool is easy to use by classroom teachers with no formal training, its authors hope that it will be used to flag struggling students so that appropriate instruction can be provided.

***Oral Language Checklists.***    Teachers need to assess oral language competence to ensure that children can accomplish the tasks required in school settings (see Chapter 2). School tasks demand language use that is quite different from the language used in homes and among peers. Thus, even if children have language development appropriate to their home environment, they may not have acquired language appropriate for functioning in a school setting.

Researchers and educators have come to realize that language is difficult to evaluate through short, controlled samples. Therefore, people who study language acquisition now frequently recommend evaluating language in naturalistic settings (see Lund & Duchan, 1988). This means talking and listening to children engaged in everyday school activities. However, if children's primary language differs in important ways from school English, observations may be conducted in other settings as well to distinguish generalized linguistic problems from issues of context and culture.

What is needed is an inclination to notice and a willingness to make narrative notes. A framework is helpful to focus the "noticing." Previously in this chapter we described Halliday's taxonomy of language functions. Halliday's categories are drawn from actual observations of children and can be used fairly easily as the basis for an evaluation checklist. This will provide information about students' functional use of language.

For more specific aspects of oral language, you might use Rubin's (2000) diagnostic checklist to focus attention (see Figure 7.7). As you observe the child, note the time, setting, materials, and activity and indicate which functions of language are being used. In addition, specific examples of language used should be noted next to each function; the child's actual word usage and syntax can be quite revealing. This approach works well in most classrooms for young children, because there are often times when children are in several centers around the room. Teachers can target one or several children for observation on a particular day. Many teachers find sticky-backed notepads useful.

***Writing Samples.***    Student writing samples can provide information about several aspects of emergent literacy. They provide teachers with information about children's knowledge of the sound-symbol system and about their understanding of the functions of writing.

If the child's classroom includes many opportunities for writing, spontaneous samples of children's work can be gathered easily. This is desirable because it permits an evaluation of not only what the child *can* do, but also of what he or she *does*. Genishi and Dyson (1984) suggest a number of questions that can be considered as various aspects of children's written work are observed (see Figure 7.8).

Not all young children come from homes where reading and writing are modeled. More seriously, not all children enter school settings that support the relations between reading and writing. The writing of five- and six-year-old children:

> is often not acceptable in schools, where conventional, adult-like writing may be the only writing of interest. As *Freddy* remarked, 'I used to write, but not anymore . . . I come to school now.' *Freddy* reported that he stopped writing when he started kindergarten. . . . (Genishi & Dyson, 1984, p. 173)

**FIGURE 7.7**
Oral Language and
Speech Diagnostic
Checklist

| Student's Name: Grade: Teacher: Diagnostic Checklist for Oral Comunication and Speech Improvement | | |
|---|---|---|
| | **YES** | **NO** |
| *Speech* (general): The child's speech is | | |
| 1. distinct | | |
| 2. inaudible | | |
| 3. monotonous | | |
| 4. expressive | | |
| *Nonverbal Communication:* The child | | |
| 1. uses facial expressions effectively | | |
| 2. uses hands effectively | | |
| 3. uses body movements effectively | | |
| *Vocabulary* (general): The child's vocabulary is | | |
| 1. meager | | |
| 2. rich | | |
| 3. accurate | | |
| 4. incorrect | | |
| *Sentences:* | | |
| 1. The child uses incomplete sentences. | | |
| 2. The child uses simplistic sentences. | | |
| 3. The child uses involved sentences. | | |
| 4. The child uses standard English. | | |
| 5. The child uses a variation of English. | | |
| 6. English is not the dominant language of the child. | | |
| The child engages in conversation freely. | | |
| The child respects other persons when he or she is speaking. | | |
| The child enters into class discussions. | | |
| The child can describe in his or her own words an event that has occurred. | | |
| The child freely engages in these activities: | | |
| 1. creative drama | | |
| 2. role playing | | |
| 3. choral speaking | | |
| 4. finger play (primary grades) | | |
| 5. puppetry | | |
| 6. pantomime | | |
| 7. "show and tell" (primary grades) | | |
| 8. informal reports | | |
| 9. formal reports (intermediate grades) | | |
| 10. debates (intermediate grades) | | |
| 11. storytelling | | |

*Source:* Rubin, D. (2000). *Teaching Elementary Language Arts: A Balanced Approach* (6th ed.) (pp. 113–114). Copyright © 2000. Boston: Allyn & Bacon. Reprinted by permission.

When observing (watching, listening to, talking to children about) their writing, you might consider the following questions:

### The Message

1. Does the child believe that he's written a message? If so,
2. Does the child know what the message is? That is, can he read it? If so,
3. Did the child freely formulate his own message? Or, did the child simply copy something? Or, was the message confined to a small set of words which the child could easily spell?
4. How long was the message?
   - one word or a list of unrelated words
   - a phrase
   - a sentence
5. How does the child's written message relate to other graphics on the page?

### The Writing System

1. Can you read the child's message? If not,
2. Does there seem to be any system to how the child went from the formulated message to the print? For example, the child may have:
   - put down a certain number of letters per object
   - rearranged the letters in his name
   - written a certain number of letters per syllable
3. If you can read the child's message, can you tell how the child wrote it?
   *For example, the child may have:
   - recalled the visual pattern (e.g., *COOW,* child intended to write *moo*)
   - based spelling on letter names (e.g., *PT,* which is read *Petie*)
   - requested spellings from peer or adult
   - based spelling on phonological analysis (e.g., *APL,* which is read *apple*)

### The Written Product

1. How conventional are the child's written symbols? (Do they look like letters?)
2. Did the child follow the left-to-right directionality convention?
3. Is there any order to the way the letters or words are arranged on the page? Or, does it appear that the child simply put letters where there was empty space?

### Message Reading

1. Does the child appear to have written without any particular intended message? If so,
2. Did the child attempt to decode the written message?
3. If so, how did the child go from text to talk? The child may have:
   - engaged in apparent fantasy behavior
   - requested that an adult read the unknown message (e.g., "What does this say?")
   - based the decoding on the perceived text segments (i.e., matched a number of oral syllables to the perceived number of segments in text)
   - used a letter-name strategy (i.e., "read" a word containing the name of a written letter, as reading "Debbie" for *PARA NB*)
   - based decoding on visual recall of a word similar in appearance

**FIGURE 7.8**
(Continued)

---

**Writing Purpose**

Why did the child write? Possible reasons include:

- Simply to write: no clearly identifiable purpose exists beyond this (e.g., "I'm gonna' do it how my Mama does it.")
- To create a message: the meaning of the message is unknown to the child (e.g., "Read this for me.")
- To produce or to practice conventional symbols (e.g., the *ABC*s, displayed written language) without concern for a referent
- To detail or accurately represent a drawn object (e.g., the *S* on Superman's shirt)
- To label objects or people
- To make a particular type of written object (e.g., a book, a list, a letter) without concern for a particular referent
- To organize and record information (e.g., to write a list of friends)
- To investigate the relationship between oral and written language without concern for a particular referent (e.g., "If I do [add] this letter, what does it say?")
- To express directly feelings or experiences of oneself or others (i.e., direct quotations, as in writing the talk of a drawn character), and
- To communicate a particular message to a particular audience

*Note:* It may be that the child is using one of these methods, but you simply cannot read it. After asking the child to read the paper, you may be able to detect patterns in the child's encoding system.

---

*Source:* From *Language Assessment in the Early Years* by Celia Genishi and Anne Haas Dyson. Ablex Publishing Corporation.

Writing samples provided by Teddy at the end of kindergarten and the end of first grade provide dramatic evidence of the difficulties that can develop because of classroom practice. Teddy's work at the end of kindergarten is exemplified in Figure 7.9a. One year later, to the month, he was producing journal entries like those in 7.9b. During a portfolio review, another teacher was struck by the fact that there was virtually no evidence of *writing* in the most recent samples, so she asked Teddy to look at the two pieces and talk about them. He seemed impressed by his own production, as represented in the kindergarten sample, but did not offer an explanation. When the teacher remarked that he had done a lot of writing in kindergarten but there wasn't any in the first grade sample, Teddy sighed and commented, "You always have to be so *neat*—and spell the words right too." Clearly, his sample was less representative of what he knew how to do than what he chose to do, given the context.

***Checklists for Concepts about Print.***    Although there are several contrived ways to assess students' knowledge about the functions of literacy, evaluation in this area can be accomplished largely through observation. Many kindergarten and first-grade classrooms are print-rich environments. Print appears on labels, charts, schedules, and so on. In this type of environment, it is possible to observe how often and how well children employ print in their daily activities. As children use print to label, describe, and follow directions, teachers can document the growing competence of each child. For example, the teacher might watch children as they reread familiar books, charts, and papers. The following examples are suggestive of the types of events that are noteworthy:

**FIGURE 7.9a**
Teddy's
Kindergarten
Journal

This is picture of the Big Apple Circus.

Example A: Four-and-a-half-year-old Nora picks up a newspaper and opens it appropriately, remarking: "Oh, here's some news."

Example B: Five-year-old Joel works intently to make a label to describe his show-and-tell object so that people who see it on the science table "will know what it is."

These children clearly are acquiring a sense of the functional nature of print. Observations should focus on behaviors that demonstrate that children understand the various functions and conventions of literate behavior, not on accuracy (do they read/write correctly?).

As teachers watch for specific behaviors that will inform them about their students' emergent literacy, they should keep the following questions in mind:

- How well does the child distinguish print from pictures?
- How well does the child recognize the functions of print in the environment (signs, posted information, and so on)?

**FIGURE 7.9b**
Teddy's First
Grade Journal

- How does the child reread familiar books (for example, does she or he "talk like a book," using the structure and vocabulary of book language)?
- What distinctions does the child make among pictures, scribbling, and print?
- In what ways does the child attempt to read familiar books, labels, charts, and so on?
- What distinctions can the child make among different forms of print (labels versus stories)?

Continuous observations of these types of behaviors yield a much richer picture of literacy knowledge than is permitted by formal measures alone.

Despite the usefulness of observation, relying on spontaneous use of knowledge and skill cannot ensure that we have gathered information about all that students can do. Thus, systematic task structuring can be helpful.

## Structured Interviews and Observations

In this section we describe several techniques for conducting informal but structured interviews with very young children. We have used these techniques ourselves and found that they are manageable and also that they do discriminate among children who are more or less aware of the demands of beginning reading.

*"Word" Reading.*   Ferreiro (Ferreiro & Teberosky, 1979/1982) has devised a number of ingenious tasks that are quite easy to administer and that yield a number of insights into children's understanding of the conventions of print. The tasks are administered in a structured interview format that includes probing and discussing children's responses to elicit more information about their print concepts. The interviews are designed specifically to explore children's ideas about what is readable and what can be written.

The word-reading task involves sorting word cards. The stimulus cards should include letter strings, real words, "possible" words, repeated strings, and numbers. Some sample items include:

> two     5     zzzz     me     n     iiio     PIE     jot     butterfly

To administer this task, simply ask the child:

1. Which are something to read?
2. Which are not something to read?
3. Can you read the cards that are "good for reading?"
4. What do they say?

The examiner should also probe to determine what criteria the child is using to classify the cards.

In evaluating the child's responses, the following questions should be considered:

- What distinctions does the child make between words and numerals and words and letters?
- What distinctions does the child make based on the length of the display?
- How sensitive is the child to repeated elements?
- How do uppercase and lowercase letters influence the child's decisions?

Patterns of response can indicate how aware the child is of the forms and conventions of written words.

Working with kindergarten children, we found that some children argue that all the cards are "good for reading." As we noted above, an interview of this type allows us to explore responses. In defending this response, two explanations are common. Some children assert that although they could not read the cards, other "older" or "bigger" people could. Other children demonstrate that all the cards are "good for reading" by reading the letter names. Thus, the card "iiio" is read "i" "i" "i" "o," and the card *jot* is read "j-o-t." In neither case do these children appear to have satisfactory ideas about the forms and functions of reading and writing.

***Finger-Point Reading.***    Ferreiro and others (Ehri & Sweet, 1991; Morris, 1993) have developed an assessment strategy designed to assess students' developing concept of word. It combines pictures and word reading. The examiner should prepare cards or book pages that contain pictures with strong action cues. Below the picture, write a sentence about the action (e.g., "The girl is walking in the rain" or "The boy eats"). The examiner/teacher engages in an open-ended dialogue with the child by asking the following questions:

1. Is there something to read on this card/page? (Have children point to it.)
2. What does it say? or What do you think it says?
3. (Using a portion of the child's response) Where does it say _____?
4. Do you think it might say _____?

A fairly typical exchange between Nicole and her teacher took place when Nicole's teacher showed her a card with a picture of a dog chasing a cat up a tree. Also printed on the card was the sentence: *"The dog runs."*

> TEACHER:    Where is there something to read on this card?
>
> NICOLE:    [Points to the words and runs her hands along the print.]
>
> TEACHER:    What does it say?
>
> NICOLE:    I don't know.
>
> TEACHER:    What do you think it says?
>
> NICOLE:    The dog is chasing the cat.
>
> TEACHER:    Where does it say "The"?
>
> NICOLE:    [Points to "The."]
>
> TEACHER:    Where does it say "cat"?
>
> NICOLE:    [Points to "dog."]
>
> TEACHER:    Where does it say "dog"?
>
> NICOLE:    [Points to "runs."]
>
> TEACHER:    Where does it say "chasing"?
>
> NICOLE:    [Laughs] There aren't any more of those . . . things.
>
> TEACHER:    That's right. What do we call those "things"?
>
> NICOLE:    Letters . . . Or, numbers.

This conversation reveals a great deal about six-year-old Nicole's concepts of print. We find out, for example, that she knows that the print is what is read. She also has a well-established sense of directionality. However, she clearly lacks a sense of speech–print match. She also lacks clarity about the terminology associated with reading instruction.

It is helpful to consider the following questions in evaluating a child's performance on this task.

- How well does the child understand the speech–print match?
- How well does the child appear to understand word boundaries?

- How well does the child appear to understand directionality?
- Is the child able to use initial or final consonants to mark word boundaries?

The purpose of these types of structured interviews is to delve into children's understanding and to gather instructionally useful information. Some of these same components are explored in the Concepts About Print test, discussed in the following section.

***Structured Observations about Print Concepts.***    Some years ago, Clay (1985) created an informal test designed to assess young children's knowledge and use of print concepts. In its most recent form, the Concepts About Print (CAP) test is part of a diagnostic survey designed to detect reading difficulties among young children (Clay, 1985). Two books, *Sand* and *Stones,* are used to assess children's knowledge of print conventions.

Using an interactive exchange, the examiner reads the book (*Sand* or *Stones*) asking twenty-four questions along the way. The child is told to help read the book by pointing to features in the book. These questions are designed to provide assessment opportunities related to the following concepts: how to hold a book for reading; print orientation; print, not pictures, carries the message; uppercase and lowercase letters; punctuation marks; and directionality.

A recent review of the available research suggests that the CAP test is a valid measure of emergent literacy independent from intelligence (Day & Day, 1986). For the classroom teacher, the CAP has the advantage of structuring observations. It can provide teachers with a place to start, and it also increases reliability, since the same tasks and materials are used for each child. In general, it can provide you with a quick assessment of children's experiences with books.

Of course, teachers can obtain similar information in more natural settings from regular picture books. Genishi and Dyson (1984) describe an adaptation that is quick and easy to use. Teachers select their own materials, including several different types of materials, for purposes of comparison. To implement this basic book-reading procedure, simply select a book and ask the child to do the following:

1. Show me the front of this book.
2. I'll read you this story. You help me. Show me where to start reading; where do I begin to read?
3. Show me where to start. Which way do I go? Where do I go after that?
4. Point to what I am reading. (Read slowly and fluently.)
5. Show me the first part of the story. Show me the last.
6. (On a page with print on both the left and right sides.) Where do I start reading?

Figure 7.10 provides a checklist of the concepts (distinctions between print and pictures, directionality, speech-to-print match) that can be used as a guide in evaluating the child's responses to these requests.

***Early and Emergent Reading Surveys.***    Recently, several educator-researchers have developed useful assessment tools for evaluating the early or emergent skills of young students. Two particularly useful tools are the Emerging Literacy Survey (ERSI) (Pikulski,

**FIGURE 7.10**
Print Concepts
Checklist

| Name: _____ Date: _____ |
|---|
| **Directions:** Using a book the child has never seen before, test the following concepts. |

| | Yes | No | Some-times |
|---|---|---|---|
| 1. Identifies front/back of book | ☐ | ☐ | ☐ |
| 2. Can indicate title | ☐ | ☐ | ☐ |
| 3. Identifies print as "what is read" | ☐ | ☐ | ☐ |
| 4. Can indicate picture | ☐ | ☐ | ☐ |
| 5. Knows where to start reading | ☐ | ☐ | ☐ |
| 6. Shows correct direction of print display | ☐ | ☐ | ☐ |
| 7. Indicates beginning of story on a page | ☐ | ☐ | ☐ |
| 8. Can show return sweep for a line of print | ☐ | ☐ | ☐ |
| 9. Indicates end of story | ☐ | ☐ | ☐ |
| 10. Identifies bottom of page | ☐ | ☐ | ☐ |
| 11. Identifies top of page | ☐ | ☐ | ☐ |
| 12. Can locate a word (by cupping, etc.) | ☐ | ☐ | ☐ |
| 13. Can locate two words that appear together | ☐ | ☐ | ☐ |
| 14. Can locate the space between words | ☐ | ☐ | ☐ |
| 15. Can locate a letter | ☐ | ☐ | ☐ |
| 16. Can locate two consecutive letters | ☐ | ☐ | ☐ |
| 17. Can indicate a period | ☐ | ☐ | ☐ |
| 18. Can indicate a comma, question mark | ☐ | ☐ | ☐ |

1999) and the Early Reading Screening Instrument (Lombardino, Morris, Mercado, DeFillipo, & Sarisky, 1999; Morris, 1992, 1999). Each of these includes tasks that evaluate a more comprehensive range of early literacy abilities than most older tools (see Figure 7.11).

The Early Reading Screening Instrument (ERSI) is "a method for identifying at-risk beginning readers which is short, yet comprehensive, and allows for adaptations cross-culturally" (Lombardino et al., 1999). The ERSI assesses students' letter knowledge, concept of word (using a finger-pointing task), phonological awareness (using inventive spelling), and word recognition for decodable and high-frequency words. When the ESRI is administered in kindergarten, it is a good predictor of first grade word recognition, word analysis, and comprehension; thus, it is an effective screening tool. The two best predictors of subsequent reading performance were the phonological awareness and word recognition components.

*Phonemic Segmentation.* The phoneme segmentation component of the ERSI is especially interesting because it employs an inventive spelling task and involves a scoring system that could be adapted and used by most teachers. On the ERSI, children are asked to try to spell twelve words, of which each contains three or four phonemes. Then you award one point for each phoneme identified by the child.

**FIGURE 7.11**
Emerging Literacy
Survey Summary
Form

Child's Name _____ Child's Date of Birth _____

Examiner _____

| Phonemic Awareness | Area Assessed | Assessment 1 Date _____ | Assessment 2 Date _____ | Assessment 3 Date _____ |
|---|---|---|---|---|
| | Rhyme | _____/8 | _____/8 | _____/8 |
| | Beginning Sounds | _____/8 | _____/8 | _____/8 |
| | Blending Onsets and Rimes | _____/8 | _____/8 | _____/8 |
| | Segmenting Onsets and Rimes | _____/8 | _____/8 | _____/8 |
| | Phoneme Blending | _____/8 | _____/8 | _____/8 |
| | Phoneme Segmentation | _____/8 | _____/8 | _____/8 |
| Familiarity with Print | Concepts of Print | _____/8 | _____/8 | _____/8 |
| | Letter Naming | _____/52 | _____/52 | _____/52 |
| Beginning Reading & Writing | Word Recognition | _____/40 | _____/40 | _____/40 |
| | Word Writing | _____(words) | _____(words) | _____(words) |
| | Sentence Dictation | _____/67 | _____/67 | _____/67 |
| | Comments | | | |

*Source:* From *Emerging Literacy Survey,* K–2 in *Houghton Mifflin Reading: A Legacy of Literacy* by J. David Cooper and John J. Pikulski et al. Copyright © 2001 by Houghton Mifflin Company. Reprinted by permission of Houghton Mifflin Company. All rights reserved.

**RIDE:**  (1 phoneme: R = 1 point, 2 phonemes: RD = 2 points, 3 phonemes: RID = 3 points)

**MEAT:**  (1 phoneme: M = 1 point, 2 phonemes: MT = 2 points, 3 phonemes: MET = 3 points)

**CATS:**  (1 phoneme: K OR C = 1 point, 2 phonemes: CS or CZ or KT, etc. = 2 points, 3 phonemes: CTZ or CAT, etc. = 3 points, 4 phonemes: CATS, CATZ, or KATZ, etc. = 4 points)

> **DUMP:** (1 phoneme: D or P = 1 point, 2 phonemes: DP, DM, etc. = 2 points, 3 phonemes: DUP, DOP, etc. = 3 points, 4 phonemes: DUMP, DAMP, etc. = 4 points)

It is important to recognize that kindergarten children are not likely to be able to complete all of these items with a full phonological analysis. In the validation study for the ESRI, for example, the average kindergarten child identified just over half of the phonemes. However, this type of assessment would provide excellent information for instructional purpose, especially when children do very poorly.

Another widely used assessment of phonemic segmentation was developed by Hallie Yopp (1988) and revised for classroom use as the Yopp-Singer Phoneme Segmentation Test (Yopp, 1995). We have added an additional blending task to the test for a bit more comprehensive examination of this component area (see Figure 7.12).

*Word Recognition.* As we have seen, students' ability to recognize some words by the end of kindergarten is a good predictor of subsequent reading success. We would like to emphasize again that the particular words do not matter. Rather, it is important to know that students are at the stage at which they are sufficiently attentive to print that they have begun to recognize some words in print. Obviously, opportunity has a major impact on the specific words that children learn first. Therefore, it is important to examine what materials have been used with young children, especially if a particular list of structured inventory will be used to assess this ability. Both the ERSI and the Emerging Literacy Survey evaluate students' recognition of some high-frequency sight words (the, and, is, etc.), although only a few of the specific words are the same.

Both of these assessments (and many others) also evaluate students word recognition of decodable words. The ERSI generally uses three-letter words that follow regular, short-vowel rules (e.g., cap, mop, dig) to assess this ability. The Emerging Literacy Survey, in contrast, uses nonsense words that represent recurrent spelling patterns, with a greater range of samples (e.g., "zan" and "dit" but also "rame" and "strime"). We will return to the issue of assessing word recognition in Chapter 8. In terms of the assessment of early or emergent readers, it is important to keep in mind the impact of the assessment tools being used. In the very earliest stages of learning to reading, when children know only eight to fifteen words, the particular words being tested can make a big difference in the conclusions drawn about students' abilities. We recommend exploring this ability broadly, and writing assessments can help.

## Structured Writing Assessments

***Dictated Stories.*** Dictated stories are a rich source of information about oral language, print awareness, knowledge of the conventions of print, and story structure (Agnew, 1982). Dictated writing samples are generally collected in one of two ways. In some classrooms children produce journal entries several times a week. For very young children this usually involves drawing a picture and "writing" any portion of the accompanying story that is possible. Then, the child dictates the message to the teacher, who writes it down exactly as produced. Alternatively, the teacher may set a topic for a child (or group of children) and then proceed as above. Some children provide only a label, while others generate text-length stories, sometimes continuing their story for several days.

**FIGURE 7.12**
Yopp-Singer
Phonemic
Segmentation
Assessment

Student: _____ Age: _____ Date: _____
Examiner: _____ Score (number correct): _____

### Part I (Original Yopp-Singer Assessment)

**Directions:** Today we're going to play a word game. I'm going to say a word and I want you to break the word apart. You are going to tell me each sound in the word in order. For example, if I say "old," you should say "/o/–/1/–/d." (*Administrator: Be sure to say the sounds, not the letters, in the word.*) Let's try a few together.

*Practice items:* (*Assist the child in segmenting these items as necessary.*)
  ride          go          man

*Test items:* (*Circle those items that the student correctly segments; incorrect responses may be recorded on the blank line following the items.*)

| | |
|---|---|
| 1. dog | 12. lay |
| 2. keep | 13. race |
| 3. fine | 14. zoo |
| 4. no | 15. three |
| 5. she | 16. job |
| 6. wave | 17. in |
| 7. grew | 18. ice |
| 8. that | 19. at |
| 9. red | 20. top |
| 10. me | 21. by |
| 11. sat | 22. do |

### Part II (Adaptation—Not part of the Yopp-Singer Assessment)

**Directions:** Let's change the rules. Now I'll say the sounds, and you tell me the word I am saying. Sample items: /c/–/a/–/t/ and /ch/–/i/–/p/

| | |
|---|---|
| 1. /f/–/i/–/g/    (fig) | 6. /b/–/a/–/t/    (bait) |
| 2. /p/–/e/–/t/    (pet) | 7. /l/–/i/–/f/–/t/    (lift) |
| 3. /s/–/oo/–/n/    (soon) | 8. /n/–/i/–/t/    (night) |
| 4. /o/–/p/–/e/–/n/    (open) | 9. /u/–/p/    (up) |
| 5. /sh/–/o/–/p/    (shop) | 10. /f/–/l/–/a/–/m/    (flame) |

*Source:* From Yopp, H. (1995, September). A test for assessing phonemic awareness in children. *The Reading Teacher, 49* (1), 20–29. Reprinted with permission of the International Reading Association. All rights reserved.

As children dictate and reread their stories, information about each component of emergent literacy can be gathered, using the type of form shown in Figure 7.13. After a dictation is completed, it is possible to gather information about other aspects of emergent literacy (Agnew, 1982). Using the dictated story, simply ask the child:

- To find a word (by circling or framing it)
- To match a story word on a card to the story itself
- To find a letter and/or a sentence
- To find a word that begins the same as another
- To point "to the letters you can name"
- To point "to the words you can read"
- To "reread" the story

Collected over time, these dictated stories and journal entries can provide strong evidence regarding children's growth in many areas of emergent literacy.

***Prompted Writing Activities.***   If spontaneous writing samples are not available, assessment information can be gathered by simply asking the child to write anything she or he knows how to write. It may be necessary to provide additional structure, because many young students balk at this. Two tasks that can be used to help generate writing samples are *All the Words I Know* and *Supported Writing.*

We have found that children often know how to write some words, even if they believe they are not yet writers. Thus, a paper headed *All the Words I Know* can sometimes produce results when the more generalized request to write has failed. Most children, for example, can write their own names, the names of some other people, and a few other high-potency words (Clay, 1985). It also helps to probe further by asking the child to attempt to write specific words such as his or her mother's name, color names, the name of the month, the words on street signs or logos, and so forth. Such samples provide information about the child's word knowledge, phonemic awareness, and attention to recurring environmental print.

Eliciting writing samples of connected text is important for assessing the child's awareness of text organization, directionality, or concept of word boundaries. In addition, the connected writing sample generally permits observation of the child's strategy for spelling unknown words.

Children will often be able to write some connected discourse if they are provided with a little support. *Supported writing* can be done in several ways. For example, the child can be asked to draw a picture, then write about it. Alternatively, it is possible to brainstorm with the child, generating several possible topics (see also the discussion of shared writing in Chapter 12).

An analysis of children's writing strategies can provide much information about the status of emergent literacy. Questions you might want to ask about the student's writing include the following:

- Does the child write from left to right?
- Does the child use letters to represent words?
- Does the child show an awareness of word boundaries and spacing?

**FIGURE 7.13**
Dictated Story
Record Form

**Dictated Experience Story Summary Form**

Name: _____ Date: _____

**Directions:** Present topic, object, or experience for student to discuss or experience directly. Ask them to tell you something about it.

**Dictated Story:**




**Assessment:**

*Language Development*

- Does the child speak in sentences, in single words, or word clusters?
- Does the child use descriptive names for objects and events or many ambiguous terms such as "it," "that," "this thing"?
- Does the child provide adequate information to reconstruct the experience?
- Does the child use appropriate grammatical structure?
- How does the child use language appropriate to the task?
- How easily and fluently does the child dictate?

*Literacy Development*

- Does the child speak clearly and pace the dictation to allow the teacher to record?
- What does the child do as the story is transcribed?
- Does the dictation have clarity and organization (does it make sense)?
- Does the child provide a title that reflects the major ideas or themes of the dictation?
- How does the child (attempt) to read back his or her dictation?

At the conclusion of a dictated story activity, it is helpful to reflect on the following:

- What evidence is there that the child understands the concepts of word, sentence, paragraph, and story?
- What aspects of the speech-to-print relationship does the child understand?
- In what ways does the child use memory for text as an aid to reading?
- What sight vocabulary does the child appear to have mastered?
- How does the child use graphophonic information to read?

**Comments:**

- Is the child able to represent the phonemes in words?
- Does the child use punctuation (e.g., periods, capitals)?
- Is there a relationship between the print and the oral story that is "read"?

Students' development can be traced from scribbling through invented spelling to conventional orthography.

## Using Stories to Assess Emergent Abilities

Because young children read or listen to many stories, it is relatively easy to embed this aspect of assessment into the regular instructional program.

***Story Retelling Guides.***    Story retelling can provide a wide range of assessment information. Because this assessment strategy is discussed at length elsewhere (see Chapters 8 and 9), the discussion in this chapter is limited to two aspects of emergent literacy that can be assessed using retelling procedures: sense of story and oral language development.

The ability to recognize and use story structure clearly aids in comprehension. As we assess children's retellings, we are looking for evidence that children have made use of the major components of stories to understand the text and to aid their recall. For young children it is important to determine whether they have noted characters, events, and resolutions. In addition, the children should make at least some sequential and causal connections between events and resolutions explicit and clear.

To conduct a story retelling, simply ask the child to retell a story that he or she has just heard or read. Ask the child specifically to retell the entire story just the way the author did. When the retelling has stopped, ask the child whether there is anything else he or she can remember about the story. Record the child's retelling in writing and/or by audiotaping.

The form presented in Figure 7.14 can be used as a guide for evaluating the retelling with regard to the child's language and sense of story structure. In addition, it may be helpful to collect retelling data from children on both familiar and unfamiliar stories. Repeated exposure to the same material should also permit the child to capture the language of the text. If the quality and quantity of the retelling do not improve with repeated exposures, it is likely that the child needs more story-reading opportunities or that oral language development (and experience) is not well-matched to the text. When used over time, retellings can help us evaluate and document a child's growth in a number of areas, including language fluency, complexity, vocabulary, usage, and knowledge about story structures. Children who need greater support in comprehending stories may be evaluated on the Directed Listening Thinking Activity.

***Directed Listening Thinking Activity (DLTA).***    Throughout this section we have encouraged a type of assessment that can be embedded in daily classroom exchanges. Indeed, most of these assessments can and should be done as a part of regular classroom routines. The Directed Listening Thinking Activity (DLTA) was developed by Stauffer (1980) as an instructional strategy, but it is easy to use on a continuous basis for assessment because it fits naturally in the classroom routine.

Child: _____ Date: _____ Story Title: _____

## Language

| | Yes | No | Some-times |
|---|---|---|---|
| 1. A variety of sentence patterns to express ideas | ☐ | ☐ | ☐ |
| 2. Complete sentences | ☐ | ☐ | ☐ |
| 3. Grammar, conventions | ☐ | ☐ | ☐ |
| 4. Precise, descriptive words | ☐ | ☐ | ☐ |
| 5. Vocabulary is well developed | ☐ | ☐ | ☐ |
| 6. Overall fluency | ☐ | ☐ | ☐ |

Word count: _____

## Story Structure

| | Yes | No | Some-times |
|---|---|---|---|
| 1. All basic structural elements present | ☐ | ☐ | ☐ |
| • Setting | ☐ | ☐ | ☐ |
| • Initiating event | ☐ | ☐ | ☐ |
| • The goal or problem | ☐ | ☐ | ☐ |
| • One or more attempts or, all major events | ☐ | ☐ | ☐ |
| • The resolution | ☐ | ☐ | ☐ |
| 2. Oral retelling is accurately sequenced | ☐ | ☐ | ☐ |
| 3. Student can recall the "big idea" | ☐ | ☐ | ☐ |
| 4. Student can sustain a train of thought | ☐ | ☐ | ☐ |

## Comments

The strategy simply involves the teacher reading a well-crafted story aloud to children. Before the story is read, the teacher asks children to make predictions about what the story will be about, what will happen in the story. Then, as the read-aloud proceeds, the teacher stops periodically to solicit predictions. The children are also directed to monitor their predictions to see if they were correct. Retellings can also be incorporated into the DLTA. Throughout the activity the teacher asks the children questions such as the following:

1. What do you think this story will be about?
2. What clues did you use to help you?
3. Were your predictions right?
4. What do you think will happen next?

To assess an individual child's participation in a DLTA, you should ask yourself the following types of questions:

- Can the child predict from the title, cover, pictures?
- Are these predictions plausible?
- Are these predictions based on prior knowledge?
- Are these predictions based on an understanding of story structure?
- Is the child able to monitor predictions?
- Is the text used to revise predictions?

Teachers can evaluate change in students' knowledge and ability to perform various types of school tasks if they use and summarize DLTA data regularly.

## The Diagnostic Portfolio and Evidence of Emergent Literacy: The Case of Kyle

In Step 3 of the assessment-instruction process we ask questions about the learner's knowledge of reading and writing, application of reading and writing skills, motivation, and independence and ownership. As we have noted, diagnostic portfolios have exceptional potential in the assessment and documentation of a child's emergence into conventional literacy. This emergence is, by definition, dynamic: We get an ever-changing view of children's emerging knowledge, skill, and affect. The portfolio, with its focus on continuous assessment, authentic tasks, and student involvement, is especially appropriate and well-suited for work with young children.

The diagnostic portfolio should contain a subset of work samples and evidence that had been collected in a classroom portfolio. Schools that use portfolios at all levels and/or settings that contain multi-age classrooms are ideal for collecting information over time; even information about the youngest learners. The samples we use in this section come from such a classroom—Kyle's multi-age teacher begins collecting information in kindergarten and continues to gather additional documentation and information for the three years that children are with her.

The rich portfolios that Ms. McIntyre and her class keep contain evidence and information about each aspect of the learner's development. You might remember that some of this information was used to "get started" with Kyle (see Chapter 4). For example, we noted that Kyle's self-evaluations (prompted by Ms. McIntyre's periodic requests for reflection) suggested that Kyle was a very active child who enjoyed making things. In addition, he was aware that his writing was improving.

Samples of the extensive written work, including Kyle's self-selected "best pieces," also go into a diagnostic portfolio (see Figures 7.15 and 7.16). Although many other children

**FIGURE 7.15**
Kyle's Writing:
Kindergarten

**FIGURE 7.16**
Kyle's Writing:
Grade 1

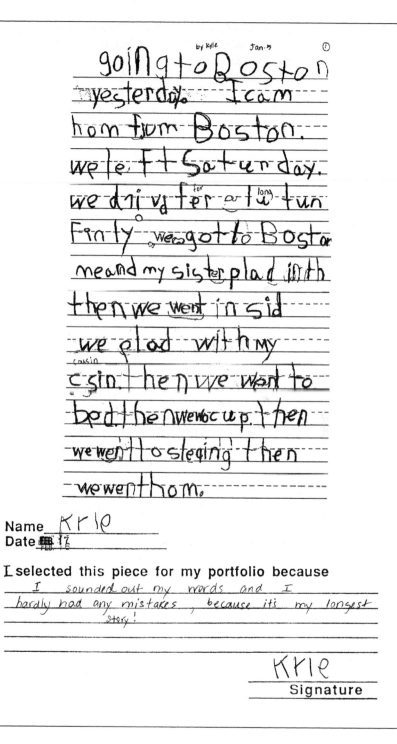

going to Boston yesterday. I cam hom fum Boston. we left Saturday. we driv fer a long tun Finly we got to Bostor me and my sister plad inth then we went insid we plad with my cusin. then we went to bed then we woc up. then we went o sleeing then we went hom.

Name Kyle
Date Feb 17

I selected this piece for my portfolio because

I sounded out my words and I hardly had any mistakes, because it's my longest story!

Kyle
Signature

in this classroom are writing more and more skillfully, Kyle's progress from kindergarten to the end of grade 1 is obvious and clearly demonstrates his ability to apply his growing knowledge and skill.

In addition to these work samples, Ms. McIntyre summarizes his progress using a "Stages of Spelling Development" form developed by teachers in her district. Throughout kindergarten she noted his progress:

| | |
|---|---|
| Pictures no words | 9/21 and 10/5 |
| Scribble or imitative writing | 10/29 |
| Random letters to represent words | 9/21; *throughout fall* |
| Initial consonants to represent words | 11/29 *"started making connection with teacher"* |
| Initial/final consonants for each word | 3/8 *jp* for *jump* 3/25 *dk* for *duck* |
| Initial, final and medial consonants for each word | 3/30 *sph dr* for *spider smt* for *cement* |
| Vowels used as place holders | |
| Approaching standard spelling | 2/26 *my, dog, mom, me* |

In combination the evidence of the portfolio suggests steady progress in the area of developmental spelling.

Kyle continues to prefer action and choice to sitting and "paying attention." Not surprisingly, he readily notes in a casual conversation that he really doesn't like to read. On the other hand, his book logs reveal the rather large amount of reading that he does do under the strong encouragement of Ms. McIntyre.

To summarize, at the end of kindergarten, Kyle was at the early phonemic stage of spelling development and had not yet begun to read conventionally. He was able to reread familiar books and could recognize many high-potency words from his environment (labels, planning time choices, names, etc.). By the end of first grade, Kyle has begun to read and to write. His spontaneous writing suggests that he has arrived at the phonetic stage of spelling development. Observations by the teacher indicate that he has made steady but slow progress in reading. He can still read only a few familiar books, although his knowledge of sight words and phonics has increased. Although he is easily distracted, he has many opportunities to learn about interesting information and to do projects, which he likes to do. His oral language development is exceptionally strong, and his retellings of both familiar and unfamiliar stories are detailed, accurate, and insightful. In the next chapters we follow Kyle's progress as he moves toward conventional reading and writing, documenting and evaluating these changes using a wide array of tools and strategies.

# Chapter Summary

In this chapter we describe the current conceptualization of reading and writing as emergent literacy. The gradual emergence of written literacy skills in the context of oral language development provides the perspective adopted for this chapter. We detailed two major areas of competence necessary for literacy learning: oral language development and literacy experiences. Oral language development was described in terms of what children must learn about language, how language is learned, and the importance of language development in literacy learning. Essential literacy experiences were defined as developing print awareness; understanding the forms and functions of print, including the language of books and story structure; analyzing print, including the concept of a word, phonemic segmentation, and the speech-to-print match; and controlling reading and writing processes, including the form and functions of writing and invented spelling. We noted that most children acquire many important literacy abilities long before they enter school.

The next section of this chapter described a variety of informal assessment procedures. These informal strategies can be used to gather information about a variety of different emergent literacy abilities. For example, dictated stories can be used to gather information about children's language development, sense of story, awareness of the speech-to-print match, and phonemic awareness. Other strategies include guidelines for using structured observations and interviews, checklists, retellings, and writing samples.

Consistent with the guidelines for assessment provided in Chapter 4, the techniques described in this chapter allow for meaningful, unobtrusive, systematic, and continuous assessment of emergent literacy. Recognizing that readiness must be viewed within the context of the instructional program and tasks that children are going to encounter in school, many of the techniques described here are designed to be used with children during instruction and/or as they engage in tasks like those they will be expected to accomplish.

Finally, we provided examples of student work and observational records that contribute to a diagnostic portfolio. For young children, the collection over time can provide vivid and immediate diagnostic information.

# 8 Informal Classroom-Based Assessment

The information obtained through interviews and observations provides the background for further evaluation of the learner, using formal and informal assessment instruments. As a practical matter, students have always been referred for more specialized assessment on the basis of at least some informal classroom-based assessment. Until recently, few professionals viewed classroom assessment information as essential to the assessment and instruction of disabled readers and writers. Now, however, there is a recognition of the importance of classroom-based assessment, in part because research findings indicate that when teachers engage in on-going assessment, student achievement improves (Black & William, 1998; Falk & Ort, 1998).

This chapter focuses on assessment strategies that are selected and/or created by teachers and clinicians who are interested in gathering information about each component of reading and writing. These classroom-based approaches differ from the norm-referenced standardized tests introduced in a later chapter because they tend to be more informal and because the content and tasks can be closely fitted to the type of knowledge and skill promoted by an individual teacher or school.

After a brief discussion of the role of the teacher in assessing students' reading and writing, we identify some critical issues in the development and use of informal assessment strategies. Finally, a wide range of strategies and tools are described for assessing component areas of literacy: word recognition, vocabulary, comprehension, studying, and writing. The assessment strategies described are almost exclusively *performance* measures. These are techniques for evaluating students' ability to *apply* their knowledge and skill. The variety of assessment strategies presented in this chapter are designed so that teachers can select from among a repertoire to examine some particular component area more closely and in an ongoing way. Many of these can (and should) be done as a routine part of the instructional program.

Finally, we describe how to use student portfolios that document their progress and provide the basis for instructional decision making.

## Understanding Informal Classroom-Based Assessment

The assessment-instruction process described in this text relies very heavily on the knowledge and skill of the teacher/examiner. Extensive description of formal tests, the traditional heart of reading and writing "diagnosis," is not the centerpiece of the process. Instead, we acknowledge the complexity of the reading and writing processes and of learning to read and write. Like Simmons and Resnick (1993), we recognize that more *informal* assessment can often provide powerful and flexible evaluation strategies: "The most authentic and reliable estimate of students' capabilities comes from work they do over extended periods of time under the guidance of teachers" (Simmons & Resnick, 1993, p. 11).

By virture of their daily contact with students in a variety of reading situations, classroom teachers are in a position to incorporate the adaptations that form the basic assessment strategies described in this chapter directly into their regular reading instruction. Teachers can collect and interpret performance data, information about students' skills and strategies, as they read and respond to various school tasks.

One of the most serious problems with traditional assessment practices is that they often lead teachers to believe that assessment and evaluation are someone else's job. When teachers rely too heavily on standardized test results, they may stop using their own good judgment (Valencia & Pearson, 1987). The overreliance on formal tests may also cause teachers to discount or become inattentive to the high-quality information they themselves have. Teachers need the information they have before them because it provides evidence about students' ability to perform the actual tasks required in their instructional settings.

Teachers gather information from multiple samples on a daily basis as a function of the different types of texts, tasks, and methods that are employed as a part of their regular reading activities. The opportunities are great but often go undetected. As Pinnell (1991, p. 81) has argued, "teachers need assessment tools that help them become 'noticing teachers.'" This chapter describes many tools and strategies that will help teachers to "notice" the information available to them on an ongoing basis. It is more a matter of knowing what to attend to than a matter of having indefinite amounts of time to work one-on-one with students. Lipson (1996) has described ways in which conversations, even casual ones, with children can provide useful assessment information. "Noticing requires not only that teachers engage in careful observations of reading and writing as they occur in their own classrooms but also that they assign importance or significance to what they note" (Lipson, 1995, p. 167).

The strategies suggested in this chapter should probably become a part of the repertoire of all teachers. Classroom-based assessments also allow us to examine students' performance using familiar text forms and tasks. Of course, the quality and nature of these in-school tasks needs to be examined closely as well (see Chapters 5 and 6). However, there is increasing agreement among researchers and educators that "the most productive and useful way to assess, or examine, rather than simply test what students understand, is to 'situate' assessment in the classroom, closest to the child and to instruction" (Valencia, 1997, p. 64).

Another advantage of classroom-based assessment is that evaluations can be responsive to the specific cultural and/or linguistic characteristics of individual students. This is critical because standardized tests can distort information for some students as they tend "to reflect the language, culture, or learning style of middle- to upper-middle-class" students (Neill & Median, 1989). To make good instructional decisions, teachers must come to trust that assessment is a continuous process that takes place within the instructional program. It should be designed to increase the goodness of the fit between each child and the materials and methods of instruction.

According to Johnston (1997), teachers can—indeed, they must—become expert evaluators. We have already noted one of the most important attributes of an expert evaluator: the ability to listen. Another important characteristic of an expert evaluator is the ability to recognize patterns. Expert evaluators are not concerned about an isolated event or behavior but are able to connect pieces of information to create an integrated vision of the student's knowledge and skill. Informal, classroom-based assessment can provide exceptionally powerful and helpful information. Johnston reminds us that

> The concept behind a "good" reading assessment, whether it is a standardized test or alternative classroom assessment, is the same. First it should be authentic; it should assess what we have defined and value as real reading. Second, it should be trustworthy; it should have clearly established procedures for gathering information and for evaluating the quality of that information. (Johnston, 1997, p. 60)

Classroom-based assessment requires reflection and planning. As teachers turn to more informal assessment options, they should proceed cautiously. Informal tests offer no guarantee of excellence. Many common informal assessment tools need to be considered carefully. For example, skills mastery tests are a common feature in many classrooms, often used to place students in reading groups.

A major problem with these measures is that they frequently assess skills in isolation on a series of discrete subtests. For example, they often evaluate a skill such as main idea recognition under highly restricted conditions (e.g., short, unfamiliar, informational passages with initial topic sentences) that do not reflect the complexity and variety of factors that are likely to influence students' ability to grasp a main idea under real reading conditions. In addition, mastery tests presume that the order of skill acquisition is invariable; that students must master a specific skill before proceeding to other skills and/or materials. Neither the assumption that reading skills are hierarchical nor the assumption that reading skills can be evaluated in discrete parts is warranted, given current knowledge about the reading process (Mason, Osborn, & Rosenshine, 1977; Valencia & Pearson, 1987).

To summarize, although informal tests can be a potent form of assessment, the techniques employed must be carefully examined for evidence that these capture what we know about skilled reading and writing. A serious problem in many existing tests, both formal and informal, is the lack of relationship between how reading and writing are measured and what we expect children to do during reading and writing. The truth is that we do *not* want children to know how to complete workbooklike pages or complete grammar exercises. Rather, we want children to be able to employ their skills during the reading and writing of real texts. In reviewing comments by the legendary educator Ralph Tyler, Horowitz (1995) noted that alternative assessment is not a panacea and that "all evaluation must be guided by a purpose and be sensitive to the uniqueness of the individual being assessed."

This means that we need to develop assessment procedures that assess more clearly the major goals of reading and writing instruction and the factors that are known to influence authentic reading and writing. As Wood (1988) notes, what is needed is a structured approach to determine how an individual handles the reading of actual textbook material under conditions that simulate the classroom situation. The guidelines for assessment offered in Chapter 4 should be reconsidered as guiding principles in teacher-designed assessment.

These guidelines are important for *both* standardized and teacher-designed assessment. However, classroom-based assessment is too often discounted as haphazard or unreliable. Consequently, teachers need to be especially careful to attend to important principles of assessment. Well-crafted informal assessment can assess meaningful reading and writing activities in a nonintrusive way, and teachers can ensure that it is systematic, continuous, and well organized.

# Strategies and Tools for Teacher-Initiated Assessment

In the remainder of this chapter we describe specific techniques for evaluating the various components of reading and writing performance (see Figure 8.1). These techniques—some old, some newer—can provide the initial repertoire for both classroom teachers and clinicians who want to expand their assessment practices. They are only suggestions, however. There are many other ways to evaluate performance informally. As teachers develop more refined skills for assessing students' knowledge and application of reading- and writing-related abilities, their confidence in making good assessment decisions will also develop.

Each of the strategies is designed to provide for ongoing student assessment during instruction. Throughout, we also provide forms that can be used to summarize and display this information. If a diagnostic portfolio is being used, these forms can facilitate analysis and interpretation. If this documentation is providing support or confirmation within a more traditional case evaluation, the summary forms are equally helpful in making sense of the documents.

## Evaluating Word Recognition

Rapid and automatic word recognition, using a combination of strategies, is a hallmark of skilled reading. Not surprisingly, many poor readers have a limited repertoire of word recognition and word analysis strategies (see Chapter 7 for assessments related to phonological awareness and early word recognition). Of course, the most effective way to assess children's word recognition and word analysis skills is to do so as children read aloud. It is possible to achieve a very detailed picture of students' word recognition and monitoring abilities by using the Reading Miscue Analysis (RMI) procedure (see Chapter 9). Because the RMI procedure is so time-consuming, few classroom teachers use it with any frequency. The running record, however, is tailored for classroom use.

***Running Records during Oral Reading.*** The *running record* is a method of assessment that is ideally suited to continuous assessment. An adaptation of the RMI, "this task requires the teacher to observe and record the strategies the child uses 'on the run' while attempting to read a whole text" (Pinnell, 1985, p. 74). The technique was originally described by Clay (1979, 1985) and is based on the work of the Goodmans and their associates (K. S. Goodman & Goodman, 1977; Y. M. Goodman, Watson, & Burke, 1987).

Although the running record might seem complex at first, it is especially useful for classroom teachers because no special preparation is required ahead of time. A running record can be created as long as the text being read by a child is visible to the teacher. Therefore it

FIGURE 8.1 Summary Chart of Classroom-Based Assessments

| Component and Strategy | Assessment Condition | Administration Notes | Age/Grade Level |
|---|---|---|---|
| **Word Recognition** | | | |
| Running Records | Individual (or individual within small-group setting) | Data gathered during any oral reading event. Advantage is on-the-spot performance data | Most appropriate for students reading at grade levels PP–grade 3 |
| Informal Miscue Assessment | Individual (or individual within small-group setting) | Uses data from running records or other records of oral reading | Any |
| Word Sorts | Individual or small group | Time varies. Students can complete independently if they record their sorts | Any |
| **Vocabulary** | | | |
| Word Sorts | Individual or small group | Time varies. Students can complete independently if they record their sorts | Any. Results may be confounded with decoding difficulties |
| Self-Assessment and Yes–No | Individual or whole group | Very little time. Students may overestimate or underestimate their word knowledge | Any |
| Free Recall | Individual or small group | Very little time | Young readers may find the unstructured tasks difficult |
| Word Association | Individual or small group | Teacher must select words ahead of time, but otherwise cuick to administer | Any, although less-verbal students may not fare well |
| Structured Questions | Individual, small or large group | Time consuming to prepare, although they yield good information. | Any |
| Recognition | Whole group | Time consuming to prepare, although they yield good information. | Very effective for students with retrieval difficulties |
| Unstructured Discussion | Individual, small or large group | Yields least information but easy to use | Any |
| PReP | Individual, small or large group | Used in conjunction with pre-reading preparation for reading. Some additional time needed to analyze responses | Any |

## Comprehension

| | | |
|---|---|---|
| Story Maps | Can be used with whole groups (written retellings) or individuals (oral retellings) | Use with narrative text. Students can create maps or their oral and written retelling is compared to the map | Any age, although mapping more long or complex narratives for older children may be problematic |
| Concept Maps | Can be used with whole groups (written retellings) or individuals (oral retellings) | Use with expository text. Students' oral and written retelling is compared to the map; or students create maps | Most appropriate for grades 3 and up |
| Retelling | Can be used with whole groups (written retellings) or individuals (oral retellings) | Use retellings *before* asking questions | Any age, although summary is preferable for older readers |
| Questioning | Groups or individuals | Craft questions carefully so as to elicit the desired information | Any |
| Think-Aloud | Individual | Focus is on processes versus content | Any age, although most appropriate for grades 3 and up |

## Studying

| | | |
|---|---|---|
| Observation Checklist | Individual | Use as student(s) is engaged in study activity | Intermediate and middle grades |
| Open Book Reading Assessment (OBRA) | Individual | Use as student(s) is engaged in study activity | Intermediate and middle grades |

## Writing

| | | |
|---|---|---|
| Holistic Scoring | Individual | Use to analyze student's written work | Any |
| Analytic Scoring | Individual | Use to analyze student's written work | Any |
| Observation Checklist | Individual | Use as student(s) is engaged in writing activities | Any |
| Self-Assessment Questionnaire | Individual | Students reflect on their own writing abilities | Any |

is possible to collect data any time you are listening to a child read aloud. It does take time and practice to do running records accurately. But it is well worth the investment because of the wealth of assessment information they provide, especially for younger and/or disabled readers. In Figure 8.2 you will find a sample running record of Kyle's reading in grade 2, along with a key to the various markings.

After the record has been taken, the teacher uses it to analyze oral reading performance. Although a full miscue analysis can be done (see Chapter 9), classroom teachers usually generate more global, less specific inferences about what the child is doing to construct meaning from text and which strategies seem to be used most often to accomplish this (Pinnell, 1987). A teacher's summary of the small sample you have examined in Figure 8.2 might read something like this:

> Kyle's most consistent miscues (oral reading "errors") are word substitutions. These substitutions are made using both language structure (syntax) and meaning (semantics) ("I tied it around a doorknob . . ."). Kyle also monitors quite effectively for problems caused by weak graphophonic skills (he tries, for example, to self-correct mispronunciations of the words *winced. shuddered. admired.* etc.). He regularly uses rereading when meaning seems distorted. What Kyle does not do is to make full and effective use of the graphophonic information available, nor does he appear to have mastered all high-frequency sight words. Miscues in this area ("emperted," "winkered") are tolerated even when they result in loss of meaning. Kyle often rereads, but his self-correction attempts too often fail due to lack of sound–symbol information and decoding skill. Although he generally seems to "read for meaning," his comprehension is affected by word recognition.

Rhodes and Shanklin (1990) have devised a simplified assessment strategy for analyzing students' miscues in the classroom, and it serves as a useful companion to the running record. The Classroom Reading Miscue Assessment (CRMA) (see Figure 8.3) is used as students read a whole text. Rather than analyze each oral reading miscue, teachers get an overall picture of the student's reading proficiency. First, the teacher determines the extent to which a reader is constructing meaning. To do this, each sentence in the text is considered separately. The teacher determines whether each sentence read by the child (after self-correction) is semantically acceptable or not. Then a percentage of semantically acceptable sentences is computed by dividing the total number of semantically acceptable sentences by the total number of sentences read. Teachers record their observations about reading behaviors using a five-point scale (see Figure 8.3).

Although the CRMA originally included a brief framework for evaluating retellings, we examine comprehension assessment in greater detail later in this chapter and again in Chapter 9. Instead, we have adapted the strategy somewhat so that teachers can also make note of the word-reading strategies used by students. In this way teachers can focus first on children's attempts to construct meaning, but they can also examine word recognition and identification strategies during authentic reading (see Figure 8.3).

As with any "test," running records provide a *sample* of behavior that may or may not be representative of the way a student interacts with different types of texts under different reading conditions. Students' miscue patterns vary depending on a number of factors (Wixson, 1979). The best way to address the problem of variability in oral reading patterns is to obtain repeated samples of a particular reader's miscues under a variety of conditions.

**FIGURE 8.2**

Sample Running Record for *Norman Fools the Tooth Fairy*

Norman was the only kid in his class who hadn't lost a baby tooth. One was sort of loose now. Instead of finishing his worksheet, Norman wiggled the tooth with his finger.

Later, while his teacher, Miss Harp, read them a story, Norman waggled the tooth with his tongue. How else was he going to get a tooth to put under his pillow for the tooth fairy?

His friends gave him lots of advice. "I tied a string around my loose tooth," said Toby. "Then I tied the other end to a doorknob, and my sister slammed the door." Norman winced.

"My dad pulled mine out," said Matt, "with his pliers."

Norman shuddered, but he admired the empty space between their teeth when they smiled. It showed that the tooth fairy had already paid them a visit.

"Try biting into an apple," said Sarah, "or eat lots of caramels."

Norman didn't have any caramels, but he did have a piece of licorice in his lunch bag.

Key for running record:

Accurate Reading ✓ ✓ ✓

Substitution  substitute / text word

Appeal  A

Told  T

Self-Correction  sc

Omission  text word

Insertion  inserted word

Repetition  ✓R

Return & Repetition  ✓✓✓ R

*(continued on next page)*

**FIGURE 8.2**
(Continued)

Detailed analyses of miscues is important in a complete assessment and we discuss this more fully in Chapter 9. However, running records provide classroom teachers with a practical assessment strategy and information about students' reading of multiple samples, since teachers can (and often do) collect information several times a week.

Because it can be a challenge to do running records, and because we feel so strongly that they are a useful classroom tool, a word about management is in order. We have found

**FIGURE 8.3**   Classroom Reading Miscue Assessment

| Classroom Reading Miscue Assessment |
|---|

Name: _____ Date: _____

Grade: _____ Teacher: _____

Text level read: _____

**I. What percent of the sentences read make sense?**   Sentence by sentence tally   Total

___ Number of semantically acceptable sentences

___ Number of semantically unacceptable sentences

___ % Comprehending score: $\dfrac{\text{Number of semantically acceptable sentences}}{\text{Total number of sentences read}} \times 100$   TOTAL _____

| | Seldom | Sometimes | Often | Usually | Always |
|---|---|---|---|---|---|
| **II. Constructive Meaning** | 1 | 2 | 3 | 4 | 5 |
| **Successful strategies for constructing meaning** | | | | | |
| A. Monitors miscues and knows when meaning is disrupted | | | | | |
| B. Makes sensible substitutions | | | | | |
| C. Self-corrects miscues when meaning is disrupted | | | | | |
| D. Uses semantic cues (context, pictures, visuals, etc.) to support comprehension | | | | | |
| E. Uses rereading and predicting to enhance comprehension | | | | | |
| **Reading behaviors that disrupt meaning** | | | | | |
| A. Makes nonsense-word or other substitutions that distort comprehension | | | | | |
| B. Skips words or makes omissions that distort comprehension | | | | | |
| C. Relies too heavily on graphic cues | | | | | |
| **III. Word Recognition** | | | | | |
| **Successful strategies for reading words** | | | | | |
| A. Looks at the entire word and makes effective use of graphophonic information | | | | | |
| B. Attends to spelling patterns and to morphemes (endings, prefixes, etc.) | | | | | |
| C. Recognizes high-frequency sight words | | | | | |
| D. Can use syllabication for longer words | | | | | |
| E. Uses a decoding-by-analogy strategy | | | | | |
| F. Uses rereading to clarify and correct | | | | | |
| G. Monitors word recognition for meaning (see above) | | | | | |
| **Less successful strategies for reading words** | | | | | |
| A. Uses only limited word features (e.g., initial or final consonants) | | | | | |
| B. Overrelies on context and pictures | | | | | |
| C. Skips words without rereading and/or makes refusal miscues | | | | | |
| D. Tries to use letter–sound decoding for all words, even high-frequency words | | | | | |

*Source:* From Rhodes, Lynn K., Shanklin, Nancy L., & Valencia, Shelia W. (1990, November). Miscue analysis in the classroom. *The Reading Teacher, 44* (3), 252–254. Reprinted with permission of the International Reading Association. All rights reserved.

it useful to buy cheap spiral-bound notebooks in volume and use them for all running records. Each time we do a running record, we simply date the page, write the student's name on each new page, and note what text is being read (see Figure 8.4). Before starting, we take a minute to organize ourselves by writing the page numbers and numbering the lines for each page we are going to have the child read. That way, we can keep track of exactly what the child has read even if the child reads quickly or we git a bit lost along the way. Using this approach, we have all our running records in one place, and they are organized sequentially. This reduces the amount of paper shuffling and record keeping. If we want to focus on a particular child, we can always tear those pages out and put them in a file.

*Word Sorts.*    The *word sort* (Gillet & Temple, 1990) is a flexible assessment strategy that can be used to assess a variety of word level abilities. Gillet and Temple suggest using the word sort as a way to assess word recognition and/or word analysis, but we have also found it useful for evaluating vocabulary as well (see the next section). This technique capitalizes on the fact that words are organized in human memory by patterns or relationships.

 There are two types of word sorts: *open* and *closed*. In an open sort, no criteria for sorting the words are provided. Because students must impose their own organization on the words, it is possible to observe the types of relationships available to students. In a closed sort, the teacher establishes the criteria for sorting in advance. Using word cards prepared in advance (or selected by students from their own word bank), the teacher asks the student to:

- Put the words that go together in the same pile (open sort);
- Put all the words together that have the same beginning letter. Then, name the group (closed sort);
- Put all the words together that have something the same and label the characteristic; and
- Put all the words together that have the same feature (for example, rhyme or spelling pattern).

**FIGURE 8.4**
Running Record
Notebook

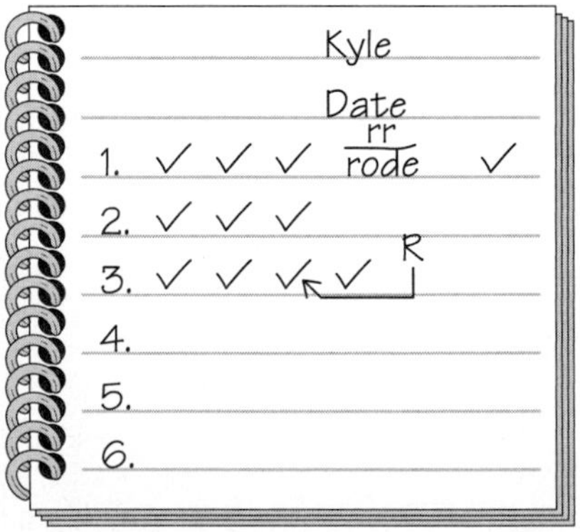

As the student's performance is evaluated, it is helpful to consider the following questions:

- Does the child attend to meaning features or graphic features?
- Does the child recognize and use initial, medial, and final sounds?
- Does the child recognize and use structural cues (compounds, base words)?
- Can the child generate categories based on visual patterns (spelling patterns)?
- Does the child recognize multiple ways to represent sounds (the several ways to spell the short *e* sound)?

Some teachers we have worked with keep a class summary chart of the ways children choose to sort the words they provide. It provides important information on students' growing knowledge and flexibility in using aspects of phonics, categorization, and/or content information.

## Evaluating Vocabulary

Knowledge of word meanings clearly influences reading performance. This fact has been unchallenged for decades, yet surprisingly few assessment techniques have been suggested for validating individual differences in this area. Most diagnosticians employ one of the available standardized tests to estimate relative vocabulary strength, and we describe several of these in Chapter 10. Most of them involve word-level assessments (finding definitions, picture associations, etc.).

A word is a label for a concept or idea. It has recently been suggested that vocabulary words are important, not because they are directly helpful in understanding text, but because the individual words reflect generalized knowledge about a topic and because a critical mass of vocabulary may trigger a student's metalinguistic analysis of words (Nagy & Scott, 2000; Whitehurst & Lonigan, 2001). When a reader knows a word, he or she probably knows many other related words. For example, a knowledgeable sailor generated in a few seconds the following words when asked what she thought of when she heard the word *spinnaker:*

> spinnaker: jib, fore, aft, mainsail, port, bow, sheets, heel, winch, cleat, starboard, heading, gaff, sloop, schooner, 12-meter, galley, tack

It should be apparent that simply learning a definition for the word *spinnaker* would not be as helpful as the knowledge base that results in knowing *spinnaker* but also knowing all those other words. As Nagy and Scott (2000) explain, word knowledge is extremely complex. In their review of research, they conclude that word knowledge has several characteristics that contribute to this complexity: (1) incrementality—"knowing a word is a matter of degrees, not all-or-nothing"; (2) polysemy—"words often have multiple meanings"; (3) interrelatedness—knowing a word often depends on our knowledge of other words; and (4) heterogeneity—"what we know about words often depends on the type of word" (Nagy & Scott, 2000, p. 270). Word meanings are related in such a way that they form concepts that are organized in a network of relationships. When asked to think about one word related to a concept, people generate many associated words.

The richness and flexibility of students' vocabulary is important to assess because vocabulary has such a strong impact on comprehension.

Of course, it is important to make sure that students' word level difficulties actually result from vocabulary problems, not decoding problems (Blachowicz & Fisher, 2002). Not infrequently, struggling readers demonstrate word-level difficulties and appear to have weak vocabulary knowledge when in fact they cannot decode or recognize target words. Needless to say, students who cannot identify the word will have difficulty assigning meaning! If you are at all concerned that decoding might be a factor in students' vocabulary scores, you should simply ask students to read the words aloud. You can provide any words that are mispronounced. Remember, the goal is to evaluate meaning vocabulary. If students still do not appear to comprehend the word, the problem is likely a vocabulary difficulty. Of course, many struggling readers exhibit *both* problems.

*Word Sorts.*   It is possible to get a general idea of the range and flexibility of students' vocabulary knowledge using word sorts. As the student's performance is evaluated, it is helpful to consider the following questions:

- Does the student attend to meaning features or graphic features?
- Can the student generate relational categories?
- Does the student recognize multiple meanings for words?
- Does the student recognize and use affixes?
- Does the student recognize and use root words?
- Can the student generate superordinate categories?

Word sorts can easily be embedded in instruction and used repeatedly. This type of assessment strategy can be especially helpful if you are selecting content-area texts, you are examining students' ability to understand basal texts, or you want to compare your students' knowledge of some new theme or topic. In these cases effective assessment can be done with word sorts using preselected words that capture the central ideas and key concepts of the new material and highlight the relationships between and among those concepts.

*Multiple Measures of Prior (Vocabulary) Knowledge.*   Although general measures of vocabulary knowledge can be helpful, teachers also need to know how vocabulary is interacting with specific reading demands. As we have seen, word knowledge is incremental. For instructional purposes it is generally acknowledged that students have three levels of knowledge: unknown, acquainted, and established (Beck, McKeown, & Omanson, 1987). Because prior knowledge can and does produce variation in reading performance, we suggest evaluating students' vocabulary within the context of specific texts. Concerns about vocabulary knowledge and development are especially critical for English language learners (ELL). These students might very well understand the concepts under consideration but not have the English vocabulary to understand the reading or to communicate their comprehension.

Fortunately, vocabulary measures are relatively easy to incorporate into regular assessment-instruction efforts. Children's self-assessments can be useful, because they can provide information before, during, and after reading events (see Figure 8.5). Interestingly, there is evidence that even a simple yes–no test (which could be done as a "thumbs up/thumbs

**FIGURE 8.5**
Self-Assessment of
Vocabulary about
Volcanoes

| Word | I Have Never Heard This Word | I Have Heard This Word and I Know Something about What It Means | I Am Very Familiar with This Word |
|---|---|---|---|
| molten | | | |
| lava | | | |
| crater | | | |
| crust | | | |
| magma | | | |
| eruption | | | |
| plate | | | |
| composite | | | |
| extinct | | | |
| explosion | | | |

down" activity for the whole class) is an effective way to assess students' vocabulary knowledge (White, Graves, & Slater, 1990).

Holmes and Roser (1987) identify and compare five techniques for evaluating prior knowledge that can be used during instruction and assessment: free recall, word association, structured questions, recognition, and unstructured discussion. The special value of the work of Holmes and Roser (1987) is that they have actually collected data to determine the utility and efficiency of these assessment strategies. The five strategies are easily adaptable to any assessment or instructional setting. Each approach requires only an observant teacher who understands his or her purpose in gathering such information.

- *Free recall.* The teacher says to students, "Tell me everything you know about ____," and records the responses. Free recall provides the most information in the least time, but can pose problems for young and/or disabled readers who have retrieval problems and/or disorganized information.
- *Word association.* This is much like the Prereading Plan (PReP) (see below). Teachers select several key words and ask children what comes to mind when they hear each one. These are quick to prepare and administer and generally yield more information than free recall.
- *Structured questions.* They are posed to determine what students know before reading. This technique is both the most effective and the most efficient, yielding by far the most information. However, they are time-consuming to prepare.
- *Recognition.* This requires that the teacher prepare several statements or key terms beforehand. Then students select the words, phrases, or sentences they believe are related to the key terms or would be present in a particular selection. Recognition is

second only to structured questions for efficiency and to free recall in effectiveness and is helpful for children who have trouble retrieving information in production tasks.

- *Unstructured discussion.* This is most like what is traditionally done in reading instruction, since students freely generate their own ideas about a topic, with no focusing from the teacher. However, this approach might not be worth the effort, since it is the least effective and efficient procedure of the five.

Each of these techniques is designed to gather information that can be used to inform instruction and to provide quick, on-the-spot assessments of students' conceptual base regarding specific text information.

*PReP.* The Prereading Plan, or PReP, is a word association procedure designed to assess both the quality and quantity of students' prior knowledge. Developed by Langer, (1982, 1984), it has been well researched. PReP is a particularly effective strategy because it can be used for assessment purposes at the time of instruction.

To implement this procedure, preview the materials to be used and list two to four key concepts. The following questions are then used as the basis for a discussion:

What comes to mind when you hear/read . . . ?
(Write the students' responses on the board.)
What made you think of . . . ?
Given our discussion, can you add any new ideas about . . . ?

After the discussion students' responses are evaluated by using the following classification scheme:

*Much prior knowledge:* precise definitions, analogies, relational links among concepts.

*Some prior knowledge:* examples and characteristics, but no connections or relations.

*Little prior knowledge:* sound-alikes or look-alikes, associated experiences, little or no meaning relations.

The technique can be used to generate diagnostic conclusions about how students' vocabulary (conceptual) knowledge is contributing to their reading difficulties, to make decisions about grouping and pacing, or to make decisions about appropriate instructional adaptations. If this information is needed for a group of students, Langer advocates creating a matrix. Students' names appear down one side, and the three categories (*Much, Some, Little*) appear across the top.

To summarize, vocabulary assessment can, and probably should, be done in association with the demands of reading selections. Teachers will obviously need to make decisions about which of these vocabulary assessment strategies is most effective for their purposes. However, it is also important to note that different procedures may actually provide different types of information. Valencia et al. (1987) found that different measures seem to assess different aspects of vocabulary (prior) knowledge. Here again, it is important to recognize the value of multiple measures of prior knowledge. This is obviously most easily accomplished by a skilled teacher during actual instruction.

## Evaluating Comprehension

The assessment of comprehension requires a dual focus. First, we are concerned with students' comprehension of a specific selection. Second, and more important, we need to assess students' growing comprehension *ability* (Johnston, 1985). In this section the descriptions of tools and strategies for assessing comprehension are designed to evaluate whether students have understood what they have just read and to reveal whether they are developing the tools needed to understand other texts.

As we have already seen, a number of factors can influence reading performance. For example, students' ability to recall information and answer questions can be affected by the type and quality of the text (see Chapters 2 and 6). Therefore it is important to assess students' comprehension of materials that are similar to those they are expected to read every day. These are likely to be much longer, more complex selections than any that appear on most commercially available tests. Because reading materials can exert such a strong influence on comprehension performance, we suggest becoming somewhat adept at analyzing the selections to be used for assessment purposes.

***Comprehension Materials: Selecting and Analyzing Long Passages.*** An important first step in developing comprehension measures is constructing maps for the reading selections. The purpose of these maps is to identify important elements within each of the reading selections to ensure that test questions (or recall evaluations) are focused on important information. Stories and informational texts will, of course, differ. We expect students to recall the sequence of events from narrative texts, for example. On the other hand, recalls of informational text might not rely as heavily on sequence. Students' recall should reflect an understanding of the relationships between and among key facts and ideas.

*Story Maps: Analyzing Narrative Text.* Story maps reveal the underlying relationships between characters, events, and settings in a given story. They create a visual representation of the elements of setting, problem, goal, events, and resolution (Beck & McKeown, 1981). As a result, they can provide the basis for assessment strategies that inform us about both the students' comprehension of a particular text and their literacy knowledge. Story mapping generally begins with the identification of the problem, the attempt (or plan), and the resolution. The characters, events, and setting revolve around these elements. Sometimes, of course, these other elements are more important. For example, in many books by Ezra Jack Keats the setting plays a central role (e.g., *Snowy Day, Evan's Corner*). Once completed, the maps are used to generate assessment questions (see below) and/or to generate alternative assessment tasks.

For *assessment* purposes it is important to remember that the map should reveal the central ideas and should also capture the underlying relationships among events. To do this, teachers might need to use somewhat more elaborate maps. The more complex maps reveal how events are organized and how they are related to each other. In Figure 8.6, the map of a fourth grade basal story reveals its problem-solution framework.

**FIGURE 8.6**   Story Map for "The Sociable Seal"

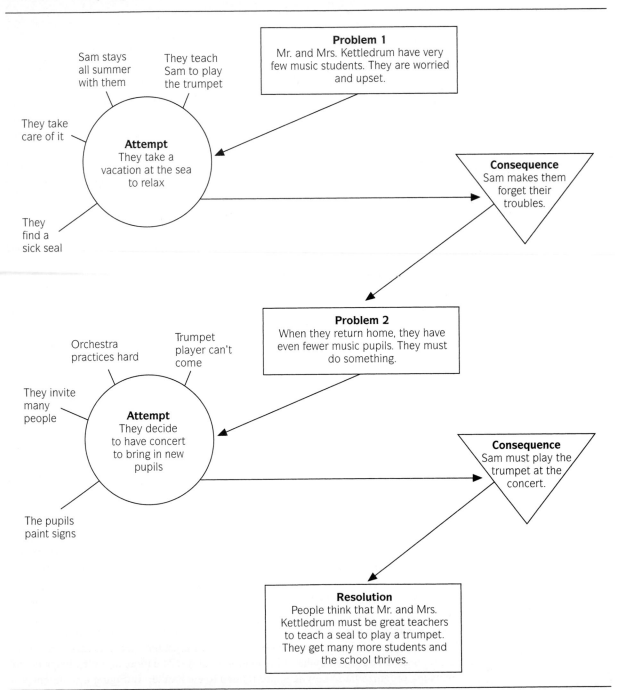

Although text mapping might seem time-consuming, we have found that teachers (even preservice teachers) can learn to do this with just a little practice. Careful analysis of texts is likely to increase both the reliability and validity of informal assessments. Structuring our assessment tasks around carefully analyzed reading material is likely to increase the degree they provide us with *trustworthy* information (Valencia, 1990a). In addition, most teachers report that they begin to view comprehension differently when they analyze selections carefully. They are much less likely to ask trivial, detail questions and much more likely to pose thought-provoking, theme-related questions. We recommend that teachers choose some stories that they will use only for informal assessment. A small set of stories (one to three) from the current basal program, for example, could be analyzed and then used for assessment rather than instructional purposes. Certainly, a battery of such selection maps could be developed by a small group of teachers working together, or teachers could work together to evaluate a set of benchmark books for use in classroom assessment (see the discussion of benchmark books in Chapter 9 for more information).

*Conceptual Maps: Analyzing Expository Text.*   Few assessment instruments provide sufficient information about students' abilities to read nonfiction materials. Yet older students and adults read disproportionately more informational text than they do fictional material. There are simply no available commercial materials that provide good diagnostic information about this critical area of reading ability. For the purposes of evaluating comprehension in general, and studying in particular, it will be necessary to examine actual textbook passages closely (see Chapter 6).

A conceptual map is used to analyze informational selections, identifying relationships in the same way that story maps do for narrative selections. Conceptual maps visually display important elements such as central purpose, main and supporting ideas, and text organization. In Figure 8.7 you will see a conceptual map of a nonfiction selection from a second grade basal reader.

Wixson and Peters (1989, pp. 29–30) provide a functional description of the steps involved in creating a conceptual map:

> Concept mapping begins with the identification of major concepts within the text, through reading and an examination of important text features such as headings and photographs. These concepts are then arranged hierarchically to form the first two levels of the concept map—central purpose(s) and major ideas. Then the map is expanded to include a third level of information—supporting ideas. Relations between concepts are highlighted by adding relational links specifying how the concepts are connected. The more clearly organized the text, the more coherent the concept map. If the relation between two concepts is not clear, a link cannot be established.

It is important to identify any major organizational patterns and use these to guide your comprehension assessment.

The conceptual map in Figure 8.7 reveals a well-organized text. The ideas are linked together very clearly and each concept is connected by a linking concept which appears in parentheses (for example, first, types, steps). The map also shows that the relationships among the levels of information in this selection are clearly hierarchical. The first level

**FIGURE 8.7**    Concept Map for "The Sea Otter"

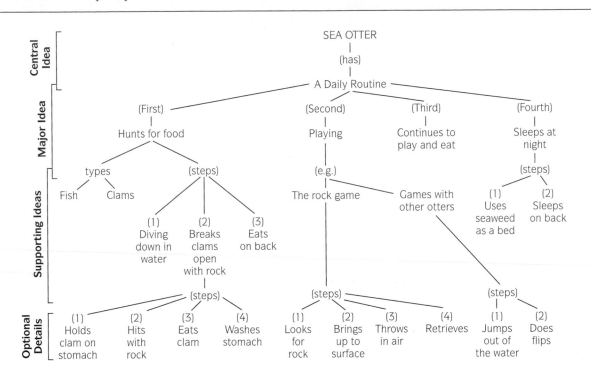

(central purpose) involves describing the daily routine of the sea otter. Then the second level (major ideas) describes the sequence of sea otter activity during one day (hunting, eating, playing, and sleeping). Finally, the third level (supporting ideas) details the steps or provides examples of these activities. Not all of the information provided in the text needs to be displayed in a concept map. But if it is not on the map, the implication is that it is not high in importance. Thus although the text includes details about how the otter plays the rock game, these are considered insignificant to understanding the selection. Of course, this also signals the teacher to avoid asking questions about this information or to expect students to recall it. The organizational pattern should be visible to, and used to support, students' comprehension of the text. It will also be used to evaluate the retellings generated by students after they have read the selection.

***Retellings.***    Armed with a representation of the important elements of a particular text, it is possible to elicit recalls and assess lengthy selections with high levels of reliability. Readers' understanding of textual materials has traditionally been evaluated by using question response scores. Indeed, the practice of answering questions is so pervasive that it is sometimes difficult for teachers to recognize that the ability to answer questions is not the same thing as understanding.

Retellings can add immeasurably to our understanding of readers' comprehension because they allow us to get a view of the quantity, quality, and organization of information constructed during reading. Readers' initial responses to the material should involve free recall of the text, without the interference of the teacher. Text recall is natural for children and does not necessarily bias them to process text in a particular way, as questions do. Because it is important to influence student response as little as possible, initial requests for retelling should be intentionally open-ended. The teacher can initiate the retelling of text with questions such as these:

- Tell *me* that story.
- Tell me what you have read, using your own words.
- What is the text about?
- Tell me as much information as you can about what you have just read. (Ringler and Weber, 1984)

Students should be allowed ample time to recall and relate information. This free recall can provide valuable insight into how the student processes text. Following the uninterrupted retelling, probing statements or questions can be used to elicit further information and to probe readers' understanding of the text. Probes constructed by the teacher should be based directly on the students' retelling. An effective initial prompt is to say, "You said _____ _____ ; tell me more about that."

Some young or less-skilled readers have had little experience in retelling. In fact, they may be surprised that you are not asking them questions. For them the novelty of the task may influence results, and you might want to attempt another retelling shortly after an initial attempt.

In addition to free and probed retelling, teachers and clinicians may also want to consider using structured questions. Then, teachers can distinguish among information generated freely, information elicited with minimal cueing, and information generated through direct cueing. The teacher should avoid their use until *after* students have provided all possible information during free and probed retelling, since structured questions impose someone else's view of what is important on an evaluation of text understanding.

*Eliciting Narrative Recalls.* For stories it is often desirable to ask probe questions, using elements of story grammar. Using specific prompts, teachers can gather information about a child's ability to recall and infer important story information. The following are examples of probe questions students might be asked for thematic stories (Lipson & Wixson, 1989):

- Where did _____ happen? (setting)
- How is the setting of the story important? (setting)
- What happens to get the story started? (initiating event)
- What did _____ do about _____ ? (attempt)
- What is the main problem the characters face? (problem)
- What makes it difficult for the characters to solve their problem? (conflict)

- How is the problem solved? (resolution)
- What lesson(s) are there in the story? (theme)
- What is the main thing that happens in the story? (theme)
- What do you learn about the main characters? (characterization)
- Which event is a turning point in the story? (events)

Collecting and interpreting retelling information can be messy. Valencia (1997) suggests that teachers use a form to guide their thinking and to enhance their systematic evaluation of comprehension over time (see Figure 8.8). Classroom teachers might find it helpful to organize the retelling information with a checklist, which provides more analytic information (see Figure 8.9).

*Eliciting Informational Recalls.*   Of course, the prompts for nonfiction, exposition text need to reflect the structure of those texts:

- What is the central idea (big idea) of this selection? (central purpose)
- Why do you think the author wrote this? (purpose)
- Using the headings to divide the text into sections, tell the main ideas in each smaller section. (major ideas)
- What details does the text provide to tell more about the important main ideas? (supporting details)
- How does the author organize the information to tell you about the central and major ideas? (structure)

If concept maps were generated, they will be exceptionally helpful as you prompt students' recall and evaluate the quality of that recall.

*Analyzing Recall Information.*   Gathering retelling data is the easy part of this assessment strategy, resulting in a wealth of rich information about students' ability to comprehend and about what they choose to share. The problem is less in the gathering than in the interpretation. How to make sense of and evaluate this wealth of information is an altogether different (and more difficult) job. It may be helpful to reflect on the following:

- What does the child recall about this selection?
- How does this recall compare with the map of the text (quantity and quality)?
- How does the student organize the recall?
- How does the recall rate as a whole?

Of course, some system for analyzing and interpreting recall data is needed to answer questions like these. Both quantitative and qualitative systems are available, some easier to use than others (Kalmbach, 1986a; Morrow, 1988).

The retelling guidelines suggested by Morrow (1989) involve a point system. The student's retelling is compared to an analysis of the original selection. To use this retelling procedure, point values are assigned to various aspects of the maps created earlier (setting, characters, problem statements, etc.). Then the student's recall is evaluated according to how

**FIGURE 8.8** Reading Summary Record

Student _____ Teacher _____

Date _____ Name of text _____

Response mode:     ☐ oral                    ☐ written                    ☐ picture
Level of passage:  ☐ easy                    ☐ average                   ☐ difficult
Type of passage:   ☐ narrative               ☐ informational
Level of support:  ☐ read independently      ☐ teacher guided reading    ☐ partner reading
Presentation mode: ☐ listening               ☐ reading

Check the appropriate description for each item.

1. **Recalls important information**
   Includes most of the important information (e.g., plot, characters, resolution *or* supporting details and
       concepts)
   Includes some of the important information
   Includes little, if any, important information

2. **Draws inferences**
   Includes conclusion, ideas that are not explicitly stated in the text
   Suggests understanding of ideas that are not explicitly stated in the text
   Includes only information explicitly stated in the text

3. **Understands the gist, main idea, theme**
   Includes theme, problem, main concept/idea, statement of synthesis of the critical content of the passage
   Includes a weak or partial synthesis
   Unable to construct a synthesis of the passage

4. **Constructs a personal response (relate to personal experience, background knowledge)**
   Includes a personal response to the major concepts, theme of the text
   Includes a personal response to surface elements of the text or a simple statement of preference
   Unable to construct a personal response

5. **Coherence and comprehensibility**
   Includes a richness, coherence, and comprehensibility that communicates the essence of the text
   Includes some coherence but is not complete or does not flow
   Includes bits of information without much organization or flow

6. **Other observations**

*Source:* "Authentic classroom assessment of early reading: Alternatives to standardized tests" by S. Valencia in *Preventing School Failure*, 1997, *41* (2), p. 67. Reprinted with permission of the Helen Dwight Reid Educational Foundation. Published by Heldref Publications, 1319 Eighteenth St., NW, Washington, DC 20036-1802. Copyright © 1997.

well it reflected these major components. Each retelling yields a score, with the total possible equaling ten points.

Figure 8.10 shows the transcript of Marvin's retelling of a full-length short story, *The Sociable Seal* (mapped in Figure 8.6). In Figure 8.11, you will find an analysis of this retelling using Morrow's (1989) system. Although Marvin did note the main characters, he did not refer to them by name (and, in fact, seems uncertain that "Sam" is the seal during probed

Key:  0   Not Yet
      ✓   Sometimes
      +   Under Control

## Students' Names

| Retelling Attributes | | | | | | | | | | | | | | |
|---|---|---|---|---|---|---|---|---|---|---|---|---|---|---|
| Setting | | | | | | | | | | | | | | |
| Characters | | | | | | | | | | | | | | |
| Problem | | | | | | | | | | | | | | |
| Character Response | | | | | | | | | | | | | | |
| Attempts | | | | | | | | | | | | | | |
| Major Events | | | | | | | | | | | | | | |
| Resolution | | | | | | | | | | | | | | |
| Theme | | | | | | | | | | | | | | |
| Maintains Narrative Organization | | | | | | | | | | | | | | |
| Coherent | | | | | | | | | | | | | | |
| Other | | | | | | | | | | | | | | |

**Comments:**

**FIGURE 8.10**
Sample Retelling

| Marvin's Retelling of "The Sociable Seal" |
|---|

They were at their house. They went to the beach and saw a seal on the shore. When they first found it they took it, a boat, and went out to the sea. They left him and he came back and went to the shore as fast as he could. They couldn't believe it so they said they'd keep him 'til the end of the summer and they did. He wanted to stay. He took baths at night and they took baths at daytime in the morning. They had a music store and she needed people to play and one kid didn't show up so they went to get the deal to play the trumpet and he played it better than ever and they decided to keep him for as long as they wanted. They had a musical seal and he played good and everyone else did and they had sign-ups so you can play with him and all the people who wanted to sign up for practice with the seal and everybody signed up so they had enough people to play so they were happy and . . . um . . . that's the end.

| Probe Questions and Marvin's Responses |
|---|

1. Who found the seal?
   *The people, Mr. and Mrs. Kettledrum.*
2. What did they do for a living?
   *They had a school music store.*
3. What problem did the Kettledrums have?
   *They couldn't find a . . . A boy was sick and he couldn't play so they had to get somebody else so they picked the seal.*
4. What was Sam like?
   *Funny.*
5. Where did the story take place?
   *At the ocean and the music store.*
6. What problem was the story trying to solve?
   *That they couldn't keep the seal and they did because he didn't want to leave.*
7. What do you think the story was telling you?
   *That seals play just as good as people, if not better.*
8. Why do you think they took Sam out to sea?
   *So they could have him find his family, but he didn't want to. He swam back to shore and they saw him and decided to keep him.*
9. Why did the Kettledrums go to the beach?
   *Because they wanted to get away from all their problems.*
10. What kind of problems were they having?
    *They had problems with their orchestra and their school. Ummm. I don't know.*
11. Why do you think they had the musical?
    *To get money.*
12. Why were they happy at the end?
    *Because the seal could play the instrument and they liked the seal so they kept him.*

questioning). In addition, his grasp of character development was very weak. More seriously, Marvin focused on events that were not central to the story. This significantly weakened his recognition of the plot and the theme. Note that when asked what the story was telling, Marvin concluded, "That seals can play just as good as people, if not better," a theme that is not supported by the text analysis (see Figure 8.11).

The advantages to this type of system are that it is relatively easy to use and that it reduces large amounts of data into manageable and reportable pieces. The disadvantage to any quantitative system is that it is possible to miss the qualitative aspects of the retellings.

FIGURE 8.11
Evaluation of
Marvin's Retelling

## Story Retelling Analysis

Student's Name: _____Marvin_____ Date: _____

Title of Story: _____The Sociable Seal_____

**General Directions:** Place a 1 next to each element if the child includes it in his or her presentation. Credit gist as well as obvious recall.

### Characters and Setting

    A. Begins story with an introduction          0

    B. Names main character(s)          0

    C. Describes character traits          0

    D. Includes statement about time and/or place          1

### Theme

    Refers to main character's primary goal or problem to be resolved.          0

### Plot Episodes

    A. Recalls main events and episodes          1

    B. Retells story in order and makes connections across text          1

### Resolution

    A. Names the problem solution/goal attainment          1

    B. Ends story          1

### Response to Literature

    Includes a personal or critical response to the literature          0

**Highest Score Possible** (10)      **Child's Score:** 5

*Comments:*

*Source:* Adapted from Morrow, Lesley Mandel. (1989). Using story retelling to develop comprehension. *Children's comprehension of text: Research into practice,* K. Denise Muth, Editor, chapter 2, pp. 37–58. Reprinted with permission of the International Reading Association. All rights reserved.

Irwin and Mitchell (1983) have proposed a more holistic scoring system, borrowing from approaches used to assess writing, that is especially appropriate for evaluating students' recall of expository text. This system attends to the "richness of retellings," assessing not only such features as the inclusion of major points and details, but also the degree to which students have gone beyond the text to generate cohesive generalizations and create a comprehensible whole.

The system employs a five-point scale. The criteria for assigning retellings to one of these levels are displayed in Figure 8.12. When Irwin and Mitchell's holistic scoring system is applied to Marvin's retelling, we would rate the richness of his retelling somewhere between 2 and 3. Marvin did include some major ideas and included appropriate supporting details. There is a cohesiveness and coherence to his recall. However, he did not include the major thesis (problem) of the selection in his retelling and, even with probing, failed to make appropriate connections between episodes, events, and problems.

To extend the diagnostic value of a qualitative assessment even further, specific aspects of the retelling can be summarized and evaluated (see Figure 8.13). The qualitative analysis in Figure 8.13 clearly demonstrates that Marvin had difficulty generating inferences from text, especially with regard to major ideas and themes. His abilities to summarize, generalize, and organize the text information were all weak. On the other hand, Marvin did recall detailed information from text and clearly responded affectively to what he read.

**FIGURE 8.12**
Guidelines for Evaluating the Richness of Retellings

| Judging Richness of Retellings | |
|---|---|
| Level | Criteria for establishing level |
| 5 | Student generalizes beyond text; includes thesis (summarizing statement), all major points, and appropriate supporting details; includes relevant supplementations; shows high degree of coherence, completeness, comprehensibility. |
| 4 | Student includes thesis (summarizing statement), all major points, and appropriate supporting details; shows high degree of coherence, completeness, comprehensibility. |
| 3 | Student relates major ideas; includes appropriate supporting details and relevent supplementations; shows adequate coherence, completeness, comprehensibility. |
| 2 | Student relates a few major ideas and some supporting details; includes irrelevant supplementations; shows some degree of coherence; some completeness; the whole is somewhat comprehensible. |
| 1 | Student relates details only; irrelevant supplementations or none; low degree of coherence; incomplete; incomprehensible. |

5 = highest level    1 = lowest level

*Source:* Irwin, P. A., & Mitchell, Judy Nichols. (1985). A procedure for assessing the richness of retellings. *Classroom strategies for secondary reading* (2nd ed.), W. John Harker (Ed.), International Reading Association, chapter 2, 10–16. (Chart-Judging Richness of Retellings.) Reprinted with permission of the International Reading Association. All rights reserved.

**FIGURE 8.13**   Diagnostic Summary of Marvin's Retelling

**Directions:** Indicate with a checkmark the degree to which the reader's retelling includes the reader's comprehension in terms of the following criteria:

|  | None | Low Degree | Moderate Degree | High Degree |
|---|---|---|---|---|
| 1. Retelling includes information directly stated in text. | | | | ✓ |
| 2. Retelling includes information inferred directly or indirectly from text. | | ✓ | | |
| 3. Retelling includes what is important to remember from the text. | | ✓ | | |
| 4. Retelling provides relevant content and concepts. | | | ✓ | |
| 5. Retelling indicates reader's attempt to connect background knowledge to text information. | | | ✓ | |
| 6. Retelling indicates reader's attempt to make summary statements or generalizations based on the text which can be applied to the real world. | | ✓ | | |
| 7. Retelling indicates highly individualistic and creative impressions of or reactions to the text. | | | ✓ | |
| 8. Retelling indicates the reader's affective involvement with the text. | | | | ✓ |
| 9. Retelling demonstrates appropriate reader's language fluency (vocabulary, sentence structure, language conventions, etc.) | | | ✓ | |
| 10. Retelling indicates reader's ability to organize or compose the retelling. | | ✓ | | |
| 11. Retelling demonstrates the reader's sense of audience or purpose. | | | ✓ | |
| 12. Retelling indicates the reader's control of the mechanics of speaking or writing. | | | ✓ | |

**Interpretation:** Items 1–4 indicates the reader's comprehension of textual information; items 5–8 indicate reader's response, and involvement with text; items 9–12 indicate facility with language.

Source: Mitchell, J. N., & Irwin, P. A. The reader retelling profile: Using retellings to make instructional decisions. Cited in *Reexamining Reading Diagnosis: New Trends and Procedures,* edited by S. M. Glazer, L. Searfoss, and L. M. Gentile. Copyright © 1988. Reprinted by permission of Dr. Pi A. Irwin.

With older students written recalls may be employed. In either case however, the task must be absolutely clear to students. As with all assessment procedures, task demands will most likely influence results. When written retellings are to be used, it is especially important that you differentiate a *retelling* from a *summary*. Although the evidence is slim, it does appear that written retellings are likely to generate more limited productions than oral ones. On the other hand, written retellings are frequently more coherent and better organized. Using brief written recalls that focus attention on important story components, we have arrived at high degrees of reliability between teachers using holistic ranking methods. When used over time, students' progress can be assessed and the effects of instruction can be demonstrated.

These techniques can be used to gather information about the child's ability to recall and infer important text information. In addition, affective responses to readings can be checked regularly with questions such as: Did you learn anything from reading this? Did you find this selection interesting? Did you enjoy reading this? Kalmbach (1986b, p. 331) suggests that careful analysis of the retellings themselves can provide important information about students' responses to the text. "The way students structure a retelling will often tell you more about what they thought of the story than they can themselves." Although Kalmbach offers no specific suggestions, the following questions may focus evaluation:

- Is the child's personal interpretation evident from the retelling?
- Does the child make evaluative statements about the characters or events?
- Does the child attend to the language of the text, using it to support his or her interpretation?

Before making final judgments about students' ability to retell passages, be sure that the samples gathered represent the students' best efforts. The selections used for assessment should provide a good match for the students' interests, prior knowledge, and developmental ability. Of course, teachers can decide to gather information regarding performance on materials that are routinely assigned to the reader, regardless of appropriateness. The point to remember is that these procedures are sampling the reader's abilities, not measuring them in some definitive way. The goal is to learn more about the reader, and the selections teachers make should reflect their assessment purpose(s).

*Questioning.*   Perhaps the most common form of informal reading assessment is questioning. Although we believe that retellings enrich the picture, careful questioning can reveal much about students' understanding of a particular selection and about their ability to comprehend in general.

The comprehension that is revealed through questioning is, at least in part, a function of the questions that have been asked. Children's ability to answer questions is influenced by both the type and content of the questions they are asked (Pearson et al., 1979; Raphael, Winograd, & Pearson, 1980). In addition, both the type and content of questions influence what children recall and the types of inferences they make (Wixson, 1983a, 1984) (see Chapter 6).

Because structured questions impose someone else's view of what is important, they should be asked *after* students have provided all possible information during free and probed retelling. In this way distinctions can be made between the information generated freely, information elicited with minimal cueing, and information generated through direct probing.

Many commercially available assessments (such as those that accompany basal programs) use a classification scheme to label comprehension questions. These classification schemes are typically based on one of several well-known taxonomies (for example, Barrett, 1976; Bloom, 1956). However, there is little evidence that these taxonomies represent real differences in comprehension skills or in the level of difficulty of different questions. As an alternative to these question taxonomies, Pearson and Johnson (1978) suggested that question types should be determined by the source of the answer. They originally devised a three-level taxonomy that captured the relationship between a question and its answer source: text-explicit questions, text-implicit questions, and scriptally implicit questions.

This taxonomy has been extended and used widely as an instructional tool by Raphael (1982, 1986). Her latest refinement of these *question-answer-relationships* (QARs) includes the following categories:

I. *Right There QARs.* The answer is explicitly stated in the text, usually easy to find. The words used to make up the question and words used to answer the question are right there in the same sentence.

II. *Think and Search QARs.* The answer can be inferred from text information. The answer is in the story, but you need to put together different story parts to find it. Words for the question and words for the answer are not found in the same sentence.

III. *In My Head QARs.* These scriptally implicit questions (the question must be answered by referring to prior knowledge) have been divided into two types:

A. *Author and You.* The answer is not in the story. You need to think about what you already know, what the author tells you in the text, and how it fits together.

B. *On My Own.* The answer is not in the story. You can even answer the question without the story. You need to use your own experience.

Distinguishing between questions on the basis of the source of the answer is extremely important in assessment. If we are not sure what is required to answer the questions we ask, then it will be difficult to make instructional decisions about comprehension. For example, if we think the answer is right there, when in fact the answer requires connecting text information through inference, then we may incorrectly assume that students cannot locate detail information in text while the problem is actually related to inferential skills. Therefore the first task in assessing students' comprehension with questions is to determine the task demands of the questions themselves (see Chapter 6).

The placement of questions also affects students' performance and consequently our judgments about their abilities. Most teachers regularly ask questions after the selection has been read. Questions in this position place a premium on student recognition of important information. It is easy to underestimate students' comprehension, especially if the end-of-selection questions focus on details and text-explicit information. Therefore teachers may want to ask questions before reading. This permits evaluation of students' ability to read for differing purposes and/or to locate key information.

Questions asked during reading can help to determine whether students are making connections and integrating relevant information. By refining the questioning strategies, important instructional information can be gathered.

Issues surrounding the quality and placement of questions in general are important, but so are concerns about the content and focus of questions. Maps or outlines like those we described earlier can serve as the basis for constructing comprehension questions. Teachers may find it useful to create a matrix like that in Figure 8.14. When the matrix is completed, an array of possible questions has been generated about important aspects of text (Wixson, Peters, Weber, & Roeber, 1987). In addition, teachers can check to make sure that they are

**FIGURE 8.14**
Narrative
Question Grid

| Story Components | Text Explicit | Text Implicit | Scriptally Implicit |
|---|---|---|---|
| **Themes**<br>Main idea<br>Level<br>Abstract<br>Level | | | |
| **Plot**<br>Setting<br>(Location and relation to theme) | | | |
| **Characters**<br>(Traits and functions) | | | |
| **Setting**<br>(Location and relation to theme) | | | |
| **Problem** | | | |
| **Conflict** | | | |
| **Resolution** | | | |
| **Major Events** | | | |

assessing students comprehension on a range of questions (the three types correspond directly to the three types of QARs described above).

Although these strategies may seem time-consuming, the instructional value of assessment information is enhanced. Students do not have to be characterized simply as "good comprehenders" and "poor comprehenders." Instead, teachers can describe quite precisely what and how they understand.

***Evaluating Comprehension Processes.*** We have described a variety of ways to gather information about the products of comprehension. Analyzing students' recall and question responses can provide information about *how* students comprehend, but this information is indirect; it must be inferred. Recently, educators have tried a number of newer assessment strategies designed to uncover the activity that goes on "inside the head."

*Think-Alouds.* In a think-aloud procedure, readers are asked to stop at various points during their reading and "think aloud" about the processes and strategies they are using as they read. Wixson and Lipson (1986; see also Afflerbach, 2000; Loxterman, Beck, & McKeown, 1994) suggest that think-alouds can produce insights into readers' approaches to text processing.

The following verbal report demonstrates this (Wixson & Lipson, 1986, pp. 139–140):

STACY:    (reads title) Space Ship Earth.

TUTOR:    What were you thinking about when you read that title?

STACY:    A space trip to earth. (reads first portion of text, haltingly and with many repetitions) Boy! I had a lot of trouble with that one.

TUTOR:    What makes you think you had trouble with it?

STACY:    I kept messing up.

TUTOR:    What do you mean by "messing up"?

STACY:    I kept reading sentences twice.

TUTOR:    What do you think caused you to read sentences twice like that?

STACY:    Not understanding it.

TUTOR:    Okay, did any of the words give you trouble?

STACY:    No.

Stacy's verbal report reveals a view of reading that is governed by attempts to understand. "Although miscues were obvious during this segment, Stacy's 'fixup' strategy was driven by a desire not to sound good but to construct a sensible text representation" (Wixson & Lipson, 1986, p. 140).

Procedures for eliciting students' reports of mental activity generally include the following (Afflerbach, 2000; Lipson, Bigler, Poth, & Wickizer, 1987; Wade, 1990):

1. Teacher/evaluator selects a text (generally about 200 words, but longer selections have been used).
2. The text is segmented and marked so that students will stop at predetermined spots.
3. The teacher/evaluator reminds students to think aloud about the text and/or their thoughts as they read the text.

Sometimes students are asked to provide text-based think-alouds. Wade (1990), for example, has designed a think-aloud procedure that requires students to generate hypotheses about the text as they read. Students are told to "tell what is happening," and they are then asked to detail the portions of text that led to their hypotheses. Student reports are analyzed in terms of the information they yield about the reader's ability to make hypotheses and integrate and revise information during reading.

On the other hand, Lipson et al. (1987) focused on readers' use of mental processes. Consequently, they asked students "to tell what you were *doing* and *thinking* as you read that part." Using this approach, students' verbal reports are analyzed for evidence that they employed various strategies known to enhance comprehension (see Chapter 15). Paris (1991) describes a more prompted think-aloud which revolves around a specially created think-aloud passage, or TAP. In Figure 8.15, you see an example of a TAP, that can be used to observe students' strategy use during comprehension. During a think-aloud assessment it is

**FIGURE 8.15**
An Example of a
Think-Aloud
Passage

## The Peabody Ducks

The Peabody Hotel in Memphis, Tennessee, is a very famous place. The Peabody is a beautiful hotel. It has large, nice rooms and fancy decorations. It is not famous for its looks, though. It is famous for its ducks!

Mallard ducks have been performing for guests of the Peabody for over 50 years. Every morning at 11:00 A.M., hotel workers roll out the red carpets in the lobby of the Peabody. Then they begin to play a marching tune.

The audience starts to smile and clap as the ducks waddle into the lobby. The ducks march down the carpet and into the fountain in the middle of the lobby.

The ducks swim in the fountain all day. At 5:00 P.M., they leave the fountain and follow their trainer, Edward Pembroke. They march to the elevator and ride back up to the roof of the Peabody. The hotel has built them a large cage on the roof. It is known as the Royal Duck Place. The place has fountains, pools, food, and even a fancy purple trat where the ducks sleep.

Edward Pembroke has trained ducks for the Peabody for almost 50 years. He teaches them to listen to his voice as he tells them what to do. He also teaches them to follow signals that he gives with a cane. Pembroke usually trains groups of five ducks at a time. Each duck only performs for three months. After three months, the trained ducks are sent back to farms. New ducks take their place. This way, the ducks don't get bored and neither does Pembroke!

As you can see, the Peabody Hotel is an unusual place! Maybe someday you'll get a chance to visit Memphis. Then you too can get a look at the famous Peabody ducks!

*Source:* Figure from Assessment and remediation of metacognitive aspects of children's reading comprehension by S. G. Paris in *Topics in Language Disorders*, 1991, 12:1, pp. 4–8.

useful to make observation notes using the form provided in Figure 8.16, which also provides an excellent summary of students' strategy use.

It is important to understand that verbal reports reflect what readers are doing as they read a specific text with specific task directions. There is good evidence that students' reading behaviors may vary as texts and tasks change (Afflerbach, 2000; Olshavsky, 1978). Maria (1990) has pointed out that think-aloud assessment procedures are very intrusive and require considerable teacher time. In addition, single think-aloud excerpts will not capture the

**FIGURE 8.16**
Summarizing
Strategy Used from
Think-Aloud

Name _____ Grade _____ Date _____
Teacher _____ School _____

| Comprehension Strategies | | |
|---|---|---|
| | Observed | Comments/notes |
| **Predict**<br>Uses title<br>Uses pictures<br>Uses prior knowledge<br>Skims | | |
| **Infer**<br>Makes text-based inferences<br>Makes personal connections<br>   (prior knowledge)<br>Connects to other texts<br>Connects to big ideas and themes | | |
| **Monitor**<br>Notices meaning disruptions<br>Miscues retain meaning<br>Uses rereading<br>Skips and rereads | | |
| **Clarify**<br>Uses rereading and reading ahead<br>Uses word recognition strategies<br>Uses context and morphological<br>   analysis for meanings<br>Uses text aids and illustrations | | |
| **Question**<br>Generates text-based questions<br>   to clarify<br>Generates questions based on<br>   prior knowledge<br>Generates questions about purpose | | |
| **Summarize**<br>Distinguish important versus unimpor-<br>   tant information<br>States mostly important information<br>Provides organized recall<br>Uses summarization to aid<br>   comprehension | | |
| **Evaluate**<br>Make jusgments and draw conclusions<br>   about significance<br>Form opinion | | |

variability we noted above. Both concerns can be addressed if teachers turn to careful observations of strategy use during normal instruction.

*Continuous Comprehension Assessment.* The value of think-alouds can be improved significantly by "specifying the factors related to text and varying them systematically (Wixson & Lipson, 1986, p. 140). This generally requires regular, ongoing assessment of students as they read and interact with a variety of texts and tasks. Good assessment should capture the full range of students' comprehension ability, not just their best or worst efforts.

A versatile assessment procedure, designed by Wood (1988), is the individual comprehension profile. As described by Wood, a profile, or matrix, is created by using the results from information that has been gathered by the teacher/evaluator. The information is recorded as students read from their basal under conditions that parallel the daily expectations in the classroom. Although Wood provides a sample profile, the matrix is meant to be teacher-made, allowing teachers to enter columns for whatever conditions appear most important for their program and student(s).

We have used a variation on this procedure to create an individual reading record (see Figure 8.17). As students read, information relevant to their performance can be recorded. If students are thinking aloud (see above), for example, the information generated would probably be used to fill the "Process Knowledge/Strategy Use" column. The data recorded, coupled with specific information about the texts and tasks (see Chapters 5 and 6), provide a very complete picture of a reader's knowledge, skills, and abilities, and how this varies across texts.

*Studying.* Studying is a specialized type of comprehension (Anderson & Armbruster, 1984b). Studying involves intensive reading for specific purposes, typically to organize, retain, and retrieve information. Often the purposes for reading have been imposed by others. However, many of the skills required for studying in the school context are also required in work settings. Even students who have a good foundation in the skills and strategies of reading through the elementary years may find the special demands of study and work reading difficult. We recommend assessing the study skills and habits of all students who

**FIGURE 8.17** Individual Reading Record

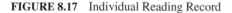

Name: _____  Teacher: _____
Grade: _____  School : _____

|  | Date | Text Description | Topic Familiarity | Attitudes and Interest | Reading Task(s) | Process Knowledge/ Strategy Use | Reading Performance | Level of Support |
|---|---|---|---|---|---|---|---|---|
| Text 1 | | | | | | | | |
| Text 2 | | | | | | | | |
| Text 3 | | | | | | | | |

have reached the sixth grade or beyond, since weaknesses in this area often cause serious academic problems.

Although it is helpful and important to assess all components of reading ability in natural contexts, it is absolutely critical to do so when assessing study skills. If they are to provide any useful information, assessments of studying ability must be specific to the content to be learned and related to the materials to be studied (Rakes & Smith, 1986).

Assessment of students' studying abilities should move forward cautiously. Clearly, students may be aware of these skills and strategies but not use them during studying. In addition, many of these skills can be executed passively (for example, outlining by copying headings and subheadings). It should be apparent how important it is to determine what is really required to understand a particular text or accomplish a specific task.

In planning an assessment of study skills, Estes and Vaughan (1978) suggest the following steps:

1. Identify the study skills that students will need for success in their studying activities.
2. Construct a diagnostic checklist to record your assessments of students' studying abilities.
3. Prepare a student self-appraisal survey based on the study skills you consider important.
4. Construct informal activities to assess the study skills you have identified as critical.
5. Informally observe students' ability to use their study skills as they perform tasks during daily classroom activities.

*Developing a Checklist of Critical Studying Skills and Strategies.*   The specification of skills and strategies as reading-studying abilities is somewhat problematic, since many of these might arguably be considered generic comprehension skills. Rogers (1984, p. 346) has made a distinction between casual and study reading that is helpful: "Deliberate procedures for retaining or applying what is read are called study-reading skills. They permit people to complete tasks which they would not do as successfully if they read only casually." Long lists of study skills generally include specialized abilities such as alphabetizing, skimming, note taking, outlining, scanning, and reading maps, graphs, tables, and diagrams. Such lists are not entirely helpful, however, because the use of these studying skills does not ensure good comprehension, nor do all good readers use all of these skills (Armbruster & Anderson, 1981).

There are many checklists available to guide observations of students as they engage in studying activities. Rogers (1984) has collapsed the long lists of reading-study skills into three large categories: (1) special study-reading comprehension skills, (2) information location skills, and (3) study and retention strategies, and has designed a comprehensive checklist of discrete abilities (see Figure 8.18). As always, this checklist should be adapted to specific settings. As students are observed engaged in study activity, the teacher should consider the following questions:

- Does the student have an organized approach to the task?
- Does the student seem to know what to do and how to use the text to accomplish the task?

**FIGURE 8.18**
Study-Reading
Skills Checklist

| Degree of Skill | Absent | Low | High |
|---|---|---|---|
| **I. Specific study-reading comprehension skills** | | | |
|    A. Ability to interpret graphic arts | | | |
|      Can the student interpret these graphic aids? | | | |
|       1. maps | | | |
|       2. globes | | | |
|       3. graphs | | | |
|       4. charts | | | |
|       5. tables | | | |
|       6. cartoons | | | |
|       7. pictures | | | |
|       8. diagrams | | | |
|       9. other organizing or iconic aids | | | |
|    B. Ability to follow directions | | | |
|      Can the student follow . . . | | | |
|       1. simple directions? | | | |
|       2. a more complex set of directions? | | | |
| **II. Information location skills** | | | |
|    A. Ability to vary rate of reading | | | |
|      Can the student do the following? | | | |
|       1. scan | | | |
|       2. skim | | | |
|       3. read at slow rate for difficult materials | | | |
|       4. read at average rate for reading level | | | |
|    B. Ability to locate information by use of book parts | | | |
|      Can the student use book parts to identify the following information? | | | |
|       1. title | | | |
|       2. author or editor | | | |
|       3. publisher | | | |
|       4. city of publication | | | |
|       5. name of series | | | |
|       6. edition | | | |
|       7. copyright date | | | |
|       8. date of publication | | | |
|      Can the student quickly locate and understand the function of the following parts of a book? | | | |
|       1. preface | | | |
|       2. foreword | | | |
|       3. introduction | | | |
|       4. table of contents | | | |
|       5. list of figures | | | |
|       6. chapter headings | | | |
|       7. subtitles | | | |
|       8. footnotes | | | |
|       9. bibliography | | | |
|      10. glossary | | | |
|      11. index | | | |
|      12. appendix | | | |

**FIGURE 8.18**
(Continued)

| Degree of Skill | Absent | Low | High |
|---|---|---|---|
| C. Ability to locate information in reference works | | | |
|    1. locate information in a dictionary | | | |
|       a. using the guide words | | | |
|       b. using a thumb index | | | |
|       c. locating root word | | | |
|       d. locating derivations of root word | | | |
|       e. using the pronunciation key | | | |
|       f. selecting word meaning appropriate to passage under study | | | |
|       g. noting word origin | | | |
|    2. locate information in an encyclopedia | | | |
|       a. using information on spine to locate volume | | | |
|       b. using guide words to locate section | | | |
|       c. using index volume | | | |
|    3. use other reference works such as: | | | |
|       a. telephone directory | | | |
|       b. newspapers | | | |
|       c. magazines | | | |
|       d. atlases | | | |
|       e. television listings | | | |
|       f. schedules | | | |
|       g. various periodical literature indices | | | |
|       h. others (    ) | | | |
| D. Ability to locate information in the library | | | |
|    Can the student do the following? | | | |
|    1. locate material by using the card catalog | | | |
|       a. by subject | | | |
|       b. by author | | | |
|       c. by title | | | |
|    2. find the materials organized in the library | | | |
|       a. fiction section | | | |
|       b. reference section | | | |
|       c. periodical section | | | |
|       d. vertical file | | | |
|       e. others (    ) | | | |
| **III. Study and retention strategies** | | | |
| A. Ability to study information and remember it | | | |
|    Can the student do the following? | | | |
|    1. highlight important information | | | |
|    2. underline important information | | | |
|    3. use oral repetition to increase retention | | | |
|    4. ask and answer questions to increase retention | | | |
|    5. employ a systematic study procedure (such as SQ3R) | | | |
|    6. demonstrate effective study habits | | | |
|       a. set a regular study time | | | |
|       b. leave adequate time for test or project preparation | | | |

**FIGURE 8.18**
(Continued)

| Degree of Skill | Absent | Low | High |
|---|---|---|---|
|    c. recognize importance of self-motivation in learning | | | |
| B. Ability to organize information Can the student do the following? | | | |
|    1. take notes | | | |
|    2. note source of information | | | |
|    3. write a summary for a paragraph | | | |
|    4. write a summary for a short selection | | | |
|    5. write a summary integrating information from more than one source | | | |
|    6. write a summary for a longer selection | | | |
|    7. make graphic aids to summarize information | | | |
|    8. write an outline of a paragraph | | | |
|    9. write an outline of a short selection | | | |
|   10. write an outline for longer selections | | | |
|   11. write an outline integrating information from more than one source | | | |
|   12. use an outline to write a report or make an oral report | | | |

*Source:* Chart from Rogers, Douglas B. (1984, January). Assessing study skills. *Journal of Reading, 27* (4), pp. 353–354. Reprinted with permission of the International Reading Association. All rights reserved.

- Does the student exhibit enthusiasm and/or interest?
- Does the student appear to be using appropriate study skills and strategies?
- Does the student appear to read with a flexible rate?

Ideally, checklists like this one would become a part of the continuous and ongoing assessment (portfolio) for each student, an idea implied by Rogers (1984, p. 347): "It (the checklist) can be completed as opportunities arise for observing each student and it can be kept in the student's records." As a matter of practicality, however, it may be necessary to create planned opportunities or informal tests to make these observations efficient.

*Open Book Reading Assessment.* In the Open Book Reading Assessment (OBRA) (Bader, 1980), as its name suggests, students have access to the text throughout. The OBRA is based on the following assumptions: "To determine the skills to be evaluated, one must give consideration to (a) the nature of the tasks to be performed with the material and the levels of comprehension required and (b) the enabling skills required to perform the tasks or comprehend the information." Bader suggests creating items about such things as technical vocabulary, use of context clues, using charts, and using book parts. In addition, she suggests testing students' ability to answer questions that require making inferences and interpreting text information.

To create an OBRA tailored for specific settings, examine the textbook carefully and consider the types of tasks generally expected of students (see Chapters 5 and 6). The OBRA is a very flexible assessment strategy, since it can accommodate almost any type of text-task context. Expository text chapters often contain features like the following:

- Chapter preview,
- List of objectives,
- Clearly labeled section headings (for example, 53.3, Fuel Flow System),
- Complex figures with detailed labeling,
- A new terms section, with new vocabulary in boldface and brief definitions,
- Marginalized concept notes,
- Chapter review,
- A discussion topics and activities section.

To create an OBRA, you ask conventional questions focused on content (e.g., "Circle the components of an airflow system") but also items that help you to see what students know about studying their specific content-area textbooks (e.g., "In my textbook, to find _____ I would turn to _____, on page _____.

After the students have completed the OBRA, the following questions should be considered in evaluating students' performance:

- Do the students recognize the parts of the text?
- Are students able to make use of graphic materials?
- When the text is available, can students locate specific information?
- Can students use the text to figure out unfamiliar, specialized vocabulary?
- Does the problem appear to be ability to use the text or ability to retain information?

This information is summarized and used to plan and adapt instruction. Bader (1980) suggests using a chart to display the information for the class. The chart in Figure 8.19 was completed by a secondary vocational education teacher with students in an auto mechanics class. He learned, to his surprise, that most of his students were unable to make effective use of the diagrams and charts in their textbook. Similarly, few of them were adept at using the helpful features of the book to derive information. Whereas he had previously attributed the students' poor performance to lack of effort and/or motivation, he now realized that at least some students were unable to learn the information using the text. Instruction in textbook use and/or additional support for reading and studying would be needed.

Again, teachers may be concerned about the time-consuming nature of these assessment strategies. Although short-cuts are possible, the information gathered will not be as useful. As Rogers (1984, p. 352) has noted, "students' use of study-reading can best be assessed by observing them while they are engaging in studying-reading for some personal interest or need. Contrived situations such as often occur when students are asked to complete worksheet pages from published materials are not as effective for assessing and teaching study-reading."

FIGURE 8.19 Open Book Reading Assessment Summary Form

| | Content Details | | | | | | | | | | | | Using Diagrams and Charts | | | | | | | | | | | | | | Using Book Parts | | | | | | | | | |
|---|---|---|---|---|---|---|---|---|---|---|---|---|---|---|---|---|---|---|---|---|---|---|---|---|---|---|---|---|---|---|---|---|---|---|---|---|
| | 1 | | | | | | | | | | | | 2 (Diagrams) | | | | | | 3 (Charts) | | | | | | | | | | | | | | | | | |
| | a | b | c | d | e | f | g | h | i | j | k | l | a | b | c | d | e | f | a | b | c | d | e | f | g | h | 4 | 5 | 6 | 7 | 8 | 9 | 10 | 11 | 12 | 13 |
| Lorie | | | | | ✓ | | ✓ | | | | | | | | | | | | | ✓ | ✓ | | | | | | | | | | | | | | | |
| Jack | | | | | ✓ | | ✓ | | | | | | | | | | | | | | | | | | | | ✓ | | ✓ | ✓ | | | | | | ✓ |
| Mark | | | | | ✓ | | ✓ | ✓ | | | | | | | | | | | | | | | | | ✓ | | | | | | | | | | | |
| Judy | | | | | ✓ | | ✓ | | | | | | | | | | | | | | | ✓ | ✓ | | | | | | | | | | | | | |
| Shane | | | | | ✓ | | ✓ | ✓ | | | | | | | | | | | | | | | | | ✓ | | | | | | | | | | | |
| Mike | | | | | ✓ | | ✓ | ✓ | | | | | | | | | | | | | | | | | ✓ | | ✓ | | ✓ | ✓ | | ✓ | | | | |
| Greg | | | ✓ | | | | | | | | | ✓ | | ✓ | | | ✓ | | | | | | | | | | | | | | | | | | | |
| Jack R. | | | | ✓ | ✓ | | | | | | | | | | | | | | | | | | | | | | | | ✓ | | ✓ | ✓ | | ✓ | | |
| Keith | | | | | ✓ | | ✓ | ✓ | | | | | | | | | | | | | | | | | | | | | ✓ | ✓ | | | | | | |

*Source:* Adapted from *Reading Diagnosis and Remediation in Classroom and Clinic* by Lois A. Bader. Copyright © 1980 by Lois A. Bader. New York: Macmillan Publishing Company.

## Writing

Traditionally, writing has been evaluated by examining written *products,* just as reading has traditionally been evaluated by examining the products of reading (for example, question responses). Product assessments have generally consisted of evaluating two aspects of written work: composition and mechanics (Cramer, 1982). Increasingly, educators and linguists are concerned with students' grasp of the writing *process.* Clearly, it is possible to make inferences about students' growing knowledge and control of the process by examining written products. However, students' behavior as they engage in writing is also of concern. Most experts suggest that the writing process involves several stages: a planning stage, for clarifying purpose and audience; a composing stage, which involves writing, reading, and attention to mechanics; and a revision stage, during which rereading and editing occur.

*Evaluating Written Products.* Folders, or portfolios, of ongoing and completed work are a normal part of classrooms where a process writing approach is used. According to most experts, what distinguishes portfolios from folders is an emphasis on reflection (Jenkins, 1996; Valencia, 1998). "Samples of written work should be gathered and provide exceptionally good evidence of both the products children create and the process they use" (Tompkins, 2000, p. 136). Daily work samples, journal entries, and work from writers' workshop all provide rich information about students' developing knowledge, skill, and motivation.

Graves (1983) recommends that evaluation start with a *folder/portfolio observation.* This entails evaluating the written work in preparation for other types of observation. "Trends in children's writing will be important observation points, along with the specifics that make up the trends" (Graves, 1983, p. 287). In completing a folder/portfolio observation, it may be helpful to reflect on the following:

- What types of writing is the student producing?
- What topics seem to fuel his/her writing?
- What new ideas are being generated?
- Is there evidence of topic or theme change/growth?
- What skills can and does this child employ?

These overall trends and patterns are very important, but teachers often need/want to evaluate students individual writing samples more closely. Written work can be evaluated holistically or analytically. Many norm-referenced tests of writing involve analytic evaluations of written products (see Chapter 10). Holistic scoring of written products is quite common both in classroom assessment and in large-scale assessment (even statewide assessment of writing) and can be especially useful for screening purposes. Holistic scoring involves assigning a piece of writing a score after examining it *as a whole* (Cockrum & Castillo, 1991).

*Holistic Scoring.*    Holistic scoring involves evaluating a composition as a whole piece of writing. Unlike analytic scores (see below), holistic scores "depend on comparisons with other pieces of writing rather than on comparisons against a predetermined scale" (Bratcher, 1994, p. 52). These comparisons may be done in two ways: by comparing the piece to other pieces (called "anchors" or "benchmarks") or by comparing a piece to papers in a set of compositions.

In the first case a teacher (or better yet a group of teachers) would collect a great deal of writing. For example, all fifth grade teachers might collect research papers for the whole year from all their students. They would then read them and agree on an exemplary paper or two—considered "high." Similarly, one or two very poor exemplars would be selected—considered "low." Finally, several papers considered to be "middle" would be identified. These pieces of writing become the "anchor" papers. Whenever a teacher evaluates a student's research paper in future, it is compared, holistically, to these anchors and classified in terms of its similarity to one or another of these types of writing.

As described by Bratcher (1994), the other type of holistic scoring occurs when teachers read an entire set of papers through one time and place them in three piles: good, poor, and somewhere in between. Then the papers are read a second time to validate the first impression. Papers can be moved from one stack to another, and then they receive a holistic score of +, ✓, or −.

Occasionally, holistic scoring proceeds using a scale to guide the evaluation. Millett (1986) provides the following example of a scale used in holistic scoring:

**0**—This score is given to papers that cannot be scored for one reason or another. Papers may be blank, unrelated to the assignment, or illegible.

**1**—This score is given to papers that do address the assignment but do so inadequately. Papers may be too short, too general, or only tangentially related to the assignment.

**2**—This score is given to papers that are incomplete, inconsistent, or too general. Organization and details may be problematic.

**3**—This score is given to papers that are generally well organized and address the assignment. There may be lapses in organization or areas of confusion, but the author's message is understandable.

**4**—This score is given to papers that are complete, well organized, and detailed. The style and vocabulary add clarity and interest.

*Analytic Scoring.* Sometimes, teachers or other evaluators want to analyze writing in terms of its component parts. When using an analytic scoring approach, teachers attend to specific writing skills and/or features of written products (traits) and judge the whole piece in terms of the subcomponents. Generally, scores or points are assigned to the various component areas and then totaled to obtain a score or grade. From a diagnostic viewpoint it can be helpful to analyze students' writing so that instruction can be tailored to the particular aspects that are causing a student difficulty. On the other hand, Bratcher (1994, p. 155) cautions that attention to subskills or components may not reflect what's really important about writing: "Analytic scoring is subjective and the categories may not be appropriate for some writing forms or may not reflect what children are learning about writing. . . ." Written products are typically evaluated in four major areas: context, content, structure, and mechanics (Bratcher, 1994). In Figure 8.20, you see a sample from this type of analytic scoring sheet.

A related but more theoretically refined scoring procedure is called *primary trait scoring.* As described by Tompkins (2000, p. 153), primary trait scoring focuses on assessing compositions in relation to specific purposes or audiences so that students' work is "judged according to situation-specific criteria." Thus students would not be expected to be equally proficient writers in all settings on all modes of writing.

Analytic or holistic evaluations of written products can certainly provide rich information about students' writing abilities. However, it is extremely difficult (perhaps impos-

**FIGURE 8.20**
Analytic
Scoring Sheet

TOTAL POINTS POSSIBLE: 100        TOTAL POINTS EARNED: _____

**Content (20 pts.)**        Points Earned: _____
     topic is narrowed
     ideas are complete
     main idea is clear
     details are tailored to the main idea

**Mechanics (20 pts.)**        Points Earned: _____
     completion of thoughts as sentences
     use of transitions and conjunctions to connect ideas
     subject-verb agreement
     conventional spelling
     punctuation
     capitalization
     sentence variety (simple, compound, and complex)

*Source:* From *Evaluating Children's Writing* by Suzanne Bratcher, p. 45. Copyright © 1994. Reprinted by permission of Lawrence Erlbaum Associates.

sible) to evaluate students' control of the writing process by considering only final products. Evaluation of student control over the process of writing requires that students be observed, over time, in a classroom that values process writing and encourages author development.

***Observation Checklists.***    An effective observation framework should include examination of written work, but it should also provide for examining the writer at work. Kemp (1987) has proposed an observational checklist of behaviors to watch for as children write. The results of these observations can be used to evaluate children's developmental progress and also to identify areas that might require instructional attention. The form, which appears in Figure 8.21, parallels the major stages of writing, focusing on the student during planning, composing (drafting), and revision phases. In addition, this checklist addresses the critical affective outcomes addressed by creating good written products and provides for evaluation of student attitudes.

Finally, teachers need ways to summarize the information they have about students' writing. Temple and Gillet (1989) suggest that in addition to the assessments of the writer in the writing process, students' written work should be evaluated in terms of the functions of the writing, writing style, writing fluency, and mechanics. The checklist devised by Temple and Gillet (1989) delineates the kinds of questions to ask during the evaluation of students' writing. These include the following:

### Functions of Writing
- What types of writing have been produced? (stories, expressive writing, descriptive writing, etc.)
- What topics have been selected by the writer? Who is the audience for this child's writing? (teacher, classmates, etc.)
- How sophisticated is the writer's awareness of audience?

### Qualities of Writing Style
- Does the writing reflect good choices in language use?
- Does the writer make good use of descriptive language?
- Does the writer maintain a focus throughout the work?
- Are papers well organized, given the purpose of the work?
- Are the written products defined by effective openings and endings?
- Is the writer developing and maintaining a personal voice?

### Mechanics of Writing
- How much control of standard English usage/grammar is reflected in the written works of this writer?
- What stage of spelling is reflected?
- Are complete idea units (sentences) used throughout?
- Are punctuation and capitalization used appropriately (for the age/grade)?

These examples demonstrate how teachers can focus on and gather evidence of the writer's reading interests, knowledge, and skill. It is possible to conduct much more extensive analyses of students' writing abilities.

**FIGURE 8.21** Checklist of The Writing Process

Name of Child: _____ Date of Assessment: _____

Name of Teacher: _____

Title of Sample: _____

(attached, if to be used in discussion with parent or teacher)

**A. Orientation to Writing**

1. Is able on most occasions to engage in discussion of a theme or topic.
2. Is positive on most occasions when given writing opportunities.
3. Responds well to 'conferencing' or seeks out others for trying out ideas or words.
4. Engages in writing without need of persuasion or direction.

**B. Drafting**

5. Manages, when motivation is high, to produce a draft.
6. Contributes drafts to a personal journal or writing folder.
7. 'Rehearses' with drawing, talking, verbal composing
8. Takes risks in using words when their spelling or precise meaning are not known.
9. Aims to write.
10. Responds to conferencing whilst composing drafts.
11. Reflects on efforts so far.
12. Avoidance strategies are rare.
13. Appears on most occasions to have purpose, that is, to write for an audience and/or a publication or self.

**C. Revising, Rewriting, Editing**

14. Makes judgments about own writing.
15. Submits drafts for others' comments.
16. Can 'see the words as temporary' (and) 'the information as manipulable.'
17. Is prepared to work over drafts.
18. Is careful in final stages about mechanics, such as spelling.
19. Revisits 'risk' areas to work over them.
20. Understands that own writing can be manipulated for better effects and to match changing intentions.
21. Seeks information, facts, opinions to strengthen writing.

**D. Production**

22. Produces sustained writing effort from time to time.
23. Takes pride in a completed work.
24. Is sensitive towards the writing efforts of others.
25. Achieves a 'voice' in some writing.
26. Achieves completeness of some writing.
27. Final presentation is accurate in mechanics, such as spelling and handwriting.
28. Reads own and others' writing.

**E. Additional Observations**

*Comments*

*What signs are there of the child's self-direction, self-monitoring, and incentive to write?*

*What kinds of freedom does the child show in engaging in the first writing stages?*

*Is s/he an "explorer" with words, styles, structures, ideas?*

*What successful changes have taken place between drafting and final writing?*

*What are some of your perceptions of the writer's recent development?*

*What does the writer do with the final products?*

*Are the final products valued/re-read? With whom?*

*What were the most successful strategies used this time to sustain the writing?*

*Source:* From *Watching Children Read and Write* by Max Kemp. Copyright © 1987 Nelson Australia Pty Limited. Reprinted by permission of Thomas Nelson Australia/Thomson Learning.

## Student Self-Evaluation

According to Valencia, McGinley, and Pearson (1990), one of the characteristics of newer perspectives on assessment is the realization that it should be *collaborative*. "The essence of collaborative criterion lies in collaboration with students. When we work *with* students in developing assessments, we communicate our support of their learning process" (Valencia et al., 1990). This means that students should share some responsibility for monitoring their own progress, but this also means that they must have access to information. They need to be clearly informed of the purposes for various work assignments, and important evaluative criteria will need to be shared with them as well. Collaboration necessarily involves at least some student self-evaluation. Indeed, the ability to evaluate one's own work should be viewed as an important goal in most literacy programs, since it is a necessary requirement of independence (Johnston, 1997).

In writing, teachers use teacher–student and peer conferences to establish criteria for evaluating success and/or progress (see previous section). Then students are invited to contribute by evaluating their own efforts (see Figure 8.22). These self-evaluations must be taken seriously and must become part of the total assessment process.

For our purposes it is especially important to note the extent to which students' self-evaluations reflect their development and progress as writers. Comments such as the following reflect differences that are important to recognize: "I liked this story because it's long"; "I tried to make a good beginning to this story and I think I did"; "I was trying to

**FIGURE 8.22**
Self-Assessment
Questionnaire

---

### A Self-Assessment Questionnaire

Name: _____ Date: _____
Title: _____

As you publish your writing, reflect on your writing processes and this piece of writing. Please respond briefly to at least three questions in each section.

#### Part 1: Your writing processes
➤ What part of the writing process was most successful for you?
➤ What writing strategies did you use?
➤ What part of the writing process was least successful for you?
➤ What do you need help with?

#### Part 2: This piece of writing
➤ What pleases you most about this piece of writing?
➤ Are you comfortable with this topic and genre?
➤ How did you organize your writing?
➤ Does your lead grab your readers' attention?
➤ Which type of mechanical errors cause you the most trouble?

---

*Source:* Tompkins, Gail E. (1992, November). Assessing the processes students use as writers. *Journal of Reading, 36* (3), 244–246. Reprinted with permission of the International Reading Association. All rights reserved.

make people understand how the boy in this story felt." We want to attend as well to changing self-evaluations. Students can help us understand their purposes in this way, but they also show us whether they have begun to take risks in writing or have internalized new standards for their work and can set their own goals.

# The Diagnostic Portfolio: Evidence from the Classroom

## Marvin

Marvin's new teacher (remember that he had only recently transferred schools, with very little information) used the end-of-level basal skills tests as her primary assessment. Marvin had been placed in a grade 3–2 basal (the lowest group). The one set of tests he had completed indicated that Marvin was weak in most areas of word analysis. His comprehension appeared stronger, and he clearly enjoys reading. As we have seen, Marvin's comprehension of long text tends to miss the point. He attends well to details although he can be diverted by entertaining subplots.

Overall, however, not a great deal of assessment information is available from the classroom. Marvin's teachers (old and new) relied quite heavily on formal tests and basal inventories. In the next chapters we see how structured inventories and diagnostic teaching provided a much fuller picture of Marvin's knowledge and skill.

## Kyle

Kyle's teacher, by contrast, engages in fairly continuous classroom assessment. Running records had been collected on Kyle since late kindergarten. These reveal a struggling reader who nevertheless has gained considerable knowledge. By fall of second grade Kyle is gaining ground on his age peers. As we have seen, he is still struggling with word level skills, both graphophonic and sight. His comprehension is very good except when his serious word recognition difficulties limit his ability to use his excellent language and prior knowledge.

Kyle's writing is similarly filled with good ideas, but it is difficult to read. His purpose is generally clear, and the content is good, but the mechanics are weak. For example, in mid-grade 2, Kyle's writing folder contained the following story:

> Once there was a eagle. He was different than the others. Some of the others teased him. He didn't have any friends. But he had one. He was a hawk. His name was Eric. One day they went fishing. They saw some poachers. They flew back and warned the others. They all were saved! They were always kind from then on.

This captivating and well-structured story was difficult to read because Kyle's writing is large and ill-formed and because his spelling is still at the phonetic level. On the other hand, sentences were marked by periods and some capitals.

About the same time, Kyle reflected on his own writing. He noted that "I used to. . . . *write one santins, only the bgining of werds, and no detal in pichers*" "But now I . . . *put mor santosis, sownd it out, and more dtal in pichers.*" Kyle is clearly developing in all areas of literacy, although his teacher and parents remain concerned.

# Chapter Summary

In this chapter we described the role of the teacher in an effective program of assessment, arguing that high-quality information about students requires knowledgeable teacher/evaluators. We described a number of informal assessment strategies for evaluating specific components of reading competence. We suggested ways to gather information as students engage in actual reading and writing activities. For example, we described methods for gathering information about students' vocabulary knowledge, using strategies such as free recall and PReP. In the area of comprehension assessment we suggested techniques for enhancing the information that can be gathered using traditional techniques like questioning and retelling. In addition, we described a verbal report, or think-aloud, procedure for assessing students' comprehension abilities. Strategies for gathering information about students' studying abilities were also discussed, stressing the need to assess this area in naturalistic contexts. Finally, several informal techniques for assessing writing were described, and a section of student self-assessment was provided as well.

In each case the assumption has been made that the information will become a part of a systematic, continuous, and well-organized assessment designed by well-informed teacher/evaluators. Assessment is an ongoing process. Each encounter with a child must be seen as an opportunity for interactive assessment. In this manner, teaching and testing become integral events focused on providing instructional programs that are responsive to the needs of all children.

Educators must continue to press for assessment instruments and methodologies that provide instructionally useful and contextually valid information. The assessment efforts described in this chapter can and should provide much more specific information about how and what to teach, but they are suggestive only. Ingenious teachers will find many other ways to evaluate their students' performance for the purpose of making placement and curricular decisions.

Most of the assessment strategies we have suggested can be easily incorporated in daily instructional programs. Indeed, the strategies described may be difficult for a teacher in a pull-out program to implement without the cooperation of the classroom teacher. It does little good to evaluate component skills if we do not observe them in action. Students can, and often do, perform differently on tests of isolated skill or on tasks in constrained and artificial environments than they do in real classrooms accomplishing real assignments.

Certainly, support personnel, who may have more time to analyze task demands or observe students in action, may want to engage in more systematic assessment for various audiences. We turn our attention to these strategies in the next chapters.

# 9 Structured Inventories and Assessments

Although the informal classroom-based assessments described in the previous chapter provide extensive diagnostic information, there are times when structured assessments are desirable or necessary. We pursue the evaluation of the learner in this chapter with a discussion of structured assessments—including informal reading inventories (IRIs), writing rubrics, informal word recognition tests, and school-based assessment "packages." In the hands of a skilled examiner these structured assessments can yield exceptionally useful information about a student's knowledge and application of reading skills and strategies. Informal structured assessments generally capture the interactive nature of reading in ways that more formal tests cannot.

This chapter presents an overview of various structured procedures. The presentation of information about the IRI is extensive, since it represents the most commonly used structured, informal assessment. We discuss construction, administration, scoring, and interpretation of IRIs, as well as issues and problems with traditional IRIs. Also in this chapter are sections that describe innovations among some newer IRIs and how the addition of retelling, miscue analysis, and fluency ratings can expand the utility of older IRIs. Other assessment tools and strategies include tests of phonics, word recognition, and spelling. Finally, tools and strategies for evaluating classroom writing are explained, including the development and use of rubrics.

## Understanding Structured Inventories and Assessments

When teachers want only to inform their own instruction, the tools and strategies described in the preceding chapter are what is likely to be most useful. However, sometimes we are concerned about individual children and want to take a closer look. At other times parents want specific information, and at still other times we are required to share information about students at the school or district level. In these cases the very informal "on-the-run" assessments that were so useful for planning and adapting daily instruction are not quite as appropriate.

The overriding issue concerns the interpretive accuracy of the information. There are many ways in which others might not interpret the results appropriately, including the following: (1) They may not understand how the information was collected; (2) they may be unfamiliar with the book or passage that was selected for running records, for example; (3) they may use different scoring conventions to record student responses; or (4) they may use different criteria for judging performance.

Classroom-based reading and writing performance is likely to provide the most authentic picture of a student's knowledge and skill because the tasks and texts will be familiar, the procedures more or less school-like, and the context informal. For all these reasons informal assessment is a good idea. On the other hand, we want our information to be trustworthy (Valencia, 1990a). When we communicate with other professionals, with parents, or with the larger community, the tasks and conditions used in collecting information must be clear, and the criteria used to interpret the information must be commonly understood.

Teachers whose work is funded by external sources (Chapter 1 and Special Education) are generally required to collect and communicate information based on systematic assessment practices. Until recently, most were required to use norm-referenced tests to gather this information (see Chapter 10). Now, however, a defensible system of informal assessment is often acceptable, but the tools and strategies need to be carefully considered.

The structured assessments described in this chapter share several common characteristics. They contain the procedures and/or materials for creating consistent, systematic assessment tools that allow a student's performance to be compared across selections or to be compared to a commonly established standard or set of criteria. Thus anyone using these tools will know that others are employing the same procedures, materials, or techniques for evaluating student performance.

Formal tests are designed to compare a student's score to that of other students (see Chapter 10). Standardized procedures are used to administer these tests to large numbers of students to establish the standards for comparison. Teachers or test examiners must administer formal tests in exactly the same way as they were administered in the standardization process for the scores to be valid. In contrast, IRIs and other structured assessments are designed to evaluate a student's scores against some criteria for acceptable performance (e.g., 99 percent word recognition and 90 percent comprehension) that have been established independently of how any particular group of students might perform on the same test.

A key feature of all these structured assessments is that the activities involved closely approximate the activities found in daily classroom reading instruction. For this reason the results that are obtained are more likely to be generalizable to classroom performance than results obtained from formal tests using activities that are farther removed from classroom practice. In addition, because they are informal measures, they can be used more flexibly than formal tests.

In short, these tools are designed to create assessment conditions that are as trustworthy as possible while still retaining an informal assessment environment. We start with the informal reading inventory because it is probably the most widely known form of systematic informal reading assessment.

# Strategies and Tools for Structured Assessment

## Informal Reading Inventories

*Overview.* An informal reading inventory is an individually administered reading test composed of a series of graded word lists and graded passages that the student reads aloud to the examiner. The examiner notes oral reading errors as the student reads and asks comprehension questions when the student has finished reading each passage. Most informal reading inventories also include silent reading passages, and some provide passages that are read to the student to determine a listening comprehension level, along with comprehension questions for each. When the student has finished, reading errors are analyzed and percentage scores are calculated for word recognition performance on the graded word lists and the oral reading passages. In addition, the examiner tallies performance on the comprehension questions for the various reading passages.

Betts (1946) and Kilgallon (1942) are frequently credited with the development of the IRI, although similar techniques were suggested by others even earlier (for example, Gray, 1920). As originally designed by Betts (1946), the IRI was to be constructed by the *teacher,* using reading materials in which the students might actually be placed and procedures for administration that were similar to those used in classroom reading instruction, such as silent reading followed by oral rereading. The intent was to evaluate students' reading performance under circumstances that were as similar to classroom reading conditions as possible.

Today, there are many types of IRIs and a variety of administration procedures. Some teachers still construct their own IRIs, but many prefer to use IRIs that have been prepared by a publisher to accompany a particular basal reading series. Others use IRIs that have been prepared commercially, independent of any particular reading series (see annotated list of commercially prepared IRIs beginning on p. 373).

The two primary purposes for administering an IRI are to place students in materials at the appropriate levels by establishing their *independent, instructional,* and *frustration* reading levels and to identify strengths and weaknesses in the areas of word recognition and comprehension by analyzing the amount and type of word recognition and comprehension errors.

Four different levels of reading can be identified by applying established criteria to a student's word recognition and comprehension performance:

1. *Independent level:* This is the level at which students read fluently and make very few word recognition or comprehension errors. The reader can handle material at this level easily without the assistance of the teacher. Free or recreational reading materials should be at this level, as should reading assignments such as homework, tests, and seatwork that the student is expected to complete independently.

2. *Instructional level:* At this level the reader makes some errors; however, word recognition errors are not excessive, and comprehension is adequate. This is the level at which the student will benefit most from direct instruction. For each child the materials used for direct instruction—such as basal readers, subject area textbooks, and skill activities—should be at this level.

3. *Frustration level:* This is the level at which reading is often slow and halting, and the reader makes an excessive number of errors. Materials at this level are too difficult for the reader, even with assistance. Students should not be placed in materials at this level because effective learning is unlikely to occur.

4. *Listening comprehension level:* This is the level at which the student can satisfactorily comprehend material that has been read aloud. This level provides a rough estimate of the student's receptive language comprehension and is often used as a measure of the student's potential reading level.

Many different procedures have developed since the IRI was first introduced. To avoid giving the mistaken impression that there is only one way to construct and/or use an IRI, we present a description of various traditional IRI procedures in the next section.

***Components of an IRI.***    The basic components of an informal reading inventory are graded word lists, graded reading passages, comprehension questions, and a summary/analysis sheet. To help illustrate some of these components, examples of an examiner's copy of graded word lists, a graded passage, and a summary sheet are presented in Figure 9.1.

*Graded Word Lists.*    Most IRIs begin with lists of words that have been graded to correspond with the grade levels in basal reading series. Although not originally included in the IRI, graded word lists have become a standard part of today's IRIs. Graded word lists are used to determine accuracy of word recognition in isolation and to assist the examiner in determining the level at which the student should begin reading the graded passages.

Each graded word list typically contains between ten and twenty words and includes different types of words ranging from a large number of function words, such as *the* or *want* at the lower grade levels, to multisyllabic content words, which may or may not be easily decoded, at the upper grade levels. Series-linked IRIs generally, but not always, choose selections from the anthologies at each level. It is often unclear how the word lists have been generated for commercially prepared IRIs (Jongsma & Jongsma, 1981). Some are created from previously published lists of graded words or word frequency lists such as *Dolch* (Dolch, 1942a) or *New Instant Word List* (Fry, 1980). However the lists are created, there is generally an effort to represent high-frequency features in the language, sampling words that students who read a great deal would not find difficult to recognize.

*Graded Reading Passages.*    The graded word lists are followed by a series of graded reading passages. Most IRIs have two or three passages at each grade level, so comparisons can be made among oral, silent, and listening comprehension. Alternatively, the various forms for each level may be used as pretests and posttests. The graded reading passages are used for evaluating comprehension and for examining oral reading accuracy in context.

Graded reading passages range in length from 25 to 350 words. Typically, the length of the passages increases gradually, from the lowest to the highest grade levels, along the following lines: preprimer and primer, 25–60 words; grade 1, 75–100 words; grades 2 and 3, 75–150 words; grades 4, 5, and 6, 150–200 words; grades 7 through 10, 200–350 words. The authors of commercially prepared IRIs often construct their own passages or select excerpts from children's materials found in the library. When teachers or publishers construct

**FIGURE 9.1a**
Sample IRI
Components

Eighth
Edition

**BASIC READING INVENTORY PERFORMANCE BOOKLET**
Jerry L. Johns, Ph.D.

B
Oral
Reading

Student _____  Grade _____  Sex   M   F   Date of Test _____

School _____  Examiner _____  Date of Birth _____

Address _____  Current Book/Level _____  Age _____

| | | | | | | | | | | | |
|---|---|---|---|---|---|---|---|---|---|---|---|
| **SUMMARY OF STUDENT'S READING PERFORMANCE** |||||||||||| |

| Grade | Word Recognition |||| | Comprehension |||| |
|---|---|---|---|---|---|---|---|---|---|---|
| | Isolation (Word Lists) |||| Context (Passages) || Oral Reading Form B || Silent Reading Form D || |
| | Sight | Analysis | Total | Level | Miscues | Level | Questions Missed | Level | Questions Missed | Level |
| PP | | | | | | | | | | |
| P | | | | | | | | | | |
| 1 | | | | | | | | | | |
| 2 | | | | | | | | | | |
| 3 | | | | | | | | | | |
| 4 | | | | | | | | | | |
| 5 | | | | | | | | | | |
| 6 | | | | | | | | | | |
| 7 | | | | | | | | | | |
| 8 | | | | | | | | | | |
| 9 | | | | | ESTIMATE OF READING LEVELS |||||| |
| 10 | | | | | | | | | | |
| 11 | | | | | | | | | | |
| 12 | | | | | Independent _____  Instructional _____  Frustration _____ |||||| |

| LISTENING LEVEL ||| GENERAL OBSERVATIONS |
|---|---|---|---|
| Grade | Form _____ Questions Missed | Level | |
| PP | | | |
| P | | | |
| 1 | | | |
| 2 | | | |
| 3 | | | |
| 4 | | | |
| 5 | | | |
| 6 | | | |
| 7 | | | |
| 8 | | | |
| **ESTIMATED LEVEL:** ____ || | |

| INFORMAL MISCUE ANALYSIS SUMMARY |||||| |
|---|---|---|---|---|---|
| Types of Miscues | Frequency of Occurrence ||| General Impact of Miscues on Meaning ||| |
| | Seldom | Sometimes | Frequently | No Change | Little Change | Much Change |
| Substitutions | | | | | | |
| Insertions | | | | | | |
| Omissions | | | | | | |
| Reversals | | | | | | |
| Repetitions | | | | | | |

*Source:* From *Basic Reading Inventory: Pre-primer through Grade Twelve and Early Literacy Assessments,* Eighth Edition by Jerry Johns. Copyright © 2001 by Kendall/Hunt Publishing Company. Used with permission.

**FIGURE 9.1b**
Sample IRI
Components
(Continued)

Form B • Graded Word Lists • Performance Booklet •

| List B-B (Pre-Primer) | Sight | Analysis | List B (Primer) | Sight | Analysis |
|---|---|---|---|---|---|
| 1. we* | | | 1. they* | | |
| 2. and* | | | 2. she* | | |
| 3. house | | | 3. will* | | |
| 4. the* | | | 4. of* | | |
| 5. duck | | | 5. blue* | | |
| 6. one* | | | 6. it* | | |
| 7. street | | | 7. are* | | |
| 8. happy | | | 8. his* | | |
| 9. lost | | | 9. now* | | |
| 10. first* | | | 10. dress | | |
| 11. do* | | | 11. if* | | |
| 12. at* | | | 12. from* | | |
| 13. very* | | | 13. morning | | |
| 14. find* | | | 14. father | | |
| 15. out* | | | 15. ask* | | |
| 16. party | | | 16. back | | |
| 17. goat | | | 17. green* | | |
| 18. wish | | | 18. time | | |
| 19. know* | | | 19. who* | | |
| 20. sing | | | 20. cookie | | |

*denotes basic sight word from Revised Dolch List       *denotes basic sight word from Revised Dolch List

| | | | | | |
|---|---|---|---|---|---|
| Number Correct | | | Number Correct | | |
| Total | | | Total | | |

### Scoring Guide for Graded Word Lists

| Independent | Instructional | Frustration |
|---|---|---|
| 20  19 | 18  17  16  15  14 | 13 or less |

**FIGURE 9.1c**
Sample IRI
Components
(Continued)

Student Copy is on page 180.

**B-B** (Pre-Primer) Activating Background: Look at the picture and read the title to yourself. Then tell me what you think will happen.

Background: Low ├───────┤ High

Birds

| | MISCUES | | | | | | |
|---|---|---|---|---|---|---|---|
| Substitution | Insertion | Omission | Reversal | Repetition | Self-Correction of Unacceptable Miscue | Meaning Change (Significant Miscue) | |

| | | | | | | | |
|---|---|---|---|---|---|---|---|
| I can look for birds. I look up in | | | | | | | |
| a tree. I see a big bird. It is brown. | | | | | | | |
| I see a baby bird. It is little. It is | | | | | | | |
| brown too. | | | | | | | |
| The big bird can fly. The baby | | | | | | | |
| bird can not fly. It is little. I like to | | | | | | | |
| see birds. | | | | | | | |
| **TOTAL** | | | | | | | |

**Word Recognition Scoring Guide**

| Total Miscues | Level | Significant Miscues |
|---|---|---|
| 0 | Independent | 0 |
| 1–2 | Ind./Inst. | 1 |
| 3 | Instructional | 2 |
| 4 | Inst./Frust. | 3 |
| 5 + | Frustration | 4 |

Total Miscues ☐        Significant Miscues ☐

_____ WPM
)3000

**B-B** (Pre-Primer)
Comprehension Questions

F 1. _____ Where did the person in the story look for the birds?
(in a tree)

F 2. _____ What kind of birds did the person see?
(big bird; baby bird; brown; little [any 2])

E 3. _____ Besides being too little, why do you think the baby bird could not fly?
(any logical response)

I 4. _____ Why do you think the person looked up in a tree to find birds?
(any logical response; birds live there)

V 5. _____ What does "little" mean?
(small; tiny; baby)

**Retelling Notes**

☐ Questions Missed

**Comprehension Scoring Guide**

| Questions Missed | Level |
|---|---|
| 0 | Independent |
| 1 | Ind./Inst. |
| 1½ | Instructional |
| 2 | Inst./Frust. |
| 2½ + | Frustration |

**Retelling**
Excellent
Satisfactory
Unsatisfactory

IRIs to accompany a particular series, the passages are selected excerpts from the readers in the series.

Passage difficulty is determined by the level of the material from which it is taken and/or through the use of readability formulas (see Chapter 5 for a detailed explanation). A review of commercially prepared IRIs indicated that two of the eleven inventories reviewed included illustrations along with their passages (Jongsma & Jongsma, 1981), though this has probably changed somewhat with the addition of new IRIs. It is also accepted practice to vary the size of the print type in a manner that is consistent with the grade level of the passage.

*Comprehension Questions.*    The graded passages are accompanied by a series of open-ended comprehension questions. Most commercially prepared IRIs have between five and ten questions per passage. Most IRIs categorize the comprehension questions according to types, such as main idea, detail, literal, inferential, vocabulary, sequence, and cause–effect. Guidelines for constructing IRIs recommend that different types of questions be used (for example, Johnson & Kress, 1965; Silvaroli, Kear, & McKenna, 1982).

***Administering an IRI.***    IRIs are administered individually and require 30–90 minutes for administration. They can be administered in more than one session. IRIs typically are administered in a quiet place, with the examiner and the student sitting at different sides of a table. It is usually a good idea to audiotape the administration for later reference. As with all aspects of the IRI, there is no one right way to administer it. Decisions about how to administer the IRI must be based on the purpose for administration and the types of information desired.

*Graded Word Lists.*    The word lists are introduced by saying something like, "I have some words I would like you to read for me today. Please read carefully, and if you come to a word you don't know, just try your best." The word lists are then presented, either as a whole or one word at a time, through a window cut in a manila folder or on individual index cards. Administration of the word lists begins with the list that is at least two years below the student's grade placement. If the student misses any words in the first list that is administered, the examiner drops to lower lists until the student achieves 100 percent accuracy. As the student reads, the examiner tallies all words read correctly and records exactly what the student says when a word is misread. The student is encouraged to read words that are unfamiliar, and the administration of the word lists continues until the student makes some specified number of errors (for example, five errors in a list or three consecutive errors).

Some published IRIs have only a timed administration of the word lists, in which the student is given anywhere from two to ten seconds to respond. Some have only untimed presentations, in which the student is given unlimited time to respond. Still others have some combination of the two; for example, a timed administration followed by an untimed administration of the words that were missed the first time. The combined administration provides the greatest amount of information.

*Oral Reading Passages.*    Administration of the oral reading passages begins with the passage that is at the same level as the word list on which the student achieved some specified criterion (for example, 100 percent). If the student does poorly on the first passage, the examiner drops down one level at a time until performance is satisfactory. The examiner begins the administration by saying something like, "Now I have some passages I would like you to read out loud to me. Please read carefully, because I will ask you some questions when you are finished. If you come to a word you don't know, just try your best." Then the examiner reads the motivation statement, if there is one, and asks the student to begin reading. The examiner may also wish to begin timing the student's reading to calculate the oral reading rate.

As the student reads, the examiner uses a code to mark every deviation from the printed text on the teacher's response sheet. If the student stops reading at a difficult word, the examiner waits some specified amount of time (for example, five seconds) and then either pronounces the word or directs the student to skip it and continue. The administration of the oral reading passages is stopped when the student is visibly frustrated or is making excessive word recognition and comprehension errors. Because it is not always possible to score the test immediately, the decision to suspend testing is frequently based on the examiner's judgment.

The oral reading errors that are commonly coded include *omissions, insertions, substitutions, repetitions, hesitations, ignoring punctuation, prompts, reversals,* and *self-corrections.* The sample coding system presented in Figure 9.2 is just one of many that can be used. Which particular system is used is not as important as becoming familiar enough with one system so that it can be used quickly and consistently. It is important to code all deviations from the text, so the student's performance can be reconstructed at a later time. Audiotaping the session helps with this, of course.

*Silent Reading and Listening Passages.*   In addition to oral reading passages, the examiner can administer silent and/or listening comprehension passages and may also want to time the silent reading to determine the student's silent reading rate. There are a number of variations in the order of administration for oral, silent, and listening passages. Several of these variations are listed below:

1. Oral reading only.
2. An oral reading passage followed by a silent reading, and possibly a listening comprehension passage, all at the same grade level before going on to higher levels.
3. Oral reading passages until frustration level is achieved, followed by silent reading passages starting at that level or one level below until frustration level is achieved, which is then followed by listening comprehension passages.
4. Silent reading followed by oral rereading of all or parts of the same passage.

A review of commercially prepared IRIs indicates that many inventories either disregard silent reading or make it optional, probably to shorten administration time (Jongsma & Jongsma, 1981).

*Comprehension Questions.*   After the student finishes reading, the passage is removed and the examiner says something like, "Now I am going to ask you some questions about the passage you just read." The examiner reads each question and provides ample time for the student to make a response. If the student does not respond or appears to have misunderstood

**FIGURE 9.2**   Oral Reading Errors

| Error | Sample Notation | Remarks |
|---|---|---|
| SUBSTITUTIONS—mispronunciations or word replacements | *cars   dogs*<br>I saw cats and dogs. | *May suggest lack of word recognition skills, carelessness, or language differences/dialect usage. Students with consistent mispronunciations usually require help in any or all word analysis skills, but especially phonics and structural analysis.* |
| INSERTIONS—letters, syllables or words added to the text | *the*<br>I saw cats and dogs.<br>^ | *These errors may signal carelessness or an oral language ability that surpasses reading ability. Comprehension is assumed when insertions are contextually appropriate.* |
| OMISSIONS—words, letters, or syllables deleted from the text | I saw cat(s)and dogs. | *Generally not serious errors if meaning is kept intact. Students may skip word parts of longer words indicating a need for instruction in word analysis. Some omissions, particularly those of word endings, may be due to language differences or difficulties.* |
| REVERSALS—reversed order of words | I saw cats and dogs. | *May be result of many factors. In beginning readers, due to inexperience with important perceptual distinctions. Reversals may accompany more serious problems in severely disabled readers.* |
| PROMPTS—words pronounced by the examiner | *P*<br>I saw cats and dogs. | *Usually due to lack of sight vocabulary and/or word analysis skills. May also be due to lack of self-confidence in ability to identify strange words.* |
| PUNCTUATION—obvious omission of punctuation | I saw cats and dogs⊙ | *May simply indicate need to work on the meaning of various punctuation marks. In some cases may be symptomatic of more serious word recognition or comprehension problems.* |
| HESITATIONS—obvious pause | *#*<br>I saw cats and dogs. | *A student with many hesitations usually lacks either sight vocabulary or word analysis skills, has formed a habit of word-by-word reading, or is experiencing difficulty of some kind.* |
| REPETITIONS—part of word, a word, or words repeated | I saw cats and dogs.<br>ᴜᴜ | *May indicate that student is trying to figure out a word or phrase. Sometimes repetitions are due to nervousness. Some believe that repetitions are a sign of normal, effective processing. Others believe they indicate some type of reading difficulty.* |
| SELF-CORRECTIONS—spontaneous corrections by the reader | *cars ✓*<br>I saw cats and dogs. | *Generally considered to be the sign of effective processing and attention to meaning. Students who must self-correct too frequently may not have acquired automatic word recognition skills and may be overrelying on context as a decoding strategy.* |

*Source:* Adapted from Ekwall, E., & Shanker, J. L. (1983). *Diagnosis and remediation of the disabled reader* (2nd ed.). Boston: Allyn & Bacon.

a question, the question may be asked again or rephrased. Additional information may be elicited by neutral questions, such as "Can you tell me more?" However, leading questions that provide information related to the answer should be avoided.

***Scoring an IRI.*** Preliminary scoring occurs while the IRI is being taken, because scores are needed to make decisions about subsequent steps in administration. The final scoring is completed when the student has finished the IRI, and the scores are entered on a summary sheet. Most published IRIs provide a type of summary sheet for recording student performance on word lists, oral reading, and oral, silent, and listening comprehension at each grade level. These scores are used to determine a student's independent, instructional, and frustration reading levels, which are recorded on the summary sheet. Many summary sheets also provide for recording the numbers and types of oral reading and comprehension errors made by the student. Increasingly, IRIs also provide guidance in scoring students' prior knowledge and fluency.

*Graded Word Lists.* The examiner determines the percentage correct on each word list and enters the number and the placement level on the examiner's response sheets. Unfortunately, this is not quite as easy as it may at first appear. As soon as we attempt to score an IRI, we are confronted with the question "What is an error?" or, conversely, "What is an acceptable response?" Once again, there is no one correct way; it depends on the situation.

The biggest decisions that have to be made in scoring the word lists are how to handle self-corrections and the time factor. In other words, does a student know a word if it takes ten seconds to identify the word or if it is misread and then self-corrected? Some commercially prepared IRIs provide no guidelines for time limits or how to score self-corrections. Those that do recommend time limits for acceptable responses suggest time limits ranging from ten to fifteen seconds. Some IRIs suggest that all deviations, self-corrected or not, count as errors, while others do not count self-corrections as errors. Clearly, when there are only ten to twenty words in a list, decisions about what constitutes an error are not trivial. Each error translates into a 5–10 percent difference in the scores, which can have a significant impact on decisions about placement levels and the entry level into the reading passages.

*Oral Reading Passages.* The examiner counts the oral reading errors and determines the percentage of word recognition accuracy. The percentage of word recognition accuracy can be either determined from a scoring guide or calculated by hand using the following procedure:

1. Subtract the number of errors from the total number of words in the passage to obtain the total number of words correct.
2. Divide the total number of words correct by the total number of words in the passage.
3. Multiply the result by 100 to convert to a percentage.

The percentage of word recognition accuracy and the placement level, if provided by a scoring guide, are entered on the summary sheet. In addition, the number of errors of each type is calculated and recorded on the summary sheet.

The question of what constitutes an error becomes even more complex in scoring the oral reading passages. Guidelines for scoring oral reading range from counting every deviation from the text as an error to the other extreme, counting only those deviations that alter the meaning of the text. Most scoring guidelines lie somewhere between these two extremes.

A review of the scoring guidelines of eleven commercially prepared IRIs indicates that the majority consider omissions, insertions, substitutions, reversals, prompts, and repetitions to be scorable errors. Self-corrections, hesitations, and punctuation are to be noted but not counted as errors (Jongsma & Jongsma, 1981).

*Comprehension Questions.*   The examiner determines whether the answers to each comprehension question are correct, incorrect, or partially correct on the basis of the suggested answers and on an awareness of acceptable alternatives. The percentage comprehension score is calculated using a scoring guide or by dividing the number of questions that were answered correctly by the total number of questions and then multiplying by 100. The percentage comprehension score and the placement level, when provided by a scoring guide, are then recorded on the summary sheet. In addition, the number of each type of questions missed is calculated and entered on the summary sheet. Because there are often as few as five comprehension questions per passage, scoring decisions have a major impact on the final results of the IRI.

*Rate.*   The examiner determines the number of words read per minute for silent and/or oral reading using the following procedure:

1. Convert the amount of time it took to read the passage to seconds.
2. Divide the number of seconds by the number of words in the passage.
3. Multiply the resulting number by 60 to reconvert it into words per minute.

When the rate in words per minute has been calculated, it is entered on the examiner's response sheets and the summary sheet, when appropriate.

**Interpreting an IRI.**   The information on the summary sheet regarding the percentage of word recognition accuracy and comprehension at each level is evaluated to determine the student's independent, instructional, and frustration reading levels. In addition, the information on the summary sheet regarding different types of oral reading and comprehension errors is used to determine specific strengths and weaknesses.

*Placement/"Achievement" Levels.*   As we have noted, IRIs have been used traditionally to place students in commercial materials (basals) that have corresponding grade level notations. Increasingly, these so-called placement levels are being used by teachers who use a literature-based approach. These teachers do not necessarily place students in reading materials according to these results, but they do use the levels as indications of student *achievement.* This is especially true in schools that are no longer using norm-referenced achievement tests and that have also abandoned basal reading programs. Lacking easily available numeric indicators of students' reading levels, they are using IRIs to communicate with parents and with each other.

Some IRIs provide placement-level criteria for the graded word lists; others do not. There is no general agreement among those that do provide placement levels as to what the criteria should be. A review conducted by the authors of a limited sample of commercially prepared IRIs provided the following range of placement criteria for lists of 10–20 words: independent level, 90–100 percent (0–2 errors); instructional level, 80–90 percent (2–4 errors); and frustration level, 80 percent and below (2–4+ errors).

Determining the criteria for a student's general independent, instructional, and frustration levels on the reading passages is a complex issue. The original criteria, established by Betts (1946) and still the most widely accepted today, are presented in Figure 9.3.

Reviews of commercially prepared IRIs indicate that the majority continue to use Betts's criteria. Several problems are associated with the use of these criteria. First, the procedures for administering IRIs have changed somewhat from those under which Betts's criteria were first developed. Most guidelines for administering either published or teacher-constructed IRIs call for oral reading at sight rather than Betts's procedure of silent reading followed by oral rereading. Second, the criteria leave a scoring gap between the frustration and instructional levels that can make interpretation fairly difficult (for example, what happens to the student who scores 65 percent in comprehension?). Third, they were developed on the basis of a study with fourth grade students, and subsequent research suggests the need for criteria that account for the differential effects of age, grade, and/or the difficulty of the materials (Cooper, 1952; Powell & Dunkeld, 1971).

As a result of the problems with Betts's criteria, some believe that different placement criteria should be used. Powell (1980) has suggested the criteria presented in Figure 9.4 to account for both the grade level of the materials and two methods of administration: oral reading at sight and silent reading followed by oral rereading. Clearly there is considerable disparity between the Betts and Powell criteria, and the majority of commercially prepared IRIs have converged in the following range, which may be used as a guide for establishing reasonable placement criteria (Figure 9.5).

The traditional interpretation of oral reading errors is based on a preponderance of errors of a particular type (see Figure 9.2), which are often noted separately on the summary form. The interpretation of a student's comprehension skills is based on an analysis of errors on different types of comprehension questions. Students with a preponderance of errors on a particular type of comprehension question are believed to have difficulty with certain types of comprehension. Depending on the types of comprehension questions included on the IRI,

**FIGURE 9.3**
Betts's Placement
Criteria

| | Word Recognition | | Comprehension |
|---|---|---|---|
| **Independent** | 99% + | and | 90% + |
| **Instructional** | 95% + | and | 75% + |
| **Frustration** | 90% or less | or | 50% or less |
| **Listening Comprehension** | | | 75% + |

**FIGURE 9.4**
Powell's Placement
Criteria

| Reading Levels | Reading at Sight | | Oral Rereading | |
|---|---|---|---|---|
| | Word | | Word | |
| By Grade | Recognition | Comprehension | Recognition | Comprehension |
| **Independent** | | | | |
| 1–2 | 94% + | 80% + | 94% + | 80% + |
| 3–5 | 96% + | 85% + | 96% + | 85% + |
| 6+ | 97% + | 90% + | 97% + | 90% + |
| **Instructional** | | | | |
| 1–2 | 88–94% | 55–80% | 92–94% | 70–80% |
| 3–5 | 92–96% | 60–86% | 95–96% | 75–85% |
| 6+ | 94–97% | 65–90% | 97–97% | 80–90% |
| **Frustration** | | | | |
| 1–2 | 86% or less | 55% or less | 91% or less | 70% or less |
| 3–5 | 92% or less | 60% or less | 91% or less | 75% or less |
| 6+ | 94% or less | 65% or less | 96% or less | 80% or less |

these problems might include understanding literal ideas or factual information, drawing inferences, identifying main idea, and so on.

Students' rate of reading is reported in terms of the number of words read per minute during oral and/or silent reading. A slow reading rate may indicate a reading problem, but an acceptable rate does not guarantee that the material is being comprehended at a satisfactory level. Desired silent reading rates are similar to oral reading rates at first- and second-grade instructional levels but begin to increase sharply at the third-grade instructional level when word identification becomes more automatic. It is also important to remember that reading rates will vary according to the conditions of the reading situation and that norms or standards are good only for the conditions under which they were obtained. Guidelines provided by Powell (n.d.) for evaluating the oral and silent reading rates obtained on IRIs for students at different instructional levels are presented in Figure 9.6. When using these guidelines, it is important to remember that students' instructional levels may be different than their grade levels.

**FIGURE 9.5**
Criteria Used by
Published IRIs

| | Word Recognition | Comprehension |
|---|---|---|
| Independent | 96–99% | 75–90% |
| Instructional | 92–95% | 60–75% |
| Frustration | 90–92% or less | 60–75% or less |

**FIGURE 9.6**
Reading Rate in
Words per Minute

| Instructional Reading Level | Oral Reading Rate at Sight | Silent Reading |
|---|---|---|
| Grade 1 | 45–65 | 45–65 |
| Grade 2 | 70–100 | 70–100 |
| Grade 3 | 105–125 | 120–140 |
| Grade 4 | 125–145 | 130–180 |
| Grade 5 | 135–155 | 165–205 |
| Grade 6 | 140–160 | 190–220 |

*Issues and Problems: Evaluating and Selecting IRIs.* Whether teachers are constructing their own or using available commercial versions, serious attention must be given to the issues and problems surrounding the use of IRIs. The information gleaned from them can be useful, but because the decisions made about children can be quite serious, it is important to understand fully how to evaluate or construct IRIs for ethical use.

*Construction.* The major area of concern regarding the construction of IRIs focuses on the representativeness of the reading selections. When a passage is selected from a basal reader for use in an IRI, it is assumed to represent the materials the student will find in that reader. This may have been an accurate assumption when IRIs were first suggested and the vocabulary and content of basal readers were more highly controlled than they are today. However, in today's basal readers, passages taken from a single level can vary from first to twelfth grade readability (Bradley & Ames, 1977). A student's reading performance within an anthology may vary considerably depending on the passage selected for use in the IRI. In fact, Bradley and Ames (1977) used several passages from the same reader and found that approximately 40 percent of the students tested had scores that ranged from the independent to the frustration level. In addition, many teachers today do not use basals at all, choosing instead from a wide range of literature. Representing this literature can pose serious challenges.

A second problem related to the reading selections involves the comparability of alternate passages at each grade level. Although there is a clear advantage to having several alternate passages at each grade level, it is difficult to be certain that these passages are comparable. Some authors suggest creating different passages by using different portions of the same selection. However, there is also variability in readability within selections, although perhaps not as great as that within a book. When passages from the same selection are used, there is also the problem of accumulated prior knowledge affecting performance from one passage to the next.

Most IRIs do not account for the fact that there are *many* text factors that are likely to influence a student's performance. For example, it has been found that the effects of interest are sufficiently strong to cause comprehension scores to vary between the frustration and instructional levels (Estes & Vaughan, 1973). Another finding is that the type and length of the passage influences the number and types of oral reading errors (see Wixson, 1979). Other factors, discussed in Chapters 5 and 6, include text organization and topic familiarity.

A third major area of concern in the construction of IRIs focuses on the nature of the comprehension questions. Peterson, Greenlaw, and Tierney (1978) constructed three sets of questions for a single IRI according to a popular set of guidelines that called for one vocabulary, two literal, and two inferential questions. When these three sets of questions were used in testing, approximately 65 percent of students examined were assigned two different instructional levels, and 10 percent were assigned three instructional levels. This suggests that different questions for the same passages can produce different results. Finally, we must also be concerned with the degree to which comprehension questions are *passage dependent*. Questions that are passage dependent have answers that depend on information provided in the passage rather than on the reader's prior knowledge about the topic. To illustrate this problem, read and answer the following questions taken from Johns (1988):

1. Skyscrapers are different from other buildings because they are: a. bigger; b. higher; c. cleaner; d. prettier.
2. A person who "operates with a frying pan" uses the pan for: a. cutting fish; b. cooking fish; c. hitting fish; d. cleaning fish.

How did you do? Johns found that 134 of 160 fourth and fifth grade students answered the first item correctly, and 131 answered the second one right *without* reading the passages. These questions were part of a study in which students scored significantly better than chance when they answered the reading comprehension questions from a test *before* they read the passages.

Studies of IRI-type tests suggest that results may be influenced by questions that are passage independent. For example, an analysis of the comprehension questions on four IRI-type tests indicated that 23–31 percent of the questions were passage independent (Allington, Chodos, Domaracki, & Truex, 1977). In addition, the analysis demonstrated that there was a large degree of variability in the number of passage-independent items from one passage to the next within each test. In other words, the results of these studies suggest that in some cases the variability in scores observed between passages may be attributable to differences in the comprehension questions, not to real differences in ability.

*Administration.*    The major issue in the administration of an IRI is the effect that different procedures might have on students' scores. For example, Brecht (1977) reports a study in which children were administered IRIs both with oral reading at sight and with silent reading followed by oral rereading. Only 20 percent of the students obtained the same instructional level under both types of administration. When the rereading format was used, 70 percent scored at least one grade level higher, and 10 percent scored at least one grade level lower.

Another factor in administration that may influence students' scores is the directions provided to both students and teachers. According to Jongsma and Jongsma (1981), some inventories clearly emphasize the importance of reading accurately and not making mistakes. Although this might seem trivial, they point to evidence that directions can influence the number and type of oral reading errors, the degree of comprehension, and the rate of reading. One inventory actually directs the students to decrease their speed for subject-area material and to reread sections or words on which they made "careless mistakes." Two inventories direct the teacher to start all students, regardless of age or reading ability, at the lowest levels on both the word lists and passages. This practice could result in boredom and fatigue for both the student and the teacher.

A final issue to be considered in the administration of an IRI is the effect of different procedures for administering oral, silent, and listening passages. If passages are only administered orally, is it safe to assume that performance can be generalized to silent reading? Research has yet to provide a definitive answer to this question. However, an interactive view of reading suggests that there will be differences in performance under different reading conditions. This means that performance may vary when students are asked to read a passage orally, as opposed to silent reading followed by oral rereading. Therefore caution is urged in generalizing from one reading situation to another. It may also be necessary to administer an IRI under various conditions that are representative of those the student encounters frequently in the classroom to obtain a complete understanding of a student's reading abilities (see Chapter 11).

*Scoring.* A major area of concern regarding the scoring of an IRI is that decisions about what gets counted as an error are going to make a difference in the scores used for determining placement levels. Betts (1946) was not entirely clear about what constituted an error; however, an examination of the summary sheets he used suggests that all deviations from the text were counted as errors. Much of the controversy about scoring oral reading errors centers on so-called good errors, that is, errors that do not disrupt the meaning of the text and appear to arise from the reader's meaningful processing of the text rather than from some faulty skill or strategy.

Repetition errors have received the most attention. Some argue that repetitions should not be counted as errors, because they represent the reader's attempt to preserve the meaning of the text (K. S. Goodman, 1973). Others argue that repetitions should be counted as errors, because failure to do so will result in readers becoming physiologically frustrated before they reach the percentage of errors normally recognized as the student's frustration level. Ekwall and Shanker (1985, p. 374) sum up the situation as follows: "Although it may not seem 'fair' to a student to count repetitions because the student ends up with more errors, it is in reality less fair not to count these errors. If the student appears to be a better reader than is actually the case, the student will be given reading material that is too difficult."

For our part, it is difficult to make a single rule that accommodates all situations satisfactorily. In general, we do not consider repetitions, especially those that are accompanied by self-corrections, to be scorable errors. However, there are instances when repetitions are so disruptive that they are clearly interfering with effective reading. In these cases repetitions should be taken into account in scoring.

A second area of concern focuses on the practice of aggregating different types of oral reading errors across passages and looking for patterns. Research has shown that the type of errors that readers make is directly related to the difficulty of the material. In fact, Kibby (1979) found that including frustration-level errors in an analysis can give a distorted view of the reader's skills and strategies. Our position on this is that oral reading errors should not be aggregated across passages. If some aggregation is necessary, then errors should be aggregated only for passages on which the student's performance was relatively comparable.

A related problem is that many commercially prepared IRIs analyze oral reading errors in isolation (Jongsma & Jongsma, 1981). The focus of this type of analysis is on letter–sound differences, without any attention to context, the effects of previous errors, and/or the reader's background knowledge. We believe that oral reading errors should be analyzed both in terms of letter–sound differences and in relation to the contexts in which they occurred (see the discussion of miscue analysis below).

Finally, traditional IRI scoring procedures do not provide any mechanism for evaluating the interaction between oral reading and comprehension errors. Oral reading accuracy affects various types of comprehension differently. Nicolsen, Pearson, and Dykstra (1979) report the results of research that revealed the following:

1. Accurate word recognition is important for comprehension of specific information, but relatively unimportant for global interpretation.
2. Errors that make sense in a sentence (for example, *giant* for *gorilla*) are more likely to disrupt comprehension of specific information than errors that clearly do not make sense (for example, *wall* for *gorilla*), because students are more likely to maintain a faulty interpretation that makes sense than one that is unreasonable.
3. Comprehension questions that require students to relate the ideas in two sentences are affected more by the word recognition error rate than questions that require responses based primarily on prior knowledge.

Therefore, it is important that oral reading and comprehension errors be examined in tandem to determine the interaction between word recognition and comprehension abilities for a particular reader.

*Placement and Achievement.*    The biggest problem confronting those who use IRIs for placement and related purposes is that there is no evidence that reading levels established through IRI testing actually correspond to classroom performance. The validity of IRI placement levels hinges entirely on readability estimates of the IRI passages. The results of an IRI must be interpreted cautiously when placing a student in appropriate instructional materials, given the variability among commercially prepared IRIs (Jongsma & Jongsma, 1981). Of course, even more caution should be exercised if the uses extend to communicating outside the classroom. Most IRIs, administered traditionally, simply are not constructed well enough to be used as indicators of overall student achievement in reading. In addition, the issues described below raise serious concerns about the use of IRIs (alone) to communicate about achievement.

Even if IRI levels are indeed indicative of classroom performance, the next problem is to decide on the criteria for placement (achievement). The decision about which placement criteria to use seems not so much a question of which are best but rather which are most appropriate, given the administration procedures, criteria for scoring, and purposes for administering the IRI. Decisions about the appropriateness of placement criteria should not be made independently of decisions about administration and scoring.

For example, a decision to administer an IRI using oral reading at sight, to count all deviations from the text as errors, and to use the Betts criteria for placement would be the strictest test and is the most commonly used set of procedures in commercially prepared IRIs. A decision to administer an IRI with silent reading preceding oral reading, to count only those errors that alter meaning, and to use the Powell criteria would provide very different results, and a much less strict test of reading proficiency. Although the majority of published IRIs use the Betts criteria, there is still enough variability to make this an important concern. Variability in placement criteria *can* result in different placement levels. This is one reason why we are much less enthusiastic about using IRIs for placement as opposed to the evaluative purposes discussed in the next section of the chapter.

A second area of concern is how well traditional error analysis reveals students' strengths and weaknesses in word recognition and comprehension. The major problem with these types of analyses is that they treat each error type as a separate entity, as though they occurred independently of each other. Research has demonstrated again and again that this is not the case; rather, error types are all interrelated and cannot be separated in this manner.

There are similar problems with using question types as a means of finding a student's relative strengths among an array of subskills (McKenna, 1983; Schell & Hanna, 1981), since we lack objective standards for classifying questions by subskill. In addition, IRIs have such a small number of questions per subskill that it is difficult to reliably classify a reader's comphension problems by using these question types. Perhaps the most damaging of all is evidence that suggests that all questions are measuring the same skill (Drahozal & Hanna, 1978). Therefore traditional analyses of oral reading and/or comprehension errors should not be relied on to produce a complete picture of a student's strengths and weaknesses in these areas.

*Guidelines for Traditional Usage of IRIs.* The significant concerns that have been raised about the construction, administration, scoring, and interpretation of IRIs indicate that caution needs to be exercised in developing or selecting IRIs for use in placing students in appropriate grade-level materials. The following guidelines, based on the information in this chapter and the recommendations of Jongsma and Jongsma (1981), McKenna (1983), and Pikulski and Shanahan (1982), are provided to assist those who choose and/or need to use IRIs for placement purposes. However, "keep in mind that when using an IRI, as with any test, you're just sampling behavior. On another set of passages, given on another day, you might get different results" (Jongsma & Jongsma, 1981, p. 704).

1. Look for selections that correspond to regularly used instructional materials with regard to content, difficulty, style, and length. Be alert to differences in the interest level of passages for different groups of students.
2. Stay alert to readability problems. Don't assume that texts are representative of classroom materials, or that texts on alternate forms are comparable.
3. Ensure the passage dependency of questions by field testing them. Do not assume that questions on published instruments are passage dependent, and do not hesitate to replace some of them with your own.
4. In writing questions, limit the number of types. In using commercial tests, be wary of summary sheets that break down student responses into a large number of comprehension subskills.
5. Determine procedures for administering and scoring and placement criteria within the context of the purpose(s) for using the IRI.
6. Consider carefully how the oral, silent, and listening passages will be presented.
7. Be sure that instructions for administering, scoring, and interpreting are clear and complete. Consider carefully what student directions communicate to the students.

8. Carefully consider what constitutes an error on the word lists and oral reading passages.
9. Consider which factors should be weighed most heavily in establishing placement levels, that is, word recognition, comprehension, or rate.
10. Do not aggregate oral reading and comprehension errors across passages. Differentiate errors that occur at students' independent, instructional, and frustration levels.

In summary, we do not believe that the primary strength of IRIs and IRI-like measures lies in their use as placement procedures—and certainly not for use as every-pupil achievement measures. Furthermore, we object most strenuously to the use of a single (usually commercially prepared) IRI as the sole criterion for placement/achievement. Having said this, we also believe that the informal procedures embedded in IRIs, coupled with the addition of more contemporary strategies like miscue analysis and retelling, can provide valuable information. The following section addresses the use of IRIs and IRI-like procedures for the evaluative and diagnostic purposes for which they are best suited.

## Contemporary IRIs: A Look at What's New

The close critical examination of IRIs that has occurred over the past two decades has resulted in changes. Several older IRIs have completed major revisions, and several new IRIs have appeared. In some cases authors have addressed criticisms related to passage selection, scoring ambiguities, quality of comprehension items, and/or difficulties related to content. In other cases authors have worked from an interactive, constructive perspective and have attempted to create inventories that reflect a contemporary model of reading. For example, *The Analytic Reading Inventory,* an IRI with considerable history, has added new dimensions to its most recent assessment (Woods & Moe, 2003). Thus users can evaluate comprehension questions in terms of "Reader Text Relationships," examining students' ability to retell explicitly stated facts, put information together, connect author and reader ("from head to text"), and evaluate and substantiate information with more personal response. In the next section we describe one IRI in some detail, using it as a prototype for examining contemporary IRIs.

*Qualitative Reading Inventory.*   The recently revised *Qualitative Reading Inventory-3* or QRI-3 (Leslie & Caldwell, 2001) is a contemporary IRI that responds to many of the concerns described above. The QRI-3 is an IRI "designed to provide diagnostic information about (1) conditions under which subjects can identify words and comprehend text successfully, and (2) conditions that appear to result in unsuccessful word identification, decoding and/or comprehension" (Leslie & Caldwell, 2001, p. 1).

The QRI-3 has undergone extensive pilot testing to develop the procedures used to answer the following diagnostic questions:

- Can the student identify words automatically? more words in context than in isolation?
- When reading orally, does the student correct oral reading errors that do not make sense? use meaning clues? use graphic or letter clues?

- Can a student successfully comprehend narrative but not informational material? familiar but not unfamiliar text?
- What is the quality of the student's comprehension?
- Does the student organize recall in stories according to elements of story structure?
- Does the student organize recall in informational texts according to main idea and supporting details?
- Can the student answer questions that require inferences as well as those whose answers are explicitly stated in the text?
- Does prior knowledge influence the student's performance?
- Does the student have a low knowledge base overall?

*Innovations.* Although a complete description of the QRI-3 is not possible here, there are important differences between the QRI-3 and other IRIs that should be highlighted. First, the QRI-3 provides both narrative and expository texts at each level. A significant improvement in the QRI involves the use of pictures at the preprimer through second-grade levels. One narrative and one exposition at each level contain supportive pictures so that the examiner can explore the impact of pictures on print-reading but also so that teachers can assess students using more authentic materials. At each level from grade 3 through junior high, there are three narrative and three expository passages. Both narrative and expository selections are intact texts, not excerpts, and are highly representative of the structure and topics of selections found in basal readers and subject area texts.

Next, the passages were developed or selected to provide intentional variation in familiarity, with some topics likely to be familiar to most students at that grade level and others likely to be unfamiliar. The QRI-3 provides two ways to assess a student's familiarity with passage content; each reading selection includes a conceptual questions task and a prediction activity that may be used to determine a student's familiarity with the topic of the selection. These tasks allow the examiner to identify each passage as either familiar or unfamiliar to each individual student. The use of passages that vary in familiarity enables the examiner to arrive at a more complete description of a student's reading ability.

In addition to evaluating prior knowledge, the QRI-3 assesses comprehension using both questions and retellings. Each selection has an accompanying text map for recording and evaluating the student's unaided recall. The comprehension questions are of two kinds: explicit and implicit. Answers to explicit questions are directly stated in the text, and answers to implicit questions require the reader to make inferences from textual clues.

The QRI-3 also includes two other optional vehicles for evaluating students' comprehension. At grades 3 through high school, teachers may add look-backs to the assessment, and for the new high school–level passages examiners may ask students to think aloud while reading. When using look-backs, the examiner first scores the comprehension using the normal procedures but then asks students to return to the text to correct or elaborate on their responses. According to Leslie and Caldwell (2001, p. 18), "look-backs allow the examiner to differentiate between comprehension during reading and memory after reading." During the think-aloud procedure the reader is encouraged to stop at predetermined points and think aloud about what he or she is doing. The administrator's materials includes a useful summary form on which the examiner can indicate whether the student's think-aloud statements fell into any of several defined categories. As with other aspects of the QRI, this section is well documented and consistent with recent research.

**FIGURE 9.7a**    Qualitative Reading Inventory-3

| Student Profile Sheet | | | | | | | | | | |
|---|---|---|---|---|---|---|---|---|---|---|
| Name ___ Kyle ___ Birthdate __ 3/27/94 __ Grade __ 2→3 __ | | | | | | | | | | |
| Sex __ M __ Date of Test ___ Examiner ___ | | | | | | | | | | |
| **Word Identification** | | | | | | | | | | |
| Grade | 1 | | | | | | | | | |
| Level/% Automatic | | | | | | | | | | |
| Level/% Total | | | | | | | | | | |
| **Oral Reading** | | | | | | | | | | |
| Passage Name | Bear/ Rabbit | Trip to Zoo | Wool: Sheep to You | Johnny Appleseed | Amelia Earhart | | | | | |
| Readability Level | 1 | 3 | 3 | 4 | 4 | | | | | |
| Passage Type | N | N | Exp | N | Exp | | | | | |
| Level/% Total Accuracy | 94% | 97% | 95% | 93% | 95% | | | | | |
| Level/% Total Acceptability | 100% | 99% | 98% | 99% | 92% | (skipped line) | | | | |
| Familiar/Unfamiliar: % | 80% | 75% | 66% | 66% | 33% | | | | | |
| Retelling: % | | | | | | | | | | |
| # Explicit Correct | 4/4 | 4/4 | 2/4 | 4/4 | 2/4 | | | | | |
| # Implicit Correct | 2/2 | 4/4 | 4/4 | 4/4 | 3/4 | | | | | |
| Level/% Comprehension | IND | IND | INST | IND | INST | | | | | |
| # Explicit Correct: Look-backs | | | | | | | | | | |
| # Implicit Correct: Look-backs | | | | | | | | | | |
| Level/% Comprehension: Look-backs | | | | | | | | | | |

*Source:* Lesley, Lauren, & Caldwell, Joanne. *Qualitative Reading Inventory-3.* Copyright © 2001. Reprinted by permission of Allyn & Bacon.

*(continued on next page)*

Another innovative feature of the QRI-3 is that the word lists contain words taken from the reading selections. As a result, the examiner can assess students' use of context by comparing their word recognition during passage reading to their performance on the word lists. Finally, like some other contemporary IRIs, the QRI-3 includes materials that support alternative analyses of oral reading errors (see the discussion of miscue analysis below).

*Scoring and Interpreting.*    Although the QRI-3 does provide quantitative scores, they will vary for many students as a function of the type of text read, the familiarity of the passage content, and the manner in which comprehension is assessed. The interpretation of the scores must therefore be qualified by the above factors. This is what sets the QRI-3 apart from other IRIs and the reason it has been called *qualitative.*

## Student Profile Sheet (continued)

| | The Friend | Where Do People Live | Cahokia | | | | | | | | |
|---|---|---|---|---|---|---|---|---|---|---|---|
| **Oral Reading** (continued) | | | | | | | | | | | |
| Rate | | | | | | | | | | | |
| Total Passage Level | | | | | | | | | | | |
| **Silent Reading** | | | | | | | | | | | |
| Passage Name | The Friend | Where Do People Live | Cahokia | | | | | | | | |
| Passage Section (High School) | | | | | | | | | | | |
| Readability Level | 3 | 3 | 4 | | | | | | | | |
| Passage Type | N | Exp | Exp | | | | | | | | |
| Familiar/Unfamiliar: % | 80% | 40% | 25% | | | | | | | | |
| Retelling: % | | | | | | | | | | | |
| # Correct Explicit | 3/4 | 4/4 | 4/4 | | | | | | | | |
| # Correct Implicit | 3/4 | 4/4 | 4/4 | | | | | | | | |
| Level/% Comprehension | INST | IND | IND | | | | | | | | |
| # Correct Explicit: Look-backs | | | | | | | | | | | |
| # Correct Implicit: Look-backs | | | | | | | | | | | |
| Level/% Comprehension. Look-backs | | | | | | | | | | | |
| Rate | | | | | | | | | | | |

As the authors of the QRI-3 suggest (Leslie & Caldwell, 2001, p. 21):

> While it was once common, it is now simplistic to talk about a single independent, instructional, or frustration level for an individual. The act of reading is highly complex and contextual.

The variety of passages on the QRI-3 allows the examiner to evaluate the effects of topic familiarity, text structure, and reading mode on the independent, instructional, and frustration levels of the student. "It is not inconceivable that a single reader may have different levels for familiar and unfamiliar text, for narrative and expository material, and for oral and silent reading modes" (Leslie & Caldwell, 2001, p. 21).

The authors further note that the major strength of the QRI-3 is that it provides a profile of an individual reader's strengths and weaknesses across different types of text and in relation to the familiarity of the reading selections. These comparisons are facilitated by the inclusion of two summary sheets: the Subject Profile Sheet and the Comparison Sheet. Kyle's performance on the QRI (between grades 2 and 3) is summarized in Figure 9.7. The Subject Profile Sheet is designed to provide the examiner with maximum flexibility in the amount

**FIGURE 9.7b**   Comparisons: Describing Specific Reading Behaviors

| | |
|---|---|
| Student _____ Kyle _____ | |

**WORD IDENTIFICATION**
**How Accurate Is the Student in Identifying Words?**
Word-Lists Total Score: Level                     —
Passage Reading
   Word Identification: Level               —

**How Automatic Is the Student in Identifying Words?**
Word-Lists Timed Score: Level               —
Oral Passage Reading: WPM                     
Silent Passage Reading: WPM

**What Strategies for Word Identification in Context Are Used by the Student?**
Percent: Graphically Similar Miscues:
   Initial Position                             yes
   Final Position                              yes
Percent: Acceptable Miscues            74% ⎫
Percent: Self-corrected Miscues        24% ⎬ = 98%

**Is There a Difference between a Student's Ability to Identify Words in Isolation and Words in Context?**
Word-Lists Total Score: Level               NA
Passage Reading
   Word Identification: Level               NA

**COMPREHENSION**
**Which Types of Text Can the Student Handle Most Successfully?**
Narrative Text: Level                    No Difference
Expository Text: Level
Text with Pictures: Level                 NA
Text without Pictures: Level           NA

**Which Modes of Reading Represent a Strength for the Student?**
Oral Reading: Level                   3-IND      4-INST
Silent Reading: Level                 ⎰ Slight Advantage
                                    ⎱ 3-IND      4-IND

**How Does the Student Perform in Familiar and Unfamiliar Text?**
Familiar Text: Level                   Oral-gr. 4 IND (INST)
Unfamiliar Text: Level                Silent-gr. 4 IND

**How Does the Student Perform with Look-Backs and without Look-Backs?**
Without Look-Backs: Level
With Look-Backs: Level

**What Comprehension Strategies Does the Student Employ While Reading?**

**What Is the Extent of the Student's Reading Problem?**
Highest Instructional Level             4
Chronological Grade Placement       3

*Source:* Lesley, Lauren, & Caldwell, Joanne. *Qualitative Reading Inventory-3.* Copyright © 2001. Reprinted by permission of Allyn & Bacon.

of information to be recorded for a given student. The Comparison Sheet is designed to facilitate comparison of a subject's reading ability across different contexts. Kyle's results, summarized in Figure 9.7, suggest generally very strong oral reading accuracy and comprehension on all materials through grade 3. Familiarity does not appear to influence his comprehension. Kyle does show particularly strong comprehension abilities on exposition. His comprehension is really influenced only by oral reading accuracy (a tendency to skip lines in print).

In summary, the QRI-3 provides a set of procedures that is both conceptually and psychometrically sound and that represents a major step forward in the development of interactive assessment devices.

***Other Special Features.***   Another new IRI designed to address earlier criticism is the *Stieglitz Informal Reading Inventory* (SIRI) (1997). It contains all of the major components described above and suggests scoring using traditional error categories (see Figure 9.2) but refers to these errors as "miscues." There are several aspects of the inventory that highlight the wide range of contemporary IRIs. First, the SIRI offers both narrative (Forms B and D) and expository (Forms A and C) selections. Second, the author suggests using *free recall* as one means of evaluating comprehension. The SIRI also suggests evaluating both *familiarity* and *interest.* The prior knowledge scale and the level of interest scale (ranging from 1 to 5) are self-reported measures that are administered *after* reading. The utility of these tools is tempered somewhat by the fact that there are few suggestions for interpreting the information that is generated, nor is there evidence of the extent to which these self-reports are reliable.

The SIRI also offers tools for *evaluating emergent literacy* using a dictated story method and includes checklists for evaluating the abilities of early readers. Similarly, the revised *Bader Reading and Language Inventory* (BRLI) (2002) also includes an "Emergent Literacy Assessment" that contains concepts about print, an interview, and an expanded phonemic awareness assessment with tests of blending and segmenting sounds in words. Another important addition to the most recent BRLI is the inclusion of a screening assessment for English language learners. This "ESL checklist" provides a way for teachers to informally assess students' English language development.

Other IRIs have included more exposition and texts appropriate for middle- and secondary-level students. The revised *Classroom Reading Inventory* (CRI) (Silvaroli & Wheelock, 2001), for example, provides separate forms for elementary, junior high/middle school, and for high school/adults. At the elementary level, the CRI also offers the unusual contrast of passages in a "traditional subskills format," accompanied by questions and a separate form of passages in a "literature format" with retellings.

The newer and revised IRIs also tend to offer more options for examining word level difficulties. For example, on the SIRI the graded word lists can be evaluated in *context* or in isolation, and in the revised *Ekwall-Shanker IRI* (2000) there are provisions for evaluating both phonics and structural analysis skills in context. The BRLI also contains a test of spelling that includes solid interpretive information.

***Specialized Inventories: Using Informal Study Skills Assessments.***   There are many commercially available informal tools that assess study skills and habits. For example, the *Shipman Assessment of Work-Study Skills* (SAWS) (Warncke & Shipman, 1984) contains a number of subtests for evaluating alphabetizing, dictionary usage, ability to use reference sources, use of graphic materials, and organizing skills. The *Content Reading Inventories: English, Social Studies, Science* (McWilliams & Rakes, 1979) contains a similar battery of informal tests. These commercial materials permit teachers to gather a wide variety of information about groups of students quickly. Therefore they are quite useful if screening data are needed. However, these tests are not generally linked to the books or curriculum used in the classroom. Thus the amount of information generated about students' ability to actually perform in that setting is somewhat limited.

To collect information about students' application of knowledge and skill, teachers will need to construct their own inventories. A *Group Reading Inventory* (GRI) is designed for use in the classroom and is helpful for gathering information about how well students can read their textbooks (Rakes & Smith, 2001). A GRI typically has two components: a book-handling component and a comprehension section. Both parts of the GRI are constructed by using the actual textbook employed in the classroom. Resource room teachers, of course, will need to construct an inventory that samples several types of texts.

Part I of the GRI is constructed by generating ten to twelve questions about the various parts of the text (see Figure 9.8 for sample items). Part II of the GRI is akin to an IRI. A relatively short selection (about 500 words) is drawn from a chapter in the text. Ten or fifteen questions are generated to test comprehension. Whereas students are directed to complete Part I of the GRI while using their textbook, the questions in Part II are to be answered without referring to the book. The information gleaned from this type of assessment can be used to complete an observation checklist like the one proposed in Chapter 8.

In summary, many of the commercial IRIs have recognized the variable nature of reading performance and have made some attempts to offer tools for collecting multiple samples under some varied conditions. The extent to which these are useful depends heavily on the orientation of the instructional program and the beliefs of the teacher. In the next sections we describe various techniques designed to create a structured assessment for (1) analyzing oral reading miscues, (2) analyzing fluency, (3) analyzing comprehension, and (4) analyzing written language.

**FIGURE 9.8**
Excerpt from a
Group Reading
Inventory

| **Using Book Parts** |
| --- |
| *Introduction:* These questions are designed to help you understand the organization of your text and to enable you to use it more effectively. You may use your text in answering the questions. |

1. Where would you look to locate a short story in the text if you could not recall the title or the author?
   a. Glossary
   b. Table of Contents
   c. Literary Terms and Techniques
   d. Index of Authors and Titles

2. If you came across the word "demagoguery" in your reading in the text, where would you look *first* for a definition?
   a. Table of Contents
   b. Literary Terms and Techniques
   c. Glossary
   d. The Composition and Language Program

*Source:* From *Content Area Literacy: An Integrated Approach,* 7th ed., by John E. Readence, Thomas W. Beam, and R. Scott Baldwin. Copyright © 2001 by Kendall/Hunt Publishing Company. Used with permission.

When used in conjunction with each other, the procedures described here form an assessment system that provides a great deal of information about the reader in a fairly parsimonious fashion. Miscue analysis of a student's oral reading is used to evaluate word recognition strategies in relation to text comprehension. The Fluency Scale (see pages 346–347) is then applied to the same oral reading samples to evaluate the student's oral reading fluency. Retellings are then used to evaluate various aspects of a student's oral, silent, and/or listening comprehension. Many of the new or revised IRIs have included some means of gathering retelling information, and many have replaced the more traditional error analysis with a focus on miscue analysis (or added it to the traditional summary).

## Retellings of IRI Selections

We discussed retellings at some length in Chapter 8. The overarching guidelines for evaluating retellings of full-length selections are no different from those already described, so we will not reiterate them here. However, it is important to remember to start with open-ended requests to recall as much as possible.

*Selecting and Analyzing Short Passages.* Although the addition of retellings can enhance the diagnostic value of an IRI tremendously, some cautions are in order. As we have already suggested, a number of factors can influence the comprehensibility—and recall—of textual material. Both the quantity and quality of student recalls can be affected by the type and quality of the text. For example, when students recall stories, we would expect to see appropriate recall of sequence and story line. In contrast, recalls of informational text might not rely so heavily on sequence but should reflect an understanding of the relationships among key facts and ideas. The coherence of a text can also affect recall. Many IRI passages read more like fragments of text than intact stories or informational selections. This can hamper student recall because it may be difficult for students to organize and retrieve the content presented. Finally, remember that reader interest in or familiarity with passage content can affect understanding, memory, and recall. Familiarity appears to influence the content of recall, and both interest and familiarity seem to have an effect on the amount of inferential comprehension achieved during reading (Lipson, Mosenthal, & Mekkelsen, 1999).

Before making final judgments about a student's ability to retell passages, it is important to be sure that samples of the student's best efforts have been gathered. To do this, the selections that are used should provide a good match for the student's interests, prior knowledge, and development ability. It is, of course, desirable to gather information regarding performance on materials that are routinely assigned to the reader in class (see the discussion of benchmark books below). The point is that we are simply sampling the reader's abilities, not measuring them in some definitive way. The selections we make should reflect our assessment purposes.

*Scoring and Interpreting Short Passages.* A number of systems for scoring and interpreting passage recall have been proposed in the past several years. One of the most useful and straightforward systems was designed by Clark (1982, 1993—revised, personal correspondence) specifically for use with IRIs. The steps in this "Free Call" procedure are as follows:

1. Break the passages to be used for retelling into pausal units by placing a slash wherever a good reader would normally pause during oral reading. The boundaries for these units typically fall at punctuation marks and at connectives such as *and, but,* and *because.*
2. Make a numbered list of the separate pausal units in the order in which they occur.
3. Rate the level of importance for each pausal unit by assigning a "1" to the most important units, a "2" to the next most important units, and a "3" to the least important units. To simplify this process, read through the units and assign a "1" to the major units, read through the units again and assign a "3" to the least important information, and then assign a "2" to all remaining units.
4. Record the order in which the pausal units are recalled by numbering them in the order in which they are retold. Give the student credit for responses that capture the gist of the unit.

Three types of information result from this technique: the amount recalled, the sequence of recall, and the level of recalled information. The assessment of sequence is purely subjective. A judgment should be made about whether the order of the retelling was reasonable. The amount recalled is determined by dividing the number of units recalled by the total number of units in the passage. The score is then converted to a percentage by multiplying by 100. There are no available guidelines to evaluate the amount recalled. Clark reports that generally acceptable levels will be below the 75–90 percent criterion level of the IRI, and numerous research studies have reported average recall levels ranging between 33 percent and 50 percent depending on the level of the students and the nature of the materials.

Finally, to get an indication of the level of information that was recalled, compute the percentage of ideas recalled for each level of importance. These are perhaps the most significant scores to result from the Free Call procedure. To compute these scores, add all the recalled units at a given importance value and divide by the total number of units *rated at that level.* The resulting average scores show if the most significant information (as judged by the examiner) has been remembered. For example, if a total of twenty idea units were rated as level 1 importance and the reader recalled ten of these, the percentage of recall would be 50 percent for level 1. The same method is used to determine percentages for levels 2 and 3. Of this earlier revision Clark notes that an ideal recall would be, in effect, a summary of the most important information.

> As a summary, it should contain virtually all of the important level 1 idea units and none of the level 3 units. The percentages for level 1 should therefore approach 100, while the percentages for level 3 should approach zero. I have also found that the recalls which I subjectively feel are best contain approximately 50% of the material from level 2. The nature and length of the text, the background of the reader, and the purpose for the reading all affect this distribution. (Clark, 1993, personal communication)

Clark cautions that it is important to remember that there is a normal developmental tendency; older, better readers recall more information at higher levels of importance and in better sequence, so comparisons among individuals of different ages and abilities is inappropriate.

A sample of Marvin's recall has been scored using this system and is provided in Figure 9.9. As can be seen, Marvin has recalled a reasonable amount of the text in good sequence. However, he has recalled only 33 percent of the possible level 1 material, 67 percent of the level 2 information, and 22 percent of level 3 content. In addition, the mean importance level of units recalled is good. It is also important to note that he has failed to recall any of the last portion of the text. This failure to report crucial information from throughout the text and, in particular, about the resolution of the problem presented in the early part of the passage is serious. It suggests that Marvin might not be sensitive to the overall text structure of the passage or that he has trouble separating important from unimportant information. It certainly warrants further investigation with additional samples, using this and other procedures.

## Miscue Analysis

Miscue analysis describes procedures that attempt to identify how readers process print by analyzing their oral reading errors. Interest in the ideas underlying miscue analysis dates back to Huey (1908/1968) but is most often associated with Kenneth and Yetta Goodman (K. S. Goodman, 1969; K. S. Goodman & Y. M. Goodman, 1977) and their colleagues. The fundamental assumption underlying miscue analysis is the idea that readers use their knowledge of language to sample, predict, and confirm the meaning of a text. Therefore oral reading provides a means for examining readers' use of the language systems that cue meaning—graphophonic, syntactic, and semantic.

Miscue analysis procedures provide a structure for analyzing students' oral reading behaviors, with special attention to times when oral reading deviates from the text. Oral reading "errors" have been renamed miscues because it is believed that they are not random errors but rather are mis-"cued" by the graphophonic, syntactic, and semantic systems the reader uses to process written material. It is assumed that both expected and unexpected oral reading responses are produced by the same process. Therefore miscues are viewed as a "window on the reading process" (K. S. Goodman, 1973). The concept of miscues has become so popular that the term is commonly used when referring to oral reading errors, even when they are analyzed in a traditional manner.

***Reading Miscue Inventory (RMI).*** The miscue analysis procedures developed by the Goodmans and their colleagues were simplified for research purposes and published as the *Reading Miscue Inventory* (Y. M. Goodman & Burke, 1972). A further revision and a set of alternative procedures for administration, depending on the purposes for which the inventory is to be used, were published more recently (Y. Goodman et al., 1987). The RMI is designed specifically to identify and evaluate the strategies used by a particular reader to process written material. The following is a summary of the basic procedure:

1. A coherent reading passage is selected for the reader. The selection must be somewhat difficult and long enough to elicit a minimum of twenty-five miscues.
2. The reader is asked to read aloud and is informed that the reading will be unaided. A code sheet is marked as the selection is read. The reading is tape-recorded for future reference.

**FIGURE 9.9**
Sample Retelling
Evaluation

| Importance Number | Pausal Unit | Recall Sequence |
|:---:|:---|:---:|
| 3 | 1. Joe sat down | 2 |
| 3 | 2. on the sidewalk | |
| 2 | 3. in front of the trading post | 3 |
| 3 | 4. with his buckskin jacket thrown over his shoulder. | |
| 1 | 5. He felt worried | 1 |
| 1 | 6. because it was difficult to know what to do. | |
| 1 | 7. "Grandfather told me | 4 |
| 1 | 8. to sell these blue beads. | 5 |
| 2 | 9. He said they would bring | |
| 2 | 10. me good fortune and good health. | |
| 2 | 11. Grandfather is a wise | 12 |
| 2 | 12. and understanding man. | 13 |
| 1 | 13. He is proud | |
| 1 | 14. to be an American Indian. | |
| 2 | 15. He remembers | 6 |
| 2 | 16. when his grandfather | 7 |
| 2 | 17. gave him these same beads. | 8 |
| 2 | 18. He has often told me | 9 |
| 2 | 19. many interesting stories | 10 |
| 2 | 20. of how his grandfather | |
| 3 | 21. rode horses and hunted buffalo | 11 |
| 3 | 22. on the plains. | |
| 3 | 23. Joe held the string of beads | |
| 3 | 24. high into the air toward the sunlight. | |
| 3 | 25. "These are | |
| 2 | 26. perfectly beautiful beads," | |
| 3 | 27. he said out loud. | |
| 1 | 28. "I can't sell them | |
| 1 | 29. because I am too proud of my great past. | |
| 1 | 30. Yes, I will keep the beads." | |

Total number of units = 30
Number of units recalled = 13
Percentage recalled = 43%
Sequence Evaluation = Good
Percentage of important units recalled = 3/9 (33%)
Percentage of moderate units recalled = 8/12 (66%)
Percentage of unimportant units recalled = 2/9 (11%)

3. The substitution miscues are coded.
4. Miscue patterns are studied, interpreted, and translated into instruction.

The reader is encouraged to guess after a thirty-second hesitation. If hesitations are continuous, the reader is told to continue reading even if it means skipping a word or phrase. The

RMI procedures also include a retelling of the selection, which is scored subjectively by the examiner. More will be said about retellings in the next section.

Although all types of miscues are marked, only substitution (including mispronunciation) miscues are coded, according to RMI procedures. Each substitution miscue is coded on the basis of the answers to a specific set of nine questions.

1. *Graphic similarity.* How much does the miscue look like what was expected?
2. *Sound similarity.* How much does the miscue sound like what was expected?
3. *Correction.* Is the miscue corrected?
4. *Grammatical acceptability.* Does the miscue occur in a structure that is grammatically acceptable? Does intonation signal author's syntactic intent?
5. *Semantic acceptability.* Does the miscue occur in a structure that is semantically acceptable? Does intonation signal author's semantic intent?
6. *Meaning change.* Does the miscue result in a change of meaning? Is a dialect variation involved in the miscue? (Optional) *Grammatical function.* Is the grammatical function of the miscue the same as the grammatical function of the word in the text? (Y. M. Goodman et al., 1987)

There is also some variation in how these questions are used within each of the alternative procedures presented in the revised RMI.

The major advantage of miscue analysis over traditional analyses of oral reading errors is that it recognizes that some errors are better than others. Miscue analysis emphasizes the quality of errors as a reflection of the quality of strategies students are using to process text. Quality exists along a continuum, from not-so-good to good, with a focus on how closely the miscues maintain meaning within the text.

Errors that focus on the meaning of the text are considered "better" than errors that focus on the letters and sounds, especially if the latter results in nonsense word substitution or substitutions that do not make sense within the context of the passage (Hood, 1978). Of course, the best errors are those that reveal attention to the multiple cueing systems; that is, they demonstrate that the reader is attending to the meaning of the *entire* passage and also to the print cues. For example, when reading aloud, good readers may substitute words that mean the same as the text, such as reading "frightened" for "afraid." In addition, they may omit unessential words, for example, by reading "told what he heard" instead of "told what he had heard." Words may be inserted, such as reading "the little old lady" for "the old lady." The writer's exact words may be read correctly but in different order, such as reading "put the tent up" for "put up the tent." Unlike other errors, which do not sound sensible, these specific examples are all good errors because they represent the same meaning as the words in the text. More important, they reflect the use of effective strategies to process the text.

There are no normative data to guide the interpretation of readers' miscue patterns. However, miscue analysis research does suggest the existence of several trends. A summary of these trends provided by Wixson (1979) includes the following:

1. Most readers, regardless of age or proficiency, produce a greater number of contextually acceptable miscues than graphophonically similar miscues.
2. As readers become more proficient, the proportion of graphophonically similar miscues stabilizes and the proportion of contextually acceptable miscues increases.

3. Less proficient readers make fewer attempts to correct their miscues than more proficient readers.

4. Less proficient readers tend to correct acceptable and unacceptable miscues at almost an equal rate, whereas more proficient readers tend to correct unacceptable miscues at a higher rate than acceptable miscues.

*Problems with the RMI.*    Miscues should be interpreted with caution, however, because there is evidence that patterns vary as a result of the complex interaction among factors such as the instructional method; the reader's background, skills, and purpose for reading; and the specific nature of the written material. As with any test, miscue analysis provides a sample of behavior that may or may not be representative of the way a student interacts with different types of texts under different reading conditions. Miscue patterns are best regarded as a reflection of the particular strategies employed by a particular reader to satisfy his or her purpose for reading a particular passage.

The best way to address the problem of variability in miscue patterns is to obtain repeated samples of a particular reader's miscues under a variety of predetermined conditions (see the discussion of running records in Chapter 8). The nature and content of the reading selections should be varied with regard to each individual reader's skills and background in an attempt to present the reader with a range of reading tasks and materials. An analysis of the miscues generated by a particular reader under a variety of conditions may reveal any pervasive problems the reader may have, as well as the particular conditions that present the reader with the greatest difficulty.

In addition to the problem of variability, the RMI often diverts attention away from a word-level analysis of miscues. Although the primary object of reading is, of course, comprehension and the maintenance of meaning, many struggling readers have decoding or word analysis difficulties, and an analysis of miscues can provide valuable insight into readers' knowledge and skill in these areas. This is especially problematic because the RMI is designed to be used with materials that are at least one grade level above the student's reading placement level, and reading miscues may vary across texts of various levels of difficulty. Finally, the administration and scoring are too complex and time consuming to make them practical for either classroom or clinical use. Procedures that we advocate to simplify miscue analysis are provided in the next section.

*Modified Miscue Analysis Procedures.*    The first step is to select text materials at what is believed to be the student's instructional level of difficulty so that information is being collected about the way the student is likely to perform during real classroom reading situations. Next, the substitution miscues are analyzed within the context of the following questions:

1. Does the miscue change the meaning of the sentence?
2. Is the miscue contextually acceptable within the context of the whole passage?
3. Was the miscue self-corrected?
4. Is the miscue graphophonically similar to the intended word?
5. If the miscue is graphically similar, does it reveal a pattern of difficulty in some component area?

In reflecting on the answers to these questions, we can begin to discover patterns of performance. In particular, we can begin to determine whether the student is attending to the meaningfulness of text (Are most of the miscues acceptable? Does the student self-correct most of those miscues that are not acceptable?).

The chart in Figure 9.10 illustrates Marvin's miscues on several sentences from a level 3 selection on the Burns and Roe *Informal Reading Inventory* (1985). One or two miscues of a particular type might not be significant. It is the *patterns* of performance that we are looking to reveal.

One of the most important findings of miscue research focuses on the self-correction patterns of skilled and less-skilled readers. Skilled readers tend to self-correct miscues that are contextually unacceptable and to leave uncorrected errors that are contextually acceptable. Less-skilled readers are just as likely to correct acceptable as unacceptable miscues.

If we examine Marvin's self-correction behavior, we see that there are six contextually unacceptable errors that we would expect a skilled reader to correct (2, 4, 5, 7, 9, and 10). Marvin corrected two of these (7 and 10) and left four uncorrected (2, 4, 5, and 9). There were also four contextually acceptable errors (1, 3, 6, and 8) that we would expect a skilled reader to leave uncorrected. Marvin corrected one of these (1) and left the other three uncorrected (3, 6, and 8). Although not entirely random, Marvin's pattern of self-correction for this text is more like that of a less-skilled than a skilled reader.

**FIGURE 9.10** Modified Miscue Analysis (Marvin)

| Text | Marvin | Meaning Change? | Contextually Acceptable? | Self-Corrected? | Graphophonic Similarity? | Word-Level Component? |
|---|---|---|---|---|---|---|
| 1. *me* | him | no | yes | yes | no | High-frequency sight word |
| 2. *these* | this | no | no | no | yes | High-frequency sight word |
| 3. *beads* | bands | yes | yes | no | yes | Medial vowel combination |
| 4. *would* | were | no | no | no | no | High-frequency sight word |
| 5. *me* | my | no | no | no | yes | High-frequency sight word |
| 6. *fortune* | future | no | yes | no | yes | |
| 7. *gave* | came | yes | no | yes | some | High-frequency sight word |
| 8. *beads* | beds | yes | yes | no | yes | Medial vowel combination |
| 9. *has* | was | no | no | no | yes | High-frequency sight word |
| 10. *rode* | told | yes | no | yes | some | |

Additional information can be obtained by examining the graphophonic similarity of the errors to the text word. Eight of Marvin's ten miscues have at least some graphophonic similarity to the word in the text (2, 3, and 5–10). Even the two errors that are not graphophonically similar (1 and 4) are common sight word confusions. This pattern, coupled with the fact that only four of his ten errors were contextually acceptable, suggests that Marvin is relying heavily on the graphophonic cues in this text.

Finally, it is important to consider the effect of the errors on the meaning of the passage. In most cases, when an error is contextually acceptable, it will not change the meaning of the text, and when an error is contextually unacceptable, it will change the meaning of the text. However, occasionally, unacceptable errors do not change the meaning of the text, and acceptable errors do. There are several examples of this among Marvin's errors. Errors 2, 4, 5, and 9 are contextually unacceptable, yet they do not change the meaning of the text. In Marvin's case these errors are all examples of common sight word substitutions, adding to the evidence that Marvin still has not mastered the orthographic structure of high-frequency words.

Marvin also has two errors (3 and 8) that are contextually acceptable but *do* change the meaning of the text. The first time he encounters the word *beads* he calls it *bands,* and the second time he calls it *beds.* This is a good error in that it suggests that Marvin is using both contextual and graphophonic cues and he does not correct it, because it makes sense in the passage. However, it is clear that this error is also likely to have a profound effect on his comprehension of this passage. Therefore the meaning change column can provide further insight into readers' miscue patterns.

The QRI-3, administered to Kyle between grades 2 and 3 (see Figure 9.6), provides support for summarizing and interpreting oral reading miscues. The summary form is presented in Figure 9.11 with Kyle's results from two instructional level passages.

Unlike Marvin's, Kyle's profile is more similar to a good reader than to a poor one. Sixteen of twenty-two miscues were semantically acceptable. Kyle attempted to self-correct four of the six remaining miscues. Only twice did Kyle leave uncorrected a miscue that was both syntactically and semantically unacceptable; substituting *then* for *when* and mispronouncing the word *formed.* In other words, Kyle is attending quite carefully to the semantic and syntactic cues in text. He also is making use of the graphophonic cues (only five of twenty-two miscues was not graphically similar). Kyle's miscues fall into two large categories: He frequently makes substitutions of high-frequency sight words (*the* for *it; there* for *where, to* for *of*), and he has problems with morphemes, frequently dropping or adding endings (*knit* for *knitted, dries* for *dry, class* for *classes*).

Before going on, it is important to remember that, for both Kyle and Marvin this is a very small sample of miscues taken from one or two texts. To make generalizations or predictions about Marvin's reading in particular, we must examine a large number of miscues taken from a variety of texts under a variety of conditions. This issue will be considered further in Chapter 11 as we examine multiple samples of Marvin's reading.

## Oral Reading Fluency Scale

There has been an increased interest in fluency among both educators and researchers, in part because there appears to be such a strong relationship between oral reading fluency and

**FIGURE 9.11** Miscue Analysis Worksheet (Kyle)

Subject _____Level 3_____ Level of Miscues: (Independent/Instructional) Frustrational

| Miscue | Text | Graphically Similar | Semantically Acceptable | Syntactically Acceptable | Self-Corrected | Word-Level Component |
|---|---|---|---|---|---|---|
| *Wool* | | | | | | |
| knit | knitted | yes | yes | no | — | word ending |
| clothes | clothing | yes | yes | yes | | word ending |
| then | when | yes | no | no | — | high-frequency sight word |
| the | it | no | no | no | yes | sight word |
| looks | locks | yes | no | no | yes | vowel combination |
| dries | dry | yes | yes | no | — | word ending |
| com bed | combed | yes | no | no | attempted, unsuccessful | silent letter |
| form-at | formed | yes | no | no | — | word ending |
| wove | woven | yes | yes | no | — | word ending |
| clothes | clothing | yes | yes | yes | — | word ending |
| hands | hand | yes | yes | yes | — | word ending |
| *Zoo* | | | | | | |
| the | their | yes | yes | yes | — | sight word |
| class | classes | yes | yes | no | yes | word ending |
| Mar | Maria | yes | yes | yes | — | |
| Angelina | Angela | yes | yes | yes | — | |
| want | wanted | yes | yes | no | yes | word ending |
| the | one | no | yes | no | — | sight word |
| Lipoz | Lopez | yes | yes | yes | — | |
| there | where | partial | yes | yes | — | sight word |
| to | of | no | no | no | yes | sight word |
| Luzpa | Lopez | yes | yes | yes | — | |
| He | and | no | yes | yes | — | sight word |
| Column Total Total Miscues Column Total/Total Miscues = % | | ___ ___ ___ | ___ ___ ___ | ___ ___ ___ | ___ ___ ___ | |

comprehension of orally reading text (Carnine, Silbert, & Kameenui, 1997) and because diverse students require attention to fluency to reach high levels of reading achievement (Chard, Simmons, & Kameenui, 1998). One commonly recommended approach is the *one-minute read*, in which students' oral reading accuracy is evaluated during one minute of reading. Students read unfamiliar text, and the number of words read correctly per minute is computed. Of course, many educators are concerned about these procedures because they seem open to questions of reliability. The primary concern about such measures (sometimes called curriculum-based measurements) is that proponents suggest that this measure alone can be used to evaluate students' reading achievement. Although critically important, students' rate of accurate reading is only one aspect of mature reading.

Other issues that should be addressed in using a one-minute read include the level of text difficulty (generally *grade*-level text is used, regardless of the reading level of the student) and questions of interpreting results. Although a number of rates have been suggested, none is sufficiently well developed to advocate as the benchmark for fluent reading, and most are very similar to the rate ranges in Figure 9.6. We suggest using those rates as a guideline for collecting data on students over time using multiple passages so that your estimates will have greater reliability.

In addition, most experts consider fluency to be more than just accuracy and rate. Oral fluency also involves readers' ability to group words into meaningful phrase units. Smoothness and the maintenance of comprehension are important as well (Harris & Hodges, 1995). "Fluent readers can read text with speed, accuracy, and proper expression" (National Reading Panel, 2000, p. 3-1).

An assessment procedure used by the National Assessment of Educational Progress (NAEP) evaluates fluency by providing an estimate of whether or not a student consistently reads sentences predominantly word by word, in two-word groups with occasional word-by-word reading, in phrase groups with some two- or three-word groups, or in phrase groups.

***Selecting Materials.***    Research with good and poor readers in grades 1 through 6, using a procedure similar to the one described here, suggests that word grouping strategies change as a function of the difficulty of the material, reading ability, and years of exposure to reading and reading instruction (see Aulls, 1982). Most good readers in grades 5 and 6 read consistently in phrase groups when reading instructional level and even frustration level material. However, good readers in grades 1 through 4 typically read material at the independent level with better word grouping strategies than they do material at the instructional or frustration level. What appears to be unique about poor readers at any grade level is that they group words in material at the independent and at the instructional level in the same fashion.

We recommend using material at the student's instructional level, since most instruction is carried out at the instructional level, and because poor readers perform similarly at all levels, instructional level materials seem acceptable. The materials should be no less than 250 words in length. The longer the text, the better the estimate. Texts of 500–1,000 words are equally appropriate and have the advantage of offering a highly confident estimate of the student's ability to consistently organize words into groups when reading texts of similar readability and text organization or type.

***Scoring.*** It is difficult to do a holistic scoring of fluency as you listen to students read. We recommend taping the oral reading sample that will be used for scoring. The Oral Reading Fluency Scale used by NAEP (Pinnell et al., 1995) is described in Figure 9.12. As the teacher listens to the oral reading sample, there are several key elements to consider. The first is *phrasing*. Phrasing patterns result from pitch sequences and pauses during oral reading. For the examiner, pauses provide the primary signal of the division of words into groups. Pitch provides a secondary signal of the meaning assigned to each group. Teachers who are assigning levels to fluency should also attend to how closely the reader *follows the author's syntax and/or sentence structure*. Stress placements and intonation can provide clues to guide the scoring. In addition, readers often insert pauses to signal meaning implied by the author. Finally, the fluency rating should consider the reader's *expressiveness* during reading. However, the degree of expressiveness expected will vary according to age and/or grade of the reader. Only in the later elementary grades would we expect students to exhibit consistently good expressiveness during oral reading.

If a student rereads a phrase or sentence, the word grouping used in the first reading is scored. This provides the best estimate of how the student typically and spontaneously performs. Students can and do self-correct word groupings, but the intent is to characterize their spontaneous patterns for organizing text information fluently, not their self-corrections of disfluent reading.

To determine the fluency rating, you might wish to mark the phrase boundaries as students read. The samples listed at the top of page 348 characterize different students' ability to organize words into groups:

**FIGURE 9.12**
NAEP Fluency
Scale Levels

| NAEP's Integrated Reading Performance Record Oral Reading Fluency Scale |
| --- |
| **Level 4—** Reads primarily in larger, meaningful phrase groups. Although some regressions, repetitions, and deviations from text may be present, these do not appear to detract from the overall structure of the story. Preservation of the author's syntax is consistent. Some or most of the story is read with expressive interpretation. |
| **Level 3—** Reads primarily in three- or four-word phrase groups. Some smaller groupings may be present. However, the majority of phrasing seems appropriate and preserves the syntax of the author. Little or no interpretation is present. |
| **Level 2—** Reads primarily in two-word phrases with some three- or four-word groupings. Some word-by-word reading may be present. Word groupings may seem awkward and unrelated to larger context of sentence or passage. |
| **Level 1—** Reads primarily word-by-word. Occasional two-word or three-word phrases may occur—but these are infrequent and/or they do not preserve meaningful syntax. |

*Source:* Pinnel et al. (January, 1995). *Listening to children read aloud.* OERIA U.S. Dept. of Education, "Nation's Report Card." Report #23-FR-04. Washington, D.C.

1. Word-by-word: *The/brown/pony/galloped/toward/the fence. /It/was* . . .
2. Beyond word-by-word reading, but not consistently in phrases: *The brown pony/ galloped/toward/the fence. /It was/*. . .
3. Consistently in phrases: *The brown pony/galloped toward the fence./ It was/*. . .

In the first example all words except two were read word by word. The words *the fence* were organized into a two-word group. Because the majority of words were read word by word, the student must be considered to be a word-by-word reader. In the second example only two of seven words in the sentence were read word by word, and other words were grouped in two-word groups. In the third example the entire text was read in phrase groups. Even if *galloped* had been read as part of the first word group (*The brown pony galloped/toward the fence*), it would still be an acceptable phrase group. The exact phrase grouping is not as important as the preservation of sensible word groupings.

To obtain an overall estimate of a student's word grouping during reading, the examiner considers the fluency across sentences, and assigns a holistic score that captures reading of this student. A sample of Marvin's fluency rating using this scoring procedure is provided in Figure 9.13. Marvin does read some small portions of the passage fluently (sentences 6 and 12, for example). Overall, however, two-word phrasings were Marvin's most consistent pattern of grouping words. He is beyond word-by-word reading the majority of the time, is able to read some sentences in complete phrases, but is not consistent in doing so. In addition, his phrasing is not fluent, and he has not maintained the author's syntax or sentence structure. Finally, Marvin reads in a monotone, with little expression to signal his understanding. We would place Marvin at a fluency level of 2.

**FIGURE 9.13**
Sample Fluency
Rating: Marvin

---

**Introductory Statement**

"Joe wanted more than anything in the world to buy the electric train set in the trading post window. But should he do this? Please read the following story."

---

1. Joe sat down/ on the sidewalk in front of/ the/ trading post with his/ buckskin jacket/ thrown over his shoulder.
2. He/ felt worried/because/ it was difficult/ to know/ what to do.
3. "Grandfather told me/ never to/ sell/ these blue/ beads.
4. He/ said they would/ bring me/ good furtune and/ good health.
5. Grandfather is/ a wise/ and understanding man.
6. He is proud/ to be an American Indian.
7. He remembers/ when his grandfather/ gave/ him these/ same beads.
8. He/ has often told/ me/ many interesting stories/ of/ how his grandfather rode/ horses/ and hunted buffalo/ on the plains."
9. Joe/ held the/ string of/ beads/ high into the air/ toward the/ sunlight.
10. "These/ are perfectly beautiful/ beads,"/ he said/ out loud.
11. "I can't sell them/ because/ I too am proud/ of/ my great past.
12. Yes,/ I will keep the beads."

---

*Source:* From "Introductory Statement" in *Analytic Reading Inventory* by Mary Lynn Woods and Alden J. Moe, 1985, Grade 3. Reprinted by permission of Pearson Education, Inc., Upper Saddle River, NJ.

*Interpreting the Score.*   Aulls (1982) suggests that students at different levels of fluency are characteristically different from one another. For example, he notes that all readers whose scores are not completely fluent (level 4) represent students who are acquiring word grouping strategies. A major distinction probably exists between levels 2 and 3. At levels 3 and 4 students seem to be able to give much more attention to the development of the more advanced strategies for processing sentence meaning (Aulls, 1982).

Students at level 1 need to become more fluent before moving on. They might need to be provided with easier materials until they have learned to group words better. Those students at level 2 will be much more likely to be ready to refine the less complex sentence processing strategies involved in confirming word identification cues or integrating them. Once the student has attained a score at level 3, the teacher should begin stressing the development of more sophisticated sentence-processing strategies.

It appears that Marvin is just on the verge of becoming a fluent reader. His ratings here are encouraging, given the large numbers of miscues present in his readings. This score sheds light on his performance because it suggests greater fluency (and potential comprehension) than a simple miscue analysis would suggest. However, Marvin is in fifth grade, and the passage described is a third-level selection from an IRI. His plight highlights the caution noted by Aulls (1982, pp. 622–623):

> When a poor reader is an older, intermediate grade pupil who cannot read material beyond third-grade difficulty at the independent level, it is very likely that all or part of the reading problem is inability to read words in phrase groups and/or inadequately developed strategies, or the lack of use of them, for processing sentence meaning. A teacher who cannot or does not assess the sentence processing strategies of poor readers may incorrectly conclude that teaching word identification cues will be sufficient to enable a poor reader to become a fluent reader.

## Tests of Word Recognition, Phonics, and Spelling

Word-level difficulties are very common among poor readers and writers. Indeed, most students who are identified as having reading or writing difficulties will have some weaknesses in the area of decoding, word identification, and/or spelling. Classroom teachers generally observe and assess students' performance informally and then bring their concerns to a staffing meeting or make a formal request for further evaluation. There are a number of structured, but still informal, evaluation tools that can be used to assess word-level skills and strategies. In general, information is needed regarding three areas of word-level performance: *sight word recognition, word analysis,* and *spelling.* The limitations of most structured word recognition tests is that they do not involve reading words in connected text. The results from these tests must, of course, be considered against information about students' word recognition performance during reading (see the discussions of running records and miscue analysis). Similarly, although spelling tests can and do provide important information, students' spelling should be examined during writing.

*Word Lists.*   As we have already noted, it is generally wise to evaluate component skills in use, rather than in isolation. Clearly, using a word list to test word recognition skills is a

**FIGURE 9.14**
The Fry Instant
Word List

| First Hundred Instant Words | | | | Second Hundred | |
|---|---|---|---|---|---|
| First 25 Group 1a | Second 25 Group 1b | Third 25 Group 1c | Fourth 25 Group 1d | First 25 Group 2a | Second 25 Group 2b |
| the | or | will | number | new | great |
| of | one | up | no | sound | where |
| and | had | other | way | take | help |
| a | by | about | could | only | through |
| to | word | out | people | little | much |
| in | but | many | my | work | before |
| is | not | then | than | know | line |
| you | what | them | first | place | right |
| that | all | these | water | year | too |
| it | were | so | been | live | mean |
| he | we | some | call | me | old |
| was | when | her | who | back | any |
| for | your | would | oil | give | same |
| on | can | make | now | most | tell |
| are | said | like | find | very | boy |
| as | there | him | long | after | follow |
| with | use | into | down | thing | came |
| his | an | time | day | our | want |
| they | each | has | did | just | show |
| I | which | look | get | name | also |
| at | she | two | come | good | around |
| be | do | more | made | sentence | form |
| this | how | write | may | man | three |
| have | their | go | part | think | small |
| from | if | see | over | say | set |
| Common suffixes: *s, ing, ed* | | | | Common suffixes: *s, ing,* | |

*Source:* Fry, Edward B. (1980, December). The new instant word list. *The Reading Teacher, 34* (3), 284–289. Reprinted with permission of the International Reading Association. All rights reserved.

very constraining procedure. However, one attribute of skilled reading is *automaticity* in word recognition. Good readers are able to recognize large numbers of words rapidly. Allington and McGill-Franzen (1980) found that the scores generated by isolated word recognition tests were markedly different from those generated by in-context word recognition tests. The scores were especially divergent for less-able readers. It appears that context does facilitate word recognition, but it is used more heavily by poor readers than by able ones. Thus students' ability to recognize high-frequency sight words should be evaluated both in isolation and in context.

There are many lists of high-frequency sight words. One of the most widely used is the *Dolch Basic Sight Word Test* (Dolch, 1942a). This test consists of 220 high-frequency

| Instant Words | | Third Hundred Instant Words | | | |
|---|---|---|---|---|---|
| Third 25 Group 2c | Fourth 25 Group 2d | First 25 Group 3a | Second 25 Group 3b | Third 25 Group 3c | Fourth 25 Group 3d |
| put | kind | every | left | until | idea |
| end | hand | near | don't | children | enough |
| does | picture | add | few | side | eat |
| another | again | food | while | feet | face |
| well | change | between | along | car | watch |
| large | off | own | might | mile | far |
| must | play | below | close | night | Indian |
| big | spell | country | something | walk | real |
| even | air | plant | seem | white | almost |
| such | away | last | next | sea | let |
| because | animal | school | hard | began | above |
| turn | house | father | open | grow | girl |
| here | point | keep | example | took | sometimes |
| why | page | tree | begin | river | mountain |
| ask | letter | never | life | four | cut |
| went | mother | start | always | carry | young |
| men | answer | city | those | state | talk |
| read | found | earth | both | once | soon |
| need | study | eye | paper | book | list |
| land | still | light | together | hear | song |
| different | learn | thought | got | stop | leave |
| home | should | head | group | without | family |
| us | America | under | often | second | body |
| move | world | story | run | late | music |
| try | high | saw | important | miss | color |
| *ed, er, ly, est* | | Common suffixes: *s, ing, ed, er, ly, est* | | | |

sight words, grouped into lists deemed appropriate from preprimer to third grade. The list has generated controversy, and many prefer to use one of the more recently created lists (for example, Fry, 1980; Johnson, 1971). The *New Instant Word List* (Fry, 1980) appears in Figure 9.14. Fry's analysis suggests that one-half of all written material comprises the first 100 of these instant words. The complete list of 300 instant words makes up 65 percent of all written material, and studies by a variety of researchers have confirmed the utility of various high-frequency core words (Durr, 1973).

Assessment of sight word skill is essential, since students will find fluent reading difficult if they do not master these words. Students can be expected, as a general rule, to have instant recognition of the entire list by the end of grade 3. Sight word lists are generally administered on flash cards. The cards are used to control the rate of presentation, so that students' instant recognition can be evaluated. Most specialists suggest presenting cards or words at a rate of one second per word. After the initial presentation is completed (or stopped due to frustration), the words that were missed can be presented again to assess students' word *analysis* abilities.

Most people suggest a criterion level of 90 percent or better for each list; however, Botel (1982) suggests a mastery level of 70 percent, arguing that because reading words in isolation is more difficult than reading words in context, the scoring procedure should be adjusted accordingly. In evaluating the student's responses to the word list task, the following questions should be considered:

- Does there appear to be any consistent pattern to the errors?
- Is the pattern of these errors comparable at each level, or does it change with increasing difficulty?
- Does the student substitute initial consonants? final consonants?
- Does the student attend to the medial portions of words?
- Does the student reverse letters or words?
- What is the student's overall level of mastery of high-frequency sight words in isolation?

Although some authors recommend equating the results from a sight word list with reading level ability, we caution against this practice. All that can reasonably be accomplished by administering a word list is an appraisal of the reader's instant recognition of words, without benefit of context. This can provide a quick, efficient clue as to the student's in-text reading and perhaps an idea of what may be impeding progress. Of course, it does not yield direct information about the student's word recognition during reading. Remember, children often misread different words in context and in isolation (Allington & McGill-Franzen, 1980).

An important next step, then, is to compare students' word recognition during reading to word recognition in isolation. Different patterns of response can be suggestive. For example, some children perform much better during reading than on isolated lists. This suggests good use of context and is frequently accompanied by better comprehension than word recognition. When there is a large discrepancy, it can be expected that students are actually *over*relying on context. The student may not have achieved automaticity in word recognition and reading may proceed very slowly.

Other children demonstrate exactly the opposite pattern. That is, they perform better on isolated word lists than they do in context. There may be several reasons for this, but often these students have too little experience with real reading. This limited reading experience often occurs in classrooms where students learn words in isolation (by completing workbook tasks, using flash cards, or playing games). Thus these students have competence in recognizing words (or analyzing them; see below) but have not learned to transfer this skill to reading continuous text.

Of course, students' sight recognition of other words can be assessed as well. For example, word lists can be prepared from the instructional materials used in classroom or clinic. Lists created from basal readers or required trade books can be helpful in evaluating readiness to read specific materials and/or in assessing progress. If students are participating in a literature-based reading program, it may be advisable to examine high-frequency words derived from the literature commonly used in such programs. To this end, Eeds (1985) has analyzed 400 books appropriate for grades K–3 and identified the high-frequency words in those books (see Figure 9.15). The 227 words listed account for 73 percent of all words in her sample of books. Specialists or other teachers who are assessing students who are learning to read in a literature-based classroom program should find this list more helpful in evaluating sight word knowledge. The booklist from which this list was generated appears in Chapter 13.

***Informal Tests of Phonics and Structural Analysis.*** Although we favor analyzing knowledge and application of phonics during reading of actual text, most diagnostic batteries include some form of isolated assessment of phonics skill. Teachers sometimes find it helpful to use these commercial materials as they build their own knowledge base and increase their ability to reliably identify important phonic elements that may be influencing students' reading. Once information has been gathered about the student's knowledge and skill in phonics, it will be important to generate record-keeping forms that summarize the patterns of strength and weakness that were observed (see Figure 9.16). These may also be used to aid analysis of writing samples, which can provide powerful information about phonics skill (see below).

Both informal and formal tests of phonic and structural analysis typically contain lists of nonsense words that embody one or more of the sound–symbol patterns. A sample test might look something like the following:

1. fload
2. zam
3. drowt
4. dispount
5. strabble
6. mait
7. glavorful
8. kneef
9. jarf
10. bluther

The advantage of nonsense words is that it is possible to evaluate students' knowledge and application of word analysis strategies as they are used with totally unfamiliar "words." The disadvantage of this practice is that reading nonsense words is a more difficult task than reading real words in context (Harris & Sipay, 1990).

Cunningham (1990) devised a test that is designed to take advantage of the nonsense word approach while tempering concerns about it. The Names Test (see Figure 9.17) comprises a list of names that are "fully decodable given commonly taught vowel rules and/or analogy approaches to decoding" (Cunningham, 1990, p. 125). Readers are told that they represent the names of students in a fictitious class and are asked to pretend to be the teachers and to "take attendance." Students' attempts are counted as correct if they correctly decode all of the syllables, regardless of the stress or accent. For example, both "West-MORE-land" and "West-more-LAND" would be scored as correct.

Although this test is an improvement over a list of nonsense words, these words still appear in isolation, and it will be necessary to contrast performance on this type of test with performance during reading. This is especially important because some children consistently

**FIGURE 9.15**
Bookwords High-
Frequency Sight
Words

### Final Core 227 Word List Based on 400 Storybooks for Beginning Readers

| word | count | word | count | word | count | word | count |
|---|---|---|---|---|---|---|---|
| the | 1334 | good | 90 | think | 47 | next | 28 |
| and | 985 | this | 90 | new | 46 | only | 28 |
| a | 831 | don't | 89 | know | 46 | am | 27 |
| I | 757 | little | 89 | help | 46 | began | 27 |
| to | 746 | if | 87 | grand | 46 | head | 27 |
| said | 688 | just | 87 | boy | 46 | keep | 27 |
| you | 638 | baby | 86 | take | 45 | teacher | 27 |
| he | 488 | way | 85 | eat | 44 | sure | 27 |
| it | 345 | there | 83 | body | 43 | says | 27 |
| in | 311 | every | 83 | school | 43 | ride | 27 |
| was | 294 | went | 82 | house | 42 | pet | 27 |
| she | 250 | farther | 80 | morning | 42 | hurry | 26 |
| for | 235 | had | 79 | yes | 41 | hand | 26 |
| that | 232 | see | 79 | after | 41 | hard | 26 |
| is | 230 | dog | 78 | never | 41 | push | 26 |
| his | 226 | home | 77 | or | 40 | out | 26 |
| but | 224 | down | 76 | self | 40 | their | 26 |
| they | 218 | got | 73 | try | 40 | watch | 26 |
| my | 214 | would | 73 | has | 38 | because | 25 |
| of | 204 | time | 71 | always | 38 | door | 25 |
| on | 192 | love | 70 | over | 38 | us | 25 |
| me | 187 | walk | 70 | again | 37 | should | 25 |
| all | 179 | came | 69 | side | 37 | room | 25 |
| be | 176 | were | 68 | thank | 37 | pull | 25 |
| go | 171 | ask | 67 | why | 37 | great | 24 |
| can | 162 | back | 67 | who | 36 | gave | 24 |
| with | 158 | now | 66 | saw | 36 | does | 24 |
| one | 157 | friend | 65 | mom | 35 | car | 24 |
| her | 156 | cry | 64 | kid | 35 | ball | 24 |
| what | 152 | oh | 64 | give | 35 | sat | 24 |
| we | 151 | Mr. | 63 | around | 34 | stay | 24 |
| him | 144 | bed | 63 | by | 34 | each | 23 |
| no | 143 | an | 62 | Mrs. | 34 | ever | 23 |
| so | 141 | every | 62 | off | 33 | until | 23 |
| out | 140 | where | 60 | sister | 33 | shout | 23 |
| up | 137 | play | 59 | find | 32 | mama | 22 |
| are | 133 | let | 59 | fun | 32 | use | 22 |
| will | 127 | long | 58 | more | 32 | turn | 22 |
| look | 126 | here | 58 | while | 32 | thought | 22 |
| some | 123 | how | 57 | tell | 32 | papa | 22 |
| day | 123 | make | 57 | sleep | 32 | lot | 21 |
| at | 122 | big | 56 | made | 31 | blue | 21 |
| have | 121 | from | 55 | first | 31 | bath | 21 |
| your | 121 | put | 55 | say | 31 | mean | 21 |
| mother | 119 | read | 55 | took | 31 | sit | 21 |
| come | 118 | them | 55 | dad | 30 | together | 21 |
| not | 115 | as | 54 | found | 30 | best | 20 |
| like | 112 | Miss | 53 | lady | 30 | brother | 20 |
| then | 108 | any | 52 | soon | 30 | feel | 20 |
| get | 103 | right | 52 | ran | 30 | floor | 20 |
| when | 101 | nice | 50 | dear | 29 | wait | 20 |
| thing | 100 | other | 50 | man | 29 | tomorrow | 20 |
| do | 99 | well | 48 | better | 29 | surprise | 20 |
| too | 91 | old | 48 | through | 29 | shop | 20 |
| want | 91 | night | 48 | stop | 29 | run | 20 |
| did | 91 | may | 48 | still | 29 | own | 20 |
| could | 90 | about | 47 | fast | 28 | | |

*Source:* Eeds, Maryann. (1985, January). Bookwords: Using a beginning word list of high-frequency words from children's literature K–3. *The Reading Teacher, 38* (4), 418–423. Reprinted with permission of the International Reading Association. All rights reserved.

**FIGURE 9.16**
Summary Chart of
Phonic and
Structural Analysis

| **Directions:** As the child reads note how frequently she or he: | | | |
|---|---|---|---|
| | **Always** | **Sometimes** | **Never** |
| Recognizes major sounds of consonants | ☐ | ☐ | ☐ |
| Uses onsets and rimes (analogies) | ☐ | ☐ | ☐ |
| Uses major CVC vowel patterns | ☐ | ☐ | ☐ |
| Recognizes consonant influenced pattern | ☐ | ☐ | ☐ |
| Uses major CVVC clusters | ☐ | ☐ | ☐ |
| Uses other patterns (clusters/phonograms) | ☐ | ☐ | ☐ |
| Uses major syllable patterns | ☐ | ☐ | ☐ |
| Uses morphemic analysis | ☐ | ☐ | ☐ |
| Uses a combination of context/decoding | ☐ | ☐ | ☐ |

attempt to make real words from nonsense words. Their attempts to make meaning override the visual display. Consequently, they may appear to have limited sound–symbol knowledge when, in fact, they regularly employ word analysis strategies during reading, in combination with their meaning-seeking strategies.

## Spelling Inventories

Virtually all experts in the area of English language arts agree that teachers should evaluate students' level of spelling and target instruction appropriately. To do that, of course, we need tools to help us. More important, we need to be clear about what content to teach. We discuss spelling instruction later in the text (see Chapter 13). For assessment purposes there are basically three sources of words to use in evaluation. Earlier educators advocated teaching students, through rote memorization, the most frequent words in the language (Dolch, 1942b).

Although it is important for students to learn to spell these words, they don't really provide useful information about students' overall spelling development. Consequently, some authors suggest using any one of the available graded spelling lists from a commercial program to determine grade level performance. Structured spelling tests are then created by selecting a sample of perhaps twenty-five words from each level. The word lists are administered to determine the level of difficulty at which students should be receiving instruction.

A different approach was suggested by Henderson (1992). He created a listing of words that reflected the recurrent spelling patterns of the English language. Building on this work, both Henderson, and later Templeton (1995) argue that spelling knowledge proceeds through several developmental stages, and effective assessment should be focused on determining which of these stages represents a student's present level of knowledge. We discussed the earliest of these stages in Chapter 7. However, many students have difficulty in the next phases, which Templeton calls "syllable juncture" and "derivational constancy" (see Chapter 13 for additional discussion). In the syllable juncture phase, children make errors at the juncture of syllables (for example, *hury* for *hurry* or *capcur* for *capture*). Some of the spelling errors of students in the syllable juncture phase may include syllable junctures involving

**FIGURE 9.17**   The Names Test

| The Names Test | | | |
|---|---|---|---|
| Jay Conway | Gus Quincy | Wendy Swain | Ned Westmoreland |
| Tim Cornell | Cindy Sampson | Glen Spencer | Ron Smitherman |
| Chuck Hoke | Chester Wright | Fred Sherwood | Troy Whitlock |
| Yolanda Clark | Ginger Yale | Flo Thornton | Vance Middleton |
| Kimberly Blake | Patrick Tweed | Dee Skidmore | Zane Anderson |
| Roberta Slade | Stanley Shaw | Grace Brewster | Bernard Pendergraph |
| Homer Preston | | | |

**Procedures for Administering and Scoring the Names Test**

*Preparing the Instrument*
1. Type or print legibly the 25 names on a sheet of paper or card stock. Make sure the print size is appropriate for the age or grade level of the students being tested.
2. For students who might perceive reading an entire list of names as being too formidable, type or print the names on index cards, so they can be read individually.
3. Prepare a protocol (scoring) sheet. Do this by typing the list of names in a column and following each name with a blank line to be used for recording a student's responses.

*Administering the Names Test*
1. Administer the Names Test individually. Select a quiet, distraction-free location.
2. Explain to the student that she or he is to pretend to be a teacher who must read a list of names of students in the class. Direct the student to read the names as if taking attendance.
3. Have the student read the entire list. Inform the student that you will not be able to help with difficult names, and encourage him or her to "make a guess if you are not sure." This way you will have sufficient responses for analysis.
4. Write a check on the protocol sheet for each name read correctly. Write phonetic spellings for names that are mispronounced.

*Scoring and Interpreting the Names Test*
1. Count a word correct if all syllables are pronounced correctly regardless of where the student places the accent. For example, either Yŏ/lan/da or Yo/lan'/da would be acceptable.
2. For words where the vowel pronunciation depends on which syllable the consonant is placed with, count them correct for either pronunciation. For example, either Ho/mer or Hom/er would be acceptable.
3. Count the number of names read correctly, and analyze those mispronounced, looking for patterns indicative of decoding strengths and weaknesses.

*Source:*  Chart from Cunningham, Patricia M. (p. 127, 1990, October). The Names Test: A quick assessment of decoding ability. *The Reading Teacher, 44* (2), 124–129. Copyright © International Reading Association. Reprinted with permission. All rights reserved.

simple affixes, such as -ing or -less. Students in the derivational constancy phase, however, understand these aspects of spelling and instead make errors involving more advanced morphological processes, often including changes in pronunciation or involving an embedded base word (e.g., *compisition* for *composition*).

Templeton (1995) describes a structured inventory for evaluating students' stage-level knowledge of spelling. The Qualitative Inventory of Spelling Knowledge (see Figure 9.18) is designed for individual administration. Students are asked to spell words as best they can. If a student spells the first ten words on a list correctly, testing moves to the next level.

**FIGURE 9.18**
Qualitative
Inventory of
Spelling Knowledge

| Level I | Level II | Level III | Level IV | Level V | Level VI |
|---------|----------|-----------|----------|---------|----------|
| bump | batted | find | square | enclosed | absence |
| not | such | paint | hockey | piece | civilize |
| with | once | crawl | helmet | novel | accomplish |
| trap | shop | dollar | allow | lecture | prohibition |
| chin | milk | knife | skipping | pillar | pledge |
| bell | funny | mouth | ugly | confession | sensibility |
| shade | start | fought | hurry | aware | official |
| pig | glasses | comb | bounce | loneliest | inspire |
| drum | hugging | useful | lodge | service | permission |
| hid | named | circle | fossil | loyal | irrelevant |
| father | pool | early | traced | expansion | conclusion |
| track | stick | letter | lumber | production | invisible |
| pink | when | weigh | middle | deposited | democratic |
| drip | easy | real | striped | revenge | responsible |
| brave | make | tight | bacon | awaiting | accidental |
| job | went | sock | capture | unskilled | composition |
| sister | shell | voice | damage | installment | relying |
| slide | pinned | campfire | nickel | horrible | changeable |
| box | class | keeper | barber | relate | amusement |
| white | boat | throat | curve | earl | conference |
| | story | waving | statement | uniform | advertise |
| | plain | carried | collar | rifle | opposition |
| | smoke | scratch | parading | correction | community |
| | size | tripping | sailor | discovering | advantage |
| | sleep | nurse | wrinkle | retirement | cooperation |
| | | | dinner | salute | spacious |
| | | | medal | treasure | carriage |
| | | | tanner | homemade | presumption |
| | | | dimmed | conviction | appearance |
| | | | careful | creature | description |

*Source:* From *How to become a better reading teacher: Strategies for assessment and intervention* by Lillian R.
Putnam. Copyright © 1996 by Prentice-Hall. Reprinted by permission of Pearson Education, Inc., Upper Saddle
River, NJ.

Teachers are advised to stop testing when a student misspells more than 60 percent of the
words on a list. Templeton (1995, p. 322) suggests interpreting results about levels using the
following guidelines:

- Independent Level: Over 90 percent of the words are spelled correctly
- Instructional Level: Between 40 percent and 90 percent of the words are spelled
  correctly
- Frustrational Level: Fewer than 40 percent of the words are spelled correctly.

Of course, teachers can do a more qualitative analysis of the spelling errors to determine
which aspects of spelling are controlled by the student and which are still problematic (see
Figure 9.19).

**FIGURE 9.19**   Qualitative Spelling Checklist

---

Student _____     Observer _____

Use this checklist to help you find what stages of spelling development your students are in. There are three gradations within each stage—early, middle, and late. The words in parentheses refer to spelling words on the first Qualitative Spelling Inventory.

This form can be used to follow students' progress. Check when certain features are observed in students' spelling. When a feature is always present check "Yes." The last place where you check "Often" corresponds to the student's stage of spelling development.

Date: _____  _____  _____

### Emergent Stage
*Early*
- Does the child scribble on the page?                                   ☐ Yes   ☐ Often   ☐ No
- Do the scribbles follow the conventional direction? (*left to right in English*)   ☐ Yes   ☐ Often   ☐ No

*Middle*
- Are there letters and numbers used in pretend writing? (*4BT for ship*)   ☐ Yes   ☐ Often   ☐ No

*Late*
- Are key sounds used in syllabic writing? (*P for ship*)                ☐ Yes   ☐ Often   ☐ No

### Letter Name—Alphabetic
*Early*
- Are beginning consonants included? (*B for bed, S for ship*)           ☐ Yes   ☐ Often   ☐ No
- Is there a vowel in each word?                                         ☐ Yes   ☐ Often   ☐ No

*Middle*
- Are some consonant blends and digraphs spelled correctly? (*ship, when, float*)   ☐ Yes   ☐ Often   ☐ No

*Late*
- Are short vowels spelled correctly? (*bed, ship, when, lump*)          ☐ Yes   ☐ Often   ☐ No
- Is the *m* included in front of other consonants? (*lump*)            ☐ Yes   ☐ Often   ☐ No

### Within Word Pattern
*Early*
- Are long vowels in single-syllable words "used but confused"? (FLOAT for *float*, TRANE for *train*)   ☐ Yes   ☐ Often   ☐ No

*Middle*
- Are most long vowels in single-syllable words spelled correctly but some long vowel spelling and other vowel patterns "used but confused"? (SPOLE for *spoil*)   ☐ Yes   ☐ Often   ☐ No
- Are most consonant blends and digraphs spelled correctly?             ☐ Yes   ☐ Often   ☐ No
- Are most other vowel patterns spelled correctly? (*spoil, chewed, serving*)   ☐ Yes   ☐ Often   ☐ No

### Syllables and Affixes
*Early*
- Are inflectional endings added correctly to base vowel patterns with short vowel patterns? (*shopping, carries*)   ☐ Yes   ☐ Often   ☐ No
- Are consonant doublets spelled correctly? (*cattle, cellar*)          ☐ Yes   ☐ Often   ☐ No

**FIGURE 9.19**  (Continued)

| | | | |
|---|---|---|---|
| **Syllables and Affixes** (continued)<br>*Middle*<br>• Are inflectional endings added correctly to base words? (*chewed, marched, shower*) | ☐ Yes | ☐ Often | ☐ No |
| *Late*<br>• Are less frequent prefixes and suffixes spelled correctly? (*confident, favor, ripen, cellar, pleasure*) | ☐ Yes | ☐ Often | ☐ No |
| **Derivational Relations**<br>*Early*<br>• Are most polysyllabic words spelled correctly? (*fortunate, confident*) | ☐ Yes | ☐ Often | ☐ No |
| *Middle*<br>• Are unaccented vowels in derived words spelled correctly? (*confident, civilize, opposition*) | ☐ Yes | ☐ Often | ☐ No |
| *Late*<br>• Are words from derived forms spelled correctly? (*pleasure, civilize*) | ☐ Yes | ☐ Often | ☐ No |

*Source:*  From *Words Their Way,* 2nd edition, by D. R. Bear, M. Invernizzi, S. Templeton, and F. Johnston, p. 289. Copyright © 2000, 1996 by Prentice-Hall, Inc. Reprinted by permission of Pearson Education, Inc., Upper Saddle River, NJ.

The recent development of various inventories in recent years provides teachers with excellent new tools to evaluate and interpret students' spelling and phonics knowledge. Bear, Invernizzi, Templeton, and Johnston (2000), for example, provide several inventories in their excellent book *Words Their Way.* Different inventories focus specifically on early elementary grades, later elementary grades, upper-level spelling, and specialized vocabulary for content areas. Importantly, they provide examples of alternative spellings and detailed error analysis guides to aid in interpreting students' spelling productions.

## Evaluating Writing Samples

In today's classrooms children write more than they ever have, and teachers have more information available to them about how to evaluate students' writing. The available options range from the very informal (see Chapter 8) to the very formal (see Chapter 10). Many norm-referenced tests of writing involve analytic evaluations of written products (see Chapter 10). Using an analytic approach, specific aspects of the writing press are judged: syntax, vocabulary, and so on. Holistic scoring of written products is quite common both in classroom assessment and in large-scale assessment (even statewide assessment of writing). Using a holistic scoring system, you arrive at a rating that represents a global judgment about the overall quality of the written product.

Ideally, evaluators first read a set of "anchor papers" to establish the criteria clearly. These compositions represent various points on the scale and increase the reliability of the evaluations considerably (Tompkins, 2000). It is essential that teachers have a clear sense of what constitutes a high-quality piece of writing if holistic scoring is to be useful. As Jenkins (1996, p. 23) so aptly notes, "when teachers are tossed into a sea of children's writing samples without a compass, they tend to bob aimless on the surface of children's work," often attending primarily to mechanics and little organization, genre attributes, or ability to communicate meaningfully.

These judgments must be guided by criteria, which are established before scoring begins. The tool that is used is called a *rubric*. According to Marzano and his colleagues, "a scoring rubric consists of a fixed scale and a list of characteristics describing performance for each of the points on the scale" (Marzano, Pickering, & McTighe, 1993, p. 29). Similarly, Garcia and Verville (1994, p. 238) describe a rubric as a "hierarchy of acceptable responses. It identifies the qualities one would expect to see in a response at several points along a scale."

Using these rubrics, general evaluations are made about the written work, typically using a three- or four-level scale (High, Middle, Low or 1–4, for example). An example of a rubric that is applied holistically to a specific type of writing is presented in Figure 9.20. Generally, these types of rubrics are task-specific. That is, the performance assessment, or genre of writing, is clearly specified and the attributes of excellent performance in that mode are identified. Other attributes are identified for other tasks. Of course, some guidelines may be used both holistically or analytically to judge writing samples (see Figure 9.21). As you can see, a composition is judged separately for narrative and exposition, whereas mechanical skills are judged together.

One of the advantages of rubrics and other similar assessment strategies is that they "promote learning by offering clear performance targets to students for agreed-upon standards (Marzano et al., 1993, p. 29). Students can use these or specially designed checklists to engage in more effective self-evaluation. Valencia and her colleagues (1998) provide persuasive evidence of the potential benefits of developing students' self-reflection and self-evaluation abilities. For example, students are more likely to take charge of their own learning when they participate in self-assessment activities. Not surprisingly, they are also more likely to take responsibility for it and to set reasonable goals for themselves, at least in part because they have a better understanding of reading and writing processes (see Valencia & Bradley, 1998). Teachers can convey to students important aspects of competent performance using well-defined self-assessments. Combs (1997) provides an example of an appropriate intermediate-grade rubric (see Figure 9.22). In this case the five criteria are listed, and levels of competence are defined for each one. Everyone is a winner in this situation. Assessment is proceeding with authentic tasks, and the assessment criteria provide useful instructional targets and a focus for learning. In addition, these rubrics provide the systematic structure that allows teachers across classrooms to discuss and evaluate students' work with a common vision and a uniform set of standards.

## A Classroom System: Benchmark Book Events

Despite the relatively informal nature of these tasks and despite the vastly improved nature of the texts and procedures among IRIs, many educators are still concerned that they represent a contrived set of materials and tasks that don't fully reflect the kinds of reading their students are doing. As a result some schools and school districts have begun to create their own assessment events, systematic assessment procedures to be carried out with real books using classroom-based techniques (Au, 1994; Bembridge, 1994; Valencia & Place, 1994).

What distinguishes these assessments from the strategies described in Chapter 8 is the extent to which procedures and policies are prescribed and the whole process made more

**FIGURE 9.20**
Sample Scoring
Rubric for Writing

| Writing to Inform | |
|---|---|
| 4 | These responses are well-developed and have provided more than enough information to inform the reader about the topic. The information is extended and expanded through specific details.<br>A. These responses contain numerous specific details that more than adequately explain the topic.<br>B. The organizational plan is established and consistently maintained.<br>C. The writer addresses the intended audience.<br>D. The writer fluently uses language choices to enhance the text in a manner consistent with the purpose. |
| 3 | These responses are adequately developed and have provided enough information to inform the reader about the topic. The information is presented clearly, and irrelevant information does not interfere with clarity.<br>A. These responses contain some specific details that adequately explain the topic, although some details may not contribute to the development of the explanation.<br>B. An organizational plan is established and generally maintained.<br>C. The writer addresses the intended audience.<br>D. The writer uses language choices to enhance the text in a manner consistent with the purpose. |
| 2 | These responses contain little development and have a minimal amount of information. The information included does not clearly explain the topic, and irrelevant information interferes with clarity.<br>A. These responses have details, but the details may be inaccurate or may not adequately explain the topic.<br>B. An organizational plan is established and minimally maintained.<br>C. The writer addresses the intended audience.<br>D. The writer seldom uses language choices to enhance the text in a manner consistent with the purpose. |
| 1 | These responses provide sufficient evidence that the writer saw the prompt and attempted to respond to it. The responses lack development and have little information. The information included may be vague or inaccurate.<br>A. These responses lack sufficient details to explain the topic.<br>B. An organizational plan, if established, is not maintained.<br>C. The writer may not address the intended audience.<br>D. The writer does not use language choices to enhance the text in a manner consistent with the purpose. |
| NSR | A. Blank<br>B. Off topic/off task<br>C. Unscorable |

*Source: Prince George's County Scoring Guide for Reading/Writing/Language Usage* (p. 54). Prepared by Rojulene Norris and Patricia Miller. Reprinted by permission of the authors.

**FIGURE 9.21**  Standards for Analytic Scoring: Narrative and Expository Writing

| Standards for Evaluating Composing Skills for Narrative Writing | | | |
|---|---|---|---|
| | **Low** | **Middle** | **High** |
| Story structure | No identifiable beginning, middle, or end. Story problem unclear. Action and characters not developed or related. Essential details missing or confusing. Story problem not solved, or resolution unrelated to events. | Beginning, middle, and end present, but not always identifiable. Story problem identifiable. Story problem presented, but not completely developed. Some conversational or descriptive details included. End may not show logical resolution of problem. | Identifiable beginning, middle, and end. Characters introduced and problem presented. Characters and problem well-developed with appropriate conversational or descriptive detail. Story ends with believable resolution of problem. |
| Story setting | Setting of the story not identifiable. Details inappropriate and confusing. | Time and place of story are hinted at. But uncertain. Further references to setting may be inconsistent with original time or place. | Time and place of story clearly set. Specific details related to setting given in appropriate context. Setting consistent throughout. |
| Story characters | Characters not believable. Details related to character development are inconsistent, inappropriate, or missing. Difficult to distinguish one character from another. Action of characters unrelated to problem. | Characters somewhat believable. Some descriptive or conversational details given. Details may not develop character personality. Action of characters not always related to problem. Major and minor characters not clearly discernable. | Characters believable. Descriptive or conversational detail develops character personally. Action of characters relates to problem. Major characters more fully developed than minor ones. |
| Story conversation | Conversation among characters haphazard, incomplete, or muddled. Much of the conversation inappropriate to circumstances and to personality of story characters. Conversation seems unrelated to story being told. | Conversation sometimes appropriate to circumstances and to characters. Conversation may reveal character personality or relationships among characters. Conversation sometimes not clearly related to story. | Conversation appropriate to story circumstances and to personality of each character. Conversation used to reveal character and develop interrelationships among characters. Conversation clearly relates to story. |
| Story idea | Story idea is trite or otherwise uninteresting. Story lacks plot or plot is vague. Story ends abruptly or reaches no definite conclusion. | Story idea is interesting. Idea may lack freshness or imaginativeness. Story has a plot. Plot may not be well-developed or entirely consistent. Story ending may not be satisfying or interesting. | Story idea is fresh or imaginative. Story plot is well-developed, is consistent, and comes to a satisfying, surprising, or otherwise highly effective ending. |

| Standards for Evaluating Composing Skills for Expository Writing | | | |
|---|---|---|---|
| | Low | Middle | High |
| Quality of ideas | Most ideas vague, incoherent, inaccurate, underdeveloped, or incomplete. Details often unrelated to topic. Nothing imaginative or thoughtful about the ideas. | Unevenness in completeness and development of ideas. Most ideas related to the topic; a few unrelated. Sound, but unimaginative ideas. | Ideas relevant to the topic, fully developed, rich in thought and imagination, and clearly presented. |
| Quality of organization | Introduction, development, and conclusion unclear. Emphasis of major and minor points indistinguishable. Sentences and paragraphs seldom related by transitions. Overall lack of coherence and forward movement. | Introduction, development, or conclusion not easily identified. Emphasis on major and minor points sometimes not well-balanced. Transitions between sentences and paragraphs used, but without consistency. Forward movement variable. | Introduction, development, and conclusion well-structured, complete, and easily identified. Emphasis of major and minor points well-balanced. Sentences and paragraphs clearly related by transitions. Logical forward movement. |
| Selection of words | Word selection inexact, immature, and limited. Figurative language seldom used. | Word selection usually suitable and accurate. Over-used words and clichés somewhat common. Figurative language may lack freshness, when used. | Facility and flair in word selection. Writer experiments with words in unusual and pleasing ways. Figurative language used, often in interesting and imaginative ways. |
| Structure of sentences | Not variety in sentence structure; often only simple sentences are used. Transitions limited to such words as **then**; conjunctions to **and**. Awkward and puzzling sentences common. Run-on sentences and fragments often appear. | Some variety in sentence length and structure. Transitions used when necessary. Few sentence constructions awkward and puzzling. Run-on sentences and sentence fragments appear, but do not predominate. | Sentence length and structure varied. Sentences consistently well-formed. Smooth flow from sentence to sentence. Run-on sentences and sentence fragments rarely appear. |
| Structure of paragraph | Topic sentences seldom used. Irrelevancies common. Order of details haphazard. Little or no command of the four common paragraph types. | Topic sentences usually stated. Irrelevancies uncommon. Order of details usually suitable. Limited ability to use the four common types of paragraphs. | Topic sentences stated and supported with relevant details. Appropriate variety used in ordering details (chronological, logical, spatial, climatic). Four types of paragraphs used when appropriate (narrative, explanatory, descriptive, persuasive). |

*(continued)*

**FIGURE 9.21** (Continued)

## Standards for Evaluating Mechanical Skills for Narrative or Expository Writing

| | Low | Middle | High |
|---|---|---|---|
| Grammar and usage | Frequent errors in the use of nouns, pronouns, modifiers, and verbs. | Grammatical conventions of inflections, functions, modifiers, nouns, pronouns, and verbs usually observed. Grammatical errors sometimes occur. | Grammatical conventions of inflections, functions, modifiers, nouns, pronouns, and verbs observed. Grammatical errors infrequent. |
| Punctuation | End punctuation often used incorrectly. Internal punctuation seldom used. Uncommon punctuation is almost never used correctly. | Sentences usually end with appropriate punctuation. Internal punctuation used, with occasional errors. Uncommon punctuation sometimes used, but often innaccurately. | Sentences consistently end with appropriate punctuation. Internal punctuation and other less common punctuation usually correctly used. |
| Capitalization | First word of sentence often not capitalized. Pronoun/often a small letter. Proper nouns seldom capitalized. Other capitalization rules usually ignored. | First word of sentences nearly always capitalized. I always capitalized. Well-known proper nouns usually capitalized. Other capitalization rules used, but not consistently. | First word of a sentence and the pronoun/always capitalized. Well-known proper nouns nearly always capitalized. Good command of other capitalization rules regarding titles, languages, religions, and so on. |
| Spelling | Frequent spelling errors. Shows a frustration spelling level (less than 70%). Unable to improve spelling accuracy in edited work without help. Misspellings often difficult to recognize as English words. | Majority of words spelled correctly. Shows an instructional spelling level (70 to 80%). Approaches 90% accuracy in edited work. Misspellings approximate correct spellings. | Nearly all words spelled correctly. Shows an independent spelling level (90%). Approaches 100% accuracy in edited work. Misspellings close to correct spellings. |
| Handwriting/ neatness | Handwriting difficult or impossible to read. Letters and words crowded. Formation of letters inconsistent. Writing often illegible. | Handwriting usually readable, but some words and letters difficult to recognize. Some crowding of letters and words. | Handwriting clear, neat, and consistent. Forms all letters legibly with consistent spacing between letters and words. |

*Source:* From *Language Structure and Use. Teacher's Edition 8* by Ronald L. Cramer et al. Copyright © 1981 Scott, Foresman and Company.

**FIGURE 9.22**
Rubric for
Evaluating
Writing Traits

## Evaluating the Traits of My Writing

### Ideas and Content

5 = I know a lot about my topic, my ideas are interesting, the main point of my paper is clear, and my topic is not too broad.

3 = The reader usually knows what I mean. Some parts will be better when I tell just a little more about what is important.

1 = When someone else reads my paper, it will be hard for them to understand what I mean or what it is all about.

### Organization

5 = My beginning gets the reader's attention and makes the reader want to find out what's coming next. Every detail adds a little more to the main idea. I ended at a good place and at just the right time.

3 = The details and order of my story/paper makes sense most of the time. I have a beginning but it may not really grab the reader. I have a conclusion but it seems to sum up my paper in a ho-hum way.

1 = The ideas and details in my paper are sort of jumbled and confused. I don't really have a beginning or an end.

### Voice

5 = My paper has lots of personality. It really sounds like me. People who know me will know it is my paper.

3 = Although readers will understand what I mean, they may not "feel" what I mean. My personality comes through sometimes. I probably need to know a little more about my topic to show, rather than tell, the reader about it.

1 = I can't really hear my voice in this paper. It was hard for me to write this paper. I really need to know much more about my topic or be more willing to take a risk about what I say.

### Use of Language

5 = The sentences in my paper are clear and sound good when read aloud. Words fit just right.

3 = Some of my sentences are choppy or awkward, but most are clear. Some words are very general, but most readers will figure out what I mean.

1 = Even when I read this paper, I have to go back, stop, and read over, just to figure out the sentences. A lot of my sentences seem to be the same. The words I chose don't seem to be very interesting.

### Use of Conventions

5 = There are very few errors in my paper; it wouldn't take long to get this ready to publish.

3 = My spelling is correct on simple words, most of my sentences begin with capital letters and end with the right punctuation.

1 = There are a lot of spelling and grammar errors in my paper. Punctuation and capital letters seem to be missing. My paragraphs are not indented.

*Source:* From *Developing Competent Readers and Writers in the Middle Grades* by Martha Combs, p. 237. Copyright © 1997. Reprinted by permission of Pearson Education, Inc., Upper Saddle River, NJ.

systematic. These events are intended to be used to inform instruction in the classroom but also to report results to audiences *outside* of the classroom. Teachers want to make sure they and their colleagues are evaluating students in a comparable way, using agreed-upon materials and assessment tools. In this section the system devised by one such school is described. Teachers there worked for two years to improve the consistency and trustworthiness of the information they pass along to colleagues and parents.

The teachers in the school determined early on in the process to use portfolios in their classroom. In Kyle's classroom the collections began in kindergarten, but by first grade all the teachers in the building had agreed to a set of core items that they would all document in the portfolios. After much discussion the teachers in this primary building determined that each teacher/child would collect writing samples three times a year, collect continuous information about independent reading using a book log, evaluate students' word recognition using the Bookwords list (see Figure 9.15), and document students' oral reading using running records (see Chapter 8) three times a year. Many other work samples were placed in the portfolios optionally.

Teachers felt strongly that they would like to have a means of evaluating students' growth in reading *in relation to* a set of increasingly difficult reading materials. These texts would provide benchmarks for estimating the appropriateness of students' progress as compared with students that age and might also serve as a means of identifying students who were in difficulty.

They began the process of identifying a set of benchmark books that could be used for examining accuracy (running records) and could also provide important information about students' comprehension abilities. The word *benchmark* was used to indicate designated points in reading development that are characterized by specific criteria and books and that are associated with increasing degrees of proficiency. A student's ability to read a particular benchmark book would provide information about his or her progress in reading and about developmental reading ability in terms of a series of stages.

Two primary concerns drove the identification of these materials. First, teachers wanted the books to reflect the authentic literacy abilities that children were acquiring in their classrooms. The basic materials for instruction in this building are trade books of children's literature. Therefore they wanted an assessment that relied on book reading.

A second concern was that the books represent an accurate estimate of increasing difficulty. The benchmarks needed to be trustworthy. Teachers spent a year establishing criteria and selecting books that exemplified those criteria (see Figure 9.23). They also created assessment items to accompany the books. The books were "protected" from circulation and instructional use and saved for assessment purposes.

New options are available today. First, you might refer to a credible leveling system and the lists of books provided (i.e., Fountas & Pinnell, 1996, 2001). For your benchmarking system you would choose specific books and then remove them from circulation so that they could be used for assessment purposes (see Chapter 6). Alternatively, you might use an IRI or a set of commercially leveled assessment materials such as the Developmental Reading Assessment (DRA).

The DRA is a set of level stories of graduated difficulty appropriate for use in kindergarten through grade 3. From level A, 1 through 20, the materials closely parallel the difficulty levels of the Reading Recovery Program. From level B, 24 to 40, the stories become

**FIGURE 9.23**
Benchmark Books:
Criteria and Samples

| Level | Descriptors | Example |
|-------|-------------|---------|
| A | Picture book with 1–3 words/page. Reptition of words and patterns. Picture clues drive recognition of unknown or unique content words. | *Baby Chimp* (R. Williams, The Wright Group, 1990) |
| B | Picture book with 4–25 words/page. High frequency Bookwords #1–60. Repetition of words, phrases, and events. Picture clues for unique words. Some phonically regular, decodable words. More difficult books may appear IF there's a familiar storyline (i.e., Little Red Hen). | *Good Morning Bears* (J. Hollands, Houghton Mifflin Read Alone, Lev. A, 1991) |
| C | Text-to-picture ratio changes (more text). Print is still enlarged. Average number of words/page variable but may go as high as 20–40. High frequency Bookwords #1–120. Less repetition and an increase in decodable words. Story structure with dialogue. | *Beef Stew* (Brenner, Random House, Step 1, STEP into Reading book, 1990). |
| D | Fully developed narrative stories and exposition. Smaller print size. All Bookwords (#1–227) may be used. Longer sentences (8–10 words/sentence). Books are longer and more dense, with 48–60 pages/book and 45–80 words/page. Pictures support comprehension vs. word ID. | *Molly and the Slow Teeth* (J. Cole, Houghton Mifflin, 1993). |
| E | Smaller print size, 90–120 words/page. Longer sentences in a longer book: 10–13 words/sentence and 20–40 pages/book. More complicated concepts and narratives. Developed dialogue, events, and characters. | *Christina Katarina and the Time She Quit the Family* (P. Gauch, Putnam, 1987). |
| F | This level builds on the others. Most distinctive feature: much longer and denser text, with more challenging vocabulary. Require that students have the "stamina" to stick with these longer, more complicated materials. | *The Knight at Dawn* (M. Osborn, First Stepping Stone Book, 1993). |

increasingly complex and much longer. Among the attractive features of this assessment system are the varying (and increasing) length of the texts, the fact that the assessment materials are designed as "little books" with full-color illustrations, and the fact that many (although not all) of the stories are engaging narratives much like those children would read in a literature-based program. We have done considerable research on these materials and have found the leveling system very reliable in terms of word recognition difficulty, though less so in terms of comprehensibility (see Lipson et al., 1999).

In either case, if these systems are to be used schoolwide or for some other systematic assessment purpose, teachers will need to engage in careful consideration of the assessment tasks that accompany the text. What criteria will be used to evaluate accuracy? How will

**FIGURE 9.24**
Kyle's Results on
Benchmark Book,
Level E

Kyle—Spring, Grade 2

*Christina Katarina,* by P. Gauch

This delightful story tells the tale of a strong-willed girl, Christina, who, having become fed-up with her family (younger brother bothering her, mom and dad yelling at her) decides to "quit the family." She changes her name to Agnes, and with the tacit approval of her mother, occupies half of the house. At first Agnes enjoys her new-found freedom, but she quickly finds that being on her own means that there is no one to help with chores and small disasters. She also finds that she misses her family. In the end, mom "convinces" her that the rest of the family really cannot get along without her and Christina returns to the family.

***Oral Reading Accuracy:*** 96% accuracy

***Comprehension:***

1. Would you like to read more stories about Christina? Is she anything like you? (personal response)
   Kyle: *No. I wouldn't want to quit the family. I wouldn't put things all over the place.*

2. Why did Christina quit her family? (text explicit)
   Kyle: *Because she didn't like how her mother nagged too much. Her brother followed her too much. She liked her dad, but he got angry at her too much.*

3. How could Christina quit the family and still stay in the house? (text implicit)
   Kyle: *She quit the family, not the house. Her mother wanted her to stay. They put places for her to be in the house and places for her not to be.*

4. Who is Agnes? (text implicit)
   Kyle: *Her, but she changed her name in the old part of the house.*

5. Name three things that Agnes did in the story. (text explicit)
   Kyle: *She marked her areas out. She started to get missing with her family. She ate underneath the table.*

6. Did she enjoy herself when she quit the family? (text explicit)
   Kyle: *In the beginning, yes. They didn't tell her what to do, she could do what she wanted.*

7. Was there any time in the story when being on her own was not a good idea? When? (text implicit)
   Kyle: *No, I guess not.*

8. What happens at the end of the story? (text implicit)
   Kyle: *She joined back the family because she missed getting helped tucked in.*

9. During the week that Christina quit the family, what did Christina learn? (theme)
   Kyle: *That you can't just do it all by yourself because you need other people.*

***Total Comprehension:*** 8/9 (89%)

comprehension be assessed? The DRA has always had well-articulated word recognition criteria, and it has recently added a helpful comprehension rubic to aid in evaluating students' retelling.

The benchmark books provide a structured assessment system that yields useful information about students. As we have seen, Kyle's progress was monitored during grade 2 by his teacher, who made regular notations of his progress using running records (see Chapter 8). In addition, however, she evaluated him three times using benchmark books. In November Kyle's word recognition accuracy on a level C book was 99 percent, so Ms. McIntyre had him read from a level D book, which yielded an accuracy score of 95 percent. Coupled with his good comprehension for the portion read, she judged this to be his instructional level. At the end of the year Kyle was evaluated on one of the challenging level E books. Figure 9.24 contains a summary of Kyle's oral reading and comprehension at that level. His total accuracy, 96 percent, makes this a comfortable instructional level for Kyle. He corrected two of six miscues, and two others were mispronunciations of proper nouns. In addition, his comprehension, as measured on the comprehension questions, was very strong, revealing his excellent verbal skills and response to literature.

The benchmark system demonstrates how the basic strategies and frameworks of IRIs, miscue analysis, and retellings can be applied to everyday materials to create a structured-assessment system for use at the school or district level.

## The Diagnostic Portfolio: Evidence from Structured Inventories

### Marvin

Marvin's performance on the informal reading inventory (Burns & Roe, 1985) suggested that his word recognition abilities were weak. Although he was a fifth grade student, the test yielded an instructional level at grade 2 and a frustrational level at grade 3 (see Chapter 11 for further details). The miscue analysis suggests some ability to self-correct and an inclination to attend to meaning. It also reveals an overreliance on graphophonic cues coupled with poor abilities in this area. Finally, Marvin's orthographic knowledge is very weak, resulting in limited sight word recognition.

The results also suggested that his comprehension is somewhat stronger than his word recognition, although that also was below grade level. He had a difficult time comprehending implicit main ideas and inferences in general, which posed particular problems. His ability to recall was less developed than his ability to answer questions. The analysis of his retelling indicated that he remembered less-important information than would be expected of a good reader, supporting the findings of retelling discussed in Chapter 8. His writing was meager, and he was reluctant to participate. Marvin is clearly struggling in many areas of literacy.

### Kyle

The new assessment system in Kyle's school generated good information. Benchmark book results during fall and early winter suggested that Kyle was still struggling. However, his

**FIGURE 9.25a**
Edited Writing:
Grade 2, Kyle

*Dear Animals of the Earth*

*Kyle*

May 10

Dear Animals of the Earth,

   I give you your mountains. I give you your habitats. I am
your mother. I am the earth. I am just as small as you are in
this big universe of planets and galaxies. The people are your
brothers and sisters even though they pollute my skies and
oceans. I am working on a letter to the humans to tell them
that you are their brothers and sisters and the beauty they
are destroying and soon, I will be so sick. I will die and there
will be no more earth.

                                        Love,
                                        Mother Earth

comprehension was often very good, and his word recognition abilities were growing. He
had not yet acquired the more complex consonant–vowel patterns of the language.

   Then, in late winter, Kyle began to show real progress. He had been reading vora-
ciously during the past two months and was now tackling much more difficult and lengthy
"chapter books" (*Ralph R. Mouse,* by Beverly Cleary). The end-of-the year benchmark book
assessment indicated that Kyle's word recognition accuracy was instructional for easy grade
3 material, that his ability to stay with a longer book had improved, and that his comprehension was flourishing with the more complicated ideas in these new books. The miscue
analysis conducted at that time clearly revealed a dramatically increased ability to self-
correct and an ability to read materials without benefit of picture cues. The only remaining
difficulties in word recognition involved longer, multisyllabic words. In short, Kyle's word
recognition abilities were reaching independence.

   The Bookwords Assessment revealed the same increasing abilities to recognize
high frequency words at sight. At the end of grade 2, Kyle missed only one word of 227
Bookwords.

**FIGURE 9.25b**
Self-Initiated
Writing:
Grade 2, Kyle

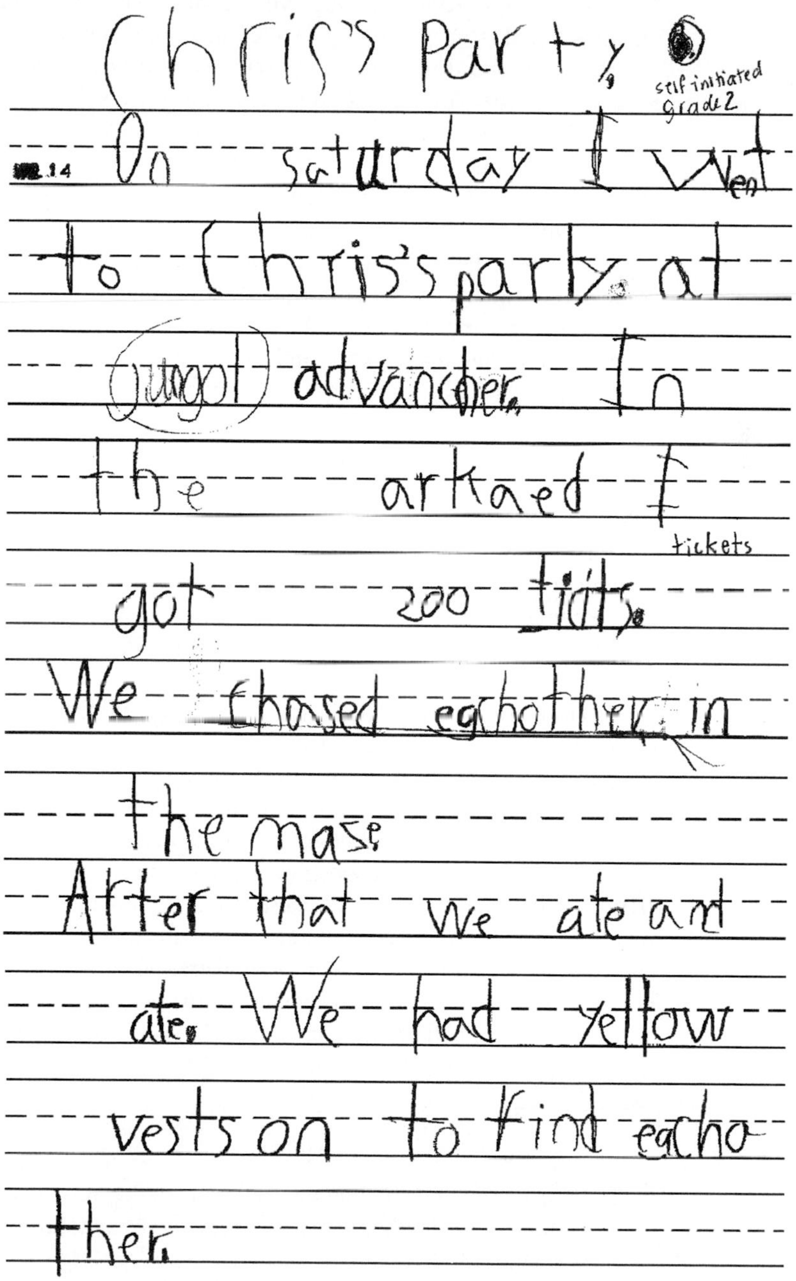

Chris's Party

On Saturday, I went to Chris's party at Jungle Adventure. In the arcade I got 200 tickets. We chased one another in the maze. After that we ate and ate. We had yellow vests on to find each other.

At this time Kyle's writing, while conceptually very interesting, had not yet reached the transitional stage of spelling development. In Kyle's diagnostic portfolio are two pieces of writing produced by Kyle in the same two-week period in May that show this clearly. Kyle's earth letter (Figure 9.25a) is the result of a conference and teacher-editorial support during the writing stage. It reflects his significant interest in nonfiction topics and his willingness to stick with difficult writing tasks. Kyle's self-initiated writing (see Figure 9.25b) reveals that he is still struggling with the mechanics of writing.

At the end of the year Kyle's teacher administered an IRI, required for all students (Spache, 1981). Both his word recognition accuracy and his comprehension were above grade level. Finally, Kyle's performance at the end of the university summer school clinic was evaluated using the QRI-3. These results clearly show that Kyle has become a strong and still improving reader who can handle material at and above his grade placements. His written language abilities are more problematic.

## Chapter Summary

An *Informal Reading Inventory* (IRI) was described as an individually administered informal reading test designed to place students in materials at the appropriate levels and to identify their strengths and weaknesses in the areas of word identification and comprehension. Traditionally, IRIs are used to identify students' independent, instructional, and frustration reading levels.

The components of an IRI include graded word lists, graded passages, comprehension questions, and separate materials for the student and the examiner. There are a variety of procedures that can be used for administering and scoring an IRI, and different procedures produce different test results. Similarly, the criteria used for interpreting students' placement levels can have a significant effect on the results of the IRI.

The first half of the chapter concludes with some guidelines for the traditional use of IRIs for placement purposes. These include looking for selections that correspond to regularly used instructional materials, evaluating the passage dependency of the comprehension questions, and determining administration and scoring procedures and placement criteria, together and within the context of the purpose for using the IRI.

The second half of the chapter describes additional tools and strategies, some of which may be used to adapt IRI administration. The techniques described in this section include the following:

1. Procedures for evaluating a reader's comprehension using retellings.
2. Procedures for analyzing readers' oral reading miscues to determine the language cue systems (i.e., graphophonic, syntactic, and semantic) they are using as they process a particular text.
3. A fluency scale designed to identify the extent to which a reader organizes the words in sentences in a manner that preserves the author's syntax and signals the relations among word meanings.
4. Informal but structured tools for evaluating sight word and phonics knowledge.
5. Procedures for using rubrics to evaluate student writing.

**6.** Strategies for using IRI-like procedures to create study inventories and for creating benchmark books to evaluate students' studying and also their word identification and comprehension skills.

IRIs and IRI-like procedures are potentially high-utility techniques for both classroom teachers and clinical personnel. For placement purposes it is important that anyone using IRIs understands the issues associated with the representativeness of the reading selections to the materials in which a student is being placed. Although some might argue that IRIs should not be used for placement purposes, in reality there is no one measure that can serve this purpose adequately. The key to successful placement, both in the classroom and in the clinic, is the use of multiple indicators of performance on materials comparable to those in which the student is to be placed.

For the purpose of evaluating reader strengths and weaknesses the issues of IRI usage differ somewhat between the classroom and the clinic. Classroom teachers obviously do not have the time to administer a traditional IRI individually to each student in their class. Even if they did, it is not clear that this would be entirely appropriate or necessary. However, using classroom materials and IRI-like techniques (as in benchmark books) can create the sort of structured assessment that can be useful to others.

In contrast to classroom teachers, specialists and clinical personnel often do not have the amount of regular contact with individual students necessary to successfully implement the classroom-based strategies described in Chapter 8. However, the interactive nature of the QRI-3 makes it an excellent alternative for clinicians and resource personnel. The QRI-3 also fits well with the purposes for which resource personnel are likely to find IRI-like procedures most useful. Whereas classroom teachers are likely to find procedures for ongoing assessment and instructional decision making most useful, clinical personnel and specialists are most likely to find these procedures useful for making programmatic curricular and instructional decisions for a given student.

Resource personnel must be particularly sensitive to the potential abuses of IRIs, given the limited amount of time that they are likely to come in contact with individual students. In particular, it may be difficult to predict a student's performance in the classroom from a small sample derived from administering just one IRI. However, in the hands of a skilled specialist, IRIs can provide a great deal of valuable information about the reader within a relatively short time period.

## ANNOTATED BIBLIOGRAPHY OF IRIs

Bader, L. A. (2002). *Bader reading and language inventory* (4th ed.). Upper Saddle River, NJ: Prentice Hall. Includes passages for grades K–12. In addition to traditional graded passages and word lists, there are tests of emergent reading, word identification and phonics, spelling, writing, and oral language. A checklist to assess English language development is a new feature.

Burns, P. C., & B. D. Roe (2002). *Informal reading inventory* (6th ed.). Boston: Houghton Mifflin. Grades 1–12. Two graded word lists and four sets of graded passages per grade level (preprimer–grade 12). Eight questions at preprimer to grade 2 levels and ten at the other grade levels.

Ekwall, E. E., & J. L. Shanker (2000). *Ekwall/Shanker reading inventory* (4th ed.). Boston: Allyn & Bacon. Grades 1–9. Each of four forms consists of eleven graded word lists (preprimer–grade 9). Five comprehension questions at the preprimer level and ten at the other grade levels. Also contains tests of letter knowledge, basic sight words, the San Diego Quick Assessment (graded word list) and the El Paso Phonics Survey, as well as tests of phonics and structural analysis in context.

Johns, J. J. (2000). *Basic reading inventory* (8th ed.). Dubuque, IA: Kendall/Hunt. Grades 1–8. Each of three forms consists of ten graded twenty-word lists (preprimer–grade 8). Four comprehension questions at preprimer level; ten at other grade levels.

Leslie, L., & Caldwell, J. (2001). *The qualitative reading inventory-3*. Boston: Allyn & Bacon. Reviewed extensively in this chapter.

Silvaroli, N. J., & Wheelock, W. H. (2001). *Classroom reading inventory* (9th ed.). Monterey, CA: McGraw-Hill. Grade 1–adult. There is a "subskills" format (Form A, levels PP–8) and a Literature format (Form B, levels 1–5) for elementary level passages. There are also separate forms (Subskills format, levels 1–8) for use with junior high and with high school students–adults. Five comprehension questions on all forms but the Literature format, which uses a retelling to evaluate comprehension. No guidelines are provided for using the retelling rubric.

Spache, G. D. (1981). *Diagnostic reading scales*. Monterey, CA: CTB/McGraw-Hill. Criterion and norm-referenced battery for Grades 1–7. Three word lists (forty to fifty words each), two sets of eleven graded passages (preprimer–grade 7) with seven to eight comprehension questions each. Twelve supplementary decoding tests yielding grade-equivalent scores.

Steiglitz, E. L. (1997). *The Steiglitz Informal Reading Inventory* (2nd ed.). Boston: Allyn & Bacon. Summarized in this chapter.

Woods, M. A., & Moe, A. J. (2003). *Analytical reading inventory* (7th ed.). Upper Saddle River, NJ: Prentice Hall. Grades 1–9. Each of three forms consists of seventeen graded twenty-word lists (primer–grade 6) and ten graded passages (primer–grade 9). Six comprehension questions for primer and grade 1; eight for the other grade levels. Two expository subtests consist of graded social studies and science passages. A separate booklet of reading passages enhances ease of administration, while an audio CD provides effective teacher support.

# 10 Formal Assessment

Formal assessment devices typically are published tests that provide standardized methods of administration, scoring, and interpretation and are often at the heart of the procedures used in traditional diagnoses of reading and writing problems. That these types of measures have not been considered until more than halfway through this text is intentional. The reason is simply that most formal tests do not reflect current definitions of reading and writing. Despite this fact, most professional educators are required to evaluate, use, and interpret both formal and informal assessment instruments. This chapter is intended to provide teachers and specialists with information about the properties of formal instruments that are important for intelligently evaluating the usefulness of available tests in light of their purposes for assessment.

The first half of the chapter describes the aspects of standardized testing that are essential for evaluating formal tests, including issues of type and purpose, important statistical concepts, validity, reliability, the characteristics of norming populations, test fairness, and the interpretation of test scores. The second half of this chapter provides detailed examples of formal reading and writing tests of different types, including survey, diagnostic, emergent literacy, and other areas related to reading and writing performance.

## Understanding Formal Assessment

In many districts, classroom teachers annually administer achievement batteries that survey several subject areas as a measure of student progress. When these tests are administered at the beginning of the year, they are often used to assist in placing students into groups or materials and to screen for referral to special programs. When they are administered at the end of the school year, they may be used for decisions about promotion and retention and about placing students in summer programs or fall classes. Many districts also involve kindergarten and first grade teachers in the administration of tests of readiness and emergent literacy for screening and program placement.

Teachers are also likely to encounter formal diagnostic and psychological tests when dealing with students who are participating in special programs, such as Title I (Chapter 1), or receiving special education services. Classroom teachers are unlikely to actually administer these tests, but they are likely to receive reports describing the results of the administration of these types of tests by the reading specialist, special education personnel, or school psychologist. Because the classroom teacher often spends considerably more time with these students than any specialist, the teacher shoulders a major portion of the responsibility for understanding the nature of these students' special needs and addressing them through classroom activities. This is why it is extremely important that classroom teachers are knowledgeable about the tests being administered to their students so that they can follow up the results with informal measures in the classroom that will lead to appropriate classroom practice.

Specialists are more likely to have direct contact with diagnostic tests and those focusing on other language arts and related areas than are classroom teachers. Resource personnel are most likely to use these tests to demonstrate program effectiveness with individual students, to identify specific strengths and weaknesses as an aid to program planning, and as an aid in the identification of students with special needs. Even when the limitations of formal tests in these areas are recognized, there is still a need for their administration because of legislative mandates and the need to have common measures that cut across schools, districts, and states. This makes it that much more important that the individuals who administer and interpret these tests have a clear understanding of what the tests can and cannot tell us.

## Concerns

Important information can be obtained from formal tests of reading, writing, and related areas. Many of the most serious problems with formal testing involve test abuse, that is, people using test information inappropriately. It is absolutely essential that both teachers and resource personnel be critical consumers of formal tests to ensure that they are used properly.

It is our belief that instructional decisions should never be made solely on the basis of formal assessment instruments. It is absolutely essential that formal tests be followed up with informal measures that are more reflective of classroom demands before decisions are made about placement or about instructional programs.

The public appetite for numerical answers to literacy questions has been fed by the educational community. Classroom teachers and clinic personnel are often caught in the middle, forced to teach content they do not believe is useful so that students can perform well on standardized tests. We need to help the public understand both the uses and limitations of test information. Educators need to be especially alert to the types of information that is *not* available from traditional standardized tests, especially information about students' abilities to read and write the different types of complex tests that are important in today's society.

Much of what we know to be important in reading and writing processes is not reflected in formal assessment devices. We know that reading and writing are holistic, constructive processes that vary as a function of the interaction among learner, text, and contextual factors (see Chapter 1). However, most existing formal instruments treat reading and writing as aggregates of isolated skills. As noted in *Becoming a Nation of Readers* (R. C. Anderson et al., 1985, p. 100):

> If schools are to be held accountable for performance for reading test scores, the tests must be broad-gauged measures that reflect the ultimate goals of instruction as closely as possible. Otherwise, the energies of teachers and students may be misdirected. They may concentrate

on peripheral skills that are easily tested and readily learned. Holding a reading teacher accountable for scores on a test of, say, dividing words into syllables is like holding a basketball coach accountable for the percentage of shots players make during the pre-game warm up.

Most existing formal reading and writing assessments also imply that reading and writing are static processes—that students can be evaluated under one set of conditions and this performance will be representative of their performance under all conditions. For example, formal tests evaluate students on passages that are much shorter than the ones students are expected to read in their classroom texts and on tasks that do not represent authentic writing activities. It is then assumed that the results will generalize to reading and writing both within and outside the classroom. These tests do not take into account differences in genre or the purposes for the reading and writing activities. Nor do they consider how students' reading and writing performance is affected by their background knowledge or their attitudes and motivation toward reading and writing. Teachers need to be aware of these limitations and take them into account in interpreting the results of these tests.

The widespread use of formal reading and writing tests makes it important to understand a number of different aspects of standardized testing in order to become a critical consumer of these types of assessment devices. The information in this section of the chapter provides the basis for guidelines for test evaluation that are discussed in the second section of the chapter.

## General Test Characteristics

Test selection and evaluation begin with an understanding of the purpose for which a test is being given. Information relative to a particular test must always be examined in relation to the purpose(s) for which it is being used.

The title, author, publisher, and date of publication reveal information about a test's quality and the appropriateness of its purpose and content for different students or testing situations. For example, a test with the word *survey* in the title suggests that the test will provide general information about a student's achievement rather than specific information about strengths and weaknesses. Similarly, the reputation of the test author and/or publisher in reading, writing, or testing may suggest something about both the content and quality of the test. A recent date of publication or revision increases the likelihood that the test reflects the most recent theory and research and that any norms used for scoring are current.

Other general characteristics of a formal test that are important for determining its appropriateness for specific students or testing situations include the level of difficulty and type of administration. Some tests are intended for a wide range of age, grade, and ability levels; others are intended only for restricted levels. Still others have different forms for different levels. Therefore it is important to determine that a test is appropriate for the age, grade, and ability of the student with whom it will be used.

The appropriateness of the test administration for specific students and purposes depends on factors such as whether the test is group or individually administered and whether it is timed or untimed. Group tests are efficient to administer but tend to provide more general information than individual tests and do not allow for the variety of response formats (e.g., oral reading, extended writing activities) that are allowed by individual tests. Individual tests require significantly more time to administer than group tests but tend to provide more specific information about the student. Timed or speed tests determine what a student can do under specified time constraints, whereas untimed or power tests evaluate a student's performance without any time constraints.

The two basic types of test interpretations that we discuss in this chapter are norm-referenced and criterion-referenced. Criterion-referenced interpretations are designed primarily to provide information that relates easily and meaningfully to specific objectives and specific standards of performance that are often determined independently of the measurement process. The emphasis is on describing the level of performance of individuals and groups on the behavior that a test is measuring.

Norm-referenced interpretations examine a given student's performance in relation to the performance of a representative group. The emphasis in norm-referenced testing is on the individual's relative standing rather than on absolute mastery of content (Salvia & Ysseldyke, 2001). Although the term *standardized* is often used synonymously with tests emphasizing norm-referenced interpretations, tests that emphasize criterion-referenced interpretations can be, and often are, standardized. *Standardized* means only that all students perform the same tasks under uniform directions (Swanson & Watson, 1989).

The difficulty of test items and the manner in which items are selected also differ between tests emphasizing norm-referenced and criterion-referenced interpretations. Test items that produce a wide range of scores and discriminate well between high-scoring and low-scoring individuals are desirable for norm-referenced interpretations that determine an individual's relative position in comparison to a group of his or her peers. Therefore the best norm-referenced items are those that 40–60 percent of the students answer correctly, because they produce the greatest variance in test scores. In well-constructed tests using norm-referenced interpretations, half of the population will score above the average, and half will fall below the average.

According to Swanson and Watson (1989), there is a shift in emphasis between criterion- and norm-referenced interpretations from items that best measure performance in a domain of knowledge to items that provide the greatest diversity in scores. They further note Popham's (1978) conclusion that the procedures used to construct tests emphasizing norm-referenced interpretations are likely to result in the exclusion of items that measure the major instructional emphases of the schools.

## Important Statistical Concepts

Tests use statistics to describe and summarize data. As a result, there are several statistical concepts that must be understood to evaluate the utility of formal tests for specific purposes. In this section we briefly summarize several major statistical concepts: normal distribution, measures of variation and centrality known as the standard deviation and the mean, and a measure of relatedness known as correlation.

*Normal Distribution.*    One way of summarizing test data is to describe the distribution of test scores. The two characteristics of a distribution that are most important for the interpretation of educational tests are the mean and the standard deviation. The mean is the arithmetic average of the scores and provides a central value or representative score to characterize the performance of the entire group. The standard deviation is a unit of measurement based on the degree to which the scores deviate from the mean. A large standard deviation indicates greater spread around the mean than a smaller one. Test scores can be referred to in terms of the number of standard deviations they are above (+) or below (–) the mean, depending on whether the score is greater than or less than the mean.

A normal distribution of the behaviors or psychological characteristics we are interested in observing means that scores are distributed symmetrically around the mean. The normal curve is symmetrical and bell-shaped and has many useful mathematical properties. One of the most useful for test interpretation is that when it is divided into standard deviation units, each unit under the curve contains a fixed percentage of cases (see Figure 10.1). This means that in any normal distribution,

- Approximately 68 percent of the population will be between +1 and –1 standard deviations from the mean;
- Approximately 95 percent of the population will fall between +2 and –2 standard deviations from the mean; and
- Approximately 99.7 percent of the population will fall between +3 and –3 standard deviations from the mean.

Raw scores from two different tests have been placed beneath the row marking the standard deviations in Figure 10.1 to illustrate how knowing the standard deviation and the mean contribute to the understanding of relative position within a group. Test 1 has a mean of 61 and a standard deviation of 4. Test 2 has a mean of 78 and a standard deviation of 7. Therefore a score of 65 is equivalent to +1 standard deviation on test 1 and a score of 85 is equivalent to +1 standard deviation on test 2. Knowing the mean and standard deviation permits us to convert raw scores to a common scale that has equal units and can be interpreted readily in terms of the normal curve.

**FIGURE 10.1**
Normal Distribution and Sample Test Scores

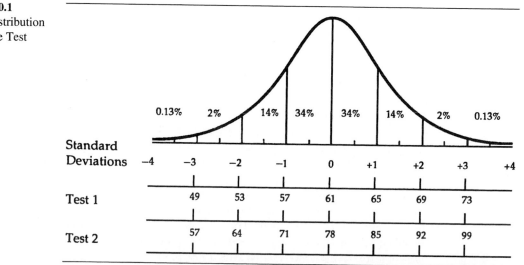

*Correlation.*    Another statistical concept that is important in the interpretation of test data is correlation. Whereas the mean and standard deviation describe a single distribution of scores, correlations describe the degree of association between two or more sets of scores. This measure is important in describing the relationship of test scores to other variables of interest and is critical to the evaluation of reliability and validity.

The strength of the correlation is expressed using a *correlation coefficient.* The values of correlation coefficients range from +1.00 to .00 to −1.00. A positive correlation (+) indicates that high scores on one variable are associated with high scores on the other variable. A negative correlation (−) indicates that high scores on one variable are associated with low scores on the other variable. A correlation coefficient of .00 between two variables means that there is no relationship between the variables; the variables are independent, and changes in one variable are not related to changes in the other variable. A correlation coefficient of either +1.00 or −1.00 indicates a perfect relationship between two variables (Salvia & Ysseldyke, 2001).

Measures of correlation provide useful information about the various components of tests and can also be used as an index of test validity and reliability (see below). However, educators must use correlational information sensibly, which means, in part, understanding that correlation is not the same as causation. Correlation is a necessary but insufficient condition for determining causality. The mere presence of a correlation between two variables does not imply that one causes the other. An extreme example of this principle is the likelihood that there is a positive correlation between the contents of a family's garbage can and their children's early reading success. It is well known that early success in reading is correlated with socioeconomic status, which will likely also result in differences in the contents of one's garbage can. However, this does not mean that a certain type of trash causes success or failure in reading.

Salvia and Ysseldyke (2001, p. 80) point out that "for any correlation between two variables (A and B), there are four possible interpretations." The relationship could occur by chance, a third variable could cause both A and B, A could cause B, or B could cause A. Correlational data do not tell us which of these four possible interpretations are true; therefore we must never draw causal conclusions from such data. So, for example, the simple fact that there is a positive correlation between reading achievement and factors such as balance-beam walking or alphabet knowledge does not, by itself, mean that these factors cause skilled reading.

## Validity

Validity is the most important concern in evaluating formal tests according to the 1985 and 1999 *Standards for Educational and Psychological Testing,* which were jointly prepared by the American Educational Research Association (AERA), the American Psychological Association (APA), and the National Council on Measurement in Education (NCME). The 1985 and 1999 standards represent the most current consensus among measurement experts on the topic of validity. According to the 1985 standards, the concept of validity is defined as "the appropriateness, meaningfulness, and usefulness of specific inferences made from test scores" (AERA, 1985, p. 9). The 1999 standards explain, "Validity refers to the degree to which evidence and theory support the interpretations of test scores entailed by proposed uses of tests" (AERA, APA, & NCME, 1999, p. 9).

Given these recent definitions of validity, it is inappropriate to talk about the validity of a test; rather, validity refers to a particular inference, interpretation, or action based on a test score. Validity is related to the claims made by users of the test information. The valid use of tests is the responsibility of both the test author and the test user. We agree with Salvia and Ysseldyke (1988, p. 145) that issues of validity are in essence "local, asking whether the testing process leads to correct inferences about a specific person in a specific situation for a specific purpose." A major factor in the valid use of tests is the extent to which there is a match between the test's and the test user's conceptualization of the domain being measured. But inferences that are valid for the majority of students might not be valid for all. Salvia and Ysseldyke (2001) point out judgments about students who are not steeped in American culture based on their performance on tests written for a general U.S. audience may be unfounded. Similarly, some tests assume that students have been given certain instruction. If a student has not been given such instruction, inferences about that student's ability to learn the material may be invalid.

Tests may be used and interpreted in a variety of ways, and evidence must be collected to support each interpretation and use. For example, standardized achievement tests are used both to provide accountability information to the public about schools and districts and to place students in particular classes and programs. Each of these purposes implies a different interpretation and use of test scores, which must be validated by accumulating appropriate evidence.

The 1985 and 1999 standards both indicate that tests should include evidence of validity that specifies what inferences can be made reasonably. In addition, these documents argue that test consumers should be warned against making specific kinds of inferences if the evidence that these inferences are warranted is not available. Again, it is the range and accuracy of possible inferences to other real-world phenomena (other tests, classroom performance, future success, etc.) that constitute evidence for the validity of a particular interpretation or use of a test score.

The 1999 standards represent a new direction in the educational testing field's conceptualization of validity and the sources of evidence that may help to build support for the validity of inferences made from test results. This new conceptualization will be discussed at the end of this section. Test publishers and the field in general may respond to these new standards, but they have had little time to do so. For this reason we explain and rely on the 1985 conceptualization in our review of assessments contained in the second part of this chapter.

***Content-, Criterion-, and Construct-Related Evidence of Validity.*** The following sections describe the three categories of evidence the 1985 standards indicate should be considered in the process of test validation: content-, criterion-, and construct-related evidence of validity. These three categories of evidence are often treated separately, giving the false impression that they are alternatives or options. Rather, they are intended as aspects of a unified view of validity, which integrates evidence across categories.

*Content-Related Evidence of Validity.* Content-related evidence of validity "demonstrates the degree to which the sample of items, tasks, or questions on a test are representative of some defined universe or domain of content" (AERA, 1985, p. 10). For example, the universe or domain of content may be an academic curriculum, a description of the behaviors required to perform a job, and a description of the psychological or educational characteristic being evaluated. The evidence usually involves professional judgments of the fit between the test items and the description of the domain.

Content validation involves a careful examination of the content of a test, in relation to the universe or domain of content being assessed. This is often done by the test developer and described in the test manual. Walsh and Betz (2001, p. 58) indicate that the most common type of evidence "presented in support of content validity is the judgment of those who construct the test or of other experts familiar with [the domain of interest]." Given that this type of evidence is usually somewhat subjective, they assert that it should be accompanied by a detailed definition of the domain being measured and a clear specification of the methods used to select items.

The test user can also gather content-related evidence of validity. Salvia and Ysseldyke (2001) identify three considerations that should be addressed in gathering content-related evidence of validity. The first deals with the appropriateness of the types of items included on the test. To examine this factor we must ask, "Is this an appropriate test question?" and "Does this test item really measure the domain?" So, for example, one should question the validity of items on a reading and writing test that require the use of skills that are not used in real reading and writing contexts outside the testing situation or the use of skills that are not age-appropriate.

The second consideration is the completeness of the item sample. For example, one would reasonably expect a test of writing achievement to include a far broader sample than would be found in a multiple-choice test of grammar and spelling. The third area concerns the representativeness of the task demands imposed by the format of the items. For example, reading skills can be evaluated in a variety of ways, including multiple-choice items, open-ended questions, retellings, oral reading samples, and so forth, and multiple formats may be required to adequately test the domain.

As models of literacy have changed, the match between the definitions of reading and writing and the content and methodology of standardized tests has become weaker (Wixson et al., 1987). Indeed, the degree of mismatch between theory, instruction, and assessment has become quite alarming. Valencia and Pearson (1987) provide a summary of some of the ways in which information about the reading process is poorly aligned with testing (see Figure 10.2).

Inferences about reading and writing achievement may be unwarranted or invalid when test content is a poor reflection of the reading and writing processes as we understand them. Literacy professionals must understand these issues and carefully evaluate the content-related evidence of validity provided by test developers. Too many of the existing standardized tests of reading, writing, and language arts distort the process by testing nothing more than subskills or by requiring students to answer only multiple-choice questions. Instructional interventions aimed at improving the reading and writing abilities of poor readers must be evaluated by using tests that do not trivialize the process.

*Criterion-Related Evidence of Validity.*    Criterion-related evidence of validity "demonstrates that test scores are systematically related to one or more outcome criteria" (AERA, 1985, p. 11). The criterion refers to the behavior or performance of primary interest for which test scores are intended to be used as a predictor. Consider the example of college admissions

**FIGURE 10.2**
Issues in Reading
Assessment

| A Set of Contrasts between New Views of Reading and Current Practices in Assessing Reading | |
|---|---|
| New views of the reading process tell us that . . . | Yet when we assess reading comprehension, we . . . |
| Prior knowledge is an important determinant of reading comprehension. | Mask any relationship between prior knowledge and reading comprehension by using lots of short passages on lots of topics. |
| A complete story or text has structural and topical integrity. | Use short texts that seldom approximate the structural and topical integrity of an authentic text. |
| Inference is an essential part of the process of comprehending units as small as sentences. | Rely on literal comprehension test items. |
| The diversity in prior knowledge across individuals as well as the varied causal relations in human experiences invite many possible inferences to fit a text or question. | Use multiple choice items with only one correct answer, even when many of the responses might, under certain conditions, be plausible. |
| The ability to vary reading strategies to fit the text and the situation is one hallmark of an expert reader. | Seldom assess how and when students vary the strategies they use during normal reading, studying, or when the going gets tough. |
| The ability to synthesize information from various parts of the text and different texts is a hallmark of an expert reader. | Rarely go beyond finding the main idea of a paragraph or passage. |
| The ability to ask good questions of text, as well as to answer them, is a hallmark of an expert reader. | Seldom ask students to create or select questions about a selection they may have just read. |
| All aspects of a reader's experience, including habits that arise from school and home, influence reading comprehension. | Rarely view information on reading habits and attitudes as being as important as information about performance. |
| Reading involves the orchestration of many skills that complement one another in a variety of ways. | Use tests that fragment reading into isolated skills and report performance on each. |
| Skilled readers are fluent; their word identification is sufficiently automatic to allow most cognitive resources to be used for comprehension. | Rarely consider fluency as an index of skilled reading. |
| Learning from text involves the restructuring, application, and flexible use of knowledge in new situations. | Often ask readers to respond to the text's declarative knowledge rather than to apply it to near and far transfer tasks. |

*Source:* Valencia, Sheila W., & Pearson, P. David. (1987, April). Reading assessment: Time for a change. *The Reading Teacher, 40* (8), 726–732. Reprinted with permission of the International Reading Association. All rights reserved.

tests, which are used to predict success in college as measured by first-year grade-point average. Success in college is the behavior of interest, and the strength of the relationship between scores on admissions tests and success in college is important evidence of the validity of the test.

There are two types of criterion-related evidence of validity: concurrent and predictive. Concurrent evidence refers to the relationship between a person's score and an immediate criterion. Salvia and Ysseldyke (2001) suggest, for example, that if we were developing a test of achievement, the basic question would be "How do we know that our new test really measures achievement?" To establish concurrent evidence of validity for this new achievement test, we would first have to find a valid criterion measure of achievement. Because there are no perfect measures of achievement, we can use other achievement tests that are presumed to be valid, and/or teacher judgments of achievement. If our new test presents concurrent evidence of validity and elicits test scores corresponding closely to teacher judgments and scores from other achievement tests that are presumed to be valid, we can conclude that our new test is a valid measure of achievement.

The second type of criterion-related evidence is predictive. Predictive evidence refers to the relation between a person's score and performance on some measure at a later time. It is used when there is interest in how present status on the test predicts future status on the criterion measure. If we were developing a test to determine reading placement, for example, we would ask, "Does knowledge of a student's score on our reading placement test allow an accurate estimation of the student's ability to perform successfully in certain materials?" Successful placement in reading materials can be evaluated by another assessment (presumed valid) or by teacher judgments. If our placement test has adequate content-related evidence of validity and corresponds closely with either subsequent teacher judgments of appropriateness of placement or validly assessed ability to read certain materials, we can conclude that reading placement is a valid use of our test.

The nature of the criterion is extremely important in gathering both concurrent and predictive evidence of validity. In effect, the value of the test is being established by comparing it to another measure. To do this, the other measure must be appropriately effective or representative of the behavior under investigation. Therefore the criterion measure clearly must be valid itself (Salvia & Ysseldyke, 2001). The 1985 standards urge test developers to provide thorough, accurate descriptions of the criterion measures and a rationale for using them. Finally, test developers and publishers are expected to provide complete, accurate statistical information regarding the degree of relationship between the target test and the criterion measure(s).

*Construct-Related Evidence of Validity.*   Construct-related evidence of validity is more complicated to describe because it can encompass a variety of types of evidence (Moss, 1994). The 1985 standards indicate that construct-related evidence of validity "focuses on the test scores as a measure of the psychological characteristic of interest" (AERA, 1985, p. 9). Examples of constructs provided in the 1985 standards include reasoning ability, reading comprehension, and endurance. The process of construct validation is characterized as follows.

The construct of interest for a particular test should be embedded in a conceptual framework, no matter how imperfect that framework may be. The conceptual framework specifies the meaning of the construct, distinguishes it from other constructs, and indicates how measures of the construct should relate to other variables. The process of compiling construct-related evidence for test validity starts with test development and continues until the pattern of empirical relationships between test scores and other variables clearly indicate the meaning of the test score (AERA, 1985, pp. 9–10).

The 1985 standards then cite examples of the many different kinds of evidence that can support construct validation. These include relationships among responses to test items, the relationship of test scores to other measures of the same and different constructs and to other nontest variables, questioning test takers about the strategies they used in responding, questioning judges of constructed responses about their reasons for their ratings, and collecting content- and criterion-related evidence. In each case the evidence is evaluated in terms of its consistency with the proposed interpretation.

Most theorists now argue that all validity research should be conducted within a construct validity framework (Moss, 1994). This means that validity research requires an explicit conceptual framework, testable hypotheses deduced from it, and multiple lines of relevant evidence to test the hypotheses.

Construct validity begins with descriptions of the purpose for which the assessment is being developed and one or more constructs appropriate to the purpose. The construct is the proposed interpretation or meaning for the test score (e.g., reading comprehension), and the purpose is the use to which it will be put, such as certification for high school graduation. The construct description should locate the construct in a conceptual framework, no matter how informal, that defines the construct and distinguishes it from other constructs. The description of the purpose should specify the desired outcomes of test use, the population of individuals for whom the test is intended, and the situations in which the test will be used. Hypotheses to be tested in subsequent studies concern the fit between the descriptions of construct and purpose and the evidence collected. Construct validation rarely results in a summative decision about whether or not a given interpretation is justified. More typically, the outcomes of a given study or line of research result in the modification of the test, the construct, the conceptual framework surrounding the construct, or all three. Thus construct validity is as much an aspect of test development as it is of test evaluation (Moss, 1994, p. 1104).

In evaluating construct-related evidence of validity, both convergent and discriminant evidence should be considered (Moss, 1994). Convergent evidence indicates that test scores are related to other measures of the same construct and to other variables that they should relate to as predicted by the conceptual framework. Discriminant evidence indicates that test scores are not unduly related to measures of other, distinct constructs. For example, within some conceptual frameworks, scores on a multiple-choice test of reading comprehension may be expected to be more "convergent" with other measures of reading comprehension, perhaps using other passages; conversely, test scores may be expected to relate less closely to measures of the specific subject matter knowledge reflected in the passages on the text.

Construct validation is most efficiently guided by the testing of rival hypotheses that suggest alternative explanations or meanings for the test score (Moss, 1994). Prominent rival hypotheses or threats to construct validity include construct underrepresentation and construct-irrelevant test variance (Linn & Gronlund, 2000). Construct underrepresentation refers to a test that is too narrow in that it fails to capture important aspects of the construct.

Construct-irrelevant test variance refers to a test that is too broad in that it requires capabilities that are irrelevant or extraneous to the intent of the test. Continuing with the above example, a potential rival hypothesis to the claim that a test measures reading comprehension is that it reflects "test-irrelevant variance" because it depends unduly on specific subject-matter knowledge.

The utility and value of tests rely on evidence of their validity. No matter what else is true, if the behavior or performance is not characteristic of the student in other related settings or tasks, then the scores are misleading.

*New Directions in Validity.*   The 1999 standards define validity as "the degree to which evidence and theory support the interpretations of test scores entailed by proposed uses of tests" (p. 9). They explain, "Validity is, therefore, the most fundamental consideration in developing and evaluating tests" (AERA, APA, & NCME, 1999, p. 9). The basic idea of validity as a "unitary concept" (p. 11) related to specific intended uses of tests is consistent with that explained in the 1985 standards. What is most different, however, is the breadth of evidence that may be important to claims that a test is used in a valid way.

The three categories of evidence explained in the 1985 standards have been either subsumed or expanded. Construct-related validity is no longer a separate category because it is redundant; since every "proposed interpretation refers to the construct or concepts the test is intended to measure" (AERA, APA, & NCME, 1999, p. 9), construct validity is synonymous with the concept of validity itself. Building a case that the test scores provide an indication of students' reading achievement, for example, is the same as building a case that the test measures the construct of reading. The concepts of content- and criterion-related evidence of validity, in contrast, are included in the categories of evidence outlined in the 1999 standards, but they have been expanded.

As explained in the 1999 standards, validity evidence might be gathered from a range of sources: test content, response processes, internal structure, relations to other variables, and the consequences of testing. Test content "refers to the themes, wording, and format of the items, tasks, or questions on a test, as well as the guidelines for procedures regarding administration and scoring" (AERA, APA, & NCME, 1999, p. 11). A test's content should be carefully analyzed as to whether and how it is related to the construct it is intended to measure.

Response processes, the second source of validity evidence, get at what students actually do as they take the test and whether they indeed engage in the activity at which the test is aimed. For example, do students taking a test designed to measure reading comprehension actually *use* comprehension skills, or are they able to answer the test questions without actually reading the passages?

A third source of validity evidence involves an analysis of a test's internal structure. This analysis is designed to determine whether the test components and their organization might support or compromise the validity of the test (AERA, APA, & NCME, 1999). These analyses may consider whether items or groups of items function in the way expected, for example, whether they are equally difficult for examinees of similar ability from different racial groups.

The fourth type of validity evidence involves a test's relationship to variables beyond the test. For example, you might examine the relationship between this test and another measure of the same construct. Alternatively, you might evaluate how well the test score predicts performance in some other setting. Finally, it might include how well the test differentiates among groups if that is an important aspect of the construct. For example, a test of emergent reading ability should distinguish students who are not yet reading conventionally from those who are.

Finally, the intended and unintended consequences of testing may be an important source of evidence for validity. As regards differential test performance among groups, "evidence about consequences may be directly relevant to validity when it can be traced to a source of invalidity such as construct underrepresentation or construct irrelevant components. Evidence about consequences that cannot be so traced—that in fact reflects valid differences in performance—is crucial in informing policy decisions but falls outside the technical purview of validity" (AERA, APA, & NCME, 1999, p. 16). More generally, if tests are administered to produce some benefit—for example, improved instruction or student motivation to learn—validation should consider whether the benefit is indeed likely to result.

The 1999 standards recommend that the available evidence from a variety of these sources be integrated to build a solid account of the extent to which the data support the proposed interpretations and specific uses of a test. The sources of evidence and the conception of validity they buttress reflect the thinking of many, many prominent researchers and testing professionals. As tests continue to be revised, it will be interesting to see how the validity arguments for formal tests of reading and writing are reworked to accommodate these changes in the field.

## Reliability

Reliability is another major consideration in evaluating a test. Reliability refers to the consistency or stability of test scores and involves the extent to which some attribute has been measured in a systematic and therefore repeatable way. When we administer a test, we need to be confident that those taking the test would earn similar scores if tested again with the same instrument. Test results would have little meaning if they fluctuated wildly from one occasion to the next. We would not administer a test if we knew that the student's score might be fifteen or twenty points higher or lower if the student were retested. For a test to be useful it must be reliable.

The 1985 standards indicate that "reliability refers to the degree to which test scores are free from errors of measurement" (AERA, 1985, p. 19), and the 1999 standards are consistent with this definition. Differences between scores from one administration to another or from one form to another may be attributable to errors of measurement. These differences are *not* attributable to errors of measurement if factors such as maturation or instructional intervention have made these differences meaningful or if inconsistency of response is a characteristic of the construct being measured. Measurement errors reduce the reliability and, as a result, the generalizability of a test score.

The importance of a particular source of error and other information about reliability depends on the specific use of the test. According to the 1999 standards (AERA, APA, & NCME, 1999, p. 27):

> The critical information on reliability includes the identification of the major sources of error, summary statistics bearing on the size of such errors, and the degree of generalizability of

scores across alternate forms, administrations, or other relevant dimensions. It also includes a description of the examinee population to whom the foregoing apply, as the data may accurately reflect what is true of one population but misrepresent what is true of another.

The reliability of a test is usually expressed as a correlation coefficient (reliability coefficient), which provides an estimate of how much error there is in the test. Different reliability coefficients can be based on various types of evidence, and each type of evidence suggests a different meaning. It is essential that the method used to estimate reliability takes into account the sources of error of greatest concern for a particular use and interpretation, such as random response variability, changes in the individuals taking the tests, differences in the content of the forms, and differences in administration. Not all sources of error are expected to be relevant for any one test.

Estimates of the reliability of a test should consider not only the relevant sources of error, but also the types of decisions that are anticipated to be based on the test scores and on their expected levels of aggregation, that is, individual versus groups. Test developers and publishers have primary responsibility for obtaining and reporting evidence concerning reliability and errors of measurement related to the intended uses. Although the test users usually do not conduct separate reliability studies, they do have a responsibility to determine that the available information is relevant to their intended uses and interpretations.

***Reliability Measures.*** There are several methods of estimating a reliability coefficient, depending on the intended uses and interpretations of the test. The two that we describe here are test–retest reliability and alternate form reliability. Test publishers should report reliability estimates and the methods used to obtain them. Test users should look for reliability information in test manuals in order to evaluate the adequacy of the test for a particular purpose.

*Test–Retest.* Test–retest reliability measures the stability of tests' scores over time. It assesses the degree to which test scores are similar after a time delay versus the degree to which they change or fluctuate with repeated testing (Walsh & Betz, 2001). If test scores are relatively stable across repeated testings, there is some basis for believing that the test is measuring something in a consistent manner. The procedures for establishing test–retest reliability usually involve two administrations of the same test to the same individuals, with a time interval of at least one week between the administrations. The test–retest reliability coefficient is the correlation between the sets of scores obtained at the two administrations of the test.

*Alternate Form.* Alternate form reliability assesses the degree to which two different forms of the same test yield similar or consistent results. If scores on one form of a test are similar to scores on an alternate form of the same test, we have increased confidence that the test forms are measuring some common domain in a relatively consistent manner (Walsh & Betz, 2001). The procedures for establishing alternate form reliability involve developing two equivalent forms of the same test and then administering both forms to a single sample of students. The reliability coefficient is the correlation between the scores obtained on the two forms of the test.

It is important to keep in mind that equivalent or parallel forms of a test are never perfectly correlated or reliable. Errors of measurement occur because the two tests differ somewhat in item sampling. This can be an important factor in interpreting pretest and posttest scores using alternate forms of the same test. Slight increases or decreases in scores are more likely to reflect measurement error than real gains or losses in the area being tested.

*Standard Error of Measurement.* One of the primary reasons for obtaining a reliability coefficient is to be able to estimate the amount of error associated with an individual's obtained score (Salvia & Ysseldyke, 2001). The standard error of measurement (SEM) permits the test user to do this. The SEM provides information about the certainty or confidence with which a test score can be interpreted. When the SEM is relatively large, the uncertainty is great. When the SEM is relatively small, the uncertainty is minimized.

The SEM can be used to suggest the distance between individuals' true scores, with all the sources of error removed, and their actual scores. An individual's true score actually may be either above or below the obtained score. Using the SEM, we can define a range, or confidence interval, within which we can be relatively certain the individual's true score lies. Several options are available, depending on how "confident" we wish to be.

Because the SEM is based on a normal distribution of scores, we can say that 68 percent of the time the individual's true score will fall within +1 or −1 SEM of his or her obtained score. Therefore, if an individual's obtained score is 60 and the SEM is 4, the person's true score is somewhere between 60 +4 or −4, or between 56 and 64. This means that an individual's score fluctuates within four points on either side of the true score 68 times out of 100. This also means that the obtained score is likely to either underestimate or overestimate the student's true score about 30 percent of the time. If we want a higher degree of confidence, we can expand the size of the interval. A 95 percent confidence band is represented by +2 or −2 SEM and provides the interval within which an individual's true score will lie 95 out of 100 times.

It is important to realize what the SEM means for the interpretation of test results. When we say that someone's raw score corresponds to a grade equivalent of 4.5 (see the section on scores), it sounds very precise. But consider the SEM and the confidence intervals. If the SEM is .3, we are only 68 percent certain that the true score falls between 4.2 and 4.8 and 95 percent certain that it falls somewhere between 4.0 and 5.1—a range of over one year. A larger SEM would mean even larger intervals. Swanson and Watson (1989) offer a related example of a child who has scored 75 on an IQ test with an SEM of 5. A 68 percent confidence level represents an interval of 70–80, and a 95 percent confidence level represents an interval from 65 to 95. Even though the student's score was at a level typically labeled as mentally retarded, it is possible that the true score was in fact in the low-normal range.

*Desired Standards.* As Salvia and Ysseldyke (2001) indicate, no test can be said to measure what its authors say that it measures unless it is reliable, and no score is interpretable unless it is reliable. Therefore it is important for test authors and publishers to present sufficient information about test reliability for the test user to interpret test results accurately. Reliability information for each type of score should be reported for each age and grade.

In terms of the level of error that is acceptable, Salvia and Ysseldyke (2001) recommend three standards or cutoff points for reliability coefficients. If test scores are to be reported for groups rather than individuals and are to be used for general administrative purposes, a reliability coefficient above .60 is acceptable. If test scores are to be used to make decisions about individual students, the standard should be much higher. For important educational decisions, such as placing a student in a Title I (Chapter 1) class, a reliability coefficient of .90 should be considered minimum. For more general purposes such as initial screening, a reliability of .80 is acceptable.

## Test Interpretations

The raw score, or the number of points received on a test, is usually the basic score in tests emphasizing either norm- or criterion-referenced interpretations. These raw scores alone tell us very little, since we know neither how other individuals performed nor how many total points might be reasonable or possible on the test. As Linn and Gronlund (2000, p. 477) note, "we can provide meaning to a raw score either by converting it into a description of the specific tasks that the student can perform (criterion-referenced interpretation) and a comparison of that performance to specified performance standards or by converting it into some type of derived score that indicates the student's relative position in a clearly defined reference group (norm-referenced interpretation)." Each of these modes of interpreting test performance can be useful under some circumstances, and occasionally both are reasonable.

*Criterion-Referenced Interpretations.*   Criterion-referenced test interpretation permits us to describe an individual's test performance on some preestablished standard, or *criterion.* In this method it is not necessary or even desirable to refer to the performance of others. Students' performance might be described in terms of the speed with which a task is performed, the precision with which a task is performed, or the percentage of items correct on some clearly defined set of learning tasks.

Although percentage correct scores are often used as the standard for judging whether a student has mastered each of the instructional objectives measured by a criterion-referenced test, there are many ways to report these scores. Swanson and Watson (1989, p. 58) present five measures, or *metrics,* that are commonly accepted as appropriate for criterion-referenced interpretation, several of which are basically raw scores:

1. A rate metric simply refers to the time it takes to complete the specified task.
2. A sign metric indicates the mastery or nonmastery of the task.
3. An accuracy metric gives the proportion of times the examinee is successful.
4. A proportion metric specifies the portion or percentage of the items in a domain on which the student performs accurately.
5. A scaling metric describes the point along a continuum at which the student's performance occurs.

Linn and Gronlund (2000) point out that criterion-referenced interpretation of test results is most meaningful when the test has been designed to measure a specific set of clearly stated learning tasks. In addition, there is sufficient coverage to make it possible to describe test performance in terms of a student's mastery or nonmastery of each task. The value of criterion test results is enhanced when the domain being measured is delimited and clearly specified and the test items are selected on the basis of their relevance to the domain being measured. There should be a sufficient number of test items to make dependable judgments concerning the types of tasks a student can and cannot perform.

Performance on the items on tests emphasizing criterion-referenced interpretations can range in difficulty from 0 to 100 percent accuracy, depending on the nature of the specific learning tasks to be measured. If the learning tasks are easy, the test items should be easy. Little attempt is made to modify item difficulty or to eliminate easy items from the test to obtain a range of test scores. On a test emphasizing criterion-referenced interpretations, we would expect all or nearly all students to obtain high scores when the instruction has been effective (Gronlund, 1985)

Although standardized tests typically have been designed for norm-referenced interpretations, it is possible to apply criterion-referenced interpretations to the test results. This simply involves analyzing each student's test responses item by item and summarizing the results with descriptive statements. Some test publishers aid this type of interpretation by providing a list of objectives measured by the test, with each item keyed to the appropriate objective, and by arranging the items into homogeneous groups for easy analysis.

But if the test was designed to be norm-referenced, interpretations of the criterion-referenced results must be made very cautiously. Linn and Gronlund (2000, p. 479) provide the following guidelines for making criterion-referenced interpretations of norm-referenced tests:

**1.** Is each achievement domain (objective or content cluster) homogeneous, delimited, and clearly specified? If not, avoid specific descriptive statements that distinguish it from other domains.

**2.** Are there enough items (say, ten) for each type of interpretation? If not, make tentative judgments and/or combine items into larger content clusters for interpretation.

**3.** In constructing the test, were the easy items omitted to increase discrimination among individuals? If so, remember that the descriptions of what low achievers can do will be severely limited.

**4.** Does the test use selection-type items only? If so, keep in mind that a proportion of correct answers may be based on guessing. (This is especially crucial when only a few items are used to measure a specific content domain.)

**5.** Do the test items provide a directly relevant measure of the objectives? If not, base interpretation on what the items actually measured (e.g., "ability to identify misspelled words" rather than "ability to spell," which are related but are not the same process).

***Norm-Referenced Interpretation.*** Norm-referenced interpretations indicate how an individual's performance compares to that of others who have taken the same test. According to Linn and Gronlund (2000), the simplest type of comparison is to rank-order the raw scores from highest to lowest and to note where an individual's score falls. Noting whether a particular score is second from the top, about in the middle, or one of the lowest scores in relation to a particular reference group provides a meaningful report to both teachers and students. If a student's score is second from the top in a group of ten or more, it is a relatively high score whether it represents 95 percent or 60 percent of the items correct. The fact that a test is relatively easy or difficult for the students does not alter the interpretation of test scores in terms of relative performance.

Although the simple ranking of raw scores may be useful for reporting the results of a classroom test, it is of limited value beyond the immediate situation. To obtain a more general framework for norm-referenced interpretation, raw scores are typically converted into some type of derived score based on norms. The concept of comparing one person's test score to the scores of other people is the basis for test norms, that is, the test scores of a representative sample of people. Test norms are usually obtained by using a standardization sample representative of the people for whom the test is designed to be taken. On the basis of the responses of this standardization, or normative sample, raw scores obtained from any subsequent examinee can be converted into a measure of relative standing in comparison to the normative group.

There are two important points related to the fact that test scores are based on the performance of individuals in the normative sample. First, even the slightest variation of the administration procedures for norm-referenced tests from those used with the standardization sample will render the norms—and therefore the test scores—invalid.

The second point is that norms are applicable only to individuals of the same age and/or grade as the students in the normative sample. This can be a major problem when testing students with serious academic difficulties. If a test at the student's age or grade level is administered, the norms are of questionable value because the student is at the extreme end of the distribution (not to mention the student's frustration at taking a test that is far too difficult). However, if a test designed for younger or lower-grade students is administered, the norms are inappropriate because older students were not included in the normative sample. To get around this problem, some tests provide norms for out-of-level testing that make it possible to obtain valid scores for students on tests that approximate their skill level more closely than their age or grade level.

According to Salvia and Ysseldyke (2001), norms are important because the normative sample may be used to obtain the various statistics on which the final selection of test items is based, and an individual's performance is evaluated in terms of the performance of the individuals in the normative sample:

> in evaluating a test's norms, users should consider not only whether the norms are generally representative, but also the age of the norms (that is, Are the norms current?), the relevance of the norms (that is, Is it appropriate to compare the performance of a specific test taker with the performances represented by the norm sample?), and the appropriate use of the norms (that is, Are the inferences derived from the comparisons appropriate?). (Salvia & Ysseldyke, 2001, pp. 118–119)

An evaluation of representativeness requires particular attention to demographic variables because of their theoretical and/or empirical relationship to what the test is intended to measure. According to Salvia and Ysseldyke (2001), representativeness hinges on two questions: "Does the norm sample contain individuals with the same characteristics as the population that the norms are intended to represent?" and "Are the various kinds of people present in the sample in the same proportion as they are in the population represented by the norms?" Among the factors that must be considered in answering these two questions are the age, grade, sex, acculturation of parents (SES and education), geographic factors, race, and intelligence of the individuals in the norm sample in relation to the characteristics of the population for whom the test is designed.

Another, often overlooked, consideration in ensuring representativeness is the date the norms were collected (Salvia & Ysseldyke, 2001). Ours is an age of rapidly expanding knowledge and rapidly expanding communication of knowledge. Children of today know more than the children of the 1930s or the 1940s and probably less than the children of tomorrow. "For a norm sample to be representative, it must represent the current population" (Salvia & Ysseldyke, 1988, p. 114). Finally, tests that are used to identify children with particular problems should include children with such problems in their standardization sample.

According to Salvia and Ysseldyke (2001, p. 113), the number of subjects in a norm sample is important for several reasons. First, the sample "should be large enough to guarantee stability." If the size of the sample is small, the norms will be undependable because another group might produce significantly different results. The larger the sample, the more stable the norms. Second, the sample should be large enough that infrequent elements in the population can be represented. Third, the sample should be large enough to produce a full range of scores. As a rule of thumb, the norm sample should contain a minimum of 100 subjects per age or grade, although in practice the sample should have more than 100 cases.

A third factor related to the adequacy of norms is the extent to which individuals in the norm sample can provide relevant comparisons in terms of the purpose for which the test was administered (Salvia & Ysseldyke, 2001). For some purposes national norms are the most appropriate; in other circumstances norms developed on a particular portion of the population may be more meaningful.

The appropriate use of norms requires that users ensure that the test taker can be compared to the test takers in the norm sample. For example, if a test manual contains tables for converting raw scores to percentile ranks based on both grade and age, the test administrator should use the grade table if the norm sample was selected on the basis of grade. Similarly, she should use the age table if the norm sample was selected on the basis of age (Salvia & Yssledyke, 2001). A final note concerns the ethical issues associated with reporting and using tests with inadequate norms. If the test publisher or author recognizes that the test norms are inadequate, the test user should be explicitly cautioned (AERA, 1985). "The inadequacies do not, however, disappear on the including of a cautionary note; the test is still inadequate" (Salvia & Ysseldyke, 2001, p. 118). Inadequate norms can lead to serious misinterpretation of test results.

## Test Scores

The following are descriptions of the most common types of derived scores: percentile ranks, standard scores, and grade and age equivalents.

***Percentile Ranks.***    A percentile score or rank indicates a student's relative position in a group in terms of the percentage of students scoring below a given raw score. For example, if we consult a table of norms and find that a student's raw score of 31 equals a percentile rank of 70, we know that 70 percent of the students in the reference group obtained a raw score lower than 31 and that this student's performance surpasses that of 70 percent of the reference group.

Percentiles should not be confused with the familiar percentage scores. The latter are raw scores, expressed in terms of the percentage of correct items. Percentiles are derived scores, expressed in terms of percentage of persons scoring below a given raw score. A raw score of 90 percent could have either a low or a high percentile rank depending on the performance of the other individuals in the group. We must always refer to the norm group used for comparison when interpreting a percentile rank.

A student does not have a percentile rank of 75. It is a percentile rank of 75 in some particular group. For example, a raw score on an achievement test may be equivalent to a percentile rank of 88 in a general group of high school seniors, 66 in a group of college-bound seniors, and 27 in a group of freshmen in a highly selective college. Relative standing varies with the reference group used for comparison. Therefore a test must have separate norms for each group to which students are to be compared.

The major limitation of percentile ranks is that they are not equal units on all parts of the scale. A percentile difference of 10 near the middle of the scale (e.g., forty-fifth to fifty-fifth percentile) represents a much smaller difference in test performance than the same percentile difference at either end of the scale (e.g., fifth to fifteenth or eighty-fifth to ninety-fifth percentiles). This is because the largest number of scores fall in the middle of the scale and relatively few scores fall at the extreme upper or lower ends of the scale. The difference between the forty-fifth and fifty-fifth percentiles represents fewer raw score points than the difference between the fifth and fifteenth or eighty-fifth and ninety-fifth percentiles (see Figure 10.3). Percentiles show each individual's relative position in the normative sample but not the amount of difference between scores.

***Standard Scores.***    Standard scores express individuals' scores in terms of standard deviation units from the mean. A number of different types of standard scores are used in testing; however, only the most common ones are discussed here. These are deviation IQs, stanines, and normal curve equivalents.

*Deviation IQ.*    One widely used standard score is the deviation IQ, in which the mean is set at 100 and the standard deviation at 15 or 16, depending on the particular intelligence test. Thus a score of 100 has been taken to indicate the average IQ, an individual with an IQ score of 84 or 85 falls one standard deviation below the mean, and an individual with an IQ score of 115 or 116 falls one standard deviation above the mean.

*Stanines.*    Stanines are standard-score bands that divide a distribution into nine parts with a mean of 5 and a standard deviation of approximately 2. The fifth stanine is located precisely in the center of the distribution and includes all scores within one fourth of a standard deviation on either side of the mean. The remaining stanines are evenly distributed above and below stanine 5. Each stanine, with the exception of 1 and 9, that cover the tails of the distribution, includes a band of raw scores the width of one half of a standard deviation unit.

**FIGURE 10.3**
Score Comparison

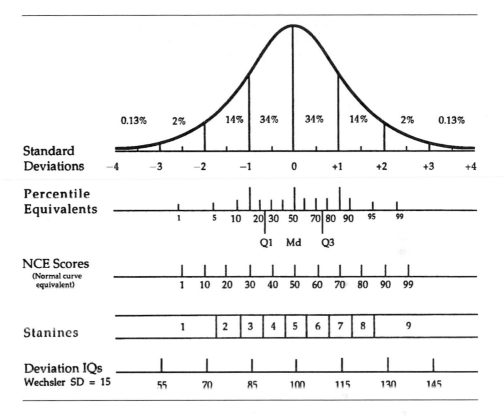

*Normal Curve Equivalents (NCEs).* NCEs are like percentile ranks with equal units. The NCE scale has been set with a mean of 50 and a standard deviation at 21.06. NCEs of 1, 50, and 99 correspond to percentiles of the same values. However, unlike percentiles, NCEs are equal units of measure whether they are at the low, middle, or high range of the distribution. A gain of five NCEs represents the same amount of improvement in performance for students at the extremes of the distribution as it does in the middle of the distribution. Federal education programs such as Title I (Chapter 1) often use NCEs for evaluation.

*Grade- and Age-Equivalent Scores.* Grade norms are widely used with standardized achievement tests, especially at the elementary school level. They are based on the average scores earned by students in each of a series of grades and are interpreted in terms of grade equivalents expressed in years and months (i.e., a grade equivalent of 4.7 indicates the fourth grade, seventh month). For example, if students in the norming groups who are beginning the fifth grade earn an average raw score of 24, this score is assigned a grade equivalent of 5.0. Tables of grade norms are made up of such pairs of raw scores and their corresponding grade equivalents.

The popularity of grade norms is due largely to the fact that test performance is expressed in common units with which we are all familiar. Unfortunately, this familiarity often leads to interpretations that are misleading or inaccurate. The most serious limitation of grade equivalents is that the units are not equal on different parts of the scale or from one test to another. For example, a year of growth in reading achievement from grade 3.0 to 4.0 might represent a much greater improvement than an increase from grade 1.0 to 2.0 or from grade 7.0 to 8.0.

A related problem is the uncertain meaning of high and low grade-equivalent scores. Raw scores, corresponding to grade equivalents at the extremes of the distribution of test scores, are usually estimated rather than determined by direct measurement of a norming sample. More precisely, they are *extrapolated* by "projecting the average performance of students at grade levels that were tested to performance of students at grade levels that were not tested" (Baumann, 1988, p. 37). In interpreting grade equivalents at the extremes, therefore, it is well to remember that they do not represent the actual performance of students at these levels. Indeed, because of the widespread misinterpretation of grade equivalents, the International Reading Association recommended that their use be discontinued in reading assessment (IRA, 1981), and several major diagnostic tests discontinued the use of these scores. In several tests' most recent revisions, however, the use of age- and grade-equivalent scores has been reinstituted because some government agencies require them. Wisely, many test authors warn that the scores should be interpreted cautiously if at all (see for example, Reid, Hresko, & Hammill, 1989, p. 44).

A common misinterpretation is that grade norms are equivalent to performance standards. It is especially important to remember that grade equivalents indicate the *average* score obtained by the students in the standardization sample at a particular grade level. This means that half the students in the norming group at this grade level scored above and half the students scored below this norm. Therefore we should not interpret a particular grade norm as something all of our students should achieve. It is important to remember that the norm represents the typical performance of average students in average schools and should not be considered a standard of excellence to be achieved by others (Linn & Gronlund, 2000).

A related misconception is that students who earn a certain grade-equivalent score in a subject are ready to do work at that level. For example, we might conclude that a fourth grade student, Sara, should be doing sixth grade work if she earns a grade equivalent of 6.0. However, students at different grade levels who earn the same grade-equivalent score are apt to be ready for quite different types of instruction. It certainly could not be assumed that Sara has the prerequisites for sixth grade reading. This would be especially true at the outer reaches of scores when no individuals from the grade group were included in the norming sample.

Age norms operate on the same principles as grade norms. Therefore, they have essentially the same characteristics and limitations as grade equivalents. Specifically, they are based on the average scores earned by students in the norming group at different ages and are interpreted in terms of age equivalents. Thus if students who are 10 years and 2 months of age earn an average raw score of 25, their score is assigned an age equivalent of 10.2. Conversely, a student with a reading age of 11.6 has earned a score on the reading test equal to that of the average 11½-year-old in the norming sample (assuming that age group was represented).

The major differences between age- and grade-equivalent scores are that test performance is expressed in terms of age levels instead of grade levels, and the expression of months in age equivalents runs from 0 to 11 months to reflect the calendar year, as opposed to a range of 0 to 9 months, which reflects the school year in grade equivalents. As with grade equivalents, age equivalents present test performance in units that are apparently easy to understand but can be misleading. Literal interpretations of either should be avoided.

***Comparison of Scores.***    Assuming a normal distribution and comparable norm group, we can compare different types of scores to the normal curve as presented in Figure 10.3. This figure illustrates the interrelated nature of various types of scores for reporting relative position in a normally distributed group. For example, a raw score that is one standard deviation above the mean can be expressed as a percentile rank of 84, a deviation IQ of 115, or a stanine of 7. Various scoring systems provide different ways of presenting the same information and, again, if we assume a normal distribution and comparable norm groups, we can convert back and forth from one scale to another.

The selection of which particular type of score to use depends on the purpose of testing and the sophistication of the consumer. In the opinion of many, grade and age equivalents should never be used because they are so easily misinterpreted (Salvia & Ysseldyke, 2001). Standard scores are convenient because they allow test authors to give equal weight to various test components, can be converted easily to percentile ranks if the distribution is normal, and are useful in developing individual profiles. Percentile ranks require the fewest assumptions for accurate interpretation and present test results in terms that are easily understood (Salvia & Ysseldyke, 2001).

## Test Fairness

Linn and Gronlund (2000) describe well the increasing attention in recent years to the issue of test fairness to racial and cultural minorities. Concern with the fairness of tests parallels the general public's concern with providing equal rights and opportunities to all citizens. Critics have charged that tests are biased and discriminatory and provide barriers to educational and occupational opportunities for minorities. The charge of test bias, or lack of fairness, can be examined from two perspectives: the possible presence of bias in the test content and the possible unfair use of test results.

Much of the concern with bias in test content focuses on the fact that minority group members frequently earn lower test scores than their more advantaged peers. At the most fundamental level is the fact that tests are, almost by definition, culture-bound. It is impossible to construct a test that is independent of a cultural content, and to assume that tests can be made culture-free is as erroneous as the assumption that behavior and attitudes can be made culture-free (Walsh & Betz, 2001).

According to Linn and Gronlund (2000), standardized tests of the past typically emphasized content and values that were more familiar to white, middle-class students than to members of racial or cultural minorities and students of lower socioeconomic status. For example, Garcia (1991) compared the English reading test performance of Hispanic children with the performance of Anglo children enrolled in the same fifth and sixth grade classrooms. The results of this investigation suggest that the Hispanic students' reading test scores seriously underestimate their reading comprehension potential. Their test performance was adversely affected by their limited prior knowledge of certain test topics, their poor performance on certain types of comprehension questions, their lack of familiarity with vocabulary terms used in the test questions and answer choices, and their tendency to interpret the test literally when determining their answers.

Special efforts are now being made to correct preexisting problems. Major test publishers employ staff members representing various racial and cultural minorities, and new tests being developed are routinely reviewed for content that might be biased or offensive to minorities. Statistical analyses are also being used to detect and remove biased test items. It is important, however, to distinguish between the performance the test is intended to measure and factors that may distort the scores in a biased manner. As explained in the 1999 standards (AERA, APA, & NCME, 1999, p. 74),

> The idea that fairness requires equality in overall passing rates for different groups has been almost entirely repudiated in the professional testing literature. A more widely accepted view would hold that examinees of equal standing with respect to the construct the test is intended to measure should on average earn the same test score, irrespective of group. Unfortunately, because examinees' levels of the construct are measured imperfectly, the requirement is rarely amenable to direct examination.

Linn and Gronlund (2000) indicate that the most controversial problems concerning the fair use of tests with minority groups are encountered when tests are used as a basis for educational and vocational selection or placement. Much of the difficulty lies in the definition of fair test use. One view is that a test is fair or unbiased if it predicts as accurately for minority groups as it does for the majority group. This traditional view, which favors a common standard for selection, has been challenged as unfair to minority groups because they often earn lower test scores; thus a smaller proportion of individuals tends to be selected. Alternative definitions of test fairness favor some type of adjustment for minorities such as separate cutoff scores or bonus points.

Walsh and Betz (2001) remind us of the importance of understanding that the quality of a test and the uses of test scores are two separate issues. The existence of bias in tests is a psychometric issue involving the concern about how tests are constructed and evaluated, whereas questions about how and when tests should be used are social issues. A test can be valid and relatively free of bias yet still produce scores that have negative effects for minorities. In short, answers to validity and test bias questions do not provide answers to social policy issues.

Taylor, Harris, Pearson, and Garcia (1995) note a fairness issue related specifically to reading assessments that is often overlooked. Because most poor readers are also poor test takers, formal tests might not fully reveal the competence and knowledge of these students, since they might be penalized by the way in which they are asked to display their knowledge. Similarly, the total test score for a poor reader might have little to do with what he or she actually knows or can do. As Taylor et al. (1995) point out, the majority of the items on norm-referenced tests are geared to the level being tested. Although a few easy and a few hard items are included, not enough of either are included to provide a reliable spread among students at the extreme ends of the distribution. As a result, the tests are likely to fail to measure what low-achieving students do know.

Some teachers believe that it is best to give students who have reading and writing problems a standardized test that matches their achievement level rather than their age or grade level. However, there are also certain problems inherent in this procedure. First, there might not be a content or format match with the student. Second, great care must be taken in interpreting the results. The scores have been determined on age or grade peers and are not appropriate for use unless the publisher has also developed out-of-level norms. Even when out-of-level norms are available, teachers should study the population on which these norms were developed to determine whether there is a match with their students.

### Guidelines for Evaluating Standardized Tests

In the sections to follow, we consider a variety of formal assessment tools. The quality and usefulness of these tools should be considered in terms of the information we have just presented. Informed educators need to be critical consumers of assessment information. To do so, they must consider a variety of test characteristics within the context of its use and interpretation. Specifically, they must consider evidence of the validity and reliability of the assessment tools for the purposes for which they are used. In addition, they must consider the methods for reporting and interpreting test scores. Finally, concerned educators need to evaluate tests for potential sources of bias, and exercise care in administering and interpreting results with special populations. The outline in Figure 10.4 can be used to guide the evaluation of formal assessment tools.

## Formal Assessment Tools

Educators do not need to be experts on the technical or psychometric properties of formal tests, but they can and should be careful consumers of test information. They should be able to evaluate critically the information provided by the tests themselves and know where to find critical reviews if necessary. In this portion of the chapter we describe several types of formal assessment tools in the area of language arts and provide detailed descriptions and evaluations of exemplars of each test type. The tests described in this section are grouped according to the primary purposes for which they were intended to be used: survey, diagnostic, tests of general cognitive and verbal abilities, and readiness/emergent literacy assessment.

Each type of test is described briefly before we begin the description of specific tests. No effort has been made to evaluate all published tests. Instead, the most commonly used tests are used as prototypes, and the guidelines for test evaluation (see Figure 10.4) are used to focus the discussion. At the end of this chapter there is a special test resources section that lists sources of information on tests and test reviews.

### Survey Tests

Survey tests emphasize norm-referenced interpretations of global achievement in a variety of academic areas, including the language arts. Generally speaking, the purpose of survey tests is to compare the performance of students or groups of students. They are most

**FIGURE 10.4**
Guidelines for
Text Evaluation

| General Information |
|---|

Name: _____ Publication date: _____

Authors: _____ Focus area(s): _____

Target ages: _____ Type of administration: _____

Scores: _____

*Interpretation of results:* (Criterion-referenced, norm-referenced, or both?)

| Type and Purpose |
|---|

*Type:* Note if a survey or diagnostic test and subtest areas
*Purpose:* What purposes are stated by the author(s)?

| Validity |
|---|

*Content-related, criterion-related, and construct-related evidence of validity:*
    Definition of domain assessed; Are items representative of defined domain?;
    concurrent and/or predictive evidence; evidence of support for testable
    hypotheses derived from defined domain

| Reliability |
|---|

*Measurement:* Are reliability coefficients, test-retest, and alternate form data
    acceptable for intended use?
*Standard error of measurement:* Is this acceptable?
*Other factors:* Sufficient numbers of items to test specific components, to determine
    a year's growth, etc.?

| Norms and Scores |
|---|

*Norming:* Consider whether the norms and norming procedures are acceptable and
    the norming sample comparable to your students
*Scores:* Note the types of scores generated and interpretations provided

| Special Considerations |
|---|

*Test fairness:* Consider both content and use in terms of examinee's background
*Provisions for students with special problems:* Consider administration flexibility,
    content, and interpretation (e.g., provision for out-of-level testing)

| General Evaluation |
|---|

*Special features/problems of this test:* Consider length, novel formats, etc.
*Appropriateness for purposes and students:* Consider ease of administration, time to
    score/interpret, difficulty, etc.
*What do others say about this test?* If possible, consult specialized colleagues, written
    reviews, etc.

| Recommendations |
|---|

Would you use this test?
For what? With whom?
What cautions should be exercised?

commonly used to screen large numbers of students for approximate levels of achievement in specific academic areas and to identify those who may have serious problems.

Survey tests are easy to administer and score and are useful screening devices. Although survey tests are generally designed for group administration, this is not always the case. Because of their general nature, survey tests often lack content depth; they evaluate language arts in a most cursory fashion, using limited samples of behaviors. Also, because survey tests are intended for large general populations, they tend to estimate more accurately the ability of average students than those who are either very skilled or very unskilled. The general scores do little to indicate specifically what a student knows or has trouble with. A low score indicates only that a difficulty exists but does not reveal the nature or degree of difficulty.

## Group Survey Tests

Group survey tests are also often used to make general judgments about program success. For example, many Title I (Chapter 1) programs use a global test of achievement in reading or mathematics for program evaluation purposes. Under these circumstances educators should be especially concerned that the evidence of validity supports the use of a test for this purpose. Average scores on these tests should parallel acceptable performance on the tasks assigned or expected in that age bracket.

***Gates-MacGinitie Reading Tests.*** One of the most commonly used group survey tests of reading is the Gates-MacGinitie Reading Tests (MacGinitie, MacGinitie, Maria, & Dreyer, 2000). Consistent with its purpose as a survey test, the authors indicate that the Gates-MacGinitie Reading Tests (GMRT) is useful for teachers and schools to know the general level of reading achievement of individual students throughout their entire school careers.

The fourth edition of the GMRT is substantially revised and includes several new features. At test level PR (Pre-reading) the four subtests address Literacy Concepts, Oral Language Concepts (Phonological Awareness), Letters and Letter/Sound Correspondences, and Listening (Story) Comprehension. At test level BR (Beginning Reading) the four subtests consist of Initial Consonants and Consonant Clusters, Final Consonants and Consonant Clusters, Vowels, and Basic Story Words. There are no time limits for either level PR or level BR.

Levels 1 and 2 are designed to provide a general assessment of early independent reading achievement. Grades 1 and 2 contain Comprehension and Word Decoding subtests, and the grade 2 tests include a subtest of word knowledge as well. All subtests are timed, ranging from twenty to thirty-five minutes. In a significant departure from earlier editions, the fourth edition includes much longer texts, including both exposition and narrative. Students respond by choosing among three pictures depicting the content of each segment (see Figure 10.5).

At grades 3 through AR (Adult Reading) the test contains two subtests, Vocabulary and Comprehension, designed to provide a general estimate of students' reading achievement. The vocabulary subtest measures students' ability to identify synonyms in a multiple-choice format, and the comprehension subtest requires students to read brief passages and answer multiple-choice questions.

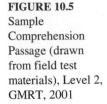

**FIGURE 10.5**
Sample
Comprehension
Passage (drawn
from field test
materials), Level 2,
GMRT, 2001

## The Newspaper

Jane used to deliver newspapers. She carried them on her bike and threw them onto people's porches.

One day, Mr. Ross went outside to get his paper, but he couldn't find it.

He called Jane. "Did you bring my paper today?" he asked.

"I'm sure I did," Jane answered. So Mr. Ross looked again. Where did he find it?

*Source:* "The Newspaper" from *Linking Testing to Teaching,* p. 35 by W. H. MacGinitie, Ruth K. MacGinitie, K. Maria, and Lois Dreyer. Copyright © 2001. Reprinted by permission of Riverside Publishing, a Houghton Mifflin Company.

There are two parallel forms for each grade from 2 through 6, 7/9, 10/12, and AR. The administration of this test is timed, with the vocabulary tests taking twenty minutes and the comprehension tests taking thirty-five minutes. As with the earlier levels, these materials have been completely revised. Comprehension passages are longer and more coherent than earlier versions and are taken from authentic trade books and text materials. Although still much shorter than the texts read by students in these grades, they are a significant improvement over most norm-referenced multiple-choice passages, permitting at least some degree of inferential assessment (see Figure 10.6).

**FIGURE 10.6**
Sample
Comprehension
Passage (drawn
from field test
materials), Level 3,
GMRT, 2001

On a tiny island in a vast blue sea, in a circle of stones, sits a little white egg. Pepe is born.

The first thing he sees is a pair of bright blue feet. His mama and papa are blue-footed boobies. They feed Pepe fish from the sea, and soon he is a little cloud of downy feathers.

There is danger in the sky. Big, hungry frigate birds and sharp-eyed hawks are watching. But Pepe is lucky. He and his world grow bigger.

Pepe looks up at the wide, blue sky and flaps his wings. But his feet will not leave the ground. Not yet.

Then one day he flaps his wings and this time they lift him high on the wind to join a flock of his kind.

**10. What was Pepe's nest like?**

O Hard

O Feathery

O Wet

O White

**11. The cloud was really**

O A white egg

O Blue feet

O Danger

O Pepe

O Wet White

**12. What does the danger come from?**

O Sharks

O Other birds

O The sun

O A strong wind.

**13. Why don't Pepe's feet leave the ground at first?**

O His world is too big

O He is tied down

O He is too young

O He looks up too quickly

*Source:* From *Linking Testing to Teaching,* pp. 15–16 by W. H. MacGinitie, Ruth K. MacGinitie, K. Maria, and Lois Dreyer. Copyright © 2001. Reprinted by permission of Riverside Publishing, a Houghton Mifflin Company.

The authors describe specific efforts to provide evidence of the content validity of the GMRT, including careful selection of vocabulary and balancing passage content across several disciplines by developmental level. They provide readable and reasonable arguments regarding the nature of reading and the way in which it changes over time. Data related to construct-related validity describe selection procedures for word items, passages, and questions. However, they do not directly provide any criterion-related evidence of validity, although this may be forthcoming in the new technical report.

Evidence of the reliability of the GMRT suggests that it ranges from acceptable to very good. Measures of internal consistency were determined for each level and each subtest, yielding reliability coefficients above .90 for all subtests and totals. Alternate form reliabilities are also excellent for the total scores, but somewhat less so for subtests and one grade level (grade 11).

Similarly, the norming procedures for this test are good. Norms were established for the GMRT during the 1998–1999 school year using a national sampling procedure and data from more than 40,000 students. At grades K–6, approximately 5,000 students per grade were assessed and the norming sample includes a representative proportion of black and Hispanic students. At grades 7 through 10 there were approximately 3,000 students per grade level. The numbers for grades 11 and 12 were much smaller. Norms are available for all times of the year, and a broad range of out-of-level norms is also available. For example, for the grade 5 test level, norms are available for 3.1 through 12.9.

Finally, the authors have made extensive efforts to remove bias from the test items and from both the content and the scoring. During field testing, responses that favored one racial group over another were removed or revised. Similarly, gender-biased responses were eliminated or balanced with other items.

A feature new to the fourth edition of the GMRT is *Linking Testing to Teaching: A Classroom Resource for Reading Assessment and Instruction,* developed and written by the same authors. These exceptionally helpful manuals provide information about how to interpret the results of the GMRT; information about how to extend the assessment information through informal, classroom-based assessments such as retelling and think-aloud; and excellent instructional guidance focused on aspects of reading tapped by the GMRT. These materials increase the likelihood that teachers will use the test results in appropriate ways.

***Nelson-Denny Reading Test, Forms G and H.*** The Nelson-Denny Reading Test (Brown, Fishco, & Hanna, 1993) is a timed test designed to measure high school and college students' ability as regards vocabulary, reading comprehension, and reading rate. The test has been in use since 1929. The basic format has remained the same, but the test has been revised several times and is now available on CD-ROM. The latest revision, contained in Forms G and H, was completed in 1993 and attempts to reduce the time pressure students may feel as they complete the test. The test contains two sections: Vocabulary and Comprehension. The vocabulary section includes eighty items, twenty fewer than the previous test forms, and Comprehension consists of seven short reading passages and thirty-eight multiple-choice questions. Previous forms included eight passages and thirty-six questions. To obtain a measure of reading rate, students are given one minute during which they begin reading the first passage in the Comprehension section. They are asked to record the number of the line they are reading at the end of the minute. Students are given a total of thirty-five minutes to complete the test. The latest revision, however, also includes directions for administration and norms for students who are provided extended time (a total of fifty-six minutes) to complete the test. Test scores can be converted into percentiles, grade equivalents, standard scores, and stanines.

The selection of items and passages for the most recent form seems reasonable. The vocabulary words and passages in the comprehension section represent a range of difficulty and are taken from high school and college social studies, science, and humanities texts that were in use in the 1990s. Care was taken to support the assertion that the test does not systematically favor students of a particular racial group. However, the norms are perhaps biased. Middle-income students were overrepresented in the normative sample, so care should be taken in interpreting the norms of students from lower SES levels (Murray-Ward, 1998; Smith, 1998).

Beyond the ample description of test fairness, little evidence of validity is offered. The standard error of measurement and related reliability coefficients reported for Forms G and H appear adequate, as do the alternate forms reliabilities. Some estimates of reliability appear low, however. For example, the reliability of reading rate scores obtained from students who took both Form G and H ($r = .68$) calls into question interpretation of these scores. This could very well be because the reading rate score does not take into account differences in purposes for reading and type and complexity of the text. Because of these issues, the Nelson-Denny Reading Test is probably best used for screening purposes.

***Individually Administered Survey Tests.*** Reading and writing achievement are commonly surveyed in batteries of general academic achievement. Both the *Peabody Individual Achievement Test—Revised,* or PIAT-R (Markwardt, 1989), and the *Wide Range Achievement Test 3,* or WRAT3 (Wilkinson, 1993), have been used extensively, because they are easy to administer and provide a general measure of achievement in several academic areas. Tests such as these are often used to determine whether there is a discrepancy between ability (usually IQ) and achievement sufficient to establish eligibility for placement in special education programs.

*Peabody Individual Achievement Test—Revised.* The PIAT-R is a general achievement battery containing six subtests in the following areas: general information, reading recognition, reading comprehension, math, spelling, and written expression. Scores are available as percentile ranks, stanines, grade and age equivalents, standard scores, and normal curve equivalents (NCEs) for the all subtests except written expression and for total reading and total test, which also excludes written expression. Grade-based stanine and developmental scaled scores are available for the written expression subtest. The 1998 edition of the test includes new norms developed from testing completed in 1995–1996. Norms can now be obtained for students through age 22.11. The new normative group appears adequate in number and is representative of the nation in the mid-1990s in terms of gender, gifted or special education status, sociodemographics, and geographical region. As compared to the previous norms, collected nearly ten years before, the updated norms indicate that the average raw score on total reading has declined for kindergartners, first graders, and second graders. At grades 1 through 12, the total reading raw scores of students scoring in the bottom half of the distribution have declined. Generally, raw scores on written expression have declined in kindergarten and first grade and remained stable at the other grade levels.

The PIAT-R is designed for use with students from kindergarten through grade 12 and is considered a screening tool, although the author also suggests that it can be used for individual evaluation and program planning. It is an untimed test that is estimated to take one hour to administer.

The content- and criterion-related evidence of validity for the PIAT-R are somewhat suspect. For example, on the reading comprehension subtest, students read isolated sentences, then turn the page and match the sentence from memory to one of four picture choices. No contextualized story comprehension is involved, nor are students expected to answer questions or summarize information. As an illustration, students read, "See the boy with a hat," and select from one of the four pictures displayed as in Figure 10.7.

In addition, the spelling subtest is a series of multiple-choice items that progresses from tasks such as identifying a specific letter to words that begin with a specified sound to identifying the correctly spelled word. The written expression subtest involves writing a story from a picture prompt without any opportunity for prewriting or editing. Furthermore, the only criterion-related validity that is offered is a correlation with the *Peabody Picture Vocabulary Test—Revised* (Dunn & Dunn, 1981), a test of verbal ability that seems an inappropriate benchmark for comparison. Other construct-related evidence of validity comes from data on developmental changes and factor analyses on test intercorrelations.

The evidence of reliability of the PIAT-R is substantially improved from the PIAT. A new reliability study was not undertaken when the norms were updated with the 1989 edition. The descriptions of reliability, then, reflect the performance of the normative group tested in the mid-1980s. On the basis of these data, both the test–retest and internal consistency

**FIGURE 10.7**
PIAT-R Item

*Source:* "See the boy with a hat." *Peabody Individual Achievement Test–Revised; PIAT–R Manual* by Frederick G. Markwardt, Jr. Copyright © 1989 American Guidance Service, Inc. Reprinted by permission.

coefficients are generally well within the acceptable boundaries for such an instrument. Test–retest reliability composite scores range from the low to the upper .90s. Most subtest correlations fall in the mid-.80s to high .90s, with low values at grade 6 in reading comprehension (.78). Separate reliability data are reported for written expression, which suggest lower reliability for this subtest. For grades 2 through 12 the coefficients range from .69 to .91. Interrater correlations for each grade range from .30 to .81, and alternate form coefficients range from .44 to .61 for the five grade levels investigated.

Although there are generally at least seven items per year's growth on the test, reading comprehension is a notable exception. This is especially problematic at the upper grades, where the limited item pool restricts its utility. With a SEM of 3.8 for reading comprehension and 2.6 for reading recognition, there is reason to exercise caution.

In summary, the PIAT-R is a generally reliable screening instrument that can provide some information to teachers who know very little about the student being tested. Because of serious concerns about the validity of the reading comprehension subtest, however, teachers might find more useful survey data on which to rely.

*Wide Range Achievement Test 3.* The PIAT-R is most often compared to another individual achievement battery, the *Wide Range Achievement Test 3,* or WRAT3 (Wilkinson, 1993). The 1993 edition of the WRAT is intended for use with individuals aged 5–75 and is designed to measure the basic academic skills of word recognition (written decoding), spelling from dictation (written encoding), and arithmetic computation. It has two alternate forms and takes fifteen to thirty minutes to administer.

The WRAT3 was given to a norm sample of approximately 5,000 individuals selected to represent the appropriate mix of gender, ethnicity, regional residence, and socio-economic level for each age group as indicated by the 1990 Census data. The median reliability coefficients range from .85 to .95 over all the WRAT3 tests. Alternate form correlations across the age groups range from .87 to .99 for reading and from .86 to .99 for spelling. Corrected test–retest coefficients range from .91 to .98. The SEM for most age levels is 5 for reading and spelling for the separate forms and 3 and 4, respectively, for the combined form.

Although content- and construct-related evidence of validity is provided, many continue to criticize the WRAT Reading test for its emphasis on letter and word recognition in isolation from any supporting context. The manual indicates that the WRAT was intentionally designed to eliminate the effects of comprehension. In so doing, it suggests, the WRAT can be used to determine whether a student's problem is due to an inability to learn the codes necessary to acquire the skill or to an inability to derive meaning from the codes and is intended to help prevent teaching errors that arise from the failure to differentiate these problems. We still agree with what Salvia and Ysseldyke (1988, p. 343) said about an earlier edition of the test: "A teacher who adjusted a student's reading curriculum on the basis of scores obtained on the Reading subtest of the WRAT-R would be on shaky ground indeed."

## Diagnostic Tests

Diagnostic tests are designed to provide a profile of a student's relative strengths and weaknesses. According to Gronlund (1985), diagnostic tests differ from survey tests in three major ways: They have a larger number of subtest scores and a larger number of items; the items are devised to measure specific skills; and difficulty tends to be lower in order to provide adequate discrimination among students with problems. For example, rather than providing one or two general scores that represent a student's overall performance in reading, diagnostic tests break the domain of reading into various components such as knowledge of phonics, structural analysis, literal comprehension, inferential comprehension, and reading rate, and provide scores for each of these areas. The rationale underlying diagnostic tests is that instruction can be planned to help a student improve in areas where performance is low.

To have confidence in a diagnostic test, test users must satisfy their concerns for construct-related evidence of validity. It is entirely possible that a subtest is measuring nothing of consequence or that it measures something that does not lend itself to instruction. Ultimately, the utility of diagnostic tests relies entirely on the relationship between the subtests and the prevailing conceptions of what is important to learn in a particular area or discipline—both the users' views and those of the school curriculum.

Diagnostic tests can be individually or group administered and provide either norm- or criterion-referenced interpretations or both. For example, the 1995 *Stanford Diagnostic Reading Test* (Karlsen & Gardner, 1995) is designed for group administration, while the *Woodcock Reading Mastery Test—Revised* (Woodcock, 1987) is an individually administered diagnostic reading test. Others include IRI-type oral reading tests such as the *Gray Oral Reading Test—4* (Wiederholt & Bryant, 2001). Finally, some diagnostic tests are embedded in criterion-referenced skills management systems. *The Brigance Diagnostic Inventories* (Brigance, 1981, 1984, 1991, 1994, 1995, 1999) provide an example of this type of testing.

### *A Group Administered Diagnostic Test: The* Stanford Diagnostic Reading Test.    The fourth edition of the *Stanford Diagnostic Reading Test,* or SDRT4 (Karlsen & Gardner, 1995) is the latest version of a widely used group diagnostic test. There are six test levels from first grade through junior college: Red, grades 1.5 and 2.5; Orange, grades 2.5 and 3.5; Green, grades 3.5 and 4.5; Purple, grades 4.5–6.5; Brown, grades 6.5–8.9; and Blue, grades 9–12.9. It is a multiple-choice test, with a single form at each of the first three levels and two alternate forms at each of the upper three levels.

The manual indicates that the SDRT4 views reading as a developmental process that encompasses four major components: decoding, vocabulary, comprehension, and scanning. The subtests of the SDRT4 reflect this view. For example, auditory vocabulary is assessed only at the lowest two levels and phonetic analysis at the lowest three levels. Reading vocabulary is measured at all levels but the lowest, and scanning is measured only at the top three levels. Reading comprehension is measured at all levels but with some variations, such as the use of cloze in addition to comprehension questions at the lowest two levels.

The stated purpose of the SDRT4 is to diagnose students' strengths and weaknesses in the major components of the reading process. The SDRT4 results can be used to help teachers challenge students who are doing well and provide assistance for others who lack some of the essential reading skills. Although the manual suggests that this test is appropriate for evaluating program effectiveness, for measuring student gains, and for reporting to the community, we believe that most people prefer a more global test of reading behavior for these purposes.

The SDRT4 is a timed test, requiring from one and a half to two hours, depending on the level. Raw scores, for both subtests and total tests, are easily converted to percentile ranks and stanine scores. Schools may also choose scoring options that include scaled scores, grade equivalents, and normal curve equivalents (NCEs). In addition, criterion-referenced interpretation is offered.

Salvia and Ysseldyke (2001) conclude about the SDRT4, "The device was exceptionally well standardized and is reliable enough to be used in pinpointing specific domains of reading in which pupils demonstrate skill-development strengths and weaknesses. Validity for the SDRT4, as for any achievement measure, must be judged relative to the content of local curricula. The test is one of the more carefully designed and developed diagnostic reading measures available" (p. 440).

***Individually Administered Diagnostic Reading Tests.*** The individually administered diagnostic reading tests described here are the *Woodcock Reading Mastery Test—Revised,* or WRMT-R (Woodcock, 1987), the *Gray Oral Reading Test, Fourth Edition,* or GORT-4 (Wiederholt & Bryant, 2001), and the *Test of Reading Comprehension, Third Edition,* or TORC-3 (Brown, Hammill, & Wiederholt, 1995).

*Woodcock Reading Mastery Test—Revised.* The *Woodcock Reading Mastery Test—Revised,* or WRMT-R (Woodcock, 1987) is a battery of individually administered tests designed to diagnose students' readiness for reading and their mastery of various components of the reading process. The six distinct subtests are grouped and reported as the readiness cluster, a basic skills cluster, and a comprehension cluster. There are two parallel forms of the WRMT-R. Form G contains all three clusters, and Form H is used to measure basic skills and comprehension only (see Figure 10.8). Although the test itself is unchanged from the 1987 edition, the 1998 edition includes new norms and new components on several record forms.

The WRMT-R is untimed, requires between forty-five and ninety minutes to administer, and emphasizes norm-referenced interpretations. It is designed for use with students from kindergarten through college. This test provides several options for scoring and interpretation. Included among these are percentile ranks for total reading score and relative performance indices (RPIs) for subtests. RPIs indicate the individual student's percentage of mastery for tasks that the norming group performed with ease (90 percent mastery). With somewhat more effort, it is also possible to generate grade and age equivalents, a variety of standard scores, and confidence bands for the RPIs.

The test manual provides little documentation of validity, and it will be left to users to decide whether reading has been appropriately tested by the subtests. The Readiness Cluster contains two subtests: Visual-Auditory Learning and Letter Identification, and Word Identification. The Visual-Auditory Learning subtest, taken from the *Woodcock-Johnson Psychoeducational Battery* (Woodcock, 1978), requires students to learn rebuslike graphics for familiar words and use them to read sentences. On the Letter Identification subtest, students are asked to name twenty-seven capital letters and thirty-six lowercase letters written in several different typefaces; this is the only criterion-referenced portion of the WRMT-R.

**FIGURE 10.8**   Table of the WRMT-R Subtests and the Clusters

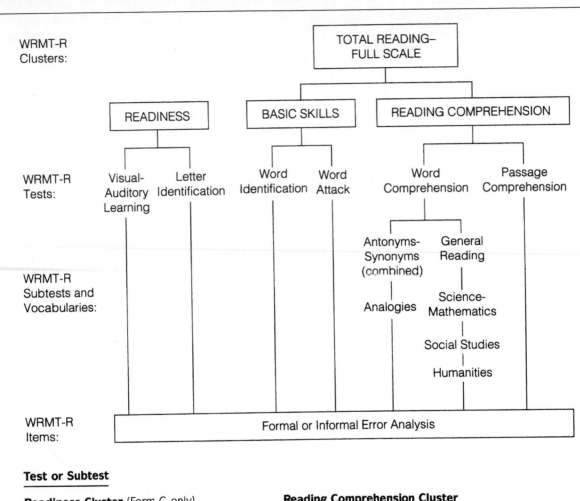

**Test or Subtest**

**Readiness Cluster** (Form G only)
  Test 1: Visual-Auditory Learning
  Test 2: Letter Identification

Supplementary Letter Checklist
  Capital Letters
  Lowercase Letters

**Basic Skills Cluster**
  Test 3: Word Identification
  Test 4: Word Attack

**Reading Comprehension Cluster**
  Test 5: Word Comprehension

  Subtests
    Antonyms-Synonyms (combined)
    Analogies

  Vocabularies
    General Reading
    Science-Mathematics
    Social Studies
    Humanities

  Test 6: Passage Comprehension

The Basic Skills Cluster also contains two subtests: Word Identification and Word Attack. The Word Identification subtest requires students to read real words in isolation. On the Word Attack subtest, students encounter forty-five nonsense words used to measure phonic and structural analysis skills. This subtest is among the most controversial, since many critics feel that reading nonsense words in isolation does not parallel normal reading. Clearly, the reader can neither check the approximation against known vocabulary words nor use the syntactic and semantic clues available in connected text. The WRMT-R authors defend its use, however, arguing that this does approximate real-life decoding (Woodcock, 1987, p. 6).

The Comprehension Cluster comprises Word Comprehension and Passage Comprehension. The Word Comprehension test has been expanded in this latest edition, and students are now required to display word knowledge by generating antonyms, synonyms, and analogies on three separate sections on the test. The Passage Comprehension subtest consists of sixty-eight sentences or short paragraphs, each containing a missing word (a modified cloze activity). Students are required to read each segment and supply the missing word.

Norming procedures for the WRMT-R are reasonable. As compared to the previous normative group, the students studied for the 1998 edition whose performance was below-average scored lower in most grades on most subjects. Generally speaking, this means that below-average scores will earn higher percentile ranks and standard scores than they would under the norms of the past edition. Grade- and age-equivalent scores, however, will be very similar. None of the validity and reliability studies were revised with the normative update. Particularly given this fact, the manual reports somewhat dated information asserting acceptable evidence of concurrent validity with unspecified editions of the *Iowa Test of Basic Skills, PIAT* reading subtest, and the *WRAT* reading subtest (see Woodcock, 1987, p. 100). Internal consistency reliability coefficients are reporter for all subtests and range from .34 on letter recognition to .98 on word identification. The reliabilities for all clusters are above .80, and most are above .90. No test–retest reliability data are provided.

The results of the WRMT-R will be most helpful to teachers with a skills approach to teaching reading. In addition, general areas of difficulty can be highlighted by using the clusters, making it useful in identifying students for special and remedial services. However, we believe that this test should be used cautiously, recognizing that it provides little new information to those who have extensive diagnostic information from other sources.

*Gray Oral Reading Test, Fourth Edition.* First published in 1915 as the *Gray Oral Reading Standardized Paragraphs,* this test has been revised and published most recently as the *Gray Oral Reading Test, Fourth Edition,* or GORT-4 (Wiederholt & Bryant, 2001). The GORT-4 has two alternate equivalent forms. Each form contains fourteen passages of increasing difficulty, one more than was included in the previous edition, GORT-3 (Wiederholt & Bryant, 1992). Five comprehension questions follow each passage, and each passage is timed. The authors suggest four purposes for using the GORT-4 that involve identifying students with oral reading problems, evaluating the strengths and weaknesses of individual students, documenting progress in remedial programs, and measuring reading ability in research investigations.

Targeted for ages 7–18, the test is similar to an informal reading inventory in format and construction. However, norm-referenced interpretations of scores are available for reading rate, accuracy, a combination of rate and accuracy called the passage score, and comprehension. Standard scores and percentile ranks are both reported. In addition an oral reading quotient is generated that is a combination of the oral passage reading score and the comprehension score. Finally, guidelines and scoring aids are provided to conduct a miscue analysis of oral reading behaviors.

The three types of content-related evidence of validity provided for the GORT-4—a detailed rationale for the structure and content of the passages and comprehension questions, the procedures used to select items, and an analysis of comprehension item bias with respect to gender and race—appear reasonable. Criterion-related evidence of validity was not updated with the GORT-4. Correlation coefficients (median = .64) from a series of smaller studies comparing GORT-3 (Wiederholt & Bryant, 1992) or its predecessor, GORT-R (Wiederholt & Bryant, 1986), with a variety of other assessment instruments are provided. Construct-related evidence of validity is provided through a procedure that first identifies constructs that are presumed to account for test performance, then generates hypotheses based on these constructs, and finally, tests these hypotheses either logically or empirically. An aspect of this test that concerns some is oral reading without any preparation or opportunity to read silently.

Norming procedures for the GORT-4 appear representative of the nation in 2000, although the number of individuals sampled at both ends of the age span is minimal. The evidence of reliability appears acceptable for the purposes for which it is intended. Internal consistency estimates of reliability include subtest coefficients are greater than .87. Alternate form reliability coefficients for thirteen age levels range from .73 to .97; comprehension scores are lower than the others. The SEM at each age level is reported as 1 for subtest scores. Test–retest correlations, delayed alternate form correlations, and interscorer correlations are also acceptable. Again, the correlations for the comprehension scores were the lowest.

The GORT-4 is relatively easy to administer and can provide guidance to a novice diagnostician, since the record form is quite comprehensive and helps to organize information (see Figure 10.9). Although most of the information provided can also be obtained by using an IRI (see Chapter 9), the availability of normative data is desirable when reporting of standardized scores is necessary.

*Test of Reading Comprehension, Third Edition.*    The TORC-3 (Brown et al., 1995) is a silent reading test designed for use with students ages 7–17. The test should be administered individually, although group administration is possible. The four subtests of the TORC-3 are General Vocabulary, Syntactic Similarity, Paragraph Reading, and Sentence Sequencing. Optional subject area vocabulary subtests are available as well. Scores from required subtests are combined to determine a basic comprehension core, expressed as a Reading Comprehension Quotient (RCQ). Raw scores can also be converted to standard scores, percentile ranks, and grade equivalents.

In addition to information about general reading comprehension ability, diagnostic information of a sort can be generated by comparing results from the various subtests. Other than Paragraph Reading, the subtests represent fairly unusual assessment formats and techniques. General Vocabulary, for example, requires students to read and consider three words that are related in some way by meaning. Then the students read four other words, selecting two of the four that are most closely related to the original three. The Syntactic Similarity test requires students to select two sentences that have the same meaning expressed

**FIGURE 10.9**
Summary Form
for *Gray Oral
Reading Test*
(GORT-4)

## Profile/Examiner Record Booklet
### Form A

## Gray Oral Reading Tests

**Fourth Edition**

### Section I. Identifying Information

Name _____ _____  School _____ Grade _____

Male ☐   Female ☐   Examiner's Name _____

Examiner's Title _____

|  | Year | Month | Day |
|---|---|---|---|
| Date of Testing | ___ | ___ | ___ |
| Date of Birth | ___ | ___ | ___ |
| Test Age | ___ | ___ | ___ |

Referred by _____

Reason for Referral _____

### Section II. Record of GORT-4 Scores

Pretest ☐   Posttest ☐

| Story # | Rate Score | Accuracy Score | Fluency Score | Comprehension Score |
|---|---|---|---|---|
| 1 | ___ | + ___ | = ___ | ___ |
| 2 | ___ | + ___ | = ___ | ___ |
| 3 | ___ | + ___ | = ___ | ___ |
| 4 | ___ | + ___ | = ___ | ___ |
| 5 | ___ | + ___ | = ___ | ___ |
| 6 | ___ | + ___ | = ___ | ___ |
| 7 | ___ | + ___ | = ___ | ___ |
| 8 | ___ | + ___ | = ___ | ___ |
| 9 | ___ | + ___ | = ___ | ___ |
| 10 | ___ | + ___ | = ___ | ___ |
| 11 | ___ | + ___ | = ___ | ___ |
| 12 | ___ | + ___ | = ___ | ___ |
| 13 | ___ | + ___ | = ___ | ___ |
| 14 | ___ | + ___ | = ___ | ___ |
| Total Scores | ☐ | ☐ | ☐ | ☐ |
| Standard Scores | ◯ | ◯ | ◯ + ◯ = ◯ |  |
| %ile | ◯ | ◯ | ◯ | ◯ |
| Age Equivalent | ___ | ___ | ___ |  |
| Grade Equivalent | ___ | ___ | ___ |  |

Sum of Fluency and Comprehension Standard Scores ◯

%ile ◯

Oral Reading Quotient (ORQ) ◯

### Section III. Record of Other Test Scores

| Test Name | Date | Test Score | GORT-4 Score Equivalent |
|---|---|---|---|
| 1. | | | |
| 2. | | | |
| 3. | | | |
| 4. | | | |

### Section IV. Profile of Scores

**GORT-4 Scores**

| Standard Score | Rate Score | Accuracy Score | Fluency Score | Comprehension Score | Standard Score | Quotient | Oral Reading Quotient | 1. Other | 2. Other | 3. Other | 4. Other | Quotient |
|---|---|---|---|---|---|---|---|---|---|---|---|---|
| 20 | · | · | · | · | 20 | 150 | · | · | · | · | · | 150 |
| 19 | · | · | · | · | 19 | 145 | · | · | · | · | · | 145 |
| 18 | · | · | · | · | 18 | 140 | · | · | · | · | · | 140 |
| 17 | · | · | · | · | 17 | 135 | · | · | · | · | · | 135 |
| 16 | · | · | · | · | 16 | 130 | · | · | · | · | · | 130 |
| 15 | · | · | · | · | 15 | 125 | · | · | · | · | · | 125 |
| 14 | · | · | · | · | 14 | 120 | · | · | · | · | · | 120 |
| 13 | · | · | · | · | 13 | 115 | · | · | · | · | · | 115 |
| 12 | · | · | · | · | 12 | 110 | · | · | · | · | · | 110 |
| 11 | · | · | · | · | 11 | 105 | · | · | · | · | · | 105 |
| 10 | — | — | — | — | 10 | 100 | — | — | — | — | — | 100 |
| 9 | · | · | · | · | 9 | 95 | · | · | · | · | · | 95 |
| 8 | · | · | · | · | 8 | 90 | · | · | · | · | · | 90 |
| 7 | · | · | · | · | 7 | 85 | · | · | · | · | · | 85 |
| 6 | · | · | · | · | 6 | 80 | · | · | · | · | · | 80 |
| 5 | · | · | · | · | 5 | 75 | · | · | · | · | · | 75 |
| 4 | · | · | · | · | 4 | 70 | · | · | · | · | · | 70 |
| 3 | · | · | · | · | 3 | 65 | · | · | · | · | · | 65 |
| 2 | · | · | · | · | 2 | 60 | · | · | · | · | · | 60 |
| 1 | · | · | · | · | 1 | 55 | · | · | · | · | · | 55 |

Additional copies of this form (#9483) may be purchased from
PRO-ED, 8700 Shoal Creek Blvd., Austin, TX 78757-6897
800/897-3202, Fax 800/397-7633, www.proedinc.com

*Source:* "Gray Oral Reading Tests" from *GORT–R Profile/Examiner Record Booklet,* 4th ed., Form A. Copyright © 2001, 1992, 1986, 1967 by PRO-ED, Inc. Reprinted by permission.

with different syntactic structure, and the Sentence Sequencing test requires students to reorder randomly presented sentences into meaningful paragraphs.

Two types of content-related evidence of validity are provided for the TORC-3: a rationale for the content and format of the subtests and the procedures used to select items. Criterion-related evidence of validity is provided in the form of correlation coefficients from six studies comparing the TORC-3 with other measures of reading comprehension. Median correlations for the subtests across measures range from .45 to .60. Construct-related evidence of validity is provided through a procedure that first identifies constructs that are presumed to account for test performance, then generates hypotheses based on these constructs, and finally, tests these hypotheses either logically or empirically. Despite this evidence, some are still concerned that this test does not adequately represent the types of abilities necessary to read and understand connected text (see Perlman, 1998).

All new normative data were collected in 1993–1994 for the TORC-3. The sample appears to be representative based on the 1990 Census data and included students with disabilities who were enrolled in general classes. The reported reliability coefficients of the RCQ are above .90 for all age groups and range from .85 to .97 on the subtests. The test–retest reliability coefficients reported for a small sample of high school students are .85 for the RCQ and range from .79 to .88 on the subtests. The SEMs are 1 for the subtests and 3 for the RCQ at every age level.

The TORC-3 provides reasonable evidence of the overall reading comprehension ability of individual students using the RCQ score. However, diagnostic information derived from subtest analysis is likely to be both less reliable and less valid. The information generated from the TORC will be most useful in meeting federal or state guidelines for screening purposes.

***Individually or Group Administered Diagnostic Writing Tests.***    The examples of diagnostic writing tests described in this section are the *Test of Written Language 3,* or TOWL-3 (Hammill & Larsen, 1996), and the *Test of Written Spelling, Fourth Edition,* or TWS-4 (Larsen & Hammill, 1999). Both can be administered to individual students or to groups of students.

*Test of Written Language, Third Edition.*    The TOWL-3 (Hammill & Larsen, 1996) is a test of both receptive and expressive language designed for use with students ages 7–17. Students are asked to read, listen, and write in response to several stimuli. Both contrived and spontaneous writing formats are employed. With the exception of the fifteen minutes allocated to story writing, the TOWL-3 has no set time limits. Much shorter than the TOWL-2 (Hammill & Larsen, 1988), the TOWL-3 takes approximately an hour and a half to administer and score. Inexperienced examiners should allow considerable additional time for scoring.

The TOWL-3 has two alternate forms and includes eight subtests that can be reported as raw scores, percentiles, subtest and composite standard scores, written language quotients, and age and grade equivalents. Three of the subtest scores are generated by analyzing a spontaneous writing sample, a story that is written in response to a picture stimulus: Contextual Conventions, Contextual Language, and Story Construction. Extensive checklists are provided for this purpose.

The other five subtests involve more contrived writing tasks. For example, subtest 4, Logical Sentences, requires students to rewrite sentences that have something wrong with them so "that it makes perfect sense" (Hammill & Larsen, 1996, p. 20). Spelling and Style are both evaluated by using the same dictation task, and the Vocabulary subtest requires students to write twenty-eight stimulus words in sentences.

The content-related evidence of validity of the TOWL-3 is derived from the theoretical orientation of the test and from examination of the types of tasks generally required of students in school settings. Item development and selection seem adequate, and scores appear similar for male and female, white and nonwhite, and Hispanic and non-Hispanic students. The only criterion-related evidence of validity offered is a correlational study of seventy-six students' performance on the TOWL-3 and a teacher rating scale, The Writing Scale of the Comprehensive Scales of Student Abilities (Hammill & Hresko, 1994, as cited in Hammill & Larsen, 1996). Correlations of averages of performance on both test forms and the Writing Scale yield coefficients for the subtests that range from .34 to .68. Many of these can be considered to be of only moderate size, as can the correlations with intelligence and other tests reported as evidence of construct validity. We believe that additional studies of the relationship of the TOWL-3 to other measures of writing ability are called for. Test–retest coefficients range from .72 to .94, with most in the high .80s. Interscorer reliabilities are reported ranging from .83 to .97.

The norming procedures for the TOWL-3 are carefully described and appear acceptable. The stratified standardization sample included over 2,000 students, distributed in a representative fashion across geographic areas and other demographic factors. The authors provide reasonable evidence regarding the reliability of the TOWL-3. The overall reliability of the test, using interscorer reliability, content sampling, and time sampling, ranged from .82 to .95.

In general, the TOWL-3 is a reasonable standardized measure of writing. Teachers and students who are accustomed to a writing process approach, however, will find this a somewhat limited view of writing competence, given that students are given the opportunity only to write one story with no prewriting or editing allowed. Although the TOWL-3 does not really generate any information that could not be collected by a knowledgeable teacher during classroom instruction and observation, the standardized information can be used to document and substantiate students' weaknesses in written language.

*Test of Written Spelling, Fourth Edition.* The TWS-4 (Larsen & Hammill, 1999) is a standardized measure for students ages 6–18. Unlike the TWS-3 (Larsen & Hammill, 1994), the TWS-4 contains two parallel forms to facilitate retesting after additional instruction has been given. The authors indicate that the TWS-4 may be used to identify students who might need interventions designed to improve spelling, to document overall progress in spelling, and to provide a measure for research but is insufficient as the basis for instructional planning.

The TWS-4 uses a dictated word format, and results are reported as standard scores, percentile ranks, spelling ages, and grade equivalents. Content-related evidence of validity for the TWS-4 is derived from the content of the subtests and from the results of item analysis procedures used during item selection. Item development and selection seem adequate, and items do not seem biased toward students of a particular gender or race. On the basis of evidence of the equivalence of the 1976 and the 1999 TWS, criterion-related evidence of validity is provided from studies of performance on the 1976 TWS correlated with the spelling subtests of four other tests. Total score correlations range from .59 to .97, and most scores are .85 or above. A moderate correlation between teachers' 1998 ratings of eighty-two students' spelling ability and their scores on the TWS-4 provides more criterion-related evidence of validity.

Construct-related evidence of validity is provided through a procedure that first identifies constructs that are presumed to account for test performance, then generates hypotheses based on these constructs, and finally tests these hypotheses either logically or empirically. Given the constructs and hypotheses presented, the TWS-4 presents reasonable construct-related evidence of validity for use as indicated in the manual.

The TWS-4 uses the same norms that were developed for the TWS-2 (Larsen & Hammill, 1986) and reinforced for the TWS-3 (Larsen & Hammill, 1994). Appropriate demographic characteristics of the sample were keyed to the 1990 Census data. Reliability studies indicate that the TWS-4 is relatively free from error resulting from irrelevant or biased content, the passage of time, and differences in scorers, although it is unclear when and on whom these studies were conducted. The new alternate forms appear parallel: Coefficients for each age level range from .86 to .98. The TWS-4 is easy to administer and interpret (see Figure 10.10). Also, the availability of normative data is helpful in evaluating students' general performance in this area.

***Individually Administered Diagnostic Language Tests.***    In this section we describe three individually administered diagnostic tests of language: the *Test of Oral Language Development, Third Edition, Primary,* or TOLD-3 Primary (Newcomer & Hammill, 1997); the *Comprehensive Test of Phonological Processing,* or CTOPP (Wagner, Torgesen, & Rashotte, 1999); and the *Clinical Evaluation of Language Fundamentals, Third Edition,* or CELF-3 (Semel, Wiig, & Secord, 1995).

*Test of Oral Language Development, Third Edition, Primary.*    The TOLD-3 Primary (Newcomer & Hammill, 1997) is an individually administered test designed for use with children ages 4.0–8.11. Norm-referenced interpretations are provided for scores on six core subtests and three supplemental subtests evaluating a student's skills in specific language areas. The semantic aspects of language are tested in the Picture Vocabulary, the Relational Vocabulary, and the Oral Vocabulary subsets; and the syntactic aspects of language are represented in the Grammatic Understanding, Sentence Imitation, and Grammatic Completion subtests. The Relational Vocabulary and Phonemic Analysis subtests are new with the third edition. The first was added to capture organizational ability and the second to measure awareness of phonemes. The phonological aspects of language are evaluated in the supplemental subtests: Word Articulation, Phonemic Analysis, and Word Discrimination. The TOLD-3 Primary is intended for use in identifying children whose language development is atypical, providing information about the strengths and weaknesses of individual children, documenting progress in specialized programs, and serving as a measure for research purposes. Administration time ranges from thirty minutes to an hour. Raw scores can be converted to percentile ranks, age equivalents, and standard scores for both subtests and composites.

**FIGURE 10.10**
Summary and
Response Form
from *Test of Written
Spelling, Fourth
Edition* (TWS-4)

# TWS–4

## Test of Written Spelling
### Fourth Edition

## SUMMARY/RESPONSE FORM

Form A ☐
Form B ☐

### Section I. Identifying Information

Name _____

Male ☐     Female ☐

School _____

Examiner's Name _____

Referred by _____

Reason for Referral _____

|  | Year | Month |
|---|---|---|
| Date Tested | _____ | _____ |
| Date of Birth | _____ | _____ |
| Age | _____ | _____ |

### Section II. Record of TWS—4 Scores

Raw Score        _____

Standard Score   _____

Percentile       _____

Spelling Age     _____

Grade Equivalent _____

### Section III. Other Test Scores

| Test Name | Date | Test Score | TWS-4 Score Equivalent |
|---|---|---|---|
| 1. | | | |
| 2. | | | |
| 3. | | | |
| 4. | | | |

### Section IV. Profile of Scores

| Standarc Score | TWS-4 Form A | TWS-4 Form B | Other Tests 1 | 2 | 3 | 4 | Standard Score |
|---|---|---|---|---|---|---|---|
| 150 | · | · | · | · | · | · | 150 |
| 145 | · | · | · | · | · | · | 145 |
| 140 | · | · | · | · | · | · | 140 |
| 135 | · | · | · | · | · | · | 135 |
| 130 | · | · | · | · | · | · | 130 |
| 125 | · | · | · | · | · | · | 125 |
| 120 | · | · | · | · | · | · | 120 |
| 115 | · | · | · | · | · | · | 115 |
| 110 | · | · | · | · | · | · | 110 |
| 105 | · | · | · | · | · | · | 105 |
| 100 | · | · | · | · | · | · | 100 |
| 95 | · | · | · | · | · | · | 95 |
| 90 | · | · | · | · | · | · | 90 |
| 85 | · | · | · | · | · | · | 85 |
| 80 | · | · | · | · | · | · | 80 |
| 75 | · | · | · | · | · | · | 75 |
| 70 | · | · | · | · | · | · | 70 |
| 65 | · | · | · | · | · | · | 65 |
| 60 | · | · | · | · | · | · | 60 |
| 55 | · | · | · | · | · | · | 55 |

### Section V. Test Conditions

A. Testing Location _____

B. Environmental Characteristics

|  | Interfering | Noninterfering |
|---|---|---|
| Noise level | _____ | _____ |
| Interruptions | _____ | _____ |
| Distractions | _____ | _____ |
| Lighting | _____ | _____ |
| Temperature | _____ | _____ |
| Other _____ | _____ | _____ |

C. Notes and other considerations _____

_____

_____

_____

### Section VI. Comments and Recommendations

_____

_____

_____

_____

_____

Additional copies of this form (#8887) may be purchased from
PRO-ED, 8700 Shoal Creek Boulevard, Austin, TX 78757-6897
512/451-3246, Fax 512/451-8542
800/897-3202, Fax 800/397-7633
Order online at http://www.proedinc.com

*Source:* "Summary/Response Form" from *TWS–4 Test of Written Spelling*, 4th ed. Copyright © 1999, 1994, 1986, 1976 by PRO-ED, Inc. Reprinted by permission.

Criterion-related evidence of validity for the TOLD-3 Primary includes moderate to high correlations between 30 students' performance on the TOLD-3's subtests and those of the *Bankson Language Test, Second Edition* (Bankson, 1990, as cited in Newcomer & Hammill, 1997). In addition, fairly extensive criterion-related evidence of validity for the similar TOLD-2 Primary is offered in the manual. The authors compared the subtests of the TOLD-2 to nine criterion tests, with the correlation coefficients for all students ranging from .69 to .84. The coefficients for subtest scores for various age groups were smaller, however. Content-related evidence of validity is presented in the form of expert judgment. Although the tasks are similar to those used on many formal tests of language, Westby (1988, pp. 236–237) asks of the TOLD-2, "Do the test tasks represent anything that the child actually does with language in the real world?" She concludes that the test has serious flaws in this area and suggests using it for screening only, supplementing it with language samples gathered in more natural language contexts. The same suggestion may be made for use of the TOLD-3.

The authors provide a good discussion of reliability and provide coefficients that consistently exceed .80. Using a measure of internal consistency, the composites range from .89 to .96, with subtests somewhat lower. These results suggest that the test has adequate reliability at both the subtest and composite levels for screening purposes. Test–retest reliability information is limited to a small sample but appears adequate.

New norms were created for the third edition, and the norming procedures appear acceptable, with representative stratified sampling of acceptable numbers of students. The TOLD-2 was criticized because the norms were based on speakers of mainstream English only, and there is some evidence that dialect speakers and bilingual speakers may perform poorly on this test (Westby, 1988). There is no evidence that this issue has been addressed in the TOLD-3. The TOLD-3 is most likely to be useful in providing normative screening data to language arts professionals, especially when they are considering a referral to a language specialist. However, test users should be especially careful about possible dialect usage and should also be alert to evidence of acceptable language use in normal daily discourse.

*Comprehensive Test of Phonological Processing.*   The CTOPP (Wagner et al., 1999), is a new addition to the available assessment tools. According to the test, it is designed for use in identifying individuals who are significantly below their peers in phonological abilities, determining their strengths and weaknesses, and documenting progress in the development of phonological processes.

There are two versions of the CTOPP, one for use with students ages 5–6 and one for use with individuals ages 7–24. Both versions contain three composite components and related subtests:

| *Composites* | *Subtests* |
|---|---|
| **Phonological Awareness Quotient (PAQ)** measures an individual's awareness and access to the phonological structure of oral language | Elision, Blending Words, Sound Matching |

**Phonological Memory Quotient (PMQ)** measures ability to code information phonologically for temporary storage in short-term memory

Memory for Digits, Nonword Repetition

**Rapid Naming Quotient (RNQ)** measures ability to retrieve phonological information from long-term memory and ability to execute a sequence of operations quickly

Rapid Color Naming, Rapid Object Naming, Blending Nonwords

Both versions also have a supplemental subtest called "Blending Nonwords," and Version 2 has the following additional supplemental composites and subtests:

| *Composites* | *Subtests* |
| --- | --- |
| Alternate Phonological Awareness | Blending Nonwords, Segmenting Nonwords |
| Alternate Rapid Naming | Rapid Color Naming, Rapid Object Naming |

Two additional subtests are not included in the composites: Phoneme Reversal and Segmenting Words.

As evidence of content-related validity, the authors describe a theoretical framework for evaluating phonological processing and use the framework to provide a rationale for the three composites in each of the two versions. The authors also provide a discussion of relevant research that supports the inclusion of content for each subtest. In addition, the authors provide statistical data to support the appropriateness of items using an item analysis procedure. Finally, they examine the relationship between content and external factors, specifically bias associated with particular groups, to demonstrate that the test items contain little or no bias. Items that appeared to be biased against one group were removed.

Evidence of criterion-related validity was provided for several indicators. Correlations between the CTOPP and the Woodcock Reading Mastery Tests—Revised (WRMIT-R) indicate the validity of the test with regard to decoding, word identification, and word analysis. There were also high correlations between the CTOPP and the Test of Word Reading Efficiency (TOWRE) with regard to sight word efficiency and phonetic decoding. Confirmatory factor analysis results support the construct validity of the CTOPP, although the correlations for some subtests are modest at best. Memory for digits, for example, is consistently lower than most other subtests in its relation to other criteria.

The average reliability coefficient ranged from .77 to .90 on subtests and from .83 to .95 for the composites, suggesting acceptable levels of reliability for most purposes. However, subtest scores are less reliable than the composite scores and should be interpreted very cautiously, if at all. The authors caution users against using CTOPP results for individual instructional planning, suggesting instead that they be used as part of a more comprehensive assessment of the students. Although the CTOPP was normed on more than 1,600 individuals ranging in age from 5 through 24, more than half of the norming sample came from students in grades K–5, so it could be expected to be more reliable at those ages or grades. The norming sample was representative of the population of the United States as reported by the 1997 Census data and was stratified by using age and demographic characteristics.

Although the authors make a persuasive case for the assessment of phonological processing, including the specific processes they evaluate, they provide less compelling evidence that such extensive consideration of phonological processing has validity for individuals beyond grade 3, even individuals with reading difficulty. The available research on phonological processes has been done almost exclusively with young children or early emergent readers. In short, there is little reason to believe that among older readers, performance on this assessment will provide important distinctions among readers and reading abilities. For younger, struggling readers this test is a welcome addition to the toolbox.

*Clinical Evaluation of Language Fundamentals, Third Edition.*    The CELF-3 (Semel et al., 1995) is intended to identify, diagnose, and further evaluate students aged 6–21 who have language skill deficits. The test contains eleven subtests that measure particular receptive and expressive language skills. Only six of the subtests are required to calculate receptive, expressive, and total language scores, and the required subtests differ according to the student's age. Required receptive subtests include Linguistic Concepts, Sentence Structure, Oral Directions, Word Classes, and Semantic Relationships. Required expressive subtests include Word Structure, Recalling Sentences, Formulated Sentences, and Sentence Assembly. Supplementary subtests for all ages are Listening to Paragraphs, Word Associations, and Rapid, Automatic Naming. In comparison to the CELF-R (Semel et al., 1989), the more recent CELF-3 includes updated stimuli that are now in color, a wider age range, and new norms. The software scoring program has been updated, and communication checklists have been added to provide another look at a student's communication and the effects any language disorder may have. The new norms are based on a sample of English-dominant students who were demographically representative of the nation in the 1980s. Of concern, however, is the fact that students who had been diagnosed with a language difficulty or were receiving language therapy were excluded from the sample. As one reviewer explained, "This poses interpretation problems for those who wish to use the test for identifying children with language impairments. If only normally achieving children were tested, and the entire range of scores presented in the manual were obtained by children who were "normal," what would constitute an abnormal score?" (Gillam, 1998, p. 261).

As evidence of content-related validity, the authors explain that the language skills sampled are well documented in the literature on language and language disorders. A factor analysis and a discriminant analysis are offered as evidence of construct-related validity. The factor analysis reveals that approximately 50 percent of the variance in students' scores is explained by one factor that the authors call *language ability.* In the discriminant analysis both students who had been identified by their school districts as language disordered and those who had not took the CELF-3. There was fairly substantial overlap between the scores of the language-disordered and non-language-disordered students, and the CELF-3 classified

29 percent of the students differently than their school districts. Criterion-related evidence of validity presented indicates that the CELF-3 correlates moderately with the *Wechsler Intelligence Scale for Children, Third Edition* ($r = .75$). Taken together, these findings suggest that the CELF-3 measures general verbal ability (Gillam, 1998). Tests of reliability reveal that the subtest scores are less reliable than the composite scores and should be interpreted very cautiously, if at all. We agree with Gillam (1998, p. 262), who concludes, "Use of the CELF-3 should be limited to contexts in which the examiner wishes only to determine a student's overall language ability with reference to a large sample of "normal" children. The CELF-3 should not be used to diagnose language impairment."

### A *Criterion-Referenced Diagnostic Test: The* BRIGANCE Diagnostic Inventories.

As we have already noted, tests emphasizing criterion-referenced interpretations (CRTs) are designed to assess students' abilities and describe their strengths and weaknesses without making comparisons to other students. CRTs have proliferated since their initial appearance in the 1960s. The success and utility of a CRT depend on the degree to which the tasks and behaviors that are sampled on the test are closely related to a reasonable view of skilled performance and are like the tasks and behaviors teachers intend to address.

The *Brigance Diagnostic Inventories* provide an example of this type of testing. There are five different Brigance inventories aimed at evaluating a wide range of ages and skills: Inventory of Early Development—Revised (Brigance, 1991), Comprehensive Inventory of Basic Skills—Revised (Brigance, 1999), Inventory of Essential Skills (Brigance, 1981), Life Skills Inventory (Brigance, 1994), and Employability Skills Inventory (Brigance, 1995). A sixth inventory is the Assessment of Basic Skills—Spanish Edition (Brigance, 1984). Separate from the inventories, there is also a series of tests designed to screen early childhood students. The inventories focus on a variety of skill areas, including oral reading, reading comprehension, word analysis, vocabulary, listening, spelling, writing, and areas in mathematics and life skills. Each of the inventories contains a listing of 100 or more skills to be tested. The tests produce grade-level scores for each of the skills, and teachers are encouraged to plan their instructional programs on the basis of the specific items missed.

The revised edition of the Comprehensive Inventory of Basic Skills includes norm-referenced scores in addition to criterion-referenced scores. A technical manual for this test (Glascoe, 1998) includes the process by which norms were obtained, some minimal and inadequate evidence of validity (Cizek, 2001), and no evidence of reliability. Unfortunately, with the exception of an insufficient study of the validity and reliability of the Diagnostic Inventory of Early Development—Revised (Enright, 1991), the tests provide no information regarding the validity of the tested skills for developing competent readers and writers. The assumption is made that if children master each of the subskills in the hierarchy, they will be successful. This near absence of validity information is especially troubling because the Brigance Inventories have enjoyed wide use, in part because the results are so easily translated into instructional objectives of the sort used by many special educators to write IEPs. Indeed, any item that is not mastered on this test is likely to be listed as a desirable outcome on an IEP.

The Brigance Inventories also provide scant information about either the reliability or developmental appropriateness of the tests. As a result, it is not reasonable to use them as a placement tool, a purpose suggested by the author (Smith in Mitchell, 1985, p. 216). The most defensible use of the Brigance Inventories is to reveal fairly quickly to the uninformed or busy teacher some of the areas that may require further testing or evaluation. However, Brigance himself notes that the test should be used together with other information, such as classroom observational data and work samples.

## Tests of General Cognitive and Verbal Abilities

Educators often require information about student performance in areas other than language arts. This may include information related to the learner factors contributing to reading and writing performance (see Chapter 2), such as general cognitive ability or emotional/physical development. Assessments in these areas may be necessary to eliminate or identify these factors as central in understanding performance.

The role of general cognitive development in influencing reading and writing achievement is well documented. As measured by standardized tests, the relationship between verbal ability and literacy learning is very strong. It is important for educators to examine the issues surrounding intelligence testing and to use this information cautiously, since test scores are obviously influenced by what is measured and by students' opportunity to learn what is expected (see Chapters 2 and 6). However, limited verbal ability *can* contribute to problems in reading and writing, and in the case of students who have significant limitations in verbal ability, special placements and provisions should be considered.

In addition to the usual cautions about test use and misuse, one major caveat regarding intelligence test information is in order. Many schools continue the practice of routinely collecting IQ data using group tests of intelligence. Sometimes the tests are piggybacked onto the group achievement tests used by the district or school, and at other times schools use the available independent group intelligence tests. A wide range of problems are associated with the use of these tests (see Salvia & Ysseldyke, 2001). Most of the tests are not adequately normed and have limited evidence of validity as measures of intelligence. In addition, the reliability coefficients for individual test scores are often low. For these reasons, group intelligence data are not permissible as data when making major placement and eligibility decisions (e.g., special education determinations). Given the limited utility of this information and the volatile nature of the data, it is hard to understand why schools persist in this practice.

Although we cannot possibly review all of these types of instruments in this text, some are administered or encountered so frequently by educators working in the language arts areas that they need to be addressed here. Specifically, we describe two tests that are commonly used to make decisions about students' cognitive abilities: the *Beery-Buktenica Developmental Test of Visual-Motor Integration,* or VMI (Beery, 1997), and the *Peabody Picture Vocabulary Test,* or PPVT-III (Dunn & Dunn, 1997). Both have serious limitations that are also described to help school personnel evaluate these and other similar tools used to make judgments about students.

***Beery-Buktenica Developmental Test of Visual-Motor Integration, Fourth Edition, Revised.*** Originally published in 1967 and essentially the same today, the VMI (Beery,

1997) requires students only to imitate or copy a series of geometric forms that are increasingly difficult. The twenty-seven-item test or a shortened version of it can be used with students aged 3–18. The primary purpose of the VMI is to screen and identify students who may benefit from special assistance. Other purposes include providing evidence to secure such assistance for a child, testing the success of interventions, and research. In 1996 two supplemental tests—one of visual perception and the other of motor coordination—were made available. These supplemental tests attempt to break the skills necessary for successful performance on the VMI into its component parts. Both supplemental tests utilize the series of forms used in the VMI. In the visual perception test, students are asked to choose the identical form among forms that are bigger or smaller or otherwise altered. In the motor coordination test, students imitate the examiner's drawing or draw within the boundaries of the outlines of the forms. The VMI takes approximately ten or fifteen minutes to administer, and children older than kindergarten may be tested in small or large groups. The supplemental tests are probably more successfully administered individually. Students are allowed three minutes for the visual perception test and five minutes for the motor coordination test. Normal curve equivalents, percentile ranks, age-equivalent scores, and other derived scores are available.

Interscorer reliability scores suggest that it is possible to score the VMI reliably. Test–retest and internal consistency coefficients are sufficient for the screening purposes for which the test is recommended. Content-related evidence of validity includes an explanation of the selection of items or forms. In part by studying the 600 students' copies of seventy-two forms, the author determined the twenty-seven forms used in the test as well as sequence in which children were developmentally able to copy them. The VMI correlates moderately well with intelligence tests and other tests of copying.

Despite the author's admonitions that the VMI is a screening device and should never be the sole evidence on which evaluations are made, the suggestion that perceptual-motor skills such as copying can predict success in reading, writing, or other academic areas is difficult to justify. Indeed, the available evidence now suggests that there is no causal relationship between perceptual-motor abilities and reading/writing success (see Chapter 2).

***Peabody Picture Vocabulary Test, Third Edition.*** The PPVT-III (Dunn & Dunn, 1997) is an individually administered test of receptive vocabulary that provides norm-referenced interpretations of scores. It is designed for use with people aged $2\frac{1}{2}$ and older and contains two parallel forms. Each form consists of an easel-booklet of stimuli plates. Each plate page contains four pictures, one of which illustrates the meaning of the stimulus word that is read by the examiner. Students need only point or gesture toward the correct picture. Administration and scoring time is approximately twenty minutes.

Raw scores can be converted to standard scores (mean of 100, SD of 15), percentile ranks, stanines, normal curve equivalents, and age-equivalent scores. In addition, confidence bands for these derived scores are provided. The norming procedures for the PPVT-III are good, in terms of both representativeness and stratified sampling methods. The norms for the group aged $2\frac{1}{2}$–18 are more reliable than those for adults because there were fewer adults in the standardization sample. The authors advise users that people with uncorrected vision or hearing problems and those whose proficiency with English was limited were not included in the normative sample. The norms should not be considered valid for students with these characteristics.

Criterion-related evidence of validity consists of correlational studies of small groups of examinees' performance on the PPVT-III and four intelligence or language tests. Correlations were at least moderate and seem acceptable despite the small number tested. The authors offer little information about content validity. Although procedures for item development appear to be adequate, Jongsma (1982) once noted that no evidence is offered for the curricular relevance of these words, and this is still true. The manual reports reliability coefficients for internal consistency, test–retest, and alternate forms. Most of these are in the .90s and are acceptable for screening purposes. As the authors advise using this test for those purposes only, the reliabilities seem reasonable.

The PPVT-III is a reasonably reliable test that is quick and easy to administer and score. The authors suggest that it serves as a measure of achievement when viewed as a test of receptive vocabulary and can also be considered to be a quick global measure of one aspect of verbal ability. Previous versions of this test resulted in so-called intelligence quotients, and the test was frequently—but wrongly—viewed as an IQ test. In this latest version the authors are careful to characterize the test as a receptive vocabulary test only and to caution against using it as a comprehensive test of intelligence. Like the TOLD-3, however, it can help educators to decide whether they wish to recommend further testing.

## Readiness/Emergent Literacy Assessment

Gathering dependable and useful information about the literacy abilities of young children can be a very tricky business. We have addressed many of the salient issues in previous portions of this text (see Chapters 5 and 7). Traditional tests of reading readiness are intended to determine whether students are ready to learn to read. As a result, they are judged useful if they predict students' subsequent success in reading or appropriately place students in beginning instructional programs. Indeed, many school systems continue to use readiness tests for both screening and placement purposes, often as the basis for recommending special classes or delayed entry into school.

Most existing readiness tests share several significant problems. First, test results of very young children are often unreliable, and existing readiness tests are no exception. Second, few such tests provide sufficient evidence of predictive validity to warrant making judgments about students' future performance. As Shepard and Smith (1986, p. 83) note,

> The lack of high correlations with later school success is caused by the instability of the very traits we are seeking to measure. Four- and five-year-olds experience developmental bursts and inconsistencies that defy normative charts. In addition, the cognitive domains that can be sampled at younger ages are only moderately related to the cognitive skills demanded later by reading and other academic tasks.

A third problem relates to the degree to which readiness tests reflect recent advances in our knowledge of literacy development. Many commercially available readiness tests were first developed fifty years ago and generally do not provide information regarding the foundations of literacy that may be used to differentiate among students in instructionally meaningful ways.

More recently, tests developed in response to an emergent literacy view of reading and writing development have begun to appear. In fact, some tests that we classified as traditional readiness tests in the first edition of this text have been revised in a manner more consistent with current views of emergent literacy. For example, in 1991 we described the Metropolitan Readiness Test, or MRT (Nurss & McGauvran, 1976/1986), as a prototype of a subskills readiness test. The current MRT6 (Nurss & McGauvran, 1995) is part of a larger Metropolitan Early Childhood Assessment Program (M-KIDS). Level 1 of MRT6 is now individually administered, and the list of subtests for level 2 appears far more representative of areas that are key to emergent literacy than in the previous edition. Although the newer tests of emergent literacy are not without flaws, they offer different types of information than traditional readiness tests. Tests such as the *Test of Early Reading Ability—3* (Reid, Hresko, & Hammill, 2001) attempt a global assessment of emergent literacy. Many school systems continue to use developmental tests, most often to make judgments about whether children are ready to enter school programs (Durkin, 1987). These tests are also commonly used to make decisions about placement into special programs (e.g., transitional kindergarten/first grades) or to limit entrance into kindergarten (who should stay home for a year). These tests often evaluate readiness using global data regarding physical and cognitive development. Alternatively, developmental readiness is often evaluated using measures of conceptual achievement. The *Boehm Test of Basic Concepts, Third Edition* (Boehm, 2001) is an example of this type. Other tests in this category not discussed here include the *Test of Early Written Language, Second Edition,* or TEWL-2 (Hresko, Herron, & Peak, 1996) and the *Test of Phonological Awareness,* or TOPA (Torgensen & Bryant, 1994).

***Metropolitan Readiness Test, Sixth Edition.*** The sixth edition of the *Metropolitan Readiness Test* (Nurss & McGauvran, 1995) is intended to assess prekindergarten, kindergarten, and beginning first grade students' readiness for reading and math instruction, specifically to provide "an assessment of emerging literacy concepts with an emphasis on reading and writing in context." As we mentioned previously, the test includes two levels; level 1 is administered individually and is intended for younger and lower achieving students. The reading subtests for level 1 are Visual Discrimination, Beginning Consonants, Sound-Letter Correspondence, and Story Comprehension. The reading subtests for level 2 are the same, except that Aural Cloze with Letter replaces Visual Discrimination. Content-referenced scores and associated performance ratings as well as norm-referenced scores (percentile ranks, stanines, scaled scores, and normal curve equivalents) are available. However, the performance ratings of students' levels of proficiency are based solely on the authors' judgments. Also, the interpretation of results for students who have limited proficiency with English is given only cursory attention. The norms are representative of the nation in 1990–1991, but the sample is not broken down by grade level.

The authors present very little evidence of validity. In fact, they present no content-related evidence of validity beyond a claim that research was done to determine relevant measures of prereading skills development. Criterion-related evidence of validity is absent for level 1, and two tests of predictive validity show moderate correlations between students' performance on level 2 of the MRT6 and their performance a year later on two other achievement tests. Moderate correlations between subtest performance might be seen as construct validity, but this too is inadequate. Perhaps worse, there are no studies of test item bias toward particular groups. One reviewer asserts that the general lack of attention to issues of fairness "makes the MRT6 inadequate by modern standards" (Kamphaus, 2001, p. 749).

Reliability evidence consists of calculations of internal consistency, test–retest coefficients, and standard errors of measurement. Internal consistency and test–retest coefficients seem reasonable for the most part, but estimates of measurement error are troubling. Standard errors of measurement are given "for skill areas and composites ranging from 1–4 raw score points (with larger SEMs associated with the composite scores). Using this information, a prekindergarten child obtaining a raw score of 18 on Story Comprehension could be said to perform anywhere from the 60th to 98th percentile; the same score for a midyear kindergarten results in an even larger confidence interval from the 34th to 95th percentile" (Novak, 2001, p. 750). Novak concludes sensibly that the MRT6 could help to determine readiness skills but that results for individual students, particularly as regards the analysis of performance strengths and weaknesses, should not be overinterpreted.

***Test of Early Reading Ability–3.***     The *Test of Early Reading Ability–3,* or TERA-3 (Reid, Hresko, & Hammill, 2001), is designed to identify students who are below the average in reading development and to monitor progress in intervention programs. It is individually administered and takes fifteen to thirty minutes to complete. The TERA-3 test items relate to three component areas of early reading behavior: constructing meaning, alphabet knowledge, and conventions of print.

The original TERA, published in 1981, was "a significant departure from current readiness tests in that it provides a norm reference for the direct measurement of reading behaviors of preschool children" (S. E. Wixson, 1985, p. 544). The revised edition (TERA-3) has maintained the strong features of the previous edition test while remedying some of the problems. For example, illustrations in the students' picture book are now in color, and test administrators no longer have to prepare items. Current normative data were collected, and studies that search for gender, racial, and disability bias have been added. Because they are required in many jurisdictions, age- and grade-equivalent scores are now provided, and the authors wisely caution users against their misuse. In addition, standard scores, percentile ranks, and stanine scores are available.

Normative data from a large sample tested during 1999 and 2000 are provided in the manual and generally seem adequate. The TERA-3 has been improved by the addition of new items designed to capture the performance of students at the upper and lower ages covered. Also, the ages covered by the test have been reduced from 3.0–9.11 to 3.6–8.6. The reliability of this test is supported by using internal consistency coefficients for each of the three subtests at six age levels. The reliability coefficients are sufficiently high, except perhaps for the conventions subtest at ages 3 and 8.

The item selection and test construction of the TERA-3 appear reasonable, but its validity really rests on its theoretical orientation. The TERA-3 is notable for its attempt to assess areas of emergent literacy that have been identified by recent research. The Meaning portion of the test contains items designed to assess environmental print awareness, knowledge of relationships among vocabulary words, print awareness in connected discourse, and the ability to anticipate written language (a cloze test). On the Alphabet portion students are required to name letters, read orally, and determine the number of syllables in words. Conventions measure students' knowledge of left–right orientation, punctuation, spatial presentation of the story on a page, and general book-handling ability.

Students respond to retelling a story, choosing correct answers, comparing answers, filling in a missing word, or finding a mistake in printed material. The test manual suggests entry points for various ages of children and procedures for finding their basal and ceiling levels. Unfortunately, the score sheet does not permit notation regarding specific components of each item passed or failed. This limits the amount of diagnostic information that is targeted, and even a sophisticated examiner has no place to organize the data.

The TERA-3 has acceptable levels of reliability for testing concepts related to emergent reading. Of the available readiness tests reviewed in this chapter, the TERA-3 is the best match with current models of readiness. Several traditional aspects of readiness (e.g., letter knowledge) are assessed, as well as several aspects of metalinguistic awareness. The test is reliable, and young children seem to enjoy it and find the format nonthreatening.

### Boehm Test of Basic Concepts, Third Edition.

Estimates of verbal and conceptual readiness are less controversial than estimates of physical and emotional development but no less difficult to evaluate in young children. One advantage to tests of basic concepts is that they are often simple to give and score. For example, the *Boehm Test of Basic Concepts–3,* or Boehm-3 (Boehm, 2001), is a group-administered test that takes only fifteen to twenty minutes to administer and provides normative data.

The Boehm-3 is designed to measure students' knowledge of concepts that are thought to be important for school achievement. According to the author, it can be used to identify children who are at risk for learning problems and children who have not mastered basic concepts, so that remedial instruction can be planned. The test evaluates students' understanding of fifty concepts representing various relationships (e.g., *next to, inside,* or *several*) by having them mark pictures that reflect concepts read by the teacher. The author provides documentation that these concepts are generally important to school settings. Alternate test forms are available for pretesting and posttesting. Pass–fail scores are generated for each item, and percentile ranks are available for total scores.

In comparison to its predecessor, Boehm-R (Boehm, 1986), the Boehm-3 includes a fourth response choice for each item, more current and appealing illustrations, a parent report form, updated norms, a Spanish edition for which separate norms were developed, and an observation form (see Figure 10.11). The normative sample includes special education students who were mainstreamed in the tested classrooms, but the authors do not report the number of such students. In addition, reliability coefficients are somewhat weak for test–retest estimates.

**FIGURE 10.11**
Example of a
Completed
Test Summary
and Teacher
Observation
Form, from
*Boehm-3*

# Boehm·3    *Test Summary and Teacher Observation Form*
Boehm Test of Basic Concepts · Third Edition

Child's Name ___Julie Martinez_____ Age __6_____ Grade __K_____

Teacher/Evaluator ___Mr. Thompson_____ School ___Lincoln Elementary_____

Language the child speaks at home ___English_____

Date Tested __10/13__ (Form E) Form F    Raw Score __45__ % Correct __90__ Performance Range __I__ Percentile __80__

Date Tested _____ Form E  Form F    Raw Score ____ % Correct ____ Performance Range ____ Percentile ____

## —— *Child's Performance Summary* ——

Place an X in the blank next to the number of the item missed. Use this form for more than one administration by using a different color of ink each time. (**Space** *Where* = Red; **Quantity** *How many?* = Green; **Time** *When* = Blue; **Other** = Orange)

| Item | Concept | Item | Concept | Item | Concept |
|---|---|---|---|---|---|
| ____ | 1. Top | ____ | 18. First | ____ | 35. As Many |
| ____ | 2. Center | ____ | 19. Row | ____ | 36. Third |
| ____ | 3. Whole | ____ | 20. Few | ____ | 37. Other |
| ____ | 4. Side | ____ | 21. Next | ____ | 38. Starting |
| ____ | 5. Last | ____ | 22. Every | ____ | 39. Most |
| ____ | 6. Medium-sized | ____ | 23. Bottom | ____ | 40. Behind |
| ____ | 7. Always | ____ | 24. Never | ____ | 41. Left |
| ____ | 8. Right | ____ | 25. Beginning | ____ | 42. Between |
| ____ | 9. Corner | ____ | 26. Second | ____ | 43. Different |
| ____ | 10. Before | ____ | 27. Front | ____ | 44. Pair |
| ____ | 11. End | ____ | 28. Widest | ____ | 45. Below |
| ____ | 12. Farthest | ____ | 29. Away | __X__ | 46. Skip |
| ____ | 13. Part | ____ | 30. Half | ____ | 47. Forward |
| ____ | 14. Through | ____ | 31. Alike | ____ | 48. Least |
| ____ | 15. Some | __X__ | 32. Fewest | __X__ | 49. Backward |
| ____ | 16. Above | ____ | 33. Match | __X__ | 50. Equal |
| __X__ | 17. Separated | ____ | 34. Over | | |

## *Teacher Observations of Basic Concepts Used Across Curriculum Areas*

| Curriculum Area | Concept | Observed | Comments/Examples |
|---|---|---|---|
| Following teacher directions and classroom activities | top*–bottom* <br> over–under* <br> next to* <br> through <br> first*–last* <br> above–below <br> corner <br> side <br> in front of—behind <br> away from* <br> nearest*–farthest* <br> separated <br> alike (same)–different* <br> match <br> left–right <br> center <br> forward–(backward) <br> always–never <br> (skip) <br> every <br> row <br> between* <br> beginning–end <br> other | <br><br><br><br><br><br><br><br><br><br><br><br><br><br><br><br>11/15<br><br>12/3 | <br><br><br><br><br><br><br><br><br><br><br><br><br><br><br><br>Used the concept "backward" during storytime.<br><br>Demonstrated understanding of skip by skipping lines on her paper when directed to. |

*Source:* "Test Summary and Teacher Observation Form" from the *Boehm-3*. Reprinted by permission of The Psychological Corporation, a Harcourt Assessment Company.

# Chapter Summary

The chapter began by emphasizing that much of what we know to be important in reading and writing processes is not reflected in formal assessment devices. However, the widespread use of formal tests in reading and writing makes it important to understand a number of different aspects of standardized testing. The general information necessary to become a critical consumer of formal assessment devices was the focus of the first half of the chapter. The topics discussed were general test characteristics, important statistical concepts, validity, reliability, test interpretations, test scores, and test fairness.

The discussion of general test characteristics included information such as the importance of determining the appropriateness of the level of difficulty and type of administration for the students with whom the test will be used and the purposes for which it is intended. Important statistical concepts for understanding normal distribution and correlation such as mean and standard deviation were also discussed.

Validity was described as the most important concern in evaluating formal tests as specified by the 1985 and 1999 *Standards for Educational and Psychological Testing*. Validity is related to the claims made by users of the test information, and the valid use of tests is the responsibility of both the test developer and the test user. The three categories of evidence that should be considered in the process of test validation were described as content-, criterion-, and construct-related evidence of validity after the 1985 standards.

Content-related evidence of validity refers to the extent to which the test's content is representative of the universe of content being sampled by the test and requires that we have a precise definition of the domain the test items are intended to reflect. Criterion-related evidence of validity demonstrates that test scores be systematically related to one or more outcome criteria. The two types of criterion-related evidence of validity are concurrent and predictive. Concurrent evidence refers to the relationship between a person's score and an immediate criterion. Predictive evidence refers to the relationship between a person's score and performance on some measure at a later time.

Construct-related evidence of validity focuses on test scores as a measure of the psychological characteristic of interest. Most theorists now argue that all validity research should be conducted within a construct validity framework that requires an explicit conceptual framework, testable hypotheses deduced from it, and multiple lines of relevant evidence to test the hypotheses.

Reliability was also described as a major criterion of test acceptability. Reliability refers to the consistency or stability of a test and involves the extent to which some attribute has been measured in a systematic and therefore repeatable way. The two types of reliability discussed here were test–retest and alternate form. The standard error of measurement (SEM) was also described as helpful to the test consumer in determining the confidence with which a test score can be interpreted.

Norm-referenced test interpretations were described in terms of the adequacy of the test norms. The size and representativeness of the norm sample are important because an examinee's performance is evaluated in comparison to the performance of the individuals in the normative sample. On the basis of the responses of the normative sample, raw scores obtained from any subsequent examinee can be converted into a variety of derived scores designed to measure relative standing. For example, grade and age equivalents are derived from the average scores earned by students in the normative sample at a particular grade or age level. Other types of derived scores that were discussed include percentile ranks and standard scores.

Criterion-referenced test interpretations were described as evaluating an individual's test performance on some preestablished standard or criterion. The issue of test fairness to racial and cultural minorities was discussed in terms of the possible presence of bias in the test content and the possible unfair use of test results. The first half of the chapter concluded with summary guidelines for evaluating formal assessment instruments.

The second half of the chapter described several types of formal assessment tools and provided detailed descriptions and evaluations of exemplars of each type of test. Survey tests were described as norm-referenced tests of global reading achievement used to screen large numbers of students for approximate reading levels and to identify those who may have serious reading and/or writing problems.

Diagnostic tests were described as designed to provide a profile of an individual's relative strengths and weaknesses. Tests of general cognitive and verbal abilities were also described. Finally, traditional tests of reading readiness were described, as were more recent tests of factors associated with emergent literacy.

In conclusion, this chapter suggested that formal tests should be used with a great deal of caution and that they should be used primarily as general estimates of various aspects of reading and writing, to be followed up by more in-depth, instructionally valid, informal measures such as those described elsewhere in this text.

## ASSESSMENT SOURCES AND RESOURCES

Professionals in the fields of reading, writing, special education, and psychology often find it helpful to refer to test reviews and critical analyses completed by experts in these fields. Perhaps the most commonly used referenced is a series of books called the *Mental Measurements Yearbooks.* Developed and edited for almost fifty years by Oscar Buros, these references are often called simply *Buros.* These volumes are unique because they provide independent, critical analyses of the tests by knowledgeable professionals. These and other critical reviews or descriptions can be helpful to those who need to evaluate tests.

### Tests Cited

Beery, K. E. (1997). *The Beery-Buktenica Developmental Test of Visual-Motor Integration.* Parsippany, NJ: Modern Curriculum Press.

Boehm, A. E. (2001). *Boehm Test of Basic Concepts* (3rd ed.). San Antonio, TX: The Psychological Corporation.

Brigance, A. H. (1981). *Inventory of Essential Skills.* North Billerica, MA: Curriculum Associates.

Brigance, A. H. (1984). *Assessment of Basic Skills—Spanish Edition.* North Billerica, MA: Curriculum Associates.

Brigance, A. H. (1991). *Inventory of Early Development—Revised.* North Billerica, MA: Curriculum Associates.

Brigance, A. H. (1994). *Life Skills Inventory.* North Billerica, MA: Curriculum Associates.

Brigance, A. H. (1995). *Employability Skills Inventory.* North Billerica, MA: Curriculum Associates.

Brigance, A. H. (1999). *Comprehensive Inventory of Basic Skills—Revised.* North Billerica, MA: Curriculum Associates.

Brown, J. I., Fishco, V. V., & Hanna, G. H. (1993). *Nelson-Denny Reading Test.* Itasca, IL: Riverside Publishing.

Brown, V. L., Hammill, D. D., & Wiederholt, J. L. (1995). *Test of Reading Comprehension* (3rd ed.). Austin, TX: PRO-ED.

Dunn, L. M., & Dunn, L. M. (1981). *Peabody Picture Vocabulary Test—Revised.* Circle Pines, MN: American Guidance Service.

Dunn, L. M., & Dunn, L. M. (1997). *Peabody Picture Vocabulary Test* (3rd ed.). Circle Pines, MN: American Guidance Service.

Hammill, D. D., & Larsen, S. C. (1988). *Test of Written Language—2.* Austin, TX: PRO-ED.

Hammill, D. D., & Larsen, S. C. (1996). *Test of Written Language—3.* Austin, TX: PRO-ED.

Hresko, W. P., Herron, S. R., & Peak, P. K. (1996). *Test of Early Written Language* (2nd ed.). Austin, TX: PRO-ED.

Karlsen, B., & Gardner, E. (1995). *Stanford Diagnostic Reading Test* (4th ed.). San Antonio, TX: Harcourt Brace.

Larsen, S. C., & Hammill, D. D. (1986). *Test of Written Spelling* (2nd ed.). Austin, TX: PRO-ED.

Larsen, S. C., & Hammill, D. D. (1994). *Test of Written Spelling* (3rd ed.). Austin, TX: PRO-ED.

Larsen, S. C., & Hammill, D. D. (1999). *Test of Written Spelling* (4th ed.). Austin, TX: PRO-ED.

MacGinitie, W. H., MacGinitie, R. K., Maria, K., & Dreyer, L. G. (2000). *Gates-MacGinitie Reading Test* (4th ed.). Itasca, IL: Riverside Publishing.

Markwardt, F. C. (1989). *Peabody Individual Achievement Battery—Revised.* Circle Pines, MN: American Guidance Service.

Newcomer, P. & Hammill, D. D. (1988). *Test of Oral Language Development—2 Primary.* Austin, TX: PRO-ED.

Newcomer, P. & Hammill, D. D. (1997). *Test of Oral Language Development—3 Primary.* Austin, TX: PRO-ED.

Nurss, J. R., & McGauvran, M. E. (1976/1986). *Metropolitan Readiness Test (MRT).* San Antonio, TX: The Psychological Corporation.

Nurss, J. R., & McGauvran, M. E. (1995). *Metropolitan Readiness Test* (6th ed.). San Antonio, TX: The Psychological Corporation.

Reid, D. K., Hresko, W. P., & Hammill, D. D. (2001). *The Test of Early Reading Ability—3 (TERA-3).* Austin, TX: PRO-ED.

Semel, E., Wiig, E. H., & Secord, W. A. (1989). *Clinical Evaluation of Language Fundamentals, Revised.* San Antonio, TX: The Psychological Corporation.

Semel, E., Wiig, E. H., & Secord, W. A. (1995). *Clinical Evaluation of Language Fundamentals* (3rd ed.). San Antonio, TX: The Psychological Corporation.

Torgeson, J. K., & Bryant, B. R. (1994). *Test of Phonological Awareness.* Austin, TX: PRO-ED.

Wagner, R. K., Torgesen, J. K., & Rashotte, C. A. (1999). *Comprehensive Test of Phonological Processing.* Austin, TX: PRO-ED.

Wiederholt, J. L., & Bryant, B. R. (1986). *Gray Oral Reading Test—Revised.* Austin, TX: PRO-ED.

Wiederholt, J. L., & Bryant, B. R. (1992). *Gray Oral Reading Test—3.* Austin, TX: PRO-ED.

Wiederholt, J. L., & Bryant, B. R. (2001). *Gray Oral Reading Test—4.* Austin, TX: PRO-ED.

Wilkinson, G. S. (1993). *Wide Range Achievement Test 3.* Wilmington, DE: Wide Range, Inc.

Woodcock, R. W. (1987). *Woodcock Reading Mastery Test—Revised.* Circle Pines, MN: American Guidance Service.

Woodcock, R. W., & Johnson, M. B. (1977). *Woodcock-Johnson Psychoeducational Battery* (1977). Allen, TX: DLM Teaching Resources.

# SECTION FOUR

# Interactions:
# Assessment as Inquiry

This section is central to understanding the relationship between assessment and instruction. As we noted previously, the interactive nature of the assessment-instruction process requires careful observation of the ways in which the various factors may be influencing reading, writing, and learning in individual students. The single chapter in this section stands alone because it focuses exclusively on the relationship between assessment and instruction—on that moment in the assessment process when informed decision making is required of the teacher and when that teacher's expertise and knowledge will determine how the instructional planning to follow will proceed. Because reading and writing abilities are not viewed as static, teachers must be prepared to describe the variability observed within the individual student under different conditions and to engage in continued explorations of this variability through diagnostic teaching.

The steps of the assessment-instruction process that are addressed in this section are shaded in the figure on the following page. They are Step 4, Evaluating the Match Between Learner and the Context; Step 5, Reflection, Decision Making, and Planning; and Step 6, Identifying a Better Match: Diagnostic Teaching.

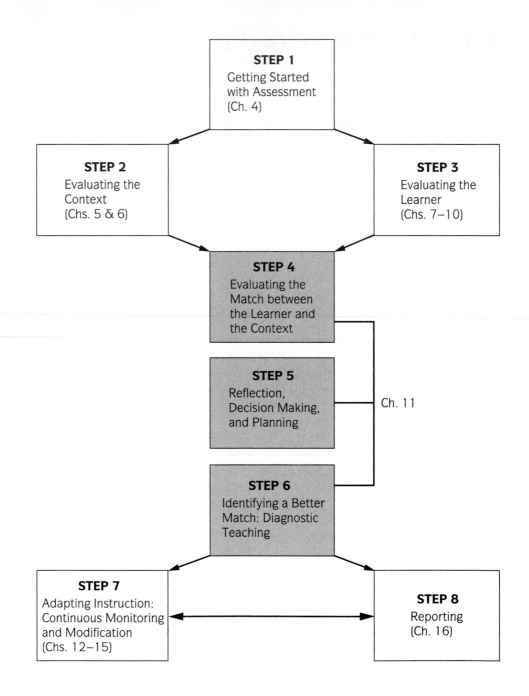

**STEP 1**
Getting Started
with Assessment
(Ch. 4)

**STEP 2**
Evaluating the
Context
(Chs. 5 & 6)

**STEP 3**
Evaluating the
Learner
(Chs. 7–10)

**STEP 4**
Evaluating the
Match between
the Learner and
the Context

**STEP 5**
Reflection,
Decision Making,
and Planning

Ch. 11

**STEP 6**
Identifying a Better
Match: Diagnostic
Teaching

**STEP 7**
Adapting Instruction:
Continuous Monitoring
and Modification
(Chs. 12–15)

**STEP 8**
Reporting
(Ch. 16)

# 11 Interactive Decision Making

Assessment is not simply the gathering of information. The success of the assessment-instruction process depends on the teacher's ability to make informed, effective decisions. Although we can provide guidance in decision making, we cannot prescribe it. Ultimately, the quality of decision making relies on the professional knowledge, experience, and judgment of the decision maker. Therefore it is incumbent on teachers and specialists to learn as much as possible about all aspects of development, learning, and teaching in order to make informed decisions.

Informed decision making also requires a clear sense of the desired outcomes of the assessment-instruction process. We agree with Johnston (1987, p. 744) when he writes, "the most fundamental goal of all educational evaluation is optimal instruction for all children and evaluation practices are only legitimate to the extent that they serve this goal." Similarly, Duffy and Rochler (1989, p. 16) note that the first characteristic of teachers who are instructional decision makers is that they "think in terms of what students should learn, not in terms of assignments for students to complete." We would also like to emphasize the value of experience in implementing the assessment-instruction process for becoming an expert evaluator and decision maker. One of the most important characteristics of expert evaluators is their ability to recognize patterns. They know not only what patterns to look for, but also the conditions under which the patterns are most likely to occur.

This chapter addresses the understanding and implementation of three steps in the assessment-instruction process: Step 4, evaluating the existing match between the learner and the context; Step 5, reflection and generating hypotheses about what the learner needs, making decisions, and implementing a plan; and Step 6, determining how to (re)establish learning through diagnostic teaching. The first half of the chapter addresses the understanding of the procedures involved in these three steps. The second half of the chapter illustrates the implementation of these three steps through the use of three case studies.

## Understanding Step 4: Evaluating the Match between Learner and Context

Using the information gathered in Steps 1–3, we are now ready to evaluate the match between the knowledge, skills, and motivation of the learner and the instrucitonal environments, settings, practices and resources within the instructional context. This step provides the answer to the question "What is the current status of the interaction between the learner and the instructional context?" Our job in this stage of the assessment-instruction process is to pull together all that we know as the result of our professional efforts and experience and to evaluate how well existing demands, expectations, and supports of the context match the learner's abilities, interests, knowledge, and level of independence. Using our framework, Vogt and Shearer (2003) have recently proposed what they call a Contextualized Assessment Cycle. In their modified plan they noted that professionals need to think of assessment as inquiry, asking questions such as:

> What do I know?
> What do I observe?
> What questions do I need to ask?
> What data do I need to collect?

The match between the learner and the instructional context includes information about areas in which the fit is both good and poor. The information in this section comes both from an evaluation of interactions between these two sets of factors and from an evaluation of the interactions observed within the assessment itself, that is, how the student performed differently under different conditions during assessment.

By the time we get to this step in the process, many of the successful and unsuccessful interactions will be obvious. If we are still uncertain about how the learner and the context interact in ways that either facilitate or inhibit learning and performance, we can examine the information in each of the categories of learner factors (background, knowledge about reading or writing, skills application, and attitudes and motivation) and ask ourselves how it fits with what we know about the contextual factors (settings, methods, and materials and tasks) and vice versa.

For example, the information about skills application might suggest that a particular reader does not fully analyze decodable words, failing to look through all of the letters and to make use of orthographic patterns. The information about methods indicates that the reader's teacher focuses on helping students to acquire strategies and promote a decoding-by-analogy approach to word recognition (see Chapter 13). This is a good match, because this instruction is likely to meet the reader's need to develop her abilities to fully examine words in print and enhance fluency. Conversely, in the case of a particular writer, information about materials may suggest that writing instruction relies almost exclusively on drill sheets with brief sentences and that the writer performs better when producing stories to be shared with an audience. This is not a good match because the writer needs different materials to facilitate learning. Other examples of poor matches that might be observed include the following:

- A third grade student who has recently arrived in the United States, with limited English proficiency and limited native-language literacy, and who is placed in a program that addresses only English acquisition and vocabulary development with no focus on building print skills in either language
- An eighth grade student who does not read independently in or out of school, whose sight vocabulary and word analysis skills are below grade level on tests of isolated skills but closer to grade level when reading coherent, full-length selections, and

who is receiving isolated word analysis skill-drill and is not permitted to advance beyond these isolated practices because of his weak performance on criterion tests of those skills

■ A highly verbal first grade student who does not have the concept of a word, nor can he voice-point, whose instruction does not include writing with invented spelling or any explicit explanation about the conventions of print, and the purposes of learning to read or write

Although it will often be quite clear how effectively the instruction and the students' needs are matched, there are times when conclusions remain ambiguous. In these cases we need to carry our questions and concerns into the next step. In other cases we will have concluded that aspects of the match are clearly inappropriate, and in these cases our questions and concerns will involve generating hypotheses about ways to remedy the mismatch. In either case it is time to step back and really think about what we know or suspect and what can be done about it.

## Understanding Step 5: Reflection, Decision Making, and Planning

After the match between the learner and the context has been evaluated, we need to reflect on this information and generate hypotheses about the second question guiding the assessment-instruction process: What does the learner need? What needs to be continued? What needs to be changed? At this point in the process, not everything will be guesswork. We already know some things about what the learner needs as a result of our previous analyses. Other things will still be unclear, however, and we need to begin to make some decisions about the relative importance of the various problems or needs we have identified.

Remember that we can always find a problem if we are looking for one but that not every problem is of equal importance to the student's progress. In evaluating the importance of the problem(s) we have identified, we should ask ourselves, "If I changed (the source of interference), is this student likely to become a better reader or writer?" If the answer is "no" or we suspect that this intervention is unlikely to go very far in solving the problem, the problem we have identified is probably not a primary source of difficulty.

Another guide to determining what the learner needs is to reexamine the information gathered about the learner and the instructional context to determine whether any of the materials, methods, or settings were more effective than others. It is important to remember that we cannot decide what the learner needs without knowing the context in which the problem exists. Otherwise, we look only to the learner for the source of the problem, when in fact it is more often the interaction between learner and context.

For example, a writer with sufficient skill and major anxiety or attitude problems may display skill deficiencies but does not need more skill instruction. What is needed instead is instruction that takes the pressure off and/or motivates the practice and application of skills. Additional examples of different types of learner needs include instruction that capitalizes on strengths while attending to weaknesses; changes perceptions of the purposes and goals of reading and writing; or explains the how, when, and why of strategy usage rather than simply providing practice.

Generating hypotheses about students' needs is always a matter of informed decision making. It requires the use of all our knowledge and experience. Examples of specific student-needs hypotheses that we have generated are as follows:

- A third grade student with adequate word recognition skill who believes that the purpose of reading is saying all the words right needs instruction that promotes understanding of the goals of reading and practice with outside reading that focuses on fluency.
- A highly verbal first grade student who does not understand print concepts needs exposure to written language in a variety of contexts.
- A fifth grade student with adequate reading skills who is uninterested and unmotivated to complete assigned reading activities and to read in or out of school needs instruction that interests and motivates him.
- A fourth grade student who functions normally at a second grade level but is placed in a fourth grade reader needs opportunities to read easy materials.
- A second grade student whose cultural background promotes reticence in public interactions and who has not engaged in challenging discussions of books needs models of how to reflect on familiar stories in nonthreatening ways, perhaps initially in a reading response log.

It is also important to recognize that many of these needs would never be identified if students were not examined within the instructional contexts in which their problems exist. Once hypotheses about learner needs have been generated and prioritized, we can begin planning the diagnostic teaching activities that will be used to evaluate the hypotheses.

# Understanding Step 6: Diagnostic Teaching

Following Steps 4 and 5, in which we reflected on the existing match and generated some preliminary hypotheses about what the learner needs, we need to address the third question guiding the assessment-instruction process: What is most likely to (re)establish learning? At this point in the process we are concerned with identifying a better or optimal match between the learner and the instructional context. To accomplish this goal, we rely primarily on the technique of diagnostic teaching. The following sections describe the purposes and procedures of diagnostic teaching.

## Definition and Purposes

The idea that we might use sample lessons as a diagnostic procedure is not a new one. According to Harris and Sipay (1985), the procedure was developed first by Harris and Roswell in 1953. Current interest in interactive views of learning has resulted in significant advances in the development and implementation of these techniques. These types of procedures are referred to variously as *trial teaching* (Tzuriel, 2000), *dynamic assessment* (Feuerstein, Rand, & Hoffman, 1979), *intervention assessment* (Paratore & Indrisano, 1987), *clinical diagnosis* (Chall & Curtis, 1987), and *diagnostic teaching* (Harris, 1977; Wixson &

Lipson, 1986). Although there are differences among these related procedures, they do share a critical feature: They are interactive assessments that provide for systematic modification of the instructional situation to observe what a student does under specified conditions.

We prefer the term *diagnostic teaching* because it reflects the dual purposes for which we use this procedure. First, the procedure is *diagnostic* because it allows us to collect additional information to clarify and test the hypotheses generated during the initial steps of the assessment-instruction process. Second, the procedure is *instructional* because it provides opportunities to try out methods that may be successful alternatives for working with a student. This last is a critical feature of diagnostic teaching because it allows us to explore a student's performance under circumstances that are more like those encountered in the classroom on a regular basis.

Throughout this book we have introduced numerous cautions, caveats, and concerns about traditional assessment practices. Diagnostic teaching procedures are flourishing, in part, as a response to these difficulties. The failure to test students under a range of conditions that represent authentic reading and writing events can result in both inaccurate diagnoses and erroneous conclusions about the focus for intervention.

Another reason why diagnostic teaching is enjoying such prominence is its utility in assessing students from linguistically and/or culturally diverse backgrounds (see Brice, 2002; Lapp, Fisher, Flood, & Cabello, 2001; O'Malley & Valdez-Pierce, 1996). Problems with the static, product-oriented results of traditional assessments have raised serious questions about *equity* issues in assessment, particularly with the use of standardized tests of achievement and intelligence. For example, Campione and Brown (1987) note that although the scores individuals attain on static tests represent only estimates of competence, all too often the unwarranted inference is made that they are measures of ability level that are relatively permanent and resistant to change (see Sternberg, 1999). In many cases, particularly for children from culturally different backgrounds, these scores provide a dramatic underestimate of the potential level of performance under different circumstances. Clearly, most conventional assessments provide flawed information about bilingual students and others from diverse cultural communities, leading to a disproportionate representation of these students in special education (NASDSE, 1994a, b). According to Wilson-Portuondo and Hardy (2001, p. 1), "It is important during the process of evaluation to understand and recognize normal difficulties resulting from the process of acculturation or to learning a second language from a disability." There is a growing body of evidence to support the conclusion that diagnostic teaching/dynamic assessment procedures provide better measures of learning potential by evaluating how a student can and will perform under different conditions (Day & Cordon, 1993; Spector, 1992).

The assessment procedures described in the preceding chapters are predicated on the assumption that we need to collect information about a range of learner and contextual factors. Until now, we have not really suggested gathering information specifically to confirm predictions about the nature of the problem and how to address it. However, diagnostic teaching is hypothesis-driven. It assumes that teachers are intentionally setting out to examine more closely something that has come to their attention.

Most instruction can be viewed as diagnostic teaching, particularly if it is carefully planned using our best predictions about what may work for a given student and if we are prepared to monitor our work continually to see how adjustments have affected learning and performance. Diagnostic teaching permits the teacher to manipulate in a planned way any of the factors that are suspected to be contributing to or inhibiting reading and writing achievement. In addition, diagnostic teaching allows us to explore the "conditions that call forth learning" (Hunt, 1961).

Skilled teachers consistently engage in diagnostic teaching. However, because this technique is so fluid and nonstandardized, most teachers undervalue the assessment information that is generated and fail to document it. At the same time they recognize the significant value of the instructional information it yields. Without diagnostic teaching we have few alternatives but to believe that all students with similar presenting problems will benefit from the same instructional program. Diagnostic teaching provides an opportunity for truly integrating instruction and assessment.

## Diagnostic Teaching Procedures

The procedures used for diagnostic teaching vary considerably from situation to situation. Because each situation is unique, it is impossible to provide step-by-step procedures for conducting diagnostic teaching sessions. However, we can describe the process of diagnostic teaching, including its characteristics and tasks. The process we describe below involves three related tasks: planning, executing, and evaluating the diagnostic teaching effort.

*Planning.*    When we reach the diagnostic teaching stage of the assessment-instruction process, we are ready to focus our efforts rather than continue gathering more general information. We have noted elsewhere in this text that assessment should be continuous and that diagnostic information is available any time we work with a student. However, we are using "diagnostic teaching" here to describe specific, intentional activity rather than a general mind-set for observing instructional interactions.

It is important to keep in mind that we are attempting to verify hunches about both the source of the problem and the instructional manipulations that are most likely to call forth learning. Because of this dual focus, diagnostic teaching requires modification and manipulation of learners and instructional contexts. To identify the student's potential for learning under different instructional conditions or the factors and conditions that facilitate or inhibit learning, we need to view diagnostic teaching as "an interaction between an examiner-as-intervener and a learner-as-active-participant, which seeks to estimate the degree of modifiability of the learner and the means by which positive changes in cognitive functioning can be induced and maintained" (Lidz, 1987, p. 4).

During planning, we need to determine how we will focus the diagnostic teaching to address the hypotheses generated in Step 5. As we have stated, the problems learners experience often lie in the interaction between knowledge, skills, and motivation of the learner and the settings, methods, and materials of the instructional context. Although the problem usually lies in the interaction between learner and contextual factors, when it comes to diagnostic teaching, it is easier to think about the contextual factors that can and should be altered than about manipulating learner factors. This is why Step 5 focuses on "what the *learner* needs"; it helps to place the emphasis in diagnostic teaching (Step 6) on the instructional environents, settings, practices and resources that are amenable to modification and manipulation (Campione & Brown, 1987; Paratore & Indrisano, 1987; Walker, 2000).

*Changing the Setting.* Using the elements of the context described in Chapters 5 and 6, the first area we might consider manipulating is the instructional setting. For example, we might consider attempting to alter the student's goals for literacy learning, acquired from the instructional context. We might also consider altering the organization of instructional activities and groups (for example, from lecture to discussion; from a teacher-led group to a cooperative work-group or individual instruction). Finally, we might consider altering the interaction patterns or "participation structures" used during instruction (e.g., from asking "known-answer" questions to more student-centered open discussion or peer writing conferences).

*Changing the Methods.* The methods of instruction make up a second element of the instructional context we might consider manipulating. Within this area we might consider altering what is being taught (focus) and/or how it is being taught (approach). For example, we might consider changing the focus of writing lessons from a heavy emphasis on individual skill instruction to the practice and application of skills in the service of writing for real audiences.

We might also wish to consider altering the methods of instruction being used to create motivated and/or strategic learning. For example, we might wish to change from extrinsic motivational techniques to those that are designed to enhance a student's desire to understand rather than simply comply with directions. We might also consider moving from methods that rely heavily on independent student practice to those that provide increased teacher support during the initial stages of learning. Some authors have suggested systematically varying the level of teacher support in the administration of traditional assessment procedures as a means of obtaining better instructional information. For example, Cioffi and Carney (1983) suggest a variety of modifications for administering an IRI, including eliminating time constraints, providing appropriate prereading instruction, observing miscues under prepared and unprepared conditions, and introducing instructional aids as needed.

*Changing the Materials and Tasks.* The third area of the instructional context we might consider manipulating in diagnostic teaching consists of materials and tasks. The characteristics of the texts a student is reading can have a profound effect on learning and performance and are therefore serious candidates for manipulation. Those that are easily modified include text type (for example, various types of stories and/or informational materials), length, readability, familiarity, organization (temporal sequence, cause–effect), coherence/unity, and structural characteristics (headings/subheadings, illustrations, charts, italics, etc.). Similarly, the type of writing that students are asked to produce may influence their performance. Again, familiarity with the mode and experience with the process can be powerful predictors of success.

It is also important to consider how the task demands that are being placed on the learner might be manipulated. Specifically, we might consider altering the content (that is, cognitive complexity) and/or the form (purpose and procedural complexity) of the tasks in which a student is asked to engage. This might include alterations such as changing from recognition tasks to open-ended or discussion tasks, or from low- to high-level tasks, or altering factors such as the quantity, mode of presentation and response (oral, written), and/or the clarity of task directions.

Generally, we should anticipate using multiple setting, method, materials and task options as we engage in diagnostic teaching. We are really attempting to set up the diagnostic teaching to represent or test certain interactions. However, not all interactions will be tested. It is important to recall that diagnostic teaching is hypothesis-driven. Only those factors and influences that appear to be likely candidates for improving learning and performance need be attempted.

***Investigating.***     It is clear that there are many ways to proceed with diagnostic teaching. However, it is important to keep in mind that designing the diagnostic teaching to provide information about how a student performs under several different or contrasting conditions can help us clarify our hypotheses about what the student needs. The many options described above suggest at least two ways that this might be accomplished. The first is to conduct diagnostic teaching sessions that try out several distinct alternatives to solving a particular problem. For future reference, we are calling this the *alternative methods* approach.

In contrast to the alternative methods approach, we can conduct diagnostic teaching sessions in which a particular procedure is modified by providing different levels of support to the learner. This approach uses the instructional technique of scaffolding described in Chapter 5 as an assessment device and will be referred to subsequently as the *scaffolding* approach. Whichever approach is selected, the procedures need to be viable instructional techniques that are appropriate for the setting in which they will be used on a regular basis.

*Alternative Methods Approach.*     The alternative methods approach involves a comparison of two or more different instructional procedures for teaching the same content or skill. An example of the alternative methods approach can be seen by rereading the case of Seth in Chapter 3, in which we described how we explored possible teaching interventions. Recall that Seth was experiencing serious word recognition problems, and, in addition, he seemed to have difficulty learning either new words or the skills needed to learn new words. Therefore our diagnostic teaching efforts involved trying out three distinct instructional approaches: phonics instruction that taught him to break the whole into component parts, phonics instruction that taught him to blend parts into wholes, and sight word instruction.

As was noted in Chapter 3, Seth recalled the words he was taught using each approach equally well. However, he learned the new words in the part-to-whole phonics approach and the sight word approach in a fraction of the time it took him to learn the words using the whole-to-part phonics approach. These results, combined with Seth's perception that he had learned most easily in the part-to-whole method, led to the recommendation that he be taught to recognize words using a part-to-whole phonics approach.

Although the alternative methods approach has been used for many years (Mills, 1956), current innovations in pedagogy have led to broader applications. For example, this approach was used in one of the authors' clinics with an articulate six grader who, despite excellent word recognition skills, was struggling with comprehension. His teachers were very worried that his increasingly negative attitude toward learning would hamper his success in middle school. The alternative approaches that were tried during diagnostic teaching included prereading discussion coupled with vocabulary instruction and an alternative questioning approach called Question the Author (QtA; see Chapter 15).

*Scaffolding Approach.* This approach involves the teacher or examiner presenting the student with a reading or writing activity, observing the response, and then introducing modifications of the task. These modifications are really hypotheses about "the minimal instructional adjustments necessary for the child to succeed in materials at or near his or her grade placement" (Cioffi & Carney, 1983, p. 768).

The predominant form of these modifications is introduction of "layered" prompts, or increasingly explicit hints (Day & Cordon, 1993). The prompts continue until the student can perform the desired task and it becomes clear how much support is needed. Consider the case of a reader who is not able to answer questions about a grade-level passage, even though word recognition is acceptable. We could plan an intervention that provided for activating background knowledge, preteaching vocabulary, focusing purpose setting, and guided reading questions. This type of instruction represents a heavy dependence on the teacher, however. As an alternative, we could teach a lesson providing only the one component of this instructional plan that we believe is crucial to improving the match so that the reader can perform effectively. For a very young or inexperienced child this might involve just the preteaching of vocabulary. For another child who has limited stamina for long texts it might involve providing only the guided reading questions.

The point is that we would start with one type of minimal support and increase it only as we see that the child requires it. We would prioritize, or layer, the prompts or supports so that we can clearly identify the intervention of least assistance. It is sometimes even possible to generate a highly specified set of ordered hints (Brown & Campione, 1986; Campione & Brown, 1987). These hints go from least support to most support and can be documented for assessment passages as we begin to use diagnostic teaching. Imagine, for example, that a student cannot edit her own writing for spelling and mechanical errors. We can add a sequence of ordered hints such as the ones in the following lists and record the point at which the student *can* answer the question(s).

### For reading:
1. Did that make sense?
2. Can you find the "tricky" (difficult) part of this text?
3. Can you figure it out?
4. Reread that and think about _____ .
5. (Continue increasing the specificity of the prompts directing students at word level or text level elements)

### For writing:
1. What could you do to make your story easier to read/understand?
2. Where is the part that you think needs work?
3. Can you figure it out?

If the student still cannot respond appropriately,

- Ask the student to reread his or her story to find any problems.
- If the student's response is inadequate, ask the student to reread a specific piece of the text to identify a problem (that is, misspelling, word left out, punctuation missing).

- Narrow the search to a sentence or two if necessary.
- Finally, provide direct feedback if that is required.

The next steps would involve planning mini-lessons and/or strategic sessions designed to help students make connections across the text, summarize, locate spelling errors, recognize run-on sentences, or clarify meaning (whatever is required by the text and task). At each stage you would describe how much support is necessary for this student to perform under the various conditions that have been explored.

These approaches are not mutually exclusive. In fact they can be, and often are, apparent in combination within a diagnostic teaching session. An example of this comes from a diagnostic teaching session for a fourth grade student with poor vocabulary knowledge in one of the author's clinics. The diagnostic teaching session employed vocabulary development activities both within and outside the context of reading connected text. In addition, the procedures that accompanied the text reading included the use of layered prompts to determine the level of support necessary to enable the student to identify, learn, and apply unknown words in the context of the student's reading.

Thus far, we have emphasized the intentional, well-planned nature of diagnostic teaching. Before leaving this section, it is important to understand that diagnostic teaching is also *opportunistic* and *flexible*. This means that a knowledgeable teacher who is able to set aside his or her own preconceived ideas about what will happen, and who can listen, is likely to gather a wealth of information from which to confirm hypotheses and plan instruction (Lipson, 1996). The following exchange occurred during a diagnostic teaching session in which the tutor was using a think-aloud procedure (see Chapter 8) to explore more carefully her hunch that Andrew did not have many comprehension strategies available for use during reading.

> **TEACHER:**   Tell me what you were doing and thinking as you read that part.
>
> **ANDREW:**   Not much.
>
> **TEACHER:**   Did that part make sense to *you?*
>
> **ANDREW:**   Not really.
>
> **TEACHER:**   Well, do you think it would be helpful to go back and reread that part to see if you can understand it?
>
> **ANDREW:**   I don't know. You tell me. You're the teacher!

This rather extraordinary, and unexpected, exchange demonstrates how much students can tell us about their reading and writing if we will listen. It is true that Andrew uses few comprehension strategies during reading, but this exchange demonstrates the more serious fact that he is willing to be compliant but not responsible for his behaviors during reading. It appears that he approaches reading and reading instruction passively rather than as an active participant (see Johnston & Winograd, 1985).

Good diagnostic teaching requires flexibility in order to take advantage of opportunities as they arise. Over time we develop a repertoire of both assessment and instruction procedures which can be used to respond to unexpected results or remarks. They will only be useful, however, to the extent that we recognize what is happening when it occurs and are prepared to revise our plans on the spot. This is opportunistic assessment-instruction. In the case we just described, the teacher decided to follow-up this exchange by asking Andrew what he thought it meant to be a good reader. She confirmed her new hypothesis; he believed good reading was flawless word calling and he relied heavily on the teacher to set purposes and to monitor both word recognition and comprehension. Consequently, he paid no attention whatsoever to meaning and could not set purposes for reading. In subsequent sessions she pursued a line of diagnostic teaching aimed at discovering how he might learn to be a more active participant in generating meaning from text.

***Evaluating.*** The examples provided above suggest that diagnostic teaching is not usually a one-time event. Diagnostic teaching is cyclical and continuous. Generally, the results of diagnostic teaching will be used either to establish a new focus for diagnostic teaching or to plan an instructional program or sequence.

> Optimal methods of instruction and levels of difficulty suggested by trial teaching thus provide the initial approaches that teachers use in remediation. However, as students progress and their needs in reading change, additional tryouts of methods and materials occur. (Chall & Curtis, 1987, p. 786)

The thrust of the evaluation of the diagnostic teaching is to determine the impact of the manipulations on the student's learning, performance, attitude, motivation, and/or knowledge. When alternative methods have been used, this involves noting similarities and differences in a student's performance, motivation, and/or knowledge during and after the administration of the different interventions.

In the case of Seth, described above, this might mean several different types of evaluation. First, we would probably want to posttest his learning of new words under the different instructional methods to compare the relative effectiveness of the different interventions. Second, we would want to observe the extent to which he participated actively in each of the interventions. Other things being equal, the extent to which he was willing to engage in the instructional activities—that is, the extent to which the techniques "made sense" to him—is perhaps the most important criterion for future success. No matter how good the instructional technique, it is unlikely to be successful if the learner resists, rather than participates actively.

When the scaffolding approach has been used, the evaluation would focus on a comparison of the student's learning, performance, knowledge and/or motivation at various levels of support from unaided to the greatest amount of support provided. The purpose of this comparison is to find an optimal level of support; that is, the level at which the student is challenged enough to learn, but not so much that he or she gives up in frustration or so little that he or she does not have to become actively involved. Regardless of the nature of the diagnostic teaching, comparisons can and should be made with information about a student's performance, skill, and motivation obtained through the observations, interviews, and formal and informal measures used in Steps 1–3.

We should also not overlook the invaluable information that can be gained by interviewing the student during and/or after the intervention. We have found the following types of questions to be extremely useful indicators of student learning and knowledge:

1. What do you think we are trying to learn and why? Why am I asking you to do _____ ?
2. Tell me how you figured out _____ .
3. What would you have done differently if you were (I asked you to) _____ ?
4. Which procedure/activity did you like best and why? Which did you think helped you the most and why?
5. What did you learn, how do you do it, and when would you use it/how would it help you to read better (to write better)?

These simple but powerful questions can reveal a great deal about students' understanding of how to use a new skill or strategy, as well as *their* attitudes and motivation for engaging in particular activities. These questions also serve an instructional purpose in that they convey to the student the need to consider when and why a skill would be used during other reading and writing events (Paris et al., 1983).

The need to accomplish both the implementation and evaluation of diagnostic teaching as efficiently as possible is obvious. The tremendous advantage to diagnostic teaching, as we have already noted, is that it melds assessment and instruction so that we need not take a great deal of time away from teaching. At the same time, it can save months that might be wasted implementing an instructional program that has little or no impact on the learner.

# Implementing Steps 4, 5, and 6 of the Assessment-Instruction Process

## Thumbnail Sketch

We introduced the thumbnail sketch in Chapter 4. It is a useful way to summarize information from the various steps of the assessment-instruction process. The first column of the Thumbnail Sketch summarizes the information gathered about the learner as part of Step 1 (Chapter 4, Getting Started). The second column summarizes the information gathered about the context in Step 2 (Chapters 5 and 6). In the third column, we summarize information gathered about the learner (Chapters 7–10).

Whenever possible, the information summarized in this part of the chart should describe the actual statements, behavior, or performance of the student rather than making interpretations about these events. When generalizations or interpretations are necessary, it is helpful to indicate the sources of the information on which they are based. It should also be noted that it is not necessary to include every piece of evidence that has been gathered. It may already be clear that certain pieces of information are irrelevant and should be disregarded. However, if there is uncertainty as to the importance of the information, it is probably best to include it. The thumbnail sketch for Marvin, summarizing information from Steps 1–3, is displayed in Figure 11.1.

The procedures necessary for completing the third and fourth columns of these charts are described in this chapter. The fourth column summarizes the decisions made about the

**FIGURE 11.1** Thumbnail Sketch: Marvin, Steps 1–3

| Getting Started (Step 1) | About the Reading and Writing Context (Step 2) | About the Learner (Step 3) |
|---|---|---|
| **Background** <br><br> Name: Marvin <br> Age: 11    Grade: 5 <br><br> Key Correlates: <br> • Above average IQ <br> • Normal vision, hearing, and overall health <br> • Interests are science, sports, "taking things apart" <br><br> **Information about the Learner** <br><br> Knowledge about Reading and Writing: <br> • Reports that people read to learn and for recreation: reports adjusting rate for text difficulty <br> • Reports that own reading problem is comprehension <br> • Names, "breaking words down" and "asking someone" as the only strategies for reading words that are unfamiliar <br><br> Motivation: <br> • Pleasant, cooperative demeanor during the classroom and clinic sessions <br> • Talks freely about affective responses to text and persists without prompting on difficult tasks <br><br> **Information about the Context** <br><br> School History: <br> • School-administered achievement tests place him in the 35th percentile in reading <br> • Multiple moves and family disruptions during K–1 <br> • English spoken in home <br><br> Instructional Approaches: <br><br> Experiences, Linguistic and Cultural Context: | **Resources** <br> • Outdated basals and workbooks <br> • Until recently, no recreational reading at all <br><br> **Instruction** <br> • Instruction focused on isolated phonics <br> • Reading assignments and practice without modeling <br> • No provision for development of motivation or strategies <br> • Whole group basal instruction; little prereading support <br> • No cooperative work, book sharing and little discussion, especially promoting higher order thinking <br> • Limited reading outside the basal <br><br> **Tasks** <br> • In both old and new school, most tasks are closed. Workbooks; seatwork repetitive and isolated from instruction. Questions used infrequently, most are text explicit, focused on detail. Almost no writing, except grammar worksheets and skills <br><br> **Methods** <br> • Practice without modeling <br> • Focus on lower-order thinking <br> • No cooperative or collaborative groups <br> • Little connection to outside <br><br> **Settings** <br> • English spoken in the home. Few reading materials, limited interest in reading at home <br> • Placed in private parochial school from grades 2–4 <br> • Large student-teacher ratio, no support services. Policy of placing *all* students in grade appropriate materials | **Knowledge about Reading and and Writing** <br> • Reports that people read for recreation; reports rate adjustment for text difficulty <br> • Reports misperception of own problem (believes it is comprehension) <br> • Names "breaking words down" and "asking" as the only strategies for reading unfamiliar words <br> • Good phonics knowledge but poor structural analysis and sight vocabulary <br><br> **Performance in Reading and Writing** <br> • Achievement test results (end of grade 4): PR-33; Stanine-4 <br> • Word recognition lower than comprehension <br> • Comprehension poor for complex, ambiguous, or symbolic texts <br> • Has difficulty inferring main ideas, problem-solution, and linking events to self-generated theme <br><br> **Motivation** <br> • Pleasant, cooperative demeanor during instructional sessions <br> • Talks freely about affective responses to text and persists without prompting on difficult tasks <br> • When reading in the "instruction comfort range," laughs and comments on text <br><br> **Strategic Abilities** <br> • Uses prior knowledge to aid comprehension <br><br> **Self-reflection** <br> • Unclear |

nature of the existing match (Step 4), and hypotheses about what the learner needs (Step 5). The fifth, and last, column summarizes information about the nature and results of the diagnostic teaching used with the student (Step 6).

The types of information provided in the last two columns of the chart are of necessity more interpretive than descriptive. However, whenever possible, it is still desirable to note the evidence leading to a particular conclusion. The remainder of this chapter is devoted to illustrating the implementation of Steps 4, 5, and 6 and the thumbnail sketch through the description of three case studies.

## The Case Study of Marvin

Figure 11.1 presents a summary of the information gathered on the learner and contextual factors involved in Marvin's case, most of which has been discussed extensively throughout the text. Normally, we would proceed to evaluate the match between Marvin and his instructional context and to attempt promising interventions. In Marvin's case, however, the information seemed inadequate. Very little information was available from the classroom context. In addition, we suspected that his weak performance on the one IRI might itself have been the result of a poor match. Therefore our next step was to continue assessing, this time with the explicit intent to explore the circumstances under which he might perform well and less well.

*Adding Information.*   Two additional IRIs were added to the one already used. Taken together, the three IRIs used in Marvin's case are the Burns and Roe *Informal Reading Inventory,* the *Analytic Reading Inventory,* or ARI, by Woods and Moe, and the *Classroom Reading Inventory,* or CRI, by Silvaroli. These three IRIs were selected because they vary considerably in several important ways that offer possible insights into Marvin's performance (see Figure 11.2).

*ARI.*   In Forms A, B, and C of the ARI, the passages are narrative excerpts. In the version used by Marvin all passages are preceded by introductory statements that compensate for incomplete texts and provide useful purpose-setting information. The selections gradually increase in length, from approximately 50 words per passage to 250 words at level 7. Eight questions of variable quality follow each selection. Most are reasonable and require a range of text processing, but some passages are weighted fairly heavily toward recall of details.

*CRI.*   The Silvaroli and Wheelock CRI has been revised in its latest edition (2001). Marvin read selections from an older edition. All passages except the primer selections were very short exposition (the longest is only 118 words in length). Each is prefaced by a motivational statement and accompanied by a picture. The selections are straightforward presentations of factual information, followed by five questions of varying quality. Most questions require recall of stated details, but many questions can be answered without reference to the text. For example, two of the five questions in the level 3, Form C selection of this IRI are "What does the word 'sip' mean?" and "Where do baby birds grow up?"

**FIGURE 11.2**
Marvin's Results
(Multiple
Administration
of IRIs)

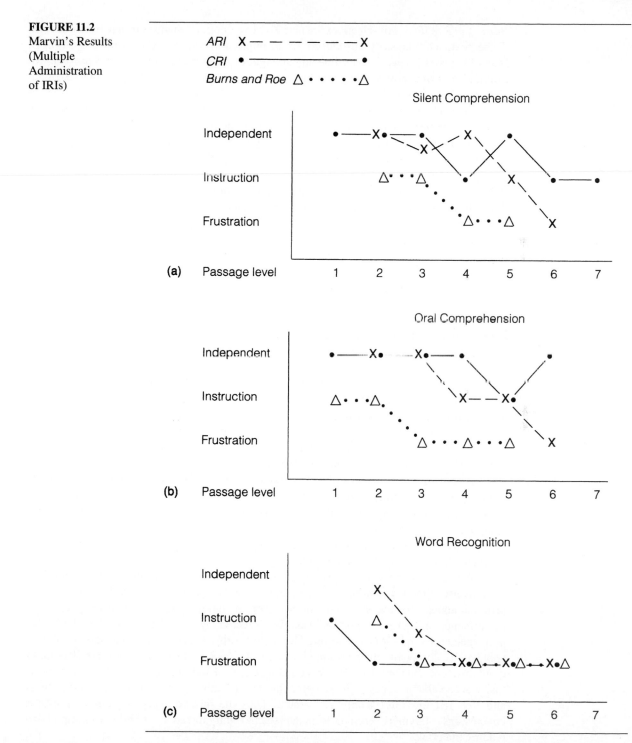

*Burns and Roe IRI.*    All selections are narrative excerpts, and many continue from one form to the next, with the story introduced, for example, in Form A and continued in Form B. Many have a rather weak story line and ambiguous story events. One level 4 passage, for example, describes how a little girl comes to understand death by watching a snowflake melt. The introductory sentences are central to student performance because in some cases the selection can be understood only with reference to the introductory remarks. In a few cases questions are posed about information that is presented only in the introductory remarks. The selections at the lowest levels are relatively long (65–100 words), but they increase in length only slightly over the reading levels (for example, level 7 has 171 words).

*Patterns and Variations.*    Figures 11.2a, b, and c compare Marvin's performance on the three IRIs in the areas of silent reading comprehension, oral reading comprehension, and word recognition. Both the similar patterns and the considerable variability provide important information about Marvin's reading. Regardless of text, for example, his word recognition scores are consistently poor, and he reaches frustration level on word recognition at level 3 on all three IRIs (see Figure 11.2c). On the other hand, his comprehension scores are consistently higher than his word recognition scores, and on two IRIs he does not reach frustration level in comprehension until grade 6 or 7. The disparity between his word recognition and his comprehension performance is substantial. However, he also demonstrates differential ability across texts and tasks. Note both his peak (silent reading at level 5 on the CRI) and his valley (frustration comprehension at level 3 on the oral reading, Burns and Roe).

To make interpretive sense of these results, we need to consider what we know about the text and task attributes of these IRIs. Although Marvin's comprehension abilities are quite good, it is obvious that the Burns and Roe IRI was more difficult for him than any others. Marvin's weakest performances occurred while reading several of these rather ambiguous passages. All three were fragments from longer texts, and none had very strong story grammar structures (see McConaughy, 1985).

Although neither the type of text (narrative versus exposition) nor the type and number of questions significantly affected Marvin's performance, his performance *was* affected by factors such as coherence and conformity to expected story structure. In particular, Marvin's comprehension performance appears to have been affected by the degree to which he could generate a meaningful framework for interpreting a text (using introductory statements, prior knowledge, pictures, text structure, etc.).

An analysis of Marvin's miscues across these texts is also helpful. Marvin's miscues were overwhelmingly similar in graphic appearance to the text. He clearly attends to the print but appears to have somewhat limited word recognition abilities. However, Marvin's performance in word recognition was also affected by different texts. Recall that his performance overall was not strong. But when self-correction rate and the percent of contexually acceptable miscues are computed, his performance on these three IRIs looks quite different. On the CRI, Marvin's combined rate of self-corrected miscues and contextually acceptable miscues is 70 percent. On the ARI this rate is 55 percent. On the Burns and Roe IRI this rate is only 29 percent. Thus the miscue analysis parallels previous conclusions. Marvin's overall performance seems tightly linked to his ability to comprehend reading materials.

This new information from several IRIs indicated that his word recognition skills were weaker than his comprehension skills and that he did not always seem to use the phonic knowledge he possessed during reading. Although generally strong, his comprehension was variable under different reading conditions, with areas of strength that had not been apparent earlier.

With this information in hand we were ready to proceed with making some decisions about the appropriateness of the existing match, the nature of Marvin's needs, and how to change the match in ways that would lead to improvement in his learning and performance. The first step in this process was evaluating the existing match between Marvin's strengths and weaknesses as a learner and the characteristics of the settings, methods, and materials in which he was placed.

***Evaluating the Existing Match and Generating Hypotheses (Steps 4 and 5).*** A summary of our evaluation of the existing match (Step 4) and of the hypotheses we generated about what Marvin needed (Step 5) is provided in the left column of the thumbnail sketch presented in Figure 11.3. Recall that we said one way to evaluate the existing match between a learner and the characteristics of the context in which he must operate is to examine the information in each of the categories in the learner column and ask ourselves how it fits with what we know about the context and vice versa. Using this technique, we found more weaknesses than strengths in the existing match.

**FIGURE 11.3**
Thumbnail Sketch: Marvin, Steps 4 and 5

| Decision Making (Steps 4 and 5) | Diagnostic Teaching (Step 6) |
| --- | --- |
| ***Evaluating the Match (Step 4)***<br>What is the match?<br>a. Reading level placement below potential performance; below grade placement.<br>b. Better reading in text is poor match to isolated phonics approach.<br>c. Has trouble reading long/complex selections but receives no instruction in this area.<br>d. Is expected to read long texts in science and social studies without preparation. | ***Planning and Implementing***<br>What is most likely to (re)establish learning? |
| ***Reflection and Generating Hypotheses (Step 5)***<br>What does the reader need?<br>a. Increased practice in reading connected text<br>b. Better prereading preparation for reading complex or lengthy selections<br>c. Additional skill and practice in WR to improve fluency | ***Evaluating the Diagnostic Sessions*** |

First, we noted that his approximate reading level (grade 3–2) was considerably below his grade placement level (grade 5). Second, his knowledge about and ability to use phonics skills during reading, combined with his lack of familiarity and ability with other word attack strategies, did not match well with his current instructional emphasis on isolated phonics. Third, his problems comprehending complex texts and dealing with high-level comprehension tasks were not well matched to an instructional method that contained no teacher modeling or explanation of comprehension. Finally, the lack of cooperative work assignments and authentic reading and writing tasks in his instructional environment did not capitalize on his knowledge about the purposes of reading or his positive attitude toward reading. In short, there were a number of areas in which the match between learner and reading context might be improved in an effort to promote Marvin's learning and performance in reading.

Step 5 provided the opportunity to reflect on the existing match and generate hypotheses about what Marvin needed if he was to become a better reader and writer. This meant setting some priorities among the various needs that had been identified. As a result of this reflection, the following priorities were established for Marvin. First, he needed to acquire much more fluency in applying the word recognition and word analysis skills he already possessed. Marvin also needed additional knowledge and skill in word analysis, particularly in the area of structural and morphemic analysis.

Second, Marvin needed to learn more about how complex stories and expositions are organized and needed many instructional opportunities to read such materials with guidance and support. These two problems converged in the need for Marvin to acquire skill in reading the type of lengthy reading assignments often expected of middle-grade students. With our priorities established, we were now ready to move on to more focused assessment using diagnostic teaching.

***Diagnostic Teaching (Step 6).***   Once we had generated and prioritized our hypotheses, we were then ready to plan, implement, and evaluate the diagnostic teaching to be used to confirm or deny our hypotheses and identify a match that would promote Marvin's learning and performance (see Figure 11.4).

*Planning.*   Marvin's strength was comprehension. However, his performance in comprehension was not universally strong. Marvin's consistently poor performance was limited to selections with unstated main ideas or problems, ambiguous themes, or complex text structures (the Burns and Roe IRI) and longer texts (see Chapter 8). These types of selections seem to embody what caused Marvin difficulty. We suspected that he could perform better if he were provided with more information before reading, since he seemed to make such good use of all available information in constructing meaning. Indeed, he even appeared to make use of information available *after* reading (better performance on questioning tasks than retelling ones). Therefore one focus for diagnostic teaching involved looking at the interaction between text, prereading support, and Marvin's ability to comprehend. Because Marvin also clearly needed additional decoding skills and a great deal of attention directed toward increasing his automaticity, a second focus for diagnostic teach-

**FIGURE 11.4**
Thumbnail Sketch:
Marvin, Step 6

| Decision Making (Steps 4 and 5) | Diagnostic Teaching (Step 6) |
|---|---|
| *Evaluating the Match (Step 4)*<br>What is the match?<br>a. Reading level placement below potential performance; below grade placement.<br>b. Better reading in text is poor match to isolated phonics approach.<br>c. Has trouble reading long/complex selections but receives no instruction in this area.<br>d. Is expected to read long texts in science and social studies without preparation. | *Planning and Implementing*<br>What is most likely to (re)establish learning?<br>a. Use difficult texts with appropriate prereading preparation.<br>b. Practice in reading connected text to build fluency.<br>c. Additional skill in word recognition.<br><br>Question:<br>Direct instruction or<br>• Try layered prompts w/IRI<br>• Try Talking Dictionary. |
| *Reflection and Generating Hypotheses (Step 5)*<br>What does the reader need?<br>a. Increased practice in reading connected text<br>b. Better prereading preparation for reading complex or lengthy selections<br>c. Additional skill and practice in WR to improve fluency | *Evaluating the Diagnostic Sessions*<br>Increased work in reading should improve fluency<br>Performs better with preparation<br>Can read grade-appropriate text with support |

ing involved testing out an approach to this problem. As we reflected on Marvin's needs and on what we could manipulate to "call forth learning," the following seemed to invite consideration:

### What Can/Should Be Changed to Improve the Match?
1. Amount of prereading support
2. Type of prereading instruction/support
3. Length of text
4. Knowledge about structural analysis
5. Ability to infer main ideas
6. Reading fluency (automaticity in word recognition)

Not all of our conclusions about ways to improve Marvin's performance needed to be pursued through diagnostic teaching. Although diagnostic teaching is an invaluable addition to our assessment-instruction repertoire, it is not required in all situations. For example, there was no real reason to use diagnostic teaching to confirm that Marvin lacked knowledge about how to analyze multisyllabic words. We had very good evidence about this from previous assessment efforts.

*Investigating Comprehension Focus.*    Because the Burns and Roe IRI selections caused Marvin difficulty, our first diagnostic teaching efforts were focused on these selections. Of course, we could have selected passages that were similar in text structure and theme. However, our major concern during this diagnostic session was to confirm our hypothesis that Marvin's comprehension was influenced by ambiguity or complexity of theme and main idea and that it could be improved by instructional support.

Marvin had reached frustrational level on a selection without a title that dealt with a young boy's concern about a test (see Figure 11.5). Marvin missed the subtle main idea and construed the selection to be about imminent war. Having construed the selection that way, he missed several related questions, resulting in a frustration level comprehension performance. Because it appeared that Marvin might be able to understand material (even at this level of difficulty) if he had some organizational support, he was asked to reread the selection, this time imagining that the story was entitled "Peter Worries about a Test." Given that much support, Marvin answered all the questions posed correctly and was able to provide a coherent and accurate summary of the selection. The exercise was repeated with two other selections, and each time Marvin was totally successful in his comprehension efforts.

Given a general idea of the topic, Marvin had no difficulty linking ideas, locating information, or supporting inferential conclusions. Our evaluation of this diagnostic teaching effort led us to conclude that Marvin could benefit from rather minimal supports in comprehending text. Next, of course, we would need to teach him to generate and use structural supports independently. This required recycling to establish a new focus, one designed to try out instructionally powerful interventions for accomplishing this. In the meantime we wanted to attempt a trial teaching lesson directed at his rather significant word recognition/automaticity problems.

*Investigating Word Recognition Focus.*    In this diagnostic teaching session we tried a variation on a repeated reading strategy, Talking Dictionary (see Chapter 12). This technique

**FIGURE 11.5**
Sample IRI
Selection

> **About the story:** Read this story to find out about a boy named Pete and a problem that he has.
>
> "I see in the papers that the world is coming to an end," said Mr. Peters, reading the newspaper at the breakfast table. He chuckled.
>
> Pete swallowed his bit of toast. "When?" he said.
>
> His mother look at his father and frowned, warningly.
>
> "Not this afternoon," she said hastily to Pete.
>
> Mr. Peters shrugged. "It doesn't say this afternoon," he agreed.
>
> Peter munched his crisp cereal thoughtfully. If it wasn't this afternoon it wouldn't do him much good, he thought. For the test would be this afternoon— the test the substitute teacher had prepared for them.
>
> Thinking about the test, Pete plopped into his seat at school with an unnecessary plunk. Miss Dingley frowned at him.

*Source:* Burns, Paul C., and Betty D. Roe, *Informal Reading Inventory,* Second Edition. Copyright © 1985 by Houghton Mifflin Company. Used with permission.

was used for two reasons: First, we believed that Marvin's poor word recognition efforts during reading might result from limited reading practice; and second, we hoped to arrive at an approach that would permit him to use his good comprehension abilities to read grade appropriate text. The supported oral reading activity that we tried permits students to ask how a word is pronounced during a first reading and evaluates the extent to which they remember these words and build fluency during a second reading of the same material. Using grade level material (grade 5), Marvin read seventy-six words correctly in a two-minute period during the first read-through (asked for eight words, misread five). During the second two-minute read of the same material, Marvin read 115 words correctly, mispronouncing only three words and correctly reading all eight words that he had requested during the first read.

*Evaluating.* As we evaluated our diagnostic teaching efforts for Marvin, we examined the impact of our manipulations on his performance. In the first instance it was apparent that our instructional manipulation during the prereading phase had produced better performance than we had observed in the unaided condition. Similarly, our hypothesis that Marvin could benefit from greater exposure to print in a supported context seemed worth continuing. The word recognition/fluency manipulation was repeated in a second session during which Marvin read sixty-four words correctly in the first two-minute read and 127 words correctly in the second two-minute period. Given the effectiveness of this approach, we then integrated it into his instructional program.

The diagnostic teaching sessions generated several instructional options. In the second case the diagnostic teaching resulted in a decision to include a specific instructional method into his ongoing program. We incorporated the repeated reading activity into every session to encourage Marvin to use his word recognition knowledge more automatically and to build fluency. In the first case our diagnostic teaching resulted in a recycling to establish a new focus. We determined that Marvin could work, with support, in grade-level material and used it whenever possible.

Because he obviously needed more understanding of complex stories, we also initiated a new series of diagnostic teaching lessons designed to help Marvin recognize and impose story structure on lengthy narratives. Story maps (see Chapters 8 and 14) were used to guide him through text. They both supported him during reading and forced him to reconstruct meaning (generating connections) during a postreading retelling. After each of these sessions Marvin's response to the three evaluative questions was recorded. After the first of these sessions, Marvin responded:

| What did you learn? | I learned about story maps. |
| How do you use it? | You think about the people in the story and what they do and put it down on the chart. |
| When would you use it? | During reading, you look for this information. Then you don't panic. |

Clearly, continuous assessment will be necessary. However, the results of just two small diagnostic interventions yielded exceptionally good information about what types of instruction would benefit Marvin.

## The Case Study of Kyle

Kyle is unusual in the sense that we have been able to follow his progress over a relatively long period of time because of the strong assessment system in place in his school and classroom. At many intervals along the way Ms. McIntyre had made decisions about how and what to teach. The end of second grade was an important time to stop and take stock because he was moving on to a different school for grade 3 and because he would be attending a university literacy clinic during the summer. The thumbnail sketch in Figure 11.6 summarizes the information that had been gathered about Kyle's reading and writing development. Using this summary of the information gathered in Steps 1–3, we turned our attention to the decision making steps in the assessment-instruction process.

***Evaluating the Existing Match and Generating Hypotheses (Steps 4 and 5).*** A summary of the existing match (Step 4) and of the hypotheses we generated about Kyle's strengths and needs (Step 5) is provided in the excerpt of Kyle's thumbnail sketch (see Figure 11.7). First, we celebrated the fact not only that Kyle's reading performance had improved considerably, but also that both his word recognition and his comprehension were age and grade appropriate. Indeed, his reading comprehension was quite exceptional. The match between his rapidly changing (growing) abilities and the classroom had been an exceptionally good one. When Kyle's emerging abilities converged with the motivation to read a whole series of books, he had a teacher who was alert to the moment and waiting to make the most of it and a classroom structure that supported his exceptional growth during the last half of grade 2. In addition, Kyle's classroom had provided him with opportunities to be highly active and personally engaged in various literacy (and other) activities.

The only area of significant need remained his weak skills in the conventions of writing and spelling. Kyle needed to acquire a better sense of conventional spelling and learn to manage, edit, and revise his own writing for better readability. In the normal course of Kyle's developmental reading program he would also need instruction in some additional areas. For example, given the difficulty of the material he was now capable of reading, he needed better word analysis skills for longer and multisyllabic words. In addition, he needed instructional support for monitoring his reading of these more complex materials.

***Diagnostic Teaching (Step 6).*** We noted earlier that diagnostic teaching is not required in all situations. We really did not need to use diagnostic teaching to confirm Kyle's areas of ongoing need or the type of instruction to which he would be responsive. For the most part his remaining difficulties could and would be addressed in the course of a good responsive literacy program. Both his teachers and his parents were aware that his placement for third grade could be critical. Kyle continued to require a flexible classroom context that encouraged self-control and focused on authentic reading and writing tasks. Self-selection and activity remained central to maintaining Kyle's motivation and momentum. Acting as advocates, Ms. McIntyre and Kyle's parents helped to place Kyle in a classroom where he would, in all likelihood, continue to flourish.

Over the summer Kyle participated in a summer literacy clinic sponsored by the local university. The work there focused on adjusting rate for text difficulty and on encouraging a self-control strategy for spelling and writing. With very little tutor support, Kyle was able

**FIGURE 11.6** Kyle's Thumbnail Sketch; Steps 1–3

| Getting Started (Step 1) | About the Reading and Writing Context (Step 2) | About the Learner (Step 3) |
|---|---|---|
| **Background**<br><br>Name: Kyle<br>Age: 7½   Grade: 2<br><br>Key Correlates:<br>• Normal vision, hearing, and overall health/development<br>• Difficult time "paying attention"<br><br>**Information about the Learner**<br><br>Knowledge about Reading and Writing:<br>• Reports that own reading problem is knowing the words<br>• Is able to reflect on his own reading and writing abilities<br><br>Motivation:<br>• Says he doesn't really like to read, would rather play and build<br>• Cooperative and willing to work both in school and in extra sessions<br><br>**Information about the Context**<br><br>School History:<br>• Successful preschool experience<br>• Same multi-age K–2 classroom since kindergarten<br>• Lack of progress in reading and writing noted at end of grade 1<br><br>Instructional Approaches:<br>• Literature-based instruction in an inquiry-oriented classroom<br>• Daily reading and writing<br><br>Experiences, Linguistic, and Cultural Context:<br>• English spoken in the home<br>• Both parents college graduates | **Resources**<br>• Beginning readers: "little books" and own writing<br>• Emerging readers: commercially controlled vocabulary and then trade books, children's literature<br>• Journals, portfolios, theme booklets<br>• Process writing folders<br>• Many read-alouds—literature<br><br>**Instruction**<br>• Child-centered curriculum<br>• Individual conferences and whole group meetings<br>• Inquiry-based theme work and choice time each day<br>• Cooperative and collaborative groups<br>• Problem-solving focus<br><br>**Settings**<br>• English only language spoken in home<br>• Considerable home emphasis on reading and writing<br>• Well-stocked library at school and home<br>• School and community emphasize achievement<br><br>**Tasks**<br>• Almost all tasks are open<br>• Reading time spent in reading continuous texts, conferencing with teacher, responding in many ways<br>• Writing time spent writing original texts and revising for publication—in books, on walls, in class<br>• Additional writing in journals, theme booklets, and correspondences<br>• Students reflect on own work as select portfolio entries and evaluate own learning | **Knowledge about Reading and Writing**<br>• Reports that people read for enjoyment and to find out things<br>• Can articulate ways to improve written work<br><br>**Performance in Reading and Writing**<br>• By end of grade 2, instructional reading level at grade 3–4 (Spache results, QRI-2, Benchmark Books)<br>• Ability to answer questions and recall passages better than word recognition, but gap closing<br>• Excellent comprehension of complex stories and materials<br>• In writing, good control of topic, purpose and voice<br>• Spelling at phonemic level (approaching transitional)<br>• Slow and illegible handwriting<br><br>**Motivation**<br>• Highly motivated to improve reading, less interested in actually reading<br>• Easily distracted, but cooperative and funny<br>• By beginning of grade 3, able to manage difficult tasks with perseverance<br>• Enjoys writing about personal events and activities and also about science topics<br><br>**Strategic Abilities**<br>• Highly developed strategies in reading; uses picture cues, context, and graphophonic information; uses prior knowledge, monitoring, and rereading<br>• In writing, strategies for managing lengthier texts and for revision are not developed<br><br>**Self-reflection**<br>• Exhibits exceptional self-evaluation and goal setting behaviors.<br>• Provides specific information about task difficulty and can identify areas of growth |

**FIGURE 11.7**
Kyle's Thumbnail
Sketch: Steps 4
and 5

| Decision Making (Steps 4 and 5) | Diagnostic Teaching (Step 6) |
|---|---|
| *Evaluating the Match (Step 4)*<br>What is the match?<br>a. His reading level is grade appropriate.<br>b. Reading materials change as Kyle's skills/abilities develop.<br>c. He is showing more interest in reading now that he can handle more difficult and lengthy "chapter" books.<br>d. In these longer books, though, he sometimes fails to monitor word recognition failures and has some word/sentence tracking problems.<br>e. Has difficulty paying attention during more academic tasks, but his preference for action is addressed in his present classroom.<br>f. Both his spelling and written language abilities are still weak. | *Planning and Implementing*<br>What is most likely to (re)establish learning? |
| *Reflecting and Generating Hypotheses (Step 5)*<br>What does the learner need?<br>a. Continued support for self-selected, high-interest reading<br>b. A literacy program that focuses on authentic reading and writing<br>c. Some flexibility about activities<br>d. A more structured spelling program<br>e. Instruction in editing and revising his own written work | *Evaluating the Diagnostic Sessions* |

to talk through some strategies for editing his written work. He generated the following description: "You write and check the spelling. You reread and see if it makes sense. Make sure it says what you want it to say." In spelling, his work focused on spelling patterns and an analogy strategy (see Chapter 13). Ms. McIntyre had provided all her students with self-addressed stamped postcards so that they could write to her over the summer. At the end of August Ms. McIntyre received a postcard from Kyle that said, "I am a reader!"

## The Case Study of Yasmin

Yasmin moved to the United States from Mexico during the spring of kindergarten. Yasmin's first and dominant language is Spanish. Her parents speak only Spanish, and it is the only language spoken at home. Yasmin had not attended any school before her arrival in the United States and had extremely limited literacy experiences and knowledge. At the time of school entry she recognized only eight letters out of fifty-two uppercase and lowercase letters combined and scored 3/24 on the Concepts about Print Assessment (Clay, 1993). Consequently, the school and her teachers were concerned from the very beginning and attended carefully to her development.

During mid-second grade her teachers determined that a closer examination of Yasmin's literacy development was appropriate. At that time Yasmin was a 7-year-old who was reading at Reading Recovery level 20. She was making steady progress but was not meeting the pupil progression standards established for her school district. A summary of the information gathered on the learner and contextual factors involved in Yasmin's case is presented in the thumbnail sketch in Figure 11.8.

The context for Yasmin's school achievement was complex. The majority (70 percent) of Yasmin's schoolmates spoke a language other than English, primarily Spanish or Haitian Creole. Hers was an urban school with approximately 900 students that had been targeted by the state because of its students' low performance in reading (scores on measures of writing were consistently higher). During Yasmin's first and second grade years the school had received a large federal grant and was engaged in considerable professional development aimed at school improvement. Most of the teachers were highly committed and eager for students to do well.

Yasmin's teachers had taken their training seriously and developed classrooms that were rich in books, where student progress was carefully monitored. Her school and classroom teachers had been strongly influenced by the Reading Recovery program, shared reading (Holdaway, 1979), and guided reading (Fountas & Pinnell, 1996). Teachers used running records to track reading development and attended to students' strategy use as they reviewed these records. In addition, students were placed in increasingly difficult texts using leveled books. Less attention had been directed toward writing, in part because the performance of the school's ELL students had been stronger in writing than in reading. Yasmin's instructional program had not included much writing at all.

In terms of possible physical, linguistic, or cognitive correlates, Yasmin's status as an English Language Learner (ELL) was the major factor. She attended an English as a second language class to promote English acquisition for her entire school experience. She received sixty minutes per day of instruction in this pull-out program.

Yasmin's interviews and performance suggested that she had acquired considerable knowledge and understanding of initial reading and writing. Her performance on the *Concepts of Print* test, for example, placed her among the most capable students of her age (22/24) and indicated that she had developed significant print-related skills and abilities, although she was not able to change letter and word order. Similarly, she was able to read seventeen of twenty high-frequency sight words on the test administered in mid second grade (Ohio Word Test). There were areas that concerned her teachers, however. First, she scored poorly on the school-administered test of oral language development (a measure of the structure of English language), and although she had acquired a corpus of sight words, her ability to decode using knowledge of word families was not strong. Indeed, a miscue analysis suggested that she relied too heavily on the visual cueing system and on meaning. For example, a running record taken early in grade 2 included miscues such as these:

**TEXT:** Deep in the jungle, alone in the river, swam a friendly crocodile.

**YASMIN:** Deep in the jungle a-a-an-al-alony in the r-i-v a friend crocodile . . .

**FIGURE 11.8**  Yasmin's Thumbnail Sketch: Steps 1–3

| Getting Started | About the Reading and Writing Context | About the Learner |
|---|---|---|
| **Background** | **Resources** | **Knowledge about Reading and Writing** |
| Name: Yasmin | • School has extensive book room and media center with multiple copies of leveled text along with quality children's literature | • Understands purpose of reading |
| Age: 7    Grade: 2 | | • Knows letters and sounds |
| Key Correlates: ESOL student | | • Hears discrete sounds in words which she uses in both reading and writing (stretching words) |
| • Spanish first language | | |
| • Arrived in U.S. in kindergarten | • Use of running records and lexile levels for matching text to readers | • Knows reading should make sense |
| • Normal vision, hearing | | |
| **Information about the Learner** | | **Performance in Reading and Writing** |
| Knowledge about Reading and Writing: | • Shared reading texts (big books and charts) | • Reading Recovery Level 20 (running record) |
| • Loves to be read to | • Books on tape | |
| • Enjoys looking at books (browsing) | • Journals, portfolios | • Scored 21 on Record of Oral Language (measure of the structure of English language) |
| • Has letter sound knowledge in Spanish and English | • Classroom libraries | |
| | • Computers with reading and writing software | • 17 out of 20 sight words (Ohio word test) |
| Motivation: | | • CAP: 22/24, not able to change word and letter order |
| • Likes books and stories | • Extensive teacher training in using assessment to plan instruction | |
| • Chooses to "read" during choice time but does not always engage | | • Gentry Spelling test: 29/39 words |
| | | • Peters Spelling in context: 55/100 |
| • Cooperative, feels successful, completes tasks | | • Score of 4 (rubric possible 6 points) on county writing prompt, first-draft piece |
| **Information about the Context** | **Instruction** | |
| School History: | • Driven by assessment data | **Strategic Abilities** |
| Entered U.S. in spring of kindergarten, no previous schooling. Closely observed due to lack of school experience and lack of literacy knowledge when entered (Letter identification: 8 out of 52 letters, uppercase and lowercase combined) CAP: 3/24 | • Whole group, small group, whole group that includes modeled and guided instruction | • Has overreliance on visual cueing system, using it in place of language structure (which is low as measured on the ROL) and meaning. However, even with using visual cues, does not read through words and search further for all visual information, relies on beginning visual cues. |
| | • Literacy learning centers | |
| | • Individual practice | |
| **Instructional Approaches** | **Settings** | • Is beginning to develop rereading, self-correcting and self-monitoring strategies. |
| • 1 hour reading block (whole, small whole group) | • 60 minutes daily of pull-out ESL instruction | |
| • 1 hour writing block (whole, small whole group) | • Only Spanish spoken in the home | • Has limited retelling ability (this has increased with development of English language). |
| • Includes modeled, shared and guided groups | • Well-stocked classroom library | • Does not have flexibility with words and word families (CAP and when writing words she knows in the Ob. Survey writes sight words but not obvious word families). |
| • ESOL class for English language development | • Manipulatives available | |
| | • Class size 22:1 | |
| **Experiences** | | |
| • Spanish first and dominant language | | • Developing greater fluency. |
| • Parents speak Spanish only | | • Needs to develop cross checking strategy. |
| • Extended family | | |

TEXT: "Will you be my friend, Parrot?" smiled the friendly crocodile.

YASMIN: Will you be my friend? **parrot**[R] swiled the friend crocodile.

Yasmin did demonstrate a positive attitude toward listening to stories and was cooperative during instruction. During the exploratory period we discovered that though Yasmin's parents had limited formal education, they were very committed to her schooling, they read to her often in Spanish, and she had a well-developed sense of story.

Given this summary of the information gathered in Steps 1–3, we were then ready to proceed to Step 4, an evaluation of the existing match between Yasmin's strengths and weaknesses and key features of the reading context

*Evaluating the Existing Match and Generating Hypotheses (Steps 4 and 5).* A summary of our evaluation of the existing match (Step 4) and of the hypotheses we generated about what Yasmin needed (Step 5) is provided in the third column of the thumbnail sketch presented in Figure 11.9. In Yasmin's case the match between her knowledge, skills, and attitudes and the settings, methods, and materials that confront her within the reading context was mixed. Generally, the organization, methods, and materials of her instruction appeared to be having a positive effect on both her general language development and her reading development. Her print-rich classroom environment, for example, had promoted and supported a love of books and improved vocabulary. Yasmin had developed good emergent skills and had proceeded through appropriately difficult texts.

It was clear, however, that her strong phonemic awareness ability had not developed into a strong use of the orthographic spelling patterns of English. This weakness showed up in both her writing and her decoding of unknown words. She did not appear to be poised to read more fluently or write more extensively because she was neither fully analyzing unknown words nor using her memory for word features to write longer pieces. In addition, there appeared to be too few opportunities to link reading and writing and not much authentic writing.

Our evaluation of the existing match provided us with the information necessary to generate hypotheses about what Yasmin needed to progress as a beginning reader and writer. Although there were many uncertainties still, it seemed likely that Yasmin needed two things. First, she needed instruction that encouraged her to examine all of the letters in a word. In the long term she would also need to use writing to strengthen her print knowledge. The second thing Yasmin needed was to increase her flexibility in using her word knowledge to acquire a strategy for decoding unfamiliar words (see Chapter 13).

*Diagnostic Teaching (Step 6).* At this point in the process we were ready to engage in diagnostic teaching as a means of confirming our hypotheses and identifying possible instructional interventions. A summary of Yasmin's diagnostic teaching and its results is presented in the thumbnail sketch in Figure 11.9.

*Planning.* In the planning phase of diagnostic teaching, we needed to determine the specific nature of the interventions that would address the needs identified in Step 5. To do this, as we noted previously, it is easiest to think in terms of the features of the settings, methods,

**FIGURE 11.9**
Yasmin's
Thumbnail Sketch:
Steps 4–6

| Decision Making (Steps 4 and 5) | Diagnostic Teaching (Step 6) |
|---|---|
| **_Evaluating the Match (Step 4)_**<br>What is the match?<br>• Reading level is within a second grade range.<br>• Strong match between classroom structure and learning expectations, i.e., teacher modeling, small group work determined by assessment information.<br>• Poor match between student choice of reading material and student reading level.<br>• Writing, specifically spelling and content, not matched to reading level. Writing is much less developed especially in areas of language structure than reading.<br>• Flexibility in decoding similar words (decoding using analogy) does not match.<br>• Strong knowledge of letter sounds and ability to hear sounds in words does not match application of visual cueing system. Can hear all sounds in words but does not search further in words (uses only first letter with unknown words) and does not stretch words when writing.<br><br>**_Reflecting and Generating Hypotheses_**<br>What does the learner need?<br>• Support in self-selection of appropriate reading materials.<br>• Own collection of books for reading practice.<br>• Continuing in a classroom that provides explicit teaching of strategies through modeling, oral language practice, small group work based on assessment information.<br>• Strong oral language models.<br>• Activities in making words, working with onsets and rimes to develop more flexibility and knowledge of word families.<br>• More writing instruction with emphasis on developing supporting details. Language experience for practice in writing correct English structures.<br>• Rereading own writing to begin knowledge of revising process. | **_Planning and Implementing_**<br>What is most likely to (re)establish learning?<br>Examine affect of two decoding strategies on word recognition and generation<br>• Teaching making/breaking words using onsets and rimes<br>• Teaching decoding by analogy<br><br>**_Evaluating the Diagnostic Sessions_**<br>• Word sorts are challenging but do encourage her to look through whole words<br>• Enjoyed and was successful with decoding by analogy<br><br>Posttesting suggests some increases spontaneous generation of word building with rimes<br><br>**_Next Steps_**<br>Explore ways to increase her fluency and stamina: perhaps have her read to younger student (easy text that she can read fluently to keep her from choosing harder text that she wants to read but can't quite do yet). |

and materials that can and should be modified and manipulated. In Yasmin's case there was a genuine commitment on the part of the classroom teacher to improving Yasmin's instructional program and a willingness to try new things. The reading coach for Yasmin's classroom conducted the diagnostic teaching sessions, keeping in mind a variety of options that could be implemented in her everyday reading program.

The characteristics of the methods, materials, and tasks of Yasmin's instructional context offered several alternatives for diagnostic teaching. Specifically, the instructional method used for word work could be modified to include methods and tasks that focused her more clearly on the orthographic patterns of words. In addition, her reading materials could be altered to provide her with more frequent opportunities for fluency practice.

After considering the various alternatives, we decided to try out two alternative approaches to word recognition instruction, one directing Yasmin's attention to onset and rime and the other to the application of this knowledge in decoding unknown words. These approaches are variations on the "making words" approach promoted by Cunningham (1995) and the "decoding-by-analogy" strategy described in the Benchmark program (Gaskins, Ehri, Cress, O'Hara, & Donnelley, 1996/97).

*Investigating for Further Assessment.* The session began with a making words lesson (*Systematic Sequential Phonics They Use* by Patricia Cunningham). This technique was not being used by her second grade teacher, but Yasmin was familiar with it because her first grade teacher had used it occasionally. The steps used were as follows:

1. Using movable letters and a tray, Yasmin was directed to make *at, ate, rat, mat, mate, rate, rake, take,* and *make,* and the secret word was *market.*
2. Yasmin was then asked to sort the words that she made into rhyming words.
3. A series of layered prompts was used to help her accomplish the sorting task successfully.
   a. She said that she did not understand "sort," and so the task was explained, and she began to sort by first letter.
   b. She was reminded to sort by rhyming families, and she put the *-ate* and *-ake* words together and the *-at* words in a separate pile.
   c. Then the words were displayed in columns sorted by ending. She was given two words, date and cake, and was asked to put them with the group that had the same ending.
4. The rhyming and sorting tasks were repeated to test for transfer.

During the making words strategy Yasmin was able to make the words but had some difficulty with the secret word (*market* in this case), which required putting all the letters together to make a word. She knew what the word was but did not know how to spell it (even with all the letters) until she was told to say the word slowly, listen to the sounds, and point to the letters.

Yasmin had significant difficulty sorting words using either rhyming or orthographic patterns. Even when reminded to sort by rhyming families, she still did not sort the words correctly. She was able to match words to correctly sorted lists, however. When this task was repeated with other words, Yasmin was unable to generate rhyming words, although she was capable of isolating individual vowel sounds.

*Investigating Using Trial Teaching.*    The next lesson involved a trial teaching session with decoding by analogy. Yasmin was taught to use a framing sentence: "If I know this word: _____ , then it can help me read this word: _____ ." The lesson demonstrations used words she knew to help her decode unknown words. For example, the teacher used color words that she knew were very familiar to Yasmin and then showed her another much more difficult word with the same word part, such as *black* and *attack.* Yasmin caught on quickly and enjoyed the activity. After several attempts, Yasmin was able to read all the new words using the words she knew. She even remarked, "I think that I can use this when I read, its like finding little words in big words!"

*Evaluating.*    In all examples Yasmin had difficulty sorting by rhyming words and generating new rhyming words. The making words strategy seemed to be a good strategy to encourage Yasmin to move letters around and help her become more flexible in transferring what she knows about some letters and words to other letters and words. Making words encouraged Yasmin to look at all the letters in words, and in creating the secret word, she had to stretch out the word and listen to the sounds, something she needed to do to move her toward more conventional (and less invented) spelling when writing. Although the making words strategy was helpful, the difficulty she demonstrated suggested that she would need support to be successful.

On the other hand, during the decoding-by-analogy activity, Yasmin quickly began using the approach to read unknown words. In addition, she enjoyed the work and appeared to learn something about how to approach unknown words. In this case the difficulty lies in Yasmin's inability to generate her own rhyming words. Thus an approach that provides her with "key words" to use for making analogies would be important (see Gaskins et al., 1996/97).

These sessions were evaluated by using an "All the Words I Know" task. In the past Yasmin had demonstrated an inability to use orthographic spelling patterns to generate words. After these two thirty-minute sessions, Yasmin was given five minutes to write the words she knew. She still mostly wrote random sight words, but she did write two families of words: *may, lay, say* and *ring, sing.*

As a result of this diagnostic teaching experience, we devised a support program based on explicit instruction in the close examination of entire words and the introduction of key vocabulary to use in decoding by analogy. Because the teacher noted that many of her ELL students were having the same types of difficulties that Yasmin was experiencing and because these activities had not been done in her grade 2 class, they were introduced to the whole class and used regularly throughout the week.

In addition, it was clear that Yasmin needed more print experience and practice reading easy books. Her teacher had already begun to provide some of this, but the reading coach suggested that Yasmin might enjoy practicing and preparing to read books to younger children. (See also Chapter 12 for repeated readings.) Finally, additional writing experience was introduced by the literacy coach and supported by the teacher.

For both Marvin and Yasmin the benefits of diagnostic teaching were both immediate and long-term. Each was quickly engaged in an instructional program that held promise of addressing their needs. Our first diagnostic teaching sessions do not always yield so rich a reward. One thing is abundantly clear, however. The quality of these sessions was directly related to two factors: the quality of the assessment information that was gathered before diagnostic teaching and the thoughtfulness of the planning that went into the diagnostic teaching segment.

# Diagnostic Portfolios: Making Diagnostic Teaching Work

Diagnostic teaching requires a solid knowledge base, a willingness to explore variation in student performance, and a repertoire of activities and materials for creating instructional adaptations. In the chapters that follow we provide many suggestions for planning, adapting, and delivering good reading instruction. Many of these ideas can be incorporated into diagnostic teaching. Decision making and diagnostic teaching require that classroom teachers and clinicians make their hunches (hypotheses) explicit, set priorities, and use them to plan and execute instructional adaptations. Maintaining a diagnostic portfolio and reviewing the contents periodically can set the stage for this reflective teaching. When students' work and performance is reviewed over time and across multiple tasks and texts, it is often easier to inform instruction—to think about what might work or what should be attempted.

Good teaching requires that teachers establish and maintain their focus to accomplish assessment or instructional purposes. However, good teaching is also opportunistic and flexible. Interactive decision making during instruction is a hallmark of effective instruction (Duffy & Roehler, 1989). This requires careful listening and refocusing.

To capitalize on the diagnostic teaching procedures we have described in this chapter, classroom teachers and clinicians will need to acknowledge the strengths and limitations of their own settings. Few classroom teachers will find the time to engage in continuous full-blown diagnostic sessions such as the ones we have described, and clinicians may even find it difficult to make this a part of their regular routine. Therefore we suggest two specific practices that may prove helpful, depending on the setting.

## Target Selections for Diagnostic Teaching

Classroom teachers who are using a basal reading system can designate specific selections in each level for use as diagnostic teaching selections. In this way, conditions can be set up that reflect the focus of classroom instruction. For example, predetermined selections can be used to:

1. conduct an individual assessment that examines students' progress outside their usual group setting;
2. set up conditions that are analogous to classroom instruction and compare those to students' unaided reading of the selection;
3. manipulate aspects of the lesson that are critical for student(s) in a particular classroom; and
4. select texts that make different demands as a means of exploring student flexibility.

If selections are targeted periodically, it is possible to do more elaborate assessment from time to time, rather than attempting it on a daily or even weekly basis.

You might use the form in Figure 11.10 to organize these diagnostic sessions. Over time you will establish a collection of books and diagnostic assessment conditions that are especially effective for assessing one or another aspect of literacy. For example, one of the authors frequently uses *Dogger,* by Shirley Hughes (1989), to explore young students' comprehension abilities because it is an appropriate but complex narrative story with multiple character motivations. At the same time the wonderful illustrations support comprehension without revealing the entire story line. Similarly, we often use *Just Like Daddy,* by Frank Asch (1981), to investigate a wide array of early and emergent print skills with students. These books are rich enough to be used flexibly, and consequently, the diagnostic manipulations are several. *Just Like Daddy,* for example, can be adjusted to examine students' concepts of word, their abilities to match speech to print, their abilities to read a few high-frequency sight words, and their abilities to anticipate upcoming text at the both word and idea levels. Teachers who may be concerned about compromising the entertainment value of these books must remember that students need practice reading for a variety of different purposes. Furthermore, if the student's personal affective response to reading is an important goal of classroom instruction, then it should be included as part of the assessment.

## A Collection of Diagnostic Teaching Selections

For both classroom teachers and clinicians the time and attention demands are so great that diagnostic teaching is more likely to be employed if the materials and tasks are readily available. Paratore and Indrisano (1987) have developed a set of materials they use for diagnostic teaching that include graded (or progressively more difficult) passages and a set of tasks and prompts to accompany these passages. These materials permit them to explore a range of student responses "on the spot." To be effective, a collection of diagnostic teaching selections must be organized and grouped for easy use and clearly labeled so that adjustments can be made during the assessment session. In addition, we recommend using a set of clearly tabbed task cards to facilitate administration. The following types of materials should be considered for inclusion in a diagnostic teaching collection:

- Selections ranked by difficulty or a list of books to be used for assessment purposes.
- A listing of the types of tasks that can and should be used and the order in which these will be presented.
- A series of statements for each selection or book that could be expected in an adequate retelling of the text, and a place to note these.
- A summary sheet that includes key words to be used for assessment of vocabulary and/or word recognition.
- A place to make notes about student comments.

These ideas are, of course, only suggestions. Once started, a well-organized collection can and will grow. Furthermore, teachers who are committed to a portfolio approach to assessment find this type of organization absolutely essential to the effective implementation of ongoing assessment activities.

**FIGURE 11.10**
Diagnostic
Teaching
Planning Guide

Text: _____ Level: _____
Key Features of Text: _____

| Possible Elements for Diagnostic Teaching | Notes |
|---|---|
| Prereading preparation<br>• Introduce key vocabulary<br>• Build background<br>• Structured overviews | |
| Introduction of title and/or main theme/idea | |
| Jump-start activity (see Chapter 15)<br>• Picture walk<br>• Disussion | |
| Provide access to text<br>• Talking Dictionary (see Chapter 12)<br>• Guided reading (see Chapter 12)<br>• Teacher read-aloud<br>• Taped read-along<br>• Technology (e.g., CDs) | |
| Other provided support<br>• Guided reading (see Chapter 12)<br>• Computer-assisted text<br>• Story frameworks<br>• K-W-L (see Chapter 12) | |
| Change task<br>• Questions<br>• Retellings<br>• Story maps<br>• Structured overviews<br>• Visual representations<br>• Performance | |
| Change text<br>• Quality of narrative<br>• Narrative versus exposition<br>• Exposition<br>• Interest<br>• Picture support<br>• Length, size, etc. | |
| Comments: | |

## Chapter Summary

This chapter focused on the point in assessment when informed decision making is required to determine how instructional planning will proceed. Specifically, this chapter dealt with understanding and implementing the steps in the assessment-instruction process that involve evaluating the match between learner and context (Step 4), reflection and generating hypotheses (Step 5), and diagnostic teaching (Step 6).

Evaluating the match between the learner and the instructional context (Step 4) involves using the information gathered in Steps 1–3 to determine the fit or match between the knowledge, skills and strategies, motivation and reflectivity of the learner and the settings, instruction, resources, and tasks within the instructional context. After the match between the learner and the instructional context has been evaluated, we need to reflect on this information and generate hypotheses (Step 5) about what the learner needs. This step is designed to help us make decisions about the relative importance of the various problems/needs we have identified.

Following Steps 4 and 5, in which we reflect on the existing match and generate some preliminary hypotheses about what the learner needs, we need to identify a better or optimal match between the learner and the context in order to (re)establish learning. To accomplish this goal, we rely primarily on the technique of *diagnostic teaching*. This procedure is both diagnostic, because it allows for the collection of additional information in order to clarify and test hypotheses, and instructional, because it provides opportunities to try out methods that may be successful alternatives for working with a student.

The process of diagnostic teaching involves three related tasks: planning, executing, and evaluating. During planning we need to determine how we will focus the diagnostic teaching to verify our hunches about both the source of the problem and the instructional interventions that are most likely to call forth learning. Executing involves administering diagnostic teaching sessions using either the alternative methods or scaffolding approach to gain information about how a student performs under several different or contrasting conditions. Successful execution also requires the flexibility necessary to be able to take advantage of opportunities as they arise.

The primary thrust of the evaluation of the diagnostic teaching is to determine the impact of the manipulations on the student's learning, performance, attitude, motivation, and/or knowledge. Diagnostic teaching activities can be facilitated in both the classroom and the clinic through procedures such as using targeted selections in basal reading programs or preselecting a collection of diagnostic teaching materials.

# SECTION FIVE

# Instruction

$T$he preceding chapters have focused on assessment and diagnostic teaching as a means of gathering information and gaining insight into individual learners. Decisions about how and what to teach are based on the resulting knowledge and understanding. Good decision making also requires an awareness of available instructional strategies and tools. Fortunately, there has been an upsurge of interest in recent years in advancing and promoting best practices in reading and writing instruction. Thoughtful teachers now have a wide array of effective instructional interventions from which to select their own preferred methods.

This section is divided into two subsections. The first subsection, Getting Started in Instruction, contains Chapter 12. It provides guidelines for creating effective literacy environments and planning good initial instruction. In the second section, Adaptations, we deal directly with Step 7 of the Assessment-Instruction Process. In these chapters we describe instructional interventions that address specific components of literacy. Chapter 13 is devoted to adapting instruction to focus on word recognition, fluency, and spelling; Chapter 14 to adapting instruction to focus on vocabulary; and Chapter 15 to comprehension, writing, and studying. Consistent with the focus throughout this text, these specific instructional techniques have been selected for discussion because they are a close match to the theoretical perspective of this text or because they have demonstrated their utility.

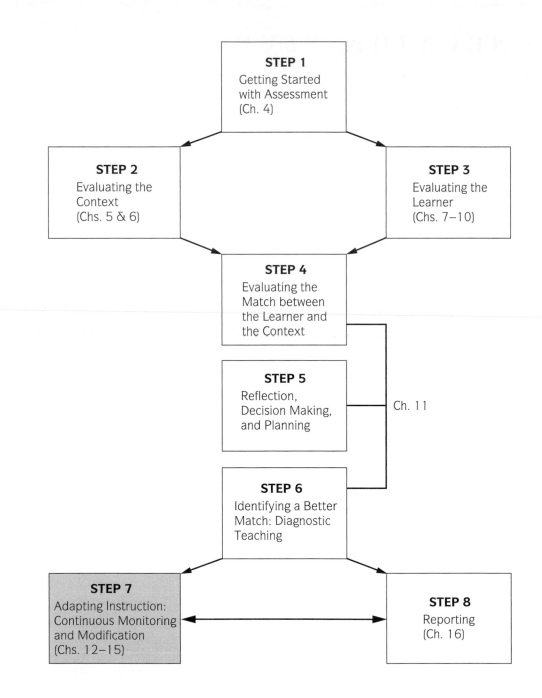

STEP 1
Getting Started
with Assessment
(Ch. 4)

STEP 2
Evaluating the
Context
(Chs. 5 & 6)

STEP 3
Evaluating the
Learner
(Chs. 7–10)

STEP 4
Evaluating the
Match between
the Learner and
the Context

STEP 5
Reflection,
Decision Making,
and Planning

Ch. 11

STEP 6
Identifying a Better
Match: Diagnostic
Teaching

STEP 7
Adapting Instruction:
Continuous Monitoring
and Modification
(Chs. 12–15)

STEP 8
Reporting
(Ch. 16)

# 12 Getting Started in Instruction

Effective reading and writing instruction relies heavily on the decision-making powers of individual teachers. To make good decisions, teachers must orchestrate knowledge and skill in endlessly changing ways. In previous chapters we provided information about how to begin making good decisions using high-quality assessment information. In this chapter we point out the types of instructional decisions that must be made and describe some effective instructional strategies for getting started.

Like assessment, instruction must begin somewhere. Of course, the multiple types of information that have been gathered, summarized, and examined quite closely in earlier steps of the assessment-instruction process (see Chapter 11) can now be used to plan an instructional program. However, it is often necessary to launch an instructional program before the assessment picture is completely clear. As we have already noted, the assessment-instruction process is continuous and requires adaptive teaching. Consequently, the issues addressed in this chapter are on the beginnings of instruction. This chapter lays the foundation for several chapters that follow, in which we offer more specific ideas about instructional intervention.

In the next three sections of this chapter we provide information that will help you get started with instruction. First we discuss several key characteristics of an instructional program, including goals and objectives, the literate environment, organizational patterns, and materials. Next, we describe a general instructional framework that consists of familiar reading, guided reading, guided writing, word study, and sustained reading and writing. We also describe some specific instructional activities that can be used within the context of this framework and have such high general applicability that it makes sense to use them with nearly all students. Using this framework and these techniques, it is possible to get started with a student or students even when there is still some doubt about the details of the instructional program. In the final section of this chapter we address the issue of lesson planning for individual students, providing guidance in specifying objectives and selecting activities. Individual lesson planning must eventually take place to make good decisions about when and how to use the more focused instructional strategies described in Chapters 13–15.

## Key Characteristics of the Instructional Program

Studies of school effectiveness suggest that instruction has the most impact when goals are clear and student progress is frequently monitored (Edmonds, 1980; Rupley, 1976). It is well established that teachers and the programs they implement are central to student learning (see Chapters 5 and 6). The basis for effective instruction is, of course, careful planning and preparation. Teachers make both general decisions about their instructional programs and specific decisions about individual students. In this section of the chapter we describe some of the general, overarching decisions and plans that teachers must make regarding goals and objectives, organizational patterns, and materials.

## Goals and Objectives

There are always a variety of ways to help students learn information and acquire competence. Effective teachers control a wide range of instructional tools that they can use flexibly. However, specific instructional activities that might be used to teach students are of far less importance than knowing what is to be accomplished. Teachers devise their goals as they consider what they know about reading and writing processes, skilled performance, and student(s).

Even without exceptionally focused information about individual students, it is possible to make some judgments about appropriate practice based on an understanding of reading and writing processes. The curricular goals described in Chapter 5 also provide important guidance in initial planning. As we stated there, the goal of reading and writing instruction should be to create and encourage knowledgeable, strategic, motivated readers and writers. In applying these goals to instructional planning, we noted the need for specific lesson objectives to address attitude, process, and content objectives.

The first step toward accomplishing these ambitious long-term goals is to create a context for success—an environment in which learning important outcomes is possible. We will return to the issue of planning for specific students in the final section of this chapter.

## Establishing a Literate Environment

The instructional context can and does influence learning and performance (see Chapters 5 and 6). Attempts to separate a particular learner's problems from settings, instructional practices, and resources are fruitless, since this separation ignores the interactive nature of reading and writing. Similarly, instruction is most effective when the texts and tasks involve authentic reading and writing and the teaching occurs in integrated contexts. For example, there is evidence to suggest that students' reading achievement is enhanced by reading connected text with the support and guidance of a teacher, whereas there is little relationship between reading achievement and students' attention to games or workbook activities (Leinhardt, Zigmond, & Cooley, 1981; Zigmond, Vallecorsa, & Leinhardt, 1980). Similarly, there is no evidence to support teaching formal rules of grammar as a means of improving speaking or writing (Hillocks & Smith, 1991). Rather, researchers such as Stotsky (1983) suggest that the abstract knowledge that proficient writers have about text comes from wide reading and writing experiences.

The first step in effective instruction, especially for less skilled readers or writers, is the creation of a literate environment. Below, we provide guidelines for establishing a literate environment using descriptors related to three aspects of classroom contexts suggested by Duffy and Roehler (1989): the print environment (the physical environment), meaningful enterprise (the intellectual environment), and social exchange and interaction (the social-emotional environment).

***The Print Environment.*** The first step in establishing a literate environment is establishing accessible, inviting, and well-trafficked reading and writing areas within the classroom. The reading center or library corner should invite students to read. Rug(s), cushions, and/or soft chair(s) establish this as an area of comfortable interaction with print. Characters from books may be prominently displayed in the form of stuffed animals, drawings, illustrations, or book covers, depending on the age of the group. The available print matter should offer students a wide range of reading options. Stocking a classroom library requires some knowledge and commitment on the part of teachers. Many teachers are well informed about books, but others have not developed knowledge and expertise in this area.

The print materials should include all manner of real texts and reading materials used by literate individuals both in and out of school. The classroom reading collection might contain several books by the same author, books and stories created by students in the class, information about authors, and reference materials such as maps, atlases, and schedules. Materials that reflect a variety of cultural perspectives, especially those of the students in the class, are also important. These materials can help students feel accepted and promote understanding of and respect for the language and the historical and personal heritage of different cultures.

Some materials will be intended for recreational, self-selected reading; others will be used more selectively by students as they complete projects or require information. The materials in reading/writing centers or libraries should be consulted whenever possible. When a map is needed, students should be aware that they can consult the atlas in the reading center. When they need a good book for silent reading time, they should expect to find one there as well, along with written critiques of books by children who have already read them. In addition, this area would ideally contain newspapers, magazines, and other everyday print materials.

A literate environment also contains a well-stocked and accessible writing/publishing center. Students' writing folders may be kept in this area, but it should also contain writing materials, dictionaries, and, for older students, a thesaurus. Writing conference guidelines should be posted here. Many teachers and students like to have a word wall in this area. The word wall is simply a large, blank sheet of paper on which the students or teacher can write words that are frequently needed but difficult to spell, words that someone has found interesting and wants to share, or theme-related words that will be useful only for a particular period. If possible, this area should also contain at least one computer with word-processing software and materials for illustrating and publishing books (paper, book bindings, markers, and so on). Samples of writing can also be posted, for inspiration or sharing.

***Meaningful Enterprise.*** A key feature of any setting that promotes literacy is the provision for meaningful enterprise. In describing the attributes of a literate environment, Raphael and Englert (1989) note that students need to read and write for "real purposes and audiences" and that they need many experiences that invite sharing and extending self-generated work. This is especially true for students of diverse backgrounds who don't understand the significance of schooling or becoming a good reader and writer for future life opportunities. Ladson-Billings (1994) and Delpit (1995) report that when students' real-life experiences are legitimized and curricula are connected to their background knowledge, they are capable of learning complex ideas and skills that far exceed their reading grade-level expectations. Alternatively, when classroom activities are uninteresting or are structured in ways that are irrelevant to students' lives, students are likely to tune out or become uncooperative (Au, 1993; D'Amato, 1987)

The point is that students must have opportunities to use their literacy skills for their own purposes, as well as the purposes of others. Classrooms where students read and write only for the teacher, using teacher-generated topics and guidelines, are less likely to produce people who read or write for their own purposes as lifelong learners. Using activities and materials that promote a meaningful approach to literacy, students are more likely to see the purpose behind them as genuine. As a result, they are more likely to transfer the knowledge and skill to new settings.

Much of the instructional and practice material designed for remedial work has been excessively contrived. The temptation is great to get started in instruction by using one of the packaged remedial programs involving extensive isolated skills work. However, remedial students are generally those who have the least appreciation for reading and writing as meaningful activities. Therefore the first approach should focus squarely on the communicative nature of reading and writing, and students should be encouraged to use their skills in authentic ways. Students may find it rewarding to do any or all of the following:

- Read/write to younger students;
- Share humorous or moving portions of stories with others;
- Read/write to find out specific information or answer a question;
- Read/write to report to others;
- Read/write to compile information;
- Read to learn how to do something or to follow directions;
- Read to find out how others feel or react;
- Read/write for emotional support and guidance;
- Write to tell a personal story;
- Read/write for enjoyment.

Whenever possible, the materials and tasks students use to learn to read and write should permit them to advance in their appreciation of the purposes for which they are acquiring these skills. Mastering a skill so that you can use it at the next level in a program is not a good enough reason for learning. Students and teachers both should understand how the new skill or knowledge can be used in real world reading and writing activities.

***Social Exchange and Interaction.***    Another critical feature of literate school environments is the degree of social exchange and interaction. To become literate—that is, to acquire the language and thinking skills needed to read and write effectively—students need many opportunities to discuss, collaborate, assist, and present information and ideas. Although we will be focusing our attention on techniques that are especially useful for working with individual students, the general environment in the school and classroom is critically important. We assume that all of the specific techniques to be discussed in this and future chapters are undertaken in an environment that involves large amounts of speaking, listening, reading, and writing.

According to Au (1993), research indicates that it is important to encourage nonnative speakers of English to use their native language to help them learn to read and write in English. For example, Moll and Diaz (1985) found that fourth grade students whose native language was Spanish could deal with grade-level texts and produce answers to comprehension questions comparable to their English-speaking peers when they were allowed to respond in Spanish. Building on students' native language abilities enhances their confidence and self-esteem by showing respect for their home languages and cultures.

In many classrooms there needs to be much more dialogue, as opposed to lecture and formal presentation, than is generally present in classroom settings (see Chapter 5 and the discussion of reciprocal teaching in this chapter). There needs to be a better balance between student and teacher talk (Raphael, 1998). The smaller, less formal environments that are often characteristic of remedial instructional settings provide the perfect opportunity to promote a very dialogic, interactive mode of instruction. Unfortunately, many teachers of less-skilled students believe that they must deliver a specific skills-based program of instruction, and they often miss opportunities to promote literacy acquisition in a socially meaningful context.

Raphael and Hiebert (1996) define four different roles that teachers employ: explicit instructor, scaffolder, facilitator, and participant. These roles represent, in decreasing order, the degree to which the teacher is "in charge." Opportunities for teachers to engage in these different roles and for achieving a better balance between teacher and student talk come from the use of different participation structures. Students' and teachers' talk differs when work is undertaken in one-to-one settings, small groups, and large groups and when the teacher is present or not. The next section considers further the matter of organizational patterns.

## Organizational Patterns

There are many ways to organize students for instruction. The range of acceptable practice is quite extensive, including classrooms with individualized arrangements, learning centers and open space, team teaching with cross-class groupings, multi-age groupings, and whole-class instruction in self-contained settings. In remedial settings, one-to-one tutoring is occasionally used. However, one of the most common ways to meet individual differences, as discussed in Chapter 5, is to organize students into ability groups (Shake, 1989) or to form homogenous ability groups in remedial settings. This type of arrangement has prevailed since the 1920s (Otto, Wolf, & Eldridge, 1984), and there is extensive but conflicting evidence of its effectiveness. Although the research suggests that students *do* benefit from placement in groups (Rosenshine & Stevens, 1984), there is less evidence that these groups need to be formed on the basis of ability (Reutzel, 1999). Indeed, an increasingly strong body of research suggests that students of all abilities benefit from organizational patterns that involve cooperative groups (Dansereau, 1985; Johnson & Johnson, 1986; Slavin, 1983; Slavin, Stevens, & Madden, 1988).

A widely recognized approach to cooperative grouping for reading and writing is Cooperative Integrated Reading and Composition (CIRC). Based on the cooperative learning principles developed by Slavin (1983; Stevens, Madden, Slavin, & Farnish, 1987), this approach has students belonging to two groups: their own reading group (a traditional basal program) and a mixed-ability team that is composed of members from two reading groups. Within the second group, students work cooperatively in a variety of supportive ways: reading to one another, summarizing stories, responding to stories, and practicing a variety of reading-related tasks. The result has been fairly dramatic reading achievement gains for students of all abilities.

Reutzel (1999) presents several different options for use within the cooperative grouping concept adapted from others, including Wood (1987). For example, dyads is a strategy in which a pair of students reads two pages of text silently or orally in unison; one student then verbally recounts what the two have read, and the other acts as listener and clarifier for the recaller. As an alternative to traditional patterns, the dyad strategy is worth a close look, to be used either in concert with other planned arrangements or as a substitute. Reutzel (1999) also describes a variety of other grouping strategies, including flexible groups and literature circles.

There is also evidence that elementary students of diverse backgrounds may benefit from the opportunity to learn in peer work groups (D'Amato, 1988; Jordan, 1985). Like other instructional approaches, however, the effectiveness of peer work groups may be strongly affected by cultural differences. Teachers need to "understand that peer work groups may need to be organized differently, and that peer teaching-learning interactions may take different forms, depending on the students' cultural background" (Au, 1993, p. 87). It is important to build on cultural patterns of interaction to further literacy learning. Specialists and support teachers are confronted with a wide array of choices about how to deliver reading and writing instruction. In some contexts it is undoubtedly better to provide in-class instruction (inclusion), especially if students join a mixed ability cooperative group after leaving their reading support group. In other cases students will receive more focused and effective instruction in pull-out programs involving small groups of like-ability students. However, specialists need to be sure that their grouping arrangements are not promoting negative attitudes and/or dependency behaviors in poor readers or writers.

Executing any alternative grouping patterns requires careful consideration and planning. Long-term planning is required to alter the delivery of instruction in any significant way. However, given the rapidly changing knowledge base regarding grouping practices, teachers should remain open to the development and evolution of different approaches as the evidence of successful interventions or arrangements grows.

## Materials

Selecting materials is always something of a challenge for teachers of less-skilled readers and writers. The challenge becomes even greater when we demand that the texts and tasks students encounter be high-quality, authentic ones. In reading, students need whole texts that offer authentic reading models. Stories should offer strong narrative structures that entertain and speak to students' personal experience or interests. Expository texts should be accurate and considerate, providing students with opportunities to learn and remember important information.

Careful examination of the materials to be used for direct instruction is absolutely essential. We strongly recommend that available materials be evaluated using the guidelines suggested in Chapter 6. In addition, it will be helpful to refer to a variety of resources to build a collection of materials. For example, the World Wide Web provides information on award-winning fiction through the American Library Association (www.ala.org) and on multicultural literature through the Internet Public Library (www.ipl.org/ref/QUE/PF/kid-multilit.html). In addition, the International Reading Association (www.reading.org/choices/) publishes annotated booklists each year that describe children's, young adults', and teachers' choices of their favorite recently published books.

Comprehensive lists of leveled books by author, genre, publisher, and level as determined by the Fountas and Pinnell (1996, 2001a) leveling system can be found in *Matching Books to Readers (K–3)* (Fountas & Pinnell, 1999) and in *Leveled Books for Readers, Grades 3–6* (Fountas & Pinnell, 2001b). These resources include books representing a wide range of genre, which is important because not all students are excited by reading stories or poetry; some prefer nonfiction. Magazines and periodicals written by and for young people, such as *Ask, Cobblestone, Click, Cricket, Highlights, National Geographic World, Ranger Rick, Sesame Street, Spider, Stone Soup,* and *Your Big Backyard,* should also be available in classroom settings. The World Wide Web is also a good resource of information on children's magazines (e.g., www.monroe.lib.in.us/childrens/kidsmags.html).

Teachers who work with struggling readers or writers need a variety of these texts so that students can acquire and/or practice their reading and writing skills in a supported print environment. Materials especially designed for less-able readers and writers should be examined carefully to make sure that the text resulting from application of readability formulas or vocabulary control is not terribly stilted. The literary quality of these books is very uneven, but poor readers can often find a satisfying story between the covers.

Establishing an environment that promotes and encourages literacy is of the utmost importance. The materials and tasks that are provided for in the environment and the organizational patterns that are used will influence students' attitude and motivation for learning and most likely what they learn about reading and writing as well. However, the instructional activities that take place in that environment also affect what students learn. In the following section we describe a generic instructional framework that can be used to get started and several high-utility instructional strategies that can be used within the context of this framework.

# Getting Started with a Lesson Framework and High-Utility Strategies

As a practical matter, teachers often want or need to begin instruction even without a complete assessment picture. Teachers can and do need to implement the steps and use the techniques of the assessment-instruction process in a variety of ways. The need to be flexible and to exercise professional judgment, however, is an ever-present mandate in working with students and schools. In this section we describe a general instructional framework and several high-utility strategies that can be used within the context of this framework. Teachers can use this framework and these techniques to get started with instruction even when there is still some doubt about the details of the instructional program.

The strategies that we describe here are admittedly selective; we might have chosen others. However, we consider these to be high-utility because they are theory driven, have at least some empirical base to support their efficacy, have broad-based applicability, and address significant literacy outcomes. These strategies generally share the following key features relative to current theory and research:

1. They provide for reading and/or writing in meaningful contexts for meaningful purposes.
2. They encourage social exchange or interaction focused on reading and writing activities.
3. They integrate skills and strategies in whole text reading and authentic writing activities.
4. They offer flexibility in terms of what can be done with the activities and the types of materials that can be employed.

Although many activities have been developed to promote reading and writing improvement, few provide evidence of their effectiveness. Most teachers are shocked to find that long-established practices often have no empirical base. For those strategies that we expect to use with all or most students (e.g., high-utility strategies), we should demand demonstrated worth. In addition to empirical evidence supporting the efficacy of the strategies described here, we have used them in our own work with less-skilled readers and writers. These techniques are manageable for teachers who have not used them before and effective for students.

In the Getting Started phase of instruction the flexibility of instructional activities is especially important, and the techniques described below offer almost unlimited adaptability. Together, these activities encompass the full range of reading and writing abilities, offering a rich context for any other instruction that might be required. The fact that each technique is designed to promote knowledgeable, strategic, and motivated reading and/or writing is also important. Instructional strategies must be planned to embody good practice but also to address the important goals denoted in long-term planning.

## A Lesson Framework

A literacy lesson framework developed by Tancock (1994) specifically for low-achieving readers and writers offers a guide to instruction that can be adapted to the needs of individuals or small groups. Our adaptation of this framework includes the following five components:

> Familiar reading
> Guided reading
> Guided writing
> Word study
> Sustained reading and writing

This is a generic literacy lesson framework that can be used with large and small groups as well as individual students. These five components cover the range of reading and writing activities that are essential to skilled performance, including attention to word recognition, fluency, comprehension, writing process, and independent reading and writing. The following sections discuss each lesson component and offer descriptions of high-utility strategies that can be used to implement the framework.

## Familiar Reading

The first component of the lesson framework calls for familiar reading. This portion of the lesson serves as a confidence builder and warm-up for the instruction to follow and provides opportunities for the teacher to model and teach fluency. In this part of the lesson the teacher selects several familiar, independent level texts for the student to choose from. The student reads and rereads, both orally and silently, these books during many successive lessons, practicing the strategies learned in previous lessons.

*Repeated Readings.*    Although very young children often hear the same story many times, once they enter school they are generally expected to read a story just once, with good fluency and comprehension, and then move on to another. Educators have too often missed the value of repeated experiences with books and stories. The point of repeated reading is simply to persuade and induce children to read a particular text several times so that they can improve fluency through increased familiarity and additional practice. As such, it has proven to be an extremely useful tool for teachers working with less-skilled readers.

One of the most potent reasons for revisiting reading materials is to build fluency. We agree with Allington (1983b, p. 560), who notes, "Limitations (of the research) aside, a preponderance of empirical and clinical evidence supports the relationship of fluent oral reading and good overall reading ability." Although there are a variety of procedures for developing oral reading fluency (see Smith, 1979), the most widely tested technique involves *repeated readings* (Allington, 1977; Chomsky, 1978; NRP, 2000).

Like the other high-utility strategies presented here, repeated reading offers both ease and flexibility in implementation. Many teachers expect resistance from students when they are asked to reread material because on the surface this seems to be such a mechanistic and repetitive task. However, young children often choose to reread material themselves as they try to read real texts (Rasinksi, 1986). They will return to the same piece until it is familiar and can be read with understanding. Less skilled readers generally do not get the opportunity to read much at all, much less reread material for control and fluency (Allington, 1977). Repeated readings offer them this opportunity.

Finally, repeated readings permit students to experience reading something that is (or has become) relatively easy for them to read. Allington (1983b) has suggested that this experience of reading relatively easy material may be essential in the development of fluency. Whatever the reason, we have not only found limited resistance to a repeated reading strategy, but we have also generally found that this is a favored activity. Repeated readings focus specifically on one aspect of the reading process, but the strong success experiences that are evoked often produce positive attitude outcomes as well.

*Launching Repeated Readings.*    The easiest way to initiate repeated reading is to select a little book or mark off a segment of print in a text that the student is already reading and to ask the student to read and reread that section until he or she has reached some predetermined level of fluency. For example, Samuels (1979) suggested that students read repeatedly until they could read the section at a rate of 85 words per minute. Others have suggested that speed is not a sufficient criterion. For example, Allington (1983b) suggests lightly marking segments of text in phrase units. Students' repeated readings are then judged in terms of improved phrasing. Still another possibility is simply to dictate how many rereadings of a text will be required (Ballard, 1978). In any event it is necessary to decide what students will be told about how the technique will be used and when they can move on to new material.

Some sensible guidelines for the beginning stages of repeated readings might include the following:

**1.** *Select materials that lend themselves to fluent oral reading.* Material that is too choppy or artificial as commercial beginning materials can be probably will not result in rewarding renderings of the text or in increased fluency.

**2.** Be sure to *talk to students about why they are doing this activity.* They should be helped to see that they are practicing a *part* of reading, much the way an athlete or musician might practice a small part to improve the overall performance. Emphasize that increased expression, knowledge of words, use of context, and so on will help them to comprehend text more easily. Students must see that the goal isn't exceptionally fine oral reading.

**3.** Because the student will be rereading the material several times, *do not hesitate to select material that will be somewhat challenging.* Clearly, it is also necessary to use good judgment about task difficulty as it affects individual students.

**4.** *Students should be encouraged to practice (reread) silently as much as possible.* The only real danger of repeated readings is that they may supplant other productive silent reading experiences.

*Maintaining and Adapting Repeated Readings.*    Samuels (1979) suggests several ways to maintain interest in repeated reading. One of the easiest is to keep track of the experience by graphing or logging the results (see Figure 12.1). Students, especially discouraged students, find this simple practice extremely gratifying and are often eager to share their progress with family and friends. Indeed, graphing or visually displaying progress is an excellent practice for young or less-skilled students, one that can be used with many activities and goals.

A caveat is in order, however. Feedback in the form of graphs and other displays should be individual and private. The purpose is to compare the student's performance with his or her earlier performance; any competitive comparison or public display is probably not helpful. Public competition is rewarding only for those who are highly successful. However, individual progress forms can help students to see their growth even when it has been slow. Other adaptations can be initiated as practical considerations and student needs dictate (Samuels, 1979, 1988). For example, students can be encouraged to practice rereading by reading along with an audiotape. This is especially helpful for students who require a fluent model to guide them. Alternatively, students can work in peer groups to practice with a buddy (see Chapter 13).

As we have suggested, there are many ways to involve students in repeated readings. One of these, Talking Dictionary (Ballard, 1978), has been especially successful for students

**FIGURE 12.1**
Repeated Reading
Chart

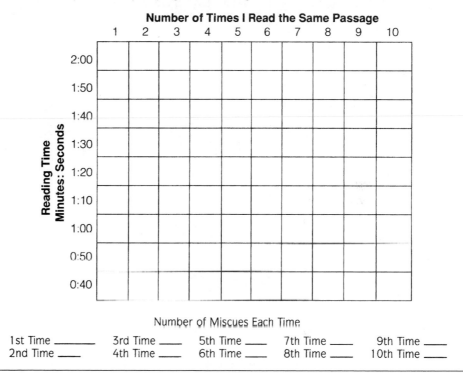

If you repeatedly read the same passage, you will soon read it smoothly and easily. This sheet will help to record your progress in reading.

**Number of Times I Read the Same Passage**

Number of Miscues Each Time

| 1st Time _____ | 3rd Time ____ | 5th Time ____ | 7th Time ____ | 9th Time ____ |
| 2nd Time ____ | 4th Time ____ | 6th Time ____ | 8th Time ____ | 10th Time ____ |

*Source:* From *Quest: Desert Magic,* Unit 1. Copyright © 1985 by Scholastic Inc. Reprinted by permission of Scholastic Inc.

who require high levels of support in repeated readings. Talking Dictionary involves reading and then rereading a specific piece of text with the help of a "talking dictionary"—the teacher. Talking Dictionary is implemented as follows (see Figure 12.2):

### *First Read:*

1. The procedure is explained to the student.
2. The teacher selects, or helps the student to select, material that is too long to be read in a single two- or three-minute sitting.
3. The student is asked to begin reading the selected portion of text aloud and continues reading for two or three minutes.
4. Whenever the reader encounters an unknown word, he or she asks for the pronunciation ("word please") and the teacher provides it *without comment.* The reading continues.
5. The teacher's job is to keep track of time, to provide unknown pronunciations, and to count the number of words read correctly.

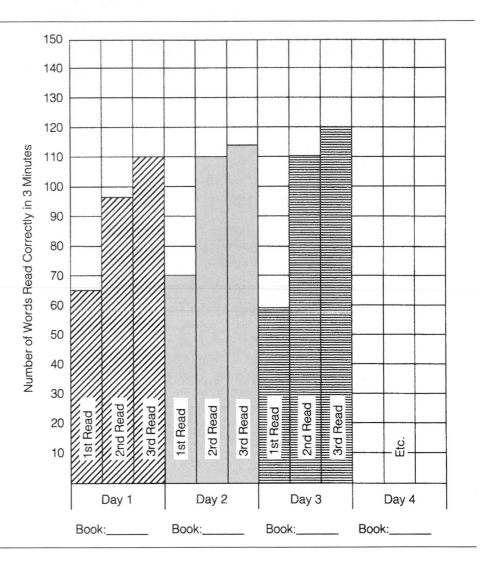

***Second Read:***
1. The student returns to the starting point and repeats the process, again asking for any unknown words.
2. Once again, the teacher provides all requested words without comment, keeps track of time, and tallies correctly read words.

***Third Read:***
1. The process is repeated.
2. When the third reading is completed, the results of the three reading attempts are graphed.

The procedure can be used quite easily by parents, who are often searching for an activity that will support their child's reading growth. One advantage of Talking Dictionary is that it permits only positive and helpful responses. In every way the technique communicates to the student that the adult is there to provide support and will also celebrate the increased fluency that invariably results. Students not only have an opportunity to practice reading connected text but also to do so in a supportive environment.

Generally speaking, teachers should expect that during the second and third renderings, students will recognize at least *some* of the words that were requested and read further into the text. If, after several attempts (graphed along the model presented in Figure 12.2), there is still *no* improvement, some adaptation should then occur. The most common adaptations involve the need to choose an easier (or more difficult) text, remind the student that it is desirable to request help when print does not make sense, or examine the role of anxiety in the student's oral reading fluency.

Although increased fluency is the most straightforward benefit to be enjoyed from repeated reading activities, it is not the only one. For example, there is evidence that young students' recognition of sight vocabulary improves when they are encouraged to reread texts (Bridge & Burton, 1982; Bridge, Winograd, & Haley, 1983; Chomsky, 1978). There is also evidence from teacher read-aloud research that when students have repeated opportunities to hear the same stories again, their comprehension improves. Martinez and Roser (1985) report four changes that occur as students become increasingly familiar with a story:

1. Students produce more verbal responses.
2. The nature of these responses changes such that self-initiated comments and judgments become more frequent.
3. The focus on discussion changes so that students "tended to talk more about story language, events, settings, and titles as the stories became familiar" (Martinez & Rosen, 1985, p. 785).
4. Students appear to gain greater insights into some segments of stories.

Because of these other benefits, teachers should find the practice of revisiting texts potentially powerful even if they do not use one of the more structured repeated reading procedures. We will describe some other ways to repeatedly use text later in the chapter.

## Guided Reading

The guided reading portion of the lesson provides opportunities for the teacher to support the student in the development of new reading knowledge and skills and for student(s) to practice using strategies that they are beginning to develop. As we note in Chapters 6 and 15, there are a number of guided reading frameworks, but most of these are organized around a Before–During–After Reading pattern. Although guided reading has traditionally been associated with the directed reading activity (DRA) found in basal reading programs (see Chapter 6), more recently it has been promoted through the work of Fountas and Pinnell (1996, 2001a).

Text selection and analysis are important steps to be taken before initiating the guided reading phase of the lesson. We have already discussed the issue of materials selection and analysis for guided reading instruction in considerable detail (see Chapters 6 and 8). In this section we wish to emphasize the need to select and analyze materials for more specific purposes.

Because of the rich variety of available texts, teachers need to think about print materials as they might be used in teaching. Different books, authors, and genres invite and permit varying instructional efforts. For example, young children often enjoy the *Curious George* books by H. A. Rey, a series of books that invites discussions of cause-and-effect. Effective comprehension work might be done with causal relations, because the stories generally revolve around a series of events that are related only by George's curiosity and the trouble that results. On the other hand, these books would not be a good choice for teaching students about story structure, because the traditional structure of stories is not obvious in them.

Once the text has been chosen, it is important to analyze the text so that the key concepts and relationships are revealed (see Chapters 6 and 8). For stories it is important to examine the characteristics of text that may cause problems for students or suggest powerful response opportunities for students. These might include recognizing various plot patterns or looking for challenging character, setting, or theme characteristics. The text should also be scrutinized for interesting or potentially troubling uses of words and illustrations. In analyzing expository text, teachers will need to consider different issues. Central purposes, major ideas, and supporting ideas must be identified so that teachers can see what content is present and how difficult it will be for students to read and learn from this material (Hayes & Peters, 1989; Wixson & Peters, 1989).

The following sections describe two different high-utility guided reading strategies: reciprocal teaching and K-W-L. These strategies are well researched and are frequently used to enhance students' comprehension.

***Reciprocal Teaching.***    Reciprocal teaching, like several techniques that have been validated in recent years, is focused on process outcomes. The strategy was devised to promote the effective use of complex comprehension knowledge and skill and has proved effective in studies with remedial readers in middle school (Palincsar, 1984; Palincsar & Brown, 1984). It has also been used successfully to enhance the listening comprehension instruction of first grade students whose test scores indicated that they were at risk for reading problems (Palincsar, 1986). The effectiveness of reciprocal teaching is evident from the improvement in the dialogue during instruction, the improvement in scores on measures of comprehension including standardized tests, the continuation of improvements for up to six months after training, and the improvement on classroom tasks that are similar to but distinct from the instructed activity.

Palincsar and Brown (1984) identified several major activities that are generally accepted as integral to comprehension ability. Skilled comprehenders understand a variety of explicit and implicit purposes for reading, activate prior knowledge, focus on important versus trivial content, and maintain this focus throughout the selection. In addition, they make critical judgments about the relationships between and among ideas in text, judge the content against prior knowledge, monitor reading for comprehension, and make inferences for the purposes of predicting, interpreting, and drawing conclusions about reading material.

Reciprocal teaching is intended to teach students to accomplish these activities as they read connected text.

*Launching Reciprocal Teaching.* This strategy requires that teachers have selected several expository passages and that they are prepared to work collaboratively with their students. The following steps describe the basic pattern of interaction in reciprocal teaching.

*Step 1.* The teacher meets with a small group (five to fifteen students) and models four comprehension-fostering strategies (predicting, self-questioning, clarifying, and summarizing). Then the teacher applies these strategies while reading a paragraph or segment from content area materials. After the procedure has been modeled by the adult teacher with several segments of text, the students take over the role of teacher.

*Step 2.* If the passage is new to the group, the adult teacher asks students to predict what the text will be about on the basis of the title. If the passage is familiar, students are asked to recall and state the topic of the passage as well as the important points already covered.

*Step 3.* The adult teacher assigns a segment of the passage to be read (usually a paragraph) and either tells the students that she will be the teacher (especially for the initial days of instruction) or assigns one of the students as teacher for the first segment.

*Step 4.* When the group finishes reading the segment silently, the teacher for that segment proceeds to ask a good question or two, clarify the hard parts, summarize the paragraph or segment in a sentence, and then (starting the cycle all over again) predict what the next paragraph or segment will discuss.

*Step 5.* Whoever is in the role of teacher for each segment must help to answer the questions or suggest alternative questions, clarify the unclear parts of the text, revise the summary, and agree or disagree with the prediction.

*Step 6.* The adult teacher provides the guidance necessary for the student teachers to complete the preceding activities through a variety of techniques:

**PROMPTING:** "What question did you think a teacher might ask?"

**INSTRUCTION:** "Remember, a summary is a shortened version, it doesn't include a lot of detail."

**MODIFYING the activity:** "If you're having a hard time thinking of a question, why don't you summarize first?"

**REQUESTING the help of other students:** "Who can help us out with this one?"

*Step 7.* The adult teacher provides praise and feedback specific to the student teachers' participation: "That was an excellent summary. You provided the most important information" or "You worded that question well, but it was about a minor detail. Can you ask us about some more important information?" After this feedback the adult teacher models any activity that continues to need improvement: "A question I would have asked is . . ." or

"I would summarize by saying . . ." The procedure continues in this manner with the teacher supporting and modeling as needed.

*Maintaining and Adapting Reciprocal Teaching.*   The dialogic and interactive nature of reciprocal teaching demands a commitment on the part of teachers to engage in discussion and to respond to students' knowledge and skill. Over time we would hope that students would not need teachers to help them craft good questions or clarify text. However, many students will need this support during difficult text reading, even after they have mastered the general approach. It is important to remember that reciprocal teaching is a *simulation* of the process of reading and comprehending. The specific strategies are not as important as the process itself. These should not be viewed as discrete activities to be trained and mastered. Instead, students (and teachers) should approach the task as a cognitive activity that is being launched interactively.

The original activity was designed for students who had adequate word identification skills but poor comprehension. It has been demonstrated to be effective with this group. However, Palincsar has subsequently adapted the technique to be used with very young or very unskilled students. In the adapted form, the text is read to students, and they are encouraged to think it through during a listening task. This approach has provided benefits for these students as well.

**K-W-L.**   Many students who require additional help in reading have particular difficulties reading and studying expository text. Reading for informational and/or study purposes may be unfamiliar for many less-skilled readers, and too often they approach reading passively, as simply a word recognition task. Carr and Ogle (1987, p. 626) provide a vivid description of the problem:

> When they (middle school and secondary readers), begin to read, they do not perceive that they should learn, rather than simply "look at text." They are unaware of basic techniques, such as identifying key ideas and summarizing. When we asked one sophomore what she did when she read, she responded, "I try to take in the words and hope the teacher won't call on me."

Ogle (1986, 1989) has developed a simple teaching strategy known as K-W-L that has high utility for many students across disciplines and is an appropriate choice for students who need support in accomplishing specific content outcomes. K-W-L is a three-step procedure to promote thinking and active reading; the name stands for What I know (K), What I want to know (W), and What I have learned (L) (see Figure 12.3).

K-W-L can easily be used to adapt the traditional Directed Reading Activity (see Chapter 6), since the technique parallels the Before, During, and After phases of the DRA. However, teachers who are accustomed to high levels of teacher control and direction will need to guard against too much interference. With too much teacher direction students will quickly realize that they are really just reading for the teacher's purpose, in which case there is little point in using the K-W-L strategy. Remember that the point of K-W-L is to help students become more actively involved in reading and to enhance their memory for information that is personally important.

**FIGURE 12.3**
K-W-L Strategy
Sheet

| K-W-L Strategy Sheet | | |
|---|---|---|
| **K**—What we know | **W**—What we want to find out | **L**—What we learned and still need to learn |
| 1. Brainstorming<br><br>2. Categories of information we expect to use<br><br>A. _____<br>B. _____<br>C. _____<br>D. _____ | | |

*Source:* Adapted from Ogle, Donna M. (1986, February). K-W-L: A teaching model that develops active reading of expository text. *The Reading Teacher, 39*(6), 564–570. Reprinted with permission of the International Reading Association. All rights reserved.

*Launching K-W-L.* In the first step (K), the teacher helps students to activate prior knowledge about a topic and organize it into useful categories. In the second step (W), the teacher helps students to ask themselves questions and set purposes for reading on the same topic. As students read, however, they are permitted to add questions to their list. In the final step (L), students record answers to questions they have asked, and the group discusses the questions and answers. Of course, students may be jotting down answers to questions as they read.

It should be apparent that K-W-L requires no special training. It does require that a teacher be willing to help students identify what they know and permit them to pursue questions of their own determination. When introducing K-W-L, teachers should prepare a large sample worksheet so that all members of the group can see how the procedure is done. During subsequent experiences with K-W-L, students can complete their own strategy sheets with diminishing amounts of teacher guidance.

Teachers can help to shape students' question-asking behavior through skillful modeling and discussion. For example, teachers are expected to model the categorization process during the K step. Similarly, in the final discussion students should be encouraged to see that some questions were not answered in the piece just read or, alternatively, to see that they now have new questions as a result of reading:

> The teacher helps students keep the control of their own inquiry, extending the pursuit of knowledge beyond just the one article. The teacher is making clear that learning shouldn't be framed around just what an author chooses to include, but that it involves the identification of the learner's questions and the search for authors or articles dealing with those questions. (Ogle, 1986, p. 569)

Because of these features of K-W-L, an excellent time to introduce the strategy is at the beginning of a new content-area unit in which students are expected to pursue some topic for a report or presentation.

*Maintaining and Adapting K-W-L.*   Maintaining K-W-L requires some investment in time. As Ogle (1986) notes, however, the increase in acquired knowledge makes the technique worthwhile. In addition, Ogle reports some evidence to suggest that repeated use of K-W-L encourages students to use the technique spontaneously during the reading of informational text. To increase the likelihood that students will transfer the strategy to other settings, the K-W-L technique has been adapted (Carr & Ogle, 1987). The revised technique, K-W-L Plus, adds concept mapping and summarization components to the original strategy to enhance its power and utility, especially for secondary students.

Both concept mapping and summarizing are helpful techniques for studying and are natural outgrowths of K-W-L (see Chapter 15). For example, concept mapping requires students to categorize information—something that has already been done as part of the basic K-W-L activity. Carr and Ogle suggest that students use the text title as the central portion of a concept map and the category labels developed during K-W-L as the major concepts in the map (see Figure 12.4). In this way students can visually display the information, helping them to understand and organize it for subsequent study.

The final step in K-W-L Plus involves using the concept map as an outline for a text summary. Carr and Ogle ask students to number the portions of the concept map in the order in which they wish to present information in their summary. Because the information is already quite concisely displayed, writing a summary is a relatively straightforward matter.

The important thing about K-W-L Plus is how clearly it demonstrates the value of linking *any* instructional strategy to important learning tasks. Furthermore, the adaptation combines several separate learning tools into one generally useful and powerful technique that teachers can use flexibly, focusing on the aspects of K-W-L Plus that will be most helpful to their students. For example, students who approach text passively, without engaging their own preexisting knowledge base, can be encouraged to spend considerable time on step K. Other students will require significant help in answering their questions and identifying additional ones.

## Dictated Stories as an Alternative to Guided Reading

As an instructional technique, the dictated story has its roots in the Language Experience Approach (LEA) to reading (Allen, 1976; Stauffer, 1969, 1980). As a beginning reading method, LEA promotes student awareness of the relationship between oral and written language by having students produce a "language experience story." This story then becomes the reading material that is used for the delivery of instruction. Because this eliminates problems of a mismatch between the student's language and the reading materials, the technique has been widely used for very beginning learners, for bilingual students (Wilson & Cleland, 1989), with middle-school remedial reading students (Sharp, 1990), and with adults (Mulligan, 1974; Newton, 1977). Clearly, LEA addresses process outcomes while attending closely to both attitude and motivation.

LEA stories have traditionally been created by individuals or collaboratively by groups. For example, one of the authors was assigned to work with seventeen fifth and sixth grade boys whose reading level was below first grade. Collaborative LEA stories revealed the group's consuming interest in football, specifically the local professional team. Using this topic and the weekly game results, students wrote, revised, and worked with football

**FIGURE 12.4**
K-W-L Plus
Worksheet on Killer
Whales

| **K** (Know) | **W** (Want to Know) | **L** (Learned) |
| --- | --- | --- |
| They live in oceans.<br>They are vicious.<br>They eat each other.<br>They are mammals. | Why do they attack people?<br>How fast can they swim?<br>What kind of fish do they eat?<br>What is their description?<br>How long do they live?<br>How do they breathe? | D—They are the biggest member of the dolphin family.<br>D—They weigh 10,000 pounds and get 30 feet long.<br>F—They eat squids, seals, and other dolphins.<br>A—They have good vision underwater.<br>F—They are carnivorous (meat eaters).<br>A—They are the second smartest animal on earth.<br>D—They breathe through blow holes.<br>A—They do not attack unless they are hungry.<br>D—Warm blooded.<br>A—They have echo-location (sonar).<br>L—They are found in the oceans. |

Final category designations developed for column L, information learned about killer whales. A, abilities; D, description; F, food; L, location.

## Concept Map of Killer Whales

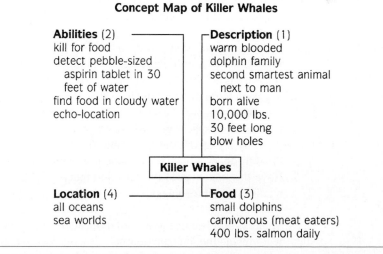

(1) through (4) indicate the order of categories the student chose later for writing a summary.

*Source:* Carr, Eileen M., & Ogle, Donna M. (1987, April). K-W-L Plus: A strategy for comprehension and summarization. *Journal of Reading, 30*(7), 626–631. Reprinted by permission of the International Reading Association. All rights reserved.

stories all fall. Newspapers, sports magazines, and special edition sports periodicals were brought into the classroom, and the students began to realize that they could read the specialized accounts of football activity. In the process, they learned to analyze the patterns of print; to recognize letter combinations, compound words, and base words; and to master some high-frequency sight vocabulary. The average reading gain for this group was over two grade levels in nine months' time. Most were still not exceptionally strong readers, but they had made good progress, had control over some essential skills, and, most important, believed that they could read and saw at least a few reasons for doing so.

As a practical matter, classroom teachers are likely to generate group stories when they have shared an experience (e.g., a field trip) or are planning an activity (e.g., a class party). Indeed, the first step in an LEA story is the provision of an experience (e.g., the unexpected appearance of a skunk on the playground or a fire in a nearby building). Rich group stories can result from such experiences.

For the purposes of working with very unskilled readers or writers, individual stories may be preferred. Individual dictated stories need not be prefaced by some formal experience. In fact, sharing personal stories, memories, and moments is an important way for students, especially those of diverse backgrounds, to feel part of the classroom community (Mikkelsen, 1990).

***Launching the Dictated Story.***    As the name suggests, these stories are created as a student dictates to a recorder (teacher, parent, more skilled student). Always start by talking with students about what they would like to say. Some students will be ready to dictate, and a brief discussion will quickly reveal this. Other children will be floundering or have little idea about what they wish to say. The youngest or most unskilled students might want only to label. Like the other activities already suggested, dictated stories permit a range of responses and all students should be able to participate, although the responses may vary profoundly. Bridge (1989) offers the following guidelines for the dictation process:

1. Students should be able to read back the story, so it shouldn't be too long.
2. If possible, wait until the student's thought is complete, then record exactly what the student says.
3. Say each word as you write it, asking the student to watch.
4. As you record, provide some reading instruction appropriate for this student (e.g., note that there are spaces between words, that certain words begin the same way, and that the story has an excellent beginning).
5. Read the story aloud for the student, encouraging students to join as they are able.
6. Have the student read the selection independently when he or she is able (this may require several readings).

Students will become more and more adept at producing dictated stories, and like the silent reading and the dialogue journals described above, this can form the core of a set of regular instructional activities. Simply producing a dictated story will be beneficial for less-able students.

The goal is to allow students to role-play themselves as successful students, even in the early stages of becoming readers and writers. Through repeated readings of the words in the familiar context of the dictated stories, students will add the words to their sight vocabularies and develop oral reading fluency and confidence in themselves as readers. (Bridge, 1989, p. 195)

***Adapting and Using Dictated Stories.*** Once the dictated story has been created, it can become the focus of all kinds of effective instruction. As we noted above, it can be the reading material that is used to deliver reading instruction. The stories can be retyped or copied for instructional purposes. Students can then underline, highlight portions, or cut the stories apart. Dictated stories around the same or similar themes can provide opportunities to develop rich vocabulary and repeated exposure to some words.

Ideally, the use of dictated stories will be reduced and a more student controlled version of writing will be initiated as soon as students are able to take over the mechanics of writing (see Graves, 1983; Temple, Nathan, Burris, & Temple, 1993). Student-produced writing should not replace dictated stories until students can produce with some ease as much as they can dictate in a comparable period of time. Until then, students should create personal journals and drawings as well as dictated stories. This is true for both native and nonnative speakers of English; research suggests that the writing development of ESL students parallels the writing development of students who speak English as a first language and that ESL students can begin writing in English before they have complete control over the systems of English (Hudelson, 1986).

Dictated stories can provide the basis for remedial or basic instructional work of the following sort:

1. Create cloze passages using these stories to provide practice in using context and writing frequently used or favorite words.
2. Select words to focus on: sight words that appear in repeated frames, words that have the same initial sound, base words used in interesting ways—whatever is appropriate for the student.
3. Look for themes that are worth pursuing with the student. Some themes may require the teacher to read aloud, but others may offer reading options for the student.
4. Look for opportunities to link the dictated story to something that has been read. One way to introduce new vocabulary and linguistic patterns is to encourage students to explore, using book models.

If the stories are placed on a classroom computer, these types of multiple revisitings for various instructional purposes are obviously made much easier. Students may also be able to manage the transition from dictated stories to some independent writing if a program with voice synthesis is available.

## Guided Writing

The guided writing portion of the lesson provides opportunities for the teacher to support the student in the development of new writing knowledge and skills and for student(s) to practice using strategies that they are beginning to develop. A common framework for writing instruction is to develop a text over several lessons, moving from planning to composing, revising, and publishing. These activities may be linked to texts the student has read in the guided or familiar reading phases of the lesson or can be completely independent of the text-reading activities. An example of an independent guided writing activity is the Interactive Writing Lesson described by Lyons and Pinnell (2001), which is described below.

***Launching Interactive Writing.***    Interactive Writing is an instructional strategy in which a teacher shares a pen, both literally and figuratively, with one or more students as they collaboratively create a written text. The components of Interactive Writing are described by Lyons and Pinnell (2001) as Identifying a Text, Preparing to Write, Composing the Text, Writing the Text, and Extending the Text.

The text in Interactive Writing arises from the students' real experiences and is negotiated with the teacher. The text in Interactive Writing can take any form including lists, class notes, letters, and stories. It is most important, however, that the text has a real purpose and audience that serves as a guide to the writing.

Once the type of text has been identified, then there may be a variety of activities that will help prepare students for writing. Preparing to write encompasses any activity that naturally leads to composing the text. For example, the teacher and students may discuss something they have learned or some experience they have had in preparation for writing a letter or a story. The conversations around preparatory activities are important, as they highlight language that can be used to compose the text.

After the preparatory activities have been completed, the teacher and students are ready to make decisions about the content of the text. The teacher guides the composition of each sentence so that it conforms to the standards of good writing. As words are chosen for the text, students are asked to think about the exact meaning that they want to convey to their audience. The focus, even for beginning work, is on clarity, cohesion, and voice. It is expected that the teacher and students will move back and forth between discussing and composing several times in the course of creating even a simple text.

Once the teacher and students have composed the content of the text, it is time to write it down. Again, a lot of discussion and sharing take place as the teacher and students decide how to write the text word by word and letter by letter. The teacher prompts students to think about letters and sounds, parts of words, and how words are connected. During the writing of the text, students reread frequently to keep the whole message in mind in terms of audience, purpose, and meaning.

The extending phase of the lesson refers to how students use the texts they have created through interactive writing. Although it is not always possible to anticipate the variety of ways in which a particular text might be used, examples include rereading in shared and independent reading situations and using them for reference in thinking about other writing projects.

***Adapting Interactive Writing.***    Students who are just learning about print can be guided to create short, simple texts, whereas those who are more sophisticated about print can create much longer texts. Also, depending on the students' level of sophistication with written language, the teacher may write many of the words to keep the process moving, asking the student to "share the pen" only to write in a letter, a part of a word, or a word.

The writing portion of the lesson may also take the form of a shared writing procedure followed by a cut-up sentence activity, a more general writing process activity, or independent writing. Shared writing is adapted from the work of Clay (1985) and is used with emergent writers who are not yet fluent in developing content or in the mechanics of writing. The student generates a message by saying the words slowly, listening to the sounds, and encoding them with the appropriate letters. When the student needs help, the teacher writes a known word that contains the same spelling pattern and shows the students how to figure out the unknown from the known. New words are added to a writing vocabulary inventory. The student continually rereads the sentence as more words are added, which allows for checking the message for errors in content.

After the message has been written, the teacher copies it onto a sentence strip while the student reads it. The teacher then cuts apart the words in the sentence, and the student reassembles and reads it without looking at the original sentence. The teacher can also cut the sentence into segments that provide practice with certain letters or sounds.

## Word Study

In the word study portion of the lesson students learn how words are structured and practice using this knowledge to improve as readers and writers. It is important to plan systematic work that focuses on letters, letter sound relationships, and other features of words. The more students explore words as they talk, read, write, or play, the more likely it is they will develop the understanding and flexibility necessary to decode words while reading and encode words in writing. The following section describes a high-utility strategy known as *word sorts* that can be used in the word study phase of the lesson.

***Launching Word Sorts.*** According to Fountas and Pinnell (2001b), word sorting helps students compare and contrast words to discover their key features. It encourages students to form hypotheses about the essential properties of words and to make connections among them. These abilities are useful for both decoding in reading and encoding in writing, making word sorts a high-utility strategy.

Word sorts can be used to teach students about a variety of word features, including sound, spelling, and meaning. Within the context of these general categories of sorts, there are various ways to organize word sorting activities to accomplish different goals (see Figure 12.5). Among the characteristics of the task that must be determined is the nature of the items to be sorted (e.g., pictures, letters, or words). It must also be decided whether items will be sorted for a particular purpose (single sort) or for different purposes and in different categories (multiple sort). It is also good to remember that items can be sorted for both their similarities and their differences. Furthermore, it is important to determine whether the word sort is to be open (categories are created by the students as they notice features such as common endings) or closed (categories of features are identified for the student).

There are also a number of variations on the sorting task itself (see Figure 12.5). For example, in a blind sort, one partner reads the words aloud without showing the print, and the partner has to indicate where to place the word or write it. Alternatively, in a visual sort, one partner reads the word and shows the word to the other, who indicates where to place it in the column. Once the type of sort and the nature of the task have been determined, the

**FIGURE 12.5**    Organizing Word Sorts

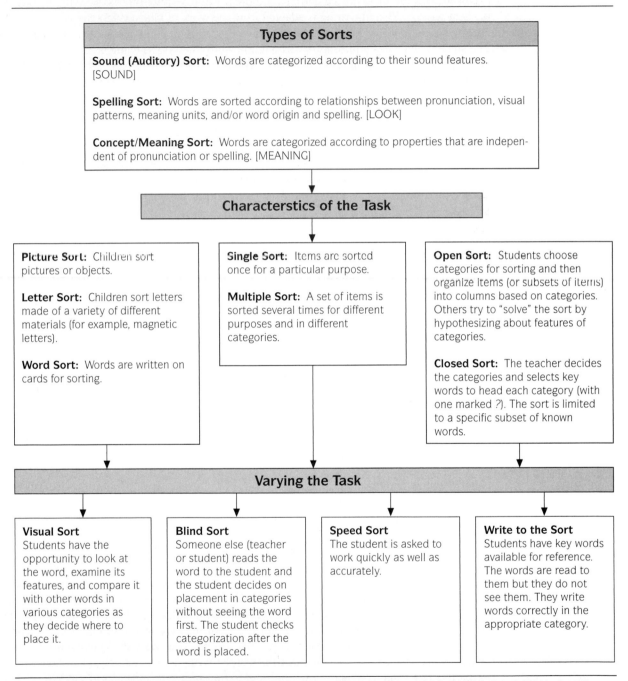

### Types of Sorts

**Sound (Auditory) Sort:** Words are categorized according to their sound features. [SOUND]

**Spelling Sort:** Words are sorted according to relationships between pronunciation, visual patterns, meaning units, and/or word origin and spelling. [LOOK]

**Concept/Meaning Sort:** Words are categorized according to properties that are independent of pronunciation or spelling. [MEANING]

### Characterstics of the Task

**Picture Sort:** Children sort pictures or objects.

**Letter Sort:** Children sort letters made of a variety of different materials (for example, magnetic letters).

**Word Sort:** Words are written on cards for sorting.

**Single Sort:** Items are sorted once for a particular purpose.

**Multiple Sort:** A set of items is sorted several times for different purposes and in different categories.

**Open Sort:** Students choose categories for sorting and then organize items (or subsets of items) into columns based on categories. Others try to "solve" the sort by hypothesizing about features of categories.

**Closed Sort:** The teacher decides the categories and selects key words to head each category (with one marked ?). The sort is limited to a specific subset of known words.

### Varying the Task

**Visual Sort**
Students have the opportunity to look at the word, examine its features, and compare it with other words in various categories as they decide where to place it.

**Blind Sort**
Someone else (teacher or student) reads the word to the student and the student decides on placement in categories without seeing the word first. The student checks categorization after the word is placed.

**Speed Sort**
The student is asked to work quickly as well as accurately.

**Write to the Sort**
Students have key words available for reference. The words are read to them but they do not see them. They write words correctly in the appropriate category.

*Source:* Reprinted by permission from *Guiding Readers and Writers* by Irene Fountas and Gay Su Pinnell. Copyright © 2001 by Irene Fountas and Gay Su Pinnell. Published by Heinemann, a division of Reed Elsevier, Inc., Portsmouth, NH.

pictures, letters, and/or words to be used must be identified and placed on cards for use in the sorting. It is best to use familiar items that students can recognize out of context in word sorts (Bear & Barone, 1998). The items that are used for sorting can be gathered from a variety of sources, including familiar and guided reading texts and the student's own writing.

In conducting the word sort, students should work with a partner (the teacher or another student), because this method promotes discussion about the words. Teachers should watch for both accuracy and fluency in a student's sorting. If the student makes three or four errors, then it is probably a good idea to back up and focus on easier activities that allow for greater accuracy. The variety of options available in creating word-sorting activities makes it possible to accommodate a wide range of student knowledge and skill.

***Adapting Word Sorts.*** Bear and Barrone (1998) provide some guidelines for using word sorts with students in the very early stages of learning to read and write. Semiphonemic students usually have a rudimentary concept of word and use their knowledge of initial and final consonants to help them identify words. They can identify a few sight words from little books, rhymes, and dictated texts, and these can be collected for use in word study and sorts. For example, on the second or third day of working with a text, have the students underline words that they *really* know. The words from the current week's reading are placed in a short-term word bank. Words from previous readings are collected in a long-term word bank. Students should review the words in their word banks frequently and discard words they cannot read easily.

Students in this phase acquire words slowly. At first these students will collect just one or two words from their reading texts. Bear and Barrone (1998) suggest that students need to collect twenty or more words before they are ready to begin word sorts. Until then, they should be asked to sort pictures with an emphasis on initial consonants.

## Sustained Reading and Writing

Sustained reading and writing activities promote power and fluency and help students to develop positive attitudes toward reading and writing. It is also likely that sustained reading and writing activities have a positive effect on vocabulary development (see Chapter 14) and on students' abilities to read and write complex texts for their own purposes. These types of activities are easy to implement in any school setting and at any grade level and should be part of every student's general instructional program.

***Sustained Silent Reading.*** Hunt (1970) provided the first descriptions of this practice, dubbing it Uninterrupted Sustained Silent Reading (USSR). In recent years variations on the practice have been offered, including SQUIRT (Sustained Quiet Reading Time), DEAR (Drop Everything and Read), and SSR (Sustained Silent Reading). Across all adaptations, however, the heart of the technique remains the same: Students read silently from self-selected materials for extended periods of time for their own purposes. The benefits of SSR are most clearly evident at the level of increased interest in, and motivation for, reading (Allington, 1975; Cline & Kretke, 1980; Sadowski, 1980).

When students are permitted to read from materials that they choose *and* when teachers model silent reading themselves, insisting that no student interfere with that experience, everyone benefits. Despite the ease of implementation of SSR and the demonstrable positive effects, some teachers abandon the practice after an initial attempt, and others are reluctant to try it. These teachers say that there is so little time in the day that they feel guilty if they are not "teaching." This is especially true for reading support teachers, such as special educators and Title I (Chapter 1) teachers, and for high school teachers, because they see students for so little time. This concern is obviously rooted in the idea that teaching occurs only during direct instruction. Although direct instruction *is* important, it is not the only way to teach. Indeed, some important literacy outcomes simply cannot be achieved via direct instruction. Such is the case with reading stamina and motivation.

With indirect instruction such as SSR, however, teachers must understand the importance of modeling (McCracken & McCracken, 1978). Although it is tempting to use this period for other things (grading papers, conferencing, etc.), it is critical that students see teachers and other adults reading. This communicates that teachers think reading is important—so important that other things are put aside for the serious, albeit pleasurable, business of reading real books.

*Launching SSR.*    The process of starting and monitoring SSR time is like implementing any other important aspect of the curriculum. There is no substitute for careful planning and good preparation. Teachers need to take time to create interest among students, on the one hand (Gambrell, 1978), and to clearly specify rules on the other (McCracken & McCracken, 1971). Unfortunately, some students will never have been expected to read for sustained periods of time and will not know how to do it. Teachers must carefully prepare students and then be aware that some will need time to become proficient silent readers. The following steps should be considered before starting and during the initial stages:

**1.** *Talk to your students.* Clearly describe to them what will happen and what types of behavior you expect of them. The rules for SSR should include provisions that everyone read a book that he or she has chosen, that everyone is quiet, and that there is no moving around during SSR.

**2.** *Help your students select books.* Do not assume that all of your students know how to choose a book that is good for them. Some younger or very unskilled students might need to have several books with them during silent reading period so that they do not need to move around to get a different book when they have chosen badly or finish a short picture book.

**3.** *Start with success.* Initially, choose a short block of time (as little as five minutes for young or less-skilled readers) during a period of the day that is generally quiet and productive. One of the goals of SSR is that students begin to realize that they *can* stick with books and that they can read and enjoy longer selections. The first periods should be so short that children should have no difficulty meeting the challenge (Mork, 1972). Do not launch SSR during a period of transition. Using SSR to quiet students after recess or lunch period, for example, works only after both teachers and students are experienced at reading silently for sustained periods. The silent reading period should gradually be extended so that primary-grade students are reading for fifteen to twenty minutes daily. Intermediate-grade students should read for thirty to forty-five minutes. Aim for this length of time even if this means that SSR cannot occur every day at the upper grades.

**4.** *Remember that you must read during this period also.* Select a book that you are currently reading or are genuinely interested in.

**5.** *Plan for it, include it in the schedule, and treat it seriously.* Recently, a first grade child told one of the authors that she did not do silent reading because her "work" was not done. Sustained silent reading is "work," and students will value its importance only if teachers do.

*Adapting SSR.* At first some students will not use the period wisely—a fact that should tell the teacher how much this period is needed. Teachers must be patient with students while insisting that no individual disrupt the period. However, some students, including very young or very unskilled readers, may experience such difficulty that adaptations are needed. The most obvious adaptation is in the time provided. Some students might be unable to sustain even the initial five minutes of time. Teachers should not hesitate to start with as little time as one minute! Some teachers find that it is helpful to set a goal together with the students and then use a kitchen timer in the beginning.

Guiding students in book selection can take care of many difficulties. Indeed, Hong (1981) has suggested that the key to success during SSR is the quality of the books. Other ways to adapt SSR that still retain the emphasis on book reading include the following:

**1.** Institute a *recreational reading time* (Morrow, 1989) or *booktime* (Hong, 1981) instead of SSR. This is a time when students are permitted some interaction and movement. For example, buddy reading might be permitted, students might be allowed to select new books, or the teacher might be available to provide some reading help. Morrow also suggests that any book-related activity might be permitted during this period.

**2.** Introduce books to students so that they can choose a book based on some knowledge. All teachers have experienced the rush of enthusiasm for a book that has just been read aloud. Reading aloud is one of the best ways to introduce books to students. Other ideas for introducing books include doing book talks, preparing puppet shows using the characters and events from a book, and making book–tape combinations available to students.

We do not find that these adaptations are necessary in remedial settings, because there are generally fewer students. Occasionally, we have had to remind students about how to read silently and how to attend to print during silent reading, and we have sometimes had to constrain students' choices so that they select appropriately. These adaptations are removed as soon as students have some experience successfully sustaining themselves with print. Students with any significant experience reading connected text do not generally need these supports.

Students who cannot sustain themselves in print may have had too much experience with isolated skills. There *are* students who have no experience reading ordinary books and, as a result, have little idea that reading is a sense-making process. The benefits of SSR for these students include recognizing the purposes of reading, providing practice and transfer opportunities, and providing experiences with meaningful reading material.

Finally, SSR must be maintained in the curriculum, with its usefulness and purpose reviewed periodically. Although students should not be interrogated about the materials they read during SSR, they can be encouraged to keep a record of their reading. Teachers can then use this to shape the rest of the reading program. Hunt (1970) suggests that student self-evaluation is an important feature of SSR, allowing students and their teachers to monitor progress (see Figure 12.6). Other methods also provide this type of continuous assessment information. Graphing the number of words or pages read or keeping reading logs of all selections read can provide excellent documentation of the instructional program and rewarding feedback to students who need visible proof of their growing competence.

**FIGURE 12.6**
Questions for
Readers and Writers

| **How Well Did I Read and/or Write Today: A Self-Check** |
|---|

Today's Date: _____ My Name: _____

Title of Books Read: _____ Authors: _____

Titles of My Writing(s): _____

This sheet contains sample questions to be used with students in evaluating progress in individualized reading and writing programs. The questions are designed for two purposes: (1) to have the student be more reflective about his/her own reading and/or writing processes; and (2) to provide a check for the teacher on the student's attitudes toward his/her own performance.

Any or all questions can be used to fit a particular program regardless of level of student and teacher needs. Each teacher is free to select those items of greatest worth.

| **Part One** |
|---|

 1. Did you have a good reading/writing period today? Did you read/write well?
 2. Did you read/write better today than yesterday?
 3. Were you able to concentrate today on your silent reading? On your writing?
 4. Did the ideas you were reading/writing about hold your attention?
 5. Were you constantly moving ahead with the ideas you were reading/writing about?
 6. Was it hard for you to keep your mind on what you were reading/writing today?
 7. Were you bothered by others or by outside noises?
 8. Could you keep the ideas in your reading/writing straight in your mind?
 9. Were there words you did not know? How did you figure them out?
10. What did you do when you got to the good parts? Did you read/write faster? Or slower?

| **Part Two** |
|---|

 1. Why did you read this particular book/write this piece?
 2. Was this a good choice?
 3. Could you tell what was happening all the time you were reading/writing?
 4. Was this book/piece of writing hard or was it easy for you to read/write?
 5. What made it hard or easy?
 6. Would you choose the same kind or a different kind of book/piece of writing next time?
 7. Did you want to keep on reading/writing? Or did you have to force yourself to keep going?

*Source:* Adapted from Hunt, Lyman, C. Jr. (Dec. 1996/Jan. 1997). The effect of self-selection, interest, and motivation upon independent, instructional, and frustrational levels. *The Reading Teacher, 50*(4), 278–282. Reprinted by permission of the International Reading Association. All rights reserved.

***Dialogue Journals.*** Dialogue journals are a high-utility strategy that encourages students to engage in sustained writing. As the name suggests, dialogue journals involve written exchanges between a teacher and his or her students, or, less often, among students in a group (Atwell, 1998; Fulwiler, 1980). A dialogue journal contains a genuine conversation, written rather than spoken. The interactive format of equal turns on the same topics is quite different from the traditional personal student journals, in which a teacher may sometimes make some kind of marginal comment on a student's entry, but often days or weeks after the student wrote it. The distinguishing characteristics of dialogue journals are their interactive, functional nature and the creation of mutually interesting topics (Staton, 1987).

Dialogue journals are frequently used to encourage students to reflect on specific content to be learned, books that have been read, or ideas that are triggered by recent reading/writing activities. As teachers respond to students' journal entries, the written dialogue becomes more sophisticated. Responses often include exchanges involving plot and action, authors and authors' craft, genre, applications to students' own writing, reading strategies and students' affective responses, judgments regarding book recommendations, and editorial topics and mechanical advice (see Figure 12.7).

Like SSR, dialogue journals are useful for most students because they are aimed at addressing broad reading/writing goals. They are especially well suited for working with less-skilled students and have been used to help bilingual students develop their English skills (Flores & Hernandez, 1988). In addition, they are easy to initiate and, with commitment, easy to sustain.

*Launching Dialogue Journals.* The success of dialogue journals will probably rely on the teacher's commitment to read and respond honestly to students' entries. Because many students (and many teachers too) have had little experience with writing, it is important to think about how to get students started. Although a dialogue journal can be as simple as several sheets of notebook paper stapled together, we have found that something more substantial invites students to take the activity seriously. Fulwiler (1987b) suggests that students use a small looseleaf notebook for all journal entries so that any writing too personal to share can be extracted before it is turned in to the teacher.

Inexperienced students will need more than an attractive journal to overcome their reluctance to write, however. The following ideas should help the teacher launch the dialogue journal.

**1.** *Provide students with material or questions that invite response.* Reading a provocative book aloud or sharing something interesting or compelling about an author will be enough for some students. Others will need a specific question that prompts thoughtful response, such as this one offered by Staton (1987, p. 49):

> **KELLY:** I like to read. Ev'ry time I woth a skery movy I have a drem.
>
> **TEACHER:** Scary movies give me bad dreams, too, Kelly. Maybe we shouldn't watch them. What good books have you read?
>
> **KELLY:** The little red hen and Dick and Jane. I have problems some times well I hav this problim it is I am not very god on my writeing.

**FIGURE 12.7**
Sample Dialogue
Journal between
Kyle and Third
Grade Teacher

Kyle moved to the intermediate school after second grade. His teacher for kindergarten through grade 2, Ms. McIntyre, had introduced dialogue journals to her students (see Figure 6.13). Kyle's third grade teacher, Mrs. Rather, also uses dialogue journals in her literature-based reading program. Within the first month of school, Mrs. Rather has helped Kyle move to a more sophisticated level of reading response. During the last week of August, Kyle is reading Farley Mowat's *Lost in the Barrens*.

8/28/96
Two boys go on a trip with a Indin trib to Eskimo land. When they go to see a stone house the canoe hits a rock and brakes. Now they have too find food to survive.

                                        Kyle

Mrs. Rather writes back, identifying some things she wants to support:

*Kyle, you've done an excellent job! You've written good information about the book. You've used good sentences, spelling, and penmanship! Keep up the great work!*

A week later, Kyle's dialogue journal includes this entry:

9/5/96      Lost in the Barrens
I would like to live in the wilderness because it would be a challenge to survive and to find food. I also like the woods and animals and also advencher. I Like woods because it's quite and pecefol.

In response, Mrs. Rather writes back:

*Kyle, you've done an excellent job of answering the question with detail and making a connection to your own life.*

By December, Kyle's entries have grown as has the sophistication of his reading. He is engrossed in Lloyd Alexander's books.

9/2/96      The Book of Three
The setting is in a castel that has a dungen and secret passages. The dungen cells have smelly straw in them and they have thick walls. There are many cells in the castel but some are deeper down in the grownd than others. The tunnels are not very high and are sort of skinny except for the tunel that Taran found when he fell down in to a pit. The tunnels leads to a secret room which held lots of jewels and armor. The castel belanged to a mean Queen that had put Taran in the cell. Taran is let out by a girl who lives there. I would like tto live there because I could live in the secret room and steal food to eat. Also it would be a challenge to serve and I could help people who are in the dungean. Plus I would like to explore runnels and cstel because I could learn lots of new stuff and I could do what I try to do and not have to do anything on time. I think it would be interesting to live in the time of the knights and castels. It would an adventure every day. I like adventure.

*Wow! Kyle, I'm very impressed by the work you put into this log. You should be very proud. You included many important details and supported your opinion on the setting very well. It sounds like a great book. Would you recommend it? Keep up the excellent work!*

**2.** *Provide students with some model or idea of what is expected.* Gambrell (1985) suggests that students think about a format similar to letter writing and that they ask the teacher a question. Alternatively, teachers can start by asking the students a question that requires them to respond. Then, in the teacher's response, appropriate dialogue exchange is modeled over several entries.

**3.** *Respond in ways that encourage individual students.* This encouragement will be based on knowledge of specific students and is likely to vary. According to Atwell (1998, p. 279):

> My responses grow from what I've learned about a reader and how I hope to move the readers' thinking. In general my comments do three things, to *affirm, challenge,* or *extend* the reader's thinking. These comments take various forms: gossip, questions, recommendations, jokes, restatements, arguments, suggestions, anecdotes, instruction, and "nudges."

Probably the most important key to maintaining the success of dialogue journals is the teacher's commitment to respond to students' entries. As a result, it is important to give some consideration to the management of journals. Many teachers, for example, find that they cannot read everyone's journal every night. Gambrell (1985) suggests starting dialogue journals with only a small group of students so that it is not necessary to juggle an entire class initially. After students have some experience with this activity, some teachers require that everyone write each day but the teachers respond to only one third of the journals each day. If a student really wants or needs a response on a particular day, however, the system should allow for this.

*Maintaining and Extending Dialogue Journals.*   Once teachers have made the commitment to read and react to students' writing, dialogue journals can add immeasurably to the instructional program. They can "provide a 'window' into the students' cognitive activities during writing and reading . . . giving teachers opportunities to highlight students' idea generation, planning, predicting, and monitoring" (Raphael & Englert, 1989, p. 238). Teachers' skills in this area are typically not well developed, so they should not expect to feel comfortable making responses initially. However, Atwell (1998, p. 280) offers some lessons that are worth sharing:

1. *"One good, thoughtful question is more than enough."* Atwell's experience suggests that students' least interesting or insightful responses came when she asked didactic questions that sounded as though she were testing the students.
2. *Respond "as a curious human being."* Dialogue journals seem to work best when they are genuine dialogues between two people who are really expressing their own ideas and sharing their own experiences.
3. *"Make no corrections on students' letters."* Dialogue entries are not final writing samples. Atwell suggests responding to mechanics only when journals cannot be read.
4. *"The journals contribute to class grades."* The grades are based on a minimum quantity (one entry per week), thoughtfulness of the responses, "use of classroom

independent reading time, and progress made toward a few, individual goals set at the beginning of each quarter."

Dialogue journals can be adapted for use across the curriculum (see Fulwiler, 1987b). Classroom teachers should look for opportunities to use journal entries during nonlanguage arts periods. It is becoming increasingly clear that when writing is used in content-area disciplines, everyone benefits. "Journal writing in class stimulates student discussion, starts small group activity, clarifies hazy issues, reinforces learning experience, and stimulates imaginations" (Fulwiler, 1982, p. 15). Resource teachers should consider asking students to write about topics that are being studied in their regular classrooms.

# Getting More Focused on Individual Students

Setting the stage for literacy instruction and getting started with some effective activities are important first steps. It is possible to make these initial decisions using the knowledge base established throughout this text. However, a repertoire of techniques, no matter how good, is not sufficient. Skilled teachers and specialists need to consider programs and planning simultaneously in a more systematic fashion. In this section we consider instructional planning in greater detail.

## Lesson Planning

Students, especially less skilled readers and writers, cannot afford to waste instructional time engaged in activities that they do not need or that will not help them to become more proficient. The goals and objectives that are designed for specific students must be clearly related to the assessment that has gone before. The most important thing to keep in mind is that there should be a clear relationship between the information that has been gathered through assessment and diagnostic teaching, the tentative conclusions about areas of need and action, and the instructional activities devised. Indeed, this is the heart of good planning: the matching of information about individual students with appropriate objectives that are, in turn, used to decide upon appropriate activities and materials.

Most teachers have been taught to use some type of generic lesson plan format. A typical lesson plan format has the following major components: (1) topic or focus, (2) objectives, (3) materials, (4) activities or procedures, and (5) evaluation plan. Clearly, writing the lesson plan following this or some other format is not what leads to success in teaching. Successful lesson planning rests on careful reflection. Using the information that has been gathered about the particular student(s) we are working with, we decide on some specific objectives. These objectives are in turn used to adapt and refine the instructional program, with changes being made in either the delivery or content of instruction as appropriate for individual students.

*Objectives.*   The available evidence suggests that effective teachers establish goals and objectives for students (Rupley, 1976). In addition, informing students of lesson objectives before reading and writing improves students' performance (Duell, 1974; Maier, 1980).

Despite both empirical and practical evidence that students benefit from carefully considered objectives, there is some misunderstanding about the role and function of objectives. The objectives that are developed for a student should be clearly related to the diagnostic assessment that has gone before. It should also be evident how the objectives promote the larger important outcomes of skilled reading and writing.

It is important that an objective be focused on what students will learn or be able to do as the result of instruction. It *is not* a statement of instructional activities.

Following is a good example of an objective:

OBJECTIVE: Jerry will increase his interest in, and his ability to sustain himself during, silent reading.

This objective provides guidance about what to focus attention on and how to accomplish the instructional jobs that are required. Because it is not a statement of the activities to be used, it is possible to imagine a variety of activities that might address Jerry's needs. Jerry's increased knowledge and skill, not the particular program or tasks, are what is important.

The use of objectives sometimes generates concern among educators. Indeed, some believe that objectives constrain teaching and limit teachers' ability to be creative or student-centered. It is true that more mechanistic models of teaching have sometimes reduced teaching and learning to easily measured, relatively trivial behaviors. However, good objectives make it more, not less, likely that students' needs will be noticed and that important outcomes will receive attention. The format of the objective is less important than the extent to which it focuses instructional attention. There are just two principles to keep in mind in writing objectives:

1. Objectives should define what the student will do and learn, not what you will do as teacher.
2. Objectives must be clearly related to some demonstrated need as determined by sound assessment.

The types of objectives that are generated for a particular student are heavily dependent on what we have learned about that student and our assessment of the match (see Chapter 11). The objectives established for some students may be largely attitude objectives; for others the objectives that are generated will be more clearly process objectives, while a third group of students might need content information. Despite these variations, all students require some balance among the three types of objectives, and their programs should reflect this.

*Activities.*    After the objectives have been determined, teachers can turn their attention to planning the specifics of the lesson they believe will best address these outcomes. This involves selecting specific materials and tasks and/or designing activities that will promote learning in identified areas. Some teachers select activities simply because they enjoy using them or think that their students will like them. Similarly, many novice teachers base their judgments of lesson success on the smoothness of execution or the degree to which students exhibit enthusiasm. These are not trivial issues because they may influence student learning.

However, the central criterion for making instructional decisions is the degree to which students make some progress toward becoming more skilled and/or motivated readers and writers.

We start with a general lesson framework and an array of instructional strategies that are useful to many students (see previous sections). Variations of these, as well as additional techniques, are then considered (see Chapters 13 and 14). Major considerations in planning and selecting activities include the following:

1. Is this activity closely linked to the student's needs? Does it address the objectives that have been established?
2. Do the tasks, in combination, form a comfortable flow of activity?
3. How close is the fit between this activity and what is expected of the student during normal reading, writing, and content-area instruction?
4. What level of support is required for the student to participate, and how does that fit with the total instructional setting?

It is particularly important to think about what level of support needs to be provided to ensure that students can learn what is being taught. Expect that efficient use of learned skill and knowledge will take considerable time and that the level of teacher support should diminish as students become more adept. This often entails adapting activities or existing programs to meet the individual needs of students.

Although some activities have high utility and are very flexible, planning must also involve selecting specific approaches or techniques to use with the particular student(s). It is important to recall that we are not describing a developmental literacy program for all students. Although a balanced program is always desirable, the instruction for some individuals may reflect a more constrained focus. Some students, for example, simply have greater needs in the area of word analysis and word recognition than in comprehension or composition.

It is also important to realize that activities are not important in themselves. Teachers must guard against viewing their instruction as merely the management of activities (see Chapter 5). The instructional program should always be designed to provide the best possible fit for specific students. In the chapters that follow we describe specific techniques that permit teachers to make adaptations in a basically effective program to focus more closely on one or another aspect of reading and/or writing.

## Example: Getting Started with Marvin

As we noted earlier, there are many ways in which students might come to work with teachers and many contexts in which this occurs. In this section we describe the Getting Started phase of working with Marvin. This instructional program was started in the university clinic setting of one of the authors. Unlike many of our students, Marvin came to this setting with a great deal of assessment information already complete.

## Background and Setting

At the time of the original referral Marvin was placed in a regular classroom, receiving no special support or services in reading or writing. His parents referred him for assessment because of their concerns about his academic problems. The assessment-instruction process was initiated by one of the authors, who was working with the school. As a result, Steps 1–6 of the assessment process were executed outside of the regular classroom setting by someone other than the teacher. Marvin's instructional program, the context for literacy, and, to some extent, the materials he would use in that setting were already determined.

In the university clinic setting, the decision was made to pair Marvin with another student. It was thought that there were benefits to an arrangement that was not one-to-one tutoring. Specifically, we believed Marvin needed opportunities to discuss reading and writing in a socially supportive environment. He was himself a gregarious young man, and many of his interests revolved around people and social interaction. In addition, his reading difficulties and the subsequent instruction he received had tended to isolate him from his peers.

## Selecting High-Utility Strategies

The information derived from the assessment and the diagnostic teaching sessions (see Chapter 11) suggested that there was merit in selecting at least two high-utility strategies to begin Marvin's program: SSR and Talking Dictionary. Indeed, except for students who require teacher read-aloud as the only way to interact with books, SSR is a standard part of all our students' programs.

Although fairly extensive and focused individual information was available about Marvin, these two high-utility strategies have merit for a wide range of students in many programs, and Marvin's case was no exception. Marvin needed to increase his ability to handle longer segments of text; reading fluency was a significant problem as well. Although it seemed likely that Marvin could benefit from K-W-L (and we might have used this had we had less information initially), the decision to use this technique was deferred until later.

## Selecting Materials

It is our experience that the appropriateness of text and task materials can have a significant effect on the success of the instruction. In Marvin's case all of the materials were chosen with two major criteria in mind. Only full-length stories or books were to be used, since this constituted an area of need for Marvin, and these would involve fully developed complex stories with a strong goal structure. *Bones on Black Spruce Mountain* is a strongly evocative narrative involving two male characters and a strong adventure/suspense series of episodes. It was among several choices offered to Marvin during the first instructional setting and one that sustained his interest over several weeks. In later sessions it provided a rich source of multisyllabic words from which to teach and practice structural and morphemic analysis.

The selections in the *Quest* materials are all fully developed short stories or expository narratives (two to six pages long) of high interest. Marvin found these challenging, but he retained an interest in them. Only stories were selected initially, and we chose those with a sophisticated story structure. These short stories were used for direct instruction to develop both fluency and comprehension. In later sessions these selections provided excellent material for use with both story mapping activities and a think-aloud strategy (see Chapter 15).

## Planning for Marvin

The substantial amount of information available on Marvin could be used almost immediately to establish objectives, decide on materials, and begin to select activities. The objectives grew directly out of the diagnostic teaching sessions described in Chapter 11 and the specific activities are essentially adaptations of the high-utility activities we have already described. The specific objectives and activities established for Marvin's initial sessions were:

1. *Objective:* To develop reading fluency and motivate recreational reading.
   *Activity:* SSR for five minutes without interruption using *Bones on Black Spruce Mountain* (Budbill, 1978).
2. *Objective:* To increase word recognition and reading fluency.
   *Activity:* Fifteen-minute taped read-along of connected text with fluency support using "Something Queer Is Going On" from *Electric Butterfly, Quest* (Aulls & Graves, 1985).
3. *Objective:* To increase comprehension.
   *Activity:* Identify characters and the goal structure (including problem-solution) of a complex story using taped read-along of "Something Queer Is Going On" from *Electric Butterfly, Quest* coupled with a story map.

Marvin's case illustrates what happens over time as planning and instruction proceed. The high-utility strategies that are used initially are sometimes retained (e.g., SSR). However, as students develop increased competence, some aspects of the initial plans are changed and adapted. The combination of initial instructional intervention and strong assessment information permits careful planning for an individual student like Marvin. The interweaving of assessment and instruction and a commitment to continuous assessment result in subtle, yet sometimes major, adjustments in the instructional program. Most often, the program becomes more and more focused as the teacher/tutor adapts to growing competence or finds that a more and more refined focus is appropriate. These more refined techniques for building an instructional repertoire are described more fully in the following chapters.

# Chapter Summary

In this chapter we provided information that will help teachers get started with instruction. First, we identified several key characteristics of an instructional program and discussed the issues related to establishing a literate environment, setting goals and objectives, establishing organizational patterns, and selecting materials. Next, we described a general instructional framework that is appropriate for low-achieving readers and writers that can be adapted to the needs of individuals or small groups. The components of this instructional framework are familiar reading, guided reading, guided writing, word study, and sustained reading and writing.

We also described some specific high-utility instructional activities that can be used within the context of the suggested instructional framework. Repeated reading was the high-utility strategy recommended for the Familiar Reading component of the instructional framework. Reciprocal teaching and K-W-L were recommended for the Guided Reading component. Dictated stories were described as an alternative to Guided Reading. Interactive writing was suggested for the Guided Writing component. Word sorts were presented for the Word Study component. Finally, sustained silent reading and dialogue journals were described for the Sustained Reading and Writing component of the framework.

The high-utility strategies presented in this chapter were selected because they are consistent with current views of reading and writing, have been proven effective, can be shaped to meet individual needs, and can be used to address some aspect of the attitude, process, and content objectives of a literacy program. In discussing each of these, we provided a description of the technique, guidelines for launching the technique in the classroom and then discussed ways to adapt and/or maintain the technique for special purposes of groups.

In the final sections of the chapter we provided information about planning for individual students using the specific, focused assessment information that has been gathered in earlier steps of the assessment-instruction process. Specifically, we addressed the issue of lesson planning for individual students, providing guidance in specifying objectives and selecting activities. Finally, we returned to Marvin to provide an example of how the instructional program was initiated with him.

By using this framework and these techniques, it is possible to get started with a student or students even when there is still some doubt about the details of the instructional program. This approach can serve as a bridge to the individual lesson planning, which must eventually take place to make good decisions about when and how to use the more focused instructional strategies described in the remaining chapters of the book (see Chapters 13–15).

# CHAPTER

# 13 Adapting Instruction to Focus on Word Recognition, Fluency, and Spelling

The various components of reading and writing are intertwined in complex ways. However, it is often necessary to focus attention more closely on a particular component of skilled reading or writing. In this chapter and the next chapter we describe the instructional approaches and materials that may be used to adapt instruction so that it provides increased instruction and support in the areas of word identification and/or vocabulary strategies. Word recognition, spelling, and vocabulary are *word-level aspects* of reading and writing. Of course, knowledge and skill in these areas often affect comprehension, composition, and studying.

Problems at the word level, in either pronunciation or meaning association, generally pose major obstacles to wide reading and effective writing. These difficulties may influence students' rate, fluency, comprehension, or enjoyment of reading. They may also influence students' fluency, effectiveness, or willingness in writing. It is important to understand that in skilled reading and writing, the boundaries between difficulties in word recognition, meaning, vocabulary, and spelling, can be blurred. With regard to reading, Wilson and Hall (1990, p. iii) note:

> Meaning must be the focus of all reading and word analysis must be viewed in conjunction with helping readers derive meaning from printed language. Sometimes word analysis is erroneously interpreted as being merely the use of sound–letter correspondences for deciphering unknown words. However, sentence structure (syntactic information) and the stock of word meanings and concepts (semantic information) are key elements in deriving meaning from printed language and in figuring out unfamiliar written words.

The information about word recognition and spelling in this chapter is presented in three large sections. First, we provide a more detailed discussion of the nature of word recognition, fluency, and spelling ability and the debates surrounding the appropriate way to help children become competent. We also detail the ways in which students' word recognition, fluency, and spelling needs may vary along a developmental continuum. Next, we provide guidelines for instruction that focuses on word recognition and analysis, fluency, and spelling. Finally, we describe promising instructional techniques for focusing on these areas.

# Understanding Word Recognition, Fluency, and Spelling Instruction

A sizeable number of disabled students have difficulty with some aspect of word identification. Many of them also struggle with other aspects of written language, particularly spelling. Recently, decades of reading research have been synthesized (Snow et al., 1998; National Reading Panel, 2000). Although these summaries have not put all the disputes about reading instruction to rest, they have provided considerable common ground on which to build a word-level program in reading for both normally developing and less-skilled readers.

## The Nature of Word Identification, Fluency, and Spelling

Rapid and efficient word recognition requires that readers know a number of words instantly at sight and that they have acquired a repertoire of word identification techniques for analyzing words that are unfamiliar to them in print. In Chapter 2 we described the various components of word identification and spelling. Competent readers and writers possess knowledge and skill in using sight word recognition, meaning-based analysis, graphophonic analysis, and structural analysis. Effective students possess a repertoire of skills and strategies that are used in concert to pronounce words and retrieve their meanings, resulting in fluent reading and accurate spelling.

***Word Identifcation, Word Analysis, and Decoding.*** These are all terms that have been used to describe a reader's ability to pronounce words. Skilled readers of English attend closely to the letters within words and process them very quickly. They do not, as many have thought, rely on context to identify words (Ehri, 1994; Share & Stanovich, 1995). Although context is critical for comprehension, its purpose at the word level is primarily a monitoring one (Snow et al., 1998).

Mature readers are capable of "reading" (pronouncing) large numbers of words without assigning meaning. Indeed, they can read "pseudo-words" with equal ease (Ryder & Graves, 1980), demonstrating the degree to which good readers have internalized the sound–symbol system and structural aspects of our language. However, when readers have meaning associations for a word, that meaning is almost always activated when the word is pronounced (Stanovich, 1991). The melding of word meanings with word pronunciation is at the heart of word identification and distinguishes the ability from simple decoding.

The tools of word identification can be placed in several large categories, with supporting skills employed as necessary:

> Phonological segmentation
> Sight word recognition
>> High frequency
>> High potency
> Phonics
> Structural analysis—syllabication
> Meaning-based word analysis
>> Contextual analysis (using syntax and semantics)
>> Morphemic analysis (structural analysis)

In a balanced reading program, provisions are made for ensuring the development of each of these components of word identification and for applying these skills in authentic contexts. Phonic analysis, or the use of letter–sound correspondences, is one tool among several available to the skilled reader (see Figure 13.1 for the content of phonics instruction).

**FIGURE 13.1**
Phonics Content

---

**Consonants** are sounds that are produced when you stop or slow the breath coming through your mouth. There are roughly twenty-five consonant sounds (phonemes) in English.

| Sound | Examples |
|-------|----------|
| / b / | **b**all, sca**b** |
| / d / | **d**og, ba**d** |
| / f / | **f**og, gra**ph**, rou**gh** |
| / g / | **g**ame, **gh**oul, fi**g** |
| / h / | **h**at, **wh**o |
| / hw / | **wh**ite |
| / j / | **j**am, **g**em, wa**ge**, we**dge** |
| / k / | **c**ar, **k**itten, ta**ke**, bla**ck**, anti**que** |
| / l / | **l**ake, wa**ll** |
| / m / | **m**onkey, sli**m**, ca**me**, li**mb** |
| / n / | **n**ame, **pn**eumonia, **gn**at, fi**n** |
| / p / | **p**ail, sa**p** |
| / r / | **r**ain |
| / s / | **s**un, **c**ereal, u**s**, ba**ss**, mi**ce** |
| / t / | **t**ap, ca**t**, clap**ped** |
| / v / | **v**ote, li**ve** |
| / w / | **w**ink |
| / y / | **y**oke |
| / z / | **z**oo, wa**s**, whi**z**, fi**zz**, ma**ze** |
| / ch / | **ch**ain, mu**ch**, hu**tch**, lec**ture**, ques**ti**on |
| / sh / | **sh**eet, **s**ugar, **ch**aise, ma**sh**, fic**ti**on |
| / th / | **th**imble, my**th** |
| / *th* / | **th**em, la**the** |
| / zh / | mea**s**ure |
| / ng / | ri**ng** |

**Vowels** are sounds that are produced when air flows in an unrestricted way through your throat and opened mouth. There are approximately sixteen vowel phonemes in English.

| Sound | Examples |
|-------|----------|
| *Long* | |
| / a / | m**a**ke, b**ai**t, fr**ay**, t**a**ble |
| / e / | b**ee**t, s**ea**m, m**e**, pon**y**, k**ey**, rec**ei**ve |
| / i / | b**i**ke, f**igh**t, tin**y**, l**ie** |
| / o / | d**o**me, s**oa**p, n**o**, m**ow**, s**o**ld, t**o**tal |
| / u / | f**u**se, p**u**ny |

**FIGURE 13.1**
(Continued)

| | |
|---|---|
| *Short* | |
| / a / | cat |
| / e / | bed, meadow |
| / i / | fit |
| / o / | top |
| / u / | cup, come |
| | |
| *r-controlled* | |
| / ar / | car |
| / i r / | fir, her, fur |
| / or / | for, more, pour, door |
| / air / | hair, bare |
| / eer / | fear, leer |
| | |
| *Other vowels* | |
| Schwa (ə) | button, about, model |
| / oi / | foil, boy |
| / ow / | owl, mouth |
| / aw / | awful, taught, fall, air, bare, balk, scoff |
| / oo / | food, suit, flew, sue |
| / oo / | book, should |

**Consonant digraphs and consonant blends** require attention because they need to be visually identified by readers during words analysis, especially in more advanced decoding.

| | |
|---|---|
| Digraphs | Consonant digraphs are two consonants that work together to represent one sound (phoneme) (e.g., sh, ch, gh). |
| Blends | Consonant blends are two consonants that work together, but each continues to represent its original sound (e.g., br, fl, kw, scr, st, sp, ld). |

Knowledge and skill in using the graphophonic cueing system are essential but not in themselves sufficient for good reading. As Figure 13.1 demonstrates, the forty to forty-four phonemes of English are represented by a variety of spelling patterns. Although they are reasonably predictable, they are also complex. R. C. Anderson et al. (1985, p. 41) concluded that "all that phonics can be expected to do is help children get approximate pronunciations of written words." Similarly, Groff (1986, p. 921) notes that phonics is not an exact science. Instead, application of phonics knowledge results in "rough estimates of the sounds that letters represent." Because the use of phonics may result in inexact renderings and because reading comprehension requires more than word calling, students must attend to several aspects of print at once.

*Fluency.* Although accurate word recognition is fundamental to reading proficiency, "teachers need to know that word recognition accuracy is not the end point of reading instruction. Fluency represents a level of expertise beyond word recognition accuracy, and reading comprehension may be aided by fluency" (NRP, 2000, p. 3-3). Fluency involves reading words accurately with appropriate rate in such a way as to maintain and construct meaning. As described by Barr, Blachowicz, and Wogman-Sadow (1995, p. 65):

> The capability to read fluently depends on two conditions: (1) instantaneous recognition of an extensive set of printed words and (2) considerable practice reading contextual selections. Some skillful young readers achieve fluency in their first year of reading. Many, however, require several years of reading experience before they acquire sufficient word knowledge and contextual practice to read unfamiliar material fluently.

Thus the instructional techniques and strategies used to promote fluency will inevitably include those that draw readers' attention to the appearance of words so that they can be recognized rapidly and accurately. However, instruction must also include supported reading of appropriately difficult texts because "fluency develops as a result of multiple opportunities to practice reading skills with a high rate of success" (Honig, Diamond, & Gutlohn, 2000, p. 11.3).

***Spelling.***    Although many people believe that accurate spelling relies on "sounding out," the evidence is clear that "beyond its most primitive stage, learning to spell has little to do with sounding a word out" (Henderson, 1992, p. 88). Correct spellings rely on knowledge of sight words, morphemic and structural analysis, and an emerging awareness of spelling patterns. Experts agree that knowledge of spelling patterns and vocabulary should be built on a foundation of experiences in reading and writing. They also agree, however, that experience alone is not enough and needs to be supplemented with explicit instruction and purposeful practice (Bear et al., 2000). This practice should focus on the alphabet, on the orthographic patterns of English, and on meaning (see later discussion in this chapter).

## Issues

Clearly, knowledge of the ways in which the sound–symbol system works is critical to becoming a skilled reader and writer. Similarly, it is clear that students must be able to use their knowledge of the graphophonic cueing system and the orthographic structure of the language with ease and efficiency to read fluently and write competently. As Adams (1990) points out, the fact that students need to acquire this knowledge and skill is really not an area of dispute. How they should acquire this knowledge and skill and what knowledge is essential to becoming a skilled reader are far more contentious questions.

***Types of Instruction.***    The overwhelming evidence from American researchers indicates that students learn basic sound–symbol correspondence more efficiently when they receive systematic and intensive phonics instruction (NRP, 2000; Snow et al., 1998). In addition, the research suggests that students who receive direct instruction in segmenting sounds and in blending are generally more adept at word recognition than are students who do not receive this training (see Adams, 1990; O'Connor, Jenkins, & Slocum, 1995). Many teachers have resisted the idea of systematic phonics instruction because it has traditionally involved isolated skill and practice in contrived materials unrelated to mainstream reading instruction,

However, it is becoming increasingly clear that within the large umbrella of systematic instruction, no one method or program of teaching phonics is necessarily better than another.

The National Reading Panel (2000) reviewed three types of systematic phonics programs. The first and most common type of program involved *synthetic* phonics instruction. Students were taught "to transform letters into sounds (phonemes) and to blend the sounds to form recognizable words" (NRP, 2000, p. 2-110). The programs that were examined in this category included Orton Gillingham, Open Court, and DISTAR.

A second type of systematic instruction reviewed by the NRP was *larger-unit* phonics programs "that emphasized the analysis and blending of larger subparts of words (i.e., onsets, rimes, phonograms, spelling patterns)" (NRP, 2000, p. 2-124). These types of programs have generally been called *analytic* phonics programs. In most of these programs writing was used as a complement. Programs examined in this category included a modified Chapter 1 program (Hiebert, Colt, Catto, & Gury, 1992), three Reading Recovery programs modified to include systematic phonics, and a variation of the Benchmark Word Identification program (Gaskins et al., 1996/1997; Lovett & Steinbach, 1997). The third, or miscellaneous, type of systematic program is less clearly defined.

After an exhaustive meta-analysis, the NRP concluded that "specific systematic phonics programs are all more effective than non-phonics programs and they do not appear to differ significantly from each other in their effectiveness" (NRP, 2000, p. 2-124). In other words, students benefit from an orderly introduction and conscious support of phonic elements in learning to read English, but they do not require a particular sort of program to enjoy this benefit.

It is important to note that the authors of the National Reading Panel also concluded that systematic phonics programs were much less effective in improving the reading performance of students beyond grade 2, although there were individual programs that had an impact (discussed later in the chapter). These findings support our conclusion that word-level concerns among students should be considered from within a developmental framework and that no one approach is likely to help all students.

Unless students are showing no growth in word recognition using a more integrated approach to reading instruction, we would argue for instruction that provides very young students with opportunities to see words in connected text first. Poor readers too often do not transfer the information they received during isolated skill instruction to more realistic reading materials and settings; many never receive sufficient practice in using the various component skills together. Consequently, they never achieve the high levels of automatic word identification that are the hallmark of skilled adult readers (West & Stanovich, 1978).

As with phonics instruction, one of the persistent issues surrounding sight word instruction is the debate regarding the appropriate presentation of new words. Although the evidence is not conclusive, there is reason to believe that students benefit from the presentation of new words in meaningful contexts (Ehri & Wilce, 1980). In addition, it appears that poor readers recognize more high frequency sight words during connected text reading than they do in isolation (Krieger, 1981), and they should have opportunities to practice in these relatively more successful settings.

As children move through different stages of word recognition, they may attend to somewhat different aspects of words. Ultimately, however, we want all children to reach the stage of sight word reading (Ehri, 1994, 1995) or automatic word recognition (Spear-

Swerling & Sternberg, 1996). Although it is clear that students benefit from isolating words for examination and that students need many opportunities to encounter these words in print, this can be done within a program that employs meaningful, even predictable, contexts for reading (Bridge et al., 1983; Leu, DeGroff, & Simons, 1986). In addition, the research in writing and inventive spelling suggests that opportunities to write provide students with natural contexts for analyzing sound–symbol correspondence. Writing focuses students' attention on segmenting and isolating speech sounds (Snow et al., 1998).

Isolated, fragmented instruction with limited opportunity to read and write real material seems doomed to failure, especially for children who are experiencing reading difficulty. On the other hand, teachers should not hesitate to provide students with information about sounds, symbols, and patterns and to pull individual words and sounds out of meaningful text experiences to help students notice key features. Timely, systematic, and focused information about how to decode should be available to all students.

The parallels in spelling instruction are striking. Spelling instruction has traditionally remained separate from both reading and writing in the elementary curriculum and has involved presenting students with isolated lists of words. Although older lists were questionable, most contemporary lists contain words that have been selected for their age or grade appropriateness and that are united either by frequency or by spelling pattern. This does not, of course, ensure that students know these words or are motivated to learn to spell them.

In particular, students who are struggling are often asked to study lists that they cannot read and learn to spell words they are unlikely to use. As Henderson (1990, p. 92) notes, "strange words, even nonsense words, may be memorized by anyone for a short period, but unless words are used in writing, they are likely soon to slip beyond recall."

***Identifying Areas of Instructional Need.***   Using the information gathered in previous stages of the assessment-instruction process, teachers can determine which aspects of word identification or spelling are posing the most serious difficulties for students. It is not uncommon for students to demonstrate difficulties in more than one arena. For example, a student with extremely limited print skills may have weak phonics skills and limited graphophonic knowledge but also a weak repertoire of sight vocabulary. This should not be too surprising, since a student with few print skills tends not to try reading. Over time, students who don't read fail to acquire other abilities that result from repeated exposure to texts (Snider & Tarver, 1987; Stanovich, 1986).

It is particularly important to recognize when direct instruction in sound–symbol associations is unlikely to be beneficial for many *older,* struggling readers (NRP, 2000). Cohn and D'Alessandro (1978) studied the word recognition errors of 100 students referred to their clinic and concluded that "only in a small percentage of cases is it true that poor word analysis performance in decoding a list of words is attributable to a lack of knowledge of the sound–symbol relationship involved" (Cohn & D'Alessandro, 1978, p. 343). In this study, students received some on-the-spot diagnostic teaching probes, such as "Please look at that word carefully and try it again." Given just this much prompting, students corrected roughly 50 percent of all initial miscues. If this prompt did not elicit a correct response, students were asked, for example, to examine the first letter(s) and produce the sound. This type of prompt resulted in the correction of another 29 percent of the miscues.

Thus at least 79 percent of all miscues resulted from something other than lack of sound–symbol knowledge.

Of the errors that remained uncorrected, there appeared to be three sources of difficulty: words with irregular phonic patterns (e.g., *tongue, guard*); lack of control over sound–symbol information, which resulted in students sometimes pronouncing the phonic element correctly and other times not; and appearance on a word list versus in context. Like Allington and McGill-Franzen (1980), these authors found that less-skilled readers made errors on lists that they did not make in context. Cohn and D'Alessandro (1978, p. 343) sensibly conclude that it is dangerous and foolish to reteach sound–symbol relationships, since it would be an attempt to "correct a situation that does not exist." These students do need help, however, and might benefit from instruction that was designed to promote fluency, control, or flexibility.

***Developmental Differences in Word Identification and Spelling.*** The issues surrounding instruction in word identification are often confounded by age and developmental stage. Teachers must recognize that differences exist among learners at different developmental stages. The very beginning stages of reading and writing involve somewhat different tasks and behaviors than later stages, and certain types of instruction are much more likely to have an impact at some stages than others. For example, a developmental study by Shanahan (1984) suggests that the overall reading abilities of beginning readers are influenced most strongly by the word-level skills of word identification and spelling, whereas range of vocabulary affected older readers to a great extent.

One of the biggest problems facing teachers of struggling readers and writers is that much of what we know about word identification instruction and spelling is based on studies of young, normal learners. Students who are experiencing difficulty do not generally parallel the general population in their reading and writing achievement or progress. Therefore describing word recognition or spelling techniques in terms of the normal stages of reading development can be problematic.

As a practical matter, students with word identification problems who appear in clinical or remedial settings generally fall into three categories: students with no or almost no print skills, students who have some print skills, and more advanced students whose print skills are not fully developed for reading multisyllabic words or specialized texts. In the following sections we will highlight the major word identification tasks of these groups.

*Word Recognition and Spelling for Students with No Conventional Print Skills.* Literacy professionals often are called on to work with students who have acquired no functional print skills. This stage of development is sometimes call the *logographic* (Ehri, 1991, 1994) or the *visual cue reading stage* (Spear-Swerling & Sternberg, 1996). They respond to words as visual wholes without using a phonological analysis. The primary job for these students is to acquire insight into the alphabetic principle, recognizing that individual phonemes are represented in English writing by one or more letters. Some children in this group may also be moving toward the partial alphabetic (Ehri, 1991, 1994) or phonetic recoding stage (Spear-Swerling & Sternberg, 1996), in which they match some letters and sounds, usually the initial consonants, but continue to rely heavily on picture and context cues for word identification. At this stage, the primary challenge is to learn to fully examine the letters in a words, attending in particular to vowels and the spelling patterns that represent larger chunks of words.

There are also some individuals who are not young but who have acquired virtually no functional print skills. Children who are bilingual or have limited English proficiency (LEP) in particular require special consideration.

In terms of word recognition, perhaps the major hurdle for bilingual or LEP students is the fact that "even if the student can sound out a word more or less accurately, the word may not be recognized because it is not a part of the student's oral vocabulary" (Chamot & O'Malley, 1994, p. 89). In addition, these authors note, bilingual or LEP students are likely to employ some of their own first-language phonemes as they read, leading to confusions about pronunciation versus understanding of sound–symbol correspondence. Like other struggling young readers, bilingual and LEP students must learn to decode English print. Unlike other students, however, they do not have control over the language used to read.

Perhaps the most critical instructional issue for this group of students is whether they are literate in their first language. One of the best predictors of students' second-language reading performance is their first language literacy development (see Garcia, 2000). Children who are literate in their first language are likely to learn to read in English, once they have acquired sufficient oral language competence (Goldenberg, 1994).

There is relatively strong evidence to suggest that students possess an underlying language competence that can be used when learning a new language (Bernhardt, 2000). Proficient speakers of one language use their knowledge of how languages work to learn a second one. Similarly, the skills used to become literate in a native language are available when one is learning to read and write a second language. Of course, students who are illiterate in their native language do not have these resources to draw on. When the school is not in a position to teach children to read and write in their own first language, learning spoken English is the appropriate first step. However, wherever possible, students benefit from learning to read and write in their native language (Snow et al., 1998).

Some programs, such as ESL (English as Second Language), have assumed that students must acquire proficiency in Standard English prior to literacy instruction. However, research certainly suggests that children can learn to read as they are acquiring oral competence (Barrera, 1984). May (1990, p. 479) concluded there is no evidence that learning to speak Standard English fluently is required to learn to read. "It is likely that they need abundant *exposure* to Standard English before they are expected to read it well, but fluent *speech* in Standard English is probably not necessary."

There are differences of opinion about how to proceed with the instruction of bilingual and LEP students. Common sense would suggest that the educational programs of bilingual and LEP students should incorporate the attributes of effective instruction (see Freeman & Freeman, 2000). Suggestions for instruction are generally consistent with the kinds of practices that are suggested for *all* students acquiring initial print skills (Garcia, 2000; Goldenberg, 1994):

1. Build background knowledge by reading aloud every day and providing other concept-developing activities.
2. Provide an academic focus for reading instruction that provides information about the graphophonic system as well as extensive vocabulary development.

3. Provide metacognitive and strategy instruction
4. Provide ample opportunity for students to develop oral language proficiency. Cooperative work groups and paired groupings work best.
5. Permit students to make limited verbal responses initially, and provide guided support for increased proficiency.
6. Support and use the home culture and language.

Spelling, like reading, is developmental in nature. These issues were discussed in detail in Chapter 7. Students in the earliest stages of spelling development might not attend to relationships between sound and print at all, but they quickly begin to represent some sounds in print. It is at this stage that students' knowledge of reading and their knowledge of spelling are most aligned. As students move toward greater skill in reading, the relationship between their word recognition and spelling knowledge and skill will weaken (Henderson, 1990).

*Word Recognition and Spelling Instruction for Students with Some Conventional Print Skills.* Most students who receive specialized reading instructional support have some print skills. Indeed, it is generally the case that a referral is made only after some significant attempts have been made to teach the student to read and it has become apparent that the pace or efficiency of learning is problematic. Students with some conventional print skills are likely moving through the partial alphabetic/phonetic cue state (see above) and are approaching or experiencing the consolidated, alphabetic (Ehri, 1991, 1994) or controlled word reading stages (Spear-Swerling & Sternberg, 1996). Readers at this point can attend to vowel patterns and both consonants and consonant combinations. For example, they would identify and use both the *br-* and the *–ake* in the word *brake*. At this stage, though, students are still struggling for control over their knowledge and skill, and they generally lack fluency in reading.

Although the majority of remedial students have some, but not all, of the print skills required for skilled reading or writing, this is definitely not a homogenous group. It will typically be impossible to predict which print skills have been learned, which are underused, what cueing system is used most often, or whether students have generated any systematic approaches to dealing with print. Again, a careful review of assessment information is required.

The major differences between these students and those who have no print skills are that these students have demonstrated their ability to learn some aspects of the reading process and their skills can be used as the basis for additional learning.

Sometimes students do not exhibit a specific area of difficulty. Rather, they may have what appears to be a general weakness in all aspects of word identification (and generally, in these cases, spelling also). An examination of the students' miscues, for example, would suggest that there is no single major area of difficulty. Miscues appear in many component areas (high-frequency sight words and several different phonic patterns), and effectiveness in using meaning-based strategies for self-correction is erratic. Such a profile suggests that the student has not achieved control over the knowledge and skills that have been taught. Lack of experience with print or haphazard instruction is the likely source of difficulty.

For young, poor readers it makes a great deal of sense to intensify the reading experience but to mimic developmental reading programs wherever possible. These students have time in their future school lives to become proficient and, with support, to practice sufficiently to regain some of the ground that was lost in the early years. Indeed, effective congruent programming may have the greatest payoff for these students.

Limited or inadequate word identification abilities are not the exclusive domain of young students, however. Many older disabled readers have partial knowledge or mastery of word identification. This partial knowledge can be troublesome, since these students generally know that they are supposed to use sound–symbol information to "sound out" unknown words. They often attempt to do so, relying on inadequate or underdeveloped information. We frequently encounter young people who have a jumble of half-known rules and homilies stored away but little ability to identify the regularities of print or to recognize the familiar words they have seen many times. They understand sound–symbol correspondence as a general proposition but do not fully analyze words and tend to guess using only partial information. These same students have typically failed to internalize the regular spelling patterns of the English language. For somewhat older students it is important to analyze performance and knowledge in terms of opportunities to learn. If the student has already received substantial experience with one type of instruction but failed to thrive, it may be especially important to consider alternatives. This might include intensive, nontraditional training in some aspect of word recognition (e.g., the ABD program developed by Williams (1980), described in the next section). It might also include supported reading of connected text (e.g. the Heckelman Impress, discussed on p. 530) and will, most certainly, need to include some specialized programs to attending to the spelling patterns to learn new words.

Although it is clear that the most desirable situation involves early acquisition of decoding skill, the appropriate intervention is not always apparent for students who have not become skilled readers. Some of these students may not have received good initial instruction; others may not have been positioned to take advantage of traditionally successful programs (e.g., LEP children and students with poor phonemic segmentation abilities). "Jenny" is an example worth noting. Jenny was a 9-year-old second grader when she came to our clinic. She had repeated both kindergarten and first grade and had been receiving specialized remedial help for several years. She had extremely limited mastery of phonics and an uncertain ability to associate sounds and symbols (the likely result of a long history of ear infections that had reached the critical stage between the ages of 4 and 6). In addition, she was exceptionally unreliable in her recognition of high-frequency sight words. Finally, neither she nor her teachers could read back the invented spellings she used during writing.

She had been receiving intensive phonics instruction as well as isolated practice on sight vocabulary for over a year. She had also been placed in a controlled vocabulary reader for application and practice. During our first session Jenny was asked to read one of these simple stories aloud. She had read, haltingly, only a few words when she came to the word *there.* She stopped abruptly, held her head, and said, "That's one of *those* words—the ones I can't remember." Her intensive isolated instructional program had certainly sensitized her. She was exceptionally skilled at locating, if not pronouncing, high-frequency sight words; she had also become convinced that the task was an impossible one. Her two most frequent responses to an encounter with these words were to give up in exasperation and remark on "those" words or to begin a fairly random run through a short list of high-frequency words, hoping to hit on the correct one. Although it is obviously desirable for Jenny to learn these words, any direct assault on them seemed doomed to failure in the immediate future.

Students like Jenny have some print skills, but these skills are not controlled and accessible for use. Other students have a much larger repertoire but have not practiced them enough in coordinated settings involving connected text reading. Fluency is almost always a problem for students with some, but not all, of the word recognition abilities. Indeed, specific instructional attention should be routinely directed to children who have not consolidated their word-level skills but who seem to have an adequate repertoire to read easy text of some length (see later in this chapter).

The spelling of students who have some print skills is also often problematic. Students may have some ability to spell sight words and often produce phonemically correct spellings for words. They have not, however, acquired the repertoire of memorized and patterned words that tell them that "kiten" or "slamed" are misspelled.

It is especially important to recognize that many of these students may also appear to be unmotivated. Many older students who have some print skills also have a history of school failure (Stanovich, 1986; Torgesen, 1977). Effective teachers and clinicians will be alert to the possibility that limited print skills have diminished the student's pleasure in reading and writing. If this is the case, motivation will be increased only when reading is supported or skill is improved. For this large group of students with some, but inadequate, word recognition, word analysis, and spelling skills, differentiated instruction delivered by a thoughtful teacher is absolutely essential.

*Word Recognition and Spelling Instruction for Students Who Need More Advanced Print Skills.* There is a third distinctive group of students who present themselves as having reading problems somewhat later in school life. These students may have experienced reading difficulties earlier, but often they were considered adequate or even good readers in the early years. These students generally have reasonably good phonics skills and are able to use phonic principles to decode unfamiliar words. Indeed, they may have arrived at the sight word stage of reading (Ehri, 1991), also called *automatic word recognition* (Spear-Swerling & Sternberg, 1996) for single syllable words. Ryder and Graves (1980) found that even less-skilled seventh-grade students have more sound–symbol knowledge than was previously assumed. Indeed, there was relatively little difference between less-skilled and above-average secondary readers, in terms of their ability to identify letter–sound relationships.

The problem for these secondary students does not appear to be lack of knowledge of individual sounds and symbols. Memory (1986, p. 195) argues that many of these students do have the requisite knowledge and skill but do not apply it during assigned content-area reading tasks:

> Possibly one reason that less-able readers in the secondary grades often do not apply their existing decoding knowledge is that the way they were taught to use that knowledge is not the way skilled readers decode words. Rather than use individual grapheme–phoneme relationships and phonic generalizations to sound out words, good readers pronounce words by putting together the sounds of familiar clusters of letters (Baron, 1977; Glass & Burton, 1973).

Students at this stage *do* lack sufficient knowledge and pattern recognition of syllables and awareness of morphemes. They make errors in the areas of syllable juncture—recognizing where syllables begin and end—and in "derivational constancy," what Templeton (1995) calls the "spelling-meaning connection." This lack of knowledge results in mispronunciations of multisyllabic words such as *predetermined* and in misspellings that result from lack of sensitivity to the underlying morphemes, for example, a misspelling like "compasition" that could be corrected if the student understood the derivational root, *compose*.

Skilled and less-skilled readers in the more advanced stages of reading development differ in other ways. Poor readers, for example, frequently do not read for meaning, and they are notably weak in their ability to read multisyllabic words. Less-skilled middle-level and secondary students often do not have a solid repertoire of skills that can be used flexibly. These problems may be related to poor meaning vocabulary (see Chapter 14) or weak comprehension abilities (see Chapter 15). In terms of word recognition, students' inability to read "long words" often stands in the way of attempts at wider reading that would, in turn, promote better vocabulary and comprehension.

Unfortunately, the evidence regarding the most productive approach to instruction in multisyllabic words is mixed at best. What does seem unequivocal is the effectiveness of teaching students some technique for identifying elements and patterns within words. Johnson and Baumann (1984, pp. 596–597) describe assumptions underlying syllabication instruction: "The rationale for teaching syllabication is based on the belief that if children can segment unknown words into more manageable parts, decoding will be facilitated; that is, phonics, phonogram identification, or structural skills can then be effectively applied."

Researchers and educators are divided about the utility of teaching dictionary rules for syllabication. Although there is no evidence that traditional syllabication instruction improves vocabulary or comprehension, most of these studies have not demonstrated that students had difficulty in this area. The evidence does suggest an improved ability to pronounce words, precisely the area of need for many less-skilled readers (see Johnson & Baumann, 1984). In addition, instruction in both syllabic analysis and dictionary usage is effective in improving *spelling* for students at these levels (Henderson, 1990).

## Guidelines for Instruction Focused on Word Recognition, Fluency, and Spelling

In thinking about word recognition or spelling instruction, decisions about what and how to teach should be informed by the more complex model we have used throughout the text. In particular, we assume that many of the basic conditions for effective teaching described in Chapter 12 have already been established and that careful assessment has suggested that the student will benefit from instruction focused on word recognition, analysis, fluency, and/or spelling. Before considering specific techniques, we offer guidelines that provide general frameworks for thinking about the content and delivery of word identification and spelling instruction.

***Focus on the Goal of Increased Ability and Fluency during Reading and Writing.***
The close approximation of skilled reading and writing should be the goal of all literacy activities. This does not mean that students will never receive instruction focused on discrete aspects of reading or writing. Students must be able to decode and recognize almost all of the words they encounter in text if they are to read with comprehension and enjoyment.

Teachers should be certain that they provide systematic instruction in phonics early in reading development, but they must also remember to teach only high-utility decoding skills (Adams, 1990).

Wherever possible, teachers should develop instructional approaches that include ample application of taught skills in authentic, connected text. In addition, teachers need to signal the importance of reading (versus worksheets) and writing (versus spelling lists) in every possible way. As the National Reading Panel (2000, p. 2-128) notes:

> Systematic phonics instruction should be integrated with other reading instruction to create a balanced reading program. Phonics instruction is never a total reading program . . . Phonics should not become the dominant component in a reading program, neither in the amount of time devoted to it nor in the significance attached.

The dangers inherent in reducing reading or writing to the acquisition of isolated bits and pieces are abundantly clear. The first danger is that a steady diet of isolated, fragmented instruction distorts the reading/writing process so that some students (and some teachers) find it impossible to remember that the goal is purposeful, self-directed learning and enjoyment.

A second danger in oversimplifying is that we may make reading more difficult and writing impossible. Highly controlled vocabulary usually does not make reading easier, because students are forced to apply their skills without the benefit of good information for self-checking (see Chapters 5 and 6). Students' well-developed sense of syntax may actually cause them difficulty in highly contrived and controlled text. Although such controlled, or decodable, texts may be useful in practicing recently taught phonic elements, they are not effective for building fluency. Similarly, much early attention on accurate spelling can both limit students' acquisition of phonemic awareness skills and dampen their enjoyment of the communicative purposes for writing.

Teachers should also evaluate students as they apply their knowledge and skill during reading and writing. In particular, teachers need to understand that students do not need to know the labels for phonic elements (blends, diphthongs, etc.), nor do they need to be able to provide an explicit rationale (rule) to decode or spell effectively. Indeed, the available evidence suggests that students' ability to decode far outstrips their ability to explain what they are doing. Similarly, the knowledge of spelling patterns that good spellers possess is often tacit knowledge that they cannot typically describe.

Tovay (1980) designed a study to examine how well children in grades 2 through 4 understood common phonic terms such as *consonant, syllable,* and *diphthong.* In addition, she examined the relationship between explicit knowledge of terms and students' ability to apply phonics in decoding words. "The results showed that elementary grade children have a poor grasp of the meaning of phonics terms yet a far better grasp of applied phonics" (Tovay, 1980, p. 431). Tovay recommends that teachers place less emphasis on knowledge of phonics terms and instead use a procedure that involves making comparisons with known words.

### *Teach Phonemic Awareness and Phonics in Appropriate Ways, but Do It Early and Efficiently.*

The largest benefits for phonics instruction occur among very young children in the first two years of schooling. The rapid decay of the need for explicit information about sound–symbol relationships caused R. C. Anderson et al. (1985, p. 43) to conclude, "The right maxims for phonics are: Do it early. Keep it simple. Except in cases of diagnosed individual need, phonics instruction should have been completed by the end of second grade." These conclusions have been reaffirmed in each of the recent research summaries over the past decade (Adams, 1990; Hiebert & Taylor, 2000; NRP, 2000).

In addition, the overwhelming evidence from three decades of research indicates that systematic phonics approaches are more beneficial than more opportunistic ones for most students. Having said this, the evidence also indicates that a wide range of programs can be used with more or less the same results. The NRP (2000) review, for example, included diverse phonics programs, ranging from synthetic programs that emphasized teaching individual phoneme–grapheme correspondences and blending to much more eclectic programs.

Finally, in terms of phonics instruction it appears that less is more. For example, there is almost universal consensus that phonics instruction should be largely completed by the end of grade 2. Similarly, it appears that short, focused phonemic awareness programs (involving between five and eighteen hours of teaching) have a greater impact on students than those that lasted longer (NRP, 2000, pp. 2-42).

It is important to note that there is little evidence that phonics instruction has benefited older, disabled, or low-achieving readers (see NRP, 2000, Chapter 2). It is likely that these students' difficulties result from several different factors, and they would not necessarily benefit from phonics or phonics-only instruction.

***Teach Students to Examine Words for Familiar Patterns and to Make Analogies.***
Extremely disabled and beginning readers seem to benefit from direct instruction in careful word analysis, blending, and decoding of individual letters and phonemes in unfamiliar words (Gaskins et al., 1996/1997; Williams, 1980). However, after a very brief initial stage of acquisition, good readers appear to move to more coordinated strategies: identifying familiar patterns in words, assigning sound relationships to those patterns, and blending elements when necessary. More proficient readers rely quite heavily on spelling patterns and other familiar chunks of letters to rapidly identify words. As good readers become even more skilled, they decode words by attending to larger and larger groupings of letters (Marsh, Desberg, & Cooper, 1977) and by using known spelling–sound patterns to decode unknown words—for example, using the known word *brake* to read a new word that shares the same spelling pattern, such as *shake*.

Memory (1986, p. 195) argues that "if poor readers are to become even average readers, they too, must learn to see the phonetically important groupings of letters in words and take advantage of their existing knowledge of those groupings." The recognition of reliable letter clusters or known phonograms that remind readers of familiar words or sound–symbol patterns has proven to be effective in instruction for many years (Wylie & Durrell, 1970), and recent revisions of decoding through analogy with known words has proven equally effective. Goswami (2000) has synthesized research demonstrating that training in the use of analogy improves reading performance among a wide range of students, including beginning readers, "dyslexic" readers, and students acquiring English.

The same systematic attention to clusters and patterns seems to be required in spelling. Students who are struggling need to examine, and attend closely to, the patterns and configurations of words. "Children need to study words so that spelling principles that they have been using intuitively become clarified, brought to the level of consciousness" (Stewig & Nordberg, 1995, p. 354).

***Provide Early Intervention.***   Several programs have been developed and tested recently that focus on the very early ages and stages of reading and writing, recognizing that early intervention is likely to be both more successful and more economical than is remediation later on (see Hiebert & Taylor, 2000; Pikulski, 1995). Generally, these programs are designed to accelerate reading development among young students by adding high-quality supplemental instruction to the regular schedule (Allington & McGill-Franzen, 1989). Among the most familiar of these programs are Reading Recovery (Pinnell et al., 1994); Success for All (Slavin, Karweit, Wasik, Madden, & Dolan, 1994); and Early Intervention in Reading (Taylor, Strait, & Medo, 1994). These programs share a number of attributes.

Two characteristics of these programs are especially important to note. First, all these programs increase the amount of time students spend reading and writing. Second, all these programs focus considerable attention on the reading and writing of connected text, as opposed to a single focus on phonics or decoding.

Pikulski (1994) has reviewed five of these programs and summarized the attributes common to all of these successful programs. The following characteristics are noted by Pikulski as especially important:

- Intervention is frequent and lengthy.
- Student–teacher ratios are small.
- Fluency is an important outcome.
- Text difficulty is controlled, so students read many easy books.
- Instruction focuses on building phonemic awareness and print skills.
- Writing is used to promote word recognition and spelling.
- There is a well-established pattern for instructional sessions.
- Instruction is fast paced.
- Assessment is frequent, ongoing, and used to inform instruction.
- Communication between home and school is critical.
- Teachers receive (sometimes extensive) training.

Finally, the accomplished teachers in these programs hold high standards for students and believe that they will achieve. Certainly, many of these characteristics can and should be present in all classrooms and available to all students. Indeed, there is good evidence to suggest that the gains enjoyed by students in early intervention programs will not be sustained without ongoing attention to excellent instruction with increasingly complex texts and tasks (Hiebert & Taylor, 2000).

## Instructional Techniques Focused on Word Recognition and Analysis

In this section we provide detailed descriptions of instructional techniques designed to focus attention on word recognition and word analysis. The instructional strategies have been categorized according to their utility for use with students in the three developmental phases described above. First, we provide suggestions for working with students who have no print skills. Next, we turn our attention to students who have acquired some knowledge and skill in word recognition. Finally, we suggest some instructional approaches for working with older, more skilled readers.

## Instructional Strategies and Tools: Students with No Print Skills

Some students have virtually no conventional print skills. Because these students may be very diverse (very young, very disabled, bilingual, etc.), the range of techniques that might be employed with this group is also great. Some techniques involve merely tightening the focus on traditional good practice. Other strategies involve much more systematic intervention.

***Establishing the Foundational Abilities.***    Age alone does not determine whether students have acquired the prerequisite knowledge and skill to become a mature reader. Although older readers are hardly ever permitted the time it would take to acquire some of the underpinnings of literacy (see Chapter 7), this is precisely what some need. In addition, most young, poor readers need at least some work on the foundations of literacy.

*Developing Phonemic Awareness and Segmentation.*    It has become increasingly clear that students must learn to segment speech into constituent parts and manipulate the segments within words (Stahl & Murray, 1994, 1998). Most students develop the ability to isolate individual sounds rapidly as they encounter typical beginning reading instruction. There are some students, however, who do not seem to learn this early and easily. For them the likelihood of reading failure is quite high (Juel et al., 1986; Snow, Burns, & Griffin, 1998; Stanovich, 1986).

The notion that sound analysis and writing may actually precede reading is a difficult idea for most educators to grasp. Traditionally, schools have stressed learning letter names first and moving from letters to sounds. However, research does suggest that children's attempts to analyze words into component sounds, essential to early writing attempts, likely promotes and develops phonics knowledge and skill.

An early emphasis on inventive, or developmental, spelling (see Chapter 7) seems critical in helping children to understand the alphabetic principle (Ehri, 1988; Snow et al., 1998). As Clay (1979, p. 66) notes, early writing "forces children to carry out a splendid sound analysis of the words they want to write—a first to last segmenting of the sounds in the word. They pay attention to the sounds of words and search for a visual way of representing these." First grade children who are encouraged to use invented spellings made more progress in both spelling and decoding than did children who were not encouraged to use invented spelling (Clarke, 1988). Similarly, Torgeson and Davis (1996, p. 18) found that "a pretest measure of kindergarten children's ability to engage in invented spelling was the strongest and most consistent predictor of their progress in a phonological training curriculum."

The strong encouragement students receive for analyzing words for the constituent sounds should be buttressed by activities that help students to identify orally rhyming words and to separate words that rhyme from those that don't and by activities that provide information about sound-symbol patterns. Indeed, the combination of invented spelling and explicit phonological instruction appears to be especially potent.

Instruction should be sensitive to the increasing complexity of phonologic tasks and vary work according to students' needs and abilities. Experts generally agree that children's abilities on common phonological awareness tasks develop in the following way (increasing in difficulty):

- Identify and produce rhyming words.
- Identify and group by initial phoneme; generally using pictures.
- Segment by syllable.
- Blend onsets and rimes to form real words ("Blend /s/ and –*it* together to make the word 'sit.'").
- Blend phonemes into real words ("If I say /b/ /a/ /t/ and blend them together, what word is it?").
- Delete a phoneme in the initial or final position ("Say 'rat' without the /r/.").
- Substitute a phoneme in the initial or final position ("Say 'rat'; now say it with /f/ instead of /r/.").
- Segment words into individual phonemes ("lake" would be segmented into /l/ /a/ /k/).
- Identify letter–sound correspondences.

Although sequences like this are often used in commercial programs, normally developing children may be experimenting with several of these abilities at the same time, especially if they are engaged in writing as well as reading. Some early phonemic training programs, such as Elkonin's (1963, 1973) approach in Russia, were completely auditory and quite removed from reading and writing. In Elkonin's program, children do not interact with print at all until they have mastered certain aspects of phonological segmentation. Markers are used to designate individual phonemes. Students are shown pictures with spaces beneath the picture that represent the total number of phonemes in that word. Students say the word, and then they separate the word into discrete phonemes, placing a marker in each space as they say it. Over time, students are expected to do this orally, without markers or pictures. More recent research has suggested that the effects on students' reading performance are much greater when phonological information is coupled with print:

> In the rush to teach phonemic awareness, it is important not to overlook the need to teach letters as well. The NRP analysis showed that phonemic awareness instruction was more effective when it was taught with letters. Using letters to manipulate phonemes helps children make the transfer to reading and writing. (NRP, 2000, p. 2-33)

Among very young readers, a variety of engaging songs and oral games are typically used to develop phonemic awareness (see, e.g., Honig et al., 2000). Activities such as *making and breaking words* are common in primary classrooms today (Iverson & Tunmer, 1993). Students word with magnetic letters or tiles and arrange letters following the teacher's directions:

1. Students are given a set of letters (e.g., "a," "c," "s," and "t."
2. The teacher directs students to use some of the letters to make the word "cat."

3. Then students are told to add a letter to make the word "cats."
4. Next, students are told to move a letter so that the word is "scat" and so on.

For somewhat older students with significant reading difficulties other approaches may be needed.

The ABDs of Reading is a word identification program for learning-disabled students designed and evaluated by Williams (1980). It focuses on teaching students to analyze, blend, and decode, using both oral training and contextual support. Williams has demonstrated that this type of program has a significant impact on the decoding abilities of older learning-disabled students. Its success is probably rooted in the combination of direct instruction and supported practice. The ABDs of Reading involves the following steps:

1. Direct instruction is provided regarding the concept of word segmentation. Students are taught to identify the syllable as an element.
2. Students receive direct instruction in phoneme analysis. Nine phonemes (seven consonants and two vowels) are used for *auditory* analysis and practice.
3. Students receive instruction in blending phonemes into two- and three-phoneme units.
4. Students are taught letter–sound relationships for the nine phonemes.
5. Students manipulate letters to learn to decode phonograms made from the nine phonemes.
6. Six additional letter–sound relationships (five consonants and one vowel) are introduced and practiced.
7. More complex patterns are introduced involving consonant combinations (e.g., CCVC).

Williams (1980, p. 4) is careful to note that "this was a decoding program, not a complete reading program" and emphasizes the need to provide experience with words in context and the need to provide instruction in comprehension as well. However, it seems safe to say that the instructional program of students who cannot reliably isolate sounds and blend them together should contain some focus on segmentation and blending.

*Using Sense and Syntax.*    To take full advantage of any word identification instruction, students must be able to use sense and syntax to test out their graphophonic approximations. Students who have limited language proficiency or have had few experiences with book print should be read to extensively. Teachers, peers, older students, and parent volunteers should all be enlisted to aid in this effort.

In addition, daily oral language experiences (shared books, chants, chart stories, etc.) and opportunities to speak should be provided. From time to time, students should also be encouraged to create dictated stories using the frameworks or language of some read-aloud books. Remember that, in general, the focus of these instructional efforts should be to promote oral comprehension, develop vocabulary, and develop the ability to use text structure to support reading.

**Developing Sight Word Recognition.**    One of the major accomplishments of skilled reading involves recognizing large numbers of words instantly *at sight*. Some of these words have become old friends—sight words—because they occur so frequently in print that the well-read student has encountered them many times. Others have been acquired as instantly recognizable words because they have very high value (high-potency words) for the reader.

In the very early stages of formal, or conventional, reading development there are two ways in which teachers can help students recognize words at sight: embed the new word(s) in a highly familiar and strongly supported print context or provide direct instruction of the new word(s). Both methods are described below, because effective instruction typically involves each at different times. Because the embedding method will require the least adaptation from the types of instruction started in Chapter 12, we address those procedures first.

*Embedded Exposure: Supported Book Experiences.* It is clear that readers' sight word recognition depends on frequent exposure. "Automatic recognition of a word from its graphic form is a consequence of extensive experience seeing that word in context and building up a complete linguistic identity around it" (Ehri, 1987, p. 15).

Using as a model the types of heavily supported print encounters provided by parents in literate environments, Holdaway (1979) described a cycle of activity that has been dubbed the *shared book experience.* Shared reading in the classroom often involves enlarged print books, called Big Books. Big Books allow teachers and students in a group environment to read a piece of text together in a manner that mimics the intimacy and give-and-take of home lap reading but also makes the print display available to students. After the teacher reads the book aloud with the students, children can engage in repeated readings of the texts. Because the books have been become less difficult by virtue of the shared experience, students often have the opportunity to read and experience sight vocabulary within the context of much more challenging words.

Using predictable books and language experience stories, Bridge et al. (1983) expanded on the shared books approach. They designed a program for teaching the basic sight words to beginning readers and examined its effect on students' recognition of high-frequency sight words. Their results indicate that students reading at a beginning primer level learned more basic sight words through this approach than did students using a regular basal with controlled vocabulary.

The instructional strategy involves selecting predictable books that contain the high-frequency sight words you wish students to learn. Using these materials, the teacher employs the following strategy:

*Step 1:* The teacher reads the book aloud and then rereads the book, encouraging students to join in when they can predict what will come next.

*Step 2:* The story is transferred to a chart, without pictures to aid the reading. Students reread the story from the chart. Then students match sentence strips from the story to sentences on the chart. Finally, students match individual words to the words in the story.

*Step 3:* Students engage in choral rereading of the story from the chart. Word cards are presented randomly and the children match them to words in the story.

In addition to these activities students regularly contributed to group language experience stories (see Chapter 12) that also focused on sight word recognition and matching.

Like the repeated reading techniques described in Chapter 12, supported book experiences rely on repeated exposure to high-frequency words to build sight word recognition. Big Books and charts have the additional advantage of providing opportunities to focus on individual words in the context of a whole text. Flaps or *masks* (Holdaway, 1979; Salinger, 1988) can be used to cover all or part of words so that teachers and students can work instructionally on features of interest (see Figure 13.2).

More recently, teachers have used similar strategies with a guided reading approach (Fountas & Pinnel, 1996, 2001) to support students' reading of increasingly difficult (and leveled) texts (see Chapter 12).

*Word Banks and Word Walls.* Some students, especially very young or struggling readers, seem to need more explicit instruction focused clearly on the orthographic features of words:

> Successful readers learn to attend to the orthographic features of words, while poor readers continue to require the syntactic and semantic cues of a sentence or phrase to recognize a word. To develop facility in recognizing highly frequent words, beginning readers benefit from occasions where they can study the features of particular words—what distinguishes *here* from *have* (Adams, 1990). Such focused attention is difficult to develop while reading a text; even when the text is made up only of high frequent words. (Hiebert, 1999, p. 555)

Similarly, students learn more words and learn them more completely when they examine the words out of context (Bear et al., 2000).

Individual word banks are one of the most flexible and instructional powerful techniques for working with high-frequency words. A word bank is a collection of words that

**FIGURE 13.2** Masking Techniques for Word Identification

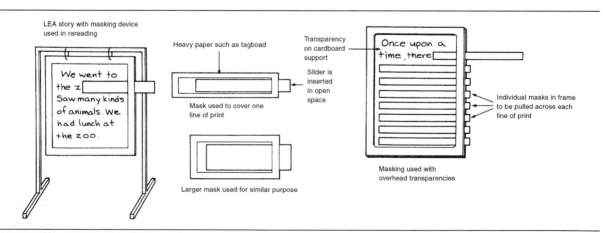

students have written on small cards and store together, usually in a file box. Generally speaking, these should be words that students can read in isolation, although they may not read them correctly each time. The words in the bank must be used for a variety of activities—sorting, games, riddles, spelling, and so on. When teachers use them instructionally, review them frequently, and help students to examine and reexamine their distinctive features, they can be effective word-learning tools.

A word wall, in contrast, is a classroom-based strategy with real potential for clinical settings as well. Although teachers use word walls for different purposes, they are especially useful for learning high-frequency sight words. According to Cunningham and Allington (1999), students generally learn to read and write all the words on a word wall as long as the word wall is well organized and the students have daily practice in finding, writing, and working with the words. A word wall is organized in sections, with a section for each letter of the alphabet. Teachers and students place words on the word wall, grouping them according to their first letter. The word wall is created throughout the year, with words added as they are encountered and needed.

*Direct Instruction.* There are students who have such a difficult time learning new words that they require unusually intensive instructional efforts. One of the most comprehensive of such approaches is described by McNinch (1981). He devised a framework for providing direct instruction in sight word recognition that includes some key characteristics of effective teaching. Words are introduced in sentences first and are then isolated so that students may examine them more closely. The steps in the McNinch procedure are as follows:

1. The teacher chooses an unknown sight word and uses it orally in the context of discussion, introducing it to or reinforcing it in the students' oral vocabulary.
2. The teacher presents the word in written context, making sure the new word appears in a sentence with words that are already in the students' sight vocabulary. The teacher reads the sentence and highlights the unknown sight word by underlining, circling, outlining in color, and so on.
3. The new word is isolated from the sentence and read by the teacher, who then asks a series of questions designed to focus students on critical features of the word. For example, students are asked to compare the word to the one in the sentence, to recall how many letters appear in the word, to tell what letter appears in the initial position, and so on.
4. Students read the new words in novel sentences that contain no other unknown words. McNinch applies a *very* strict criterion at this stage of the process. Teacher guidance and feedback are offered until students can read their sentences with 100 percent accuracy.
5. Students apply and practice by reading other materials containing the word(s) for meaningful purposes.
6. Students are then given practice with the word in the form of games designed to achieve mastery of the word.

The McNinch procedure acknowledges that some students might need extraordinary help and focuses on critical aspects of print (see Step 2). Once students have even a small number of words that can be recognized at sight, the instructional program should include large doses of supported practice in ways like those described in the next section.

## Instructional Strategies and Tools: Students with Some Print Skills

As we have already noted, the vast majority of students who are referred with reading difficulties in the area of word recognition have some print skills. The array of teaching strategies is quite varied, because the needs of this group can be diverse.

***Building on the Known: Providing Supported Practice.***   Students with some print skills, no matter how limited, should be supported in using those skills during authentic reading and writing events. This will frequently mean providing extensive scaffolding (see the previous chapters). Although some of this can be provided by careful materials, for the least-skilled readers in the early stages, teachers will need to plan and execute heavily supported reading opportunities. Supported practice allows students to interact with texts that would be too difficult to read independently but that provide important text exposure. There is evidence that supported practice is most effective when students are reading texts that are somewhat challenging for them (Kuhn & Stahl, 2000).

*Assisted Reading Strategies.*   There are any number of variations on supported or *assisted* reading for struggling readers. Some require one-on-one support; others are appropriate for small-group or even whole-group settings. In one of its earliest forms, the impress method (Heckleman, 1969) was conducted with one student in a clinical setting. The teacher reads a designated text with good fluency and moderate rate, and the student chimes in and attempts to keep pace with the teacher's reading. Although successful, this approach is time consuming, and there is little evidence that it is more effective than other assisted reading approaches that can be used in small groups. *Echo reading,* for example, requires only that students emulate (echo) the teacher's reading of a segment of text (B. Anderson, 1981). In *choral reading,* everyone reads together, making it an effective substitute for round-robin oral reading, because the teacher's voice can lead the reading and provide a strong model. As the National Reading Panel (2000, p. 3-111) concluded, "it is evident that with round robin procedures students receive little actual practice in reading because no child is allowed to read for very long."

*Paired and Partner Reading Techniques.*   *Partner,* or *peer, reading* offers additional opportunities to provide supported practice. A variation on the impress method (see above) was designed by Eldredge (1990). Children were paired up, with one student designated the *lead reader* and the other designated the *assisted reader.* The lead reader's job was to read the text fluently, using phrase appropriate phrasing. The partner reading strategy was highly effective for assisted readers; approximately 85 percent of the "poor" readers were able to read grade level material by the end of the school year (as opposed to 19 percent of students who participated in basal reading instruction only. *Paired reading* is a procedure described and evaluated by Topping (1987) that involves parents. The child and parent read together at the same time from a book that the child has selected. When the child feels ready, he or she reads alone. Topping reports significant gains made by students who have participated in a paired reading program, reporting progress three to five times the average on both word recognition and comprehension (Topping, 1987). The activity is meant to be done for approximately 15 minutes every day.

1. Child selects a book to be read.
2. Child and adult read together until the child, using a prearranged signal (e.g., a nudge), indicates that he or she is ready to read alone.
3. The child reads independently until an error is made or a word is encountered that is not read correctly in five seconds.
4. The adult immediately rejoins the child in reading together.
5. Reading together continues until the child gives the signal again, and the procedure is repeated or the session ends.

Parents are encouraged to praise children for appropriate signaling, self-correcting, fluent reading, decoding difficult words independently, and thinking about the story while reading.

The advantages to Topping's paired reading procedure are several. First, the student receives substantial practice with an important person in a low-risk context. Second, the student self selects the reading material, so interest should remain reasonably high. Finally, the procedure can accommodate both extensive support and independent practice.

*Developing Fluency.*  These assisted reading strategies are generally effective in building fluency. Certainly, the repeated reading procedures described in Chapter 12 provide an important base for fluency development. However, adaptations can also be introduced to add additional practice in word identification or to focus and support students' development in this area for struggling readers. For example, a method proposed by Chomsky (1978) involves the student listening to a tape-recorded version of the text while reading along. Then the student practices until he or she can read it fluently.

*Readers' theater* is another strategy that enhances students' fluency (Martinez, Roser, & Strecher, 1999). Readers' theater uses intact stories, not plays, but allows children to perform or interpret through oral reading. The strategy is useful because it provides the critical elements of repeated reading and assistance (feedback and correction) within the framework of a pleasurable group activity.

1. Select stories with a strong story structure, multiple characters, and plenty of dialogue.
2. Either make a script that specifies what the narrator and the various characters say or, preferably, make a copy of the story for each reader and highlight the portions to be read for each child.
3. Read and reread the story until it is ready for presentation.
4. Perform.

It is important to keep this simple. Readers' theater does not involve props or costumes. The focus should be on reading and rereading the material so that it can be effectively shared.

Finally, several researchers have demonstrated that integrating fluency work within the framework of ongoing reading instruction is beneficial. Hoffman (1987), for example, designed an *oral recitation* strategy that is embedded in basal reading lessons:

1. The teacher reads the story aloud.
2. Using echo reading, the teacher and students reread the story.
3. Each child practices reading a different segment of the text until the child can read fluently to the group.
4. The group moves on to a new story.

Like other assisted repeated reading strategies, the oral recitation lesson has been proven effective in developing students' fluency and, in some reports, word recognition ability (see Kuhn & Stahl, 2000).

***Teaching and Extending Word Analysis.***    Systematic and carefully planned instruction is important in word analysis. Many students need explicit instruction in substituting initial consonants and consonant clusters as they create rhyming patterns and work with phonograms (see Figure 13.3). However, there is generally no magic in the exact sequence or program. What does seem to be especially potent is the decoding-by-analogy strategy that has been well documented (see Adams, 1990; Cunningham, 1975–76; Gaskins et al., 1996/1997), although children are not likely to benefit from this strategy until they have reasonable control over vowel and consonant sounds (Juel & Minden-Cupp, 2000). Clearly, mature readers decode unknown words by relating them to spelling patterns in words they do know. For example, skilled readers might think of known words *paint* or *faint* when encountering the unknown word *tainted.* As Cunningham (1995, p. 57) explains, "Children who learn many common word families also learn something more important—to look carefully at the spelling pattern of a new word and search through the words they already know for words with the same pattern." As we will see. this tack also helps students become good spellers.

Students will need to be introduced to word families or phonograms. Lists are available from many sources (see, e.g., Cunningham, 1995), but all include recurrent spelling patterns such as the following:

| | | | | |
|---|---|---|---|---|
| bed | rain | cake | kick | boat |
| red | gain | rake | pick | coat |
| fed | pain | fake | tick | goat |
| led | chain | brake | chick | moat |

*The Benchmark Word Identification Program* (Gaskins, Gaskins, & Gaskins, 1992) is a program designed to capitalize on this approach. Students are gradually taught a set of 120 key words representing examples of these spelling patterns. At the same time, students are taught a compare/contrast strategy that relies on their ability to delete initial phonemes and substitute others. When they come to an unknown word, students are taught to examine its spelling pattern (or rime) and then refer to the previously taught key word (e.g., *make* for

**FIGURE 13.3**
Sample Word
Analysis Lessons

| A Demonstration Lesson on Initial Consonant Clusters | |
| --- | --- |
| Instructional Steps | Lesson for *cl-cl/* |
| 1. Review the initial sound. | 1. Ask the children to identify the initial sound in "can" and "cup." |
| 2. Review the other phoneme. | 2. Ask the children to identify the initial sound in "loud" and "lap." |
| 3. Provide auditory experiences having combined consonant phonemes. | 3. Ask the children to listen to the combined sound in "cloud," "clam," "close," etc. |
| 4. Provide visual identification. | 4. Present the children with the written words "cloud," "clam," "close," etc., and have the youngsters identify graphic similarities. |
| 5. Ask the children to find *cl* words in their word banks. | 5. Have the children supply new examples. |
| 6. Present new *cl* words in sentence context. | 6. Apply new concepts to new words. |
| **A Demonstration Lesson for Phonograms** | |
| Instructional Steps | Lesson for *cl-an* |
| 1. Present known words in a pattern. | 1. Remind children that they know the words "pan" and "Dan." |
| 2. Recognize rhyme and graphic similarity. | 2. Encourage children to identify two common elements of -an: rhyme and letters. |
| 3. Make a new word. | 3. Write "fan": have the children identify graphic similarity; have them use rhyming and pronounce the word. |
| 4. Supply new and additional words. | 4. Let the children suggest another word like "man," and then have them search for more examples from their word banks. |
| 5. Make application to new words. | 5. Have each child pronounce new words: for example, "ran" and "tan." |

*Source:* From *Development of Language and Literacy in Young Children* by Susanna W. Pflaum. Copyright ©
1986 by Bell & Howell Company. Reprinted by permission of Pearson Education, Inc., Upper Saddle River, NJ..

*rake*) that represents the same spelling pattern. Using the strategy, students are taught to make
analogies. Their self-talk looks like this: "*Rake* has the same spelling pattern as *make*. If
m-a-k-e is *make,* then r-a-k-e must be *rake.*" Recently, the program has been adapted in two
ways. A second version of the original program has been revised so that it provides more
explicit instruction in letter–sound analysis in the earliest stages (see Gaskins et al.,
1996/1997). In this program, *Word Detectives: Benchmark Word Identification Program for*

*Beginning Readers,* students examine key words carefully, spelling and writing the words so that the orthographic patterns are well established. This type of instruction and that revealed in Figure 13.3 should, of course, be followed closely (or accompanied) by ample opportunities to read and write.

## Instructional Strategies and Tools: Print Skills for More Advanced Readers

Students who are generally skilled in word identification but who have specialized difficulties are often among the most difficult to instruct. Both students and teachers are frequently confused about where to focus attention. Indeed, there are several possible reasons for such difficulties. Students might not have acquired a balanced repertoire of word recognition and word analysis skills, or they might have difficulty using both word analysis and meaning-based strategies together. Alternatively, students might not have gained control over reading, especially reading that involves complex materials with a significant number of multisyllabic words. Of course, students might not have adequate meaning vocabulary, an issue that we will take up in the next chapter (see Chapter 14).

*Multisyllabic and Content Words.*    Cunningham (1975–76, 1979) used the same compare/contrast strategy described above to promote word identification of multisyllabic words. By being taught to make analogies with known words (see above), elementary school children (grades 2–5) improved their ability to read unfamiliar words and to transfer this knowledge to reading two-syllable words. The compare/contrast technique proceeds as follows:

1. Familiar sight words are placed on cards for students to manipulate.
2. Using these word cards, students are taught to compare and contrast known two-syllable words to known one-syllable words that rhyme with individual syllables of the two-syllable words (e.g., *banter—can, her*).
3. Students practice pronouncing the polysyllabic word and the two separate words.
4. Students practice the technique, adding other known sight words to cards for manipulation and matching them to additional two-syllable words.
5. Students receive extensive practice in executing this matching in their heads, without cards.
6. The technique is expanded to three-syllable words.

The great advantage of this technique is that it depends on flexible application of the analogy strategy. Students do not need to learn rules, but rather learn to approximate words, using sound and sense together. In the National Reading Panel's synthesis of phonics programs, this type of instruction was among the only successful approaches for older, struggling readers (Lovett & Steinbach, 1997).

Of course, more advanced students readers are often unclear about either the syllabic or morphemic boundaries of words (see the section on spelling later in this chapter). Teaching students some basic syllabication patterns can often be helpful (see Figure 13.4). Shefelbine (1991) suggests working with syllable transformations to help students gain flexibility with longer words. He advocates teaching "transformation syllables," which are basically sets of open and closed syllables such as su/suf and flo/flom, and word parts, which are generally morphemes. Students then engage in word-building activities, constructing such words as *establishment, standardization,* and *digestible.* Vogt (1999) reports that this approach, one of the few strategies specifically designed for young adolescents, was motivating for students. In addition, they were more likely to attempt unknown, multisyllabic words. We

**FIGURE 13.4**
Syllable Types
and Patterns

| The Six Most Common Types of Syllable | |
|---|---|
| Type | Example |
| open | Open syllables end with a single vowel and make the long sound of that vowel: go, ba/by |
| closed | In a closed syllable, a single vowel is followed by a consonant and the vowel sound is short: met, lot/to |
| r-controlled | This is a specialized form of the closed syllable in which the vowel is followed and "controlled" by the "r": farm, bor/der |
| vowel combinations | In these syllables, vowel combinations (dipthongs and digraphs) make one sound, which may be long (sea/son), short (read/y), or a dipthong (pound) |
| vowel–silent e | These syllables involve vowel–consonant–silent e, and the first vowel is typically long |
| consonant–le | In syllables that end in -le, the consonant accompanies the -le and produces the schwa sound (unaccented vowel): battle, ruble |

| Common Syllable Patterns | |
|---|---|
| Pattern | Example |
| VCCV | Words with this pattern are divided VC/CV: bon/net, tab/let |
| VCV | Words with this pattern are usually divided V/CV: mo/tor, ba/by. Sometimes the words are divided VC/V as in rap/id |
| VCCCV | Words with this pattern typically contain a consonant blend or digraph. The word is divided before the consonant combination if it involves a blend: pil/grim. If, however, the combination is a digraph, it is usually divided after: laugh/ter |
| VV | When two vowels adjoin, but are not vowel teams, each vowel produces a sound: li/on, fu/el |

*Source:* Adapted from *Words Their Way,* 2nd edition, by D. R. Bear, M. Invernizzi, S. Templeton, & F. Johnston. Englewood Cliffs, NJ: Prentice Hall.

will return to this issue in Chapter 14 when we consider morphological analysis in vocabulary development.

***Teaching Strategies for Independence.***    Some students need to be taught how to approach and analyze multisyllabic words, but others need help in pulling together the skills and strategies they already know. They need to be encouraged to become independent. There is growing evidence that struggling intermediate and middle grade students benefit from strategy instruction (V. Anderson, Chan, & Henne, 1995).

*Guide for Attacking Unknown Words.*    Students, even very young ones, should be encouraged to attain some degree of independence and control in using their existing knowledge and skill. Most authors recommend teaching students a general strategy for word recognition and helping them to use it regularly during reading of connected text. The following steps seem reasonable:

1. Look at all the letters from left to right.
2. As you look at the letters, look for words parts you know:
   - For one-syllable words, compare the word to other known words: CVC, CVCe, CVVC.
   - For two-syllable words, identify the parts and compare each syllable to a known word: CVC + CVC.
   - For words with more than one morpheme, identify the root and then add the affixes.
3. Use the sound-plus-sense strategy. (Get an approximation by sound–symbol, and then monitor to make sure it makes sense.) Correct or adapt, using the context of the sentence.
4. If the word is important and you're still not sure, ask someone.

As is the case with any aspect of reading competence, independence in word identification takes substantial time and effort to accomplish on the part of both readers and teachers. Sometimes students need a copy of this guide to refer to until the steps become automatic. Teachers should teach this type of independent strategy just as carefully as they teach students the component skills.

*Student Monitoring and Highlighting.*    Many less-skilled readers have difficulty transferring and coordinating their word analysis skills. In addition (perhaps consequently), they often have trouble attending to the meaningfulness of text. Pflaum and Pascarella (1980) developed a program designed to help students monitor their reading miscues, paying particular attention to those that distort meaning. In addition, these authors taught students to correct these miscues to retain meaning.

Reinforcing the developmental nature of some reading abilities, the program improved the reading level of learning disabled students (ages 8–13) but only if they had previously attained a reading level of second grade or higher. Thus, it appears that explicit training in monitoring and repair strategies may depend for its success on a certain level of word identification ability.

An important part of the program is that students were informed about what they were learning and the teacher discussed when to use the strategy in their own reading. The activities were modeled by the teacher, students received guided practice at each step, and then they received help in applying the strategy to their own reading.

Students received instruction in two phases; half of the lessons focused on helping students to identify miscues that affect meaning, and half focused on teaching students to self-correct miscues. During the first set of lessons students listen to an audiotape of a child who is making miscues. Students are repeatedly advised to think about whether a miscue (substitution) is "serious" (meaning-changing) or not. Specifically, the program involves the following steps:

1. Students listen to ten sentences, underlining the miscue made in each.
2. Students read five short paragraphs, underlining the two miscues in each. They discuss the seriousness of each miscue, using meaning change as the criterion.
3. Students read an instructional selection and record their own performance.
4. Students listen to their tape, underlining their own miscues. They then practice reading and recording additional passages until they reach 70 percent accuracy in noting miscues.
5. Students again listen to five short recorded paragraphs, underlining "serious" miscues twice. Students underline miscues once that do not distort meaning.
6. Students repeat Step 5 using their own recorded reading (underline serious miscues twice and less serious miscues once).

In the second set of lessons, students focus on learning to self-correct miscues that do not make sense. They are taught to use both context and graphophonic cues to self-correct.

1. Students listen to an audiotaped child, marking that child's self-corrections on a worksheet copy of the text.
2. Students discuss the self-corrections, noting especially the technique used to self-correct and the reason underlying the self-correction (e.g., "that doesn't make sense").
3. Students practice and discuss replacements for blanks in fifteen sentences (use context).
4. Students practice choosing replacement words using initial letter cues, then final letter cues.
5. Students continue practice, first listing possible words for a cloze replacement (using only context), then narrowing the choices using first initial letter information, then finally letter information.
6. Students read their own material, record it, and analyze their own miscues and self-corrections. Students are taught to correct uncorrected miscues as they listen by stopping the tape.

# Instructional Techniques Focused on Spelling

Instructional recommendations for students who are experiencing spelling difficulty parallel those for word recognition in important ways. First, spelling ability is developmental in nature. Second, the specific strategies for developing spelling ability include provisions for both explicit instruction and ample opportunities for practice.

## Instructional Focus at Various Developmental Spelling Levels

It will be no surprise to teachers that a great many students who are struggling readers are also having trouble in spelling. Many of the recommendations just suggested for instruction in word recognition will inevitably aid spelling also. Indeed, Templeton (1995) has made a persuasive case for the mutuality of word recognition and spelling instruction:

> Words need to be examined in their own right. The resulting development and understanding of underlying spelling structures will guide rapid and efficient word identification in reading as well as more rapid spelling of words in writing. This is particularly true for struggling readers. (Templeton, 1995, p. 317)

As we have already noted, reading and writing ability and knowledge are closely aligned in the earliest stages and ages of literacy development. As they progress, these abilities diverge somewhat. In the struggling reader, however, the underlying phonological and orthographic knowledge required is quite similar. The developmental overlap between word identification and spelling ability is made clear by this progression. In addition, the knowledge (both phonological and orthographic) that students must acquire at various stages clearly fuels both word identification and spelling abilities.

Templeton (1995) recommends that teachers plan their instructional program around a core list or group of words and that spelling patterns be identified that relate to the various spelling levels of students. In Figure 13.5 the instructional content of a developmental spelling program is fully described.

To be useful, however, teachers must have a clear sense of students' needs. Templeton (1995; Bear et al., 2000) has described a progression of spelling, or orthographic knowledge, that provides excellent guidance for spelling assessment (see Chapter 9). Using that information and the content descriptions in Figure 13.5, teachers can plan the appropriate program for struggling students. If students are regularly trying to memorize words that are too difficult for them, they may be successful on the posttest, but they will continue to spell words incorrectly at point of use.

## Instructional Strategies and Tools for Spelling

Specialized spelling instruction, like word recognition instruction, should take place within the context of a literacy program that includes effective overall instruction. That means first and foremost that students are encouraged to write continuously for a variety of purposes.

**FIGURE 13.5** Spelling Features That Are Examined at Each Developmental Phase

## Letter Name

1. Students should be guided to examine and to learn the correct spelling of selected words they are being taught to read.
2. Through activities involving recognition, grouping, substitution, and spelling, beginning consonant elements are examined in the following order: single consonants, common consonant digraphs, and common blends.
3. Short vowel patterns (phonograms) are examined systematically.
4. "Continuant" or nasal consonants that precede other types of consonants are examined (wi*n*ter, ca*m*p).
5. The most common long vowel patterns, or phonograms, are examined (m*a*ke, r*i*de). A phonogram is the vowel and what follows within a single syllable.

## Within-Word Pattern

1. Additional common long vowel patterns are examined (/ā/ in b*ai*t, w*ei*ght; /ī/ in l*i*ght; /ē/ in m*ea*t, fr*ee*ze).
2. R- and l-influenced vowel patterns are studied (c*ar*d, f*er*n, f*a*ll, p*u*ll).
3. Common diphthongs are introduced (h*ow*, b*oi*l).
4. Compound words are studied.
5. Through the examination of common homophones, students begin to develop an awareness of the meaning principle in spelling.

## Syllable Junction

1. Common and less frequent vowel patterns in stressed syllables continue to be examined.
2. Common inflections and the ways in which they are joined to base words are examined (-*ed*, -*ing*, -*ly*).
3. The sound and the meaning of common prefixes and suffixes are analyzed (*un-, re-, -ment, -ness*).
4. The role of stress or accent is introduced in the context of homographs.
5. Unstressed syllables are examined, first in two-syllable words and later in polysyllabic words.
6. More complex prefixes and suffixes are examined.
7. The principle of consonant doubling is examined as it applies to a broader range of vocabulary.

## Derivational Patterns: The Spelling-Meaning Combination

1. Silent and sounded consonant patterns are studied (colum*n*/colum*n*ist, resi*g*n/resi*g*nation).
2. Considerable attention is given to the different vowel alternation patterns, sequenced for study as follows:
   a. Long-to-short (extr*e*me/extr*e*mity, rev*i*se/rev*i*sion)
   b. Long-to-schwa (infl*a*me/infl*a*mmation, def*i*ne/def*i*nition)
   c. Short-to-schwa (ex*ce*l/ex*ce*llent, l*e*gal/l*e*gality)
   d. Predictable sound/spelling alternation (consume/consumption, receive/reception)
3. While the vowel-alternation patterns are studied, other accompanying consonant alternation patterns are examined:
   a. Sound change/spelling stable (musi*c*/musi*c*ian, constitu*t*e/constitu*t*ion)
   b. Predictable sound/spelling alternation (explo*d*e/explo*s*ion, absen*t*/absen*c*e, permi*t*/permi*ss*ion)
4. The role of Greek and Latin forms in spelling and in meaning is explored.
5. "Absorbed" or "assimilated" prefixes are examined (*ad* + tract = *at*tract; *in* + luminate = *il*luminate).

It also means that there are explicit conversations that encourage students to note patterns and orthographic regularities.

***Spelling and Writing.***    In the context of a rich writing community there will be many opportunities to use invented spelling, where appropriate, and to attend more closely to conventional spellings as work is edited and revised for publication. At least some of the spelling words that struggling writers are learning should be drawn from their own writing, although few teachers find that they can plan their entire spelling program using this individualized approach.

Spelling instruction can become more visible during writing in the following ways:

1. Create charts and/or lists of commonly misspelled words in a central place for students to refer to. Alternatively, have students create a word wall on which they place words that they use often and that others would find helpful.
2. Use mini-lessons to highlight specific spelling difficulties, particularly when these revolve around various patterns (i.e., phonograms at the earliest levels and rules for adding affixes at the upper levels).
3. When students request a spelling for a word, do not provide it out loud. Instead, either write it down (requiring the student to compare/contrast as she or he rewrites it) or encourage use of the dictionary, when appropriate.
4. Encourage students to write first and worry about spelling later. But later, be sure to offer good support for editing.
5. Encourage students to use what they know. This means spelling by analogy with known words and it also means writing two or three versions of the word to see which one "looks right". There is evidence to suggest that both strategies improve spelling (Templeton, 1995).

Even with a strong writing program, many students need additional attention to spelling (Ganske, 2000). As Henderson (1990, p. 92) has noted, "writing provides sound exercise of spelling knowledge but only modest information for a memorized spelling vocabulary."

***Word Sorts.***    The word sort strategy (described in Chapter 12) has already been suggested for assessment. It can also have powerful instructional value. Of course, when used for spelling, instruction will focus on the orthographic structure of the words and on recurrent spelling patterns. Most researchers agree that struggling spellers do not attend closely enough to the print display and, as a result, do not acquire the sensitivity to patterns that good spellers have.

Both the words selected and the directions for sorting will, of course, vary by developmental level (see Bear et al., 2000; Ganske, 2000). For example, as students move into the "within-word pattern" stage of spelling development, word sorts might include words such as *make, train, state,* and *paint.* Such words will encourage students to distinguish the spelling (orthographic) pattern from the sound (phonological) appearance of the words.

***Spelling Lists.***   There are a number of lists from which teachers might choose a master spelling list. Indeed, the words in most commercial programs are selected from such reasonable sources as high-frequency word lists and/or lists of common elements (Henderson, 1990). A relatively small number of words (5,000) accounts for 95 percent of all the words that adults use in writing, so, of course, it makes sense to encourage children to acquire these spellings.

Two guidelines should guide a teacher's use of spelling lists. First, students must be able to read the words. If they cannot, they will not retain their spellings even if they do well on weekly tests. Similarly, the list should contain words that relate to the relative spelling knowledge (stage of development) that has most currency for that child. Second, there is considerable evidence that students should correct their own pretest spellings using a compare/contrast method (Henderson, 1990). This dramatically improves the likelihood that the spelling will be retained.

# A Final Note

In summary, what teachers must do is help students develop the ability to tell when a word "looks right" (see Cunningham, 2000). Both experience and direct instruction will probably be required for students with reading and writing difficulties to accomplish this.

Classroom teachers and clinical teachers must be especially careful to provide coherent word recognition, word analysis, and spelling instruction to children who are struggling to master print skills. These students are most likely to receive fragmented instruction with a heavy emphasis on isolated skills. Indeed, many of the specialized commercial programs on the market are designed to provide instruction in the components of sound–symbol correspondence to the exclusion of meaningful practice. Although some of these programs and materials may be useful tools in the hands of a knowledgeable teacher, they certainly should not be mistaken for a total reading/literacy program.

# Chapter Summary

In this chapter we reexamined the components of word recognition and spelling ability and discussed several issues related to teaching word-level instruction. In particular, we described the debate surrounding the appropriate way to help students acquire effective word analysis strategies, noting that views have tended to be polarized. Some educators argue that word identification strategies will not be acquired without direct instruction; others argue that they cannot be taught at all unless students are helped to learn them as they engage in extensive reading and writing in meaningful settings. Similar, though less strident, arguments have surrounded spelling instruction. Recent advances in knowledge and expertise permit a balanced perspective that acknowledges the importance of both positions. There are at least three stages in the acquisition of word identification and spelling competence, and instructional approaches will be most beneficial if teachers differentiate among students who have no conventional print skills, students who have some ability to recognize words, and students with more advanced knowledge and skill in this area.

In the next major section of the chapter we provided guidelines for teaching word-level skills to students. We emphasized the importance of providing instruction in service to meaningful activity, reminding teachers that the goal of instruction should be improved fluency during reading and writing, not better knowledge and skill of phonics or spelling. In addition, we pointed out that instruction should help students to recognize familiar patterns in words; it appears that this is a particularly effective approach to the teaching both word analysis and spelling. In the final portion of the chapter we provided instructional techniques and strategies for word recognition and then for spelling. The word recognition strategies were divided into three categories, paralleling the three developmental stages of word recognition described earlier. We described techniques for embedding word analysis instruction in meaningful book experiences, and we described two direct instruction models for teaching word identification. For students with some print skills we described ways to improve students' fluency and instructional frames for teaching students to extend and consolidate their word recognition abilities. For students with more advanced skills we described some ways to help them become more facile in attacking multisyllabic words and ways to teach students to be somewhat more independent in their word reading abilities.

Finally, in a section of instructional strategies for spelling, we reviewed the developmental nature of spelling, suggested content for each level, and described several strategies that have proved effective in addressing the spelling difficulties of some students.

# 14 Adapting Instruction to Focus on Vocabulary

Words help us organize life experiences, because they represent ideas or concepts in the environment and the interrelationships among those concepts (Searfoss & Readence, 1989). As such, words facilitate our thinking processes. Reading and writing are thinking processes; therefore it is not surprising that vocabulary is a prime contributor to effective reading and writing. Text cannot be understood unless the meanings of most of the words are known, nor can it be created without a large store of vocabulary knowledge.

A wealth of research has demonstrated a strong relationship between vocabulary and reading comprehension (Nagy & Scott, 2000). For example, Davis (1968) found that word knowledge was the single most important factor that accounted for variability in comprehension. Similarly, the proportion of difficult words in a text has been found to be the single most powerful predictor of text difficulty, and a reader's general vocabulary knowledge is one of the best predictors of how well that reader can understand text (R. C. Anderson & Freebody, 1981; Nagy, 1988).

As Nagy (1988) points out, the lack of adequate vocabulary knowledge is already a serious obstacle to literacy for many students, and the numbers can be expected to rise as an increasing proportion of students fall into categories whose members are considered educationally at risk. For example, there is some evidence that the reading difficulties of students in the United States with limited English proficiency may be related directly to vocabulary knowledge (Garcia 1991, 1993). At the same time advances in knowledge are creating an ever-larger pool of concepts and words that a person must master to be literate and employable. As a result, considerable attention to vocabulary and teaching students to derive word meanings and attach personal associations to them is vital to instruction at all levels and to success in reading, writing, and learning.

The first half of this chapter discusses the issues surrounding the discussion about when and how vocabulary should be taught. In addition, goals and guidelines for vocabulary instruction are presented. The second half of the chapter describes instructional techniques that correspond to these established goals and guidelines. First, we present basic strategies for independent vocabulary learning during reading and methods for teaching the techniques needed to support these strategies. Second, we describe techniques for providing direct instruction of key terms related to students' assigned reading. Finally, we discuss methods for promoting general vocabulary development and building interest in vocabulary learning that have relevance for success in both reading and writing.

# Understanding Vocabulary Instruction

This section of the chapter discusses the issues related to when and how vocabulary should be taught and presents goals and guidelines for vocabulary instruction.

## Issues

Although there is widespread consensus that vocabulary knowledge is fundamental to comprehension and composition, there is some debate about when and how vocabulary should be taught. The issues surrounding this controversy are summarized in the following discussion.

***Direct Instruction versus Incidental Learning.***    The debate about the best way to develop students' vocabulary focuses on the question of the degree to which learners develop vocabulary through incidental learning as they are exposed to unfamiliar words in context, as opposed to direct instruction. Nagy, Herman, and Anderson (1985) have argued that direct instruction in specific words is a slow and inefficient method of vocabulary development and that incidental learning is the primary source of vocabulary growth (see also Fielding, Wilson, & Anderson, 1986). Nagy (1988) makes the case for incidental learning as follows. Very few people have received the type of intensive and prolonged vocabulary instruction that would guarantee gains in reading comprehension. However, many people have acquired extensive vocabularies. Few vocabulary programs, no matter how ambitious, cover more than several hundred words a year. Yet research indicates that the vocabularies of school-aged students grow at the rate of 3,000 new words each year (Nagy & Herman, 1987). Nagy (1988) acknowledges that a single encounter with a word does not provide in-depth knowledge. However, he also maintains that because "many people do develop in-depth knowledge of large numbers of words apart from much vocabulary instruction, wide reading must be able to produce the kind of word knowledge necessary for reading comprehension" (Nagy, 1988, p. 31).

In contrast, others have argued that direct instruction in vocabulary is essential for good vocabulary growth (*Put Reading First,* 2001; Stahl & Kapinus, 2001). For example, a review by Stahl and Fairbanks (1986) concluded that over the long term, students who were taught word meanings significantly outperformed students who were not given instruction, indicating that sustained attention to vocabulary may produce better comprehension. According to this view, the process of learning new words incidentally through repeated exposures in context is a slow and difficult method of vocabulary development.

The research cited in support of direct instruction indicates that skilled readers frequently skip over unfamiliar words as they read (Freebody & Anderson, 1983) and that intermediate-grade students are not very skilled at using context to determine the meanings of unfamiliar words (Carnine, Kameenui, & Coyle, 1984). In addition, it has been found that certain unfamiliar words are learned better through direct instruction than through incidental exposures in reading material (Beck, McKeown, & McCaslin, 1983; Omanson, Beck, McKeown, & Perfetti, 1984).

***Contradictory Conclusions.*** Nagy (1988) presents the apparent contradiction regarding the degree of in-depth vocabulary knowledge necessary for comprehension as follows. On the one hand, it appears that comprehension of text depends on more in-depth knowledge than simply knowing the definitions of words. This implies that in at least some cases, vocabulary instruction must be rich enough to teach students new concepts in depth. An extreme response to this point of view might be to devote large portions of the school day to intensive vocabulary instruction. On the other hand, it appears that comprehension of text does not require in-depth knowledge of *every word* in the text. Indeed, reading itself is the major avenue of acquiring in-depth knowledge of words. An extreme response to this point of view would be to abandon vocabulary instruction in favor of increased reading time.

According to Nagy (1988), this contradiction is more apparent than real. If students are to achieve both the depth and the breadth of vocabulary knowledge that they need to become proficient adult readers and writers, a balance between direct instruction and incidental learning is clearly necessary. Most growth in vocabulary knowledge must necessarily come through reading, because there is no way that vocabulary instruction alone can provide enough experiences with enough words to produce the necessary depth and breadth of vocabulary knowledge. Increasing the amount of students' reading is the single most important thing a teacher can do to promote large-scale vocabulary growth. However, vocabulary instruction is also necessary in cases in which context does not provide essential information and knowledge of specific words is crucial to comprehension.

Teachers should also guide students in the development of strategies that promote independent word learning. There is no doubt that skilled word learners use context and their knowledge of word parts to deal effectively with new words. Independent word learning is enhanced when these techniques are taught as strategies by modeling how the knowledge of context and word parts can be used to determine the meanings of unfamiliar words encountered while reading and by providing ample opportunity for guided practice in the use of these strategies.

***When Direct Instruction Is Appropriate.*** Direct vocabulary instruction is needed to produce in-depth word knowledge. However, because only a fraction of the potentially unfamiliar words in a text can be taught directly, we need to determine when this type of instruction is most appropriate.

Direct vocabulary instruction is most appropriate for conceptually complex words that are not likely to be part of the students' everyday experience (Nagy, 1988). In addition, direct instruction is most worthwhile when the words to be taught are important to the understanding of the central ideas in the reading selection and to language development in general.

According to Nagy (1988) the single most important question for the teacher who is trying to determine when direct instruction is most appropriate is which words are likely to be conceptually difficult for the reader. Furthermore, the conceptual difficulty of the entire text, not just the individual words, must be taken into account in determining when direct instruction is necessary. Finally, the greater the proportion of unfamiliar words in a text, the more intensive is the instruction that is required to improve comprehension.

In terms of the most effective means of direct instruction, reviews of the literature indicate that not all types of vocabulary instruction result in improved reading comprehension (Mezynski, 1983; Stahl & Fairbanks, 1986). Nagy (1988) suggests that one reason vocabulary instruction often fails to increase comprehension is that it does not produce in-depth word knowledge. At a minimum, in-depth vocabulary knowledge involves at least two types of information about words: definitional information and contextual information (Stahl & Kapinus, 2001). Definitional information refers to the knowledge of the logical relations between a word and other known words as provided in dictionary definitions. Contextual information refers to knowledge of the core concept the word represents and how that core concept changes in different contexts (Stahl, 1986).

A large proportion of vocabulary instruction involves the use of definitions: some combination of looking them up, writing them down, and memorizing them. Stahl and Fairbanks (1986) report that when these approaches are used alone, they have no significant effect on comprehension. Nagy (1988, p. 7) suggests that definitional approaches fail because "reading comprehension depends on a wealth of encyclopedic knowledge and not merely on definitional knowledge of the words in the text."

Another commonly used method involves teaching students to infer the meaning of a new word from the context. Again, Stahl and Fairbanks (1986) report that when a word is used only in context without the definition, there are no significant effects on comprehension. The biggest problem with contextual approaches appears to be that although a context might appear to be quite helpful to those who already know what the word means, it rarely supplies adequate information for those who have no other knowledge about the meaning of a word (Nagy, 1988).

It appears that neither definitional nor contextual methods, taken by themselves, are especially effective ways to improve reading comprehension (Nagy, 1988). Stahl and Fairbanks (1986) report that the strongest effects are found when there is a combined emphasis on definitional and contextual information or when the balance is tipped toward contextual information. However, Nagy (1988) maintains that supplying both definitions and contexts does not necessarily guarantee gains in reading comprehension; rather, "methods of vocabulary instruction that most effectively improve comprehension of text containing the instructed words go far beyond providing definitions and context. Such methods can be referred to as intensive vocabulary instruction" (Nagy, 1988, p. 9).

## Goals

Given the evidence regarding what, when, and why vocabulary instruction is desirable, it appears that we need multiple goals for engaging students in activities designed to increase their vocabulary knowledge (Blachowicz & Fisher, 2002). The following are three primary goals for vocabulary instruction:

1.  *Teach independent vocabulary learning.* Our first goal is to teach students strategies to learn vocabulary independently as they read. We cannot possibly teach students all the unfamiliar words they will encounter in the course of their reading; however, we can provide them with a repertoire of strategies that will enable them to identify and learn the meanings of unfamiliar words as they read.
2.  *Teach concepts important for comprehension.* Our second goal is to teach directly those concepts that are essential for comprehending specific written materials. It is important to provide intensive vocabulary instruction when in-depth knowledge of complex

concepts is critical to the understanding of reading assignments, because it is unlikely that this level of knowledge can be obtained by the student independently from context.

3. *Create an environment that promotes general vocabulary development.* Our third goal is to promote general vocabulary development by providing a vocabulary-rich environment with frequent opportunities to learn through reading and writing. Because a major factor distinguishing between more- and less-skilled readers and writers is their level of vocabulary knowledge, a primary goal of instruction must be the continual development and expansion of students' vocabulary knowledge.

In short, we need vocabulary instruction that teaches students strategies for acquiring new vocabulary as they read and write and increases their knowledge of both general vocabulary and vocabulary specific to their reading materials.

## Guidelines

To accomplish the goals set forward in the previous section, research suggests that vocabulary instruction must embody the characteristics outlined in the following guidelines.

*Guideline 1: Relate the New to the Known.*   The first property of powerful vocabulary instruction is that it integrates knowledge of instructed words with other, previously acquired knowledge. This emphasis in instruction is an outgrowth of schema theory which has shown us that knowledge is structured into sets of relationships, and we understand new information by relating it to what we already know (Nagy, 1988).

Vocabulary instruction is effective when it helps students relate new vocabulary to their previous experience. In the case of limited-English-proficient students it appears that relating unknown English vocabulary to known Spanish words with obvious orthographic and semantic similarities is likely to overcome problems with English reading vocabulary (Garcia, 1993). By relating the new to the known, new vocabulary becomes personally meaningful, and students' understanding is enhanced in ways that lead to increased skill in reading and writing. This practice also leads to improved learning and retention of the meanings of new words.

*Guideline 2: Promote Active, In-Depth Processing.*   Effective vocabulary instruction involves students in constructing the meanings of new words. This principle can be related to the depth-of-processing framework used in memory research (cf. Craik & Lockhart, 1972). This framework suggests that the harder one "works" to process information to be learned, the better is one's retention. For example, retention will be better if one works to construct a relationship rather than simply memorizing a stated relationship.

Stahl (1986) identifies three levels of processing for vocabulary instruction. The first level is *association processing.* At this level a student simply learns an association for a word, such as a synonym or a particular context. At the second level, *comprehension processing,* the student applies a learned association to demonstrate understanding of the word. This involves doing something with the association, such as finding an antonym, fitting the word into a sentence, or classifying the word that requires the student to go beyond just giving back the association or something similar. The third level, *generation processing,* involves taking the comprehended association and generating a novel product using it. This product could be a restatement of the definition in one's own words, comparing the definition to one's own experiences, making up a novel sentence that demonstrates the word's meaning clearly, and so on.

These three increasingly deep levels of processing produce increasingly strong effects on comprehension. When students are actively processing information about each word's meaning, their comprehension of texts using those words improves. Generation could involve having students make their own sentence or definitions, developing semantic maps, breaking words down into semantic features, and so forth. What appears to be most important is not only that learners comprehend a word's meaning, but also that they take that comprehension one step farther and make the word their own by interacting with it (Stahl & Kapinus, 2001).

***Guideline 3: Provide Multiple Exposures.***    Another important factor for vocabulary instruction to affect comprehension is the number of times the student is exposed to a word and what types of information are given each time. According to Kapinus and Stahl (2001), providing the student with multiple repetitions of the same information about each word's meaning and providing the student with multiple exposures to the word in different contexts or settings both significantly improve comprehension. Providing only one or two exposures to a word does not have a positive effect on comprehension.

It is also important to recognize that limited or superficial knowledge of word meanings can have a detrimental effect on comprehension (Nagy, 1988). Being able to identify or produce a correct definition for a word does not guarantee that one will be able to access its meaning quickly and effortlessly during reading. Vocabulary instruction must therefore ensure not only that readers know what the word means, but also that they have had sufficient practice using it to make its meaning quickly and easily accessible during reading. In short, it appears that both the amount of time and the way time is spent in vocabulary instruction have a measurable effect on reading comprehension.

***Guideline 4: Teach Students to Be Strategic.***    Effective vocabulary instruction teaches students to be strategic in their acquisition of new vocabulary. Students need to understand how to learn the meanings of new words they encounter in oral and written communication. This guideline can be related to the concept of a strategic reader as described by Paris, Lipson, and Wixson (1983). Strategic readers are those who are responsible for their knowledge, cognizant of that responsibility, and motivated to learn. In the context of vocabulary instruction, being strategic includes awareness of a variety of methods to acquire word meanings, the ability to monitor one's understanding of new vocabulary, and the capacity to change or modify strategies for understanding new words if comprehension is not forthcoming.

Teachers can help students become more strategic by teaching different methods of vocabulary learning as strategies rather than as isolated activities. This type of instruction involves modeling and explanation of how particular techniques can help students deal with unfamiliar words encountered while reading, and providing ample opportunity for guided practice, using these strategies with authentic materials.

## Summary

In this first section of the chapter we describe several key issues in understanding vocabulary instruction. We conclude that vocabulary instruction requires careful reflection, since neither direct instruction nor incidental learning accounts for the complex interplay of learning, vocabulary, and comprehension issues. However, it is possible to conclude that wide reading contributes to vocabulary learning in important ways and that direct instruction in vocabulary can improve students' word knowledge under some circumstances. To be effective, vocabulary instruction must foster independence and focus on conceptually difficult words that are central to understanding the reading selection.

# Strategies for Vocabulary Instruction

This section of the chapter describes instructional techniques that correspond to the three goals of vocabulary instruction presented previously. First, we present basic strategies students can learn to use during reading and methods for teaching the techniques needed to support these strategies. Second, we describe techniques for providing direct instruction in specific target words related to students' assigned reading. Finally, we discuss methods for promoting general vocabulary development and building interest in vocabulary learning. The various strategies and techniques adhere to the guidelines presented previously. They focus on relating the new to the known, promoting active, in-depth processing, providing repeated exposures, and promoting the acquisition of independent learning strategies.

## A General Framework for Independent Vocabulary Learning

Consistent with our first goal for vocabulary instruction, we are concerned here with the ways in which we can provide the student(s) with a general framework or strategy that can be used independently to identify and learn unknown words during reading. This means that we need to teach them how to employ this type of strategy or framework. To this end, we describe here a general framework for independent vocabulary learning, a specific strategy for implementing this framework, and several techniques that can be used to support the development of the students' ability to use this framework.

The framework described below requires intentional effort and is designed to address vocabulary learning explicitly. The use of such a framework is necessary if vocabulary acquisition in new areas of study is to become habituated.

***Phases of the Framework.*** The general framework we recommend has four phases that involve different types of reading/thinking activities:

Phase 1: Reading and identifying unknown vocabulary and activating prior knowledge regarding the words in relation to the reading

Phase 2: Applying a repertoire of techniques to identify and learn the meanings of the unfamiliar words including the use of context, word parts, and the dictionary

Phase 3:     Relating the meanings of new words to previous knowledge as an aid to learning and memory

Phase 4:     Repeatedly studying and reviewing the meanings of new words in a variety of contexts

This framework serves as a guide for students in independently identifying and learning unfamiliar words as they read. There are a number of ways in which this framework might be implemented, including the Vocabulary Overview Guide described in the next section.

***Vocabulary Overview Guide.***     One strategy that embodies many of the features of the general framework is the Vocabulary Overview Guide developed by Carr (1985) and emphasized by Blachowicz and Fisher (2002). This strategy is intended to teach students a series of steps for self-selecting and defining vocabulary terms from natural text. This teaches students to learn unknown words in their reading materials by establishing a network of relationships among words and relating these words to personal experiences. The students gain greater control over their reading and increase motivation to learn. It also can be used with a variety of reading materials.

The Vocabulary Overview Guide is completed by the students as they read a text. It helps them to organize terms and indicate the relationships among the terms, passage concepts, and their personal experience. The steps in the strategy are designed to encourage the students to self-monitor as a means of becoming independent learners. Initially, however, teacher modeling is essential to ensure mastery of the strategy. The three basic parts of this strategy are: defining the vocabulary through the use of context, completing the guide, and studying the vocabulary.

*Defining the Vocabulary in Context.*     The steps involved in defining the vocabulary require the students to do the following:

1. Survey the text (titles, headings) to determine the nature of the material and consider what they already know about the topic.
2. Skim the materials to identify unknown or confusing vocabulary words and underline them.
3. Read the selection and try to figure out the meaning of the word from the context of the sentences around it combined with personal experience. Check the accuracy of these definitions by asking someone or using a dictionary.
4. Write the definition in the text or on paper so that it will be available during reading.
5. Reread the passage with the defined vocabulary to ensure understanding.

*Completing the Guide.*     After the students have reread the selection, have them fill in the guide for use in studying the selected terms. Demonstrate this procedure by presenting a sample guide, such as the one in Figure 14.1. Instruct the students to do the following:

1. Write the title of the passage on the top line.
2. Select categories of words from the text and place them on the second row of lines. Categories should be selected by studying the vocabulary words and the text to

**FIGURE 14.1**
Sample of
Vocabulary
Overview Guide

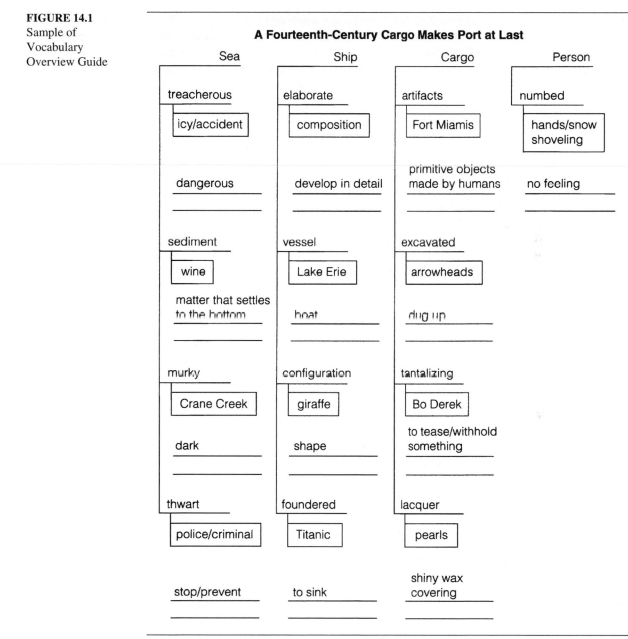

### A Fourteenth-Century Cargo Makes Port at Last

| Sea | Ship | Cargo | Person |
|---|---|---|---|
| treacherous | elaborate | artifacts | numbed |
| icy/accident | composition | Fort Miamis | hands/snow shoveling |
| dangerous | develop in detail | primitive objects made by humans | no feeling |
| sediment | vessel | excavated | |
| wine | Lake Erie | arrowheads | |
| matter that settles to the bottom | boat | dug up | |
| murky | configuration | tantalizing | |
| Crane Creek | giraffe | Bo Derek | |
| dark | shape | to tease/withhold something | |
| thwart | foundered | lacquer | |
| police/criminal | Titanic | pearls | |
| stop/prevent | to sink | shiny wax covering | |

determine what the unknown words describe or discuss. The number of categories will vary according to the vocabulary to be learned and what the words describe.

3. Fill in the vocabulary under the appropriate category on the next line.
4. Write a definition and/or synonym underneath each vocabulary word, leaving space to add more synonyms as new words are learned.
5. Add a personal clue in the box below the vocabulary word that relates the word to a personal experience or a quality or trait of someone or something that is familiar. The meaning of the word is thus related to the student's background knowledge and more clearly understood.

*Studying the Guide.*    After the guide has been filled in, the students are ready to study the vocabulary using the following procedures:

1. Read the title to activate background knowledge and recall words associated with the text.
2. Try to recall the meanings of the words in each category with the personal clue and definition of the word covered by a sheet of paper. If the meaning is not recalled, uncover the personal clue to jog the memory. If the meaning still cannot be recalled, uncover the definition for further study.
3. Use the guide to review the words every day until they are well known; then review them once a week as new words are learned.
4. Add synonyms to old vocabulary words as new words are learned, as a way to connect the old and the new and to refine and extend meanings.

The steps in this procedure can be summarized in a chart and given to the students as an aid until the strategy has become automatic. To ensure that the students are able to construct vocabulary overviews independently, it is important to provide frequent opportunities for practicing this strategy with a variety of reading materials. After demonstrating the strategy, complete several additional guides together, providing direction and feedback to the students. After the students understand how to create the guide, they should create several of them independently to ensure that they can monitor the correct use of the strategy.

The Vocabulary Overview Guide is one strategy for implementing the framework for independent vocabulary learning introduced previously. There are a number of other techniques that can be helpful in teaching students how to apply the framework successfully. Several of these supporting techniques are described in the next section.

## Supporting Techniques

This section describes several techniques that can be used to help students learn to apply various parts of the general framework independently. These techniques are not intended to be used in isolation from the larger context of the general framework, nor are they intended to be used for extended periods of time. They are intended to be used as initial supports in teaching students how to apply the general framework.

***Teaching Students to Use Context.*** We agree with Searfoss and Readence (1989) that the best way to teach students to use context clues is by talking through how to use these clues to gain meaning of an unknown word. Toward this end we describe briefly the *Preview in Context* and *Contextual Redefinition* approaches developed by Readence, Bean, and Baldwin (1985) and the *GLURK* technique developed by Kendall and Mason (1980).

*Preview in Context.* This technique uses the students' experiences and teacher questioning to discover the meaning of unknown vocabulary in context. It is a very informal technique that requires little teacher preparation and lends itself to normal classroom interaction. The four steps in this procedure are as follows:

1. Select words from the material to be read that are both important to central ideas in the text and may present difficulties for the students as they read.
2. Direct the students to the words in context. Read the material aloud as the students follow along in their own texts. Then ask the students to read the material silently.
3. Use questioning and discussion to talk the students toward a probable meaning for each word in its immediate context.
4. When the students have an understanding of a word's meaning in its immediate context, extend their understanding through discussion of alternative contexts, synonyms and antonyms, and the like. Encourage the students to use a dictionary or thesaurus to expand their understanding of each word. Word cards or a personal dictionary can be used as a permanent place to put words for later study and review.

Instruction of this type will have a significant cumulative effect. If students are shown how to use contextual analysis for only two words per week over the course of the school year, they will have eighty experiences with the process. This leads the student(s) to develop a habit of trying to discover the meanings of words through their own experiences and knowledge gained from the context.

*Contextual Redefinition.* This technique was developed by Readence et al. (1985) to assist students in learning how to use context as an aid to understanding unfamiliar words. This procedure involves the following steps:

1. Select words from the assigned reading that are necessary to understand the important ideas in the text and are likely to be unfamiliar to the students.
2. Provide a written context for each word that includes appropriate clues to the word's meaning. Sentences from the text can be used if they provide such a context.
3. Present the words in isolation and ask the students to provide a meaning for each word. The students defend their guesses and come to consensus on the best definition.
4. Present the words in context, using the sentences developed previously. Once again, the students should be asked to offer their best guesses as to the meaning of each word and to defend their definitions. Borrowing from a technique developed by Gipe (1978–79), we would suggest adding to this step the posing of a question that requires the student to relate the word to their own experience. For example, if the word is

*surplus,* the question might be "What do you or your family have a surplus of in your house?"

**5.** Verify the meaning of the words using a dictionary.

*GLURK.*     Many words have multiple meanings, so we need to help students have a flexible attitude toward word meanings to enable them to recognize the appropriate meanings of words in context. Kendall and Mason (1980) developed a technique called GLURK to help students attend to context so that they will select the proper meaning of polysemous words. As a first step the teacher constructs sentences that use the less common meanings of polysemous words. After the sentences have been constructed, the polysemous word is replaced by the word GLURK (for example, "John's knees GLURKED from carrying the heavy weight." "The music had a clear GLURK.").

After writing the GLURK sentences on paper or a chalkboard, the students are asked what GLURK might mean in each sentence, as well as what it could not mean. For example, they might say that John's knees "hurt" or that the music had a clear "sound." The teacher then replaces GLURK with the target word, and the students discuss the intended meaning of the polysemous word *(buckled* and *heat* in our examples). This should lead to a discussion of how words can have more than one meaning and how context can be used to identify and learn new and appropriate meanings.

After the students have worked through a number of GLURK exercises, they should be shown how to apply this technique in actual reading. Using sentences from their reading that contain less common meanings of polysemous words, ask the students to identify the polysemous word and its appropriate meaning from context without first substituting the word GLURK. As a follow-up the teacher can provide a practice activity consisting of a pair of sentences representing both a primary and a secondary meaning of a polysemous word. The students must then use the sentence context to identify the appropriate meaning for each underlined word. Responses can also be verified using a dictionary.

***Teaching Students to Use Word Parts.***     A word itself provides information about its meaning. Analyzing a word's structure is another tool that students can use to predict meaning. When readers use word parts in combination with context, they have a powerful meaning-getting strategy at their command.

Mason and Au (1990) describe a technique that teaches students to apply their knowledge of familiar roots and affixes to word learning. This technique has the students determine whether a new word is related in meaning to any words they already know. From a knowledge of affixes, root words, and how compound words are formed, the students can get some idea of a word's meaning. They can check their initial hypotheses about it by considering the context provided by the surrounding sentence or passage.

The first step of this technique is to familiarize the students with the concept of the *word family.* Word families consist of words that are so similar that they are closely related in meaning, as in the following lists:

theory, theorist, theoretical, theorem

sense, senseless, sensitive, sensation

For instructional purposes teachers can think of a word family as all those words derived from the same root and related in meaning. The goal, then, is to enable the students to make the connection between root words they already know and the obvious variations formed from inflections and affixes. Common prefixes and suffixes can also be introduced as part of this technique, using the following steps:

1. Write a short list of familiar words in a column on paper or a chalkboard (for example, *preview, predetermine, predate, premature*).
2. Have the students explain how the words are similar and then add some examples of their own.
3. Have the students think about how the meaning of each word is affected by the prefix and generate a rule that explains how the prefix changes the meaning.
4. Post the list and encourage the students to add to it from their reading.

At some point the students are likely to come up with words that appear to fit the pattern, but do not (for example, *prefer, preen, present*). These are opportunities to provide the student with more information about the kinds of words that do and do not have affixes and to show that certain affixes have more than one meaning.

After the students have become familiar with a number of prefixes and suffixes, it is important to help them develop a more general understanding of affixes. This can be done by asking the students to review several lists of words with either prefixes or suffixes and to determine how affixes change the meanings of words. Add one or two new examples for each affix, and see whether the students can figure out the meanings of these new words. Discuss how knowledge of prefixes and suffixes can be used to determine word meanings. When the students are ready to move on, introduce new words with both prefixes and suffixes. Ask the students to find the root words and identify the affixes, and see whether they can figure out the meanings from reading the words in sentences.

A related technique is recommended by Readence et al. (1985), in which known parts of familiar words are transferred to parts of unfamiliar words. They recommend the following procedures:

1. Select unfamiliar words that may be troublesome for conceptual understanding of a text and that lend themselves to an analysis of word parts.
2. Identify other words with identical word parts so that the students can associate the new words with known words.
3. Present the unknown words along with the similarly constructed known words in a manner that encourages comparison and provides the basis for predictions about the meaning of the roots or affixes in question.
4. Look up the word in the dictionary to verify predictions about the meanings of the unknown words.

***Teaching Students to Use a Dictionary.***    The use of context and the use of word parts are techniques that usually yield approximate meanings, rather than precise definitions, of unknown words. There are times, however, when context and word parts reveal very little about a word's meaning. At these times, or when a precise definition is needed, a dictionary is a reasonable alternative and a valuable resource for the students.

Knowing when to use a dictionary is just as important as knowing how to use one. One way to make the dictionary a functional resource is to use it to confirm predictions about word meaning that were arrived at through the use of context and/or word parts. To use a dictionary effectively, the students may require some direction. Dictionary skills that may require some assistance include the following:

1. Alphabetizing words
2. Locating words
3. Using the pronunciation key
4. Identifying the correct entry for different word forms
5. Determining which of several definitions is appropriate for a particular context

***Teaching Students to Put It Together.***    After the students have become familiar with the various techniques that can be used to determine the meanings of unfamiliar words in context, it may be helpful to conduct a series of strategy lessons to assist them in deciding when these techniques are most appropriately applied. The procedure described here is an adaptation of the Context-Strategy Lessons presented by Searfoss and Readence (1989) and involves analyzing the text to determine how much help it provides in determining the meanings of unknown words in context.

Strategy lessons teach the students to select an appropriate technique for identifying the meanings of unknown words in a text by analyzing the material to determine the amount of help it provides in understanding the unfamiliar words. The students are taught to look first for direct help in the form of context clues that provide definitions, synonyms, and/or comparisons, as in the following examples:

1. *Context clues of definition.* The *ecologist,* a scientist who studies the environment, is usually quick to attack new sources of air pollution.
2. *Context clues of comparison.* Unlike Len, who was flattering in his actions with people, John was stubbornly flippant.

When no direct help is provided, the students are taught to look for indirect help from familiar root words and/or affixes. Searfoss and Readence (1989) provide an example of such a situation from a text with the sentence "John's mother has *hydrophobia.*" The teacher helps the students recognize that since there is no direct help from the context, they need to look for indirect help from familiar root words and affixes. The teacher then guides the students in breaking down the word and identifying the meanings of its component parts by comparing the parts to other known words and their parts (for example, *phobia, hydroplane, hydroelectric*).

Finally, when the text provides neither direct nor indirect help, the students are taught to consult a dictionary to identify a meaning that is appropriate to the context. Thus these lessons focus on analyzing the amount of help provided by the text as a means of deciding which techniques should be applied to determine the meanings of unknown words. Naturally, the number and variety of techniques (and therefore the strategy lessons) may be varied according to the needs of the individual student.

Consistent with the gradual release model of instruction described in Chapters 6 and 12, the amount of support provided by the teacher in the use of the techniques described in this section should depend on the students' level of development. Students in the initial stages of acquisition require a great deal of teacher support in the form of modeling and explanation. Students who have acquired some knowledge and skill in vocabulary learning may require only a brief period of guided instruction before they are ready to work independently. Finally, students who have mastered the integrated use of vocabulary learning strategies should be given opportunities for independent application.

## Strategies for Teaching Specific Vocabulary for a Text

Consistent with our second goal for vocabulary instruction, it is important to provide direct vocabulary instruction when in-depth knowledge of complex concepts is critical to the understanding of reading assignments. The following techniques can be used for this purpose.

*List–Group–Label.* The list–group–label lesson was originally developed by Hilda Taba (1967) and is still popular (see Blanchowicz & Fisher, 2002) to assist students in dealing with the technical vocabulary in subject-area reading. Although the foundation of these procedures is in subject area reading, the concept can be broadened to all areas and levels of vocabulary learning.

To implement the procedure, the teacher selects a one- or two-word topic as a stimulus word and writes it at the top of a chalkboard or large sheet of paper. Topics may be drawn from either literary themes (e.g, fear, trust) or subject-area content (e.g., a social studies unit on independence). Although general topics such as events of the school year (Martin Luther King Day, President's Day, etc.) or places (e.g., school, home) could be used, we are recommending this procedure primarily for development of specific vocabulary in preparation for reading a particular text.

After the topic is presented, the students are asked to think of related words or expressions. For example, the teacher might ask, "What comes to mind when you think about this topic?" All responses are recorded until a reasonable list has been compiled (that is, between fifteen and twenty-five words). Then the teacher rereads the list orally or asks the students to do so. The students are then asked to break the larger list into smaller lists of three words or more that have something in common. The students are also asked to give each group of words a label indicating the characteristics they share. The students must then explain why the words have been grouped in a certain manner. All groupings should be accepted and recorded, although the teacher should point out that meaningful associations are preferable to groupings based on surface-level features such as spelling.

A number of variations of this procedure are possible for students who might need more assistance. For example, the teacher might provide the initial list of words and ask the students to group and label them. Alternatively, the teacher could provide the groups of words and ask the students to label them, or the teacher could supply the list and the label and have the students group the words.

***Semantic Mapping.*** Another well-practiced version of the list–group–label strategy is called *semantic mapping* (Johnson & Pearson, 1984; Blachowicz & Fisher, 1996). Semantic maps are graphic representations of text concepts that typically consist of three levels of information about the main topic in a central hub, spokes labeled to indicate major ideas or categories, and branches containing specific supporting details. Maps can be used either to organize the students' brainstorming before reading a text or as the basis for summarizing ideas after reading.

To implement this procedure, begin by placing the topic in a central hub and eliciting major category labels related to the topic. Then ask the students either to brainstorm or search the selection for supporting information within each of the categories. After the supporting information has been categorized, the teacher can bring up any important ideas the students have not suggested and ask them to try to place the ideas in an appropriate category. With students who require more structure, a prestructured map with empty slots can be supplied, and the students can be asked to fill these in as the material is discussed. Figure 14.2 presents a semantic map constructed before reading an expository selection on wolves.

List–group–label and semantic mapping procedures can also be used as a measure of how well the students have learned the vocabulary from a particular lesson. They can be used at different points in a lesson or unit to determine whether the students are beginning to use and categorize the key vocabulary. Each time a list–group–label lesson or semantic map has been completed, the categories can be compared to the previous ones as a means of evaluating progress. Figure 14.3 presents a semantic map for *wolves* that was created after the students read, embellished, and made corrections as necessary. A comparison between this postread-

**FIGURE 14.2**
Prereading
Semantic Map

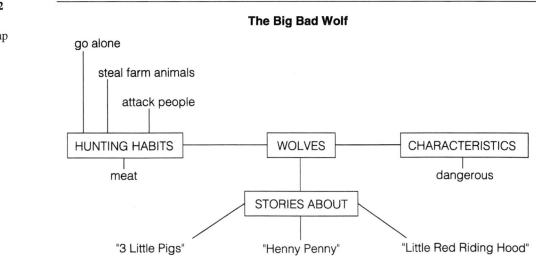

*Source:* Reprinted by permission of the publisher from Winograd, P. N., Wixson, K. K., and Lipson, M. Y., editors, *Improving Basal Reading Instruction* (New York: Teachers College Press © 1989 by Teachers College, Columbia University. All rights reserved.) p. 157.

**FIGURE 14.3**
Postreading
Semantic Map

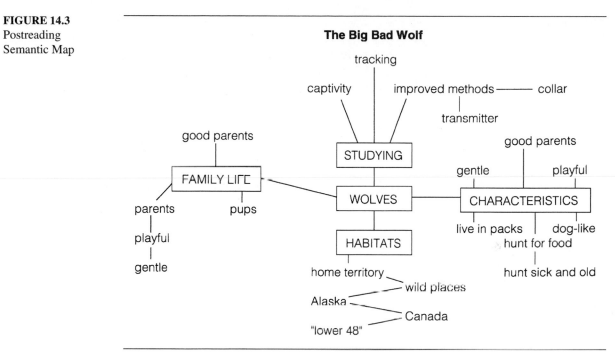

**The Big Bad Wolf**

*Source:* Reprinted by permission of the publisher from Winograd, P. N., Wixson, K. K., and Lipson, M. Y., editors, *Improving Basal Reading Instruction* (New York: Teachers College Press © 1989 by Teachers College, Columbia University. All rights reserved.) p. 158.

ing map and the prereading map reveals increased knowledge about the general attributes and specific characteristics of wolves.

***Structured Overview or Graphic Organizer.*** Structured overviews or graphic organizers are visual representations of the relationships among important vocabulary terms and concepts in a text. They are generally more structured than semantic maps and more tied to the hierarchical structure of the information presented in a text. For this reason they are particularly well suited for subject-area texts.

According to Nelson-Herber (1986), these overviews or organizers have three purposes: to help students expand their knowledge of vocabulary by building from the known to the new, to help students refine their understanding of word meanings and the ways in which words interrelate, and to support students in the use of their word knowledge in reading, writing, and speaking. They are also used to introduce vocabulary in a way that helps students relate new material to what they already know and to provide an advance organizer for the reading assignment.

The overview or organizer itself is a tree diagram with the most inclusive concepts subsuming subordinate ones. Relationships among the concepts are indicated by the connecting lines between terms (see Figure 14.4). These diagrams can be designed by the teacher prior to instruction or can be developed jointly by the teacher and the students during

**FIGURE 14.4**
Structured
Overview

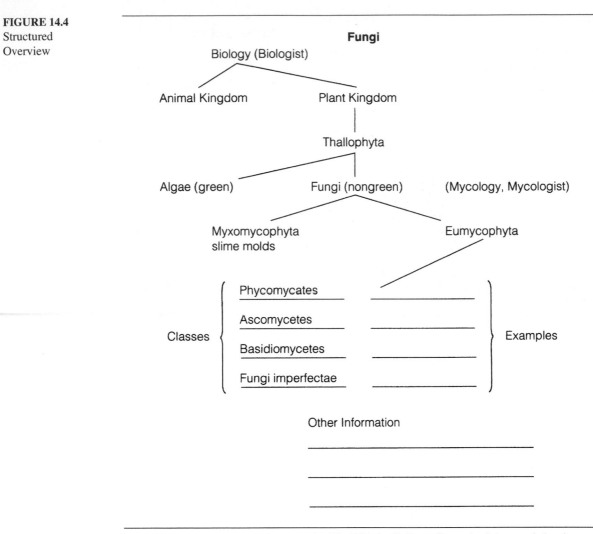

instruction. As the students work with the text, they refer to the diagram and use it to organize and learn key concepts as presented in their reading.

The following steps are suggested for developing the diagram and introducing it to students (cf. Barron, 1969; Herber, 1978; Nelson-Herber, 1986):

1. Analyze the text and list the major concepts and key terms that are to be stressed in instruction and therefore are important for students to understand.
2. Arrange the list of words into a diagram that shows the interrelationships among the concepts in a manner that relates to and expands on what the students already know.

The arrangement depends on the teacher, the number of concepts to be learned, and the students' prior knowledge of the concepts.

**3.** Evaluate the overview. Are the major relationships shown clearly? Can the diagram be simplified and still effectively communicate the key ideas? Add to the diagram any vocabulary necessary for students to understand the relationships between the text information and the discipline as a whole.

**4.** Introduce and talk the students through the diagram. Encourage them to apply previously learned knowledge by adding to the diagram. Engage students in the construction of word meanings from context, experiences, and reasoning in small-group interactive discussions of words and meanings.

**5.** After discussing the concepts and their interrelationships, leave the diagram in full view of the students as a reference point during reading and/or discussion following reading.

Nelson-Herber (1986) also recommends the use of follow-up activities to provide contexts for students to construct, refine, and reinforce word meanings. Using the concepts from the diagram shown in Figure 14.4, she provides the following sample activities:

I. Directions: Work together to choose the word that best completes the analogy.
  A. Green: chlorophyllous as nongreen:
    1. phyla  2. achlorophyllous  3. mycology
  B. Green: nongreen as algae:
    1. protist  2. mycologist  3. fungi
II. Directions: Circle the word in each set that does not belong and be ready to explain why the other three go together.
  A. fungi, heterotrophic, vascular, achlorophyllous
  B. algae, chlorophyllous, nongreen, autotrophic

***Semantic Feature Analysis.*** Semantic feature analysis (SFA) is a procedure for helping students see how words within a category are alike and different and to relate the meanings of new words to previous knowledge and experience. The guidelines presented here are recommended by Anders and Bos (1986) as an adaptation of the SFA teaching strategies proposed by Johnson and Pearson (1984). These guidelines were designed and tested for use with subject-area reading material.

The first step in the SFA procedure is to read the text thoroughly and make a list of the major ideas that students will encounter. Next, examine the list and determine which ideas represent the superordinate concepts. Then identify words that represent the supporting or subordinate ideas related to the superordinate concepts. This information should then be organized into a relationship chart with the superordinate concepts as column headings across the top and the related vocabulary as row headings down the side (see Figure 14.5).

Each student should receive a copy of the relationship chart before reading the assignment. Then, using a copy of the chart, either on the board or on an overhead projector, the students should be introduced to the topic of the assignment and the meaning of each superordinate word or phrase. Following the discussion of the superordinate concepts, introduce each subordinate concept, giving a simple definition. Students should be encouraged to add their personal experiences or understandings of the terms during these discus-

| The Fourth Amendment | | | | | |
|---|---|---|---|---|---|
| | Important Ideas | | | | |
| **Important Vocabulary** | Citizen's right to privacy versus | Society needs to keep law and order | Police search with a search warrant | Police search without a search warrant | Evidence allowed in court |
| Search and seizure | | | | | |
| Unreasonable search and seizure | | | | | |
| Probable cause to search | | | | | |
| Your property and possessions | | | | | |
| Absolute privacy | | | | | |
| You give consent | | | | | |
| Hot pursuit | | | | | |
| Moving vehicle | | | | | |
| Stop-and-frisk | | | | | |
| Plain view | | | | | |
| During an arrest | | | | | |
| Evidence | | | | | |
| Exclusionary rule | | | | | |

*Source:* Chart from Anders, Patricia L., & Bos, Candace S. (1986). Semantic feature analysis: An interactive strategy for vocabulary development and text comprehension. *Journal of Reading.* Reprinted by permission of the International Reading Association. All rights reserved.

sions. One key to a successful discussion is to ask students how and why they arrived at a certain relationship rating.

Next, lead a discussion with the students to determine the relationship between each superordinate term or phrase and each subordinate concept. Fill in the relationship chart using the following symbols to signify the nature of the relationship: a plus sign (+) for a positive relationship, a minus sign (−) for a negative relationship, a zero (0) for no relationship, and a question mark (?) when no consensus can be reached without further information.

After completing the relationship chart, the students read to confirm their predictions and to determine the relationship between the terms for which no agreement could be reached. Following the reading, review with the students the relationship chart, changing any of the relationships if necessary, and reach consensus on the previously unidenti-fied relationships.

A more general, less text-specific application of semantic features analysis uses a group of words that are closely related. These words serve as the headings for the rows, whereas the headings for the columns are the semantic features or phrases describing components of meaning shared by some of the words or that distinguish a word from other meanings. In this way SFA can be used to promote general vocabulary development in addition to specific vocabulary learning for a particular text.

In concluding this section of the chapter, we would like to reiterate Nagy's (1988) observation that the procedures described above for teaching vocabulary for specific texts serve several purposes. First, they activate appropriate background knowledge, encouraging students to think about experiences in their own lives that relate to the central concepts of the reading. Second, they help students understand the semantic relations and organization of the concepts in their text. Third, they allow the teacher to identify and assess the specific background knowledge of their students. The teacher can then clear up misconceptions and make sure that new concepts and words are related to experiences that are meaningful to those particular students. Finally, these techniques provide a rich basis for further reading, writing, and discussion.

## General Vocabulary Development

Consistent with our third goal, it is important to promote general vocabulary development in a variety of ways. One that has been mentioned frequently throughout this chapter is extensive reading, both in and out of school (Nagy, 1988). In addition to wide reading, this section presents a well-documented method for teaching general vocabulary and sev-eral suggestions for building interest in and enthusiasm for vocabulary learning as a life-long process.

*Teaching General Vocabulary.* Beck and McKeown (1983) describe a vocabulary-learn-ing program based on introducing words by semantic categories. This program emphasizes the development of word consciousness, with the aim of making students more aware of words in general. Grouping the words into meaningful sets helps students learn and remember subtle differences in word meanings.

The program is designed to give students an in-depth knowledge of word meanings through a carefully planned sequence of activities using groups of eight to ten words at a time. For example, a category of words about moods would include words such as *cautious, jovial, glum, placid, enthusiastic, envious,* and *impatient.* Words are grouped in this manner to allow the students to build relationships among them.

The students receive a five-day cycle of instruction on each set of words. Each day's lesson lasts about thirty minutes. The first few lessons are designed to be fairly easy; the later lessons are more demanding. Each cycle covers a range of tasks, including defining, sentence generation, oral production, and games calling for rapid responding. The point of presenting students with a variety of tasks is to help them develop a rich understanding of the words and the ability to use them flexibly.

Beck and McKeown (1983) use a variety of activities for teaching semantically related words. For example, students are asked to compare the features of two new words and consider whether the two are mutually exclusive. They are asked questions such as "Could a *virtuoso* be a *rival?*" or "Could a *philanthropist* be a *miser?*" In another activity a clue word is used to elicit a newly defined word (for example, *crook* is used to elicit *accomplice*). Then the students are required to explain why these two terms should be associated with each other.

In a word association activity the teacher says a familiar word, and the students are supposed to respond with a closely related word selected from among those being taught. If the day's words are *virtuoso, accomplice, philanthropist,* and *novice,* the teacher might say *crook.* The students are expected to respond with the word *accomplice* and to be able to defend their choice.

A final activity is completion of sentences containing the target words, for example: "The *accomplice* was worried because. . . ." The use of sentence completion, rather than the more open-ended task of "using the word in a sentence," helps steer students in the direction of sentences that really use the meaning of the word instead of producing stereotyped answers such as "I saw *X* yesterday."

As Nagy (1988) suggests, the exact activity is not the issue, and any of these or similar activities can be adapted for particular classrooms, words, and/or students. What is important is that students be given practice at tasks that require them to *use,* rather than state, the meanings of words they are learning in natural sentence contexts.

### Building Interest and Enthusiasm for Vocabulary Learning.

In the final analysis, the students who are interested in words are likely to be the most motivated to attend to vocabulary learning. It is important to try to instill in students a sense of excitement about word learning that will compel them to make vocabulary learning a part of their daily life. A good way for teachers to build students' enthusiasm for words and word learning is to engage them in vocabulary games and other interesting activities.

*Creating an Environment for Word Learning.* Students often enjoy sharing with others new words they have learned outside of school (Taylor, Harris, & Pearson, 1988). The teacher simply sets aside a few minutes once or twice a week for the students to present and define new words. The students share how they came across the word and the context in which it was used. Students' attention to unfamiliar words often increases if they know they have the opportunity to share them.

As an additional incentive, the students can be responsible for making a bulletin board display to present new words they have encountered outside of school. Bulletin board displays can also be used by the teacher to stimulate interest in key concepts from the students' reading materials through items such as pictures, cartoons, advertisements, and magazine or newspaper articles. Student committees can also be formed to preview reading assignments for new or unusual words and to explain them. An example from Vacca and Vacca (1989, p. 331) illustrates this type of activity nicely:

An English class committee called the Word Searchers found this passage from *Flowers for Algernon:* "Sculpture with a living element. Charlie, it's the greatest thing since junkmobiles and tincannia." The Word Searchers introduced the terms *junkmobiles* and *tincannia* to the class. They explained that the two words would not be found in the dictionary. Then the committee challenged the class to come up with definitions that would make sense. To top off the presentation the committee prepared Exhibit A and Exhibit B to demonstrate the words—a mobile made of various assortments of junk and an *objet d'art* made from tin cans, jar lids, and the like.

*Playing with Words.* There are a variety of ways students can be encouraged to play with words that are likely to enhance their interest and understanding of new vocabulary. Blachowicz and Fisher (2003, p. 187) suggest the following guidelines for selecting and using word games:

1. Games should be simple to use without teacher intervention;
2. Vocabulary level should be appropriate;
3. Play should call on students to use the words in some meaningful way;
4. Games should utilize outside resources (e.g., a dictionary or class notebook) for self-checking;
5. Games should limit the number of players so that all players are involved.

Examples of useful games include crossword puzzles, which can be used to develop vocabulary and increase interest in words. In addition to the crossword puzzles that are already available for students to use, many students enjoy constructing their own crossword puzzles for others to complete.

Adapted versions of vocabulary games such as Spill-and-Spell, Scrabble, Bingo, and Concentration also can be valuable for increasing students' interest in and learning of new vocabulary. To adapt these games for this purpose, simply include new rules about giving definitions and/or examples of the words that are constructed, identified, or matched as part of each game.

Goldstein (1986) has suggested that cartoons and comics can be used as an inexpensive source for developing interest in and knowledge of vocabulary. Both the teachers and the students locate cartoons and comics that illustrate the use of new vocabulary or old vocabulary used in new ways. The teacher and the students discuss the meanings of the words and expressions both in and out of the humorous context provided by the cartoon or comic. Then the students keep a record of the vocabulary or expressions in notebooks, journals, or on cards according to categories such as figurative language, colloquial expressions, puns, and palindromes. The students can also use their notes to make humorous constructions of their own.

*Word Histories.* Brief discussions of word derivations or histories often increase students' interest in words and make the words more memorable. Teachers can collect word origins that have a clear connection to the current meaning of a word and use them as mnemonic devices. Examples provided by Vacca and Vacca (1989) from *Picturesque Word Origins* (1933) include the following:

*Muscle.* Metaphorically, the scurrying of a mouse. A Latin word *musculus* means "mouse." The French adapted it because they associated the rippling of a muscle with the movement of a mouse.

*Calculate.* Originally, the counting stones of the Romans. The Latin word *calx* means "limestone." The ancient Romans used little stones called *calculus* to add and subtract. From this derived the English word *calculate* and its many derivatives.

Vacca and Vacca (1989) suggest that interest and enthusiasm also can be created by discussions of *eponyms* and *acronyms.* Eponyms are words originating from persons or places such as *pasteurize, maverick,* or *chauvinistic.* Acronyms are words formed from the beginning letters or groups of letters that make up phrases. For example, *scuba* is the acronym for *s*elf-*c*ontained *u*nderwater *b*reathing *a*pparatus, and *snafu* stands for *s*ituation *n*ormal— *a*ll *f*ouled *u*p. As Vacca and Vacca (1989, p. 333) note, "interesting words abound. If they appear in a text assignment, don't miss the opportunity to teach them to students."

# Chapter Summary

This chapter discussed the role of vocabulary and vocabulary instruction in reading comprehension and presented a variety of strategies for teaching vocabulary. Vocabulary knowledge has long been recognized as a significant factor in reading comprehension; however, how this relationship works and what it implies for instruction are still open to debate.

The first half of the chapter discussed the issues related to when and how vocabulary should be taught and presented goals and guidelines for vocabulary instruction. The major issues that were addressed were the debate about whether students learn vocabulary best through direct instruction or incidental learning, when direct vocabulary instruction is most appropriate, and which types of direct vocabulary instruction (e.g., definitional, contextual, intensive) are most effective. These issues were then translated into the following goals and guidelines for vocabulary instruction.

### Goals
Teach independent vocabulary learning.
Teach concepts important for comprehension.
Create an environment that promotes general vocabulary development.

### Guidelines
Guideline 1: Relate the new to the known.
Guideline 2: Promote active, in-depth processing.
Guideline 3: Provide multiple exposures.
Guideline 4: Teach students to be strategic.

The second half of the chapter described strategies for three different types of vocabulary instruction that correspond to the established goals and guidelines: (1) strategies for teaching independent vocabulary learning during reading, (2) strategies for teaching key vocabulary in preparation for reading specific texts, and (3) strategies for creating an environment that promotes general vocabulary development. A general framework for independent vocabulary learning during reading was presented that consisted of four phases: reading and identifying unknown vocabulary, applying a repertoire of techniques to identify and learn the meanings of the words, relating the meanings of the new words to previous knowledge to aid learning and memory, and reviewing and studying the meanings of the new words in a variety of contexts. This was followed by a description of the Vocabulary Overview Guide, a strategy that embodies the features of the general framework, and of methods for teaching the techniques (for example, using context or word parts) needed to support independent vocabulary learning.

Strategies for teaching vocabulary for specific texts and for general vocabulary development were also presented. The four strategies described for direct instruction of vocabulary related to specific reading assignments were list–group–label, semantic mapping, structured overviews or graphic organizers, and semantic feature analysis. Finally, methods for using semantic categories to teach general vocabulary and for building interest and enthusiasm for vocabulary learning (for example, word play, word histories) were described.

# 15 Adapting Instruction to Focus on Comprehension, Composition, and Studying

The abilities to read with comprehension and to communicate effectively in writing for age-appropriate purposes are the hallmarks of a literate person. In the past, however, prevailing views of reading provided little reason to devote attention to comprehension instruction, because comprehension was thought to be the natural by-product of accurate word recognition. Similarly, until recently, writing instruction was focused more on mechanics and grammar than on creating engaging and effective writing. The view of reading and writing presented throughout this text differs considerably from those earlier, skills-based models.

Now, however, there is an impressive agreement among researchers and educators of many stripes that comprehension is the primary goal and purpose of reading and reading instruction: "reading comprehension has come to be viewed as the 'essence of reading'" (National Reading Panel, 2000, p. 4-1). There is also agreement that comprehension, like word recognition and vocabulary, requires focused instructional attention. Readers and writers unquestionably need skills and strategies to attain high levels of ease and efficiency in word-level aspects of literacy, but these abilities are the means, not the end itself, and good decoding skills are no assurance of good comprehension or study strategies (Rand Reading Study Group [RRSG], 2002). Effective readers and writers *use* skills and strategies to comprehend and compose, but it is the reader's response and comprehension that are important, not the acquisition of the skills and strategies themselves. Similarly, students need to acquire high levels of knowledge and skill in spelling, mechanics, grammar, and usage to facilitate effective writing. But the real purpose is composition and communication of an effective message.

The focus of this chapter is on providing instruction that improves students' ability to understand (learn, enjoy, and/or remember) information from different types of texts read under a variety of different conditions and to compose different types of texts for a variety of purposes. First, we describe the nature of comprehension instruction, discussing issues and providing guidelines. Then we turn to a variety of instructional techniques designed to focus on comprehension and composition. Finally, we describe instructional techniques for addressing the special case of studying.

# Focusing Instruction on Comprehension, Composition, and Studying

Reading and writing are functional skills. This means that people engage in reading and writing for a variety of purposes that include enjoyment and the completion of work tasks, both academic and nonacademic. Some students have difficulty comprehending texts for *any* purpose. More commonly, students can read and understand some materials, but not all, and can read for some purposes, but not many. This is also true for composition. Students may write acceptable fictional or personal narratives, for example, but be unable to produce persuasive essays or informational pieces. The consequences of this problem become more and more serious as students move through each subsequent grade in school. To succeed in school and work settings, "students must learn to think in such a way that they can tackle, unravel, and understand any author's communication" (Sardy, 1985, p. 216). In the following sections we discuss some issues surrounding comprehension and comprehension instruction as well as composition and writing instruction; we also provide some guidelines for instruction.

## The Nature of Instruction in Comprehension and Composition

With regard to comprehension instruction, educators have traditionally taken one of two views (see Kameenui & Shannon, 1988). Some argue for structured programs involving direct instruction in various comprehension skills (Carnine, Silbert, & Kameenui, 1990). In this case comprehension instruction has often involved teaching fairly discrete skills from a long list, often provided by commercial publishers. Others suggest that students will learn to comprehend without any direct instruction at all (Goodman, 1989). In this case students are often expected to generate knowledge and skill through repeated exposure to texts and questions (Durkin, 1978–79).

The situation with regard to writing instruction is entirely analogous. Thus students have generally experienced one of two writing approaches also: a skills program involving discrete tasks, assigned topics, and an emphasis on form or open-ended writing opportunities with little or no teacher direction (often resulting in students not completing many or any written pieces).

Although deficiencies in underlying skills and strategies may account for many students' inability to comprehend, some young or disabled readers simply do not understand when or why they should use the skills and knowledge they do possess (Paris, Lipson, & Wixson, 1983). Without sufficient understanding of the functional value of these skills, students are unlikely to use them during reading. Other students do not realize that reading demands attention to meaning. For example, when Susan, a seventh grade student, was asked to talk about what she had been thinking as she read a portion of text she responded, "Oh, I don't usually *think* while I read." Clearly, Susan misunderstands the purpose of reading and cannot be successful.

Research points to the conclusion that the types of instruction typically offered to disabled readers or writers contribute to the problem. A recent review of comprehension research conducted by the RAND Corporation in conjunction with a group of highly regarded experts (RRSG, 2002, p. 103) concluded, for example, that

reading instruction in schools serving poor children is more likely to be more exclusively skill focused and to incorporate less focus on text interpretation (Allington & McGill-Franzin,

1989; Nystrand, 1990). Schools serving poor children are much less likely to have lengthy texts widely available in classrooms, and instruction in such schools is more likely to require students to read and write single words and brief texts than longer units (Duke, 2000a).

This is especially troubling because research suggests that extensive amounts of reading and writing practice are a feature of successful comprehension instruction (Mosenthal et al., 2001). In focusing on understanding specific texts or writing correct sentences, teachers may have inadvertently denied students the instruction they need to learn how to be independent and strategic.

Regarding this issue, we argue for balance. Students need ample opportunities to practice comprehending and composing, but many also require accurate, accessible information about how to comprehend or compose a text (see Figure 15.1). In many classrooms teachers guide or support students through text, making sure they understand the particular story or chapter that has been assigned. Although this approach is very appropriate under specific circumstances (when the content of the selection is critically important), it has several disadvantages for helping students learn to comprehend. First, it often keeps students dependent on the teacher and undermines the development of independence. Second, students rarely have the opportunity to discover how to identify and manage comprehension failures, because teachers may "understand it for them." Finally, teachers may inadvertently adopt an approach that focuses too strongly on content versus process, thereby failing to teach the skills and strategies necessary for improved comprehending ability.

Precisely the same difficulties occur in many process writing classrooms (see Lipson et al., 2000). Teachers guide and direct students in the editing of their work, with the result that the final product may be improved, but students might not acquire appropriate knowledge and skill to enhance their writing ability.

## Becoming Strategic

Good readers and writers are "planful." They understand and think about their purpose for reading or writing. They preview materials and determine how difficult the task will be.

**FIGURE 15.1**
Dual Focus for
Instruction in
Comprehending and
Composing

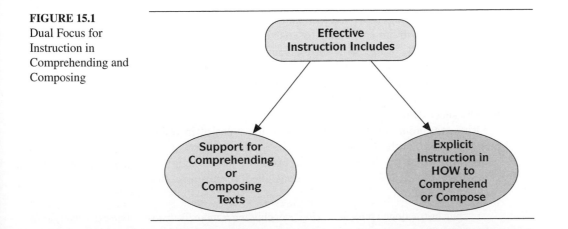

Using their own knowledge and experience, they make predictions and brainstorm ideas, and they consider how much time they have. Then strategic readers and writers select, from a wide repertoire, the skills and approaches they will use. Sometimes they scan quickly; at other times they read closely, even highlighting important information. In writing, sometimes they brainstorm many ideas first, sometimes they take painstaking notes from source material before they ever begin to write, and sometimes they quickly begin to write about powerful ideas and experiences that do not need revision because they are for personal use.

Again, the important distinction here is the intentional or planful nature of the activity. Sometimes readers are reasonably successful but not because they have behaved strategically. The student who gets a correct answer by chance (e.g., by circling all the "A's" on a multiple-choice tests) is lucky but not strategic. Similarly, the student who writes descriptive sentences at the teacher's direction but cannot or will not use those same techniques during independent writing is compliant but not strategic (see Paris, Lipson, & Wixson, 1983).

Finally, strategic readers and writers change their approach to reading and writing depending on difficulty, purpose, and task. "Strategies are inherently flexible and adaptable" (Dole et al., 1991, p. 242). Strategies require using several skills or abilities in concert. Individual skills can be very important under some circumstances, but they are generally not, by themselves, sufficient to accomplish the complex jobs required of mature readers and writers.

The obvious next question is "Are there some strategies that really help readers and writers to be more competent—to read and write better?" The answer is clearly "Yes," although the particular list of essential strategies frequently varies slightly from one educator or researcher to another. There are two things that most experts agree are essential to understand about strategies. First, the number of these strategies is small—it isn't a long list of discrete abilities. Second, these strategies, individually, are not as important as a strategic approach. As Dole et al. (1991, p. 242) have argued, "The goal of instruction would be to develop (in students) a sense of conscious control, or metacognitive awareness, over *a set of strategies* that they can adapt to any text they read" (emphasis added). In Figure 15.2 we have listed the generally accepted group of strategies that have been found useful for improving students' reading comprehension (Dole et al., 1991; Harvey & Goudvis, 2000; Keene & Zimmerman, 1997; National Reading Panel, 2000).

Many of these have analogues in the writing process. According to Tompkins (2000, p. 76), "Students learn and use strategies for writing, too. 'Writing strategies are deliberate thinking procedures writers use to solve problems that they counter while writing' (Collins, 1998, p. vii)" (see Figure 15.3).

Effective readers and writers activate existing knowledge before reading or writing. During reading, they make connections between this prior knowledge and the text content, using personal experience and beliefs, knowledge about other texts, and knowledge about the world. They also fill in the gaps and connect information in text by making inferences. In writing, they brainstorm and plan their writing, thinking about both the content and the organization of the work.

Many skilled readers and writers use visualization to improve comprehension and enhance the quality of their writing. These visualizations allow readers and writers to create mental images that often deepen involvement.

**FIGURE 15.2**
Research-Based
Reading Strategies

| Make Connections | Text–self: Link prior knowledge and experience to current text in terms of character traits/motivations, events, settings, or personal interest<br>Text–text: Link current text with other texts in terms of characters, events, themes, or concepts<br>Text–world: Link current text to big ideas or issues outside the classroom |
|---|---|
| Infer and Predict | Connect ideas across parts of the text<br>Fill in information not provided by the author<br>Construct meaning<br>Use prior knowledge and previous text information to anticipate content or draw conclusions |
| Question | Increase engagement<br>Focus reading<br>Encourage problem solving<br>Improve search for answers and information<br>Clarify confusions |
| Visualize | Increase engagement<br>Create mental images<br>Use prior knowledge and text to construct pictures (meaning)<br>Promote creative thinking<br>Enhance comprehension<br>Encourage personal response |
| Monitor/Clarify | Attend to the meaningfulness of text<br>Identify difficulties<br>Promote problem-solving stance<br>Promote use of "repair" strategies<br>Encourage readers to adjust rate, pace, etc.<br>Attend to the interconnectedness of text ideas |
| Summarize | Pause and reflect<br>Distinguish important from unimportant ideas<br>Identify main points or major themes<br>Organize information so that it highlights superordinate and subordinate ideas |
| Evaluate | Make judgments about reading<br>Personalize reading by forming new ideas, opinions, and perspectives<br>Determine the author's purpose<br>Make judgments about ideas and presentation |

Periodically, most readers and writers also stop to summarize the text. This periodic reflection helps both readers and writers to organize their thoughts, maintain the threads of the text meaning, and identify key concepts.

Skilled readers and writers also monitor to check the sensibleness of the text. They ask themselves whether there is any portion of text that does not make sense. Poor readers and

**FIGURE 15.3**
Strategies That
Writers Use

| Strategy | Explanation | Sample Activities |
|---|---|---|
| *Tapping prior knowledge* | Students think about what they already know about the topic about which they will write. | Brainstorm ideas<br>Draw pictures<br>Talk with classmates |
| *Organizing ideas* | Students group and sequence ideas before writing. | Cluster ideas<br>Make data charts<br>Make an outline |
| *Visualizing* | Students use description and sensory details to make their writing more vivid. | Add sensory words<br>Write dialogue<br>Use metaphors and similes |
| *Summarizing* | Students write the main ideas or events in a text they have read or written. | Take notes<br>Write journal entries |
| *Making connections* | Students recall similar experiences or similar books they have read as they write. | Brainstorm ideas<br>Write pattern books |
| *Revising meaning* | Students add words and sentences, make substitutions and deletions, and move text around to communicate more effectively. | Reread<br>Participate in a writing group<br>Make revisions |
| *Monitoring* | Students coordinate all writing-related activities, check on how well they are communicating, and ask self-questions. | Reread<br>Ask self-questions |
| *Playing with language* | Students incorporate figurative and novel uses of language in their writing. | Use metaphors and similes<br>Use idioms<br>Write alliterations<br>Create invented words |
| *Generalizing* | Students draw out main ideas and details and use main ideas to direct readers through the compositions. | Cluster ideas<br>Write topic sentences<br>Write conclusions |
| *Evaluating* | Students make judgments about, reflect on, and value their writing. | Self-assess the writing<br>Use rubrics<br>Write reflections |

*Source:* From *Teaching Writing: Balancing Process and Product,* 3rd edition, by Gail E. Tompkins. Copyright © 2000 by Prentice-Hall, Inc. Reprinted by permission of Pearson Education, Inc., Upper Saddle River, NJ.

weak writers, by contrast, rarely reflect on the meaning of the text. More often, they believe that the goal is simply to say the words (Paris & Myers, 1981), and they focus their revisions on proofreading, not meaning (Graham & Harris, 1994). Similarly, effective readers check to see whether their initial (and interim) predictions were accurate or their topic was maintained. Finally, skilled readers attempt to accommodate new information by checking to see whether it is necessary to change the meaning they have constructed. Poor readers often fail to monitor their reading efforts and therefore are typically insensitive to their comprehension failures (Kennedy & Miller, 1976).

Successful comprehension and composition require students to evaluate new (text) information and to integrate information from several parts of text to form a coherent whole. Younger and less-skilled readers often fail to use textual information to acquire new information or change their minds (see Lipson, 1983) and may also fail to evaluate their own writing for meaningfulness (Graham & Harris, 1994).

Finally, effective readers ask themselves questions about the text. Self-questioning can help to promote active involvement and establish purposes for reading and writing, help students to determine the most important information in a selection, encourage students to monitor their own reading (or writing progress), and prompt students to engage in self-evaluation.

Self-questioning can be directed at the content of the reading (for example, "Who was Matthew Henson and what did he do?"), or it can focus on reading or writing processes ("Did I use humor effectively in this part?"). Students appear to require careful instruction in question asking if they are to be successful at it. With good teaching, however, students can use this strategy to improve comprehension (Palincsar & Brown, 1984; see Pearson & Fielding, 1991, for a review). In addition, students who pose their own questions show more improvement in comprehension than students who answer teachers' questions (Singer & Donlan, 1982). Similarly, students who engage in self-questioning during composition produce both more and better writing (Graham & Harris, 1994). As one student remarked, "(In writing) I had to get my thoughts and opinions together on the subject and also try to find out how much I knew about it" (O'Flahavan & Tierney, 1991, p. 47).

As students read the text that they and others create, they reread portions of it as necessary to clarify ideas and relationships. People who read with good comprehension and write effectively use a variety of skills and strategies. But they don't really recruit these strategies individually, making them appear like so many rabbits out of a hat. Instead, they use a strategic approach to reading and writing, often using several strategies at one time. The hallmark of truly effective readers and writers is that they are able to use their strategic knowledge flexibly, coordinating and adapting the various skills and strategies to fit a particular reading or writing task and purpose (Dole et al., 1991; Duffy, 1993; Paris, Lipson, & Wixson, 1983).

> Being strategic is much more than knowing individual strategies. . . . A good strategy user uses sets of strategies, coordinates those strategies, and shifts strategies when appropriate. If one thing does not work, good strategy users try something else. . . . One must also have an overall idea of what it means to be strategic, that is, how to adapt and combine individual strategies within an overall plan. (Duffy, 1993, p. 232)

The thoughtful reader or writer needs to understand when and why to use a repertoire of more sophisticated approaches, strategies that do not run on automatic pilot as skills do (Paris, Lipson, & Wixson, 1983).

## Deepening Understanding through Discussion and Writing

Current thinking suggests that reading and writing are actually two facets of the same process and that they emerge simultaneously in terms of literacy development (Kucer, 1985; Squire,

1983). Researchers have almost unanimously concluded that reading and writing should be developed together from an early age, and on the basis of their review of relevant research, O'Flahavan & Tierney (1991, p. 47) concluded that "The results suggest that reading and writing in combination are more likely to promote critical thinking than when reading is separated from writing." There appear to be many ways in which these relationships fuel each other:

> Children borrow ideas from reading stories and incorporate them into their own stories. Through reading, they build a richer store of meanings from which to write. Reading their own writing provides practice in reading. Writing helps children to see how written and oral language are related and expands their understanding of the parts of print: phonics, spelling, syntax, and semantics. As they write, children begin to think of themselves as writers just as they think of themselves as readers when they read. (Jewell & Zintz, 1990, p. 102)

This reading and writing cycle has specific effects. For example, when children read or hear good literature, they "use what they have learned about the literary aspects of children's literature in their writing and their speech" (Galda, Ash, & Cullinan, 2000, p. 370). Indeed, researchers have consistently shown how children's language moves closer to the "literary register" of books when they are exposed to high-quality literature and that their writing is more likely to make effective use of literary elements such as character development, plot development, and setting (Dressel, 1990; Lancia, 1997). Despite these realizations it is still much more common for reading and writing to be taught in separate blocks of time and as completely separate and unrelated activities.

Most teachers are comfortable with writing that is focused on the generation of a product, whether narrative or exposition. Students may write original narrative stories to entertain themselves and others; they may write poetry to share thoughts and feelings; or they may write research reports to tell others about what they have learned about a topic. Indeed, most of the writing that elementary students do is designed to communicate with others, and an explicit rationale for using the writing process with young students involves the focus on audience and revision for other. Teachers who promote and support a diversity of responses help students acquire the range of reading abilities required outside of school settings.

To encourage strategic reading for a wide range of purposes, teachers will need to encourage responses that are richer and more complex than past practice has dictated. Group discussions clearly improve students' comprehension. They stimulate students thinking, help them to clarify misconceptions, encourage deeper processing of text, and help students to consider alternate points of view (Almasi, 1995; Alvermann, 1991; Fall, Webb, & Chudowsky, 2000).

The teacher's role in these discussions is worth considering, since it differs from the typical interaction patterns (especially for struggling readers). Generally speaking, the teacher will (1) briefly introduce the idea/concepts to be considered, (2) introduce and/or review strategies that the group has been learning, (3) monitor and observe the students during discussion, and (4) debrief following the discussion (Wiencek & O'Flahavan, 1994). The debriefing would focus on both the content of the discussion and the process of discussion.

**FIGURE 15.4**
Prompts for
Group Discussion

I was surprised by/when . . .

I wonder why . . .

This made me think of . . .

I was confused when/by . . .

I wish . . .

I was hoping . . .

When I think about ____(character)____ , I feel . . .

These characters reminded me of . . .

The part of this book that reminds me of my own life is . . .

I think the author is trying to . . .

I really did not like . . .

Engaging discussion can often be prompted by the right question (see Figure 15.4). These types of prompts allow for a range of responses, and there is no one correct answer. There is evidence that literature discussions that rely on student response have great potential for developing the comprehension abilities of a wide range of students, including those with learning disabilities or limited English proficiency (see Fall et al., 2000; Goatley, Brock, & Raphael, 1995). Both teachers and students will need to develop discussion skills that promote exploration of divergent interpretations.

## Guidelines for Instruction Focused on Comprehension and Composition

Effective instruction does not happen spontaneously. It requires thoughtful preparation, careful execution, and continuous monitoring and adjustment. Just as isolated practice in word identification and vocabulary seem inadequate, isolated comprehension activities completed with small, fragmented texts do not seem to result in improved ability to read real books, poems, newspapers, or brochures for authentic purposes. Nor do writing exercises involving unrelated sentences and paragraphs appear to improve students' ability to write narratives, reports, speeches, and the like. Therefore before turning our attention to specific instructional practices, in this section we will review and expand on some guiding principles for comprehension and composition instruction.

***Provide Information (Explicit Instruction).*** It is clear that students' writing and comprehension abilities can be improved. The key aspects of direct instruction appear to be clear, specific teacher explanation, conveying information about when and why to use the skills; feedback on the effectiveness of the action; and scaffolded instruction with dialogue. Teacher provision of this type of information and structure appears to aid in comprehension and composition.

Explicit instruction provides poor readers and/or writers with information about skills and strategies in terms of how these would be helpful during authentic literacy tasks. Because strategies are more complicated cognitive activities, they take time and (often) explicit instruction for students to acquire (Center for the Improvement of Early Reading Achievement, 2002; Duffy, 1993; Harris & Pressley, 1991). This explicit instruction should make clear to students the value of using a particular strategy(ies) and should model for students appropriate mental processes. Then teachers should let students know when to use these strategies during reading and writing tasks (Paris, Lipson, & Wixson, 1983; Raphael et al., 1989). Teachers need to be sure that students receive reinforcement for the right kind of reading behaviors as well as the right answers.

***Develop Independence and Self-Control.*** Research paints a picture of the learning-disabled child as an inactive learner (Torgeson, 1990). Students in remedial settings often seem willing to be compliant but not responsible readers or writers of text. They often appear willing to do what we ask, but they might not demonstrate any independent ability to apply skills in transfer settings. Often, these children seem to use skills and strategies (in both reading and writing) only when they are explicitly directed to do so (see Wong, Wong, & Blenkisop, 1989). To become mature readers and writers, students need more than skills; they need to learn to use them.

Too often, children do not use their available skills because they have not practiced or acquired the skills in authentic reading/writing situations. They might not know when to use their skills and under which circumstances they would be helpful. Alternatively, students might have learned specific skills or strategies using only one type of text or with one sort of task. Students must practice using skills and strategies in a variety of text–task combinations if they are to acquire the ability to use them spontaneously and flexibly (Fielding & Pearson, 1994). Teachers must also provide instructional supports so that students can gradually acquire the competence they need to be successful in many contexts (Pearson & Gallagher, 1983).

***Provide Support (Make Reading and Writing as Easy as Possible).*** Although students should receive clear, direct information, this will be most effective when teachers view the information (both content and delivery) as a means of supporting students' performance. When teachers provide information that is not needed or for which students are not ready, no learning occurs. The hallmark of effective teaching is thus for teachers to listen and observe carefully so that they identify what information and guidance students might use to become more proficient and strategic.

It is attractive to imagine an area that prescribes the content, difficulty, and pace of instruction appropriate for a given student. The Russian psychologist Vygotsky advanced the idea that students' readiness might be described as "the zone of proximal development"

(Campione, Brown, Ferrara, & Bryant, 1984; Vygotsky, 1978). This zone is thought to be the distance between a student's unaided performance and his or her performance when supported and guided by someone with greater knowledge and expertise. When there is little difference between these two, the child is not likely to take advantage of the proffered support and guidance. On the other hand, the distance is sometimes much greater. "Here, the implication is that with proper input, she could be expected to perform much more capably than her current level would indicate" (Campione et al., 1984, p. 265).

The notions of scaffolded instruction, dialogue, and release of responsibility were described in earlier chapters. It is important for teachers to acquire a strong sense of the importance of supportive teaching, both in the environment and in their interactions with students. Vygotsky strongly believed that learning occurs as a collaborative effort between adults and children, with competence acquired gradually. "What a child can do in cooperation today he can do alone tomorrow. Therefore, the only good kind of instruction is that which marches ahead of development and leads it" (Vygotsky, 1962, p. 104). In classrooms this means that students are not left at a level of lesser performance. Instead, as they become able to read and write some things for some purposes, they are asked to perform increasingly challenging tasks and are supported in doing so.

This type of instruction cannot be scripted, and it relies heavily on the judgments of knowledgeable teachers. However, the past two decades have produced several specific instructional techniques that conform in important ways to this type of teaching. The reciprocal teaching technique introduced in Chapter 12 is one such approach. We will describe others later in this chapter.

***Create Extensive Opportunities for Practice and Personal Response.***    In Chapters 5, 6, and 12 we described the characteristics of classrooms that develop high levels of success in literacy. A substantial convergence of research data show that a print-rich environment, active student involvement with reading, and adult–child interactions focused on literature contribute to students' comprehension of text (Morrow, 1989; Mosenthal et al., 2001). Similarly, student-centered writing programs that focus on creating and revising authentic texts contribute to students' composing abilities (Englert, 1992; Lipson et al., 2000).

No matter how skillful the instruction, students probably cannot become mature, competent comprehenders, skillful at studying and effective at written communication, unless they have extensive opportunities for practice in connected text (Pressley, 2000). Students should have opportunities to retell, judge, and write a wide range of materials. Discussions and projects that promote a personal relationship with characters and/or books are essential.

Teachers also need to take responsibility for directing students to texts and setting tasks that will ensure experiences with a wide range of materials, read or written for a variety of purposes. Extensive exposure to literature improves students' knowledge—they get "smarter" (Stanovich, 1992). The literacy program must also include a wide range of writing tasks and materials. Although they are often engaging, student narratives on self-selected topics are only one type of writing for one purpose. Students should have extensive opportunity to read and write nonfiction as well. The use of writing as a vehicle for expression, persuasion, and learning is essential to the acquisition of written language competence. In both reading and writing, practice and skill in one type of mode or purpose do not ensure success and expertise in other types.

***Integrate Reading and Writing.*** The research results of the past two decades leave little room to question the desirability of providing more unified experiences in reading and writing. Whereas reading and writing had been defined as opposite processes, current thinking suggests that competence in reading and writing are acquired in an interrelated fashion.

Educators in a variety of disciplines have been exploring the use of writing as a tool for learning and thinking. According to Fulwiler (1987, p. 1), "Writing is basic to thinking about, and learning, knowledge in all fields as well as to communicating that knowledge." Interestingly, children who are offered many opportunities to write seem aware of this potential. Nine-year-old Naomi was voluntarily writing on the weekend, creating a paper called "Should Women Be Allowed to Fight in War?" When asked why she would write such a piece on a sunny Sunday, she explained: "Well, on TV some people were arguing about whether women should be allowed to fight in war and I knew that if I *wrote* about it, I'd know what I thought."

Many teachers have begun to capitalize on the promise of writing as a tool for thinking and learning (see Alvermann & Phelps, 2002; Atwell, 1998; Holliday, Yore, & Alvermann, 1994). Frequently, the writing is spontaneous and unedited, as when teachers ask students to do free writing to activate prior knowledge or jot down reflections as they discuss ideas in a cooperative group. Tchudi (1994) lists several of the reasons why teachers should use writing to advance content goals:

1. Writing about a subject helps students learn better.
2. Writing about content helps students acquire skills they will need in real-world contexts.
3. Nonfiction writing supports unmotivated writers, since they may be more interested in writing about content even if they have no interest in writing narrative fiction.
4. Teaching writing teaches thinking.

Teachers must help struggling readers to integrate their abilities with continuous instructional support. In addition to this general promotion of the relationships between reading and writing, various researchers and educators have developed specific suggestions for improving students' abilities in these areas. We discuss some of these in the following sections.

## Instructional Techniques Focused on Comprehension and Composition

Students who are having difficulty comprehending and composing generally need support in two areas. They need help completing reading and writing tasks for school and recreational purposes, and they need to learn to comprehend these and other materials. Reading professionals need to know how to adapt the instructional context, and they need skill in teaching students strategies for reading and learning. Consequently, they are almost always engaged in a balancing act, trying to respond to the sometimes competing demands of these two needs.

## Providing Explicit Instruction

There is ample evidence that students can be taught to comprehend—that teachers can intentionally develop readers' comprehending abilities. The key elements of explicit instruction are clear explanation of the focus, modeling, guided practice, and feedback. This type of instructional model has been used to great effect in both reading and writing.

***Teaching Comprehension Strategies.***   There is considerable evidence that the strategies described earlier in this chapter can be taught to students and that this instruction will improve students' comprehension. A number of recent books provide very useful examples of how to develop expertise and control over the major strategies (see Harvey & Goudvis, 2000; Keene & Zimmerman, 1997; Wilhelm, 2001). Each of these emphasizes using teacher think-alouds to model how to use the various strategies. The several steps suggested by Wilhelm can provide an initial framework for the explicit instruction of strategies:

Step 1.    Choose a short section of text (or a short text).
Step 2.    Decide on a few strategies to highlight.
Step 3.    State your purposes.
Step 4.    Read the text aloud to students, and think aloud as you do.
Step 5.    Have students underline words and phrases related to the use of the strategy (alternatively, discuss these with students).
Step 6.    List (or discuss) the cues and strategies that are used to comprehend.
Step 7.    Ask students to identify other situations in which they could use these strategies.

Although all students benefit from instruction in strategies (NRP, 2000), this intentional approach is especially important for students who have not had extensive literary opportunities outside of school. Short texts and picture books are especially effective for introducing strategies (see Harvey & Goudvis, 2000, who provide an extremely helpful listing of books that they have matched to particular strategies for the purposes of instruction).

Subsequently, of course, you will gradually release the amount of responsibility you take and will extend the types of reading students do. As teachers release responsibility for the use of strategies to students, support is important. The work featured in Figure 15.5 comes from a strategy journal created by a fourth grade teacher after she had spent considerable time explicitly describing how to use this strategy (and others). She expects students to make quite specific responses, drawing on text information, not just general responses that don't really require students to dig deeply. Because many of her students speak English as a second language or have had limited literacy experiences before coming to school, she provides substantial support and feedback before she expects students to use these strategies by themselves. Different pages in the journal support different strategies.

**FIGURE 15.5**
Sample from a
Strategy Journal

Book Title __Junie B. Jones__

Page # __10__       Date __1/24/02__

### Predicting

While reading, use a sticky to mark a sentence or picture with P when you find yourself making a prediction. Write down the sentence or describe the picture that spurs your prediction, and then record the prediction below. After you finish reading, explain what finally happened at the bottom of the page.

Quote or Picture from Text "No dogs or cats will be allowed at school at all."

My Prediction That Junie B. Jones will bring a fish in school because her best firend will bring it in.

What Happened Junie B. Jones wants to cetch a racoon for pet Day.

*Source:* Materials created by Robin Hood, a fourth-grade teacher at John F. Kennedy School in Winooski, Vermont. Adapted from *Strategies that work: Teaching comprehension to enhance understanding* by Stephanie Harvey and Anne Goudvis. Copyright © 2000. Reprinted with permission of Stenhouse Publishers.

*Techniques for Using Text Structure and/or Identifying Patterns.* According to Lapp and Flood (2000, p. 142), "at risk students particularly benefit from instruction in text structure because it becomes a useful aid when content is unfamiliar." Readers create *mental maps* when they have multiple experiences with certain types of texts. When students become highly familiar with particular text structures or genres, reading is easier because those frameworks help them to anticipate text and make rapid, accurate inferences, which frees them to attend to other, more novel aspects of the text. This is, of course, one of the reasons children love series books so much: They become familiar enough with the structures that they can enjoy (comprehend) the text more easily.

When students do not have these mental maps, teachers can help improve students' comprehension abilities by teaching them what to expect and how to read particular texts. Story maps for narrative fiction have become quite common in elementary classrooms (see Chapter 8) and are often used to support students' retellings. We have already discussed in some detail the elements of narrative and exposition and the issue of mapping to reveal important ideas and themes in text (see Chapters 8 and 9). A good map will help children to see the relationships between the events in a story or informational piece. Students are guided to understand the selection because the map directs their attention. In addition, students generally find it easier to recall information when it has been organized coherently, and maps help here as well. Creating text-specific maps is a great deal of work, and many classroom teachers will not be able to find the time to do this. Fowler (1982) suggests a somewhat more generic technique for supporting students in text. He developed the idea of *story frames,* featuring the common characteristics of stories that could be used with elementary students (see Figure 15.6). "Once a frame is constructed it can be used with new passages so long as the passage can support the line of thought or argument implied with the frame" (Fowler, 1982, p. 176).

Fowler suggests using story frames after reading, in place of questions. Students can be guided to complete the frames, and the frames themselves can be shaped to focus on particular elements. Fowler provides copies of frames for focusing on plot, setting, character, and character comparison. He also suggests that students work together to clarify and complete their early frames. We have found that some students with very weak comprehension abilities benefit from being introduced to the frames before reading so that they can use

**FIGURE 15.6**
Sample Story Frame

| Story Summary with One Character Included |
|---|
| Our story is about _____ |
| _____ . _____ is an |
| important character is our story. _____ |
| tried to _____. |
| The story ends when _____ |
| _____ |
| _____. |

*Source:* Chart from Fowler, Gerald. (1982, November). Developing comprehension skills in primary students through the use of story frames. *The Reading Teacher, 36*(2), 176–179. Reprinted with permission of the International Reading Association. All rights reserved.

the frames to guide them through text. When coupled with explicit instruction about the nature of texts, this strategy can lead to improved comprehension of many texts.

As Fowler notes, the same story frames can be used with students of widely varying abilities, because they permit open-ended responses. In addition, they are generic enough so that they provide routine structure and students can do new stories without new instructions. This is especially helpful in working with young or less-skilled readers.

A close relative to story maps are *pattern guides,* which are designed to help students identify important ideas and see how concepts are related in informational text. McNeil (1992) described steps for generating expository guides, which we believe are useful in generating all types of maps:

1. Identify the key idea or generalization to be gained from reading the material.
2. Identify the predominant pattern used in the material: cause and effect, compare/contrast, or other.
3. Illustrate the pattern, and tell the class how you identified it.
4. Make clear to the students that their task is to place relevant information from the text within the pattern. If, for example, you have identified a compare/contrast pattern, students should know what is to be compared and contrasted (the central idea) and then look for information that can be used in making the comparison.
5. Provide the pattern guide, consisting of key concept or generalization, the pattern to be used, and directions.

The directions should indicate the kind of information to be placed within the pattern.

As useful as maps can be, it is important to remember that they are intended to help students comprehend specific materials. As soon as students have control over the various structures and can use them to help understand difficult or unfamiliar text, then the maps should be abandoned in favor of more usual school or work-response modes. According to Buehl (2001), students need to learn to identify the appropriate frame (of mind) to read various types of materials. He suggests using a framework to identify the type of text frame for a specific piece of reading. This is important because different text frames require different reading processes (see Figure 15.7).

These text frames are especially useful for helping students to read exposition. Armbruster, Anderson, and Ostertag (1989) have demonstrated that students' comprehension and writing improved when they were instructed in the use of text structure and taught to write summaries using these frames. They have developed quite sophisticated frames to be used with middle-grade students (see Figure 15.8). Using these frames, students are taught the general frame (e.g., compare/contrast pattern) and are taught to recognize and summarize text that exemplify these structures.

***Teaching Students to Ask and Answer Questions:.*** As we have already noted, the process of asking and answering questions is perhaps the most pervasive activity in formal school settings. We have also seen that the quantity, quality, and placement of questions all influence students' performance and learning. Although teachers often receive vast amounts of advice about how to become better at asking questions (see Chapter 9), relatively little

**FIGURE 15.7**
Framework for
Identifying Text
Frames

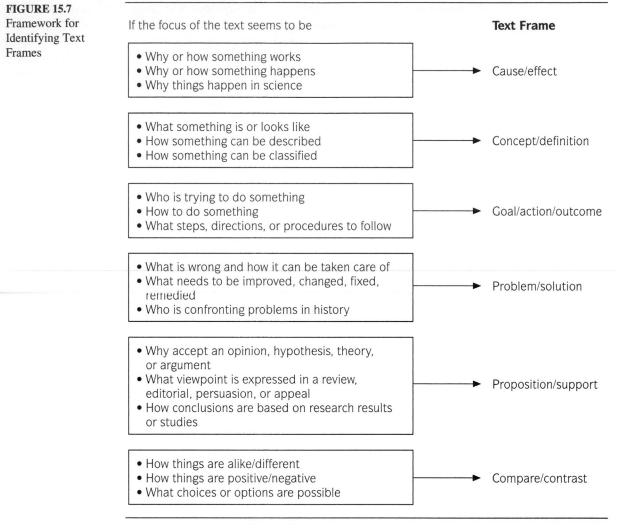

If the focus of the text seems to be                                    **Text Frame**

- Why or how something works
- Why or how something happens
- Why things happen in science

→ Cause/effect

- What something is or looks like
- How something can be described
- How something can be classified

→ Concept/definition

- Who is trying to do something
- How to do something
- What steps, directions, or procedures to follow

→ Goal/action/outcome

- What is wrong and how it can be taken care of
- What needs to be improved, changed, fixed, remedied
- Who is confronting problems in history

→ Problem/solution

- Why accept an opinion, hypothesis, theory, or argument
- What viewpoint is expressed in a review, editorial, persuasion, or appeal
- How conclusions are based on research results or studies

→ Proposition/support

- How things are alike/different
- How things are positive/negative
- What choices or options are possible

→ Compare/contrast

*Source:* Figure from Buehl, Doug. (2001). *Classroom strategies for interactive learning,* 2nd ed. Newark, DE: International Reading Association. Reprinted by permission. All rights reserved.

attention has traditionally been directed at ways to help students become better at answering them.

Students need to gain control over answering the types of questions that are often asked in schools, and teachers need to help them learn this skill. In addition, if students are to grow into competent adults, they must become highly skilled at asking their own questions and knowing how to answer them, using one or more sources of printed material.

Using Pearson and Johnson's (1978) taxonomy, Raphael (1982, 1986) developed a training program that has proven effective in improving students' abilities to answer comprehension questions.

## Compare/Contrast Frame

### Example [contrast]:

Marsupials are either meat eaters or plant eaters. Generally speaking, one can tell what type of food a marsupial eats by looking at its teeth. Meat-eating marsupials have a great many small sharp teeth designed to tear flesh. In contrast, the front teeth of the plant eating marsupials are large and designed for nipping and cutting. The feet of meat-eating marsupials also differ from those of plant-eating marsupials. The meat eaters have feet that look rather like a dog's or cat's foot. The plant eater's feet are quite different. The second and third toes on the hind feet are joined together and the big toe is opposed to the other toes, just as a person's thumb is to their fingers.

### General frame:

|  | Concept A | Concept B |
|---|---|---|
| Feature 1 |  |  |
| Feature 2 |  |  |
| · · · | · · · | · · · |
| Feature *n* |  |  |

### Frame for example:

|  | Meat-eating marsupials | Plant-eating marsupials |
|---|---|---|
| Teeth | Many small sharp teeth | Large front teeth, designed for nipping and cutting |
| Feet | Look like dog's or cat's foot | Second and third toes joined; big toe opposed |

### Summary pattern:

A. Comparison

_____ and _____ are similar in several ways. Both _____ and _____ _____ , _____ and _____ have similar _____ . Finally, both _____ and

_____ _____ .

B. Contrast

_____ and _____ are different in several ways. First of all, _____ , while _____ . Secondly, _____ but _____ . In addition, while _____ , _____ . Finally, _____ _____ , while _____ .

*Source:* Chart from Armbruster, Bonnie B., Anderson, Thomas H., & Ostertag, Joyrce. (1989, November). Teaching text structure to improve reading and writing. *The Reading Teacher, 43*(2), 130–137. Reprinted by permission of the International Reading Association. All rights reserved.

*Question–Answer Relationships (QARs).*   These relationships involve teaching children how to answer questions by recognizing the relationships between the question and possible answers (see Chapter 8). As with other effective teaching strategies, Raphael suggests using effective instructional features such as feedback, gradual release of responsibility and increasing independence, and movement toward longer and more complex texts. In addition, the QAR training program suggests structuring lessons in the following way.

*Lesson 1.* Introduce QARs using a chart or transparency to help students focus attention (see Figure 15.9). Particular attention should be paid to helping students understand how QAR knowledge will help them answer questions more effectively. Following this lesson,

**FIGURE 15.9**
Illustrations to
Explain QARs
to Students

| In the Book QARs | In My Head QARs |
|---|---|
| **Right There** | **Author and You** |
| The answer is in the text, usually easy to find. The words used to make up the question and words used to answer the question are Right There in the same sentence. | The answer is *not* in the story. You need to think about what you already know, what the author tells you in the text, and how it fits together. |

| **Think and Search** | **On My Own** |
|---|---|
| (Putting It Together) | The anwer is not in the story. You can |
| The answer is in the story, but you need to put together different story parts to find it. Words for the question and words for the answer are not found in the same sentence. They come from different parts of the text. | even answer the question without reading the story. You need to use yur own experience. |

*Source:* Figure from Raphael, Taffy E. (1986, February). Teaching question-answer relationships, revisited. *The Reading Teacher, 39*(6), 516–522. Reprinted by permission of the International Reading Association. All rights reserved.

in which each type of question is clearly described, students engage in practice activities that increase in complexity. First students receive two- or three-sentence passages that are accompanied by questions, answers, and QARs. Teacher and students discuss and provide a rationale for each of the QARs. The next practice session involves using the same short passages plus questions and answers, but the students must identify the QAR. Finally, students practice with short passages and questions, answering the questions and identifying the QAR.

*Lesson 2.* Students receive passages of 75–150 words with questions representing each of the types of relationships. The students read the passage(s), answer the questions and assign a QAR to it. Students must be able to defend their choices, though responses may vary. In this part of the training, teachers should be prepared to help students correct wrong decisions about question–answer relationships. However, they must also respond to incorrect answers.

*Lesson 3.* Students work with a basal-length passage that has been divided into at least four segments, with six questions for each segment (two of each type). The first segments should be done as a group; later sections can be done independently if students seem able.

*Lesson 4.* The QAR training is applied to normal reading material as used in the classroom. Students identify the QARs and then answer the questions.

*Maintenance.* For young children (grades 4 and below) Raphael suggests periodic sessions with shorter passages.

Teachers should use QAR training cautiously. Although many students will benefit from the types of discussion that can occur in this program, the training is not explicitly designed to ensure correct question-answering results. Of course, students who know where to look for an answer are at least part of the way toward success.

*Reciprocal Questioning (ReQuest).* Another type of approach to teaching students about questioning was developed by Manzo (1969). *Reciprocal questioning*, or ReQuest, addresses a slightly different aspect of skilled reading: the ability to formulate and pursue reasonable questions and purposes for reading. ReQuest is often used in regular classrooms as an adaptation to the DRA, but it was originally designed for use in clinical, remedial settings, and it is ideally suited for work with inactive readers who comprehend poorly. It can be used with any instructional materials being read by the students, but teachers should ensure that the text is appropriate for the students. As with any new activity, careful introduction is essential. Manzo (1969, p. 124) suggests that students are told the following:

> The purpose of this lesson is to improve your understanding of what you read. We will each read silently the first sentence. Then we will take turns asking questions about the sentence and what it means. You will ask questions first, then I will ask questions. Try to ask the kind of questions a teacher might ask, in the way a teacher might ask them. You may ask me as many questions as you wish. When you are asking me questions, I will close my book. When I ask questions, you close your book.

Both students and the teacher read the material silently; then the students begin questioning the teacher. The teacher responds to all questions to the best of his or her ability. Teachers should not pretend a level of ignorance or fail to answer a question because they wish a student to answer it.

Similarly, when the roles are reversed and the students are questioned, they are not permitted to respond with "I don't know." Instead, they can provide an explanation for their inability to answer or ask for additional information to respond. Question clarification and/or reworking is permissible if either the teacher or the student does not understand the question itself. Finally, when answering questions, individuals should refer to their source of information (the text or their own experience) as a way to justify answers. Clearly, many students will initially have a difficult time with this, but teachers are participating, providing models and responding to questions (see also the discussion of reciprocal teaching in Chapter 12) if students have many comprehension problems.

### Teaching Students How to Write

*Mini-Lessons.*   Many teachers make effective use of mini-lessons to help students become better writers. Mini-lessons are short instruction sessions during which teachers introduce, describe, or show how to accomplish some writing skill or strategy, some aspect of process writing, or some element of author's craft. Virtually anything that might improve students' writing ability could become the focus of a mini-lesson, and teachers can use the approach as needed. Tompkins (2000) describes the steps involved in effective mini-lessons:

*Step 1.*    Introduce the topic.
*Step 2.*    Share examples of the topic.
*Step 3.*    Provide additional information about the topic.
*Step 4.*    Create a poster of other visual for students to refer to.
*Step 5.*    Have children reflect on their learning.

An example of a mini-lesson focused on revision is available in Figure 15.10.

*Strategy Instruction.*    Just as strategies have been devised to help students gain control over their comprehending abilities, some educators have developed approaches to help students develop and regulate their writing abilities. The clear conclusion of this research is that explicit instruction with supportive feedback improves students' writing abilities, especially students who are struggling (see Gersten, Baker, & Edwards, 1999; Gersten, Schiller, & Vaughn, 2000).

The best-documented of these is a program called Cognitive Strategy Instruction in Writing (CSIW), developed by Raphael and Englert (1989, 1990; Englert et al., 1995). As they explain it, "the CSIW program combines principles of process writing with principles underlying the teaching of cognitive strategies such as those used during reading writing" (Raphael & Englert, 1989, p. 242). CSIW relies heavily on helping students to cope with text organization. Students use a variety of *think sheets* to help them plan, draft, monitor, and revise their texts. For example, students use one think sheet to get started on the first phases of prewriting and planning. They are directed to ask themselves questions such as "Why am I writing this?" and "What do I already know about my topic?" Then students are

**FIGURE 15.10**
A Mini-Lesson on
Revising for a Small
Group of Sixth
Graders

**1. Introduce revising.** Mrs. Hernandez gathers together seven students and explains they will spend approximately 15 minutes in a minilesson on revising. She reminds them that revising is the third stage of the writing process and it is the stage when students revisit their rough drafts. They reread and make revisions to make their writing better. By the word *better* she means both clearer and more complete. She shares this quote from children's author Roald Dahl about revision: "By the time I am nearing the end of a story, the first part will have been reread and altered and corrected at least 150 times. I am suspicious of both facility and speed. Good writing is essentially rewriting. I am positive of this" (qtd. in Murray, 1990, p. 182). 150 times! The students are shocked, but Mrs. Hernandez assures them that she does not expect that much revision.

**2. Share examples of revision using students' writing samples.** Mrs. Hernandez shares a classmate's rough draft and final copy of a piece of writing (with that classmate's permission, of course). She asks students to identify changes they noted between the drafts. They also look at the classmate's rough draft to see how the changes were made by crossing out and adding words and phrases and using arrows to move text. They also notice that the classmate's rough draft was double-spaced and written in pencil. The revisions were written in the spaces between lines in blue pen. (They also notice the editing corrections made in red pen.)

**3. Provide information about revising.** Mrs. Hernandez explains that there are four kinds of revisions students can made in their writing: adding, deleting, substituting, and moving. She points to a wall chart with this information. Then students look at the classmate's rough draft and classify his revisions into the four categories.

**4. Have students make notes about revising in their writing notebooks.** Mrs. Hernandez asks students to list the four kinds of revisions in their writing notebooks. She also asks them to return the next day with a composition (rough draft and final copy) that they have written so that they can analyze their own revisions.

**5. Ask students to reflect on how they revise and how they can use this information in revising.** The next day the small group of students gathers together for another 15-minute minilesson and they examine their own revisions. Students notice that they have made only one or two revisions and that most changes are either adding or deleting. One student finds an example of moving text. Mrs. Hernandez asks students to write a plan of action in their writing notebooks under the list of kinds of revisions they added yesterday. She wants students to recognize the value of revising and plan to pay more attention to revisions they make in the writing they are doing now. Mrs. Hernandez also notes in her conference notebook to check with these seven students next week during independent writing time about their revising.

*Source:* From *Teaching writing: Balancing process and product,* by Gail E. Tompkins. Copyright © 2000.

introduced to another think sheet that helps them to plan how they will organize their ideas. The think sheets in this second stage reflect the various types of text structure and are similar to pattern guides described earlier in the chapter.

Components that were added to CSIW to support a greater focus on independence involved more student engagement and a more dialogic approach. The program calls for teachers to model the writing process, and think sheets are provided to guide writing and editing (see Figure 15.11). It should be apparent that although the process is similar to the writing procedures described above, the focus for this writing is content and structure. Thus students' attention is drawn to the specialized features of expository writing. In addition, students are then encouraged to take control themselves (see Figure 15.12). During revision students are clearly expected to make judgments and decide what and how they will shape their writing. Such explicit instruction in writing exposition apparently provides substantial

**FIGURE 15.11** Think Sheet for Editing Comparison/Contrast

**Writing Conference Guides**

Author's Name ____________________ Editor's Name ____________________

**Read to check information**

What is the paper mainly about?

What do you like best? Put a * next to the part you liked best and tell here why you like it: What parts are not clear? Put a ? next to the unclear parts, and tell what made the part unclear to you.

**Question yourself to check organization**

Did the author:

| | | | |
|---|---|---|---|
| Tell what two things are compared and contrasted? | YES | SORT OF | NO |
| Tell the things that they are being compared to and contrasted with? | YES | SORT OF | NO |
| Tell how they are alike? | YES | SORT OF | NO |
| Tell how they are different? | YES | SORT OF | NO |
| Use key words clearly? | YES | SORT OF | NO |

**Plan revision**

What two parts do you think should be changed or revised? (For anything marked "sort of" or "no," tell whether the author should add to, take out, or reorder.)

1. ____________________________________________
____________________________________________
2. ____________________________________________
____________________________________________

What could help make the paper more interesting?

**Talk**

Talk to the author of the paper. Talk about your comments on this think sheet. Share ideas for revising the paper.

*Source:* Reprinted by permission of the publisher from Raphael, T. E., and Englert, C. S., "Integrating writing and Reading Instruction" in Winogard, Peter N., Wixson, Karen K. & Lipson, Marjorie Y., eds., *Improving Basic Reading Instruction* (New York: Teachers College Press, © 1989 by Teachers College, Columbia University. All rights reserved), p. 248.

**FIGURE 15.12**
Think Sheet
for Revision

---

**Think Sheet for Revision**

Author's Name _____

*List suggestions from your editor.*

List all the suggestions your editor has given you:

a. _____

b. _____

c. _____

d. _____

e. _____

*Decide on the suggestions to use.*

Put a * next to all the suggestions that you will use in revising your paper.

*Think about making your paper more interesting.*

List ideas for making your paper more interesting to your reader:

_____

_____

_____

Return to your first draft.

On your first draft, make all changes that you think will improve your paper. Use ideas from the lists you have made on this think sheet.

---

*Source:* "Acquisition of expository writing skills" by T. Raphael, C. S. Englert, & B. Kirschner. In *Reading and Writing Connections,* J. Mason (ed.), p. 280. Copyright © 1989 Allyn and Bacon. Reprinted by permission.

benefits for reading exposition as well and improves students' attitudes toward writing (Raphael, Kirschner, & Englert, 1988).

## Providing Support

Although it is critically important, the directive aspects of explicit instruction are not, in themselves, sufficient to ensure that all students will develop effective comprehension abilities. Teachers must also introduce texts and tasks that will challenge their students and provide the support to help them respond to the text and/or acquire needed information from it. In this section we describe first some strategies for supporting comprehension and then make similar suggestions for supported writing.

*Lesson Frameworks That Support Comprehension Before, During, and After Reading.* There is certainly nothing new in the idea that good teachers help students comprehend and learn from their reading materials (see Graves & Graves, 1994). For over forty years, teachers have been trained to use standard lesson frames that provide extensive support for understanding texts. Almost all approaches to comprehension lesson planning involve a basic before–during–after pattern of instruction. Over the years this basic pattern of the teacher-guided reading has been altered and changed to meet new challenges or to provide different kinds of teacher guidance (Cooper, 1986; Fountas & Pinnell, 1996, 2001a; Spiegel, 1981). The fundamental soundness and flexibility of the before–during–after framework has been demonstrated many times. In the following subsection we use the framework to describe a variety of ways in which teachers can support students as they construct meaning.

*Before Strategies.*    What teachers and students do before reading should obviously help students prepare to read a particular text. This typically involves one of several goals:

- Activate or build prior knowledge;
- Participate in an activity that is likely to help students become more deeply and actively engaged in reading; or
- Remove any barriers to comprehension.

Several common guided reading approaches have well-articulated before-reading procedures. For example, the Directed-Reading-Thinking Activity (DRTA) developed by Stauffer (1969, 1980) is designed to promote students' ability to set purposes for reading and to help them monitor their comprehension. One of the major contributions of the DRTA is its focus on actively involving students in their reading through prediction. The following steps are generally followed in using the DRTA:

1. Elicit student predictions about the outcomes (for fiction) or topic (for nonfiction) of the selection. If students have not done this sort of activity before, they might need help in surveying the title, pictures, and other print clues that can help in making focused predictions.
2. Students read silently to confirm, alter, or reject predictions. This may involve reading the whole or any part of the selection, depending on student skill and text difficulty.
3. The cycle of predict–read–monitor predictions continues, with the teacher helping as little as possible.
4. After-reading activities include student summarization, student–teacher discussion, evaluation of the DRTA process, and involvement in any vocabulary or skills work that the teacher deems important.

Today, many teachers encourage students to make predictions as they read, and there are well-developed guides for helping students make use of text features (pictures, titles, etc.) to promote predicting. What is often missing is the sense of monitoring that was a part of the original DRTA. In our clinics we often ask students to record the page number and their prediction as they read, and then, after each page (or section) they indicate whether the events they predicted have happened, still might happen, or won't ever happen. Most suitable for younger students and for fiction, these prediction guides can even be used as a listening activity if the teacher is willing to record the predictions and the prediction checks. We have also used more focused prediction guides with success.

Several authors have devised prediction guides that work well with expository material. One of these, the Extended Anticipation Guide (Dufflemeyer, Baum, & Merkley, 1987), is displayed in Figure 15.13. The teacher prepares an anticipation guide ahead of time by listing statements about the selection to be read. Some of the statements accurately state information conveyed in the selection; some are misleading, wrong, or simply not supported by the text. Before reading, students predict the topics or content that they think will appear in their reading. During and after reading, students complete the section portion of the guide, which requires them to read the text carefully to support or refute ideas.

The DRTA and prediction guides help students to realize that they already have some ideas about the topic to be considered. Both also provide help and support during reading, so students are encouraged to monitor and check their comprehension. Prediction guides

**FIGURE 15.13**
Extended
Anticipation
Guide

| Extended Anticipation Guide |
| --- |

**Directions:** Read each statement in Part 1. If you believe that a statement is *true*, place a check in the Agree column. If you believe that a statement is *false*, place a check in the Disagree column. Be ready to explain your choices.

**Part 1**

| Agree | Disagree | |
| --- | --- | --- |
| [✓] | | 1. Worms die when they are cut in half. |
| [✓] | | 2. Some living things don't need sunlight. |
| | [✓] | 3. Some animals can grow a new body part after it has been cut off. |
| | | 4. Animals that don't have noses can't smell. |
| | | 5. Laying eggs and giving live birth are the only ways that animals can reproduce. |
| | | 6. All worms have round bodies. |

**Directions:** Now you will read information related to each of the statements in Part I. If the information you read supports your choices above, place a check in the Support column in Part 2. If the information does *not* support your choices above, place a check in the No support column and write what the selection says in your own words.

**Part 2**

| | Support | No support | In your own words |
| --- | --- | --- | --- |
| 1. | | [✓] | [Some flatworms split apart and become two flatworms.] |
| 2. | [✓] | | |
| 3. | | [✓] | [If you cut off a flatworm's head, it will grow a new one.] |
| 4. | | | |
| 5. | | | |
| 6. | | | |

*Source:* Chart from Duffelmeyer, Frederick A., Baum, Dale D., & Merkley, Donna J. (1987, November). Maximizing reader-text confrontation with an Extended Anticipation Guide. *Journal of Reading, 31*(2), 146–150. Reprinted by permission of the International Reading Association. All rights reserved.

especially can be useful for students who require quite structured support. They work best when students' ideas about the text are reasonably congruent with the text information and when students have sufficient prior knowledge to facilitate reading (Spiegel, 1981).

The *Vocabulary-Language-Prediction* (VLP) offers another approach for prereading. The VLP provides support for students in several ways (Wood & Robinson, 1983). There is extensive prereading support, and the activity combines vocabulary and oral language development with prediction and monitoring. The VLP is especially attractive because it can so easily be embedded in typical reading lesson frameworks. It requires some preparation by the teacher; indeed, Steps 1–3 have to do with selecting and preparing the vocabulary:

### Vocabulary

*Steps 1–3:*  Select vocabulary, determining which words are important and will cause students difficulty (see Chapter 13). Decide what skill(s) will be addressed in this lesson and how vocabulary is related to the skill(s). The words are then written on individual cards with the page number from the story on them.

*Step 4:*  The words are displayed for the students; students are told they will see these words in the selection and that they will do some activities with the words.

Students can point to or pick up the cards that contain the correct word during the following steps.

### Oral Language

*Step 5:*  The teacher asks questions about the structural and conceptual features of the words. Other activities may include discussions of categories, context, synonyms, and so on.

### Prediction

*Step 6:*  The teacher directs children to use these words to predict what the story will be about, and predictions are written on the board. Wood and Robinson (1983, p. 394) suggest the following as possible prediction questions: Characterization: "Which words probably tell you about the main character?" Setting: "Which words tell where she/he lives?" Events/outcomes: "Which words give clues about events in the story?"

*Step 7:*  Children are asked to confirm, reject, or modify their predictions during reading.

Because of the focus on vocabulary and prereading preparation, the VLP can be used with English language learners as well as students reading highly unfamiliar material. In addition, the link between story vocabulary and prediction helps students to see other ways to generate hypotheses about the text besides using the title and pictures. Finally, the focus on monitoring in Step 7 helps students to connect the prereading instruction and the postreading discussion, an important feature of the next framework.

When students' prior knowledge is a significant factor, other adaptations may be needed. Au (1979) developed a lesson framework that focuses on the experience-text-relationship (ETR). In ETR teachers take an active role in discussing the text and text-related ideas with students, and they also model skilled reading for students, helping them to build a concept of reading as a meaningful activity. Thus before reading, the teacher must preview the reading material and identify concepts or themes that might be especially interesting or relevant for students. Before reading, teachers should also identify places where silent reading can be stopped for students who need to read in smaller segments. The Experience (E) phase occurs before reading. The teacher evaluates students' prior knowledge of the themes, concepts, or ideas central to reading the selection. The teacher guides the discussion in two ways: leading discussion toward the selection by showing pictures or using ideas and helping students to see the relationships between their knowledge and the text. Then students make predictions about the selection. During the Text (T) phase teachers support students in a typical guided reading of the text, and in the Relationship (R) phase of ETR the teacher leads students to make connections between the selection and their own knowledge and experience.

This focus on connecting past experience and knowledge with text information needs to be done quite explicitly for some students. Teachers should be aware of these connections as well and should actively seek ways to focus students on the important ideas in text. The underlying relationships describing how people feel when they do not get the help or cooperation they desire do not require such specific prior knowledge.

Fountas and Pinnell (1996) remind us that the prereading portion of the plan should be brief and varied. They suggest that the teacher *not* preteach words. Instead, they suggest using a *picture walk* to "debug" the text for students: naming pictures and parts of pictures to remove word-level boundaries. Although this might work very well with young children, some students will require even more help in the area of prior knowledge. Some may benefit from additional instruction in the area of vocabulary (see Chapter 14). Others may benefit from instructional support that focuses on combining the areas just described.

*During Strategies.*    Some strategies or activities are useful at all three phases of the before–during–after plan. That is true of story maps. Maps can be used to accommodate a wide range of student abilities by altering the degree of prereading and during-reading support that is provided. Maps and other text frames are especially effective in guiding students through text, even when they are introduced prior to reading. For example, students can be given a blank but fully structured story map so that their task is to read for the purpose of completing the network. For some children this will provide the right degree of support. For others, who have comprehension abilities that are even less well developed or who are reading especially difficult material, portions of the map can be filled in, leaving only a few blanks to be completed.

Although this support for comprehending the story content is important, teachers also need to support students as they apply the strategies they are learning. *Supported Think Aloud during Reading* (STAR) is an instructional strategy designed to focus students on the *processes* of effective comprehension whenever they are reading (Lipson & Wickizer, 1989; Lipson et al., 1987). STAR is a technique that involves student–teacher dialogues about a reading selection. The purpose of these dialogues is to encourage students to actively use the skills and strategies they have available but often do not use. The key to STAR is the teacher's ability to elicit student talk about reading and then to respond with supportive remarks about the value of the student's approach. To do this, students are stopped periodically as they read and are encouraged to talk about what they had been doing and thinking as they read each portion of text.

These interruptions open dialogues that provide teachers with instructional opportunities. These exchanges are guided by a checklist that summarizes the comprehending behaviors used by skilled readers (see Figure 15.14). Teachers ask questions that focus on the process versus the products of reading to lead students toward self-control and encourage them to take increased responsibility for their own learning.

The following specific guidelines should be considered:

1. *Keep instruction focused.* Many students must first become aware of the reading behaviors that are likely to improve comprehension. When students do not use a range of appropriate reading strategies, teachers can prompt them to become more active in one of the component areas: pause and reflect, hypothesize, monitor, integrate, and clarify (see Figure 15.14).

2. *Provide appropriate feedback.* Because many teachers are not accustomed to teaching with extensive dialogue, Lipson and Wickizer (1989) found that most needed some guidance about how to conduct these teacher-student exchanges. When using STAR in the early stages of instruction:

    *Listen* carefully to what the child is saying.
    *Attend* to what the child is *doing* as well as to the accuracy of the response.
    *Acknowledge* (by naming) the strategy used to understand the text.
    *Affirm* use of the strategy with praise or feedback. (Lipson & Wickizer, 1989, p. 30)

Often students' statements suggest, but do not explicitly name, a strategy, and it appears that they are relatively unaware that they have employed a useful approach to the task. Under these circumstances it is even more important that the teacher use acknowledgement and affirmation. For example, in the following exchange, the student does not name the strategy himself and must be informed of its use:

STUDENT:   I didn't get that. I couldn't understand it because of that word there.

TEACHER:   Okay. It's really helpful to try to make sense out of what you're reading. It's important to ask yourself if it makes sense or not, and I'm glad you're doing that. Okay, Mitchell, when that happened, what did you do?

This teacher is helping Mitchell to become aware of his reading strategies and to see which ones are productive. These patterns of interaction are essential for many older and disabled readers. It appears that middle-school students, even very disabled ones, can benefit from these procedures, improving their comprehension during teacher-supported reading activities but also during silent unsupported reading (see Lipson et al., 1987).

FIGURE 15.14
Supported
Think-Aloud
Checklist

| Prompts | Stop 1 | Stop 2 | Stop 3 | Stop 4 | Stop 5 |
|---|---|---|---|---|---|
| **Pause and Reflect** 1. Does this part make sense? | ✓ | ✓ | ✓ | ✓ | ✓ |
| 2. Do the words and sentences in this section make sense together? | | ✓ | ✓ | ✓ | ✓ |
| **Hypothesize** 3. What do you think will be presented next? (or what will the next part talk about?) | | | ✓ | ✓ | |
| 4. What do you think this story is going to be about? | ✓ | | | | |
| **Monitor** 5. Is there any part you didn't understand? | | | ✓ | | ✓ |
| 6. Did this part talk about what you predicted (expected)? | | ✓ | | ✓ | ✓ |
| 7. Did you change your mind about anything? | | ✓ | | ✓ | |
| **Integrate** 8. Does the information in this part fit with what you knew before reading? | | ✓ | | | |
| 9. Does the information in this part fit with the information presented earlier in the text? | | | ✓ | ✓ | |
| 10. What's the most important thing(s) in this part? (or what is the main idea of this part?) | | | | ✓ | ✓ |
| 11. Did you get any pictures in your head about this part? | | | ✓ | | ✓ |
| **Clarify** 12. Did you ask yourself questions about this part? | | ✓ | | ✓ | |
| 13. Do you need to go back in the text to clarify anything? (or do you need to reread anything?) | | | ✓ | ✓ | ✓ |
| 14. What did you do when you didn't understand a word, a sentence, or a part of a sentence? | | | ✓ | | ✓ |

*After Strategies.*    There are many attractive and useful books on the market today to help teachers create frameworks and patterned responses to text (see Blachowicz & Ogle, 2001; McLaughlin & Allen, 2002). However, most teachers still rely on questioning as a major tool in supporting students' comprehension. Too often, the questions become a sort of interrogation, and the teacher is conducting assessment, not instruction. Certainly, the research suggests that "the questions that teachers pose in discussions or incorporate on their tests are highly influential in guiding students' learning" (Alexander & Jetton, 2000, p. 302).

*Question the Author* (QtA), developed by Beck and McKeown and their colleagues (Beck, McKeown, Sandora, Kucan, & Worthy, 1996; Beck & McKeown, 2001), is a strategy designed to help students build understanding of text, to become more engaged with texts, and to consider ideas deeply. The important thing about QtA is that it reminds both the teacher and the students that comprehending requires figuring out what the author is meaning. As Beck and McKeown (2001, p. 16) note, "initial questions may not bring forth meaningful responses from young children. Yet simply asking more questions will not necessarily prompt richer comments." Teachers might think that because students can respond to their questions, they have understood the text, but they often are reciting elements from the text without really understanding the significance of the words.

QtA is conducted during guided reading in small or large groups. It relies on queries, or prompts, that teachers use to help students build understanding and engage with the text. These queries are of two types: queries that help students deal with text or queries that advance group discussion and promote student–student interaction. Note that queries that are designed only to check students' memory are not allowed. Instead, the queries are designed to help students think, "What is the author talking about? Why does the author tell us this now? Why did the author choose these words?"

Many of the queries suggested by Beck and McKeown sound like the answers to our old questions. For example, Beck and McKeown (2001, p. 15) suggest questions that might be used to promote comprehension of *Harry the Dirty Dog* (Zion, 1994):

*They called Harry, "This little doggie." What does that tell us?*

*It says, "Mrs. Bobbin . . . was tired and had a bad headache, but she still managed to sew the last stitches in the gown she was making." What's going on?*

*How does what Harry did fit in with what we already know*

The research suggests that teachers who use QtA are more likely to support and sustain the kinds of discussion that appear to help students understand the text more deeply and also learn how to approach other texts in the future.

***Providing Support for Writing.***    Programs that promote a process (versus product) view of writing have great potential for enhancing students' reading as well as writing abilities. Ours is an admittedly slim review of the issues and techniques. This text is designed to help teachers consider specialized practices designed for struggling students and to identify ways to adapt practice. Ideally, the specialized program is being designed to complement a preexisting developmental program of high quality. Interested readers are referred to one of the many fine books on this topic for more information (e.g., Calkins, 1994; Graves, 1983, 1994; Tompkins, 2000).

Generically called "process writing programs," these approaches to teaching writing have grown out of a clearer understanding of writing and writers. Elsewhere in the book, we have generally described the writing process. In the following discussion we suggest some ways to help support students as writers and ways to manage writing and reading activities in the classroom so that writing will be sustained as an important daily activity. Then we describe one approach designed to provide extra support for the struggling writer.

Many students experience considerable difficulty in writing. After reviewing the available research, Graham and Harris (1994, p. 209) concluded:

> In addition to the low quality of their writing, many poor writers, especially students with learning or behavioral problems, are not especially productive. . . . The papers they produce are often impoverished in their detail and inordinately short. They further have difficulty completing writing assignments and may resist well-intentioned efforts to get them to write regularly.

These extensive difficulties are especially troubling because of the reciprocal nature of the reading/writing processes. Students who have had opportunities to write continuously and to confer with others about their work bring the knowledge they acquire about writing, structure, and communication to their reading. To complete the work expected of them, many struggling students need considerable support. There are several suggestions for supporting students as they write and read.

*Support the Classroom Writing Program.* Many special teachers do not have the types of schedules that allow for a full-blown writing workshop approach. In that case it is often better to try to support students in the classroom during the regularly scheduled writing time. If the classroom is not using these approaches, your job as a language arts professional may be to help organize and initiate such an approach. Then support (i.e., flexible grouping for skills or extra support for revision) can be planned within this framework.

There are also ways in which the classroom context can be adapted to support many different students. Block (1993), for example, describes a cooperative strategy that would be useful in helping students to get started and also provides a fun way to experience different writing styles. The strategy uses a progressive dinner format and involves students in each phase of the writing process. Students are grouped and placed at tables. On each table is the same small set of objects (e.g., a food item, a ball, a map, and an item of clothing) and five sheets of chart paper (for the first five steps of the activity). Other ways to prompt writing may be used. One person in each group serves as a recorder.

| | |
|---|---|
| Step 1 (prewriting): | Students brainstorm ideas about the objects on the table. Then they move to the next table. |
| Step 2 (writing): | Each group uses the ideas from the previous group to write a story draft. After twenty minutes, they move to the next table. |

| | |
|---|---|
| Step 3 (revising): | The group revises the previous group's story by adding, deleting, or reorganizing content. After ten minutes the group moves to the next table. |
| Step 4 (editing): | The group edits the story as it was left by the previous group. The have seven minutes to attend to grammar, usage, and mechanics. They move to the next table. |
| Step 5 (final draft): | The group creates a final draft of the edited story. After seven minutes, they return to their writing (Step 2) and read the final version of their story, paying particular attention to the changes that were made. The group writes a title for the story. |
| Step 6 (sharing). | |

*Maintain Writing Folders.*    Students (and teachers) should understand that not all pieces of writing will proceed smoothly from prewriting to publication. Many good ideas will go dry after writing has begun; others will be derailed by a more pressing topic. Still others require more time to develop. Therefore students should keep a folder, not only for their current writing, but also as a place to keep other story ideas, notes on topics to be pursued, and early drafts of any project that has not been completed. Teachers and students together should review this folder periodically for ideas and decide on pieces that should really be brought to completion. These folders can also be used by support personnel to identify areas of need or places where extra support is required and to plan instruction.

*Help Students Select Topics.*    Encourage students to write about things that interest them. Try to ensure that they have more than one topic idea so that they can turn to a different one if the first doesn't seem to be working. Atwell (1987) suggests the following ways to help students in topic selection. Students should interview each other and keep a list of "My Ideas for Writing." Be sure that students know that they can ask for a conference to discuss ideas for generating and selecting topics, and be ready to provide stimulus questions such as "What is special about you?" or "Who's your best friend? What's special about him or her?" Teachers who are unhappy with the topics of students' writing need to take responsibility for helping students choose more wisely.

*Develop and Teach Conference Skills.*    For students to advance in a writers' workshop or process writing approach, teachers must confer regularly with students. This may require that teachers develop some new skills or resurrect and refine dormant ones. Florio-Ruane worked with novice teachers as they engaged in teacher-student conferences and has remarked (1991, p. 381),

> Many beginning teachers assume a vision of knowledge as a commodity to be transferred. Clearly the theory of cognitive development underlying dialogic approaches to teaching assumes, in contrast, a view of knowledge development as a continuing process of negotiation and transformation. This difference has profound implications for teaching by conference. . . . Showing, telling, and evaluating are transformed into diagnostic listening, asking, and responding.

Florio-Ruane (1991, p. 382) goes on to suggest several maxims that teachers should use as they engage in conferences with young or struggling writers:

- Assume competence.
- Know the learner.
- Follow the learner.
- Capitalize on uncertainty.

These ways of interacting might seem especially alien to many reading teachers and special educators. For a very long time, the skills model has encouraged the older view, and the idea that disabled learners would negotiate and discuss their work is not a common one. To capitalize on uncertainty both students and teachers will need to believe that it is all right not to be sure about something and then use these as opportunities for learning.

Students, even primary-age children, can and should be taught to have productive conferences with their peers (Lipson et al., 2000). To have effective and fruitful writing conferences, students need to know what is expected and how to behave. General guidelines for how the conference should proceed include the following:

1. The author should have a clear goal in mind, such as seeking advice about the title, requesting help on a difficult section, or soliciting an overall reaction to the ideas in a piece.
2. Meaning discussions should always precede mechanics discussion, although mechanical difficulties may account for difficulties in conveying meaning.
3. First, the author reads his or her draft aloud to the conference partner. During this read-aloud the author is likely to find areas that require revision.

Students need clear guidelines for responding, and many teachers find it helpful to provide a conference guide, with a few easy prompts or reminders to students about their role(s). This can either be placed in the students' folder or posted on the wall of the writing center.

Some teachers have found it helpful to make a videotape that demonstrates effective conferencing so that students can see others working through the process. Teachers will find it easier to maintain process writing programs if they invest in conference training with their students, and students will benefit from the opportunity to think about other students' writing and provide feedback to them.

*Provide Opportunities for Sharing.* Students should not be expected to share all their pieces of writing. However, there is no clearer motivation for taking writing and revising seriously than to make sure that authors have opportunities to share their work. This may involve bookmaking activities or word processing and desktop publishing. Some children's magazines regularly publish written work of young people, and these may be interesting for some teachers and students (see Chapter 12).

Teachers should find ways to celebrate students' writing outside of the classroom. However, these activities can become quite elaborate projects, and for struggling writers, specialized teachers should make sure that there is ample time for writing. There are less involved and, in some cases, equally gratifying ways to share writing. For example, many teachers have long known the power of having older students read to younger ones. This can be extended to having students read their own stories and descriptions to younger students. Many teachers and students have been attracted to the idea of an *author's chair* (Graves & Hansen, 1983). This special chair provides a place for authors to sit as they read their work to the class. Teachers may also sit there to read trade books for the purpose of author discussion. These less formal forums for sharing can be powerful social forces for literacy acquisition. They also provide additional models for students who need topic ideas or suggestions for new ways to express themselves.

Quite often, struggling students find writing both difficult and painful. Even for these students, though, writing can occasionally provide the key to reading. For example, Justin came to a university reading clinic several years ago. At 10 years of age he was an extremely reluctant and unskilled reader who nevertheless discovered that he loved to write. His own explanation for this is interesting: "I like to make my own ideas for what will happen. I don't like reading because you have to get the ideas *they* wrote." The dialogue journal that had been started early took shape as a prewriting idea log. In addition, Justin avidly listened as his tutor read *Dear Mr. Henshaw* (Cleary, 1983), a book about a young boy who wanted to be an author. Over time, he found that there were things he liked to read as well, and although still struggling, he is no longer stalled.

*Provide Opportunities for Doing Different Types of Writing.*   Many struggling writers lack skill but they also lack a sense of the functional value of writing. Teachers should remember the many writing forms and formats that people use everyday and encourage students to explore as many of these as seems reasonable (see Figure 15.15). Many of these forms will seem easier for a struggling student and will also provide the authenticity that many conventional writing tasks lack.

The Cognitive Strategy Instruction (CSIW) discussed earlier also provides supportive frameworks for struggling writers. The program is designed to help students as they are engaged in creating whole texts versus sentence writing and worksheets (see Englert, 1992). Scaffolding is provided in the CSIW program through a series of *think sheets*. "One think-sheet was developed to guide thinking during each phase of writing: planning, drafting, reflecting on the first draft and preparing to edit it, editing, revising, and second or final drafts" (Raphael et al., 1989, p. 269).

Figure 15.16 shows one of these think sheets, this one focused on the planning phase of the writing process. Raphael et al. (1989) report that students who had used these supports made significant gains in free writing and that they outperformed students in a more conventional language arts/writing program. Of course, students who require a great deal of support will need an interactive or shared writing approach (Chapter 12; see also Button, Johnson, & Furgerson, 1996).

## Developing Independence

It is extremely important for teachers to help students comprehend the specific texts they must read. However important these supporting tasks may be, permanent maintenance is not desirable. Students need to learn how to read and how to learn so that they can do so across

**FIGURE 15.15**
Discourse Forms
for Content-Area
Writing

| | | |
|---|---|---|
| Journals and diaries (real or imaginary) | Commentaries | Practical proposals |
| Biographical sketches | Responses and rebuttals | Interviews: |
| Anecdotes and stories | Newspaper "fillers" | actual |
| from experience | Fact books or fact sheets | imaginary |
| as told by others | School newspaper stories | Diections: |
| Thumbnail sketches: | Stories or essays for | how-to |
| of famous people | local papers | school or neighborhood |
| of places | Proposals | guide |
| of content ideas | Case studies: | survival manual |
| of historical events | school problems | Dictionaries and lexicons |
| Guess who/what | local issues | Technical reports |
| descriptions | national concerns | Future options, notes on: |
| Letters: | historical problems | careers, employment |
| personal reactions | scientific issues | school and training |
| observations | Songs and ballads | military/public service |
| public/informational | Demonstrations | Written debates |
| persuasive: | Poster displays | Taking a stand: |
| to the editor | Reviews: | school issues |
| to public officials | books (including | family problems |
| to imaginary people | textbooks) | state or national issues |
| from imaginary places | films | moral questions |
| Requests | outside reading | Books and booklets |
| Applications | television programs | Informational monographs |
| Memos | documentaries | Radio scripts |
| Resumés and summaries | Historical "you are there" | TV scenarios and scripts |
| Poems | scenes | Dramatic scripts |
| Plays | Science notes: | Notes for improvised |
| Stories | observations | drama |
| Fantasy | science notebook | Cartoons and cartoon |
| Adventure | reading reports | strips |
| Science fiction | lab reports | Slide show scripts |
| Historical stories | Math: | Puzzles and word searches |
| Dialogues and | story problems | Prophecy and predictions |
| conversations | solutions to problems | Photos and captions |
| Children's books | record books | Collage, montage, mobile, |
| Telegrams | notes and observations | sculpture |
| Editorials | Responses to literature | |
| | Utopian proposals | |

*Source: Teaching Writing in the Content Areas: Elementary School* by Stephen N. Tchudi and Susan J. Tchudi. Copyright © 1983 National Education Association of the United States. Reprinted by permission.

many settings over a lifetime. To accomplish this often requires different types of instructional activity.

***A General Plan to Teach for Independence.*** A recurrent finding among researchers and educators over the past two decades is that students need explicit instruction to acquire reading competence (Paris et al., 1984; RRSG, 2002). In addition, teachers need to be sure

**FIGURE 15.16**
Think Sheet
for Planning

| Plan Think Sheet |
| --- |

Name: _____ Date: _____

Topic: _____

***WHO:*** Who am I writing for?

_____

_____

***WHY:*** Why am I writing this?

_____

_____

***WHAT:*** What do I know? (Brainstorm)

1. _____

2. _____

3. _____

4. _____

5. _____

6. _____

7. _____

8. _____

_____

_____

*Source:* From Englert, C. S. (1992, March). Writing instruction from a sociocultural perspective: The historic, dialogic, and social enterprise of writing. *Journal of Learning Disabilities, 25*(3), p. 156. Copyright © 1992. Reprinted by permission of Sage Publications, Ltd.

that they provide for a release of responsibility if they hope that students will transfer and apply newly acquired skills and strategies (Pearson & Gallagher, 1983). Using research evidence from several research efforts, Palincsar (1986) concluded that effective comprehension instruction should include *metascripts,* or action plans, that involve general suggestions for instruction but also allow teachers to be responsive to the students' behaviors during teaching.

The metascripts suggested by Palincsar (1986) involve several stages in instruction, and it seems reasonable to suggest that teachers' long-term planning should include three instructional phases: Heavy Coaching, Supported Reading (Working Together), and Independent Application (On Your Own).

*Heavy Coaching.* When students are learning brand-new skills and strategies or transferring newly acquired skills to difficult material, they need teachers to guide their reading and provide significant coaching. During this phase of instruction teachers have responsibility for much of the reading or learning event (see Palincsar, 1986, for examples). Teachers should do the following:

- Make explicit statements of lesson focus and content;
- Model the skill or strategy (Teacher Talk Thru);
- Support students' contributions;
- Use students' ideas and link them to new knowledge; and
- Maintain focus and direction.

*Supported Reading (Working Together).* As students become increasingly competent, they should begin to gain more control over the knowledge and skill they are acquiring. During this phase teachers should encourage students to take responsibility but provide guidance and maintenance functions to support successful reading and learning. Teachers should take primary responsibility for maintaining the focus and direction of the reading or studying event. In other respects, however, there is a shared responsibility:

- Students (with teacher support) state the lesson focus;
- Students (with teacher support) model the skill or strategy (Student Talk Thru);
- Students and teacher support students' contribution; and
- Students and teachers use each others ideas and link them to new knowledge.

*Independent Application (On Your Own).* Student independence is the goal of the reading instructional program. Success in this area results from careful and supportive instruction that includes an explicit self-control component (Brown, Campione, & Day, 1981; Dewitz, Carr, & Patberg, 1987; Paris, Newman, & McVey, 1982). In this phase students are encouraged to generalize their learning to unstructured settings. In addition, students and teachers troubleshoot so that the various components work in concert for the desired purposes.

*Teaching Students to Monitor and Manage Their Own Comprehension.* Instruction should not be limited to those periods when reading is being taught directly. The first step in empowering students and helping them gain control over their reading is to help them use and control their skills as they read in a variety of contexts. Because poor readers often do not understand when and why to use their skills and strategies, teachers need to teach students about the functional value of these behaviors during all reading events.

To this end, educators frequently suggest an integrated or thematic approach to instruction that is more likely to help students see the interrelatonships between and among knowledge, skills, and content (Gavelek, Raphael, Biondo, & Wang, 2000; Lipson, Valencia, Wixson, & Peters, 1993). For specialized reading or writing educators, of course, this poses a considerable difficulty because they might not work with students throughout the day. Certainly, if we are to take the idea of self-regulated, motivated learning seriously, we will all need to work together to create a coherent and engaging learning environment.

# Studying: A Specialized Case of Reading and Writing

## Explicit Instruction

Studying can be improved through explicit instruction in several of the areas we have already discussed. For example, when students are taught to map the text, identifying the text structures and organizational patterns, their performance improves (Bernard & Naidu, 1992). Similarly, several of the strategies discussed earlier are especially helpful for studying. Question generation, text summarization, and comprehension monitoring have all been shown to improve students' study results (Nist & Simpson, 2000; NRP, 2000).

## Supported Studying

Students must learn to set their own purposes and decide what they want or need to know from specific materials. However, educators must acknowledge that studying places very specific demands on students, demands that are not always consistent with the student's own goals. Studying usually requires students to identify or recognize an external purpose. Learning in school texts often demands that students know not only what to read but also what the associated tasks are or will be.

Because teachers often set purposes for students in school settings and decide what tasks must be accomplished with the information acquired, it would be helpful if they supported students' content study. Although there are relatively few empirically validated study approaches (Nist & Simpson, 2000), teachers can help all students to learn the information they have identified as important by employing techniques like those described in the following sections.

***Lesson Frameworks in Content Text.***     Using a before–during–after approach to reading specific texts will often help students learn the content of informational texts. Before reading, teachers should take care to introduce any content-specific words or to note cases in which vocabulary usage varies from everyday meanings. Structured overviews (see Chapter 14) and other prereading activities can also help students focus and prepare. In addition, teachers can either set a purpose for reading themselves or elicit purpose-setting ideas from the group, thereby assessing students' ability to identify appropriate purposes.

During reading, students can be provided with embedded guided reading questions (Weir, 2000) or text frameworks that many find helpful as an aid to comprehension. These can, of course, be used later as a study guide. After reading, students can be helped to revisit the text to organize information or gather ideas that were missed on an initial read through of the text.

When working with students who need additional guidance and conceptual support, teachers might wish to employ the modifications suggested by the *concept–text–application* (CTA) approach developed by Wong and Au (1985). The CTA, like the ETR, is a variation on the traditional guided reading framework that places particular emphasis on students' prior knowledge. During the concept (C) phase teachers assess students' knowledge of the major concepts to be encountered in text. Where appropriate and necessary, unfamiliar vocabulary or concepts are pretaught. Students read predetermined segments silently during the text (T) phase, and teachers lead discussions that help students build background knowledge and/or fit new information to older concepts.

It might seem obvious that this teacher-guided lesson framework would be useful in reading the types of dense, unfamiliar texts that students often encounter for study. Unfortunately, many teachers, even those who use a DRA during reading instruction, do not apply the principles of this plan during the reading of other texts (see Alvermann, 1989). As a result, reading teachers and other support personnel might need to help students acquire important content. Creating study aids such as study guides is one option, but so is helping regular teachers to adapt their reading expectations. Both techniques are described next.

***Study Guides.***   Studying from content-area textbooks is challenging for even the most able school-aged students. It requires students to recognize important information and to locate it in dense, often poorly written text. Even when studying from considerate text, students must be able to make use of complex text structures, using these to help identify major ideas and supporting details. One of the best-documented techniques for helping students maintain their focus in text is the study or reading guide (see Wood, Lapp, & Flood, 1992, for a review of these):

> Study guides—or reading guides, as they are sometimes called—are teacher-developed devices for helping students understand instructional reading material. Research and experience show that study guides can help students understand their content area texts by focusing their attention on the major areas of importance within a given chapter or chapter segment. (Wood, Lapp, & Flood, 1992, pp. 2–3)

These guides generally involve segmenting text into smaller pieces and interspersing checkpoints throughout that are designed to help students check their comprehension or monitor their progress. This level of support has generally proved helpful for readers of all abilities (Armstrong, Patberg, & Dewitz, 1988).

A wide array of study guide models is currently available to teachers. Herber's (1970) *three-level guide* focuses students' attention on different levels of meaning. Herber contended that three levels of comprehension are required of students in content-area reading:

literal, interpretive, and applied. Therefore he designed the three-level guide to help students interact with the text in three fairly distinct stages. The three questions students are guided to answer in a three-level guide are as follows:

- What does the author say?
- What does the author mean?
- How does this relate to your own life? How can you use this information?

Preparation is obviously very important (see the sample guide Figure 15.17). It proceeds in the following way for both three-level and study guides (Brozo & Simpson, 1999; Herber, 1978):

1. Analyze the text. Identify the major text organization pattern and specify the relationships between ideas. Decide what inferences or conclusions can be made from the ideas presented in the text.
2. Make decisions. Decide what knowledge and abilities your students have and what your objectives are.

**FIGURE 15.17**
Levels-of-
Comprehension
Guide
(Science, Middle
Level)

---

**Food Chains and Food Webs**

**I. *Literal Level***
As you read "Food Chains and Food Webs," decide which of the statements below are clearly stated in the text. Mark each statement that is clearly stated in the text and be prepared to support your choices.

_____ 1. When a mouse eats a grain, energy is passed from the grain to the mouse.
_____ 2. A food chain is the transfer of energy, in food form, from one organism to another.
_____ 3. The sun is an important source of light.

**II. *Interpretive Level***
Read the following statements. Mark each statement that expresses an idea that can be supported with information in the text section you have just read. Be prepared to discuss the supporting evidence.

_____ 1. Owls eat mice, snakes, and rabbits; this makes them all part of a food web.
_____ 2. Only some consumers are part of a food web.
_____ 3. When mice eat grain, they are receiving energy from the sun.

**III. *Applied Level***
Read the following statements. Mark each statement that you think is reasonable and that can be supported with information from the text combined with what you already know.

_____ 1. Humans are major consumers in a food chain.
_____ 2. We could live without energy from the sun.
_____ 3. The early bird gets the worm.

---

*Source:* Wood, Karen D., Lapp, Diane, & Flood, James. (1992). *Guiding readers through text: A review of study guides,* p. 28. Newark, DE: International Reading Association. Reprinted by permission. All rights reserved.

**3.** Decide what quantity and quality of comprehension you require for this reading assignment.

Once these steps have been completed, teachers create a guide. This is done by writing statements for each level of the guide. According to Ruddell (1993, p. 150), "It is better to have too few rather than too many statements. A few well-chosen statements will serve to launch the interesting, animated small-group discussions you're attempting to stimulate."

The three-level guide, like the study guide (see Figure 15.17), requires significant amounts of teacher time and effort, and although these are intended to help students acquire independence in studying, they are heavily teacher-directed.

***Discussion Webs.***    We have already noted how helpful classroom discussion can be to improve students' comprehension of text. Good discussions are difficult to initiate, however, and even more difficult to maintain. During whole-class discussions it is often the case that only a few students participate. During small-group discussions the teacher often takes over, and it becomes a question–answer period. Alternatively, when teachers use peer-led groups, they are often unhappy with the results. A strategy that is helpful here is the discussion web. Alvermann (1991) designed the approach to enhance students' active engagement with text and improve their participation in discussion. The discussion web is especially useful when you want students to consider more than one perspective or when there may be more than one correct answer. Drawing on other strategies, Alvermann described five steps:

*Step 1.*   Use your typical prereading preparation plan. This might include vocabulary development and purpose setting.

*Step 2.*   After reading, introduce the discussion web and the discussion question you want the students to address (see Figure 15.18). Students use the Yes and No columns to write key retrieval words to help them keep track of the ideas that are being discussed.

*Step 3.*   Initially, you might find two-person partnerships the most workable because students are encouraged to come to group consensus about the issue. They are encouraged to entertain diverse perspectives as they talk, and some students might need to grow into this type of exchange.

*Step 4.*   Once the group has reached consensus, they select a spokesperson. The group reviews the reasons for their conclusion and helps to prepare the spokesperson for reporting to the whole group. Whole-group sharing occurs.

*Step 5.*   Individual students write their own responses to the issue.

Although the discussion web was originally designed for use with narrative literature, Buehl (1995) has adapted it for use with content-area materials. Because it is clear that student engagement promotes studying effectiveness, this is an approach that should help students grapple with complex texts.

**FIGURE 15.18**
A Discussion Web

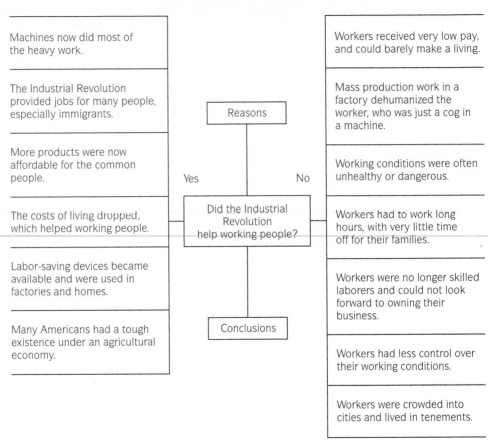

Discussion Web for
The Industrial Revolution

| | Reasons | |
| --- | --- | --- |
| Machines now did most of the heavy work. | | Workers received very low pay, and could barely make a living. |
| The Industrial Revolution provided jobs for many people, especially immigrants. | | Mass production work in a factory dehumanized the worker, who was just a cog in a machine. |
| More products were now affordable for the common people. | Yes      No | Working conditions were often unhealthy or dangerous. |
| The costs of living dropped, which helped working people. | Did the Industrial Revolution help working people? | Workers had to work long hours, with very little time off for their families. |
| Labor-saving devices became available and were used in factories and homes. | | Workers were no longer skilled laborers and could not look forward to owning their business. |
| Many Americans had a tough existence under an agricultural economy. | Conclusions | Workers had less control over their working conditions. |
| | | Workers were crowded into cities and lived in tenements. |

## Teaching Students to Study

Teachers generally believe that students who understand will perform well on their tests, problems, and projects. Although this is often true, there is a sizable group of students who do not know how to respond to the demands of teachers or tasks and therefore do not demonstrate the knowledge and skill they actually possess. A much larger group of students do not understand the content but could if they were provided with tools for learning and remembering important information.

There are some troubling trends in this regard. Although many content-area teachers recognize their students' inability to read and comprehend their textbooks, they often respond by circumventing the books altogether.

> Limited as it is, the research on the use of textbooks in helping students learn from text has several implications. First, it suggests that students will not read their content-area textbooks if teachers fail to expect them to learn from text. Second, the research suggests that teachers rarely spend time teaching students how to use their content area texts. (Alvermann, 1989, p. 257)

**SQ3R.** The grandfather of study strategies, SQ3R (Survey, Question, Read, Recite, Review) was developed by Robinson in 1946. SQ3R is meant to be taught to students as an organized method for dealing with study and learning tasks in assigned textbook reading. Students are taught to approach their textbook reading/studying using the following procedures.

*Survey.* Students are told to preview the material to get a general overview of the chapter. This step will be most helpful if students are provided with information about how to preview a text effectively. For example, they should be taught to ask themselves questions such as "What appears to be the main topic of this chapter?" and "How has the author organized the information?" In addition, students should be taught to survey any maps, figures, captions, and so on for useful information about the topics.

*Question.* The information students have gained by surveying the text is used to generate questions to guide their reading. Students are specifically directed to restate boldface headings as questions. For example, when using this step of the technique to study the present chapter, a reader might pose the question "What is SQ3R?"

*Read.* Using the questions and purposes established in the first steps to guide them, students read the assigned material.

*Recite.* Students are expected to pause periodically and "recite," or think about, their reading. Students are encouraged to try to provide answers to their questions given the reading they have done.

*Review.* When students have completed the assigned reading, they are expected to stop, review the material, and summarize or take notes on the important information. Many variations of SQ3R have been proposed, some designed for study in specific content areas. SQ3R is still widely taught and appears to be an effective technique for students who use it. The biggest concern expressed by critics involves the relatively low incidence of student use (Adams et al., 1982). This is probably related to the failure of teachers to provide explicitly for careful instruction in how or why to employ the technique. The next strategy addresses this concern.

**SMART.**     A *Self-Monitoring Approach to Reading* (SMART) comprises a series of steps that students are taught to use. Developed by Vaughan and Estes (1986), the strategy is especially helpful for students who need help attending to meaning in reading.

*Step 1:*     Students are taught to keep track of their comprehension by putting a $\approx$ or a ? in the margins as they read. The $\approx$ indicates understanding, the ? confusion.

*Step 2:*     Students self-check, explaining in their own words the concepts or ideas they have understood.

*Step 3:*     Students are taught to deal with comprehension failures: reread, identify the problem (e.g., word?, relationships?), generate possible solutions, review the text, and so on.

*Step 4:*     Students continue using Steps 1–3 as a cycle of activity to read long passages. Then they self-check and review.

It should be apparent that none of these specific activities is new. All are often suggested to students. What is different is that the students would be taught these steps as a systematic approach to the problem of reading and understanding. In addition, students are encouraged to think about solutions to their problems and to use the skills and strategies they possess. According to Irvin (1990):

> Successful study skills training programs have three main components: (1) training and practice in the use of task-specific strategies (knowing *what* to apply); (2) instruction in the monitoring of these skills (knowing when and how to apply strategies); and (3) information concerning the significance and outcomes of these activities and their range of utility (knowing why we apply strategies). (Paris et al., 1982, p. 140)

***Underlining, Note Taking, and Outlining.***     Although both note taking and outlining are generally perceived to be helpful for studying, few students in grades 1–8 are skilled enough in these areas to use the techniques effectively. Because these activities are useful in studying, they should be taught as tools for independence. However, the evidence suggests that although students are often told to use these strategies, they seldom receive instruction in them (Irvin, 1990), and when they do, it might not be helpful.

For example, a well-executed outline is a helpful study tool (Anderson & Armbruster, 1984b) but only if the content of the outline is reasonable. Outlining is often taught structurally. That is, students are taught the mechanics of outlining, such as where to put Roman numerals, letters, and so on. Students rarely receive help in the difficult tasks of identifying important ideas, recognizing supporting details, and generating large themes or main ideas. These same problems and criticisms apply to summarization and note-taking activities in most schools.

Effective note taking and underlining, like outlining, require that students be able to distinguish important from unimportant information. Most students, of course, will require some instruction and discussion in these areas before they will be able to manage successfully. Yet one researcher reports that only 17 percent of college students ever received any instruction in how to take notes!

If students merely copy information verbatim from the text, as many research results suggest they typically do (Bretzing & Kulhavy, 1981), then the benefits of note taking may be quite weak. Indeed, it is possible that students who simply reread or underline effectively will do at least as well under those circumstances. They could spend more time thinking about the material, since a read–reread strategy takes less time than recording information that they might recall anyway:

> Research has shown that people tend to remember the most important information anyway. Therefore, note takers may be learning main ideas very well, but at the expense of learning other information. On the other hand, subjects who use less time-consuming studying techniques (e.g., read-reread and underline) are able to distribute their attention and effort more evenly over the passage. (Anderson & Armbruster, 1984b, p. 668)

It is possible to teach one of the available systems of note taking such as the Cornell Notetaking Method (Pauk, 1974) or the Notetaking System for Learning (Palmatier, 1973). The format of the note-taking system and the specifics are less important than the guidance students receive in learning to note important information and use notes to study. Irvin (1990) suggests that the following guidelines be applied in teaching note taking:

1. Students should be asked to preview the chapter before beginning, attending especially to the structure of the material.
2. Textbooks with clear headings and subheadings should be used during initial instruction.
3. Practice with shorter texts should precede work with longer assignments.
4. Students should be provided with examples and feedback, and their initial attempts at notetaking should be reviewed.
5. Students should receive instruction and practice in using notes to accomplish others tasks—to write a summary, make outlines, etc.
6. Finally, students' notes should be used to study for a test.

In reviewing students' notes with them and helping them to use them for study, teachers should be asking the following questions (Tierney, Readence, & Dishner, 1985, p. 203):

- Has this student noted the essential concepts and supporting detail emphasized in the unit?
- Is the material organized in a way that will lead to successful study of the material for testing purposes?

When students are having difficulty with either of these aspects of note taking, additional instruction will be needed. It is also possible that students will benefit from instruction designed to focus them more clearly on the central information in texts or in summarizing.

*Summarization.*    To summarize means to eliminate extraneous information so that only the main points remain. As a study strategy, summarizing is useful only under some circumstances. First, students must be well-equipped to engage in summarization. This often (always with poor readers) involves specific instruction in how to write a summary. A second condition is that the subsequent tasks students are required to perform demand the kind of information and thinking that is represented in a summary. Clearly, writing a good summary is not likely to enhance performance on a short-answer/multiple-choice objective test.

To summarize effectively, students need to learn how to identify the prevailing text structure, how to recognize or generate important ideas and connections, and how to produce an overarching statement of topic. Fortunately, several effective instructional programs have been designed to teach students how to summarize information in texts. For example, Brown et al. (1981) taught students five rules for generating summaries:

1.  Delete irrelevant or trivial information.
2.  Delete redundant information.
3.  Select topic sentences.
4.  Substitute a superordinate term or event for a list of terms or actions.
5.  Invent topic sentences when none are provided by the author.

Using rules very much like these and feedback and practice with modeling, Hare and Borchardt (1984) successfully taught high school students to summarize texts. Similarly, sixth grade students who were taught rules for summarizing and learned to use them effectively showed improvement in comprehension (Bean & Steenwyk, 1984).

## Needed: A Functional, Integrated Approach to Study Skills Instruction

Teachers have always bemoaned the apparent absence of study skills on the part of their students. Until recently, however, only a meager array of tools and strategies were passed along, and students were more often admonished to engage in them than they were taught to employ them. The situation has begun to change quite rapidly in recent years, as educators have demonstrated that study strategies and studying approaches can be taught, although it is less clear that these abilities are generally transferable. Instead, it appears that strategic behavior, content knowledge, and text features interact to influence students' performance—in the just the way that our model would predict (see Nist & Simpson, 2000; Pressley, Wharton-McDonald, Hampson, & Echevarria, 1998).

The wide array of available techniques does not, however, ensure that students will use them appropriately or voluntarily (Garner, 1990; Pressley, 1995). The increasing interest in this area has revealed what earlier examinations of comprehension in general did: that studying is a complex cognitive activity that involves knowledge, skills, and motivation in at least equal parts . If students are going to become effective studiers, they will need an integrated and well-conceived repertoire of knowledge and skills.

Paris (1988) has summarized the characteristics of successful strategy instruction. Not surprisingly, many of these parallel the characteristics of effective comprehension instruction, including the need for explicit instruction and transfer of responsibility from teachers to students. He notes several other characteristics that seem especially important in the promotion of independent study behaviors:

1. Students must believe in the utility and necessity of using the strategies.
2. Teachers must provide a demonstration of how the strategies can be used and when and why they are valuable.
3. The strategies must be appropriate for the student in terms of his or her abilities and willingness to expend effort.
4. Strategy instruction should result in improved student confidence and belief in their own competence.

The ability to study effectively is merely a specialized type of reading and writing ability. As with all aspects of comprehension and composition ability, studying ability emerges over time and in response to need and instruction. Teachers must provide much more intentional, focused, and continuous instruction in studying if students are going to become independent in this area.

## Reading, Writing, and Studying across the Curriculum

Every developmental or remedial reading teacher and special educator knows that transfer from one setting to another is painfully difficult unless there is a close approximation of the classroom texts and tasks. Students and teachers need to learn and use strategies at the point of need. Students will probably never acquire good, independent comprehending, composing, or studying strategies if they do not receive at least some encouragement and direction from content teachers.

Similarly, classroom teachers must concern themselves with providing appropriate adaptations and supports for students so that they can read and/or study the materials they are using in their classrooms. Teachers might find it especially helpful to review the general guidelines for comprehension instruction and then to become quite comfortable with a range of the strategies provided in the sections of this chapter on supporting students' comprehension and studying. The lesson frames, in particular, are easily adapted to most classrooms.

On the other hand, clinical teachers must be absolutely focused on providing students with instruction aimed at improving their ability to comprehend, compose, and study. The array of techniques provided in this chapter should be helpful here. However, specialized language arts personnel should also consider carefully the implications of the general plan to teach for independence. The intentional planning for self-controlled learning is of the utmost importance and will be difficult to achieve in an isolated clinical setting. Specialized teachers and classroom teachers must find ways to collaborate to advance this primary goal.

## Chapter Summary

After a brief introduction we reviewed several issues related to literacy instruction. Specifically, we noted that research has provided persuasive evidence of the interrelationships between reading and writing and had also resulted in considerable knowledge about effective teaching and productive learning. We argued that teachers should strike a balance, providing rich literacy contexts as well as good explicit instruction regarding the reading and writing processes. Next, we described one particularly important issue related to literacy instruction: the acquisition of strategic abilities. Then we provided information about the ways in which discussion and written response deepen students' comprehension. Finally, five key guidelines were provided to shape teachers' thinking about instruction, including a strong suggestion that reading and writing instruction need to be more closely aligned.

In the next major section of this chapter we provided detailed descriptions of instructional techniques for focusing on comprehension and composing. These were divided into two classes of technique: those designed to provide explicit instruction for students in the skills and strategies of reading/writing and those that support students as they read and write particular texts. Explicit instructional guidelines were described generally and then linked to comprehension strategies such as making connections, inferring, questioning, visualizing, monitoring and clarifying, and summarizing. We also provided information about the explicit introduction of text structures and patterns. In addition, we described specific techniques for helping students ask and answer questions with QAR training and ReQuest and provided information about explicit instruction in writing, using a specific approach (CSIW) to demonstrate how cognitive development instruction can work in writing also.

In the next section we introduced lesson frameworks for supporting students before, during, and after reading using approaches such as DRTA, text mapping, and Question the Author. Next, we described a general plan for teaching students to become independent. In the fourth major section of the chapter we discussed studying as a specialized purpose for reading and writing. Again, this was approached in terms of strategies that support students in studying particular texts (e.g., lesson frames and study guides) and those approaches designed to help students learn how to study (SQ3R and summarizing, for example). Finally, guidelines for developing a more integrated approach to reading and writing in the curriculum were provided.

# Professional Roles and Responsibilities

Teachers who conduct effective assessment and thoughtful, well-designed instruction may feel that they have completed their responsibilities. However, work in assessment and instruction always requires accountability to a wide array of groups and individuals (such as administrators, other teaching professionals, parents, and community members). Consequently, the final step in the assessment-instruction process emphasizes the need to effectively communicate with others about the students and the curriculum (see the figure on the following page).

The single chapter in this section contains a focus on the responsibilities of English language arts professionals that extend beyond working with an individual student or client. We discuss the importance of skillful communication with parents and the need for accurate reporting procedures. Teachers will be guided with samples of exemplary written reports. Finally, we discuss the ethics and responsibilities of literacy professionals.

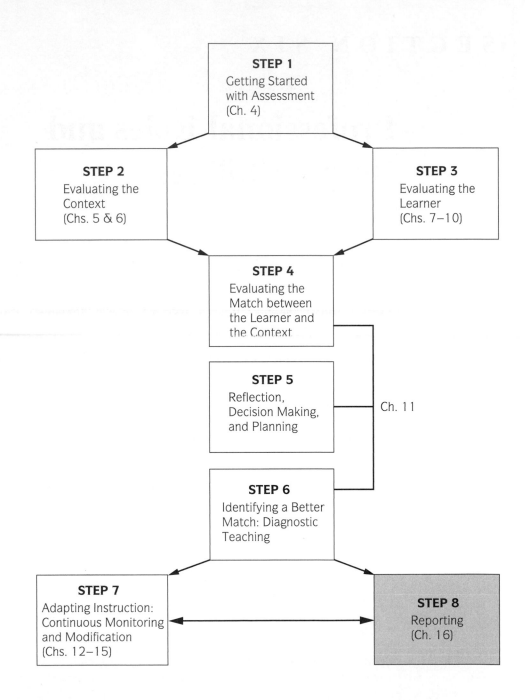

STEP 1
Getting Started
with Assessment
(Ch. 4)

STEP 2
Evaluating the
Context
(Chs. 5 & 6)

STEP 3
Evaluating the
Learner
(Chs. 7–10)

STEP 4
Evaluating the
Match between
the Learner and
the Context

STEP 5
Reflection,
Decision Making,
and Planning

Ch. 11

STEP 6
Identifying a Better
Match: Diagnostic
Teaching

STEP 7
Adapting Instruction:
Continuous Monitoring
and Modification
(Chs. 12–15)

STEP 8
Reporting
(Ch. 16)

# 16 Professional Roles and Responsibilities

In this text we have focused on some specific roles that are important to literacy leaders, roles involving assessment and instruction. However, most language arts professionals are actually expected to fulfill many roles. Certainly, they are expected to be preeminently knowledgeable in reading and writing instruction (Radencich, 1995), but there are many other expectations of literacy professionals as well, including consulting, supervising, grant writing, and providing in-service functions (Vogt & Shearer, 2002).

Skillful communication with parents and community is absolutely essential to the assessment-instruction process. Sophisticated assessment and well-designed instruction must be accompanied by clear and accurate reporting procedures. Otherwise, it is possible for laypeople, as well as other professionals, to be confused or to misunderstand the implications of the work done with students or clients.

Throughout the text we advocated an approach to assessment that valued multiple sources of information collected fairly continuously. Converting the instructionally useful information that is gathered in a portfolio into information suitable for communicating with others is one issue facing teachers, especially classroom teachers. Similarly, it can be challenging to communicate the results of diagnostic teaching and other innovative approaches to assessment and instruction. Finally, teachers must also be able to convey the results of standardized tests in a clear and concise manner.

In this chapter, we describe the range of functions and responsibilities that may be associated with the various roles of literacy leaders. A listing of abilities helpful for professionals in the English language arts is provided.

Among the most important of these is the ability to communicate effectively. Consequently, we provide a major section on reporting to others that includes some general guidelines and some suggestions for organizing and reporting on the contents of portfolios. In addition, teachers are guided through the process of writing formal reports and are provided with samples of exemplary written reports. We describe how different types of reports may be appropriate for different purposes and discuss conferences as well as written reporting. In the final section of this chapter we describe the professional and ethical responsibilities associated with providing literacy assessment and support to students and clients.

## The Role(s) of the English Language Arts Professional

There is a rather wide range of ideas about the appropriate roles and functions of reading and writing teachers. Traditionally, these professionals have provided direct service for individual students and, in some settings, have provided support for individual teachers and some schoolwide professional development (Bean, 1979). However, the roles of reading teachers have changed in the past decade in response to changed legislative actions.

Confusion over the appropriate functions led the International Reading Association (IRA) (1998, 2000) to identify roles and responsibilities of various reading professionals. The list includes the following three categories: Category I, Classroom Teachers; Category II, Specialized Reading Professionals; and Category III, Allied Professions. Category II is the largest category, encompassing all roles involving consulting, coordinating reading programs, and delivering diagnostic-remedial services. The Allied Professions category includes special educators, administrators, and others such as counselors and psychologists.

Within the broad category of Classroom Teachers there are differentiated roles for classroom teachers at different developmental levels (early child and middle level, for example). Within the category of Specialized Reading Professionals are the roles and responsibilities most likely to be relevant for readers of this text. The International Reading Association has defined the competencies for three levels of preparation: reading specialist, reading coordinator, and teacher educator. At all levels, specialized reading professionals are expected to be able to conduct individualized reading assessments and plan instructional programs for struggling students. The competencies that are acknowledged also describe the other common roles and responsibilities of professionals at these levels, including organizing and administering school reading programs, providing staff development, and coordinating reading specialist and other specialist activity.

According to Gupta and Oboler (2001, p. 6), "the changing dynamics of the school culture continue to shape the responsibilities of educators, including Reading Teachers. New responsibilities create new roles with different expectations." Many of these roles are new for reading professionals and may require them to acquire new abilities. In Figure 16.1 we have compiled a list of abilities that are suggested by a variety of authors and that seem essential to professional success (see IRA, 2000; Vogt & Shearer, 2002). Whatever the formally designated role, there is a need for school-level leadership surrounding literacy and reading-writing disabilities. No matter what the title, professionals who are well versed in literacy and literacy instruction will have a responsibility to function as an educational leader in the school or school district.

## Reporting to Others

English language arts professionals are often expected to report to a wide range of people regarding the literacy abilities and progress of students. There are a number of ways professionals communicate with others. Reporting may be as informal as a chat in the teachers' lounge, as routine as a parent–teacher conference, or as formal as a complete case

**FIGURE 16.1**
Desirable Abilities
for Literacy
Professionals

| Ability and Skill In: |
| --- |
| 1. Teaming with other professionals, including classroom teachers and special educators to plan appropriate assessment and instruction opportunities for students who need additional support in reading and/or writing. |
| 2. Helping teachers together and interpreting assessment data |
| 3. Mentoring other teachers through modeling and discussion |
| 4. Providing research-based information and resources to teachers to accommodate individual differences and meet the needs of all students |
| 5. Evaluating and/or diagnosing individual students |
| 6. Analyzing and evaluating instructional materials |
| 7. Providing staff development for colleagues |
| 8. Initiating schoolwide programs and/or introducing reforms |
| 9. Supervising and training paraeducators |
| 10. Administering federal guidelines and local mandates |
| 11. Providing leadership in the development of schoolwide or districtwide language arts curriculum |
| 12. Program evaluation, including the development and implementation of data collection and summary tools |

report. Its purpose should always be to communicate or solicit information about an individual student.

In this section we provide some guidelines for effective reporting, describe some ways to use the portfolio in reporting to others, and discuss several types of written reports. Finally, specific procedures for writing formal reports are detailed.

## General Guidelines

No matter what form the reporting takes, there are some guidelines that should be considered:

1. *Provide a clear summary* of what has been done in both assessment and instruction. The tools, strategies, and techniques should be clear, and the results should be understandable, apparent, and reasonable. Effective reports provide detailed descriptions so that others can understand the learner and the instructional context with little chance of confusion.
2. *Include only relevant information.* No matter how interesting, information should not be included unless there appears to be a close link to reading, writing, or overall academic performance. When sensitive personal information is discussed, this should be treated as discreetly as possible.
3. *Highlight the most important information* about the learner and the context. Always make sure that the student's most salient strengths and obvious difficulties are described as priorities. Similarly, critical positive supports in the instructional context should be noted along with suggestions for instruction that is likely to be effective for the student. Less central information should be discussed later in the reporting session or at the end of any written report. It is not necessary or desirable to report the same

information about all individuals; the report should reflect the particular needs and abilities of the learner.

   **4.** *Use language and format appropriate for the audience.* When reporting to parents, it is important to keep discussions free of jargon and as straightforward as possible. When specialized terms seem necessary to use, be sure to define them. If there is any reason at all to suspect the literacy skills of parents or guardians, all information should be communicated orally. On the other hand, in reporting to teachers, schools, or other agencies, the form and language should be professional and technical terms should be used to ensure precision.

In deciding on the form of reporting, it is important to consider the needs of the audience as well as the purposes for communicating. Too often, professionals believe that reporting must always involve transmitting and interpreting formal test data. Yet parents often would prefer periodic meetings that inform them about their children's general progress. This is where assessment portfolios are particularly powerful tools in reporting.

## Reporting via Diagnostic Portfolio Summaries

Throughout this text we have described how diagnostic portfolios may be created and maintained. A diagnostic portfolio, unlike some others, probably should contain *all* types of available information about an individual student. It will include *at least* three types of information:

   **1.** Formal, standardized test information, where available (see Chapter 10);
   **2.** The results of intentionally planned assessments of reading/writing ability such as retellings (see Chapters 8 and 9); and
   **3.** Work samples collected as representative of the activities and abilities of that student/classroom.

These pieces of evidence are themselves relatively uninformative, however. They are essentially raw data unless a knowledgeable teacher organizes the information and interprets its significance.

When preparing to report the contents of portfolios to others, it is helpful to organize the information in some way so that it takes on meaning for others who are less well-informed. Even a simple cover sheet stapled to a folder can systematize the information (see Figure 16.2).

Listing the pieces of information in the portfolio and the dates collected can help the teacher and any others to see the range of information available. If, in addition, the teacher writes a narrative periodically (for example, at conference time), then the information can be even more accessible to others.

For the purposes of reporting to others it may be important to organize the information and the patterns of literacy behavior to an even greater extent. In such cases, teachers can use a portfolio analysis sheet (see Figure 16.3). The example provided is only suggestive, since teachers should use an analysis system that parallels the types of assessment and instruction that are most central to their program.

**FIGURE 16.2**
Portfolio Cover
Sheet

Name _____     Teacher(s) _____

Grade _____     Birthdate _____

| CONTENTS | DATE |
|---|---|
| 1. _____ | |
| 2. _____ | |
| 3. _____ | |
| 4. _____ | |
| 5. _____ | |
| 6. _____ | |
| 7. _____ | |
| 8. _____ | |

**COMMENTS**                                    **DATE**

_____

_____

_____

_____

It is important that the portfolio analysis offer systematic evaluation of the contents of the portfolio—analysis that could be replicated by others who are interested in this student's performance. Although the contents may be helpful to classroom teachers as they work with students, they are unlikely to be informative to others (or considered valid and reliable) unless some additional effort is made to interpret and formalize the results. If this effort is made, however, both parents and administrators are likely to be pleased with the specificity of information and the depth of knowledge available. In Chapters 8 and 9 we described a variety of ways to strengthen organizational aspects of gathering informal data (see also Valencia, Hiebert, & Afflerbach, 1994; Valencia, 1998).

There are times, of course, when the information about students must be interpreted and summarized for other purposes or in other ways. Written reports vary in both type and purpose and are discussed in the next section.

## Report Writing: Different Types for Different Purposes

Writing reports is an essential part of the job of most English language arts professionals. However, these may vary from very brief reports to extensive formal case reports. Parents generally want to know what is happening in the clinical or classroom setting, especially when the student is receiving specialized help for an identified problem. Brief reports about the student's program and progress can and should be sent periodically to parents and other involved professionals. This kind of report can alert parents and teachers to special accomplishments that have occurred or to problems that have been identified. At other times, this report may be used to enlist the help of parents and classroom teachers (see Figure 16.4).

**FIGURE 16.3**
Portfolio Analysis
Sheet

| Observations of Reading and Writing | |
|---|---|
| **Date** | **Student Interview** |
| | Summarize results |
| | **Observations** |
| | Record observations of student's development in reading/writing |

| Reading Materials/Tasks | |
|---|---|
| **Date** | |
| | Books/selections read (assigned) and level of difficulty |
| | Books/selections read (self-selected) and level of difficulty |
| | Books/reading-related written work completed |
| | Group activities |

| Reading Performance (Note materials, task, level of support) | |
|---|---|
| **Date** | |
| | Word recognition ability |
| | Oral reading fluency |
| | Comprehension: Question answering |
| | Comprehension: Retelling |
| | Strategy use |
| | Studying strategies |

**FIGURE 16.3**
(Continued)

| Writing Development | |
|---|---|
| **Date** | |
| | Describe writing samples (include all drafts) |
| | Note types of writing represented |
| | Summarize writer's development of written mechanics (spelling and writing conventions) |
| | Student-selected "best piece" (describe) |
| | Evaluate writing development (progress over time and in terms of age-appropriateness) |
| **Summary** | |
| **Date** | |
| | Student's reading development |
| | Student's writing development |

**FIGURE 16.4**
Parents/Teacher
Report Form

Student _____ Date _____
Teacher _____

Summary of the following instructional periods (dates/times of sessions):
_____

Summary of reading/writing abilities: _____
_____
_____

Summary of instructional program (materials, activities): _____
_____
_____

Summary of progress: _____
_____
_____

Comments: _____
_____
_____

It is also important for classroom teachers and specialized personnel to communicate with each other. Issues of congruence discussed earlier (see Chapters 5 and 6) have obvious implications for reporting. As Shake (1989) has noted,

> It seems safe to say that remedial teachers cannot provide instruction that either introduces or reinforces the classroom literacy curriculum if they do not know what that curriculum contains. Both classroom and remedial teachers report concern regarding the lack of time for communication about programs and target students. (Allington & Shake, 1986; Johnston, Allington, & Afflerbach, 1985, p. 74)

Clearly, the type of reporting that is called for in this situation is somewhat different, though no less important. Shake suggests that teachers and specialists keep a record form (see Chapter 5) that travels with the student. This type of documentation can diminish the need for extensive formal reporting at a later date and also increases the likelihood that instruction will have some coherence across settings. Of course, if a portfolio system is being employed, then the student as well as all teachers can and should contribute samples, observations, and evaluations.

Just as the audience and format for reporting may vary, so may the content. For example, all of the specially funded programs for reading, writing, and related difficulties require some sort of reporting procedures. These programs often require the teacher only to report program data; extensive individual reporting is not necessary. Even when formal individual case reports are expected, they may vary depending on the audience and the program. For many school-based purposes, the literacy report format outlined in Figure 16.5 would be appropriate. Teachers and specialists alike should think about using this

**FIGURE 16.5**
Literacy Report
Format

| Development |
| --- |
| Emergent Abilities (where appropriate)<br>Reading Strategies<br>Response to Literature<br>Comprehension of Content Area Text<br>Writing: Content, organization, voice, coherence, range<br>Writing: Grammar, usage, mechanics |
| **Attitudes and Motivation** |
| Ownership/Engagement<br>Self-Reflection<br>Work Habits<br>Effort |
| **Text Levels** |
|  |
| **Individual Goals** |
| Teacher Comments<br>Parent Comments or Questions<br>Student Comments |
| **Next Steps** |
|  |

fairly streamlined approach that focuses on important literacy goals and outcomes (see Figure 16.5).

Sometimes it is important to write much more comprehensive case reports that include summaries of all available standardized test information and interpretations of the results for specific uses. A written report of a student's reading and writing ability generally includes all or some of the following: background information, summary of assessment information, summary of factors influencing performance, and implications for instruction or future placement (or summary of instructional progress).

Formal reports about individual students in public school settings are used most often when the student has been referred for special services or for a determination of eligibility for special education (see Chapter 1). These often make recommendations regarding the student's eligibility for services but are less helpful regarding the specific implications for instructional programs.

As we have seen, literacy leaders may be asked or required to perform in a variety of contexts and may need to be responsive to different people and their needs. Perhaps the most frequent responsibility, however, involves the need to pull together an array of assessment information and use it to plan an instructional program. This type of reporting, something we call the *case report,* is described in much greater detail in the next section.

## Procedures for Writing Diagnostic Case Reports

Fully executed case reports are very time consuming to write, and few settings require such extensive documentation. Although it is not the most frequent format for reporting and communicating about students, it is the format that professionals often use as the vehicle for learning how to report. A formal, written report requires discipline in organizing information, ability to interpret results, and well-developed writing skills. It demands careful examination of all information regarding a student and involves learning to communicate that information to others in a much more public forum than many teachers typically experience.

Choosing and using a fairly standard format for writing case reports saves time. A wide array of formats are used. Several factors need to be considered in selecting a format. First, it should accommodate and support reporting of the types of information that you wish to communicate. Second, it should be flexible enough that it can be shaped to take the focus appropriate to the particular individual and purpose. Third, it should offer a format that is convenient for the consumer of the report—both considerate in terms of what is expected and familiar and clearly organized for ease of reading. Finally, there is a political consideration. Although the situation is changing rapidly, the educational community still has a bias toward data gathered from standardized, norm-referenced tools. Because we include large amounts of nontraditional information in our reports, we are particularly sensitive to the ways in which we display these data.

The format described in this section has an overall appearance that is similar to traditional case reports and provides for formally reporting all existing assessment information. We want readers to take the information seriously and to consider it as reliable and valid as the more familiar test scores (see Figure 16.6). The format also offers flexibility in accommodating the types of information we have advocated throughout this text. If the thumbnail sketch was done earlier (see Chapter 11), this information will be very useful in preparing the case report.

The case of Marvin, discussed periodically throughout this text, is now used to illustrate the sections in a diagnostic case report (another full case report is presented in the appendix). Each of the procedures described below parallels a major component of the diagnostic case report (see Figure 16.7).

***Display the Assessment Information.***    The cover sheet should contain a concise yet complete description of the assessment information. To the extent possible, all available information about the reader should be displayed on a cover sheet (see Figure 16.6). This includes identifying information such as name, age, and school. It should also clearly indicate the date of the report, who has prepared the report, and who administered the tests (if this was different). The date and source of the report should be easy to find. Remember, these

**FIGURE 16.6**
Cover Sheet

## Confidential Diagnostic Report

NAME _____Marvin B._____ DATE _____December 27, 1998_____
EXAMINER _____Marjorie Y. Lipson, Ph.D._____
NAME OF PARENT/GUARDIAN ____Joan and Phillip B._____
ADDRESS __15 East View_____ PHONE _____923-6570_____
_____Lakeview, VT_____ BIRTHDATE _____
SCHOOL ___Apple Elementary School_____ AGE _____11_____ GRADE _____5_____
_____Lakeville, Vermont_____

### Previous Test Information

WISC-R (Administered 4/98 by M. Hawkins, Psychologist):
    Verbal: 109        Performance: 114        Full scale: 112

Metropolitan Achievement Tests (Administered 4/98, 4th grade)
        Total Reading:            37th percentile (4th stanine)
        Word Identification:      23rd percentile (3rd stanine)
        Comprehension:            45th percentile (5th stanine)

### Summary of Assessment Results

| Woodcock Reading Mastery (Form B) | Relative Mastery | Percentile Rank |
|---|---|---|
| Letter Identification | 93% | 58 |
| Word Identification | 7% | 10 |
| Word Attack | 32% | 9 |
| Word Comprehension | 55% | 15 |
| Passage Comprehension | 29% | 8 |

| Analytic Reading Inventory | Independent Reading Level | Instructional Reading Level | Frustrational Reading Level |
|---|---|---|---|
| Word Recognition | 2 | 3 | 5–6 |
| Oral Comprehension | 2 & 3 | 4 & 5 | 6 |
| Silent Comprehension | 2–4 | 5 | 6 |
| Classroom Reading Inventory | | | |
| Word Recognition | NA | 1 | 2–6 |
| Oral Comprehension | 1–4 & 6 | 5 | 7 |
| Silent Comprehension | 2, 3, & 5 | 4 | 6 |
| Burns and Roe, Informal Reading Inventory | | | |
| Word Recognition | NA | 2 | 3–5 |
| Oral Comprehension | NA | 2 | 3–5 |
| Silent Comprehension | NA | 2 & 3 | 4 & 5 |

### Summary

Comprehension Scores:
        Highest Instructional/Independent Level: (7-Ind. Silent)
        Lowest Instructional:  1 (Oral and Silent)
        Lowest Frustrational : 2 (Oral)

Listening Comprehension: (Analytic Reading Inventory)
        Independent: Grades 2–6; Instructional: Grade 7

Relevant Instruction Information
        Grades K–1:    Conrad Elementary, Lakeville Public Schools Readiness and Primer
                       levels of Ginn 360 (1992)
        Grades 2–4:    St. Mary's School, Lakeville, Vermont
                       Basal books for Grades 2–4, synthetic phonics series
        Currently:     Fifth grade, recently placed in Apple School, Lakeville Public Schools.
                       Literature-based individualized reading program.

**FIGURE 16.7**
Diagnostic Case
Report Format

| | |
|---|---|
| **Cover Sheet(s)** | **Diagnostic Teaching** |
|   Identifying information for student |   Strategies |
|   Name of reporter and date of report |   Results |
|   Summary of assessment results | **Diagnostic Statement** |
| **Background Information** |   Summarize major findings |
|   Reason for referral |   Summarize learner's strengths/ |
|   Distinctive developmental history |     weaknesses |
|   School history |   Note factors that influence |
|   Results of initial student, parent, |     performance (peaks/valleys) |
|     teacher interviews | **Suggestions for Instruction** |
| **Summary of Assessment Results** |   Content of instruction |
|   Reader factors (areas discussed as |   Delivery of instruction |
|   appropriate for individual) |   Materials |
|     Emergent literacy development |   Level of support |
|     Word recognition | **Other Suggestions/Recommendations** |
|     Vocabulary |   Home involvement |
|     Comprehension |   Additional assessment |
|     Studying |   Special placement |
|     Writing | |
|     Integrated discussion of results | |
|   Instructional factors | |
|     Results of classroom/other | |
|       observation | |
|     Analysis of text and task demands | |

reports end up in files and often follow students for some time. It can be both irritating and confusing to find a report in a file and be unable to tell when the results were generated.

Previous results may be included on the cover sheet when they are recent and the data are useful in the total report (e.g., a recent psychological report and an existing IEP). In such cases both the examiner and the date of testing should be clearly labeled. School achievement test data can also be provided when they demonstrate a pattern or are relevant to the referral or the summary.

The remainder of the cover sheet involves presenting both formal and informal data in brief numerical or descriptive form. This serves two purposes. First, the report reader can get an overview of what has been done and what pattern of results is emerging without reading the entire report. Second, it eliminates the need to include extensive numerical data in the body of the report, thus focusing attention on the interpretation of these results.

***Describe Background Information.***     This section should open with a clear statement about who referred the student for special evaluation and instruction, and the reason for this referral. The content of the remainder of this section of the report will vary. For some students it is important to describe rather extensive amounts of relevant background information. Critical aspects of health history, notable school factors, or particularly disruptive emotional incidents need to be included. There are other students for whom this section is brief, because there are no factors that seem related to the reading/writing difficulties. In these cases simply noting that the student's development appears normal and the school history uneventful should be sufficient.

It is also helpful to convey in this background section both the student's and the family's attitude toward reading/writing activities and toward the student's particular problems. Information gleaned from interviews and from observations should be summarized here and used to support any statements made about attitudes, motivation, or the influence of correlational factors (see Figure 16.8).

***Summarize the Assessment Information.*** The section called Summary of Assessment Results is designed to convey critical aspects of student performance as clearly as possible. There are a number of ways to do this, and the emphasis and focus should reflect the *particular* reader being described. In some cases, the reader will be the focus of the summary and analysis; in other cases, instructional factors will loom large.

**FIGURE 16.8**
Case Report:
Background
Information Section

### Reason for Referral
Marvin has just returned to a public school setting, having been enrolled in a private parochial school for three years. Concerns about Marvin's reading abilities, expressed by both school and parents, led to a referral for reading assessment.

### Observation and Interview Information
Neither Marvin's mother nor the available records suggest any remarkable health or development problems. Throughout the current series of assessment activities, Marvin appeared to be an engaging, friendly, and open fifth-grade boy. His manner was quite easy-going and he appeared to have excellent self-confidence. He approached each task with vigor, never tired of the activities, and always appeared ready for the next one. He smiles easily and does not appear ruffled by even the most difficult tasks. Marvin has extraordinary stamina for reading activities, especially given his slow pace and rate.

These observations are somewhat at odds with Marvin's case history (see Confidential Psychological Report in files). Marvin's mother reports that the family has experienced significant disruption for the past two years as a result of a separation and impending divorce between Marvin's parents. A psychologist's report suggests that Marvin's reading difficulties may result from his inability to attend to school tasks and from high levels of anxiety related to these family problems. At the present time, the family appears to have settled into a more regular routine and Marvin regularly visits with his father and he reports enjoying these visits.

When asked to reflect on reading in general and his own abilities in particular, Marvin offered very little. He could neither think of anything to say about how he viewed reading nor describe what a good reader was like. With regard to his own reading ability he believes he is a "medium" reader and that his biggest problem is "understanding what I read." On the other hand, Marvin believes that people read "to learn and to get away from things." He suggests that he reads because "it's fun—but, not all the time."

Marvin exhibits enthusiastic curiosity about a wide range of topics and he brings this interest to bear on his reading. He becomes actively involved with reading, stopping to comment and/or chuckle over parts of the text. He indicated an interest in reading books with a high degree of action and humor and also said he likes to read

**FIGURE 16.8**
(Continued)

books about his hobbies and about machines and the outdoors. He is not, however, interested in reading about American heroes, biographies, or sports. Marvin builds model cars as a hobby and he says he generally likes to "take stuff apart."

### School/Instructional History

Due to family moves, Marvin attended two different schools during kindergarten and first grade. During these early years, Marvin was reported to be struggling with reading. Because his parents were concerned about his limited reading abilities after first grade, they decided to send him to a private parochial school for second grade. He remained there throughout the second, third, and fourth grades. During Marvin's fourth-grade year, his teacher reported that Marvin was experiencing serious difficulties in reading: precipitating a psychological evaluation (see file). At least partly because this private school does not have any remedial services, Marvin's parents decided to return him to the public school in their neighborhood and he was referred for reading assessment at that time.

Marvin has received reading instruction with a basal reading program since kindergarten. In Grades K–1, the program was an eclectic one published in the 1980s and he progressed as a member of the lowest reading group. From Grades 2 through 4, he was placed in the phonics-oriented basal used in his new school. No grouping or special support was employed in this school, so he progressed through the materials at the pace determined appropriate for the whole class. The reading methods of the school appear to revolve around daily oral reading of assigned basal selections followed by independent completion of assigned workbook pages. Neither silent reading time nor process writing activities were provided on a regular basis. Starting in fourth grade, the school used textbooks for science and social studies, although it is not clear how often students received reading assignments in these materials.

Marvin has only just been placed in the fifth grade of a public school. Although the classroom program is a literature-based individualized one, with individual work folders assigned to each student, the least-able readers are often placed in a dated basal series. The teacher is anxious to receive information about Marvin's reading abilities in order to make some instructional decisions. Oral reading occurs in this classroom during one-to-one conferences with the teacher and generally involves student-selected and prepared excerpts from books of stories. Silent reading is a daily activity although writing activities are more irregular and generally involve writing book reports and research reports.

In summary, Marvin presents himself as a vigorous, active, and undaunted boy who is remarkably at ease in new settings.

*Summarize the Instructional Factors.* This portion is the least common in traditional reports. In some cases it would make more sense to include observations and information about the instructional factors in the Background Section (see p. 630). In others the information is included as a part of the discussion regarding the test results. In still other cases it is important only to state that the instructional context has included appropriate instruction and literacy experiences for the student. However, there are times when the information collected in the assessment-instruction process warrants separate commentary.

In Marvin's case there seemed to be little point in conducting a classroom observation, since he had only just transferred to the school/classroom. Critical information about instructional history was placed here in the Background Section (see Figure 16.8). It was important to note that he had received no individualized instruction in his program and that the methodologies were quite sparse. Specific information about texts and tasks that influence Marvin's performance was placed in the Summary of Assessment Results section (see Figure 16.9).

*Information about the Reader.* This section is not designed to reiterate tests scores that have already been summarized, although these can be used when needed for clarity. Rather, it is designed to interpret and pull into clear view the overall performance patterns of the reader. As the various components of reading and writing are discussed, all pieces of evidence about that component are described (see Figure 16.7). When the test or some aspect of the assessment task contributes strongly to the results, they should also be discussed and interpreted. In Marvin's case this type of description was offered to help interpret the results of the various IRIs (see Figure 16.9).

It is important to point out again that the reports of specific students may vary considerably from this. Effective reporting describes the reader and focuses attention on important aspects of his or her performance. In some cases this may be done more effectively by using subheads that parallel the various components of reading and writing that are posing

**FIGURE 16.9**
Case Report:
Summary and
Interpretation of
Results

---

### Summary of Assessment Results

The pattern of Marvin's performance is quite stable. An examination of the pattern of results for the various informal reading inventories (IRIs) demonstrates that his word recognition scores are consistently poor and he reaches frustrational level on word recognition at Level 3 on all three IRIs (see Cover Sheet). On the other hand, his comprehension scores are consistently higher than his word recognition scores and, on two IRIs, he does not reach frustrational level in comprehension until Grade 6 or 7.

Marvin's performance on the word analysis subtest reflects his limited ability to decode nonmeaningful words out-of-context. He does, however, demonstrate adequate knowledge of the basic phonic relationships. There are two possible phonic components that may also require additional instruction: (1) consonant blends and digraphs, and (2) complex vowel combinations like "ea," "ou," and "oi." Marvin's miscues on these ("tragic" for "task," "find" for "friend," etc., and a persistent problem with "ea" words) suggest that he has not yet mastered these phonic elements. It should be noted, however, that his phonics skills *overall* appear to be adequate except as he fails to apply these skills to multisyllabic words.

An analysis of Marvin's miscues (see Chapter 5) demonstrates the large number of word recognition difficulties he experiences during reading. Many of these miscues appear on high-frequency sight words ("the" for "our," "and" for "the," "the" for "her," etc.). Thus, it would appear that Marvin needs continued opportunities to practice these high-frequency words. Many of Marvin's remaining miscues involve word endings—inflectional endings and suffixes (for example: "safe" for "safer," "means" for "meant," "quick" for "quickly," etc.) Marvin consistently deletes such endings, and occasionally adds endings not present. There is also evidence that Marvin has underdeveloped syllabication skills ("enginical" for "energetic," "detoof" for "develop," etc.) and it would appear that direct instruction in structural analysis as a word recognition strategy would be helpful to Marvin.

**FIGURE 16.9**
(Continued)

The disparity between his word recognition and comprehension performance is substantial. Marvin demonstrated good to excellent comprehension of most materials read. He was able to answer questions following both oral and silent reading with ease and he appears capable of answering a broad range of question types. Analysis of his rate of self-correction and the proportion of meaningful miscues (see Chapter 5) provide additional evidence of Marvin's substantial comprehension abilities. His rate of self-correction is extremely high (especially at lower levels), suggesting that he actively monitors his reading progress and attempts to construct meaning from text. Indeed, when his rate of self-correction is coupled with the percentage of meaningful miscues (i.e., the "error" does not affect the meaning of the text), it becomes apparent how impressive Marvin's efforts to understand really are. He rarely produces nonsensical substitutions or "wild guesses" and, often, his substitutions could go undetected since they do not significantly affect the meaning of the selection.

Though Marvin's comprehension abilities are quite robust (note the overall pattern of performance), he also demonstrates differential ability across the texts and tasks. (Note both his "peak"—silent reading on the CRI (instructional at Grade 7) and his "valley" (frustrational comprehension at Grade 3 on the oral reading Burns and Roe). It is obvious that the Burns and Roe passages were more difficult for him than any others. In fact, if only the Burns and Roe IRI had been administered, it would have appeared that limited power and automaticity in decoding skills was the sole source of his comprehension problems, so that as decoding accuracy decreased, so did comprehension.

This explanation obviously cannot account for Marvin's performance at other times. His performance on the other two IRIs in fact suggests exactly the opposite—that comprehension ability drives his reading efforts and that he is likely to perform poorly overall only when the reading process cannot be driven from a position of understanding. Marvin's weakest performance occurred while reading several rather ambiguous texts in the Burns and Roe IRI. Two are set in a foreign country and are guided almost entirely by a type of lyrical internal response structure. All three are fragments from longer texts and none have a very strong story structure. While Marvin often understood all the relevant explicit information in these texts, he did not always make the inferences necessary to answer the question. Thus, while neither the type of text (exposition versus narrative) nor the type and number of questions significantly affect Marvin's performance, other factors such as coherence and conformity to expected story structures did. The diagnostic teaching pursued with Marvin supports this conclusion and this segment of the assessment is described in the next section.

problems for that student. For example, there might appear within the Summary of Results section a subsection on Emergent Literacy Development, another on Vocabulary, and another on Word Recognition, but no separate heads for Studying or Writing, if those were less critical areas for the student.

On the other hand, the reports for other students seem to be more straightforward and coherent when the various tests are discussed and the results interpreted. This format is likely to be most helpful when the tests themselves contribute to a student's performance and a discussion of the test or assessment strategy is needed. This organization can be helpful when there are important anecdotal aspects to the student's interactions.

*Describe and Report the Results of Diagnostic Teaching.* In this section specific manipulations of the literacy event should be described. Because diagnostic teaching is not included in most traditional assessment plans, it is important to describe briefly the purpose of such activity. The reader should understand both what was done and why this was attempted. In addition, the section should conclude with a summary that interprets the results.

In Marvin's case (see Figure 16.10) the specific procedures were developed using a framework like that described earlier (see Chapter 11) . The evaluation was conducted by someone other than school personnel and for very specific purposes. The descriptions of

**FIGURE 16.10**
Case Report:
Diagnostic Teaching

**Diagnostic Teaching**

In order to clarify Marvin's problem, diagnostic teaching was attempted with him. Diagnostic teaching involves manipulating the assessment process in any of a number of ways. The purpose of manipulating the assessment process is twofold: to collect additional information to clarify and test the hypotheses about Marvin's reading problems, and to try out potential methods of instruction.

Marvin clearly needs additional decoding skills and a great deal of attention directed toward increasing his automaticity. Marvin's strength is comprehension. However, his performance in comprehension was not universally strong and it was in this area that more information might be useful.

Because he had performed poorly on the Burns and Roe IRI, these selections were used in the diagnostic teaching. Marvin had reached the frustration level on a selection without a title that dealt with a young boy's concern about a test. The main idea of this selection was subtle and Marvin constructed a different main theme for the selection. Marvin also asked several questions related to the main theme. It seemed likely that Marvin might be able to understand challenging material if some organizational support were provided. Therefore, he was asked to reread the selection, this time imagining that the story was entitled, "Peter Worries About a Test." Given that much support, Marvin answered all the questions posed correctly and was able, in addition, to provide a coherent and accurate summary of the selection. The exercise was repeated with two other selections and each time Marvin was totally successful in his comprehension efforts. Given a general idea of the topic, Marvin has no difficulty linking ideas, locating information, or supporting inferential conclusions.

It is clear that Marvin's forte involves responding to questions after reading coherent or well-structured text (even when his percentage of miscues is extremely high). However, Marvin also will need to be able to comprehend text on his own. Thus, a final activity was employed. Marvin was asked to silently read a very lengthy (5-page) narrative story written at the high third/low fourth-grade readability and to do a retelling of the story. Marvin appeared very interested in the selection and launched into the retelling with enthusiasm. Despite this obvious interest, Marvin's reconstruction of the story left out vital events and concepts and his recount involved no sound sequence. In addition, his recount failed to name the important characters, to identify their problem in the story, or to accurately identify the final solution to the problem. On the other hand, when Marvin was asked specific questions about the selection, he was able to demonstrate a far clearer understanding of the text or, perhaps more accurately, he was able to use the questions asked to reorganize his understanding of the story.

diagnostic teaching may be a much more substantial part of some reports. This is especially true when the reports are written after significant instructional contact (see Progress Reports, p. 638).

***Provide a Diagnostic Summary Statement.***    This section provides a brief, coherent statement of the student's strengths and weaknesses (see Figure 16.11). In a straightforward way the report reader is reminded of the ground that has been covered and helped to see the big picture. Because no assessment data are specifically cited here, it is especially important that there be no surprises. This is not the time to introduce new information. In addition, what is concluded in this section should be clearly related to the earlier data that were described.

The diagnostic statement should synthesize information across the various assessment and instructional contexts. The results of the diagnostic teaching are embedded to inform the conclusions drawn. The summary statement should contain enough information to function as an overview of the entire report so that individuals who cannot read or reread the whole document can read an accurate statement that captures the reading or writing process for that student/client.

**FIGURE 16.11**
Case Report:
Diagnostic Summary

**Diagnostic Summary**

Marvin has a great many strengths, not the least of which is his interest in reading and his obvious enjoyment of it. Marvin makes an excellent showing in silent reading comprehension, especially as measured by ability to answer questions. In addition, Marvin has good to excellent memory skills which he uses to aid his understanding. He uses all pre-reading information (introductory statements, for example) to the greatest possible extent to drive his reading efforts. In addition, Marvin actively attends to his reading. He self-corrects frequently, does not produce "wild guesses," and is able to respond effectively to what he reads. He uses context very effectively to aid his word recognition and to derive meaning from text.

Marvin has serious word recognition difficulties, including limited sight-word recognition. He also has difficulty reading multisyllabic words and has not acquired a strategy for coping with words that require structural analysis (including syllabication). He also demonstrates limited ability to apply knowledge of consonant blends and digraphs and vowel digraphs and dipthongs. He will need to improve his word recognition skills if he is not to be overwhelmed by lengthy reading assignments, since his lack of automaticity slows him down.

While comprehension is generally a strength for Marvin, his ability to impose structure and meaning on longer, denser, or less-considerate text is limited. He seems to lack experience reading different types of materials. In addition he has had limited opportunities to read for a variety of purposes or for different tasks.

Marvin is capable of handling much of the material at his grade level, although he will not sound fluent in oral reading situations. His performance is improved significantly when relevant pre-reading supports are provided. Narrative selections are easier for Marvin to read than expository ones. In addition, dense, poorly organized texts of all types are more difficult for him to read and should be avoided wherever possible.

***Describe Recommendations for Instruction.*** In this section the specific implications for instruction are described. Again, there should be no surprises. Suggestions for improving word identification cannot be offered when no evidence for a problem in this area was provided earlier. There should be a clear link between the assessment portions of the report and these instructional suggestions.

There are several types of instructional advice that can be offered in this section, both of which are evident in Marvin's report (see Figure 16.12). Suggestions often include ideas for shaping literacy instruction and/or offering instructional support (Recommendations 1, 3, and 4). Of course, instructional recommendations should also specify the component areas to be emphasized in instruction (Recommendations 2 and 3).

Other suggestions for instruction may involve naming particular instructional strategies or techniques (Recommendation 3). In these cases it is important to make sure that teachers reading the report are familiar with the techniques. If there is any doubt about the familiarity of the method, strategy, or text suggested, the information should be provided as a part of the report. This can be done in the body of the report for brief recommendations. For instructional techniques that require greater additional explanation, an appendix works best.

**FIGURE 16.12**
Case Report:
Recommendations
for Instruction

---

**Recommendations**

Marvin is a very able, hard-working, eager boy who should progress in reading if offered the opportunity. It is entirely possible that his history (see Confidential Psychological Report in school files) has slowed his progress in reading and that he is currently in a position to take advantage of some remedial help.

1. Marvin needs to have his reading assignments structured for him. Wherever possible, pre-reading questions will help Marvin significantly. In addition, visual story "maps," structured overviews, etc. would be very helpful to Marvin, and he should be able to learn to construct them for himself in a very short time.

2. Some direct instruction in structural analysis skills (specifically, syllabication and recognizing suffixes) is essential. This instruction should be coupled with a reminder to Marvin that he can employ his rather good phonics skills after he has analyzed the structure of the words (thus, this provides the opportunity for review in phonics as well). Since Marvin enjoys "taking things apart," he should be able to employ these skills to good effect once he understands how this will aid his reading.

3. Marvin could benefit from a holistic approach to his word recognition problems. I would recommend two strategies for Marvin (as opposed to more isolated work in phonics or word recognition): [a] Repeated Readings Approach, or its variation, the Talking Dictionary; and [b] taped read-alongs requiring Marvin to read in a book along with an oral rendition that has been taped for him. Several commercial companies produce good tape-book combinations. The Neurological Impress (NIM) might also be a good approach to use with Marvin in a tutorial or other one-on-one setting.

4. Every effort should be made to sustain Marvin's positive attitude and cooperation in any remedial program. At the moment he has an excellent approach to reading and school and he should be encouraged to develop his substantial strengths.

***Note Any Additional Suggestions and/or Recommendations (Optional).***    There are times when the literacy professional completes an assessment and is aware that there is more to be done. Often, it would be desirable to collect information from other professional sources. For example, medical services might be needed to explore health, vision, or auditory contributions to the reading or writing difficulties. Alternatively, it might be concluded that a psychologist and/or special educator should become involved to determine eligibility for special services. Referrals to other professionals should be done generally; specific recommendations should be avoided.

The reporter may also wish to recommend that the student receive additional support services. Again, the nature and/or duration of the support should be described, but the report should avoid recommending specific sources of service. The obvious exception is the case in which the person reporting is also responsible for delivering the type of service recommended, although in that case the reporter might wish to summarize the planned services so that everyone is clear about what will happen next (see Figure 16.13).

Finally, it is often desirable to specify what types of activities would be appropriate in the home environment (see Figure 16.14). It is not possible to ensure home involvement and support, but parents often welcome specific suggestions for helping their children. We often attach some parent information to each report, since many parents are unaware of the importance of some simple ways they can help. Tips about reading to children, ideas for writing at home, local sources of good books, guidelines for controlling TV watching, and directions for supporting students with specific techniques are generally welcomed.

## Progress Reports

The procedures described above are appropriate for an initial and complete diagnostic assessment. Students often become involved in special programs or receive special instructional services as the result of such reports. In such cases periodic reports may be very desirable, but there is no need to write such a comprehensive diagnostic report. The format for progress reports is somewhat different, with a focus on instruction rather than assessment (see Figure 16.15).

The first two sections of a progress report are almost identical to a diagnostic report. Only minor variations in the cover sheet and background information components are obvious. For example, the cover sheet may include both test and retest information. Because the progress report is written after some period of instructional intervention, it is important to date and note this information carefully. Similarly, the background information component may contain information that has been gathered over a considerable period of time. Thus it is important to note if an observation was made early in the program or was made more recently.

In a progress report, one of the most important components is the diagnostic summary. This section should be written carefully, because it essentially provides the rationale for the instructional program that is described. This brief, accurate, and focused statement is usually not more than a page in length. It may refer to earlier assessments (by date and examiner) but should not be viewed as a complete diagnostic report.

The Summary of the Instructional Program is also a critical component of the progress report. It should describe exactly what was done and why. The excerpt in Figure 16.16

**FIGURE 16.13** Special Services Scheduling Survey

| Student _____ Teacher _____ Date _____ | Reading | Math | Writing |
|---|---|---|---|
| 1. Student will fully participate in regular classroom without any Special Services support (specially designed instruction). | | | |
| 2. Student will fully participate in regular classroom with direct Special Services support (Specialist staff in regular classroom). | | | |
| 3. A combination of 2 and 4 (student may receive support in classroom some of the time and receive services out of the classroom sometimes). | | | |
| 4. Student will fully participate in regular classroom with supplementary support outside of classroom (student brings regular classroom materials). | | | |
| 5. Student will work at a program similar to that in the regular classroom, but doncuted entirely out of classroom by Special Services staff. | | | |

Specific areas of concern:

_____

_____

_____

_____

_____

If there were a mixed-grade Writer's Workshop in the Resource Room, would this student be a good candidate for that group?

☐ Yes    ☐ No

Check any Special Services currently received by the student:

☐ Developmental K      ☐ Chapter 1      ☐ ESL      ☐ Resource Room      ☐ Highly Capable

What is your "best guess" as to the times these subjects will fit into your classroom schedule for this student? (e.g. from 10:00 to 10:45)

Reading _____    Math _____    Writing _____

Would you be willing to have within your class a small group of students who require similar Special Services, if a member of the appropriate Special Services staff was scheduled to be in your room for the part of each day when students would need support?

☐ Yes    ☐ No

*Source:* From *Authentic Assessment* by B. Hill and C. Ruptic. Copyright © 1994 Christopher Gordon. Reprinted by permission.

**FIGURE 16.14**
Case Report:
General
Recommendations

**Additional Recommendations**

Marvin could benefit from additional individualized or small group instruction. A tutorial or clinical setting would be beneficial to him. Additional testing does not, however, seem necessary at this time.

At home, Marvin should set aside a short period each day for silent reading. Marvin's mother reads regularly herself and might consider setting aside a "family reading time" each evening. It might be helpful if Marvin were encouraged to read aloud (after practice) to his younger brother and sister as well.

Marvin could also benefit from doing the Talking Dictionary at home several times a week. This should be a relaxed, enjoyable time for both Marvin and whomever he is reading with. Family participation in word and memory games could be helpful to Marvin. Games such as Scrabble and Memory could increase Marvin's word analysis skills.

Finally, Marvin should be encouraged to write as often as possible. Letters and notes to family and friends should be actively encouraged. He might also be charged with making lists of activities and notes to remind family members of special events.

_____          _____
Marjorie Y. Lipson, Ph.D.                   Date

demonstrates how instructional goals are linked to specific activities. These activities are either described in the body of the report or descriptions can be provided in an appendix. If there were changes in the instructional program, these should be noted also. It is obviously quite common for student progress to occur that results in refocusing the program or changing the activities. The rationale for program decisions should be carefully described.

The Summary of Progress section should contain a description of the student's performance at the current time. Quantitative and/or qualitative evidence should be provided

**FIGURE 16.15**
Progress Report
Format

**Cover Sheet(s)**
  Identifying information for student
  Name of reporter and date of report
  Summary of existing assessment
    information
  Summary of new or retest information
**Background Information**
  Summary of relevant referral
    information
  Summary of continuing observation
    or interview data
**Diagnostic Summary**
  Brief summary of relevant assessment
    information
  Conclusions re: major instructional
    implications

**Summary of Instructional Program**
  Description of instructional goals
  Description of instructional activities/
    program
**Summary of Progress**
  Description of areas of improvement
    (with evidence)
  Description of areas that remain
    problematic
**Recommendations**
  Further intervention and instructional
    programs
  Parental support

**FIGURE 16.16**
Excerpt from
Summary of
Instructional
Program

Much of Jason's instruction this term has focused on two main areas: foundation skills, designed to help him see the purposes of reading, and comprehension. Comprehension activities were designed to help Jason see reading as a process of getting meaning from text and to help him acquire strategies for understanding.

The Think Aloud activity has been used several times with Jason to encourage more active comprehension. The first time he did this activity, it was clear that word recognition greatly affected his performance. He offered very little in response to the initial prompt of, "What were you doing and thinking as you read that part?" Jason's main concern centered around how well he was going to read. Since then, Jason's responses to prompts have been more focused on comprehension. He prefaces his responses with, "Well, I was thinking about . . ." or, "That makes sense." Recently, during a Think Aloud selection, when he was asked what he had been doing or thinking as he read, Jason responded: "I wasn't thinking about nothing, but I made a picture in my mind about a cave with stone pictures." When he was asked if he had to think to make a picture in his mind, Jason paused and said, "Yeah—I guess I do think!"

regarding areas of improvement. In addition, there should be clear descriptions of the types of texts, tasks, or skills that require continued attention. Finally, the report should contain recommendations about changes in instructional focus, the desirability of continued support services, and the need for continued support at home.

## Conferences

Conferences are a common format for reporting to others. They differ somewhat from other forms of reporting because they are generally less formal. The skills and strategies for conducting interviews (see Chapter 4) are helpful in conducting conferences. Whereas the purpose of an interview is to gather information, the purpose of a conference is to report or clarify information.

As in all forms of reporting, there are a variety of reasons why conferences are conducted. For example, professionals are frequently expected to confer with classroom teachers, administrators, and other specialized professionals about the abilities or progress of individual students. English language arts professionals are also often expected to participate in formal conferences like those conducted for IEP hearings. And, of course, there are usually regularly scheduled conferences for parents.

The different types of conferences are likely to be focused on slightly different issues, and often require slightly different skills. A conference with a classroom teacher sometimes involves specific issues about which there has been ongoing communication prior to the conference. Perhaps, for example, the classroom teacher and the English language arts teacher have been keeping an eye on the progress of one young girl, Krista. They have set a conference time to examine all the pieces of information they have about her and to review her progress and performance in the classroom. As a result, they may decide to continue observing, or they may decide that Krista should be evaluated more fully by the literacy professional.

Conferences can also focus on solving problems or sharing perceptions. The classroom teacher may report, for example, that Jay is having trouble with some task in the classroom. The conference may involve:

- Evaluating the appropriateness of that task for the child;
- Examining the task itself;
- Other evidence that the child has problems in a particular area;
- Developing ways to work on this problem in the support program;
- Developing ways to address the problem in the regular classroom.

In some parts of the country these prereferral conferences have become a formal part of the process to be used in responding to students with special needs. The school designates Student Support Teams (SSTs) that meet to discuss students when teachers are concerned. The format presented in Figure 6.17 is used by one school district to guide the work of the SST. Only after the teacher and support personnel have tried a variety of options discussed and described during the "staffing" can children be referred for further evaluation or eligibility determination.

Parents are not generally part of an SST conference, but if it is decided that further assessment is needed they would, of course, be consulted (see Chapters 1 and 4). Particular care must be taken when conferring with parents. Parents can react emotionally to information about their children, and this may prevent them from receiving the information as you intended. It is important to help parents understand the significance of what you are saying. In addition, you should always be sensitive to different cultural modes of interacting. Every effort should be made to communicate in the language most comfortable to the parents and to use interactional styles appropriate to them. If that is not possible, then it will be important to maintain contact and to follow up on any requests for parental action.

It is important to provide clear, concise information during a conference. It is also important to listen carefully and attend to the other individual(s). Be especially alert to the possibility that the parent or teacher has not clearly understood what you are saying. Also be sure to request new or additional information about the student or the situation. Finally, be sure to enlist the support of these individuals. Be as specific as possible about the ways in which they can help.

# Ethical Responsibilities

Like all those who work with people, literacy professionals must be careful to attend to their ethical responsibilities. Because they often work with young or vulnerable people, these responsibilities must be taken particularly seriously. The International Reading Association Code of Ethics (see Figure 16.18) should be given careful consideration by all English language arts professionals. The portion regarding ethical standards in reading services has critical implications for teachers and clinicians who work with disabled readers or writers.

This statement conveys most of what we believe to be important professional conduct, but there are two other responsibilities that we believe literacy professionals should shoulder. First, they should be advocates for students and their families. This means ensuring that

**FIGURE 16.17**
Preconference
Questionnaires and
SST Report Form

## I. Student Support Team Questionnaire

*Please consider these questions prior to the STT meeting.*
*Bring work samples to the meeting.*

What materials are you using with this student?

Do you think other materials could be more effective?

What are some instructional strategies that you've found effective with this student?

What doesn't work?

What are this student's areas of strength?

Could you use these strengths to increase learning?

What methods have you used to reach the above conclusions?

How do you prepare the student for a lesson?
    Do you use preteaching methods?
    Do you consider prior knowledge?

Does the student work well with a group?

Does the student work well independently?

Does the student complete work in the time allowed?

What services are presently provided for this student?

What is your most important learning goal for this student?

What information can the S.S.T. help you with?

## II. Student Support Team Minutes and Plan for Intervention

Student's name _____

Date of meeting _____

Present at meeting _____

_____

_____

_____

**Reason for referral:**




**Ideas for intervention:**




With thanks to Mrs. Anne Browne, Principal of Orchard Elementary School, South Burlington, VT.

**FIGURE 16.18**   IRA Code of Ethics

The members of the International Reading Association who are concerned with the teaching of reading form a group of professional persons obligated to society and devoted to the service and welfare of individuals through teaching, clinical services, research, and publication. The members of this group are committed to values which are the foundation of a democratic society—freedom to teach, write, and study in an atmosphere conducive to the best interests of the profession. The welfare of the public, the profession, and the individuals concerned should be of primary consideration in recommending candidates for degrees, positions, advancements, the recognition of professional activity, and for certification in those areas where certification exists.

**Ethical Standards in Professional Relationships**

1. It is the obligation of all members of the International Reading Association to observe the Code of Ethics of the organization and to act accordingly so as to advance the status and prestige of the Association and of the profession as a whole. Members should assist in establishing the highest professional standards for reading programs and services, and should enlist support for these through dissemination of pertinent information to the public.
2. It is the obligation of all members to maintain relationships with other professional persons, striving for harmony, avoiding personal controversy, encouraging cooperative effort, and making known the obligations and services rendered by professionals in reading.
3. It is the obligation of members to report results of research and other developments in reading.
4. Members should not claim nor advertise affiliation with the International Reading Association as evidence of their competence in reading.

**Ethical Standards in Reading Services**

1. Professionals in reading must possess suitable qualifications for engaging in consulting, clinical, or remedial work. Unqualified persons should not engage in such activities except under the direct supervision of one who is properly qualified. Professional intent and the welfare of the person seeking services should govern all consulting or clinical activities such as counseling, administering diagnostic tests, or providing remediation. It is the duty of the professional in reading to keep relationships with clients and interested persons on a professional level.
2. Information derived from consulting and/or clinical services should be regarded as confidential. Expressed consent of persons involved should be secured before releasing information to outside agencies.
3. Professionals in reading should recognize the boundaries of their competence and should not offer services which fail to meet professional standards established by other disciplines. They should be free, however, to give assistance in other areas in which they are qualified.
4. Referral should be made to specialists in allied fields as needed. When such referral is made, pertinent information should be made available to consulting specialists.
5. Reading clinics and/or reading professionals offering services should refrain from guaranteeing easy solutions or favorable outcomes as a result of their work, and their advertising should be consistent with that of allied professions. They should not accept for remediation any persons who are unlikely to benefit from their instruction, and they should work to accomplish the greatest possible improvement in the shortest time. Fees, if charged, should be agreed on in advance and should be charged in accordance with an established set of rates commensurate with that of other professions.

*Breaches of the Code of Ethics should be reported to IRA Headquarters for referral to the Committee on Professional Standards and Ethics for an impartial investigation.*

*Source:* (1987, November). IRA Code of Ethics, *The Reading Teacher, 41*(2), 143. Reprinted by permission of the International Reading Association. All rights reserved.

parents and clients understand forms they must sign and that those who cannot read are provided with information to make informed decisions about their programs and options.

Being an advocate involves much more, of course. It means insisting that inadequate programs are revised, that misleading test results be reconsidered, and that instructional programs respond to students' needs. It means being concerned with issues of equity, funding, and politics. Clearly, this is not easy, and an in-depth discussion is beyond the scope of this text. However, disabled readers often need strong voices, and the families of poor readers frequently need an advocate as well. Institutions are not always responsive to the needs of individuals; literacy professionals must be, to the fullest extent possible.

A second responsibility that English language arts professionals should accept is the responsibility to remain current regarding developments and research in the field. They must make a commitment to read and communicate about the important advances and techniques available. In doing so they should advance high standards in assessment and instruction for all students. This responsibility extends beyond working with children to providing literacy leadership across the educational community. A growing body of research suggests that literacy success depends heavily on the expertise and collegial support that reading specialists provide at the school and district level (see Allington & Cunningham, 2002; Mosenthal et al., 2001a, 2001b). There is every reason to believe that the field will remain dynamic for several years to come. New information, better practice, and fresh approaches are all likely to emerge. The effective professional must take as an ethical responsibility the responsibility to be informed and to inform others.

## Chapter Summary

In the first section of this chapter we described the various roles that literacy professionals are expected to perform. These range from direct instructional contact with students to consultative roles with teachers. We noted that these critical roles all share a common requirement for effective communication. We argued that literacy leaders must be able to interact with a wide array of people, sharing information and advocating effective assessment and instructional practices.

We described several modes for reporting including summaries of portfolios and the most formal type of communication, case reports. We detailed the contents of a formal case report, using the case of Marvin (see earlier chapters) to exemplify each section. These sections include descriptions of background information, summaries of assessment information, descriptions and reports of the results of diagnostic teaching, a diagnostic summary statement, and recommendations for instruction. In addition to formal case reports, we described progress reports, noting the similarities and differences between various reporting forms. Finally, we described the role of conferences in the reporting process.

In the final portion of this chapter we presented the International Reading Association Code of Ethics. Several aspects of this code were elaborated to focus on issues of particular importance to professionals who work with disabled students.

# Sample Case Report: Seth

## College of Education Reading Clinic Progress Report

*Name:*  Seth C.                                      *Date of Report:*  May 19, 2002

*Address:*  Route 390
            Pleasantville, Vermont
*Phone:*  624-0111
*Birthdate:*  6/26/92
*Age:*  9 years, 11 months      *Grade:*  3 (R1)
*School Name:*  Pleasantville Elementary      *School Address:*  Pleasantville, Vermont
*Parent's/Guardian's Name:*  Mr. & Mrs. C.
*Tutor:*  W. Jorgan
*Attendance for Tutoring*

    A. *Times present:*  12
    B. *Times absent:*  2
    C. *Reasons for absences:*  NA
    D. *Attitude toward tutoring:* Seth appears highly motivated to work hard in those areas where he feels he is competent and/or where he is succeeding. Seth appears tired much of the time. He yawned several times during the classroom observation and yawns and rubs his eyes three to five times during each clinic session. Seth is an open and friendly child who smiles often, is animated in discussions, makes eye contact when working with the examiner, and likes to laugh.

## Summary of Assessment Results

Dolch Word List (2–27–02)                    *Recognized 192/220*
   Post Test (4–24–02)                       *Recognized 196/220*
Peabody Picture Vocabulary
   Test (form M)                            *Standard Score Equivalent: 95*
   Date of Testing: 2–13–02                 *Percentile Rank: 37*
   Age: 9 years, 8 months                   *Age Equivalent: 8 years, 11 months*
El Paso Phonics Survey                        *Frustrational level errors: 2.9*
   Date of Testing: 2–20–02                 *Level 1.9 errors: 19/30*
   Post Test (4–24–02)                      *Retest of skills taught at grade*
                                 *1.9: 22/30 correct*

Analytical Reading Inventory
　　by Mary Lynn Woods and
　　Alden J. Moe
　　Date of Testing: 2–6–02
Auditory Discrimination of Pairs (Bader)
　　Date of Testing: 2–13–02
Hearing Letter Names in Sounds (Bader)
　　Date of Testing: 2–13–02
Woodcock Reading Mastery Tests-Revised
　　(Form G)

*Instructional: primer–1*
*Frustrational: 2*
*Hearing Capacity: 2*

*29/30 items correct (competent)*

*9/12 items correct (competent)*

| | *Relative Mastery* | *Percentile Rank* |
|---|---|---|
| Letter Identification | 93% | 58 |
| Word Identification | 7% | 10 |
| Word Attack | 32% | 9 |
| Word Comprehension | 55% | 15 |
| Passage Comprehension | 29% | 8 |

Specified Areas of Reading Difficulty: Despite a reading expectancy of 4.1, Seth demonstrates difficulty in skills taught as early as first grade. Specific areas needing attention are vowels, reversals, visual discrimination, blending, sight words, fluency in oral reading, the graphemes *g, ch, sch, sp, str, squ, spl, qu,* and *s,* ending consonant sounds, and comprehension strategies.

# Background Information

## Reason for Referral

Seth's reading level is considerably below his grade placement. The Chapter 1 reading teacher in Seth's school requested that Seth be tested for further data and insight.

## Family and Medical History

Seth lives at home with both parents, who are farmers. When asked to tell the examiner something about himself, the first thing Seth mentioned was that he lived on a farm. At the beginning of nearly every clinic session, when asked how he's been doing, Seth invariably tells a story about something that has happened on the farm. Seth's primary interest beyond the farm is his four-wheeler; the friend he plays with most is a 12-year-old from down the road with whom he rides his four-wheeler. Seth has mentioned special days he has spent in the fields and woods as well.

　　　　Seth says that he doesn't like television that much; he says that he doesn't like "being cooped up" and would rather play outside. He watches television about 1/2 hour after school and 1 to $1\frac{1}{2}$ hours in the evenings—usually movies on his VCR.

　　　　Seth indicated that no one in his family reads and that only occasionally does either his mother or his sister read to him. Despite this, there is obvious concern about Seth's reading difficulties on the part of the family, and the commitment that they have made to drive him the considerable distance to the clinic each week is indicative of this. In addition, the interview with Seth's mother and sister revealed that despite Seth's contention that he does not read at home, he has been reading as part of a Pizza Hut promotion, his family is aware of his favorite kind of book, he does read a farm journal occasionally, and he receives *Humpty-Dumpty* magazine.

Seth was $11\frac{1}{2}$ pounds at birth and several weeks late. Forceps were used as a result of a difficult delivery, pinching nerves in his left arm. It is shorter than the right arm, and because of a lack of mobility, he receives physical therapy. Beyond this Seth's health has been normal except for a series of ear infections suffered during his first year in the first grade. Tubes were inserted to rectify his problems.

Seth goes to bed between 8:00 and 8:30 on weeknights and gets up at 7:00. He goes to sleep with the radio playing.

## School History and Teacher Comments

Seth is in a third grade classroom with Mrs. Garvey, an experienced teacher who replaced Seth's regular teacher when the latter went on maternity leave in February. Seth repeated first grade after a difficult year of health and academic problems. Mr. Williams, the Chapter 1 reading teacher with whom Seth works, feels that the phonetic approach used by Seth's teacher that first year was inappropriate, given Seth's ear problems. Presently, Seth receives help from Mr. Williams in reading and math.

Mrs. Garvey reports that Seth seems much younger than the other children in the class and that he sometimes asks questions or makes comments that are "babyish"; she says at times even the other children react negatively to his immaturity. She feels that Seth acts "cute" when he can't do something or wants help. Seth is required to complete all assigned tasks before going out to recess. Mrs. Garvey reports that he really likes recess and doesn't like to miss it.

# Summary of Assessment Results

## Reader Factors

On the Metropolitan Achievement Tests (most recently administered in Seth's school in the fall of 2001) Seth scored in the first percentile in reading comprehension. No other subtest scores were available.

Seth underwent an extensive psychoeducational evaluation in November, 2001, at the request of the Special Educator at his school. The results of the Weschler Intelligence Scale for Children—Revised (WISC-R) indicate a Full Scale score of 88. Results of the Bender Visual Motor Gestalt Test and the Visual Aural Digit Span Test appear to demonstrate a preference for visual processing; however, his score on the former reflects a slightly more than one-year delay, and his scores on visual processing subtests of the latter placed him in the 25th to 50th percentile.

Seth's standard score equivalent on the Peabody Picture Vocabulary Test-R (PPVT-R) was 95, and, consistent with the WISC-R results, his score places Seth in the low-average to average range of ability.

Observations made by the examiner during the administration of the *Analytic Reading Inventory* indicate that Seth only sporadically attempts to construct meaning from the text. On a primer-level selection Seth omitted the word "I" at the beginning of three different sentences, rendering them semantically and syntactically incorrect. Other miscues as early as the primer level reflect an inattention to meaning; for example, "I can run as fast as a turn (train)."

Some miscues, however, do reflect an effort on Seth's part to construct meaning from the passage. This was particularly evident on a passage about a boy's dog being hit by a car. "Hit" was misread as "hurt" twice, "pup lying" became "puppy laying," and "badly hurt" was misread as "belly hurt." On this selection, Seth's miscues (sixteen) rendered a score of frustrational level. However, he had only two comprehension errors, both of which may be construed as logical on the basis of Seth's experience. When asked how the child felt seeing his pet hurt, Seth answered, "Sad" (the correct answer being "Scared"). In answer to the question "What does the child say to make you think he loved the dog?" Seth answered, "I'll hurry right home" (to get help for the dog). The writers of the inventory consider the answer to be "Shep is my best friend."

The nature of many of Seth's miscues on this story and his level of comprehension appear to be a result of the structure and content of the story. Both primer-level selections and one of the first-grade passages appear to begin in the middle of stories; they lack a strong structure and interesting plot. The story about the dog getting hit by a car (Level 2) had no clear resolution, but elements of the story (i.e., the subject, the clear statement of a problem, Seth's ability to relate to a child with a hurt pet) may have encouraged him to construct meaning from it. Seth's other strong comprehension performance was on a Level 1 passage with a clear story line (about a child who brings home stray animals) and a conclusion (his mother puts a halt to it). Not only did Seth answer four out of six questions competently, he retold the story in detail and made a well-formulated statement of the main idea.

Despite Seth's performance on the second-grade passage about the hurt dog, the examiner weighed the large number of miscues (16) as well as his comprehension on a second-grade passage that he read silently (42 percent) to determine this level as frustrational. Seth's listening level was determined by weighing his answers to traditional postreading questions and the quality of his retellings. Seth was tested at the third grade level twice. In both cases he answered a percentage of questions correctly, which placed this level on the instructional/frustrational border for him. However, his retellings in both cases lacked organization and missed the main ideas. On the basis of this the examiner determined Seth's instructional listening level to be second grade.

Analysis of Seth's miscues reveals strong attention to initial letters, such as *hit–hurt* (with any pair of words or phrases listed in this case report, the first word or phrase will represent the text and the second will represent Seth's word calling). Other miscues demonstrate use of both beginning and ending sounds (*drop–drip, thud–tried, anyway–always*). Seth also appears to rearrange letters in the medial portions of words to create new words (*felt–flat, still–sitting, train–turn*). Miscues on the Word Identification subtest of the

Woodcock Reading Mastery Tests-Revised (WRMT-R) reflect these patterns as well (*grow–grew, happen–hope, heart–hurt*).

Except for the Letter Identification subtest, all of the other subtests of the WRMT-R indicate that Seth is far below the norm in these tasks. Seth's word comprehension score reveals this as an area of some strength. Seth's only errors before reaching a ceiling level were with analogies in which Seth could not read one or more of the words. For diagnostic purposes the examiner gave Seth those words. In all cases Seth was able to complete the analogies. The results of the Passage Comprehension subtest confirm observations made by the examiner during clinic sessions. The cloze exercise requiring Seth to use context to determine the meanings of words is especially difficult for him.

Word analysis skills were tested with two different instruments. The results of both the Word Attack subtest of the WRMT-R and the El Paso Phonics Survey indicate difficulties in a number of decoding skills. The validity of tests requiring children to read nonsense words has been questioned; indeed, Seth did miscall a number of the nonsense words as legitimate words. A second weakness of the testing situation—the tendency for Seth's eyes to wander to letters above and below the word which he was reading—was eliminated when the El Paso Phonics Survey was readministered with the words written on cards.

Despite the drawbacks of these kinds of tests, the skill difficulties that surfaced consistently are worth noting. Although Seth is capable of reading the phonograms *up, in,* and *am,* in four out of twenty-two cases he had difficulty blending one of these with an initial consonant. Vowels, both long and short, surfaced as an area of weakness for Seth on the Word Attack subtest of the WRMT-R. Other error patterns include adding an *m* before a final *p* (*shup–shump*), changing the initial sound entirely despite a correct pronunciation of it prior to word analysis (*quam–cume*), adding ending consonants (*blin–blant*), and separating the letters of blends (*plip–pilip*). It should be noted, however, that Seth performed accurately on 26/32 blends taught as late as grade 3.5.

The Bader auditory tests were administered because of Seth's history of ear problems. No deficiencies in discrimination surfaced.

A second testing of the Dolch Word List demonstrated that Seth lacks automaticity on many of the words which he read correctly on the first testing. Although he had only twenty-four errors on the second testing, eighteen of these were not repeat errors.

## Instructional Factors

Seth receives instruction both in a regular classroom and in a Chapter 1 reading program outside the classroom. Seth is not part of a regular reading group within the classroom, although workbook tasks are assigned frequently. He is rarely expected to read full-length texts in either setting. In the Chapter 1 classroom his reading instruction has focused largely on word analysis, and work is assigned from a program that emphasized visual and auditory perception of letter clusters in words. The method of instruction used by this particular program emphasized the analysis of words into their constituent parts.

The classroom teacher indicated that Seth was responsible for the same assigned work required of all other children in the class and that there was no differentiation of tasks among students. The language arts, spelling, and social studies books used in Seth's classroom are standard third grade texts with readability estimates ranging from a 2.5 to a 5.0 grade level. Seth is expected to complete all classroom assignments before going to recess. The teacher reported that Seth really likes recess and does not like to miss it, although he frequently does because his work is incomplete.

The examiner observed Seth in his classroom for approximately one hour in April. At the beginning of the observation period Mrs. Garvey was phasing children into a painting project. Seth was one of the first students done with his project. While the majority of the class continued to paint, Seth washed his hands and returned to his desk.

Throughout the period during which Seth painted, as well as during the work period, no other children initiated an interaction with him. Seth appears to enjoy the other children, often responding and laughing at general comments made by others to the group as a whole.

Only occasionally did Seth look up from his work after returning to his desk. Six children were coloring on the floor near him, two children were painting at the table behind him, and except for three other children working, the rest of the class was engaging in one of these activities around the room. Despite the noise level and the proximity of two groups of children chatting, Seth seemed undistracted.

Although Seth appears to work well independently, he is very reliant on his teacher. He asks questions frequently, requiring her help on nearly every individual task on which the examiner observed him working.

## Diagnostic Teaching

Using three different approaches to instruction and three groups of five words, Seth was systematically taught to recognize the words instantly. The instructional sequence was timed to determine how long it took under each set of instructional circumstances for him to learn the five words in each set. He was retested on these words after $1\frac{1}{2}$ hours to see how many he had retained from each sequence. Thus both effectiveness and efficiency were evaluated. Finally, Seth was asked to tell which method he thought had been most effective for him.

At delayed retesting, Seth knew all fifteen new words at sight (two-second flash). Thus the three instructional approaches were equally effective. However, using one approach he learned the five new words in $1\frac{1}{2}$ minutes, whereas using a different approach, it took ten minutes for him to learn the words! In terms of efficiency Seth is likely to benefit from a phonics program that blends parts into wholes, as opposed to a phonics program that breaks the whole into component parts. It should be noted, however, that he learned the words with equal ease when they were presented as sight words. The approach that was least efficient for Seth was the whole-to-part phonics approach, similar to his current instructional program. Seth's perception confirmed these conclusions. He felt he had learned the words most easily in the part-to-whole phonics approach.

To clarify issues related to approach and content, we initiated a language experience activity designed to allow Seth to read and write about topics of interest to him. During the first diagnostic teaching segment we were chagrined to find that, while Seth was enthusiastic about discussing a personal encounter with a "coydog" (half dog, half coyote), the story he dictated was sparse and incoherent. Subsequent work with a conference partner did nothing to improve the quality of the product. Two additional trials, yielding similar results, led to the conclusion that this was not the most effective method for improving Seth's word recognition or comprehension skills at the present time.

## Diagnostic Statements and Suggestions for Instruction

Structuring concepts for Seth will be valuable in all remedial activities. Evidence indicates that he is not grasping the whole and that parts-to-whole instruction may be helpful in improving comprehension as well. Seth needs to acquire a *story schema,* including a knowledge of story grammar. By focusing Seth's attention on the elements of story structure with prereading and postreading questions and activities, he will begin to acquire a sense of the parts of a well-written story. Given Seth's limited independent reading, it is suggested that this be done initially with books read aloud by the teacher.

Another vehicle for structuring reading selections for Seth is concept mapping. This spatial visualization task may fit his learning style, given his preference for visual processing as indicated on the psychoeducational report. A variety of models exist. For story structure a map can be constructed to show the flow of the problem/resolution pattern, completed initially with teacher direction. Other models can be specifically used to map expository writing. Mapping can also be used to help Seth structure his own writing. As with expository maps, he could begin with his superordinate concept and extend his map with subordinate details.

To further expand instruction in the concept of the whole as a sum of its parts, *writing* can be taught through conventional parts of a piece of writing. In the clinic Seth has generated ideas for a piece of writing through discussion with the examiner. After Seth has written what he believes is a finished product, the examiner rewrites it with an introduction, episode, and conclusion. It is read to Seth and the parts of a strong piece of writing are discussed, as is the importance of writing for an audience. One of the examiner-written parts is then excluded and Seth composes that part. This process is continued until Seth has rewritten the entire piece within this framework. Thus far, it has been a successful technique, although repetition and reinforcement are indicated. Seth's revisions have become more detailed, but his initial drafts are still only two or three sentences about the episode.

Of extreme importance are instructional programs that would teach Seth to think about what he is reading. By attending to the meaning of what he is reading, Seth will correct miscues that are not appropriate to the text. A number of strategies can be employed to improve Seth's *thinking/reading skills.* Think-Aloud, a program that requires the reader to discuss what she or he is thinking about while reading, has been used, as have teacher-directed cloze activities. Cloze exercises that are guided and directed by the teacher will encourage Seth to look for contextual cues for a word that he doesn't know, improve his understanding of the structure of language, inform the teacher of his instructional needs, and allow the teacher to provide activities that are specifically designed to fill those needs.

In addition to monitoring his reading comprehension, Seth needs to attend to the word display. An analysis of Seth's errors on the El Paso Phonics Survey indicated that at times he retrieves letters from lines above and below where he is reading. Specific decoding exercises that require that Seth attend to the symbols and sounds will provide less opportunity for his eyes to wander. Seth's lack of progress and his demonstrated difficulties with the whole (both words and concepts) indicate that a parts-to-whole approach is needed.

Seth's concept of reading and of himself as a reader would improve with more *fluency* in his oral reading. In addition, fluency and phrasing facilitate comprehension by redirecting the child's focus from the individual words to the flow of writing as "talk written down." Neurological impress is a method for improving fluency with which Seth has met success in the clinic. He is eager to try reading the practice passage himself and likes to bring it home to read to his parents. Also appended is an article describing ways to improve comprehension by using this technique.

As the test results indicate, Seth has specific areas of instructional need. His *sight vocabulary* is adequate, but the results of the posttest indicate a lack of automaticity on at least eighteen words (read correctly on the pretest but incorrectly on the posttest) in addition to the twenty-eight he missed on the pretest. It is critical in this, and in all of Seth's instruction, that a variety of techniques be employed. Initial presentation of each word should be in a variety of modes; Seth should say the word, write it, hear it said and used in a sentence, and use it himself. Suggesting that he note configuration and providing opportunities for him to experience the word kinesthetically (such as tracing or building the word) would also be helpful.

There are other methods that can encourage Seth to attend to all parts of the word. Because of the wide range of vowel errors, it is suggested that *vowel instruction* include all vowel sounds and be concurrent with instruction in *phonograms*. Activities should require Seth to say, hear, write, read, and feel the vowels and phonograms taught.

Seth's tendency to rearrange letters in the medial portions of words and add letters near the end suggests a need for instruction in structural analysis and in the close examination of all the letters in a word. Initially, instruction in this area needs to focus on the parts of simple words. Instruction could build on vowel and phonogram instruction with the teacher asking Seth to identify in what part of a word he hears a sound (i.e., when teaching the long *o* have him hold up a card with the word *middle* on it to demonstrate that he heard the *o* in the middle of the word *boat*). Written exercises can be designed on this same premise.

Seth's miscues indicate that he lacks skill in *blending*. While teaching any of the skill areas, the teacher could include activities that provide practice in blending the sound taught to produce a word. Many enjoyable and productive oral and kinesthetic activities can be employed to aid Seth in learning to blend all parts of a word. The teacher can point to each part of a word, having Seth say and hold the sound represented until the teacher moves his or her finger to the next word part. Letters could be placed on the floor, and Seth could "skate" from one phoneme of a word to the next while saying the word aloud. These and other activities would be especially beneficial when teaching Seth vowels and *ending consonant sounds* that testing identified as weak.

A technique that might be of benefit to Seth in seeing the whole and its parts is that of using one book in all reading exercises in a given day. There is added power in doing this. It will be easier for him to operate within a familiar and consistent context, and to be working on varying skills toward one purpose: to complete and understand the story.

## Suggestions and Recommendations

The above are specific skill areas in which Seth needs instruction. Other strategies can be employed both in school and at home to improve his reading.

1. The lack of self-reliance that Seth demonstrated in the classroom indicates a need to provide assignments and tasks on which he can become self-directed. Seth must fulfill the high standards set for him; however, he will benefit from a quantity of work that he can complete and a level of work at which he can succeed.

2. An accompanying shift of responsibility to Seth at home may benefit him. Perhaps he could do more chores in the barn or around the house to help build an image of himself as a mature and helpful member of the family.

3. Goal setting is a technique that might be employed to encourage responsibility for himself and his work at both school and home. If Seth is exhibiting difficulty in completing tasks, he can set a goal for himself (i.e., finishing a number of math problems before recess).

4. As was noted above, Seth will benefit tremendously from using one book in all reading exercises in a given day.

5. Seth needs help choosing books that are appropriate for his reading ability and interests. His performance on the passage about a dog who gets hit by a car indicates an interest in exciting stories that he can relate to personally. In conversations with the examiner Seth had indicated an interest in horse stories as well. These interests are one of Seth's strengths in reading, a major part of what he brings to the process, and it will be to his benefit to capitalize on them.

6. Seth needs more exposure to reading and language. At home this could be accomplished by trips to the library, a family reading time, and a time during which Seth is read to daily. It is recommended that Seth be read to daily at school as well. Only with repeated exposure to story structure will Seth utilize it as a comprehension strategy.

7. Seth's parents may employ the Talking Dictionary approach to oral reading. Seth enjoyed his success in this activity at the clinic and loved to graph his progress.

8. It is recommended that Seth go to bed earlier. He seemed very tired in school and at the clinic. It is also recommended that Seth receive complete physical and eye examinations. Some of his fatigue may be due to health problems.

9. It is recommended that objectives be stated for Seth. He will benefit from clear direction in instruction.

Seth brings to the reading process specific interests and a positive attitude toward most tasks asked of him. The examiner believes that with opportunities to succeed, more exposure to literature that meets his interests, and most importantly, a unified instruction plan across all of Seth's academics, his reading will improve.

_____     _____

Clinician                                                      Date

# REFERENCES

Adams, A., Carnine D., & Gersten, R. (1982). Instructional strategies for studying content area texts in the intermediate grades. *Reading Research Quarterly, 18,* 27–55.

Adams, M. J. (1990). *Beginning to read: Thinking and learning from print.* Cambridge, MA: The MIT Press.

Adelman, H., & Taylor, L. (1977). Two steps toward improving learning for students with (and without) "learning problems." *Journal of Learning Disabilities, 10,* 455–461.

Afflerbach, P. (2000). Verbal reports and protocol analysis. In M. L. Kamil, P. B. Mosenthal, P. D. Pearson, & R. Barr (Eds.), *Handbook of reading research* (Vol. 3, pp. 163–180). Mahwah, NJ: Lawrence Erlbaum.

Agnew, A.T. (1982). Using children's dictated stories to assess code consciousness. *The Reading Teacher, 35,* 450–454.

Alexander, L. (1964). *The book of three.* New York: Holt.

Alexander, P. A., & Jetton, T. L. (2000). Learning from text: A multidimensional and developmental perspective. In M. L. Kamil, P. B. Mosenthal, P. D. Pearson, & R. Barr (Eds.), *Handbook of reading research* (Vol. 3, pp. 285–310). Mahwah, NJ: Lawrence Erlbaum.

Allen, R. V. (1976). *Language experience in communication.* Boston: Houghton Mifflin.

Allington, R. L. (1975). Sustained approaches to reading and writing. *Language Arts, 52,* 813–815.

Allington, R. L. (1977). If they don't read much how they ever gonna get good? *Journal of Reading, 21,* 57–61.

Allington, R. L. (1980). Teacher interruption behaviors during primary grade oral reading. *Journal of Educational Psychology, 72,* 371–377.

Allington, R. L. (1983a). Fluency: The neglected reading goal. *The Reading Teacher, 36,* 556–561.

Allington, R. L. (1983b). The reading instruction provided readers of differing reading abilities. *Elementary School Journal, 83,* 548–558.

Allington, R. L. (1984). Content coverage and contextual reading in reading groups. *Journal of Reading Behavior, 16,* 85–96.

Allington, R. L. (1991a). Children who find learning to read difficult: School responses to diversity. In E. H. Hiebert (Ed.), *Literacy for a diverse society: Perspectives, practices, and policies* (pp. 237–252). New York: Teachers College Press.

Allington, R. L. (1991b). The legacy of "slow it down and make it more concrete." In J. Zutell & S. McCormick (Eds.), *Learner factors/teacher factors: Issues in literacy research and instruction* (pp. 19–30). Chicago: National Reading Conference.

Allington, R. L. (1994). Critical issues: What's special about special programs for children who find learning to read difficult? *Journal of Reading Behavior, 26,* 95–115.

Allington, R. L., Chodos, L., Domaracki, J., & Truex, S. (1977). Passage dependency: Four diagnostic oral reading tests. *The Reading Teacher, 30,* 369–375.

Allington, R. L., & Cunningham, P. M. (2002). *Schools that work: Where all children read and write* (2nd ed.). Boston: Allyn & Bacon/Longman.

Allington, R. L., & Johnston, P. (1989). Coordination, collaboration, and consistency: The redesign of compensatory and special education intervention. In R. Slavin, M. Madden, & N. Karweit (Eds.), *Preventing school failure: Effective programs for students at risk* (pp. 320–354). Boston: Allyn & Bacon.

Allington, R. L., & McGill-Franzen, A. (1980). Word identification errors in isolation and in context: Apples vs. oranges. *The Reading Teacher, 33,* 795–800.

Allington, R. L., & McGill-Franzen, A. (1989). Different programs, indifferent instruction. In D. Lipsky & A. Gartner (Eds.), *Beyond separate education: Quality education for all* (pp. 75–98). Baltimore: Brookes.

Allington, R. L., & Shake, M. C. (1986). Remedial reading: Achieving curricular congruence in classroom and clinic. *The Reading Teacher, 39,* 648–654.

Allington, R. L., Stuetzel, H., Shake, M., & Lamarche, S. (1986). What is remedial reading? A descriptive study. *Reading Research and Instruction, 26,* 15–30.

Almasi, J. F. (1995). The nature of fourth graders' sociocognitive conflicts in peer-led and teacher-led discussion of literature. *Reading Research Quarterly, 30,* 314–351.

Altwerger, B., Diehl-Faxon, J., & Dockstader-Anderson, K. (1985). Read-aloud events as meaning construction. *Language Arts, 62,* 476–484.

Alvermann, D. E. (1989). Creating the bridge to content-area reading. In P. Winograd, K. Wixson, & M.Y. Lipson (Eds.), *Improving basal reading instruction* (pp. 256–270). New York: Teachers College Press.

Alvermann, D. E. (1991). The discussion web: A graphic aid for learning across the curriculum. *The Reading Teacher, 45*(2), 92–99.

Alvermann, D. E., Dillon, D. R., & O'Brien, D. G. (1987). *Using discussion to promote reading comprehension.* Newark, DE: International Reading Association.

Alvermann, D. E., & Phelps, S. F. (2002). *Content reading and literacy: Succeeding in today's diverse classrooms* (3rd ed.). Boston: Allyn & Bacon.

American Educational Research Association (AERA) (1985). *Standards for educational and psychological testing.* Washington, DC: American Psychological Association.

American Educational Research Association, American Psychological Association, and National Council on Measurement in Education. (1999). *Standards for educational and psycho-*

*logical testing*. Washington, DC: American Educational Research Association.

Anders, P. L., & Bos, C. S. (1986). Semantic feature analysis: An interactive strategy for vocabulary development and text comprehension. *Journal of Reading, 29,* 610–616.

Anders, P. L., & Evans, K. S. (1994). Relationship between teachers' beliefs and their instructional practice in reading. In R. Garner and P. A. Alexander (Eds.), *Beliefs about text and instruction with text* (pp. 137–153). Hillsdale, NJ: Lawrence Erlbaum.

Anderson, B. (1981). The missing ingredient: Fluent oral reading. *Elementary School Journal, 81,* 173–177.

Anderson, L. M. (1981). Short-term student responses to classroom instruction. *Elementary School Journal, 82,* 97–108.

Anderson, L. M. (1984). The environment of instruction: The function of seatwork in effective commercially developed curriculum. In G. G. Duffy, L. R. Roehler, & J. Mason (Eds.), *Comprehension instruction: Perspectives and suggestions* (pp. 93–104). New York: Longman.

Anderson, L. M., Brubaker, N. L., Alleman-Brooks, J., & Duffy, G. G. (1985). A qualitative study of seat-work in first-grade classrooms. *Elementary School Journal, 86,* 132–140.

Anderson, R. C., & Freebody, P. (1981). Vocabulary knowledge. In J. T. Guthrie (Ed.), *Comprehension and teaching: Research perspectives* (pp. 71–117). Newark, DE: International Reading Association.

Anderson, R. C., Hiebert, E. H., Scott, J. A., & Wilkinson, I. G. (1985). *Becoming a nation of readers: The report of the Commission on Reading.* Washington, DC: The National Institute of Education.

Anderson, R. C., Wilson, P. T., & Fielding, L. G. (1988). Growth in reading and how children spend their time outside of school. *Reading Research Quarterly, 23,* 285–303.

Anderson, T. H., & Armbruster, B. B. (1984a). Content area textbooks. In R. C. Anderson, J. Osborn, & R. J. Tierney (Eds.), *Learning to read in American schools: Basal readers and content texts* (pp. 193–226). Hillsdale, NJ: Lawrence Erlbaum.

Anderson, T. H., & Armbruster, B. B. (1984b). Studying. In P. D. Pearson, R. Barr, M. Kamil, & P. Mosenthal (Eds.), *Handbook of reading research* (pp. 657–679). New York: Longman.

Anderson, V., Chan, C., & Henne, R. (1995). The effects of strategy instruction on the literacy models and performance of reading and writing delayed middle school students. Perspectives on literacy research and practice (44th Yearbook of the National Reading Conference). Chicago: NRC.

Anthony, R. J., Johnson, T. D., Mickelson, N. I., & Preece, A. (1991). *Evaluating literacy: A perspective for change.* Portsmouth, NH: Heinemann.

Applebee, A. (1974). *Tradition and reform in the teaching of English: A history.* Urbana, IL: National Council of Teachers of English.

Applebee, A. N., Langer, J. A., Mullis, I. V. S., & Jenkins, L. B. (1990). *The writing report card, 1984–1988* (Report No. 19-W-01). Princeton, NJ: Educational Testing Services

Argiro, M. (1987). The development of written language awareness in black preschool children. *Journal of Reading Behavior, 19,* 49–67.

Armbruster, B. B. (1984). The problem of "inconsiderate text." In G. G. Duffy, L. R. Roehler, & J. Mason (Eds.), *Comprehension instruction* (pp. 202–217). New York: Longman.

Armbruster, B. B., & Anderson, T. H. (1981). Research synthesis on study skills. *Educational Leadership, 39,* 154–156.

Armbruster, B. B., Anderson, T. H., & Ostertag, J. (1989). Teaching text structure to improve reading and writing. *The Reading Teacher, 43,* 130–137.

Armstrong, D. P., Patberg, J., & Dewitz, P. (1988). Reading guides: Helping students understand. *Journal of Reading, 31,* 532–541.

Asch, F. (1981). *Just like daddy.* New York: Simon and Schuster.

Ash, B. H. (1990). Reading assigned literature in a reading workshop. *English Journal, 79,* 77–79.

Ashton-Warner, S. (1963). *Teacher.* New York: Simon & Schuster.

Atwell, N. (1998). *In the middle: New understandings about writing, reading, and learning* (2nd ed.). Portsmouth, NH: Boynton/Cook.

Au, K. H. (1979). Using the experience-text-relationship method with minority children. *The Reading Teacher, 32,* 677–679.

Au, K. H. (1980). Participation structures in a reading lesson with Hawaiian children: Analysis of a culturally appropriate instructional event. *Anthropology and Education Quarterly, 11,* 91–115.

Au, K. H. (1993). *Literacy instruction in multicultural settings.* Fort Worth: Harcourt Brace.

Au, K. H. (1994). Portfolio assessment: Experiences at the Kamehameha Elementary Education Program. In S. W. Valencia, E. H. Hiebert, & P. P. Afflerbach (Eds.), *Authentic reading assessment: Practices and possibilities* (pp. 103–133). Newark, DE: International Reading Association.

Au, K. H. (1997). Ownership, literacy achievement, and students of diverse cultural backgrounds. In K. T. Guthrie & A. Wigfield (Eds.), *Reading engagement: Motivating readers through integrated instruction* (pp. 168–182). Newark, DE: International Reading Association.

Au, K. H. (1998). Social constructivism and the school literacy learning of students of diverse backgrounds. *Journal of Literacy Research, 20,* 297–319.

Au, K. H. (2000). A multicultural perspective on policies for improving literacy achievement: Equity and excellence. In M. L. Kamil, P. B. Mosenthal, P. D. Pearson, & R. Barr (Eds.), *Handbook of reading research* (Vol. 3, pp. 835–851). Mahwah, NJ: Lawrence Erlbaum.

Au, K. H., & Carrol, J. H. (1996). Current research on classroom instruction: Goals, teachers' actions, and assessment. In D. Speece & B. Keogh (Eds.), *Research on classroom ecologies: Implications for inclusion of children with learning disabilities* (pp. 17–37). Mahwah, NJ: Lawrence Erlbaum.

Au, K. H., & Carrol, J. H. (1997). Improving literacy achievement through a constructivist approach: The KEEP demonstration school project. *Elementary School Journal, 97,* 203–221.

Au, K. H., & Kawakami, A. J. (1986). The influence of the social organization of instruction on children's text comprehension ability: A Vygotskian perspective. In T. E. Raphael (Ed.), *The contexts of school-based literacy* (pp. 63–77). New York: Random House.

Au, K. H., & Kawakami, A. J. (1994). Cultural congruence in instruction. In E. R. Hollins, J. E. King, & W. Hayman (Eds.), *Teaching diverse populations: Formulating a knowledge base* (pp. 5–23). Albany: State University of New York Press.

Au, K. H., & Mason, J. (1981). Social organizational factors in learning to read: The balance of rights hypothesis. *Reading Research Quarterly, 17,* 115–167.

Au, K. H., Mason, J. M., & Scheu, J. A. (1995). *Literacy instruction for today.* New York: HarperCollins.

August, D., & Hakuta, K. (1994). *For all students: Limited English proficient students and Goals 2000* (NCBE Focus, Occasional Papers in Bilingual Education, no. 10). Washington, DC: National Clearinghouse for Bilingual Education.

August, D., & Hakuta, K. (1997). *Improving schooling for language-minority children: A research agenda.* Washington, DC: National Academy Press.

Aulls, M. W. (1982). *Developing readers in today's elementary school.* Boston: Allyn & Bacon.

Aulls, M. W., & Graves, M. S. (Eds.). (1985). *Electric butterfly and other stories (Quest series).* New York: Scholastic.

Bader, L. A. (1980). *Reading diagnosis and remediation in classroom and clinic.* New York: Macmillan.

Bader, L. A. (2002). *Bader reading and language inventory* (4th ed.). Upper Saddle River, NJ: Prentice Hall.

Baker, L., & Brown, A. L. (1984). Metacognitive skills and reading. In P. D. Pearson, R. Barr, M. Kamil, & P. Mosenthal (Eds.), *Handbook of reading research* (pp. 353–394). New York: Longman.

Baker, L., Scher, D., & Mackler, K. (1997). Home and family influences on motivations for reading. *Educational Psychologist, 32,* 69–82.

Balajthy, E. (1989). *Computers and reading: Lessons from the past and the technologies of the future.* Englewood Cliffs, NJ: Prentice Hall.

Ballard, R. (1978). *Talking dictionary.* Ann Arbor, MI: Ulrich's Books.

Bangert-Drowns, R. (1993). The word processor as an instructional tool: A meta-analysis of word processing in writing instruction. *Review of Educational Research, 63,* 69–93.

Bankson, N. W. (1990). *Bankson Language Test—2.* Austin, TX: PRO-ED.

Barker, T. A., Torgesen, J. K., & Wagner, R. K. (1992). The role of orthographic processing skills on five different tasks. *Reading Research Quarterly, 27,* 335–345.

Baron, J. (1977). Mechanisms for pronouncing printed words: Use and acquisition. In D. LaBerge & S. J. Samuels (Eds.), *Basic process in reading: Perception and comprehension* (pp. 175–216). Hillsdale, NJ: Lawrence Erlbaum.

Barr, R., Blachowicz, C. L. Z., & Wogman-Sadow, M. (1995). *Reading diagnosis for teachers: An instructional approach.* New York: Longman.

Barr, R., & Sadow, M.W. (1989). Influence of basal programs on fourth-grade reading instruction. *Reading Research Quarterly, 24,* 44–71.

Barrera, R. (1984). Bilingual reading in the primary grades: Some questions about questionable views and practices. In T. H. Escobedo (Ed.), *Early childhood bilingual education: A Hispanic perspective* (pp. 164–184). New York: Teachers College Press.

Barrett, T. C. (1976). Taxonomy of reading comprehension. In R. Smith & T. C. Barrett (Eds.), *Teaching reading in the middle grades* (pp. 53–58). Reading, MA: Addison Wesley.

Barron, R. (1969). The use of vocabulary as an advance organizer. In H. L. Herber & P. L. Sanders (Eds.), *Research in reading in the content areas: First report* (pp. 29–39). Syracuse, NY: Syracuse University Reading and Language Arts Center.

Bateman, J. A., & Rondhuis, J. K. (1997). Coherence relations: Towards a general specification. *Discourse Processes, 24,* 3–49.

Baumann, J. F. (1986). Effect of rewritten content textbook passages on middle grade students' comprehension of main ideas: Making the inconsiderate considerate. *Journal of Reading Behavior, 28,* 1–21.

Baumann, J. F. (1988). *Reading assessment: An instructional decision-making perspective.* Columbus, OH: Charles E. Merrill.

Baumann, J. F., & Kameenui, E. J. (1991). Research on vocabulary instruction: Ode to Voltaire. In J. Flood, J. M. Jensen, D. Lapp, & J. R. Squire (Eds.), *Handbook on research on teaching the English language arts* (pp. 604–632). New York: Macmillan.

Baumann, J. F., Ro, J. M., & Duff-Hester, A. M. (2000). Then and now: Perspectives on the status of elementary reading instruction by prominent reading educators. *Reading Research and Instruction, 39,* 236–264.

Bean, R. M. (1979). Role of the reading specialist: A multifaceted dilemma. *The Reading Teacher, 32,* 409–413.

Bean, T. W., & Steenwyk, F. L. (1984). The effect of three forms of summarization instruction on sixth graders' summary writing and comprehension. *Journal of Reading Behavior, 16,* 297–306.

Bear, D. R., & Barone, D. (1998). *Developing literacy: An integrated approach to assessment and instruction.* Boston: Houghton Mifflin.

Bear, D. R., Invernizzi, M., Templeton, S., & Johnston, F. (2000). *Words their way: Word study for phonics, vocabulary, and spelling instruction.* Upper Saddle River, NJ: Merrill.

Bear, D. R., & Templeton, S. (1998). Explorations in developmental spelling: Foundations for learning and teaching phonics, spelling, and vocabulary. *The Reading Teacher, 52,* 222–242.

Beck, I., & McKeown, M. (2001). Text talk: Capturing the benefits of read-aloud experiences for young children. *The Reading Teacher, 55,* 10–20.

Beck, I., McKeown, M., Sandora, C., Kucan, L., & Worthy, J. (1996). Questioning the author: A year-long classroom implementation to engage students with text. *Elementary School Journal, 96,* 385–414.

Beck, I. L., & McKeown, M. G. (1981). Developing questions that promote comprehension: The story map. *Language Arts, 58,* 913–918.

Beck, I. L., & McKeown, M. G. (1983). Learning words well: A program to enhance vocabulary and comprehension. *The Reading Teacher, 36,* 622–625.

Beck, I. L., McKeown, M. G., & McCaslin, E. S. (1981). Does reading make sense? Problems of early readers. *The Reading Teacher, 34,* 780–785.

Beck, I. L., McKeown, M. G., & McCaslin, E. S. (1983). Vocabulary development: All contexts are not created equal. *Elementary School Journal, 83,* 177–181.

Beck, I. L., McKeown, M. G., & Omanson, R. (1987). The effects and uses of diverse vocabulary instructional techniques. In M. G. McKeown & M. E. Curtis (Eds.), *The nature of vocabulary acquisition.* Mahwah, NJ: Lawrence Erlbaum.

Beers, J., & Henderson, E. H. (1977). A study of developing orthographic concepts among first graders. *Research in the Teaching of English, 11,* 133–148.

Beery, K. E. (1997). *The Beery-Buktenica Developmental Test of Visual-Motor Integration.* Parsippany, NJ: Modern Cirriculum Press.

Bembridge, T. (1994). A multi-layered assessment package. In S. W. Valencia, E. H. Hiebert, & P. P. Afflerbach (Eds.), *Authentic reading assessment: Practices and possibilities* (pp. 167–196). Newark, DE: International Reading Association.

Bernard, R. M., & Naidu, S. (1992). Post-questioning, concept mapping, and feedback: A distance education field experiment. *British Journal of Educational Technology, 23,* 48–60.

Bernhardt, E. B. (2000). Second-language reading as a case study of reading scholarship in the 20th century. In M. L. Kamil, P. B. Mosenthal, P. D. Pearson, & R. Barr (Eds.), *Handbook of reading research* (Vol. 3, pp. 791–812). Mahwah, NJ: Lawrence Erlbaum.

Betts, E. A. (1946). *Foundations of reading instruction.* New York: American Books.

Bialystok, E., & Ryan, E. (1985). A metacognitive framework for the development of first and second language skills. In D. L. Forrest-Pressley, G. E. MacKinnon, & T. G. Waller (Eds.), *Metacognition, cognition, and human performance* (pp. 207–252). New York: Academic Press.

Binkley, M. R. (1988). New ways of assessing text difficulty. In B. L. Zakaluk & S. J. Samuels (Eds.), *Readability: Its past, present, and future* (pp. 98–120). Newark, DE: International Reading Association.

Blachman, B. A. (2000). Phonological awareness. In M. L. Kamil, P. B. Mosenthal, P. D. Pearson, and R. Barr (Eds.), *Handbook of reading research* (Vol. 3, pp. 483–502). Mahwah, NJ: Lawrence Erlbaum.

Blachowicz, C., & Fisher, P. (1996). *Teaching vocabulary in all classrooms.* Englewood Cliffs, NJ: Prentice Hall.

Blachowicz, C., & Fisher, P. (2002). *Teaching vocabulary in all classrooms* (2nd ed.). Upper Saddle River, NJ: Pearson Education.

Blachowicz, C., & Ogle, D. (2001). *Reading comprehension: Strategies for independent learners.* New York: Guilford Press.

Black, P., & William, D. (1998). Inside the black box: Raising standards through classroom assessment. *Phi Delta Kappan, 80,* 139–148.

Block, C. C. (1993). *Teaching the language arts: Expanding thinking through student-centered instruction.* Boston: Allyn & Bacon.

Bloom, B. S. (Ed.). (1956). *Taxonomy of educational objectives. Handbook I: Cognitive domain.* New York: David McKay.

Blumenfeld, P. C., Mergendoller, J. R., & Swarthout, S.W. (1987). Task as a heuristic for understanding student learning and motivation. *Journal of Curriculum Studies, 19,* 135–148.

Boehm, A. E. (1986). *Boehm Test of Basic Concepts—Revised.* San Antonio, TX: The Psychological Corporation.

Boehm, A. E. (2001). *Boehm Test of Basic Concepts* (3rd ed.). San Antonio, TX: The Psychological Corporation.

Boggs, S. T. (1985). *Speaking, relating and learning: A study of Hawaiian children at home and at school.* Norwood, NJ: Ablex.

Borich, G. D. (1994). *Observation skills for effective teaching* (2nd ed.). New York: Merrill.

Bosman, A. M. T., & Van Orden, G. C. (1997). Why spelling is more difficult than reading. In C. A. Perfetti, L. Rieben, & M. Fayol (Eds.), *Learning to spell: Research, theory, and practice across languages* (pp. 173–194). Hillsdale, NJ: Lawrence Erlbaum.

Botel, M. (1982). New informal approaches to evaluating word recognition and comprehension. In J. J. Pikulski & T. Shanahan (Eds.), *Approaches to the informal evaluation of reading* (pp. 30–41). Newark, DE: International Reading Association.

Bowey, J. A., & Frances, J. (1991). Phonological analysis as a function of age and exposure to reading instruction. *Applied Psycholinguistics, 12,* 91–121.

Bowman, B. T., Donovan, M. S., & Burns, M. S. (2000). *Eager to learn: Educating our preschoolers.* Washington, DC: National Academy Press.

Bowles, S., & Gintis, H. (1976). *Schooling in capitalist America.* New York: Basic Books.

Bradley, J. M., & Ames, W. S. (1977). Readability parameters of basal readers. *Journal of Reading Behavior, 9,* 175–183.

Bransford, J. D., Goldman, S. R., & Vye, N. J. (1991). Making a difference in people's abilities to think: Reflections on a decade of work and some hopes for the future. In L. Okagaki & R. J. Sternberg (Eds.), *Directors of development: Influences on the development of children's thinking* (pp. 147–180). Hillsdale, NJ: Lawrence Erlbaum.

Bransford, J. D., & Johnson, M. K. (1972). Contextual prerequisites for understanding: Some investigations of comprehension and recall. *Journal of Verbal Learning and Verbal Behavior, 11,* 717–726.

Bratcher, S. (1994). *Evaluating children's writing.* New York: St. Martin's Press.

Brecht, R. D. (1977). Testing format and instructional level with the informal reading inventory. *The Reading Teacher, 31,* 57–59.

Brennan, A. D., Bridge, C. A., & Winograd, P. N. (1986). The effects of structural variation on children's recall of basal reader stories. *Reading Research Quarterly, 21,* 91–104.

Bretzing, B. B., & Kulhavy, R.W. (1981). Note-taking and passage style. *Journal of Educational Psychology, 73,* 242–250.

Brice, A. (Ed.). (2002). *The Hispanic child: Speech, language, culture, and education.* Boston: Allyn & Bacon.

Bridge, C., & Hiebert, E. H. (1985). A comparison of classroom writing practices, teachers' perceptions of their writing instruction, and textbook recommendations on writing practices. *The Elementary School Journal, 86,* 155–172.

Bridge, C. A. (1989). Beyond the basal in beginning reading. In P. Winograd, K. Wixson, & M. Lipson (Eds.), *Improving basal reading instruction* (pp. 177–209). New York: Teachers College Press.

Bridge, C. A., Belmore, S., Moskow, S., Cohen, S., & Matthews, P. (1984). Topicalization and memory for main ideas in prose. *Journal of Reading Behavior, 16,* 27–40.

Bridge, C. A., & Burton, B. (1982). Teaching sight vocabulary through patterned language materials. In J. A. Niles & L. A. Harris (Eds.), *New inquiries in reading research and instruction* (31st Yearbook of The National Reading Conference, pp. 119–123). Washington, DC: National Reading Conference.

Bridge, C. A., & Winograd, P. N. (1982). Readers' awareness of cohesive relationships during cloze comprehension. *Journal of Reading Behavior, 14,* 299–312.

Bridge, C. A., Winograd, P. N., & Haley, D. (1983). Using predictable materials vs. preprimers to teach beginning sight words. *The Reading Teacher, 36,* 884–891.

Brigance, A. H. (1981). *Inventory of Essential Skills.* North Billerica, MA: Curriculum Associates.

Brigance, A. H. (1984). *Assessment of Basic Skills—Spanish Edition.* North Billerica, MA: Curriculum Associates.

Brigance, A. H. (1991). *Inventory of Early Development—Revised.* North Billerica, MA: Curriculum Associates.

Brigance, A. H. (1994). *Life Skills Inventory.* North Billerica, MA: Curriculum Associates.

Brigance, A. H. (1995). *Employability Skills Inventory.* North Billerica, MA: Curriculum Associates.

Brigance, A. H. (1999). *Comprehensive Inventory of Basic Skills—Revised.* North Billerica, MA: Curriculum Associates.

Brophy, J. E. (1983a). Conceptualizing student motivation. *Educational Psychologist, 18,* 200–215.

Brophy, J. E. (1983b). Research on the self-fulfilling prophecy and teacher expectations. *Journal of Educational Psychology, 75,* 631–661.

Brown, A. L., Armbruster, B. B., & Baker, L. (1986). The role of metacognition in reading and studying. In J. Orasanu (Ed.), *A decade of reading research: Implications for practice* (pp. 49–75). Hillsdale, NJ: Lawrence Erlbaum.

Brown, A. L., & Campione, J. C. (1986). Psychological theory and the study of learning disabilities. *American Psychologist, 14,* 1059–1068.

Brown, A. L., Campione, J. C., & Day, J. D. (1981). Learning to learn: On training students to learn from texts. *Educational Researcher, 10,* 14–21.

Brown, J. I., Fishco, V. V., & Hanna, G. H. (1993). *Nelson-Denny Reading Test.* Itasca, IL: Riverside Publishing.

Brown, J. S., Collins, A., & Duguid, P. (1989). Situated cognition and the culture of learning. *Educational Researcher, 18,* 32–42.

Brown, V. L., Hammill, D. D., & Wiederholt, J. L. (1995). *Test of Reading Comprehension* (3rd ed.). Austin, TX: PRO-ED.

Brozo, W. G., & Simpson, M. L. (1999). *Readers, teachers, learners: Expanding literacy across the content areas* (3rd ed.). New York: Prentice Hall.

Bruce, B. (1984). A new point of view on children's stories. In R.C. Anderson, J. Osborn, & R. J. Tierney (Eds.), *Learning to read in American schools: Basal readers and content texts* (pp. 153–174). Hillsdale, NJ: Lawrence Erlbaum.

Bruner, J. S. (1964). The course of cognitive growth. *American Psychologist, 19,* 1–15.

Bryant, P. E., MacLean, M., Bradley, L. L., & Crossland, J. (1990). Rhyme and alliteration, phoneme detection, and learning to read. *Developmental Psychology, 26,* 429–438.

Budbill, D. (1978). *Bones of black spruce mountain.* New York: Dial Press.

Buehl, D. (1995). *Classroom strategies for interactive learning.* Schofield: Wisconsin State Reading Association.

Buehl, D. (2001). *Classroom strategies for interactive learning.* Newark, DE: International Reading Association.

Burne, J. (2000). *Assessment of culturally and linguistically diverse students for special education eligibility* (ERIC EC Digest #E604). Arlington, VA: ERIC Clearinghouse on Disabilities and Gifted Education.

Burns, P. C., & Roe, B. D. (1985). *Informal reading inventory* (2nd ed.). Boston: Houghton Mifflin.

Bus, A. G. (2001). Joint caregiver-child storybook reading: A route to literacy development. In S. B. Neuman & D. K. Dickinson (Eds.), *Handbook of early literacy research* (pp. 179–191). New York: Guilford Press.

Bus, A. G., van Ijzendoorn, M. H., & Pellegrini, A. D. (1995). Joint book reading makes for success in learning to read: A meta-analysis on intergenerational transmission of literacy. *Review of Educational Research, 65,* 1–21.

Buss, K., & Karnowski, L. (2000). *Reading and writing literary genres.* Newark, DE: International Reading Association.

Butkowsky, I. S., & Willows, D. M. (1980). Cognitive-motivational characteristics of children varying in reading ability: Evidence for learned helplessness in poor readers. *Journal of Educational Psychology, 72,* 408–422.

Button, K., Johnson, M. J., & Furgerson, P. (1996). Interactive writing in a primary classroom. *The Reading Teacher, 49,* 446–454.

Calfee, R., Lindamood, P., & Lindamood, C. (1973). Acoustic-phonetic skills and reading: Kindergarten through twelfth grade. *Journal of Educational Psychology, 64,* 293–298.

Calfee, R. C. (1987). The design of comprehensible text. In J. R. Squire (Ed.), *The dynamics of language learning.* Urbana, IL: ERIC Clearinghouse on Reading and Communication Skills and the National Conference on Research in English.

California Instructional Technology Clearinghouse (1998–2000). *Appendix C: Screening criteria for interactive technology resources* [Online document]. Stanislaus County Office of Education, California. Available: www.clearinghouse. k12.ca.us/c/@B0DvQuqHKTomU/dev/appendc.htm.

Calkins, L. (1991). *Living between the lines.* Portsmouth, NH: Heinemann.

Calkins, L. M. (1983). *Lessons from a child.* Exeter, NH: Heinemann.

Calkins, L. M. (1994). *The art of teaching writing.* Portsmouth, NH: Heinemann.

Cambourne, B., & Turbill, J. (1994). *Responsive evaluation.* Portsmouth, NH: Heinemann.

Campione, J. C., & Brown, A. L. (1987). Linking dynamic assessment with school achievement. In C. S. Lidz (Ed.), *Dynamic assessment* (pp. 82–109). New York: Guilford.

Campione, J. C., Brown, A. L., Ferrara, R. A., & Bryant, N. R. (1984). The zone of proximal development: Implications for individual differences and learning. In B. Rogoff & J. Wertsch (Eds.), *New directions for child development: Children's learning in the "zone of proximal development"* (Vol. 23, pp. 265–294). San Francisco: Jossey-Bass.

Carew, J. V., & Lightfoot, S. L. (1979). *Beyond bias: Perspectives on classroom.* Cambridge, MA: Harvard University Press.

Carnegie Corporation. (1994). *Starting points: Meeting the needs of our youngest children.* New York: Carnegie Corporation.

Carnine, D., Silbert, J., & Kameenui, E. J. (1990). *Direct instruction reading* (2nd ed.). Columbus, OH: Charles E. Merrill.

Carnine, D. W., Kameenui, E. J., & Coyle, G. (1984). Utilization of contextual information in determining the meaning of unfamiliar words. *Reading Research Quarterly, 19,* 188–204.

Carnine, D. W., Silbert, J., & Kameenui, E. J. (1997). *Direct instruction reading* (3rd ed.). Upper Saddle River, NJ: Merrill/Prentice Hall.

Carr, E. (1985). The vocabulary overview guide: A metacognitive strategy to improve vocabulary and retention. *Journal of Reading, 28,* 684–689.

Carr, E., & Ogle, D. (1987). K-W-L Plus: A strategy for comprehension and summarization. *Journal of Reading, 30,* 626–631.

Cazden, C. B. (1986). Classroom discourse. In M. C. Wittrock (Ed.), *Handbook of research on teaching* (3rd ed., pp. 432–463). New York: Macmillan.

Center for the Improvement of Early Reading Achievement. (2001). *Improving the reading achievement of America's children: 10 research-based principles.* Ann Arbor, MI: Author.

Center for the Improvement of Early Reading Achievement. (2002). *Improving the reading comprehension of America's children: 10 Research-based principles* [Online document]. Available: www.ciera.org/library/instresrc/compprinciples/ index/html.

Chall, J. S. (1984). Readability and prose comprehension: Continuities and discontinuities. In J. Flood (Ed.), *Understanding reading comprehension* (pp. 233–246). Newark, DE: International Reading Association.

Chall, J. S., & Curtis, M. E. (1987). What clinical diagnosis tells us about children's reading. *The Reading Teacher, 40,* 784–789.

Chamot, A. U., & O'Malley, J. M. (1994). Instructional approaches and teaching procedures. In S. Spangenberg-Urbschat & R. Pritchard (Eds.), *Kids come in all languages: Reading instruction for ESL students* (pp. 82–107). Newark, DE: International Reading Association.

Chard, D. J., Simmons, D. C., & Kameenui, E. J. (1998). The primary role of word recognition in the reading process: Curricular and instructional implications. In D. C. Simmons & E. J. Kameenui (Eds.), *What reading research tells us about children with diverse learning needs: The bases and the basics* (pp. 169–181). Mahwah, NJ: Lawrence Erlbaum.

Chittenden, E. (1991). Authentic assessment, evaluation, and documentation of student performance. In V. Perrone (Ed.), *Expanding student assessment.* Alexandria, VA: Association for Supervision and Curriculum Development.

Chomsky, C. (1978). When you still can't read in third grade: After decoding, what? In S. J. Samuels (Ed.), *What research has to say about reading instruction* (pp. 13–30). Newark, DE: International Reading Association.

Cioffi, G., & Carney, J. J. (1983). Dynamic assessment of reading disabilities. *The Reading Teacher, 36,* 764–768.

Cizek, G. J. (2001). Review of Brigance Diagnostic Comprehensive Inventory of Basic Skills, Revised. In B. S. Blake and J. C. Impara (Eds.), *Fourteenth mental measurements yearbook.* Lincoln, NE: Buros Institute of Mental Measurements.

Clark, C. H. (1982). Assessing free recall. *The Reading Teacher, 35,* 434–439.

Clark, C. H. (1993). Personal communication.

Clarke, L. K. (1988). Invented versus traditional spelling in first graders' writings: Effects on learning to spell and read. *Research in the Teaching of English, 22,* 281–309.

Clay, M. M. (1979). *Reading: The patterning of complex behavior* (2nd ed.). Auckland, New Zealand/Exeter, NH: Heinemann.

Clay, M. M. (1985). *The early detection of reading difficulties* (3rd ed.). Auckland, New Zealand: Heinemann.

Clay, M. M. (1993). *An observation survey (of early literacy achievement).* Portsmouth, NH: Heinemann.

Cleary, B. (1983). *Dear Mr. Henshaw.* New York: Bantam Doubleday Dell Publishing.

Clifford, G. (1984). Buch und lesen: Historical perspectives on literacy and schooling. *Review of Educational Research, 54,* 472–500.

Clifford, M. M. (1991). Risk taking: Theoretical, empirical and educational considerations. *Educational Psychologist, 26,* 263–297.

Cline, R. L., & Kretke, G. L. (1980). An evaluation of long-term SSR in the junior high school. *Journal of Reading, 23,* 503–506.

Cockrum, W. A., & Castillo, M. (1991). Whole language assessment and evaluation strategies. In B. Harp (Ed.), *Assessment and evaluation in whole language programs* (pp. 73–86). Norwood, MA: Christopher Gordon.

Cohn, M., & D'Alessandro, C. (1978). When is a decoding error not a decoding error? *The Reading Teacher, 32,* 341–344.

Cole, M. (1990). Cultural psychology: A once and future discipline? In J. Berman (Ed.), *Nebraska's symposium on motivation: Cross cultural perspectives, 37.* Lincoln: University of Nebraska Press.

Coles, G. S. (1978). The learning disabilities test battery: Empirical and social issues. *Harvard Educational Review, 48,* 313–340.

Coles, G. S. (1987). *The learning mystique.* New York: Pantheon.

Collins, James L. (1998). *Strategies for struggling writers.* New York: Guilford Press.

Combs, M. (1997). *Developing competent readers and writers for middle grades.* Upper Saddle River, NJ: Prentice Hall.

Commins, N. L., & Miramontes, O. B. (1989). A descriptive study of the linguistic abilities of a selected group of low achieving Hispanic bilingual students. *American Educational Research Journal, 26,* 443–472.

Conrad, S. S. (1984). *On readability and readability formula scores* (Ginn Occasional Papers No. 17). Columbus, OH: Ginn and Co.

Cooley, W. W., & Leinhardt, G. (1980). The instructional dimensions study. *Educational Evaluation and Policy Analysis, 2,* 7–25.

Cooper, J. D. (1986). *Improving reading comprehension.* Boston: Houghton Mifflin.

Cooper, J. L. (1952). *The effect of adjustment of basal reading materials on reading achievement.* Unpublished doctoral dissertation, Boston University, Boston, MA.

Corno, L., & Mandinach, E. B. (1983). The role of cognitive engagement in classroom learning and motivation. *Educational Psychologist, 18,* 88–108.

Covington, M. V., & Omelich, C. L. (1979). Effort: The double-edged sword in school achievement. *Journal of Educational Psychology, 71,* 169–182.

Craik, F., & Lockhart, R. (1972). Levels of processing: A framework for memory research. *Journal of Verbal Learning and Verbal Behavior, 11,* 671–684.

Cramer, R. L. (1982). Informal approaches to evaluating children's writing. In J. J. Pikulski & T. Shanahan (Eds.), *Approaches to the informal evaluation of reading* (pp. 80–93). Newark, DE: International Reading Association.

Crawford, J. W. (1997). *Best evidence: Research on language-minority education.* Washington, DC: National Clearinghouse on Bilingual Education.

Cremin, L. (1989). *Popular education and its discontents.* New York: Harper & Row.

Critchley, M. (1975). Specific developmental dyslexia. In E. H. Lenneberg & E. Lenneberg (Eds.), *Foundations of language development* (Vol. 2, pp. 361–366). New York: Academic Press.

Cullinan, B., & Fitzgerald, S. (1984). *Statement on readability.* Joint statement by the Presidents of the International Reading Association and the National Council of Teachers of English.

Cummins, J. (1996). *Negotiating identities: Education for enpowerment in a diverse society.* Los Angeles: California Association for Bilingual Education.

Cummins, J. (1998). *Negotiating identities: Education for empowerment in a diverse society.* Ontario, CA: California Association for Bilingual Education.

Cunningham, A. E. (1990). Explicit vs. implicit instruction in phonemic awareness. *Journal of Experimental Child Psychology, 50,* 429–444.

Cunningham, P. (1990). The Names Test: A quick assessment of decoding ability. *The Reading Teacher, 44,* 124–129.

Cunningham, P. (1995). *Phonics they use: Words for reading and writing* (2nd ed.). New York: HarperCollins.

Cunningham, P. M. (1975–76). Investigating a synthesized theory of mediated word identification. *Reading Research Quarterly, 11,* 127–143.

Cunningham, P. M. (1979). A compare/contrast theory of mediated word identification. *The Reading Teacher, 32,* 774–778.

Cunningham, P. M. (2000). *Phonics they use: Words for reading and writing.* New York: Longman.

Cunningham, P. M., & Allington, R. A. (1999). *Classrooms that work: They can all read and write* (2nd ed.). New York: Longman.

Cunningham, P. M., & Allington, R. L. (1996). *Classrooms that work: They can all read and write.* New York: HarperCollins.

Cunningham, P. M., & Cunningham, J. W. (1992). Making words: Enhancing the invented spelling-decoding connection. *The Reading Teacher, 46,* 106–113.

Cunningham, P. M., Moore, S. A., Cunningham, J. W., & Moore, D.W. (1989). *Reading in elementary classrooms* (2nd ed.). New York: Longman.

Curry, L. (1993). *Educating professionals: Responding to new expectations for competence and accountability.* San Francisco: Jossey-Bass.

Cutler, R. B., & Truss, C. V. (1989). Computer aided instruction as a reading motivator. *Reading Improvement, 26,* 103–109.

Daiute, C. (1983). *Writing and computers.* Reading, MA: Addison Wesley.

Daiute, C. (1986). Physical and cognitive factors in revising: Insights from studies with computers. *Research in the Teaching of English, 20,* 141–159.

Dale, E., & Chall, J. (1948). A formula for predicting readability. *Educational Research Bulletin, 27,* 11–20, 37–54.

D'Amato, J. (1987). The belly of the beast: On cultural differences, castelike status, and the politics of school. *Anthropology and Education Quarterly, 18,* 357–361.

D'Amato, J. (1988). "Acting": Hawaiian children's resistance to teachers. *Elementary School Journal, 88,* 529–544.

Dansereau, D. F. (1985). Learning strategy research. In J. Segal, S. Chipman, & R. Glaser (Eds.), *Thinking and learning skills: Relating instruction to basic research* (Vol. 1, pp. 209–240). Hillsdale, NJ: Lawrence Erlbaum.

Darling-Hammond, L. (1995). Inequality and access to knowledge. In J. A. Banks & C. A. M. Banks (Eds.), *Handbook of research on multicultural education* (pp. 465–483). New York: Macmillan.

Darling-Hammond, L., Ancess, J., & Falk, B. (1995). *Authentic assessment in action.* New York: Teachers College Press.

Davis, F. B. (1968). Research in comprehension in reading. *Reading Research Quarterly, 3,* 499–545.

Davison, A. (1984). Readability: Appraising text difficulty. In R. C. Anderson, J. Osborn, & R. T. Tierney (Eds.), *Learning to read in American schools: Basal readers and content texts* (pp. 121–140). Hillsdale, NJ: Lawrence Erlbaum.

Davison, A., & Kantor, R. N. (1982). On the failure of readability formulas to define readable texts: A case study from adaptations. *Reading Research Quarterly, 17,* 187–209.

Day, J. D. (1992). *Population projections of the United States by age, sex, race, and Hispanic origin: 1992–2050.* Washington, DC: U.S. Bureau of the Census.

Day, J. D., & Cordon, L. A. (1993). Static and dynamic measures of ability: An experimental comparison. *Journal of Educational Psychology, 85,* 75–82.

Day, K. C., & Day, H. D. (1986). Tests of metalinguistic awareness. In D. B. Yaden & S. Templeton (Eds.), *Metalinguistic awareness and beginning literacy: Conceptualizing what it means to read and write* (pp. 187–198). Portsmouth, NH: Heinemann.

DeFord, D. (1991). Using reading and writing to support the reader. In D. E. DeFord, C. A. Lyons, & G. S. Pinnell (Eds.), *Bridges to literacy* (pp. 77–95). Portsmouth, NH: Heinemann.

DeFord, D. E. (1980). Young children and their writing. *Theory into Practice, 19,* 157–162.

DeFord, D. E. (1986). Classroom contexts for literacy learning. In T. E. Raphael (Ed.), *The contexts of school-based literacy* (pp. 163–180). New York: Longman.

Delpit, L. (1995). *Other people's children.* New York: New Press.

Dewitz, P., Carr, E. M., & Patberg, J. P. (1987). Effects of inference training on comprehension and comprehension monitoring. *Reading Research Quarterly, 22,* 542–546.

Dickinson, D., & McCabe, A. (1991). A social interactionist account of language and literacy development. In J. Kavanaugh (Ed.), *The language continuum,* Parkton, MD: The York Press.

Dickinson, D. K. (1986). Cooperation, collaboration, and a computer: Integrating a computer into a first-second grade writing program. *Research in the Teaching of English, 20,* 357–378.

Dickinson, D. K., McCabe, A., & Sprague, K. (2001). *Teacher rating of oral language and literacy (TROLL): A research-based tool* (CIERA Report #3–016). Ann Arbor, MI: Center for the Improvement of Early Reading Achievement.

Dillon, J. T. (1988). *Questioning and teaching: A manual of practice.* New York: Teachers College Press.

Doctorow, M., Wittrock, M. C., & Marks, C. (1978). Generative processes in reading comprehension. *Journal of Educational Psychology, 70,* 109–118.

Dolch, E. W. (1942a). *Basic sight word test.* Champaign, IL: Garrard Press.

Dolch, E. W. (1942b). *Better spelling.* Champaign, IL: Garrard Press.

Dole, J. A., Duffy, G. G., Roehler, L. R., & Pearson, P. D. (1991). Moving from the old to the new: Research on reading comprehension instruction. *Review of Educational Research, 61,* 239–264.

Donly, B., Henderson, A., & Strang, W. (1995). *Summary of bilingual education state education agency program survey of states' limited English proficiency persons and available educational services, 1993–1994.* Arlington, VA: Development Associates.

Donovan, M. S., & Cross, C. T. (Eds.) and the Committee on Minority Representation in Special Education. (2002). *Minority students in special and gifted education.* Washington, DC: National Academy Press.

Downing, J. (1978). Linguistic awareness, English orthography and reading instruction. *Journal of Reading Behavior, 10,* 103–114.

Doyle, W. (1983). Academic work. *Review of Educational Research, 53,* 159–199.

Doyle, W. (1986). Classroom organization and management. In M. C. Wittrock (Ed.), *Handbook of research on teaching* (3rd ed., pp. 392–431). New York: Macmillan.

Drahozal, E. C., & Hanna, G. S. (1978). Reading comprehension subscores: Pretty bottles for ordinary wine. *Journal of Reading, 21,* 416–420.

Dreeben, R. (1968). The contribution of schooling to the learning of norms. In *Socialization and schools* (Harvard Educational Review Reprint Series No. 1). Cambridge, MA: Harvard University Press.

Dressel, J. H. (1990). The effects of listening to and discussing different qualities of children's literature on the narrative writing of fifth graders. *Research in the Teaching of English, 24,* 397–444.

Duell, O. K. (1974). Effect of types of objective, level of test questions, and judged importance of texted materials upon posttest performance. *Journal of Educational Psychology, 66,* 225–232.

Dufflemeyer, F. A., Baum, D. D., & Merkley, D. J. (1987). Maximizing reader-text confrontation with an extended anticipation guide. *Journal of Reading, 31,* 146–150.

Duffy, G. G. (1993). Rethinking strategy instruction: Four teachers' development and their low achievers' understandings. *Elementary School Journal, 93,* 231–247.

Duffy, G. G., & Roehler, L. R. (1989). *Improving classroom reading instruction: A decision making approach* (2nd ed.). New York: Random House.

Duffy, G. G., Roehler, L. R., Meloth, M. S., Vavrus, L. G., Book, C., Putnam, J., & Wesselman, R. (1986). The relationship between explicit verbal explanations during reading skills instruction and student awareness and achievement: A study of reading teacher effects. *Reading Research Quarterly, 21,* 237–252.

Duke, N. K. (2000). For the rich it's richer: Print environments and experiences offered to first-grade students in very low and very high SES school districts. *American Educational Research Journal, 37,* 441–478.

Dunn, L. M., & Dunn, L. M. (1981). *Peabody Picture Vocabulary Test—Revised.* Circle Pines, MN: American Guidance Service.

Dunn, L. M., & Dunn, L. M. (1997). *Peabody Picture Vocabulary Test* (3rd ed.). Circle Pines, MN: American Guidance Service.

Durkin, D. (1978–79). What classroom observations reveal about reading comprehension instruction. *Reading Research Quarterly, 14,* 481–533.

Durkin, D. (1981). Reading comprehension instruction in five basal reader series. *Reading Research Quarterly, 16,* 515–544.

Durkin, D. (1983). *Teaching them to read* (4th ed.). Boston: Allyn & Bacon.

Durkin, D. (1984). Is there a match between what elementary teachers do and what basal reader manuals recommend? *The Reading Teacher, 37,* 734–749.

Durkin, D. (1987). Testing in kindergarten. *The Reading Teacher, 40,* 766–770.

Durr, W. K. (1973). Computer study of high frequency words in popular trade journals. *The Reading Teacher, 27,* 37–42.

Dweck, C. S. (1975). The role of expectations and attributions in the alleviation of learned helplessness. *Journal of Personality and Social Psychology, 31,* 674–685.

Dyson, A. H. (1999). Transforming transfer: Unruly children, contrary texts, and the persistence of the pedagogical order. In *Review of research in education* (Vol. 24, pp. 141–172). Washington, DC: American Educational Research Association.

Eckhoff, B. (1983). How reading affects children's writing. *Language Arts, 60,* 607–616.

Edmonds, R. (1980). *A discussion of the literature and issues related to effective schooling.* St. Louis: Cemrel.

Eeds, M. (1985). Bookwords: Using a beginning word list of high frequency words from children's literature K–3. *The Reading Teacher, 38,* 418–423.

Ehri, L. (1979). Linguistic insight: Threshold of reading acquisition. In T. G. Waller & G. E. MacKinnon (Eds.), *Reading research: Advances in theory and practice* (Vol. 1, pp. 63–114). New York: Academic Press.

Ehri, L. (1987). Learning to read and spell words. *Journal of Reading Behavior, 19,* 5–32.

Ehri, L. (1991). Development of the ability to read words. In R. Barr, M. Kamil, P. Mosenthal, & P. D. Pearson (Eds.), *Handbook of reading research* (Vol. 2, pp. 383–417). New York: Longman.

Ehri, L. (1994). Development of the ability to read words: An update. In R. Ruddell, M. Ruddell, & H. Singer (Eds.), *Theoretical models and processes of reading.* Newark, DE: International Reading Association.

Ehri, L. (1995). Phases of development in learning to read words by sight. *Journal of Research in Reading, 18,* 116–125.

Ehri, L., & Sweet, J. (1991). Fingerpoint-reading of memorized text: What enables beginning readers to process print? *Reading Research Quarterly, 26,* 442–462.

Ehri, L., & Wilce, L. S. (1980). Do beginners learn to read function words better in sentences or in lists? *Reading Research Quarterly, 15,* 451–476.

Ehri, L. C. (1988). Movement into word reading and spelling: How spelling contributes to reading. In J. M. Mason (Ed.), *Reading and writing connections* (pp. 65–81). Needham Heights, MA: Allyn & Bacon.

Ekwall, E. E., & Shanker, J. L. (1985). *Teaching reading in the elementary school.* Columbus, OH: Charles E. Merrill.

Eldredge, J. L. (1990). Increasing the performance of poor readers in the third grade with a group-assisted strategy. *Journal of Educational Research, 84,* 69–77.

Elkins, J. (1986). Self-help for older writers with spelling and composing difficulties: Using the word processor and spelling checker. *Exceptional Child, 33,* 73–76.

Elkonin, D. E. (1963). The psychology of mastering the elements of reading. In B. Simon & J. Simon (Eds.), *Educational psychology in the U.S.S.R.* (pp. 165–179). London: Routledge.

Elkonin, D. E. (1973). U.S.S.R. In J. Downing (Ed.), *Comparative reading: Cross-national studies of behavior and processes in reading and writing* (pp. 551–579). New York: Macmillan.

Elley, W. B. (1989). Vocabulary acquisition from listening to stories. *Reading Research Quarterly, 24,* 174–187.

Elley, W. G., & Mangubhai, F. (1983). The impact of reading on second language learning. *Reading Research Quarterly, 19,* 53–67.

Ellis, N., & Cataldo, S. (1990). The role of spelling in learning to read. *Language and Education, 4,* 1–28.

Ellis, W., & Cramer, S. C. (1994). *Learning disabilities: A national responsibility* (Report of the Summit on Learning Disabilities in Washington, DC. September 20–21). New York: National Center for Learning Disabilities.

Englert, C. S. (1992). Writing instruction from a sociocultural perspective: The holistic, dialogic, and social enterprise of writing. *Journal of Learning Disabilities, 25,* 153–172.

Englert, C. S., Garmon, A., Mariage, T., Rozendal, M., Tarrant, K., & Urba, J. (1995). The early literacy project: Connecting across the literacy curriculum. *Learning Disability Quarterly, 18,* 253–275.

Englert, C. S., & Palincsar, A. S. (1991). Reconsidering instructional research in literacy from a sociocultural perspective. *Learning Disabilities Research and Practice, 6,* 225–229.

Enright, B. E. (1991). *Brigance Diagnostic Inventory of Early Development—Revised Technical Report.* North Billerica, MA: Curriculum Associates.

Entin, E. B., & Klare, G. R. (1985). Relationships of measures of interest, prior knowledge, and readability to comprehension of expository passages. In B. Hutson (Ed.), *Advances in reading/language research* (Vol. 3, pp. 9–38). Greenwich, CT: JAI Press.

Ericsson, K. A., & Simon, H. A. (1980). Verbal reports as data. *Psychological Review, 87,* 215–251.

Ertmer, P. A., Gopalakrishnan, S., & Ross, E. M. (2001). Technology-using teachers: Comparing perceptions of exemplary technology use to best practice. *Journal of Research on Technology in Education, 33*(5). [Online article]. Available: http://www.iste.org/jrte/33/5/ertmer.html.

Estes, T. H., & Vaughan, J. L. (1973). Reading interest and comprehension: Implications. *The Reading Teacher, 27,* 149–153.

Estes, T. H., & Vaughan, J. L. (1978). *Reading and learning in the content classroom.* Boston: Allyn & Bacon.

Falk, B., & Ort, S. (1998). Sitting down to score: Teacher learning through assessment. *Phi Delta Kappan, 80,* 59–64.

Fall, R., Webb, N. M., & Chudowksky, N. (2000). Group discussion and large-scale language arts assessment: Effects on students' comprehension. *American Educational Research Journal, 37,* 911–941.

Fass, W., & Schumacher, G. M. (1978). Effects of motivation, subject activity, and readability on the retention of prose materials. *Journal of Educational Psychology, 70,* 803–808.

Feitelson, D., Kita, B., & Goldstein, Z. (1986). Effects of listening to series stories on first graders' comprehension and use of language. *Research in the Teaching of English, 20,* 339–356.

Ferreiro, E. (1978). What is written in a written sentence? A developmental answer. *Journal of Education, 160,* 25–39.

Ferreiro, E. (1980, May). *The relationship between oral and written language: The children's viewpoints.* Paper presented at the 25th Annual Conference of the International Reading Association, St. Louis, MO.

Ferreiro, E., & Teberosky, A. (1979/1982). *Literacy before schooling.* Exeter, NH: Heinemann.

Feuerstein, R., Rand, Y., & Hoffman, M. B. (1979). *The dynamic assessment of retarded performance.* Baltimore: University Park Press.

Fielding, L., & Pearson, P. D. (1994). Reading comprehension: What words? *Educational Leadership, 51,* 62–67.

Fielding, L. G., Wilson, P. T., & Anderson, R. C. (1986). A new focus on free reading: The role of trade books in reading instruction. In T. E. Raphael (Ed.), *The contexts of school-based literacy* (pp. 149–160). New York: Random House.

Figueroa, R., & Garcia, E. (1994). Issues in testing students from culturally and linguistically diverse backgrounds. *Multicultural Education, 2*(1), 10–23.

Fillion, B., & Brause, R. S. (1987). Research into classroom practices: What have we learned and where are we going? In J. R. Squire (Ed.), *The dynamics of language learning* (pp. 201–225). Urbana, IL: ERIC Clearinghouse on Reading and Communications Skills and the National Conference on Research in English.

Finders, M. (1997). *Just girls.* New York: Teachers' College Press.

Firth, U. (1980). Unexpected spelling problems. In U. Firth (Ed.), *Cognitive processes in learning to spell.* London: Academic Press.

Fisher, C. W., Berliner, D. C., Filby, N., Marliave, R., Cohen, L., Dishaw, M., & Moore, J. (1980). Teaching behaviors, academic learning time, and student achievement: An overview. In C. Denham & A. Lieberman (Eds.), *Time to learn* (pp. 7–32). Washington, DC: National Institute of Education.

Flavell, J. H., & Wellman, H. M. (1977). Metamemory. In R. Kail, Jr., & J. W. Hagen (Eds.), *Perspectives on the development of memory and cognition* (pp. 3–33). Hillsdale, NJ: Lawrence Erlbaum.

Fleming, S. (1995). Whose stories are validated? *Language Arts, 72,* 500–596.

Flesch, R. (1948). A new readability yardstick. *Journal of Applied Psychology, 32,* 221–233.

Flores, B., & Hernandez, E. (1988). A bilingual kindergartener's sociopsychogenesis of literacy and biliteracy. *Dialogue, 3,* 43–49.

Florio-Ruane, S. (1991). Instructional conversations in learning to write and learning to teach. In L. Idol & B. F. Jones (Eds.), *Educational values and cognitive instruction: Implications for reform* (pp. 365–386). Hillsdale, NJ: Lawrence Erlbaum.

Flower, L., & Hayes, J. (1981). Plans that guide the composing process. In C. H. Frederiksen & J. Dominic (Eds.), *Writing: The nature, development, and teaching of written communication* (pp. 39–58). Hillsdale, NJ: Lawrence Erlbaum.

Fountas, I. C., & Pinnell, G. S. (1996). *Guided reading: Good first teacher for all children.* Portsmouth, NH: Heinemann.

Fountas, I. C., & Pinnell, G. S. (1999). *Matching books to readers (K–3).* Portsmouth, NH: Heinemann.

Fountas, I. C., & Pinnell, G. S. (2001a). *Guiding readers and writers grades 3–6.* Portsmouth, NH: Heinemann.

Fountas, I. C., & Pinnell, G. S. (2001b). *Leveled books for readers grades 3–6.* Portsmouth, NH: Heinemann.

Fowler, G. L. (1982). Developing comprehension skills in primary students through the use of story frames. *The Reading Teacher, 36,* 176–184.

Fowler, J. W., & Peterson, P. L. (1981). Increasing reading persistence and altering attributional style of learned helpless children. *Journal of Educational Psychology, 73,* 251–260.

Fox, B., & Routh, D. K. (1976). Phonemic analysis and severe reading disability in children. *Journal of Psycholinguistic Research, 9,* 115–119.

Fraatz, J. M. (1987). *The politics of reading: Power, opportunity, and prospects for change in America's public schools.* New York: Teachers College Press.

Francis, H. (1973). Children's experience of reading and notions of units of language. *British Journal of Educational Psychology, 43,* 17–23.

Freebody, P., & Anderson, R. C. (1983). Effects on text comprehension of differing proportions and locations of difficult vocabulary. *Journal of Reading Behavior, 15,* 19–40.

Freeman, D. E., & Freeman, Y. S. (2000). *Teaching reading in multilingual classrooms.* Portsmouth, NH: Heinemann.

Fry, E. (1968). A readability formula that saves time. *Journal of Reading, 11,* 513–516, 578.

Fry, E. (1980). The new instant word list. *The Reading Teacher, 34,* 284–289.

Fulwiler, T. (1980). Journals across the disciplines. *English Journal, 69,* 14–19.

Fulwiler, T. (1982). The personal connection: Journal writing across the curriculum. In T. Fulwiler & A. Young (Eds.), *Language connections: Writing and reading across the curriculum* (pp. 15–32). Urbana, IL: National Council of Teachers of English.

Fulwiler, T. (Ed.). (1987a). *The journal book.* Portsmouth, NH: Boynton/Cook.

Fulwiler, T. (1987b). *Teaching with writing.* Portsmouth, NH: Boynton/Cook.

Gaffney, J. S., & Anderson, R. C. (2000). Trends in reading research in the United States: Changing intellectual currents over three decades. In M. L. Kamil, P. B. Mosenthal, P. D. Pearson, & R. Barr (Eds.), *Handbook of reading research* (Vol. 3, pp. 53–74). Mahwah, NJ: Lawrence Erlbaum.

Gage, N. L., & Berliner, D. C. (1988). *Educational psychology.* Boston: Houghton Mifflin.

Galda, L. (1982). Assessment: Responses to literature. In A. Berger & H. A. Robinson (Eds.), *Secondary school reading: What research reveals for classroom practice* (pp. 111–125). Urbana, IL: National Council of Teachers of English and ERIC Clearinghouse on Reading and Communications Skills.

Galda, L., Ash, G. E., & Cullinan, B. E. (2000). Children's literature. In M. L. Kamil, P. B. Mosenthal, P. D. Pearson, & R. Barr (Eds.), *Handbook of reading research* (Vol. 3, pp. 361–379). Mahwah, NJ: Lawrence Erlbaum.

Gallagher, J. (1984). Policy analysis and program implementation/PL 94–142. *Topics in Early Childhood Special Education, 4*(1), 43–53.

Gallego, M., & Hollingsworth, S. (1992). Research directions: Multiple literacies: Teachers' evolving perceptions. *Language Arts, 69,* 206–213.

Gambrell, L. B. (1978). Getting started with sustained silent reading and keeping it going. *The Reading Teacher, 32,* 328–331.

Gambrell, L. B. (1985). Dialogue journals: Reading-writing interaction. *The Reading Teacher, 38,* 512–515.

Gambrell, L. B. (1996). Creating classroom cultures that foster reading motivation. *The Reading Teacher, 50,* 14–25.

Ganske, K. (2000). *Word journeys: Assessment-guided phonics, spelling, and vocabulary instruction.* New York: Guilford Press.

Garan, E. M. (2001). What does the report of the National Reading Panel really tell us about teaching phonics? *Language Arts, 79,* 500–506.

Garcia, G. E. (1991). Factors influencing the English reading test performance of Spanish-speaking Hispanic children. *Reading Research Quarterly, 26,* 371–392.

Garcia, G. E. (1993). Spanish-English bilingual students' use of cognates in English reading. *Journal of Reading Behavior, 25,* 241–259.

Garcia, G. E. (2000). Bilingual children's reading. In M. L. Kamil, P. B. Mosenthal, P. D. Pearson, & R. Barr (Eds.), *Handbook of reading research* (Vol. 3, pp. 813–834). Mahwah, NJ: Lawrence Erlbaum.

Garcia, G. E., & Pearson, P. D. (1991). The role of assessment in a diverse society. In E. H. Hiebert (Ed.), *Literacy for a diverse society* (pp. 253–278). New York: Teachers College Press.

Garcia, M. W., & Verville, K. (1994). Redesigning teaching and learning: The Arizona state assessment program. In S. W. Valencia, F. Hiebert, & P. P. Afflerbach (Eds.), *Authentic reading assessment: Practices and possibilities* (pp. 228–246). Newark, DE: International Reading Association.

Gardner, E. F. (1978). Bias. *Measurement in Education, 9,* 1–4.

Gardner, H. (1983). *Frames of mind.* New York: Basic Books.

Gaskins, I. W., Ehri, L. C., Cress, C., O'Hara, C., & Donnelly, K. (1996/1997). Procedures for word learning: Making discoveries about words. *The Reading Teacher, 50,* 312–327.

Gaskins, R. W., Gaskins, J. C., & Gaskins, I. (1992). Using what you know to figure out what you don't know. *Reading & Writing Quarterly, 8,* 197–221.

Gavelek, J. R., & Palincsar, A. S. (1988). Contextualism as an alternative worldview of learning disabilities: A response to Swanson's "Toward a metatheory of learning disabilities." *Journal of Learning Disabilities, 21,* 278–281.

Gavelek, J. R., Raphael, T. E., Biondo, S. M., & Wang, D. (2000). Integrated literacy instruction. In M. L. Kamil, P. B. Mosenthal, P. D. Pearson, & R. Barr (Eds.), *Handbook of reading research* (Vol. 3, pp. 587–608). Mahwah, NJ: Lawrence Erlbaum.

Gee, J. P. (1989). Commonalities and differences in narrative construction. *Discourse Processes, 12,* 287–307.

Gee, J. P. (2001). A sociocultural perspective on early literacy development. In S. B. Neuman & D. K. Dickinson (Eds.), *Handbook of early literacy research* (pp. 30–42). New York: Guilford Press.

Geertz, C. (1983). Blurred genres: The refiguration of social thought. In C. Geertz (Ed.), *Local knowledge: Further essays in interpretive anthropology.* New York: Basic Books.

Genishi, C., & Dyson, A. H. (1984). *Language assessment in the early years.* Norwood, NJ: Ablex.

Gentry, J. R. (1981). Learning to spell developmentally. *The Reading Teacher, 34,* 378–381.

Gentry, J. R. (1982). An analysis of developmental spelling in GYNS AT WORK. *The Reading Teacher, 36,* 192–200.

Gernsbacher, M. A. (1997). Two decades of structure building. *Discourse Processes, 23,* 265–304.

Gersten, R., Baker, S., & Edwards, L. (1999). *Teaching expressive writing to students with learning disabilities.* (ERIC/OSEP Digest #E590).

Gersten, R., Schiller, E. P., & Vaughn, S. (Eds.). (2000). *Contemporary special education research: Syntheses of the knowledge base on critical instructional issues.* Mahwah, NJ: Lawrence Erlbaum.

Gillam, R. B. (1998). Review of the Clinical Evaluation of Language Fundamentals, Third Edition. In J. C. Impara and Plake,

B. S. (Eds.), *Thirteenth mental measurements yearbook.* Lincoln, NE: Buros Institute of Mental Measurements.

Gillet, J., & Temple, C. (1982). *Understanding reading problems.* Boston: Little, Brown.

Gillet, J., & Temple, C. (1990). *Understanding reading problems* (3rd ed.). Glenview, IL: Scott, Foresman.

Gipe, J. (1978–79). Investigating techniques for teaching word meanings. *Reading Research Quarterly, 14,* 624–644.

Glascoe, F. P. (1999). CIBS-R Standardization and Validation Manual. North Billerica, MA: Curriculum Associates.

Glass, G. G., & Burton, E. H. (1973). How do they decode? Verbalizations and observed behaviors of successful decoders. *Education, 94,* 58–64.

Gleason, J. B. (1997). *The development of language* (4th ed.). Boston: Allyn & Bacon.

Goatley, V. J., Brock, C. H., & Raphael, T. E. (1995). Diverse learners participating in regular education "Book Clubs." *Reading Research Quarterly, 30,* 352–380.

Goetz, E., & Armbruster, B. (1980). Psychological correlates of text structure. In R. J. Spiro, B. C. Bruce, & W. F. Brewer (Eds.), *Theoretical issues in reading comprehension* (pp. 201–220). Hillsdale, NJ: Lawrence Erlbaum.

Goldenberg, C. (1993). Instructional conversations: Promoting comprehension through discussion. *The Reading Teacher, 46,* 316–326.

Goldenberg, C. (1994). Promoting early literacy development among Spanish-speaking children: Lessons from two studies. In E. H. Hiebert & B. M. Taylor (Eds.), *Getting reading right from the start* (pp. 171–199). Boston: Allyn & Bacon.

Goldenberg, C., & Gallimore, R. (1991). Changing teaching takes more than a one-shot workshop. *Educational Leadership, 49,* 69–72.

Goldenberg, C., & Patthey-Chavez, G. (1995). Discourse processes in instructional conversations: Interactions between teacher and transition readers. *Discourse Processes, 19,* 57–73.

Goldman, S. R., & Rakestraw, J. A. (2000). Structural aspects of constructing meaning from text. In M. L. Kamil, P. B. Mosenthal, P. D. Pearson, & R. Barr (Eds.), *Handbook of reading research* (Vol. 3, pp. 311–336). Mahwah, NJ: Lawrence Erlbaum.

Goldman, S. R., & Saul, E. U. (1990). Flexibility in text processing: A strategy competition model. *Learning and Individual Differences, 2,* 181–219.

Goldstein, B. S. (1986). Looking at cartoons and comics in a new way. *Journal of Reading, 29,* 657–661.

Gonzalez-Edfelt, N. (1990). Oral interaction and collaboration at the computer. *Computers in the Schools, 7,* 53–90.

Good, T. (1983). Research on classroom teaching. In L. S. Shulman & G. Sykes (Eds.), *Handbook of teaching and policy* (pp. 42–80). New York: Longman.

Good, T. L., & Brophy, J. E. (2000). *Looking in classrooms* (8th ed.). Boston: Allyn & Bacon.

Good, T. L., & Marshall, S. (1984). Do students learn more in heterogeneous or homogeneous achievement groups? In P. Peterson, L. Cherry-Wilkinson, & M. Hallinan (Eds.), *The social context for instruction* (pp. 15–38). New York: Academic Press.

Goodman, K. S. (1969). Analysis of oral reading miscues: Applied psycholinguistics. *Reading Research Quarterly, 5,* 9–30.

Goodman, K. S. (1973). Miscues: Windows on the reading process. In K. S. Goodman (Ed.), *Miscue analysis: Applications to reading instruction* (pp. 3–14). Urbana, IL: ERIC Clearinghouse on Reading and Communication Skills and the National Council of Teachers of English.

Goodman, K. S. (1989). Whole language *is* whole: A response to Heymsfeld. *Educational Leadership, 46(6),* 69–70.

Goodman, K. S., & Goodman, Y. M. (1977). Learning about psycholinguistic processes by analyzing oral reading. *Harvard Educational Review, 47,* 317–333.

Goodman, K. S., Shannon, P., Freeman, Y. S., & Murphy, S. (1988). *Report card on basal readers.* New York: Richard C. Owen.

Goodman, Y. M. (1986). Children coming to know literacy. In W. H. Teale & E. Sulzby (Eds.), *Emergent literacy: Writing and reading* (pp. 1–14). Norwood, NJ: Ablex.

Goodman, Y. M., & Burke, C. L. (1972). *Reading miscue inventory.* New York: Richard C. Owen.

Goodman, Y. M., Watson, D. J., & Burke, C. L. (1987). *Reading miscue inventory: Alternative procedures.* New York: Richard C. Owen.

Gordon, C., & Pearson, P. D. (1983). *The effects of instruction in metacomprehension and inferencing on children's comprehension abilities* (Technical Report 269). Urbana: University of Illinois, Center for the Study of Reading.

Goswami, U. (1986). Children's use of analogy in learning to read: A developmental study. *Journal of Experimental Child Psychology, 42,* 73–83.

Goswami, U. (2000). Phonological and lexical processes. In M. L. Kamil, P. B. Mosenthal, P. D. Pearson, & R. Barr (Eds.), *Handbook of reading research* (Vol. 3, pp. 251–268). Mahwah, NJ: Lawrence Erlbaum.

Gough, P. B. (1972). One second of reading. In J. F. Kavanagh & I. G. Mattingly (Eds.), *Language by ear and by eye* (pp. 331–358). Cambridge, MA: MIT Press.

Grabe, M., & Grabe, C. (1996). *Integrating technology for meaningful learning.* Boston: Houghton Mifflin.

Graesser, A. C., Golding, J. M., & Long, D. L. (1991). Narrative representation and comprehension. In R. Barr, M. L. Kamil, P. Mosenthal, & P. D. Pearson (Eds.), *Handbook of reading research* (Vol. II, pp. 171–205). New York: Longman.

Graesser, A. C., & Riha, J. R. (1984). An application of multiple regression techniques to sentence reading times. In D. Kieras & M. Just (Eds.), *New methods in comprehension research* (pp. 183–218). Hillsdale, NJ: Lawrence Erlbaum.

Graham, S., & Harris, K. R. (1994). The role and development of self-regulation in the writing process. In D. H. Schunk & B. J. Zimmerman (Eds.), *Self-regulation of learning and performance* (pp. 203–228). Hillsdale, NJ: Lawrence Erlbaum.

Graves, D. H. (1983). *Writing: Teachers and children at work.* Portsmouth, NH: Heinemann.

Graves, D. H. (1994). *A Fresh Look at Writing.* Portsmouth, NH: Heinemann.

Graves, D. H., & Hansen, J. (1983). The author's chair. *Language Arts, 60,* 176–183.

Graves, M., & Graves, B. (1994). *Scaffolding reading experiences.* Norwood, MA: Christopher Gordon.

Graves, M. F., Cooke, C. L., & LaBerge, M. J. (1983). Effects of previewing short stores. *Reading Research Quarterly, 18,* 262–276.

Gray, W. S. (1920). The value of informal tests of reading achievement. *Journal of Educational Research, 1,* 103–111.

Gray, W. S., & Leary, B. E. (1935). *What makes a book readable?* Chicago: University of Chicago Press.

Greaney, V. (1980). Factors related to amount and type of leisure reading. *Reading Research Quarterly, 15,* 337–357.

Green, G. (1984). On the appropriateness of adaptations in primary-level basal readers. In R. C. Anderson, J. Osborn, & R. J. Tierney (Eds.), *Learning to read in American schools: Basal readers and content texts* (pp. 175–191). Hillsdale, NJ: Lawrence Erlbaum.

Green, J., & Bloome, D. (1983). Ethnography and reading: Issues, approaches, criteria, and findings. In *Searches for meaning in reading/language processing and instruction* (32nd Yearbook of The National Reading Conference, pp. 6–30). New York: National Reading Conference.

Groff, P. (1986). The maturing of phonics instruction. *The Reading Teacher, 39,* 919–923.

Gronlund, N. E. (1985). *Measurement and evaluation in teaching* (5th ed.). New York: Macmillan.

Gump, P. V. (1969). Intra-setting analysis: The third grade classroom as a special but instructive case. In E. Willems & H. Rausch (Eds.), *Naturalistic viewpoints in psychological research* (pp. 200–220). New York: Holt, Rinehart & Winston.

Gunning, T. G. (2002). *Assessing and correcting reading and writing difficulties* (2nd ed.). Boston: Allyn & Bacon.

Gupta, A., & Oboler, E. (2001, September). Changing roles of Title I reading teachers in light of new provisions and team teaching models. *The Reading Matrix, 1*(2), 1–6.

Guthrie, J. T. (1980). Research reviews: Time in reading programs. *The Reading Teacher, 33,* 500–502.

Guthrie, J. T., & Wigfield, A. (2000). Engagement and motivation in reading. In M. L. Kamil, P. B. Mosenthal, P. D. Pearson, & R. Barr (Eds.), *Handbook of reading research* (Vol. 3, pp. 403–422). Mahwah, NJ: Lawrence Erlbaum.

Gutierrez-Clellen, V. F., Pena, E., & Quinn, R. (1995). Accommodating cultural differences in narrative style: A multicultural perspective. *Topics in Language Disorders, 15,* 54–67.

Guzzetti, B., & Hynd, C. (Eds.). (1998). *Perspectives on conceptual change: Multiple ways to understand knowing and learning in a complex world.* Hillsdale, NJ: Lawrence Erlbaum.

Halliday, M. A. K. (1975). *Learning how to mean: Explorations in the development of language.* New York: Elsevier North Holland.

Halliday, M. A. K., & Hasan, R. (1976). *Cohesion in English.* London: Longman.

Hammill, D. D., & Hresko, W. P. (1994). *Comprehensive scales of student abilities.* Austin, TX: PRO-ED.

Hammill, D. D., & Larsen, S. C. (1988). *Test of Written Language— 2.* Austin, TX: PRO-ED.

Hammill, D. D., & Larsen, S. C. (1996). *Test of Written Language– 3.* Austin, TX: PRO-ED.

Hansen, J. (1981). The effects of inference training and practice on young children's reading comprehension. *Reading Research Quarterly, 16,* 391–417.

Hare, V. C. (1984). What's in a word? A review of young children's difficulties with the construct of "word." *The Reading Teacher, 37,* 360–364.

Hare, V. C., & Borchardt, K. (1984). Direct instruction of summarization skills. *Reading Research Quarterly, 20,* 62–78.

Hare, V. C., Rabinowitz, M., & Schieble, K. M. (1989). Text effects on main idea comprehension. *Reading Research Quarterly, 24,* 72–88.

Harris, A. J. (1977). Ten years of progress in remedial reading. *The Reading Teacher, 31,* 29–35.

Harris, A. J., & Sipay, E. R. (1985). *How to increase reading ability* (8th ed.). New York: Longman.

Harris, A. J., & Sipay, E. R. (1990). *How to increase reading ability* (9th ed.). New York: Longman.

Harris, K. R., & Pressley, M. (1991). The nature of cognitive strategy instruction: Interactive strategy construction. *Exceptional Children, 57,* 392–404.

Harris, T. L., & Hodges, R. E. (1995). *The literacy dictionary.* Newark, DE: International Reading Association.

Harste, J., Woodward, V. A., & Burke, C. (1984). *Language stories and literacy lessons.* Portsmouth, NH: Heinemann.

Harvey, S., & Goudvis, A. (2000). *Strategies that work.* York, ME: Stenhouse.

Haskins, R., Walden, T., & Ramey, C. (1983). Teacher and student behavior in high- and low-ability groups. *Journal of Educational Psychology, 75,* 865–876.

Hayes, B., & Peters, C. W. (1989). The role of reading instruction in the social studies. In D. Lapp & J. Flood (Eds.), *Handbook of instructional theory and practice* (pp. 152–178). Englewood Cliffs, NJ: Prentice Hall.

Hayes, J. R., & Flower, L. S. (1980). Identifying the organization of writing processes. In L. W. Gregg & E. R. Steinberg (Eds.), *Cognitive processes in writing* (pp. 3–30). Hillsdale, NJ: Lawrence Erlbaum.

Heath, S. B. (1981). Questioning at home and at school: A comparative study. In G. Spindler (Ed.), *Doing ethnography: Educational anthropology in action* (pp. 102–131). New York: Holt, Rinehart & Winston.

Heath, S. B. (1983). *Ways with words: Language, life, and work in communities and classrooms.* Cambridge, England: Cambridge University Press.

Heath, S. B. (1991). The sense of being literate. In R. Barr, M. Kamil, P. Mosenthal, & P. D. Pearson (Eds.), *Handbook of reading research* (Vol 2). White Plains, NY: Longman.

Heckleman, R. G. (1969). Neurological impress method of remedial reading instruction. *Academic Therapy Quarterly, 4,* 277–282.

Henderson, E. H. (1980). Developmental concepts of word. In E. H. Henderson & J. W. Beers (Eds.), *Developmental and cognitive aspects of learning to spell: A reflection of word knowledge* (pp. 1–14). Newark, DE: International Reading Association.

Henderson, E. H. (1992). *Teaching spelling* (2nd ed.). Boston: Houghton Mifflin.

Hendley, B. (1986). *Dewey, Russell, Whitehead: Philosophers as educators.* Carbondale: Southern Illinois University Press.

Henkin, R. (1995). Insiders and outsiders in first-grade writing workshops: Gender and equity issues. *Language Arts, 72,* 429–434.

Herber, H. L. (1970). *Teaching reading in the content areas.* Englewood Cliffs, NJ: Prentice Hall.

Herber, H. L. (1978). *Teaching reading in the content areas* (2nd ed.). Englewood Cliffs, NJ: Prentice Hall.

Herman, P. A., Anderson, R. C., Pearson, P. D., & Nagy, W. E. (1987). Incidental acquisition of word meaning from expositions with varied text features. *Reading Research Quarterly, 22,* 263–284.

Hiebert, E. H. (1981). Developmental patterns and interrelationships of preschool children's print awareness. *Reading Research Quarterly, 16,* 236–260.

Hiebert, E. H. (1983). An examination of ability grouping for reading instruction. *Reading Research Quarterly, 18,* 231–255.

Hiebert, E. H. (1994a). Becoming literate through authentic tasks: Evidence and adaptations. In R. R. Ruddell, M. R. Ruddell, H. Singer (Eds.), *Theoretical models and processes of reading* (4th ed., pp. 391–413). Newark, DE: International Reading Association.

Hiebert, E. H. (1994b). Reading Recovery in the United States: What difference does it make to an age cohort? *Educational Researcher, 23,* 15–25.

Hiebert, E. H. (1999). Text matters in learning to read. *The Reading Teacher, 52*(6), 552–566.

Hiebert, E. H., Colt, J. M., Catto, S. L., & Gury, E. M. (1992). Reading and writing of Grade 1 students in a restructured Chapter 1 program. *American Educational Research Journals, 29,* 545–572.

Hiebert, E. H., & Fisher, C. W. (1991). Task and talk structures that foster literacy. In E. H. Hiebert (Ed.), *Literacy for a diverse society* (pp. 341–356). New York: Teachers College Press.

Hiebert, E. H., & Martin, L. A. (2000). The texts of beginning reading instruction. In S. B. Neuman & D. K. Dickinson (Eds.), *Handbook of early literacy research* (pp. 361–376). New York: Guilford Press.

Hiebert, E. H., Pearson, P. D., Taylor, B. M., Richardson, V., & Paris, S. G. (Eds.). (1998). *Every child a reader: Applying reading research in the classroom.* Ann Arbor, MI: Center for the Improvement of Early Reading Achievement.

Hiebert, E. H., & Raphael, T. E. (1998). *Early literacy instruction.* Fort Worth: Harcourt Brace.

Hiebert, E. H., & Taylor, B. M. (2000). Beginning reading instruction: Research on early interventions. In R. Barr, M. L. Kamil, P. B. Mosenthal, & P. D. Pearson (Eds.), *Handbook of reading research* (Vol. 3, pp. 455–482). Mahwah, NJ: Lawrence Erlbaum.

Hiebert, E. H., Winograd, P. N., & Danner, F. W. (1984). Children's attributions for failure and success in different aspects of reading. *Journal of Educational Psychology, 76,* 1139–1148.

Higgins, K. M., Harris, N. A., & Kuehn, L. L. (1994). Placing assessment into the hands of young children: A study of student-generated criteria and self-assessment. *Educational Assessment, 2,* 309–324.

Hillocks, G. (1986). *Research on written composition: New directions for teaching.* Urbana, IL: National Conference on Research in English.

Hillocks, G., & Smith, M. W. (1991). In J. Flood, D. Lapp, & J. Squire (Eds.), *Handbook of research on teaching the English language arts* (pp. 591–603). New York: Macmillan.

Hine, M., Goldman, S. R., & Cosden, M. A. (1990). Error monitoring by learning handicapped students engaged in collaborative microcomputer-based writing. *Journal of Special Education, 23,* 407–422.

Hoffman, J. (2001, December). *Words.* Review of research at the annual meeting of the National Reading Conference, Austin, TX.

Hoffman, J. V. (1987). Rethinking the role of oral reading. *Elementary School Journal, 87,* 367–373.

Hoffman, J. V., McCarthey, S. J., Abbott, J., Christian, C., Corman, L., Curry, C., Dressman, M., Elliott, B., Matherne, D., & Stahle, D. (1994). So what's new in the new basals? A focus on first grade. *Journal of Reading Behavior, 26,* 47–73.

Hoffman, J. V., McCarthey, S. J., Elliott, B., Bayles, D. L., Price, D. P., Ferree, A., & Abbott, J. A. (1998). The literature-based basal in first grade classrooms: Savior, Satan, or same-old, same-old? *Reading Research Quarterly, 33,* 168–197.

Hoffman, J. V., Roser, N. L., Salas, T., Patterson, E., & Pennington, J. (2000). *Text leveling and little books in first-grade reading.* CIERA Report #1–010. Ann Arbor, MI: Center for the Improvement of Early Reading Achievement.

Holdaway, D. (1979). *Foundations of literacy.* Sydney, Australia: Ashton Scholastic.

Holliday, W. G., Yore, L. D., & Alvermann, D. E. (1994). The reading-science-learning-writing connection: Breakthroughs, barriers, promises. *Journal of Research in Science Teaching, 31,* 877–894.

Holmes, B. C., & Roser, N. L. (1987). Five ways to assess readers' prior knowledge. *The Reading Teacher, 40,* 646–649.

Hong, L. K. (1981). Modifying SSR for beginning readers. *The Reading Teacher, 34,* 888–891.

Honig, B., Diamond, L., & Gutlohn, L. (2000). *Teaching reading sourcebook.* Novato, CA: Arena Press.

Hood, J. (1978). Is miscue analysis practical for teachers? *The Reading Teacher, 32,* 260–266.

Horowitz, R. (1995). A 75-year legacy on assessment: Reflections from an interview with Ralph W. Tyler. *The Journal of Educational Research, 89*(2), 68–75.

Hoskisson, K., & Tompkins, G. E. (1987). *Language arts: Content and teaching strategies.* Columbus, OH: Merrill.

Howell, K. W., & Morehead, M. K. (1987). *Curriculum-based evaluation for special and remedial education.* Columbus, OH: Charles E. Merrill.

Hresko, W. P., Herron, S. R., & Peak, P. K. (1996). *Test of early written language* (2nd ed.). Austin, TX: PRO-ED.

Hudelson, S. (1986). ESL children's writing: What we've learned, what we're learning. In P. Rigg & D. S. Enright (Eds.), *Children and ESL: Integrating perspectives* (pp. 23–54). Washington, DC: Teachers of English to Speakers of Other Languages.

Hudelson, S. (1987). The role of native language literacy in the education of language minority children. *Language Arts, 64,* 827–834.

Huey, E. B. (1908/1968). *The psychology and pedagogy of reading.* Cambridge, MA: MIT Press. (Republished: Cambridge, MA: MIT Press, 1968).

Hughes, S. (1989). *Dogger.* Boston: Houghton Mifflin.

Hunt, J. M. (1961). *Intelligence and experience.* New York: Ronald.

Hunt, L. C. (n.d.). *Vocabulary development is a simple dumbbell operation.* Burlington: University of Vermont.

Hunt, L. C. (1970). Effect of self-selection, interest, and motivation upon independent, instructional, and frustration levels. *The Reading Teacher, 24*(2), 146–151.

Hynd, C. R., & Alvermann, D. E. (1986). Prior knowledge activation in refutation and non-refutation text. In J. A. Niles & R. Lalik (Eds.), *Solving problems in literacy: Learners, teachers, and researchers* (35th Yearbook of The National Reading Conference, pp. 55–60). Rochester, NY: National Reading Conference.

International Reading Association (IRA). (1981, April). Misuse of grade equivalents. Resolution passed by the Delegates Assembly of the International Reading Association, April 1981. Published in *The Reading Teacher, 35,* 464.

International Reading Association (IRA). (1998). *Standards for reading professionals.* Newark, DE: International Reading Association.

International Reading Association (IRA). (2000). Teaching all children to read: The roles of specialists. *Journal of Adolescent and Adult Literacy, 44*(1), 99–104.

Invernizzi, M., Abouzeid, M., & Gill, T. (1994). Using students' invented spelling as a guide for spelling instruction that emphasizes word study. *Elementary School Journal, 95*(2), 1655–1657.

IRA/NCTE (1994). *Standards for the assessment of reading and writing.* Newark, DE: International Reading Association/National Council of Teachers of English.

Irvin, J. L. (1990). *Reading and the middle school student.* Boston: Allyn & Bacon.

Irwin, J. W., & Davis, C. (1980). Assessing readability: The checklist approach. *Journal of Reading, 24,* 124–130.

Irwin, M., & Lipson, M. Y. (1985). Guidelines for evaluating reading. *The Michigan Reading Journal, 18*(4), 23–26.

Irwin, P. A., & Mitchell, J. N. (1983). A procedure for assessing the richness of retellings. *Journal of Reading, 26,* 391–396.

Iverson, S., & Tunmer, W. (1993). Phonological processing skills and the Reading Recovery Program. *Journal of Educational Psychology, 85,* 112–126.

Jaggar, A. (1985). On observing the language learner: Introduction and overview. In A. Jaggar & M. T. Smith-Burke (Eds.), *Observing the language learner* (pp. 1–7). Newark, DE: International Reading Association.

Jenkins, C. B. (1996). *Inside the writing portfolio: What we need to know to assess children's writing.* Portsmouth, NH: Heinemann.

Jewell, M. C., & Zintz, M. V. (1990). *Learning to read and write naturally* (2nd ed.). Dubuque, IA: Kendall/Hunt.

Johns, J. J. (1988). *Basic reading inventory* (4th ed.). Dubuque, IA: Kendall/Hunt.

Johnson, D. D. (1971). A basic vocabulary for beginning reading. *The Elementary School Journal, 72,* 29–34.

Johnson, D. D., & Baumann, J. F. (1984). Word identification. In P. D. Pearson, R. Barr, M. Kamil, & P. Mosenthal (Eds.), *Handbook of reading research* (Vol. 1, pp. 583–608). New York: Longman.

Johnson, D. D., & Pearson, P. D. (1984). *Teaching reading vocabulary* (2nd ed.). New York: Holt, Rinehart & Winston.

Johnson, D. W., & Johnson, R. T. (1986). *Learning together and alone* (2nd ed.). Englewood Cliffs, NJ: Prentice Hall.

Johnson, M. S., & Kress, R. A. (1965). *Informal reading inventories.* Newark, DE: International Reading Association.

Johnson, M. S., Kress, R. A., & Pikulski, J. J. (1987). *Informal reading inventories* (2nd ed.). Newark, DE: International Reading Association.

Johnston, P., & Rogers, R. (2001). *Assessment of literacy development in early childhood: Handbook for early childhood practices.* New York: Guilford Press.

Johnston, P. H. (1985). Teaching students to apply strategies that improve reading comprehension. *Elementary School Journal, 85,* 635–645.

Johnston, P. H. (1987). Teachers as evaluation experts. *The Reading Teacher, 40,* 744–748.

Johnston, P. H. (1992). *Constructive evaluation of literate activity.* New York: Longman.

Johnston, P. H. (1997). *Knowing literacy: Constructive literacy assessment.* York, ME: Stenhouse.

Johnston, P. H., Allington, R. L., & Afflerbach, P. (1985). The congruence of classroom and remedial reading instruction. *Elementary School Journal, 85,* 465–477.

Johnston, P. H., & Winograd, P. N. (1985). Passive failure in reading. *Journal of Reading, 17,* 279–301.

Jones, B. F. (1983, April). *Integrating learning strategies and text research to teach higher order thinking skills in schools.*

Paper presented at the Annual Meeting of the American Educational Research Association, Montreal, Canada.

Jongsma, E. A. (1982). Test review: Peabody Picture Vocabulary Test-Revised (PPVT-R). *Journal of Reading, 20,* 360–364.

Jongsma, K. S., & Jongsma, E. A. (1981). Test review: Commercial informal reading inventories. *The Reading Teacher, 34,* 697–705.

Jordan, C. (1985). Translating culture: From ethnographic information to educational program. *Anthropology and Education Quarterly, 16,* 105–123.

Juel, C. (1988). Learning to read and write: A longitudinal study of fifty-four children from first through fourth grade. *Journal of Educational Psychology, 80,* 437–447.

Juel, C. (1996). What makes literacy tutoring effective? *Reading Research Quarterly, 31,* 268–289.

Juel, C., Griffith, P. L., & Gough, P. B. (1986). Acquisition of literacy: A longitudinal study of children in first and second grade. *Journal of Educational Psychology, 78,* 243–255.

Juel, C., & Minden-Cupp, C. (1998). *Learning to read words: Linguistic units and strategies* (CIERA Report #1-008). Ann Arbor, MI: Center for the Improvement of Early Reading Achievement.

Juel, C., & Minden-Cupp, C. (2000). Learning to read words: Linguistic units and instructional strategies. *Reading Research Quarterly, 35*(4), 458–492.

Kalmbach, J. R. (1986a). Evaluating informal methods of assessment of retellings. *Journal of Reading, 30,* 119–129.

Kalmbach, J. R. (1986b). Getting to the point of retellings. *Journal of Reading, 29,* 326–333.

Kameenui, E. J., & Shannon, P. (1988). Point/counterpoint: Direct instruction reconsidered. In J. Readence, R. Baldwin, J. Konopak, & P. O'Keefe (Eds.), *Dialogues in literacy research* (37th Yearbook of the National Reading Conference, pp. 35–44). Chicago: National Reading Conference.

Kamil, M. L., & Intrator, S. (2000). Technology and literacy. In M. L. Kamil, P. B. Mosenthal, P. D. Pearson, & R. Barr (Eds.), *Handbook of Reading Research* (Vol. 2, pp. 771–788). Mahwah, NJ: Lawrence Erlbaum.

Kamphaus, R. W. (2001). Review of the Metropolitan Readiness Tests, Sixth Edition. In B. S. Blake & J. C. Impara (Eds.), *Fourteenth mental measurements yearbook.* Lincoln, NE: Buros Institute of Mental Measurements.

Kane, C. (1994). *Prisoners of time research: What we know and what we need to know.* Washington, DC: National Education Commission on Time and Learning.

Karlsen, B., & Gardner, E. (1995). *Stanford Diagnostic Reading Test* (4th ed.). San Antonio, TX: Harcourt Brace.

Kastler, L. A., Roser, N. L., & Hoffman, J. V. (1987). Understanding the forms and functions of written language: Insights from children and parents. In J. E. Readence & R. S. Baldwin (Eds.), *Research in literacy: Merging perspectives* (36th Yearbook of the National Reading Conference, pp. 85–92). Rochester, NY: National Reading Conference.

Katz, M. (1987). *Reconstructing American education.* Cambridge, MA: Harvard University Press.

Keene, E., & Zimmerman, L. (1997). *Mosaic of thought.* Portsmouth, NH: Heinemann.

Kemp, M. (1987). *Watching children read and write.* Portsmouth, NH: Heinemann.

Kendall, J., & Mason, J. (1980). *Comprehension of polysemous words.* Paper presented at the Annual Meeting of the American Educational Research Association, Boston, MA.

Kennedy, B. A., & Miller, D. J. (1976). Persistent use of verbal rehearsal as a function of information about its value. *Child Development, 47,* 566–569.

Kibby, M. W. (1979). Passage readability affects the oral reading strategies of disabled readers. *The Reading Teacher, 32,* 390–396.

Kilgallon, P. A. (1942). *The study of relationships among certain pupil adjustments in reading situations.* Unpublished doctoral dissertation, Pennsylvania State University, State College, PA.

Kim, S. A. (1995). Types and sources of problems in L2 reading: A qualitative analysis of the recall protocols of Korean high school EFL students. *Foreign Language Annals, 28*(1), 49–70.

King, L. H. (1983). Pupil classroom perceptions and the expectancy effect. *South Pacific Journal of Teacher Education, 11,* 54–70.

Kintsch, W., & van Dijk, T. (1978). Toward a model of text comprehension and production. *Psychological Review, 85,* 363–394.

Klare, G. (1984). Readability. In P. D. Pearson (Ed.), *Handbook of reading research* (pp. 681–744). New York: Longman.

Klare, G. (1988). The formative years. In B. L. Zakaluk & S. J. Samuels (Eds.), *Readability: Its past, present, and future* (pp. 14–34). Newark, DE: International Reading Association.

Klenk, L., & Kibby, M. W. (2000). Re-mediating reading difficulties: Appraising the past, reconciling the present, constructing the future. In M. L. Kamil, P. B. Mosenthal, P. D. Pearson, & R. Barr (Eds.), *Handbook of reading research* (Vol. 3, pp. 667–690). Mahwah, NJ: Lawrence Erlbaum.

Kremers, M. (1990). Sharing authority on a synchronous network: The case for riding the beast. *Computers and Composition, 7,* 69–77.

Krieger, V. K. (1981). Differences in poor readers' abilities to identify high-frequency words in isolation and context. *Reading World, 20,* 263–272.

Kucer, S. (1985). The making of meaning: Reading and writing as parallel processes. *Written Communication, 2,* 317–336.

Kuhn, M. R., & Stahl, S. A. (2000). *Fluency: A review of developmental and remedial practices* (CIERA Report #2-008). Ann Arbor, MI: Center for the Improvement of Early Reading Achievement.

Labbo, L. D. (2000). 12 things young children can do with a talking book in a classroom computer center. *The Reading Teacher, 53*(7), 542–546.

LaBerge, D., & Samuels, J. (1974). Toward a theory of automatic information processing in reading. *Cognitive Psychology, 6,* 293–323.

Ladson-Billings, G. (1994). *The dreamkeepers.* San Francisco: Jossey-Bass.

Lancia, P. J. (1997). Literary borrowing: The effects of literature on children's writing. *The Reading Teacher, 50,* 470–475.

Langer, J. A. (1982). Facilitating text processing: The elaboration of prior knowledge. In J. Langer & M. T. Smith-Burke (Eds.), *Reader meets author/bridging the gap* (pp. 149–162). Newark, DE: International Reading Association.

Langer, J. A. (1984). Examining background knowledge and text comprehension. *Reading Research Quarterly, 19,* 468–481.

Langer, J. A. (1991). Literacy and schooling: A sociocognitive perspective. In E. H. Hiebert (Ed.), *Literacy for a diverse society* (pp. 9–27). New York: Teachers College Press.

Lapp, D., Fisher, D., Flood, J., & Cabello, A. (2001). An integrated approach to the teaching and assessment of language arts. In S. R. Hurley & J. V. Tinahero (Eds.), *Literacy assessment of second language learners.* Needham Heights, MA: Allyn & Bacon.

Lapp, D., & Flood, J. (2000). Reading comprehension instruction for at-risk students: Research-based practices that can make a difference. In D. W. Moore, D. E. Alvermann, & K. A. Hinchman (Eds.), *Struggling adolescent readers: A collection of strategies* (pp. 138–147). Newark, DE: International Reading Association.

Larsen, S. C., & Hammill, D. D. (1986). *Test of written spelling* (2nd ed.). Austin, TX: PRO-ED.

Larsen, S. C., & Hammill, D. D. (1994). *Test of written spelling* (3rd ed.). Austin, TX: PRO-ED.

Larsen, S. C., & Hammill, D. D. (1999). *Test of written spelling* (4th ed.). Austin, TX: PRO-ED.

Leinhardt, G., Zigmond, N., & Cooley, W. (1981). Reading instruction and its effects. *American Educational Research Journal, 18,* 171–177.

Lemann, N. (1997). The reading wars. *The Atlantic Monthly, 280*(5), 128–134.

Lepper, M., & Chabay, R. (1985). Intrinsic motivation and instruction: Conflicting views on the role of motivational processes in computer-based education. *Educational Psychologist, 20,* 217–230.

Lepper, M., & Malone, T. W. (1987). Intrinsic motivation and instructional effectiveness in computer-based education. In R. E. Snoth & M. J. Farr (Eds.), *Aptitude, learning and instruction* (pp. 255–296). Hillsdale, NJ: Lawrence Erlbaum.

Leslie, L., & Caldwell, J. (2001). *Qualitative Reading Inventory–3.* Boston: Allyn & Bacon.

Leu, D., DeGroff, L. C., & Simons, H. D. (1986). Predictable texts and interactive-compensatory hypothesis: Evaluating individual differences in reading ability, context use, and comprehension. *Journal of Educational Psychology, 78,* 347–352.

Leu, D. J., Jr. (2000). Literacy and technology: Deictic consequences for literacy education in an information age. In M. L. Kamil, P. B. Mosenthal, P. D. Pearson, & R. Barr (Eds.), *Handbook of reading research* (Vol. 2, pp. 743–770). Mahwah, NJ: Lawrence Erlbaum.

Liberman, I. Y., & Shankweiler, D. (1979). Speech, the alphabet, and teaching to read. In L. B. Resnick & P. A. Weaver (Eds.), *Theory and practice of early reading* (Vol. 2, pp. 109–134). Hillsdale, NJ: Lawrence Erlbaum.

Lidz, C. S. (1987). Historical perspectives. In C. S. Lidz (Ed.), *Dynamic assessment* (pp. 3–34). New York: Guilford Press.

Linn, R. L., & Gronlund, N. E. (2000). *Measurement and assessment in teaching* (8th ed.). Upper Saddle River, NJ: Merrill.

Lipson, M. Y. (1982). Learning new information from text: The role of prior knowledge and reading ability. *Journal of Reading Behavior, 14,* 243–262.

Lipson, M. Y. (1983). The influence of religious affiliation on children's memory for text information. *Reading Research Quarterly, 18,* 448–457.

Lipson, M. Y. (1995). Conversations with children—and other classroom-based assessment strategies. In L. Putnam (Ed.), *How to become a better reading teacher: Strategies for diagnosis and remediation* (pp. 167–179). Columbus, OH: Merrill/Macmillan.

Lipson, M. Y. (1996). Conversations with children and other classroom-based assessment strategies. In L. R. Putnam (Ed.), *How to become a better reading teacher: Strategies for assessment and intervention* (pp. 167–179). Englewood Cliffs, NJ: Merrill.

Lipson, M. Y., Bigler, M., Poth, L., & Wickizer, B. (1987, December). *Instructional applications of a verbal report methodology.* Paper presented at the 37th Annual Meeting of the National Reading Conference, St. Petersburg, FL.

Lipson, M. Y., Irwin, M., & Poth, E. (1986). The relationships between metacognitive self-reports and strategic reading behavior. In J. Niles & R. Lalik (Eds.), *Solving problems in literacy: Learners, teachers, and researchers* (35th Yearbook of the National Reading Conference, pp. 460–476). Rochester, NY: National Reading Conference.

Lipson, M. Y., Mosenthal, J. H., Daniels, P., & Woodside-Jiron, H. (2000). Process writing in the classrooms of eleven teachers with different orientations to teaching and learning. *Elementary School Journal, 101*(2), 209–231.

Lipson, M. Y., Mosenthal, J. H., & Mekkelsen, J. (1999). The nature of comprehension among grade 2 children: Variability in retellings as function of development, text, and task. In T. Shanahan & F. V. Rodriguez-Brown (Eds.), *Forty-eighth yearbook of the National Reading Conference* (pp. 104–119). Chicago: National Reading Conference.

Lipson, M. Y., Valencia, S., Wixson, K. K., & Peters, C. (1993). Integration and thematic teaching: Integration to improve teaching and learning. *Language Arts, 70,* 252–263.

Lipson, M. Y., & Wickizer, E. (1989). Promoting reading independence through instructional dialogue. *Teaching Exceptional Children, 21*(2), 28–32.

Lipson, M. Y., & Wixson, K. K. (1986). Reading disability research: An interactionist perspective. *Review of Educational Research, 56,* 111–136.

Lipson, M. Y., & Wixson, K. K. (1989). Student evaluation and basal instruction. In P. Winograd, K. K. Wixson, & M. Y.

Lipson (Eds.), *Improving basal reading instruction* (pp. 109–139). New York: Teachers College Press.

Liu, M., & Reed, W. M. (1995). The effect of hypermedia assisted instruction on second language learning. *Journal of Educational Computing Research, 12,* 159–175.

Lodge, H. C., & Trett, G. L. (1968). *New ways in English.* Englewood Cliffs, NJ: Prentice Hall.

Lomax, R. G., & McGee, L. M. (1987). Young children's concepts about print and reading: Toward a model of word reading acquisition. *Reading Research Quarterly, 22,* 237–256.

Lombardino, L. J., Morris, D., Mercado, L., DeFillipo, F., Sarisky, C., & Montgomery, A. (1999). The Early Reading Screening Instrument: A method for identifying kindergarteners at risk for learning to read. *International Journal of Language and Communication Disorders, 34,* 135–150.

Loughlin, C. E., & Martin, M. D. (1987). *Supporting literacy: Developing effective learning environments.* New York: Teachers College Press.

Lovett, M., & Steinbach, K. (1997). The effectiveness of remedial programs for reading disabled children of different ages: Does the benefit decrease for older children? *Learning Disability Quarterly, 20,* 189–210.

Loxterman, J., Beck, I., & McKeown, M. (1994). The effects of thinking aloud during reading on students' comprehension of more or less coherent text. *Reading Research Quarterly, 29*(4), 352–367.

Lund, N. J., & Duchan, J. F. (1988). *Assessing children's language in naturalistic contexts.* Englewood Cliffs, NJ: Prentice Hall.

Lyons, C. A., & Pinnell, G. S. (2001). *Systems for change in literacy education.* Portsmouth, NH: Heinemann.

MacArthur, C. A. (1998). Word processing with speech synthesis and word prediction: Effects on the dialogue journal writing of students with learning disabilities. *Learning Disability Quarterly, 21,* 151–166.

MacGinitie, W. H., MacGinitie, R. K., Maris, K., & Dreyer, L. (2000). *The Gates-MacGinitie reading tests* (4th ed.). Itasca, IL: Riverside Publishing.

Maier, A. A. (1980). The effect of focusing on the cognitive processes of learning disabled children. *Journal of Learning Disabilities, 13,* 143–147.

Malmstrom, J. (1968). *Introduction to modern English grammar.* Rochelle Park, NJ: Hayden Press.

Mandler, J. M., & Johnson, N. S. (1977). Remembrance of things parsed: Story structure and recall. *Cognitive Psychology, 9,* 111–115.

Manzo, A.V. (1969). The request procedure. *Journal of Reading, 13,* 123–126.

Maria, K. (1986, December). *Refuting misconceptions: Its effect on middle grade children's comprehension.* Paper presented at the 35th Annual Meeting of the National Reading Conference. Austin, TX.

Maria, K. (1990). *Reading comprehension instruction: Issues and strategies.* Parkton, MD: York Press.

Markwardt, F. C. (1989). *Peabody Individual Achievement Battery—Revised.* Circle Pines, MN: American Guidance Service.

Marsh, G. P., Desberg, P., & Cooper, J. (1977). Developmental changes in reading strategies. *Journal of Reading Behavior, 9,* 391–394.

Marshall, H. H., & Weinstein, R. S. (1984). Classroom factors affecting students' self-evaluations: An interactional model. *Review of Educational Research, 54,* 301–325.

Marshall, N., & Glock, M. (1978–79). Comprehension of connected discourse: A study into the relationship between the structure of text and information recalled. *Reading Research Quarterly, 14,* 10–56.

Martinez, M., & Roser, N. (1985). Read it again: The value of repeated readings during storytime. *The Reading Teacher, 38,* 782–786.

Martinez, M., Roser, N., & Strecker, S. (1999). I never thought I could be a star: A reader's theater ticket to fluency. *The Reading Teacher, 50,* 326–334.

Marzano, R. J., Pickering, D., & McTighe, J. (1993). *Assessing student outcomes.* Alexandria, VA: ASCD.

Mason, J., Osborn, J., & Rosenshine, B. (1977). *A consideration of skill hierarchy approaches to the teaching of reading* (Technical Report No. 42). Urbana: University of Illinois, Center for the Study of Reading.

Mason, J. M., & Au, K. H. (1990). *Reading instruction for today* (2nd ed.). Glenview, IL: Scott, Foresman.

Mathews, M. (1966). *Teaching to read: Historically considered.* Chicago: University of Chicago Press.

May, F. (1990). *Reading as communication: An interactive approach.* Columbus, OH: Charles E. Merrill.

McAuliffe, S. (1993). Toward understanding one another: Second graders' use of gendered language and story styles. *The Reading Teacher, 47,* 302–310.

McCabe, A. (1992, December). All kinds of good stories. Paper presented at the 42nd Annual Meeting of the National Reading Conference, San Antonio, TX. ERIC document: ED355474.

McCloughlin, M. (1987). *Parent-teacher conferencing.* Springfield, IL: Charles Thomas.

McConaughy, S. H. (1982). Developmental changes in story comprehension and levels of questioning. *Language Arts, 59,* 580–589, 600.

McConaughy, S. H. (1985). Good and poor readers' comprehension of story structure across different input and output modalities. *Reading Research Quarterly, 20,* 219–232.

McConnell, C. R. (1982). Readability formulae as applied to college economics textbooks. *Journal of Reading, 26,* 14–17.

McCracken, R. A., & McCracken, M. (1971). Initiating sustained silent reading. *Journal of Reading, 14,* 521–524, 582–583.

McCracken, R. A., & McCracken, M. (1978). Modeling is the key to sustained reading. *The Reading Teacher, 31,* 406–408.

McDermott, R. P. (1977). The ethnography of speaking and reading. In R. W. Shuy (Ed.), *Linguistic theory: What can it say about reading?* (pp. 153–185). Newark, DE: International Reading Association.

McGill-Franzen, A. (1992). Early literacy: What does "developmentally appropriate" mean? *The Reading Teacher, 46,* 56–58.

McGill-Franzen, A. (1994). Compensatory and special education: Is there accountability for learning and belief in children's potential? In E. H. Hiebert & B. M. Taylor (Eds.), *Getting reading right from the start: Effective early literacy interventions* (pp. 13–35). Boston: Allyn & Bacon.

McGill Franzen, A. (2000). Policy and instruction: What is the relationship? In M. L. Kamil, P. B. Mosenthal, P. D. Pearson, & R. Barr (Eds.), *Handbook of reading research* (Vol. 3, pp. 889–908). Mahwah, NJ: Lawrence Erlbaum.

McGinnis, D. J., & Smith, D. E. (1982). *Analyzing and treating reading problems.* New York: Macmillan.

McKenna, M. C. (1983). Informal reading inventories: A review of the issues. *The Reading Teacher, 36,* 670–679.

McKenna, M. C., Kear, D. J., & Ellsworth, R. A. (1995). Children's attitudes toward reading: A national survey. *Reading Research Quarterly, 30,* 934–956.

McLaughlin, M., & Allen, M. B. (2002). *Guided comprehension: A teaching model for grades 3–8.* Newark, DE: International Reading Association.

McNeil, J. D. (1992). *Reading comprehension: New directions for classroom practice* (3rd ed.). New York: HarperCollins.

McNinch, G. H. (1981). A method for teaching sight words to disabled readers. *The Reading Teacher, 35,* 269–272.

McWilliams, L., & Rakes, T. A. (1979). *Content reading inventories: English, social studies, science.* Dubuque, IA: Kendall/Hunt.

Medley, D. M. (1985). Systematic observation schedules as measuring instruments. In R. A. Weinberg & F. H. Woods (Eds.), *Observation of pupils and teachers in mainstream and special education settings: Alternative strategies* (pp. 97–106). Minneapolis: University of Minnesota, Leadership and Training Institute/Special Education.

Meisels, S. J. (1998). *Assessing readiness* (CIERA Report #3-002). Ann Arbor, MI: Center for Improvement of Early Reading Achievement.

Meisels, S. J., Marsden, D. B., Wiske, M. S., & Henderson, L. W. (1997). *Early screening inventory—revised.* Ann Arbor, MI: Rebus, Inc.

Memory, D. M. (1992). Guiding students to independent decoding in content area classes. In E. K. Dishner, R. W. Bean, J. E. Readence, & D. W. Moore (Eds.), *Reading in content areas* (3rd ed., pp. 210–218). Dubuque, IA: Kendall/Hunt.

Meyer, B. J., & Freedle, R. O. (1984). Effects of discourse type on recall. *American Educational Research Journal, 21,* 121–143.

Mezynski, K. (1983). Issues concerning acquisition of knowledge: Effects of vocabulary training on reading comprehension. *Review of Educational Research, 53,* 253–279.

Michaels, S. (1981). "Sharing time": Children's narrative styles and differential access to literacy. *Language in Society, 10,* 423–442.

Michaels, S. (1991). The dismantling of narrative. In A. McCabe & C. Peterson (Eds.), *Developing narrative structure* (pp. 303–351). Hillsdale, NJ: Lawrence Erlbaum.

Michigan Reading Association. (1993). *Computers in the reading program* (2nd ed.). Grand Rapids: Michigan Reading Association.

Mikkelsen, N. (1990). Toward greater equity in literacy education: Storymaking and non-mainstream students. *Language Arts, 67,* 556–566.

Miller, J. D. (1993). Script writing on computer network: Quenching the flames or feeding the fire. In J. Kreeft Peyton, B. C. Bruce, & T. Batson (Eds.), *Network-based classrooms: Promises and realities* (pp. 124–137). Cambridge, England: Cambridge University Press.

Miller, L., & Olson, J. (1995). How computers live in schools. *Educational Leadership, 53,* 74–77.

Miller, P., & Goodnow, J. J. (1995). Cultural practices: Toward an integration of culture and development. In J. J. Goodnow & F. Kessel (Eds.), *Cultural practices as contexts for development, No. 67: New directions in child development.* San Francisco: Jossey-Bass.

Miller, P., & Mehler, R. (1994). The power of personal storytelling in families and kindergartens. In A. H. Dyson & C. Genishi (Eds.), *The need for story: Cultural diversity in classroom and community* (pp. 38–56). Urbana, IL: National Council of Teachers of English.

Millett, N. C. (1986). *Teaching the writing process: A guide for teachers and supervisors.* Boston: Houghton Mifflin.

Mills, R. E. (1956). An evaluation of techniques for teaching word recognition. *Elementary School Journal, 56,* 221–225.

Minami, M., & McCabe, A. (1991). Haiku as a discourse regulation device: A stanza analysis of Japanese children's personal narratives. *Language in Society, 20*(4), 577–599.

Minami, M., & McCabe, A. (1995). Rice balls and bear hunts: Japanese and North American family narrative patterns. *Journal of Child Language, 22,* 423–445.

Mitchell, J. V. (1985). *Ninth mental measurements yearbook.* Lincoln, NE: Buros Institute of Mental Measurements.

Moffett, J. (1985). Hidden impediments to improving English teaching. *Phi Delta Kappan, 67,* 50–56.

Moje, E. B., Willes, D. J., & Fassio, K. (in press). Constructing and negotiating literacy in a seventh-grade writer's workshop. In E. G. Moje & D. G. O'Brien (Eds.), *Constructions of literacy: Studies of teaching and learning in secondary classrooms and schools.* Mahwah, NJ: Lawrence Erlbaum.

Moll, L. C., & Diaz, E. (1987). Change as the goal of educational research. *Anthropology and Education Quarterly, 18,* 300–311.

Moll, L. C., & Diaz, S. (1985). Ethnographic pedagogy: Promoting effective bilingual instruction. In E. Garcia & R. V. Padilla (Eds.), *Advances in bilingual education research* (pp. 127–149). Tucson: University of Arizona Press.

Moll, L. C., Estrada, E., Diaz, E., & Lopes, L. M. (1980). The organization of bilingual lessons: Implications for schooling. *The Quarterly Newsletter of the Laboratory of Comparative Human Cognition, 2,* 53–58.

Moll, L. C., & Gonzalez, N. (1994). Critical Issues: Lessons from research with language-minority children. *Journal of Reading Behavior, 26,* 439–456.

Montague, M., Cleborne, D., Maddux, D., & Dereshiwsky, M. I. (1990). Story grammar and comprehension and production of narrative prose by students with learning disabilities. *Journal of Learning Disabilities, 23,* 190–197.

Mork, T. A. (1972). Sustained silent reading in the classroom. *The Reading Teacher, 25,* 438–441.

Morris, D. (1981). Concept of word: A developmental phenomenon in the beginning reading and writing processes. *Language Arts, 58,* 659–668.

Morris, D. (1992). What constitutes at-risk: Screening children for first-grade reading intervention. In W. A. Secord & J. S. Damico (Eds.), *Best practices in school speech language pathology* (pp. 43–51). Orlando, FL: Harcourt Brace & Jovanovich.

Morris, D. (1993). The relationship between children's concept of word in text and phoneme awareness in learning to read: A longitudinal study. *Research in the Teaching of English, 27,* 133–153.

Morris, D. (1999). *The Howard Street tutoring manual: Teaching at-risk readers in the primary grades.* New York: Guilford Press.

Morrow, L. M. (1983). Home and school correlates of early interest in literature. *Journal of Educational Research, 76,* 221–230.

Morrow, L. M. (1986). Encouraging voluntary reading: The impact of a literature program on children's use of library centers. *Reading Research Quarterly, 21,* 330–346.

Morrow, L. M. (1987). Promoting voluntary reading: Activities represented in basal reader manuals. *Reading Research and Instruction, 26,* 189–202.

Morrow, L. M. (1988). Retelling stories as a diagnostic tool. In S. M. Glazer, L. W. Searfoss, & L. M. Gentile (Eds.), *Reexamining reading diagnosis: New trends and procedures* (pp. 128–149). Newark, DE: International Reading Association.

Morrow, L. M. (1989). Creating a bridge to children's literature. In P. Winograd, K. Wixson, & M. Lipson (Eds.), *Improving basal reading instruction* (pp. 210–230). New York: Teachers College Press.

Morrow, L. M., Tracey, D. H., Woo, D. G., & Pressley, M. (1999). Characteristics of exemplary first-grade literacy instruction. *The Reading Teacher, 52,* 462–476.

Mosenthal, J., Lipson, M., Sortino, S., Russ, B., & Mekkelsen, J. (2001a). Literacy in rural Vermont: Lessons from schools where children succeed. In B. Taylor & P. D. Pearson (Eds.), *Teaching reading: Effective schools and accomplished teachers.* Mahwah, NJ: Lawrence Erlbaum.

Mosenthal, J. H., Lipson, M. Y., Sortino, S., Russ, B., & Mekkelsen, J. (2001b). *Elementary schools where children succeed in literacy.* Providence: The Northeast and Islands Regional Laboratory.

Mosenthal, P., & Na, T. (1980). Quality of children's recall under two classroom testing tasks: Towards a socio-psycholinguistic model of reading comprehension. *Reading Research Quarterly, 15,* 504–528.

Moss, M., & Puma, M. (1995). *Prospects: The congressional mandated study of educational growth and opportunity.* Cambridge, MA: ABT Associates. (Eric Document: ED 394334).

Moss, P. A. (1994). Validity. In R. J. Sternberg (Ed.), *Encyclopedia of human intelligence* (Vol. 2, pp. 1101–1106). New York: Macmillan.

Mowat, F. (1985). *Lost in the barrens.* New York: Bantam Books (paperback reissue, original copyright 1956).

Mulligan, J. (1974). Using language experience with potential high school dropouts. *Journal of Reading, 18,* 206–211.

Murray, D. H. (1990). *Shoptalk: Learning to write with writers.* Portmouth, NH: Heinemann.

Murray-Ward, M. (1998). Review of the Nelson-Denny Reading Test, Forms G and H. In J. C. Impara & Plake, B. S. (Eds.), *Thirteenth mental measurements yearbook.* Lincoln, NE: Buros Institute of Mental Measurements.

Muter, W., Hulme, C., Snowling, M. J., & Taylor, S. (1997). Segmentation, not rhyming, predicts early progress in learning to read. *Journal of Experimental Child Psychology, 65,* 370–396.

Nagy, W. E. (1988). *Teaching vocabulary to improve reading comprehension.* Urbana, IL: ERIC Clearinghouse on Reading and Communication Skills and the National Council of Teachers of English.

Nagy, W. E., & Anderson, R. C. (1984). How many words are there in printed school English? *Reading Research Quarterly, 19,* 304–330.

Nagy, W. E., & Herman, P. (1987). Breadth and depth of vocabulary knowledge: Implications for acquisition and instruction. In M. G. McKeown & M. E. Curtis (Eds.), *The nature of vocabulary acquisition* (pp. 19–36). Hillsdale, NJ: Lawrence Erlbaum.

Nagy, W. E., Herman, P. A., & Anderson, R. C. (1985). Learning words from context. *Reading Research Quarterly, 20,* 233–253.

Nagy, W. E., & Scott, J. A. (2000). Vocabulary processes. In M. L. Kamil, P. B. Mosenthal, P. D. Pearson, & R. Barr (Eds.), *Handbook of reading research* (Vol. 3, pp. 269–284). Mahwah, NJ: Lawrence Erlbaum.

Naslund, J. C., & Schneider, W. (1996). Kindergarten letter knowledge, phonological skills, and memory processes: Relative effects on early literacy. *Journal of Experimental Child Psychology, 62,* 30–59.

National Assessment of Educational Progress (NAEP). (1996). *1994 reading report card for the nation and the states.* Washington, DC: U.S. Department of Education.

National Association of State Directors of Special Education (NASDSE). (1994a). *Disproportionate representation of culturally and linguistically diverse students in special educa-*

*tion: A comprehensive examination.* Prepared by Project Forum. Alexandria, VA: Author (ED379812).

National Association of State Directors of Special Education (NASDSE). (1994b). *Disproportionate representation of students from minority ethnic/racial groups in special education: A policy forum to develop action plans for high priority recommendation* (Final Report. Project Forum). Proceedings of a Policy Forum in Disproportionate Representation (ED378716).

National Reading Panel. (2000). *Teaching children to read: An evidence-based assessment of the scientific research literature on reading and its implications for reading instruction.* Washington, DC: National Institute of Child Health and Human Development.

Neill, D. M., & Median, J. (1989). Standardized tests: Harmful to educational health. *Phi Delta Kappan, 70,* 688–697.

Nelson-Herber, J. (1986). Expanding and refining vocabulary in content areas. *Journal of Reading, 29,* 626–633.

Neuman, S. B., & Dickinson, D. K. (Eds.). (2001). *Handbook of early literacy research.* New York: Guilford Press.

Newcomer, P., & Hammill, D. D. (1997). *Test of Oral Language Development—3 Primary.* Austin, TX: PRO-ED.

Newmann, F. M., & Associates. (1996) *Authentic achievement: Restructuring schools for intellectual quality.* San Francisco: Jossey-Bass.

Newmann, F. M., & Wehlage, G. G. (1993). Five standards of authentic instruction. *Educational Leadership, 22*(2), 4–13, 22.

Newton, E. S. (1977). Andragogy: Understanding the adult as learner. *Journal of Reading, 20,* 361–363.

Nicolsen, T., Pearson, P. D., & Dykstra, R. (1979). Effects of embedded anomalies and oral reading errors on children's understanding of stories. *Journal of Reading Behavior, 11,* 339–354.

Nist, S. L., & Simpson, M. L. (2000). College studying. In M. L. Kamil, P. B. Mosenthal, P. D. Pearson, & R. Barr (Eds.), *Handbook of reading research* (Vol. 3, pp. 645–666). Mahwah, NJ: Lawrence Erlbaum.

North, S. (1987). *The making of knowledge in composition.* Portsmouth, NH: Heinemann.

Novak, C. (2001). Review of the *Metropolitan Readiness Tests* (6th ed.). In B. S. Blake & J. C. Impara (Eds.), *Fourteenth mental measurements yearbook.* Lincoln, NE: Buros Institute of Mental Measurements.

Nurss, J. R. (1979). Assessment of readiness. In T. G. Waller & G. E. MacKinnon (Eds.), *Reading research: Advances in theory and practice* (Vol. 1, pp. 31–62). New York: Academic Press.

Nurss, J. R., & McGauvran, M. E. (1976/1986). *Metropolitan Readiness Tests (MRT).* San Antonio, TX: The Psychological Corporation.

Nurss, J. R., & McGauvran, M. E. (1995). *Metropolitan Readiness Test, Sixth Edition.* San Antonio, TX: The Psychological Corporation.

Nystrand, M. (1990). High school English students in low-achieving classes: What helps? *Newsletter: National Center for Effective Secondary Schools,* 5, 7–8, 11. Madison: Wisconsin Center for Education Research, School of Education, University of Wisconsin–Madison.

Oberlin, K. J., & Shugarman, S. L. (1989). Implementing the reading workshop with middle school learning-disabled readers. *Journal of Reading, 32,* 682–687.

O'Connor, R. E., Jenkins, J., & Slocum, T. A. (1995). Transfer among phonological tasks in kindergarten: Essential instructional content. *Journal of Educational Psychology, 87,* 202–217.

O'Flahavan, J. F., & Tierney, R. J. (1991). Reading, writing, and critical thinking. In L. Idol & B. F. Jones (Eds.), *Educational values and cognitive instruction: Implications for reform* (pp. 41–64). Hillsdale, NJ: Lawrence Erlbaum.

Ogle, D. M. (1986). K-W-L: A teaching model that develops active reading of expository text. *The Reading Teacher, 39,* 564–570.

Ogle, D. M. (1989). The know, want to know, learn strategy. In K. D. Muth (Ed.), *Children's comprehension of text: Research into practice* (pp. 205–223). Newark, DE: International Reading Association.

Okagaki, L., & Sternberg, R. J. (1991). Cultural and parental influences on cognitive development. In L. Okagaki and R. J. Sternberg (Eds.), *Directors of development: Influences on the development of children's thinking* (pp. 101–120). Hillsdale, NJ: Lawrence Erlbaum.

Oken-Wright, P. (1998). Transition to writing: Drawing as a scaffold for emergent writers. *Young Children, 53,* 76–81.

Ollila, L. O., & Mayfield, M. I. (1992). Home and school together: Helping beginning readers succeed. In J. Samuels & A. E. Farstrup (Eds.), *What research has to say about reading instruction* (pp. 17–45). Newark, DE: International Reading Association.

Olshavsky, J. E. (1978). Comparison profiles of good and poor readers across materials of increasing difficulty. In P. D. Pearson & J. Hansen (Eds.), *Reading: Disciplined inquiry in process and practice* (27th Yearbook of The National Reading Conference, pp. 73–76). Washington, DC: National Reading Conference.

Olson, M. W. (1985). Text type and reader ability: The effects of paraphrase and text-based inference questions. *Journal of Reading Behavior, 17,* 199–214.

Olson, R. K., Wise, B., Connors, F., Rack, J., & Fulker, D. (1989). Specific deficits in component reading and language skills: Genetic and environmental influences. *Journal of Learning Disabilities, 22,* 339–348.

O'Malley, J. M., & Valdez-Pierce, L. V. (1996). *Authentic assessment for English language learners: Practical approaches for teachers.* White Plains, NY: Addison Wesley Longman.

Omanson, R. C., Beck, I. L., McKeown, M. G., & Perfetti, C. A. (1984). Comprehension of texts with unfamiliar versus recently taught words: An assessment of alternative models. *Journal of Educational Psychology, 76,* 1253–1268.

Onosko, J. J., & Newmann, F. M. (1994). Creating more thoughtful learning environments. In J. N. Mangieri & C. C. Block

(Eds.), *Creating powerful thinking in teachers and students* (pp. 27–49). Fort Worth: Harcourt Brace.

Opitz, M. (1998). *Flexible grouping in reading.* New York: Scholastic Professional Books.

Osborn, J. H. (1984). The purposes, uses, and contents of workbooks and some guidelines for publishers. In R. C. Anderson, J. Osborn, & R. J. Tierney (Eds.), *Learning to read in American schools: Basal readers and content texts* (pp. 45–112). Hillsdale, NJ: Lawrence Erlbaum.

Osborn, J. H. (1989). Summary: Improving basal reading programs. In P. Winograd, K. Wixson, & M. Y. Lipson (Eds.), *Improving basal reading instruction* (pp. 203–226). New York: Teachers College Press.

Otto, W., Wolf, A., & Eldridge, R. (1984). Managing instruction. In P. D. Pearson, R. Barr, M. Kamil, & P. Mosenthal (Eds.), *Handbook of reading research* (pp. 799–828). New York: Longman.

Ovando, C. J. (1988). Language diversity and education. In J. A. Banks & C. A. McGee Banks (Eds.), *Multicultural education: Issues and perspectives* (pp. 208–227). Boston: Allyn & Bacon.

Ovando, C. J. (1993). Language diversity and education. In J. A. Banks & C. A. McGee Banks (Eds.), *Multicultural education: Issues and perspectives* (pp. 215–235). Boston: Allyn & Bacon.

Page, W. D., & Pinnell, G. S. (1979). *Teaching reading comprehension: Theory and practice.* Urbana, IL: ERIC Clearinghouse on Reading and Communication Skills and the National Council of Teachers of English.

Palincsar, A. S. (1984). The quest for the meaning from expository text: A teacher-guided journey. G. Duffy, L. Roehler, & J. Mason (Eds.), *Comprehension instruction: Perspectives and suggestions* (pp. 251–264). White Plains, NY: Longman.

Palincsar, A. S. (1986). The role of dialogue in providing scaffolded instruction. *Educational Psychologist, 21,* 73–98.

Palincsar, A. S., & Brown, A. L. (1984). Reciprocal teaching of comprehension-fostering and monitoring activities. *Cognition and Instruction, 1,* 117–175.

Palmatier, R. A. (1973). A notetaking system for learning. *Journal of Reading, 17,* 36–39.

Pany, D., & Jenkins, J. (1978). Learning word meanings: A comparison of instructional procedures and effects on measures of reading comprehension with learning disabled students. *Learning Disabilities Quarterly, 1,* 21–32.

Pappas, C. C., Kiefer, B. Z., & Levstik, L. S. (1995). *An integrated language perspective in the elementary school* (2nd ed.). New York: Longman.

Paratore, J. R., & Indrisano, R. (1987). Intervention assessment of reading comprehension. *The Reading Teacher, 40,* 778–783.

Paris, S. G. (1988). Models and metaphors of learning strategies. In C. Weinstein, E. T. Goetz, & P. A. Alexander (Eds.), *Learning and study strategies: Issues in assessment, instruction, and evaluation* (pp. 299–321). San Diego: Academic Press.

Paris, S. G. (1991). Assessment and remediation of metacognitive aspects of children's reading comprehension. *Topics in Language Disorders, 12,* 32–50.

Paris, S. G., Cross, D. R., & Lipson, M. Y. (1984). Informed strategies for learning: A program to improve children's reading awareness and comprehension. *Journal of Educational Psychology, 76,* 1239–1252.

Paris, S. G., & Jacobs, J. (1984). The benefits of informed instruction for children's reading awareness and comprehension. *Journal of Educational Psychology, 76* 1239–1252.

Paris, S. G., Lipson, M. Y., & Wixson, K. K. (1983). Becoming a strategic reader. *Contemporary Educational Psychology, 8,* 293–316.

Paris, S. G., & Myers, M. (1981). Comprehension monitoring in good and poor readers. *Journal of Reading Behavior, 13,* 5–22.

Paris, S. G., Newman, R. S., & McVey, K. A. (1982). Learning the functional significance of mnemonic actions: A microgenetic study of strategy acquisition. *Journal of Experimental Child Psychology, 34,* 490–509.

Paris, S. G., Olson, G., & Stevenson, H. (Eds.). (1983). *Learning and motivation in the classroom.* Hillsdale, NJ: Lawrence Erlbaum.

Paris, S. G., Wasik, B. A., & Turner, J. C. (1991). The development of strategic readers. In R. Barr, M. Kamil, P. Mosenthal, & P. D. Pearson (Eds.), *Handbook of reading research* (Vol. 2, pp. 609–640). New York: Longman.

Paris, S. G., Wasik, B. A., & Van der Westhuizen, G. (1988). Meta-cognition: A review on research on metacognition and reading. In J. E. Readence & R. S. Baldwin (Eds.), *Dialogues in literacy research* (37th Yearbook of the National Reading Conference, pp. 143–181). Chicago: NRC.

Paris, S. G., & Wixson, K. K. (1987). The development of literacy: Access, acquisition, and instruction. In D. D. Bloome (Ed.), *Literacy and schooling* (pp. 35–54). Norwood, NJ: Ablex.

Paris, S. G., Wixson, K. K., & Palincsar, A. S. (1986). Instructional approaches to reading comprehension. In E. Rothkopf (Ed.), *Review of research in education* (pp. 91–128). Washington, DC: American Educational Research Association.

Parsons, L. (1990). *Response journals.* Portsmouth, NH: Heinemann.

Patton, J. M. (1998). The disporportionate representation of African Americans in special education: Looking behind the curtain for understanding and solutions. *The Journal of Special Education, 32,* 25–31.

Pauk, W. (1974). *How to study in college.* Boston: Houghton Mifflin.

Pearson, P. D. (1993). Standards for the English language arts: A policy perspective. *Journal of Reading Behavior, 25,* 457–475.

Pearson, P. D., & Fielding, L. (1991). Comprehension instruction. In R. Barr, M. Kamil, P. Mosenthal, & P. D. Pearson (Eds.), *Handbook of reading research* (Vol. 2, pp. 815–860). New York: Longman.

Pearson, P. D., & Gallagher, M. (1983). The instruction of reading comprehension. *Contemporary Educational Psychology, 8,* 317–344.

Pearson, P. D., Hansen, J., & Gordon, C. (1979). The effect of background knowledge on young children's comprehension of explicit and implicit information. *Journal of Reading Behavior, 11,* 201–209.

Pearson, P. D., & Johnson, D. (1978). *Teaching reading comprehension.* New York: Holt, Rinehart & Winston.

Pellegrini, A. D. (2001). Some theoretical and methodological considerations in studying literacy in social context. In S. Neuman & D. Dickinson (Eds.), *Handbook of early literacy research* (pp. 54–65). New York: Guilford Press.

Pellegrini, A. D., Perlmutter, J., Galda, L., & Brody, G. (1990). Joint reading between black Head Start children and their mothers. *Child Development, 61,* 443–453.

Perfetti, C. A., Beck, I., Bell, L., & Hughes, C. (1987). Phonemic knowledge and learning to read are reciprocal: A longitudinal study of first grade children. *Merrill-Palmer Quarterly, 33,* 283–319.

Perfetti, C. A., & Hogaboam, T. (1975). The relationship between single word decoding and reading comprehension skill. *Journal of Educational Psychology, 67,* 461–469.

Perlman, C. (1998). Review of the *Test of Reading Comprehension,* third edition. In J. C. Impara & Plake, B. S. (Eds.), *The thirteenth mental measurements yearbook.* Lincoln, NE: Buros Institute of Mental Measurements.

Peters, C. W., & Wixson, K. K. (in press). Unifying the domain of K–12 English language arts curriculum. *Handbook of English language arts.* New York: Macmillan.

Peterson, C., Jesso, B., & McCabe, A. (1999). Encouraging narratives in preschoolers: An intervention study. *Journal of Child Language, 26,* 49–67.

Peterson, J., Greenlaw, M. J., & Tierney, R. J. (1978). Assessing instructional placement with an IRI: The effectiveness of comprehension questions. *Journal of Educational Research, 17,* 247–250.

Pflaum, S. W., & Pascarella, E. T. (1980). Interactive effects of prior reading achievement and training in context on the reading of learning-disabled children. *Reading Research Quarterly, 16,* 138–158.

Philips, S. U. (1982). *The invisible culture: Communication in classroom and community on the Warm Springs Indian Reservation.* New York: Longman.

Piaget, J. (1960). *Language and thought of the child.* London: Routledge & Kegan Paul.

Pikulski, J. J. (1994a). Preventing reading failure: A review of five effective programs. *The Reading Teacher, 48,* 30–39.

Pikulski, J. J. (1994b). Preventing reading failure in young children. *The Reading Teacher, 46,* 30–39.

Pikulski, J. J., & Shanahan, T. (1982). Informal reading inventrories: A critical analysis. In J. J. Pikulski & T. Shanahan (Eds.), *Approaches to the informal evaluation of reading* (pp. 94–116). Newark, DE: International Reading Association.

Pinnell, G. S. (1985). Helping teachers help children at risk: Insights from the Reading Recovery Program. *Peabody Journal of Education, 62,* 70–85.

Pinnell, G. S. (1987). Helping teachers see how readers read: Staff development through observation. *Theory into Practice, 26,* 51–58.

Pinnell, G. S. (1991). Interactive assessment: Teachers and children as learners. In J. A. Roderick (Ed.), *Context-responsive approaches to assessing children's language* (pp. 79–96). Urbana, IL: National Conference on Research in English.

Pinnell, G. S., Lyons, C. A., DeFord, D. E., Bryck, A., & Selzer, M. (1994). Comparing instructional models for the literacy education of high-risk first graders. *Reading Research Quarterly, 29,* 8–39.

Pinnell, G. S., Pikulski, J. J., Wixson, K. K., Campbell, J. R., Gough, P. B., and Beatty, A. S. (1995). *Listening to children read aloud.* Washington, DC: U.S. Department of Education, National Center for Education Statistics.

Plass, J. L., Chun, D. M., Mayer, R. E., & Leutner, D. (1998). Supporting visual and verbal learning preferences in a second-language multimedia learning environment. *Journal of Educational Psychology, 90,* 25–36.

Popham, W. J. (1978). *Criterion-referenced measurement.* Englewood Cliffs, NJ: Prentice Hall.

Popham, W. J. (1993). Circumventing the high costs of authentic assessment. *Phi Delta Kappan,* February, 470–473.

Poplin, M. (1984). Summary rationalizations, apologies and farewell: What we don't know about the learning disabled. *Learning Disabilities Quarterly, 7,* 130–134.

Porter, J. (1974). Research report. *Elementary English, 51,* 144–151.

Powell, W. R. (n.d.). *The finger count system for monitoring reading behavior.* Unpublished paper, University of Florida, Gainesville.

Powell, W. R. (1980). Measuring reading performance informally. *Journal of Children and Youth, 1,* 23–31.

Powell, W. R., & Dunkeld, C. G. (1971). The validity of IRI reading levels. *Elementary English, 48,* 637–642.

Pressley, M. (1995). Reading comprehension strategies. In M. Pressley & V. E. Woloshyn (Eds.), *Cognitive strategy instruction that really improves children's academic performance.* Cambridge, MA: Brookline Books.

Pressley, M. (2000). What should comprehension instruction be the instruction of? In M. L. Kamil, P. B. Mosenthal, P. D. Pearson, & R. Barr (Eds.), *Handbook of reading research* (Vol. 3, pp. 545–561). Mahwah, NJ: Lawrence Erlbaum.

Pressley, M., Wharton-McDonald, R., Hampson, J. M., & Echevarria, M. (1998). The nature of literacy instruction in ten grade–4/5 classrooms in upstate New York. *Scientific Studies of Reading, 2,* 159–194.

Puma, M. J., Karweit, N., Price, C., Icciuti, A., Thompson, W., & Vaden-Kiernan, M. (1997). *Prospects: Final report on student outcomes.* Washington, DC: U.S. Department of Education, Planning and Evaluation Services.

*Put reading first.* (2001). Jessup, MD: National Institute for Literacy.

Radencich, M. C. (1995). *A handbook for the K–12 reading resource specialist.* Boston: Allyn & Bacon.

Rakes, T. A., & Smith, L. (1986). Assessing reading skills in the content areas. In E. K. Dishner, T. W. Bean, J. E. Readence, & D. W. Moore (Eds.), *Reading in the content areas: Improving classroom instruction* (2nd ed., pp. 145–159). Dubuque, IA: Kendall/Hunt.

Rakes, T. A., & Smith, L. (2001). Assessing reading skills in the content area. In J. Readance, T. Bean, & R. Baldwin (Eds.), *Content area literacy* (7th ed., pp. 399–413). Dubuque, IA: Kendall/Hunt.

RAND Reading Study Group (RRSG) (Catherine Snow, chair). (2002). Reading for understanding: Toward an R & D program for reading comprehension. Santa Monica, CA: RAND.

Raphael, T. E. (1982). Question-answering strategies for children. *The Reading Teacher, 36,* 186–190.

Raphael, T. E. (1986). Teaching question-answer relationships, revisited. *The Reading Teacher, 39,* 516–522.

Raphael, T. E. (1998). Balanced instruction and the role of classroom discourse. In J. Osborn & F. Lehr (Eds.), *Literacy for all* (pp. 134–169). New York: Guilford Press.

Raphael, T. E., & Englert, C. S. (1989). Integrating writing and reading instruction. In P. Winograd, K. Wixson, & M. Lipson (Eds.), *Improving basal reading instruction* (pp. 231–255). New York: Teachers College Press.

Raphael, T. E., & Englert, C. S. (1990). Writing and reading: Partners in constructing meaning. *The Reading Teacher, 43,* 388–400.

Raphael, T. E., Englert, C. S., & Kirschner, B. W. (1989). Acquisition of expository writing skills. In J. M. Mason (Ed.), *Reading and writing connections* (pp. 261–290). Boston: Allyn & Bacon.

Raphael, T. E., & Hiebert, E. H. (1996). *Creating an integrated approach to literacy instruction.* Ft. Worth: Harcourt Brace.

Raphael, T. E., Kirschner, B. W., & Englert, C. S. (1988). Expository writing program: Making connections between reading and writing. *The Reading Teacher, 41,* 790–795.

Raphael, T. E., Winograd, P., & Pearson, P. D. (1980). Strategies children use in answering questions. In M. L. Kamil & A. J. Moe (Eds.), *Perspectives in reading research and instruction* (29th Yearbook of The National Reading Conference, pp. 56–63). Washington, DC: National Reading Conference.

Rasinski, T. V. (1986). Repeated readings–naturally. *The Reading Teacher, 39,* 244–245.

Read, C. (1971). Preschool children's knowledge of English phonology. *Harvard Educational Review, 41,* 1–34.

Read, C. (1975). *Children's categorization of speech sounds in English.* Urbana, IL: National Council of Teachers of English.

Read, C. (1986). *Children's creative spelling.* London: Routledge & Kegan Paul.

Readence, J. E., Bean, T. W., & Baldwin, R. S. (1985). *Content area reading: An integrated approach* (2nd ed.). Dubuque, IA: Kendall/Hunt.

Reid, D. K., Hresko, W. P., & Hammill, D. D. (1989). *The Test of Early Reading Ability (TERA–2).* Austin, TX: PRO-ED.

Reid, D. K., Hresko, W. P., & Hammill, D. D. (2001). *The Test of Early Reading Ability—3 (TERA-3).* Austin, TX: PRO-ED.

Reid, J. F. (1966). Learning to think about reading. *Educational Research, 9,* 56–62.

Resnick, L. B., & Resnick, D. L. (1992). Assessing the thinking curriculum: New tools for educational reform. In B. R. Gifford & M. C. O'Connor (Eds.), *Future assessments: Changing views of aptitude, achievement, and instruction* (pp. 37–75). Boston: Kluwer.

Reutzel, D. R. (1999). Organizing literacy instruction: Effective grouping strategies and organizational plans. In L. B. Gambrell, L. M. Morrow, S. B. Neuman, & M. Pressley (Eds.), *Best practices in literacy instruction.* New York: Guilford Press.

Rey, H. A. (1941). *Curious George.* Boston: Houghton Mifflin.

Rhodes, L. K., & Shanklin, N. (1990). Miscue analysis in the classroom. *The Reading Teacher, 44,* 252–254.

Richek, M. A., Caldwell, J. S., Jennings, J. H., & Lerner, M. W. (2002). *Reading problems: Assessment and teaching strategies.* Boston: Allyn & Bacon.

Ringler, L. H., & Weber, C. K. (1984). *A language-thinking approach to reading.* San Diego: Harcourt Brace Jovanovich.

Roberts, P. (1962). *English sentences.* New York: Harcourt Brace Jovanovich.

Robinson, F. (1946). *Effective study.* New York: Harper Brothers.

Robinson, V. M. K. (1998). Methodology and the research-practice gap. *Educational Researcher, 27,* 17–26.

Rock, E., Fessler, M., & Church, R. (1997). The concomitance of learning disabilities and emotional/behavioral disorders: A conceptual model. *Journal of Learning Disabilities, 30,* 245–263.

Rodino, A. M., Gimbert, C., Perez, C., Craddock-Willis, K., & McCabe, A. (1991, October). Getting your point across: Contrastive sequencing in low-income African American and Latino childen's personal narratives. Paper presented at the 16th annual Boston University Conference on Language Development, Boston.

Roehler, L., & Duffy, G. (1984). Direct explanation of comprehension processes. In G. G. Duffy, L. R. Roehler, & J. Mason (Eds.), *Comprehension instruction: Perspectives and suggestions* (pp. 265–280). New York: Longman.

Rogers, D. B. (1984). Assessing study skills. *Journal of Reading, 27,* 346–354.

Rogers, V. R., & Stevenson, C. (1988). How do we know what kids are learning in school? *Educational Leadership, 45*(5), 68–75.

Rosenbaum, J. E. (1980). Social implications of educational grouping. In D. C. Berliner (Ed.), *Review of Research in Education* (Vol. 8, pp. 361–401). Washington, DC: American Educational Research Association.

Rosenblatt, L. (1978). *The reader, the text, and the poem: The transactional theory of literary work.* Carbondale: Southern Illinois University Press.

Rosenblatt, L. (1982). The literary transaction: Evocation and response. *Theory into Practice, 21,* 268–277.

Rosenshine, B. V., & Stevens, R. (1984). Classroom instruction in reading. In P. D. Pearson, R. Barr, M. Kamil, & P. Mosenthal (Eds), *Handbook of reading research* (pp. 745–798). New York: Longman.

Rosenthal, R., & Jacobson, L. (1968). *Pygmalion in the classroom: Teacher expectation and pupils' intellectual development.* New York: Holt, Rinehart & Winston.

Rowe, M. B. (1974). Wait time and rewards as instructional variables, their influence on language, logic, and fate control. Part one—Wait time. *Journal of Research in Science Teaching, 11,* 81–94.

Rubin, D. (2000). *Teaching elementary language arts: A balanced approach* (6th ed.). Boston: Allyn & Bacon.

Ruddell, M. R. (1993). *Teaching content reading and writing.* Boston: Allyn & Bacon.

Ruddell, R. B. (1965). Effect of the similarity of oral and written language structure on reading comprehension. *Elementary English, 42,* 403–410.

Rumelhart, D. (1977). Toward an interactive model of reading. In S. Dornic (Ed.), *Attention and performance VI* (pp. 573–603). Hillsdale, NJ: Lawrence Erlbaum.

Rupley, W. H. (1976). Effective reading program. *The Reading Teacher, 29,* 616–623.

Russell, D. (1991). *Writing in the academic disciplines, 1870–1990: A curricular history.* Carbondale: Southern Illinois University Press.

Ryder, R. J., & Graves, M. F. (1980). Secondary students' internalization of letter-sound correspondence. *Journal of Educational Research, 73,* 172–178.

Sadowski, M. (1980). Ten years of uninterrupted sustained silent reading. *Reading Improvement, 17,* 153–156.

Salinger, T. (1988). *Language arts and literacy for young children.* Columbus, OH: Charles E. Merrill.

Salvia, J., & Ysseldyke, J. E. (1988). *Assessment in special education and remedial education* (4th ed.). Boston: Houghton Mifflin.

Salvia, J., & Ysseldyke, J. E. (2001). *Assessment* (8th ed.). Boston: Houghton Mifflin.

Samuels, S. J. (1979). The method of repeated readings. *The Reading Teacher, 32,* 403–408.

Samuels, S. J. (1988). Decoding and automaticity: Helping poor readers become automatic at word recognition. *The Reading Teacher, 41,* 755–760.

Santa, C., & Hoien, T. (1999). An assessment of Early Steps: A program for early intervention of reading problems. *Reading Research Quarterly, 34,* 54–79.

Sarason, S. B, & Doris, J. (1979). *Educational handicap, public policy, and social history.* New York: Free Press.

Sardy, S. (1985). Thinking about reading. In T. L. Harris & E. J. Cooper (Eds.), *Reading, thinking and concept development* (pp. 213–229). New York: College Entrance Examination Board.

Savage, J. F. (1977). *Effective communication.* Chicago: Science Research Association.

Scarborough, H. S. (1998). Early identification of children at risk for reading disabilities: Phonological awareness and some other promising predictors. In B. K. Shapiro, P. J. Accardo, & A. J. Capute (Eds.), *Specific reading disability: A view of the spectrum* (pp. 77–121). Timomium, MD: York Press.

Scardamalia, M., Bereiter, C., & Goelman, H. (1982). The role of production factors in writing ability. In M. Nystrand (Ed.), *What writers know: The language process and structure of written discourse* (pp. 173–210). San Diego: Academic Press.

Schell, L. M., & Hanna, G. S. (1981). Can informal reading inventories reveal strengths and weaknesses in comprehension subskills? *The Reading Teacher, 35,* 263–268.

Scheu, J. A., Tanner, D. K., & Au, K. H. (1989). Integrating seatwork with the basal lesson. In P. Winograd, K. K. Wixson, & M. Y. Lipson (Eds.), *Improving basal reading instruction* (pp. 58–73). New York: Teachers College Press.

Schlagal, R. (1995). Teaching disabled spellers. In R. Putnam (Ed.), *How to become a better reading teacher* (pp. 307–316). Englewood Cliffs, NJ: Merrill.

Schmidt, W., Caul, J., Byers, J., & Buchman, M. (1984). Content of basal reading selections: Implications for comprehension instruction. In G. Duffy, L. R. Roehler, & J. Mason (Eds.), *Comprehension instruction* (pp. 144–162). New York: Longman

Schunk, D. H. (1989). Social cognitive theory and self-regulated learning. In B. J. Zimmerman & D. H. Schunk (Eds.), *Self-regulated learning and academic achievement* (pp. 83–110). New York: Springer-Verlag.

Schuyler, M. R. (1982). A readability program for use on microcomputers. *Journal of Reading, 25,* 560–591.

Scott, D., Kahlich, P., & Barker, J. (1994). Motivating at-risk students using a literature based writing unit with computers. *Journal of Computing in Childhood Education, 5,* 311–317.

Scribner, S., & Cole, M. (1981). *The psychology of literacy: A case study among the Vai.* Cambridge, MA: Harvard University Press.

Searfoss, L. W., & Readence, J. E. (1989). *Helping children learn to read* (2nd ed.). Englewood Cliffs, NJ: Prentice Hall.

Semel, E., Wiig, E. H., & Secord, W. A. (1995). *Clinical evaluation of language fundamentals* (3rd ed.). San Antonio, TX: The Psychological Corporation.

Senechal, M., LeFevre, J., Hudson, E., & Lawson, E. P. (1996). Knowledge of storybooks as a predictor of young children's vocabulary. *Journal of Educational Psychology, 88,* 520–536.

Senechal, M., LeFevre, J., Thomas, E. M., & Daley, K. E. (1998). Differential effects of home literacy experiences on the development of oral and written language. *Reading Research Quarterly, 13,* 96–116.

Shake, M. C. (1989). Grouping and pacing with basal materials. In P. Winograd, K. K. Wixson, & M. Y. Lipson (Eds.), *Improving basal reading instruction* (pp. 62–85). New York: Teachers College Press.

Shanahan, T. (1984). The reading-writing relation: An exploratory multivariate analysis. *Journal of Educational Psychology, 76,* 466–477.

Shanahan, T. (1998). Effectiveness and limitations of tutoring in reading. In P. D. Pearson & A. Iran-Nejad (Eds.), *Review of Research in Education* (Vol. 23, pp. 217–234). Washington, DC, American Educational Research Association.

Shanahan, T. (2001). A rebuttal to Garan: What does the report of the National Reading Panel really tell us about teaching phonics? *Language Arts, 79,* 500–506.

Shanahan, T., & Barr, R. (1995). Reading Recovery: An independent evaluation of the effects of an early instructional intervention for at-risk learners. *Reading Research Quarterly, 30,* 958–997.

Shanahan, T., & Lomax, R. (1986). An analysis and comparison of theoretical models of the reading-writing relationship. *Journal of Educational Psychology, 78,* 116–123.

Shannon, P. (1983). The use of commercial reading materials in American elementary schools. *Reading Research Quarterly, 19,* 68–85.

Share, D., & Stanovich, K. E. (1995). Cognitive processes in early reading development: Accommodating individual differences into a mode of acquisition. *Issues in Education: Contributions for Educational Psychology, 1,* 1–57.

Sharp, S. J. (1990). Using content subject matter with LEA in middle school. *Journal of Reading, 33,* 108–112.

Shefelbine, J. L. (1991). *Encouraging your junior high student to read.* Newark, DE: International Reading Association.

Shepard, L. A., & Smith, M. L. (1986). Synthesis of research on school readiness and kindergarten retention. *Educational Leadership, 20,* 78–86.

Shimmerlik, S. (1978). Organization theory and memory for prose: A review of the literature. *Review of Educational Research, 48,* 103–121.

Silvaroli, N. J., Kear, D. J., & McKenna, M. C. (1982). *A classroom guide to reading assessment and instruction.* Dubuque, IA: Kendall/Hunt.

Silvaroli, N. J., & Wheelock, W. H. (2001). *Classroom reading inventory* (9th ed.). Monterey, CA: McGraw-Hill.

Simmons, W., & Resnick, L. (1993). Assessment as a catalyst of school reform. *Educational Leadership, 50,* 11–15.

Singer, J., & Donlon, D. (1982). Active comprehension: Problem-solving schema with question generation for comprehension of complex short stories. *Reading Research Quarterly, 17,* 166–168.

Slavin, R. (1991). *Educational psychology.* Englewood Cliffs, NJ: Prentice Hall.

Slavin, R. E. (1989). Students at risk of school failure: The problem and its dimensions. In R. E. Slavin, N. L. Karweit, & N. A. Madden (Eds.), *Effective programs for students at risk* (pp. 3–19). Boston: Allyn & Bacon.

Slavin, R. E., Karweit, N. L., Wasik, B. A., Madden, N. A., & Dolan, L. J. (1994). Success for all: A comprehensive approach to prevention and early intervention. In R. E. Slavin,

N. L. Karweit, & B. A. Wasik (Eds.), *Preventing early reading failure* (pp. 175–205). Boston: Allyn & Bacon.

Slavin, R. E., Stevens, R. J., & Madden, N. A. (1988). Accommodating student diversity in reading and writing instruction: A cooperative learning approach. *Reading and Special Education, 9,* 60–66.

Smith, D. D. (1979). The improvement of children's oral reading though the use of teacher modeling. *Journal of Learning Disabilities, 12,* 39–42.

Smith, D. K. (1998). Review of the Nelson-Denny Reading Test, Forms G and H. In J. C. Impara & B. S. Plake (Eds.), *Thirteenth mental measurements yearbook.* Lincoln, NE: Buros Institute of Mental Measurements.

Snider, V. E., & Tarver, S. G. (1987). The effect of early reading failure on acquisition of knowledge among students with learning disabilities. *Journal of Learning Disabilities, 20,* 351–356, 373.

Snow, C. E., Burns, M. S., & Griffin, P. (Eds.). (1998). *Preventing reading difficulties in young children.* Washington, DC: National Academy Press.

Spache, G. D. (1981). *Diagnostic reading scales.* Monterey, CA: CTB/McGraw-Hill.

Spear-Swerling, L., & Sternberg, R. J. (1998). *Off track: When poor readers become "learning disabled."* Boulder, CO: Westview.

Spector, J. E. (1992). Predicting progress in beginning reading: Dynamic assessment of phonemic awareness. *Journal of Educational Psychology, 84,* 353–363.

Spiegel, D. L. (1981). Six alternatives to the Directed Reading Activity. *The Reading Teacher, 34,* 914–923.

Spiro, R., & Myers, A. (1984). Individual differences and underlying cognitive processes. In P. D. Pearson, R. Barr, M. Kamil, & P. Mosenthal (Eds.), *Handbook of reading research* (Vol. 1, pp. 471–504). New York: Longman.

Squire, J. (1983). Composing and comprehending: Two sides of the same basic process. *Language Arts, 60,* 581–589.

Squire, J. (1991). The history of the profession. In J. Flood, J. Jensen, D. Lapp, & J. Squire (Eds.), *Handbook of research on teaching the English language arts.* New York: Macmillan.

Stahl, S., & Kapinus, B. A. (2001). *Word power: What every educator needs to know about vocabulary.* Washington, DC: NEA Professional Library.

Stahl, S. A. (1986). Three principles of effective vocabulary instruction. *Journal of Reading, 29,* 662–668.

Stahl, S. A., & Fairbanks, M. (1986). The effects of vocabulary instruction: A model-based meta-analysis. *Review of Educational Research, 56,* 72–110.

Stahl, S. A., & Murray, B. A. (1994). Defining phonological awareness and its relationship to early reading. *Journal of Educational Psychology, 86,* 221–234.

Stahl, S. A., & Murray, B. A. (1998). Issues involved in defining phonological awareness and its relation to early reading. In J. L. Metsala & L. C. Ehri (Eds.), *Word recognition in beginning reading* (pp. 65–87). Mahwah, NJ: Lawrence Erlbaum.

Stallings, J., Needels, M., & Sparks, G. M. (1987). Observation for the improvement of classroom learning. In D. C. Berliner & B. V. Rosenshine (Eds.), *Talks to teachers* (pp. 129–158). New York: Random House.

Stanovich, K. E. (1986). Matthew effects in reading: Some consequences of individual differences in the acquisition of literacy. *Reading Research Quarterly, 21,* 360–406.

Stanovich, K. E. (1991). Word recognition: Changing perspectives. In R. Barr, M. L. Kamil, P. B. Mosenthal, & P. D. Pearson (Eds.), *Handbook of reading research* (Vol. 2, pp. 418–452). New York: Longman.

Stanovich, K. E. (1992). Are we overselling literacy? In C. Temple & P. Collins (Eds.), *Stories and readers: New perspectives on literature in the elementary classroom* (pp. 209–231). Norwood, MA: Christopher-Gordon.

Stanovich, K. E., Cunningham, A. E., & Cramer, B. B. (1984). Assessing phonological awareness in kindergarten children: Issues of task comparability. *Journal of Experimental Child Psychology, 38,* 175–190.

Staton, J. (1987). The power of responding in dialogue journals. In T. Fulwiler (Ed.), *The journal book* (p. 63). Portsmouth, NH: Heinemann.

Stauffer, R. (1969). *Teaching reading as a thinking process.* New York: Harper & Row.

Stauffer, R. (1980). *Directing the reading-thinking process.* New York: Harper & Row.

Stein, N. L., & Glenn, C. G. (1979). An analysis of story comprehension in elementary school children. In R. O. Freedle (Ed.), *New directions in discourse processing* (Vol. 2, pp. 53–120). Norwood, NJ: Ablex.

Stein, N. L., & Nezworski, M. T. (1978). The effects of organization and instructional set on story memory. *Discourse Processes, 1,* 177–193.

Stein, N. L., & Policastro, M. (1984). The concept of a story: A comparison between children's and teachers' viewpoints. In H. Mandl, N. L. Stein, & T. Trabasso (Eds.), *Learning and comprehension of text* (pp. 113–158). Hillsdale, NJ: Lawrence Erlbaum.

Sternberg, R. J. (1999). Ability and expertise: It's time to replace the current model of intelligence. *American Educator, 23,* 1–30, 50.

Stevens, R. J., Madden, N. A., Slavin, R. E., & Farnish, A. M. (1987). Cooperative integrated reading and composition: Two field experiments. *Reading Research Quarterly, 23,* 433–454.

Stewig, J. W., & Nordberg, B. (1995). *Exploring language arts in the elementary classroom.* Belmont, CA: Wadsworth.

Stotsky, S. (1983). Research on reading/writing relationship: A synthesis and suggested directions. *Language Arts, 60,* 627–642.

Sulzby, E. (1986). Children's elicitation and use of metalinguistic knowledge about "word" during literacy interactions. In D. B. Yaden & S. Templeton (Eds.), *Metalinguistic awareness and beginning literacy* (pp. 219–234). Portsmouth, NH: Heinemann.

Sundbye, N. (1987). Text explicitness and inferential questioning: Effects on story understanding and recall. *Reading Research Quarterly, 22,* 82–98.

Swanson, H. L., & Watson, B. L. (1989). *Educational and psychological assessment of exceptional children* (2nd ed.). Columbus, OH: Merrill Publishing Company.

Taba, H. (1967). *Teacher's handbook for elementary social studies.* Reading, MA: Addison Wesley.

Taberski, S. (2000). *On solid ground: Strategies for teaching reading K–3.* Portsmouth, NH: Heinemann.

Tancock, S. M. (1994). A literacy lesson framework for children with reading problems. *The Reading Teacher, 48,* 130–140.

Taylor, B. M., Harris, L. A., & Pearson, P. D. (1988). *Reading difficulties: Instruction and assessment.* New York: Random House.

Taylor, B., Harris, L. A., Pearson, P. D., & Garcia, G. (1995). *Reading difficulties: Instruction and assessment* (2nd ed.). New York: McGraw-Hill.

Taylor, B. M. (1982). A summarizing strategy to improve middle grade students' reading and writing skills. *The Reading Teacher, 36,* 202–205.

Taylor, B. M. (1986). Teaching middle grade students to summarize content textbook material. In J. F. Baumann (Ed.), *Teaching main idea comprehension* (pp. 195–209). Newark, DE: International Reading Association.

Taylor, B. M., Pearson, P. D., Clark, K. F., & Walpole, S. (2000). Effective schools and accomplished teachers: Lessons about primary-grade reading instruction in low-income schools. *The Elementary School Journal, 101*(2), 121–165.

Taylor, B. M., & Samuels, S. J. (1983). Children's use of text structure in the recall of expository material. *American Educational Research Journal, 20,* 234–237.

Taylor, B. M., Strait, J., & Medo, M. A. (1994). Early intervention in reading: Supplemental instructions for groups of low-achieving students provided by first-grade teachers. In E. H. Hiebert & B. M. Taylor (Eds.), *Getting reading right from the start* (pp. 107–121). Boston: Allyn & Bacon.

Tchudi, S. (1994). *Integrated language arts in the elementary school.* Belmont, CA: Wadsworth.

Teale, W. H., Hiebert, E. H., & Chittenden, E. A. (1987). Assessing young children's literacy development. *The Reading Teacher, 40,* 772–777.

Teale, W. H., & Sulzby, E. (Eds.). (1986). *Emergent literacy: Writing and reading.* Norwood, NJ: Ablex.

Temple, C., & Gillet, J. W. (1989). *Language arts: Learning processes and teaching practices* (2nd ed.). Glenview, IL: Scott, Foresman.

Temple, C., Nathan, R., Burris, N., & Temple, F. (1988). *The beginnings of writing.* Boston: Allyn & Bacon.

Temple, C., Nathan, R., Temple, F., & Burris, N. A. (1993). *The beginnings of writing* (3rd ed.). Boston: Allyn & Bacon.

Templeton, S. (1995). Spelling: The foundation of word knowledge for the less proficient reader. In M. L. Putnam (Ed.), *How to become a better reading teacher* (pp. 317–329). Englewood Cliffs, NJ: Merrill.

Templeton, S. (1997). *Teaching the integrated language arts.* Boston: Houghton Mifflin.

Templeton, S., & Bear, D. (1992). *The development of orthographic knowledge and the foundations of literacy: A memorial Festschrift for Edmund H. Henderson.* Hillsdale, NJ: Lawrence Erlbaum.

Templeton, S., & Morris, D. (2000). Spelling. In M. Kamil, P. Mosenthal, P. D. Pearson, & R. Barr (Eds.), *Handbook of reading research* (Vol. 3, pp. 525–543). Mahwah, NJ: Lawrence Erlbaum.

Thorndyke, P. W. (1977). Cognitive structures in comprehension and memory of narrative discourse. *Cognitive Psychology, 9,* 77–110.

Tierney, R., Readence, J. E., & Dishner, E. (1985). *Reading strategies and practices: A compendium* (2nd ed.). Boston: Allyn & Bacon.

Tierney, R. J. (1992). Ongoing research and new directions. In J. W. Irwin & M. A. Doyle (Eds.), *Reading/writing connections: Learning from research* (pp. 247–259). Newark, DE: International Reading Association.

Tierney, R. J., Carter, M. A., & Desai, L. E. (1991). *Portfolio assessment in the reading-writing classroom.* Norwood, MA: Christopher-Gordon.

Tikunoff, W. J., & Ward, B. A. (1983). Collaborative research on teaching. *Elementary School Journal, 83,* 453–468.

Tompkins, G. E. (2000). *Teaching writing: Balancing process and product* (3rd ed.). Upper Saddle River, NJ: Prentice Hall.

Topping, K. (1987). Paired reading: A powerful technique for parent use. *The Reading Teacher, 40,* 608–614.

Torgeson, J. (1990). The learning disabled child as an inactive learner. In P. Cole & L. Chan (Eds.), *Methods and strategies for special education.* Englewood Cliffs, NJ: Prentice Hall.

Torgeson, J. K., & Bryant, B. R. (1994). *Test of Phonological Awareness.* Austin, TX: PRO-ED.

Torgeson, J. K., & Davis, C. (1996). Individual difference variables that predict response to training in phonological awareness. *Journal of Experimental Child Psychology, 63,* 1–21.

Torgeson, J. K. (1977). The role of non-specific factors in the task performance of learning disabled children: A theoretical assessment. *Journal of Learning Disabilities, 10,* 24–34.

Torgeson, J. K., & Davis, C. (1996). Individual difference variables that predict response to training in phonological awareness. *Journal of Experimental Child Psychology, 63,* 1–21.

Tovay, D. R. (1980). Childen's grasp of phonics terms vs. sound-symbol relationships. *The Reading Teacher, 33,* 431–437.

Tucker, M. S., & Codding, J. B. (1998). *Standards for our schools: How to set them, measure them, and reach them.* San Francisco: Jossey-Bass.

Tunmer, W. E., Herriman, M. L., & Nesdale, A. R. (1988). Metalinguistic abilities and beginning reading. *Reading Research Quarterly, 23,* 134–158.

Turner, J., & Paris, S. G. (1995). How literacy tasks influence children's motivation for literacy. *The Reading Teacher, 48,* 662–673.

Turner, J. C. (1995). The influence of classroom contexts on young children's motivation for literacy. *Reading Research Quarterly, 30,* 410–441.

Tzuriel, D. (2000). Dynamic assessment of young children: Educational intervention perspectives. *Educational Psychology Review, 12*(4), 385–434.

Vacca, R. T., & Padak, N. D. (1990). Who's at risk in reading? *Journal of Reading, 33,* 486–488.

Vacca, R. T., & Vacca, J. L. (1989). *Content area reading* (3rd ed.). Glenview, IL: Scott, Foresman.

Valdes, G. (1996). *Con respeto: Bridging the distances between culturally diverse families and schools.* New York: Teachers College Press.

Valencia, S. (1990a). A portfolio approach to classroom assessment; The whys, whats, and hows. *The Reading Teacher, 43,* 338–340.

Valencia, S. (1990b). Portfolio assessment: Separating the wheat from the chaff. *The Reading Teacher, 44,* 60–61.

Valencia, S., McGinley, W., & Pearson, P. D. (1990). Assessing reading and writing: Building a more complete picture. In G. Duffy & P. Anders (Eds.) *Reading in the middle schools* (pp. 124–153). Newark, DE: International Reading Association.

Valencia, S., & Pearson, P. D. (1987). Reading assessment: Time for a change. *The Reading Teacher, 40,* 726–733.

Valencia, S., Stallman, A. C., Commeyras, M., Hartman, D.K., Pearson, P. D., & Greer, E. A. (1987, December). Three methods of assessing prior knowledge: A validation study. Paper presented at The National Reading Conference, St. Petersburg, FL.

Valencia, S. W. (1997). Authentic classroom assessment of early reading: Alternatives to standardized tests. *Preventing School Failure, 41*(2), 63–70.

Valencia, S. W. (1998). *Literacy portfolios in action.* Fort Worth: Harcourt Brace.

Valencia, S. W., & Bradley, S. (1998). Engaging students in self-reflection and self-evaluation. In S. W. Valencia (Ed.), *Literacy portfolios in action* (pp. 174–218). New York: Harcourt.

Valencia, S. W., & Calfee, R. (1991). The development and use of literacy portfolios for students, classes, and teachers. *Applied Measurement in Education, 4*(4), 333–345.

Valencia, S. W., Hiebert, E., & Afflerbach, P. P. (Eds.). (1994). *Authentic reading assessment: Practices and possibilities.* Newark, DE: International Reading Association.

Valencia, S. W., & Place, N. A. (1994). Literacy portfolios for teaching, learning, and accountability: The Bellevue literacy assessment project. In S. W. Valencia, E. H. Hiebert, & P. P. Afflerbach (Eds.), *Authentic reading assessment: Practices and possibilities* (pp. 134–166). Newark, DE: International Reading Association.

Valencia, S. W., & Wixson, K. K. (2000). Policy-oriented research on literacy standards and assessment. In M. L. Kamil, P. B. Mosenthal, P. D. Pearson, & R. Barr (Eds.), *Handbook of reading research* (Vol. 3, pp. 909–935). Mahwah, NJ: Lawrence Erlbaum.

Vandervelden, M. C., & Siegel, L. S. (1995). Phonological recoding and phoneme awareness in early literacy: A developmental approach. *Reading Research Quarterly, 30,* 854–875.

Vaughan, J. L., & Estes, T. H. (1986). *Reading and reasoning beyond the primary grades.* Boston: Allyn & Bacon.

Vellutino, F. R., Scanlon, D. M., & Sipay, E. R. (1997). Toward distinguishing between cognitive and experiential deficits as primary sources of difficulty in learning to read: The importance of early intervention in diagnosing specific reading disability. In B. A. Blachman (Ed.), *Foundations of reading acquisition and dyslexia: Implications for early intervention* (pp. 347–379). Mahwah, NJ: Lawrence Erlbaum.

Vellutino, F. R., Scanlon, D. M., Sipay, E. R., Small, S. G., Pratt, A., Chen, R., & Denckla, M. B. (1996). Cognitive profiles of difficult-to-remediate and readily remediated poor readers: Early intervention as a vehile for distinguishing between cognitive and experiential deficits as basic causes of special reading disability. *Journal of Educational Psychology, 88*(4), 601–638.

Vernon-Feagans, L., Hammer, C. S., Miccio, A., & Manlove, E. (2001). Early language and literacy skills in low-income African American and Hispanic children. In S. B. Neuman & D. K. Dickinson (Eds.), *Handbook of early literacy research* (pp. 192–210). New York: Guilford Press.

Villa, R. A., & Thousand, J. S. (Eds.). (1995). *Creating an inclusive school.* Alexandria, VA: ASCD.

Villaume, S. K., Worder, T., Williams, S., Hopkins, L., & Rosenblatt, C. (1994). Five teachers in search of a discussion. *The Reading Teacher, 47,* 480–487.

Vogt, M. E. (1999). *Read-2-Succeed: An intervention model for middle and high school students.* Paper presented at the Annual Meeting of the National Reading Conference, Orlando, FL.

Vogt, M. E., & Shearer, B. A. (2003). *Reading specialists in the real world: A sociocultural view.* Needham Heights, MA: Allyn & Bacon.

Vygotsky, L. S. (1962). *Thought and language.* Cambridge, MA: The MIT Press.

Vygotsky, L. S. (1978). *Mind in society: The development of higher psychological process.* Cambridge, MA: Harvard University Press.

Vygotsky, L. S. (1986). *Thought and language.* Cambridge, MA: MIT Press.

Wade, S. E. (1990). Using think alouds to assess comprehension. *The Reading Teacher, 43,* 442–453.

Wade, S. E., & Moje, E. B. (2000). The role of text in classroom learning. In M. Kamil, P. Mosenthal, P. D. Pearson, & R. Barr (Eds.), *Handbook of reading research* (Vol. 3, pp. 609–627). Mahwah, NJ: Lawrence Erlbaum.

Wagner, R. K., Torgeson, J. K., & Rashotte, C. A. (1999). *Comprehensive Test of Phonological Processing.* Austin, TX: PRO-ED.

Wagner, R. K., Torgeson, J. K., Rashotte, C. A., Hecht, S. A., Barker, T. A., Burgess, S. R., Donahue, J., & Garon, T. (1997). Changing relations between phonological processing abilities and word-level reading as children develop from beginning to skilled readers: A 5-year longitudinal study. *Developmental Psychology, 33,* 468–479.

Walker, B. (2000). *Diagnostic teaching of reading* (4th ed.). Upper Saddle River, NJ: Prentice Hall.

Walmsley, S., & Allington, R. (1965). Redefining and reforming instructional support programs for at-risk readers. In R. Allington & S. Walmsley (Eds.), *No quick fix: Rethinking literacy programs in America's elementary schools* (pp. 19–44). Newark, DE: International Reading Association.

Walp, T. P., & Walmsley, S. A. (1989). Instructional and philosophical congruence: Neglected aspects of coordination. *The Reading Teacher, 42,* 364–368.

Walsh, S. B., & Betz, N. E. (2001). *Tests and assessment* (4th ed.). Upper Saddle River, NJ: Prentice Hall.

Walters, J., Seidel, S., & Gardner, H. (1994). Children as reflective practitioners. In J. N. Mangieri & C. C. Block (Eds.), *Creating powerful thinking in teachers and students* (pp. 289–303). Fort Worth: Harcourt Brace.

Wang, M. C., Haertel, G. D., & Walberg, H. J. (1994). What helps students learn? *Educational Leadership, 51,* 74–79.

Warncke, E. W., & Shipman, D. A. (1984). *Group assessment in reading: Classroom teacher's handbook.* Englewood Cliffs, NJ: Prentice Hall.

Wasik, B. A. (1998). Volunteer tutoring programs in reading: A review. *Reading Research Quarterly, 33,* 266–292.

Watson, R. (2001). Literacy and oral language: Implications for early literacy acquisition. In S. B. Neuman & D. K. Dickinson (Eds.), *Handbook of early literacy research* (pp. 43–53). New York: Guilford Press.

Weiner, B. (1992). *Human motivation: Metaphors, theories, and research.* Newbury Park, CA: Sage.

Weinstein, R. S. (1976). Reading group membership in first grade: Teacher behaviors and pupil experience over time. *Journal of Educational Psychology, 68,* 103–116.

Weinstein, R. S. (1986). Teaching reading: Children's awareness of teacher expectations. In T. E. Raphael (Ed.), *The contexts of school-based literacy* (pp. 233–252). New York: Random House.

Weir, C. (1998). Using embedded questions to jump-start metacognition in middle school remedial readers. *Journal of Adolescent and Adult Literacy, 41,* 458–468.

Weir, C. (2000). Using embedded questions to jump-start metacognition in middle school remedial readers. In D. W. Moore, D. E. Alvermann, & K. A. Hinchman (Eds.), *Struggling adolescent readers: A collection of strategies* (pp. 138–147). Newark, DE: International Reading Association.

Wells, G. (1982). Story reading and the development of symbolic skills. *Australian Journal of Reading, 5,* 142–152.

Wells, G. (1986). *The meaning makers: Children learning language and using language to learn.* Portsmouth, NH: Heinemann.

Wepner, S. B., & Feeley, J. T. (1993). *Moving forward with literature: Basals, books, and beyond.* New York: Merrill.

West, R. F., & Stanovich, K. (1978). Automatic contextual facilitiation in readers of three ages. *Child Development, 49,* 717–727.

Westby, C. (1988). Test Review: Test of Language Development—2. Primary. *The Reading Teacher, 42,* 236–237.

White, T. G., Graves, M. F., & Slater, W. H. (1990). Growth in vocabulary in diverse elementary schools: Decoding and word meanings. *Journal of Educational Psychology, 82,* 281–290.

Whitehurst, G. J., & Lonigan, C. J. (2001). Emergent literacy: Development from prereaders to readers. In S. B. Neuman & D. K. Dickinson (Eds.), *Handbook of early literacy research* (pp. 11–29). New York: Guilford Press.

*Wide Range Achievement Test 3* (1993). Wilmington, DE: Wide Range Inc.

Wiederholt, J. L., & Bryant, B. R. (1986). Gray *Oral Reading Test—Revised.* Austin, TX: PRO-ED.

Wiederholt, J. L., & Bryant, B. R. (1992). Gray *Oral Reading Test–3.* Austin, TX: PRO-ED.

Wiederholt, J. L., & Bryant, B. R. (2001). Gray *Oral Reading Test—4.* Austin, TX: PRO-ED.

Wiencek, J., & O'Flahavan, J. (1994). From teacher-led to peer discussions about literature: Suggestions for making the shift. *Language Arts, 71,* 488–497.

Wigfield, A., & Asher, S. R. (1984). Social and motivational influences on reading. In P. D. Pearson, R. Barr, M. Kamil, & P. Mosenthal (Eds.), *Handbook of reading research* (pp. 423–452). New York: Longman.

Wiggins, G. (1989). Teaching to the (authentic) test. *Educational Leadership, 46,* 141–147.

Wilhem, J. (2001). *Improving comprehension with think-aloud strategies: Modeling what good readers do.* New York: Scholastic.

Wilkinson, G. S. (1993). *Wide Range Achievement Test 3.* Wilmington, DE: Wide Range Inc.

Wilkinson, L. C., & Silliman, E. R. (2000). Classroom language and literacy learning. In M. L. Kamil, P. B. Mosenthal, P. D. Pearson, & R. Barr (Eds.), *Handbook of reading research* (Vol. 3, pp. 337–359). Mahwah, NJ: Lawrence Erlbaum.

Will, M. (1986). *Educating students with learning problems: A shared responsibility.* Washington, DC: Office of Special Education and Rehabilitation Services, U.S. Department of Education.

Williams, J. P. (1980). Teaching decoding with an emphasis on phoneme analysis and phoneme blending. *Journal of Educational Psychology, 72,* 1–15.

Williams, J. P., Taylor, M. B., & deCani, J. S. (1984). Constructing macrostructure for expository text. *Journal of Educational Psychology, 76,* 1065–1075.

Wilson, R. M., & Cleland, C. J. (1989). *Diagnostic and remedial reading for classroom and clinic.* Columbus, OH: Charles E. Merrill.

Wilson, R. M., & Hall, M. (1990). *Programmed word attack for teachers.* Columbus, OH: Charles E. Merrill.

Wilson-Portuondo, M. L., & Hardy, P. R. (2001). *When is a language difficulty a disability? The assessment and evaluation process of English language learners.* The New England Equity Assistance Center, Providence: The Education Alliance, Brown University. [Online Document]. Available: www.alliance.brown.edu/eac/spedMTSL101.shtml.

Winograd, P., Wixson, K. K., & Lipson, M. Y. (Eds.). (1989). *Improving basal reading instruction.* New York: Teachers College Press.

Winograd, P. N., & Johnston, P. (1987). Some considerations for advancing the teaching of reading comprehension. *Educational Psychologist, 22,* 213–230.

Wittrock, M. C., Marks, C., & Doctorow, M. (1975). Reading as a generative process. *Journal of Educational Psychology, 67,* 484–489.

Wixson, K. K. (1979). Miscue analysis: A critical review. *Journal of Reading Behavior, 11,* 163–175.

Wixson, K. K. (1983a). Postreading question-answer interactions and children's learning from text. *Journal of Educational Psychology, 30,* 413–423.

Wixson, K. K. (1983b). Questions about a text: What you ask about is what children learn. *The Reading Teacher, 37,* 287–293.

Wixson, K. K. (1984). Level of importance of postquestions and children's learning from text. *American Educational Research Journal, 21,* 419–434.

Wixson, K. K., Bosky, A. B., Yochum, M. N., & Alvermann, D. E. (1984). An interview for assessing students' perceptions of classroom reading tasks. *The Reading Teacher, 37,* 354–359.

Wixson, K. K., & Dutro, E. (1999). Standards for primary-grade reading: An analysis of state frameworks. *Elementary School Journal, 100,* 89–110.

Wixson, K. K., & Lipson, M. Y. (1986). Reading (dis)ability: An interactionist perspective. In T. E. Raphael (Ed.), *Contexts of school-based literacy* (pp. 131–148). New York: Random House.

Wixson, K. K., & Peters, C. W. (1989). Teaching the basal selection. In P. Winograd, K. K. Wixson, & M. Y. Lipson (Eds.), *Improving basal reading instruction* (pp. 21–61). New York: Teachers College Press.

Wixson, K. K., Peters, C. W., Weber, E. M., & Roeber, E. D. (1987). New directions in statewide reading assessment. *The Reading Teacher, 40,* 749–755.

Wixson, K. K., Valencia, S., & Lipson, M. Y. (1994). Critical issues in literacy assessment: Confronting the realities of external and internal assessment. *Journal of Reading Beahavior, 26,* 315–337.

Wixson, S. E. (1985). Test review: The Test of Early Reading Ability (TERA). *The Reading Teacher, 38,* 544–547.

Wong, B. Y. L., Wong, R., & Blenkisop, J. (1989). Cognitive and metacognitive aspects of learning-disabled adolescents' composing problems. *Learning Disabilities Quarterly, 12,* 300–323.

Wong, F. L. (1991). Second-language learning in children: A model of language learning in social context. In E. Bialystok (Ed.),

*Language processing in bilingual children* (pp. 49–69). Cambridge, England: Cambridge University Press.

Wong, J., & Au, K. H. (1985). The concept-text-application approach: Helping elementary students comprehend expository text. *The Reading Teacher, 38,* 612–618.

Wong-Fillmore, L. (1991). Language and cultural issues in the early education of language minority childen. In S. Kagan (Ed.), *The care and education of American young children: Obstacles and opportunities.* The 90th yearbook of the National Society for the Study of Education. Chicago: University of Chicago Press.

Wood, D. J., Bruner, J. S., & Ross, G. (1976). The role of tutoring in problem solving. *Journal of Child Psychology and Psychiatry, 17,* 89–100.

Wood, K. D. (1987). Fostering cooperative learning in middle and secondary school classrooms. *Journal of Reading, 31,* 10–19.

Wood, K. D. (1988). Techniques for assessing students' potential for learning. *The Reading Teacher, 41,* 440–447.

Wood, K. D., Lapp, D., & Flood, J. (1992). *Guiding readers through text: A review of study guides.* Newark, DE: International Reading Association.

Wood, K. D., & Robinson, N. (1983). Vocabulary, language, and prediction: A prereading strategy. *The Reading Teacher, 36,* 392–395.

Woodcock, R. W. (1987). *Woodcock Reading Mastery Test—Revised.* Circle Pines, MN: American Guidance Service.

Woods, M. L., & Moe, A. J. (1999). *Analytical reading inventory* (6th ed.). Columbus, OH: Merrill.

Woods, M. A., & Moe, A. J. (2003). *Analytical reading inventory* (7th ed.). Upper Saddle River, NJ: Prentice Hall.

Wylie, R. E., & Durrell, D. D. (1970). Teaching vowels through phonograms. *Elementary English, 47,* 787–791.

Yopp, H. K. (1992). Developing phonemic awareness in young children. *The Reading Teacher, 45,* 696–703.

Yopp, H. K. (1995). A test for assessing phonemic awareness in young children. *The Reading Teacher, 49,* 20–29.

Yopp, H. T. (1988). The validity and reliability of phonemic awareness tests. *Reading Research Quarterly, 23,* 159–177.

Young, J. P., & Brozo, W. G. (2001). Conversations: Boys will be boys, or will they? *Reading Research Quarterly, 36*(3), 316–325.

Ysseldyke, J., & Christenson, S. (2002). *Functional assessment of academic behavior.* Longmont, CO: Sopris West.

Ysseldyke, J. E., & Christenson, S. L. (1987). *The Instructional Environment Scale (TIES).* Austin, TX: PRO-ED.

Ysseldyke, J. E., & Christenson, S. L. (1993). *TIES-II: The instructional environment system.* Longmont, CO: Sopris West.

Zakaluk, B. L., & Samuels, S. J. (1988). Toward a new approach to predicting text comprehensibility. In B. L. Zakaluk & S. J. Samuels (Eds.), Readability: Its past, present, and future (pp. 121–144). Newark, DE: International Reading Association.

Zigmond, N., Vallecorsa, A., & Leinhardt, G. (1980). Reading instruction for students with learning disabilities. *Topics in Language Disorders, 1,* 89–98.

Zion, G. (1976). *Harry the dirty dog.* New York: HarperCollins.

# NAME INDEX

# SUBJECT INDEX

Note: An italicized letter *f* following page numbers indicates a figure.

morpheme - Smallest unit of meaning
root words; affixes; inflections

page 183